D1449708

BIOGRAPHICAL DICTIONARY OF AMERICAN JOURNALISM

BIOGRAPHICAL DICTIONARY OF AMERICAN JOURNALISM

Edited by Joseph P. McKerns

GREENWOOD PRESS
New York • Westport, Connecticut • London

Library of Congress Cataloging-in-Publication Data

Biographical dictionary of American journalism / edited by Joseph P. McKerns.

p. cm.

Includes index.

ISBN 0–313–23818–9 (lib. bdg. : alk. paper)

1. Journalists—United States—Biography—Dictionaries.
2. Journalism—United States—History—Bio-bibliography.
I. McKerns, Joseph P., 1950–

PN4871.B56 1989

070'.92'2—dc19

[B] 88–25098

British Library Cataloguing in Publication Data is available.

Library of Congress Catalog Card Number: 88–25098
ISBN: 0–313–23818–9

First published in 1989

Greenwood Press, Inc.
88 Post Road West, Westport, Connecticut 06881

Printed in the United States of America

The paper used in this book complies with the Permanent Paper Standard issued by the National Information Standards Organization (Z39.48–1984).

10 9 8 7 6 5 4 3 2 1

To My Parents,
Jean and Joseph McKerns
and
To My Teacher,
Edwin Emery

CONTENTS

INTRODUCTION ix

ABBREVIATIONS xv

THE DICTIONARY 1

APPENDIX 771

News Media and Professional Fields 771

Columnists 771

Editorial Cartoonists and Illustrators 772

Foreign Correspondents 772

Humorists 773

Magazines 773

Newspaper Editors, Managing Editors, and Publishers 775

News Services and Syndicates 778

Photography, Documentary, and Newsreels 780

Radio and Television 780

Sports Journalism 781

War Correspondents 781

Washington Correspondents 782

Women in Journalism 783

Minority and Ethnic Journalism 784

DuPont and Peabody Awards in Broadcasting 784

Pulitzer Prizes 784

INDEX 787

ABOUT THE CONTRIBUTORS 807

INTRODUCTION

This biographical dictionary brings together within the covers of one volume the richness and diversity of American journalism from 1690 to the present. It offers biographical sketches of nearly 500 persons who contributed to the development of American journalism through their work in the various media—newspapers, magazines, radio and television—and in various occupational roles—reporter, editor, publisher, war, Washington or foreign correspondent, commentator, columnist, humorist, editorial cartoonist, illustrator, photographer, documentary film or television producer, sports journalist, and wire service and press association personnel. Also, because the development of American journalism was not only affected by those working for the mainstream media of daily newspapers, national magazines, and broadcasting networks, this volume includes those who made significant contributions in the women's, ethnic, minority, and dissident media. These latter subjects are not "tokens" offered in an attempt to right ancient wrongs, but instead they are a reflection of my personal conviction that the true significance and development of American journalism cannot accurately be measured and understood by examining only the mainstream media in the nation's major cities. The texture of American journalism is as rich and diverse as the texture of its population with its many hues and colors, races, creeds, and nationalities.

The biographical sketches in this volume are organized alphabetically by the subject's last name (alphabetical lists of the subjects by categories of media and professional fields are included in the appendix). Each sketch, or entry, follows the format of such standard biographical dictionaries as the *Dictionary of American Biography*, and begins with the subject's name and dates of birth and death (or only the former if the subject is still living). This is followed by a paragraph summarizing the subject's significance in the history of American journalism. The succeeding paragraphs offer a chronological narrative of the subject's life and achievements.

The emphasis in each entry is on the important career details of the subject's life. Also included are data on the names of parents, spouses, siblings, children; dates of marriage; details of education; and important nonjournalistic activities, for example, government service. The final paragraph offers information about the subject's death, or, if the subject is still living, what his or her current activity is. Most of the subjects included who are still living have retired, and the date of retirement is noted in the entry, usually in the last paragraph.

Following each entry is a brief bibliography on the subject, which is divided into two parts. Part A lists those significant published works by the subject not incorporated into the chronological narrative. Most often these are memoirs, autobiographies, or works of an autobiographical nature. Part B lists books, articles, and other printed material about the subject, including references to the obituary published in the *New York Times*, when appropriate, and citations to other biographical dictionaries.

For a number of entries, most often those whose subject is a regional, woman, or minority journalist, biographical references are scarce. There may not have been an obituary published in the *Times*, or other accessible major newspaper, nor an entry in any of the standard biographical dictionaries. For some subjects, their appearance in this volume marks the first time they have been included in a major reference work. Among such entries are those on Howard Rock, a native Eskimo editor, and James P. Newcomb, an important regional journalist.

The name of the author of the entry follows the bibliography. More information about the authors is offered in the ''About the Contributors'' section at the back of this volume. Most of the contributors have a research interest in the subject of the entry, or in the subject's category of journalism. All of the contributors have a strong personal interest in the subject matter of the entries they wrote.

This work differs from other biographical dictionaries in that it includes subjects who are living, of whom some are still active in a facet of journalism. The decision to include subjects who are still living was a subjective one, but, nevertheless, a decision necessitated by the history of American journalism itself. While the history of American newspapers dates back to 1690, the other major mass media have emerged only during the past century. Mass-circulation national magazines are scarcely 100 years old; radio broadcasting scarcely 65 years old; and television roughly 40 years old.

Additionally, the historical age of the several professional fields varies greatly, for example, while newspaper editors have been around since Benjamin Harris in 1690, editorial cartoonists first appeared around the time of Thomas Nast in the mid- to late-nineteenth century. A career field making an even more recent appearance is the syndicated political columnist, such as Walter Lippmann or Joseph Kraft, whose heyday dates only to the 1930s. Because many of the most significant figures in the development of the newer media and professional fields are still living, it seemed only logical to include them. Therefore, the selection of living subjects was weighted in favor of persons involved in the development of broadcasting and magazines, and from the newer professional fields such as political columnists and commentators.

However, the decision to include living subjects prevented the kind of closure possible when the selection of subjects is limited to those who are dead. Therefore, I decided to weight the selection of subjects who are living in favor of those who have retired, thus achieving closure to an extent. But, "retirement" is a slippery concept in a profession such as journalism. For example, a significant journalist may formally retire from his or her position, as Walter Cronkite did when he retired as anchor of the "CBS Evening News," and yet remain active in the field afterward, as Cronkite also has done with his various broadcasting projects and special assignments. Furthermore, there have been others who never formally retired, but who moved into a different realm of activity, sometimes in journalism, sometimes outside of it. Theodore H. White is an example of this. The decision to include White was made long before he died because of his great importance as a China correspondent and political journalist. White never formally retired from magazine journalism, but he did move on to other activities, most notably his *The Making of the President* series of books.

For subjects like Cronkite, the decision to include them was a relatively easy one to make given that other criteria (discussed below) were met. For subjects like White, or Nancy Dickerson, who is a successful producer of syndicated television documentaries but who is included in this volume because she was the first woman White House correspondent for a major television network, the decision was more subjective and it reflects my interpretation of the development of journalism based upon nearly two decades of study and research. Taken as a whole, this work reflects an understanding of the history of journalism and those who contributed to it in a significant way from the perspective of the mid–1980s.

Before turning to an explanation of the criteria used to select subjects for this volume, it is necessary to clarify how the term *American journalism* was interpreted in this work. Does "American" mean that only native-born citizens of the United States are included? No. Instead it means any journalist, whether native-born, naturalized, or foreign national, whose work was significant in the development of journalism in the United States. For example, some naturalized citizens, such as Joseph Pulitzer, began their journalism careers only after immigrating to the United States and are included. Others, such as W. T. Stead, were journalists in their native countries and never became citizens of the United States, but their work in this country significantly influenced American journalism and they are included because of that.

"Journalism" is interpreted to reflect the many-faceted activities of gathering, processing, and disseminating information about politics, culture, and society that are journalism in its reality, in other words, what a reader or viewer commonly expects to find in newspapers, magazines, or on broadcast news and public affairs programs. Journalism is more than just the timely reporting of current events or what is called "news"; it includes the work of columnists, editorial cartoonists, photographers, television documentary producers, and others. Their work also feeds the pool of public knowledge about politics, culture, and society as does the work of reporters and editors.

Nevertheless, even though the way in which the term "American journalism" is interpreted here tends toward a holistic view, there still is closure. This volume does not include significant figures from the history of advertising or public relations. Each of those professions deserves full treatment in its own volume first, and then perhaps a truly holistic volume covering American mass communication would be in order.

Also, this volume does not attempt to be exhaustive of its subject. That would be impossible short of a commitment to a multi-volume series. Therefore, criteria were established at the beginning of the project to guide the selection of subjects. These criteria were adapted from the *Encyclopedia of American Biography*, edited by John A. Garraty and Jerome L. Sternstein, a work similar to this in that it is a one-volume biographical reference that includes entries on living subjects and covers a range of activities and career fields.

The criteria for selection were the following: *Significance*. Did the person influence journalism in his or her own time or later? *Achievement*. Did the person reach a level of competence in journalism that was recognized by peers and contemporaries, or later by biographers and historians? *Fame (or Notoriety)*. Was the person widely known by peers or contemporaries, or by later generations? *Typicality*. Does the person merit selection because he or she reflects some broad trend or is representative of some large group? The order of the criteria indicates their priority; is significance alone enough to merit selection? Yes, regardless of whether or not the person's significance was recognized in his or her own lifetime or later.

Most of the subjects included in the volume easily met the significance criterion, and many of them met all four criteria. Any biographical dictionary of American journalism would be incomplete without entries on Joseph Pulitzer, the elder James Gordon Bennett, Edward R. Murrow, Horace Greeley, Frederick Douglass, Henry R. Luce, Margaret Fuller, and others like them. Selection was more difficult and became more subjective as subjects met three or fewer of the criteria notwithstanding significance. Some subjects met only one of the criteria, other than significance, but were included nonetheless. For example, James Gordon Bennett, Jr., the editor who sent Stanley to find Livingston in order to sell more newspapers, is included for his notoriety primarily, and also because he controlled a very important American newspaper of the time, the *New York Herald*.

Some of the early radio correspondents are included not because they were especially significant individually, but because they are representative of an important, emerging career field in their time, and because information about them was more accessible than information about others who were not included. Surely, there will be disagreement with some of the close decisions made in this volume, but such is the nature of biographical reference works and of the discourse on historical significance. I respect criticism based upon informed opinion. A number of difficult choices had to be made, and the decisions made in those cases reflect my own subjective, but informed, opinion regarding historical significance.

Finally, a few points regarding the importance of the person versus the importance of the specific journalistic organization the person was affiliated with need to be made. Having held a specific position with an organization did not automatically qualify a person for selection, for example, having been the editor or publisher of a major metropolitan newspaper, or the president of one of the three major television networks. Adolph Ochs is included because his genius and leadership resurrected the *New York Times* after 1896 and made it the great newspaper that it is, and not because he was the publisher of the *Times*. Likewise, William S. Paley, who has never been a journalist, is included because his managerial leadership and determination to make CBS a leader in broadcast news is largely responsible for that network's excellent journalistic reputation through the decades, and not because he has been the chief executive officer of CBS.

Also, having received a Pulitzer Prize in print journalism or a DuPont or Peabody award in broadcasting did not automatically qualify a person for selection. Most often these prestigious awards are given to individuals in recognition of an outstanding, but specific, achievement in journalism, such as excellence in coverage of a major news event, or for an outstanding series of articles or programs on an important political or social issue. They are seldom awarded in recognition of the long-term significance of a person's contributions to journalism. However, a number of the subjects in this volume received a Pulitzer Prize, or DuPont or Peabody award, and their names are listed in the appendix at the end of this volume.

Given the above criteria and guidelines for selection, the process of selection involved surveying those works considered standard histories of American mass communication, such as the works of Frank Luther Mott, Edwin Emery, Erik Barnouw, Sidney Head, and even Isaiah Thomas (who is among the subjects included), whose *History of Printing in America* was the first major work on journalism history published in the United States. Also consulted were the works of historians and other scholars who specialize in one of the many facets of American mass communication history, such as women in journalism, the black press, the ethnic and immigrant press, and so on. A number of the contributors to this volume also offered helpful suggestions about persons to be added to the list of subjects. All such suggestions were appreciated, and a number of the names suggested were added if they met the criteria established for selection.

This volume is dedicated to three people who are very important to me, and who have had a profound influence on my life and work. It is dedicated to my parents, Jean and Joseph McKerns, who worked very hard for many years to give me the best they could, and whose love and concern for me I shall always cherish and never forget. I suppose the same could be said of all good parents, but they are my parents and they are special.

It is also dedicated to Edwin Emery, Emeritus Professor of Journalism and Mass Communication at the University of Minnesota, who was my doctoral adviser and dissertation chairman. He gave freely and unselfishly of his time and knowledge, and tolerated the sometimes annoying, sometimes naive questions that all doctoral students are prone to ask. We may disagree in our interpretations of journalism history, but he taught me to be independent and he encouraged the discourse we enjoyed at Minnesota. I shall always feel privileged to have studied with Edwin Emery whose knowledge of the history of journalism is unsurpassed.

I am indebted to each of the contributors to this volume for their hard work and patience, and for their expertise. I am especially indebted to Dwight Jensen of Syracuse University who unselfishly volunteered to write a bushel of entries very late in the project after several contributors were unable to complete their assignments.

A sincere "Thank You" is extended to Cynthia Harris, my editor at Greenwood Press, for her patience with the sometimes slow progress of my work, and for her timely advice and suggestions; and to Paul Kobasa and Mary Sive, acquisition editors at Greenwood Press, whose encouragement and suggestions were invaluable in the early stages of this project.

Finally, my heartfelt appreciation and affection goes to my wife, Annamae, and my three sons, Michael, Evan, and Douglas, for their support and understanding during the years I worked on this volume. They have had to live with it every day as I have, and are not any less happier than I am that it is finally finished.

ABBREVIATIONS

ACAB	Appleton's Cyclopaedia of American Biography
AWW	American Women Writers
BARB	Black American Reference Book
BHB	Biographical History of Blacks
CA	Contemporary Authors
CB	Current Biography
DAB	Dictionary of American Biography
DANB	Dictionary of American Negro Biography
DLB	Dictionary of Literary Biography
DNB	Dictionary of National Biography
EAB	Encyclopedia of American Biography
FAN	Famous American Negroes
NAW	Notable American Women
NCAB	National Cyclopaedia of American Biography
NYT	New York Times

b.	date of birth
d.	date of death
q.v.	also included in the dictionary

A

ABBOT, WILLIS JOHN (b. 16 March 1863; d. 19 May 1934) was a nationally recognized newspaper journalist, author, and peace advocate. He worked for the *Christian Science Monitor*, the *New York Journal*, and *Chicago Times*, and other newspapers. His journalistic career is something of a paradox, moving successfully from William Randolph Hearst's (q.v.) "yellow" press to the idealistic and responsible *Christian Science Monitor*. In addition to his newspaper work, Abbot authored more than twenty books. He was influential as an articulate spokesperson and leader in debates about political and social issues of the day because of his intense activity to promote individual political candidates and world peace.

Abbot, the only child of Waldo and Julia (Holmes) Abbot, was born in New Haven, Connecticut. Young Abbot's mother was widowed in 1864 when his father, a collector at the port of Key West, Florida, died of yellow fever. Abbot's mother married Sabin Smith and the family moved to Chicago, Illinois. There Abbot's interest in social and political issues was sparked and nurtured as he listened to radical labor speakers and observed their activities. In 1880 he attended the first of twenty-one national political conventions in which he would participate during his lifetime.

Abbot studied literature at the University of Michigan from 1881 to 1883, but transferred to the law school where he earned a LL.B. in 1884. Moving to New Orleans for his health, Abbot accepted an offer to work as a cub reporter at the *Times-Democrat*. While there he also worked as a correspondent for the *New York World*.

In 1886 he took his second reporting job, writing for the *New York Tribune*. In 1887 he and some newspaper associates launched what he called the most expensive school of journalism in the country. Their *Kansas City Evening News*, of which Abbot was editor in chief, folded in 1889 because of fierce competition with William R. Nelson's (q.v.) *Star*, and the collapse of Kansas City's economic boom. On 30 November 1887 Abbot married Marie Amanda Mack, daughter of a merchant, Christian Mack, of Ann Arbor, Michigan.

After the collapse of the *News*, Abbot returned to his boyhood home of Chicago to become an editorial writer for the *Chicago Evening Mail*, becoming managing editor in 1892. He refined his journalistic skills and nurtured his political interests by helping the *Mail*'s owner, Carter Henry, to be reelected mayor of Chicago.

It was during this period that Abbot developed an interest in, and admiration for, the populist movement. Endorsing "people's" candidates and causes, Abbot became preoccupied with political problems and issues of silver, taxes, and peace that would demand his attention the rest of his career.

Attracted to the rising fortunes of Hearst, Abbot went to work as editor in chief for Hearst's *New York Journal* in 1895, beginning an association that lasted for nearly two decades. He continued to be engrossed in politics and actively served as chairman of Henry George's (q.v.) campaign for reelection as mayor of New York in 1897.

The National Democratic Convention of 1896 was one of the most memorable events Abbot covered. His admiration for William Jennings Bryan motivated him to promote Jennings's election among other journalists. Abbot continued his active involvement in politics by managing the Democratic national press bureau for the presidential campaign of 1900, and again in 1908, and by writing a very effective pro-Democratic newspaper column for the Republican *Chicago Tribune*.

Marie Abbot died in 1903, leaving Abbot with a son, Waldo Mack. On 12 April 1905 Abbot married a Detroit banker's daughter, Elsie Maples, who survived him without children.

After 1890 Abbot contributed prolifically to magazines such as *Review of Reviews*, *Literary Digest*, *New Republic*, *Outlook*, *Forum*, *Munsey's*, and *Harper's Weekly*, writing about domestic and foreign public affairs, travel, and interesting people. He was editor and part owner of the Battle Creek, Michigan, *Pilgrim* monthly magazine from 1900 to 1903; chief editorial writer for Hearst's *New York American* from 1905 to 1916 with a brief respite from 1908 to 1911; special political writer for the *Chicago Tribune* in 1908; a writing editor for the *New York Sun* from 1916 to 1917; and political writer for the *Chicago American* in 1917. He also served as correspondent for *Collier's Weekly*, the *London Times*, and the *Washington Herald*. He was vigorously pro-Ally during 1914–17, and withdrew from Hearst's *Chicago American* staff when the newspaper reported that the sinking of the *Lusitania* was a legitimate military incident.

On 30 January 1921 Abbot became the third editor of the *Christian Science Monitor*. A Christian Scientist since experiencing a cure for nervous prostration and insomnia, he worked with great devotion to rebuild the *Monitor*, which had suffered from reduced circulation because of in-fighting for control between the church's board of directors and the publishing society's board. Within five years the newspaper's circulation approached 130,000. The staff was revitalized, overseas bureaus strengthened, and the editorial policy changed to more effectively promote "ideals of decency and constructiveness."

Abbot took particular interest in working with peace advocates from both sides of the Atlantic and in promoting the *Monitor*'s peace plan, suggested in 1923 and 1924. The plan proposed a constitutional amendment subjecting property to conscription for war along with citizens. It was formally introduced into both houses of Congress and seriously explored in hearings. He also took great satisfaction in the newspaper's enthusiastic fight against repeal of the Eighteenth Amendment.

In 1927 he became a member of the governing board of the *Monitor* and a contributing editor to the paper, posts he held until his death. During this period he spent much of his time traveling in Europe, writing about international relations and events for his regular column entitled "Watching the World Go By."

The many political and social groups to which he belonged were generally dedicated to tireless promotion of responsible journalism and world peace. He was one of the founders of the American Society of Newspaper Editors. Abbot was honored by Greece and Romania for international service. His alma mater, the University of Michigan, conferred on him an honorary doctor of laws degree in 1927. In 1943 a Liberty ship was named in his honor.

Abbot died in Brookline, Massachusetts, of undiagnosed causes. He was cremated and his ashes were interred at Mount Auburn Cemetery in Cambridge, Massachusetts.

BIBLIOGRAPHY:

A. *Headlining Happiness* (Boston, 1925); *Watching the World Go By* (Boston, 1933).

B. DAB 11, 1–2; DLB 29, 3–11; NYT 20 and 21 May 1934; E. D. Canham, *Commitment to Freedom: The Story of the "Christian Science Monitor"* (Boston, 1958).

J. DOUGLAS TARPLEY

ABBOTT, LYMAN (b. 18 December 1835; d. 22 October 1922) was a liberal theologian, author, and editor of semireligious magazines for fifty years. He was famous in his time as a popularizer of the doctrine that it is more important to have faith in oneself and in one's fellow men than faith in God.

Abbott, third and youngest son of Jacob and Harriet (Vaughan) Abbott, was born in Roxbury, Massachusetts, just west of Boston. His father, a professor and author of the Rollo series of children's books, became controversial in the 1830s for declaring that Christ was man but not God. Abbott's mother, often infirm, died in childbirth when he was seven. He spent the next several years under the care of his aunts, "a lonely, homeless, outcast boy," as he later recalled in *Reminiscences*.

Abbott received an A.B. from New York University in 1853, then passed the bar exam and joined his two brothers in a New York law firm. He also became a law reporter for the *New York Times*. On 14 October 1857 Abbott married his second cousin, Abby Frances Hamlin, and settled in Brooklyn. Influenced by his father and by the popular liberal minister Henry Ward Beecher (q.v.), Abbott studied theology and was ordained in 1860. From 1860 to 1868 he presided over churches in Indiana and New York, but dissension within his last congregation helped him to realize his future was as a writer. He began contributing regularly to *Harper's*, and to Beecher's magazine, *Christian Union*. From 1868 to 1876 Abbott wrote a biography of Jesus and commentaries on the four Gospels and the Acts of the Apostles while editing a small newspaper, the *Illustrated Christian Weekly*.

Abbott's big break came at age forty-one. When Beecher was charged with adultery the circulation of *Christian Union* dropped sharply, and Abbott was made editor in 1876. He rescued the magazine by having it appeal to those who looked upon the Bible as fable rather than fact. Abbott eventually took Christianity out of the journal's title as well as its pages. The magazine was renamed *Outlook* in 1893. In political matters Abbott argued for the establishment of a national citizens' committee comprised of 50–100 lawyers, educators, ministers, and merchants. Like latter-day Platonic philosopher kings, they supposedly would know where the public interest lay even when the public was confused. In economics, Abbott championed what he called "industrial democracy," which included federal ownership of the telephone and telegraph, and the power to take over other industries.

Abbott was editor of *Outlook* until his death after a lingering respiratory attack in 1922. In the 1890s he succeeded Beecher as preacher at Brooklyn's Plymouth Church, but he became best known for books which attacked biblical Christianity in the name of evolution. In 1915, while millions were dying in European trenches, one of Abbott's *Outlook* editorials proclaimed that the world was a better world to live in than it was fifty years earlier. There was no need to stress original sin or other Christian statements, Abbott declared. As his father and Beecher had argued before him, Abbott held that there was a force in the universe which always was with humankind. His many supporters applauded his popularizing ability: One critic wrote that Abbott was a master of style, a rhetorician, but not a profound scholar, an original thinker, nor a logician.

Abbott was survived by his four sons and two daughters. His wife died in 1907 after an attack of pneumonia. *Outlook* survived him for a while, but died in 1935.

BIBLIOGRAPHY:

A. *The Theology of an Evolutionist* (Boston, 1897); *The Other Room* (New York, 1903); *The Great Companion* (New York, 1904); *Reminiscences* (Boston, 1915); *What Christianity Means to Me: A Spiritual Autobiography* (New York, 1921).

B. DAB 1, 24–25; NYT 23 October 1922; Ira V. Brown, *Lyman Abbott, Christian Evolutionist* (Cambridge, Mass., 1953).

MARVIN N. OLASKY

ABBOTT, ROBERT SENGSTACKE (b. 28 November 1868; d. 29 February 1940) probably had no idea when he founded the *Chicago Defender* in 1905 that it would become one of the few daily black newspapers in America and the flagship for the largest black newspaper chain in the United States.

Abbott was born at Fort Frederica, St. Thomas Island, off the coast of Savannah, Georgia. His father, Thomas, and mother, Flora, were former slaves and operated a grocery store on the island. Following the death of Thomas Abbott in 1869, Flora moved, with her son, to Savannah and in 1874 married John Herman Henry Sengstacke, the son of a German father and a black mother. Born in America, Sengstacke had been reared in Germany and returned to the United States in 1869. Abbott later added the Sengstacke name to his. Abbott's stepfather was a teacher, minister, and later editor of the *Woodville Times*, which served a black community on the outskirts of Savannah.

Abbott attended Hampton Institute in Virginia and later graduated from the Kent College of Law in Chicago in 1899, but he was never admitted to the bar. However, during his years as editor and publisher of the *Defender*, he was awarded honorary degrees from Wilberforce University in Ohio and Morris Brown College in Georgia. He was also elected president of the Hampton Institute Alumni Association.

After jobs as a printer, an occupation he had learned in Savannah while working for a white newspaper and had later studied at Hampton, Abbott founded the *Defender* with hardly the bare necessities. His office was rented desk space in a real estate and insurance office, and his furnishings were a card table and a borrowed kitchen chair. His total capital was twenty-five cents, which went for notebooks and pencils.

Abbott was practically a one-man show during the infant days of the *Defender*. He served as editor, publisher, reporter, and even newsboy. However, within ten years the *Defender* emerged as America's leading black newspaper with an estimated circulation of 230,000. The paper had branch offices in key cities in the United States and one in London.

Often referred to as a sensational journal for its front-page coverage of crime stories, the *Defender* also led the fight for better treatment of blacks in general and in the military. During World War I Abbott asked why blacks should fight for democracy abroad when they could not taste its fruits at home. His editorials prompted several investigations by the FBI. Abbott and his *Defender* are also credited with urging thousands of blacks to leave the South and migrate North shortly after World War I. So intense was his campaign that the *Defender* was banned from certain sections of the South.

Like most black editors of his time, Abbott was a crusader for the rights of his people. Abbott outlined seven goals for which his newspaper would push; (1) the obliteration of race prejudice; (2) racially unrestricted membership in all trade unions; (3) equal employment opportunities in all jobs, public and private; (4) true representation in all police forces; (5) complete cessation of all school segregation; (6) establishment of open occupancy in all housing; and (7) federal intervention to protect civil rights in all instances where civil rights compliance at the state level broke down. However, showing that to be ''pro-black'' did not mean ''anti-white,'' the *Defender* became the first black newspaper with an integrated staff.

Abbott was married twice. His first marriage was to Helen Thornton Morrison on 10 September 1918. At the time he was approaching his fiftieth birthday. They had no children. Following a divorce, he married Edna Brown Dennison on 7 August 1934. Abbott died from a complex of illnesses in 1940.

Control of the *Defender* was turned over to Abbott's nephew, John H. Sengstacke, the son of his brother, Alexander. Under his guidance the paper continued to grow. In 1956 he converted the weekly into one of America's few black daily newspapers. Sengstacke is also responsible for developing the Sengstacke newspaper chain, which is the largest black newspaper chain in the United States.

BIBLIOGRAPHY:

A. Robert S. Abbott, "Looking Back," *Chicago Defender*, 4 May 1935.

B. BARB, 852–859; BHB, 244–245; DAB 11, 2–3; FAN, 76–81; *Chicago Defender*, 2 and 9 March 1940; Roi Ottley, *The Lonely Warrior* (Chicago, 1955); Roland E. Wolseley, *The Black Press, U.S.A.* (Ames, 1971); "Robert Abbott: Defender of His Race," *Ebony*, June 1955.

J. WILLIAM SNORGRASS

ABEL, ELIE (b. 17 October 1920) served as a national and international correspondent for major American news organizations for a quarter of a century before becoming the fifth dean of Columbia University's Graduate School of Journalism in 1970. He covered the principal diplomatic relations stories stemming from the cold war that followed World War II, and he served as a key source of the news information which shaped American public opinion, and even policies, concerning the role of the United States in the postwar era.

Upon graduation from McGill University in 1941, Abel began as a reporter for the *Windsor* (Ontario) *Star*. During World War II, from 1942 to 1945, he served in the Royal Canadian Air Force as a radar man aboard flying boats based in Scotland, and later as a combat correspondent. After the war, he returned home to work as the assistant city editor of the *Montreal Gazette* from 1945 to 1946. Then he took two positions which gave him an opportunity to have his skills in preparation for later major diplomatic reporting posts. During 1946–47 he was a foreign correspondent in Berlin for the North American Newspaper Alliance, and from 1947 to 1949 he was the UN correspondent for the Overseas News Agency. During the second half of the 1940s, Abel covered the pivotal events shaping the present world order in the aftermath of World War II—the Nuremberg war crimes trials, the first attempts at four-power government in a divided Germany, the fledgling United Nations, and many others.

In 1949 Abel began a decade of association with the *New York Times*, for which he worked as a reporter in Detroit, Washington, Europe, and India. He directed the *Time*'s prizewinning coverage of the 1956 Hungarian uprising. Abel moved to the *Detroit News*, as Washington bureau chief, from 1959 to 1961 before switching to broadcast journalism.

From 1961 to 1969 Abel served in a series of senior positions with NBC News—first as State Department correspondent, then in 1964 as diplomatic correspondent, later, from 1965 to 1967, as London bureau chief, and finally from 1967 to 1969, as diplomatic correspondent in Washington.

In 1969 Abel was appointed Godfrey Lowell Cabot Professor of Journalism at Columbia University. On 1 February 1970 he became dean of the Graduate School of Journalism at Columbia. Since 1979 he has been the Harry and Norman Chandler Professor of Communication and chairman of the Department of Communications at Stanford University.

Abel was born in Montreal, Quebec, Canada, to Jacob Abel, a printer, and Rose Savetsky Abel. In addition to a B.A. from McGill University, he holds a M.S. in Journalism from Columbia University (1942) and an honorary doctor of laws degree which McGill awarded in 1971. Other honors include a Columbia Journalism Alumni Award for distinguished service to journalism (1966), a George Foster Peabody Award for outstanding radio news (1967), and an Overseas Press Club Award for the best interpretation of foreign news (1969).

Abel married Corinne Adelaide Prevost on 28 January 1946, and the couple have two children. Abel became a naturalized U.S. citizen in 1952. He has served as a member of the board of governors of the American Stock Exchange, beginning in 1972, and as chairman of the board of trustees of the Greater Washington Educational Television Association.

Abel's writing includes a series of books he has authored or coauthored. They include *The Kennedy Circle* (1961); *The Missile Crisis* (1966), published in England under the more descriptive title *The Missiles of October: The Story of the Cuban Missile Crisis*; a background study of America's role in Vietnam, with Marvin Kalb, *Roots of Involvement: The U.S. in Asia 1784–1971* (1971); a primary source document written with W. Averell Harriman, *Special Envoy to Churchill and Stalin, 1941–1946* (1975); and a sociological overview of the fourth estate, which Abel edited, *What's News: The Media in American Society* (1981).

BIBLIOGRAPHY:

B. CA 1961; NYT 20 December 1969; *Editor & Publisher*, 27 December 1969.

JAMES WESOLOWSKI

ADAMS, ANSEL EASTON (b. 20 February 1902; d. 22 August 1984) developed a technique of forming sharp clear photographs through the viewfinder and printing them without retouching or gimmickry to produce prints that made him probably America's best-known photographer, famous especially for his images of the American West.

Adams was born in San Francisco and trained as a concert pianist. He was making a living as a musician when, in 1930, a patron took him to Taos, New Mexico. Adams said later that Paul Strand's negatives, which he saw in Taos, profoundly influenced his concept of photography. Developing that concept, using it, and teaching it became his life's work. His work made him highly popular with artists and laymen alike. He was interested more in tone than in composition, and unified his pictures with light, which he learned to measure carefully while setting up his pictures. He worked always in black and white.

In 1916 Adams took his first photograph. He used a box Brownie camera to snap a scene in Yosemite National Park, California. He was fascinated by the park, and for four years in a row he worked summers as caretaker at the Sierra Club's lodge there. Later he served thirty-seven years as a director of the Sierra Club.

Adams practiced his photographic technique as he had practiced his piano technique. In 1933 he traveled to New York City to make his fortune and met Alfred Stieglitz (q.v.), who spent the morning in arrogant conversation with Adams and said in the afternoon that Adams's work consisted of the finest prints he had ever seen. Stieglitz gave Adams a one-man show at his American Place gallery in 1936, and Adams was successful from then on.

Adams married Virginia Best in 1928. In 1936 she inherited the photo concession at Yosemite, and the couple moved to the park, where they lived for about forty years. They had two children, Michael and Anne. Adams for a time did publicity work for the park, and he became the Sierra Club's official photographer. More mundanely, he photographed women's underwear for Stein and Company.

Adams published thirty-five books and portfolios of photographs, including a series of instructional books, the Basic Photo Series. He wrote articles on photographic technique for *Fortnightly* and *Camera Craft*. In the late 1970s Adams and his wife moved to Carmel, California. His name was so closely associated with Yosemite that one of the mountains there was informally known as Mount Ansel Adams.

In 1980 Adams received the Medal of Freedom, the highest award given by the U.S. government to a civilian. Adams died on the Monterey Peninsula at age eighty-two of heart disease. His ashes were scattered on the mountain known by his name, and about a year after his death, the mountain was officially named for him.

BIBLIOGRAPHY:

B. NYT 24 April 1984; Andrea Gray, *Ansel Adams, An American Place* (Tempe, 1982).

DWIGHT JENSEN

ADAMS, FRANKLIN PIERCE (b. 15 November 1881; d. 23 March 1960) was one of the most widely read newspaper columnists of the 1920s and 1930s. His column "The Conning Tower" was read for its gentle humor and for its insights into the genteel pleasures of New York's social life. It recorded the doings of the Round Table, the group of wits who met daily at the Algonquin Hotel and whose members included Adams, Alexander Woollcott (q.v.), Robert Benchley, George S. Kaufman, and Dorothy Parker. Parker's biographer, John Keats, has written, "To a word-struck college boy in the provinces, Mr. Adams' column was news from Olympus, and insofar as New York editors and journalists were concerned, mention in 'The Conning Tower' was the equivalent of the accolade."

"F.P.A.," as he was known to his readers, was born in Chicago, Illinois, the son of Moses Adams, a dry-goods merchant, and Clara Schlossman Adams. He attended Chicago public schools and was graduated from the Armour Institute of Technology in 1899. He attended the University of Michigan for less than a year.

After three years in the insurance business, Adams joined the staff of the *Chicago Journal* in 1903, producing a daily weather column and, later, a humor column for $25 a week. The humor column succeeded in part because of Adams's use of readers' contributions.

In 1904 he accepted a position with Henry Stoddard's *New York Evening Mail*, for which he wrote a daily humor column, "Always in Good Humor." The column consisted of informal essays spiced with wordplay (such as his characterization of a novelist's obsession with death as "cremative art") and light verse, such as his slang translations of Horace's odes and his mock elegy, "Baseball's Sad Lexicon." Beginning in 1911, the humor column alternated with his parody of Samuel Pepys's diary, a daily record of Adams's social life; his dislike of movies, ballet, and opera; and his love of good conversation, literature, and poker.

When he moved to the *New York Tribune* in 1914, he retained both columns, the diary running on Saturday, because he said he needed a day's rest from the humor column, renamed "The Conning Tower." He continued the practice begun in Chicago of accepting contributions to the column. At the end of each year he awarded the writer with the most, rather than the best, contributions because he felt that any contribution accepted by him meant that it was peerless. His unpaid contributors, many of them appearing in print for the first time, included Kaufman, Ring Lardner (q.v.), James Thurber, John O'Hara, and Parker. Their contributions and Adams's observations about topics as diverse as censorship, paper towels, and bad grammar made "The Conning Tower" popular for over thirty years.

During World War I, Adams served as a captain in the intelligence service and wrote a column for *Stars and Stripes*. His colleagues on the AEF newspaper included Grantland Rice, Harold Ross (qq.v.), and Woollcott. After the war he returned to the *Tribune* and remained until 1922, when he moved to the *New York World*. In some respects the *World* was New York's most prestigious newspaper, and Adams joined a roster on the op-ed page that came to include columnists Walter Lippmann and Heywood Broun (qq.v.), music critic Deems Taylor, and drama critic Woollcott. When the Pulitzer brothers sold the *World* in 1931, Adams moved to the *New York Herald Tribune*. He left after six years in a squabble over his salary; he argued he was worth more than publisher Ogden Reid was paying because his column was syndicated in six newspapers. Adams also wrote for the *New York Post* between 1938 and 1941.

In 1938 Adams became a panelist on the ''Information Please'' radio program, a quiz show for which listeners submitted questions to a panel of experts that included John Kieran and Oscar Levant. The program proved so popular that it was the basis for a series of movie shorts from 1939 to 1942. The series was cited by *Saturday Review* for service to literature. Adams remained with ''Information Please'' until it was canceled in 1948.

Adams was married twice. His first marriage, to Minna Schwartz, ended in divorce. He married Esther Sayles Root in 1925. They had four children: Anthony, Timothy, Jonathan, and Persephone.

Adams suffered from arteriosclerosis and spent his last years in a New York nursing home. In his funeral eulogy, playwright Marc Connelly, Adams's friend from the Algonquin days, said, ''Rejoicing in the truth, he used mockery in a civilized therapeutic way. His wit was never mean. He hated only the ugly. He stimulated more writers in the Twenties and Thirties than any other person. He was a constant, brilliant light.''

BIBLIOGRAPHY:

A. *Weights and Measures* (Garden City, N.Y., 1917); *Something Else Again* (Garden City, N.Y., 1920); *Overset* (Garden City, N.Y., 1922); *Half a Loaf* (Garden City, N.Y., 1927); *The Diary of Our Own Samuel Pepys* (New York, 1935); *Nods and Becks* (New York, 1944).

B. DAB Supp. 6, 93–96; DLB 29, 18–25; NYT 24 March 1960; Margaret Chase Harriman, *The Vicious Circle* (New York, 1951); Gerald Johnson, ''No Taste for Trivia,'' *New Republic*, 11 April 1960; John Keats, *You Might As Well Live* (New York, 1970).

HARRIS E. ROSS

ADAMS, SAMUEL (b. 27 September 1722; d. 2 October 1803) was the leading propagandist of the American Revolution. He wrote articles and editorials for several Boston papers, was an influential speaker, and organized radical committees and demonstrations.

Adams was born on his family's large estate on Purchase Street in Boston. His father, Samuel, was a man of substantial wealth and influence who dealt in real estate and owned a brewery. The elder Samuel Adams was also active in politics. Adams's mother was the former Mary Fifield. Adams was educated at Harvard, where he received a bachelor's degree in 1740 and a master's three years later. He also briefly studied law, although lawyers were then held in low esteem.

After graduation, Adams established his own business with a loan from his father, but he lost the entire investment and joined his father's brewery. Although Adams would never be a business success, he soon found a more amenable vocation, again through his father's help. The elder Samuel Adams met with a group of politically active men as the Caucus Club, which founded a newspaper, the *Independent Advertiser*, in 1748. Young Sam Adams became editor of the paper and wrote political essays for it until it folded in 1750.

After the demise of the *Independent Advertiser*, Adams concentrated his literary work on the *Boston Gazette* and later the *Massachusetts Spy*. He wrote under at least a score of pseudonyms, including "Candidus," "Vindex," "Popicola," and "Observation." His political essays were based on the philosophy of John Locke, embracing the concept of a political compact; his writings were jeremiads, full of a concentrated bitterness and increasingly radical as anti-British diatribes.

Adams also continued his political activities and served as a member of the Massachusetts General Court from 1765 to 1774. As clerk of that body he was given the task of writing certain official documents.

Adams was also a skillful organizer, politician, public speaker, and writer of polemics, and his activities in the decade prior to the Revolution brought him increased influence and notoriety. With John Hancock he formed the Sons of Liberty in 1765, and organized the Committees of Correspondence in 1772. That same year he drafted the Boston declaration of rights, and a year later he instigated and led the Boston Tea Party. His passionate, if highly biased, accounts of British "atrocities" were circulated throughout the colonies.

Adams, along with his cousin John, served as a delegate to the First Continental Congress, and his radical activities finally became too much for the British. General Gage received orders to seize Adams and Hancock at Lexington on 19 April 1775, but they were warned by Paul Revere and Joseph Warren and escaped to Woburn. Adams then went to Philadelphia for the Second Continental Congress, in which he served until 1781.

He was a member of the committee which had drafted the Articles of Confederation, and he opposed a strong federal government. Still, his support for the Constitution was influential in the Massachusetts legislature's narrow passage of the document.

After the Revolution, Adams continued in state politics as a senator and member of the council, then as lieutenant governor from 1789 to 1793. Upon the death of Hancock, Adams succeeded Hancock as governor of Massachusetts, and was later elected to the post, serving in that role from 1794 to 1797.

Adams married twice, first to Elizabeth Checkley in 1749; she died in 1757. Eight years later he wed Elizabeth Wells. He had two children; his only son, Samuel, was a surgeon who died in 1788. Samuel Adams died in 1803.

BIBLIOGRAPHY:

A. *The Writings of Samuel Adams*, ed. Henry A. Cushing, 4 vols. (New York, 1904–1908).

B. DAB 1, 95–100; Stewart Beach, *Samuel Adams: The Fateful Years, 1764–1776* (New York, 1965); John C. Miller, *Samuel Adams: Pioneer in Propaganda* (Boston, 1936); W. V. Wells, *Life and Public Service of Samuel Adams*, 3 vols. (Boston, 1865).

CAROLYN G. CLINE

ADAMS, SAMUEL HOPKINS (b. 26 January 1871; d. 16 November 1958) muckraked the patent medicine industry and so helped—with Upton Sinclair—to bring about the Pure Food and Drug Act. He also was a hotshot crime reporter for the *New York Sun*, 1891–1900; managing editor of McClure's syndicate,

1900–1901; a staff member of *McClure's* magazine, 1903–1905; and, in the later part of his long life, a prolific producer of popular novels, sketches, biographies, and children's books.

His most controversial book was *Revelry*, a fictionalized version of the life of President Warren G. Harding—suppressed in Washington, and condemned by several state legislatures. Adams also chronicled the period in a nonfiction work, *The Incredible Era*. Another novel, *Flaming Youth*, written under the pseudonym of Walter Fabian, also characterized the 1920s. A series of works, including *Grandfather Stories*, which won the National Book Award for 1955, were careful re-creations of New York state life, from the building of the Erie Canal to the turn of the century.

Adams's chief biographical works were on his friend Alexander Woollcott (q.v.); Daniel Webster, *The Godlike Daniel*; and Margaret O'Neill, *The Gorgeous Hussy*, President Andrew Jackson's hostess.

Adams was born in Dunkirk, New York, the son of Myron Adams, a Presbyterian minister, and Hester Rose Hopkins Adams, whose father was a professor of theology in Auburn. Young Adams attended Hamilton College, doing some writing but also thinking of a medical career. But after graduation in 1891, he joined the *New York Sun*, where his knack of seizing upon little out-of-the-way incidents, in the *Sun* style, gave him assignments on sensational murders and robberies. He remained there until 1900, when the mercurial S. S. McClure hired him as managing editor of the McClure syndicate. He was with McClure, in advertising and on the staff of *McClure's*, until 1905, when he went free-lance.

That fall, *Collier's* published his series on patent medicines—what went into them, how they were marketed, and how low their medical value was. For the series, "The Great American Fraud," he drew upon personal knowledge of the industry, since some of the manufacturers were located in upstate New York. An outcome, the Pure Food and Drug Act, was stricter labeling and control over advertising claims. His prominence, because of the series, and interest in health later led to work with the Committee of 100 on National Health, the National Consumers League, and the National Conference of Charities.

In 1907 he joined with Stewart Edward White in writing a successful novel, *The Mystery*, and followed it, on his own, with *The Flying Death*. After that, his writing career flourished—over fifty books and over one hundred magazine articles and stories for leading publications, as well as movie scripts and even a play or two. He recognized that he was not producing great literature. But his books always were highly readable, and, in the series on New York life—*Canal Town*, *Banner by the Wayside*, *Dawn to Dusk*, and *Grandfather Stories*—carefully researched and entertaining. He wrote everything three times, Adams once told an interviewer.

Three of his novels, *The Clarion*, *Common Cause*, and *Success*, reflected his lifelong liberalism and ideals about journalism. In each he railed at advertisers, politicians, and corrupt newspapermen who, he felt, sought to turn newspapers from their primary task of providing factual information for society. He also investigated deceptive advertising for the *New York Tribune* in 1915–16.

A small, slight, and gregarious man, Adams maintained a summer home in Auburn, New York, and a winter home in Beaufort, South Carolina, where he died in 1958 after a long bout with heart disease. His 1898 marriage to Elizabeth R. Noyes of Charleston, West Virginia, ended in divorce. In 1915 he married Jane Peyton Van Norman, an actress, of Milwaukee, Wisconsin, and Chicago, Illinois.

BIBLIOGRAPHY:

A. *Great American Fraud* (New York, 1906); *The Mystery* (New York, 1906); *Common Cause* (New York, 1919); *Success* (New York, 1921); *Revelry* (New York, 1926); *The Godlike Daniel* (New York, 1930); *The Gorgeous Hussy* (New York, 1934); *The Incredible Era* (New York, 1939); *Canal Town* (New York, 1944); *Alexander Woollcott* (New York, 1945); *Banner by the Wayside* (New York, 1947); *Sunrise to Sunset* (New York, 1950); *Erie Canal* (New York, 1956).

B. NYT 17 November 1958; James Stanford Bradshaw, "The Journalist as Pariah: Three Novels by S. H. Adams," *Journalism History*, Spring-Summer 1983; Serrell Hillman, "Samuel Hopkins Adams," *Saturday Review*, 20 December 1958.

JAMES STANFORD BRADSHAW

ADE, GEORGE (b. 9 February 1866; d. 16 May 1944) was, in the course of his career, a respected Chicago journalist, a nationally known writer of vernacular tales, and a Broadway playwright. His comic vignettes of street life and urban characters set a model for many later American humorists. The popularity of his plays and stories made him one of the most financially successful writers of his age.

Ade was born in Kentland, Indiana, a county seat eighty miles southeast of Chicago. The fifth of six children, he grew up in a typical midwestern small-town, middle-class environment. His father, John, was a bank cashier of modest means. His mother, Adaline Bush, was an Ohio native from a Scotch-Irish family. A dreamy boy with literary ambitions and no talent for farming, Ade entered Purdue University at age seventeen, graduating with a B.S. degree in 1887.

After a brief and uneventful apprenticeship in a Lafayette law office, Ade was offered a reporting job at the *Lafayette Morning News*, a newly formed Republican party organ. When the *News* folded, Ade got a job at the *Lafayette Call*, an evening paper. He shortly left that job as well, to become an advertising writer for a patent-medicine wholesaler.

When the company Ade worked for changed hands in June 1890, he decided to move to Chicago. His good friend and fraternity brother from Purdue, John T. McCutcheon (q.v.), had recently gotten a job in the art department of the *Chicago Morning News*, later called the *News-Record* and later still the *Record*. Ade landed a job there too. At first he wrote only weather stories, but within a year and a half he had become the paper's star reporter, covering a variety of important assignments, including the Homestead steel strike, the 1892

Democratic and Republican national conventions, and the John L. Sullivan–James J. Corbett fight.

Ade truly came into his own, however, as a daily columnist during the World's Columbian Exposition, held in Chicago in 1893. From May until October, he wrote a series of columns for the editorial page under the running title "All Roads Lead to the World's Fair." These stories, accompanied by McCutcheon's illustrations, attempted to convey the mood of the fair and to characterize its participants and visitors. After the fair closed, Ade and McCutcheon continued their collaboration. Ade's "Stories of the Streets and of the Town," which ran on the same page as Eugene Field's (q.v.) "Sharps and Flats," offered finely crafted portraits of Chicago's inhabitants, their haunts, and their everyday lives. A number of these sketches were later collected in the books *Artie* (1896), *Pink Marsh* (1897), and *Doc' Horne* (1899).

In 1897 Ade published "The Fable of Sister Mae, Who Did As Well As Could Be Expected," the first of his famous "fables in slang." Cast in traditional fable form but written in colloquial language and a laconic style, the fables won Ade a reputation as a first-rate American humorist. Soon they were widely syndicated in American newspapers and magazines and collected in *Fables in Slang* (1900), *More Fables* (1900), and *Forty Modern Fables* (1901).

Leaving the *Record* in 1900 to become a free-lance writer, Ade turned his attention from journalism to theater, one of his lifelong loves. He wrote over twenty plays and musicals in the next twenty years, including his two biggest Broadway hits, *The County Chairman* (1903) and *The College Widow* (1903). In the 1920s Ade wrote a number of screenplays for films as well as a series of autobiographical sketches for *Hearst's International Magazine*, and in 1931 he published a humorous reminiscence entitled *The Old-Time Saloon*.

Ade was elected to the National Institute of Arts and Letters in 1908 and received honorary doctorates from Purdue University in 1926 and Indiana University in 1927. Never married, he traveled extensively from 1904 on and lived at his 400-acre estate in Hazelden, Indiana. Ade suffered a stroke in June 1943 and died less than a year later.

BIBLIOGRAPHY:

A. *Artie* (Chicago, 1896); *The Old-Time Saloon* (New York, 1931); with John T. McCutcheon, *Notes and Reminiscences* (Chicago, 1940); *Stories of the Streets and of the Town*, ed. Franklin J. Meine (Chicago, 1941; rpt. 1963); *The Permanent Ade*, ed. Fred C. Kelly (Indianapolis, 1947); *The America of George Ade*, ed. Jean Shepherd (New York, 1960).

B. DAB Supp. 3, 2–4; NYT 17 May 1944; Lee Coyle, *George Ade* (New York, 1964); Fred C. Kelly, *George Ade, Warmhearted Satirist* (Indianapolis, 1947); Lowell Matson, "Ade: Who Needed None," *Literary Review*, Autumn 1961; Dorothy R. Russo, *A Bibliography of George Ade, 1866–1944* (Indianapolis, 1947).

JOHN J. PAULY

ALLEN, RILEY HARRIS (b. 30 April 1884; d. 2 October 1966) was editor of the *Honolulu Star-Bulletin* from 1912 to 1918 and from 1921 until his retirement in 1960. During more than fifty years as a journalist and community activist he helped shape modern Hawaiian journalism and lead Hawaii's statehood movement.

The only son of Riley Harris and Anvaline Beck Allen was born in Colorado City, Texas. After the death of his father, his mother moved to Kentucky and then to Seattle, Washington, where Allen and his two sisters were raised. His mother, who sold real estate and taught school, encouraged Allen's interest in writing and journalism. He attended the University of Washington from 1902 to 1903, and the University of Chicago where he graduated in 1904. He worked for the *Chicago Daily News*, and the *Seattle Post-Intelligencer* (1904–1905) before going to Hawaii as a reporter for Wallace Farrington's (q.v.) *Honolulu Evening Bulletin*.

In 1906 Allen returned to the mainland to be closer to his family, but the lure of the islands and the invitation to serve as Farrington's city editor called him back in 1910. In 1912 Allen was named editor of the *Honolulu Star-Bulletin*, a merger of Farrington's *Evening Bulletin* and the *Hawaii Star*, started in 1893. With the exception of a three-year interval when he served with the American Red Cross assisting in the relocation of 800 children uprooted during the Russian Revolution, Allen was the guiding force behind the newspaper which became the largest in the territory.

An admirer of Progressive Republican editor William Allen White (q.v.), Allen promoted the ideas of education, suffrage, and self-governance in news stories and editorials on behalf of the multiracial American possessions in the Pacific. Along with Farrington, who was territorial governor from 1921 to 1929, Allen helped articulate and implement an ongoing crusade for statehood. The *Star-Bulletin*'s editorial policy contrasted with that of the islands' other major daily, the *Honolulu Advertiser*, which opposed statehood until after World War II.

Allen received national attention on 7 December 1941 for his role in mustering a staff and getting out a newspaper on the Pearl Harbor attack before the last Japanese planes had returned to aircraft carriers waiting off Oahu. He also fought against military governance and censorship in Hawaii. He was a member of the American Society of Newspaper Editors, the Hawaii Equal Rights Commission (predecessor of the Hawaii Statehood Commission), and dozens of local organizations for Hawaiian, Chinese, Japanese, Puerto Rican, and Filipino ethnic associations which he sponsored and gave credibility to in the *Star-Bulletin*.

After his retirement Allen served as a trustee of the Farrington estate, and along with Farrington's daughter-in-law, Allen opposed the merger of the *Star-Bulletin* with its competitor the *Advertiser* in a joint operating agreement. Allen was unsuccessful, however, and the publication was purchased by outside interests. The paper was eventually sold to the Gannett organization. Allen was preceded in death by his wife, Suzanne McArdle, whom he married on 6 September 1910.

BIBLIOGRAPHY:

A. *Wallace Farrington: Newspaperman* (Honolulu, 1937).

B. NYT 3 October 1966; Alf Pratte, "A History of the *Honolulu Star-Bulletin*, 1820–1966," M.A. thesis, Brigham Young Univ., 1967; Paul Alfred Pratte, "Ke Alaká i: The

Leadership Role of the *Honolulu Star-Bulletin* in the Hawaiian Statehood Movement,'' Ph.D. diss., Univ. of Hawaii, 1976.

ALF PRATTE

ALSOP, JOSEPH (b. 11 October 1910) retired from active political journalism at the end of 1974 after a distinguished career that saw him become the dean of American national columnists. He continued to write about art and archaeology, which he had pursued as hobbies.

Joseph Wright Alsop V was born in Avon, Connecticut, the son of Joseph Wright Alsop IV and Corinne Douglas Robinson Alsop. He is related to both prominent branches of the Roosevelt family, and although he came from a family of Republicans, he became a classic New Deal liberal Democrat.

He attended Groton prep school and Harvard University, and upon his graduation cum laude in 1932 he became a reporter on the staff of the *New York Herald Tribune*. He began in the city room, and in 1936 went to Washington, D.C., to cover capitol news for the *Herald Tribune*. In 1937 he and Robert E. Kintner began writing a nationally syndicated column called ''The Capitol Parade.''

In 1940 Alsop entered the U.S. Navy as an officer. He served in the Far East during World War II. Both he and his brother Stewart (q.v.), who served in the armed forces in Europe (and whose biographical sketch in this volume should be read in conjunction with Joseph's), came out of the war impressed that their preconceptions of a foreign country were much changed by their firsthand experience.

It was thus natural when the war ended and they became partners in writing a political column that they made it a point not to write about a foreign country or its leaders until at least one of them had visited that country under those leaders. Joseph invited Stewart to become his partner in the column, which they called ''Matter of Fact'' and which reached as many as 137 newspapers at a time during the twelve years they produced it. The partnership ended amicably in 1958. Joseph Alsop continued to write his column alone until he retired at the end of 1974. He said he lost the zest for his work. He considered himself the dean of American political columnists.

Alsop was a New Deal Democrat, an admirer of Franklin Roosevelt and of John Kennedy, and a combative individual who appeared to enjoy levying vigorous criticism on those he thought deserved it. He was a hawk in the Vietnam War years.

From 1971 to 1974 Joseph formed a new kind of collaboration with his brother; Stewart was dying of leukemia, and Joseph provided his brother with regular blood transfusions.

One of Alsop's advantages as a Washington reporter was that he began his career in the days when (as his brother Stewart pointed out) the reins of power still were held by the WASP establishment. He developed lines of information within it. He frequently knew the details of clandestine government operations, but thought it was improper to report them. He said it was one thing to be secretive about things everyone ought to know and another thing to be aggressive about reporting legitimate government secrets. He believed it was vital to report things that change national security. That attitude helped make Alsop a trusted man in Washington, and he had confidants at high levels. He entertained both John Kennedy and Richard Nixon in his home.

For most of his life, that was a bachelor's home. Alsop married Susan Mary Jay of Washington in 1961. They separated in 1974. They had no children.

Alsop became well known for two of his hobbies, art collecting and archaeology. He published books about both topics. His work on archaeology was critically acclaimed; his book about the history and practice of art collecting was less warmly received.

Alsop continues to work at his office in Washington, D.C.

BIBLIOGRAPHY:

A. With Stewart Alsop, *The Reporter's Trade* (New York, 1958).

DWIGHT JENSEN

ALSOP, STEWART (b. 17 May 1914; d. 26 May 1974) was a member of a distinguished New England family who carved his own distinguished career as a political commentator and concluded it by writing movingly and informatively about the leukemia that killed him.

Stewart Alsop was born in Avon, Connecticut. His father, Joseph Wright Alsop IV, was prominent in Connecticut politics. His mother, Corinne Douglas Robinson Alsop, was a relative of Franklin D. Roosevelt (and a first cousin to Eleanor) but was nevertheless a devout Republican; she made one of the seconding speeches for Alf Landon at the 1936 Republican convention.

Stewart attended Groton prep school in Massachusetts and received his B.A. from Yale in 1936. He went to work as an editor for Doubleday, Doran and Company in New York City. In his first published piece, in the *Atlantic*, he described himself as a Marxist liberal. He always voted Democratic except when George McGovern ran for president. But he was generally identified as a moderate, and he was annoyed during the 1960s when many described him as a conservative.

At the beginning of World War II Alsop was rejected by the American armed forces on medical grounds, but joined the British army as a member of the King's Royal Rifle Corps. Later he transferred to the U.S. Army and, working for the OSS, parachuted into France in 1944 to help the French resistance behind the German lines. He described his activities in the war in comic rather than heroic or dramatic terms. He claimed to have left the airplane too soon, landed in a tree, and spent more time socializing than making war.

He married an Englishwoman, Patricia (Tish) Hankey, on 20 June 1944 in England. They raised six children: Joseph Wright Alsop VI (Stewart's brother, whose biography is included in this volume, is Joseph Wright Alsop V), Ian, Elizabeth, Stewart, Richard, and Andrew.

When Stewart Alsop returned to the United States after the war his brother Joseph, already an established political journalist, invited him to be his partner in writing a political column. The pair wrote the column "Matter of Fact" from 1946 until 1958. Stewart's calm demeanor, he rarely raised his voice in public, complemented Joseph's. The coauthorship of the column was a stormy partnership that ended amicably in divorce.

While they worked together, the Alsops were strong advocates of openness in government. In 1950 they had already criticized the government for telling the American people less than one-tenth of what they ought to know about the atomic bomb. Stewart snapped at "Daddyknowsbestism," and in a joint article in *Harper's* they criticized the Atomic Energy Commission for its attack on J. Robert Oppenheimer.

In 1958 Stewart became the political editor of the *Saturday Evening Post*, a job he held until the magazine folded in 1968. He then became a political columnist for *Newsweek*. He opposed U.S. involvement in Vietnam and helped abolish the draft by saying that it operated on a fraudulent basis and that ending it would restore government authority and presidential dignity.

In 1971, Stewart Alsop was diagnosed as having a peculiar form of leukemia. The diagnosis was, in effect, a death sentence, and Alsop treated it as such. But he continued to write—not only his column, but also a book about his illness. In that book he combined memoirs and sober New England humor with anguish about his impending death and with solid reporting about his illness. Throughout his journalistic career he insisted on the importance of factual reporting—even by a columnist—and the unimportance of pontification.

Alsop (pronounced, he insisted, All-sop) is credited with originating a number of phrases that became common in American political language. He wrote first about "hawks and doves" in the debate about Vietnam, about John Kennedy's "Irish mafia," and about "eggheads" and "eyeball to eyeball" confrontations and "the Masada complex"—a phrase that drew him a scolding from Golda Meir.

After besieging him for almost three years, leukemia killed Stewart Alsop on 26 May 1974 at Bethesda, Maryland.

BIBLIOGRAPHY:

A. With Joseph Alsop, *The Reporter's Trade* (New York, 1958); *Stay of Execution: A Sort of Memoir* (Philadelphia, 1973).

B. NYT 27 May 1974.

DWIGHT JENSEN

AMES, MARY CLEMMER (b. 6 May 1831; d. 18 August 1884) was believed to be the highest-paid American newspaperwoman of the post–Civil War era. Her columns on politics and the Washington scene, titled "A Woman's Letter from Washington," appeared as a popular feature of the *Independent*, an influential New York weekly, from 1866 until her death. Ames, however, minimized her commitment to a career, always maintaining that a woman belonged in the home, although this conception of Victorian womanhood was not borne out by her own life. She divorced one husband, remarried, experimented with various forms of writing, developed contacts with leading politicians to gain material for her commentaries, and doggedly pursued success in journalism.

Born in Utica, New York, Ames took pride in her Anglo-Saxon background. She was the eldest of a large number of children, of whom seven lived to maturity. Her parents were Abraham Clemmer, of Alsatian Huguenot stock, and Margaret Clemmer, an immigrant from the British Isle of Man. Her impractical father struggled unsuccessfully to earn a living as a tobacconist, grocer, and merchant. The family moved about 1847 to Westfield, Massachusetts, where she attended the Westfield Academy and won acclaim for her poetry. It attracted the attention of Samuel Bowles (q.v.), editor of the *Springfield Republican*, who became her close friend.

The family's financial misfortunes prompted her marriage on 7 May 1851 to Daniel Ames, a Methodist minister in Enfield, Massachusetts, who subsequently held Presbyterian pastorates in New York and Minnesota. During the Civil War he took a federal job in Harpers Ferry, West Virginia, where she was imprisoned briefly by the Confederates and observed the surrender of the town to Union forces. She used her experiences as a basis for *Eirene* (1871), the best of her three novels. Her marriage, a mistake from the start, ended with a final separation in 1865 and a divorce in 1874. Following the divorce, she resumed her maiden name.

Driven by the need to support herself during a trial separation in 1859, Ames sent columns from New York City, where she was living with the acclaimed poets Alice and Phoebe Cary, to the *Utica* (New York) *Morning Herald* and to the *Springfield Republican*. The Carys presented her to Horace Greeley (q.v.) and other editors who encouraged her career aspirations. Discontinuing her efforts to write during the Civil War, she spent some time in Washington where she nursed in army hospitals. She also developed friendships with prominent men like Senator Justin S. Morrill of Vermont who later proved excellent sources for her newspaper columns.

Her first "Woman's Letter" appeared on 4 March 1866, proving a distinctive addition to Washington journalism. Declining to cover social events, Ames spent a considerable amount of time observing Congress and pinpointed lawmakers she thought guilty of ineptitude or moral failings. A Radical Republican, Ames accused President Andrew Johnson of betraying the newly freed black population. She backed suffrage for women but considered it less important than economic gains.

In her Washington correspondence Ames showed how a woman could function as a journalist by trading on the Victorian mystique that women possessed a higher spirituality than men. Thus she claimed the right to criticize public affairs in the name of morality and womanly "purity." She insisted a woman correspondent had no need to pattern herself after her male colleagues. Declining to enter the congressional press galleries, she viewed debates only from the ladies' galleries.

From 1869 to 1872 she also wrote for the *Brooklyn Daily Union*, which, like the *Independent*, was published by Henry C. Bowen. Her Brooklyn assignments, which included book reviews and even preparation of advertising copy, so impressed Bowen that in 1872 she received a salary of $5,000, thought to be the largest paid to an American newspaperwoman up to that time. Two volumes of comment on Washington drawn from her columns appeared in 1873.

In 1878 she suffered a skull fracture in a carriage accident and her literary output diminished although she wrote one book of poems (1883). On 19 June 1883 she was married to Edmund Hudson, editor of the *Army and Navy Register*. She died of a cerebral hemorrhage in Washington. She had no children.

BIBLIOGRAPHY:

A. *Outlines of Men, Women and Things* (New York, 1873); *Ten Years in Washington: Life and Scenes in the National Capital as a Woman Sees Them* (Hartford, 1875).

B. DLB 23, 3–7; NAW 1, 41; *Washington Evening Star*, 19 August 1884; "Mary Clemmer Ames: A Victorian Woman Journalist," *Hayes Historical Journal*, Spring 1978; Edmund Hudson, *An American Woman's Life and Work: A Memorial of Mary Clemmer* (Boston, 1886); Lilian Whiting, "Mary Clemmer, " in *Our Famous Women: An Authorized Record* (Hartford, 1886).

MAURINE H. BEASLEY

ANTHONY, SUSAN BROWNELL (b. 15 February 1820; d. 13 March 1906) was a reformer, active first in the temperance and abolition movements. However, as she met increasing prejudice against women's full involvement in public affairs she quickly grew more committed to the women's rights movement. *Revolution*, the suffrage newspaper that she began publishing in 1868, had an impact on the suffrage movement far beyond what its thirty-month life and small circulation list would suggest.

Born in 1820, Anthony was the second of the six children of Daniel and Lucy Read Anthony. Her father, owner of a cotton mill in Adams, Massachusetts, was a Quaker who was zealously moral, but he also occasionally rebelled against Quaker conservatism. Susan herself was rather serious, rigid, and prudish throughout her adolescence. In 1826 the Anthonys moved to Battenville, New York, where her father became managing partner of another mill. After the panic of 1838 the Anthonys ended up on a Rochester farm.

For the most part Susan, precocious as a child, was taught at home, although she briefly attended a public school and later a finishing school. She then held a number of low-paying teaching positions. She had a few gentlemen admirers in those days, but apparently had no interest, then or ever, in marriage, children, or homemaking.

Increasingly frustrated and eager to participate in reform causes, Anthony returned in 1849 to Rochester to work on behalf of temperance. After being informed that women could not address a temperance meeting, she organized the Woman's State Temperance Society of New York; Elizabeth Cady Stanton (q.v.) was president, and Anthony and Amelia Bloomer, then publisher and editor of the *Lily*, were secretaries. But in 1853 when men took over that organization, Anthony and Stanton resigned. For the next half century the two worked together closely, with the ever resourceful and politically astute Anthony always responsible for organizational and behind-the-scenes labor.

Before and during the Civil War, Anthony worked for the abolition movement. But after the war she and Stanton broke with mainstream reformers over the Fourteenth Amendment, which enfranchised black men, thereby introducing the word "male" into the Constitution; most reformers said this was "the Negro's hour."

While campaigning in Kansas for simultaneous enfranchisement of blacks and women, Stanton and Anthony met George Francis Train, an eccentric but wealthy Democrat, a Fenian and Copperhead. Train offered to finance a suffrage newspaper to be published by Anthony, and edited by Stanton and Parker Pillsbury, former editor of the *Anti-Slavery Standard*. Although they realized that the connection to Train would provoke considerable consternation among their Republican reform-minded friends, they accepted Train's money and conditions (that he be allowed to join their lecture tour, and that their paper publish a financial column by Train and his friend David Meliss, an editor of the *New York World*).

On 8 January 1868 appeared the first issue of *Revolution*. Its mottoes were "Men, their rights and nothing more; women, their rights and nothing less," as well as "Principle, not policy; Justice, not favors." Ten thousand copies were sent out under a congressional frank, and it was immediately recognized by both popular and reform papers for what it was: a self-consciously militant, aggressive, defiant paper which argued the cause of "strong-minded" women. *Revolution* crusaded for educated suffrage, coeducation, equal pay for equal work, and liberalized divorce law. Anthony, organizer of a working women's association, was responsible for *Revolution*'s advocacy of unionization of women workers and the opening up of new professions for women.

Immediately after *Revolution*'s initial publication, Train went to Ireland, where he was promptly jailed. A year later he officially severed his affiliation with the paper, ostensibly for the good of the cause. But suffragists remained divided over *Revolution*'s connection to various controversial figures, as well as over the generally radical style and highly politicized philosophy of the New York–based *Revolution* and the National Woman Suffrage Association, formed by Stanton in May 1869. In November 1869 more conservative suffragists formed a competing organization with its own paper, the Boston-based *Woman's Journal*.

Revolution attracted great attention, but it had only 3,000 subscribers and insufficient advertising. The expense of the weekly paper ultimately grew too great even for Anthony; after much agonizing, she sold the paper for a dollar to Laura Curtis Bullard, who transformed it into a genteel society journal. It took Anthony six years on the lecture circuit to pay off the $10,000 in debts the paper had incurred.

Although she preferred making history to writing it, the *History of Woman Suffrage*, begun in 1877, was Anthony's other major publishing venture. She wrote the first three volumes with Stanton and Matilda Joslyn Gage. She used the proceeds from a large bequest to distribute a fourth volume, which she wrote with Ida Husted Harper. (Harper, also Anthony's biographer, wrote a fifth and sixth volume as well.)

In 1872, in an attempt to test a theory that the Fourteenth Amendment had enfranchised women, Anthony registered to vote and cast her ballot in Rochester. For this she was arrested and convicted; having written his opinion before the trial, a hostile judge directed the jury to bring in a guilty verdict. She died of heart failure in 1906, fourteen years before women were constitutionally enfranchised. Once widely ridiculed if not denounced, Anthony came to enjoy respect and status. Between 1892 and 1900 she served as president of the National American Suffrage Association, and she was honored at women's conventions and congresses in both America and Europe.

BIBLIOGRAPHY:

A. With Elizabeth Stanton, Matilda J. Gage, and Ida H. Harper, *History of Woman Suffrage*, 4 vols. (New York, 1881–1902); "Woman's Half-Century of Evolution," *North American Review*, December 1902; "Achievement of Woman," *Collier's*, 10 January 1903.

B. DAB 1, 318–321; NAW 1, 51–57, NYT 13 March 1906; Rheta C. Dorr, *Susan B. Anthony, The Woman Who Changed the Mind of a Nation* (New York, 1928, reprinted 1970); Ida H. Harper, *The Life and Work of Susan B. Anthony*, 3 vols. (Indianapolis, 1898–1908); Elizabeth C. Stanton, "Susan B. Anthony," in *Our Famous Women: An Authorized Record* (Hartford, 1886).

LINDA STEINER

B

BACHE, BENJAMIN FRANKLIN (b. 12 August 1769; d. 10 September 1798) was the leading Republican editor in America in the 1790s. He was founder and editor of the *Aurora*, a paper strong in its opposition to the Federalist influence in the national government. He was the chief target of the Sedition Act and was arrested under it for his attacks on President John Adams.

Bache, the oldest son of Sarah Franklin—the only daughter of Benjamin Franklin (q.v.)—and Richard Bache, was born in Philadelphia, Pennsylvania. His father was a Whig merchant and succeeded Franklin as postmaster general.

In September 1776 Bache accompanied his grandfather to Europe, where he stayed nine years. He was educated in the liberal arts in France and Geneva and received instruction in printing in Paris. In September 1785 he returned to America and studied at the College of Philadelphia (now the University of Pennsylvania).

On 1 October 1790 Bache became the founder and editor of the *General Advertiser and Political, Commercial, Agricultural, and Literary Journal*. The paper's name was changed to *Aurora* (the name that had been used for a London journal) on 3 November 1794. The press and type with which the paper was begun are said to have been given to Bache by his grandfather, who died six months before the advent of the paper.

The *Aurora* contained extended accounts of European affairs and published full proceedings of Congress. It was notorious, though, for its involvement in the partisan newspaper warfare that characterized the 1790s.

Bache was friendly to the George Washington administration for a year or two, but his French sympathies soon made him a vigorous critic of the president. When Philip Freneau's (q.v.) *National Gazette* ceased publication in 1793, the *General Advertiser* assumed the role as the leading anti-Federalist journal.

In 1795 Bache accused Washington of illegally receiving advances on his salary. Federalists reacted indignantly. It was later discovered that Bache was right about the money.

In 1795 Senator George Mason of Virginia sent an advance copy of the Jay Treaty to Bache. Bache published the substance of the treaty on 29 June 1795 in the *Aurora*, and in pamphlet form on 1 July 1795. In 1796 he opened his columns to the French minister Adet who published a decree of the Directory, an address to the French in America, and sentimental appeals. In 1796 Bache also accused Washington of violating the Constitution, printed a burlesque poem for Washington's birthday, and reprinted forged letters of Washington, originally issued by the British in 1776. In Mary 1797 Bache, upon Washington's retirement, denounced him and all Federalist policies.

The Federalists tried on many occasions to silence Bache. He was barred from the House of Representatives throughout the 1797–1798 session. Bache was physically abused several times—although he never resorted to physical abuse. On 5 April 1797, while visiting a shipyard, Bache was attached by Abel Humphries, the son of a shipbuilder who had been criticized in the *Aurora*, and beaten severely around the head. On 7 May 1797, and again on 9 May, his house was attacked by mobs. With the aid of friends and neighbors, he drove them away.

The *Aurora* began to suffer financially, and Bache may have had to spend as much as $20,000 to keep it going.

On 16 June 1798 Bache printed a secret state paper from Talleyrand, French foreign minister, to American envoys in Paris attempting to solve a diplomatic crisis. Federalists claimed that publication of the letter proved that Bache was a French agent. On 26 June 1798 Bache was arrested on the charge of libeling President Adams under the Sedition Act. On 29 June he was freed on $4,000 bail. His trial was scheduled for October.

In August 1798 Bache was assaulted by John Ward Fenno, son of the Federalist editor John Fenno (q.v.). Bache continued to publish the *Aurora* in the late summer even though yellow fever had swept Philadelphia and many people had left the city. He contracted the fever on 5 September 1798 and died five days later.

On 17 November 1791 Bache had married a Danish woman, Margaret Hartman Markoe. Their son, Franklin Bache, made important contributions to the development of chemical theory. Mrs. Bache married William Duane (q.v.), the associate editor of the *Aurora*, after Bache's death.

BIBLIOGRAPHY:

A. *Truth Will Out*, a pamphlet (Philadelphia, 1798).

B. DAB 1, 462–463; Bernard Fay, "Benjamin Franklin Bache, A Democratic Leader of the Eighteenth Century," *Proceedings of the American Antiquarian Society*, October 1930; Bernard Fay, *The Two Franklins* (Boston, 1933).

C. JOANNE SLOAN

BAILLIE, HUGH (b. 23 October 1890; d. 1 March 1966) was a reporter "first, last, and always," but his administrative skills were such that he spent twenty years of his life as the chief executive officer of United Press. Even as a business executive, though, he used his picturesque writing (he said that every reporter should be a newsreel camera) to cover stories throughout the world.

Baillie was born in Brooklyn. His father, David Gemmell Baillie, was born in Scotland; he became a political journalist in New York City and, for a time, literary secretary to Andrew Carnegie. Baillie's mother was Fanny Mead Hays Baillie, the daughter of John B. Hays, a New York city hall reporter.

Baillie was educated in Brooklyn until the family moved to Los Angeles, where he completed high school. He attended the University of Southern California from 1907 to 1910, then became a sports reporter with the *Los Angeles Herald*. Later in 1910 he took a reporting job with the *Los Angeles Record*, and remained with the *Record* until 1915.

United Press had borrowed Baillie in 1912 to cover the trial of Clarence Darrow, accused of bribing a jury in another case. Baillie beat all his competition to the verdict by staying in the courtroom during the jury's deliberations. In 1915, United Press offered him a job in its San Francisco bureau. By 1920 he had been bureau chief for United Press in its Los Angeles, Portland (Oregon), New York City, and Washington bureaus. He covered Woodrow Wilson's speaking tour in support of the League of Nations in 1919. In 1920, covering the Repubican National Convention, he introduced the noiseless typewriter to the press box to get a running account of the action. The running-account technique had also served him well at the Darrow trial.

In 1921 Baillie became United Press's assistant general news manager, and the next year became its general manager. He became sales manager in 1924 and reorganized the service to put one individual in charge of both news and sales in each region. In 1927 he became vice president and general business manager; in 1931, executive vice president and general manager; in 1935, president and general manager. He retained those titles until 1955. For the next two years he served United Press as chairman of the board.

As an administrator he worked for openness of news sources at home and abroad and for the improvement of transmission facilities. He pioneered United Press's radio news service—as early as 1924 he set up the United Press radio network that carried convention coverage to radio stations throughout the United States. In 1951 he started, in cooperation with Movietonews, a newsreel supply service to television stations. He replaced the overseas United Press telegraph stations with teletypewriters.

He also served as president of United Features Syndicate, United Radio Stations, and Ocean Press, Inc. In 1937 he was honorary national president of Sigma Delta Chi.

His administrative duties did not keep him from reporting. He helped cover the abdication of Edward VIII in London, covered several of the 1930s events preliminary to and early in World War II, covered the Nuremberg trials, and took personal control of United Press coverage of the Korean War. He interviewed many of the heads of state of major countries in the 1930s and 1940s, visited both World War II battlefronts, and interviewed the top commanders. He even received answers to all thirty-one questions he cabled to Joseph Stalin.

Baillie married Constance Scott of San Francisco in 1916. They had one son, Hugh Scott Baillie.

Baillie died at home in La Jolla, California, in 1966.

BIBLIOGRAPHY:

A. *High Tension* (1959).

B. NCAB 62, 97; NYT 1 March 1966; Joe Alex Morris, *Deadline Every Minute* (New York, 1968).

LAURA NICKERSON

BAKER, RAY STANNARD (b. 17 April 1870; d. 12 July 1946) learned the craft of newspaper reporting during six years of reporting and editing in Chicago. He became nationally recognized as a muckraker and a Progressive Era reform-minded journalist. He wrote carefully detailed series for *McClure's*, then *American*, the latter which he helped found. After laboring briefly as a publicist for Progressive political leaders, he served as Woodrow Wilson's director of the American press bureau at the World War I peace conference in Paris. He became Wilson's official biographer and coedited Wilson's public papers. He also wrote nine popular volumes on the theme of emotional serenity, under the pseudonym David Grayson.

Baker, the oldest of six sons, was born in a frame house in Lansing, Michigan. His father, Joseph Stannard Baker, traced his lineage back to Alexander Baker, who arrived with his wife in Boston in 1635. Joseph Stannard attended two colleges, was a traveling book salesman, a major in the Union cavalry during the Civil War, and a real estate promoter and agent in St. Croix, Wisconsin. Baker's mother, Alice Potter Baker, was a high-strung, religious woman who despaired over the isolation of the pioneering hamlet of St. Croix. After three years of being an invalid with an enlarged liver and spleen, she died when Baker was thirteen. Baker graduated in 1889 from Michigan Agricultural College (now Michigan State University), briefly studied law, and took a pioneering journalism course at the University of Michigan in 1892.

Upon graduating from college Baker labored as a real estate clerk in his father's office for two years. After a few months at the University of Michigan, he traveled to Chicago and landed a job at the *Chicago Record* in 1892. He remained there six years, learning the folkways of big-city life as a reporter, columnist, and subeditor. Three stories, in particular, contributed to his understanding of social conditions and labor woes in the early 1890s: interviewing in depth the English reformer and editor William T. Stead (q.v.) about Chicago's vice- and graft-riddled social structure; covering the unemployment protest march of Coxey's Army to Washington, D.C.; and witnessing the bloody repression of striking workingmen during the Pullman railway strike in 1894. A man with a sensitive social conscience, Baker handled the *Record*'s relief fund for the strikers.

Baker started writing free-lance articles for Sunday newspaper magazines and various popular magazines, after his marriage to Jessie Irene Beal on 1 January 1896. They had four children: Alice Beal Hyde (b. 1898), James Stannard (b. 1899), Roger Denio (b. 1902), and Rachel Napier (b. 1901).

In February 1898 Baker traveled east to join the staff of *McClure's*, the preeminent, ten-cent popular magazine of the day. He handled the magazine's newspaper syndicate while writing articles and profiles on the side. The magazine's distinguished staffers included reporters Ida Tarbell and Lincoln Steffens, editor John S. Phillips, and the erratic but brilliant publisher S. S. McClure (qq.v.). As a muckraker, Baker was moderate, reformist, progressive, and individualistic. He contributed a noteworthy series on labor unrest and railroad rate-making to *McClure's*.

He joined the exodus to *American* magazine in 1906, and penned series on the social conditions of blacks in the South (collected into a pioneer sociological book, *Following the Color Line*, in 1908), and on the crisis of contemporary religion (also published in book form, as *The Spiritual Unrest*, 1910). Baker did not resign from the *American* until 1915, but after 1909 he began promoting the cause of progressive reform, first by backing Senator Robert M. La Follette, and later Woodrow Wilson. In 1910 Baker moved from one college town, Lansing, Michigan, to another, Amherst, Massachusetts, where he lived until his death.

In the service of Wilson, Baker gathered information for the State Department about public morale in Great Britain, Belgium, France, and Italy in 1918. Then he directed the American Commission's press bureau at the World War I peace conference in Paris. During this period he received honorary Litt.D. degrees from Michigan State College in 1917 and Amherst in 1925.

Convinced of Wilson's greatness as an examplar of democracy, Baker devoted twenty-one years of hard labor to writing Wilson's eight-volume, official biography, writing three volumes on the World War I peace settlement, and coediting six volumes of Wilson's public papers. His short book *What Wilson Did at Paris* explained the big issues of the World War I peace conference in popular form. Baker sifted through more than five tons of resource materials in these labors. He won the Pulitzer Prize in 1940 for the last two volumes of the Wilson biography.

As a respite from work pressures, Baker wrote some seventy diaries which contained his musings and philosophy of copybook maxims. In part from the diaries, he compiled and wrote under the pseudonym David Grayson nine books imbued with an Emersonian cosmological philosophy on the theme of emotional repose, which sold some two million copies. A prolific writer, Baker wrote more than 400 magazine pieces, and 19 major series of articles. During the final years of his life, Baker continued looking backward, writing three autobiographical books, including *American Chronicle* in 1945. Baker died of a heart attack at his Amherst home on 12 July 1946.

BIBLIOGRAPHY:

A. *Woodrow Wilson, Life and Letters*, 8 vols. (New York, 1927–39); *Native American* (New York, 1941); *American Chronicle* (New York, 1945).

B. DAB Supp. 4, 46–48; NYT 13 July 1946; Robert C. Bannister, *Ray Stannard Baker* (New Haven, 1966); David Mark Chalmers, *The Social and Political Ideas of the Muckrakers* (New York, 1964); Louis Filler, *Crusaders for American Liberalism* (New York, 1939); William Parmenter, ''Muckraking and Ray Stannard Baker,'' M.A. thesis, Univ. of Maryland, 1975; C. C. Reiger, *The Era of the Muckrakers* (Chapel Hill, N.C., 1932.

WILLIAM Q. PARMENTER

BARTHOLOMEW, FRANK HARMON (b. 5 October 1898; d. 26 March 1985) was a longtime executive of United Press International news service. He began his fifty-year career with United Press as bureau manager in Portland, Oregon, in 1921 and became president and general manager in 1955 and chairman of the board and director in 1962. While president of United Press Associations, he negotiated the merger of International News Service and United Press Associations to become United Press International (UPI) in 1958.

Bartholomew was the only child of John William and Kate Leigh (Schuck) Bartholomew. The couple separated and Mrs. Bartholomew moved to Portland, Oregon, with her son.

Bartholomew began his journalism career at the age of fifteen when he launched the *Portland Recorder* and called it an independent boy's paper on the masthead. The once-published issue stimulated the young man to apply for a reporting job on the *Portland Oregonian* immediately after graduation from high school. He briefly worked for the *Oregonian*, and then worked for short periods on the *Albany* (Oregon) *Evening Democrat*, the *Oregon City Courier*, the *Vancouver* (British Columbia) *Sun*, and the *Portland Evening Telegram*.

During World War I, Bartholomew entered Oregon State University and joined the Student Army Training Corps. When the war ended, Bartholomew returned to Portland to work for the *Portland Evening Telegram*. It was in 1921 that Bartholomew was hired as Portland bureau manager for United Press. The next year he managed the Los Angeles bureau.

On 18 May 1922 Antonia Luise Patzelt and Bartholomew were married. The couple had no children. They established their first home that year in Kansas City, Kansas, as Bartholomew began working the southwest territory for the business side of United Press. His next promotion was to San Francisco, where he was appointed division manager. It was in that capacity that Bartholomew covered some of the big news stories of that era—including the Roscoe (Fatty) Arbuckle murder trial. Bartholomew spent twenty-eight years as Pacific division manager. Two notable stories he supervised were the Santa Barbara (1925) and the Long Beach (1933) earthquakes.

When the Japanese attacked Pearl Harbor in 1941, Bartholomew directed the San Francisco division in war news coverage and then began his wartime duties as an accredited Pacific war correspondent. He served as correspondent in New Guinea during 1943, in the Aleutian campaign in 1943–44, in Okinawa with the Tenth Army, and in Luzon in the Philippines with the 38th Division in 1945. He covered the Japanese surrender aboard the USS *Missouri* in Tokyo Bay in 1945 and was pool correspondent for the Bikini atomic bomb tests in 1946. In 1950 he reported on the Korean War, and in 1954 he covered the war in Indochina. Bartholomew scored a major reporting scoop when he wrote the story of the U.S. Strategic Air Command's "fail-safe" concept of national defense.

He served as chairman of the board of UPI until 1972, when he retired from active service. For forty years Bartholomew made his home at the Buena Vista winery and vineyards near Sonoma, California, where he was involved in restoring the winery and vineyards and in producing varietal wines.

BIBLIOGRAPHY:

A. *Bart, His Memoirs* (Sonoma, Calif., 1983); "Putting the 'I' into U.P.I.," *Editor and Publisher*, 25 September 1982.

B. NYT 28 March 1985.

THEODORE H. CARLSON

BATES, LUCIOUS CHRISTOPHER (b. 27 April 1901; d. 22 August 1980) was the editor and publisher of the *Arkansas State Press*, published weekly from 1941 to 1959 in Little Rock, Arkansas. A black, Bates magnified instances of injustice toward blacks, and his articles and editorials called for social change and equal rights for his race. His writings agitated the white community, and he and his wife, Daisy L. Bates, were embroiled in the 1957 school integration crisis at Central High School in Little Rock. His involvement in the crisis was instrumental in the demise of his newspaper, because white merchants were pressured by segregationists to stop using the *State Press* as an advertising outlet.

Bates was the only son of a Baptist minister and farmer and had material comforts and advantages, both educationally and socially, that were not available to many blacks growing up in the early 1900s. Born on a farm in Liberty, Amite County, Mississippi, he plowed fields and gathered corn, but never chopped cotton. He attended an all-white grammar school near Indianola, Mississippi. His parents, Morris B. and Laura Brown Bates, had dreams of their son's becoming a doctor, but he became more interested in printing and newspaper work after working as a printer's devil in a printing shop in Indianola.

Following grammar school, he attended high school at Alcorn College in Alcorn, Mississippi, because there was no high school for blacks near his home. In 1919 he entered Wilberforce College, now Central State College, in Wilberforce, Ohio, near Dayton. After the first year, he dropped out of college and worked for several black-owned newspapers around the nation. His first job in 1920 was at the *Interstate Reporter* in Helena, Arkansas. In 1921 he joined the *Kansas City Call* in Kansas City, Missouri, as a reporter. While there, he was associated with the late Roy Wilkins, who later became president of the National Association for the Advancement of Colored People (NAACP). After a year at the *Call*, Bates moved to Pueblo, Colorado, and started his own newspaper, the *Western Ideal*. It folded a year later, and Bates found employment in California at the *Golden Age*, a Los Angeles newspaper. After one year in that position, he left the journalism field and sold insurance and novelty advertising for almost twenty years.

In 1924, while living in Omaha, Nebraska, Bates married Kassandra Crawford, a native of Iowa. They had one daughter, Loretta Ann Bates Carter. The couple were divorced in the early 1930s, but the exact date is not known, and he moved to Memphis, Tennessee. There, he traveled a nine-state area, selling insurance and novelty advertising.

His travels took him on numerous occasions to Little Rock, and it was there in 1941 that he began publication of the *Arkansas State Press*. He married Daisy Lee Gaston, a native of Huttig, Arkansas, 4 March 1942. They had no children; they were divorced in February 1963, but were remarried 12 July the same year.

The *Arkansas State Press* began publication with a circulation of 1,500. It reached its peak in 1952 at more than 18,000. Bates was a quiet, soft-spoken man, who preferred to stay out of the limelight, but his articles were fiery and his headlines often sensational. While Bates wrote emotionally, he never advocated violence in his editorials, yet they stirred such resentment among the white community during the Little Rock school integration crisis in 1957 that his home was the target of rocks and bombs and cross burnings. From September 1957 to December 1959, he kept an armed guard at his home. However, the bombings and threats did not stop his relentless call for social change. His editorials called for, among other things, the integration of public schools, the public library, the city bus system, and public meeting places in the city. By the time his newspaper folded, all these changes had come about.

When his newspaper ceased publication in October 1959, Bates accepted a position as field representative for the NAACP. He traveled as a troubleshooter for the organization in Arkansas and in several counties in Tennessee. He retired from the NAACP in January 1972. He died at St. Vincent Infirmary in Little Rock following surgery for an aneurism. He donated his body to science.

BIBLIOGRAPHY:

B. Daisy L. Bates, *The Long Shadow of Little Rock* (New York, 1962); Irene Wassell, "L. C. Bates: Editor of the *Arkansas State Press*," M.A. thesis, Univ. of Arkansas at Little Rock, 1983.

IRENE M. WASSELL

BAUKHAGE, HILMAR ROBERT (b. 7 July 1889; d. 13 January 1976) was a radio commentator, writer, lecturer, and newspaperman. A native of La Salle, Illinois, Baukhage was a descendant of a Prussian high court judge. His parents were Frederick Robert and Alice Blood Baukhage. Shortly after his birth, the Baukhage family moved to Buffalo, New York, where he was graduated from high school. Baukhage attended the University of Chicago, where he earned the Ph.B. degree in literature in 1911. He continued his studies abroad at universities in Bonn (1911), Kiel (1912), Jena (1912), Freiburg (1913), and the Sorbonne (1913). He became fluent in French and German, which became important in his later reporting career.

While at the University of Chicago Baukhage gained some newspaper experience on the university's *Daily Maroon* and on the *Chautauqua Daily*. While studying at the Sorbonne, he served as an assistant to the Paris correspondent of the London publication *Pall Mall Gazette*. He also filed occasional stories with the Associated Press and joined the AP staff in Washington, D.C., in 1914. His assignment was to cover the State Department and a number of embassies and legations. In 1916, Baukhage joined *Leslie's Illustrated Weekly*, a photo magazine, becoming its managing editor.

Baukhage sought to enlist in the army when the United States entered World War I in 1917; however, his poor eyesight posed a problem. Finally, he was assigned to the coast artillery as a private in 1918. Just before the war ended, he received a second lieutenant's commission in the field artillery. With his journalistic background, Baukhage obtained an assignment as a reporter for *Stars and Stripes*, arriving in Europe in time to cover the Paris Peace Conference at Versailles.

In 1919 Baukhage returned to the United States and joined the Continental Press Association, which had been established by his childhood friend, David Lawrence (q.v.). He served as business manager and later as bureau chief in Chicago, San Francisco, and Washington until 1932. He continued working for Lawrence on the *United States Daily* and the *United States News* (forerunners of *U.S. News and World Report*) until 1937.

H. R. Baukhage made his broadcasting debut in 1932; and during most of his remaining career, he was active in both broadcast and print journalism. At first, he gave a daily five-minute news commentary on "The National Farm and Home Hour," a noontime broadcast produced by the *United States News* on the NBC-Blue network. Baukhage became an NBC staff commentator in 1937, continuing his appearances on "The National Farm and Home Hour" until 1942. Simultaneously, he wrote a Washington column for the North American Newspaper Alliance in 1937; from 1940 through 1945, he wrote a weekly column, "Washington Digest," for the Western Newspaper Union syndicate.

When war became imminent in 1939, NBC sent Baukhage to Europe as a foreign correspondent. His fluency with German served him well when he broadcast direct from the Reichstag in Berlin as Hitler announced the invasion of Poland. Returning to America after hostilities began, Baukhage became the first reporter ever to broadcast directly from the White House pressroom a few minutes after the attack on Pearl Harbor.

When NBC-Blue became the American Broadcasting Company (ABC) in 1943, Baukhage remained with ABC as a Washington commentator. His slot was a fifteen-minute daily broadcast called "Baukhage Talking." It was an unusual news commentary in that on slow news days Baukhage would depart from serious matters to present light essays on nature, mankind, and the classics.

On one occasion, he is reported to have interviewed the statue of Thomas Jefferson. Baukhage continued his commentaries on ABC until 1951, when he moved to the Mutual Broadcasting System (MBS). He retired from radio in 1954. Among Baukhage's best known broadcasts were his poignant accounts of the death and funeral of President Franklin Roosevelt in 1945. For the funeral broadcast at Hyde Park, Baukhage received the National Headliners Club Award for the best domestic broadcast of the year.

After retiring from MBS, Baukhage served as an editorial consultant with the Army Times Publishing Company and wrote investment columns for the *Army, Navy*, and *Air Force Register* newspapers from 1955 until 1962. He also did occasional news commentaries on the Armed Forces Network for American troops overseas. He then returned to *U.S. News and World Report* as a special columnist from 1963 to 1967.

Baukhage married Marjorie Collins in 1922. He was a Mason and held memberships in the National Press Club, Radio Correspondents Association (president, 1941–42), Overseas Writers, and the Radio News Analysts Association. After a series of strokes, he died in Washington, D.C., at age eighty-seven.

BIBLIOGRAPHY:

A. With C. L. Baldridge, *I Was There with the Yanks on the Western Front from 1917–1919* (New York, 1919).

B. NYT 2 February 1976; Irving E. Fang, ''Baukhage,'' *Those Radio Commentators!* (Ames, Iowa, 1977); *Who Was Who* 6, 24.

HERBERT H. HOWARD

BEACH, MOSES YALE (b. 15 January 1800; d. 19 July 1868) was owner of a leading ''penny press'' daily in New York City, but unlike his contemporary rivals, he was more concerned with improving techniques to gather and distribute news than with establishing a notable editorial policy. He helped organize the New York Associated Press, is credited as being the first American publisher to syndicate news material, and was the first to print a European edition of his paper.

The son of Moses Sperry Beach, a farmer, and Lucretia Yale Beach, the future publisher was apprenticed at age fourteen to a Hartford, Connecticut, cabinetmaker. His industry was such that he was able to negotiate a new contract allowing him two cents an hour for overtime work. At eighteen he bought his freedom for $400 and had $100 left from his savings. He joined another cabinetmaker in Northampton and their work received a prize from the Franklin Institute.

Turning to mechanics, he invented an engine powered by gunpowder explosions and a rug-cutting machine used in paper mills. For this latter invention he failed to obtain a patent in time and missed large financial rewards. However, in 1829 he moved to Saugerties, New York, where his rag-cutting equipment allowed him to obtain a share in a paper mill. Lacking financial success, Beach went to New York City to become manager of the mechanical department of the *New York Sun*, in which his wife's brother, Benjamin H. Day (q.v.), had an interest. In 1835, Beach bought a partnership in the *Sun*, and in 1838 he purchased Day's share for $40,000.

The *New York Sun* during this period printed two of American journalism's most celebrated hoaxes: the Moon Hoax in late August 1835, and the Balloon Hoax in April 1844. The first told of the purported "Great Astronomical Discoveries" of lunar creatures that walked "both erect and dignified" like human beings and had faces of "a yellowish flesh color" and with "a slight improvement upon that of the large orang-utan." The whole series was invented by Richard Adams Locke (q.v.), an imaginative *Sun* reporter who drank too much with a rival journalist and disclosed the deception. The second hoax was written by Edgar Allan Poe and recited how a crew of Englishmen had crossed the Atlantic in three days in a dirigible balloon, landing near Charleston, South Carolina. Two days later Beach admitted the fake and claimed Poe had simply been satirizing the devotion to speed.

Beach and James Gordon Bennett (q.v.) of the rival *New York Herald* battled constantly to beat each other in printing the latest news. Beach built his own news service. The *Sun*'s sailing vessels greeted ships from Europe as they approached New York harbor to obtain recent news. Horse expresses from Albany and special trains from Washington allowed the *Sun* to print exclusive information frequently. The paper constructed a pigeon house on the roof of its new offices at Nassau and Fulton streets in 1842 and birds flew in with news for half a century. During the Mexican War, dispatches were delayed between Mobile, where steamers arrived, and Montgomery, so Beach set up his own special train service between the cities.

Coverage of that war demonstrated anew how expensive news gathering could be as each New York City paper tried to best its rivals. In an 1848 meeting in the *Sun* offices, representatives of the city's leading papers agreed to establish the New York Associated Press, which would gather news from such centers as Albany, Washington, Boston, and Philadelphia. The Harbor News Association also established a common fleet of news boats to replace the individual papers' activities. Thus were set up the foundations for what became the international press associations and syndicates of later eras.

Previously Beach had experimented successfully with news syndication. When the *Sun* received President John Tyler's message to Congress by special messenger in 1841, an extra edition was printed for twenty other papers, alike except for the nameplate.

Beach established two other notable innovations: a weekly journal called the *American Sun*, which sold overseas for twelve shillings a year and thus was the first American publication with a European edition; and the *Weekly Sun*, printed on Saturdays and sold among farmers around the nation for one dollar a year.

Beach turned the *Sun* over to two of his sons—Moses Sperry Beach and Alfred Ely Beach—in 1848 when the publication was fifteen years old. Its circulation then was 50,000 and it claimed "the largest cash advertising patronage on this continent." He returned to his native community of Wellingford, Connecticut, where he died of paralysis at age sixty-eight.

He married Nancy Day on 19 November 1819, and in addition to Moses S. and Alfred E. of the *New York Sun*, he was survived by three other sons—Henry, Joseph, and William—and one daughter.

BIBLIOGRAPHY:

A. *Wealth and Wealthy Citizens of New York City* (New York, 1841).

B. DAB 2, 82–84; NYT 21 July 1868; Frederic Hudson, *Journalism in the United States, From 1690 to 1872* (New York, 1873); Frank M. O'Brien, *The Story of the Sun* (New York, 1918).

HILLIER KRIEGHBAUM

BEECHER, HENRY WARD (b. 24 June 1813; d. 8 March 1887) was a noted clergyman, author, and journalist who became one of the most controversial figures of the nineteenth century. He opposed slavery and supported woman suffrage and free trade. He was a Darwinian who favored scientific biblical criticism.

He was born in Litchfield, Connecticut, one of thirteen children of Lyman Beecher, a Congregational minister. His mother, Roxanna Foote, died when he was three years old. His father married Harriet Porter, who had a profound influence on Henry's life. His sister was Harriet Beecher Stowe, the author of *Uncle Tom's Cabin*. Beecher attended the Boston Latin School and Mount Pleasant Institute. He was graduated from Amherst College in 1834 and then moved to Cincinnati, Ohio, to enroll in Lane Theological Seminary where his father was president. During his years in Cincinnati he wrote for the *Daily Evening Post*, and edited the *Cincinnati Journal*, a Presbyterian weekly, for seven months. In early 1838 he began preaching at a church in Lawrenceburg, Indiana, but he left in 1839 for the pastorate of the Second Presbyterian Church in Indianapolis, where he stayed until 1846.

In 1847 Beecher was called to the pastorate of the Plymouth Church in Brooklyn, New York. His sermons, reported by stenographers, resulted in a weekly publication, *Plymouth Pulpit*. He became a contributor to the *Independent*, a Congregational newspaper with a strong, radical antislavery position. He edited the *Independent* from 1861 to 1864. He is best remembered for founding the *Christian Union* in 1870. Also, between 1859 and 1874 he wrote for the *New York Ledger*.

The editorship of the *Christian Union* slipped from his hands after 1874 when he became involved in a scandal that affected circulation of the journal. Theodore Tilton, who worked with Beecher on the *Independent*, accused him of trying to seduce his wife. In the ensuing trial the jury failed to reach a verdict, but the scandal tarnished Beecher's career and reputation. In 1876 the editorship of the *Christian Union* passed to Lyman Abbott (q.v.), who revived the journal and renamed it *Outlook* in 1893. Beecher suffered a cerebral hemorrhage and died on 8 March 1887. He was buried in Greenwood Cemetery in Brooklyn.

BIBLIOGRAPHY:

B. ACAB 1, 219–220; NYT 8 and 9 March 1887; Lyman Abbott, *Henry Ward Beecher* (Boston, 1903); Clifford E. Clark, Jr., *Henry Ward Beecher: Spokesman for a Middle-Class America* (Urbana, 1978); Jane Shaffer Elsmere, *Henry Ward Beecher: The Indiana Years* (Indianapolis, 1973).

JOHN M. BUTLER

BELL, EDWARD PRICE (b. 1 March 1869; d. 23 September 1943) was a reporter, foreign correspondent, and writer. Known mainly for the contribution he made to the development of the *Chicago Daily News*'s renowned foreign service in the years before World War I, for his activities during that war, and for his work in the 1920s and 1930s, Bell became identified, in particular, with developing the high-level interview.

Born in Parke County, Indiana, on a farm sixteen miles north of Terre Haute, Edward was the seventh of nine children. His parents, Addison William Bell and Nancy Elizabeth Price Bell, typified the hardy breed of people who appear frequently in the history of nineteenth-century rural Indiana. His father, a farmer, was also engaged in several farm-related businesses. Edward attended a small, rural one-room school for his early education. As a young man, he worked as a reporter on a number of Indiana newspapers and for a short while published a small paper of his own, the *Rosedale Bee*. When he was twenty-four, he entered Wabash College, and after completing his final term there, he married Mary Alice Mills. They had four children: Martha, who died in infancy; Alice; Edward Jr.; and John. After finishing college, he became the editor of the *Terre Haute Express*, but because of a disagreement with its publisher, he left in 1898 and went to Chicago.

There Bell became a reporter on Victor F. Lawson's (q.v.) *Chicago Record*. It was with that paper and later with Lawson's *Chicago Daily News* that he acquired his reputation. In 1900 Lawson sent Bell to London as chief of his newly formed foreign service. It was as overseas manager of the *Chicago Daily News*'s foreign service that Bell's career reached fruition. In the years before World War I, he developed the system of original news collection that characterized the *Daily News*'s foreign coverage. During World War I, Bell conducted a number of interviews with British statesmen and military figures and became an active advocate of American entrance into the war. Afterwards, in 1922, he returned to Chicago, where he continued his long association with the *Daily News*.

The ten years following his return to the United States were rich and active ones for Bell. In the mid–1920s he conducted several world tours to interview leading public figures in Europe and Asia, and, as a result, published two books: *World Chancelleries* (1926) and *Europe's Economic Sunrise* (1927). In 1927 he began a weekly column for the *Chicago Daily News* called "The Marching

World,'' which he continued until 1931. Throughout the 1920s Bell became a familiar figure to many people in the Midwest as a public speaker and as a commentator on WMAQ, the *Daily News*'s radio station.

Long interested in the press as a vehicle for international understanding, Bell was involved in journalism at the diplomatic level several times during these years. He worked hard in behalf of a meeting between Prime Minister J. Ramsay MacDonald and President Herbert Hoover that eventually occurred in 1929. He was at the London Naval Disarmament Conference in 1930 for the *Daily News* and returned to England once again for that paper to cover the economic crisis in 1931. Later in 1931, finding it increasingly difficult to work with Frank Knox (q.v.), who was then publisher of the *Daily News*, Bell resigned and moved to his winter home in Pass Christian, Mississippi. For his efforts in behalf of world peace, he was nominated for the Nobel Peace Prize in 1930–31.

Bell remained active in journalism for many years following his retirement from the *Daily News*. In the mid–1930s, he went on another world tour, this time for the *Literary Digest*, and again interviewed many prominent leaders in Europe and Asia including Chiang Kai-shek and Adolf Hitler. His work, however, began to lose much of the sharpness and perception that had characterized it in previous years. When he returned home in 1935, his health was in shambles. He had contracted beriberi while in China. Nevertheless, he continued to pursue his writing and public speaking to the limits of his strength. During the late 1930s, however, much of his work was rejected as he grew more out of step with his times. In 1941 he found a final opportunity to contribute regularly to a paper, the *Saturday Spectator*, a weekly published in Terre Haute, Indiana. Many of his articles for the *Spectator* were polemics aimed at the interventionist policies of President Franklin D. Roosevelt.

Always a generous and helpful colleague, Bell was held in high esteem by many of his journalistic contemporaries in the United States and England. He was an imaginative and somewhat romantic writer whose creative ability surfaced not only in his journalistic work but also in a number of short stories that he wrote at various times of his life. His writings on the practice of journalism are also worthy of note. After a long illness, he died in Pass Christian, Mississippi, on 23 September 1943, as a result of heart failure.

BIBLIOGRAPHY:

B. *Who Was Who in America* 2, 55–56; *Chicago Daily News*, 24 September 1943; James D. Startt, *Journalism's Unofficial Ambassador: A Biography of Edward Price Bell, 1869–1943* (Athens, Ohio, 1979); Benedict K. Zobrist, ''Edward Price Bell and the Development of the Foreign News Service of the *Chicago Daily News*,'' Ph.D. diss., Northwestern Univ., 1953.

JAMES D. STARTT

BELL, PHILIP A. (b. 1808; d. 24 April 1889) had the distinction of establishing black newspapers on the East and West coasts of the United States during his career in journalism. He was referred to by some journalists of the time as ''The Napoleon'' of the Afro-American press.

Little background information can be found on Bell prior to his founding of the *Weekly Advocate* in New York City in January 1837. Samuel E. Cornish (q.v.) served as editor of the paper with Bell as its proprietor. The name of the paper was changed in March 1837 to the *Colored American*. When Cornish retired as editor in May 1839, Bell assumed the position of coeditor along with Dr. James McCune Smith. In 1841 Bell severed his connection with the paper. Almost twenty years later Bell arrived in San Francisco and in 1862 was chosen by Peter Anderson to be editor of his newly founded *Pacific Appeal*.

Bell left the *Appeal* after only four months as editor. Some scholars of the black press attribute this split between Bell and Anderson to severe personality conflicts. Bell was considered by some to be a "militant" and "undiplomatic" while Anderson was considered a "moderate." Bell would later establish his own paper in San Francisco and the two would become bitter rivals.

Approximately three years after leaving the *Appeal*, Bell established the *Elevator* on 7 April 1865. Bell's *Elevator* and Anderson's *Appeal* provided their readers with contrasting views for nearly fourteen years.

Probably the best black writer on the West Coast at the time, Bell made himself clear on several issues through the *Elevator*. He called for "political and civil liberties"; however, he believed these liberties should be granted only to American citizens.

Bell saw education as a major weapon against prejudice and in 1867, through his paper, called for self-help and black cooperatives to overcome poor education and economic conditions. Since labor and economics are so closely associated, he took great interest in labor developments in the San Francisco area.

Bell consistently expressed anti-Chinese and anti-Irish sentiments in the *Elevator*. He believed the Chinese were a threat to black labor in the area because they would work for cheaper wages. This, Bell believed, would bring about displacement of black workers in their "traditional" jobs. At one point he opposed further immigration by Chinese to the United States.

Bell's hostility toward the Irish was even deeper than his aversion to the Chinese. He reminded his readers of past conflicts between the Irish and blacks on the East Coast. He recalled through strong editorials in the *Elevator* the traditional hostility the Irish had shown toward blacks during the labor movement in New York and other northern cities from the 1830s to the Civil War.

On the issue of unions and organized labor, Bell believed black and white workers should unite to protect their mutual interest; however, he rejected the violence and socialism that many labor unions preached.

As most black editors of the time, Bell was strongly Republican and believed it would be through the political process that blacks would achieve some degree of elevation in American society. However, he advocated "independent" action by forming all-black pressure groups and voting blocs to bring about collective action within the party.

Bell stayed at the helm of the *Elevator* from its founding to July 1872. In financial difficulties, he sold the paper to Alexander Ferguson; however, in

November of the same year, he repurchased the paper and again became its owner, publisher, and editor. In 1885 Bell became ill and was forced to retire. The paper was published by the Elevator Publishing Company until 1899.

No family records could be found of Bell. He died in San Francisco in "destitute" condition according to one historian of the black press. He is reported to have been cared for by a group of ladies until his death.

BIBLIOGRAPHY:

B. Francis N. Lortie, Jr., "San Francisco's Black Community, 1870–1890: Dilemmas in the Struggle for Equality," M.A. thesis, Univ. of San Francisco, 1970; Philip M. Montesano, "Some Aspects of the Free Negro Question in San Francisco, 1849–1870," M.A. thesis, Univ. of San Francisco, 1967; I. Garland Penn, *The Afro-American Press and Its Editors* (New York, 1969); J. William Snorgrass, "The Philosophy of a Black Editor, Philip A. Bell 1808–1889," *Negro History Bulletin*, April–May 1981.

J. WILLIAM SNORGRASS

BENNETT, JAMES GORDON (b. 1 September 1795; d. 1 June 1872) combined personal journalism with an understanding of readers' wants and the use of innovative techniques to become a modern journalism pioneer who founded the *New York Herald*.

His newspaper catered to the public through the use of reporting rather than editorial writing, of controversial writing on taboo topics, and of covering vice and crime, all without allegiance to any political party. His tenacity and personality ostracized him from his contemporaries, but even they could not deny that his reporting skill and willingness to innovate changed the course of American journalism.

Bennett's trailblazing led him on a circuitous route for the first half of his life. Born in Keith, Banffshire, Scotland, he was the oldest son of a farm family. His devout Catholic parents sought to have him enter the priesthood, but he left the Catholic seminary at Aberdeen at nineteen. Although Bennett published some poetry in the local Banffshire County newspaper, his eyes were turned by Benjamin Franklin's *Autobiography* to the future in North America. Five years after leaving the seminary he sailed to Halifax, Nova Scotia, where he taught. After a stay in Maine, he arrived in Boston and secured a position with a publishing office as a proofreader, the beginning of his career in American print.

In 1822 Bennett went to New York and wrote items for various newspapers. By chance he met the proprietor of the *Charleston* (South Carolina) *Courier*, for whom he went to work translating from Spanish-American journals. But after a year, a desire to be on his own took him back to New York, where an attempt to start a commercial school became the first of a frustrating string of unsuccessful ventures.

He purchased the *New York Courier* in 1825, but soon resold it. Bennett then became a Washington correspondent and associate editor of the *Courier and Enquirer*. In Washington he demonstrated his talents as an innovator with spicy, pointed, and graphic reporting instead of the traditional stodgy fare. After three years, in 1832, he broke with editor James Watson Webb (q.v.) over the latter's political support of Nicholas Biddle.

He then tried publishing his own newspaper, but the ill-fated *Globe* in New York lasted only a month. He went to Philadelphia and became editor of the *Pennsylvanian*, but lack of help from his political "friends" ended that venture and soured Bennett on political party control.

With $500, two friendly printers, and a rejection of work from Benjamin Day (q.v.) of the *New York Sun*, Bennett founded the *Herald* on 16 May 1835, to begin one of the great rags-to-riches stories in American journalism. Priced at one penny, the *Herald* stressed, for the first time, the news in a newspaper. Bennett drew upon his long apprenticeship to parlay a keen news sense with a dedication to political autonomy, an understanding of what readers wanted, and the courage to tackle snobbishness, the clergy, and the financial world. His newspaper was an instant success.

Even fire could not stop him. When a fire forced him out of the cellar in which he was operating that first year, he used the opportunity to find another basement and become sole proprietor of the *Herald*. A major fire in December 1835 showed Bennett's innovativeness as he combined his brilliant reporting with a woodcut map and picture. His inventive nature was not limited to graphics like maps and portraits. He introduced financial news and stock lists personally gathered on Wall Street, ran the first direct interview, arranged with journalists in Europe to provide foreign news, organized a news staff, committed large sums of money to news-gathering activities, employed newsboys to deliver his paper, and made use of technological advances like the electric telegraph to speed news delivery.

But the innovation that brought Bennett the most readers and the greatest scorn was his use of sensationalism. Biographer Oliver Carlson has called him "the real father of 'yellow journalism.' " Beginning with the turgid coverage of the Ellen Jewett murder, Bennett made crime, vice, and sex basic ingredients of the *Herald*. He attacked prudishness and dealt with New York society in a sardonic manner. It brought him vicious criticism from his competitors, whippings from offended parties, and even a bomb attempt on his life.

Into this social barrenness created by the man whom the *New York Times* would call in his obituary "so cynical, so poiseless, so cold" came Henrietta Agnes Crean. After a whirlwind courtship they were married on 6 June 1840. The Bennetts had four children, two of whom died at an early age; Jeannette, who was a companion to her mother; and firstborn James Gordon Bennett, Jr. (q.v.), who would succeed his father as proprietor of the *Herald*. Mrs. Bennett would accept the benefits of the most prosperous newspaper in America by seeking refuge in Europe from the public scorn.

Bennett's ostracism allowed him time to devote to the *Herald*, and he continued expanding coverage by getting reporters into the galleries of Congress, setting up elaborate transportation networks, and giving comprehensive coverage to the Civil War.

But as he entered his seventies, time took its toll and his prodigious work schedule slowed. He still remained active with the *Herald* almost up until 1 June 1872, when he died of a cerebral hemorrhage. His wife died less than a year later in Europe of cancer.

BIBLIOGRAPHY:

B. DAB 2, 195–199; NCAB 7, 241–242; NYT 2 June 1872; Oliver Carlson, *The Man Who Made News, James Gordon Bennett* (New York, 1942); Richard O'Connor, *The Scandalous Mr. Bennett* (Garden City, N.Y., 1962).

SAMUEL V. KENNEDY III

BENNETT, JAMES GORDON, JR. (b. 10 May 1841; d. 14 May 1918) was designated from youth by his founding-publisher father to take command of the great *New York Herald* newspaper enterprise. He ran the *Herald* for half a century, expanding it to European influence, and taking the lead in foreign news, sporting news, and news expeditions. However, he also damaged the property through personal eccentricity, erratic behavior, and dissipation, thereby presiding over the *Herald*'s decline, as it was eclipsed by Joseph Pulitzer's (q.v.) *World* in the 1880s, and William Randolph Hearst's (q.v.) *Journal* in the 1890s.

Bennett was born in Chambers Street in New York City, the first of four children, to James Gordon Bennett (q.v.), publisher of the *Herald*, and Henrietta Agnes Crean. To avoid the atmosphere of calumny surrounding his father, young Bennett was educated by private tutors in Europe, and at the École Polytechnique in Paris. He served in the Union navy during the Civil War, a measure to mitigate criticism of the *Herald*'s Copperhead tone.

Following the war Bennett began training in each of the *Herald*'s departments. Upon the retirement of Frederic Hudson (q.v.), considered one of the nation's ablest managing editors, Bennett assumed that post in 1866. The following year the elder Bennett retired, leaving Bennett junior in charge of a newspaper business with 90,000 circulation, annual profits around $400,000, and advertising revenue second only to the *Times* of London.

The *Herald* was still riding the crest of fame attained for its unrivaled news-gathering operation during the Civil War. Bennett seized upon the public's interest in the exotic, and sponsored widely reported news expeditions. He dispatched Henry M. Stanley to cover the British army assault against Abyssinia, and sent him into deepest Africa to locate the missionary David Livingstone. Another correspondent was sent to the Crimea, to Russia on an expedition, and to Central Asia. Bennett's interest in nautical affairs found outlet in dispatching a bark to search for the Northwest Passage, and the fitting-out of the ill-fated *Jeannette* expedition to the Arctic.

In his news philosophy Bennett followed his father, devising ways to appeal to a low common denominator, and eschewing normative news values. In his early years Bennett gathered an editorial staff of unusual ability. Strains developed due to Bennett's irascible, domineering, and erratic habits and he later broke with some of the staff. However, he was enterprising, and founded fresh newspapers: the *Evening Telegram* in 1867 with his father's support, and London and Paris editions of the *Herald*, establishing European influence. He joined with John W. Mackay in 1883 and laid a cable line across the Atlantic, breaking the grip of the existing cable monopoly, and making more foreign news available to his papers.

Bennett moved in a fast set of New York bachelors. His engagement to Edith May led to the scandal of his life in 1877. The May family was so insulted by Bennett's behavior that the engagement was abruptly broken off, and Edith's brother horsewhipped Bennett. After an inconclusive duel, Bennett expatriated to Paris and remained there permanently, running his newspapers from his Paris office. Later on, he was sued for support by the daughter of a French actress who claimed Bennett was her father. Finally, in 1914 he was married to the widow Baroness de Reuter, the former Maud Potter of Philadelphia.

The *New York Herald* was hurt by a newsdealers war in 1884 and by the rise of the *World*, *Times*, and *Journal*. Nevertheless, Bennett moved the *Herald* to an impressive new building on Herald Square on Thirty-sixth Street in 1894. By 1900 the *Herald* had sunk in revenue, circulation, and prestige. In 1907 Bennett had to pay $31,000 in fines for allowing immoral ads to appear in the personal columns of the *Herald*—a humiliating episode instigated by Hearst. Through it all Bennett remained a big spender, became progressively Europeanized, and patronized sports.

He died of heart disease at Beaulieu in 1918. Most of his much reduced fortune was left, after the sale of the *Herald* to Frank Munsey in 1920, to found a shelter for indigent New York newspapermen.

BIBLIOGRAPHY:

B. NYT 19 May 1918; Richard O'Connor, *The Scandalous Mr. Bennett* (Garden City, 1962); Don C. Seitz, *The James Gordon Bennetts* (Indianapolis, 1928).

WILLIAM Q. PARMENTER

BERRYMAN, CLIFFORD "CLIFF" KENNEDY (b. 2 April 1869; d. 11 December 1949), and **BERRYMAN, JAMES "JIM" THOMAS** (b. 8 June 1902; d. 11 August 1971) were a world-renowned father-and-son team of editorial cartoonists who worked together at the Washington, D.C., *Evening Star* newspaper.

Cliff was born in Versailles, Kentucky, to James T. and Sallie C. Berryman. His father was a commission salesman and farmer in Woodford, Kentucky. Berryman graduated from Professor Henry's School for Boys in Versailles in 1886. He taught himself the rudiments of drawing. When he was seventeen he attended a political rally in Kentucky and sketched a likeness of the speaker with a piece of charcoal. Another person in the audience showed the sketch to the orator, Senator Joseph Blackburn, who asked to meet the artist. Not long afterward, Blackburn took young Berryman to Washington, where he secured a drafting job for the artist at the Patent Office in 1886.

In 1891 he was hired as a general illustrator for the *Washington Post*. He stayed with the *Post* until 1907, serving as a general illustrator until 1896 when the *Post* allowed him to specialize in editorial cartooning. Meanwhile, on 5 July 1893, he married Kate Gaddis Durfee. They had three children: Mary Belle, Florence Seville, and James Thomas.

On 1 February 1907 Berryman left the *Post* and went to work for the rival *Washington Evening Star* as an editorial cartoonist. Berryman developed the Teddy Bear figure in the Theodore Roosevelt era, and included the figure in a corner of his cartoons for a number of years, as a trademark of his work. However, he did not license the figure with the U.S. Patent Office, so he did not receive any income from the manufactured Teddy Bears of a later era.

In 1921 George Washington University awarded him an honorary M.A. degree. In 1926 Clifford Berryman was chosen president of the Gridiron Club—the first cartoonist elected to the post. In 1944 he received a Pulitzer Prize for a cartoon titled "But Where Is The Boat Going?"

He was the author of *Berryman's Cartoons of the 58th House* (1903), and became the first person to draw a cartoon of every member of any one session of the House of Representatives. He and his wife lived for a number of years in a large old house on Bancroft Place in the District of Columbia.

On the morning of 17 November 1949 he collapsed in the lobby of the *Star* on his way to work. He had worked for the newspaper for forty-two years. He died at his home on 11 December. He was eighty years old. Berryman was buried in Glenwood Cemetery in Washington, D.C.

His two children (Mary Belle preceded him in death) had long before signed on to work at the *Star*. Florence Seville Berryman was an art critic for the paper, and James Thomas Berryman followed in his father's footsteps as a cartoonist.

Jim was born on 8 June 1902 in Washington, D.C. He graduated from Central High School in 1920 and entered George Washington University as a journalism student. The next two years he took instruction at the Corcoran School of Art. In 1923 he left the university and went to work as a reporter for the *New Mexico State Tribune*. He stayed only a few months. He was hired as a staff artist by the *Washington Evening Star* in 1924. In 1931 the paper named him an editorial illustrator, and in 1934 he became a sports cartoonist for both the *Evening Star* and the *Sporting News*.

Jim married Louise Marble Rhees on 23 October 1926. They had one son, Rhys Morgan Berryman.

On assignment for the U.S. Justice Department in 1934, Berryman drew the composite sketch of the suspect in the kidnapping of the Lindbergh baby.

In addition to his work at the *Star*, Jim occasionally provided illustrations for magazines, beginning in 1936. He was the cartoonist for all of the publications of the Association of American Railroads, and during the 1937–38 academic year he taught graphic arts at Southeastern University in Washington, D.C. During World War II Jim illustrated publications for several government agencies, including the U.S. Navy.

In 1941 Jim was named an editorial cartoonist at the *Star*. The father-and-son team of Cliff and Jim Berryman, along with longtime associate Gibson Crockett, provided the lion's share of the original editorial cartoons which appeared in the *Star* in the 1940s. After his father's death Jim Berryman was chief political cartoonist at the *Star* for twelve years. When he retired in 1964 he had worked at the *Star* for forty-one years. From 1944 until his retirement his cartoons were syndicated by King Features.

In 1949 he was presented with the Freedom Foundation Award. In 1950 he received the American Legion's Distinguished Service Medal and the Pulitzer Prize for an editorial cartoon published in the *Star* on 23 July 1949 entitled "All Set For A Super-Secret Session in Washington." He thus became the first son of a Pulitzer Prize winner in cartooning to also receive the coveted award.

James Berryman died 11 August 1971 in Venice, Florida, after a brief illness.

BIBLIOGRAPHY FOR CLIFFORD BERRYMAN:

B. NYT 12 December 1949; *Newsweek*, 29 November 1948.

BIBLIOGRAPHY FOR JAMES T. BERRYMAN:

B. CA 93–96, 49; NYT 2 May 1950 and 13 August 1971; *Newsweek*, 29 November 1948.

DONALD L. MCBRIDE

BETTMANN, OTTO LUDWIG (b. 15 October 1903) established one of the first commercial picture archives in the United States. Besides amassing an immense collection of pictures, Bettmann also wrote or coauthored several illustrated histories, ranging from sports to medicine to music, organized picture filing systems, and served as editor for music and book publishers. Copies of his photographs, drawings, and other illustrations have appeared in thousands of tradebooks, textbooks, magazines, and advertisements around the world.

The older of two children, Bettmann was born in Leipzig, Germany. His father was a prosperous orthopedic surgeon who studied with Roentgen and advanced the technique of X-ray diagnosis. Bettmann's mother, Charlotte Frank, was the daughter of a well-to-do family of Leipzig. In 1923 Bettmann was graduated from Oberreal Gymnasium in Leipzig, where he studied music. In 1927 he received his Ph.D. from the University of Leipzig in art history. For a year after graduation, Bettmann was employed as an associate editor for C. F. Peters, a music publishing house in Leipzig. In 1928 he became editor for Abel Juncker Publishers in Berlin. While in that post Bettmann enrolled in the University of Leipzig School of Library Science, from which he received a master's degree in 1932.

Because he was a Jew, he was dismissed from his job on the eve of the Nazi takeover in 1933 despite having established a reputation. In 1935, leaving nearly everything behind except boxes and trunks packed with more than 20,000 photographs and illustrations that he had been collecting, Bettmann emigrated to the United States. He arrived nearly penniless. Bettmann's uncle, a prosperous lawyer in Cincinnati, financed a small office for him in New York, where he began his business of renting illustrations. Despite the depression, the growth of picture magazines such as *Life* and *Look*, and the development of photojournalism, created a heavy demand for historical pictures. The Bettmann Archive was founded in 1936, but did not achieve stability until 300 pictures for a history of the world were requested by a publisher. A request by the Columbia Broadcasting System for an illustration for an advertisement in *Fortune* furthered the fame of Bettmann's archive. The two-page advertisement won awards for CBS, and Bettmann received broader recognition for his collection and an increased number of orders from advertising agencies.

Bettmann continued to add to his collection of pictures with special attention to what is generally recognized as one of the best sets of medical illustrations in the world. In addition he began to produce, either alone or with others, a number of pictorial histories beginning with *As We Were: Family Life in America, 1850–1900* in 1946, and ending with *The Bettmann Archive Picture History of the World* in 1978. Through acquisition or merger with other collections, Bettmann enlarged his archive to more than five million pictures, allocated to fifty groups, five thousand categories, and many thousands of subcategories. It is renowned as perhaps the finest and most complete private collection of illustrations in the world. Bettmann was given the Award of Merit by the Institute of Graphic Arts three times: in 1967, 1968, and 1971.

Bettmann's stepson, Melvin Gray, became president of the archive in 1976. Bettmann sold the archive to the Kraus-Thomson Organization in March 1981. Bettmann married Anne Clemens Gray of Boston on 4 March 1938. They live in Boca Raton, Florida.

BIBLIOGRAPHY:

B. CB 1961, 51–53; John F. Baker, ''Living in the Past with Dr. Otto Bettmann,'' *Publishers Weekly*, 25 November 1974; Helen Markel, ''The Bettmann Behind the Archives,'' *New York Times Magazine*, 18 October 1981; John Tebbel, ''Picture Man on 57th Street,'' *Saturday Review*, 11 February 1961.

JACK H. COLLDEWEIH

BIERCE, AMBROSE GWINNETT (b. 24 June 1842; d. 11 January 1914?), called ''Bitter Bierce'' and ''The Wickedest Man in San Francisco,'' was among the most gifted and caustic of American satirists. He was known for the pungent humor and terse writing style of his essays, short stories, sayings, and newspaper and magazine columns.

He was born near Horse Cave Creek in Meigs County, Ohio, to Marcus Aurelius and Laura Sherwood Bierce. He enlisted in the Union army in the Civil War and rose through the ranks. He was seriously wounded at the Battle of Kennesaw Mountain and was cited for bravery. Breveted a major in 1867, he resigned his commission and settled in San Francisco, where he soon became a successful free-lance writer.

In 1868 he became editor of the *San Francisco News Letter* and began writing a column, ''Town Crier.'' His reputation as a humorist was established. On 25

December 1871 Bierce married Mary Ellen "Mollie" Day. The couple had two sons and a daughter; however, only the daughter survived Bierce. Later, Bierce would become estranged from his wife, and they would eventually divorce in 1905.

Between 1872 and 1875 Bierce and his family lived in England, where he continued his writing for publications such as *Fun*. He returned to San Francisco in 1875 and became associate editor of a weekly paper called *Argonaut* and wrote a column, "Prattle," modeled after his "Town Crier." He left San Francisco to go gold prospecting around 1880, but was unsuccessful. He returned to become editor of the *Wasp* from 1881 to 1886. His "Devil's Dictionary," which ran in the *Wasp*, was collected and published as *The Cynic's Word Book* in 1906 (also published under the title *The Devil's Dictionary*).

When the *Wasp* was sold Bierce was hired by William Randolph Hearst (q.v.) to write columns for the *San Francisco Examiner* and, later, the *New York Journal* and *Cosmopolitan* magazine. The relationship lasted for more than twenty years even though Bierce quit and was rehired several times.

Bierce left the Hearst organization in 1906, but he continued to write essays, short stories, verse, and books. Between 1909 and 1912 he published *The Collected Works of Ambrose Bierce* in twelve volumes. His death remains a mystery today. After the publication of his *Works*, Bierce left for Mexico, which was in the throes of revolution. He was last heard from in a letter dated 26 December 1913, in which he said he was going to leave Chihuahua for Ojinaga the next day. It is presumed that he died in the Battle of Ojinaga on 11 January 1914, but no evidence has ever been found to confirm that conclusion.

BIBLIOGRAPHY:

B. Richard O'Connor, *Ambrose Bierce* (Boston, 1967).

JOSEPH P. MCKERNS

BINGHAM, GEORGE BARRY (b. 10 February 1906) is chairman of the board of the Courier-Journal and Louisville Times Company, which consists of the two papers, two radio stations, a television station, and a printing operation in Louisville, Kentucky. He is former editor and publisher of the *Courier-Journal* and the *Louisville Times*. Bingham, who had a distinguished military career during World War II, also served as a U.S. government official in postwar Europe and has been prominent in civic movements on national, state, and local levels.

The third child and second son of Robert Worth Bingham and Eleanor Everett Miller Bingham, he was born in Louisville. Three generations of the Binghams, an old North Carolina family, had operated the Bingham Military School in Asheville, but Barry's father had left education for law and moved to Louisville. When Robert's first wife died, he married the widow of one of the founders of the Standard Oil Company. She died about six months later and left Robert $5 million, which he used to buy the *Courier-Journal* and the *Louisville Times* in

1918. He was U.S. ambassador to Great Britain from 1933 until his death in 1937.

Young Barry attended Richmond School in Louisville and Middlesex School in Concord, Massachusetts, before entering Harvard University in 1924. He graduated magna cum laude in English in 1928. After graduation he traveled extensively for a couple of years and did free-lance writing.

In 1930, because his father believed he should learn the business from the bottom up, Bingham started working as a police reporter for the *Louisville Times*. Next came general assignment reporting, the *Courier-Journal*'s Washington bureau, and editorial writing. Shortly after his father became ambassador in 1933, the twenty-seven-year-old Bingham was named assistant to the publisher. He was serious about making the *Courier-Journal* a top-notch paper and in 1936 hired a young Mississippian named Mark Ethridge as general manager. During the next decade the two transformed it from what had been called a business-office paper relying on circulation gags and stunts into a dignified, well-written daily. Circulation grew more than 100 percent for the *Courier-Journal* and more than 70 percent for the *Times*. A new plant was built and staffs were boosted about 50 percent. Both papers established reputations for strong coverage of foreign affairs and support for local civic and charitable activities.

When his father died in 1937, Bingham became publisher of both papers. He held that title until 1941, when he entered the service and Ethridge took over. After the war he became president of the corporation and editor of the *Courier-Journal*. In 1961 he was elected editor and publisher of both papers, and Ethridge was named chairman of the board, a new position. Bingham was sixty-five in 1971 when he stepped down as editor and publisher and became chairman of the board. Besides the two newspapers, the company owns WHAS, established by Bingham's father in 1923 to operate Kentucky's first radio station.

Bingham married Mary Clifford Caperton in Richmond, Virginia, on 19 June 1931. She was a Radcliffe student while he was at Harvard, and they had appeared in plays together. She was editor of the "World of Books" column in the *Courier-Journal* from 1942 until 1967, and has taken an active role as an officer and director in her husband's company as well as participated in countless civic and cultural activities. The couple had three sons and two daughters, but the oldest and youngest sons were killed in accidents in the mid–1960s. Their surviving son, Barry Jr., succeeded his father as publisher in 1971.

Bingham made trips to occupied Europe in 1946 and 1947 with other newspaper editors as a guest of the army to report on postwar problems. In 1949 he was appointed head of the Economic Cooperation Administration's (ECA) mission to France and deputy ambassador-at-large to all ECA member nations. In this post, which he held for a little more than a year, he was responsible for reporting on the accomplishments of Marshall Plan aid. As the result of his work, he was decorated with the rank of commander in the French Legion of Honor in 1950 and was made a commander of the Order of the British Empire in 1962.

Described in his younger days as boyishly good-looking and somewhat shy in manner, Bingham calls himself an independent Democrat. Throughout the years the Louisville papers have reflected the Bingham family's support for liberal causes and Democratic candidates. Bingham fought hard for the abolition of the poll tax and winning full franchise for blacks. Great strides also were made in improving schools, boosting Kentucky's literacy rate, opening Louisville to labor union organizers, and turning it into one of the most graft-free cities in America. A personal friend of Adlai Stevenson, Bingham spent three months touring Asia with him in 1953 and was cochairman of the Stevenson for President Committee in 1956.

Bingham is an Episcopalian and a member of several private clubs. In January 1985 Bingham was reported to be robust and active but not involved directly in the management of the companies. However, at age seventy-eight, he was still keeping a full schedule of civic and cultural activities.

BIBLIOGRAPHY:

B. NCAB J, 256; CB 1949, 54–56; "Kentucky Team," *Time*, 14 January 1946; Llewellyn White, "Papers of Paradox: The Louisville *Courier-Journal* and *Times* Confound Critics of Press Monopolies," *Reporter*, 31 January 1950.

KAY MARIE MAGOWAN

BIRCHALL, FREDERICK THOMAS (b. 1871; d. 7 March 1955) was one of the chief news executives of the *New York Times* for twenty-seven years, including six years as acting managing editor. He was also an outstanding foreign correspondent, and won the 1933 Pulitzer Prize for reporting the rise to power of Adolf Hitler.

There is no exact record of the date of his birth in Warrington, England. He was the only son of Thomas Birchall, member of a prominent county banking family. Educated in Lancashire schools, he was sent to college, but left when he realized his father intended for him to enter the ministry. He worked on several English newspapers, including the *Pall Mall Gazette*, then came to America in 1893, working first as editor of a small Philadelphia weekly for an almost nonexistent salary. After several weeks, he moved to New York and for two years covered police headquarters for a news bureau. It was at that time that he married Annie Hood, who lived in New Jersey but came from his native county in England. They had no children.

From the news bureau, Birchall moved to the *New York Tribune* as copyreader. Two years later he went to the copydesk of the *New York Sun*, where he rose to the position of assistant city editor. In 1905 he joined the *New York Times* as night city editor at the invitation of managing editor Carr Van Anda (q.v.), under whom he had worked when Van Anda was night editor of the *Sun*. In 1912 Birchall was made assistant managing editor, and he worked closely with Van Anda after the outbreak of World War I. Birchall, who worked for the English government during the war, maintained his British citizenship throughout his life and for that reason, when he was appointed to succeed Van Anda in

1926, his title was made "acting managing editor" to avoid, it was said, criticism from those who claimed the *Times* was pro-British.

Birchall had the same keen news sense as Van Anda, although he had a warmer, more outgoing personality. Described as an energetic and effective editor, he was also nervous, impulsive, excitable, and, at times, explosive when a reporter had not asked the right questions or something else had gone wrong. He was a short, stocky, bald-headed man, with a round face and pinkish-red chin whiskers, who squinted through thick-lensed glasses and always wore a green eyeshade in the newsroom.

Birchall, who felt more comfortable as a correspondent, was sent abroad in 1932 to take charge of the European news service of the *Times*. On occasion, there were difficulties, such as in 1934 at Cologne airport when he was forced to strip for German customs officials who believed he was trying to smuggle currency out of the country, an incident he reported in a humorous dispatch. His reports from Germany in 1933 described Hitler's rapid deprivation of political and social rights of communists, socialists, Catholic centrists, and Jews. He was the first American newspaper correspondent to tell the world about the concentration camps which were being set up, and in a prophetic dispatch in September 1933, he warned that Nazi policy was "persecution even to extermination—the word is the Nazis' own—of the non-Aryans, if that can be accomplished without too great world disturbance."

Summing up his journalistic experiences in 1940, Birchall wrote in *The Storm Breaks* that he had "a front seat at the greatest show in history—the spectacle of a changing world." He later accepted assignment to Ottawa, covering Canada's preparations for the defense of the empire, then retired from the *Times* to devote his energies to British war relief. He died in a Nova Scotia hospital at age eighty-four, two weeks after his wife's death.

BIBLIOGRAPHY:

A. *The Storm Breaks: A Panorama of Europe and the Forces That Have Wrecked Its Peace* (New York, 1940).

B. DAB Supp. 5, 59–60; NYT 7 March 1955; Meyer Berger, *The Story of the New York Times, 1851–1951* (New York, 1951); W. Richard Whitaker, "Outline of Hitler's 'Final Solution' Apparent by 1933," *Journalism Quarterly*, Summer 1981.

W. RICHARD WHITAKER

BLACK, WINIFRED (b. 14 October 1863; d. 25 May 1936) is usually identified by her sob-sister pen name, Annie Laurie. But she was also a crusading journalist who investigated Chicago juvenile courts, exposed New York charity racketeers, and organized disaster relief in Galveston, Texas. During her years with the Hearst organization she was society editor, drama critic, city editor, managing editor, foreign correspondent, and syndicate writer.

Born Martha Winifred Sweet in Chilton, Wisconsin, she early lost both parents and was raised by an older sister, Ada Celeste, a federal pension agent in Chicago. Early ambitions for a stage career lured her to New York, where she came under the influence of such writers as William Dean Howells (q.v.), Edwin Booth, and Mary Mapes Dodge, who encouraged her literary career.

The move to journalism was almost accidental, however. Her sister gave the *Chicago Tribune* one of Winifred's letters describing life on tour with an amateur theatrical company. The *Tribune* liked it and asked for more. Not until 1889 did she formally make journalism a career. She went west that year in search of a runaway younger brother, found him safe on an Arizona ranch and, a few days later, arrived in San Francisco, hunting a job, and was hired at the *San Francisco Examiner*. Her first major story grew out of one assignment to investigate the City Receiving Hospital and the treatment of women there. She went undercover, dressed as an indigent, and feigned a collapse on a street. Her subsequent *Examiner* story documented neglect and mistreatment, and prompted a governor's inspection, hospital staff changes, initiation of city ambulance service, and some improvement in the treatment of female patients.

She also worked undercover in a southern cotton mill, in a local fruit cannery, and as a Salvation Army angel in the Barbary Coast district. She traveled to Molokai, the Hawaiian leper colony, and her copy evoked sympathy and an outpouring of public support for the settlement. Other causes she championed included indigent children in San Francisco.

Historians usually ignore her public service stories in favor of her sob-sister reporting during the 1907 trial of Harry Thaw. Thaw, a railroad magnate, was accused of murdering his young wife's seducer, architect Stanford White. She shared the press table, and the label, with such people as Dorothy Dix, Nixola Greeley-Smith (qq.v.), and Ada Patterson, as well as several males who somehow escaped labeling.

She greatly admired Hearst and in later life reflected on his strong influence throughout her career. She was, in turn, the only woman on his staff with direct access to him. Not surprisingly, it was she who, in 1927, was assigned to write his mother's obituary, and a biography, *The Life and Personality of Phoebe Apperson Hearst* (1928).

Her personal life took second place to her career. An 1892 marriage to fellow journalist Orlow Black ended in divorce five years later. A second marriage, in 1901, to Charles Alden Bonfils, a journalist with the *Denver Post*, lasted formally until her death, but was interrupted several times by the separate newspaper involvements of husband and wife.

Lured to New York briefly when Hearst moved there in 1895, she covered William Jennings Bryan in his presidential campaign in 1896. But she loved the West and in 1897 left for the *Denver Post*, where she met Bonfils. In 1898–99 she went to Utah to cover polygamy among the growing Mormon communities. Though she remained with the *Post* for many years, her loyalties remained with Hearst. When a tidal wave crashed into Galveston, Texas, on 8 September 1900, she covered it for Hearst. Her exclusive front-page copy described the "terrible, sickening odor" of decaying bodies and the desperate need for disinfectant.

Six years later, on 18 April 1906, when San Francisco was rocked by an earthquake, she covered that disaster for Hearst as well. She went to Europe in 1918 to study the effects of the war and the rumored armistice on American soldiers. She covered the peace conference after the war, and the Washington Naval Disarmament Conference in 1921 and 1922. Despite diabetes and arteriosclerosis, she remained an active columnist until three months before her death.

BIBLIOGRAPHY:

B. John Tebbel, *The Life and Good Times of William Randolph Hearst* (New York, 1952).

SHARON MURPHY

BLAIR, FRANCIS PRESTON (b. 12 April 1791; d. 19 October 1876) edited the *Washington Globe*, the party organ of the Jackson and Van Buren administrations for fifteen years, exerting through its editorial pages an enormous influence on public opinion and Democratic party politics. A devotee and confidant of Andrew Jackson's, Blair became the mouthpiece of Jacksonian democracy.

One of seven children of James Blair, a Virginian of Scotch-Irish descent, and Elizabeth Smith Blair, Blair was born in Abingdon (Washington County), Virginia. His father moved to Kentucky with his family and was elected the state's attorney general in 1796. Francis grew up near the state capital in Frankfort and was educated at Transylvania University, where he graduated with honors in 1811. He was admitted to the Kentucky bar, but because of lung problems never practiced. Instead he attempted to farm near Frankfort while joining his father in defense of the right of a state to control the Bank of the United States. Blair married Eliza Violet Gish, the stepdaughter of Governor Charles Scott, on 21 July 1812.

Blair supplemented his farm income by being elected circuit court clerk in Franklin County, a position he held for eighteen years. Resentment over the federal bank escalated when it began to call in debts and tighten money supplies in the frontier areas. Blair became associated with the relief party in Kentucky which advocated stay and replevin laws to allow debtors to keep their land and property. In 1821 he became a director, and later president, of the Bank of the Commonwealth, created by the Kentucky legislature to help debtors. When the Kentucky Court of Appeals struck down the state's relief laws, the relief-dominated legislature reacted by creating a new court of appeals. Blair, who had opposed the antirelief position in letters under the pen name "Patrick Henry" in the Frankfort, Kentucky, *Argus of Western America*, was appointed clerk of the new court in 1824. His attempts to secure records from the old court clerk fueled public debate on the issue. When the Old Court party regained a majority in the state legislature, Blair gave up his clerkship. He joined Amos Kendall (q.v.), editor of the *Argus*, and William T. Barry, another reliefer, in shaping the New Court party into a powerful organization for Andrew Jackson in 1828.

When Kendall and Barry went to Washington as members of Jackson's Kitchen Cabinet, Blair edited the *Argus*, and developed an editorial position which opposed the Bank of the United States, attacked nullification by South Carolina opponents of the tariff, and defended Peggy Eaton, the wife of Jackson's secretary of war, against ostracism by Washington society.

When Jackson looked for an editor to replace Duff Green (q.v.), editor of the *United States Telegraph*, Kendall recommended Blair. The new party organ, the *Globe*, was financed on borrowed money with the promise of executive patronage as collateral. The *Globe* plant was located only a short distance from the White House and the house which Blair bought on Pennsylvania Avenue diagonally opposite the president's home.

The first issue of the *Globe* appeared on 7 December 1830 as a four-page semiweekly. In six months it converted to a daily. By 1835 the *Globe* had 17,000 subscribers and its columns were reprinted in over 400 newspapers. Besides being the voice of Jacksonian democracy, Blair also enjoyed almost daily access to the president and was frequently consulted on matters of policy and patronage. While receiving patronage from the executive branch of government, Blair and his partner, John C. Rives, shared Congress's printing contracts with other publishers who sought the post of House or Senate printer. Blair and Rives supplemented their income with the establishment in 1833 of the *Congressional Globe*, a weekly of sixteen pages published during sessions of Congress. Bound and sold in volumes after each session, it served as the public record of Congress.

Blair and the *Globe* maintained their influential political roles during the Van Buren administration, but began to fall into disfavor in 1840 with the election of William Henry Harrison and his successor, John Tyler, who created a new party organ. In 1845 President James Polk forced Blair out as editor, and offered him the mission to Spain, which Blair refused. The *Globe* was sold to Thomas Ritchie (q.v.) for $35,000. The deal did not include the printing equipment, and Blair and Rives continued to publish the *Congressional Globe* until Blair dissolved the partnership in 1849. Under Rives, the *Congressional Globe* continued as the record of Congress until 1873.

Blair moved to Silver Spring, his Maryland farm only five miles from Washington, where he remained active in national politics. His editorial voice reemerged as an opponent of the admission of slave states and a supporter of and adviser to Abraham Lincoln. Blair's eldest son, Montgomery, was Lincoln's postmaster general. Another son, Francis "Frank" P. Blair, Jr., was a Missouri congressman and Union general and the Democratic vice presidential candidate in 1868. Blair was the father of another son, James, and a daughter, Elizabeth Blair Lee. Two other children died in early childhood.

BIBLIOGRAPHY:

B. DAB 1, 330–332; NYT 20 October 1876; Culver H. Smith, *The Press, Politics, and Patronage: The American Government's Use of Newspapers 1789–1875* (Athens, Ga., 1977); Elbert B. Smith, *Francis Preston Blair* (New York, 1983); William E. Smith, *The Francis Preston Blair Family in Politics* (New York, 1933).

ELIZABETH FRAAS

BLAKESLEE, HOWARD WALTER (b. 21 March 1880; d. 2 May 1952) was one of the elite group of news reporters who pioneered science and medical writing during the first half of the twentieth century.

The son of Jesse Walter Blakeslee, then a missionary among the Indians in the territory of Washington, and Jennie Howard Blakeslee, who had been a Civil War nurse, he was born in New Dungeness, Washington. Several years after his birth, the family moved to Detroit, where he was graduated from high school. He attended the University of Michigan and was expelled during his senior year for reporting in the *Michigan Daily* that disturbed administrators. After he had become famous for his science news coverage, the university conferred on him an honorary M.S. degree in 1935.

Blakeslee began his professional career in 1901 as a feature writer with the *Detroit Journal*. He worked as a sports reporter on Detroit and Chicago dailies and joined the Associated Press in New York City on 4 July 1905. After serving as AP bureau chief in New Orleans, Atlanta, and Dallas, Blakeslee became news editor in Chicago and then New York. He was named AP science editor in 1928 and held the position until his death.

A small group of correspondents covered the Harvard University tercentenary, which included discussions of recent developments in various fields of knowledge and predictions about the future. Blakeslee was among five who shared the 1937 Pulitzer Prize for their articles.

Blakeslee reported extensively on testing of the atomic bomb and possible applications of atomic energy to peacetime uses. He covered the Bikini tests in 1946 and had returned from the Yucca Flats, Nevada, tests in 1952 only a few days before he died of coronary thrombosis in Fort Washington, New York.

He wrote several books on atomic energy, one of which was translated into Japanese and one provided to AP member publications in 1946 for public distribution. He joined his contemporaries on the science writing circuit during the 1930s in establishing the National Association of Science Writers, a professional organization that grew to more than 1,000 members half a century later. He served as president in 1936–37.

Blakeslee married Marguerite Alton Fortune on 19 March 1906; they had four children: John Herbert, Merlys, Alton Lauren, and Carol. After that marriage ended in divorce, he married Rosamond Robinson; they had three children: Howard W. Jr., Rosamond, and Alan Robinson.

BIBLIOGRAPHY:
B. DAB Supp. 5, 64–65; NYT 3 May 1952; Hillier Krieghbaum, *Science and the Mass Media* (New York, 1967).

HILLIER KRIEGHBAUM

BLISS, EDWARD, JR. (b. 30 July 1912) has been a newspaper reporter, a broadcast journalist for CBS, and a journalism educator. During his twenty-five-year tenure at CBS in the radio and television divisions, he wrote and edited copy for two of CBS's preeminent journalists, Edward R. Murrow and Walter Cronkite (qq.v.). Bliss was known by his colleagues for his excellent writing skills, news judgment, and integrity.

Bliss was born in Foochow, China, to Edward and May Bortz Bliss. His father was a medical missionary and his mother a teacher. Bliss received his secondary education in the United States and earned a B.A. degree from Yale in 1935. Between 1935 and 1936, Bliss worked for the *Bucyrus* (Ohio) *Telegraph-Forum* as a reporter. He moved to the *Columbus* (Ohio) *Citizen* as a reporter and state editor in 1936 and remained with the paper until 1943. Bliss married Lois Arnette, a teacher, from Raleigh, North Carolina on 26 August 1940. They had two children, Anne Bliss Mascolino and Lois Bliss Abshire.

In 1943 Bliss moved to New York, where he wrote news for CBS. He became night editor for CBS News in 1945, a position he held for ten years. Bliss began working with Edward R. Murrow in 1948 when Murrow was doing nightly commentary. Since it was CBS policy that an editor "read copy" on the scripts of even its most distinguished journalists, Bliss got to work closely with Murrow. They respected each other's writing, both recognizing the importance of clarity, simplicity, economy, and precision in preparing broadcast copy.

Murrow was so impressed with the skill of his editor that he asked Bliss to join his own staff in 1955 as a writer. Bliss worked for Murrow until 1961, first as writer-editor-producer for Murrow's nightly radio broadcasts, then as producer of Murrow's "Background" radio program. Bliss remained with Murrow until President John F. Kennedy asked Murrow to head the United States Information Agency in 1961. The high regard Murrow had held for Bliss was reflected in the choice of Bliss by Murrow's widow to edit a book of the newsman's broadcasts.

Between 1961 and 1962, Bliss worked with the CBS-TV documentary unit which produced "CBS Reports." In 1962, he worked as assistant to Richard S. Salant (q.v.), president of CBS News. By the fall of 1963, Bliss had joined the team of CBS broadcast journalists who were designing a new evening television newscast. On Labor Day, the thirty-minute "CBS Evening News with Walter Cronkite" replaced the fifteen-minute nightly news summary. Cronkite was the managing editor and anchor. Bliss was news editor. He sat an arm's length from Cronkite, just out of camera range, prepared to hand over a late-breaking story, update, or rewrite. The relationship was a close one: it was Bliss who first informed Cronkite that John Kennedy had been shot in Dallas. Bliss remained as news editor of "CBS Evening News" until 1968. He had earned the genuine respect of Cronkite who said that Bliss's copy was close to the finest professionally that could be found.

Bliss left CBS News in February 1968 to teach. He founded the broadcast journalism program at American University in Washington, D.C. He retired in 1977. After his retirement, Bliss acted as a broadcast journalism consultant for CBS, PBS, the CBC (Canadian Broadcasting Corporation), National Public Radio, and numerous local stations throughout the United States. He wrote articles on the profession for a wide variety of publications from *TV Guide* to *Television Quarterly*, and he worked on a history of American broadcast journalism for Columbia University Press. He also taught broadcast journalism as a visiting professor at the University of North Carolina at Chapel Hill in 1981.

Among the honors Bliss has received are the Distinguished Teaching Award of the Society of Professional Journalists, Sigma Delta Chi, in 1977, and the Distinguished Broadcast Journalism Educator Award from the Association for Education in Journalism and Mass Communication in 1984.

BIBLIOGRAPHY:

A. *In Search of Light: The Broadcasts of Edward R. Murrow, 1938–1961* (New York, 1967); with John M. Patterson, *Writing News for Broadcast* (New York, 1971; 2d. ed., 1978).

B. CA 41–44, 1st rev., 72–73; Jack Gould, "Radio Was His Medium," *New York Times Book Review*, 10 September 1967; Robert Metz, *CBS: Reflections in a Bloodshot Eye* (New York, 1975).

JOHN P. FREEMAN

BOK, EDWARD WILLIAM (b. 9 October 1863; d. 9 January 1930) was a creative and sometimes controversial editor of the *Ladies' Home Journal* for thirty years, a Pulitzer Prize–winning author, a philanthropist, and a peace advocate. Bok established a reputation as a bright, innovative writer-editor during a journalistic career that spanned more than fifty years and produced more than a dozen books. His willingness to tackle sensitive topics and social taboos editorially, and to promote internationalism and world peace organizations philanthropically also gained him national and worldwide recognition.

Bok was born in the Netherlands seaport city of Den Helder, the second of two sons of William John Hidde Bok and Sieke Gertrude van Herwerden Bok. His father was a minister in the court of the Dutch king, William III. After a series of serious financial setbacks, the family emigrated to the United States in September 1870. They settled in Brooklyn, where Bok entered public school not knowing how to speak English. To help family finances, Bok worked at odd jobs, including his first journalism job—he reported on children's parties for the *Brooklyn Daily Bugle*.

After his father was hired as a translator by the Western Union Telegraph Company, Bok quit school and became an office boy with his father's company at the age of thirteen. Bok continued and even expanded his writing activities while an office boy. He wrote biographies of prominent Americans, covered theatrical news for the *Brooklyn Eagle*, published theater programs, and edited the *Philomathean Review* for Henry Ward Beecher's (q.v.) Plymouth Church. For a short time, Bok served as a stenographer for Western Union. In 1882 Bok was hired as a stenographer for Henry Holt and Company, and two years later moved to Charles Scribner's Sons publishing house with a similar position.

Bok continued to edit the church magazine, which in 1884 became the *Brooklyn Magazine*, and began publishing works by well-known authors. With his excellent literary contacts, Bok left the magazine in 1886 and started his own newspaper syndicate. "Bok's Literary Leaves," containing features and reviews written by respected authors, quickly reached more than forty subscribing newspapers. Bok also assembled reading materials designed especially for women. The innovative "Bok page," as it was called, proved extremely popular and was widely imitated in the form of the "woman's page" by newspapers around the country.

Impressed by Bok's syndicated literary and women's material, Cyrus H. K. Curtis (q.v.), publisher of the *Ladies' Home Journal*, invited Bok to become editor of the six-year-old magazine. In 1889, at the age of twenty-six, Bok accepted the position. Building on the solid editorial base established by the *Journal*'s first editor, Louisa Curtis, Bok initiated several innovations. He offered prizes for the best suggestions for stories and features; he created advice columns for women of all ages; he introduced how-to stories about interior design, gardening, and other topics; and his magazine's "question and answer" column, designed to be "a great clearing house of information" for women, brought in almost a million letters annually by 1917. Bok was also able to attract the works of the greatest literary and political figures of his day, including Mark Twain (*see* Clemens, Samuel Langhorne), Rudyard Kipling, Theodore Roosevelt, and Woodrow Wilson.

On 22 October 1896 Bok married the daughter of Cyrus H. K. Curtis, Mary Louise. They had two sons, William Curtis Bok and Cary William Bok.

Bok's editorship of the *Journal* was as provocative as it was innovative. The *Journal* published frequent articles on the issues of women's rights and suffrage, public health, consumer safety, and the environment. Bok also shocked his readers on occasion with stories on "forbidden" subjects, such as venereal disease. Such stories prompted bitter protests and lost many readers, but Bok continued tackling the taboos of the time.

Following his retirement from the editorship of the *Journal* in the fall of 1919, Bok devoted his energies to writing and promoting civic and political causes. His Pulitzer Prize–winning autobiography, *The Americanization of Edward Bok*, was published in September 1920, and was followed by at least seven other books, including the biography of his father-in-law, Cyrus H. K. Curtis. Bok also endowed several awards for civic service and international peace. He created, for example, the Philadelphia Award of $10,000 for community service, and the American Peace Award of $100,000 for the "most practicable plan by which the United States may cooperate with other nations to achieve and preserve the peace of the world.'' In all, he donated more than $2 million to charitable causes.

Bok suffered a heart attack at his estate and died at the age of sixty-seven.

BIBLIOGRAPHY:

A. *The Americanization of Edward Bok* (New York, 1920).

B. DAB 21, Supp. 1, 91–93; NYT 10 January 1930; *Editor and Publisher*, 11 January 1930; *Ladies' Home Journal*, March 1930; *Publishers Weekly*, 18 January 1930.

ROY ALDEN ATWOOD

BONFILS, FREDERICK GILMER (b. 31 December 1860; d. 2 February 1933) and his partner, Harry Heye Tammen (q.v.) were two of the most successful, colorful, and vilified publishers in the history of the American press. These yellow journalists turned an unprofitable daily into the most widely read newspaper in Colorado. When Bonfils died, the *New York Times* noted that his newspaper, the *Denver Post*, had followed ''a fearless, aggressive policy'' of attacking anyone the publishers felt opposed the public good. No elected official, no public figure was safe from attacks by the newspaper ''weaned on tiger's milk.'' But if Bonfils and Tammen brought yellow journalism's social conscience to the Rockies' they also brought its unscrupulous methods, its dependence on sensationalism, and its penchant for managing the news for personal advantage. They were among the first to break the Teapot Dome story and ironically were later found to have profited from the shady oil dealings.

To account for his notorious stinginess, Bonfils recalled his impoverished boyhood near Troy, Missouri. Like much in his life, the truth behind his memories is difficult to determine. He was the fourth of eight children born to Eugene Napoleon Bonfils and Henrietta Lewis Bonfils. His father was a probate judge and, later, an insurance executive. Bonfils was educated in Troy public schools and was admitted to West Point in 1878. He said that he left without graduating because he had fallen in love with Belle Barton, whom he married in 1882. It is more likely that he left, not because of a conflict between love and honor, but because of a deficiency in mathematics.

By the time he met Tammen in 1895, Bonfils had held a number of jobs, including, ironically, a position as a mathematics instructor at a military school. He had also concocted a number of moneymaking schemes that would haunt him in later life. Bonfils had cleared at least $15,000 selling parcels of land in Texas, miles from the nearest railroad or water. Bonfils and Tammen formed a partnership, with Bonfils contributing $125,000 to purchase the *Evening Post* (Denver).

When the two took charge of the *Post* on 28 October 1895, the paper's circulation was a meager 6,000. Circulation rose steadily, reaching 83,000 by 1907, more than the combined circulations of its three competitors. Only then did Bonfils allow the partners to draw salaries—$1,000 a week each. They were less successful with the *Kansas City Post*, which they ran from 1909 to 1922, chiefly to bedevil Bonfils's old nemesis, the *Kansas City Star*.

Bonfils—handsome, irascible, and acute—handled the daily management of the paper, scrutinizing each edition until late into the night. Tammen—short, round, and jovial—handled the promotions to increase the newspaper's circulation.

Of the newspaper's freewheeling attacks on Denver's power structure, Tammen said, "We're yellow, but we're read." The publishers allowed so much editorial comment in their news stories, topped by red headlines, that they had little need for editorials, except for their column, "So the People May Know." So vehement were the attacks that many called the publishers' red conference room "the Bucket of Blood."

Many suspected that the publishers used the crusades to coerce merchants into advertising. Tammen said his paper had a heart and soul. His detractors added, "And a price." Though the publishers were taken to court a number of times—Bonfils was convicted in 1907 of assaulting the publisher of the *Rocky Mountain News*—the charges of coercion were never substantiated.

Bonfils's role in the Teapot Dome scandal received national attention and scrutiny by a Senate committee. Testimony revealed that in 1922 Bonfils had financed a lawsuit brought by his friend John Leo Stack against Harry F. Sinclair, the recipient of the controversial oil leases. Bonfils was to share in the settlement against Sinclair. While the committee never determined whether Bonfils had used his newspaper to force Sinclair to settle, the appearance of impropriety led the American Society of Newspaper Editors to order his expulsion from the organization in 1926.

On 2 February 1933, shortly after converting to Roman Catholicism, Bonfils died of toxic encephalitis, an acute inflammation of the brain. He was survived by his wife and two daughters, May and Helen. His estate was officially valued at $14,308.72.

BIBLIOGRAPHY:

B. DAB Supp. 1, 93–96; NCAB 49, 54–55; NYT 3 February 1933; Gene Fowler, *Timber Line* (New York, 1933).

HARRIS E. ROSS

BOOTH, GEORGE GOUGH (b. 24 September 1864; d. 11 April 1949) was president of the *Detroit News* and founder of the eight-city Booth newspaper chain in southern Michigan, now owned by the Newhouse group. Booth's newspaper career was concentrated on the business side of publishing; by the time of his retirement, the *News* held the largest circulation in Detroit. In the first decades of this century, Booth and his wife, the former Ellen Scripps, began building a group of educational institutions on their suburban estate, Cranbrook. The Cranbrook community grew into an unusual range of institutions, from boarding schools to a graduate school of art and design. Booth's private vision, beginning with his early interest in design, brought together architects and designers from the United States and Europe to create Cranbook's architecture and to develop a major influence on American design.

Booth was born in Toronto, Ontario, to Henry Wood Booth and Clara Gagnier Booth. Booth's father operated newspapers at Toronto and St. Catharines, Ontario, although his son initially chose other careers. Henry Booth also had moved his family frequently and had pursued other occupations, such as manufacturing copper work for distilleries. George Booth worked in an architect's office and was co-owner of an ironworks foundry in Windsor, Ontario, across the river from Detroit, when he married Ellen Scripps, daughter of James Scripps (q.v.), founder and publisher of the *Detroit News*.

A few years after Scripps started the *News* in the 1870s, he and his brothers, George H. and Edward Willis (q.v.), launched a newspaper chain which now bears the name Scripps-Howard. James Scripps eventually split with the rest of the family and chose to remain with the *News* as a nonchain publisher. Booth and Ellen Scripps were married on 1 June 1887, and in 1888 Booth went to work for the *News* at his father-in-law's request. Booth was assigned to the business office and given no further instruction by Scripps. In time, Booth acted as liaison between James and the more flamboyant E. W. Scripps. Booth saw the value of a newspaper independent of outside, chain control as well as the financial gain from chain publishing. In his career, Booth combined both attributes by staying at the independently run *News* and founding a prosperous chain of his own.

With the help of his brother, Edmund, and others, Booth founded the *Grand Rapids Press* in 1893 and established and operated newspapers in Michigan's population centers outside Detroit. In 1897 Booth became general manager of the *News*. He was named president of the newspaper in 1906, on the death of James Scripps. Booth retired from the *News* in 1929 but remained a director until his death. His support of the arts may have been spurred by Scripps's own art collection, which he brought from Europe to his Detroit home. Booth was a contributor to the Detroit Institute of Arts, to the American Federation of Arts, and to fellowship funds at the University of Michigan. He also served as president of the Detroit Society of Arts and Crafts for some twenty-three years. In 1927 the Booths established the Cranbrook Foundation to support the cultural and educational center on their estate, eventually spending more than $24 million for that purpose.

Booth's absorption with his estate and its projects, even before retirement, helped to earn him the nickname "the duke of Cranbrook," especially popular with a rival newspaper. While Booth's most visible role was that of philanthropist, there is some evidence that he may also have played a part in the daily coverage of his newspaper, the *News*. In 1912, Andrew H. Green, Jr., a Detroit businessman, wrote to the newspaper about Booth's involvement in helping to promote stories exposing city council corruption. Green credited Booth with giving him the suggestion to investigate the graft.

Booth's wife, Ellen, died in 1948. Booth died the next year. He was survived by two sons, Warren Scripps Booth, publisher of the *News* from 1952 to 1963, and Henry Scripps Booth, executive director of the Cranbrook Foundation from 1946 to 1965.

BIBLIOGRAPHY:

B. NYT 12 April 1949; William W. Lutz, *The News of Detroit* (Boston, 1973); Arthur Pound, *The Only Thing Worth Finding: The Life and Legacies of George Gough Booth* (Detroit, 1964).

JAMES BOW

BOUDINOT, ELIAS (b. ca. 1803; d. 22 June 1839), a Cherokee, was editor of the first American Indian newspaper, the *Cherokee Phoenix* of New Echota, Georgia. Having received a far better education than most Indians of his era, Boudinot was made clerk of the Cherokee Council, served as an eloquent spokesman for his people's interests, and became one of the most influential members of his tribe.

First of eight children of Oowatie, a full-blooded Cherokee, and Susannah Reese, half Cherokee and half Scot, Boudinot was born in northwestern Georgia as Galagina (pronounced Kil-ke-nah), which means "buck," or male deer. Oowatie was a member of the progressive faction of the Cherokees, and when the opportunity arose, sent Galagina to a Moravian mission school at Spring Place, near Chatsworth, Georgia. In 1817 the young Galagina was enrolled at Brainerd, Tennessee, in a school founded by the New England–based American Board of Commissioners for Foreign Missions (ABCFM). Shortly thereafter the ABCFM established a school in Cornwall, Connecticut, expressly dedicated to educating and Christianizing "heathen young men of promise." One of those selected for the Cornwall School was Galagina. On his way north with two ABCFM members, the young man visited the elderly Elias Boudinot, former president of the Continental Congress, at his Burlington, New Jersey, home. Boudinot was much taken with Galagina and suggested that the young Cherokee adopt his name. When Galagina arrived at Cornwall, he registered as Elias Boudinott, spelling the name with an extra *T* until 1831.

After completing his studies, Boudinot married Harriet Ruggles Gold, a daughter of one of Cornwall's leading citizens, on 28 March 1826. Boudinot brought his bride to the Georgia hills, where he took charge of the ABCFM's Hightower mission station. In December 1827 the couple moved to the Cherokee capital New Echota, where Boudinot became clerk of the Cherokee Council and tutored a recently arrived missionary, Samuel Worcester, in Cherokee.

Thanks to the work of a Cherokee known as Sequoyah, the tribe had been the first Indian nation to adopt a written syllabary, or alphabet. After a substantial part of the tribe had become literate, the council decided to found an official tribal newspaper and chose the lettered Boudinot as its first editor. The name chosen for the paper was the *Cherokee Phoenix*, symbolic of the tribe's desire to rise Phoenix-like from its own ashes and join the white man on equal footing. From his first issue on 21 February 1828, Boudinot editorialized against the growing specter of Indian removal to the West and wrote convincingly of his people's progress and development. Writing largely for the benefit of his non-Indian readers, Boudinot pointed to his tribe's representative form of government, court system, and prosperous agricultural base. More than 1,000 Cherokees, he wrote, were baptized Christians, and the tribe's mode of dress was much like that of the white settlers who surrounded them. The editor's overall tone was puritanical, yet a keen sense of humor shone through the piety. Most of Boudinot's weekly was printed in English, a small part in Cherokee.

Boudinot's tenure as editor was rife with difficulties; a succession of acts of the Georgia legislature made life increasingly unpleasant for the tribe. By 1829 a full-scale gold rush had materialized in the Georgia hill country, and by 1830 gold-hungry whites were illegally driving Cherokees from their property. In his editorials Boudinot appealed for fair treatment for his tribe but counseled passive resistance as opposed to bloodshed. At last he concluded that removal was inevitable and resigned as editor in September 1832. The paper's final issue was published on 31 May 1834, and subsequent attempts to revive it ended in 1835 when the *Phoenix*'s press and type were confiscated by the Georgia Guard.

In May 1836 Boudinot was one of twenty Cherokee delegates sent to Washington to negotiate the removal question. Having struck what they viewed as the best possible deal for their people, Boudinot and the others signed the New Echota Treaty, which agreed to removal, a deed that to this day many Indians regard as traitorous.

Boudinot's wife Harriet died in June 1836, having borne him six children. Of these, Elias Cornelius Boudinot, the youngest, became most prominent in a varied career as an engineer, lawyer, gentleman farmer, editor of the *Arkansian*, and editorial writer for the Little Rock *True Democrat*. William Penn Boudinot became a successful Philadelphia engraver, and Frank Boudinot died as a Union soldier in the Civil War.

Later in 1836 Boudinot married Delight Sargent, a missionary with whom he had worked; the couple had no children. In November 1837 he left his Georgia farm and moved his family to the Indian Territory in what is now Oklahoma, where they joined the Worcesters, who had established a church at Park Hill.

On 22 June 1839 a band of resentful Cherokees murdered Boudinot on his Park Hill farm. Also assassinated were his kinsmen Major Ridge and John Ridge, who had also signed the controversial removal treaty.

BIBLIOGRAPHY:

A. *An Address to the Whites* (Philadelphia, 1826); *Letters and Other Papers Relating to Cherokee Affairs* (Athens, Ga., 1837); Theda Perdue, ed., *Cherokee Editor: The Writings of Elias Boudinot* (Knoxville, Tenn., 1983).

B. DAB 1, 478; George Adams Boyd, *Elias Boudinot, Patriot and Statesman* (Princeton, N.J., 1952); Ralph Henry Gabriel, *Elias Boudinot, Cherokee, and His America* (Norman, Okla., 1941); Barbara F. Luebke, "Elias Boudinot, Cherokee Editor: The Father of American Indian Journalism," Ph.D. diss., Univ. of Missouri, 1981; Barbara F. Luebke, "Elias Boudinot, Indian Editor/Editorial Columns for the *Cherokee Phoenix*,"

Journalism History, Summer 1979; Sam G. Riley, "The *Cherokee Phoenix*: The Short, Unhappy Life of the First American Indian Newspaper," *Journalism Quarterly*, Winter 1976.

SAM G. RILEY

BOURKE-WHITE, MARGARET (b. 14 June 1904; d. 27 August 1971) was one of the world's first and foremost photojournalists and one of the first to provide both photographs and text for a story. Her pictures conveyed to Americans much of what they felt about the Great Depression and World War II. She documented the industry of America, including steel, mining, shipping, and railroads. She helped create the *Life* photo essay wherein one picture or a short series of pictures conveyed a story.

Maggie (as her colleagues called her) was born in New York to Joseph White and Minnie Elizabeth Bourke White. Her father, who designed rotary presses, was a weekend naturalist, and while Margaret was growing up in Cleveland she raised 25 turtles and 200 caterpillars, acquiring knowledge that found its way onto paper later in such photo essays as one in *Life* about the praying mantis. She spent a summer session at Rutgers University and a year at Columbia (where she studied photography under Clarence H. White), then went to the University of Michigan in 1923 where, at age nineteen, she married for the first time. Her husband, Everett Chapman, taught at Purdue, and she attended classes there. The marriage ended in divorce after two years. It was then that she added her mother's maiden name and the hyphen to her last name.

Divorced, her father dead and her money gone, she worked at the Natural History Museum in Cleveland and attended Case Western Reserve. She attended Cornell in 1926–1927—her sixth college—and completed her degree. She earned money there by photographing campus scenes and selling the pictures. In Cleveland again, she happened one day upon a man preaching in a park to an audience of pigeons. She hurried into a photo shop across the street, bought a camera and film, persuaded the man to resume his sermon, and took a picture. It was shown in several exhibits and gained her a critical reputation.

She obtained assignments to photograph architecture. On one of her first such assignments she relieved a bare, muddy landscape of a new school by placing a bouquet of asters in the foreground. Her tendency to arrange a photograph rather than shoot it candidly brought criticism. James Agee accused her in his book *Let Us Now Praise Famous Men* of arranging some of her most famous depression pictures. But the architectural pictures she took at the Otis Steel Works helped develop modern techniques for architectural and industrial photography, and added to her renown. She became a staff photographer for *Fortune*.

In 1934 she began working with Erskine Caldwell, who wrote text for many of her pictures. They traveled together, and in 1939 were married at Silver City, Idaho, a ghost town she chose because she liked the name when she saw it on a map. The marriage lasted only three years. She had no children by either of her marriages. She joined the staff of the new *Life* magazine in 1936 and took the photograph used for its first cover. The photo was typical of her work, which featured clear-cut detail and nothing extraneous.

During World War II she photographed the Big Three leaders—Churchill gave her twelve minutes, Stalin carried her bags and she managed to get him to smile for the camera. She was the only U.S. photographer in the Soviet Union during the Battle of Moscow, and was the only woman photographer accredited to war zones by the U.S. Army.

She flew on bombing raids in American aircraft, accompanied artillery spotters, and photographed the concentration camp at Buchenwald when it was liberated by the U.S. Third Army. After the war she covered South Africa and India—she took the last picture of Gandhi alive hours before he was assassinated. She covered the Hindu-Moslem fighting in India and the war in Korea, emphasizing its effect on civilians.

Korea was her last assignment for *Life*. En route home from Korea she felt a numbness that was eventually diagnosed as Parkinson's disease. She fought it for nineteen years with therapy and medication. Bourke-White asked for and got *Life*'s assignment to be the first of its photographers to go to the moon, but mortality interfered. Her disease became worse and developed into what she called a creeping rigidity. She died of the illness at the age of sixty-seven.

BIBLIOGRAPHY:

A. With Erskine Caldwell, *You Have Seen Their Faces* (New York, 1937); *Shooting the Russian War* (New York 1942); *They Call It Purple Heart Valley* (New York, 1944).

B. NYT 28 August 1971.

DWIGHT JENSEN

BOVARD, OLIVER KIRBY (b. 27 May 1872; d. 3 November 1945) reigned for thirty years as managing editor of the *St. Louis Post-Dispatch*. During that time he probably was the highest paid and was considered by many to be the ablest managing editor of a metropolitan daily in the United States. Stern in demeanor and thoroughly efficient in evaluating the significance and potential of events as well as the capabilities of reporters and subeditors. Bovard was respected by all and feared by most. His formal education ended with the eighth grade, but his reading and development of keen insight did not, and he became a shrewd judge of the holders of power in politics and business. This suited him particularly well for direction of the *Post-Dispatch*, founded in 1878 by Joseph Pulitzer (q.v.) with the mandate that it crusade for justice and reform and "never be satisfied with merely printing news."

Bovard was born in Jacksonville, Illinois, the second of five children of Charles Wyrick and Hester Bunn Bovard. His father was a printer who worked in several Illinois towns and finally in St. Louis, where he became telegraph editor of the *Post-Dispatch* in 1891. The son also wanted to be a newspaperman, and after working as a clerk in several St. Louis business offices, got a job as a reporter on the *St. Louis Star*. An avid participant in the new sport of bicycling, he also became editor of the *Star*'s bicycle pages. He left the *Star* after two years because it would not disclose a bribery scandal involving a street railway franchise. He took the story to the *Post-Dispatch*, which both printed the story and hired him as a reporter.

In 1900 Bovard became city editor, and in 1908 was made acting managing editor of the *Post-Dispatch*. In 1909 Pulitzer offered him the position of assistant managing editor of the publisher's prized *New York World*, but Bovard declined, saying he would rather be in charge in St. Louis than play "second fiddle" in New York. In 1910 he became permanent managing editor of the *Post-Dispatch*.

Bovard was instrumental in the training of many *Post-Dispatch* journalists, but none more apt than the publisher's namesake son. The young Pulitzer soon formed a high opinion of Bovard's skill as an editor even though he found him at times to be a martinette. When he became editor and publisher in 1912 following his father's death, Joseph Pulitzer II (q.v.) allowed the news operation of the paper to be largely Bovard's domain. Among the managing editor's most noteworthy achievements were establishing the paper's Washington bureau in 1918, supervising the uncovering of the Teapot Dome oil lease scandal in 1923, and exposing improper conduct on the part of U.S. District Court Judge George W. English that resulted in the judge's resignation in 1926. Reporters Paul Y. Anderson and John T. Rogers won Pulitzer Prizes for their roles in those episodes, but as Anderson wrote some years later, Bovard, who deliberately avoided the limelight, shared the reporters' credit: "Careless reporters, slovenly writers and oafish sub-editors lived in terror of his questions. To those who met his tests he gave encouragement, inspiration, and unflagging personal solicitude. He was the best friend of every good man who ever worked for him" (Markham, 1954).

Though he too had a high estimate of the man, the younger Pulitzer, by then taking a more active role as editor, would not commit the *Post-Dispatch* to a course of nationalization of key industries that Bovard saw as essential following the crisis of the Great Depression. In August 1938 Bovard resigned. Though painful for both sides, the break was clean, and the two maintained a cordial relationship until Bovard's death.

BIBLIOGRAPHY:

B. DAB 3, 91–92; NYT 5 November 1945; Paul Y. Anderson, "The Greatest Managing Editor," *Nation*, 13 August 1938; James W. Markham, *Bovard of the "Post-Dispatch"* (Baton Rouge, 1954).

DANIEL W. PFAFF

BOWLES, SAMUEL, III (b. 9 February 1826; d. 16 January 1878) edited the *Springfield* (Massachusetts) *Republican* from its birth in 1844. It became the best-known eastern daily outside of the seaboard cities in the latter nineteenth century and the weekly edition circulated nationally. His comprehensive news coverage of nearby communities was combined with independence of editorial opinion on national issues. Under Bowles, the newspaper became acknowledged as a ''school of journalism'' for its training of young journalists who went on to larger metropolitan newspapers.

One of five children, Bowles was the son of Samuel Bowles and Huldah Deming Bowles. His father had been a printer who founded the *Republican* in 1824 as an anti-Federalist weekly. His mother was a descendant of Miles Standish. He was educated in public and private schools and became an apprentice at the *Republican* at seventeen. The next year he convinced his father to put out a daily *Republican* and assumed responsibility for its news coverage. In spite of Bowles's ill health, the daily survived because of low expenses and his hard work.

Editorially, the paper was erratic at first. It began as a Whig supporter, but by 1855 Bowles boosted the early efforts to organize the Republican party and took up the abolitionist cause. After the death of his father in 1851, the weekly became more concerned with New England news and national issues and circulated throughout the country reprinting many of the daily's editorials. Bowles in later life more often supervised the weekly and delegated responsibility for editing the daily. At its peak, the weekly circulated 10,000 copies by mail throughout the nation.

From the beginning, Bowles emphasized local news. He later added correspondents in an ever-widening radius. When the telegraph came in, Bowles developed the ability to expand and supplement the meager news service. He also had the advantage that Springfield was a railroad crossroads and could receive the New York papers within hours of publication. He taught his reporters and editors to use concise, ordinary language, and to eschew the literary style of the day.

In 1846 the daily *Gazette* appeared in competition, but was absorbed by Bowles in 1848. The daily *Hampden Post* began in 1848, but lasted only six years. Bowles in 1857 became editor of a new Boston daily, the *Traveller*. Disagreements with the organizers caused him to return to the *Republican* after four months. He spurned other offers to leave Springfield thereafter.

In 1872 Bowles joined in the mugwump movement to deny Grant reelection. The dissenting editors were known as the Quadrilateral and expected to control the movement. In addition to Bowles, they included Carl Schurz (q.v.) of the *St. Louis Westliche Post*, Horace White (q.v.) of the *Chicago Tribune*, and Murat Halstead (q.v.) of the *Cincinnati Commercial*. The Liberal Republican convention met in Cincinnati and nominated editor Horace Greeley (q.v.), a candidate each member of the Quadrilateral disapproved. Their eventual support was not enough, and Greeley was soundly defeated.

In an 1872 agreement, partner Clark W. Bryan was bought out of the newspapers by taking the job-printing and book-binding business. The transaction was done in such a brusque manner that Bryan and some employees purchased the *Springfield Union* and made it into the first formidable rival of the daily *Republican*.

The daily became a magnet for younger journalists as its reputation grew. Bowles selected college graduates and supervised their rigorous training. Associate editor J. G. Holland became editor in chief of *Scribner's Monthly*; Charles R. Miller later edited the *New York Times* for decades; Charles Dow (q.v.) went on to found the *Wall Street Journal*. Anyone who worked satisfactorily under Bowles was welcomed on the biggest papers in the country.

Bowles's appetite for work and devotion to excellence often caused him ill health and strained personal relations with those around him. He suffered a stroke in December 1877 and died on 16 January 1878.

BIBLIOGRAPHY:

A. *Our New West: Records of Travel Between the Mississippi River and the Pacific Ocean* (Hartford, Conn., 1869).

B. DAB 1, 514–518; NYT 17 January 1878; Richard Hooker, *The Story of an Independent Newspaper* (New York, 1924); George S. Merriam, *Life and Times of Samuel Bowles*, 2 Vols. (New York, 1885).

SAM KUCZUN

BRACKENRIDGE, HUGH HENRY (b. 1748; d. 25 June 1816) was noted as a satirist, magazine editor, jurist, and politician in the Revolutionary and early National periods. His *Modern Chivalry* (1792–1815), a four-volume novel that satirized the new country's foibles and follies, is considered the first literary work of the American West. He was also a founder of the first newspaper west of the Alleghenies, the *Pittsburgh Gazette*.

Born near Campbeltown, Scotland, in 1748, Hugh Henry Brackenridge migrated with his parents to rural York County, Pennsylvania, when he was five years old. Encouraged by his mother and a neighboring clergyman, he read everything he could get his hands on, sometimes walking thirty miles to borrow books and newspapers. At age fifteen he became a schoolmaster in Maryland to earn money for college. He entered Princeton about 1768 and made friends there with Philip Freneau (q.v.) and James Madison. He collaborated with Freneau in 1771 in writing *The Rising Glory of America* (1772), a commencement poem that expressed the growing national feeling. After studying divinity for a time he was awarded a master's degree at Princeton in 1774 and wrote another commencement poem, *A Poem on Divine Revelation*.

With the outbreak of the American Revolution, Brackenridge entered service as a chaplain but continued his writing. He composed two plays, *The Battle of Bunker's Hill* (1776) and *The Death of General Montgomery* (1777), written in blank verse in a neoclassical mold. In 1778 he published *Six Political Discourses Founded on the Scriptures*, which exhorted readers to fight for American independence.

In 1779 Brackenridge left the service and established the patriotic *United States Magazine* in Philadelphia. But the brilliantly written magazine folded within the year, and Brackenridge began studying law with Samuel Chase in Annapolis, Maryland. Moving on to the frontier village of Pittsburgh in 1781,

Brackenridge became an important cultural catalyst, helping to establish the first newspaper, the first bookstore, a library, and the Pittsburgh Academy. He persuaded John Scull and his partner to bring a press westward from Philadelphia in 1786 and the first *Pittsburgh Gazette* appeared on 29 July of that year. Brackenridge, however, became an important leader of the Jeffersonian Republicans in the West, and when Scull's newspaper later began leaning toward the Federalists, Brackenridge established the short-lived *Tree of Liberty* as a rival.

Brackenridge served in the Pennsylvania Assembly in 1786–87 and was the foremost champion of the Federal Constitution in western Pennsylvania, satirizing the opposition in contributions to the *Gazette*. However, he failed in his bid to be elected to the state constitutional convention. Brackenridge's first wife died in 1788. Her name has been lost to history, but two years before her death she gave birth to Henry Marie Brackenridge, who later became a noted lawyer and author. In 1790 Hugh Henry married Sabina Wolfe, a farmer's daughter to whom he had proposed upon their first meeting.

During the Whiskey Rebellion of 1793–94, Brackenridge vacillated between government loyalty and community loyalty and his efforts at mediation only brought castigation by both sides. He remained an important Jeffersonian Republican, however, and in 1799 was appointed a justice of the Pennsylvania Supreme Court. He moved to Carlisle two years later and devoted much of the remainder of his life to legal writing. His chief legal contribution, *Law Miscellanies* (1814), was published two years before his death. He continued to contribute articles on public affairs to various newspapers, including the *National Gazette*. He also rode circuit as a judge, acting with such eccentricity that his name became fixed with that of Mike Fink in frontier legend.

Brackenridge's major literary contribution, *Modern Chivalry*, recounted the adventures of an American Quixote, Captain Farrago, and his comic Irish servant Teague. Brackenridge's slashing wit was unleashed through his characters against contemporary attitudes, personalities, and institutions, especially striking at ambition and ignorance. He wished to show that the new experiment in democracy could not thrive without a knowledgeable citizenry. Thus, he attacked in turn politicians, lawyers, the clergy, Philadelphia belles, frontier gamecocks, and journalists. His political activity and caustic wit had made him many enemies in his lifetime, but his honesty and ability had won the respect of most who had come into contact with him or his writings. His name lives on in the Allegheny County community of Brackenridge about twenty miles northeast of Pittsburgh.

BIBLIOGRAPHY:

A. *Incidents of the Insurrection in Western Pennsylvania* (Philadelphia, 1795); Daniel Marder, ed., *A Hugh Henry Brackenridge Reader, 1770–1815* (Pittsburgh, 1970).

B. DAB 1, 544–545; Charles Frederick Heartman, *A Bibliography of the Writings of Hugh Henry Brackenridge Prior to 1825* (New York, 1968); Daniel Marder, *Hugh Henry*

Brackenridge (New York, 1967); Claude M. Newlin, *The Life and Writings of Hugh Henry Brackenridge* (Princeton, N.J., 1932).

ROBERT M. OURS

BRADFORD, ANDREW (b. 1686?; d. 24 November 1742) was one of the earliest and most important of colonial American journalists. He published the *American Weekly Mercury* (1719–42), a typical but exceptionally long-lived colonial newspaper, and the *American Magazine* (1740/41), the first true magazine in British America.

Bradford was born in Philadelphia, eldest of the three children of William and Elizabeth Sowle Bradford. Both of Andrew's grandfathers were printers: William Bradford of Leicestershire, and Andrew Sowle of London. Sowle, well known during the Commonwealth and Restoration, was a Quaker, a friend of George Fox and William Penn, and a witness to the original charter of Pennsylvania. His apprentice and son-in-law, William Bradford, emigrated in 1685 to become the first printer in Philadelphia. In 1693 Andrew moved with his parents to New York, where on 22 February 1708/09, he was listed as a printer and freeman of that city. In 1713, having returned to Philadelphia, he began printing for both the Society of Friends and the province of Pennsylvania. He and his father, publisher of the *New York Gazette*, maintained an informal partnership for many years.

Until 1723 Andrew was the only printer in Pennsylvania, responsible for the acts of the assembly, the first collection of the laws of the province, almanacs, official proclamations, Indian treaties, Quaker books, and pamphlets. In 1717 he was made a freeman of Philadelphia. From 1727 to the end of his life he was a member of the city council; between 1728 and 1737 the postmaster of the colony; for many years a vestryman of Christ's Church; a charter member of the Fellowship Fire Company; and one of the founders of the Durham Iron Company (1728–73).

Andrew's store in Second Street, a conventional adjunct of the colonial printing shop, sold both local and imported merchandise. It offered a very large number of books, chiefly from England, on a great variety of subjects and in at least five languages. Bradford published the first Welsh and German books in the colonies, but his greatest accomplishment was the *American Weekly Mercury*, the first colonial newspaper to appear outside Boston. The *Mercury* ran continuously from 22 December 1719 to the last known issue of 22 May 1746. It circulated throughout the colonies and carried a large amount of advertising. It printed local, colonial, and foreign news, drawing directly or indirectly upon some fifty European papers and magazines and sixteen colonial journals from New England to Jamaica and Barbados. It also included literary work, both prose and poetry. Bradford's *American Magazine, or A Monthly View of the Political State of the British Colonies*, appeared on 13 February 1740/41, three days before Benjamin Franklin's (q.v.) *General Magazine*. Neither attempt was financially successful, Bradford's magazine ceasing after three months, Franklin's after six.

Little is known of Bradford's private life. He was married twice, to Dorcas Boels of Freehold, New Jersey, and after her death in 1739 to Cornelia Smith of New York. Cornelia Bradford succeeded him in his business, including the publication of the *Mercury*, and lived until August 1755. Andrew's one son, Andrew Sowle Bradford, apparently died in infancy or childhood. His nephew, William Bradford III (q.v.), who called himself William Bradford, Jr., was Andrew's partner for ten months in 1739–40.

Andrew Bradford's place in American journalism history rests mainly upon the remarkable success of the *Mercury*, but the full significance of that success is not always realized. Twice Bradford ran afoul of the provincial government for printing what was considered inflammatory criticism. Once he was let off with an apology; the second time he was jailed. Neither episode, however, changed his willingness to speak out in his paper on controversial issues.

BIBLIOGRAPHY:

B. DAB 1, 552–553; Anna Janney DeArmond, *Andrew Bradford, Colonial Journalist* (Newark, Del., 1949; reprint ed., Westport, Conn., 1969).

ANNA JANNEY DEARMOND

BRADFORD, JOHN(b. 6 June 1749; d. 20 March 1830) was the publisher of the *Kentucke Gazette*, (later changed to *Kentucky Gazette*) the first newspaper west of the Allegheny Mountains except for Pittsburgh. When delegates to Kentucky's statehood convention solicited a printer to establish a newspaper for the territory, Bradford agreed to publish the newspaper in return for a promise of printing patronage. The first issue of the *Gazette* appeared on 11 August 1787, in Lexington, Kentucky. While his ownership of the paper was interrupted several times during a career crowded with civic responsibilities, Bradford and his family were connected with the *Gazette* for most of its history. When Kentucky became a state in 1792, Bradford was designated the first state printer.

Called "The Kentucky Franklin" or "Old Wisdom," Bradford contributed more than a newspaper to the community of Lexington and the new state of Kentucky. He printed dozens of books and pamphlets, helped to organize and maintain a public library, was chairman of the board of Transylvania University and the Board of Trustees of Lexington, and encouraged the exchange and discussion of ideas on philosophy, science, literature, and politics.

Although details of his background before he came to Kentucky in 1779 are sketchy, most researchers agree that Bradford had no training as a printer. He was born in Prince William (later Fauquier) County, Virginia, the son of Daniel and Alice Bradford. His father was a surveyor, a skill that John Bradford also adopted. As deputy surveyor under George May, the chief surveyor of what was then Kentucky County, Virginia, he was able to acquire large landholdings around central Kentucky. He served in the campaign against the Indians at Chillicothe in 1779 as a member of the Kentucky militia.

Bradford married Eliza James, the daughter of Captain Benjamin James of Fauquier County, in 1771 in Virginia, but did not bring his family to Kentucky until around 1785. His brother, Fielding, and later three of his sons, Daniel, Fielding Jr., and Charles, shared ownership of the *Gazette* at various times.

The name "Kentucke" in the flag was not changed until March 1789. The *Gazette* was a four-page paper which included letters reflecting on political issues of the time and reports from the Virginia legislature and Congress. Bradford included letters from writers arguing both for and against separation from Virginia. In addition to printing the newspaper, Bradford also published and sold many books and pamphlets including, beginning in 1788, the annual *Kentucke Almanac*, and in 1789 *The Kentucky Miscellany*, the first book printed in Kentucky. As state printer, he also published *Acts Passed at the First Session of the General Assembly for the Commonwealth of Kentucky* and the first journals of the house and senate. He operated a bookstore, and his print shop served as a post office for early Lexington.

Besides his publishing career, Bradford was a state representative in 1797 and 1802, and ran unsuccessfully for lieutenant governor in 1812. He was associated with the attempt to include emancipation in Kentucky's second constitutional convention of 1799 but was defeated as a delegate from Fayette County. Intimately involved in the affairs of Lexington, Bradford helped to organize a fire department and, at the time of his death, was high sheriff of Fayette County. He was one of the founders of the city's public library and encouraged the preservation of records, including files of his own newspaper.

In his later years, Bradford began writing "Notes on Kentucky," a series of articles recounting the history of the state which were published in sixty-two installments in the *Gazette* from August 1826 to January 1829. His last editorial direction of the paper was apparently in 1827 when he wrote a farewell to his readers citing both physical and mental incapacities. He died on 20 March 1830 and was buried in Lexington. Bradford had five sons and four daughters. His wife died on 12 October 1833.

BIBLIOGRAPHY:

B. DAB 1, 557–558; *Lexington Herald-Leader*, 11 August 1937; Karen Maurer Green, *The "Kentucky Gazette," 1787–1800: Genealogical and Historical Abstracts* (Baltimore, 1983); C. Douglas McMurtrie, *John Bradford: Pioneer Printer of Kentucky* (Springfield, Ill., 1935); J. Winston Coleman, "John Bradford and his *Kentucke Gazette*," *Indiana Quarterly for Bookmen*, July 1948.

ELIZABETH FRAAS

BRADFORD, WILLIAM, III (b. 19 January 1721/22; d. 25 September 1791), known as the "Patriot Printer of 1776," founded and edited one of America's best colonial newspapers, the *Pennsylvania Journal*, and was a magazine publishing pioneer as well. Bradford was a successful businessman with interests ranging from operation of a popular Philadelphia coffeehouse to insurance to bookselling and publishing. He also served in the militia and in the Revolutionary army. Bradford's newspaper took the lead against British "oppressions" in the Stamp Act crisis of 1765 and remained a staunch advocate of American rights throughout the Revolutionary period.

Born to William Bradford and Sytje Santvoort Bradford in New York City, William Bradford III was the grandson of the William Bradford who had pioneered printing in the English middle colonies. He also was the nephew of Andrew Bradford (q.v.), whose *American Weekly Mercury* in Philadelphia was the first American newspaper published outside Boston. Andrew adopted young William and taught him the printing trade, making him a partner in 1739. But in 1741 William fled the animosity of his foster mother and went to England to visit relatives and improve his opportunities as a printer and bookseller.

Upon Andrew's death William returned to Philadelphia in 1742 with equipment and stock for a printing business and bookstore of his own. On 15 August he married Rachel Budd of Northampton, New Jersey. They had three sons and three daughters. One son, Thomas, became a noted newspaper publisher in his own right and another, William, served as U.S. attorney general under President Washington.

William Bradford issued the first edition of the *Weekly Advertiser, or Pennsylvania Journal* on 2 December 1742. It soon was known more simply as the *Pennsylvania Journal*. Well written and edited from the start, it gained a reputation as one of the best printed and most widely circulated newspapers in America. During the *Journal*'s life Bradford published pamphlets, sermons, almanacs, and the like, and in 1754 he opened the London Coffee-House in Philadelphia. That same year his newspaper was one of the most vocal in the colonies in calling for the ouster of French forces from the Ohio Valley, and in urging some sort of colonial union to deal with the French threat.

At the height of the French and Indian War, in October 1757, Bradford began issuing the *American Magazine and Monthly Chronicle*, a strongly pro-British literary periodical. One of the earliest American monthlies, and probably the best of its time, it was edited by William Smith, provost of the College of Philadelphia. In addition to political fare, it included original satirical essays and poetry. The magazine had about 1,000 subscribers but lasted only through October 1758. A decade later Bradford and his son Thomas came out with a second magazine, the *American Magazine, or General Repository*, edited by Lewis Nicola. It lasted only from January to September 1769.

By the time the French and Indian War ended in 1763, Bradford had helped found the Philadelphia Insurance Company and was involved in a number of businesses in addition to his publishing interests. The *Journal* remained a chief occupation, however, and it gained new fame with the Stamp Act crisis of 1765. On 31 October, the day before the hated stamp tax was to take effect, Bradford's *Journal* appeared with a black border fashioned in tombstone design outlining the front page. Under the nameplate was the statement: "EXPIRING: In Hopes of a Resurrection to Life again." Bradford supported American rights and advocated independence. He became a member of the Sons of Liberty, opposed the tea tax, and from 27 July 1774 until October 1775 carried the famous ''Unite or Die'' serpent cartoon in each issue of the *Pennsylvania Journal*. He and Thomas became the official printers to the Continental Congress, and in 1776 the *Journal* was the first newspaper to publish Thomas Paine's (q.v.) first ''Crisis'' essay.

Following the Declaration of Independence, William Bradford (though in his mid-fifties) joined the Patriot army and eventually rose to the rank of colonel. He suspended operation of the *Journal* for a while and took active part in the battles at Trenton and Princeton, suffering a severe wound in the latter engagement. The *Journal* was suspended again between September 1777 and June 1778 when the British occupied Philadelphia. William's health was too fragile to resume publication of the newspaper, but Thomas took it over and edited it for another fifteen years before founding a paper of his own.

William Bradford was not active in public life after the death of his wife on 25 or 26 June 1780. He suffered a series of three strokes in his latter days and died on 25 September 1791.

BIBLIOGRAPHY:

B. DAB 1, 564–566; Arthur M. Schlesinger, *Prelude to Independence* (New York, 1958); Isaiah Thomas, *The History of Printing in America*, 2 vols. (Worcester, Mass., 1810; rev. ed., Albany, 1874); John W. Wallace, *An Old Philadelphian, Colonel William Bradford, the Patriot Printer of 1776*. (Philadelphia, 1884).

ROBERT M. OURS

BRADY, MATHEW B. (b. 1823?; d. 15 January 1896) was the undisputed leader in commercial studio photography from about 1843 to about 1865 which made him a wealthy and admired pioneer in daguerreotypes in New York and Washington, D.C., but Brady's obsession with photographing important people and events, especially the Civil War, ultimately led to his death in a charity ward in a New York City hospital. His massive projects form the basis for most photographic representations of his era.

Nearly nothing is known about Brady's childhood. Biographers have been unable to ascertain when he was born (probably 1823), where he was born (either Warren County, New York, or Cork, Ireland), who his parents were (the names Andrew and Julia were on his death certificate), what they did (probably farmers), the kind or extent of his formal education (if any), or even what his middle initial stood for (probably nothing). He had one brother, about whom little is known, and one sister, whose early death brought her two children into Brady's household.

As a red-haired teenager, Brady studied under William Page, a Saratoga, New York, portrait and history painter. Around 1839, Brady and Page moved to New York City, where Brady worked as a clerk for A. T. Stewart, the department store magnate. In about 1841 Page introduced Brady to artist and scientist Samuel F. B. Morse, in whose classes in daguerreotypes at New York University Brady enrolled.

By 1843 Brady had established a small business in making and selling miniature jewelry and surgical cases. In 1844 he opened Brady's Daguerreian Miniature Gallery. Although he had about a hundred competitors, Brady's studio was a quick success. A tireless innovator, entrepreneur, and promoter of himself and his profession, Brady attracted the most fashionable and famous of American and international customers. His pet project became photographing and displaying pictures of all the notables of the day. Brady opened and closed several studios in New York and Washington, D.C., over the years, each one more luxuriously spectacular and elaborately equipped than the last. He helped develop and readily adopted new techniques in the art and science of photography. In 1851 Brady traveled to London for the World's Fair, in which he dominated the photography awards in international competition.

In 1856 Brady hired Alexander Gardner (q.v.), a Scottish immigrant who later went on to distinguish himself in photography but not before making major contributions to Brady's success through management of Brady's National Photographic Art Gallery in Washington. Brady's photographs became the primary bases for many of the linecuts and engravings in *Harper's Weekly*, *Frank Leslie's Illustrated Newspaper*, and other publications.

In 1858 Brady married Juliet Elizabeth "Julia" R. C. Handy, whose distinguished heritage could be traced to revolutionary war heroes. Educated in fine schools in Maryland and Georgia, she has been credited with part of Brady's success through her hard work and social skills. They lived at the National Hotel in Washington and at the Astor House in New York in order to make contacts and to enjoy the social life.

Brady, with great success in New York and Washington, became determined to photograph the Civil War. He obtained official approval to travel in the campaigns, trained ten photographers, established four field units in thirty-five bases of operation in three states, purchased teams of horses and specially designed wagons as traveling darkrooms, and obtained large-format cameras and extensive supplies on an unlimited account with A. T. Anthony and Company. He also established a network for buying photographs from other frontline photographers. The exploits of Brady and his photographers are legendary, although there is some doubt about how much time Brady himself actually spent near the battle lines. He was more of a businessman than an adventurer, and his coordination of operations resulted in collections of thousands of photographs of the war, unmatched in quality, completeness, and perception.

The departure of Gardner in 1862 and the financial strain of the Civil War project led Brady slowly toward financial disaster. The Washington studio was forced into bankruptcy while Brady attempted to catalog his photographs and interest Congress in buying his $100,000 investment. Brady grew bitter over public and congressional apathy about his collection and the precipitous decline of his eyesight. Temporarily resigned to recover his position in Washington, he put part of the collection in storage, but it was sold when he could not pay the storage bill. The War Department bought the collection for the amount of the debt, but Brady received nothing. Brady declared bankruptcy in Washington in 1868 and in New York in 1873. Finally in 1875, Brady received $25,000 from Congress for title to the War Department collection, which was to deteriorate in storage.

From about 1882 Julia Brady was bedridden with heart disease. She required his nearly constant attention as they moved to cheaper hotels and boardinghouses. She died 20 May 1887. Her death pushed Brady, suffering from rheumatism, blindness, and injuries from a horsecar accident, toward depression, idleness, and alcoholism. Despite his efforts to revive the declining Washington studio with his nephew, Levin Handy, the gallery was sold in 1895. Feeble with kidney disease, Brady, about seventy-three, fell gravely ill and died 15 January 1896 in the pauper's ward of a New York hospital. His personal effects were negligible, but his historically priceless collections are in the National Archives, the Library of Congress, and the New York Historical Society. Much of his work, however, has not been accounted for.

BIBLIOGRAPHY:

A. *Gallery of Illustrious Americans* (New York, 1850).

B. James D. Horan, *Mathew Brady: Historian with a Camera* (New York, 1955); Dorothy Meserve Kunhardt and Philip B. Kunhardt, Jr., *Mathew Brady and His World* (Alexandria, Va., 1977); Roy Meredith, *Mathew Brady's Portrait of an Era* (New York, 1982); Roy Meredith, *Mr. Lincoln's Camera Man: Mathew B. Brady*, 2d rev. ed. (New York, 1974).

THOMAS A. SCHWARTZ

BRANN, WILLIAM COWPER (b. 4 January 1855; d. 2 April 1898) was a flamboyant independent editor of the late nineteenth century. Brann's monthly *Iconoclast* was a nationally famous platform for his views on matters political, literary, and philosophical, always couched in his distinctive prose style, alternately florid and earthy. His notoriety was enhanced by his violent death, earning him a reputation as a martyr to independent thought.

Brann was born in rural Coles County, Illinois, the son of Noble J. Brann, a Presbyterian minister. Brann's mother died when he was just two years old; subsequently, he was placed with the family of a local farmer named William Hawkins. At the age of thirteen he left home to work as a bellboy in a nearby town, the beginning of a series of odd jobs that gave him an opportunity to travel and acquire experience. This substituted for his formal education, which had ceased before his teens. He became an avid reader, and his writings are peppered with literary allusions and exotic vocabulary. Also during this time, Brann acquired some experience in journalism, working as a printer's devil.

On 3 March 1877 Brann married Carrie Belle Martin, the daughter of an Iowa physician, in Rochelle, Illinois. The marriage produced three children: Inez Martin Brann in 1877, Grace Brann in 1886, and William Brann in 1892. Inez, also called Dottie, committed suicide by an overdose of morphine in 1890; the other two children, and Carrie, affectionately called Midget, survived Brann.

In 1883 Brann went to work for the *St. Louis Globe-Democrat*, beginning his career in journalism. But he had trouble holding down a job with any one paper because he usually found himself in disagreement with the editorial line of the newspaper's management. Brann's temperament was combative; once engaged in a controversy he refused to surrender. And so he changed employers frequently, moving from the *Globe-Democrat* to the *Galveston Evening Tribune* to the *Galveston News* to the *Houston Post*. He resigned from the *Post* in 1890. His experiences led him to become a vocal critic of the way newspapers were run; he commonly characterized his journalistic brethren as venal and corrupt, prefiguring the critique that would be developed by the muckrakers in later decades. Meanwhile, Brann had been developing his literary skills. He acquired an unusual and eclectic store of words and knowledge, and began to dabble in fiction. In 1889 he registered three plays with the Library of Congress.

But Brann's main strength was as an editorial writer. His ability to drive home a point allowed him to find employment with newspapers even as his reputation as a troublemaker grew. At the same time, his uncompromising devotion to a stand once taken made it difficult for him to work for other men. It was natural, then, that Brann would try to establish a journal of his own. After leaving the *Houston Post* in 1890, Brann moved to Austin and began the *Austin Iconoclast*, a one-man journal devoted to the currency question, an issue of urgent concern in the days of the populist movement, especially in Texas. As interest in his paper waned, though, Brann left it in the hands of an associate and went back to work for the *Globe-Democrat* in 1892, only to leave later that year to take over the editorship of the *San Antonio Express*. Shortly thereafter he left the *Express* over a disagreement with the owner and, after spending a few discouraging months on the lecture circuit, landed a position with the *Daily News* in Waco.

Waco in 1894 was a lively town of 25,000. It boasted an active cultural life, with a number of educational institutions, the most famous being Baylor University, plus a large number of newspapers and periodicals. Brann's independent nature reasserted itself in Waco. He left the *Daily News* and revived the *Iconoclast* in February 1895. A sixteen-page monthly begun on a financial shoestring, the journal achieved popular success, claiming 100,000 readers worldwide, and continuing to rise in popularity up to the time of Brann's death.

The new *Iconoclast*, unlike its predecessor, was not limited in scope. Brann used it as a pulpit from which to preach whatever thoughts crossed his mind. His frequently caustic expostulations covered the entire spectrum of social concerns, but his most controversial writings were on religion. Earlier Brann had been branded "the Apostle of the Devil" by the influential preacher and columnist T. DeWitt Talmadge, a title that Brann seemed to accept with pride; he regularly referred to himself as "The Apostle" in his columns. He took special delight in annoying the Protestant establishment: in the first issue of the revived *Iconoclast*, he struck back at Talmadge, calling him "a monstrous bag of fetid wind."

This sort of exchange was typical of Brann. He engaged in editorial battles for the simple purpose of annoying an establishment he perceived as smug and hypocritical: hence his choice of the title *Iconoclast*. But his own ideas were often just as smug: he believed in the racial inferiority of blacks, and his attitudes toward women were at best condescending. His virtue was in being an irritant.

Brann's antagonistic style led directly to his violent death. Early in his Waco career he took on the Baptists at Baylor, especially when a young Brazilian girl studying there turned up pregnant, claiming to have been raped by a relative of the university's president. Brann's exploitation of this scandal infuriated Baylor's students and friends, and their anger was intensified by the fact that Brann had a national audience. Brann's battle with the Baylor Baptists culminated in a series of violent incidents. First he was abducted from his office and beaten by a gang of students. A short while later he was led at gunpoint into the streets and horsewhipped. And finally Brann was shot fatally in a gun battle with a man named Tom Davis. The *Iconoclast* died with him, the last issue dated May 1898.

BIBLIOGRAPHY:

A. *The Works of William C. Brann, the Iconoclast*, 12 vols. (Chicago, 1903); *The Writings of Brann, the Iconoclast*, 2 vols. (New York, 1938).

B. DAB 21, 108–109; NYT 2 April 1898; Charles Carver, *Brann and the ''Iconoclast''* (Austin, 1957); Donna Dickerson, ''William Cowper Brann: Nineteenth Century Press Critic,'' *Journalism History*, Summer 1978; William Rivers, ''William Cowper Brann and His *Iconoclast*,'' *Journalism Quarterly*, Fall 1958.

JOHN NERONE

BRECKINRIDGE, MARY MARVIN (b. 2 October 1905) was the first woman correspondent for the Columbia Broadcasting System, reporting from Europe during the first year of World War II. She was also widely published as a photographer, with photos in *Life*, *Town and Country*, and the *New York Times*.

Breckinridge was born in New York City, the daughter of John Cabell Breckinridge, a lawyer from a prominent Kentucky family, and Isabella Goodrich Breckinridge. Breckinridge was graduated from Vassar with a degree in modern languages and history in 1927. She was active in national and international student groups, through which she met Edward R. Murrow (q.v.). By the time she graduated from college, Breckinridge had been abroad a half dozen times, and had been formally presented to society in London and New York. In 1928 she took classes at the New School for Social Research in New York, and studied filmmaking. In the early 1930s Breckinridge worked as a secretary for the Democratic National Committee and for a member of Congress. She was also successful as a free-lance photographer and writer, with pieces in *Vogue*, *House and Garden*, and the *Washington Post*.

Breckinridge concentrated on photography in the later part of the 1930s, and was on assignment at the Lucerne Music Festival when the Nazis invaded Poland. She went to London and got work with Black Star, an international photo agency whose New York office already represented her. Breckinridge recorded British preparations for war. Murrow, who was in London as CBS chief of European coverage, asked her to speak on one of his broadcasts to America. Breckinridge talked about the evacuation of London children to the English countryside, and Murrow, who was expanding his staff to cover the war, asked her to report again. This time the topic was a group of women who were manning a fire station in London.

Breckinridge, who has a pleasant, but formal, speaking voice, apparently impressed the CBS officials listening in New York, and a third broadcast was arranged, this time from Ireland. Breckinridge had suggested the location, for the Irish were declaring themselves neutral while Britain was at war. Murrow called immediately after that broadcast and asked Breckinridge to return to London to receive a European assignment. She was sent to the Netherlands in early December, doing her first report from Hilversum on 10 December 1939. Breckinridge continued to report from the Netherlands over the next five months, with a brief stint in Berlin as William L. Shirer's (q.v.) relief while he was on vacation and ill.

While in Berlin, Breckinridge met an old acquaintance, Jefferson Patterson, who was in charge of the prisoner of war section of the American embassy. Their marriage several months later would end her career in radio. Breckinridge covered the German buildup and subsequent blitzkrieg. She fled Amsterdam on 8 May 1940, on the last train to get through to Paris, and pitched in to help CBS cover the war from Paris. Her last report for the network was on 5 June 1940. It was about the stream of refugees passing through a small village to the south of Paris. Breckinridge left Paris after learning the government was about to flee. She went to Italy, and finally arrived in Berlin. Breckinridge and Patterson were married 20 June 1940. They had a three-day honeymoon before turning to the grim task of inspecting prisoner-of-war camps.

Breckinridge would continue to serve at her husband's side in diplomatic assignments. But she was forbidden to broadcast by U.S. officials who feared that the content of her reports would cause problems for American diplomats. Jefferson Patterson held posts in Peru, Belgium, Egypt, and Greece before serving as ambassador to Uruguay from 1956 to 1958. The couple adopted two children, and although she is no longer a broadcaster, Breckinridge (she uses her maiden name professionally) continues to publish pictures. She lives in Washington, D.C.

BIBLIOGRAPHY:

B. Harry W. Flannery, *Assignment to Berlin* (New York, 1942); David H. Hosley, *As Good As Any* (Westport, Conn., 1984); Marion Marzolf, *Up From the Footnote: A History of Women Journalists* (New York, 1977).

DAVID H. HOSLEY

BRIGGS, EMILY POMONA EDSON (b. 14 September 1830; d. 3 July 1910) was one of the foremost, best-paid women correspondents in Washington during the post–Civil War era. Her thousands of newspaper columns about political figures and Washington society were published in the *Philadelphia Press* from 1866 to 1882. Under the pseudonym "Olivia," Mrs. Briggs reported such events as the impeachment trial of President Johnson, White House festivities, the national woman suffrage movement, and the trial of President Garfield's assassin.

She was born at Burton, Ohio, one of four daughters of Robert Edson and Mary "Polly" Umberfield Edson. Mrs. Briggs's father was a blacksmith from Vermont and her mother was the daughter of pioneer settlers from Connecticut. Mrs. Briggs attended schools in Burton and in Illinois when the family moved in 1840 to a farm north of Chicago.

She taught briefly in Painesville, Ohio. Her introduction to journalism and political society was accelerated when about 1854 she married John R. Briggs, Jr., who in 1853 had served in the Wisconsin legislature. The Briggses had two sons, John Edson, who became a real estate operator, and Arthur, who died in infancy. In 1854 they moved to Keokuk, Iowa, where Briggs became part owner of the *Daily Whig*, soon renamed the *Gate City*. Through the Iowa Republican party and his coverage of the Lincoln-Douglas debates, Briggs developed a personal friendship with Lincoln. In 1861 the family moved to Washington, where Briggs served as a political adviser to Lincoln and held the position of assistant clerk of the House of Representatives under another staunch Republican newspaper owner, John W. Forney of the *Philadelphia Press* and *Washington Chronicle*. Mrs. Briggs worked during the war as a clerk in the House and came to Forney's attention as a writer when she wrote a letter in defense of women clerks accused of inefficiency. Forney asked her to write a regular column for his *Philadelphia Press*. Although she adopted the pseudonym Forney chose for her, she did not try to hide her identity.

Mrs. Briggs's columns focused on personalities in Washington political society, and she often commented on postwar politics. Like her Republican publisher, she opposed President Johnson's southern strategy. In sympathizing with freed blacks who were denied full citizenship, she noted that as an unfranchised and "feeble woman" she could "do nothing for the freedman but utter shriek after shriek for him. . . . " She was one of the first women admitted to the congressional press gallery, but she usually got her news from other vantage points where women were more welcome. She was also one of the first women to use the telegraph to send dispatches.

Mrs. Briggs was noted for her coverage of society and her "pen pictures" of senators and other Washington political figures. She reported White House festivities during five presidencies. In January 1870 she gave daily coverage to the first Washington conference on woman suffrage, noting the few male sympathizers and hailing Susan B. Anthony (q.v.). In January 1882 one of her last columns focused on the trial of Garfield's assassin and refuted the allegation that the courtroom had become a daily habit for Washington's women theatergoers. "Our ladies," she wrote, "had a desire to look upon a man who could murder a President, but the desire was gratified with one visit."

Mrs. Briggs, who earned as much as $3,500 a year, was revered by Republican loyalists, one of whom wrote at the time that there was no man or woman reporter in Washington who was more industrious and painstaking than she. Toward the end of her career, in 1882, she helped found the short-lived Women's National Press Association and was elected its first president. After 1882 she quit journalism for a second career as one of the better known Washington society hostesses. In 1872 she and her husband (who died six months later of tuberculosis) had bought the Maples, a Capitol Hill mansion which became the setting for her many parties. She died on 3 July 1910 of a cerebral hemorrhage.

BIBLIOGRAPHY:

A. *The Olivia Letters* (New York and Washington, 1906).

B. AWW 1, 232–233; NAW 1, 242–243; *Washington Evening Star*, 4 July 1910; *Washington Post*, 5 July 1910; Maurine H. Beasley, *The First Women Washington Correspondents* (Washington, D.C., 1976).

LEONARD RAY TEEL

BRISBANE, ARTHUR (b. 12 December 1864; d. 25 December 1936) had an unparalleled career in American journalism, being a major force behind the success of William Randolph Hearst's (q.v.) early New York newspaper operations. Brisbane was America's best known editorial writer during his day, an early and shrewd exploiter of debased popular news values, and a dynamic newspaper publisher. He used the money earned from newspapering to become a real estate tycoon and to practice scientific farming.

During his lifetime Brisbane traveled mentally a great distance from the social and utopian reformist ideals of his father, Albert Brisbane, to the hard, shallow, and dogmatic materialism that he came to embody. He was born to Albert and Sarah White Brisbane in Buffalo, New York. Albert was an apostle of the Fourierism brand of utopian socialism, an author and inventor. Upon the death of his mother when he was two, Arthur passed a helter-skelter boyhood in an atmosphere of books, theories, and intellectual discussions. After attending public schools, he traveled to Europe at thirteen to attain more education as his father had before him, attending schools in Ivry, Asnières, and Paris, France, and Stuttgart, Germany.

At nineteen Brisbane found his vocation in newspapering when he started as a reporter on Charles Dana's (q.v.) *New York Sun* at $15 per week. He immediately established himself as an unusually facile and gifted reporter. During his seven years on the *Sun*, from 1883 to 1890, he was successively reporter, London correspondent, and after 1887 editor of the *Evening Sun*.

Brisbane was lured from the *Sun* by Joseph Pulitzer (q.v.) to the *World*, where he stayed seven years until 1897. During this period the *World* was the world's circulation leader, and was making Pulitzer a wealthy man. Working successively as an aide to Pulitzer, a reporter, editor, and editor of the *Sunday World*, Brisbane became highly experienced and regarded. After Hearst bought the *Journal* in 1895, and raided Pulitzer's staff, Brisbane helped hold the line in maintaining the *World*'s supremacy. When Pulitzer forbade Brisbane to write front-page editorials, Brisbane went over to Hearst in 1897, where he stayed for the rest of his life, and made newspaper history.

Hearst cut Brisbane's weekly salary in half, to $150, but sweetened the deal with an incentive of $1 for each additional 1,000 circulation. Brisbane pulled out all stops to increase the *Journal*'s 40,000 circulation. He amazed the newspaper industry by pulling the *Journal*'s circulation up to that of the *Evening World* at 325,000 in only seven weeks. He did so by starting work at 4:30 A.M., radically sensationalizing the *Journal*, and getting it onto the streets hours ahead of its competitors. The *Journal* was a leader of the agitation campaign to involve America in a war with Spain over Cuba, running shrieking, inflated atrocity stories, huge red headlines, and inflammatory editorials. The *Journal* soared to one-day circulation peaks of over one million, eclipsing the *World*, but the credibility of both papers plummeted.

As Hearst expanded his newspaper operations to Chicago in 1900, Brisbane was sent there to take command of the *Chicago American*. During the 1910s Brisbane owned the *Washington* (D.C.) *Times* and the *Wisconsin News*, which he sold to Hearst in 1919. He also briefly owned two New Jersey newspapers. He helped Hearst in his tabloid battle of New York in 1934 by running the *New York Mirror*, an exercise in sleazy journalism.

Chiefly, Brisbane was known as a columnist. His "Today" column was printed in all Hearst papers, and his "This Week" column appeared in 1,200 weekly papers. He also wrote a weekly Sunday page for Hearst newspapers. Read by more people than any other living man, Brisbane's writing had a terse, driving, and cutting clarity, marked by superficial learning. Though his interpretation of the news was often provocative, it suffered from several faults; reversibility (self-contradictory), Brisbanalities (platitudes), and adjustable conscience (self-justifying rationalizations).

Brisbane's newspaper salary soared to $260,000 per year, which he invested in valuable properties, including prime New York real estate, with Hearst as his partner. His aggregate net from all sources rose to over $1 million per year in 1935. Brisbane did not marry until he was forty-seven, and then it was to the daughter of a cousin, Phoebe Cary. From their marriage issued six children: Seward, Sarah, Emily, Hugo, Alice, and Elinor. He owned four residences, including a 3,000-acre estate at Allaire, New Jersey. In late 1936 Brisbane suffered a series of heart attacks, but he kept dictating his column up to his death in December. He left an estate of $8 million. All efforts by Hearst to develop a successor columnist failed, so Hearst himself briefly wrote a daily column of news comment from 1940 to 1942.

BIBLIOGRAPHY:

B. DAB Supp. 2, 62–65; NYT 26 December 1936; Oliver Carlson, *Brisbane: A Candid Biography* (New York, 1937).

WILLIAM Q. PARMENTER

BROOKS, NOAH (b. 24 October 1830; d. 16 August 1903) gave Civil War readers of the *Sacramento Union* "inside" coverage of the White House unmatched in the history of the American press. One of the most widely quoted sources of Lincolniana, Brooks was Washington correspondent (1862–65) for the *Union*, one of several newspapers he worked for. He was also a magazine and book author of national reputation; two of his works of juvenile fiction, *The Boy Settlers* (1876) and *The Boy Emigrants* (1891), are still regarded as excellent works of their genre.

Brooks, the eighth and last child of Barker Brooks and Margaret Perkins Brooks, was born in Castine, Maine. His father was a shipbuilder; his mother was the daughter of a ship captain. In 1848 Brooks moved to Boston to study painting, but his interest waned and he went to work for the *Boston Atlas* at age twenty. He emigrated to Dixon, Illinois, in 1854, where he went into business and farming with indifferent success. In 1856 he married Caroline Fellows of Salem, Massachusetts, went to work for the *Dixon Telegraph*, and met Abraham Lincoln. The prairie-politician was stumping for the Republican presidential nominee, John C. Frémont. The reporter was completely won over and from that time on remained a warm admirer of Lincoln.

An economic slump shackled Dixon in 1859, and Brooks set out on a five-month wagon trek to California. He settled in Marysville, a bumptious river port, and in 1860 became co-owner of the *Marysville Daily Appeal*, the youngest of the city's four dailies. The *Appeal* was staunchly Republican but operated successfully despite location in a belt of pro-slavery Democrats. A career as small-town publisher seemed laid out for Brooks when death took his young wife in 1862. In escape he sold his interests in Marysville and traveled to Washington as correspondent for the *Sacramento Union*, the foremost paper in California from 1851 to 1875. During the Civil War, when many Californians favored an armistice and recognition of the Confederacy, the *Union* was an all-out supporter of the Northern cause. Many Lincoln biographers dwell on Brooks's Washington reports, but he painted a full canvas of the North at war. He also reported from ten states, covered the Republican and Democratic conventions in 1864, and took to the field to cover the army of the Potomac. His impressions of a visit to this fighting force in 1863 can be found numerous times in the Lincoln literature.

Brooks covered every corner of Washington. Although his forte was the feature story, he also wrote many cogent straight news stories of particular interest to Californians. Within a year of his arrival in Washington, Brooks had become almost a daily visitor to the White House. He got a close look at the Lincoln family at work and play. His relationship with Lincoln helped Brooks professionally and socially, but the relationship was not a one-way street. Lincoln sought the young man's advice on intricate California patronage and political matters and tapped his knowledge of congressional matters. A convivial companion and a good listener, Brooks provided his greatest service to the older man by helping him to relax. Also, Brooks was one of the few friends the high-strung Mary Todd Lincoln had in Washington. Brooks was slated to take the position of Lincoln's secretary when the president was assassinated.

Prospects dampened, Brooks tarried in Washington for a few months and then wangled a federal position in San Francisco. A year later he returned to newspapering on the *San Francisco Daily Times*. In 1867 he became managing editor of the *Alta California*, the state's oldest newspaper. When a quality magazine, the *Overland Monthly*, was established, Brooks was retained as an adviser to editor Bret Harte (q.v.).

In 1871 Brooks became night editor of the *New York Tribune*. After four years he became an editorial writer with the *New York Times*. In 1884, he was appointed editor of the *Newark Daily Advertiser*. During his stay in New York, Brooks wrote at least thirty magazine articles for such periodicals as *Scribner's Monthly*, *Century*, and the popular juvenile magazine *St. Nicholas*. In 1894 Brooks retired to Castine, Maine. He continued to contribute to magazines and wrote five books. In 1900 he became ill and returned to California, where in Pasadena he died on 16 August 1903 of chronic bronchitis.

BIBLIOGRAPHY:

A. *Washington in Lincoln's Time* (New York, 1895).

B. DAB 2, 82–83; *Los Angeles Times*, 17 August 1903; NYT 18 August 1903; *New York Herald*, 18 August 1903; *New York Tribune*, 18 August 1903; Robert E. Blackmon, "Castine, the *Sacramento Union* and Lincoln," M.A. thesis, Univ. of California, Berkeley, 1954; Frederick Evans, "Noah Brooks," *Lamp*, September 1903.

ROBERT E. BLACKMON

BROUN, HEYWOOD CAMPBELL (b. 7 December 1888; d. 18 December 1939) was, Franklin P. Adams (q.v.) said, "a lion in print but a lamb in his personal relationships." Rotund and amiable, Broun avoided confrontation in his personal life and sought it in his columns. Though outwardly even-tempered, he was beset by a number of phobias. He was tested so often for what he was convinced was heart trouble that his friend Alexander Woollcott (q.v.) suggested he stage a one-man show of his cardiograms. He had to relinquish his duties as drama critic for the *New York Tribune* because of his claustrophobia. Fearful in life, he was fearless in his column "It Seems to Me." At the urging of his wife, Ruth Hale, he tackled such controversial issues as anti-Semitism, censorship, and the Sacco-Vanzetti trial, and became a leading spokesman for liberalism during the 1920s and 1930s. Because of his concern for the working conditions of newspaper employees, he was instrumental in forming the New York Newspaper Guild and served as the first president of the national union, the American Newspaper Guild.

Broun was the third of four children born to Heywood Cox and Henriette Brose Broun. His father, a Scots immigrant, ran a successful printing and stationery business in New York. Broun attended a private school, Horace Mann, where he was voted best all-around student. In 1906 he entered Harvard University, but unlike classmates Walter Lippmann and John Reed (qq.v.), Broun took academics less seriously than poker and baseball. When he failed French his senior year, he did not graduate.

Over the objections of his teachers and family, he decided to enter journalism. He had been rejected three times for membership on the Harvard *Crimson*, but he had worked summers as a reporter on the *New York Morning Telegraph*, which specialized in horse racing and scandal. So when the *Morning Telegraph* offered him a position at $20 a week, Broun went to work, writing about baseball and Broadway starlets. After two years, with several bylines to his credit and his popularity growing, he asked for a $10 raise. He was promptly fired.

He was hired by the *New York Tribune* in 1911 as a copyreader for $25 a week. After a leave of absence to research a play in the Orient for a theatrical firm, he returned to the *Tribune* to work as a general assignment reporter and, later, a sports writer. Broun lacked the objectivity necessary for a reporter. He shocked his fellow reporters by openly rooting in the press box, and he wrote sports stories that were notable for their color, hyperbole, and fanciful literary allusions.

In 1917 Broun married Ruth Hale, a reporter who had worked for the *Washington Star* and the *New York Times*. Franklin P. Adams, the best man at their wedding, called them "the clinging oak and the sturdy vine." By Broun's admission, the strong-minded feminist often shoved her genial husband in the direction of controversy and liberal causes. They spent their honeymoon on a ship bound for Paris, where he was to serve as war correspondent for the *New York Tribune* and she was on the staff of the Paris edition of the *Chicago Tribune*. Broun was rankled by the uniforms required of correspondents and by military censorship. General John J. Pershing once spied the incurably sloppy Broun dressed in an orange tunic and black slouch hat and asked, "Did you just fall down?" (Broun, 1983; O'Connor, 1975) Convinced that military censors would not pass his stories attacking Pershing, Broun sent his dispatches directly to the *Tribune*. When he returned to New York in 1918 and wrote articles critical of the war effort, his correspondent's credentials were revoked.

Broun became the *Tribune*'s literary editor and the author of a daily column, "Books and Things." Recalling his lack of objectivity as a sports writer, he decided that the way to popularity and a higher salary was to make himself a recognizable personality through his writing. So he used his column to air his opinions on topics that ranged from politics to the rearing of his son, Heywood Hale, who was born in 1918. Broun defected to the *New York World* in 1921 because, he said, he would have more freedom of expression on the liberal Pulitzer newspaper than he had on the more conservative *Tribune*. Executive editor Herbert Bayard Swope (q.v.) assured Broun that he would be free to write what he wished; all Swope asked was that the column "It Seems to Me" be lively and controversial. Broun joined an impressive roster of columnists on the op-ed page—Franklin Adams, Deems Taylor, and Lawrence Stallings—and he became one of the most widely read and highly paid columnists, earning $25,000 a year.

Despite Swope's assurances, Broun encountered problems with newspaper management over the content of his column; similar problems would plague him throughout his career. The trouble began in 1927 over a series of columns on the Sacco-Vanzetti trial. Broun fiercely condemned the murder conviction of the two Italian immigrants, who he believed had been convicted for their nationality and their political beliefs. When a commission headed by the president of Harvard failed to find grounds for a stay of execution, Broun wrote that the two would die "at the hands of men in dinner jackets or academic gowns, according to the conventionalities required by the hour of execution." Though Broun's opinions had frequently differed from the *World*'s more moderate editorial stands, the newspaper's executives were alarmed by what they saw as Broun's inflammatory attacks on the judicial system. When Broun refused to find new subject matter for his column, editor Ralph Pulitzer suspended him.

After writing a column in the *Nation* for a few months, Broun rejoined the *World* in 1928. But his truce with management lasted only four months. When he wrote in the *Nation* that the *World* was timid and lived in "fear of shocking any reader," Pulitzer fired him for disloyalty. He was lured to Scripps-Howard's *New York Telegram* (later the *World-Telegram*) by a yearly salary of $30,000 and by Roy Howard's (q.v.) promise of freedom of expression. Broun said that the Sacco-Vanzetti trial had been a watershed in his career. His column and his private life were increasingly devoted to social issues. When unemployment soared, he used his column as an employment agency and found jobs for more than a thousand people. In 1930, over Howard's objections, he ran for Congress on the Socialist ticket. He campaigned for full employment from a rented limousine in his district, one of the wealthiest in Manhattan. Though he garnered an impressive list of supporters, including his friends from the Algonquin Round Table, he ran third in a field of three.

When the Pulitzer brothers sold the *World*, adding many of his colleagues to the growing list of the unemployed, Broun began agitating for a union of newspaper workers. Initially, his efforts were met with indifference, but in 1933 Broun and about a dozen others met in his penthouse to lay plans for what would become the New York Newspaper Guild. In December 1933 similar groups met in Washington, D.C., to form the American Newspaper Guild. Broun was elected president, a position he held until his death.

Though Ruth Hale had demanded that she and Broun live separate lives as a condition to their marriage, she felt stifled by his success and reputation. On 17 November 1933 she was granted a divorce. They nonetheless remained close, and he was at her bedside when she died the next year. In 1935 Broun married Maria Incoronata, a singer and dancer known professionally as Connie Madison. They had met during the run of *Shoot the Works*, a musical he had produced to give work to unemployed actors. He adopted her daughter, Patricia, and in 1939 converted to his wife's religion, Roman Catholicism.

Broun's political activities strained his relationship with the *World-Telegram* management, and he found that his copy was run only after heavy editing. He had no such problems with the *Connecticut Nutmeg* (later *Broun's Nutmeg*), a weekly that he ran almost single-handedly and underwrote with the $1,000 a week he was receiving from Scripps-Howard. In 1939 Broun's contract with the *World-Telegram* was not renewed because management felt it could no longer afford him. He joined the *New York Post* for about one-fourth of his old salary. After completing his first column for the *Post*, he developed pneumonia. His wife, his son, and his friends kept a vigil in the hospital corridor for two days. He died on 18 December 1939.

BIBLIOGRAPHY:

A. *It Seems to Me* (New York, 1935); *The Collected Edition of Heywood Broun* (New York, 1941).

B. DAB Supp. 2, 67–69; NCAB 30, 171–173; NYT 19 December 1939; Heywood Hale Broun, *Whose Little Boy Are You?* (New York, 1983); Frank O'Connor, *Heywood Broun* (New York, 1975).

HARRIS E. ROSS

BROWN, CECIL (b. 14 September 1907) epitomizes the fraternity of international news correspondents renowned during World War II. His reporting experiences during that time may have been unparalleled in the annals of network news. Brown was accorded the George Foster Peabody Radio Award, and awards by Sigma Delta Chi, the Overseas Press Club (of which he would become president in 1957), and the National Headliners Club. His eyewitness account of the Japanese sinking of the British warships the *Prince of Wales* and the *Repulse* was one of the journalistic scoops of the year.

Brown was born in New Brighton, Pennsylvania, to Maurice I. Brown and Jennie Broida Brown. He attended Western Reserve University from 1925 to 1927, then Ohio State, where in 1929 he received a B.S. degree. He began writing for a Warren, Ohio, newspaper, but left to try his hand at sea. He joined his brother as a stowaway on a ship to South America. After that, Brown signed on as a seaman aboard a freighter that sailed to the Black Sea. The results of his travels were chronicled in some fifteen articles published in the *Youngstown* (Ohio) *Vindicator*. Back home in the United States he went to work for United Press, then in 1933 he became editor of the *Prescott* (Arizona) *Journal-Miner*. Ten months later, however, Brown resigned in a dispute with the paper's publisher.

Over the next four years Brown held positions with the *Pittsburgh Press*, the *Newark Ledger*, and the *New York American*. The lure of free-lance writing from abroad took him to Europe in 1937, where he began sending articles back to the States. The International News Service liked his work and hired him for duty in Paris and Rome. He joined CBS in 1940 and began reporting on the German-Italian advances and the events that would lead to U.S. involvement. For his efforts, he was expelled from Italy by the Mussolini government on 1 April 1941.

Brown went on to Belgrade, Yugoslavia, arriving just as the Germans reached the city. He found it impossible to broadcast what he saw, but he wrote of his experiences there, including his escape from the Nazis. He began broadcasting again from Budapest, and was eventually sent by CBS to report from Turkey, Syria, and Cairo, where he broadcast the German parachute invasion of Crete. He received the Distinguished Service Award from Sigma Delta Chi for his broadcast of the escape of Greece's King George from German forces. Brown reported British military advances in North Africa before his assignment to Singapore in late 1941. He continued his unabashed accounts of the war's progress, which caused the British to ban his broadcasts and declare him persona non grata.

Brown headed for Sydney, Australia, where he continued his reports of the unpreparedness of the British for the Japanese invasion. He had married Martha Leaine Kohn in July 1938, and she stayed with him during the years of war coverage.

He broadcast the nightly news for CBS in 1943–44 before joining the Mutual Broadcasting System, where he was heard several times a day on the network for thirteen years. Brown moved his news broadcasts and commentary to ABC radio on 1 April 1957. He joined NBC News in 1958, and was immediately assigned to cover the Far East as that network's Tokyo correspondent.

Brown spent the next four years in Japan, moving up to bureau chief before returning to the United States in 1962 to serve as an NBC correspondent on the network's news programs. In 1964 he left NBC for public television station KCET in Los Angeles to become its director of news and public affairs, and a commentator. For his "outstanding work" there he received the Alfred I. DuPont Award as well as two Associated Press awards. Brown left broadcasting in 1967 to teach communications and international affairs at California State Polytechnic University.

BIBLIOGRAPHY:

A. *Suez to Singapore* (New York, 1942).

B. "What Kind of Radio Newspaper?," *Broadcasting*, 4 October 1943; "Cecil Brown," *ABC Biography*, 13 May 1957; "Cecil Brown: NBC News' Tokyo Correspondent," *NBC Biography*, 18 November 1958.

DAVID M. GUERRA

BROWNE, CHARLES FARRAR (b. 26 April 1834; d. 6 March 1867) was a printer, journalist, and popular humorist. He first gained public notice in the *Cleveland Plain Dealer*, writing comic letters signed Artemus Ward, the name by which he became known throughout America and England. Subsequent books and lectures were highly successful and inspired the style of future American humorists.

Browne (he added the "e") was born on a farm outside Waterford, Maine, to Levi Brown and Caroline Farrar Brown, both of old New England families. His father served in the state legislature and held a variety of jobs. When Browne was thirteen, his father died and family fortunes declined. He found work as an apprentice printer at the *Lancaster* (New Hampshire) *Weekly Democrat*, a year later at the *Norway* (Maine) *Advertiser*, edited by his brother Cyrus, and at two or three other New England newspapers until he landed in 1851 at the *Carpet Bag*, a Boston humor magazine. There he published his first paragraphs, described as "mildly funny things."

After three years in Boston, he tramped through Kentucky and Ohio, ending up at the *Toledo Commercial*, working first as printer, then as journalist. His lively anecdotes caught the attention of *Cleveland Plain Dealer* publisher Joseph W. Gray. Browne joined the *Plain Dealer* on 29 October 1857 as "local" editor, providing a column of observations and quips. Then on 30 January 1858 the newspaper published a short letter from Artemus Ward:

Sir:

i write to no how about the show bisnes in Cleevland i have a show consisting in part of a Calforny Bare two snakes tame foxies etc also wax works my wax works is hard to beat, all say they is life and nateral curiosities among my wax works is Our Saveyer Gen taylor and Docktor Webster in the ackt of killing Parkman. now mr. Editor scratch off few lines and tel me how is the show bisnes in your good city i shal have hanbils printed at your offis you scratch my back i will scratch your back, also git up a grate blow in the paper about my show don't forgit my wax works.

Much of Browne's humor may escape modern readers, but in 1858 it excited Cleveland, and much of the country beyond as other newspapers reprinted it. Why Browne named his character Artemus Ward is not known, although an Artemus Ward was an early landowner in Browne's hometown of Waterford. Over the next two years, Browne published twenty-one Artemus Ward letters in the *Plain Dealer*. Near the end of the period, *Vanity Fair*, a New York comic magazine, contracted to reprint the popular material. With that New York connection, Browne quit the *Plain Dealer*, journeyed east, and talked his way eventually into the position of managing editor at *Vanity Fair*.

At about the same time, he began to gather the Artemus Ward letters into a book and to develop a humorous lecture. He gave his first performance on 26 November 1861 at New London, Connecticut, polished his act in other New England towns, abandoned the failing *Vanity Fair*, attracted ever larger audiences and eventually carried his unique humor—as much style as substance—throughout the nation. In spite of brandy, and other spirits shared liberally with such friends as Samuel Clemens and Bret Harte (qq.v.), the winter 1863–64 tour through California, Nevada, and Utah was a success and resulted in new Artemus Ward material. In 1866 Browne took his lecture to England, generating enthusiastic crowds at Piccadilly's Egyptian Hall and writing for *Punch*, the British humor magazine. Never physically strong, Browne became ill in England, and early in 1867 he learned he had tuberculosis. He died in March at Southampton.

In his brief career, Browne was extremely popular. He combined old techniques—anecdotes, puns, parodies, misspelling, impossible grammar, disjointed dialect, mock seriousness—into a novel style to which the public of the 1860s responded. His lasting significance was his influence on a host of imitators, including Henry Wheeler Shaw (Josh Billings), David Ross Locke (q.v.) (Petroleum Vesuvius Nasby), and Charles Henry Smith (Bill Arp).

BIBLIOGRAPHY:

A. *Artemus Ward: His Book* (New York, 1862); *Artemus Ward: His Travels* (New York, 1865); *Artemus Ward in London and Other Papers* (New York, 1867).

B. DAB 3, 162–164; NYT 9 March 1867; Walter Blair and Hamlin Hill, "Charles Farrar Browne/Artemus Ward," *America's Humor* (New York, 1978); Don Carlos Seitz, *Artemus Ward (Charles Farrar Browne): A Biography and Bibliography* (New York, 1919; reprint ed., 1974).

ROBERT L. HOSKINS

BROWNLOW, WILLIAM GANNAWAY (b. 29 August 1805; d. 29 April 1877), whose fiery style earned him the nickname "the Fighting Parson," was an iconoclast, preacher, editor, and Unionist. He was Tennessee's first post–Civil War governor in 1865, and served in the U.S. Senate from 1869 to 1875. He was a leader in Tennessee and national journalism as editor of the *Knoxville Whig*, and other newspapers before and after the Civil War.

He was one of five children of Joseph A. and Catherine Gannaway Brownlow and was born in Wythe County, Virginia. His family moved to Knoxville, Tennessee, around 1810 and Brownlow was educated in local schools. In 1826 he entered the ministry of the Methodist church and was assigned to the Black Mountain circuit in North Carolina. At age thirty-one he married Eliza Ann O'Brien on 11 September 1836, and they settled in Elizabethton, North Carolina. The couple had two sons and five daughters.

Brownlow decided to supplement his preacher's income and preach the gospel through a newspaper. He started the *Elizabethton Whig* on 16 May 1839. He moved to Jonesboro, Tennessee, and from 1839 to 1849 he edited the *Jonesboro Whig and Independent*, then moved to Knoxville, where he took over the *Knoxville Whig* in 1849. Brownlow made the *Whig* into an influential political newspaper with the largest circulation in the state before the Civil War.

The *Whig* was the last Unionist paper in the South and was suppressed on 24 October 1861. Even though Brownlow preached that according to the Bible slavery was ordained of God, he advocated the preservation of the Union. His paper's motto was "Independent in all things—Neutral in nothing." Brownlow was forced to flee Knoxville, but he was captured, imprisoned, and charged with treason to the Confederacy. In March 1862 he was released into Union territory and went into Ohio. Upon his release he supposedly said, "Glory to God in the highest, and on earth, peace, good will toward all men, except a few hell-born and hell-bound rebels in Knoxville" (Coulter, 1971).

While in Ohio he wrote his *Sketches of the Rise, Progress, and Decline of Secession; with a Narrative of Personal Adventure Among the Rebels* (1862), and then left for a strenuous lecture tour of the North. When Union forces occupied eastern Tennessee in 1863, Brownlow returned to Knoxville and became the leader of the Central Committee that was reorganizing state government. In 1865 he was chosen Tennessee's governor without opposition. He served for two terms during difficult times and encouraged the investment of northern capital, immigration to the state, a free school system, and mining and manufacturing. He dealt strongly with the Ku Klux Klan, but his policies may have inadvertently encouraged the Klan.

Brownlow resumed publication of the *Whig* in October 1863 and called it the *Knoxville Whig and Rebel Ventilator*. While he was governor his son, John Bell Brownlow, edited the paper. Upon his election to the Senate in 1869, Brownlow sold the *Whig*. When he left the Senate in 1875, he bought the newspaper back and continued to edit it until shortly before his death.

BIBLIOGRAPHY:

B. DAB 3, 177–178; NYT 30 April 1877; E. Merton Coulter, *William G. Brownlow: Fighting Parson of the Southern Highlands* (Chapel Hill, N.C., 1937; reprinted with an introduction by James W. Patton, Knoxville, 1971).

WILLIAM RAY MOFIELD

BRYANT, WILLIAM CULLEN(b. 3 November 1794; d. 12 June 1878) was one of America's leading newspaper figures for fifty years, editing the *New York Evening Post* from 1829 to 1878. He had an international reputation as a poet and literary critic before he became a journalist. Known as "the father of American poetry," the author of "Thanatopsis" and approximately 160 other poems was also one of the most prolific prose writers in America. Writing about 10,000 editorials, he brought a polished style to newspapers and a higher literary plane than probably any other American newspaper has achieved. He was one of the nation's foremost advocates of free trade, free speech, low tariffs, international copyright, civic reforms, labor rights, low postage rates, abolition, and democratic philosophies. His eloquent editorials during the Civil War reflect his belief in the inviolability of the Union.

Bryant, the second of seven children, was born in Cummington, Massachusetts, a village in the western part of the state. His father, Peter Bryant, was a physician and surgeon as well as a lover of poetry and music. Bryant's mother, Sarah Snell Bryant, was the daughter of Squire Ebenezer Snell of Cummington, and traced her ancestry to the Mayflower. Bryant's early education was in the district schools. He studied Latin in Brookfield under the Reverend Thomas Snell, his uncle, and studied Greek under the Reverend Moses Hallock in Plainfield. Bryant attended Williams College for a year. Because his family could not afford to send him to Yale, he studied law from 1811 to 1814 under Mr. Howe of Worthington, Massachusetts. He was admitted to the bar in August 1815 and was a practicing lawyer in Plainfield and Great Barrington until 1825. During this period he wrote much of his poetry including "Thanatopsis" and "To a Waterfowl."

On 11 January 1821 Bryant married Frances Fairchild, daughter of a neighboring farmer. They had two daughters: Frances, born on 2 January 1822, and Julia, born on 1 June 1831.

Because Bryant disliked law, he went to New York in 1825 to edit the *New York Review*, a literary magazine. In June 1826 William Coleman (q.v.), editor of the *New York Evening Post*, was thrown from his carriage by a runaway horse. Bryant became assistant editor of the paper on 1 July 1826. When Coleman died on 13 July 1829, Bryant became editor in chief.

The *Evening Post*, founded under the auspices of Alexander Hamilton, had long been one of the country's leading newspapers. After Bryant took it over, he left it in charge of his assistants much of the time. By 1840 it had become one of the leading Democratic papers. Bryant supported Andrew Jackson and Martin Van Buren, opposed high tariffs, and advocated a complete separation between government and banking.

In 1844 Bryant kept the paper on the Democratic side even though he opposed Polk and the annexation of Texas. During this period Parke Godwin, his son-in-law, was his able assistant. In 1848 he broke with the Democratic party and supported the Free-Soil candidacy of Van Buren. In 1856 he allied the paper with the new Republican party supporting John C. Frémont and made the *Evening Post* a vigorous Republican organ. When Abraham Lincoln made his Cooper Union speech in 1860, Bryant introduced him. Although he supported Lincoln, he assailed him during the Civil War because of his moderation and reluctance to emancipate the slaves. Bryant kept the paper Republican even though he sometimes disagreed with party policies.

Bryant was an inveterate tourist and wrote three books based on his correspondence with the *Evening Post* during his travels. After Bryant's fifth trip to Europe, his wife died on 27 July 1866. After her death, he occupied himself with translating the *Iliad* and the *Odyssey*, as well as working several hours a day at the *Evening Post*.

Bryant often made formal addresses at celebrations and official occasions. On 29 May 1878 he delivered an oration at the unveiling of the Mazzini statue in Central Park. Returning after the ceremonies to the home of James Grant Wilson, he fell and sustained a concussion. After an illness of two weeks, he died at his home on 12 June 1878.

BIBLIOGRAPHY:

A. *Letters of a Traveller* (New York, 1850).

B. DAB 3, 200–205; NYT 13 June 1878; Charles H. Brown, *William Cullen Bryant* (New York, 1971); Parke Godwin, *A Biography of William Cullen Bryant with Extracts from his Private Correspondence*, 2 vols. (New York, 1883); Allan Nevins, *The "Evening Post": A Century of Journalism* (New York, 1922).

C. JOANNE SLOAN

BUTLER, BURRIDGE DAVENAL (b. 5 February 1868; d. 30 March 1948) was an early, innovative leader in agricultural publishing and broadcasting. *Prairie Farmer* magazine and WLS radio were among the journalistic properties he brought to national prominence.

Butler was born in Louisville, Kentucky, and lived there until school age. His parents, Thomas D. Butler and Marie Radcliffe Butler, moved frequently and his formal education was limited to grammar school. Thomas was a part-time minister and religion editor. Marie, who also preached, was a published poet and sometime religion editor. Butler's father was frequently absent, so when his mother died he returned, at age sixteen, to Louisville to work at odd jobs. At seventeen he was hired as a reporter for the *Louisville Evening Times*, but was fired his first week. Later that year, in the fall of 1885, he was hired as a sports writer for the *Cincinnati Enquirer*. He quit the job after two months and moved to Grand Rapids, Michigan, where in March 1886 he became a free-lance writer for the *Grand Rapids Morning Democrat*, and then a full-time reporter. Butler worked briefly in 1887 for a competing paper—the *Eagle*—but he rejoined the *Democrat* and earned national attention for his on-site coverage of the aftermath of the Johnstown, Pennsylvania, flood of 1889. He was promoted to city editor in 1890 and to state editor in 1891. During this time, on 22 December 1890, Butler married Winnie L. Whitfield of Grand Rapids.

Butler's first publishing venture, *Michigan Cyclist*, lasted from 1893 to 1898. Others edited the magazine while Butler worked as a publicist for a St. Louis stove manufacturer from 1894 to 1885, and as assistant manager of the Chicago sales office of the Scripps-McRae League from 1896 to 1899. In 1899 he joined with workers in the Scripps chain to found the *Omaha Daily News*, and was its editor until 1902. The partners formed the Clover Leaf League, which owned newspapers in St. Paul, Des Moines, Kansas City, Sioux City, and Duluth. He was head of the chain's Chicago sales office from 1902 to 1903. He was president and publisher of the chain's *Minneapolis Daily News* from 1903 until he left the group in 1909. In the meantime, Butler's wife, Winnie, died childless of a lingering illness on 26 July 1904. He married Ina Hamilton Busey on 30 July 1906. They had one stillborn son.

Butler first tasted farm publishing when the Clover Leaf League became part of an advertising sales unit called the Farm League List, a group of five farm magazines that included *Prairie Farmer* of Chicago. When Butler left the league, he took ownership of *Prairie Farmer*, which was the oldest publication of its kind in the country. By hiring editors who met the journalistic standards he had forged in the heat of daily newspaper work, Butler helped set the course for current agricultural reporting. His magazine soon spread through Illinois, Indiana, Michigan, and Iowa to become one of the three largest farm publications in the nation.

On 1 October 1928 Butler purchased WLS radio, a clear-channel station in Chicago that had been operated by the Sears-Roebuck Agricultural Foundation. Under Butler, WLS worked in tandem with *Prairie Farmer* and provided innovative programming, including educational programs for use in poor, rural schools. In the 1930s Butler began spending winters in Arizona, where he bought radio stations KOY in Phoenix and KTUC in Tucson. He bought *Arizona Farmer*, a publication similar to *Prairie Farmer*, in 1940.

On 23 March 1948 Butler fell at his Arizona estate, Casa Davenal. He entered the hospital with back and cardiac injuries but never recovered. He died of kidney failure one week later.

BIBLIOGRAPHY:

B. DAB Supp. 4, 131–132; NYT 31 March 1948; *Broadcasting*, 5 April 1948; James F. Evans, *''Prairie Farmer'' and WLS: The Burridge D. Butler Years* (Urbana, Ill., 1969).

GORDON BILLINGSLEY

CAHAN, ABRAHAM (b. 6 July 1860; d. 31 August 1951) was editor of the *Jewish Daily Forward* for nearly fifty years and a profound influence on the Jewish community of New York City's Lower East Side, especially between 1900 and 1920. He was a talented writer of fiction and nonfiction, labor organizer, thinker, and spellbinding orator.

Cahan was born in Podberezy, Lithuania, a small village near Vilna. He was the son of Schachne Cahan and Sarah Goldarbeiter Cahan. His father was too poor to give Cahan the secular education he wanted him to have, so Cahan was educated in Hebrew schools. While a teacher in Velizh, he became involved with the underground radical socialist movement opposed to the czar. Political oppression forced him to leave the country, and he arrived in the United States in June 1882.

He settled in New York's Jewish ghetto, the Lower East Side, and worked at various jobs. He became involved with the growing Jewish labor union movement and spoke out in favor of socialism as well. Cahan learned English quickly and contributed stories about the Lower East Side to the *New York World* and *New York Sun*. Cahan organized a labor union for Jewish garment workers, and in 1886 he became editor of *Neie Zeit*, a labor paper which lasted only a few months.

Cahan married Anna Bronstein of Kiev on 11 December 1886. The couple had no children. In 1891 Cahan became editor of *Arbeiter Zeitung*, a Yiddish-language labor newspaper founded in 1890, and continued as editor until 1894. In 1893 he also became editor of *Die Zukunft*, a Yiddish-language organ of the Socialist Workers party.

In the 1890s Cahan began to develop his skill as a fiction writer, and in 1896, with the encouragement of William Dean Howells (q.v.), Cahan published his first novel, *Yekl: A Tale of the New York Ghetto*. He remained active in the socialist and Jewish labor movements, and on 22 April 1897, the first issue of the *Jewish Daily Forward* appeared; Cahan was its editor. Because of internal strife he resigned after six months.

Between 1897 and 1901 Cahan was a reporter for the *New York Commercial Advertiser* and worked under the direction of its city editor, Lincoln Steffens (q.v.). He returned to the *Jewish Daily Forward* as editor for only six months in 1902 before resigning because of clashes with Jewish intellectuals who did not approve of the direction in which Cahan was taking the paper. He returned as editor in 1903 and remained in that position until his death. In 1902 Cahan had attempted to revive the dying *Jewish Daily Forward* by de-emphasizing ideology and featuring stories of life in the Jewish community. He continued this after 1903 and also continued to clash with the Jewish intellectuals who thought he had turned the paper into a Jewish version of yellow journalism. However, Cahan and the paper remained loyal to socialism and supported trade labor unions. By 1918 the circulation rose to nearly 200,000.

World War I was problematic for Cahan and the *Forward*. The paper's antiwar position brought threats of postal censorship, and Cahan eased the *Forward*'s opposition rather than risk losing the paper. The *Forward* fully supported the Russian Revolution and continued to support the Bolshevik government afterward even in the face of repressions by the communists in Russia. Later in the 1920s, after visiting the Soviet Union, Cahan dropped his support of the communist regime, and in the 1930s the *Forward* was a harsh critic of Stalin. In the 1930s Cahan moved the newspaper into the mainstream of the liberal-labor coalition and supported many of the New Deal policies of Franklin Roosevelt.

After World War II, the *Forward* began to decline due to a combination of factors, among them Cahan's advanced years. He suffered a stroke in 1946, but continued to hold the title of editor until his death in 1951. He had continued writing short stories and novels throughout his active life. *The Rise of David Levinsky* (1917) is considered his best novel.

BIBLIOGRAPHY:

A. *The Education of Abraham Cahan* (Philadelphia, 1969).

B. Irving Howe, *World of Our Fathers* (New York, 1976).

JOSEPH P. MCKERNS

CAMPBELL, JOHN (b. 1653; d. March 1727/28) was a Boston postmaster who published the first newspaper in the colonies to appear for more than a single issue. He began the *Boston News-Letter* on 24 April 1704, and was its publisher until 1722. The paper continued publication until 1776.

Campbell was born in Scotland in 1653, the son of Duncan Campbell, a Glasgow bookseller who was reported to be industrious and a fashionable dresser with an eye for young ladies of great fortune. It is not known when John Campbell came to New England, but it was some time before 1695. Isaiah Thomas reported that Campbell had written at least nine newsletters to special correspondents in other colonies before 1703. Campbell had been named postmaster in 1702, and realized that his office was a clearinghouse for news, especially dispatches from Europe, legal notices, arrivals, shipping news, and gossip. There was such a demand for his handwritten dispatches that he even enlisted his brother Duncan to help, but could not keep up. In 1704 he turned to printer Bartholomew Green to publish a new journal, the *Boston News-Letter*. Green printed the paper from 1704 to 1707, when the contract was given to John Allen. When Allen's shop was destroyed in the great fire of 1711, Green resumed printing the *News-Letter*.

The *News-Letter* was chiefly concerned with rather dated news clipped from London papers, dealing with English politics, the court, and European wars. Some of the personal gossip from Europe was slightly racy, but Campbell was careful not to offend colonial authority. Perhaps because of its relative blandness, the paper was never a financial success and Campbell wrote that he "laboured hard to get it along" and had but few subscribers and little support from advertisers. At two pence a copy, or twelve shillings a year, the paper was considered a luxury item, and even by 1719 Campbell was selling fewer than 300 impressions. He twice suspended publication for a time, until a government subsidy saved him from bankruptcy. Campbell also had problems with long delays in reprinting foreign news, so he expanded half the issues of 1719 to whole sheets in order to catch up with the events. The paper usually was a single half sheet printed on both sides. On occasion, Campbell expanded it to three or four pages.

In the summer of 1719 a new postmaster, William Brooker, was appointed, but Campbell would not relinquish the *News-Letter*. Brooker began his own paper, the *Boston Gazette*, and a newspaper war of short duration began. Campbell began to catch up on his thirteen-month backlog of foreign news, and left blank one page, "of good writing paper," so readers could fill in their own news. He reiterated his intention to publish every other week, although he admitted that he might have to suspend publication again during the winter until weather permitted the resumption of shipping from London.

With the founding of the *New England Courant* in 1721, the three Boston papers engaged in lively, if often acrimonious, debate. Campbell was irked to have the *Courant* call his paper "a dull vehicle of intelligence" and responded with an acerbic editorial from "J.C." to the *Courant*'s "Jack Dullman," who was *Courant* editor John Checkley.

But Campbell was now over seventy years old, and may have tired of publishing a paper which offered so many difficulties and so little financial reward. In 1722 he turned the *News-Letter* over to Bartholomew Green. Green and his successors continued the paper until the British evacuation of Boston in 1776.

Campbell survived only a few years more. He died in March 1727/28, a respected citizen and justice of the peace.

BIBLIOGRAPHY:
B. DAB 2, 456; Clarence S. Brigham, *History and Bibliography of American Newspapers, 1690–1820*, 2 vols. (New York, 1947); Isaiah Thomas, *The History of Printing in America*, 2 vols., rev. ed. (Albany, 1874).

CAROLYN G. CLINE

CANHAM, ERWIN DAIN (b. 13 February 1904; d. 3 January 1982) worked for the *Christian Science Monitor* most of his adult life, became its editor, and gave that newspaper its reputation for thoughtful, analytical coverage.

Canham, a practicing Christian Scientist, was born in Auburn, Maine, the only child of Vincent Walter Canham, a printer, farmer, and newspaperman, and Elizabeth May Gowell Canham, who had been a schoolteacher. Canham learned the rudiments of the news business by visiting shops where his father worked, and sometimes helping. From the age of eight he undertook such chores as copying rural dispatches over the telephone, folding papers off a flatbed press, working as a galley boy and a bill collector, and finally reporting for a local paper and stringing for eight metropolitan dailies.

In 1915 the family moved to Gardiner, then to Lewiston. He entered Bates College in Lewiston in 1921. He joined the debate team, and in 1925 led that team on a tour of seven British universities. While on that trip he received a cable from the *Christian Science Monitor* offering him a job as reporter, which he accepted.

After a year with the *Monitor*, Canham won a Rhodes scholarship, and while studying modern history at Oxford he covered the League of Nations for the *Monitor*. From 1930 to 1932 he ran the *Monitor*'s bureau in Geneva and covered the London Naval Disarmament Conference. Also, in 1930 he married Thelma Whitman Hart of Cape Cod. The couple had two daughters, Carolyn and Elizabeth. Thelma Canham died in 1967. His second wife, Patience Daltry, survived him. They were married in 1968.

In 1932 Canham became chief of the *Monitor*'s bureau in Washington, D.C. He covered Hoover's unsuccessful reelection campaign and the first seven years of the New Deal. He went overseas from time to time to report on such things as the London Economic Conference and the founding of the Philippine Commonwealth. During the 1930s Canham also appeared on a weekly radio program on CBS. In 1939 he moved to Boston as general news editor of his paper. At the end of 1940 he became the *Monitor*'s chief editorial executive, and in 1945 its editor. Beginning in 1940 he wrote a weekly column, "Down the Middle of the Road." He also contributed a quarterly article to the *Round Table*, a British publication. For two months in 1945 he substituted for Cedric Foster as a commentator on the Mutual network, and that December began a weekly commentary on ABC, sponsored by the *Monitor*.

After World War II, Canham was involved in public affairs, both inside and outside his profession. He was president of the American Society of Newspaper Editors in 1948. In 1949 he became a U.S. delegate to the United Nations and helped draft a treaty on freedom of information. In the 1950s he advised the U.S. Information Agency and the State Department about the nation's global information program. He served on President Eisenhower's Commission on National Goals and on his National Manpower Council. In 1959 he was president of the U.S. Chamber of Commerce. He served as a member of the board of directors of the Public Broadcasting System, and was a member of President Nixon's Commission on Campus Unrest. He delivered lecture series at Yale and at Stanford which became books, and wrote many articles for the *Monitor* that were later published in book form.

As editor of the *Monitor*, Canham strengthened its foreign news coverage and developed its staff. He encouraged specialization by reporters and sought reporting in breadth and in depth, leaving "mere reporting of the event" to radio and television. Canham served as editor until 1964, then as editor in chief until 1974, and then editor emeritus.

In 1966 Canham served one year as president of the Christian Science Church. From 1975 to 1978 Canham served as the resident commissioner of the Northern Marianas Islands. He died 3 January 1982 at Agana, Guam, two weeks after undergoing abdominal surgery.

BIBLIOGRAPHY:

A. *Commitment to Freedom: The Story of the "Christian Science Monitor"* (Boston, 1958).

B. NYT 4 January 1982.

DWIGHT JENSEN

CANNON, JAMES "JIMMY" (b. 10 April 1909 or 1910; d. 5 December 1973) was an accomplished reporter and wordsmith who had covered wars, trials, and politics, but who preferred sportswriting. And within sports he most enjoyed covering boxing, which he called "the red light district of sports."

Jimmy Cannon was born in Greenwich Village, the son of Thomas J. Cannon and Loretta Monahan Cannon. After one year at Regis High School he became, in 1926, a copyboy for the *New York Daily News*. He met Mark Hellinger (q.v.), the drama critic, who influenced and helped him. He was promoted to reporter in 1927, covering general assignments. In 1934 he moved to the *World-Telegram*, and in 1935 became a feature writer for International News Service.

When Cannon covered the Lindbergh kidnapping trial, he met Damon Runyon (q.v.) and became his protégé. He went to work for the *New York Journal-American* as a sportswriter in 1936, and remained a sportswriter for most of the rest of his life. But during World War II he served in the U.S. Army. He wrote columns for *PM*, which were later collected in book form as *The Sergeant Says* (1942). He was a combat correspondent for *Stars and Stripes*.

In 1946 Cannon became a sports columnist for the *New York Post*. He left sports coverage briefly to report from Korea during the war there. In 1959 the *Journal-American* hired him back as a sports columnist at a salary reported to be $1,000 a week, said to make him the highest-paid sports columnist in the United States.

Cannon became a friend of Frank Sinatra, who asked Cannon to write his biography. Cannon said he would agree only if Sinatra would tell him everything. The project fell through. Cannon concluded his career writing for King Features and the Hearst papers. He suffered a stroke in 1971, but was able to resume writing until a few weeks before he died.

The *New York Times* called him "an artisan of the language." It was Cannon who wrote of Joe Louis, "He's a credit to his race—the human race." Ernest Hemingway (q.v.) praised Cannon for his ability to convey the quality of the athlete and the excitement of sport. Cannon never married.

BIBLIOGRAPHY:

B. NYT 6 December 1973.

DWIGHT JENSEN

CAPA, ROBERT (b. 22 October 1913; d. 25 May 1954) was one of the greatest photojournalists ever to cover war. Best known for his image of a soldier caught at the moment of death in the Spanish civil war, Capa covered combat for eighteen years until he was killed on assignment in Vietnam. Guided by his belief that "if your pictures aren't good enough, you aren't close enough," Capa's photographs rarely have been equaled.

Born André Friedmann in Budapest, Hungary, Capa spent his youth in the city. At age eighteen, he moved to Berlin to study sociology and journalism at Berlin University from 1931 to 1933. While living in Berlin in 1931, Capa held a part-time job in the darkroom of Ulstein Enterprises, a group of magazines that pioneered in the art of photojournalism.

On a day when Leon Trotsky was scheduled to speak in Copenhagen, Capa was the only person in the darkroom available to cover the event. Carrying his tiny Leica camera in his pocket, Capa managed to get inside the auditorium and take a series of photographs, one of which became his first published image. Other photographers were not able to photograph the camera-shy Trotsky because they had large box cameras which were easily spotted and confiscated. Capa remained in Berlin until 1933 and then left for Paris.

For the first two years in Paris, Capa worked under his real name, but in 1935, he began using the name Robert Capa because he felt he would earn more money if editors thought he was a "famous American photographer." With the help of the woman he would marry, Gerda Taro, Friedmann shot photographs that were credited to Robert Capa.

In 1938 he was sent to cover the Spanish civil war. While waiting in a trench, watching untrained soldiers attempting to charge an entrenched machine-gun nest, Capa shot a series of images, one of which was the now famous image of a soldier caught in the moment of his death. The photograph was published around the world and credited to Robert Capa. From that time on, Friedmann became Capa, the famous combat photographer.

After the Spanish civil war, Capa photographed the Japanese invasion of China in 1938. With the outbreak of war in Europe, Capa worked as a photographer for *Life* magazine and other publications from 1941 to 1945.

One of Capa's most memorable assignments during World War II was D day. Capa went in with Company E in the first wave and shot pictures of the men trying desperately to hold onto a small strip of sand. After six hours of shooting photographs, Capa returned to the USS *Chase* and sent his film in for processing. Seven days later he learned that his photographs of the invasion were the best taken on that day, but an excited darkroom assistant made a critical mistake by using too much heat to dry the negatives. The emulsion had run down the length of Capa's film. Out of 106 pictures, only 8 were salvaged.

Capa also jumped with paratroopers into Germany, was one of the advance arrivals on Anzio, and even found himself under fire from American soldiers in Belgium who had mistaken the photographer for an enemy soldier.

With the end of World War II, Capa and other unemployed war photographers formed a new picture agency, Magnum, in 1947. Capa served as the first president and central figure of Magnum. From 1947 to 1954 Capa devoted himself to strengthening Magnum, authored several books and articles that were illustrated with his photographs, and covered the birth of Israel from 1948 to 1950. Capa returned to combat coverage in 1954 when he went to Vietnam to cover the French struggle against the Vietminh.

On 25 May 1954 Capa was working on a picture story to be entitled "Bitter Rice." It was to show the dramatic contrast between the French tanks and the peasants working in the rice paddies, of men dying in the struggle for the rice harvest. That afternoon, a jeep in which Capa was riding was stalled by an ambush up the road. Bored with the wait, Capa decided to walk ahead in search of more images. He was killed by an antipersonnel mine.

BIBLIOGRAPHY:

B. NYT 26 May 1954; Cornell Capa, *Robert Capa* (New York, 1974).

MICHAEL D. SHERER

CARTER, BOAKE (b. 29 September 1898; d. 16 November 1944) was a popular network radio commentator during the 1930s. His broadcasts were easily identified by his deep baritone voice, his British accent, and his customary closing of "Cheerio!" Carter also was known for his widely read newspaper columns and books.

Carter was born in the Soviet province of Azerbaijan in the oil port of Baku. His father, Thomas Carter, was a British oilman and consular agent. His mother, Edith Harwood-Yarred Carter, was Irish. The journalist was christened Harold Thomas Henry Carter. He was taken to England at age five, where he was enrolled in the upper-class Tunbridge Wells preparatory school for boys. Carter was educated at Christ Church, Cambridge University, and attended the Royal Air Force training school in Scotland during World War I. He also studied at the Slade School of Art in London. At Cambridge, he took an active part in sports and served as a reporter on the school newspaper, the *Cantabrian*. He also worked briefly as a reporter for the *Daily Mail* in London before coming to the United States in 1920. Carter accompanied his father in the southwestern United States, Mexico, and Central America, working in the oil fields and writing for newspapers. His employers included the *Tulsa World* and the newspaper *Excelsior* in Mexico City. In 1923 he settled with his parents in Philadelphia, where he became a rewrite man and later a copyreader for the *Evening Bulletin*. He became an American citizen in 1933.

In 1924 Carter married Beatrice Olive Richter, who was the assistant society editor of the *Bulletin*. Her father was the publisher and editor of *Sporting Life* magazine. The Carters had two children—a daughter, Gladys Sheleagh Boake Carter, and a son, Michael Boake Carter. After the couple's marriage, Carter moved to the *Philadelphia Daily News* as assistant city editor. The Carter family lived in an old farmhouse at Torresdale, just outside the city.

Carter's radio career began at WCAU, Philadelphia, in 1930, when he was asked to describe a local rugby match. He also broadcast a simulated description of a Cambridge-Oxford boat race for WCAU. A short time later, he attempted a daily radio commentary, but listeners had difficulty understanding his British accent. Unable to find a sponsor, he returned to the *Daily News* after a brief interval. However, in 1931 the newspaper assigned him to do two daily news broadcasts on WCAU under sponsorship of Hearst Metrotone newsreels. When he returned to the air, he had modified his accent and adopted the first name of Boake, a family name on his mother's side. Carter selected and rewrote his own stories, treating them in a dignified, yet frequently emotional manner. He spoke rapidly and made frequent use of clichés and dramatic phrases. He often added his own editorial comments to the stories he broadcast.

Boake Carter gained national fame in 1932 when CBS picked up his daily reports and commentary on the Lindbergh kidnapping case. These special broadcasts attracted considerable national attention and led to his joining CBS. In January 1933 Carter signed a contract with the Philco Corporation to give a fifteen-minute commentary five nights a week on CBS. On his broadcasts, Carter stressed interpretation rather than factual narration of the news, often exercising little restraint in his commentary. Characteristically, he offered simple solutions and slashing attacks upon much of the establishment. Among his targets were President Roosevelt and the New Deal, organized labor, and the British government. He accused the latter of trying to drag the United States into a war to protect its commercial interests. He crusaded on such matters as ship inspection procedures, shortcomings of the U.S. merchant marine, and the development of air power instead of a traditional buildup of naval weaponry for defense and possible warfare. During Carter's heyday at CBS, his audience was estimated at more then ten million, or roughly equal to that of Lowell Thomas (q.v.) on NBC. Ironically, he was voted the nation's most popular commentator in *Radio Guide*'s annual poll in 1938, the year that CBS dropped him because of his sensationalism.

After his release by CBS, Carter wrote a daily newspaper column called "But———." which was carried by sixty newspapers. His column, which had an estimated readership of seven million, was ranked third nationally in popularity. From September 1939 until his death in November 1944, Carter's news commentaries were heard intermittently on the Mutual Broadcasting System. He never regained his great popularity, however, because he had alienated so many groups.

He was under a severe mental strain during his last years. Carter divorced his first wife in 1941 and married Paula Nicoli in August 1944. He also embraced a mystical sect of Judaism, even though his public and broadcast statements led many people to label him as anti-Semitic. Carter died of a cerebral hemorrhage.

BIBLIOGRAPHY:

B. DAB 3, 142–143; NYT 17 November 1944; *Time*, 27 November 1944; David Culbert, *News for Everyman* (Westport, Conn., 1976); Irving E. Fang, *Those Radio Commentators!* (Ames, Iowa, 1977).

HERBERT H. HOWARD

CARVALHO, SOLOMON SOLIS (b. 16 January 1856; d. 12 April 1942) was nationally known as an outstanding executive in the William Randolph Hearst (q.v.) newspaper and magazine chain. He was also considered an expert in finance and law.

Born in Baltimore, Maryland, the youngest of four children of Solomon Nunes Carvalho and Sarah Solis Carvalho, both Sephardic Jews, he spent his childhood and youth in New York City. The elder Carvalho gained recognition when he accompanied John C. Frémont on his fifth expedition to the West as photographer and artist. In 1877 Carvalho received an A.B. degree from the City College of New York, and then read law. He was admitted to the New York State Bar, but never practiced in the courts. Beginning as a reporter for the City News Association in 1877, he soon became known for his ability to solve murder and suicide mysteries. He moved to Charles A. Dana's (q.v.) *Sun* the following year.

In 1877 he moved to the Pulitzer organization, where he helped to launch the evening edition of the *World* in reaction to the introduction of the evening edition of the *Sun* on 10 October 1887. He became known as "Loo" in the Pulitzer code list. In July 1892 Joseph Pulitzer (q.v.) called him to Paris and gave him full jurisdiction over all *World* expenditures. In May 1895 he married Helen Cusach, a reporter for the *World* known professionally as Nell Nelson.

Carvalho was made assistant vice president on 30 September 1892, but resigned 31 March 1896 because the paper lost $100,000 in one year after the per copy price was reduced to one cent at Carvalho's urging. He joined the Hearst organization, where he was known for his aggressive financial policies. It was said he spent time picking paper off the floor and turning out lights in an effort to reduce spending. He was called "Richelieu" in part because of his goatee and limp, but also because of his operating policies. The limp was believed to have been caused by a clubfoot.

Hearst began the publication of the *Chicago American*'s evening edition in 1899 in preparation for the presidential election of 1900, and assigned Carvalho to oversee its introduction. In 1903 he was assigned to organize the Hearst newspaper in Boston. Not only did Carvalho oversee the complex Hearst organization, but he is reported to have managed Hearst's personal finances. His salary reached $52,000 in the early 1900s, not long after Pulitzer is reported to have offered him a $50,000 salary as an inducement to return to the *World*.

In 1902 Hearst gave him a $25,000 bonus. In 1903, the year of Hearst's wedding to Millicent Willson at which Carvalho was one of thirty invited guests, Hearst gave him a trip to Europe, a Stearns automobile, and a collection of valuable antiques. While Hearst was on his honeymoon in Europe, he saw the British magazine *Car*, and cabled Carvalho to begin publication of a similar magazine in the United States to be called *Motor*. It was the first of Hearst's magazine ventures and was published in New York.

In December 1917 Carvalho retired from the Hearst organization, but for many years he continued as a highly paid consultant and chairman of the Hearst executive council. His later years were spent on a family farm at Metuchen, New Jersey, where he raised horses and created one of the largest blue and white china collections in the United States. Carvalho and his wife had two daughters, Helen C. Steele and Sarah Crehore. He died 12 April 1942 of arteriosclerosis. His wife died 27 October 1945.

BIBLIOGRAPHY:

B. DAB Supp. 3, 143–145; NYT 13 April 1942 and 29 October 1945.

ADRIAN L. HEADLEY

CATHER, WILLA (b. 7 December 1873; d. 24 April 1947) was an author of great literary importance who began her career as a journalist, writing reviews and critiques first for Lincoln, Nebraska, papers and later for *McClure's* magazine.

Cather was born in Back Creek Valley (later Gore), Virginia, and in 1883 moved with her family to Webster County, Nebraska, a change that had profound effects on Cather's professional and literary work. Her mother, Mary Virginia Boak Cather, was a dominant fourth-generation American; her father, Charles Fectigue Cather, ran a farm loan business. But an important early influence also came from Cather's grandmother, who spent much time reading to Cather when she was a child. Cather adopted her grandmother's maiden name, Sibert, as her middle name, although by 1920 she had dropped its use for professional purposes. Nevertheless, she is often referred to as Willa Sibert Cather.

Her literary debut was during her first year at the University of Nebraska in 1891 with a published essay on Thomas Carlyle. Later she became drama critic and columnist for the Lincoln newspaper, a job she held until earning her degree in 1895. In 1986 she moved to Pittsburgh, Pennsylvania, where she worked first as an editor for a small magazine, later as a telegraph editor and reviewer for the *Pittsburgh Daily Leader*. During the Pittsburgh years Cather also published poetry and fiction.

In 1906 S. S. McClure (q.v.) offered her a job on his muckraking journal. The year 1906 was a critical one for *McClure's* because a number of key journalists left to found their own publication. Among Cather's most important assignments was the editing of a lengthy manuscript on the life of Mary Baker Eddy (q.v.) and her Christian Science Church. The manuscript as given to Cather was of monumental importance, but vast, disorganized, and often unsubstantiated. Cather's fine editorial work led to her appointment as managing editor of *McClure's* in 1908.

However, Cather believed her crucial work was in the field of creative writing. As managing editor of *McClure's* she had little time to devote to her own literary pursuits. Thus, with publication of *O Pioneers!* in 1913, Cather left journalism, turning to fiction as her primary professional involvement. She died of a cerebral hemorrhage in New York City after a number of years of ill health.

BIBLIOGRAPHY:

B. Dorothy Tuck McFarland, *Willa Cather* (New York, 1972); Phyllis C. Robinson, *Willa: The Life of Willa Cather* (New York, 1983).

ELLI LESTER-MASSMAN

CATLEDGE, TURNER (b. 17 March 1901; d. 27 April 1983) first came to national prominence as a Washington correspondent covering depression-era politics for the *New York Times* and several national magazines. Catledge also helped launch Marshall Field's *Chicago Sun*, but soon returned to New York where he rose steadily through the executive ranks of the *Times* news department.

He was born on his paternal grandfather's 300-acre farm near New Prospect, in central Mississippi, the second child of Lee Johnston Catledge and Willie Ann Turner Catledge. His father, a railway clerk, was a political enthusiast who served as first mayor of Philadelphia, Mississippi, the cotton-ginning town 165 miles southeast of Memphis where Catledge was raised. His mother was a seamstress.

He excelled at the local public school and at Mississippi A&M, from which he was graduated in 1922 with a B.S. in business. Catledge had held various jobs since he was ten years old, including a jack-of-all-trades position at the country weekly, the *Neshoba Democrat*. Its publishers asked him to run the *Tunica Times*, but it foundered a year later after Catledge published a series of anti–Ku Klux Klan articles. He then found a similar position with the biweekly *Tupelo Journal*, and in February 1924 he moved to the *Memphis Press* as a reporter. Six weeks later, he proudly took a job with the *Memphis Commercial Appeal*, the paper his father had so avidly read.

In June 1927 Catledge joined the *Baltimore Sun* as a feature writer and was assigned to its Washington bureau in 1928. He joined the local staff of the *New*

York Times in July 1929 after Herbert Hoover, impressed with his coverage of the 1927 Mississippi floods, recommended him to Adolph S. Ochs (q.v.).

Catledge was transferred to the paper's Washington bureau only five months later. There he covered, successively, the House, the Senate, and the White House. From 1936 to 1941 he was the bureau's chief news correspondent, covering all phases of government nationwide. He had married Mildred Turpin on 19 March 1931, and they had two daughters. To supplement his income, he collaborated on articles for the *Saturday Evening Post* with Joseph Alsop (q.v.). Their series on Roosevelt's plan to expand the Supreme Court was published as a book, *The 168 Days* (1938).

Catledge left the *Times* in October 1941 to join the *Chicago Sun*, where he served first as world-correspondent and, starting in April 1942, as editor in chief. Unhappy, he returned to the *Times* in May 1942 as national correspondent; his attempts to get a foreign posting were rebuffed.

In January 1945 Catledge was named assistant managing editor of the *Times* and began his twenty-five-year quest for a more tightly edited and easily read paper. In 1946 he helped found the American Press Institute, serving as an advisory board member until 1970. Legally separated from his wife in 1949, Catledge threw himself into his work. He became executive managing editor in January 1951, and managing editor in December 1951. In 1955 he was appointed to the advisory board for the Pulitzer Prizes, a post he held for twelve years. He continued to write, both for the *Times* and several national magazines, obtaining in May 1957 an exclusive interview with Nikita Khrushchev. The Catledges were divorced on 10 February 1958; five days later he married Mrs. Abby Ray Izard, a widow from New Orleans.

Long a member of the American Society of Newspaper Editors, Catledge was president in 1960–61. In September 1964 he was named executive editor of the *Times*, a new position in which control over the news and Sunday departments was centralized. Catledge served as vice president of the New York Times Company from June 1968 to January 1970, and director from 1968 to 1973. He retired in 1970 and moved with his wife to New Orleans, where he died in 1983 after a long illness following a stroke.

BIBLIOGRAPHY:

A. *My Life and The Times* (New York, 1971).

B. NYT 28 April 1983; Harrison E. Salisbury, *Without Fear or Favor* (New York, 1980); Gay Talese, *The Kingdom and the Power* (New York, 1966).

KRISTEN DOLLASE

CHANDLER, HARRY (b. 17 May 1864; d. 23 September 1944) was born at Landaff, New Hampshire, the son of Moses Knight Chandler and Emma Jane Little Chandler. He attended Lisbon, New Hampshire, High School. Chandler married twice; the first time to Magdalena Schlador of Berlin, on 6 February 1888. They had two daughters, Frances and Alice May. Magdalena died in 1892. On 5 June 1894 Chandler married Marian Otis, the daughter of Harrison Gray

Otis (q.v.), owner of the *Los Angeles Times*. They had six children: Constance, Ruth, Norman, Harrison Gray, Helen, and Philip.

After attending Dartmouth, Chandler moved to California in 1882 for reasons of health. He bought the city circulation routes for the *Los Angeles Times*—the routes served 1,400 subscribers—and became circulation manager, then business manager, then vice president and assistant general manager of the *Times*. In1917 General Otis died and Chandler became president and general manager of the paper. In 1941 he retired to the chairmanship of its board of directors. David Halberstam credits Chandler with shrewdness, the ability to manipulate people and money without tipping his hand in public, and gives details about how Chandler's shrewdness gave him power at the *Times* and helped wipe out competition and build his newspaper in size, circulation, and influence.

Chandler built the *Times* from a four-page paper with a four-figure subscription list into a large paper with a daily circulation of 320,000 and a Sunday circulation of 615,000. The paper was not considered a good newspaper during his lifetime—in fact, it was considered by many to be unfair and unreliable—but it gained respect later, after Harry Chandler provided it with resources and his son Norman (q.v.) had added sound management.

Harry Chandler's resources came to include a fortune based on land investments in southern California and other areas. He invested in cotton and livestock, helped build the southern California aircraft industry, and built the syndicate that constructed California's first paved road outside the city. He became an officer and a director of some forty California corporations. At one time, he owned more than 1.25 million acres of land. He died in Los Angeles.

BIBLIOGRAPHY:

b. NYT 24 September 1944; David Halberstam, *The Powers That Be* (New York, 1979).

DWIGHT JENSEN

CHANDLER, NORMAN (b. 14 September 1899; d. 20 October 1973) was born in Los Angeles, the son of Harry Chandler (q.v.) and Marian Otis Chandler; the grandson of Harrison Gray Otis (q.v.).

Chandler obtained his A.B. at Stanford University in 1922, and that August he married Dorothy Buffum. They had two children; a daughter, Camilla, and a son, Otis. Also in 1922 Chandler began work for the Times-Mirror Company in Los Angeles, which had been headed by his grandfather Otis and then passed on to the leadership of his father. Norman Chandler remained active in that company the rest of his life. He also held directorships in a number of other corporations.

Chandler had been a delivery boy with the *Los Angeles Times* when he was younger. In 1922 he became secretary to his father, and during the next seven years he moved from department to department within the company, learning its operations. In 1929 he became assistant to the publisher; and in 1934 he was appointed assistant to the general manager. Two years later he was named vice president and general manager, and in 1941, president and general manager.

From 1945 to 1960 Norman Chandler was president and publisher of the *Times*. He then served a year as president of the Times-Mirror Company, and from 1961 to 1966 was president and chairman of the board of the Times-Mirror Company. During 1966–68 he was the company's chairman and chief executive officer. After 1968 he served as chairman of the firm's executive committee.

Chandler led the Times-Mirror Company in new directions in at least these respects: he took the company into other fields of publishing besides newspapers; he acquired more newspapers (the company acquired *Newsday* and the *Dallas Times-Herald*, among other papers); the company entered the fields of television, cable television, magazines, book publishing, paper manufacturing, and other lines of business.

Also, Chandler modernized and automated his newspaper and broke out of some of the customary patterns of operation. For fourteen years he published the *Los Angeles Mirror* as an afternoon paper. Finally, he attempted to make the *Times* respected and influential on more than a local level. In 1939 he was cited for contempt for publishing articles criticizing judges (the U.S. Supreme Court dismissed the citation in 1941). In 1942 the *Times* won the first of its several Pulitzer Prizes.

Chandler established the Times Charities, which evolved into the Times-Mirror Foundation. He died in Los Angeles.

BIBLIOGRAPHY:

B. NYT 21 October 1973; David Halberstam, *The Powers That Be* (New York, 1979).

DWIGHT JENSEN

CHILDS, MARQUIS WILLIAM (b. 17 March 1903) was awarded the first Pulitzer Prize for distinguished commentary in 1969 as chief Washington correspondent for the *St. Louis Post-Dispatch*. He was regarded as the dean of the Washington press corps for his writing and reporting ability over a period of nearly four decades. He was known for his use of highly placed sources including presidents, cabinet officials, Supreme Court justices, and diplomats. In addition, he authored or edited nearly twenty books.

Childs was born in Clinton, Iowa, the son of lawyer and county attorney William Henry Childs and Lilian Malissa Marquis. Childs grew up in Iowa and Milwaukee, Wisconsin. He received his bachelor's degree in 1923 from the University of Wisconsin and his master's degree from the University of Iowa two years later. He worked briefly for the United Press in 1925 before returning to academia to teach freshman English. He later rejoined the United Press and was given assignments in Chicago, Detroit, New York, and St. Louis.

He married a St. Louis schoolteacher, Lu Prentiss, in August 1926 and accepted a staff appointment with the *St. Louis Post-Dispatch* that same year. The couple had two children, Henry Prentiss and Malissa Marquis Elliot. Childs worked as a feature writer at the *Post-Dispatch* covering cornfield murders and a wide range of subjects including reports from Louisiana on the political activity of Governor Huey Long. In 1930 he requested and received a leave of absence from the newspaper to do a study of economic conditions in Sweden. He visited Sweden twice during this period and subsequently wrote two books, *Sweden: Where Capitalism Is Controlled* (1934), and *Sweden: The Middle Way* (1936). The latter was an immense critical and popular success which examined Sweden's economy and the role of cooperatives in enhancing an industrial base. Some have maintained that its publication helped establish Sweden as a role model or alternative to communism and fascism for many countries during the depression. It is also credited with having influenced the Roosevelt administration to study the use of cooperatives.

In 1934 Childs requested the position of movie critic for the *Post-Dispatch*, but managing editor O. K. Bovard (q.v.) objected, and Childs was assigned instead to the newspaper's three-man Washington bureau. He distinguished himself in this position, traveling with the Roosevelt campaign in 1936. He was sent to report on the Spanish civil war from Madrid and Valencia, and he prepared a series of articles for the *Post-Dispatch* on economic conditions in Mexico that resulted in a call for a Senate investigation. Throughout the 1940s, Childs wrote about the Roosevelt administration and the effects of the war effort on American society and abroad. He also lectured throughout the United States on political and economic problems and wrote articles for a variety of publications including the *Yale Review, New Republic, Life, Reader's Digest*, and the *Saturday Evening Post*.

Childs left the *Post-Dispatch* to work for United Features Syndicate in 1944. He continued to augment his newspaper work with major books on American government and prominent political figures. He published *Eisenhower, Captive Hero* (1958) and, along with James Reston, edited *Walter Lippmann and His Times* (1959). He stayed at the United Features Syndicate for ten years, his column appearing in 150 newspapers, before returning to the *Post-Dispatch* as a special correspondent. He served as chief of the *Post-Dispatch* Washington bureau during the turbulent 1960s.

His first wife died in June 1968. He married Jane Neylan McBain in August 1969 and continued to write on a wide variety of topics. Childs ended formal staff responsibilities with the *Post-Dispatch* in 1974, but continued to contribute columns for seven more years. His last column appeared on 28 May 1981. In it, he credited his success to pragmatism and dedication to the abatement of human suffering.

BIBLIOGRAPHY:

A. *I Write from Washington* (Cambridge, Mass., 1942); *Witness to Power* (New York, 1975); "35 years of Deadlines," *St. Louis Post-Dispatch*, 28 May 1981.

B. CA 1984, 110–111; CB 1943, 126–128; Thomas Ottenad, "News Columnist Childs 'Winding Down' Career," *St. Louis Post-Dispatch*, 28 May 1981.

MICHAEL D. MURRAY

CHURCH, FRANCIS PHARCELLUS (b. 22 February 1839; d. 11 April 1906) was the author of perhaps the most famous editorial ever written. Church, editorial writer for the *New York Sun* from 1874 to 1906, wrote "Is There a

Santa Claus?'' on 21 September 1897. Before his association with the *Sun*, Church was the cofounder of the *Army and Navy Journal* and the *Galaxy*.

Church was born in Rochester, New York. His father, Pharcellus Church, was a Baptist clergyman, editor of a religious newspaper, and writer of theological books. Church's grandfather, Willard Church, was a soldier in the revolutionary war who had been imprisoned on the ship *Jersey* for nine months. Church's mother, Clara Emily Conant Church, was a descendant of Roger Conant, governor of the Massachusetts colony.

Church attended Charles Anthon's Latin School in New York. He graduated with honors from Columbia College in 1859, and then studied law in the office of Judge Hooper C. Von Horst in New York until 1861. Church gave up law for a journalism career. In 1860 he worked as an editorial writer on his father's newspaper, the *New York Chronicle*. In 1863 Church and his brother, William Conant Church, founded the *Army and Navy Journal*. In 1866 they founded the *Galaxy*, a literary magazine. Some of the leading literary figures of the day—Henry James, Walt Whitman (q.v.), and Samuel Clemens (q.v.)—contributed articles to the magazine. The *Galaxy* was consolidated in 1878 with the *Atlantic Monthly*. The brothers were also associated with the *Internal Revenue Record*.

Church became one of the principal editorial writers for the *New York Sun* in 1874, and stayed in that position until his death. He remained a director in the corporation that owned the magazines he had founded. The *Sun* under Charles Dana (q.v.) was known for its interesting casual essays. As an editorial writer for thirty-two years, Church wrote on topics of every kind. If Church had a specialty, it was probably religious controversy.

The practice of the *Sun* was to keep anonymous the authors of its editorials. When Church died, however, the *Sun* broke its rule of anonymity, the only time it ever did so, and revealed that Church was the author of ''Is There a Santa Claus?'' written in 1897. Edward P. Mitchell, editor in chief of the *Sun*, stated that Church produced the answer to eight-year-old Virginia O'Hanlon's question ''Is There a Santa Claus?'' in a short period of time. ''Yes, Virginia there is a Santa Claus'' is America's most famous editorial quote. The editorial is without doubt the nation's best known, and has been reprinted more than any other newspaper article ever written. Yet few authors of famous works are as little known as Church.

Church died in New York City after an illness of several months. He was married to Elizabeth Wickham of Philadelphia. They had no children.

BIBLIOGRAPHY:

B. NYT 12 April 1906; William David Sloan, ''Is There a Santa Claus?,'' *Masthead*, Fall 1979.

C. JOANNE SLOAN

CLAFLIN, TENNESSEE (b. 26 October 1845; d. 18 January 1923) rose from poor white trash in Ohio to become a titled member of the British aristocracy. In between, she was a huckster, a stockbroker, a spiritualist, a publisher, an alleged murderess, a woman suffragist, a social pariah, and a wealthy philanthropist. With such an interesting life, Tennessee Claflin should have been the topic of social discourse in her own time and of historical research in ours. Unfortunately for Tennessee, she had in Victoria Woodhull (q.v.) an older sister who was even more fascinating and flamboyant. In both life and death, Tennessee's star was eclipsed by that of her more famous and infamous sibling.

The Claflin sisters were born in rural Homer, Ohio, Victoria in 1863 and Tennessee seven years later. Their father, Ruben Buckman "Buck" Claflin, was a one-eyed backcountry drifter. Their mother, Roxanna Hummel Claflin, had an equally dubious background. The two produced a squalid, uneducated brood of ten children, most of whom were attractive and all of whom had a huckster's instincts. Tennessee and Victoria had both these qualities in excess. An additional talent was the ability to go into trances at will. The sisters therefore became an integral part of the Claflin family's traveling medicine show.

As the show traveled through the Midwest, it left in its wake charges of blackmail, prostitution, and fraud. Tennessee was charged with manslaughter following the death of one of her "patients," but the Claflins hurriedly left town and avoided indictment. Tennessee also picked up a husband on that tour, a gambler named John Bartles. He, however, seems to have disappeared almost immediately after the ceremony.

The Claflins were more successful at conquering New York, largely because they were helped by Cornelius Vanderbilt. The aging Vanderbilt had an eye for beauty and an interest in spiritualism, and was deeply attracted to Tennessee (who now called herself Tennie C.). He set up the sisters in a Wall Street brokerage business that earned $300,000 in three years.

The shocking "lady brokers of Wall Street" used the profits they made off Vanderbilt's tips to establish *Woodhull and Claflin's Weekly* in 1870. This strange little paper, which eventually reached a circulation of 20,000, contained short stories, book and play reviews, fashion items, news stories, and personality profiles. The *Weekly* was not much different from other newspapers of the period, but its editorial stance distinguished it from its competitors. Under the headings "Upward and Onward," "Progress," "Free Thought," "Untrammeled Lives," and "Breaking the Way for Future Generations," the paper endorsed a variety of radical causes, such as free love, vegetarianism, licensed prostitution, birth control, woman suffrage and financial equality, and "Victoria Woodhull for President."

It is questionable whether the sisters could have produced such articles, as their education was rudimentary. The power behind the *Weekly*'s pen was said to be held by two men—Colonel James H. Blood, a spiritualist and freethinker who was Victoria's second husband; and peripatetic philosopher Stephen Pearl Andrews. Whoever was responsible, the *Weekly* left its mark—or stain—on journalism of the period. Two high points were the paper's exposés of Wall Street fraud and its publication (the first in this country) of the *Communist Manifesto*. The low point was the 1872 revelation of the affair between influential minister Henry Ward Beecher (q.v.) and Elizabeth Tilton, wife of the liberal journalist and editor Theodore Tilton. Following publication of these charges, Anthony Comstock had the sisters arrested for distributing obscene material through the mails. They were acquitted.

The *Weekly* did not long survive the scandal and the sisters fled to London. In England, both remarried well. Victoria wed a prominent banker, but Tennessee outdid her sibling. She married Francis Cook, the wealthy owner of a dry-goods business. A year after their 1885 wedding, he became a baronet.

As Lady Cook, Tennessee produced a series of pamphlets espousing her own unorthodox philosophy on such social and moral questions as eugenics, abortion, prostitution, illegitimacy, and sexual equality. She and her sister also collaborated on a book, *The Human Body as the Temple of God* (1890). Until her death, Tennessee, as well as Victoria, espoused bizarre causes. Her last was to mount an ''Amazon Army'' of 150,000 women to fight in World War I. Although her contemporaries, and our own historians, see this woman as a pale copy of her sister, Tennessee Claflin Cook never failed to come up with original ideas.

BIBLIOGRAPHY:

B. DAB 25, 493–494; NAW 3, 652–655.

LYNNE MASEL-WALTERS

CLAPPER, RAYMOND (b. 30 May 1892; d. 1 February 1944) was one of the most widely known political analysts and newspaper columnists of his time. From the latter 1920s until near the end of World War II he covered the nation's capital and national politics. His columns, ''Between You and Me'' and ''Watching the World Go By,'' were read by an estimated ten million persons; and he also served as a commentator for the Mutual Broadcasting System. His book *Racketeering in Washington* (1933) exposed a wide range of corruption in the executive and legislative branches of the U.S. government.

Clapper was born on a Kansas farm near La Cygne, in Linn County. His parents, John William Clapper and Julia Crow, found they were unable to make a satisfactory living on the farm, so they moved to Kansas City, where the father obtained a job in a soap plant in the Armourdale district. There Raymond attended the Morse school and worked in a neighborhood grocery whose owner's daughter, Olive Ewing, he married 31 March 1913. Following their marriage, the Clappers dropped out of high school. Raymond took an apprentice printer's job, but the couple decided shortly afterward to resume their education. Hitchhiking to Lawrence, Kansas, they enrolled at Kansas University, where Clapper eventually became editor of the university newspaper and a campus correspondent for the *Kansas City Star*.

Before being graduated, Clapper became a regular member of the Kansas City newspaper's reporting staff. Following a brief period on the newspaper's staff, Clapper joined that of the United Press (UP), for which he worked in Chicago, Milwaukee, St. Paul, and New York, before moving to Washington in 1918. In 1920 Clapper achieved a sensational scoop at the Republican National

Convention of that year by anticipating the nomination of Warren G. Harding (q.v.). In 1923 Clapper became night manager of the UP capital bureau and its political analyst. In 1929 he became chief of the bureau. In 1934 Clapper left UP to join the *Washington Post* as chief of its national news bureau and political columnist. In 1936 he began writing a column for the Scripps-Howard newspapers. The next year, the column was purchased by the United Features Syndicate.

In 1939 Clapper was president of the Gridiron Club and served that same year as honorary president of Sigma Delta Chi, the national society of professional journalists. In addition, Clapper was a director of the National Press Club and a member of the Overseas Press Club. In a poll taken in 1940 among members of the national press corps, Clapper's column was adjudged "the most significant, fair, and reliable." The *London Daily Mail*, that same year, described Clapper as "America's No. 1 columnist" and observed that "his articles carry more weight than those of any other writer in the United States. With the outbreak of World War II, Clapper devoted more attention to international affairs and traveled to the Near East, India, and China in 1942. In 1943 he traveled to Sweden, England, North Africa, Sicily, and then to the South Pacific, where he died the following year in the collision of two U.S. Navy airplanes engaged in the invasion of the Marshall Islands.

In an introduction to Clapper's second book, *Watching the World Go By*, published after his death, Ernie Pyle (q.v.) wrote, "More than anything else he was a crusader for the right of people to think things out for themselves . . . and he spent his life giving them information that would help them. People believed what he said because they could sense the honesty in his writing." In Clapper's memory, his associates and friends established an annual award to the U.S. capital correspondent whose writings the previous year best embody the ideals of "fair and painstaking reporting and sound craftsmanship that marked Mr. Clapper's work, and have contributed most to public enlightenment and a sound democracy." Clapper and his wife, who died 11 November 1968, had two children, Janet and Peter Raymond.

BIBLIOGRAPHY:

A. *Watching the World Go By* (New York, 1944).

B. NYT 4 February 1944; Olive Ewing Clapper, *One Lucky Woman* (New York, 1961); Olive Ewing Clapper, *Washington Tapestry* (New York, 1946); "Everyman's Columnist," *Time*, 6 July 1942; E. K. Lindley, "Clapper and White: A Personal Tribute," *Newsweek*, 14 February 1944.

JOHN DE MOTT

CLAY, CASSIUS MARCELLUS (b. 19 October 1810; d. 22 July 1903) was an editor, abolitionist, politician, author, and diplomat. As editor of the *True American* of Lexington, Kentucky, he battled slavery with a vigor matched by none in the Border States and few in the nation.

Clay was one of seven children born to Green Clay and Sally Lewis Clay at the family home called Clermont in Madison County, Kentucky. Clay was educated at the College of St. Joseph, Transylvania University, and Yale University. He was graduated from Yale in 1832. While at Yale, Clay heard abolitionist William Lloyd Garrison (q.v.) speak, and although his father was a slave owner, Clay became a convert to the abolitionist cause. He returned to Kentucky and studied law at the Transylvania Law School during the fall of 1832, but then turned toward politics. In 1835 he was elected to the state legislature, defeated in 1836, and reelected in 1837. When he moved to Lexington in 1840, he ran for the legislature again and won, but against the advice of his cousin, Henry Clay, he introduced abolitionism into his 1841 campaign and lost.

Clay first issued the *True American* in Lexington on 3 June 1845 and protected his offices with cannon and other weapons in anticipation of trouble from anti-abolitionists. In his absence, his office was captured and he was forced to move the paper to Cincinnati, but he continued to distribute the paper in Lexington. In his paper he opposed the war with Mexico, but then surprised everyone by volunteering for the army. He was appointed a colonel of a Kentucky regiment and distinguished himself in battle.

He eventually moved his newspaper operation to Louisville where the *True American* was continued as the *Examiner*. He ran as the abolitionist candidate for governor of Kentucky in 1849, but lost. He was an early supporter and friend of Abraham Lincoln. Upon Lincoln's election, Clay was named minister to Russia. He was recalled in 1862 and offered a major general's commission in the Union army, but refused it. He returned to Russia in 1863 and served there until 1869. He was instrumental in the purchase of Alaska by the United States.

On 26 February 1833 Clay had married Mary Jane Warfield. The couple had eleven children, but four died in childhood. A daughter, Laura, became a noted feminist and was nominated for the presidency at the Democratic convention of 1920. He and his wife were divorced in 1878. At age eighty-four, Clay married fifteen-year-old Dora Richardson, but the marriage soon failed. According to one of his seven wills, a son, Larney, who returned with him from Russia, was the offspring of an affair with a woman named Annie Petroff of St. Petersburg. In his last years, Clay was adjudged insane by the Madison County Court. He died at his home, White Hall.

BIBLIOGRAPHY:

B. DAB 4, 169–170; NYT 23 July 1903; William H. Townsend, *The Lion of White Hall* (Dunwoody, Ga., 1967).

WILLIAM RAY MOFIELD

CLEMENS, SAMUEL LANGHORNE (b. 30 November 1835; d. 21 April 1910), better known by the pseudonym Mark Twain, was a humorist whose novels, short stories, sketches, and lectures made him one of the best-known literary personalities in America at the time of his death. Less well known was his extensive apprenticeship as a journeyman printer, newspaper reporter, and travel correspondent, which had a profound effect upon his literary career.

Clemens was born in Florida, Missouri, where his parents and their three children had moved a few months earlier. His father, John Marshall Clemens, was educated as a lawyer, but had attempted to establish himself as a merchant in both Tennessee and Missouri. In Hannibal, where the family moved when Samuel was four years old, he abandoned business and his vision of quick wealth to resume the practice of law and was later elected as justice of the peace. He died in 1847 when Samuel was twelve years old.

Samuel's mother, Jane Lampton Clemens, was a member of a family that had an earldom in one of its English branches, including certain American claimants. Young Samuel grew up under circumstances that were to stimulate his imagination and furnish him with a wealth of literary material. His boyhood experience in Hannibal became a part of books such as *Tom Sawyer* (1876) and *Huckleberry Finn* (1884). His speculation about noble ancestors led to another book, *The American Claimant* (1891), and was reflected in two fictional characters in *Huckleberry Finn*, the duke and dauphin. His Missouri experiences are also reflected in *Life on the Mississippi* (1883).

Upon his father's death, Samuel left school to be apprenticed to a printer and was soon working at his brother Orin's newspaper, the *Hannibal Journal*. He worked also as a journeyman printer in St. Louis, Philadelphia, and New York during those years. In 1856 he planned to seek his fortune in South America but gave up that plan to become a steamboat pilot on the Mississippi between St. Louis and New Orleans until the coming of the Civil War in 1861. After a brief tour of duty with the Confederate volunteers, Clemens mustered himself out of service and went West with his brother Orin, who had been appointed secretary to the governor of Nevada. After joining the news staff of the *Virginia City Territorial Enterprise* in 1862, he adopted the pseudonym Mark Twain (a river term meaning two fathoms deep) to begin his career as a humorist in the frontier tradition. His articles during this period are collected in *Mark Twain of the "Enterprise"* (1957).

After two years in Virginia City, Clemens moved to San Francisco where he worked for the *Morning Call* and contributed articles to two other newspapers, the *Golden Era* and the *California*. During this period he met Artemus Ward (*see* Browne, Charles Farrar), Bret Harte (q.v.), and others who encouraged him in his writing. While hiding out in a mining cabin to avoid the ire of the San Francisco police, whom he had criticized in a newspaper article, Clemens wrote "The Celebrated Jumping Frog" sketch, which was to bring him national recognition as a writer and humorist. Clemens's next journalistic venture was an assignment to write a series of letters from the Sandwich Islands for the *Sacramento Union*. Upon his return to San Francisco, he lectured about the islands and later wrote about his adventures in *Roughing It* (1872). He returned to the East in December 1866 to join the *Quaker City* Holy Land excursion, reporting about the trip to the *New York Tribune* and the *Alta California*. The series of reports were published in revised form in *Innocents Abroad* in 1869 and became a widely acclaimed travel book.

During the *Quaker City* voyage, Clemens became acquainted with a young man, Charles J. Langdon of Elmira, New York, who showed him a miniature reproduction of the face of his sister, Olivia. Clemens and Livy, as he called her, were married 2 February 1870 at her father's house in Elmira. Soon afterward he became editor and co-owner of the *Buffalo Express* in New York. In little more than a year (1869–71), however, Clemens sold his interest in the Buffalo newspaper to pursue his writing, and in 1874 built a home in Hartford, Connecticut, where the family lived for seventeen years. The couple had four children: a son, Langdon, who died in infancy, and three daughters, Susy, Clara, and Jean. Both Susy and Jean preceded their father in death. Livy, whose genteel, conservative upbringing was in marked contrast to the bohemian life-style of her husband's early years, died in 1904, six years prior to the death of her spouse.

During the Hartford years, Clemens wrote most of his books upon which his literary fame rests: *Tom Sawyer, Huckleberry Finn, Life on the Mississippi*, and others. His comic energy remained at its height during the period, and his excesses were tempered by both his wife Livy and his literary associate, William Dean Howells (q.v.), then editor of the *Atlantic Monthly*. He also engaged in a book-publishing venture and invested in a typesetting machine which brought him to near bankruptcy and caused the closing of his home. For four years the Clemenses, accompanied by their daughter, Clara, lived in London and Vienna, where expenses were less and where he wrote and lectured to pay his debts. He returned to America in 1900 something of a conquering hero and celebrity.

During the last decade of his life, Clemens was repeatedly honored and was frequently called upon to deliver lectures on special occasions while working steadily at dictating his autobiography. A degree of doctor of literature was conferred upon him by Oxford University in 1907. His death from heart disease (angina pectoris) at Stormfield, his home near Redding, Connecticut, in 1910 brought an outpouring of universal regret for the loss of America's chief man of letters.

BIBLIOGRAPHY:

B. DAB 2, 192–198; NYT 22 April 1910; Van Wyck Brooks, *The Ordeal of Mark Twain* (New York, 1920); William Dean Howells, *My Mark Twain* (New York, 1910); Justin Kaplan, *Mr. Clemens and Mark Twain* (New York, 1966); Albert Bigelow Paine, *Mark Twain: A Biography*, 3 vols. (New York, 1912).

HARRY W. STONECIPHER

CLOSE, UPTON(b. 27 February 1894; d. 14 November 1960) is considered one of a group of conservative, sometimes radical, radio political commentators which included Father Charles Coughlin, Fulton Lewis, Jr., and Boake Carter (qq.v.). Close got his name from articles he wrote for the *Shanghai Weekly Review*, always concluding his work with the words "Up Close," thereby attempting to locate himself for his readers as he reported the Japanese invasion of 1916–19. The sign-off became his professional name. He may even have been a member of an American espionage team.

Close was born Josef Washington Hall in Kelso, Washington, on an Indian reservation along the Columbia River. Little is known about his mother, but his father was at one time a gold miner. Close was first educated at Washington Missionary College and eventually received a B.A. from George Washington University in 1915. That year he married the first of five wives, and in all had five sons, Marvell, Louis, Spencer, Clarence, and Josef III. His life and work found him traveling extensively throughout the world, and in particular throughout the Orient.

He worked as a newspaper correspondent during exciting times, and covered China, Japan, and Siberia. Some reports say he advised Chinese revolutionaries and served in the regime of Chinese General Wu Pei-fu. Afterwards, he was a lecturer at the University of Washington, where he remained five years. A prolific author whose experiences provided much material for his many books, Close wrote extensively about China. For about twenty years after 1925, Close produced several books and articles, among them *In the Land of the Laughing Buddha* (1924).

Called by the *Chicago Tribune* the ''Marco Polo'' of news commentators, Close continued to lecture for a living after returning from the Far East, moving with ease into the new medium of radio. His first broadcasts began in 1924 when he collaborated on one with Lowell Thomas (q.v.), then unknown. Working off and on for NBC, Close became famous for commentaries and news broadcasts made over that network on Sunday afternoons, speaking vigorously about his personal knowledge of the Far East and the significance of that area for the United States. ''Hello, Americans'' was Close's greeting to listeners.

''Close-Ups of the News'' became a regular Sunday afternoon program on NBC during World War II. Close traveled extensively and broadcast from wherever he found himself, a special event in those days of cranky land-line network connections. The war period, in fact, was one of great popularity for Close, and he apparently felt confident to go beyond the analysis of Far Eastern politics and culture for which he had become famous. His commentary now included attacks on President Roosevelt, Britain, Russia, some eastern U.S. groups, and others he regarded as less than fully patriotic.

Amid increasing controversy, Close was relieved of his work at NBC in 1944. With a small but loyal audience, Close moved to the Mutual Broadcasting System in 1945, only to retire in 1946. He left the United States to live in Mexico shortly thereafter. A series of broadcasts from Palm Beach, Florida, in 1953 lambasted fellow commentators Drew Pearson (q.v.) and H. V. Kaltenborn (q.v.) and praised Boake Carter and Gabriel Heatter (q.v.), among others. He died in 1960 in Guadalajara, Mexico, killed by a train as his car traveled over the tracks.

BIBLIOGRAPHY:
B. NYT 15 November 1960; Irving E. Fang, *Those Radio Commentators!* (Ames, Iowa, 1977).

JONATHAN L. YODER

COBB, FRANK IRVING (b. 6 August 1869; d. 21 December 1923) was editor of the *New York World*; a friend, supporter, and aide of President Woodrow Wilson; and a leader of American liberalism.

Although Frank Cobb was born in Shawnee County, Kansas, where his father was a railway contractor, his roots were in Michigan, where he spent fourteen years as a newspaperman before joining the *World*. His father, Minor H. Cobb, and his mother, Matilda Clark Cobb, were brought up on neighboring farms near Grand Rapids. Cobb attended Michigan State Normal College at Ypsilanti from 1887 to 1890. He had hoped to enter law school, but instead in 1891 took a $6-a-week job on the *Grand Rapids Telegram-Herald*. Later he became city editor of the *Grand Rapids Eagle*, and, when it folded, worked briefly on the *Grand Rapids Democrat*. In 1894 he moved to the *Detroit Evening News*. He became its political writer, covering the career of the colorful populist mayor-governor Hazen S. Pingree. His writing, flavored with humor and irony, and his analytical talents shortly led him to become editorial writer for the *News*. On 16 June 1897, in Grand Rapids, Cobb married Delia S. Bailey, an 1894 graduate of the University of Michigan. The marriage, however, later ended in divorce.

In 1900 Cobb moved from the *News* to the rival *Detroit Free Press*, as chief editorial writer. The *Free Press* long had been sympathetic to the Democratic party, and Cobb found its liberal outlook more to his taste. He remained with it, growing in stature and local reputation, until 1904, when he took a probationary $100-a-week job as editorial writer on Joseph Pulitzer's (q.v.) famed *New York World*. Cobb's friendship with Pulitzer—personally warm despite political differences—later soured over the *World*'s exposures of the Panama Canal takeover.

In New York Cobb had a number of problems. Pulitzer, a very demanding master, felt Cobb was too prolix, even giving him a little silver scale to "weigh his words." Cobb therefore had to refine and condense his articles, and the period 1904–11 probably saw his best work. Further, he had, somehow, to make himself indispensable to the perverse and austere editor. He did this by gossipy little private notes, full of humor, and by insisting, doggedly, on what he felt was right for the *World* and the nation. Some conflicts inevitably resulted. Louis Starr wrote that Pulitzer once referred to his "indegoddampendent" editor. Cobb would be fired—once even being put ashore at midnight from the Pulitzer yacht—or would quit. But always, he returned. He became, within a year or so, the undisputed editorial voice of the paper. His knowledge of history, literature, and political and foreign affairs was extensive, kept current by extensive reading.

The issues for which the *World* and he fought are impressive: against "Jim Crowism," prohibition, states' rights and excessive federal power, trusts and the "money power," and for woman suffrage, the League of Nations, and honest, intelligent, and compassionate public servants. Frequently, issues were treated in terms of personalities, and this led to Cobb's long and friendly relationship with President Woodrow Wilson.

The *World* consistently backed Wilson in his battles against privilege, and was the first to suggest his candidacy for the presidency. A Cobb editorial, "No Compromise," broke a deadlock at the Baltimore convention, and helped give Wilson the 1912 Democratic nomination.

Wilson appreciated such support, and despite differences in their natures, Cobb became one of Wilson's chief private advisers. The two carried on a voluminous correspondence, and the *World* benefited from a number of deliberate leaks of information. On the day before the United States declared war on Germany, Wilson sent for Cobb and, in an extraordinary interview, talked of his alternatives and the future. In late 1918 Wilson sent Cobb—on a short leave from the *World*—to Paris with Colonel E. M. House and Walter Lippmann (q.v.) to "interpret" the Fourteen Points. In 1919 Wilson reportedly offered to make Cobb secretary of state. But Cobb told his wife—he had married newswoman Margaret Hubbard Ayer on 2 October 1913—that such power was temporary, and that he had as much as he wanted on the *World*.

He returned to the paper as its editor under Ralph Pulitzer, but with primary responsibilities for the editorial page. He spoke occasionally, but his writing was confined almost exclusively to the *World*, and he looked forward to weekends on his farm near Westport, Connecticut. He died on 21 December 1923 of cancer, leaving his wife and two children, Jane and Hubbard Cobb. In one of his last formal statements, Wilson termed Cobb's death "an irreparable loss to journalism and to the liberal political policies which are necessary to liberate mankind from the errors of the past" (Heaton, 1924). Mrs. Cobb died 3 February 1965.

BIBLIOGRAPHY:

A. "Learned Newspaper Work 'Under Dire Compulsion,' " in *Reminiscences of Editors and Reporters*, ed. A. S. White (Grand Rapids, 1921).

B. DAB 2, 241; NYT 22 December 1923; John L. Heaton, *Cobb of "The World"* (New York, 1924); Louis M. Starr, "Joseph Pulitzer and His Most 'Indegoddampendent' Editor," *American Heritage*, June 1968.

JAMES STANFORD BRADSHAW

COBB, IRVIN SHREWSBURY (b. 23 June 1876; d. 10 March 1944) was a journalist, humorist, novelist, playwright, and actor noted for his wit and colloquial style. He capitalized on his partly rural, partly southern upbringing to become one of the most popular—and reputedly the highest paid—journalists of his time.

Cobb, the second of four children, was born in Paducah, Kentucky. His father was Joshua Clark Cobb, a veteran of the Confederate army and a worker in the local tobacco and steamboat industries. His mother was Manie Saunders Cobb, the daughter of physician Reuben Saunders, who has been credited with discovering the first successful treatment for cholera in humans. Cobb attended private and public schools in Paducah until he was sixteen. Then, on 16 January 1893, he joined the staff of the *Paducah Daily News* as a reporter and illustrator. He was gifted at both tasks. It is said that the ambidextrous Cobb could simultaneously draw different pictures with each hand. At nineteen, Cobb was named managing editor of the newspaper, an achievement that earned him the nickname "kid editor" among area editors. Beginning in 1897 he supplemented his income as a correspondent for newspapers in Louisville, Memphis, and Chicago.

In October 1898 Cobb joined the staff of the *Cincinnati Post*, but he quit after one month and took a job with the *Louisville Evening Post*. During his three years at the Louisville paper, he wrote his first series of humorous columns, which he called "Kentucky Sour Mash." He married Laura Spencer Baker on 12 June 1900, and they had one daughter, Elisabeth Cobb (later Chapman), who became a novelist, biographer, and playwright.

In May 1901 Cobb became managing editor of the new *Paducah Daily Democrat*, which resulted from a merger of the *Daily News* and the *News Democrat*. In August 1904 Cobb left for New York and through sheer pluck got a job with the *New York Evening Sun*. A year later he gained an international reputation for his humorous sidebar series, "Making Peace at Portsmouth," which poked fun at the Russo-Japanese Peace Conference being held in New Hampshire. Later in 1905, Cobb joined the *New York Evening World* where—at $165 per week—he was said to command the highest salary among journalists of his time. Columns he wrote for the *World* included "New York Through Funny Glasses," "Live Talks with Dead Ones," and "Hotel Clerk."

Cobb began contributing humorous articles to the *Saturday Evening Post* in 1910, and was on the magazine's staff from 1911 to 1922. His *Saturday Evening Post* tenure included a trip overseas as a war correspondent in World War I. From 1922 to 1932 Cobb was a staff writer for *Cosmopolitan* magazine. In all, Cobb wrote more than 60 books and more than 300 short stories that are widely published in anthologies and in collections of his work. He probably is best remembered for his tales of the old Confederate veteran Judge Priest—based on a composite of characters Cobb knew while growing up in Kentucky—which he wrote while working at the *Saturday Evening Post*.

Toward the end of his career, Cobb wrote plays for screen and stage and acted in films. A film based on Cobb's Judge Priest stories starred Cobb's friend and fellow-humorist Will Rogers (q.v.). The two men worked or starred together in several films, probably the most notable of which was *Steamboat Round the Bend* (1935). Cobb played a steamboat captain. Early in 1944 Cobb took ill with dropsy and died weeks later in his New York apartment.

BIBLIOGRAPHY:

A. *Back Home: Being the Narrative of Judge Priest and His People* (New York, 1912); *Old Judge Priest* (New York, 1916); *Stickfuls: Myself to Date* (New York, 1923); *Exit Laughing* (Indianapolis, 1941).

B. DAB Supp. 4, 170–171; NYT 11 March 1944; Elisabeth Cobb, *My Wayward Parent* (Indianapolis, 1945); Fred G. Neuman, *Irvin S. Cobb: His Life and Letters* (Emaus, Pa., 1938).

GORDON BILLINGSLEY

COBBETT, WILLIAM (b. 9 March 1763; d. 18 June 1835) was a passionate, righteous, and gifted English journalist whose vituperative writing style was described soon after his death by the *Times* of London as : ''A mingled storm of torturing sarcasm, contemptuous jocularity, and slaughtering invective.'' An early American opponent once compared him to a porcupine, and the unruly Cobbett gleefully embraced the pen name Peter Porcupine to represent his utter acerbity, recklessness, partisanship, and lust for battle in all media of writing and on virtually all topics, especially politics.

Cobbett was the third of four sons born to George and Ann Vincent Cobbett at Farnham, Surrey, England. His father began as a laborer, educated himself, and became a surveyor and the owner of a modest farm and the Jolly Farmer, an inn. The family belonged to the Church of England.

Cobbett described his youth as carefree but industrious, apolitical but religious, and uncultured but peaceful. The adventuresome young Cobbett impulsively bolted from his prosaic home several times to see the outside world, finally refusing to return from an escapade in London in 1783. He worked for several months as a clerk for an attorney, then joined the army and was shipped, at age twenty-one, to Nova Scotia, then New Brunswick. Quickly appreciating the importance of reading and writing, he was promoted within a year to sergeant-major of an infantry regiment. He became engaged in St. John to Ann Reid, then thirteen and the uneducated daughter of an artillery sergeant. Six months later she moved with her family back to England and worked as a servant. He returned to England in November 1791, obtained an honorable discharge a month later, and married her on 5 February 1792 at Woolwich.

Cobbett brought serious charges of corruption against army officers, and was threatened with revenge. In March 1792, Cobbett and his wife fled to Tilques, France, where he learned the language. Shortly before war broke out between England and France in August 1793, the Cobbetts sailed to America for a seven-and-a-half-year sojourn. They settled in Philadelphia. He offered tutoring in English to French immigrants and wrote an English grammar book that became quite popular.

Cobbett's first political tract in the United States was a response to publications based on remarks by Dr. Joseph Priestley, an English scientist who attacked England upon landing in the United States in 1794. Cobbett wrote a reply in the excessively indignant manner that was to become his trademark. By 1796 he had published dozens of translations, pamphlets, and minor writings and had started two journals. Although the pugnacious and shrewd essayist refused sponsorship from any party, he usually was perceived as a friend of the Federalists and foe of Republicans.

He opened a bookstore in 1796 and published the *Political Censor*, the proceedings of Congress with commentary (1796–97). In March 1797 Cobbett established his own daily newspaper, *Porcupine's Gazette and Daily Advertiser*. He narrowly escaped prosecution for libeling the king of Spain, but in 1799 he lost a $5,000 verdict for criticizing the treatment of copious bleeding by Dr. Benjamin Rush. Nearly bankrupt, he closed the *Gazette* and moved to New York, where he started in 1800 a fortnightly for five numbers that continued the attack on Rush. He refused to become a naturalized citizen, and he barely eluded a deportation order in 1799. Friends convinced him, his wife, and two children to return to England, but he criticized the United States in a parting open letter.

Cobbett sometimes wrote fondly of the United States later, and he returned in 1817–18 when he was threatened with legal action in England. His career in England, however, certainly exceeded that in the United States. He operated thirteen periodicals in his life, the most important probably being *Cobbett's Political Register* (1802–35). He published twelve volumes of *Porcupine's Works* (1801) and about a hundred pamphlets and other works.

When he first returned to England, he continued to defend the Tory administration but refused its offer of financial support and gradually became disenchanted, especially with movements toward peace with France. In 1806 he joined the Radical party and was imprisoned for two years for seditious libel. He crusaded for electoral and parliamentary reform and against systems of pensions, sinecures, and tithes.

His popularity became immense among the English working class, and he was elected to Parliament in 1832 and 1835 even though he could affect no legislation. His fierce independence on literally hundreds of issues hurt him financially as well, but his family was never poor. His sense of outrage served him well in successfully conducting his own defense in 1831 in the Court of the King's Bench for allegedly encouraging disorders in an article; this was the government's last overt attempt to coerce the press by legal action.

Cobbett died on 18 June 1835 at his home at Normandy Farms, still politically active and endearingly cranky, as his son described him. He was buried in a churchyard at Farnham. He was survived by his wife; three daughters, Anne (1795–1877), Eleanor (1805–1900), and Susan (1807–89); and four sons, William Jr. (1798–1878), James Morgan (1800–1877), James Paul (1803–81), and Richard Beaverbrook Brown (1814–75).

BIBLIOGRAPHY:

A. *Life and Adventures of Peter Porcupine* (London, 1927); *The Autobiography of William Cobbett, the Progress of a Plough-Boy to a Seat in Parliament*, ed. William Reiztel (London, 1947).

B. Karen K. List, "The Role of William Cobbett in Philadelphia's Party Press, 1794–1799," *Journalism Monographs* no. 82, May 1983; John W. Osborne, *William Cobbett: His Thought and His Times* (New Brunswick, N.J., 1966); James Sambrook, *William Cobbett* (London, 1973).

THOMAS A. SCHWARTZ

COCHRANE, ELIZABETH (b. 5 May 1865 or 1867; d. 27 January 1922) achieved national prominence as a stunt journalist for the *New York World* during the period 1887–95, and as such brought attention to women reporters in America. Her most famous exploits as a reporter involved feigning insanity so that she could gain entrance to a local insane asylum, and traveling around the world in an attempt to break the fictional record of Jules Verne's Phileas Fogg. She also wrote investigative pieces about the social ills that plagued the cities in which she worked and traveled.

During the late 1890s she published three books about her adventures as a reporter. At the peak of her career, Cochrane left journalism to marry a wealthy New York businessman, but she returned to journalism after her husband died. She regained some of her notoriety when in 1920, as a reporter for the *New York Evening Journal*, she sensationalized the Gordon Hamby execution at New York's Sing Sing prison.

Cochrane, the third of ten children, was born near Pittsburgh in Cochran's Mills, Pennsylvania. Early in her career she added the *e* to her last name. Her birthdate is cited by various sources as either 1865 or 1867, and the truth is further confounded by some of the same sources that say she was fifty-six years old when she died in 1922. Her father, Judge Michael Cochran, was a lawyer and a mill owner who founded Cochran's Mills. Her mother, Judge Cochran's second wife, was Mary Jane Kennedy. Except for a brief stint at a boarding school in Indiana, Pennsylvania, from 1880 to 1881, Cochrane was educated at home.

Her family moved to Pittsburgh after her father died, and in November 1885 Cochrane began her journalism career as a reporter for the *Pittsburgh Dispatch*. At the suggestion of her editor, George Madden, she adopted Nellie Bly as her pen name. The name came from the well-known Stephen Foster song. As an investigative reporter, she wrote stories that exposed poor working conditions in local factories and poor living conditions in local slums. Later, as society editor for the *Dispatch*, she wrote about the arts, the theater, and Pittsburgh's social life.

Madden sent her to Mexico for six months in 1886–87 to write about life in Mexico, and she published letters in the *Dispatch* that described the social ills in that country. Soon after she left Mexico, she moved to New York City and managed to obtain a position as a reporter on Joseph Pulitzer's (q.v.) *New York World*. It was her stunt journalism for this paper that gained her a national reputation. Her first assignment culminated in one of her most famous series about social ills in New York City. She feigned insanity in order to investigate the way the insane were treated at the Blackwells Island asylum. Her reports sparked an official investigation, which resulted in improvements at the institution.

The success with which her series was received by the public catapulted Nellie Bly into the role of a reformer, which melded nicely with Pulitzer's crusading approach to journalism. After her sensational start at the *World*, she continued to do stunt journalism and to write reform-oriented pieces about such topics as employee exploitation, prisoner treatment, and political corruption. Her most famous stunt was her seventy-two-day trip around the world, which lasted from 14 November 1889 to 25 January 1890. During her trip, she sent dispatches that described her adventure to the *World*'s readers. After she returned from the adventure, she wrote investigative stories for the *World* until she married seventy-two-year-old Robert L. Seaman on 5 April 1895. Seaman was owner and president of the American Steel Barrel Company and the Ironclad Manufacturing Company. His wealth led Cochrane to exchange her journalism career for New York's social circles. While the marriage produced no children, it is a matter of record that it bore at least one public encounter involving jealousy between the two principals.

When her husband died on 12 March 1904, she tried unsuccessfully to run his manufacturing businesses. After more than a decade of bankruptcies and litigation, she left her business interests in the hands of her brother and traveled to Austria, where she stayed until the end of World War I. Upon her return to the United States in 1919, she was hired as a reporter for the *New York Evening Journal* by her friend and former colleague at the *World*, Arthur Brisbane (q.v.), who was the *Journal*'s editor. She worked for the *Journal* until she died of bronchopneumonia on 27 January 1922.

BIBLIOGRAPHY:

A. *Ten Days in a Madhouse* (New York, 1887); *Nellie Bly's Book: Around the World in Seventy-Two Days* (New York, 1890).

B. DAB 3, 253–255; NYT 28 January 1922; *New York World*, 28 January 1922; Iris Noble, *Nellie Bly: First Woman Reporter* (New York, 1956); Mignon Rittenhouse, *The Amazing Nellie Bly* (New York, 1956).

BRUCE L. PLOPPER

COCKERILL, JOHN ALBERT (b. 5 December 1845; d. 10 April 1896) was one of the leading practitioners of the combination of democratic spirit and sensationalism known as "the New Journalism" in the latter decades of the nineteenth century. Although Joseph Pulitzer (q.v.), publisher of two of the papers Cockerill edited, generally is credited with developing and popularizing the movement, an 1886 publication refers to Cockerill as the "father of the new journalism." He gained his greatest fame as managing editor of Pulitzer's *St. Louis Post-Dispatch* and *New York World*, and as a foreign correspondent for the *New York Herald*.

Cockerill, third of five children, was born in Adams County, Ohio. His father, Joseph Randolph Cockerill, was a schoolteacher, surveyor, clerk of court, lawyer, state representative, and congressman. During the Civil War, he was a colonel in the Union army. Cockerill's mother, Ruth Eylar, was the daughter of an Adams County judge. Young Cockerill received a public school education in West Union, Ohio. He began working for the *Scion*, a weekly newspaper in West Union, when he was fourteen. He inked the press, delivered papers, and was allowed to write some minor items. He enlisted as a drummer boy in the Union army at the outbreak of the Civil War, and carried a musket at the Battle of Shiloh.

In December 1862 Cockerill became editor and part owner of another West Union weekly, the *Democratic Union*. Two years later he sold his interest in the paper and went to work for another weekly, the *True Telegraph*, in nearby Hamilton. He and a brother bought the paper in October 1865, and Cockerill bought out his brother's interest within two years.

While Cockerill was in Hamilton, his writing attracted the attention of J. B. McCullagh (q.v.), editor of the *Cincinnati Enquirer*, and the young publisher took on the additional job of Hamilton correspondent for the *Enquirer*. For four months in 1868 he was editor and part owner of the *Dayton Daily Ledger* in partnership with C. L. Vallandigham, who had been a noted Copperhead editor during the Civil War. By early 1869, Cockerill was in Cincinnati working as a reporter for the *Enquirer* under McCullagh, who would one day be a competitor in St. Louis.

Cockerill was made city editor of the *Enquirer* shortly after he arrived, and before the end of 1870 he was managing editor. Cockerill ended his tenure on the *Enquirer* with a six-month stint as a correspondent covering the Russo-Turkish War in 1877.

Instead of returning to Cincinnati, Cockerill became editor and part owner with Stilson Hutchins of the new *Washington Post*. Then slightly more than a year later, Cockerill disposed of his interest in the *Post* and became editor of the *Baltimore Gazette*. While he was in Baltimore, he was asked by Pulitzer to go to St. Louis as managing editor of the *Post-Dispatch*, only a year old but already the leading evening paper in that city.

Cockerill arrived in St. Louis in 1880 to form a newsroom team with Pulitzer that would introduce an exciting brand of journalism, first to St. Louis and later to New York. Public opinion turned against both men and their newspaper in October 1882 after Cockerill shot and killed Alonzo W. Slayback, an attorney who came to Cockerill's office to attack the editor over an insult in the paper. Cockerill resigned his position early in 1883, and by May of that year Pulitzer had bought the *New York World* and installed Cockerill as his managing editor once more.

Cockerill had considerable responsibility for the day-to-day operation of the *World* (and more than just the news side) during the paper's phenomenal rise in popularity until he resigned in 1891. During this period he also served as president of the New York Press Club for five terms from 1888 to 1892.

From May 1891 to October 1894, he was editor and part owner of the *New York Commercial Advertiser*. By February 1895 Cockerill was a foreign correspondent for the *New York Herald*. He was awarded one of Japan's most important citations, the Third Order of the Sacred Treasure, for his reporting of Japanese news to America. Only two non-Japanese, and no journalists, previously had won the award. He later scored a beat by reporting the murder of Korea's Queen Min in October 1895, even though his first dispatch was held up in Tokyo. He died of a stroke in Cairo on his way home from his Far East assignment. Cockerill married Leonora Barner, an actress, in 1884. They had no children.

BIBLIOGRAPHY:

B. DAB 4, 256; NYT 11 April 1896; Donald F. Brod, "John A. Cockerill's St. Louis Years: A Study of the Campaign that Brought Them to an End," *Bulletin of the Missouri Historical Society*, April 1970; Homer W. King, *Pulitzer's Prize Editor: A Biography of John A. Cockerill, 1845–1896* (Durham, N.C., 1965).

DONALD F. BROD

COFFIN, CHARLES CARLETON (b. 26 July 1823; d. 2 March 1896), Civil War "special" for the *Boston Journal*, was one of the few reporters—some sources say the only reporter—to cover all four years of the war. Through his 400 letters to the *Journal*, signed "Carleton," and his extensive writings and lectures after the war, he brought the fighting home to New England readers. He used a concise, detailed, modern newswriting style. As a reporter he was on good terms with officers and privates alike and was noted for his courage, energy, competitiveness, and ability to sense where the action would be next and to get there on time.

Like many members of the "Bohemian Brigade," as Civil War correspondents were called, Coffin flitted between jobs before being caught up in newspaper work. He was born in Boscawen, New Hampshire, the son of a farm couple. He attended village schools, then taught school briefly, worked in a lumber camp, clerked, surveyed, and strung telegraph wire. On 18 February 1846 he married Sally Russell Farmer. The couple, who were married fifty years, had no children.

Coffin went to Boston in 1853 and taught himself to be a reporter by working three months without pay at the *Journal*. For the next several years he worked for various Boston papers. Unlike New York editors, those in New England did not immediately make plans for covering the Civil War. Coffin's first letters from Washington about war preparation were on a free-lance basis. After his coverage of the Battle of Bull Run, the *Journal* hired Coffin as a regular correspondent for $25 a week, plus extra for transportation. He was thirty-seven.

A tall (six feet), lean, hardworking man, Coffin was seen at most of the major battles of the war, with a spyglass around his shoulder and his pockets stuffed with notebooks. His concern for accuracy was such he once rode twenty-five miles to check a fact. He was one of the few reporters to include diagrams. He used his surveying background to discuss topography and his musical background to determine the difference in ammunition from the note of the projectile whistling by. His account of the Union recapture of Charleston was the first news President Lincoln had of the battle and beat the New York papers by several hours. His description of Lincoln's visit to Richmond after it fell was so vivid that Thomas Nast (q.v.) made a famed drawing from it. Coffin was at Appomattox Courthouse for the surrender and ended that account with the thought that "the flag which traitors had trailed in the dust at the beginning of the conflict was more than ever the emblem of the world's best hopes."

After the war, Coffin returned to Boston and traveled the world for the *Journal*. He reworked his dispatches into a number of books, writing also on the revolutionary war and other topics, and delivered hundreds of lectures. He was at work and planning a speech on the recollections of a war correspondent the day he died, of apoplexy, at the age of seventy-three.

BIBLIOGRAPHY:

A. *My Days and Nights on the Battlefield* (Boston, 1864); *Following the Flag* (Boston, 1865); *Four Years of Fighting* (Boston, 1866); *The Boys of '61* (Boston, 1881); *Marching to Victory* (New York, 1888).

B. NYT 3 March 1896; J. Cutler Andrews, *The North Reports the Civil War* (Pittsburgh, 1955); Emmet Crozier, *Yankee Reporters* (New York, 1956); William Elliot Griffis, *Charles Carleton Coffin* (Boston, 1898); Louis M. Starr, *Bohemian Brigade* (New York, 1954).

JUDITH A. SERRIN

COLEMAN, WILLIAM (b. 14 February 1766; d. 14 July 1829) was a leading Federalist journalist employed by Alexander Hamilton to manage and edit the *New York Evening Post*, the leading exponent of Federalist views in print.

Coleman was born in Boston to a family in dire poverty. He was able to study at Andover Academy thanks to the benevolence of persons of wealth who were impressed with his scholarship. He served in the militia and fought against Shay's Rebellion. Later he studied law in Worcester under the tutelage of Robert Treat Paine, the attorney general of Massachusetts. In 1788 Coleman set up his own law practice in Greenfield, Massachusetts. He founded and wrote for the *Impartial Intelligencer* while continuing to practice law. He was elected to the Massachusetts General Court and served in the legislature in 1795 and 1796. He was awarded an honorary doctorate by Dartmouth College in 1796. While in Greenfield he invested heavily in the Yazoo Purchase land scheme, and lost all of his investment. Facing public disgrace, he left Greenfield and moved to New York City late in 1797.

In 1798 Coleman was admitted to the New York bar and briefly entered a partnership with Aaron Burr. Upon finding that work in Burr's law office would not support two full-time attorneys, Coleman left and entered into partnership with John Wells, an accomplished attorney and outspoken Federalist. Coleman had met Alexander Hamilton in 1796, but through social contacts made possible by Wells, Coleman renewed his acquaintance with Hamilton. They became close friends. In 1800 Hamilton secured the position of clerk of the New York Circuit Court for Coleman. However, when the Democrats swept into office in 1801, Coleman lost his job. In the summer of 1801 Hamilton, Coleman, and other Federalists held a series of meetings to plan the establishment of a party newspaper, which first appeared on 16 November 1801 as the *New York Evening Post*. In the first issue, editor Coleman said the paper would support Federalism, but not dogmatically.

The *Evening Post* was a daily, but on Saturdays a weekly edition—known as the *Herald*—was sent to out-of-town subscribers. The *Post* published vigorously worded pieces of prose elucidating and arguing for the Federalist position on every major political question which arose in the young country during the early part of the nineteenth century. Frequently Coleman would go to Hamilton's house late in the evening and have editorials for the next edition dictated to him by the old master of the Federalist cause.

Historian Allan Nevins has noted that Coleman had three faults as editor of the *Evening Post*: a diffuse style, a vituperative pen, and a poor business acumen. Coleman was physically beaten and verbally abused several times while editor of the *Post*. Many lawsuits were filed against the *Post* during Coleman's tenure as editor, but none were successful.

In June 1826 Coleman was thrown from his carriage when his horse was startled. He was unable to use his legs again, and later that year he began to lose strength slowly in the rest of his body. He died at his home on 14 July 1829 at age sixth-three. William Cullen Bryant (q.v.) succeeded Coleman as editor in chief of the *Evening Post*.

BIBLIOGRAPHY:

B. DAB 4, 294–295; Allan Nevins, *The "Evening Post": A Century of Journalism* (New York, 1922).

DONALD L. MCBRIDE

COLLINGWOOD, CHARLES CUMMINGS (b. 4 June 1917; d. 3 October 1985) a Rhodes scholar, was recruited by Edward R. Murrow (q.v.) to serve as a network correspondent for CBS radio. Collingwood covered the North African campaign and the D day invasion for CBS during World War II. Returning to the United States he was the first network correspondent assigned to the United Nations. Making the transition to television, he was newsman for "The CBS Morning Show," moderated the first "CBS Town Meeting of the Air," and succeeded Edward R. Murrow on the popular "Person to Person" program. He also hosted a documentary series on American involvement in Southeast Asia and was the first network newsman admitted into North Vietnam.

Collingwood was born in Three Rivers, Michigan, the eldest son of George Harris Collingwood and Jean Grinnell Cummings. He had two brothers and three sisters. His father, a forestry professor, moved the family from Michigan to Ithaca, New York, when Charles was a child, in order to join the faculty of Cornell University. The senior Collingwood's subsequent appointments led to Bethesda, Maryland, and Washington, D.C., when he became an official in the U.S. Forest Service.

Collingwood graduated from Central High School in Washington, D.C., in 1934, having served as president of his student council. He also was a member of the National Honor Society and received a scholarship to an unorthodox institution near Death Valley, California. He spent three years at the small school, which required students to perform ranch and farm chores. He continued his education at Cornell University and graduated in 1939 with a B.A. degree.

He was awarded a Rhodes scholarship upon graduation from Cornell, and began studies at Oxford, with the intention of pursuing a career in international law. While studying at New College, he also worked part-time for the United Press and, during holiday and vacation periods, frequently traveled on assignment throughout Europe. He withdrew from scholarly pursuits in 1940 and began working full-time for United Press. The next year he joined a group of young journalists including Howard K. Smith, Eric Severeid, and William L. Shirer (qq.v.), also recruited for CBS broadcast correspondents' positions by Edward R. Murrow.

Collingwood was sent to North Africa and reported from Radio Algiers on assassination and political intrigue. He held the rank of captain as war correspondent with the British army and earned a reputation for being able to beat his print counterparts in reporting important stories. He won a Peabody Award for best foreign reporting in 1943 and was sent back to the United States. He continued to function as a radio commentator for CBS. In May 1946 he was married to actress Louise Allbritton and that same year was assigned to the post of United Nations correspondent. He also covered the White House and joined the CBS television division in time to host an analysis of the 1952 presidential campaign entitled "Whistle-Stop, U.S.A."

Collingwood served briefly as president of the American Federation of Television and Radio Artists (AFTRA), New York chapter. He took a two-year leave of absence from the television network to aid the Mutual Security Agency under Averell Harriman. Upon his return to CBS, he was made a network bureau chief in London, and two years later he was asked to succeed his mentor, Edward R. Murrow, as host of the popular "Person to Person" series. During this period he also served as a newsman for "The CBS Morning Show," and hosted "Adventure," an educational program for children. His tenure on "Person to Person" lasted until 1961, and subsequent assignments included public affairs series such as "Eyewitness," "Portrait," and a television tour of the White House with Jacqueline Kennedy. The latter won for him a second Peabody Award in 1963. He was also responsible for hosting a CBS memorial tribute to Edward R. Murrow.

Collingwood began reporting on American involvement in Southeast Asia in 1964 as chief network foreign correspondent. He presented a major analysis, "Vietnam: The Deadly Decision," early that year and began an annual assessment of the conflict which lasted for four years. In 1968 he became one of the first U.S. newsman admitted to North Vietnam and broadcast two special programs from Hanoi.

Throughout the 1970s Collingwood continued to host CBS specials such as reports on the Middle East conflict and year-end broadcasts presenting the news in review. He announced his retirement just after his sixtieth birthday in 1977. The announcement was integrated into the concluding segment of a program devoted to the problems associated with retirement.

Collingwood died at Lenox Hill Hospital in Manhattan. Although he was retired from CBS, he had served as a special correspondent until his death. He was survived by his second wife, Swedish concert singer, Tatiana Angelini Jolin.

BIBLIOGRAPHY:

B. NYT 4 October 1985 CB 1943, 136–138; Les Brown, *The New York Times Encyclopedia of Television* (New York, 1977), 89–90; Gary Paul Gates, *Air Time: The Inside Story of CBS News* (New York, 1978); Alexander Kendrick, *Prime Time: The Life of Edward R. Murrow* (Boston, 1970); "Mission to Hanoi," *Time*, April 1968.

MICHAEL D. MURRAY

CONSIDINE, ROBERT BERNARD (b. 4 November 1906; d. 25 September 1975), had it not been for the misspelling of his name by a sportswriter, might never have become a journalist. Considine was born to James William Considine and Sophia Small Considine in Washington, D.C. He attended grammar school and Gonzaga High School in Washington, and studied journalism and creative writing in night school for four years at George Washington University. In 1923, at seventeen, Considine joined the Census Bureau as a messenger and subsequently continued government service in the Bureau of Public Health, as a typist in the Treasury Department, and as a clerk in the Department of State.

Considine's entry into newspaper work came about because of two related events. After winning a match in a Washington tennis tournament, he was irritated to find his name misspelled in accounts by the *Washington Herald*. He presented himself to the *Herald*'s sports editor, William Henry Coyle, who told him bluntly that if he wanted any tennis news in the paper, he would have to write it himself. Shortly after that, a friend asked Considine to write a review of the previous tennis season, for which he would be paid two dollars. Considine consented, and thus his journalistic career was born. Subsequently, Coyle asked Considine to write a report of a tournament Considine won, using a pen name. For this, "Bill Henry," as Considine called himself, earned ten dollars. His next foray into sportswriting was in the form of a column, "Speaking of Tennis," for the *Washington Post*, which led to his being hired in the sports department of the

Post in 1930. In July 1931, fresh with the insecurity of his new job, Considine married Mildred Anderson.

In 1931 Considine was promoted from high school sports to college sports, and in 1933 he became the *Post*'s baseball writer. Considine's work covering spring baseball in 1933 brought him to the attention of Mike Flynn, managing editor of the *Washington Herald*. Just prior to the opening of the 1933 baseball season, Considine joined the *Herald* and was named sports editor. He wrote a daily column, "On the Line with Considine," that was carried in more than 100 newspapers.

In 1936 Considine left the *Herald* to join the *New York American*, and subsequently was transferred to the *New York Daily Mirror*, another Hearst newspaper. As part of his contractual arrangement, the International News Service (INS) was responsible for half of his salary. Considine continued to write his daily sports column, but he handled other general assignments. By 1942 Considine was exclusively an INS writer, and it was as a war correspondent for INS that he covered the news of the China-Burma-India theater. Moreover, Considine's skills as an author emerged with the publication of *MacArthur the Magnificent* (1942) and *Thirty Seconds Over Tokyo* (1943).

Considine gained fame for his stories of Dwight Eisenhower's visit to Korea in 1952. He won the Overseas Press Club award in 1957 for stories based on interviews with Soviet leader Nikita Khrushchev, and in 1959 for his reporting on the death of Pope Pius XII. Considine also received the George R. Holmes Memorial Award (1947) for coverage of the hydrogen bomb test, the Catholic Writers Guild Award (1949), the Catholic Institute of the Press Award (1949), the Sigma Delta Chi Distinguished Service in Journalism Award (1949), and the Albert and Mary Lasker Foundation Award (1952).

Considine was the author, coauthor, or editor of twenty-five books, including his 1967 autobiography, *It's All News to Me*. He also was the author of five screenplays.

BIBLIOGRAPHY:

B. NYT 27 September 1975; Donald Paneth, *The Encyclopedia of American Journalism* (New York, 1983).

JOHN A. LEDINGHAM

COOPER, KENT (b. 22 March 1880; d. 31 January 1965) was an eager and creative reformer of the Associated Press news report. As AP's chief administrative officer for twenty-three years, he transformed that wire service into a competitive, diversified, international news brokerage, and, at times, in the process had to buck conservative elements in AP's membership. Also a crusader during World War II for unimpeded and uncensored flow of news in the postwar world, Cooper is credited with introducing the phrase "the right to know," a reference to journalists' and the public's right of access to governmental information.

The youngest child and only boy among four siblings, Cooper was born in Columbus, Indiana, the son of George William Cooper and Sina Green Cooper. His father, a lawyer and Democratic politician, was mayor and city attorney of Columbus before being elected to three terms as congressman between 1889 and 1895. Cooper was educated in Columbus public schools. He delivered newspapers at the age of eleven and, during high school, set type and reported for Columbus newspapers. In 1899, after attending Indiana University one year, Cooper was forced by the death of his father to leave school and take a job on the *Indianapolis Press*.

Within two years Cooper was a police reporter on the *Indianapolis Sun*, where he was introduced to the Scripps-McRae Press Association, a regional forerunner of United Press International. He joined Scripps-McRae in 1901, working first as a stringer and then as manager of the Indianapolis bureau. With this move Cooper began a half-century career of active wire service administration. The first of Cooper's many innovations was the creation in 1906 of a ''pony'' news service, by which an abbreviated news report was telephoned to small newspapers. The next year Scripps-McRae and two other regional news services merged to form United Press (UP), and Cooper was made a traveling salesman of UP news and the chief organizer of state pony service in the Midwest.

Feeling forgotten among UP's legions of aggressive and aspiring young men, Cooper on 5 December 1910 jumped to the rival Associated Press (AP), then a stodgy and antiquated organization. Although eager to modernize and expand AP, the thirty-year-old Cooper found himself constrained by the reluctance of AP's aging general manager, Melville E. Stone (q.v.), to abandon long-standing practices. Cooper had to wait fifteen years for his chance to improve the wire service.

Still dull and stagnant on 20 April 1925 when Cooper was appointed general manager, AP was being challenged by Scripps-Howard's UP and the Hearst corporation's International News Service (INS). In his first year at AP's helm Cooper introduced staff bylines, news features, livelier writing, and human-interest copy to the wire's report. He soon added a feature service, and in 1928 started a mailed news photo service that evolved into AP's pioneering Wirephoto service inaugurated on 1 January 1935. The ''disquieting truth'' about Cooper's revolution at AP, said Silas Bent, writing in *The Independent* in 1927, ''is that the AP has succumbed to what I may call United Pressure. It has bobbed its hair and got out its lipstick in order to keep up with a flapper.''

On other fronts, however, Cooper's campaign to reform AP had to move more cautiously. The general manager served at the pleasure of AP's board of directors and was restricted by the cooperative membership structure at AP and by the bylaws which granted disproportionate power to AP's members. Big-city, well-to-do, long-standing members held greater voting strength and had powers via the ''protest right'' to exclude competing local newspapers from AP membership. Such protests, in fact, had been a factor in AP's sagging growth. Between the end of World War I in 1918, and 1925, when Cooper became general manager,

AP had grown by only seventy-five members while UP had added 300 clients and INS had gained 150 clients.

Only gradually and quietly was Cooper able to coax AP members to reduce or relinquish their protest rights so AP could stay abreast of its competitors. Finally, on 18 June 1945 the U.S. Supreme Court declared the AP protest right a violation of federal antitrust laws. Cooper later boasted that the decision had not weakened AP "because of the defense [in the form of an improved news report] I built up during thirty years."

Another limitation on AP's growth was the international news cartel operating since 1870 principally for the benefit of three European news agencies, Reuters, Havas, and Wolff. A tributary of Reuters from the start, confined to distribution only in North America and required to take the cartel's international news report, AP found itself disadvantaged vis-à-vis UP and INS, which, without cartel constraints, were free to cover and distribute news throughout the world. Although Cooper received broad permission to renegotiate AP-Reuters relations in 1929, a nonexclusive news-exchange contract, freeing AP from the cartel, was not signed until 12 February 1934.

Cooper described his crusade to free AP's international operations in *Barriers Down*, published in 1942 as part of his wartime campaign for international press freedom. On 21 January 1945 Cooper, speaking in New York City, originated the phrase the citizen's "right to know," according to the *New York Times*. Cooper elaborated on the concept in *The Right to Know* (1956). Cooper stepped down as general manager in 1948, but stayed on as executive director (a title the board had given him in 1943) until his retirement in 1951.

He was married three times, first to Daisy McBride from 1905 to her death in 1920, second to Marian Rothwell from 1921 to their divorce in 1940, and third to Sara A. Gibbs from 1942 to his death. Cooper had one daughter, Jane, by his first marriage. After a heart seizure on 22 January, Cooper died on 31 January 1965 in West Palm Beach, Florida.

BIBLIOGRAPHY:

A. *Kent Cooper and the Associated Press: An Autobiography* (New York, 1959).

B. NYT 31 January 1965; Oliver Gramling, *AP: The Story of News* (New York, 1940).

RICHARD A. SCHWARZLOSE

COOPER, THOMAS (b. 22 October 1759; d. 11 May 1839) was a lifelong controversialist whose writings covered a wide range of topics, including religion, science, materialism, and government. He turned from antislavery as a young man in England to a defense of the "peculiar institution" in his later years in South Carolina and became known as the "father of nullification." Yet he had a lifetime passion for free inquiry and free speech, and was the most famous of those found guilty of libeling President John Adams under the Sedition Act of 1798.

Thomas Cooper was born in Weymouth, England, and was educated at Oxford, although he did not take a degree there. He studied medicine and practiced law in London and Manchester, and dabbled in philosophy and chemistry. For a while he was also engaged in calico printing. His first publication in 1787 called for abolition of the slave trade, and for the next seven years he wrote numerous pamphlets expounding his materialist philosophy, opposing the established church, advocating parliamentary reform, and lauding individual freedom. Joseph Priestley nominated him for membership in the Royal Society, but he was turned down because of his unpopular viewpoints. Upon visiting Paris in1792 Cooper instituted a correspondence between the Jacobins and the Manchester Constitutional Society, which drew attacks from Edmund Burke and other English opponents of the French Revolution. Cooper became disgusted with the excesses of the new French regime himself, but was equally disturbed by the conservative reaction in England. In 1794 he made an exploratory trip to the United States, which he praised for its religious and civil liberty in a tract published in England upon his return.

Cooper and Priestley emigrated to the United States that same year, Cooper settling in Northumberland County, Pennsylvania, where he farmed while practicing law and medicine. He soon began writing in support of the Jeffersonian Republicans. A statement of his published in the *Reading Weekly Advertiser* strongly indicating that President Adams was incompetent was the basis for a libel trial under the Sedition Act of 1798. Cooper was found guilty and was fined $400 and sentenced to six months in prison.

In 1800 Cooper's wife, Alice Greenwood Cooper (whom he had married in England), died. Their marriage had produced five children. Cooper had three more children by Elizabeth Pratt Hemming of England, whom he married about 1811.

With the triumph of the Jeffersonian Republicans at the beginning of the nineteenth century, Cooper served as a Pennsylvania county commissioner from 1801 to 1804 and then as a state judge from 1804 to 1811. In 1811 he was accused of arbitrary conduct by the state legislature and was removed from office by the governor. Cooper thereupon turned to education, teaching chemistry at Carlisle (now Dickinson) College from 1811 to 1815 and chemistry and mineralogy at the University of Pennsylvania from 1815 to 1819. During this period he published many scientific works and was elected to the American Philosophical Society, but Thomas Jefferson's attempt to get him appointed to the staff at the new University of Virginia did not bear fruit. Thus, Cooper took a similar position at South Carolina College (later the University of South Carolina) in January 1820.

He soon was named president of the college and also taught chemistry, mineralogy, and political economy there until 1834. Cooper helped found South Carolina's first medical school and its first insane asylum. He became embroiled with the clergy over his biblical criticisms and materialist philosophy, but held his position at the college because of his defense of states' rights, slavery, and the southern view of free trade. His extreme love of individual liberty led to his advocacy of nullification and secession under circumstances in which the union infringed on individual or states' rights. Nonetheless, he resigned as president of the college in 1834 under heavy pressure as a result of his 1833 tract that said the Bible was not an infallible guide in mineralogy and geology.

Cooper wrote the pioneer political science textbook, *Lectures on the Elements of Political Economy* (1831), among other works. He died on 11 May 1839, survived by his second wife. Cooper impressed people with his brilliant conversation as well as with his writing. His belligerent attitude, which made him numerous enemies, represented the depth of his belief in teaching the truth as he saw it.

BIBLIOGRAPHY:

B. DAB 2, 414–416; Maurice Kelley, *Additional Chapters on Thomas Cooper* (Orono, Maine, 1930); Dumas Malone, *The Public Life of Thomas Cooper, 1783–1839* (New Haven, 1926); Harry M. Tinkcom, *The Republicans and Federalists in Pennsylvania, 1790–1801* (Harrisburg, Pa., 1950).

ROBERT M. OURS

COPLEY, IRA CLIFTON (b. 25 October 1864; d. 2 November 1947) was an Illinois public utility executive, a newspaper publisher, and a congressman. Copley's business career was guided by the principle that the safest investment is a monopoly serving many customers so well that it discourages competition. In applying his principles to journalism, he was instrumental in hastening the growth of newspaper monopolies.

Copley, born in Knox County, Illinois, was the third of five surviving children and the younger of two sons of Ira Birdsall Copley, a farmer, and Ellen Madeline Whiting. His mother had moved west from Connecticut, and his father, a descendant of colonial Massachusetts settlers, had migrated to Illinois in 1854 from his native New York state. When young Copley was blinded at the age of two by scarlet fever, his parents moved to Aurora, Illinois, to be near an eye specialist. There the elder Copley became part owner and manager of the Aurora Gas Light Company. Copley regained some vision after four years of treatment, but his vision remained impaired for the rest of his life.

Copley was graduated in 1883 from Jennings Seminary in his hometown, and in 1887 was graduated from Yale University with a B.A. degree. He then studied at the Union College of Law in Chicago and was awarded the LL.B. degree in 1889. Before completing his law courses, however, he was called home to help run his father's failing company. He consolidated and developed the company over two decades until it was expanded to serve seventy-five cities and towns in Illinois. On 3 March 1892 Copley was married to Edith Strohn of Los Angeles, California. Three children by this marriage died in infancy, and later the Copleys adopted two sons, James Strohn Copley and William Nelson Copley.

Copley's publishing interests developed in 1905 when he purchased the *Aurora Beacon*, later consolidating it with the *Aurora News* to form the *Beacon News*. In 1908 he acquired the *Elgin Courier*, and in 1926 the *Elgin News*, combining them as the *Courier-News*.

As early as 1894 he was a member of the Republican state and central committees, and a lieutenant colonel in the Illinois National Guard. "Colonel" Copley, as he became known, served on the state park commission from 1894 to 1898, and as an aide on the staff of Governor Charles S. Deneen from 1905 to 1913. Politically liberal, he supported the Progressive candidacy of Theodore Roosevelt in 1912, but ran as a Progressive himself only in 1914. In Congress he introduced a bill to prevent the interstate shipment of goods produced by child labor, supported a graduated income tax and a national referendum on prohibition, and advocated the regulation of public utilities.

In 1912 Copley added the *Joliet Herald* to his acquisitions and later merged it with the *Joliet News* to form the *Herald-News*. His operations in the publishing field were further enlarged by his lease in 1928 of the *Illinois State Journal*, of Springfield, and eighteen daily newspapers in California, including the *San Diego Union* and the *San Diego Tribune*. Copley established a Washington bureau in 1944 to provide for his newspapers an on-the-spot service from the nation's capital dealing with events of national importance and of special importance to the communities where his papers were published.

Mrs. Edith Strohn Copley died in 1929. While touring France, Copley married his second wife, Chloe Davidson Worley, on 27 April 1931. Mrs. Worley, whom he had known in Aurora, had a daughter, Eleanor, by a previous marriage.

Several of Copley's properties were later disposed of and some combined with others. The Illinois newspapers were operated directly by the Copley Press, and the California papers, with the exception of those in San Diego, under the corporate name of Southern California Associated Newspapers. Recognizing that each paper and each community has a distinct identity, Copley refused to do what he called "mass thinking" for his chain. He gave his publishers considerable autonomy and insisted that they publish all local news impartially.

Copley was a complex man, friendly but formal, tolerant but authoritative. He contributed generously to several philanthropic causes including Wilmer Ophthalmological Institute at Johns Hopkins University, and the Copley Hospital in Aurora. In religion, Copley was a Universalist. He died of arteriosclerotic heart disease at Copley Hospital on 2 November 1947.

BIBLIOGRAPHY:

B. DAB Supp. 4, 180–181; NCAB 36, 118–119; NYT 3 November 1947; Walter S. J. Swanson, *The Thin Gold Watch* (New York, 1964).

JULIA CRAIN ZAHAROPOULOS

COUGHLIN, FATHER CHARLES EDWARD (b. 25 October 1891; d. 27 October 1979) was a Roman Catholic priest and political activist who gained national prominence through his weekly radio sermons attacking communism, internationalism, labor unions, Jews, Wall Street, and numerous other political and economic subjects. During the depression era he became known as the "radio priest," as his broadcasts over twenty-eight stations brought him millions of listeners. Father Coughlin also published numerous books and the magazine *Social Justice*.

Coughlin was born in Hamilton, Ontario, to an American father and Canadian mother. His father, Thomas, was a poorly educated Irish Catholic who contracted typhoid fever while a sailor on a Great Lakes steamer. He was hospitalized in Ontario, and then found a job as church sexton and later as a bakery foreman. Coughlin's mother, Amelia Mahoney, was a seamstress. The boy graduated from St.Mary's parochial school in Hamilton (1903), and St. Michael's College high school in Toronto (1907) where the principal purpose was to train priests. He entered St. Michael's College of the University of Toronto, and graduated in 1911. Coughlin seems to have been torn between his parents' wish for him to become a priest and his desire to pursue a career in politics. Coughlin entered the church and in 1916 was ordained a priest. From 1916 to 1922 he taught at Assumption College, Toronto, and then had preaching assignments in Kalamazoo and Detroit, Michigan. Coughlin was sent to erect and assume the pastorate of the Shrine of the Little Flower in Royal Oak, Michigan, in 1916. It was at Little Flower that he approached WJR radio, Detroit, with a broadcast plan designed to help the small parish and its finances.

At first his broadcasts were directed to children. Later he moved to an adult audience. Soon letters and donations were flooding his office. Coughlin bought time on the influential WLW, Cincinnati, and then negotiated with WMAQ, Chicago. By 1930 broadcasts were going out weekly over eighteen stations. In 1930 Coughlin began to lace his sermons with economic and political views. Communism, the "red serpent," and remonetization of silver became two early and frequently heard topics. With the depression, emphasis turned to the perils of "unregulated capitalism." His broadcasts are said to have gotten more emotional as he increased his criticisms of President Hoover, international bankers, and others. CBS became concerned, and asked Coughlin to temper his broadcasts and submit scripts in advance. Instead of complying, the priest used his next broadcast to ask listeners whether CBS was right in suppressing him. CBS received 1.25 million letters of protest, but Coughlin was dropped by the network in April 1931. NBC also was unavailable, but a group of radio stations, including WOR, New York, allowed him to buy time. In late 1932 Coughlin's message went out on twenty-seven stations, at a weekly cost of $14,000. By 1935 costs had risen to between $14,000 and $15,000 a week. These costs were offset by donations. For example, money orders totaling some $4 million were said to have been cashed by Coughlin's Radio League of the Little Flower at the Royal Oaks Post Office in a twenty-month period alone. Coughlin needed 106 clerks and 4 personal secretaries to answer the mail.

When the 1930s began, Coughlin was a firm supporter of Franklin D. Roosevelt and the New Deal. The priest often sent advice to the president, and on air gave the impression that he had an insider's influence with the administration. All of this changed when in 1934 the administration led an attempt to block silver legislation by targeting individuals who were said to be in a position to gain through large silver investments. Coughlin was one of those targeted. After this Coughlin's feelings toward Roosevelt shifted. He lashed out when Roosevelt proposed joining the World Court, which Coughlin thought to be a ploy of international bankers. Some 200,000 telegrams inundated Congress, and contributed to halting action on the measure. Besides his radio network, Coughlin also created the National Union for Social Justice, an interest group, and established the magazine *Social Justice* designed to help spread his views.

In 1936 Coughlin's National Union for Justice joined with the late Huey P. Long's Share the National Wealth movement and pension crusader Dr. Francis E. Townsend in supporting the establishment of the Union party which ran William Lemke, North Dakota congressman, for president. Lemke received one million votes.

By 1939 Coughlin found himself siding with the pro-Fascist Christian Front. His anti-Semitism intensified. Coughlin's politics increasingly were becoming a liability. Charges were being levied that the priest was a Nazi sympathizer. Coughlin's direct superior, Edward Cardinal Mooney, ordered him to stop his broadcasts in 1941. He obeyed this order. In 1942 the Post Office barred *Social Justice* from the mails. The National Union for Social Justice was soon dissolved. Coughlin returned to his parish and continued as pastor of the Royal Oaks church until his retirement in 1966, almost totally removed from public view. He died at his home in Bloomfield Hills, Michigan, at age eighty-eight.

BIBLIOGRAPHY:

B. EAB 231–232; NYT 28 October 1979; Alfred McClung Lee and Elizabeth Briant Lee, eds., *The Fine Art of Propaganda: A Study of Father Coughlin's Speeches* (New York, 1939); Sheldon Marcus, *Father Coughlin* (Boston, 1973); Charles J. Tull, *Father Coughlin and the New Deal* (Syracuse, 1965).

RICHARD C. VINCENT

COWLES, GARDNER (b. 28 February 1861; d. 28 February 1946) built one of the Midwest's most respected media groups with the Des Moines Register and Tribune Company, the Register and Tribune Syndicate, *Look* magazine, and the Cowles Broadcasting Company. From his start as majority owner and publisher of the Pulitzer Prize–winning *Des Moines Register* until his death, Cowles gained a reputation as an innovative and fair, yet aggressive, media-businessman. He transformed the *Register* from a small, failing paper into Iowa's largest daily (with statewide circulation) and the flagship of his media empire. He also pioneered newspaper employees' group insurance, retirement, and company stock purchase plans.

Cowles, one of four children, was born in Oskaloosa, Iowa, a small farming community about seventy-five miles southeast of Des Moines. His father, the Reverend William Fletcher Cowles, was the local Methodist minister, and his mother, Maria Elizabeth LaMonte Cowles, was a schoolteacher and the daughter of a northeastern Iowa pioneer family. Gardner went through the public schools in a succession of Iowa towns such as Muscatine and Mt. Pleasant where his father held pastorates. He attended Penn College in Oskaloosa for one year, Grinnell College in Grinnell, Iowa, for two years, and was graduated from Iowa Wesleyan College in Algona, Iowa, in 1882. Cowles also received a master's degree from Iowa Wesleyan College in 1885.

Cowles worked as a schoolteacher while in college, and following graduation became superintendent of the Algona schools, a position he held for two years. On 3 December 1884 Cowles married Florence Maud Call, a member of the Algona teaching staff and daughter of a local banker. Florence and Gardner Cowles eventually had six children, three girls and three boys, including John and Gardner Jr. (q.v.), who carried on their father's later media interests.

Cowles left teaching in 1885 and with the help of his banker father-in-law embarked on a career as a banker, investor, and real estate broker. From 1899 to 1903 Cowles served as a Republican representative in the Iowa legislature from Kossuth County. By 1903, at age forty-two, Cowles owned ten banks in northern Iowa and had amassed a sizable personal fortune.

Prior to 1903 Cowles had only scant contact with the newspaper business. As a child, he had folded papers for the *Muscatine Journal*, and as a young man, he became a partner in the weekly *Algona Republican* and edited the *Advance* in Algona part-time for about eighteen months. While associated with the *Republican*, Cowles became friends with Harvey Ingham, then editor of the *Upper Des Moines*. Ingham later became associate editor and minority owner of the *Des Moines Register and Leader* about the time Cowles entered banking and politics.

In early 1903 Ingham's minority investment in the *Register and Leader* was threatened by a takeover bid. During his search to find someone to buy out the majority stock owners to save his own investment, Ingham telegraphed Cowles with the investment proposition. Cowles came to Des Moines and examined the paper. At the time, the *Register and Leader* was the smallest of Des Moines' three dailies, $180,000 in debt and struggling with a circulation of about 15,000. Nonetheless, Cowles agreed to buy up the majority stock for $300,000.

Within five years, Ingham and Cowles turned the *Register and Leader* into a financially successful paper recognized for its nonpartisan editorial policy and its journalistic integrity. Cowles also gained a reputation for honesty and high principles from his refusal to accept liquor ads and from the fact that his Chicago advertising agent dropped the *Register* for its refusal to follow the common practice of publishing exaggerated circulation figures.

Cowles strengthened his paper's position in the Des Moines market with the purchase of an afternoon daily competitor, the *Des Moines Tribune*, in 1908. Cowles eventually bought out his remaining evening competitors, the Scripps-Howard *Daily News* and the *Des Moines Capital*, in 1924 and 1927 respectively. To avoid the stigma of a monopoly, Cowles established the Bureau of Accuracy and Fair Play to evaluate publicly the performances of his papers. He also pitted the editorial staffs of his morning and evening papers against each other to preserve the attitudes and appearances of competition.

Having firm control of the newspaper business in Des Moines by the mid–1920s, Cowles launched a series of experiments in audience surveys, photography, employees benefits, and broadcasting. In 1925 he hired George Gallup (q.v.) to survey *Register and Tribune* readers. Gallup's poll found that readers preferred pictures to text, and so the staff began experiments with the Sunday rotogravure section. Vernon Pope, who became *Look* magazine's first editor, began running news and feature photo essays. The photo pages were so successful that in 1933 the *Register and Tribune* syndicated them to twenty-six other papers. During this period, Cowles also departed from the traditional adversarial model of labor-management relations and pioneered newspaper employees' group insurance, retirement plans, and company stock purchases. In 1928 Cowles diversified his media holdings and established the Cowles Broadcasting Company with three radio stations: KRNT, Des Moines; WNAX, Yankton, South Dakota; and WOL, Washington, D.C. By the early 1930s Cowles had also introduced picture transmission by airplane, created the Register and Tribune Syndicate, and developed newspapers in Minnesota, including the *Minneapolis Star Journal*.

In 1929 Herbert Hoover appointed Cowles to the Federal Commission on Conservation and Administration of the Public Domain. During the banking crisis of 1932 he was appointed director of the Reconstruction Finance Corporation. In 1934 Cowles and his wife created the Gardner Cowles Foundation. During his lifetime, the foundation made almost $1 million in charitable contributions to private colleges and hospitals throughout Iowa. In his later years, Cowles was stricken with chronic myocarditis and eventually became deaf and blind. He died in his Des Moines home on his eighty-fifth birthday.

BIBLIOGRAPHY:

B. DAB Supp. 4, 188–190; NYT 1 March 1946; "Gardner Cowles Succumbs," *Editor and Publisher*, 9 March 1946.

ROY ALDEN ATWOOD

COWLES, GARDNER, JR. "MIKE" (b. 31 January 1903; d. 8 July 1985) not only carried his family heritage, the *Des Moines Register and Tribune*, to greater heights of journalistic prominence, but influenced such journalistic developments as readership polling and the sequence photograph technique, a precursor of today's photo essay form. He was also instrumental in expanding the Cowles family's business from its Iowa newspaper origins to the magazine world of New York City with *Look* magazine, along with radio and television stations scattered around the country.

Cowles was born in Algona, Iowa, the youngest of six children of Florence Call Cowles and Gardner Cowles, Sr. (q.v.). Shortly after Mike's birth, so-named by his father because of his Irish countenance, the family moved to Des Moines where Gardner Sr. and Harvey Ingham purchased the *Register and Leader*, the town's morning newspaper with a circulation of about 15,000. By 1927 Cowles papers, the morning *Register* and the afternoon *Tribune*, were the capital city's two remaining dailies. Cowles's early years were spent at the newspaper office—in the cashier's cage at age six, reading editorials for a quarter at age eight, and working as a summer reporter during his college years.

Cowles graduated from Phillips Exeter Academy in 1921 and then received a bachelor's degree from Harvard in 1925. At Harvard he was the editor of the *Crimson*, and a member of the Delphic and Hasty Pudding clubs. Upon graduation from Harvard, he returned to the *Des Moines Register and Tribune*, where he held the following positions: city editor (1925), news editor (1926), associate managing editor (early 1927), managing editor (1927–31), executive editor (1931–39), associate publisher (1939–43), president (1943–71), and chairman (1971–73). During the late 1920s and early 1930s Cowles shifted the family enterprises into the new medium of radio with stations in Yankton, South Dakota; Fort Dodge, Iowa; and Des Moines.

Both Cowles and his brother, John, contributed to the *Register and Tribune*'s growth during this period with Cowles's influence felt in the areas of news and pictures. Based on a readership survey by fledgling pollster George Gallup (q.v.), the *Des Moines Register* began to reflect a reader preference for photographs over words; particularly pictures that were part of a sequence which in itself told a visual story. These "picture-series" stories not only appeared frequently in the *Register*'s Sunday rotogravure section, but became the impetus for Cowles's use of airplanes in coverage of sports and news events in the 1920s. Also during this time, the *Register* established a national reputation for its liberal stance and internationalist outlook.

In 1933 Cowles began plans that ultimately lead to the appearance of *Look* magazine on 5 January 1937. From 1939 to 1971, Cowles served as editor in chief and chairman of Cowles Magazines and Broadcasting Company, later known as Cowles Communications, which included several radio and television stations round the country, and newspapers in Florida, New York, Puerto Rico, and Tennessee, along with magazines such as *Quick, Venture, Flair, Collier's, Family Circle, Lancet, Medicine Group*, and *Look*, which ceased publication in 1971. He remained active with the company until 1976.

During World War II, Cowles was domestic director of the Office of War Information (1942–43). He advised the Republican presidential campaigns of Wendell Willkie in 1940 and Dwight D. Eisenhower in 1952. He supervised the *Des Moines Register* during the time when it became one of the nation's most frequent winners of Pulitzer Prizes. He was married four times: to Helen Curtiss, Lois Thornburg, Fleur Fenton, and Jan Streate Cox; and had four children: Lois, Gardner III, Kate, and Virginia.

On 31 January 1985 the family's lengthy ownership of the *Des Moines Register and Tribune* ended when the company's board of directors accepted a $530 million cash offer from the Gannett Company. Included in the purchase package were two biweeklies in Independence and Indianola, Iowa; a daily in Jackson, Tennessee, and the *Register*, with a daily circulation of 240,000 and 390,000 for the *Sunday Register*; and a 13 percent stock holding in Cowles Media

Company of Minneapolis. One week after the transaction was finalized, Cowles died at a Long Island, New York, hospital.

BIBLIOGRAPHY:
B. NYT 9 July 1985.

MARIANNE SALCETTI

COX, JAMES MIDDLETON (b. 31 March 1870; d. 15 July 1957) was a newspaper publisher, broadcast station owner, and an Ohio politician who, in 1920, was the Democratic candidate for president.

Cox, the youngest of seven children, was born at Jacksonburg, Ohio, a village twenty miles south of Dayton. His father, Gilbert Cox, was a farmer of English descent whose ancestors originally settled in Virginia and New York. Cox's mother, Eliza Andrews Cox, grew up on a nearby farm. Cox worked on the family farm, was a janitor in the local public school, and served as sexton in the United Brethren Church where the family worshipped. He later became an Episcopalian. While attending an academy in Middletown, Ohio, young James Cox worked in the print shop of his brother-in-law's newspaper. Tutored by this relative, Cox passed the teacher certification examination at age seventeen and taught a few years in country schools in southwestern Ohio.

Cox continued his interest in newspaper work and, in 1892, achieved a major scoop about a train wreck while working for the *Middletown Signal*. This story led to his joining the *Cincinnati Enquirer* as a reporter the same year. After attracting attention as a successful journalist, Cox was offered a position as secretary to newly elected Congressman Paul J. Sorg in 1895. Cox returned to Ohio in 1898 and, with Sorg's financial backing, bought the struggling *Dayton Evening News*. With sound editorial judgment and business acumen, he developed his first newspaper into a financially successful publication and the forerunner of the important media companies known today as Cox Enterprises (newspapers), and Cox Communications (radio, television, and cable). Cox bought his second newspaper, the *Springfield Press-Register*, in 1905. Through his two Ohio newspapers, Cox built a reputation as an aggressive reform journalist.

Cox plunged into politics in 1908, when he easily won election to represent Ohio's Third Congressional District in the U.S. Congress. He was reelected to the House in 1910. As a liberal and progressive Democrat, Cox was elected governor of Ohio in 1912. Although he lost the 1914 gubernatorial election, Cox won the governorship again in both 1916 and 1918. He was the first Democratic governor of Ohio elected to serve three terms. Cox identified himself with the goals and programs of Woodrow Wilson and earned a reputation as a liberal, a friend of labor, and an opponent of prohibition. As governor, his major accomplishments included improvement of the state's public school system, prison reforms, workman's compensation and minimum wage programs, and a major highway construction program. He received the Red Cross Gold Medal of Merit for his handling of the devastating Ohio River flood of 1913.

At the 1920 Democratic National Convention in San Francisco, Cox was nominated for president on the forty-fourth ballot. He pledged continuation of Wilson's policies of domestic reform and international cooperation, including support of the League of Nations. After losing the election to Warren G. Harding (q.v.), Cox completed his governorship and returned to the private life of a journalist. Although he never again sought public office, Cox accepted an appointment by President Roosevelt as vice chairman of the U.S. delegation to the World Monetary and Economic Conference at London in 1933.

After his retirement from politics, Cox developed extensive media holdings. His acquisitions included the *Miami* (Florida) *Metropolis* (1923), *Springfield* (Ohio) *Sun* (1928), *Dayton Journal-Herald* (1948), *Atlanta Constitution* (1950), and the *Canton* (Ohio) *News*. The latter received a Pulitzer Prize in 1927 for its fight against corruption in local government. Cox acquired radio station WIOD, Miami, in 1930, and established WHIO at Dayton in 1935. With the purchase of the *Atlanta Journal* in 1939, he also acquired WSB, a 50,000-watt radio facility in Atlanta. Before his death, television stations were added at Dayton and Atlanta.

Cox married Mayme L. Harding of Cincinnati in 1893. They had three children and were divorced in 1910. In 1917, during his second term as governor, Cox married Margaretta Parker Blair of Chicago. They had one child. Cox died in Dayton, Ohio, on 15 July 1957.

BIBLIOGRAPHY:

A. *Journey Through My Years* (New York, 1946).

B. NYT 18 July 1957; *Newsweek*, 29 July 1957; *Time*, 29 July 1957; Irving Stone, "James Middleton Cox," *They Also Ran: The Story of the Men Who Were Defeated for the Presidency* (Garden City, N.Y., 1945).

HERBERT H. HOWARD

CRAIG, DANIEL HUTCHINS (b. 3 November 1811; d. 5 January 1895) systematized intercity news movement and shaped the Associated Press into a national news monopoly in the decade prior to the Civil War. A shrewd and energetic businessman and journalist, Craig was the general agent for the New York Associated Press from 1851 to 1866 and an investor in telegraph developments which were helpful to his news enterprise.

The youngest of eight children, Craig was born in Rumney, New Hampshire, the son of Daniel and Pamela Hutchins Craig. The record shows only that his father fought in the War of 1812 and his grandfather, Alexander Craig, fought in the revolutionary war. After printing apprenticeships at the *Gazette* of Plymouth, New Hampshire, and the *Gazette* of Lancaster, Massachusetts, Craig became a journeyman printer in 1832 in Boston, where he married Helena Croome of England on 6 November 1834.

Between 1840 and 1844 the Craigs lived in Baltimore where, after unsuccessfully attempting to market *Craig's Business Directory and Baltimore Almanac*, he collaborated with *Baltimore Sun* editor Arunah S. Abell in developing a system for gathering news from distant cities via carrier pigeons.

While nominally a printer until 1849, Craig devoted most of his time in the 1840s to perfecting and operating news-gathering systems for various eastern newspapers and market speculators. During the 1840s the Craigs also had three children: Ida G., born in either 1843 or 1844; Frank H., born in 1845 and died from cholera infantum on 18 August 1846; and William L., born in 1848.

In 1844 Craig moved back to Boston, applying his pigeon express to the steady flow of European news terminating in that city via transatlantic Cunard steamers. Craig carried his pigeons overland to Halifax, Nova Scotia, the westbound Cunarders' first port of call, boarded the ships, condensed on tissue paper the news from the European papers, and flew his birds from the steamers' decks fifty miles outside of Boston harbor. The first telegraph line to connect Boston and Halifax ended his pigeon service in late November 1849, but while the line was being erected, the enterprising Craig operated horse expresses from Halifax to the end of the line, regularly beating express competitors.

Impressed with Craig's success and daring, New York City's six leading dailies and the partners in the recently formed Associated Press (AP) wire service in late 1849 named him their Halifax agent, responsible for summarizing and telegraphing foreign news dispatches for their joint use. On 19 May 1851, when the New York AP's first general agent in New York City, Alexander Jones, relinquished his post, Craig succeeded him. Facing stiff competition from Abbot and Winans, a news service closely allied with the Morse telegraph system, and inheriting a lackluster and brief news report, Craig went to work to establish his Associated Press as the nation's news monopoly.

He established a network of news correspondents in most towns and cities and enlarged the news report's size and scope. Securing low telegraph rates for late-night transmission of news, Craig routed his news dispatches first to New York City for use by his patron AP newspapers there and then into the hinterlands in abbreviated form, where local, state, and regional APs distributed it to member newspapers.

Meanwhile, in order to preserve safe and friendly telegraph circuits for his news reports, Craig purchased a line between New York City and Boston, leased a line across Newfoundland, and unearthed and promoted the Hughes telegraph instrument, which assisted Craig's friends at Western Union and the American Telegraph Company to overcome the competition of the Morse telegraph companies. The Abbot and Winans news service succumbed to Craig's pressure in 1855, and by the start of the Civil War, Craig's network was so pervasive and dependable that President Abraham Lincoln relied on the AP, rather than the traditional political press, as his conduit to the public.

At the height of his career, Craig was discovered organizing a wire service for Western Union to oppose the AP, and on 5 November 1866 AP fired him. He briefly operated his new agency without Western Union's help, but an AP–Western Union alliance on 11 January 1867 put him out of business. Although he formed the National Telegraph Company in 1869 and the American Rapid

Telegraph Company in 1879, both were unsuccessful. Craig died while sitting quietly in his Asbury Park, New Jersey, home on 5 January 1895.

BIBLIOGRAPHY:

B. DAB 4, 495–496; NYT 6 January 1895 as "David H. Craig"; *New York Herald*, 6 January 1895; Peter R. Knights, *The Press Association War of 1866–67* (Austin, Texas, 1967); James D. Reid, *The Telegraph in America, Its Founders, Promoters and Noted Men* (New York, 1879); Robert Luther Thompson, *Wiring a Continent: The History of the Telegraph Industry in the United States, 1832–1866* (Princeton N.J., 1947).

RICHARD A. SCHWARZLOSE

CRANE, STEPHEN (b. 1 November 1871; d. 5 June 1900) was for much of his brief life associated with newspapers as a reporter, special writer, war correspondent, and free-lance contributor. Some scholars have said his literary apprenticeship was gained in journalism, although the journalistic and literary phases of his career were concurrent in the 1890s.

Crane was born in Newark, New Jersey, the fourteenth and last child of the Reverend Jonathan Townley Crane and Mary Helen Peck Crane. The family moved to Port Jarvis, New York, where Crane started school, and after his father died, Stephen and his mother moved to Asbury Park, New Jersey. He attended Pennington Seminary, Claverack College, and Hudson River Institute. His first reporting job was with his brother Townley's news agency, gathering news of the Jersey Coast resorts, which appeared in the Sunday edition of the *New York Tribune*. He worked for Townley during summers from 1888 to 1892. Crane attended Lafayette College and Syracuse University for a term each in 1890 and 1891. In 1892 his literary sketches about Sullivan County, New York, ran in the Sunday *Tribune*, but his association with the paper ended in August 1892 after he wrote an ironic sketch about a parade of workmen in Asbury Park.

In the fall of 1892, Crane moved to New York City, worked as a newspaper stringer, and began his novel *Maggie: A Girl of the Streets*. He published it himself in 1893 and began working on *The Red Badge of Courage*. In 1894 and 1895, Crane was a special writer for the Sunday *New York Press*, doing a number of sketches of city life. He also wrote for *Arena* magazine and did some work for *McClure's* magazine and the McClure Press Syndicate. A condensed version of *The Red Badge of Courage* was published in newspapers in December 1894, and the book came out in October 1895. Earlier that year the Bacheller, Johnson and Bacheller Syndicate had sent Crane west as a roving correspondent, and he traveled from Nebraska to Texas to Mexico, writing as he went. Back in New York in 1896, Crane continued writing for the Bacheller and McClure syndicates and was a regular contributor of features to the *New York Journal*.

In late 1896 Crane went to Florida for Bacheller so that he could travel to Cuba to cover the insurrection there. On 2 January 1897 Crane's ship sank off the coast of Florida, and Crane and three others were adrift in a dinghy for thirty hours. The experience was dramatized in "The Open Boat," which was published in *Scribner's* in June 1897. In May 1897 Crane went to Greece to cover the Greco-Turkish War for the *New York Journal*. He was accompanied by Cora Taylor Stewart, the woman he had met in Florida who became his common-law wife. After that brief war, Crane and Cora settled in England.

In April 1898 he returned to the United States to join the *New York World* as a correspondent covering the Spanish-American War. He covered the landing and combat of the U.S. Marines at Guantanamo in Cuba and was on hand for most of the major land engagements of the brief war. His physical condition deteriorated, however, and he was evacuated in early July. Crane was dismissed by the *World*, apparently because of a dispute over expenses, but was hired by the *Journal* and sent to Puerto Rico to cover that phase of the war in July and August. He stayed on in Havana after the war and continued sending dispatches to the *Journal*. After the war Richard Harding Davis (q.v.) hailed Crane as the best correspondent in the war.

He returned to England after the war. *Active Service*, his novel about war correspondents, was published in 1899. Weakened by failing health, Crane struggled to write material to sell to handle his and Cora's mounting debts. He collapsed in December 1899, and Cora took him to Badenweiler, Germany, in 1900, seeking relief for his tuberculosis. He died 5 June, five months short of his twenty-ninth birthday.

Crane's status as a figure in the history of journalism has always been uncertain, and his journalistic work has generally been unappreciated and underrated. Although not a major figure, Crane was a newspaper journalist of considerable range and skill, especially as a feature writer and war correspondent.

BIBLIOGRAPHY:

A. *Tales,Sketches, and Reports,* vol. 8 of *The University of Virginia Edition of the Works of Stephen Crane* (Charlottesville, Va., 1970); *Reports of War,* vol. 9 of *The University of Virginia Edition of the Works of Stephen Crane* (Charlottesville, Va., 1971).

B. DAB 2, 506–508; NYT 6 June 1900; *New York World*, 10 June 1900; Edwin H. Cady, *Stephen Crane* (New York, 1980); James B. Colvert, *Stephen Crane* (San Diego, 1984); R. W. Stallman, *Stephen Crane: A Biography* (New York, 1968).

RONALD S. MARMARELLI

CRAWFORD, KENNETH GALE (b. 27 May 1902; d. 13 January 1983), a liberal journalist for forty-six years, reported and commented upon wars and peaceful change for newspapers, wire service bureaus, a news magazine, and political journals, becoming a confidant of every president from Franklin D. Roosevelt to Richard M. Nixon.

Born and reared in Sparta, Wisconsin, Crawford was the son of Robert Levy Crawford and Madge Gale Crawford. Beloit College conferred on Crawford the B.A. degree in 1924 and an honorary Litt.D. degree in 1954. On 21 July 1928 he married Elisabeth Bartholomew, by whom he had two children. He died at age eighty of lung cancer in Washington, were he had lived most of his life.

Between 1924 and 1927 Crawford worked as a reporter or bureau manager for United Press (UP) in St. Paul, St. Louis, Cleveland, Lansing, and

Indianapolis. Until 1929 he served as a Washington correspondent for UP, moving to the *Buffalo Times* as a columnist. From 1932 until 1940 he wrote a column for the *New York Post*. When the liberal New York newspaper *PM* was founded, he became a Washington correspondent and bureau manager for the paper, which he left in 1943. *Newsweek* hired him as a war correspondent in 1943, and he covered war fronts in North Africa, the Middle East, England, France, and Italy. He was the first American reporter ashore in the D day landings in Normandy on 6 June 1944. Returning to the United States that year, he again became a Washington correspondent and then a senior editor at *Newsweek*. He served briefly as assistant bureau chief for the magazine in Washington and as its national affairs editor from 1949 until 1954. From then until 1961 he managed *Newsweek*'s Washington bureau. In the last decade of his career he wrote a weekly *Newsweek* column before retiring in 1970.

Crawford became the second president in the history of the American Newspaper Guild, serving out Heywood Broun's (q.v.) term in 1939–40 after the latter's death. Though it was not a matter of public record, he wrote the *New Republic*'s TRB column from 1940 to 1943. For his reportage in World War II, Crawford received the European Theater ribbon, the Navy Commendation, and the French Liberation Medal.

Throughout his career, Crawford was as well known as a fighter for his beliefs as for his indefatigability as a reporter. In the guild, he battled communists and fellow travelers. He fought reactionary Republicans and others who opposed the New Deal; isolationists in the 1930s and 1940s; and foes of the Vietnam War in the 1960s. His departure from the *New Republic* was occasioned by one of his frequent disagreements with the editors of the magazine. Long after the Vietnam War had become unpopular, he defended it in *Newsweek*. A part of Crawford's reputation, too, was based on his dashing, handsome, mustachioed appearance.

BIBLIOGRAPHY:

A. *The Pressure Boys* (New York, 1939); *Report on North Africa* (New York, 1943).

B. NYT 14 January 1983; Katy Louchheim, *The Making of the New Deal: The Insiders Speak* (Cambridge, Mass., 1983).

DAVID L. ANDERSON

CREEL, GEORGE (b. 1 December 1876; d. 2 October 1953) was a muckraking journalist and reformer who gained international fame as chairman of the Committee on Public Information during World War I. After the war he occasionally ventured into politics, but he spent much of his career as columnist and Washington correspondent for *Collier's*.

Creel was born in Lafayette County in western Missouri to southern parents. His father, Henry Clay Creel, was an ex-Confederate army officer who had once served in the Virginia House of Delegates. After the war Creel's father failed at farming in Missouri, and the family moved to Kansas City, where Creel's mother, Virginia Fackler Creel, supported them by running a boardinghouse.

Creel attended high school for a time, but spent most of his teenage years working odd jobs.

In 1896 Creel began work as a reporter for the *Kansas City World*, but soon moved to New York City to seek work as a writer. There he supported himself by writing gags and jokes for New York publications, and in 1898 he joined the staff of the comic supplement of the *New York American*. He tried twice, without success, to enlist to fight in the Spanish-American War. In 1899 he moved back to Kansas City to edit, with Arthur Grissom, a weekly paper called the *Independent*. Creel used the paper to promote a series of Progressive political reforms, including municipal ownership of utilities, child labor laws, and women's rights.

In 1909 Creel took a job as editorial writer with the *Denver Post*, but he resigned in 1911 over the *Post*'s endorsements of machine candidates in an election. Creel moved briefly to New York City again, doing some writing for *Cosmopolitan*, but in September returned to Denver to write for the *Rocky Mountain News*. In 1912, as part of Denver reformers' attempts to initiate commission government, Creel accepted an appointment as police commissioner. His attempts to regulate Denver's notorious prostitution "cribs" won enemies, however, and he was dismissed from office the following year.

Over the next few years Creel worked as a free-lancer for New York magazines and participated whenever possible in reform movements across the country. He supported the Minneapolis campaign for commission government, worked for the confirmation of Supreme Court appointee Louis D. Brandeis, and aided the investigations of the Committee on Industrial Relations. In1914 he coauthored an exposé on child labor, called *Children of Bondage*, one of the first of over fifteen books he would write during his career.

An avid supporter of Woodrow Wilson in 1912 and 1916, Creel was named chairman of the Committee on Public Information in 1917. The committee's international campaign on behalf of the American war effort was one of the most ambitious and systematic early attempts to use public relations techniques to mold public opinion. Abroad Creel's committee tried to counteract German propaganda with information on the American way of life; at home the committee distributed pamphlets, press releases, and drawings, and sponsored a speakers' bureau of 75,000 "Four Minute Men" who promoted the war effort in movie theaters, clubs, factories, and churches.

After armistice Creel traveled to Europe with Wilson, reporting to the president on conditions in Eastern Europe and Ireland. Many of his findings were published in his book *Ireland's Fight for Freedom* (1920). With the defeat of the Democrats in the 1920 presidential election, Creel returned to magazine writing. *Collier's* offered him a staff job, writing articles on political leaders as well as humorous stories featuring a cracker-barrel philosopher named Uncle Henry, loosely modeled after Finley Peter Dunne's (q.v.) Mister Dooley. After moving to San Francisco in 1926, Creel traveled East occasionally in his work for *Collier's*, but he largely retired from active politics for most of the 1920s.

In 1932, however, Creel took a leave from the magazine to support former War Secretary Newton Baker's bid for the Democratic presidential nomination. When Baker lost, Creel swung his support to Franklin Roosevelt, then returned to California to work on the Senate campaign of William G. McAdoo. Creel twice served as a volunteer in the New Deal—in 1933 as chairman of a labor board administering the National Recovery Act on the West Coast, and in 1934 as chairman of the National Advisory Committee of the Works Progress Administration. But he soon resigned each, disenchanted with the New Deal's disorganization and lack of direction. In August 1934 Creel ran against the socialist Upton Sinclair (q.v.) in California's Democratic gubernatorial primary but lost.

After his defeat Creel returned to *Collier's* as Washington correspondent and stayed out of the political spotlight. Throughout the 1930s, however, he maintained his ties to Roosevelt, who often used Creel's articles to float trial balloons. In 1942 Creel broke with the Democratic party to support Republican Earl Warren's bid for California governor, and he increasingly spoke out against crackpot demagoguery. Like so many other Progressive Era liberals, Creel by the 1950s had become a rabid anticommunist.

Creel married twice, the first time to stage actress Blanche Bates, by whom he had two children. She died in 1941, and in 1943 Creel married Alice May Rosseter. He died in 1953, following surgery for a liver ailment.

BIBLIOGRAPHY:

A. *How We Advertised America* (New York, 1920); *Rebel at Large* (New York, 1947).

B. DAB Supp. 5, 141–143; NYT 3 October 1954; James R. Mock and Cedric Larson, *Words That Won the War* (Princeton, N.J., 1939).

JOHN J. PAULY

CREELMAN, JAMES (b. 12 November 1859; d. 12 February 1915) was a leading figure in the "Golden Age of the Reporter" in the late nineteenth century. A special correspondent in war and peace for leading newspapers, Creelman gained fame for his exploits covering the major stories and interviewing the major figures of his time.

He was born in Montreal, Canada, to Matthew and Martha Dunwoodie Creelman. His parents separated, and when he was twelve, Creelman walked to New York City to live with his mother. He avoided school and went to work in the printing plant of a church newspaper, then worked briefly at the *Brooklyn Eagle*. Creelman joined the staff of the *New York Herald* as an eighteen-year-old cub reporter. His early exploits for the *Herald* included going aloft in a gas airship that crashed; covering the Hatfield-McCoy feud in Kentucky and being shot at; and interviewing Sitting Bull. Creelman went to Europe in 1889 as the *Herald*'s special correspondent and was editor of the London edition in 1889 and 1890 and of the *Paris Herald* in 1891 and 1892. His work included interviews with Pope Leo XIII, Henry Stanley, and Leo Tolstoy. He married Alice Leffingwell Buell on 3 December 1891. They had one son and two daughters.

From late 1892 to 1893 Creelman was editor of the *New York Evening Telegram*, the *Herald*'s sister paper. In 1893 he left James Gordon Bennett, Jr.'s (q.v.) employ to work as associate editor of the *Illustrated American* and manager of *Cosmopolitan* magazine's London edition. In 1893 Joseph Pulitzer (q.v.) hired Creelman for the *New York World* and sent him to Asia to cover the Sino-Japanese War. Creelman accompanied the Japanese armies in Korea and Manchuria, witnessed the battles of P'yongyang and Port Arthur, and got out an exclusive dispatch on the naval battle of the Yalu. He was injured while covering the armies in Manchuria, the first of several wounds and injuries he suffered in action during his career. In December 1894 his reports of the massacre a few weeks earlier of the Chinese population of Port Arthur by the victorious Japanese created an international sensation. The incident and his story remained a hot issue for several weeks. After Creelman returned to New York, Pulitzer provided a testimonial dinner in his honor.

In February 1896 the *World* sent Creelman to Cuba to cover the insurrection there. He publicized alleged atrocities by the Spanish, antagonized Spanish officials who were increasingly irritated by the "meddlesome scribblers" writing about the conflict for American newspapers, and was expelled from the island in May 1896. Back in the United States, Creelman openly advocated U.S. intervention. In the fall he covered William Jennings Bryan's unsuccessful presidential campaign.

Late in 1896 William Randolph Hearst (q.v.) hired Creelman away from the *World* for his *New York Journal*. Hearst sent his new star correspondent to Europe as his special representative. In April 1897 Creelman joined the troupe of *Journal* correspondents covering the Greco-Turkish War. Creelman was back in New York in the summer of that year aiding Hearst's campaign against the Spanish in Cuba. He was in London when war erupted between Spain and the United States in April 1898. Hearst assigned him the task of buying a ship and having it sunk in the Suez Canal to prevent a Spanish fleet from passage to the Philippines to attack Dewey's American fleet. The Spanish fleet turned back, making the scheme superfluous.

In June Creelman went to Cuba as one of Hearst's several correspondents covering the war there. He was wounded on 1 July 1898 leading a charge of American troops at El Caney. After the battle, Creelman dictated his story to Hearst, who filed it for his correspondent. After recovering from his wound, he was sent to the Philippines later in the year to cover the conflict between American forces and Filipino rebels and was twice wounded. Creelman rejoined the *New York World* in 1900 and worked as a special correspondent and editorial writer. He was an associate editor of *Pearson's* magazine from 1906 to 1910. Creelman also served as a special correspondent for the *New York Times* in that period.

He served on the New York City Board of Education and was president of the Municipal Civil Service Commission until he resigned in late 1912 to join the *New York Evening Mail* as an associate editor. Back with Hearst in January

1915, Creelman was sent to Europe to cover the war for the *New York American*. He died of Bright's disease shortly after his arrival in Berlin.

BIBLIOGRAPHY:

A. *On the Great Highway: The Wanderings and Adventures of a Special Correspondent* (Boston, 1901).

B. DAB 2, 533; NYT 13 February 1915; Jeffrey M. Dorwart, "James Creelman, the *New York World* and the Port Arthur Massacre," *Journalism Quarterly*, Winter 1973.

RONALD S. MARMARELLI

CROLY, HERBERT DAVID (b. 23 January 1869; d. 17 May 1930) was a noted American political writer, journalist, and magazine editor whose major contributions included the founding of the *New Republic* and authorship of *The Promise of American Life*.

Croly was born in New York City, the son of two journalists, David Goodman Croly and Jane Cunningham Croly (q.v.), both well known in their own right. Croly was brought up in an atmosphere that stressed education. Both parents were followers of Auguste Comte and they instilled in the younger Croly a positivist outlook. Croly was educated in public and private schools, attending Harvard in 1886 although he did not receive his degree until 1910 (awarded as class of 1890). Among his teachers were George Herbert Palmer, Josiah Royce, William James, and George Santayana.

Croly's Harvard career was interrupted by a variety of responsibilities. The first was to his father; in 1888 he became secretary and intellectual partner to David Croly. When his father died the following year, Croly edited the *Record and Guide*, a real estate paper where he applied his own social philosophical analysis to economic questions, unfolding a well-articulated political and social philosophy. When the *Record and Guide* created a new publication, the *Architectural Record*, Croly moved to the staff there.

Croly married Louise Emory of Baltimore on 30 May 1892. He spent the next several months at Harvard, continuing work toward his degree, but suffered a nervous collapse before the second term began. The Crolys moved to Cornish, New Hampshire, there encountering a colony of artists and intellectuals, many of whom became Croly's intimate friends and associates. The Crolys also traveled in Europe before returning once again to Harvard.

Between 1900 and 1913, Croly maintained a connection with the *Architectural Record*, six of those years as editor. With publication of *The Promise of American Life* in 1909, Croly became established as the leading political philosopher in America. Though not a popular success, the work attracted the attention of the period's leading intellectuals. Perhaps more importantly, it also attracted the attention of Willard and Dorothy Straight, the financial backers of what would become the *New Republic*. The Straights suggested publishing a Progressive journal and guaranteed editorial freedom to Croly if he would undertake the task. The *New Republic* was established in 1914 with a distinguished editorial board, and Croly as its guiding light. The journal was rumored to be the mouthpiece of Woodrow Wilson, and as such it enjoyed a period of popularity. However, Croly and the *New Republic* broke with Wilson over the Treaty of Versailles and subsequently suffered a certain loss of prestige. With the advent of Warren Harding (q.v.) and Calvin Coolidge, Croly lost interest in politics and devoted more time to philosophy. He remained with the *New Republic*, continuing to imprint it with his own brand of refined impassivity.

Croly suffered a paralytic stroke in October 1928 and remained an invalid until his death at Santa Barbara, California. His most important contribution, aside from the *New Republic*, was his *Promise of American Life* which Charles Forcey called "a political classic which announced the end of the Age of Innocence . . . and inaugurated the process of self-examination."

BIBLIOGRAPHY:

B. DAB Supp. 1, 209–210; NYT 18 May 1930; Charles Forcey, *The Crossroads of Liberalism: Croly, Weyl, Lippmann, and the Progressive Era 1900–1925* (New York, 1961).

ELLI LESTER-MASSMAN

CROLY, JANE CUNNINGHAM (b. 19 December 1829; d. 23 December 1901), journalist and author, used the pseudonym Jennie (Jenny) June professionally. She was the first woman reporter to work at a desk in the city room on a daily basis and the first woman to syndicate her work. She has been credited with establishing the women's page format and with being the forerunner of the trained woman reporter of today. However, she is best remembered for her work in establishing some of the earliest women's clubs and for her championing of working women.

Jane Cunningham was born in Market Harborough, Leicestershire, England, the fourth child of the Reverend Joseph Howes Cunningham and his wife Jane. Her father, a Unitarian minister, moved the family to America in 1841. They lived first in Poughkeepsie, New York, and later in Wappinger Falls, New York. Jane was educated at home, then attended school at Southbridge, Massachusetts. When her formal education ended, she taught district school and later became housekeeper for her brother John, a Congregational minister in Worcester County, Massachusetts.

Her father's death, when Jane was twenty-five, left her in a precarious financial position. She went to New York City to become a journalist, adopting the pen name Jennie June from a poem by Benjamin Taylor. Charles A. Dana (q.v.), then assistant editor of the *New York Tribune*, accepted her first article, launching her on a career which was to last more than forty years. She also wrote bylined articles for the *Sunday Times and Noah's Weekly Messenger*, and for the *New York Herald*. She was a popular and prolific journalist, writing for a female audience on fashion, food, manners, and feminine pastimes.

While at the *New York Herald*, she met David Goodman Croly, later to become editor of the *New York World* and the *New York Daily Graphic*, and to be credited with originating the Sunday newspaper and the illustrated daily. They were married 14 February 1856. They had five children, among them Herbert D. Croly (q.v.), first editor of the *New Republic*. Because of her popularity, Jennie had been able to sell her work simultaneously to several newspapers. In 1856 she expanded her market, selling her material to the *Democratic Review*, the *New Orleans Picayune*, the *Baltimore American*, the *New Orleans Delta*, the *Richmond Enquirer*, and the *Louisville Journal*.

In 1859 the Crolys moved to Rockford, Illinois, where David became editor and publisher of the *Rockford Daily News*. A year later they returned to New York. David joined the *New York Daily World*, and his wife became editor and chief staff writer of the *Demorest Illustrated Monthly*, a position she held for twenty-seven years. In addition, she managed the women's section of the *World* from 1862 to 1872 and wrote women's news, drama, and literary criticism for the *Messenger*, the *Graphic Daily Times*, and the *Weekly Times*.

In 1873 David Croly became editor of the *Daily Graphic*, a new illustrated newspaper, and Jennie joined him there while still syndicating to other papers. In 1887 Jennie bought a half interest in *Godey's Lady's Book*, serving as editor for two years. She also founded the *Women's Cycle*, a magazine for the General Federation of Women's Clubs.

Her pioneer work in the formation of American women's clubs began in 1868 and came about because women journalists were barred from the all-male New York Press Club's reception and banquet for Charles Dickens. The women, including Jennie June, Fanny Fern (see Parton, Sara Willis), Alice Cary, and Kate Field (q.v.), formed their own club in response. It was called Sorosis, a gathering of sisters, and it was one of the earliest women's clubs in America. Jennie was club president in 1868, 1870, 1886, 1887, and 1888. In 1889 she founded the Women's Press Club of New York City and served as its only president until her death. Her pioneer work brought about the consolidation which lead to the General Federation of Women's Clubs in 1898.

Jennie June was the author of seven books. In her later years she was awarded an honorary doctorate from Rutgers Women's College and was appointed to a new chair of journalism and literature there. She taught journalism at Rutgers and at other women's colleges, becoming the first woman to do so.

David Croly died 29 April 1889. An accident in 1898, which left Jennie crippled from a badly healed hip injury, forced her retirement from journalism. She died in New York City 23 December 1901. She was buried beside her husband in the Lakewood, New Jersey, cemetery. Jennie June was a reformer and an innovator. In addition to her work with women's clubs, she called a Woman's Congress in New York in 1856, and again in 1869. She campaigned for women's right to work, financial independence, and economic equality. Her work encompassed crusades for education, justice, and civic and social reform.

BIBLIOGRAPHY:

A. *History of the Women's Club Movement in America* (New York, 1898).

B. DAB 2, 560–561; NYT 24 December 1901; Caroline M. Morse, ed., *Memories of Jane Cunningham Croly "Jennie June"* (New York and London, 1904); Madelon Golden Schilpp and Sharon M. Murphy, *Great Women of the Press* (Carbondale, Ill., 1983).

NORA BAKER

CRONKITE, WALTER LELAND, JR.(b. 4 November 1916) inaugurated the first half-hour network television newscast and was the premier television anchorman for CBS News during the 1960s and 1970s. Cronkite was regarded as the most trusted public figure in America during part of this period due in large measure to his centrist approach to important stories and his participation in the key national and international events of his day. As anchorman for the "CBS Evening News," Cronkite fostered an image of professionalism, insisting on the title "managing editor" to augment his decision-making role in the creation of the nightly newscast. His nightly closing, "And that's the way it is . . . ," became a popular trademark.

Cronkite was born in St. Joseph, Missouri, the only son of Dr. Walter Leland Cronkite and Helen Lena Fritsche Cronkite. He spent his early years in Kansas City until his father, a dentist, decided to move the family to Houston and join the faculty of the University of Texas Dental School. It was in high school in Houston that Cronkite first showed a desire to become a journalist, working as a reporter for the *Campus Cub*. He was educated at the University of Texas from 1933 to 1935, and during this period worked as a stringer for the *Houston Post*, a sports announcer for a small radio station, and a state capital reporter for the International News Service. He left the University of Texas to work full-time for the *Houston Post*. This was followed by reporting assignments with Scripps-Howard in Austin, Texas, and a sportscasting position with WKV Radio in Oklahoma City. He also worked briefly in public relations for Braniff Airways in Kansas City before returning to wire service work in 1939.

He married Mary Elizabeth Simmons Maxwell, a women's page editor for the *Kansas City Journal Post*, in 1940, and for the next nine years he worked for the United Press. The Cronkites have three children: Nancy Elizabeth (Mrs. Gifford Cochran Whitney, b. 1949), Mary Kathleen (b. 1951), and Walter Leland Cronkite III (b. 1958).

Cronkite's national recognition began with America's entry into World War II. He was one of the first American journalists accredited to cover the war effort and was sent to London in 1942, working briefly for Harrison Salisbury (q.v.). It was also at this time that Cronkite made his first appearance in front of the camera. As a war correspondent he flew on numerous missions with Allied forces and reported eyewitness accounts of the North Africa campaign, the invasion of Normandy, and the Battle of the Bulge. At war's end, Cronkite stayed in Europe to help establish United Press bureaus in Belgium, Luxembourg, and the

Netherlands. He served as chief correspondent at the Nuremberg trials and then was sent to Moscow as United Press bureau chief.

Returning to the United States in 1948, Cronkite became Washington, D.C., correspondent for a group of midwestern radio stations headed by KMBC, Kansas City, Missouri. Two years later, with the outbreak of the Korean War, he joined the Columbia Broadcasting System (CBS) but stayed in Washington, assisting in the development of a news department at WTOP-TV, the network's affiliate in the nation's capital. In 1954 he moved to New York City to host CBS network programs including "You Are There" and "The CBS Morning Show." Beginning in 1953 he narrated series such as "Eyewitness to History," "The Twentieth Century," and "The Twenty-First Century."

Cronkite became CBS anchorman in 1962, inheriting this position from Douglas Edwards. The next year CBS introduced the first half-hour network newscast, with Cronkite at the helm. Cronkite competed, unsuccessfully at first, with the NBC-TV news team of Chet Huntley (q.v.) and David Brinkley until Huntley retired in 1970. Cronkite began coverage of national political conventions in 1952, and during his tenure at CBS he covered every major convention for the network with one exception. He was replaced briefly by CBS management in 1964 by the team of Roger Mudd and Robert Trout (q.v.).

Cronkite gained in popularity with coverage of important stories such as the Kennedy assassination and funeral—one of the few times he lost his calm composure on the air. In preparation for coverage of space exploration, Cronkite conducted a careful study and immersed himself in the story, conducting interviews with technical staff and space scientists in visits to Cape Canaveral and Houston. In 1969 he stayed on the air for twenty-four consecutive hours covering the moon landing of *Apollo 11*.

Cronkite visited Southeast Asia in 1965 and returned to Vietnam three years later, after the Tet Offensive. After this second visit, he spoke out against American involvement and questioned prospects for success. In 1968 he protested the actions of Chicago security forces during the Democratic National Convention when CBS correspondent Dan Rather was physically assaulted. He accompanied Richard Nixon to China and Moscow and is credited along with CBS News for the best broadcast coverage of the controversial grain sale to the Soviets and the Watergate story.

He served as host of a special day-long bicentennial celebration for CBS and moderated radio talks with President Jimmy Carter. Toward the end of his career, Cronkite advocated a national hour-long newscast and spoke out against the trend in television journalism toward feature stories and away from hard news. He also condemned the management practice of hiring television news staff without training in journalism. He retired in 1981 but continued, from time to time, to contribute to CBS special projects, especially those dealing with the environment.

BIBLIOGRAPHY:

A. *Challenges of Change* (Washington, D.C., 1971); *Eye on the World* (New York, 1971).

B. CB 1975, 95–98; Les Brown, *The New York Times Encyclopedia of Television* (New York, 1977), 105; Gary Gates, *Air Time: The Inside Story of CBS News* (New York, 1978); David Halberstam, *The Powers That Be* (New York, 1979).

MICHAEL D. MURRAY

CURTIS, CYRUS HERMANN KOTZSCHMAR (b. 18 June 1850; d. 7 June 1933), the founder and publisher of *Ladies' Home Journal*, created a highly successful and extremely profitable magazine business. Recognized for his sharp business acumen and his skill at picking successful editors for his publication, Curtis eventually became the publisher of the *Saturday Evening Post*, the *Country Gentleman*, and several daily newspapers in New York City and Philadelphia. Curtis's incredible wealth and his sizable donations to colleges, hospitals, and museums earned him a reputation as one of the nation's richest and most philanthropic individuals.

Curtis was born in Portland, Maine, the son of German immigrant parents, Cyrus Libby Curtis and Salome Ann Cummings Curtis. His second and third names were those of an old German organist and friend whom his father had convinced to come to Portland. As a twelve-year-old, Curtis began hawking local penny papers to contribute to the family finances. He saved enough money to buy a small, inexpensive printing press and published his first ''newspaper,'' the *Young America*, at age fifteen. Curtis attended public primary schools in Portland and completed only one year of high school. He was forced to quit school after his family lost their home and all their possessions in the Great Portland Fire of 1866.

Curtis started working in a local dry-goods store to help support his family after the Great Fire. In 1869, at age nineteen, he moved to Boston to work as a dry-goods salesman, but eventually took jobs in newspaper advertising with the *Traveller's Guide*, the *Boston Times*, and the *Boston Independent*. In 1872 Curtis started the *People's Ledger*, a weekly that specialized in short stories and features. On 10 March 1875 he married Louisa Knapp, of Boston. Their only child, Mary Louise, later became the wife of Edward W. Bok (q.v.), an editor of the *Ladies' Home Journal*. Fire struck again—this time the Boston fire—and so injured Curtis's news business that he moved his family and newspaper to Philadelphia in 1876. There he sold his presses and became advertising manager for the weekly *Philadelphia Press* in 1878.

Philadelphia, his adopted home, became the center of his publishing ventures. In 1879 Curtis took a partner, Thomas Meehan, and a $2,000 loan and started the *Tribune and Farmer*, which achieved moderate success covering agricultural topics. In the paper, Curtis also edited a column devoted to women's issues. Mrs. Curtis ridiculed her husband's column. Curtis responded by making his wife editor of the women's column. Under her editorship, the column became so popular that it expanded to a full-page section and then to an eight-page supplement called ''The Ladies' Journal'' with a picture of a little house marked ''Home'' between the words. The success of the supplement prompted Curtis to publish the *Ladies' Home Journal* as a separate magazine, and it quickly outgrew the circulation of his newspaper. By 1884 Curtis had sold his share of the *Tribune and Farmer* and devoted his entire time to his new magazine. Louisa Curtis served as editor of the *Ladies' Home Journal* from 1883 to 1889. During that period the magazine reached a circulation of 500,000 and featured some of the finest writers of the day. Edward W. Bok succeeded her as editor and built the magazine's reputation and circulation until it reached 2.6 million readers at the time of Curtis's death in 1933.

In 1891 Curtis established the Curtis Publishing Company as the umbrella organization to cover his increasingly diverse publishing ventures. In 1897 he bought the *Saturday Evening Post*, struggling with only 2,000 subscribers, for only $1,000. After five years and an infusion of $1.25 million, the *Post* became a popular general-circulation magazine. By the time of Curtis's death, the *Saturday Evening Post* reached 2.7 million readers.

In February 1910 Curtis's wife, Louisa, the real genius behind the *Ladies' Home Journal*, died. Curtis was remarried to Kate Stanwood Cutter Pillsbury, the widow of a Milwaukee lumber baron and Curtis's second cousin, on 2 August 1910. In 1911 he acquired the agricultural magazine *Country Gentleman*, then published in Albany, New York. Six years and $2 million later, the *Country Gentleman* was turning a sizable profit.

Curtis returned to the newspaper business and took almost total control of Philadelphia's daily market with a series of acquisitions between 1913 and 1930. In 1913 he bought his first morning daily, Philadelphia's *Morning Public Ledger*, from Aldoph Ochs (q.v.) for $2 million. By September 1914 he added an evening edition. In 1918 he bought the *Philadelphia Telegraph* and merged it with the *Evening Public Ledger*. In 1920 he acquired the *Philadelphia Press*. Curtis also entered the New York newspaper market in 1923 with the purchase of the *New York Evening Post*. In 1925 he purchased the *Philadelphia North American* and established, with John C. Martin as general manager, Curtis-Martin Newspapers to manage his newspaper properties. The last link and the largest morning and Sunday newspaper in Pennsylvania, the *Philadelphia Inquirer*, was finally added to the Curtis-Martin chain in 1930.

Ironically, the sweeping success of his magazines eluded his newspaper ventures. Almost all of his papers struggled with circulation and were generally financial disasters. The *Morning Public Ledger* died shortly after he purchased its competitors; the *New York Evening Post* was sold for only $300,000 after Curtis had pumped in over $10 million to revive it; and the *Philadelphia Inquirer* was bought back by its former owners three years after Curtis's death.

Despite the disappointing performance of his newspaper chain, Curtis enjoyed incredible financial success and literary prestige from his magazines. He understood the reading interests and cultural tastes of middle America and created publications with broad, popular appeal.

Curtis kept watch primarily over the business affairs of his publishing empire, and had relatively little interest in the day-to-day operations of his magazines and newspapers. But however small his role in the editorial process may have been, he clearly set the direction for his magazines. Curtis suffered a heart attack on 24 May 1932 on his yacht, and remained ill at his Wyncote estate until his death in June the following year.

BIBLIOGRAPHY:

B. DAB 21, Supp. 1, 212–213; NYT 7 June 1933; *Philadelphia Public Ledger*, 7–9 June 1933; Edward W. Bok, *A Man from Maine* (New York, 1923).

ROY ALDEN ATWOOD

CURTIS, GEORGE WILLIAM (b. 24 February 1824; d. 31 August 1892) was one of a number of late nineteenth-century intellectuals who have come to be known as embodying the "genteel tradition" in American letters. An essayist, orator, and editor, Curtis devoted his considerable talents to urging participation in public life by the educated and well-born. After achieving early fame as a man of letters, Curtis was best known for the graceful and lucid essays of his regular column, "The Editor's Easy Chair," in *Harper's Monthly*.

Curtis was born into a comfortable and loving family in Providence, Rhode Island. His father, George Curtis, was a banker with political and literary inclinations; his mother, Mary Elizabeth Burrill, died when Curtis was five years old. George William Curtis and his brother Burrill attended boarding schools in Jamaica Plain, Massachusetts, and Providence, Rhode Island. In 1838, George William Curtis applied for admission to Brown University and was rejected, though the institution later awarded him two honorary degrees. Largely self-educated, and greatly influenced by the individualism of Emerson and the transcendentalist writers, both George and Burrill Curtis joined the experimental community at Brook Farm in 1842.

In 1846 George William Curtis left the United States for a four-year tour of Europe. The letters he wrote to the *New York Tribune*, with which he was loosely affiliated, later formed the basis for two travel books, *Nile Notes of a Howadji* (1851) and *The Howadji in Syria* (1852). These books, in keeping with the nineteenth-century vogue for travel literature, gave Curtis almost immediate literary prominence.

When Curtis returned to the United States in 1850, he continued to write essays on music, art, and literature for the *New York Tribune*. In 1852 Horace Greeley (q.v.) sent Curtis on a tour of eastern summer resorts. Again he was able to publish his travel letters on the Catskills, Niagara Falls, Lake George, and Newport in a collection called *Lotus-Eating, a Summer Book* (1852).

In 1853 Curtis was invited to serve as an editor and contributor to *Putnam's Monthly*, a magazine of discriminating literary standards that published the works of American writers. Many of Curtis's sketches and satiric essays that first appeared in *Putnam's* were later collected into *The Potipher Papers* (1853) and *Prue and I* (1856). *Putnam's Monthly* failed in 1857 because, according to Curtis, it was too highbrow for the American reading public.

In 1853, while still working for *Putnam's*, Curtis began a forty-year affiliation with the house of Harper. His column "The Editor's Easy Chair," which appeared in *Harper's Monthly*, touched on a variety of political and social issues. The essays gently satirized the manners and morals of New York society, and called for greater morality and enlightened participation in public life. Also in 1853, Curtis began to develop his oratorical skills. An early member of the Republican party, he stumped for John C. Frémont in 1856, and became known as one of the party's best speakers.

In part as a result of his orations Curtis was, in 1863, appointed political editor of *Harper's Weekly*, a post that he held until his death. While occasionally in conflict with the equally talented and opinionated Thomas Nast (q.v.), Curtis transformed *Harper's Weekly* into a highly influential and popular Republican journal.

George William Curtis remained actively involved in public life after the war, his most important crusade being for the cause of civil service reform. As president of the National Civil Service Reform League, Curtis pressured the Republican party to do away with the abuses of the patronage system. In 1884 Curtis was one of the leaders of the Independent Republican (or "mugwump") bolt from the candidate James G. Blaine, and one of the early supporters of the Democratic candidate Grover Cleveland. Actively involved in education and the promotion of American scholarship, Curtis was in 1864 elected a regent of the University of the State of New York, and in 1890 became its chancellor.

Curtis married Anna Shaw, daughter of prominent Francis George Shaw, on 25 November 1856, and had three children. He died in 1892 of an ailment that was probably cancer of the stomach.

BIBLIOGRAPHY:

A. *From the Easy Chair* (New York, 1893).

B. DAB 2, 614–616; NYT 1 September 1892; Gordon Milne, *George William Curtis and the Genteel Tradition* (Indianapolis, Indiana, 1956).

JANET E. STEELE

DALY, JOHN CHARLES, JR. (b. 20 February 1914) may be best remembered as moderator of the light and entertaining CBS television program ''What's My Line?'' which began in the 1950s. Daly, however, had a long and distinguished career in broadcast journalism which started and ended in radio.

Born in Johannesburg, South Africa, the son of mining engineer John Charles Daly and Helen Grant Tennant Daly, John Charles Daly, Jr., was educated in South Africa at Marist Brothers College until his father died. Thereafter his mother took John and his older brother to the United States. There he was educated at Tilton Academy in New Hampshire, and graduated in 1930. Attending Boston College, Daly worked to pay his expenses as a part-time switchboard operator in a medical building, but had to leave school when he ran out of money. In Boston, Daly also worked as a clerk in a wool firm and appeared briefly with the Peabody Players.

Daly married his first wife, Margaret Criswell Neal, in 1937. They had three children: John Neal, John Charles, and Helene Grant. He divorced Ms. Neal in 1960 and married Virginia Warren daughter of Chief Justice Earl Warren, that year. With her he had three additional children: John Warren, John Earl Jameson, and Nina.

After a brief stint with NBC, Daly began his radio career in earnest in 1937 as White House correspondent for Washington-based CBS station WJSV. He spent the next five years reporting the activities of President Franklin Roosevelt. He also covered the Wendell Willkie campaign, and the Republican and Democratic conventions of 1940. At the other extreme, Daly once reported the hatching of penguins' eggs while he was appropriately dressed in white tie and tails.

Daly was a war correspondent for CBS during World War II, and in 1943 he joined the network's London bureau. He was featured often on the programs

''Spirit of 1941,'' ''Report to the Nation,'' and ''Transatlantic Call'' with the BBC. Daly was CBS's chief correspondent for the war in Italy and landed on Sicilian beaches during the Allied invasion. He covered the fighting at Anzio, the bombardment of Cassino, and the fall of Messina.

In 1944 Daly returned to the United States and was the first reporter to announce the death of President Roosevelt. He also covered the Nuremberg trials, and the first postwar sailing of the liner *Queen Elizabeth*. Daly was host of the radio predecessor to television's famous ''You Are There'' series entitled ''CBS Is There,'' which premiered in July 1947.

Daly is also known for television work. In particular, he appeared first on a program known as ''Celebrity Time.'' Later he became involved in CBS's ''It's News to Me'' and the famous ''What's My Line?'' For a while he also appeared in the last of the ''March of Time Through the Years,'' ''News of Tomorrow,'' and ''This Week Around the World'' for ABC radio where he was a staff news correspondent. In 1958 he hosted a new concert series on ABC, ''Voice of Firestone.'' He even once appeared in an early television version of ''The Front Page'' as Walter Burns, although he regards himself as a reporter and not an actor.

Daly quit ABC in 1960 in a policy dispute with the network president, Leonard Goldenson. At that point he was vice president in charge of news, special events, and public affairs. In 1967 Daly was named director of the Voice of America, succeeding John Chancellor, and was sworn in by his father-in-law, Chief Justice Earl Warren. However, Daly only held the controversy-ridden post for less than one year before resigning, citing ''maladministration'' and differences with U.S. Information Agency director Leonard H. Marks over personnel assignments.

For a while thereafter, Daly served as moderator and host for various broadcast programs, including WNDT's ''Critique'' series. He is past president of the Radio-Television Executives Society.

BIBLIOGRAPHY:

A. *Vital Speeches*, 15 April 1968.

B. NYT 30 May 1967 and 7 June 1968; *Newsweek*, 3 June 1967.

JONATHAN L. YODER

DANA, CHARLES ANDERSON (b. 8 August 1819; d. 17 October 1897) was probably the last great practitioner of personal journalism in New York. For the nearly thirty years he edited the *New York Sun*, the paper was noted for its sparkling wit, its condensation of the news, and its often idiosyncratic editorial views. Though nominally independent, the *Sun* under Dana's editorship generally espoused Democratic party views and attracted a largely Democratic readership. While the paper was most popular with the city's workingmen, the high quality of writing and succinct journalistic style made it notable as the newspaperman's newspaper. A staunch believer in personal journalism, in which a newspaper was intended to express the views of its strong-minded editor, Dana and the *Sun* embodied a style of newspaper writing that died out in the late nineteenth century as journalism became more professional.

Dana was born in Hinsdale, New Hampshire, one of several children of Ann Denison and Anderson Dana, a merchant distantly related to the colonial settler Richard Dana. Repeated business failures plagued Anderson Dana, eventually forcing him to scatter his children among relatives. At the age of twelve, Charles was sent to Buffalo, New York, to clerk in his uncle's general store. In 1839 he enrolled at Harvard College, where he studied for two years, until dwindling financial resources and failing eyesight forced him to leave. In 1841 he joined the experimental association at Brook Farm, and became one of its most committed members, as well as one of the leaders of American Fourierism. On 2 March 1846 he married Eunice MacDaniel, another Brook Farmer.

When Brook Farm burned to the ground in March 1846, Dana took advantage of his connection with Horace Greeley (q.v.) to secure employment on the *New York Tribune*. In 1849 Greeley promoted Dana to managing editor—a new post created expressly for him. Under Greeley's tutelage, Dana developed assumptions about the role of an "independent" editor that stayed with him long after the relationship between the two men ended in bitterness. Greeley fired Dana from the *Tribune* in 1863, ostensibly because of their differences over the paper's course during the sectional crisis, but also because Dana's skills as an editor had begun to rival Greeley's own. After he was fired, Dana used his connections with New York state Republicans to obtain a position as assistant secretary of war, and was soon assigned to the secret duty of investigating Ulysses S. Grant's Mississippi command.

As the war drew to a close, Dana attempted to parlay his Republican connections into another newspaper job. After several false starts, the most notable being the ten months during 1865–66 that he edited the *Chicago Republican*, he returned to New York. There his luck changed when Moses Beach (q.v.), the proprietor of the *New York Sun*, agreed to sell him his complete establishment for $175,000. The *Sun* was already a venerable New York institution when Dana began to publish it in January 1868; founded in 1833 by Benjamin Day (q.v.), it was the city's first "penny paper," and a loyal partisan of the Democratic party.

Most observers expected Dana, who was seemingly allied with the radical wing of the Republican party, to transform the *Sun* into a Republican journal. Instead Dana arrived at a strategy that not only kept his Democratic readers and Republican stockholders happy, but also demonstrated his brilliance as a journalist and his skill as a mediator. Dana took the familiar mid-century ideas of personal journalism and the independent press, and from them forged a daily unlike anything New Yorkers had ever seen. The *Sun* had a unique appeal in an era that was characterized by intense partisanship; by trumpeting the virtues of political independence and impartiality, Dana drew upon the deeply rooted American values of individualism and freedom of self-expression.

The *New York Sun* was the city's most popular daily newspaper during the 1870s. Its supremacy stemmed from its breezy championing of the common man, its lively reporting of the news, and its playfulness, all of which disguised a profound ability to communicate with different groups in a socially fragmented metropolis. Dana's editorials were at the heart of the paper's popularity. As his views became more closely allied with those of the Democrats as the decade wore on, the paper drew upon an ever-growing pool of immigrant and working-class readers.

Dana and the *Sun* began to lose their dominant position in the New York press in the mid–1880s. A number of factors influenced the *Sun*'s decline. Most obvious was Joseph Pulitzer's (q.v.) 1883 purchase of the *New York World*, which challenged the *Sun* for its largely Democratic readership of merchants and mechanics. Coincident with this was Dana's personal dislike of Grover Cleveland, the 1884 Democratic presidential nominee, and his support of Benjamin Butler, the Greenback-Labor candidate. By the time the election was over, the *Sun* had lost somewhere between sixty and seventy thousand readers. But probably most significant was the increasing professionalization of journalism, with its emphasis on objectivity, marketing techniques, and enshrinement of news over editorial opinion. Dana's unwillingness to relinquish his individual control of the *Sun* as a vehicle for his personal views meant that the paper's circulation steadily declined over the remainder of the century. By the time that Dana died on 17 October 1897, the *New York Sun* was but a shadowy remnant of its former self. After Dana's death, editorial control of the *Sun* passed into the hands of his son, Paul Dana.

BIBLIOGRAPHY:

A. *The Art of Newspaper Making, Three Lectures* (New York, 1895); *Eastern Journeys* (New York, 1898).

B. DAB 3, 49–52; NYT 18 October 1897; Edward P. Mitchell, *Memoirs of an Editor* (New York, 1924); Frank M. O'Brien, *The Story of the Sun* (New York, 1918); Candace Stone, *Dana and the Sun* (New York, 1938); James Harrison Wilson, *The Life of Charles Anderson Dana* (New York, 1907).

JANET E. STEELE

DANIELS, JOSEPHUS (b. 18 May 1862; d. 15 January 1948) successfully combined a newspaper career with government service. His long editorship of the *Raleigh News and Observer* in Raleigh, North Carolina, made him known nationally as a farseeing and competent journalist, and his tenure as secretary of the navy under Woodrow Wilson and as ambassador to Mexico under Franklin Roosevelt demonstrated rare ability in administration and diplomacy.

Daniels, the second of three surviving sons of Josephus Daniels and Mary Cleaves Seabrook Daniels, was born in Washington, North Carolina, as the Civil War was raging. Daniels's father, a shipwright, died in 1865 and his mother moved the family to Wilson, North Carolina, where she became a seamstress and postmaster. Daniels studied in Wilson's one-room school and in the nine-month term of the Wilson Collegiate Institute. He left school in 1880 to become local editor of the *Wilson Advance*, a weekly he bought two years later. He developed the style of a hard-hitting champion of reform and of the Democratic party. He showed deep concern for the underdog and advocated prohibition and federal aid to education, ideas that were pervasive throughout his career.

After becoming a partner in two other rural weeklies, he was elected president of the state press association at age twenty-two. His only experience with higher education came during the summer of 1885 when he studied law at the University of North Carolina. He passed the bar exam, and although he never practiced law, he believed a knowledge of law was helpful to a journalist. Daniels took over a struggling weekly, the *Raleigh State Chronicle*, in 1885 and published it for a while as a daily before selling it in 1892. After starting a small weekly, the *North Carolinian*, he left for Washington, D.C., to work in the Grover Cleveland administration, first as chief of the appointments division and then as chief clerk in the Interior Department. He remained in Washington two years, 1893–95. In 1894 he combined the *North Carolinian* with the *Raleigh News and Observer*, which he owned the rest of his life and which he used to fight special interests, demand more effective control of trusts and railroads, expose corruption, and condemn vice and the liquor traffic.

Daniels boasted on the mast of his paper that it was "the only daily paper in the world having more subscribers than population of the city in which published." His viewpoints on the need for reform were not appreciated by everyone, and some nicknamed his paper the "Nuisance and Disturber."

Beginning in 1896 he served for many years on the Democratic National Committee, and was secretary of the navy through Wilson's two terms. As secretary, he instituted many reforms, with the banning of liquor from officers' messes perhaps the most noticed. Franklin Roosevelt was assistant secretary and, upon becoming president in 1933, named Daniels as ambassador to Mexico, a position he held until late 1941. After leaving government service, Daniels returned to the editorship of his paper. He received many honorary degrees and served forty-seven years as a trustee of the University of North Carolina.

Daniels was married on 2 May 1888 to Addie Worth Bagley, the granddaughter of a North Carolina governor. They had five children, one of whom, a daughter, died in infancy. Three of his sons, Josephus Jr., Frank, and Jonathan, held positions on the *News and Observer*, and Worth was a physician. Mrs. Daniels died on 19 December 1943. Daniels was still active on the newspaper until he died of pneumonia on 15 January 1948. Among those expressing regret at Daniels's death was President Harry Truman. Daniels was remembered as a warm, friendly man who nourished a deep religious faith and a lifelong love of journalism.

BIBLIOGRAPHY:

A. *Tar Heel Editor* (Chapel Hill, 1939); *Editor in Politics* (Chapel Hill, 1941); *The Wilson Era: Years of Peace* (Chapel Hill, 1944); *The Wilson Era: Years of War and After* (Chapel Hill, 1946); *Shirt-Sleeve Diplomat* (Chapel Hill, 1947).

B. DAB Supp. 4, 215–218; NYT 16 January 1948; Joseph L. Morrison, *Josephus Daniels: The Small-d Democrat* (Chapel Hill, 1966).

DENNIE HALL

DARLING, JAY NORWOOD (b. 21 October 1876; d. 12 February 1962) was one of the world's most prolific editorial cartoonists and a staunch supporter of efforts to conserve America's natural resources. He took time out of his career with the *Des Moines Register* to serve as chief of the Bureau of Biological Survey in the U.S. Department of Agriculture while Franklin D. Roosevelt was president. He also served as president of the National Wildlife Federation.

Darling, the second child of the Reverend Marcellus W. Darling and Clara R. Woolson, was born in Norwood, Michigan, while his father was a Methodist pastor there. In the fall of 1894 Darling entered Yankton College in South Dakota but transferred in the fall of 1895 to Beloit College in Wisconsin. At Beloit he was art editor of the *Codex*, the college yearbook. He signed his artwork, "Ding," a contraction of his surname which was a nickname given to his father and his brother Frank as well. Darling was suspended from Beloit after his junior year ostensibly because of poor grades and erratic class attendance. However, the suspension came a few days after the publication of the *Codex* which contained unflattering caricatures of faculty members.

During the year away from Beloit, Darling traveled in the southeastern United States and served briefly as a reporter for the *Sioux City Tribune* in Iowa. He returned to Beloit and received a bachelor's degree in 1900. Darling returned to Sioux City upon graduation and became a reporter for the *Sioux City Journal*.

In his free moments, Darling made sketches of well-known Sioux City citizens and kept the drawings in his desk at the *Journal*. When an attorney refused to allow Darling to take a photograph to use with a trial story, Darling used a sketch he had made instead. The sketch received favorable comments and the editor began using other Darling caricatures.

On 31 October 1906 Ding married Genevieve Pendleton, a Sioux City physical therapist, and soon after he accepted an offer to become the cartoonist for the *Des Moines Register and Leader*. In November 1911 Ding left Des Moines and moved to New York City. He signed a contract to produce cartoons for the *New York Globe* and a syndicate started by the *Globe*. He was not comfortable in the metropolitan environment and with the editorial policy of the *Globe*. Early in 1913 he returned to the *Des Moines Register and Leader*, which placed his cartoons on the front page and allowed him to express any opinion without censorship.

On 21 October 1916 Darling signed a ten-year contract to produce cartoons for the *New York Tribune* syndicate in addition to his work for the *Register and Leader*. He lived in New York City for several months in 1918–19, but then returned to Des Moines. His most popular cartoon was "The Long, Long Trail," which was produced following the death of Theodore Roosevelt in January 1919. In 1924 he was awarded a Pulitzer Prize for a cartoon he drew in 1923 titled "In Good Old U.S.A." He was awarded a second Pulitzer in 1943.

Darling frequently suffered from physical problems including arthritis, bronchial asthma attacks, cataracts, deafness, heart irregularities, and soreness of the arm. In March 1925 he contracted peritonitis and it appeared for several weeks that he was near death.

From 10 March 1934 to 15 November 1935, Darling served as chief of the U.S. Bureau of Biological Survey. Later in the decade he was elected president of the National Wildlife Federation. When he returned to the *Des Moines Register and Tribune* in 1935, Darling was a stockholder and a director of the parent corporation as well as the newspaper's chief cartoonist. He retired from the *Register and Tribune* in April 1949. He died in Des Moines following a stroke. His wife died on 13 December 1968. The couple had two children: John and Mary.

BIBLIOGRAPHY:

A. *Ding's Half Century* (New York, 1962).

B. NYT 13 February 1962; David L. Lendt, *Ding: The Life of Jay Norwood Darling* (Ames, Iowa, 1979).

DONALD L. MCBRIDE

DAVENPORT, HOMER CALVIN (b. 8 March 1867; d. 2 May 1912) became famous as a political cartoonist, first on William Randolph Hearst's (q.v.) *San Francisco Examiner* and then later on Hearst's *New York Journal*. Davenport's cartoons have been credited with being a major factor in the election of Theodore Roosevelt as president.

Davenport was born near Silverton, Oregon. His father, Timothy Davenport, was a physician, surveyor, legislator, farmer, and storekeeper. His mother, Florinda Geer Davenport, crossed the plains at fourteen and settled near Silverton. She died when Homer was three-and-one-half years old. His father later remarried. Davenport had an older sister, four half-sisters, and a half-brother from his father's two marriages.

Davenport first published as a newspaper artist at age twenty-two in the *Portland Oregonian*. He worked as a free-lance artist covering the Dempsey-Fitzsimmons championship fight in New Orleans and submitted his drawings to the *Sunday Mercury*, a sporting weekly.

He was employed briefly as an artist with the *San Francisco Examiner* and, later, with the *San Francisco Chronicle*. In 1893 he worked on the *Chicago Daily Herald* before coming back to work on the *Chronicle*. Here he came to the attention of Hearst, who hired Davenport to be his chief cartoonist on the *Examiner*. His ability as an image maker and a deflator of the political figures of the day soon enhanced his reputation. But it was when Hearst bought the *New York Journal* and brought Davenport with him in 1895 that the cartoonist's reputation became international.

Davenport's cartoons, among them political boss Mark Hanna, replete with a suit of dollar signs, are classics in political cartooning. His reputation soared under the astute direction of Hearst, and he was considered the equal of Thomas

Nast (q.v.). At his peak with Hearst, Davenport was earning $25,000 a year, the largest salary a cartoonist had received to that time.

Affable and well-liked, Davenport was the confidant and friend of the rich and famous. He was married in Chicago on 7 September 1893 to Daisy Moore. The Davenports had three children: Homer Clyde, Mildred, and Gloria. The marriage lasted sixteen years, although it was troubled almost from the beginning. His unhappy marriage and separation from his children caused Davenport severe mental stress.

Davenport left the *New York Journal* and Hearst over the presidential candidacy of Theodore Roosevelt. The cartoonist had lambasted Roosevelt in the past, but a curious turnaround and a $25,000 offer for six months of work by the *Evening Mail* caused Davenport to create a drawing that was credited with helping to elect Roosevelt. The drawing showed Uncle Sam standing behind Roosevelt, one hand on the president's shoulder, with the caption ''He's good enough for me.'' The Republican party spent $200,000 to distribute the cartoon nationally, and it was dubbed the greatest vote-getting cartoon in American history. Roosevelt was later to repay the debt. Davenport, traveling to the deserts of Arabia in 1906, had made arrangements to buy Arabian horses. Encountering some difficulty, Davenport cabled the president, who saw to it that the twenty-seven Arabian horses could come to the United States. The importation of these horses was the basis for the Arabian horse industry.

Hearst invited Davenport to return to the *New York American*. On 15 April 1912 the *Titanic* sank with heavy loss of life. Davenport's drawing, depicting an arm reaching out of the sea to pull the *Titanic* under, is considered a classic. Less than a month after the *Titanic*'s sinking, Davenport died of pneumonia on 2 May 1912. It was said that the strain of illustrating the disaster was a major factor in his death.

BIBLIOGRAPHY:

B. DAB 3, 83–84; NYT 3 May 1912.

THEODORE H. CARLSON

DAVIS, ELMER (b. 13 January 1890; d. 18 May 1958), a reporter, editorial writer, magazine free-lancer, novelist, and broadcast commentator, was a man of all media. But his most important work was done for, rather than in, those media. As the director of the Office of War Information (OWI) from 1942 to 1945, Davis was responsible for getting accurate news about the war effort to the press, and through it to the American people.

Elmer Holmes Davis was born in Aurora, Indiana. The son of Elam and Louise Severin Davis, he received the B.A. (1910) and M.A. (1911) degrees from Franklin College. Davis also was a Rhodes scholar and received a second B.A. from Queens College, Oxford in 1912. It was while studying at Oxford that Davis first became interested in politics and foreign affairs, traveling extensively through Europe during school holidays and after graduation. It was on one of these trips that he met Florence MacMillan of Mount Vernon, New York. They were married in 1917 and had two children, Robert and Caroline.

Davis's travels ended when his father died in 1913. He returned home to become a writer. Davis spent a year as assistant editor of *Adventure* magazine, and then accepted a position at the *New York Times*. In the next ten years, Davis rose from cub reporter to foreign correspondent and editorial writer. Although he wrote a history of the paper in 1921, his most important work at the *Times* was a Mr. Dooley-esque creation named Godfrey Gloom. This character was resurrected to provide acerbic commentary on four presidential campaigns from 1920 to 1936.

While with the *Times*, Davis began to write novels, short stories and articles. His moderate success convinced him to become a full-time free-lancer in 1924. In the next fifteen years, Davis published nine novels and a number of essays and sketches on a variety of topics. These were printed in such magazines as the *New Yorker*, the *Saturday Review of Literature*, *New Republic, Collier's,* and *Harper's*. It was in *Harper's* that Davis published a series of articles analyzing the situation in Europe in 1937 and 1938. The perceptive pieces were so well regarded that Davis was hired by the Columbia Broadcasting System (CBS) as a political commentator to replace the Europe-bound H. V. Kaltenborn (q.v.). Davis was an immediate success at CBS. His straightforward and calm reports of the growing international crisis won him an audience of more than twelve million by 1941.

Davis's reputation for truthfulness led to his 1942 OWI appointment by President Franklin D. Roosevelt. Under Davis, OWI served as a coordinating agency and central clearinghouse for news about the war effort. In this way, he opened the lines of communication through the American media and to the people concerning developments at the front and in government war programs. The OWI also planned and executed the government's information and propaganda activities outside the United States and engaged in psychological warfare in enemy-occupied areas.

OWI was disbanded in 1945 and Davis returned to radio broadcasting as a regular commentator for the American Broadcasting Company. The number of broadcasts he did per week varied with his health, but all were characterized by calm, common sense, historical accuracy, and objectivity. As the decade drew to a close, those broadcasts began to focus increasingly on the anticommunist hysteria that was sweeping the United States. A rationalist and a libertarian, Davis was appalled by McCarthyite attacks on American individuals and institutions. In his broadcasts, Davis spoke against the House Un-American Activities Committee and for beleaguered public servants, entertainers, and academics. This defense of civil liberties won him the George Foster Peabody Radio Award in 1951. Davis also took his philosophy on the road, speaking throughout the country on the need to defend freedom of thought. His speeches were published as *But We Were Born Free* (1954). His last book, *Two Minutes Till Midnight* (1955), dealt with the threat of nuclear war.

In 1954 Davis moved from radio to television commentary, but this stage of his career was a short one. Advancing heart disease forced him to give up the microphone. He died in Washington, D.C., in 1958.

BIBLIOGRAPHY:

B. DAB Supp. 6, 148–149; NCAB 50, 13; NYT 19 May 1958; *Indiana Authors and Their Books, 1816–1916*, 82–83; Roger Burlingame, *Don't Let Them Scare You* (Philadelphia, 1961).

LYNNE MASEL-WALTERS

DAVIS, RICHARD HARDING (b. 18 April 1864; d. 11 April 1916) was a newspaper reporter, magazine writer and editor, playwright and fiction writer whose byline was one of the most popular of the 1890s and early 1900s. As one of the premier journalists of his time, he perfected the role of the gentleman reporter in search of action and adventure, establishing the world as his beat from about 1895 until his death. He scored his greatest journalistic successes as a war correspondent, and helped popularize the "glamour-boy" school of war reporting.

Davis's desire to be a writer developed early and was encouraged by his parents, both of whom were writers. His father, L. Clarke Davis, was a Philadelphia lawyer by training but a journalist and author by choice. His mother, Rebecca Blaine Harding Davis, was a pioneer of the realistic movement in fiction, having published her most significant work in the 1860s. Davis did not care much for Philadelphia, where he was born and raised, but he thought highly of his family and was strongly influenced by his mother, who remained a confidante and adviser even after he was a noted writer.

Although he attended Lehigh University and Johns Hopkins University, Davis was a poor student and failed to receive a degree. He did, however, begin writing in college and determined at that time to become a successful journalist. His first newspaper job on the *Philadelphia Record* in 1886 ended after only three months when he was fired for incompetence. But Davis took his next job, on the *Philadelphia Press*, more seriously and he made a point to learn from the veteran reporters, willingly covered a wide range of stories, and developed the personal, impressionistic style of writing that became his trademark.

While at the *Press*, he helped found, and wrote for and edited, the *Stage*, a weekly that carried news and commentary on the theater, especially actors and acting. Davis maintained a lifelong interest in the theater, and wrote dramatizations of several of his short stories. A number of his original plays, including *The Dictator* (1904), *The Galloper*, *Miss Civilization* (1905), and *Who's Who* (1913), were critical and box-office successes, but were not strong enough to win Davis acclaim as a first-rate playwright.

At the *Press*, he distinguished himself with his coverage of the aftermath of the Johnstown flood in June 1889, and by the fall of that year he was reporting for the *New York Evening Sun*, where he stayed until February 1891 when he became managing editor of *Harper's Weekly*. Davis considered the entire city his beat at the *Sun*, and covered crime and courts, but also wrote short vignettes that contained little news value but depicted human behavior. He often provided accounts of "slumming" expeditions involving his high-society friends and their ladies. He also created for the newspaper his fictional character Charlie "Rags" Raegan, a New York City tough who lived in the tenements and was always in trouble with the law.

As editor of *Harper's Weekly*, Davis favored features and news on sports and the theater, and subjects of interest to New Yorkers, and he hired bright, young reporters, such as David Graham Phillips (q.v.) and Stephen Bonsal, to write the articles. Davis frequently left his editor's chair to gather material for travel articles. In 1892, for example, he toured the West and Southwest and wrote articles that were collected and published as *The West from a Car-Window*. In the same year, he visited England and wrote about the country's social life in articles that appeared in *Our English Cousins* (1894). The Harper brothers desired a more sedentary editor, and in 1893 Davis entered into an agreement that allowed him to be an associate editor and travel and write as well. But little of his work appeared in *Harper's* in 1894, and after 1895 much of it was published in *Scribner's*.

Also in 1895, Davis wrote his first story for William Randolph Hearst (q.v.) and the *New York Journal* when he was paid the then-large sum of $500 to report on the Yale-Princeton football game. That essentially started a successful and lucrative period of free-lancing, as Davis became a much-demanded special correspondent who was called upon to cover the world's major events. From 1896 to 1897 his assignments varied, from the coronation of Czar Nicholas II in Moscow to the inauguration of William McKinley in Washington, from the Greco-Turkish War to the Cuban insurrection. The articles written at this time were collected in *A Year from a Reporter's Notebook* (1898).

Davis continued covering events and wars, finishing his career with the armies fighting World War I. His account of the German army marching into Brussels has been called his finest effort at war reporting, and a classic of the genre. Davis produced at least three nonfiction versions: a dispatch for the *New York Tribune* (24 August 1914), an article for *Scribner's*, and a part of a chapter in *With the Allies*. A fictional account is given in "Somewhere in France." Davis wrote fiction throughout his career, publishing his work in magazines and books, producing in all seven novels and eighty short stories, from *Gallegher and Other Stories* in 1891 to *The Boy Scout* in 1914.

Although some contemporaries of Davis claimed that he twisted the facts for effect and that he was more of a star writer than a "real" reporter, his reputation as the preeminent journalist of his day has stood over time, as has the stature of his war reporting. Many have testified, and others have verified, that he influenced other reporters and the period itself, and that he was truly a representative figure of his age.

Davis was married twice. His first marriage, to Cecil Clark on 4 May 1899, ended in divorce; he married Elizabeth Genevieve McCoy on 8 July 1912. The second marriage produced one daughter, Hope Harding Davis. He died suddenly just short of his fifty-second birthday at his home in Mount Kisco, New York.

BIBLIOGRAPHY:

A. *Cuba in War Time* (New York, 1897; *Notes of a War Correspondent* (New York, 1910).

B. DAB 5, 144–145; NYT 13 April 1916; Gerald Langford, *The Richard Harding Davis Years: A Biography of a Mother and Son* (New York, 1961); Scott C. Osborn and Robert L. Phillips, Jr., *Richard Harding Davis* (Boston, 1978).

THOMAS CONNERY

DAVIS, THEODORE RUSSELL (b. 1840; d. 10 November 1894) worked twenty-three years as the most traveled of the special artists for *Harper's Weekly* covering the Civil War and subsequent campaigns against American Indians. He is best known for his sketches and articles about frontier life in the late 1860s.

Born in Boston, Davis was educated at Rittenhouse Academy in Washington, D.C. At fifteen, he moved to Brooklyn, where he received some training from a wood engraver, and within a year he had exhibited a crayon drawing. He joined the staff of *Harper's Weekly* in 1861 as a traveling artist and made one trip through the South before the war. Believing that special artists must see the most dramatic scenes of a battle, Davis often exposed himself to enemy fire. He was twice wounded during the Civil War and was said to have held off at gunpoint surgeons who wanted to amputate his leg. Davis was with General Ulysses S. Grant at Vicksburg in 1863, and he was the only artist with General William T. Sherman during the Atlanta campaign in 1864. He witnessed the major battles at Shiloh and Antietam and the fight between the *Monitor* and the *Merrimac*.

Davis was one of the most prolific of the Civil War artists, and he revealed much about how he worked. He suffered many close calls and tense moments. As early as June 1861 he was searched by members of a Memphis vigilance committee, some of whom took sketches. His only revenge was to sketch and publish an illustration of the ordeal. Davis also told of having his sketchbook shot out of his hands and how one night he shared his blanket with a soldier who stopped a fatal bullet which otherwise would have claimed the artist. Jerky marks here and there on sketches, he later wrote, indicated an unsteady pencil in an unsafe position. Davis made "sketch notes" under fire which he later completed with details. A sketchbook filled during calmer times provided details on uniforms and military equipment.

En route to his postwar assignment in the West, Davis was in a mule-drawn Concord stagecoach that was attacked by Indians in late November, 1865. The account and sketch published the following April became the prototype for thousands of Wild West show, motion picture, and television reenactments of wild savages attacking the stagecoach with its frightened passengers and a colorful driver. Davis was on the first Indian campaign to be accompanied by reporters. He and Henry M. Stanley, who represented the *Weekly Missouri*

Democrat and the *New York Tribune*, accompanied General Winfield S. Hancock and Lieutenant Colonel George A. Custer on the summer 1867 campaign against Sioux, Cheyenne, Arapahoes, Kiowa, and Comanches in Kansas and Nebraska. Hancock, whom Davis knew during the Civil War, invited the special artist who was stationed in Denver. Davis described councils with the Indians, mutilated white bodies discovered by soldiers, and the cavalry's burning of an Indian village. His articles included details of daily life among both Indians and soldiers, and he consistently supported calls for a military solution. In August he left the West after spending four months in the saddle and covering 3,000 miles.

Davis continued to sketch and write about the West, apparently from memory and imagination. In 1879 he designed the Haviland state dinner service for the White House. In the 1880s he was historical consultant for large cyclorama paintings of the battles of Missionary Ridge and Atlanta. Throughout his career, he contributed articles under various names to such metropolitan newspapers as the *Rocky Mountain Weekly News* of Denver, and the *New York Tribune, Sun,* and *Herald*. His first-person narrative and eye for detail engaged readers. Unfortunately, few of his original drawings remain; the published illustrations were, of course, redrawn or traced on wood blocks which were then carved by engravers. Davis's engraving experience gave him the talent to provide sketches that required little change before publication.

In 1884 Davis retired from *Harper's* to do free-lance work. For health reasons, he had moved to Asbury Park, New Jersey, where he died in1894 after a lingering illness with Bright's disease. He left a widow and two daughters.

BIBLIOGRAPHY:

B. *Asbury Park Press*, 10 November 1894; Edgar M. Howell, ''A Special Artist in the Indian Wars,'' *Montana, the Magazine of Western History*, Spring 1965; Robert Taft, ''Theodore R. Davis and Alfred R. Waud,'' in *Artists and Illustrators of the Old West 1850–1900* (New York, 1953).

WILLIAM E. HUNTZICKER

DAY, BENJAMIN HENRY (b. 11 April 1810; d. 21 December 1989) remade American journalism ''more by accident than by design'' when he founded the *New York Morning Sun*, the nation's first successful penny paper in 1833. Yet, despite a long and prosperous publishing and printing career, he left little of a personal record. Most of what is known about him came in an 1883 interview.

Although the *Sun* was his chief achievement—he sold it in 1838 to his brother-in-law, Moses Y. Beach (q.v.), ''the silliest thing I ever did''—Day also was involved in the publication of other New York papers. These included a successful literary weekly, *Brother Jonathan* (ca. 1844–61), the *Evening Tattler* (1839–42), and the weekly *True Sun* (1843–48). He seems more a busy job printer and shrewd publisher than an editor.

A native of West Springfield, Massachusetts, Day was the son of Henry Day, a hatter, and Mary Ely, daughter of an old Connecticut family. He attended school at the Munson Academy, in Munson, Connecticut, and then was apprenticed to a printer, Samuel Bowles, Sr., who had just started the later famed *Springfield Republican*. At nineteen, he went to New York, hoping to establish his own printing office, and worked as a journeyman on the *Journal of Commerce*, the *Post*, and the *Courier and Enquirer*. Late in 1829 he was one of six practical printers who announced plans to publish the *New York Sentinel*, a daily which would support the new Workingmen's party. Before it finally emerged, however, he had dropped his involvement, and his longtime friend, George Henry Evans (q.v.), took his place. Later in the 1830s, he became printer for Frances Wright's (q.v.) *Free Enquirer*, although after she had withdrawn from it. In 1831 he married his cousin, Eveline Shepherd, a schoolteacher, who died in 1885. They had four children, Benjamin, Henry, Clarence, and Mary. The younger Benjamin, an artist, gave his name to the Benday screening process.

In early 1883 he established his own printing office in a three-story building at 222 William Street, a site now occupied by Pace University. But competition for printing work was strong. A fellow compositor, David Ramsey, Day recollected much later, had long talked about putting out a little people-oriented paper to be called the *Sun*. Day decided to put out a "handbill" type paper, to be called the *Sun*, which would both give the news of the day briefly and advertise his printing office. The first number, with a run of 1,000, was put together by Day and one assistant, with advertising and copy lifted from other newspapers. The tiny paper, three columns, four pages, sold well, but Day—never himself a writer—wanted an editor, and ultimately hired George W. Wisner (q.v.), also a young printer, who soon was specializing in police reporting. Day, in 1883, said this was his idea; yet Wisner was the one who brilliantly carried it forward. Circulation zoomed, and after two years was at the 20,000 mark. Wisner became a partner in the enterprise.

Day, as senior editor, gave the paper its editorial direction, although he admitted that he "neglected" it in late 1833 after he got a fat printing contract for the *American Museum*. He, rather than the politically minded Wisner, insisted that the paper be politically neutral; he organized the newsboy system, with youngsters "yelling" and selling the paper on the streets, under the "London plan" which provided him with an immediate cash return. He showed—as a Democrat—his sympathy with New York workingmen; and, as a shrewd business man, kept firm track of the advertisements, consistently upgrading his equipment, including a steam press. Also, probably even more than the well-read Wisner, he insisted that each edition carry educational material—poetry, essays, and book excerpts. "More by accident than by design," as he said later, he had lit on the formula for a popular press.

In 1835 Wisner sold his share in the paper to Day for $5,300. He was replaced as editor by Richard Adams Locke (q.v.), a reporter who gave the *Sun* enduring notoriety through his "Moon Hoax," a fictitious account of life on the moon. The depression of 1837, and the rise of competition, brought problems for Day. The paper was just meeting expenses, and he still had his other printing business.

He sold the *Sun* to Beach for $40,000. The Beach family continued with the paper until it was sold to Charles A. Dana (q.v.).

Day tried to get back into the newspaper business in 1839 with the *Evening Tattler*, but later sold it. He then joined with J. Gregg Wilson to bring out *Brother Jonathan*, which specialized in textual reprints, in a large format, of British novels and articles from British literary magazines. The novels subsequently were republished in pamphlet form. About 1843, he brought out the weekly *True Sun*. At its peak, *Brother Jonathan*, for which Nathaniel P. Willis at one time was editor, had a circulation of 70,000, and a monthly edition named the *Dollar*. When Day finally closed out his participation in it, he was a wealthy man and lived on his income, although he dabbled with the publication of low-priced manuals and other short works. His recounting of his publishing career came in an 1883 interview with Edward P. Mitchell for the fiftieth anniversary edition of the *Sun*. He died in 1889, after catching a severe cold, and was buried in Woodlawn cemetery.

BIBLIOGRAPHY:

B. DAB 3, 155; NCAB 12, 307; NYT 22 December 1889; *New York Sun*, 2 September 1933; Frank M. O'Brien, *The Story of the Sun* (New York, 1918).

JAMES STANFORD BRADSHAW

DAY, DOROTHY (b. 8 November 1897; d. 29 November 1980) was a major figure in twentieth-century American social radicalism and advocacy journalism. A voice of conscience in the Roman Catholic church, she championed peace and social justice in the *Catholic Worker*, the penny monthly she cofounded in 1933, then edited and published for nearly fifty years.

Day was born in Brooklyn Heights, New York, the third of five children of Grace Satterlee Day and John I. Day. Her mother came from an established Marlboro, New York, family of merchants, craftspeople, whalers, and mill workers. Mrs. Day once worked in a Poughkeepsie shirt factory and was one of the first women trained in stenography. Day's Scotch-Irish father belonged to a Cleveland, Tennessee, family of farmers and physicians. He was an itinerant newspaperman who helped found the Hialeah racetrack in Florida, and was sports editor of the *Chicago Inter Ocean*. Later he became racing editor of the *New York Morning Telegraph*. Two of Day's brothers had distinguished journalism careers: Sam Houston Day as managing editor of the *New York Journal-American*, and Donald Day as a reporter for Chicago's *Day Book*, sports editor of the *Journal-American*, and later Baltic correspondent for the *Chicago Tribune*.

In 1916, after two unsatisfying years at the University of Illinois, Dorothy Day realized that journalism was also her calling, and moved to New York with her family to find a job on a newspaper. Her father, who opposed women in careers—especially in journalism—instructed his city editor friends to send her home with a lecture on women's proper place. She then persuaded the editor of the socialist *New York Call* to hire her as a reporter. The following year she began to write for Max Eastman's (q.v.) *Masses*, almost single-handedly editing the August 1917 issue that attracted the notice of government censors. She also wrote pieces for its successor, the *Liberator*.

As a journalist for these publications during the Jazz Age, Day belonged to the New York literary and social avant-garde. Her companions included Eugene O'Neill, Michael Gold, Caroline Gordon, Allen Tate, Malcolm Cowley, John Dos Passos, and Hart Crane. Friendly with socialists, communists, and other radicals, she seemed destined for an editorial career among secular, leftist publications. But all this changed in 1927, two years after she entered into a short-lived common-law marriage with Forster Batterham. The birth of her daughter Tamar Teresa that year led Day to join the Catholic church, which she felt was the church for the poor. Thereafter, for the rest of her life, she sought to combine her profound religious faith with the equally deep compassion for the poor she had developed as a young American social radical.

In New York City during the depths of the depression, she cofounded, with Peter Maurin, the *Catholic Worker*, to popularize papal encyclicals on issues of social justice and peace. The organ of their Catholic Workers movement (which established houses of hospitality to shelter and feed the poor across the United States and abroad), the paper was also produced largely by lay people, without official ties to the Catholic church. Its contributors included Michael Harrington, Thomas Merton, Martin Buber, Jacques Maritain, Danilo Dolci, Claude McKay, Daniel and Philip Berrigan, and J. F. Powers, with illustrations by Fritz Eichenberg and Ade Bethune. Day was a frequent contributor of muckracking reports, essays, reviews, and columns.

From the beginning, the *Catholic Worker* was her paper; she chose the content, wrote much of the copy, and often designed the layout. As editor and publisher for nearly fifty years, until her death from heart disease, Day kept the *Catholic Worker* editorially consistent and absolutely pacifist through several major American wars. For this both the secular and the conservative Catholic press often attacked her. But Day never criticized Catholic teachings, only the church's failure to live up to them.

In part through her diplomacy and personal example (she lived in voluntary poverty and went to jail several times for civil disobedience), Day eventually won a following. Growing admiration for Day's ideas and activities prompted the University of Notre Dame to present her with its prestigious Laetare Medal in 1972, as an outstanding American Catholic. In their 1983 pastoral letter on war and peace, which represented a historic shift in their viewpoint, the American Catholic bishops singled out Day's contribution in sustaining the peace ideal.

Dorothy Day's impact reached far beyond the Catholic Left and Catholicism. Through her journalism she challenged several generations of Americans to scrutinize their commitment to social justice and peace. Writing in *Commonweal* in 1982, historian David J. O'Brien called Day "the most significant, interesting, and influential person in the history of American Catholicism."

BIBLIOGRAPHY:

A. *The Long Loneliness: The Autobiography of Dorothy Day* (New York, 1952); *On Pilgrimage: The Sixties* (New York, 1973).

B. NYT 30 November and 1 December 1980; Patrick G. Coy, ed., *Revolution of the Heart: Essays on the Catholic Worker* (Philadelphia, 1988); Nancy L. Roberts, *Dorothy Day and the "Catholic Worker"* (Albany, 1984).

NANCY L. ROBERTS

DEALEY, GEORGE BANNERMAN (b. 18 September 1859; d. 26 February 1946), known as the dean of American journalism at the time of his death, was unique among American journalists in terms of service to one organization. He served seventy-one years with the A. N. Belo Corporation's *Galveston News* and *Dallas Morning News*. Largely responsible for founding the *Dallas Morning News*, he helped guide development of his adopted city from a frontier settlement to a major urban center. Adolph S. Ochs (q.v.) said Dealey's gentlemanly, civic-minded journalism was the inspiration for the *New York Times*'s news policies.

Dealey, born in Manchester, England, was the second son and fourth of nine children of George Dealey and Mary Ann Nellins. His father, a shoe shop owner, moved the family to Liverpool in 1864 and, following business reversals, embarked with his family for Galveston in 1870. The elder Dealey opened a coffee and tea business in Galveston; his son, George, went to school and worked at a variety of jobs before becoming office boy for the *Galveston News* on 12 October 1874 at three dollars a week. It was the beginning of a career that would span the Reconstruction through post–World War II eras.

A younger brother, James Quayle, who held a Ph.D. from Brown University, was editor of the *Dallas Morning News* from 1 October 1929 to his death on 22 January 1937. He served as president of the American Sociological Society, and as vice president of the American Political Science Association. He served on the faculty of Brown University and was author of ten books on social science and government.

Dealey rose from office boy to owner of the *Dallas Morning News*. He was rapidly promoted through several positions with the Belo organization. It was his suggestion that the *News* be located in Dallas, which Dealey identified as the most likely site for a major city in north Texas at a time when the city had only about 10,000 residents. Dealey was named business manager of the paper when it was established on 1 October 1885.

Dealey married Olivia Allen of Lexington, Missouri, on 9 April 1884; the couple had five children. By 1895 Dealey was manager of the *Dallas Morning News* and enjoyed almost complete control of direction. He was vice president and general manager of the Belo Corporation from 1906 to 1920, and president from 1920 to 1926. In 1923 the Belo Corporation sold the unprofitable *Galveston News*. In July 1926 Dealey and associates bought a controlling interest in the company, and Dealey became publisher. In 1940 Dealey became chairman of the board; his son, E. M. "Ted" Dealey, was elected president. In 1922 Dealey, along with his elder son, Walter, began development of radio station WFAA, which became the first 50,000-watt station in the South in 1930.

Dealey's newspaper creed was that clean news and profits go hand in hand, and that journalistic ethics must supersede profits when necessary. This belief was tested in the midst of the post–World War I oil boom in west Texas when Dealey refused to accept oil stock advertising because speculation was rampant and it was impossible to distinguish between sound and unsound stock. His refusal to accept promotional copy cost his newspaper hundreds of thousands of dollars in advertising revenue.

In the 1920s he stood firm against attempts by the Ku Klux Klan to gain political power in Texas. In 1924 the *News* published a serial exposé of the Klan which had been syndicated by the *New York World*, despite growing support for, and political gains by, the Klan. At the same time the *News* supported the anti-Klan gubernatorial campaign of Miriam A. Ferguson, who won the bitterly contested election largely because of the *News*'s influence in heavily populated north-central Texas.

Dealey was committed to civic involvement. He strongly supported improvements in rural and urban living conditions. He was a tireless proponent of flood control, and soil and water conservation. Largely through his efforts, the original Dallas city plan was adopted in 1910. Additional city planning successes helped Dealey become recognized as the father of city planning in the Southwest. Dealey also was devoted to numerous philanthropic and charitable causes, and was a key figure in the founding of Southern Methodist University, which later granted him an honorary doctor of laws degree in 1921.

Dealey died of natural causes in his home at age eighty-six, still active as owner of the *News*. A twelve-foot statute of Dealey was dedicated at Dealey Plaza in Dallas on 14 November 1949. It was at this site on 22 November 1963 that President John F. Kennedy was assassinated.

BIBLIOGRAPHY:

B. DAB Supp. 4, 221–222; NYT 27 February 1946; *Dallas Morning News*, 27 February 1946; Sam Acheson, *35,000 Days in Texas: A History of the "Dallas News" and Its Forebears* (New York, 1938).

JAMES DANIEL WHITFIELD

DELANY, MARTIN ROBINSON (b. 6 May 1812; d. 24 January 1885) engaged in many activities during his life and was successful in most. Between 1843 and 1849 he made his mark in the history of American journalism as one of the most respected but least known black journalists of his time. Delany made significant contributions to the profession by founding the *Mystery* in Pittsburgh, Pennsylvania, in 1843, and was equally responsible, with Frederick Douglass (q.v.), in establishing the well-known *North Star* in Rochester, New York, in 1847.

Delany was born of free parents, Samuel and Pati Delany, in Charles Town, West Virginia. Both parents claimed, with some verification, to be of African royalty. The education of blacks, whether slave or free, was outlawed in West Virginia, and it was not until 1818 that Delany was exposed to any type of formal education. He and his brothers and sisters were taught by underground private tutors in their home. When the Delany children began to exhibit their newly acquired skills in public, the family was harassed and forced to leave Charles Town in 1822. They moved to Chambersburg, Pennsylvania, where the children could continue their elementary education.

After a short time, Delany dropped out of school and found work to help support the family. He became dissatisfied with the menial jobs at which he was forced to work, so with the consent of his family he departed for Pittsburgh, which offered more educational opportunities. With little or no money, he walked and worked on his way. In Pittsburgh, Delany worked at various jobs to support himself while he studied at a school for blacks established by an educational society in the city. He excelled in his studies; however, most doors to higher education, even in the North, were still closed to him. For a time he became involved with the Philanthropic Society of Pittsburgh, which was a direct link in the underground railroad. At the same time he began to study medicine under Dr. Andrew N. McDowell. For some unknown reason he did not complete his studies and became a dentist. He later set up a dental practice on the Sea Islands of South Carolina. In 1843 he returned to Pittsburgh and married Kate A. Richardson. They would become the parents of eleven children over the years.

Also upon his return to Pittsburgh, Delany found that blacks in the area had no platform to express their views on the injustices they suffered. Attempts by blacks to air their views in the white-owned newspapers were either refused or ignored. Unassisted, Delay founded the *Mystery*, a paper devoted to elevating the black race. For nine months Delany sustained the paper alone before transferring ownership to a committee of six. His editorials received praise even from his enemies and were frequently reprinted in their columns. One crusade by Delany concerning the aspirations and needs of black people was credited with influencing the Reverend Charles Avery to found a school for blacks, the first step toward the establishment of Avery College. Delany did not confine his *Mystery* to coverage of racial issues. His reports of the great fire in Pittsburgh in 1844 were extensively quoted by other papers.

Considered radical by some, Delany was held in high esteem and respected by blacks and whites in Pittsburgh. He also probably holds the distinction of being the first black editor sued for libel. The case resulted from his accusations that a black man in Pennsylvania had assisted slave catchers. He was found guilty and fined $200. White newspaper editors and members of the community supported Delany and a drive was started to raise the money for his fine; however, it was remitted by the governor.

After a year as editor, Delany left the *Mystery* and later became cofounder and coeditor with Frederick Douglass of the *North Star* in 1847. He traveled extensively promoting the paper and sending back dispatches for publication. In June 1849 he dissolved his connection with the *North Star*. He enrolled at Harvard University and resumed his study of medicine. After leaving Harvard and completing a successful lecture tour of the United States, he moved to Canada in 1856 and set up a medical practice.

Prior to the Civil War, Delany returned to the United States and became active in recruiting black soldiers to fill the ranks of the newly formed black militia units. He later entered the army and became the first black to be promoted to the rank of major. For a time following the war he worked with the Freedmen's Bureau.

During Reconstruction, Delany remained in South Carolina and became involved in politics. In 1874 he ran unsuccessfully for lieutenant governor as an independent. In 1875 the Republican administration in the state appointed him a justice. He was appointed to the same position in 1876 for his support of the Democratic party. In his advanced years, Delany joined his family in Xenia, Ohio, where he died at age seventy-two. He has been called the "founding father" of black cultural nationalism.

BIBLIOGRAPHY:

B. I. Garland Penn, *The Afro-American Press and Its Editors* (Springfield, Mass., 1891).

J. WILLIAM SNORGRASS

DENNIE, JOSEPH (b. 30 August 1768; d. 7 January 1812) was an essayist, magazine editor, and cultural critic who has been called the American Addison. He was best known for his "Lay Preacher" essays, which first appeared in newspapers and magazines in New Hampshire and Philadelphia, and for his skill in editing *Port Folio*, which he founded and which was the most significant magazine in America to that time. As editor of *Port Folio*, he attacked Thomas Jefferson and democracy, and consequently stood trial and was acquitted on a charge of seditious libel.

Dennie was born in Boston, the only son of Joseph Dennie and Mary Green Dennie. His father was a successful Boston merchant, and his mother was from a well-established family of printers that included Bartholomew Green. When Dennie was seven, the family moved from Boston to Lexington.

As a precocious child, Dennie read the English essayists and religious works of high literary quality, as well as classical literature, and at an early age was writing poetry modeled after that of Horace. In 1783 his family sent him to Boston to study bookkeeping for a year, after which he clerked for another year in a countinghouse. In 1785, however, he was placed under the tutelage of the Reverend Samuel West of Needham to prepare for Harvard. Under West, Dennie's love of literature was encouraged, as well as his inclination for things British rather than American. In 1787 he entered Harvard's sophomore class. He was suspended his senior year for insulting the faculty, but was reinstated in time to graduate with his class in 1790.

After six months of indecision concerning a career, Dennie began studying law in the office of Benjamin West in Charlestown, New Hampshire. While there, he wrote a series of light, satirical essays on American morals and manners.

The first of these ''Farrago'' essays appeared in 1792 in the *Morning Ray, Or Impartial Oracle*, a Windsor, Vermont, newspaper. Others appeared in the *Eagle: Or Dartmouth Centinel* in Hanover, New Hampshire, and later most of the twenty-five essays were reprinted in *Port Folio*. It also was during this period that Dennie entered into a literary partnership with Royall Tyler, and the two sold poetry and prose to newspapers under the heading the ''Shop of Colon and Spondee.''

In 1795 Dennie returned to Boston, where he started the *Tablet*, a weekly magazine that contained no advertising or news, but only essays and original criticism. The first issue appeared 19 May 1795, but the publication failed after thirteen issues, the last appearing 11 August. That fall, Dennie set up a law practice in Walpole, New Hampshire, although he still had not developed much enthusiasm for the legal profession. His literary inclinations, however, had grown stronger, and he soon began contributing the ''Lay Preacher'' essays to the *New Hampshire Journal: Or The Farmer's Weekly Museum*. These essays ran from 12 October 1795 to 24 May 1796, and then irregularly until 26 August 1799. They were at least partially inspired by his experience as a lay reader in a Congregational church in 1793.

In adopting the ''Lay Preacher'' pseudonym, Dennie established himself as a guardian of traditional English morals and manners. Essay topics varied greatly, from music, democracy, or philosophers to what it took to be a good wife, mother, or father. Eventually, 118 essays were written by Dennie. Thirty-eight of the essays were published as *The Lay Preacher, Or Short Sermons for Idle Readers* in Walpole in 1896, but the volume had a limited circulation and made no money for Dennie. Twenty-eight essays were issued in another limited edition volume in 1816, four years after his death.

In April 1796 Dennie became editor of the *Farmer's Museum*, and the publication became one of the most popular in New England. The success of the magazine and the essays led to offers to edit papers in Boston, New York,and Philadelphia, but Dennie chose instead to become personal secretary to Secretary of State Timothy Pickering in Philadelphia, assuming that post sometime in the fall of 1799. While serving as Pickering's secretary, Dennie contributed extensively to the *Gazette of the United States*, and his position with Pickering having ended in April 1800, he became the paper's literary editor from June through December of that year.

The first issue of *Port Folio*, a weekly which Dennie published with Asbury Dickens, a Philadelphia bookseller, appeared 3 January 1801. Dennie edited *Port Folio* under the name Oliver Oldschool, Esq., a pseudonym that reflected his traditional conservative literary, political, and moral views. Those Oldschool values were essentially British standards and conventions, which Dennie espoused in opposing the party and politics of Jefferson, and the Americanization of the English language and manners. It was Dennie's denunciation of democracy that led to his being charged with inflammatory and seditious libel for a paragraph that appeared in *Port Folio* on 23 April 1803. A grand jury indictment was delivered on 4 July, but his trial did not begin until 28 November 1805, and only lasted until 2 December, when he was found not guilty.

Although Dennie eagerly participated in the country's bitter partisan fights, he was not merely a political hack for the Federalists. At *Port Folio* Dennie further demonstrated that he was a skillful editor who could attract the best writers, edit with perception and verve, and produce commentary and criticism that often was bitingly ironic and satiric. Dennie insisted on lively prose on a variety of subjects and *Port Folio*'s reputation grew quickly until it became the only literary magazine in the country with a national circulation. In addition to political commentary and literary and cultural criticism, the magazine contained travel articles, essays, humor, poetry, and translations from foreign authors. Unlike previous American publications, *Port Folio* published original poetry by a number of English writers. Dennie and his magazine had a direct influence on a number of prominent Americans, such as Washington Irving, whose "Sketch of Launcelot Langstaff" was based on Dennie.

His poor health and the poor financial condition of the magazine forced Dennie to give up its ownership in late 1808 or early 1809. He remained as editor, but after this he paid less attention to the magazine, which became a monthly in 1809. He died 7 January 1812 in Philadelphia after an extended illness. *Port Folio* appeared in various forms under a number of publishers and editors until 1827.

BIBLIOGRAPHY:

B. DAB 5, 235–237; William Clapp, Jr., *Joseph Dennie* (Cambridge, Mass., 1880); Harold Milton Ellis, *Joseph Dennie and His Circle* (Austin, Texas, 1915).

THOMAS CONNERY

DE ROCHEMONT, LOUIS CHARLES (b. January 1899; d. 23 December 1978) was a pioneer in the fields of newsreel and documentary film. His career spanned making hometown newsreels with a homemade camera to travelogues made with Cinerama and Cinemiracle processes. He created the *March of Time* series for the movies and introduced the nonfiction style of presentation into feature film production. Besides producing films for Hollywood, de Rochemont also founded his own company to produce feature films and several series of educational films for schools and the government.

De Rochemont, the older of two children, was born in Chelsea, Massachusetts, a descendant of French Huguenots who came to New Hampshire in 1685. His father, Louis Leonard Guertis de Rochemont, was an attorney and city solicitor for the city of Boston. His mother was Sarah Wilson Miller de Rochemont.

De Rochemont attended public schools in Chelsea and Winchester, Massachusetts. At age twelve, he was inspired by seeing himself in a local newsreel. He built a camera from plans he purchased by mail, scrounging and fabricating the parts. He filmed local scenes and people and sold the results, *See Yourself as Others See You*, to local theaters and occasionally to newsreel companies. While still in high school, de Rochemont developed the technique of news reenactment and scooped all other newsreelmen with pictures of the imprisonment of a German saboteur who had blown up a bridge between the United States and Canada. He merely asked the marshal to reenact it.

De Rochemont attended the Naval Aviation School at Massachusetts Institute of Technology and the Naval Cadet School at Harvard before entering the navy in 1918, although he may have served a year with British military intelligence prior to his naval service. He was commissioned and served as a line officer until his resignation in 1923 as a lieutenant. During this period de Rochemont filmed the taking of Smyrna by Kemal Ataturk and the opening of Tutankhamen's tomb in Egypt.

He joined the staff of International Newsreel after leaving the navy and roamed the world as cameraman and director from 1923 to 1927, when he became assistant editor for Pathé News. During that time, he also made a series of short recruiting films for the navy. In 1929 de Rochemont moved to Fox Movietone News as a producer and director of short subjects.

After his experiences as cameraman and producer of short subject films, he independently produced and financed a feature documentary, *The Cry of the World* (1933). De Rochemont left Movietone in 1934 for Time, where he cofounded and produced for nine years *The March of Time*, a monthly series of topical films which mixed reporting and editorial commentary. He also produced two feature-length documentary films, *The Ramparts We Watch* (1940) and *We Are the Marines* (1942). He was awarded a special Academy Award for *The March of Time* series in 1936.

In 1943 de Rochemont left Time to become a feature producer for Twentieth Century-Fox. In the three years he was there, de Rochemont produced four films, the first of which, *The Fighting Lady* (1944), received a special Academy Award for distinctive achievement in documentaries and a special award from the New York Film Critics Circle. The remaining three films set the style for using documentary techniques in film drama about real events. He was insistent on "location" shooting, and avoided the studio whenever possible.

In order to buy out his contract with Twentieth Century-Fox in 1946, de Rochemont agreed not to make any commercial films for eighteen months. Therefore, he organized Louis de Rochemont Associates to begin independent production of a series of educational film shorts on geography for public schools. With *Reader's Digest*, de Rochemont formed the RD-DR Corporation in 1946 to exchange ideas and stories. A product was the award-winning *Lost Boundaries* (1949). He also produced *The Whistle at Eaton Falls* (1951).

In the 1950s, de Rochemont's work ranged from documentary-style feature films, *Walk East on Beacon Street* (1952); to biography, *Martin Luther* (1953); a feature-length cartoon, *Animal Farm* (1954); a wide-screen travelogue, *Cinerama Holiday* (1955); and an educational series. He also released a documentary about Norwegian sailing students, *Windjammer* (1956), which was done in a multi-camera wide-screen process called Cinemiracle. He received the

Order of St. Olaf for the film in 1959. Norway also awarded him the Order of Liberation for one of his *March of Time* films in 1948.

In the late 1960s, de Rochemont produced a series of films, under the general title *Job Opportunities*, for the U.S. Department of Labor and the New York Employment Service. De Rochemont died in a nursing home in York Harbor, Maine.

BIBLIOGRAPHY

B. CB 10, 13–15; NCAB 62, 183–184; NYT 25 December 1978; Richard B. Gelman, ''De Rochemont—a Pictorial Journalist Who Records the American Scene on Film,'' *Theatre Arts*, October 1951; Eugene Lyons, ''Louis de Rochemont: Maverick of the Movies,'' *Reader's Digest*, July 1949.

JACK H. COLLDEWEIH

DE YOUNG, MICHEL HARRY (b. 30 September 1849; d. 15 February 1925) published the *San Francisco Chronicle* for more than forty-five years, becoming a power in California journalism and the Republican party.

Known generally as ''M. H.,'' de Young was born in St. Louis, the son of Michel H. de Young, a banker, and Amelia Morange de Young. The family moved to California in 1854, the elder de Young dying en route. M. H. de Young attended school in San Francisco and aided his elder brother, Charles, when he published a school paper, the *School Circle*. When Charles decided on a larger venture he called on his brother for aid, and on 16 January 1865 the two boys, Charles, 19, and M. H., 17, offered the *Dramatic Chronicle: A Daily Record of Affairs Local, Critical and Theatrical* to the people of San Francisco.

Although focusing initially on theatrical advertising and events, the de Youngs intended their paper to cater to wider interests, and they offered a mix of gossip and news, using the *New York Herald* as their model. They were the first on the streets with an extra with news of Lincoln's assassination, and in the turbulent hours that followed, they reported on the mobs that attacked Democratic newspapers in town.

Described as restless and energetic, in contrast to his more contemplative brother, M. H. was the business manager of the early *Chronicle*. His ingenuity in promoting the newspaper and organizing dealers contributed significantly to the newspaper's success in the face of competition from a dozen other English-language newspapers in the city. The *Dramatic Chronicle* was distributed free; to extend their circulation the boys would collect used copies, smooth them out, and send them to hotels and restaurants in other parts of the city and state.

In 1868 the de Youngs dropped ''Dramatic'' from the newspaper's title and it became the *Daily Morning Chronicle*, with a weekly edition as well. As the publishers expanded their newspaper, they crusaded against monopolies and generally made the *Chronicle* a friend of the workingman. In 1879 theirs was the only San Francisco newspaper to support a new California constitution, one backed by the Workingman's party. This was a violent period in California journalism. Both of the de Youngs were physically attacked by irate readers, and Charles was frequently defending himself against libel suits. In 1880 Charles was fatally shot by the son of San Francisco's mayor because of political differences. M. H. was left in charge of the newspaper.

M. H. published the *Chronicle* for the next forty-five years, attracting his share of enemies—he was shot by Adolph Spreckels in 1884 after an exposé of sugar baron Claus Spreckels—but increasing the financial stability and the influence of his newspaper. In 1890 the *Chronicle* moved into a new ten-story building and in 1905 added a seventeen-story tower. When the San Francisco earthquake and fire struck in 1906, destroying the *Chronicle* building, de Young joined with other publishers for a combined issue on 19 April, printed at the *Oakland Tribune* plant. The next day the *Chronicle* was back on its feet, albeit printed at the *Oakland Herald*. By the end of July, the *Chronicle* was essentially back to pre-earthquake operation.

De Young, meanwhile, was an active Republican, serving as a delegate to the Republican National Convention in 1888, 1892, and 1908, and as a member of the Republican National Committee for eight years, four of them as vice chairman. In 1892 he sought a U.S. Senate seat, but was unsuccessful.

A commissioner for several of the expositions held around the turn of the century, he was president of the U.S. Commission to the Paris Exposition in 1900. He was a member of the executive committee of the Red Cross Fund after the 1906 earthquake, and a director of the Associated Press for twenty-five years. In 1913 de Young bought the *San Francisco Call* and suspended it.

In 1880 de Young married Katherine I. Deane of San Francisco. They had four daughters and a son, Charles, who was being groomed to take over the *Chronicle* when he died in 1913. Mrs. de Young died four years later. De Young died on 15 February 1925 in San Francisco after an emergency operation for an acute intestinal condition.

BIBLIOGRAPHY:

B. DAB 5, 283–284; NYT 16 February 1925; *San Francisco Chronicle*, 16 February 1925; *Who Was Who in America, 1897–1942*, 1, 320; John P. Young, *Journalism in California* (San Francisco, 1915).

BARBARA CLOUD

DICKERSON, NANCY HANSCHMAN (b. ca. 1927), a Milwaukee schoolteacher who came East looking for fame and fortune, broke ground for women in broadcast journalism by becoming CBS's first female Washington correspondent in 1960. While attractive enough to have worked as a model, Dickerson won her slot in the CBS lineup because of her Washington expertise and her skill at interviewing. She did graduate work in government and international relations at Harvard University and served as a staff assistant to the Senate Foreign Relations Committee before becoming a broadcast journalist. Dickerson was so good at getting congressmen to grant her interviews that she was dubbed "CBS's secret weapon."

She was the first woman in broadcasting to work on the floor of a political convention as well as the first woman to sit in the anchor booth, joining Edward R. Murrow and Walter Cronkite (qq.v.) there at the 1960 Democratic convention. She capped a distinguished career as a White House correspondent for CBS and NBC by turning to the making of television documentaries. Her Watergate documentary, "784 Days That Changed America—from Watergate to Resignation," won the Peabody and Silver Gavel awards in 1982.

Born in the Milwaukee suburb of Wauwatosa to architect Frederick R. Hanschman and Florence Conners Hanschman, Dickerson studied at Clarke College in Iowa, but finished her A.B. at the University of Wisconsin in 1948. After spending several years teaching in Milwaukee, in 1951 she moved to New York, but unable to find work, ended up in Washington, D.C. Her first job was as registrar for the Institute of Languages at Georgetown University. From there she went to work for the Senate Foreign Relations Committee, and her report on the U.S. Information Agency for the committee was the first authored by a woman in that position.

In 1954 CBS hired her as the producer for "The Leading Question." She served for six years behind the scenes as a producer for CBS, including a stint as associate producer for "Face The Nation." Determined to work in front of the camera as a correspondent, Dickerson got her chance in January 1960 when her exclusive interview with camera-shy House Speaker Sam Rayburn was aired on Douglas Edwards's CBS news show. The break came because of her success the summer before at getting high-quality interviews from European leaders as they reacted to Khrushchev's U.S. visit. Dickerson had initially gone abroad only to do a story on the Women's Army Corps. The Khrushchev story brought interviews that her male colleagues could not get.

Dickerson's status as CBS's first woman correspondent became official on 22 February 1960. She also had a five-minute radio program entitled "One Woman's Washington." Dickerson was assigned to cover the civil rights bill and then Senator Lyndon Baines Johnson. Once Johnson became president, she began to cover the White House on a regular basis. In 1962 she married real estate entrepreneur C. Wyatt Dickerson. They had five children: Elizabeth, Ann, Jane, Michael, and John, and their home, Merrywood, in MacLean, Virginia—once owned by the family of Jacqueline Kennedy Onassis—became one of the hubs of Washington entertaining. Dickerson was divorced in 1983.

In 1963 Dickerson switched from CBS to NBC after that network promised her more air time. Her interviews began appearing on both "The Today Show" and "The Huntley-Brinkley Report," and she had her own daily news show. Her salary in 1964, a reputed $40,000, was said to be the highest among women in the business then. She stayed at NBC until 1970, when she left to become a political commentator for the syndicated television show "Inside Washington." Dickerson also served as a political commentator for the Newsweek Broadcasting Service before founding Dickerson and Company in order to produce television documentaries. When she represented PBS in a live one-hour interview with President Nixon, she became the first woman to participate in such a broadcast.

She started a second production company, Television Corporation of America, in 1980. In addition to a Watergate documentary, Dickerson produced "Being With John F. Kennedy" to mark the twentieth anniversary of Kennedy's assassination. She continues to produce television documentaries in Washington, D.C.

BIBLIOGRAPHY:

A. *Among Those Present* (New York, 1976).

B. *Foremost Women in Communication* (New York, 1970).

BROOKS ROBARDS

DIX, DOROTHY (b. 18 November 1861; d. 16 December 1951) was said to have a larger readership than any other newspaper columnist in her day. Her advice to the lovelorn earned more money than was paid to any other contributor. But oddly enough, her early journalistic reputation was made in crime reporting.

She was born on a farm in Montgomery County, Tennessee, and was christened Elizabeth Meriwether. She was the eldest of three children born to William Douglas and Maria Winston Meriwether. Her mother died when the children were young, and her father married Martha Gilmer Chase.

After attending school at the Female Academy in Clarksville, Tennessee, and at Hollins Institute in Botetourt Springs, Virginia, where she won the composition medal, Elizabeth married her stepmother's brother, George Gilmer, in 1882. Her husband was emotionally unstable, and the marriage was not a happy one. She left him in 1893 and returned to her family after she suffered a nervous breakdown. They took her to the Mississippi Gulf Coast, where she recuperated at Bay St. Louis, near New Orleans. Next door to her cottage lived Mrs. E. J. Nicholson (q.v.), the owner of the *New Orleans Picayune*.

She went to work for the *Picayune*, adopting the pen name of Dorothy Dix, in 1894. There she developed "Dorothy Dix Talks"—a series of articles about domestic life in which she told women "the truth about themselves instead of flattering them, lambasting them instead of jollying them, and using the vernacular in writing instead of poetic phrases" (Kane and Arthur, 1952).

William Randolph Hearst (q.v.) wooed her away from the *Picayune* for his *New York Journal* at a salary of $5,000. For Hearst she wrote prolifically. Besides her column, she wrote short stories, beast fables, humorous pieces in black dialect, and news reports of sensational crimes. She tracked down the notorious temperance crusader Carrie Nation, and she covered the love-triangle murder involving architect Stanford White, playboy Harry K. Thaw, and show girl Evelyn Nesbit. She also began publishing collections of her work: her beast fables were published in 1902 under the title *Fables of the Elite*, some of her black dialect philosophy was published in 1914 as *Mirandy*, and in 1915 she published a collection of her advice columns as *Hearts à la Mode*.

In 1916 she signed with the Wheeler Syndicate. Her contract permitted her to concentrate on writing her advice columns and to give up the reports of murders and trials for which she had become so well known. The lucrative contract permitted her to make a trip around the world with her husband George, who had rejoined her. Her account of the trip was published in 1922 as *My Joy-Ride round the World*. The trip only worsened his emotional condition, and they were permanently separated.

In 1923 she joined the Ledger Syndicate, and in 1926 she published her most popular book. *Dorothy Dix—Her Book: Every-day Help for the Every-day People* went into three editions. She was now living in New Orleans and working out of her home. In 1927 she received the doctor of letters degree from Tulane University, and the following year she was honored in New Orleans with Dorothy Dix Day. In 1929 her husband George died at the asylum where his family had taken him several years earlier.

Despite her increasing age she continued to write her column, and in 1939 she published her last book, *How to Win and Hold a Husband*. She was with the Bell Syndicate from 1942 to 1949, when she ended her journalistic career after over a half century of column writing. When the Dorothy Dix column ended, it was the oldest column in the world with the same author. It was carried in 215 newspapers on three continents and read by thirty million people.

Elizabeth Meriwether Gilmer—better known as Dorothy Dix—suffered a stroke in 1950 and was hospitalized until her death on 16 December 1951.

BIBLIOGRAPHY:

B. DAB Supp. 5, 243–244; NYT 17 December 1951; Harnett Kane and Ella Bentley Arthur, *Dear Dorothy Dix: The Story of a Compassionate Woman* (Garden City, N.Y., 1952).

WHITNEY R. MUNDT

DODGE, MARY ABIGAIL (b. 31 March 1833; d. 17 August 1896) was a well-known journalist and writer in an era when exceptional women were seeking career opportunities as a way of broadening women's traditional role. Dodge used the pseudonym Gail Hamilton, due to personal dislike of publicity reinforced by the Victorian convention that women should be shielded from public attention. An advocate of economic independence for women, Dodge was best known for her humorous essays, frequently on New England country life, which appeared in the *Atlantic Monthly*. Related by marriage to Congressman James G. Blaine of Maine, Dodge lived in the Blaine household in Washington in the 1870s and 1880s. During this time she wrote influential political commentary for the *New York Tribune*.

Dodge was the third daughter and seventh and last child of James Brown Dodge and Hannah Stanwood Dodge, both of English ancestry. Their families had lived for several generations in Essex County, Massachusetts, where Dodge was born in the village of Hamilton. Her father was a farmer, and her mother, to whom Dodge was deeply devoted, a schoolteacher before her marriage. As a small child Dodge suffered an accident that damaged one of her eyes and made her extremely sensitive about her personal appearance. She was educated at the village school, and at twelve was sent to a boarding school in Cambridge for one year. The next year she went to the Ipswich Female Seminary, from which she was graduated in 1850. Subsequently she taught there and at the Hartford High School. In Hartford she started writing as "Gail Hamilton," using her middle name and the name of her hometown.

Prose and poetry sent to Dr. Gamaliel Bailey, editor of the *National Era*, Washington's abolitionist newspaper, so impressed him with her talent that he arranged for Dodge to move to Washington in 1858 as a governess for his children. During the next two years she wrote for the *National Era* as Gail Hamilton and for the *Congregationalist*, a Boston newspaper that included general news. She signed her *Congregationalist* pieces "Cunctare," a Latin epithet referring to hesitation or reserve. Written in a lively style, her columns included comment on antislavery issues, economy in government, and congressional proceedings.

Although Dodge returned to Hamilton on the eve of the Civil War to care for her ailing mother, her writing career was not handicapped. She sold numerous essays, based on a sharp-witted Yankee philosophy of self-reliance and belief in the Civil War as a moral crusade, to the *Atlantic Monthly* and other magazines. From 1865 to 1867 she helped edit a children's magazine, *Our Young Folks*. Her essays, collected in five books, were published by Ticknor and Fields, who also published the works of John Greenleaf Whittier, Henry Wadsworth Longfellow, Nathaniel Hawthorne, and other famous writers. She broke with the firm in a battle over royalty payments, which she wrote about in fiction.

After 1871 Dodge, who never married, spent winters in Washington in the home of Blaine, whose wife was her first cousin. Her most notable newspaper work was a series of columns opposing civil service reform that appeared in the *New York Tribune* in 1877. Rumored to be written by Blaine himself, an accusation which both Dodge and the *Tribune* indignantly denied, the series echoed Blaine's opposition to civil service legislation. It is believed, without firm evidence, that Dodge wrote Blaine's speeches and it is clear she assisted him with his autobiography, *Twenty Years of Congress*. In her last years she became increasingly conservative and devoted herself to religious themes.

It was unfortunate that she fell so completely under Blaine's sway, since the perceptiveness and originality of her early work did not flower in later years. Her relationship with Blaine was in line with her views on women's role, expressed in *Woman's Worth and Worthlessness* (1874), in which she condemned suffrage on grounds that women should exercise political influence only through their family ties. Her last major work was a eulogistic *Biography of James G. Blaine* (1895). She died of a cerebral hemorrhage in Hamilton.

BIBLIOGRAPHY:
A. H. Augusta Dodge, ed., *Gail Hamilton's Life in Letters* (Boston, 1901).
B. NAW 1, 494; *New York Tribune*, 18 and 23 August 1893; Maurine H. Beasley, *The First Women Washington Correspondents* (Washington, D.C., 1976).

MAURINE H. BEASLEY

DORR, RHETA CHILDE (b. ca. 1873; d. 8 August 1948) had already established herself as a journalist and a feminist before she became a war correspondent and foreign correspondent while in her forties.

She was born in Omaha, Nebraska, the daughter of Dr. Edward P. Childe and Lucie N. Childe. She attended the University of Nebraska for two years. In 1892 she married John Pixley Dorr. They had one child, Julian Childe Dorr. Mrs. Dorr died a widow.

From 1902 to 1906 she edited the women's pages at the *New York Evening Post*, and there gathered the material for her first book, *What Eight Million Women Want* (1910). She became editor of the *Suffragist* and an active worker for voting rights for women. She wrote for *Collier's*, *Cosmopolitan*, *Hampton's*, and other magazines.

In 1917 Dorr became a war correspondent for the *New York Evening Mail* and a syndicate of twenty-one newspapers. After the war she set up headquarters in Prague as a foreign correspondent. She worked as a contributor to the *Columbia Encyclopedia* in 1934 and 1935.

BIBLIOGRAPHY:
A. *A Woman of Fifty* (New York, 1924).
B. NYT 9 August 1948.

DWIGHT JENSEN

DOUGLASS, FREDERICK (b. February 1817; d. 20 February 1895) lived in the extremes of slavery and freedom, absolute poverty and international fame and gentility. Though he escaped from slavery, he fought for more than fifty years against that institution, using oratory and the press. His *North Star* was one of the earliest successful black newspapers in the United States.

Born Frederick Augustus Washington Bailey, in Tuckahoe, Talbot County, Maryland, he was the son of Harriet Bailey, a slave, and a white man whose name he never learned. His mother was one of very few literate slaves, and though removed from her by force at an early age, Douglass was strongly influenced by her throughout his life.

As a slave, he worked as a house servant, a shipyard worker, and a farm laborer, and exhibited such a strong spirit and evident desire for freedom that he was sent to a slave breaker to be trained, worked to death, or beaten into submission. He escaped to freedom on 3 September 1838, fleeing from Baltimore to Philadelphia with a borrowed sailor's suit and a sympathetic freedman's protection papers. He married Anna Murray, a freedwoman who had encouraged and financially supported his escape. The couple settled in New Bedford, Massachusetts, and Douglass adopted his new surname.

As a free man he tended furnaces, and often nailed a newspaper to the post near his bellows and read while working. A regular and avid reader of William Lloyd Garrison's (q.v.) *Liberator*, he soon became active in that editor's Abolitionist Society and addressed a society gathering in New Bedford's Christina Church on 12 March 1839, just six months after his escape. Despite the danger the resultant notoriety put him in, he quickly became part of a national and international team of lecturers. Between 1842 and 1847 the *Liberator* published many of his letters and lectures.

His first autobiography appeared in 1845 and put bounty hunters on his trail. He left his wife and four children that year and went to England to lecture and act as a correspondent for the *Liberator* and the *National Anti-Slavery Standard*. Admirers in England and Ireland raised £150 sterling to purchase his freedom papers, making it safe for him to return to America. This he did 20 April 1847, armed with the intention, and funded by supporters, to establish a newspaper.

The *North Star*, published in Rochester, New York, had the slogan "Right is of no Sex—Truth of no Color—God is the Father of us all, and we are all Brethren." It supported abolition, woman suffrage and education, and married women's rights. Financial problems led to the paper's death in 1848, but only after Douglass had mortgaged his home to keep it afloat. Douglass's efforts to save the *North Star* included merging it with Gerrit Smith's *Liberty Party Paper*. It was essentially a new publication, *Frederick Douglass' Paper*, which appeared in 1851. It would survive into the mid–1860s. The four-page, six-column weekly covered local and state antislavery meetings, reprints from other reformist papers, antislavery verse and essays, book reviews, novels, and advertisements. It sought freedom and self-determination for black people and opposed efforts by the Colonization Society to revive the back-to-Africa movement as a solution to the "Negro problem."

Douglass promoted job training in mechanics and farming as alternatives to traditional black occupations. *Frederick Douglass' Paper* was discontinued shortly after his return from a second forced exile in England and Scotland, this time for a six-month duration and occasioned by John Brown's raid at Harpers Ferry, Virginia. In the course of planning the raid, Brown had sought out Douglass. The latter was seen as an accomplice and fled to the British Isles.

A short-lived companion publication, *Douglass' Monthly*, appeared between 1858 and 1860, and was aimed at British readers and financial backers of the abolition movement. It was preceded by his second autobiography, *My Bondage and My Freedom* (1855), which attested to the influence his journalistic experiences had on the way he viewed and judged black existence in pre-emancipation America.

Political involvement took the place of his editorial work beginning in 1861. Following Abraham Lincoln's call to arms after the attack on Fort Sumter, Douglass urged black men to form militia companies to support the Union effort.

When Lincoln resisted black enlistments, Douglass took his grievances to the White House. Given to believe he would receive an army commission to recruit for black divisions, he formally issued a valedictory message in the *Monthly* and discontinued the publication "because I can better serve my poor bleeding country-men whose opportunity has now come, by going South and summoning them to assert their just liberty."

Though he was never commissioned, he had the ear of the president and began pressing for black suffrage. He was eventually named to minor posts in government. He was a U.S. marshal (1877–81), District of Columbia recorder of deeds (1881–86), and U.S. minister to Haiti (1888–91).

Douglass's major contributions were not in politics, however, His writing appeared in many publications in the United States and abroad. He reestablished himself as an editor in 1870 when he joined the *National Era*. He purchased the paper the next year and for four years kept it afloat in what he called a $10,000 misadventure. Renamed the *New National Era*, it was devoted to the "defence and enlightenment of the newly emancipated and enfranchised" black citizens of Washington. The paper suspended operations in 1874, but that was not the end of Douglass's writing. *The Life and Times of Frederick Douglass, Written by Himself* appeared in 1881, and was updated in 1892. Douglass died 20 February 1895, at home, of a heart attack. He had five children: Rosetta, Lewis, Frederick, Charles Remond, and Annie. Douglass's first wife died in August 1882. He married Helen Pitts on 24 January 1884.

BIBLIOGRAPHY:

A. *The Narrative of the Life of Frederick Douglass, an American Slave* (Boston, 1845).

B. Arna Bontemps, *Free at Last: The Life of Frederick Douglass* (New York, 1971).

SHARON MURPHY

DOW, CHARLES HENRY (b. 6 November 1851; d. 4 December 1902) was one of the founders of Dow Jones and Company and the *Wall Street Journal*, serving as its editor from its beginning until 1902. Under his leadership, the *Journal* became the leading daily publication of financial news. His writings in the *Journal* were compiled and became known as the Dow Theory of stock market behavior.

Dow, the youngest of three sons, was born on his father's farm in Sterling, Connecticut, near the Rhode Island border. The Dow family lineage goes back to Henry Dow, who arrived in Boston in 1637. When Dow was six, his father, Charles, died, and his two older brothers died in childhood. He was raised by his mother and educated locally. In 1872 he worked as a reporter on the daily *Springfield Republican* under famed editor Samuel Bowles III (q.v.). It was the leading provincial newspaper in the country. Bowles was one of the most respected editors of the period, and his training of journalists gave them entry to leading metropolitan dailies if they sought further challenges. Dow became a reporter and night editor in 1875 on the *Providence Star* and also wrote for the *Providence Evening Star*. He was a reporter for the *Providence Journal* from 1877 to 1879.

Dow's interest in financial journalism began in 1879 when he accompanied eastern financiers on a trip to Leadville, Colorado, to report on a silver mining boom for the *Providence Journal*. His nine "Leadville Letters" appeared in both the *Providence Journal* and *Evening Bulletin* during the summer. He offered a firsthand report on living conditions and the boom nature of Leadville as well as estimates of the magnitude of the silver find. The articles established him as a first-rate reporter and expert on mining.

In 1880 he became a business reporter for the *New York Mail and Express* and then a reporter for the Kiernan News Agency. The agency delivered handwritten news bulletins to financial institutions and individuals. With Edward D. Jones, a fellow employee at Kiernan and an acquaintance from Providence, Dow founded Dow Jones and Company in 1882 as a competitor to Kiernan. Charles M. Bergstresser was also a minority partner. In 1883 the firm began distributing a printed sheet, the *Afternoon News Letter*, which was a summary of the major items of the day. It was later enlarged, and became the *Wall Street Journal* on the afternoon of 8 July 1889. A morning edition began in 1898. As early as 1884 Dow compiled an average of selected stock prices which, with changes, became identified as the Dow Jones averages.

The financial news service expanded into offering a telegraph ticker with news to supplement the messenger delivery of news bulletins. Circulation of the morning and afternoon editions totaled 10,000 by the turn of the century, and advertising flourished. There were correspondents in Boston and Philadelphia. A Washington office was opened in 1897. From 1899 Dow authored a commentary, "Review and Outlook," which he wrote about the stock and bond markets. With the use of his price averages, he attempted to explain market behavior. Two decades after his death, a book synthesizing his writings was published identifying Dow's thoughts as the Dow Theory. Countless investment letters, stock commentary, and books since have continued to interpret his theory in light of contemporary conditions.

In addition to his everyday activity at Dow Jones and Company, Dow was from 1885 to 1891 a partner of Goodbody, Glynn and Dow and a member of the New York Stock Exchange, and had some experience on the floor executing orders. Dow suffered from ill health from 1900. Jones had left the company in 1899 to pursue other interests. As majority owner of Dow Jones, Dow arranged for its sale to Clarence W. Barron in 1902 only months before his death. He was survived by his wife, the former Lucy M. Russell, whom he had married 9 April 1881, and a stepdaughter.

BIBLIOGRAPHY:

A. "Leadville Letters," reprinted in George W. Bishop, Jr., *Charles H. Dow and the Dow Theory* (New York, 1960).

B. NYT 5 December 1902, George W. Bishop, Jr., *Charles H. Dow, Economist* (Princeton, N.J., 1967); Lloyd Wendt, *The Wall Street Journal* (New York, 1982).

SAM KUCZUN

DRAPER, MARGARET GREEN (b. 3 May 1727; d. 1804?) was born into one of the most important printing families in colonial Massachusetts. Her grandfather, Bartholomew Green, was printer of the first continuously published newspaper in colonial America, and her great-grandfather, Samuel Green, ran the Cambridge (Harvard) press. Margaret Draper is remembered as a thorn to the Patriots and the printer of the last Tory newspaper in Boston.

She was born in Boston, the daughter of Thomas and Ann Green. Little is known of Margaret Draper's parents, but because the Green clan spawned many printers, her father may have been involved in the trade. In all probability Margaret Draper was educated at home, and because she was reared in a literate environment, she was probably quite educated for the day. As was common in Europe at the time, many colonial trades were held together through intermarriage. On 30 May 1750 Margaret Green married her cousin Richard Draper. Richard and Margaret Draper were childless; however, about 1766 they adopted her niece, Margaret Draper Hamilton.

When John Campbell (q.v.) started the *Boston News-Letter*, his printer was Bartholomew Green, Margaret and Richard Draper's grandfather. Richard's father, John, inherited Bartholomew Green's printing shop and the *Boston News-Letter* when Green died in 1732. It was Richard Draper's turn to inherit when his father died in 1762. Despite being an avowed Loyalist, Richard Draper ran a balanced publication. Following Richard's death on 5 June 1774, Margaret Draper took over the operation of the newspaper, now titled the *Massachusetts Gazette and Boston News-Letter*, along with Richard's printing shop.

As a member of a prominent family and the wife of a wealthy printer, Margaret Draper had little cause for involvement in business affairs during her husband's life. Whether she needed to run the printing shop and newspaper for sustenance, as she claimed, or wished to do so to promote her own Tory sympathies, which were powerful, is unclear. However, she began to operate the newspaper as a Tory voice and Patriot critic with the 9 June 1774 issue. Richard had held a lifetime appointment as official printer to the governor, as position that Margaret Draper continued. Merely printing for the governor was sufficient for her to be mistrusted and criticized by the Patriots, but it was in her newspaper that she became their greatest thorn.

Shortly before his death Richard Draper had entered into a partnership with John Boyle, a man with Patriot tendencies. Whether Richard could have continued in partnership with someone of an opposing political bent is unclear; however, Margaret Draper could not. Barely two months after Richard's death, Margaret Draper and Boyle dissolved the partnership by "mutual consent." Margaret Draper later claimed the partnership was dissolved because Boyle wanted to make the newspaper a Patriot voice.

From the beginning Margaret Draper ran the *News-Letter* as an outspoken proponent of the Loyalist cause. She ran the *News-Letter* for only two years, but during that period the newspaper became more strident and more shrill in its espousal of the Loyalist viewpoint and in its opposition to rebellion. At the outbreak of the Revolution there were six newspapers in Boston. At one time or another Draper's competitors launched scathing attacks on the *News-Letter*. The other newspapers were not alone in their complaints about the Loyalist bias of the *News-Letter*. In fact, the newspaper was "voted to be burned by the common hangman," according to the British Commission of Enquiry looking into Loyalist losses during the Revolution.

As early as September 1774 Margaret Draper launched her attack on the Patriots with her defense of the Intolerable Acts and criticism of the nonimportation agreements. In addition she began to reprint material from New York's two Tory newspapers. The *News-Letter* even attacked the Continental Congress and predicted defeat for the Patriots. The beginning of the end for Margaret Draper and other Loyalists came with the Battle of Lexington and Concord. The situation made Boston unsafe for all newspapers, and almost immediately the number declined from six to one. The survivor was Margaret Draper's *News-Letter*.

The publication of the *News-Letter* was not continuous following Lexington and Concord. Because of difficulties with publication Margaret Draper took on a partner, John Howe, sometime in the summer of 1775. Many historians state that Draper and Howe published the *News-Letter* jointly during the next several months; others argue that Howe ran the newspaper alone. In any event, the newspaper was printed sporadically until 27 February 1776. On 6 March 1776 Margaret Draper and Howe departed Boston with the evacuating British troops, and Patriots confiscated her Boston property. So ended after seventy-one years the first continuously published newspaper in the American colonies.

Draper and Howe went to Halifax, Nova Scotia. Howe remained in Halifax, but after a few months Draper went to England. After some difficulty she was awarded a pension for service to the Loyalist cause. She never again involved herself in printing. Ironically, British authorities treated Margaret Draper's contributions to the Loyalist cause as merely an extension of her husband's work. Little is known of Margaret Draper's life in England. In fact, even the date of her death is unknown. Her pension stopped in 1804 and her will was probated in 1807.

BIBLIOGRAPHY:

B. DAB 5, 442–443; Leona M. Hudak, *Early American Women Printers and Publishers, 1639–1820* (Metuchen, N.J., 1978).

DONALD R. AVERY

DREISER, THEODORE (b. 27 August 1871; d. 28 December 1945) was a major figure in twentieth-century American letters, active in a variety of genres: newspapers, magazines, poetry, plays, travel, autobiography, sketches, essays, and naturalistic novels. He is chiefly remembered as a novelist of shattering honesty and realism who probed dark forces beneath surface morality in such works as *Sister Carrie* (1900), *The Financier* (1912), and *An American Tragedy* (1925). An active spokesman for liberal and leftist causes, Dreiser sometimes allowed his political involvements to overshadow his literary activities.

Dreiser came from outside the Protestant, Anglo-Saxon, middle-class mainstream. He was born to John Paul Dreiser and Sarah Schnepp Dreiser, one of ten children, in Terre Haute, Indiana. Both parents came from German backgrounds, the father German Catholic, the mother German Pietist. The family was impoverished and moved from place to place. Dreiser was educated in an intellectually arid parochial school, and in public schools in Sullivan, Evansville, and Warsaw, Indiana. Though the mysteries of grammar eluded Dreiser, his teachers perceived his sensitivity and intelligence. His high school teacher, Mildred Fielding, paid out of her own savings for a crucial year of higher education for Dreiser at the Indiana University in 1889.

He worked briefly in a hardware warehouse, then went to the vital and growing metropolis of Chicago, where he was briefly a real estate clerk and a collections agent. Dreiser brought the varied experiences of lower-class poverty and the immense possibilities of the metropolis to his first newspaper job on the *Chicago Daily Globe* in 1891. Features illuminated by observations of social relations were Dreiser's forte, rather than hard news stories.

Not staying in one place long, he moved about the Midwest working in St. Louis, Toledo, and Pittsburgh. He was a drama critic and traveling correspondent on the *St. Louis Globe-Democrat* in 1892, and in 1893–94 was a traveling correspondent for the *St. Louis Republic*. In 1894 he met Arthur Henry in Toledo, Ohio, who encouraged Dreiser to write fiction, and prodded and coached him as he struggled to write *Sister Carrie*.

He moved to New York in late 1894, and eked out a precarious living writing at space rates on newspapers, living in flophouses and from hand to mouth. In 1895 he proposed to his brother Paul, a successful songwriter, that his music firm publish a monthly magazine. Dreiser edited the prosperous magazine *Ev'ry Month* for two years. He broke away from that success to establish himself as a free-lancer for popular magazines such as *Munsey's*, *Cosmopolitan*, *Success*, *McClure's*, *Harper's*, and *Scribner's*, writing profiles and urban sketches.

Dreiser earned enough to marry Sara Osborne White in 1898, whom he had met five years before, a troubled marriage that ended without issue in separation around 1910. Dreiser had numerous affairs and flings, driven by a Don Juan compulsion. He established a long-term liaison with Helen Patges Richardson in 1919, and married her in 1944, the year before he died. Dreiser worked another six years in journalism, from 1904 to 1910. He was a subeditor for the *New York Daily News* in 1904, and an editor of *Smith's Magazine* and of *Broadway Magazine* in 1905. From 1907–1910 he was editor in chief of the Butterick publications, the *Delineator*, *Designer*, *New Idea*, and *English Delineator*, but he was fired for his feverish pursuit of a seventeen-year-old girl.

From 1910 Dreiser primarily devoted himself to fiction and literature. He died of a heart attack in Hollywood in 1945.

BIBLIOGRAPHY:

A. *Newspaper Days* (New York, 1922).

B. DAB Supp. 3, 232–238; NYT 29 December 1945; W. A. Swanberg, *Dreiser* (New York, 1965).

WILLIAM Q. PARMENTER

DRUMMOND, JAMES ROSCOE (b. 13 January 1902; d. 30 September 1983) was a veteran Washington correspondent and columnist who launched his journalistic career early and distinguished himself for his thorough, comprehensive, middle-of-the-road analysis of national and international affairs.

A native of Theresa, New York, he was the son of John H. Drummond and Georgia Drummond. His father was a pharmacist, and Drummond first planned to be a doctor. This changed after he became editor of his high school magazine in Syracuse, New York. From Central High School in 1920 he went on to the School of Journalism at Syracuse University. He was coxswain on the freshman crew, and a part-time reporter for the *Syracuse Journal* in his first three years. He was a journalism scholarship holder in his senior year and editor of the *Daily Orange*, the student newspaper.

While most beginning journalists hold few hopes of landing their first job on a major publication, Drummond started his career on the *Christian Science Monitor*. His rise through the editorial ranks of the *Monitor* was steady. From reporting he moved successively to assistant city editor, assistant to the executive editor, and chief editorial writer. In 1930 he was sent to London, where he served three years as European editorial manager, supervising correspondents. In 1934 he returned to Boston as executive editor, where he stayed until 1940. In that year the *Monitor* made him chief of its Washington bureau and author of a front-page column, "State of the Nation." *Look* in 1940 described his work as "balanced, penetrating analyses of national affairs."

Although he was able to cope with Washington bureaucracy, he was sobered by the ability of government to classify and cover up. He worked vigorously against censorship in its many forms and is credited with coining the phrase "creeping censorship" to describe what he and others in the nation's capital saw as the growing tendency by government to hold back information. In 1952 he was named to lead an advisory committee that worked with the Senate in an investigation of the handling of news by government agencies.

While the columns rolled from his typewriter, he also wrote frequently for general-circulation magazines and specialized periodicals. For *Reader's Digest* he wrote about Moscow's use of forgery as a propaganda weapon and the failure of the Berlin Wall to halt the flow of freedom seekers to the West. In the *Saturday Evening Post* he urged reform for a bogged-down Congress, and in the *Saturday Review* in 1962 he wrote of the growing crisis in Latin America.

With the exception of a year spent as director of information in Europe for the Marshall Plan, Drummond served the *Monitor* from Washington until 1954. The *New York Herald-Tribune* lured him away as Washington bureau chief, but fourteen months later he turned the bureau over to Walter Kerr and launched a four-times weekly column called ''Washington'' that was widely syndicated and exposed Drummond's work to millions of readers. Later he switched to the Los Angeles Times Syndicate, returning to the ''State of the Nation'' title, writing regularly until he was seriously injured in an automobile accident in 1981. He spent the last two years of his life in a Christian Science nursing home in Princeton, New Jersey. His second wife, the former Carol Cramer, described him as a ''reporter to the end'' busily working on his memoirs of a half century in global journalism, and a mystery novel. His first wife was Charlotte Bruner. He had a son, Geoffrey.

BIBLIOGRAPHY:

B. NYT 1 October 1983.

WALLACE B. EBERHARD

DRYFOOS, ORVIL EUGENE (b. 8 November 1912; d. 25 May 1963) became first a Wall Street broker and then publisher of the *New York Times*, where he gained wide recognition for directing the newspaper through the period of its 114-day strike.

Born in New York City, he was the eldest of three sons of textile merchant Jack A. Dryfoos and Florence Levi Dryfoos. Young Dryfoos attended the Horace Mann School, where he was active in sports and wrote a column, ''The Dugout,'' for the school *Record*. In 1934 he graduated from Dartmouth College and became a stock broker with Asiel and Company. Three years later, when he became a partner of Sydney Lewison Company, he purchased a seat on the New York Stock Exchange, which he retained until 1949. Soon after his marriage, at his father-in-law's urging he joined the *New York Times* on 2 January 1942.

On 8 July 1941 he married Marian Effie Sulzberger, the eldest daughter of Arthur Hays Sulzberger and Iphigene Ochs Sulzberger who had a controlling interest in the *Times*. Starting as a cub reporter, he became a legman, moved to the makeup desk and went on to become Sulzberger's assistant. One of the regrets of his reporting days was that he never received a byline for his work. He also disliked after-dinner speeches because of having once covered seventeen consecutive late-night assignments.

As an executive observer, beginning in 1944 he accompanied the *Times* team to every major political party convention. In 1955 he became vice president of the *Times* and a member of the board of directors. In 1957 he became president and was given more responsibility in decision making for the publishing empire. When Sulzberger retired as publisher in 1961, Dryfoos replaced him as the *Times*'s sixth publisher.

By 1 October 1962 his earlier decision to publish a western edition of the *Times* was in operation, and by 8 December the great newspaper strike had begun. He was under great strain, having only a skeleton crew to run the paper and keep the news flowing to the western and international editions as well as to news service customers.

Although Dryfoos was never considered a dynamic leader, he knew how to delegate responsibility to competent persons. He was also known for his informality, kindness, and thoughtfulness. Over the years he had become close to the employees, and the newspaper strike came as a shock to him. He was said to report, at the conclusion of the strike, that it was the most traumatic experience of his life. Throughout the 114–day strike, he continued to stay in contact with both staff and strikers by writing personal letters to them. On one occasion he killed a column which was said to be an attack on the union president.

Dryfoos learned he had rheumatic heart disease when he was rejected for military service in World War II. Although he had always been active in sports, he was advised by doctors to become more moderate in his activities. He limited his sports to weekend golf, fishing, and family softball games. He was an avid Yankee fan. In good weather he walked daily to work from his home on Fifth Avenue to the *Times* offices on West 43rd Street.

Following the newspaper strike, Dryfoos went to Puerto Rico for a rest. Two weeks later he was hospitalized in New York, where he died of a heart ailment on 25 May 1963. A close friend and fellow *Times* employee, James Reston, gave the eulogy at the funeral. Dryfoos and his wife had three children: Jacqueline Hays, born 8 May 1943; Robert Ochs, born 4 November 1944; and Susan Warms, born 5 November 1946.

BIBLIOGRAPHY:

B. DAB Supp. 7, 199–200; NYT 26 May 1963.

ADRIAN L. HEADLEY

DUANE, WILLIAM (b. 17 May 1760; d. 24 November 1835) was one of the editors in the early years of the United States who taught the nation what freedom of the press really meant. He was a tough, abrasive editor of the *Philadelphia Aurora* for more than twenty years, and he exhibited fierce prejudices and loyalties. He is most noted for his exposure of a Federalist plot to prevent the election of Thomas Jefferson in 1800 and for being a chief target of the odious Sedition Act, passed to silence Republican critics of the government.

Duane was born to Irish immigrant parents in Lake Champlain, New York, and when his father died in 1765, his mother took him back to Ireland. There he learned to be a printer and in 1787 went to India to establish the *Indian World* in Calcutta. He quickly irritated the owners of the East India Company with his independent editorship, and he was arrested, deported, and had his equipment confiscated. He tried to get some payment for his equipment in London, but finally despaired of this and decided to travel to America.

Duane was taken in by Benjamin Franklin Bache (q.v.), editor of the *Aurora*, and he took over the paper when Bache died of yellow fever in 1798. Duane continued and extended the editorial policies of Bache, and the Federalists turned their attention toward silencing him. Duane obtained what was perhaps the major journalistic scoop of the young republic. Sensing that the presidential election of 1800 might be a close one, the Federalists, who controlled the Congress, devised a scheme to deny the election of Jefferson. A bill introduced by Senator James Ross proposed to establish a committee of thirteen members to count the electoral votes and announce the winner; it also provided that the committee meet in secret and decide which electoral votes to accept and reject. The bill was introduced, debated, and passed by the Senate in a secret session, but Duane, probably through Republican sources, found out what was happening and even obtained a copy of the bill. The measure was later defeated by the House of Representatives.

Federalist senators were beside themselves with anger, and they turned their fury on Duane. Duane was commanded to appear before the Senate to answer charges. Part of the purpose was to embarrass Jefferson, who was presiding, but the Republicans cleverly turned the tables on their enemies. Duane appeared, requested that he be permitted to obtain counsel, and withdrew. He then asked fellow Republicans Alexander Dallas and Thomas Cooper (q.v.) to represent him, and they—by prearrangement—declined, saying they could not agree to the rules under which Duane was being tried by the Senate. Duane then submitted their correspondence to Jefferson and declined any further appearance before the Senate. That body, he said, could take whatever action it wanted.

The Senate then declared Duane guilty of contempt and issued a warrant for his arrest, but Duane evaded the warrant until the Senate had adjourned. After further wrangling, the Senate realized its own impotence and weakly requested that the president prosecute Duane under the Sedition Act. A succession of delays prevented the prosecution from taking place immediately, and the charges were dropped when Jefferson became president the next year.

Although Duane remained staunchly loyal to the president, he lost much of his influence during the Jefferson administration because of a combination of factors. One was that the capital had moved from Philadelphia to the newly created town of Washington, D.C., but the *Aurora* remained in Philadelphia. Another was that Duane fell out with many in Jefferson's government, and ultimately, he became enemies with James Madison and James Monroe. Duane maintained his influence in Pennsylvania politics, however, and he remained in close contact with the president for many years.

Jefferson appointed him lieutenant colonel of rifles in July 1808 and solicited subscriptions to relieve him of financial embarrassment in 1811. Duane was an adjutant general during the War of 1812 and continued editorship of the *Aurora* until his retirement in 1822. He made one unsuccessful attempt to revive the *Aurora* to fight the National Bank. He was appointed prothonotary of the supreme court of Pennsylvania for the eastern district and kept that position until his death in 1835.

BIBLIOGRAPHY:
B. DAB 5, 467–468; Donald H. Stewart, *The Opposition Press of the Federalist Period* (Albany, 1969).

JAMES GLEN STOVALL

DU BOIS, WILLIAM EDWARD BURGHARDT (b 23 February 1868; d. 27 August 1963) was a pivotal figure in shaping attitudes on civil rights in the United States and Africa. As a young man, he was a correspondent for the *New York Age* and the *Springfield Republican*. In the years that followed, he wrote columns for several papers, including the *Pittsburgh Courier* and the *San Francisco Chronicle*. He was the founder and editor of several publications, most notably the *Crisis*. This journal, the official organ of the National Association for the Advancement of Colored People (NAACP), provided a forum for black thought during the first half of the 1900s.

Du Bois was born in Great Barrington, Massachusetts. His father, Alfred Du Bois, was descended from French Huguenots. His mother, Mary Silvina Burghardt, was descended from an African who was stolen by Dutch slave traders. Mary was thirty-five years old and had a son, Idelbert, who was fathered by her cousin, when she met Alfred. After they married and William was born, Alfred moved to New Milford, Connecticut. He sent for the family, but Mary chose to stay with her relatives. William therefore never really knew his father. He and his mother were supported by her family and by her occasional work as a housekeeper.

Du Bois was one of few blacks in his community, and the only black in his high school class. While in high school, William contributed letters to, and earned money as a local sales agent for, the *New York Age*. By the time he was seventeen, Du Bois had also acted as a correspondent for the *Springfield Republican*, and the *New York Globe* and *Freeman*. Upon graduation, he enrolled at Fisk University, where he gained a new understanding of black culture. While there, Du Bois founded and edited a literary magazine, the *Fisk Herald*.

In 1888 he earned a B.A. and entered Harvard University. In 1890 he earned a B.A. from Harvard, graduating cum laude. After winning a fellowship for study abroad, Du Bois studied economics and history at the University of Berlin. In 1895 he earned a Ph.D. from Harvard. Du Bois taught Greek and Latin at Wilberforce University, a small black college in Ohio. While there he married Nina Gomer on 12 May 1896. The marriage lasted fifty-three years, until Nina's death. The couple had a son, Burghardt, who died at age three, and a daughter, Yolande. After two years at Wilberforce, Du Bois moved to the University of Pennsylvania for a year. He taught and studied the life-styles of blacks in the city. His research, based on his interviews with 5,000 residents, was published under the title *The Philadelphia Negro* (1899).

From 1897 to 1910 he was professor of economics and history at Atlanta University. It was during this period that Du Bois became heavily involved in civil rights and established himself as a national leader. By the turn of the century he had begun to question the racial philosophy of Booker T. Washington. As the leading spokesperson for blacks, Washington advocated a program of racial progress through skilled trades and labor. Du Bois believed that a "Talented Tenth" of blacks should be encouraged to gain knowledge to act as leaders for the race. The two became involved in a philosophical debate that caused Du Bois to become active in organizing blacks for civic progress.

In early summer 1905, Du Bois became incensed by the jailing of William Monroe Trotter (q.v.). Trotter had led heckling that escalated to a civil disturbance during a speech by Booker T. Washington. Shortly thereafter, Du Bois called a meeting of "a few selected persons for organized determination and aggressive action [for] Negro freedom and growth." The group that met became incorporated in 1906 as the Niagara Movement, and became part of the founding of the NAACP. Du Bois was named director of publications and a member of the board of directors for the young NAACP. In 1906 he briefly published a newspaper in Memphis called the *Moon*. The experience gave him some basis for starting the *Crisis* in 1910. Du Bois remained editor of the magazine and a member of the NAACP board until 1934.

Du Bois's interest in socialist causes increased over the years. In 1913 he joined the editorial board of the *New Review*, a socialist magazine. In 1926 he visited the Soviet Union. During this period, Du Bois was also a leader of the Harlem Renaissance, a literary movement by and about blacks. His books, articles, poems, and essays, written during the Renaissance and afterward, established him as the leading black intellectual during the first half of the century.

By the early 1930s Du Bois's socialist activities caused friction with the NAACP. As moves were made to limit his authority, he resigned in 1934. Between 1936 and 1948 his columns appeared in the *Pittsburgh Courier* and the *New York Amsterdam News*. He returned as a researcher for the NAACP from 1944 to 1948, but his socialist activities continued.

In November 1950 he was indicted, tried, and acquitted on charges of being an unregistered foreign agent. In 1951, when Du Bois was eighty-three years old, he married Shirley Graham, who was forty years his junior. In 1958–59 he toured the Soviet Union and China, and in 1961 he joined the Communist party. Du Bois accepted an offer by the president of Ghana to work in that country in 1961, and became a citizen there in 1963. He died in August of that year, and is buried in Accra.

BIBLIOGRAPHY:

A. *The Souls of Black Folk: Essays and Sketches* (Chicago, 1903); *The Autobiography of W.E.B. Du Bois* (New York, 1947).

B. DAB Supp. 7, 200–205; NYT 28 August 1963; Leslie Alexander Lacy, *Cheer the Lonesome Traveler* (New York, 1970).

KAREN FITZGERALD BROWN

DUNIWAY, ABIGAIL SCOTT (b. 22 October 1834; d. 11 October 1915) was the founder and longtime editor and publisher of one of the first woman suffrage newspapers in the western United States. She led the forty-year fight for women's right to vote in Oregon and traveled extensively in other western states to organize and recruit supporters for suffrage groups. She wrote the first novel commercially printed in Oregon, along with much other fiction and poetry, most of which was published in her own periodicals.

The third of twelve children, Abigail Jane Scott was born on her family's farm near Groveland, Illinois. She attended nearby schools sporadically, with most of her time occupied by tasks at home and on the farm. In 1852 her father, John Tucker Scott, decided to move his family to Oregon and assigned her diarist for the trip. The move was opposed by her mother, Ann Roelofson Scott, who was not in good health and who died on the journey. The hard lot of her mother made a lasting impression on Duniway, and she later named it as a leading cause of her involvement with women's rights.

In Oregon's Willamette Valley, near Salem, Duniway taught school for a year and then was married, on 1 August 1853, to Benjamin Charles Duniway, a farmer who also had come to Oregon from Illinois. The couple had one daughter and five sons between 1854 and 1869. Duniway marketed, cooked, washed and mended for both family and hired hands, and helped with farm chores as well until 1862, when the farm was lost because of an unpaid note her husband had endorsed for a friend. She had not been consulted before the note was signed, and she used this incident as an illustration of women's unfair treatment. However, she credited Ben with suggesting to her that only winning the right to vote would improve women's condition. Ben was injured in a wagon accident, and Duniway resorted to running a boarding school and then a millinery shop to support the family. In 1870 she founded an Equal Rights Society in Albany.

The following year the family moved to Portland, where Duniway's brother, Harvey Scott (q.v.), editor of the *Portland Oregonian* and a lifelong opponent of woman suffrage, was helpful in getting Ben a job at the Portland Customs House, and where Duniway established her weekly newspaper, the *New Northwest*. A lively combination of news, advice, editorials, humor, poetry, and fiction, the paper lasted for sixteen years. Duniway was assisted during most of this time by her children and her sister, Catherine Coburn, an important western journalist in her own right. The paper survived for only two months after Duniway sold it in 1887. Apparently weary of financial and political struggles, she yielded to her family's plea to take up ranching in Idaho, but spent only summers there. In 1891 she returned to journalism in Portland with a short-lived paper called the *Coming Century*, and from 1895 to 1897 edited the *Pacific Empire*, a temperance journal. Her husband died 4 August 1896.

Although Duniway was a firm advocate of temperance, she opposed prohibition and particularly its pairing with suffrage. This viewpoint and her outspoken independence of character led to her estrangement from the National American Woman Suffrage Association, of which she had at one time been a vice president. She withdrew from involvement in the unsuccessful 1906 Oregon suffrage battle after acrimonious disagreements with the eastern suffragists, but again led the Oregon Equal Suffrage Association, which she had founded in 1873, for the 1908 and 1910 campaigns. By 1912, when Oregon voters at last approved suffrage, she was confined to a wheelchair, but she wrote the suffrage proclamation and signed it jointly with the governor. Two years later her autobiography, *Path Breaking* (1914), appeared.

Duniway served as president of the Portland Woman's Club and the Oregon Federation of Women's Clubs and was invited in 1893 to address the Congress of Women at the World's Columbian Exposition in Chicago. She died from a persistent infection in 1915. Her daughter and one son, Willis, who had been elected Oregon state printer in 1906, died before her. Another son, Clyde, became a professor of history at Stanford University and then served successive terms as president of the University of Montana, the University of Wyoming, and Colorado College.

BIBLIOGRAPHY:

B. DAB 5, 513–514; NAW 1, 531–533; NYT 12 October 1915; Ruth Barnes Moynihan, *Rebel for Rights* (New Haven, 1983).

SHERILYN COX BENNION

DUNNE, FINLEY PETER (b. 10 July 1867; d. 24 April 1936) was one of the most brilliant and popular satirical essayists of his generation. His "Mr. Dooley" stories, written in Irish-American dialect, began in Chicago newspapers, but soon appeared in magazines and newspapers throughout the United States and England. Dunne's essays deflated the presumption of the rich and powerful and offered readers a sardonic running commentary on the important political events of the day.

Born in Chicago and baptized Peter Dunne, he was the fifth of seven children born to Peter and Ellen Finley Dunne. (In 1886 Dunne would take his mother's maiden name to commemorate her early death from tuberculosis.) Dunne's father was a carpenter who provided his family with a comfortable middle-class living, but who was generally suspect of his son's literary leanings and independent ideas. His mother inculcated in Dunne a love of literature and reading that would last his whole life. Dunne never cared for much of the rest of his schoolwork, however, and he graduated last in his class at Chicago's West Division High School in 1884.

Seeming to his father an unlikely candidate for college, Dunne went to work as an errand boy at the *Chicago Telegram*, thus beginning a newspaper career that by 1900 would take him to almost every daily in Chicago. Late in 1884 he moved to the *Chicago Daily News*, where he began writing editorials and reporting sports. In 1888 he was hired by the *Chicago Times* as a political reporter and editorial writer. He covered both the Democratic and Republican conventions that year and quickly rose to city editor. Following a change in management at the *Times* a year later, Dunne moved to the *Chicago Tribune* as a general reporter, and by January 1890 had been made editor of the Sunday edition. Later that year he took a job at the *Chicago Herald*, to return to the political reporting that he loved. In 1892 the *Herald*'s owners put Dunne in charge of the editorial page of the *Herald*'s sister paper, the *Evening Post*.

It was the *Post* that allowed Dunne the freedom to write the freewheeling, satirical editorials and dialect humor that would make him famous. His earliest dialect pieces featured a Colonel McNeery, owner of a downtown Chicago bar, who was modeled after James McGarry, a well-known Chicago tavern owner. When McGarry protested, Dunne chose a new setting—Archer Avenue in the "shanty Irish" South Side neighborhood of Bridgeport—and on 7 October 1893 introduced a new character—tavern owner Martin Dooley. In the early Dooley stories, Dunne lampooned local politics and prominent Chicagoans such as Charles Yerkes and George Pullman, but he later would take on national issues and figures such as William Jennings Bryan, Theodore Roosevelt, and Andrew Carnegie.

In 1897 Dunne became managing editor of the struggling *Chicago Journal*, and immediately improved that paper's prospects by bringing the Mr. Dooley columns with him. A year later the first of the Mr. Dooley collections appeared, *Mr. Dooley in Peace and War* (1898), followed shortly by *Mr. Dooley in the Hearts of His Countrymen* (1899).

When Dunne moved to New York City in 1900 and began writing his Dooley pieces for national syndication and for *Harper's Weekly* and *Collier's Weekly*, his stories came to focus less on Chicago life and more on national and international affairs. In 1902 he became editor of the *New York Morning Telegraph*, but severed his connection with that theatrical and sporting newspaper in 1904 when its owner died. From then on Dunne worked only for magazines and was increasingly drawn into editorial management and administration. From 1906 to 1913 he wrote dialect essays for *American Magazine* and contributed monthly editorials to a feature called "In the Interpreter's House." From 1913 to 1915 Dunne wrote political commentary for *Collier's Weekly*, and in 1917 he succeeded Mark Sullivan as editor in chief, a job he held until Crowell Publishing bought the magazine in 1919. That same year the last of eight collections of the Dooley essays appeared.

After 1920 Dunne occasionally tried to revive Dooley, but without much success, and for the most part he retired to family and club life. In 1902 he had married Margaret Abbott, and they had raised four children. When Payne Whitney died in 1924, leaving a $200 million estate, he bequeathed to Dunne $500,000, enough to let Dunne maintain his stylish way of life without ever having to work again. In 1935 Dunne discovered that he had throat cancer, and though the treatments seemed successful, he died a year later from a hemorrhage.

BIBLIOGRAPHY:

A. Philip Dunne, ed., *Mr. Dooley Remembers: The Informal Memoirs of Finley Peter Dunne* (Boston, 1963).

B. DAB Supp. 2, 158–160; NYT 25 April 1936; Elmer Ellis, *Mr. Dooley's America: A Life of Finley Peter Dunne* (New York, 1941); Grace Eckley, *Finley Peter Dunne* (Boston, 1981).

JOHN J. PAULY

DURANTY, WALTER (b. 25 May 1884; d. 3 October 1957) was one of the most prominent journalists of the 1920s and 1930s. He served as a foreign correspondent of the *New York Times* from 1913 to 1941 and gained renown as an expert on Russian affairs as a result of his long residence (1922–34) in Moscow as the *Times* correspondent. In 1932 he won a Pulitzer Prize for a series of articles on the Soviet Union. After that his reputation as a Soviet expert continued to grow. He wrote a number of books, some of which were best-sellers in their day.

Born in Liverpool, England, Duranty spent his early years in the country of his birth. He was the only son of William Steel Duranty, a merchant, and Emmeline Hutchins Duranty. His parents, who were rigidly Presbyterian in matters of both religion and discipline, were killed in a train crash when Walter was only ten. He had a public school education at Harrow and Bedford before attending Emmanuel College, Cambridge, where he received first class honors in classics. After leaving Cambridge, he spent seven years traveling about in Europe and in the United States. During that time he contributed occasionally to Frank Munsey's (q.v.) *Argosy*.

His journalism career began in 1913 when he joined the staff of the *New York Times* in Paris. During World War I, he served that paper as a correspondent not only in Paris but also at French army headquarters and later on the French front. After covering the Paris peace conference in 1919, he went to Riga to report on the political unrest and famine in the Baltic states that followed the Russian Revolution. In 1920 he returned to Paris, but in the following year he went back to Eastern Europe where he managed to enter Soviet Russia with Herbert Hoover's American Relief Administration. In 1922 he became the Moscow correspondent of the *New York Times*, a post he held until 1934.

While in Moscow, Duranty achieved his reputation as an expert on Soviet affairs. His dispatches from the Soviet capital contained vivid descriptions of Soviet life and helped to untangle the Byzantine webs of Soviet politics for Western readers. He twice interviewed Joseph Stalin. In 1933 he accompanied Maxim Litvinov, the Soviet commissar for foreign affairs, to Washington for the negotiation of American recognition of the Soviet Union. In 1934 he resigned from his position in Moscow, but he continued his association with the *Times* and returned to Russia many times in ensuing years.

Duranty's reputation rested on his ability to interpret Soviet policy and the conditions of Russian life to the Western world. Some of his contemporaries, however, questioned the validity of his interpretations. Claiming that his reporting of Soviet affairs was biased and that it departed from the truth, they charged that he was, in fact, a failure as a political analyst and that his dispatches from Moscow were too sympathetic to Soviet leaders including Joseph Stalin. His dispatches about the great man-made famine of the early 1930s in the Soviet Union seriously departed from the truth, and he even defended Stalin and his advisers during the major purge trials of the mid-thirties. Duranty always had his defenders, such as Joseph Davies, the American ambassador to the Soviet Union from 1936 to 1938. Recent research, however, has underscored the validity of his critics' charges.

After leaving Moscow as the *Times* correspondent in residence there, he remained active in journalism. Aside from his regular return visits to the Soviet Union, his most important assignment in the 1930s was in Spain, where he went in 1936 to write a series of articles on the Spanish Loyalists. During the early years of World War II, he was in the field again, in France, Sweden, the Soviet Union, the Balkans, and Japan.

Duranty was small in stature and walked with a limp. He lost his left leg in a train accident in 1924, but despite that handicap, he continued to lead an active and aggressive life with the aid of an artificial leg. In 1925 he married Jeanne Sheron. They were separated later. He died on 3 October 1957 after a short illness, just a week after marrying Mrs. Anna Enwright while a patient in a hospital in Orlando, Florida.

BIBLIOGRAPHY:

A. *I Write As I Please* (New York, 1935).

B. DAB Supp. 6, 183–185; NYT 4 October 1957; James William Crowl, *Angels in Stalin's Paradise: Western Reporters in Soviet Russia, 1917 to 1937, A Case Study of Louis Fischer and Walter Duranty* (Lanham, Md., 1982).

JAMES D. STARTT

E

EARLY, STEPHEN TYREE (b. 27 August 1889; d. 11 August 1951) was the first official White House press secretary, serving throughout Franklin D. Roosevelt's twelve years in office. As the voice of the New Deal, he announced the bank holiday and various new government programs, and as the voice of the nation at war, he announced the bombing of Pearl Harbor and various international negotiations.

Although previous presidents had press advisers, with Early's appointment the job became formalized. Early's reporting background and his long-standing friendship with Roosevelt enabled him to bridge the gap between the press and the presidency and helped Roosevelt win public support. During press conferences in the Oval Office, Early would be at the president's side and make suggestions to the president on what to say and to newspapermen on how to interpret what was said.

Early was born in Crozet, Virginia, the son of Thomas Joseph Early, a railway lerk, and Ida Virginia Wood Early. Early attended local schools and, in 1908, after high school, went to work in the Washington office of the United Press. He covered the Departments of State, War, and the Navy, where he met Roosevelt, then an assistant secretary of the Navy. The two became good friends and Early is said to have taught Roosevelt the fundamentals of the Washington publicity game. In 1913 Early switched from United Press to the Associated Press.

In 1917 Early enlisted in the army. He saw combat as an infantry officer, then was assigned to the staff of *Stars and Stripes*, the soldier's newspaper, eventually becoming the officer in charge. Upon returning to Washington in 1919, he worked briefly as director of publicity for the U.S. Chamber of Commerce. In 1920 he was advance man for Roosevelt's unsuccessful campaign for the vice presidency. Early then rejoined the Associated Press, where he was regarded as a crack spot-news man. In 1923 he scored a six-minute beat on President Warren Harding's (q.v.) death from a heart attack by slipping down the hotel stairs to find a phone before the official announcement. In 1927 Early became Washington editor for Paramount News, a newsreel company.

In 1933 Roosevelt picked Early to be assistant secretary in charge of press relations, one of several members of the working press in the administration. (Early was named press secretary in 1937.) Early had to work against formidable odds because most of the powerful newspaper publishers in the country opposed Roosevelt and the New Deal programs. But he had an advantage in Roosevelt, who enjoyed, at least at the beginning of his presidency, dealing with reporters. Early established regular press conferences for the president (twice weekly at first; 998 in all) and eliminated the written questions that President Herbert Hoover had required reporters to submit. The first news conference, on 8 March 1933, established the rules. The president could not be quoted directly unless Early issued statements in writing. Other information was for background only, and could be used but not attributed. Some information would be off the record, the reporters were warned that if they violated the president's confidence, he would make an example of them. As a result, the press conferences, while enjoyable and informative for the reporters, provided little direct news to the public.

Early also had his own daily press conferences that provided a flow of copy. He guided Roosevelt into use of radio and newsreels. He put a news ticker in his office so he would know what was going on elsewhere, and he insisted on access to the president to answer reporters' questions. Early was hardworking but short-tempered, often regarded, *Editor and Publisher* said, as an impossible grouch. His relations with reporters became strained over the years, but he was generally regarded as doing a good job for the president.

In April 1945 Early announced Roosevelt's death to the nation. In June he left the White House to become vice president of the Pullman railroad car company. He returned to government service twice: for a year, beginning in 1949, to try to shape up Defense Department press relations, and for two days, in 1950, when President Truman's press secretary, Charles Ross, died during an important international meeting. Then Early returned to Pullman. Passionately loyal to Roosevelt, Early refused all offers to write his memoirs.

At his death, of a heart attack, in 1951, Early was survived by his wife, Helen Wrenn Early, a childhood friend he had married in 1921, and their three children.

BIBLIOGRAPHY:

B. DAB Supp. 5, 196–197; NYT 12 August 1951; Stephen E. Schoenherr, "Selling the New Deal: Stephen T. Early's Role as Press Secretary to Franklin Roosevelt," Ph.D. diss., Univ. of Delaware, 1975.

JUDITH A. SERRIN

EASTMAN, MAX FORRESTER (b. 4 January 1883; d. 25 March 1969). "A man of letters," a term seldom used today but in vogue during the first quarter of this century, could be applied to few more appropriately than to Max Eastman.

Born in the upstate New York town of Canandaigua, Eastman acquired a respect for intellectual rigor and a sense of moral purpose from his parents, Samuel Elijah and Annis, both ordained ministers. He disliked the respectable but stringent life of a minister's family, and developed a taste for a more cosmopolitan setting in which to pursue his moral quest. His parents were able to send him to Williams College, from which he received his B.A. in 1905. After a year during which he considered a variety of possible careers, he entered Columbia University in 1907. He found the Columbia Department of Philosophy a congenial place in which to study and work as an assistant, and became a protégé of John Dewey and a friend of Sidney Hook. He remained at Columbia for four years. He claimed that he completed all of the requirements for the Ph.D., but, according to a quotation found in several sources, "preferred not to receive it."

In 1911 he married Ida Rauh and began a career as a journalist. In 1913 he helped found and became editor of the *Masses*, a post that brought him considerable notoriety. The magazine became a vehicle for social protest and the application of left-wing ideas he had debated at Columbia. Eastman's interest in revolution as a mechanism for social change, together with his unyielding opposition to American participation in World War I, led the government to ban the magazine from the U.S. mails. This resulted in the demise of the magazine and an increase in his revolutionary zeal. In 1918 he launched the *Liberator* and continued his political journalism. The government continued its attempts to suppress his magazine. In the eight years from the founding of the *Masses* to his departure from the *Liberator* in 1922 he became a leading spokesman for the left and, if he had cared to portray himself in this way, something of a martyr for his ideas. Had his career ended at this point he would be remembered as someone who risked prison to maintain the freedom of the press.

Eastman was not to be frozen into a historical role, however. He visited Russia to see the consequences of the revolution and was shocked to discover, not a socialist state, but rather a "totalitarian tyranny." In 1924 he married Eliena Krylenko and began work on a series of books in which he attacked the intellectual roots of Marxism. He was one of the first to travel the road, later taken by Arthur Koestler and others, that led from the revolutionary left to the repudiation of those views. His essential charge was that the scientific underpinning of Marxism could not be sustained. Having been attacked for his left-wing views a decade earlier, he now found himself attacked once again, this time by the intellectual establishment which was taking a fashionable interest in the left that he now denounced.

Although he lectured widely, appeared on network radio, and worked as a roving editor for *Reader's Digest* from 1941 until 1969, Eastman did not hold institutional positions. He devoted his time to writing. Aside from his political writing, he had a continuing interest in the psychology of art and the relation of literature to science. Perhaps his most notable characteristic was the tentative manner in which he held his opinions. Although he would fight and suffer for whatever views he held at any moment, he was never embittered by his struggles.

When he became convinced that an idea could no longer be supported, he moved on without rancor. Had he waited for the left to become fashionable in the twenties, or had he postponed his renunciation of it for a decade, his decisions might have been celebrated. His willingness to follow his own timetable rather than editorial fashion meant that he frequently appeared to be idiosyncratic and quixotic.

In 1958 Eastman married Yvette Szekely. His autobiographical book, *Love and Revolution* (1964), reveals his Edwardian fairness and directness, his enjoyment of life's many pleasures, and his genius for friendship which made him a prominent participant in American literary life for more than half a century.

BIBLIOGRAPHY:

B. NYT 26 March 1969; Sidney Hook, ''Remembering Max Eastman,'' *American Scholar*, Summer 1979; William L. O'Neill, *The Last Romantic: A Life of Max Eastman* (New York, 1978).

ROBERT RUTHERFORD SMITH

EDDY, MARY BAKER (b. 16 July 1821; d. 3 December 1910), the enigmatic woman who founded a major American church, also made a major contribution to journalism by founding the international newspaper *Christian Science Monitor*. The newspaper was started twenty-nine years after the Church of Christ, Scientist was chartered on 23 August 1879 in Boston. The first *Monitor* rolled off the press in the same city on 25 November 1908.

Although Mary Baker Eddy wanted the newspaper to help demonstrate her vision of Christian Science as something beyond sectarian, emotional, and cultural boundaries, she also wanted it to help fend off rumors about the church and about her personal condition. She recognized the value of having a respected publication that would appeal to intellectuals. She saw secular publications as too much conveying the notion that ''it is dangerous to live, so loaded seems the very air with disease'' (Beasley, 1952). She insisted on having ''Christian Science'' as part of the title, and she picked the motto for the editorial page: ''First the blade, then the ear, then the full grain in the ear.'' She wrote the newspaper's statement of purpose: ''to injure no man, but to bless all mankind.''

Before beginning the *Monitor*, Mrs. Eddy wrote several books, the most significant being *Science and Health with Key to the Scriptures* (1875). Her first publication was the *Journal of Christian Science*, an eight-page periodical. Part of the mystery of Mary Baker Eddy lies in the fact that although she founded a church based on positive thinking, whose creed included faith healing, she spent a great deal of her life ill and in pain. Undoubtedly her physical condition led her to seek spiritual help. After a stay in a sanatorium that did little for her, she consulted Dr. Phineas Parkhurst Quimby of Portland, Maine. Just months later she declared that because of Dr. Quimby her health was recovered. But the recovery was temporary. There is no doubt that Quimby was a strong influence. There is evidence that she owed a lot of her thinking to Dr. Quimby as well as to his pupil, Warren Felt Evans, who later published *The Mental Cure*. Despite her literary faults, she brought new zest and forcefulness to their shared ideas, which helped her in her ultimate success in founding the church.

Mary Baker Eddy was born in Bow (near Concord), New Hampshire, the youngest of six children. Her father, a farmer, was Mark Baker, and her mother was Abigail Barnard Ambrose Baker. Reared in a strict religious household, she became a member of the Tilton Congregational Church at seventeen, but not before she had been carefully examined about her theological beliefs, which even then differed somewhat from those of the establishment. Her early education was at private academies in Plymouth, Massachusetts, but her main education, considered sketchy by some, was from tutoring by her brother Albert, a student at Dartmouth College. Biographers have noted that she did not progress very far in her study of languages, even her own, although she claimed otherwise.

Despite the frailty and illness of her growing-up years, Mary Baker Eddy was married at twenty-two to George Washington Glover, a contractor and builder from Charleston, South Carolina, where she began writing poems and short pieces for newspapers and magazines. The wedding was in December 1843, but on 3 July 1844 she was widowed when her husband died of what was called "bilious fever." In September 1844 she gave birth to her only son, George Glover. Thereafter, she spent many unhappy years dependent upon her family, mainly her father and a sister, Abigail. She became a chronic invalid, suffering, according to her official biographer, Norman Beasley, "from a spinal weakness" and "spasmodic seizures, followed by prostration that amounted to a complete nervous collapse." When her son was four, because her family apparently could not handle both of them, he was sent away to live with her former nurse, and for a time she lost touch with him entirely.

In 1853 she married Dr. Daniel Patterson, an itinerant dentist and homeopathist who was a family friend. They lived in various New Hampshire villages until Dr. Patterson, caught up in the Civil War, was imprisoned by the Confederate army in 1862. Having been separated from him for years, she divorced him on grounds of desertion in 1873 and took back the name Mary M. Glover. On New Year's Day, 1877, at age fifty-six, she startled friends and followers by marrying Asa Gilbert Eddy, a mild-mannered man said to be of "limited" intelligence, who was devoted to her. Five years later, on 3 June 1882, Asa Eddy died of what was ruled organic heart disease, but it was Mrs. Eddy's opinion that had she herself treated him in time, she could have saved him.

Mrs. Eddy seemed always to need a man around for emotional and intellectual support as well as for business and literary advice. She was married three times, and her attachment to Dr. Quimby, though brief, was strong. After her divorce from Dr. Patterson, she and Richard Kennedy moved into an apartment that served as a lodging as well as an office. He practiced as "Dr. Kennedy," and she wrote about and taught Christian Science. Others who were her followers and supporters included Daniel H. Spofford and Calvin Frye. She came close to marrying Spofford before she married Asa Gilbert Eddy.

However, Mary Baker Eddy was no feminist, although she gave passing approval to the woman suffrage movement. She sometimes signed herself as "Mother Mary." Perhaps the desire to be a mother motivated her adoption of Ebenezer Johnson Foster, who added Eddy to his name when she formally adopted him when he was forty-one. He was, until their break, another important man in her life, and because he was legally her son, he inherited a considerable estate when she died. Perhaps she regretted not having been more of a mother to George Glover, whom she saw only seldom in his later years. She corresponded with him erratically, was concerned for his children, and loaned him money. His illiteracy worried her, but she apparently did nothing about it.

In her later life Mary Baker Eddy did much to build the church organization. She used the title "Pastor Emeritus" authoritatively to change the church manual as she saw fit. Her complex personality and her displeasures became more difficult for everyone to deal with. She suffered nocturnal seizures that increased in frequence as she aged, and some important revelations about church doctrine followed the attacks. For example, at one point she stated that "whenever the pain is too violent for mental treatment, a Scientist may call a surgeon to administer a hypodermic injection [morphine]," but when the pain stopped, "the sufferer should handle his own case mentally" (Beasley, 1952).

She spent the end of her life in the Chestnut Hill mansion prepared for her, where she was alternately described as a saint and "a shrinking, pathetic figure." There were rumors of the undue influence of Frye upon her. Frye was a young machinist and a Christian Scientist who became her steward, secretary, bookkeeper, and footman from 1882 until her death. She suffered a serious and painful illness during the last years of her life, probably gallstones, although that is not well documented. Her pain was so great that she was attended by physicians and did receive morphine injections. However, despite ill health most of her life, she lived to be eighty-nine. The cause of her death was pneumonia, according to the *New York Times*. She left an estate of more than $2.5 million.

BIBLIOGRAPHY:

B. DAB 3, 7–14; NYT 5 December 1910; Norman Beasley, *Mary Baker Eddy: The Cross and the Crown* (Boston, 1952).

JUNE N. ADAMSON

EDES, BENJAMIN (b. 14 October 1732; d. 11 December 1803) was co-owner of the *Boston Gazette*, a prime mover in the formation of the Sons of Liberty and, in the words of a contemporary, "one of the most influential and active newspaper editors and political writers of the Revolutionary War" (Cullen, 1974).

Edes was born in Charlestown, Massachusetts, the son of Peter and Esther Hall Edes. His great-grandfather, John Edes, came over from England about 1674. His father was a hatter who took an active part in the affairs of Charlestown. Early details about Benjamin Edes are scarce, but it is certain that he served an apprenticeship in printing. In May 1755 Edes married Martha Starr. They were the parents of ten children.

At the end of 1754 Edes formed a partnership with fellow apprentice John Gill and sent out subscription notices for a weekly, the *Country Journal*. Before their plans matured, Gill's father-in-law, Samuel Kneeland, announced that he was discontinuing his *Boston Gazette*. Anxious to procure a ready-made subscription list, the two young men took over the operation, producing the first issue of the *Boston Gazette, or Country Journal* on 7 April 1755.

Edes and Gill proved to be able newspaper publishers. The circulation at one time stood at 2,000, a robust figure for a colonial newspaper. From their print shop adjoining the prison on Queen Street, the pair published books, pamphlets, theological tracts, and almanacs, and carried, until their antigovernment posture began to irritate authorities, a large amount of public printing in the *Gazette*.

As the business flourished, Edes became involved in civic matters. He served as town constable in 1757, as scavenger in 1760, and as clerk of the market from 1763 to 1765. He also joined the North End Caucus, a political group that offered opportunities for debating public issues. Edes also held membership in the Loyall Nine, an exclusive group of extremists which would form the nucleus of the Sons of Liberty.

The *Gazette* became a leader in the resistance movement that flourished from 1765 to 1775. History has long given credit to its contributors, the illustrious Samuel Adams (q.v.), John Adams, James Otis, Joseph Warren, and others. The owners of the *Gazette*, however, were not mere typesetters. As Isaiah Thomas (q.v.) wrote in his *History of Printing in America* "No publisher of a newspaper felt a greater interest in the establishment of the independence of the United States than Benjamin Edes; and no newspaper was more instrumental in bringing forward this important event than the *Boston Gazette*." Edes assumed increasing responsibility in the resistance with the advent of the Stamp Act crisis. The *Gazette* became more pugnacious, Boston Loyalists referring to it as "The Weekly Dung Barge." Governor Francis Bernard tried to get the legislature to take action against the *Gazette* but without success.

When the issue of tea became explosive in 1773, Edes helped to guard the wharves against the unloading of the hated British brew. Matters deteriorated rapidly when the British brought ships with their cargo of tea to Boston despite opposition. A group of radicals met at Edes's home on 16 December 1773. They drank punch, discussed the matter, and at dark moved to the *Gazette* office. Joined by others, they assumed Indian disguises, proceeded to the harbor, boarded three ships, and dumped more than 300 chests of tea into the bay.

After the battles of Lexington and Concord, the British established martial law in Boston. On the British block list, Edes fled to Watertown, where he resumed publication of the *Gazette* on 5 June 1775. After the British evacuation, Edes returned to Boston, where he found a dispirited Gill unwilling to continue the struggle. Edes then became sole proprietor of the newspaper. But times had changed. The center of action had moved from Boston. The coterie of brilliant editorialists had died or moved. People had come to identify the *Gazette* with disruption. With Boston safe in American control, people turned to other concerns, and circulation waned. By 1797 Edes was publishing from his home and the *Gazette*'s circulation had dwindled to 400. On 17 September 1798 Edes printed the final edition. He and his wife continued to operate a print shop out of their home.

BIBLIOGRAPHY:

B. DAB 3, part 2, 17–18; Maurice R. Cullen, Jr., "The *Boston Gazette*: A Community Newspaper," *Journalism Quarterly*, Spring 1959; Maurice R. Cullen, Jr., "Benjamin Edes: Scourge of Torries," *Journalism Quarterly*, Summer 1974.

ROBERT E. BLACKMON

EISENSTAEDT, ALFRED (b. 6 December 1898) was one of the four original *Life* staff photographers when the magazine began in November 1936, and he maintained that position until it folded in December 1972. Since then, he has been a contributing photographer to *People*, an active free-lancer, and author of several photographic books. Considered by many to be the "father of photojournalism," Eisenstaedt began his career in Germany, working from 1929 to 1935 for the Pacific and Atlantic Picture Agency (absorbed in 1931 by the Associated Press).

Born in Dirschau, Germany (now Tczew, Poland), he was the older son of Regina Schoen Eisenstaedt, a homemaker, and Joseph Eisenstaedt, a department store owner. The family, which was well-to-do, moved to Berlin in 1906, and he graduated from the Hohenzollern Gymnasium there in 1912. His attendance at the University of Berlin was interrupted by World War I when he was drafted into the German army in 1916. On 12 December 1917, he sustained serious leg injuries when the rest of his artillery battery was killed. Upon returning to civilian life in Berlin, Eisenstaedt enrolled again at the university but was forced to quit to take a job as a buttons-and-belts salesman when his family's fortune was lost during the period of postwar inflation.

Eisenstaedt began photographing in the mid–1920s, selling a shot he took in 1925 on vacation to *Der Weltspiegel* two years later. Happy that he could get paid for doing something he had taught himself to do and thoroughly enjoyed, Eisenstaedt began free-lancing part-time. He was represented by the Pacific and Atlantic Picture Agency in Berlin. In December 1929 he decided to quit his sales job to free-lance full-time with the agency. During the late 1920s and early 1930s, Eisenstaedt's work appeared in such European publications as the *Berliner Illustrirte Zeitung*, *Der Weltspiegel*, *Die Dame*, the *Illustrated London News*, and the *Graphic*.

He was an established photojournalist when he emigrated to the United States near the end of 1935 in an attempt to escape the Nazis (he later became a naturalized citizen in 1943 or 1944). Leon Daniel, his boss at the Associated Press in Berlin, also emigrated to New York City, establishing a new picture agency called Pix. Eisenstaedt was associated with Daniel's agency for many years.

Early in 1936 he spent several months in Hollywood, selling photographs to *Harper's Bazaar*, *Vogue*, *Town and Country*, and other prestigious magazines. In April 1936 Eisenstaedt was hired by Time Inc. to join Margaret Bourke-White (q.v.), Peter Stackpole, and Thomas McAvoy as the original staff for Henry Luce's (q.v.) newest magazine, *Life*.

While many *Life* photographers became known as specialists in areas such as science, medicine, and architecture, Eisenstaedt remained a generalist. He is proud of the fact that he can handle all types of assignments, but clearly he excels when working with people. Of the more than ninety *Life* covers to his credit, most of them are portraits of celebrities. His work has taken him all over the world, and his stature in photographic circles is far greater than his small five-foot-four-inch frame.

Throughout his career he has been an active lecturer, and his work has been exhibited in New York, Philadelphia, Toronto, and Munich. An intensively private man, Eisenstaedt married Alma ''Kathy'' Kaye on 24 June 1949. They had no children, and lived for many years in Queens, New York. Mrs. Eisenstaedt died on 27 February 1972.

BIBLIOGRAPHY:

A. *Eisenstaedt on Eisenstaedt: A Self-Portrait* (New York, 1985).

B. Stanley Rayfield, *''Life'' Photographers: Their Careers and Favorite Pictures* (New York, 1957).

C. ZOE SMITH

EVANS, GEORGE HENRY (b. 25 March 1805; d. 2 February 1856) was a reformer who insisted that land was a right of every citizen, and so became a central figure in the homestead movement. He also was the publisher and editor of the *Working Man's Advocate*, a pioneering labor paper, and other liberal publications in New York

Evans was born in Tenbury-Bromyard, England, the son of George and Sarah White Evans. His father, a brickmaking proprietor, had been an officer in the Napoleonic wars, and his mother came from a well-to-do family. Another son, Frederick, born in 1808, later became head of the Shaker movement in the United States. George Henry probably attended grammar school at Tenbury.

In 1820 the elder Evans migrated to the United States. Ultimately, he settled on a thirteen-acre farm on the Oswego turnpike, near Ithaca, New York. At sixteen, George Henry was apprenticed to A. P. Searing, who published the weekly *Ithaca Journal*. Near the end of his apprenticeship, Evans became copublisher of the biweekly *Museum and Independent Corrector*. In 1827 he moved to New York City and was a printer and sometime writer for George Houston's free-thought *Correspondent*, subsequently establishing his own printing company. Early in 1829 he became the printer for feminist Frances Wright's (q.v.) *Free Enquirer*, which had moved from New Harmony, Indiana, and was coedited by Robert Dale Owen. Owen and Wright advocated compulsory national education, an issue in which the nascent New York Workingmen's party was also interested. With support form both, Evans, on 23 October 1829, brought out the first issue of his own weekly, *Working Man's Advocate*, a labor paper, which continued, with some breaks, until 1845. Its circulation probably never exceeded 2,000, although it was widely imitated and quoted at the time. He became an American citizen on 4 November 1829.

Earlier, in June 1829, he also served as one of six printers of the *New York Daily Sentinel*, covertly edited by Robert Dale Owen, and also devoted to the workingman's causes. The *Advocate*, in fact, became the "country" or mail edition of the *Sentinel*. The politics advocated by both included universal education, abolition of licensed monopolies, equal taxation, a lien law for laborers, end of the militia system, abolition of capital punishment, and a district system of elections. Ultimately, Evans took full responsibility for the *Sentinel*, but discontinued it in July 1833.

After the success, later that year, of the *New York Sun*, Evans on 18 February 1834, brought out his own penny daily, the *Man*. It continued for sixteen months, moderately successful, but never strong in advertising. An official union paper, the *National Trades Union*, had appeared; and other penny papers, the *Sun*, *Transcript*, and *Herald*, had a broader appeal. In August 1835 Evans moved the *Advocate* to Rahway, New Jersey, publishing it there as a liberal weekly for Essex county. It did not prosper, and in early 1836, he suspended it.

The issue of land ownership—influenced by his 1829 association with Thomas Skidmore—led him in February 1841 to begin publication at Granville, New York, of a small monthly, the *Radical*. It contained Evans's history of the New York Workingmen's party, but after one gap of eleven months—Evans had little money—it was suspended.

In February 1844, still obsessed with the land problem, he returned to New York City, and in March, with John Windt, resumed weekly publication of the *Working Man's Advocate* (new series) and a triweekly, *People's Rights*. They became the organs for the National Reform Organization, of which Evans was the moving spirit and chief ideologue. It advocated freedom of the public lands, homestead exemptions, and limitations of the purchase and ownership of land. The National Reformers, following a plan outlined by Evans, undertook a massive program of political agitation, and made themselves noticed. Money, however, remained a problem, and Evans, late that year, briefly issued the *Advocate* jointly with another liberal weekly, Mike Walsh's outspoken *Subterranean*.

In 1845, after a crisis in the movement, he finally closed out publication of the *Advocate*, replacing it with *Young America*, another weekly devoted to land reform. Ultimately, Evans's longtime acquaintance Horace Greeley (q.v.), and Greeley's much more influential *New York Tribune*, virtually co-opted the cause. *Young America* continued until 1849, when Evans discontinued it and returned to his hardscrabble farming.

He died of pneumonia at Granville (now Keansburg), New Jersey, on 2 February 1856. His death was noted only in two belated lines in the *New York*

Tribune. He was buried at Granville, next to his first wife, Laura, who had died on 18 December 1849, leaving him three children: George Henry, Jr., aged fifteen; and two daughters, Frances, aged eight, and Edwina, aged six. His second wife, Mary Ann, survived until 1876.

BIBLIOGRAPHY:

B. DAB 7, 201–202; Newman Jeffrey, ''Social Origins of George Henry Evans' *Workingman's Advocate*,'' M.S. thesis, Wayne State Univ., 1960; Richard W. Leopold, *Robert Dale Owen* (New York, 1969).

JAMES STANFORD BRADSHAW

— F —

FARRINGTON, JOSEPH RIDER (b. 15 October 1897; d. 19 June 1954) was a newspaper reporter, editor, and territorial representative from Hawaii in the U.S. Congress.

Farrington was born in Washington, D.C., before his parents, Wallace Rider Farrington (q.v.) and Catherine McAlpine Crane Farrington, returned to Honolulu, where his father had been named editor of the *Evening Bulletin*. Joseph Farrington was educated at Honolulu's exclusive Punahou Academy and at the University of Wisconsin, where he was a roommate of Phillip La Follette, son of Robert La Follette. Farrington enlisted in the U.S. Army and served as a second lieutenant in the field artillery from June to December 1918.

After his graduation in 1919, Farrington worked for the *Philadelphia Public Ledger* before being assigned to the paper's Washington bureau for four years. He married Elizabeth Pruett (q.v.), a University of Wisconsin journalism graduate, on 17 May 1920. They adopted two children: John and Beverly. In 1923 Joseph Farrington was persuaded to return to Hawaii as managing editor of the *Star-Bulletin* while his father served as territorial governor. Farrington was later named president and director of the corporation. He was also president of the *Hilo Tribune-Herald* and the Honolulu Lithographic Company.

As a consequence of efforts by the U.S. Congress to amend Hawaii's Organic Act following the sensational Massie rape trial case, Farrington became less involved in journalism and more involved in politics. In 1934 he was elected to the territorial legislature where he introduced legislation establishing the Hawaii Equal Rights Commission, a full-time body to promote statehood in Hawaii and in Washington. Farrington was reelected in 1938 on a statehood platform. In 1939 he introduced legislation which placed a statehood plebiscite on the 1940 ballot. Hawaii's voters endorsed statehood on the plebiscite by a two-to-one margin.

From 1942 until his death in 1954, Joseph Farrington served as Hawaii's nonvoting representative in the U.S. Congress. During that period, Farrington's priority both in Washington and in Hawaii was to promote the cause of statehood. In order to accomplish this goal he used his membership on committees as well as social activities to inform, to educate, and to try to influence members of Congress, the press, and other groups. He supported efforts to protect Hawaii's agriculture and defense industries as well as expand human rights in Hawaii, throughout the Pacific, and on the mainland. During his twelve years in Congress he was credited with sponsoring more bills than any other member. Although as an elected member from a territory he could not vote, he saw eighteen of his bills become law. He was known by his colleagues in Congress and in the media for his representation not only of the islands but of the entire Pacific community, which he had covered as a journalist and later as a member of congressional committees. In addition to statehood for Hawaii, Farrington urged the granting of citizenship to residents of other islands friendly to the United States as a means of countering totalitarian influence in the Pacific. He died in his congressional office from a heart attack at age fifty-six.

BIBLIOGRAPHY:

B. NYT 20 June 1954; Paul Alfred Pratte, "Ke Alaká i: The Leadership Role of the *Honolulu Star-Bulletin* in the Hawaiian Statehood Movement," Ph.D. diss., Univ. of Hawaii, 1976.

ALF PRATTE

FARRINGTON, MARY ELIZABETH PRUETT (b. 30 May 1898) was a newspaper reporter, political leader, member of Congress, and president of the *Honolulu Star-Bulletin* before resigning the position when the paper was sold to nonfamily interests.

She was born in Tokyo, Japan, the daughter of Robert Lee Pruett and Josie Baugh Pruett, American missionaries. She was educated at Hollywood High School in California, Ward Belmont Junior College in Nashville, Tennessee, and the University of Wisconsin, from which she was graduated in 1918. She married Joseph R. Farrington (q.v.) on 17 May 1920. The couple worked for newspapers in Philadelphia and Washington, D.C., where they developed professional and social contacts they were to use later as members of Congress.

In 1923 Elizabeth Farrington returned to Hawaii with her husband, who had been named managing editor of the *Honolulu Star-Bulletin*, the afternoon daily in which the Farrington family had financial holdings. Joseph Farrington was later appointed general manager of the paper while his father, Wallace Farrington (q.v.), served as Hawaii's sixth governor from 1921 to 1929. During this period and throughout her life, Elizabeth Farrington continued her interests in national and world affairs, particularly in Pan-Pacific relations.

While her husband was serving as Hawaii's territorial representative in Congress from 1942 to 1954, Elizabeth was active in community and social activities. She served as president of the Washington League of Republican

Women from 1946 to 1948, and president of the National Federation of Women's Republican Clubs in 1949. *McCall's* magazine named her one of the ten most influential women in national politics. The General Federation of Women's Clubs selected her as one of the twelve leading women in the nation.

Elizabeth Farrington was named in a special election to succeed her husband, who died in June 1954. She was reelected in November 1954, but defeated in 1956. During her tenure in Congress, she was recognized for her efforts in the reapportionment of the territorial legislature and for her work to secure the nomination of Masaji Marumoto as the first Japanese-American associate justice of the Hawaii Supreme Court. She was also well known for her contributions in Congress and through the pages of the *Star-Bulletin* to the Farrington family crusade for statehood.

After losing her seat in Congress, Mrs. Farrington returned to Honolulu to serve as president of the *Star-Bulletin*. She resigned the position in 1961 after the paper was sold to nonfamily interests. Mrs. Farrington adopted two children: Beverly (Mrs. Hugh F. Richardson) and John.

BIBLIOGRAPHY:

B. Paul Alfred Pratte, "Ke Alaká i: The Leadership Role of the *Honolulu Star-Bulletin* in the Hawaiian Statehood Movement," Ph.D. diss., Univ. of Hawaii, 1976.

ALF PRATTE

FARRINGTON, WALLACE RIDER (b. 3 May 1871; d. 6 October 1933) was a newspaper editor, publisher, community leader, and appointed governor of the Hawaiian Islands. He used the power of his political office as well as his newspaper to promote better educational opportunities and statehood for Hawaii's multiracial population.

The youngest of six children, Farrington was born in Orono, Maine, to Joseph Rider and Ellen Holyoke Farrington. His father was superintendent of a state farm and instructor of agriculture at the state college, later to become the University of Maine. After graduation from the state college in 1891, Farrington became night editor of the *Bangor News*; associate editor of the Phelps Publishing Company at Springfield, Massachusetts; and in 1894, a reporter for the *New York Commercial*.

On 2 January 1895 Farrington became editor of the *Honolulu Pacific Commercial Advertiser*, a morning newspaper controlled by the Castle family. Farrington resigned the position on 4 August 1897 and, with his wife, left for the eastern United States. His wife was the former Catherine McAlpine Crane, whom he married on 2 October 1896. They had three children: Joseph Rider Farrington (q.v.), Ruth Farrington Leavey, and Frances Farrington Whittemore.

Farrington returned to Hawaii in 1898 as the editor of the *Honolulu Evening Bulletin*, founded in 1870. On 1 July 1912 the *Bulletin* merged with the *Hawaii*

Star to form the *Honolulu Star-Bulletin* with Farrington as the paper's general business manager. Although the *Star-Bulletin* was owned by the conservative oligarchy of Hawaii, Farrington worked to promote progressive causes, such as equality in education, a stable teacher salary system, public playgrounds, beach areas for public use, local government, and statehood. He was one of the founders of what was to become the University of Hawaii. He was the first president of the Honolulu Advertising Club, and president of the Pan-Pacific Club. In 1929 he was a delegate to the Conference of the Institute of Pacific Relations in Japan.

In 1921 Farrington was appointed governor of the territory of Hawaii by President Warren G. Harding (q.v.), who had met Farrington while visiting the islands as a U.S. Senator. He was reappointed governor by President Calvin Coolidge in 1925. During his terms Farrington reorganized the territorial government, strengthened the public school system, and contributed to legislation which forwarded the statehood movement. In July 1927 Farrington was featured on the cover of *Time* magazine in an article discussing the possibilities of Hawaiian statehood.

After turning down the opportunity for a third term as governor, Farrington returned to newspaper pursuits and to travel. He never fully recovered from ailments he contracted in 1930 while visiting China and Japan. He died of heart failure in Honolulu at age sixty-two.

BIBLIOGRAPHY:

B. NYT 6 October 1933.

ALF PRATTE

FENNO, JOHN (b. 12 August 1751; d. 14 September 1798) was editor and publisher of the *Gazette of the United States*, a Federalist newspaper published in New York, from 1789 until his death in 1798.

Fenno was born in Boston, the son of Ephraim Fenno and Mary Chapman Fenno. His father was in the business of dressing leather, while selling cakes and ale on the side. He was educated at the Old South Writing School on the Boston Common. Later he became a teacher at that institution, working under the supervision of another teacher, Samuel Holbrook. It was during this period that he began a lifelong friendship with Joseph Ward, then one of the school's masters. Their correspondence during the period of Fenno's editorship reveals the political turmoil of the era and Fenno's continuing struggles to keep the publication financially afloat.

Fenno apparently left teaching about 1774; the path he followed in the next fifteen years is somewhat uncertain. He may have served as secretary to General Artemus Ward during the revolutionary war, but this is in dispute. He married Mary Curtis of Needham, Massachusetts, on 8 May 1777. He next operated an inn and livery in Boston, and then became an editorial assistant to Benjamin Russell (q.v.), editor of the *Massachusetts Sentinel*. A period spent as operator of a dry-goods business, underwritten by his wife's uncle, Obadiah Curtis, apparently ended in failure. He then enlisted the support of a group of Boston Federalists for a publishing venture in which he was engaged for the rest of his life. He left Boston for New York, then the seat of government, armed with a letter from one of his patrons, Christopher Gore, another of his wife's relatives. Gore was a member of the Massachusetts House of Representatives. Among other prominent backers were James Bowdoin, later governor of Massachusetts, and Jonathan Mason, also a member of the Massachusetts assembly.

The prospectus he prepared for potential supporters stated his political stance. His newspaper would be "a continued series of Essays in vindication and support of the Federal constitution [and] its several parts, connections and dependencies." The "production" of his publication would be under the "direction of characters who are fully in the Federal interest." The first issue of the *Gazette* hit the streets of New York on 11 April 1789. Early issues made clear to readers his Federalist partisanship.

The newspaper moved to Philadelphia when the government relocated in 1790. His first issue there was dated 3 November 1790. The paper struggled from the start, with revenues initially covering only basic printing costs. Fenno wrote General Ward that the newspaper's management employed all his time and absorbed his attention. His contributors included Alexander Hamilton—the leading supporter—as well as John Adams and Rufus King. The newspaper was less pungent politically than its partisan competition. Eventually, though, its constant harping on Federalist themes led an exasperated Thomas Jefferson to launch a rival newspaper under Philip Freneau (q.v.), the poet-patriot of the Revolution. But Freneau folded his Philadelphia newspaper, the *National Gazette*, in 1793, while Fenno kept going, even though he was forced to suspend publication for three months during that year. The hiatus was due in part to poor finances and in part to the yellow fever epidemic which swept the community and caused thousands to evacuate in panic until the disease had run its course. Fenno, his wife, and fourteen children survived, despite the tension engendered by the grim toll of victims, sometimes reaching the rate of one hundred deaths a day.

Hamilton came to the financial rescue in 1793, and the combination of outside supporters, government contracts, and a federal position kept things going. Publication was changed from semiweekly to evening daily status in December 1793; the title was changed to the *Gazette of the United States and Evening Advertiser*. Critics generally agree that in a period of clearly partisan journalism, Fenno's newspaper was editorially superior to its competitors. He was deeply and tirelessly dedicated to his party and editorial office, and insisted on staying in Philadelphia when another epidemic of yellow fever hit during the summer of 1798. He became one of its victims. His oldest son, John Ward Fenno, nineteen, took over, continuing the newspaper's strong pro-Federalist stance.

BIBLIOGRAPHY:

B. DAB 6, 235; Jerry W. Knudson, ''Political Journalism in the Age of Jefferson,'' *Journalism History*, Spring 1974; William David Sloan, ''The Early Party Press: The Newspaper Role in American Politics, 1788–1812,'' *Journalism History*, Spring 1982.

WALLACE B. EBERHARD

FIELD, EUGENE (b. 2 or 3 September 1850; d. 4 November 1895) was a newspaper columnist who gained recognition nationally for humorous and sentimental verse, including ''Little Boy Blue'' and ''Dutch Lullaby'' (''Wynken, Blynken and Nod''). For the final twelve years of his life he provided the *Chicago Morning News* (renamed the *Record* in 1890) a daily column of personal notes, tributes, quips, jingles, verses, and observations under the headline ''Sharps and Flats.'' Today his work survives in anthologies of children's verse.

Field was the son of Roswell M. Field and Frances Reed Field, New Englanders transplanted to St. Louis, Field's birthplace. His father was a successful lawyer who distinguished himself representing the slave Dred Scott. Field's mother died when he was six, and he was raised by his cousin, Mary Field French, in Amherst, Massachusetts.

Field's academic record was mediocre, the result of poor health, a lack of interest in scholarship, and a penchant for practical jokes. He attended Williams College in 1868–69. After his father's death in 1869, he entered Knox College, where he gained his first experience in journalism, writing for a local newspaper. The next year he enrolled with his brother Roswell in the junior class at the University of Missouri, but continued to express his creativity through good-natured pranks rather than academic achievement. He never graduated. Instead, at twenty-one, he invited classmate Edgar Comstock to join him in a trip to Europe.

When he returned in 1873, he joined the *St. Louis Evening Journal* as a reporter and then journeyed to St. Joseph, Missouri, to claim Comstock's young sister as his bride. Field had proposed to Julia Sutherland Comstock when she was fourteen, but her parents had persuaded them to wait until she was older. They waited two years, being wed on 16 October 1873. He and his wife had three daughters and five sons, not all of whom survived to adulthood.

Field worked for the *St. Louis Evening Journal* until 1875, served as city editor of the *St. Joseph Gazette* for one year, went back to the *Evening Journal*, now merged with the *St. Louis Times*, for four years as editorial writer and paragrapher, jumped to the *Kansas City Times* as managing editor for one year, and wound up in 1880 as managing editor of the *Denver Tribune*. Denver in the early 1880s was readily suited to Field's undisciplined humor. The record suggests that Field rarely allowed serious journalism to intrude on his irreverent attitude toward facts.

In 1883 Field accepted an invitation to join Melville Stone's (q.v.) *Chicago Morning News* as a columnist. In Denver he had written columns under various titles, and his first Chicago column was headed "Current Gossip." But on 31 August 1883 his work appeared under the title "Sharps and Flats," the head that would stand for the rest of his career. Journalism historian Frank Luther Mott in *American Journalism* said "Sharps and Flats" was "the model of many urbane and witty columns" and "has probably never been excelled by any long-continued newspaper feature for its keen satire, its genuine wit and the lightness of its literary touch."

Field considered himself a newspaper man. "I don't claim to be anything else," he said. "I never have put a high estimate upon my verse. . . . Not much of it will live." Most of what he wrote was published first in a newspaper, but some of it did live, particularly the verse for children.

While in Chicago, Field produced the bulk of his verse, wrote some undistinguished prose, participated enthusiastically in collecting rare books, labored on and off translating Horace, extended his reputation through platform appearances, and never tired of his extravagant practical jokes. He died in 1895 of heart disease.

BIBLIOGRAPHY:

A. *Works of Eugene Field*, 10 vols. (New York, 1899).

B. DAB 6, 362–364; NYT 5 November 1895; Slason Thompson, *Eugene Field* (New York, 1901).

ROBERT L. HOSKINS

FIELD, KATE (b. 1 October 1838; d. 19 May 1896) was christened Mary Katherine Keemle Field but used the name Kate throughout her career that spanned three decades. Her endeavors included journalism, lecturing, acting, and publicizing various reforms and causes. Desiring a platform for her ideas, she founded a weekly newspaper in Washington, D.C., titled *Kate Field's Washington*, which lasted from 1890 to 1895. Although she displayed talent as a writer, her importance lay less in what she accomplished than in the fact that her life symbolized the independence of path-breaking American women in the late nineteenth century.

Field was the only surviving child of Joseph M. Field, an actor, journalist, and theater manager, who had come to the United States as a child from Ireland, and Eliza Riddle Field, an actress of Philadelphia Quaker background. She was born in St. Louis, where she attended Mrs. Smith's Seminary for three years, receiving a good education for the period in spite of her family's financial problems. After the death of her father, when she was eighteen, she became the ward of a millionaire uncle, Milton L. Sanford, whose wife, Cordelia, was Mrs. Field's younger sister.

Sanford, a Bostonian, supported the young woman lavishly for several years, financing her education at Lasell Seminary in Auburndale, Massachusetts (1854–56), and then taking her to Italy in 1859. There she became the intimate friend of Anthony Trollope and other members of the writers' colony in Florence. Her sympathy for the Union in the Civil War caused Sanford, who had ties with the

Southern cotton industry, to change his mind about leaving his fortune to her, and she decided to support herself.

Dividing her time between Europe and the United States, she wrote travel letters for the *Springfield* (Massachusetts) *Republican* and other newspapers; lectured on the lyceum circuit; sold articles, often humorous, that were later collected into books; appeared on the stage; and tried writing plays. During the 1870s she wrote mildly satirical travel articles from London for the *New York Tribune*. She also published articles in the *Atlantic Monthly* on theatrical and literary personalities. As one of the first commercial publicists, she prepared a booklet for the Libby Glass Company disguised as a history of glassmaking. When she publicized the new invention of the telephone, she received valuable stock which she lost in an unsuccessful endeavor to reform the fashion industry by promoting simpler styles of dress.

Apparently hesitant to play a woman's customary role in the Victorian world, she declined opportunities to marry. According to a biographer, she distrusted marriage instinctively, although she exploited her own attractive appearance and feminine manner. Baptized a Catholic, she delved into the occult and wrote one book on spiritualism. Her intense individualism prompted her last ambitious undertaking, *Kate Field's Washington*, in an era when it was unusual for a woman to found and run a newspaper.

Eager to express her personal views on topics of the day, Field picked Washington as the logical location for her paper. She was not a strong supporter of women's rights, endorsing woman suffrage weakly in 1893. Field, however, was one of the founders of Sorosis, the first women's club. The newspaper featured political comment, book reviews, theatrical news, novelettes, and drawing-room comedies, often written by Field. Her kaleidoscopic opinions opposed arbitrary power but championed tariff and civil service reform, temperance (not abstinence), high society, and the arts. She tended to picture somewhat marginal issues as great causes, for example, championing a national marriage law, cremation, removal of taxes from imported art objects, and a national conservatory of music.

A handsomely printed publication which aimed at an upper-class audience, the newspaper ceased publication in April 1895. Reflecting little but the personality of its founder, it suffered as her interest and health began to wane. After it failed, Field moved from Washington to Hawaii, where she hoped to regain her health and write travel articles. She died in Honolulu of pneumonia.

BIBLIOGRAPHY:

B. AWW 2, 17–18; NAW 1, 612–614; NYT 31 May 1896; Maurine H. Beasley, *The First Women Washington Correspondents* (Washington, D.C., 1976); Maurine H. Beasley, "Kate Field and 'Kate Field's Washington,'" in *Records of the Columbia Historical Society, 1973–1974*; Lillian Whiting, *Kate Field: A Record* (Boston, 1899).

MAURINE H. BEASLEY

FISCHETTI, JOHN (b. 27 September 1916; d. 18 November 1980) was a nationally recognized editorial cartoonist. He drew illustrations for several major magazines and editorial cartoons for major newspapers, and was syndicated nationally. Awarded a Pulitzer Prize for his editorial cartoons, he once characterized his drawings as serious comments in comic clothing.

He was born to Pietro and Emanuela Navarra Fischetti in Brooklyn, New York. His father was a barber in Brooklyn's Little Italy. John left home at sixteen and worked at a variety of odd jobs, not unlike many other young men during this country's deep depression. He returned home at age nineteen to enter Pratt Institute. He studied commercial art there for three years.

His first professional artwork was completed at the Walt Disney Studios in Burbank, California, where he worked as an animator. During this time he also drew as a free-lance artist for the *Los Angeles Times*, and produced illustrations for *Coronet*, *Esquire*, *Saturday Evening Post*, and *Collier's* magazines, as well as the *New York Times*. His first political cartoons were drawn for the *Chicago Sun*. Between 1942 and 1946, he was an artist and editorial cartoonist for *Stars and Stripes*.

He married Karen Mortenson on 25 October 1948. They had two children, Peter and Michael.

Fischetti was a syndicated editorial cartoonist for the Newspaper Enterprise Association from 1950 to 1962. He drew for the *New York Herald Tribune* from 1962 to 1967 when it ceased publication. While he worked there, he shared editorial page duties with Bill Mauldin and Dan Dowling. He worked next for the *Chicago Daily News* as chief editorial cartoonist until it ceased publication in 1978. Soon he joined the *Chicago Sun-Times* staff and the Field Newspaper Syndicate, where he worked until age sixty-four, when he died of heart disease at Columbus Hospital in Chicago.

He was recognized in his mature years as an editorial cartoonist of national stature. In 1969 he was awarded a Pulitzer Prize "for the body of his work in 1968," produced while at the *Chicago Daily News*. He received several other awards for his artwork. He was named Best Editorial Cartoonist by the National Cartoonists Society four different times. He was awarded Sigma Delta Chi awards in 1954 and 1956; an American Civil Liberties award in 1972; the New York Newspaper Guild's Front Page Award in 1962; and recognition by the National Headliners Club.

The writer of John Fischetti's *New York Times* obituary noted, "Although his political cartoons often had a satirical bite, they avoided hard-nosed partisanship." Fischetti once described his editorial cartoons as a union of the editorial cartoon and the humor cartoon. He said that his cartoons contained serious comments even though they were dressed in comedy and humor.

BIBLIOGRAPHY:

B. NYT 20 November 1980; *Time*, 1 December 1980.

J. DOUGLAS TARPLEY

FITZPATRICK, DANIEL ROBERT (b. 5 March 1891; d. 18 May 1969) was awarded the Pulitzer Prize for editorial cartooning on two occasions. He exhibited his work in art galleries in the United States and abroad during a career that spanned forty-five years at the *St. Louis Post-Dispatch*. During this period,

1913–58, he drew over 14,000 cartoons. Regarded as a champion of the underdog, Fitzpatrick indicted local graft and corruption in the "Rat Alley" cartoon series.

Fitzpatrick was born in Superior, Wisconsin, one of three sons of machinist Patrick Fitzpatrick and Delia Ann Clark Fitzpatrick. He worked as a boy in his father's millwork factory. He was also employed as a machinist's helper and as a cook on a lake freighter. He did not graduate from high school but did support himself in studies at Chicago's Art Institute as a cafeteria worker and theater usher. He joined the staff of the *Chicago Daily News* and worked for one year as an artist for the sports department and as comic page cartoonist. He married Lee Anna Dressen, moved to St. Louis, and began work at the *St. Louis Post-Dispatch* in 1913 at age twenty-two. His first cartoon for the *Post-Dispatch* depicted a train made of coffins passing under a skull and crossbones, representing the safety hazards associated with wooden railway cars in use at that time.

Initially, Fitzpatrick drew his cartoons in pen and ink, but after extended university art studies, he used crayon and charcoal, which became his trademark. By the middle 1920s he also began contributing cartoons to the *New York World* and *Collier's* magazine. In 1924 Fitzpatrick was awarded the John Frederick Lewis Prize by the Philadelphia Academy of Fine Arts, and two years later he won his first Pulitzer Prize for a cartoon entitled "The Laws of Moses and the Laws of Today," which contrasted the tablets of Sinai with an enormous mound of statutes stacked side by side.

During this early period, Fitzpatrick's cartoon campaigns against the dry laws, fascism in Europe, anti-unionism, overcrowding and slums in the cities, and corruption in government led to the series of cartoons labeled "Rat Alley." The series began with a 1931 St. Louis bank robbery and the subsequent negotiation to return some stolen bonds by a member of the Missouri legislature—a lawyer who was never punished. One "Rat Alley" cartoon almost resulted in criminal confinement for both Fitzpatrick and Ralph Coghlan, editor of the *Post-Dispatch* editorial page in 1940. They were cited for contempt of court, fined, and sentenced to ten days in jail for two editorials and a cartoon critical of Judge Thomas J. Rowe's handling of a criminal case involving charges that a stagehands union extorted $10,000 from local theater owners. They were freed on bond, and the Missouri Supreme Court reversed Rowe's decision.

Fitzpatrick's cartoons were syndicated in thirty-five American newspapers and published in Asia, South America, and Europe. He gained an international reputation among artists, in part because of his ability to put across editorial points of view without a heavy reliance on explanatory captions. In May 1941 he presented a one-man show at the Associated Artists Galleries in New York City. At the request of the Moscow Union of Soviet Painters, eight Fitzpatrick cartoons were exhibited at the Museum of Modern Western Art in the Soviet Union.

Fitzpatrick reportedly turned down lucrative offers by other newspapers in order to stay at the *Post-Dispatch*. In spite of this dedication, relations with management were not always serene. On two occasions Fitzpatrick requested and received a leave of absence to avoid conflict over the newspaper's editorial policy regarding political endorsements. The *Post-Dispatch* supported Alfred M. Landon in 1936 and Thomas E. Dewey in 1948; Fitzpatrick favored Democratic candidates Franklin D. Roosevelt and Harry Truman. In 1954 he was awarded his second Pulitzer Prize for a cartoon critical of American involvement in Southeast Asia. He retired from the *Post-Dispatch* on 1 August 1958.

His first wife, Lee Anna, died in 1965. He married his former housekeeper, Beulah O. Hawthorne, in December 1968. He died on 18 May 1969. Death was attributed to general infirmities.

BIBLIOGRAPHY:

A. *As I Saw It: A Review of Our Times* (New York, 1953).

B. NYT 19 May 1969; *St. Louis Post-Dispatch*, 19 May 1969.

MICHAEL D. MURRAY

FLEESON, DORIS (b. 20 May 1901; d. 1 August 1970) was a newspaper political reporter and commentator. Her liberal and hard-hitting columns served as a ''personal pipeline'' to congressional and administrative news sources, and often amazed and irritated official Washington for several years. Her political column was syndicated and appeared in nearly 100 leading newspapers five times a week. Fleeson also served as a war correspondent covering the Italian and French fronts in 1943 and 1944 for the *Woman's Home Companion*, and eagerly fought for a minimum wage for reporters in the mid-thirties.

Fleeson was born in Sterling, Kansas, the daughter of William and Helen Tebbe Fleeson. She attended the University of Kansas and graduated in 1923 with a B.A. degree. She took a job as a reporter for the *Pittsburg* (Kansas) *Sun*, followed by a series of jobs including society editor for the *Evanston* (Illinois) *News-Index* and city editor of the *Great Neck* (Long Island) *News*. She eventually landed a general assignment position in 1927 at the *New York Daily News*.

She began acquiring the skills of political reporting at the *Daily News* Albany bureau. While she was thoroughly immersed in the coverage of Judge Samuel Seabury's investigation of official corruption in New York, she married fellow political reporter John O'Donnell on 28 September 1930.

Fleeson was one of the founders of the American Newspaper Guild in 1933. That year she was also named to a committee to travel to Washington, D.C., to urge the National Recovery Administration to adopt a code providing a minimum wage of $35 a week for reporters. At the Washington hearing that followed, she protested a provision in the code which had been submitted by the American Newspaper Publishers Association; it would have exempted those earning more than $35 a week from the regulations of the National Recovery Administration on the ground that they were ''professionals.'' She said newsmen objected to being classified as professionals because that deprived them of the benefits of the N.R.A.

Fleeson and her husband moved to Washington, D.C., in 1933 to work at the newly opened *Daily News* Washington bureau. With O'Donnell she wrote the newspaper's "Capitol Stuff" column. She was also named the one permanent woman member of the press group that accompanied President Roosevelt on his campaign tours.

As war brewed in Europe, Fleeson found herself drifting further away from the editorial opinions of the *Daily News*. At the same time, there were domestic problems with her husband. They divorced in 1942, thus freeing Fleeson to travel abroad to do a series of articles for the *Daily News* about wartime conditions. Upon her return from Europe she was reassigned to desk editing, radio news, and Albany coverage so as not to conflict with her former husband's Washington column. On 15 May 1943 she announced her resignation from the *Daily News* to become a war correspondent for the *Woman's Home Companion*.

After the war Fleeson returned to Washington and launched a column on political affairs for the *Washington Evening Star* and the *Boston Globe*. Her column on 16 May 1946 became front-page news when it brought into the open a feud between Supreme Court Justices Robert H. Jackson and Hugo Black. Her column was distributed by Bell Syndicate until 1954, then by United Features Syndicate until her death.

Although she considered herself a nonpartisan liberal, some readers felt she favored the Democrats. She was outspokenly critical but treated everyone in the same manner. She was a member of the Women's National Press Club and served as president in 1937.

Fleeson was honored by the New York Newspaper Women's Club in 1937 with the first of what became an annual award for outstanding reporting. She received a second award from the club in 1943. She was one of four newspaperwomen given Headliner Awards in 1950 by Theta Sigma Phi, the national fraternity of newspaperwomen. In 1953 she received a medal of honor from the University of Missouri School of Journalism. In 1954 she was honored with the Raymond Clapper Award for "exceptionally meritorious work."

In 1958 she married Dan A. Kimball, then president of the Aerojet-General Corporation of Sacramento, California, and former secretary of the navy. She had one daughter, Doris, by her first husband.

BIBLIOGRAPHY:

B. NYT 2 August 1970.

CHRISTINE M. MILLER

FLOWER, BENJAMIN ORANGE (b. 19 October 1858; d. 24 December 1918) was a social reformer and prominent editor whose *Arena* magazine served as a leading forum for reform sentiments in the last decade of the nineteenth century. Along with championing various reform causes, many of which came to fruition after 1900 in the Progressive Era, Flower pressed for a creative literature that would entertain but also expose and help abolish the evils he saw in the social system. Flower's choice of authors and subjects in the *Arena* clearly reflected his ideals and complemented 1,000 book reviews, 200 signed articles, and hundreds of editorials he also wrote.

Flower was born in Albion, Illinois, the son of the Reverend Alfred Flower and Elizabeth Orange Flower. His father was a minister with the Disciples of Christ. Flower intended to follow his father into the ministry, but he became a Unitarian and turned to journalism. From December 1880 to August 1881 he edited a social and literary weekly, the *American Sentinel*, in Albion.

Flower left the Midwest in 1881 and began work in Boston for his brother, Dr. Richard C. Flower, who had a medicine-by-mail business. The exact nature of his work is unclear. While in Boston he married Hattie C. Cloud of Evansville, Indiana, in 1885. In 1886 Flower founded and edited the *American Spectator*, which was a house organ for his brother's potions and cures.

In 1889 Flower founded the *Arena* in Boston, and for the next seven years it was one of the most lively and influential magazines in America, reaching at one point a circulation of 35,000 and making Flower an important voice decrying the concentration of wealth in too few hands. Flower's editorials were strident in their call for reform while his book reviews praised novelists who were revealing flaws in industrial capitalism.

Among the reforms that Flower sought were direct election of U.S. senators, control of trusts by the federal government, suffrage for women, nationalization of public utilities, strict child work laws, popular referenda to enact new legislation, and prohibition of liquor. Although Flower's magazine editorialized more than it exposed, it was the direct forerunner of the muckraking magazines which flourished after 1900.

In 1896 Flower resigned as editor of the *Arena* and helped edit *New Time* of Chicago. That year his wife was committed to an institution for the mentally ill where she remained for the rest of her life. Flower helped found *Coming Age* in Boston in 1899, and a year later merged it with the *Arena*. He became one of three editors, with sole responsibility for the writing of editorials. Flower became the magazine's sole editor again in 1904. He continued to urge reforms in politics, to ask novelists to support reform causes, and to agree with exponents of the Social Gospel movement that the nation needed moral reconstruction. The *Arena* ceased publication for good in 1909, the victim, some have written, of economic pressure from advertisers who were angry with its reformist outlook.

Flower subsequently edited two more magazines: *Twentieth Century Magazine* (1909–11), similar in outlook to the *Arena* but less successful, and the *Menace*, a virulent anti-Catholic publication, an anomalous ending to an otherwise progressive career. Flower died in Cambridge, Massachusetts, his death scarcely noticed.

BIBLIOGRAPHY:

B. DAB 6, 477–478; Howard F. Cline, "B. O. Flower and the *Arena*, 1889–1909," *Journalism Quarterly*, June 1940; Frank L. Stallings, Jr., "B. O. Flower and the *Arena*: Literature as an Agent of Social Protest and Reform," Ph.D. diss., Univ. of Texas, 1961.

ROBERT MIRALDI

FLYNT, JOSIAH (b. 23 January 1869; d. 20 January 1907) was one of the first muckrakers, though his name is not often mentioned in discussions of that era and its major characters—Lincoln Steffens, Ida Tarbell, David Graham Phillips, Upton Sinclair, and Ray Stannard Baker (qq.v.).

Flynt, whose real name was Josiah Frank Willard, was (in the words of Louis Filler's *Crusaders for American Liberalism*) among those who "were significant to, or central in, muckraking operations, and whose names never appear in commentary respecting the era." Flynt worked just prior to the glory days of muckraking; and when American readers were devouring the exposés of Steffens, Tarbell, and the others, Flynt was dying after a life of abuse.

Flynt was born in Appleton, Wisconsin, and grew up in Evanston, Illinois, the son of a professor. His life was comfortable, despite the fact that his father died when he was eight. But Flynt was restless, a trait that seemed to be inherited; all the members of his immediate family had the urge to wander. While Flynt attended college, his mother and sisters wandered to Germany. Flynt was too restless to stay in college, so he dropped out, turned to thievery, was caught, and sent to reform school. He escaped, lived as a hobo for some time, was arrested, and jailed again.

On his release, Flynt decided to join his family in Germany, where his mother enrolled him in the University of Berlin, but German university life pleased him no better than American university life. He dropped out and traveled the Continent and the British Isles. He befriended Aubrey Beardsley, Oscar Wilde, and Arthur Symons. The restlessness grew. Flynt submerged himself in the underside of Europe, lived as a hobo and was known as "Cigarette." His wanderings took him to Russia, where he worked on Leo Tolstoy's farm.

Flynt had begun writing about his experiences, and in the early 1890s publishers began to accept his work. He returned to America in 1898, with a lifetime of experience crammed into a few short years. One of Flynt's first sensational series was published in the *Century* in 1899, and collected in the book *Tramping With Tramps* (1899). He moved to *McClure's* in 1900 with a series on crime in America collected under the title *True Stories of the Underworld* (1901).

Flynt's extensive use of argot has been credited with loosening up journalistic style. *Underworld*, used to describe the world of organized crime, is a term credited to Flynt. His articles were lively and peppered with colorful expressions. Flynt introduced such terms as *mob* (for organized crime), *squeal*, *speakeasy*, *fix* (as in bribe), *handout*, *pull* (for influence), *pinch* (for arrest), and *joint* (for an illegal liquor establishment).

The public appetite for Flynt's exposés of life in the underworld was only whetted by his first series, and *McClure's* commissioned another series, collected as *The World of Graft* (1901). Historian Filler called that "the first genuine muckraking book." Harold S. Wilson wrote of Flynt in *"McClure's Magazine" and the Muckrakers* (1970): "Flynt's method was to submerge briefly, then emerge with an article full of evidence from the testimony of friends. During three months of 1900 he interviewed underworld figures, many of whom were personal friends, in regard to the police management of criminals. . . . "

Flynt was friends with S. S. McClure (q.v.), and the two had much in common, despite a twelve-year age difference. Both had been wanderers, although McClure's life was conventional, compared to Flynt's.

Flynt was a captivating writer, but he had a plethora of bad habits—he smoked, was an alcoholic (despite his aunt, Frances Willard, leader of the Women's Christian Temperence Union), and a drug addict. His habits wore hard on him, and he was virtually incapacitated in the last years of his life. He died at thirty-seven. An autobiography made up largely of sketches was published posthumously.

BIBLIOGRAPHY:

A. *My Life* (New York, 1908).

B. Fred C. Cook, *The Muckrakers* (New York, 1972); C. C. Reiger, *The Era of the Muckrakers* (Chapel Hill, N.C., 1932); Harold S. Wilson, *"McClure's Magazine" and the Muckrakers* (Princeton, N.J., 1970).

WILLIAM MCKEEN

FORTUNE, TIMOTHY THOMAS (b. 3 October 1856; d. 2 June 1928), who was born a slave, devoted his life to journalism, and became known as the dean of black journalism. Fortune was editor of the *New York Globe*, *New York Age*, and Marcus Garvey's (q.v.) *Negro World*. His papers are considered the best-edited black papers of their period. Fortune also wrote for white dailies, including Charles Dana's (q.v.) *New York Sum*. He concentrated on the conditions of blacks and popularized the term *Afro-American*.

Born in Marianna, Jackson County, Florida, he was the son of Emanuel and Sarah Jane, slaves of Ely P. Moore. After Emancipation, his parents took the name Fortune, because Emanuel's father was believed to be an Irishman named Thomas Fortune. Emanuel Fortune, a literate man, was a shoe maker and tanner. He was elected to the Florida House of Representatives during Reconstruction. Racial tension, however, forced Emanuel to move his wife and four children to Jacksonville. Shortly thereafter Sarah Fortune died at age thirty-six. Her death was the first of many that deeply affected Thomas.

Timothy Thomas Fortune, the third child and first son, became interested in newspapers when, as a child, he watched the printing of the *Marianna Courier*. Later he was a printer's devil for the *Jacksonville Daily Union*. During his youth, the slender, light-skinned young man also served as a page in the state senate for four terms, and worked for the post office. An avid reader, his early formal education included one term at the Freedmen's Bureau school in Marianna, two terms at the Stanton Institute in Jacksonville, and two years at Howard University in Washington, where he studied law.

Financial problems after his first year in college caused him to take a job in 1877 in the printing shop of the *People's Advocate* in Washington, a black weekly. Fortune operated the mechanical end of production and wrote a column under the name Gustafus Bert. During this period Fortune also married Carrie C. Smiley, a sixteen- or seventeen-year-old girl from Florida.

Because the *Advocate* suffered financial problems, and because Carrie wanted to be in Florida as the couple awaited the birth of their first child, the Fortunes moved to Florida. The South, however, was too restrictive for a young man of Fortune's temperament and ability. In 1881 the Fortunes moved to New York, a move that led to Fortune's most productive period as a journalist. He was hired by the *Rumor*, and stayed with the paper through changes in management and in the paper's name. Fortune was editor and sometimes sole proprietor as the *Rumor* became the *New York Globe*, then the *New York Freeman*, then the *New York Age*. In 1887, during the period in which he withdrew from the *Freeman*, he worked at the *New York Sun*. His articles covered all areas except Wall Street. Fortune also had articles in the *Boston Transcript* at the turn of the century.

By 1900 four factors began to sap his journalistic energy. The first was a series of tragedies in his life. During the last two decades of the 1800s he struggled through the deaths of two sons, his younger brother to whom he was very close, his father, a sister, and other relatives. Throughout his career he battled to keep his newspapers afloat and to support his wife and two children (a daughter, Jessie, born in 1883, and a son, Fred, born in 1890). The strain of it all contributed to his poor health and alcoholism. He was always frail, and through the years he suffered many illnesses, particularly a nervous disorder. Finally, Fortune was pressured by his very close relationship with Booker T. Washington, a relationship that cost the writer his credibility with other black leaders. Not only was the militant journalist a ghostwriter, confidant, and publicist for the accommodationist Washington, but he had also become financially dependent on Washington. In 1906 Fortune separated from Carrie. They never reconciled although they communicated until his death. In 1907 Washington's support of the *New York Age* became publicly known, and Fortune suffered a nervous breakdown.

For the next decade Fortune drifted, trying to survive by writing for various newspapers. In 1919 he began writing for the *Norfolk Journal and Guide*, and in 1923 he became editor of Marcus Garvey's *Negro World*. He retained positions with both papers until his death, and regained respectability in journalism. Fortune continued to write even though rheumatism and generally frail health hampered him. He died in the home of his son, who was a medical doctor.

BIBLIOGRAPHY:
B. Emma Lou Thornbrough, *T. Thomas Fortune: Militant Journalist* (Chicago, 1972).

KAREN FITZGERALD BROWN

FOWLER, GENE (b. 8 March 1890; d. 2 July 1960) was a florid writer, a hard drinker, and an accomplished pursuer of women when all three were considered assets to a journalist.

Eugene Fowler (but even formal indexes call him Gene) was born on the west bank of Miller's Millstream in Denver, the son of Charles Francis Devlan, Jr., and Dora Grace Wheeler Devlan. (The mother's maiden name has also been given as Parrot.) Fowler was born Eugene Parrot Devlan—the middle name sometimes spelled Parrott. Devlan deserted the family before Gene was born. When Dora married Frank Fowler, Fowler adopted the child.

As a boy, Gene Fowler worked for a taxidermist, then a greengrocer, and then became a telegraph clerk. He next landed a job as a printer's devil. He edited his high school paper, and he studied journalism in his one year at the University of Colorado. Except for one day on the *Boulder Camera*, Fowler's first newspaper job was on the *Denver Republican* in 1912. In 1913 the *Republican* merged with the *Rocky Mountain News*, which hired Fowler. In 1914 he moved to the *Denver Post*. For those newspapers he covered sports, city hall, and the crime beat. One of his leads from that era typifies his style of writing—a style well in tune with American journalism of his day:

> She laid her wanton red head on her lover's breast, then plugged him through the heart (Smith, 1977).

Fowler became acquainted with another Colorado product, Damon Runyon (q.v.), and in 1918 Runyon helped Fowler land a job as a sports writer for Hearst's *New York American*. Fowler branched out to cover a variety of other stories—his eyewitness account of the electrocutions of Ruth Snyder and Judd Gray achieved a measure of fame as an example of journalism in the Roaring Twenties.

In 1924 Fowler became sports editor of the *New York Daily Mirror*, and the next year was named managing editor of the *New York American*. He did not last out his three-year contract on that job—one biographer suggests a lack of business acumen. In 1928 he left Hearst and became managing editor of the *New York Morning Telegraph*. He hired Ring Lardner, Ben Hecht, Charles MacArthur, Walter Winchell, Norman Hapgood, Westbrook Pegler (qq.v.), Martha Ostenso, Marie Jeritza, and David Belasco, and was fired for his extravagance.

That ended Fowler's newspaper career. He began writing books and screenplays. His style as a city hall–sports–crime reporter carried over to his creative writing. He turned out fourteen books and spent more than thirty years in Hollywood grinding out motion picture scripts. His books included a biography of his close friend John Barrymore, *Good Night, Sweet Prince* (1944). He was also

Jimmy Durante's biographer, a friend of W. C. Fields, and a sort of mentor or adviser to Red Skelton.

Rumor, sometimes documented, linked Fowler romantically with a number of actresses and other prominent women, and with not a few women of no fame or ill fame, but his one marriage seems never to have been in trouble. He married Agnes Hubbard in 1916; they had two sons and a daughter. They were sitting quietly together at home in Brentwood, California, when Fowler died of a heart attack at age seventy.

BIBLIOGRAPHY:

A. *Timber Line* (New York, 1933).

B. NCAB 48, 6; NYT 3 July 1960; H. Allen Smith, *The Life and Legend of Gene Fowler* (New York, 1977).

LAURA NICKERSON

FRANKLIN, ANN SMITH (b. 2 October 1696; d. 19 April 1763) was one of the earliest printers in colonial America. She was the first female editor and printer of an almanac, the first woman to print textiles in America, and the second female to be an official colonial printer, and while the evidence is sometimes contradictory, she may have been the first woman to be involved in the printing of a colonial newspaper.

Ann (or Anne) Franklin was born in Boston, the daughter of Samuel and Anna (or Ann) Smith. Virtually nothing is known of her parents or her early life. That she was educated (to the extent women were schooled in that period) is clear from the evidence that she was able to continue her husband's printing business following his death. On 4 February 1723 Ann married James Franklin (q.v.), the publisher of the *New England Courant*. After the *Courant*'s demise in 1727, Ann and James moved to Newport, Rhode Island, where James became the first printer in that colony.

The Franklins had five children, three daughters and two sons. Two of the children, a daughter and a son, died young. The surviving daughters, Elizabeth and Mary, were trained to set type and helped their mother in the printing shop following James's death. The surviving son, James Jr., eventually became Ann Franklin's partner in the printing business. In the years before his death James printed the short-lived *Rhode Island Gazette*, the *Rhode Island Almanack* (also called *Poor Robin's Almanack*), and various pieces of business ephemera. During the latter years of his life James suffered several protracted illnesses, and if Ann Franklin were like other colonial women, she helped him in his printing business. Indeed, historians suggest that James had the practical help of his wife in Newport and that the *Gazette* was a joint enterprise. Because she was able to successfully take over the print shop following James's death, it is reasonable to conclude that she was skilled at the printing business before his death. However, there is only circumstantial evidence to suppose she actually did.

Following James's death, Ann and her daughters operated the printing shop for thirteen years until James Jr. returned from Philadelphia where he had been apprenticed to his uncle Benjamin. Ann Franklin appears to have been a more successful printer in Rhode Island than her husband. In 1736 she became the official printer for the colony, a position never held by James, making her the second women to hold a government printing license. (The first, Dinah Nuthead, was illiterate and could not set type.) However, Ann Franklin was the first to actually perform the functions of a printer. She was the official colonial printer for twenty-six years and did considerable government printing, including over 500 copies of the *Acts and Laws* of 1745, a volume of more than 300 pages. In all, some forty-seven different pieces of printing have been credited to her press during the years between her husband's death and the return of James Jr. In addition to colonial printing, her output included religious tracts and literary works.

Ann Franklin was the first woman printer of an almanac, the *Rhode Island Almanack*. It was published annually by James Franklin from 1727 to 1735. While the 1736 edition lists James Franklin as printer, he had died the previous year and Ann Franklin was the actual printer. Beginning with the 1737 edition the printer is listed as the "Widow Franklin." The almanac ceased publication with the 1739 edition. Much of the material appearing under Ann Franklin's name was rewritten or copied from James Franklin's early almanacs.

James Jr. returned to Rhode Island in 1748 to join his mother in the printing business. Ann Franklin continued to run the business, but mother and son submitted joint bills to the colonial government for printing until 1757. However, during this period all printing carried Ann Franklin's name as printer. In 1758 Ann Franklin took her son into partnership and the name of the firm became "Ann & James Franklin."

In 1758 mother and son started the *Newport Mercury*, although it is doubtful that she was much involved in the day-to-day affairs of the newspaper, being at that time sixty-two years old and in failing health. However, the newspaper was printed under the partnership name. This situation changed when James Jr. died suddenly on 21 April 1762. The newspaper did not miss an edition and Ann Franklin became publisher and, perhaps, editor and writer as well. In August 1762 she took Samuel Hall as partner and continued the *Mercury* until her death the following year. The *Mercury* survived her by 171 years.

BIBLIOGRAPHY:

B. Susan Henry, "Ann Franklin: Rhode Island's Woman Printer," in *Newsletters to Newspapers: Eighteenth Century Journalism*, ed. Donovan H. Bond and W. Reynolds McLeod (Morgantown, W.Va., 1977).

DONALD R. AVERY

FRANKLIN, BENJAMIN (b. 17 January 1706; d. 17 April 1790), statesman, natural scientist, and civic leader, took pleasure in referring to himself as "a printer by trade." Although there is a self-conscious modesty in the term, there is also a measure of truth. A printer in the eighteenth century was not merely a skilled pressman, but also a publisher, editor, and, in modern sense, a journalist.

It was in this trade that Franklin founded his fortune, honed his prose style, and entered public life.

His father, Josiah, was a dyer and tallow chandler in Boston. With little prospect of affording a university education for his son, Josiah removed him from Boston Latin School to be tutored by George Brownell. At twelve he was apprenticed to his brother, James (q.v.), who was a printer.

Benjamin wrote topical ballads for his brother's press, the first appearing in 1718 shortly after he began his apprenticeship. These might have led to little as a career had not his brother founded the *New England Courant* in 1721. Here Benjamin met other writers, learned the trade, and developed that independence and confidence of judgment which marked him throughout his life. At sixteen he published a series of letters modeled after contemporary English journalism signed "Silence Dogood." The wit and sophistication was surprising for a young writer, but when his brother discovered the identity of the author, the series ended.

James showed considerable courage by opposing Cotton Mather on the matter of smallpox inoculation. James was subsequently jailed and forbidden to publish the *Courant*. In a successful attempt to evade the ban, in 1723 James released Benjamin from his indenture (although binding him with a private agreement which he was unable to enforce) and named his younger brother publisher. It is difficult to be fair to James because we see him through the lens of Benjamin's career. Whatever the cause of friction between them, Benjamin ran away and, in search of a job, found his way to Philadelphia. Here he found fertile soil for his journalistic talents.

This period of Franklin's life must have been more difficult than his own account suggests. Separated from his family, he found work in a Philadelphia print shop but took an offer of support from the governor and, on a mission to buy equipment, found himself penniless in London. He worked for Palmers and Watts, Printers, in London and returned the next year to Philadelphia, where he founded his own firm.

The *Pennsylvania Gazette* was purchased from Samuel Keimer. An intellectually ambitious and charming man, Keimer had devoted the first page of each issue to an excerpt from Ephraim Chambers's *Cyclopaedia*. Essays Franklin contributed to the competing *Mercury* of Philadelphia helped undermine Keimer's readership and he sold out to Franklin in 1729. Confident of his skills as a printer, relatively experienced in the ways of the world, enterprising and gifted with the ability to combine public service with profit, Franklin entered the short mature phase of his life as a journalist.

His accomplishments during the next decade are astonishing in variety. In 1733 he published *Poor Richard*, an almanac that expressed the tolerant, optimistic, diligent, and practical morality that guided him. He played a crucial role in founding a circulation library in 1731; the American Philosophical Society in 1751; and an academy which became the University of Pennsylvania, in 1751; and he helped his employees to found their own print shops in other colonies as partners.

Throughout this period he revised *Poor Richard* which continued to sell more than 10,000 copies per year. In 1757, on a voyage to London, he rewrote from memory and expanded the thoughts in the almanac in *The Way to Wealth* (1758). This eventually sold some seventy editions in English and countless more in other languages. Franklin planned the first monthly magazine in America. His business rival, Andrew Bradford, was first to the readers with the *American Magazine*, but Franklin's *General Magazine*, also dated January 1741, was the first magazine to carry advertising.

In 1744, with prospects of a sizable fortune before him, Franklin sold his firm to an employee he had brought from England, David Hall. The reasons for his retirement are not clear, but the time he devoted to the study of lightning and electricity during the next few years suggests that his claim that he wanted time for "philosophical amusements" was not entirely inaccurate.

Although Franklin entered the printer's trade as apprentice to his controversial brother, Benjamin's *Pennsylvania Gazette* was not noted for disputation. Franklin resorted to pamphlets for the extended presentation of his own views. He was a prudent businessman. In 1753 Franklin and William Hunter of the *Virginia Gazette* were named deputy postmasters general for the colonies. Franklin used the post to improve communication among the colonies and initiated the policy of providing favorable rates for printed matter that continues to this day.

As a man of affairs, Franklin played a role in the Stamp Act controversy, urged Thomas Paine (q.v.) to emigrate to America, and was a key figure in the disclosure of letters by Massachusetts Governor Thomas Hutchinson. This last error cost him his London post. Franklin later negotiated the treaty with France which was crucial to the fledgling nation. He participated in the Constitutional Convention and, in his last public act, asked Congress to abolish slavery.

Although his contributions to journalism are of great significance, Franklin's career was based upon, rather than devoted to, the writer's trade. There is probably no more genial figure in this period, nor one who has entered more intimately into our daily lives. His inventions, notably the lightning rod, are daily reminders of his genius. Quotations from *Poor Richard* are the very stuff of our daily conversation. Although most Philadelphians probably identify him with the Franklin Institute, which continues his work in natural science, it is possible that Franklin's personality is best epitomized by the Franklin Inn Club, a Philadelphia club for journalists and writers where a generosity of spirit, wit, and respect for the written word is demonstrated at daily luncheon conversations.

BIBLIOGRAPHY:

B. Ronald W. Clark, *Benjamin Franklin* (New York, 1983).

ROBERT RUTHERFORD SMITH

FRANKLIN, JAMES (b. 4 February 1697; d. 4 February 1735) was a Boston printer and founder of the *New England Courant*, a rebellious journal which attacked the Boston theocracy and adopted a literary style and wit in the manner of the London *Spectator*.

Franklin was born in Boston, and a great deal is known of his early life because of the fame and the *Autobiography* of his youngest brother, Benjamin (q.v.). The Franklin family had come to New England in 1682 from the family village of Ecton, Northamptonshire. His father, Josiah, had apprenticed as a dyer, but found employment in Boston as a tallow chandler, since he was unable to earn a living at his prior trade. However, he did little better, and settled into a situation which was respectable, but also was one of poverty and obscurity, according to Ben Franklin. Josiah's second wife was Abiah Folger, the daughter of poet Peter Folger. Josiah fathered eighteen children, and only one died before maturity.

Josiah Franklin was ambitious, but his financial situation and Boston's economic distress made formal education impossible for most of his children. James was sent back to Ecton to apprentice as a printer; later he moved to London, where he worked in another printing shop. In March of 1717 the young Franklin returned to Boston, with a sixty-five-year-old press and a font of type to set up his own business. Although his family was unable to help him, Franklin did set up a small printing shop on Dorset's Lane, and took his brother Ben as apprentice, at the insistence of his father. Business was slow, and Franklin was reduced to all sorts of odd jobs—Ben's ballads, pamphlets, and even cloth.

Slowly, business improved although Franklin was no match for the powerful printing dynasties which dominated Boston. But late in 1718 a political controversy became a financial godsend for Franklin. When John Campbell (q.v.) was replaced as postmaster, he refused to relinquish the *Boston News-Letter* to his successor, William Brooker. Brooker began a second paper, the *Boston Gazette*, which was printed by James Franklin.

Criticism was heaped upon Brooker for the poor printing of the *Gazette* and Franklin was fired; a few months later, Brooker himself was replaced. Franklin was again reduced to living off an occasional odd job. He did some work for booksellers, but his share of the printing business in 1720 was only half of what it had been the previous year.

By 1721 dissent had grown in Boston, and there was increased dissatisfaction with the theocracy, personified in Cotton and Increase Mather. The dispute centered around the issue of smallpox inoculation, espoused by the Mathers and most of the physicians. Chief among the dissenters were a group of men who gathered at Richard Hall's Tavern, primarily Anglophile John Checkley and William Douglass, a Scottish-born, irascible physician. Along with James Franklin, these men founded the third Boston newspaper, the *New England Courant*, on 21 August 1721, with the avowed purpose of opposing inoculation. Checkley was dismissed as editor after three intemperate issues, and the smallpox controversy waned in 1722, but the *Courant* continued its crusades.

In 1722 Franklin accused the civil government of failing to provide adequate defense against pirate raids in the vicinity of Boston. Authorities were willing to tolerate attacks on the ministers and physicians, but not on the government, so Franklin was arrested, charged with contempt after his appearance before the council, imprisoned, and forbidden to print or publish anything without prior approval by the secretary of the province. Franklin evaded the ban by putting the paper in Ben's name, who edited the *Courant* with the help of the Hell-Fire Club.

With the publication of the *Courant*, Franklin's business dramatically improved and remained substantial until the paper's death in 1727. Franklin apparently felt secure enough to marry, for on his twenty-sixth birthday, 4 February 1723, he married Ann Smith. They had five children, three of whom lived to maturity: James Jr., Elizabeth, and Mary.

Following the end of the *Courant*, James took the advice of his brother John and moved to Newport, Rhode Island, to begin a printing business. For the next eight years, Franklin printed only a few religious books and pamphlets, an almanac, and a few other volumes. He turned to selling a variety of products from snuff to powers of attorney. He also turned bookseller and imported volumes from England.

Franklin's most ambitious venture in Newport was the founding of the *Rhode Island Gazette* in 1732. But James Franklin was unable to re-create the *Courant* success, and the paper failed after eight months. It started off as a four-page journal, but soon was reduced to two pages with few advertisements and most of it news clippings from London newspapers. Franklin advertised for ''Gentlemen of Capacity and Leisure'' to contribute articles, and he did receive some letters and essays, but in the spring of 1733, the *Gazette* folded. Franklin himself did not long survive the paper. He died in Newport on 4 February 1735—his thirty-eighth birthday and the twelfth anniversary of his marriage.

BIBLIOGRAPHY:

B. DAB 3, 599; Willard G. Bleyer, ''The Beginning of the Franklins' *New England Courant*,'' *Journalism Quarterly*, June 1927; Carolyn Garrett Cline, ''The Hell-Fire Club: A Study of the Men Who Founded the *New England Courant* and the Inoculation Dispute They Fathered,'' M.A. thesis, Indiana Univ., 1976.

CAROLYN G. CLINE

FREDERIC, HAROLD HENRY (b. 19 August 1856; d. 19 October 1898), London correspondent for the *New York Times* in the 1880s and 1890s, gained an international reputation for his articles on the cholera epidemic in southern France in 1884, on the Irish independence question, and on the persecution of Jews in czarist Russia, among many other subjects. While meeting the heavy demands of his journalism, he wrote a dozen novels and many short stories and sketches. One novel, *The Damnation of Theron Ware* (1896), a best-seller in England and America, is still in print.

Born in Utica, New York, he was the only son of Henry DeMott Frederick (the son later dropped the ''k''), a railroad freight conductor who was killed when his namesake was only two, and Frances Ramsdell Frederick. Frederic graduated from eighth grade and was a photographer's assistant for several years. At age nineteen, he went to work as a proofreader for the *Utica Observer*. He began to write and free-lance short articles, and was given reportorial assignments. On 10 October 1877 he married Grace Williams of Utica. He was promoted to news editor, and at twenty-four was made editor of the *Observer*. In 1882 he became editor of the *Albany Evening Journal*, considered the most influential Republican newspaper in upstate New York. Under his leadership, however, the paper abandoned its strict Republicanism, frequently praising New York governor Grover Cleveland, a Democrat. When the Albany paper was sold in 1884, Frederic joined the *New York Times* and was sent to London.

Almost as soon as he was abroad, he went to France to report on the cholera epidemic. Risking his own health, he visited several disease-ridden cities in the south and filed "Down Among the Dead Men" and other highly detailed stories. These were widely reprinted and praised. The rival *New York Star* commented that Frederic's reporting was "a piece of courage and enterprise that only Stanley could rival and places him among the few great newspaper correspondents of the age."

As London correspondent from 1884 until his death, Frederic ranged widely in his choice of subjects, writing extensively on politics in France and Germany as well as Britain, covering the opening of new Gilbert and Sullivan operettas in London, and even writing columns on finance and philately. At the same time he was active in London clubs and contributed occasionally to British journals.

A trip to Russia in 1891 resulted in a series of articles describing the czarist government's anti-Semitic policies and commenting caustically on Russian civilization. They earned him praise in England and America and the hostility of the Russian government. They were published as a book. A series on Wilhelm II of Germany was also published as a book, *The Young Emperor* (1891).

Frederic's early novels, on upstate New York themes, achieved only mild success, but *The Damnation of Theron Ware* was acclaimed by the critics and bought by many in America and England, where it was published as *Illumination*. A study of a disastrous year in the life of a naive and self-centered Methodist minister, *Ware* is clearly a product of a reporter's astute observations of life in a Mohawk Valley city. After *Ware*, Frederic turned to British themes exclusively, with less success.

From 1890 Frederic, who had raised four children to maturity (two died in infancy) with his wife, Grace, openly maintained a separate home with another woman, Kate Lyon. They had three children, and entertained Stephen Crane (q.v.) and other friends at their home. It was at this second residence that Frederic suffered a fatal stroke, which came only a few months after one that paralyzed his right arm.

BIBLIOGRAPHY:

B. DAB 4, part 1, 7–8; NYT 20 October 1898; Thomas F. O'Donnell and Hoyt C. Franchere, *Harold Frederic* (New York, 1961).

EDWARD A. NICKERSON

FREED, FREDERICK A. (b. 25 August 1920; d. 31 March 1974) was recognized even in death for his successes in the production of documentaries on network television, when he was honored posthumously with his third Alfred

I. DuPont–Columbia University Award in Broadcast Journalism. At the time of the award no other documentarian had won as many as Freed. He also received posthumously the University of Missouri's Honor Award for Distinguished Service in Journalism and was up for his third George Foster Peabody award. Reuven Frank, a past president of NBC News, said Freed's distinction was "in his straight-line manner of developing a subject, masking prodigies of research and sophisticated complexities of technique; in his concern for the world he lived in, and in his repugnance for extreme positions."

Freed was born in Portland, Oregon, to Edgar Freed and Elise Oberdorfer Freed. He went on to Princeton University, where he graduated in 1941. The next four years were spent in the U.S. Navy during World War II. He served as a communications officer and a gunnery officer on destroyers. After the war he met and married Judith Chenkin, and they had two children, Lisa, born in 1954, and Katherine Celia, born in 1958. The family lived in the New York borough of Manhattan.

Freed began writing for *Esquire* magazine, where he moved up to assistant managing editor before moving into broadcasting. In 1949 he joined the Columbia Broadcasting System as a writer on the staff of the CBS radio program "This Is New York." He became writer-editor of the radio series "The People Act," funded by the Ford Foundation and winner of an Ohio State University award, his first.

Freed joined the National Broadcasting Company in 1955 as managing editor of NBC's "Home" television series. However, after two years he moved to CBS where he produced such documentaries as "The Dollar Debate," "The World of Ideas," "Politics, U.S.A.," and "Woman." In 1961 he returned to NBC, where he was to finish out his career, first as producer of the "Today" program with Dave Garroway and finally as an NBC News executive producer.

During thirteen years at NBC Freed was to become one of the premier producers of documentary programs. He became producer of the successful NBC News "White Papers," which won him many of his awards. In fact NBC, on three separate occasions, preempted its three-hour prime-time television programming schedule to air a Freed "White Paper" documentary. His productions included "American White Papers: Organized Crime in the United States" (1966) and "Who Killed Lake Erie?" (1969), the latter one of three programs designed to study the urban crisis in America. The other two documentaries were "White Paper: The Ordeal of the American City" (1968–69) and "Pollution Is a Matter of Choice" (1970).

Counted among the awards Freed received for his work were the Sidney Hilman Foundation Award for Outstanding Achievement in Mass Communications, the Overseas Press Club Award, a Security World Magazine award, and a prestigious Poynter Fellowship by Yale University. Of particular note, Freed was recognized with seven Emmy awards for such documentaries as "The Blue Collar Trap," "One Billion Dollar Weapon," and part 2 of "And Now the War Is Over—The American Military in the 1970s" (all in 1972). Earlier productions included

''Cuba: Bay of Pigs,'' ''Cuba: The Missile Crisis,'' (1964), the three-and-one-half hour ''United States Foreign Policy'' (1965), and ''Summer '67: What We Learned'' (1967).

Freed considered himself ''an old-fashioned liberal, conditioned in growing up to believe that the individual can bring about change in his society.'' He chose the medium of television and the documentary format to accomplish his goal. He did it all, from formulating the idea, interviewing, researching, editing and writing to producing. He once said that the only thing he did not do was to ''appear on the screen.''

He was fifty-three when he died, suffering a heart attack in his bed at home in New York City.

BIBLIOGRAPHY:

V. NYT 1 April 1974; Reuven Frank, ''Fred Freed, 1920–1974,'' NYT 14 April 1974; David G. Yellin, *Special: Fred Freed and the Television Documentary* (New York, 1973).

DAVID M. GUERRA

FREEMAN, LEGH RICHMOND (b. 4 December 1842; d. 7 February 1915) became one of America's best known frontier editors as he moved his newspapers, collectively known as the ''Press on Wheels,'' throughout the West. A native of Culpeper, Virginia, Freeman served in the army of the Confederacy, was captured, and was eventually reassigned to Fort Kearny, Nebraska, where he established the *Frontier Index* in 1866. It was this newspaper, which he published with a brother, Frederick K. Freeman, on the westward construction route of the Union Pacific Railroad, that catered to the public's interest in the frontier.

Freeman was the son of Arthur Ryland Freeman, a Culpeper County blacksmith, and Mary Kemper Freeman, a sister of James Lawson Kemper, who served as governor of Virginia from 1875 to 1879. Freeman attended Kemper College in Gordonsville, Virginia.

Although Freeman never planned as a youth to be a journalist, his education prepared him to pick up the scattered type of the *Kearny Herald* when he arrived at the fort in the spring of 1865. A year later he turned management of the newspaper over to his brother, and he headed west to explore the Yellowstone country. His tall tales appeared in the *Frontier Index*, as the *Kearny Herald* became known, during the next two years. After leaving the fort, the paper was published at nine sites along the construction route of the Union Pacific Railway before it was burned out by a mob at Bear River City, Wyoming Territory, late in 1868.

Freeman returned home to Virginia, where he lectured in buckskin on the marvels of the West. It was on this trip that he and Ada Virginia Miller, a native of Strasburg, Virginia, were married on 6 May 1869. After a brief residence at Rock Island, Illinois, where he had been a Civil War prisoner, the young family in the early 1870s moved west to Rock Springs, Wyoming. By 1873 the Freemans were the parents of two sons, Randolph Russell, who was born at Rock Island, and Hoomes Kemper, born at Rock Springs.

Involved in telegraphy in Illinois and land speculation in Wyoming, Freeman moved on to Ogden, Utah, where he resurrected the "Press on Wheels," starting the *Ogden Freeman* on 18 June 1875. Mrs. Freeman published the first issue in the absence of her husband, who had remained in Wyoming; a month later the couple's third son, Legh Miller Freeman, was born.

After a stormy period in Ogden publishing his anti-Mormon newspaper, Freeman moved to Butte, Montana, where railroad development promised the still elusive riches he sought. But as he waited in Butte for his family to arrive from Ogden, a shotgun fell from a wagon, the discharge striking Mrs. Freeman, who died on 22 August 1879 in Butte. Freeman went on to publish several newspapers in Butte before moving on to Thompson Falls, Montana, another railroad boomtown. Finally, he pushed on to Yakima City in Washington Territory, on the Northern Pacific Railroad route. He started the *Washington Farmer* there on 20 September 1884, the newspaper which he published, under this name or others until his death in Washington thirty-one years later.

On 10 June 1886 Freeman and Janie Nicholas Ward, a native of Georgia, were married in Cuthbert, Georgia. The couple returned to North Yakima to continue publication of the *Farmer* for only three years before moving in 1889 to Fidalgo Island in Puget Sound, the site of another anticipated railroad boom. Not only did the boom fail to materialize, but the financial panic of 1893 erased any hope of profit from either newspaper publishing or land speculation. In 1894, Freeman, nearing age fifty-two and the father of a newborn daughter, Varinia Allison, returned to North Yakima, the first time the frontier journalist had to move a newspaper from west to east.

Freeman's misfortune continued. In 1897 the Freeman home burned and Mrs. Freeman died on 2 November of "typhoid malaria." His third wife, Mary Rose Genevieve Whitaker of St. Paul, Minnesota, whom he married on 11 July 1900, survived her husband, dying in Yakima in 1917.

Perhaps because he never achieved the financial success he sought in his ventures in the West, Freeman turned to politics. He became an active populist, campaigned for the U.S. Senate in 1897 and 1910, and in 1914, at age seventy-one, announced his candidacy for the position of North Yakima mayor. He polled only 158 votes, proving a failure in this race as he had in convincing the state legislature to appoint him to the Senate.

Freeman died in North Yakima of infirmities of age on 7 February 1915, a product of the country's railroad frontiers, which instilled in him a restlessness and optimism which were never fulfilled. Unlike the community publishers who were establishing permanent ventures in this era, Freeman had proved incapable of settling successfully into the life of the publisher of the farm journal; the *Washington Farmer* became profitable only after his death. In establishing it, he recognized the need of farmers and ranchers for information. More substantial than his tall tales from the Yellowstone country, this was his contribution to American journalism.

BIBLIOGRAPHY:

B. DLB 23, 131–140; Thomas H. Heuterman, *Movable Type: Biography of Legh R. Freeman* (Ames, Iowa, 1979).

THOMAS H. HEUTERMAN

FRENEAU, PHILIP MORIN (b. 2 January 1752; d. 18 December 1832) was a noted poet of the revolutionary war period who also gained notoriety as editor of the anti-Federalist *National Gazette* from 1791 to 1793. His crusade to open the doors of the U.S. Senate was based on a belief that to do otherwise was "dangerous to liberty and entirely inconsistent with the principle of a free government."

Freneau, the oldest of five children, was born in New York City. His French-American father, Pierre Freneau, was a wine merchant. Freneau's mother, Agnes Watson Freneau, was the daughter of a prosperous Scotch yeoman from Monmouth, New Jersey. Freneau attended schools in New York and New Jersey and was graduated from the College of New Jersey (now Princeton), where he was a classmate of later president James Madison, in 1771.

Upon graduation, Freneau taught school and wrote poetry. In 1772 he published his first work and by 1775 had no fewer than eight pamphlets, all burning with invective aimed at the British. In July 1776 he left the colonies to become secretary to a prominent planter in the West Indies, where he also furthered his interest in poetry. He returned to New Jersey in 1778 and joined the militia there. A year later his travel accounts of life in the West Indies first appeared in the *United States Magazine*, and in 1781 he began an association with the *Freeman's Journal* in Philadelphia. It was here that Freneau gained his reputation as "the poet of the American Revolution" while following the last years of the war through satiric verse. He occasionally turned on his rival printers, James Rivington (q.v.) of the *New York Gazette and Universal Advertiser* and Hugh Gaine (q.v.) of the *New York Mercury*.

In 1784 Freneau went to sea, but while he was away, Francis Bailey, printer of the *North American Intelligencer*, printed the first of Freneau's poetry and its popularity was such that in a short time Bailey published an additional collection. On 15 April 1790 Freneau married Eleanor Forman, and the two had four daughters. In 1790 he also became chief editor of the *New York Daily Advertiser*, but not much of his early work dealt with controversy. However, his "Rules how to compliment great Men in a proper manner" by showing the person in command as "no more than a fellow citizen" can be pointed to as the foreshadowing of an adversarial relationship between the American press and the American president. His "Occasioned by a Legislation bill proposing a Taxation upon Newspapers" was a direct attack on the Washington administration, and Freneau quickly gained the attention of a number of anti-

Federalists who were equally concerned about the direction of the new government.

Madison suggested to then Secretary of State Thomas Jefferson that Freneau be made a translating clerk in the State Department at a salary of $250 a year. On 16 August 1791 the appointment was made, and by 31 October the *National Gazette* had been set up with Freneau as editor.

Alexander Hamilton attacked Freneau, claiming that an employee of government should not be criticizing its policies. But Freneau was undaunted. He wrote that Washington was "too buoyed up by official importance to think it beneath his dignity to mix occasionally with the people." Washington called him "that rascal Freneau," but the precedent had been set for an editor to show his journalistic independence, and Freneau vigorously fought for the right of newsmen (and the general public) to attend sessions of the U.S. Senate. Jefferson claimed that Freneau's efforts on behalf of the rights of man "saved our Constitution, which was galloping fast into monarchy" (Leary, 1941). However, in less than two years after its first issue, the *National Gazette* ran out of funds and was closed down. Yet Freneau's plea to open the doors of the Senate was not forgotten, and four months after the paper's demise, a motion to open the doors to the press passed.

In 1794 Freneau established his own press in Mount Pleasant, New Jersey, and in 1795 he began the *Jersey Chronicle*, which died a year later. In 1797 he began editing the *New York Time Piece, and Literary Companion*, but left it after a year. In his last years he returned to the sea and wrote poetry, but occasionally submitted letters and essays to newspapers. He has been considered the most significant poet in America before William Cullen Bryant (q.v.). On 18 December 1832 Freneau died from exposure in a blizzard.

BIBLIOGRAPHY:

B. DAB 4, 27–28; Mary W. Bowden, *Philip Freneau* (Boston, 1976); Lewis Leary, *That Rascal Freneau* (New Brunswick, N.J., 1941); Philip Marsh, *Philip Freneau: Poet and Journalist* (Minneapolis, 1967).

ROBERT L. BAKER

FRIENDLY, FRED W. (b. 30 October 1915), one of Edward R. Murrow's (q.v.) protégés in the early 1950s, pioneered in the establishment of television as a serious journalistic medium. He played a major role in the development of the television documentary as a programming form, one used to treat socially significant issues in broad scope and in depth for the purpose of affecting public awareness and public opinion. For two decades, from the mid–1940s through the mid–1960s, Friendly, as a member of the CBS News organization, shaped news programming styles and a philosophy of journalism, both of which have been adopted throughout national television news operations. For the next two decades, he served American journalism from outside the day-to-day operations of the newsroom, as an educator, critic, and one of a handful of electronic journalism's elder statesmen. While he comes from the same generation as such on-the-air figures as Walter Cronkite and Howard K. Smith (qq.v.), Friendly is not as well known to the general public; yet his observations about the current state of television news are weighed, respected, and quoted—if not always heeded—by thoughtful observers and practitioners of television news.

Friendly's professional career began in 1937 at WEAN radio in Providence, Rhode Island, where he worked as an announcer and newscaster. There, he wrote, produced, and narrated a series of programs entitled "Footprints in the Sands of Time," which dramatized biographies of such famous historical figures as Thomas Edison, Harvey Firestone, and others.

During World War II, Friendly served in the U.S. Army Information and Education Section in the China-Burma-India theater, as well as in the Pacific and Europe. He was a reporter and writer for the military newspaper *CBI Roundup*.

After the war, Friendly returned to the States to work in radio. In 1947 he was introduced to Edward R. Murrow by J. G. Gude, who thought Friendly's idea for a record album of oral history of the years 1933 to 1945 might interest Murrow. That introduction led to a long professional association. Murrow sold the idea to Goddard Lieberson of Columbia Records, which contracted for the album, entitled *I Can Hear It Now*. The production took eighteen months to complete. Meanwhile, Friendly and his wife, Dorothy Greene, began producing a weekly information series, "Who Said That?," which first aired on the NBC radio network in July 1948. *I Can Hear It Now* was released around Thanksgiving in 1949, and proved to be an unprecedented commercial success.

In 1950 Friendly left NBC to join Murrow full-time at CBS News. The two men began with a weekly, hour-long radio documentary series, "Hear It Now," which premiered just as the Chinese entered the Korean War. The program moved to television as "See It Now" on 18 November 1951. Over the years, this half-hour documentary series caught the attention of newsmakers and the public with such sensational and controversial programs as the exposé of Senator Joseph R. McCarthy. "See It Now" was expanded to one hour during the 1955–56 season. The following season saw nine irregularly scheduled programs, and in 1958 eight were aired. The program ended in July 1958, after having received thirty-five major awards.

From 1959 to 1964 Friendly was the executive producer of the series "CBS Reports," and in 1964 he became president of CBS News. He resigned from this position on 15 February 1966, following an unsuccessful battle with the network to preempt its regular programming to air live coverage of the U.S. Senate Foreign Relations Committee's hearing on Vietnam. Friendly's resignation—which he later characterized as "the most important act of my life"—became a cause célèbre in a continuing dialogue concerning the proper balance between journalistic and commercial considerations in the television industry.

In April 1966 Friendly became television adviser to the Ford Foundation and the first Edward R. Murrow Professor of Broadcast Journalism at Columbia

University, teaching and directing the Graduate School of Journalism's television workshop.

Fred Friendly was born in New York City on 30 October 1915 as Fred Wachenheimer, the son of a Providence, Rhode Island, jewelry manufacturer, Samuel Wachenheimer, and Therese Friendly Wachenheimer. In 1937 he adopted his mother's maiden name and added a "W" as his middle initial. During the war, Friendly received four battle stars, the Soldier's Medal, and the Legion of Merit decorations. On 24 June 1947 he married Dorothy Greene, a Time-Life magazine researcher, and the two collaborated on broadcast news programming in the early years of his network career. The couple had three children before being divorced. Friendly's second marriage, in June 1966, was to educator Ruth W. Mark, who had three sons by a previous husband.

During his years in the profession, Friendly was awarded many honors. "CBS Reports" was the most decorated news series on network television, with forty major awards. Friendly himself has received ten George Foster Peabody awards.

BIBLIOGRAPHY:

A. *Due to Circumstances Beyond Our Control* (New York, 1967).

JAMES WESOLOWSKI

FULLER, SARAH MARGARET (b. 23 May 1810; d. 19 July 1850), also known as the Marchioness d'Ossoli, is noted as the first American woman foreign correspondent and the first woman war correspondent, although she is better known as an author, critic, feminist, and transcendentalist philosopher. Born in Cambridge, near Boston, Fuller's early childhood was devoted to learning. Her father, Timothy Fuller, was a lawyer and Harvard graduate, noted for being a member of the Massachusetts senate and a representative in Congress. Her mother, Margaret Crane Fuller, was a schoolteacher. But it was Fuller's father who instructed her, exposing her to Latin when she was only six years old. By the time she was eight, Fuller was reading Shakespeare, Ovid, Cervantes, and Molière.

From her precocious childhood, Fuller moved into the same intellectual circles as Bronson Alcott, Ralph Waldo Emerson, and other noted transcendentalist philosophers. She quickly became known as a leading thinker and conversationalist, eventually in 1839 establishing her famous "conversations," an educational method for instruction. She conducted these conversations through 1844, using them as the material and inspiration for *Woman in the Nineteenth Century* (1845), which focused on issues of the burgeoning women's movement. Considered a classic work on feminism, it helped lay the foundation for the Seneca Falls convention on women's rights in 1848.

Fuller began her journalistic career as coeditor of the *Dial*, a transcendentalist publication. In 1844 Horace Greeley (q.v.) hired her as the first woman staff member of the *New York Tribune*, where she was named literary critic. She spent the next two years in New York, earning a reputation as an important

American critic. She also wrote exposés of public institutions, and promoted a home for freed women convicts.

In 1846 Fuller was able to fulfill a long-held ambition by traveling to Europe as a writer for the *Tribune*. There she reported on social conditions in the British Isles, and interviewed leading political and artistic figures. After arriving in Italy, Fuller became involved in the Roman revolution, sending to the *Tribune* first-person accounts of the French bombardment. Also in Italy she met Angelo Ossoli, with whom she had a son. A year after their son's birth d'Ossoli and Fuller married. When Rome fell, the family boarded a boat for the United States. Fuller carried with her a manuscript of her history of the Roman revolution, but it along with Fuller and her family was lost in a shipwreck off the coast of Fire Island. Fuller died just weeks before her fortieth birthday.

Margaret Fuller excited much attention both during her lifetime and after her death. Horace Greeley considered her ''the most remarkable and in some respects the greatest woman whom America has yet known.''

BIBLIOGRAPHY:

B. Katharine Anthony, *Margaret Fuller: A Psychological Biography* (New York, 1920); Arthur W. Brown, *Margaret Fuller* (New York, 1964); Bell Gale Chevigny, ed., *The Woman and the Myth: Margaret Fuller's Life and the Writings* (New York, 1977).

ELLI LESTER-MASSMAN

G

GAINE, HUGH (b. 1726; d. 25 April 1807), who for thirty-one years published the *New-York Mercury* (known as the *New-York Gazette and the Weekly Mercury* from 1768 to 1783), won notoriety in the history of American journalism by switching his allegiance from the American revolutionaries to the British in 1776.

Born near Belfast in Ireland, he was apprenticed at fourteen by his father, Hugh, to the Belfast printers Samuel Wilson and James Magee. At the end of his apprenticeship in 1745 he emigrated to New York where he was hired as a journeyman in the shop of James Parker (q.v.), printer-editor of the *New York Weekly Post-Boy*.

Gaine left Parker to open his own print shop in the spring of 1752, and in August of that year he began publication of the *New-York Mercury*. The paper was undistinguished in appearance from other newspapers of the day, but it was equal, if not superior, editorially to most. Like most other printers, Gaine involved his newspaper in the political conflicts of the time.

Gaine was successful. The newspaper, his adjunct printing, and the sale of books, paper, and sundries from his print shop brought him an increasing income. Gaine married Sarah Robbins in 1759. They had two daughters, Elizabeth, born 1761, and Anne, in 1764; a son, John R., was born in 1762. Sarah Gaine died soon after Anne's birth, leaving Gaine to raise the infants. He married Cornelia Wallace, a widow, in 1769. They had two daughters, Cornelia (birth date unknown) and Sarah, born in 1772.

Gaine and the *Mercury* followed an erratic course during the long struggle in the 1760s and 1770s against the British mercantile system. He joined in the fight against the Stamp Act by publishing essays opposing the measure and by printing his paper on unstamped paper. When the act was repealed in 1766, Gaine exulted. He also opposed the subsequent Townshend Acts and supported the movement to boycott British goods. But when the duties on all goods but tea were repealed, he stood against the Whigs in advocating that the boycott be lifted.

During the two-year calm that followed the repeal of the Townshend Acts, Gaine was appointed public printer of New York province in 1768, an event he celebrated by changing the name of the paper to the *New-York Gazette and the Weekly Mercury*. The paper carried little political news during that time, but it was drawn back into the political wars when Parliament enacted the British East India Company Act in 1773. He gave perfunctory support to the resistance movement at first and then strengthened it. However, following "tea parties" in Boston and New York, he ran essays abjuring violence and advocating accommodation with Britain.

Gaine opposed another boycott of imports, but he did give space to supporters of nonimportation after the Continental Congress adopted stringent measures. But because he had not fully supported the measures, he was branded an enemy of the colonies by militant Whigs. However, after Lexington and Concord, he sided wholeheartedly with the Whigs.

A fence-straddler during the debate over independence, he accepted it readily if not enthusiastically when it was declared. On the eve of the British invasion of New York in September 1776, Gaine packed a press, a limited amount of paper and type, and fled to Newark where he enlisted the *Mercury* in the revolutionary cause. Ambrose Serle, Lord Richard Howe's secretary, took over Gaine's shop, materials, and even the nameplate of the *Mercury* to provide the British with an official organ. Gaine, in Newark, suffered the deprivations of war, and on 1 November, he returned to New York.

Gaine regained full control of the *Mercury* after Serle sailed with Lord Howe's fleet in the summer of 1777, but he did not regain the trust of the British. They gave the post of royal printer to his competitor, James Rivington (q.v.), when Rivington returned to America shortly after Gaine's defection. Nevertheless, Gaine placed the *Mercury* in the British ranks for the remaining seven years they occupied New York. When the British sailed away at the end of the war, Gaine closed his newspaper. The final issue was dated 10 November 1783.

In the years following the war, Gaine maintained his printing business and was active in civic affairs and professional activities. He was a founder of the American Booksellers Association and served as its first president. He died at age eighty-one and was buried in the Trinity Church yard in New York.

BIBLIOGRAPHY:

B. DAB 4, 91–92; Alfred Lawrence Lorenz, *Hugh Gaine: A Colonial Printer-Editor's Odyssey to Loyalism* (Carbondale, Ill., 1972).

ALFRED LAWRENCE LORENZ

GALES, JOSEPH, JR. (b. 10 April 1786; d. 21 July 1860), was an editor of the *National Intelligencer*, a Washington, D.C., newspaper which was the semiofficial organ for presidents Jefferson, Madison, Monroe, and Fillmore and the leading daily in the city for most of the first half of the nineteenth century.

With his partner and brother-in-law, William W. Seaton (q.v.), he published in book form the major documentary sources of the first fifty years of the nation's political life.

He was the son of Joseph Gales, Sr., an immigrant printer from England, and Winifred Marshall Gales. Born in Eckington, England, young Gales received an education in the classics in England and the United States and attended the University of North Carolina. He entered the newspaper business in Raleigh with his father and later studied printing. He received a diploma from the Typographical Society of Philadelphia to augment the skill at shorthand he learned from his father.

In 1807 he began reporting congressional debates for the *National Intelligencer*. On 31 August 1810, he became publisher of the triweekly. Seaton joined the newspaper in 1812, and they became partners for forty-eight years until Gales's death. The paper became a daily the next year. In the early years, the newspaper devoted most of its space to reporting debates when Congress was in session. At first, Gales reported on the House proceedings while Seaton covered the Senate. In later years other reporters were hired. Gales married Sarah Juliana Maria Lee of Virginia on 14 December 1813. They entertained many of the nation's political notables at their home.

When the British captured Washington in the War of 1812, they destroyed the paper's records and equipment. Gales and Seaton were the congressional printers between 1819 and 1829 benefiting handsomely from their political contacts. In 1825 they began printing in book form the *Register of Debates in Congress*, the first permanent record of each congressional session covering the period until 1837. In 1834, financed by the government, they began printing the *Annals of Congress* in forty-two volumes covering the years 1789 to 1824. They used the material of earlier reporters as well as the reports from the *National Intelligencer*. Other newspapers supplanted the *Intelligencer* as semiofficial organ of presidents until the practice declined.

Congress authorized the firm with financial backing to collect and print important historical documents of the young nation covering the period before 1832. Their *American State Papers* appeared in thirty-eight volumes from 1832 to 1861. Gales and Seaton oversaw the most extensive printing business in the country for decades until Congress reduced appropriations for official printing.

Although Gales and Seaton divided the work of the firm equally between them, Gales was believed to be the primary editorial writer. The paper continued to emphasize political news and documents even after most newspapers began wider coverage of society after the 1830s.

The paper was anti-Jackson, pro-Whig, against the War with Mexico, and for continued compromise on slavery. It became more independent editorially in the 1830s. The *Intelligencer* carried long columns of House and Senate proceedings until 1851, when the *Daily Globe* became the official reporter for Congress. With its emphasis on political news, its circulation declined steadily for the three editions: the daily, the triweekly, and the weekly. Gales died at his Washington home after years of declining health.

BIBLIOGRAPHY:

B. DAB 7, 100–101; NYT 27 July 1860; William E. Ames, *A History of the "National Intelligencer"* (Chapel Hill, N.C., 1972).

SAM KUCZUN

GALLAGHER, JAMES WESLEY "WES" (b. 6 October 1911) retired on 26 October 1976 from the Associated Press (AP) after thirty-nine years of service. Prior to his assuming the general manager position in 1962, Gallagher had been a reporter, war correspondent, a news executive, and author. His major contribution to the journalism world was his leadership of AP during a period of growth and turmoil for the news media, including the Vietnam War and the resignation of President Richard M. Nixon.

Gallagher was born to James Gallagher and Chispa Howard Gallagher in Santa Cruz, California. He attended schools in the state, including the University of San Francisco. After working for the *Register-Pajaronian*, in Watsonville, California, as a sports writer, he moved into general assignments in 1929 and 1930. In 1934 Gallagher entered Louisiana State University, and completed a master's degree in journalism in 1935. While going to school, he served as a correspondent for a news service, and as relief reporter and telegraph editor for the *Baton Rouge State-Times* and *Morning Advocate*. He was in another hall in the state capitol when Huey Long was shot, but he was one of the first to obtain accurate knowledge of the extent of Long's injuries.

Gallagher went from Baton Rouge to Rochester, New York, where for two years he was a reporter-photographer for the *Democrat and Chronicle*. In 1938 he went to work for AP in its Buffalo bureau, and then went to Albany. From there he was transferred to New York and was assigned as a foreign correspondent. Gallagher was sent to cover the Finnish-Russian War, but it ended while he was en route. He arrived in Copenhagen just as the German army invaded Denmark and Norway in April 1940. He covered the final phases of the Norwegian campaign and then was sent to the Budapest bureau.

When the Italians attacked Greece, Gallagher was in Belgrade, Yugoslavia. He covered the war on the Albanian front for the next four months until he became ill with jaundice. He remained in Greece until the country fell to the Germans. In 1942 he covered the invasion of North Africa as head of the AP field crew. In 1943 his back was injured and his face cut when his jeep overturned. In 1944 he was assigned to head the AP staff covering the Normandy invasion. He also coauthored a narrative of the war, *Free Men Are Fighting* (1944).

Betty G. Keeley, a New York actress, became his wife on 6 June 1946. The couple had three children: Brian, Jane, and Christine. They lived in Rye, New York, while Gallagher worked for AP. He was named general executive in charge of personnel in the New York office in 1951. In 1953 he took over direction of AP Newsfeatures. In October 1962 he was named general manager.

Under his guidance, the AP blended and broadened the news and photo report by combining the best of news features, business news, and women's news with the general news report. It expanded the use of surveys, exclusive interviews, situation stories, polls of Congress, national roundups of events, texts sent by high-speed wires, development of more specialists, task-force approaches to big news stories, and a premium on enterprise stories beyond the day's news.

In the technical field, Gallagher promoted the use of computers in the news operation. He spurred AP to obtain an exclusive leased cable for picture transmission between the United States and Europe, the first facility of its kind to be leased by a news service. An automatic wirephoto-receiving machine delivering glossy prints within twenty seconds after completion of the picture was introduced. He created a communications department as a planning instrument to explore the potentials in satellite communication, and to apply new communications developments as rapidly as possible.

In 1969 Gallagher announced a regionalization of the editing and distribution of the news in nine hub cities. A technical center was established in St. Louis to work with staff technicians in the field and with newspaper production executives.

In 1976 Gallagher was named a director of the Gannett Company. He resides in Santa Barbara, California.

BIBLIOGRAPHY:

B. *Who's Who in Finance and Industry, 1974—75*, p. 20; Saul Pett, "He Came in Like a Lion. He Goes out Like a Lion." *AP World* (1977).

JOHN M. BUTLER

GALLUP, GEORGE HORACE (b. 18 November 1901; d. 26 July 1984), although not technically a journalist, made a tremendous impact on the business and editorial sides of journalism. He pioneered research on what readers and audiences liked, and pioneered in the development of public opinion polls. What people thought could be as interesting as what people did, Gallup said in an interview several months before his death, and he was proud that he helped make opinions newsworthy.

When Gallup started political polling in Iowa in 1932, asking voters about his mother-in-law, a secretary of state candidate, the idea of measuring opinion was new. By the time of his death, a Gallup Poll showed that one in every seven American adults had been interviewed by a pollster. Through many books and articles Gallup was a salesman for polling, and he staunchly defended polling against its critics. To say that a poll changed opinion, he said, was like saying that a thermometer changed the temperature. He consistently scoffed at the idea that democracy would suffer by politicians' blindly following public opinion polls; the American people, he said, were repeatedly ahead of their leaders. He also actively promoted polling throughout the world, so much so that in some countries "to do a gallup" meant to take a poll. "Dr. Gallup was the most important person in the history of polling,'' said Irving Crespi, a polling consultant.

Born in Jefferson, Iowa, the son of George Henry Gallup, a land speculator, and Nettie Davenport Gallup, Gallup attended the University of Iowa. He was editor of the student newspaper and was awarded his B.A. in 1923. He became an instructor of journalism at the school while he earned his M.S. in psychology (1925), and his Ph.D. in journalism (1928). His dissertation dealt with a method of measuring reader interest in newspapers. In the process he determined that adults read comic strips more than realized, which led to the use of comics in advertising, and that photographs were very popular, which led his backers, Cowles Publishing, to start *Look* magazine.

Gallup taught journalism for two years at Drake University and one year at Northwestern University before being hired in 1932 as director of research for the Young and Rubicam advertising agency in New York City. He stayed until 1947, and his work contributed to the agency's rapid growth. Meanwhile, in 1935, he founded the American Institute of Public Opinion, which became headquartered in Princeton, New Jersey, where Gallup lived. The institute conducted marketing and advertising research, and from the polls, Gallup spun off a weekly newspaper report, ''America Speaks.'' His political polls, although a minor part of the operation, drew publicity, particularly when Gallup correctly called the 1936 presidential election for Franklin D. Roosevelt.

After Gallup left the advertising agency, he concentrated on running his public opinion firm. At his death, due to a heart attack, he was chairman of the board and chief executive officer. Among Gallup's contributions to polling were his work to refine a sampling method that would correctly represent the public and a question design method that would screen out people who did not have enough knowledge about a topic to form an opinion. He used his news sense to develop questions about topics that would appeal to newspaper editors, and his repetition of the same questions over the years helped chart changing American attitudes in such areas as religious beliefs and the role of women.

Gallup formed related polling organizations in Great Britain and dozens of other foreign countries, and was president, from 1947 on, of the International Institutes of Public Opinion. He also founded Quill and Scroll, an international honor society for high school journalists. Unlike many of his colleagues, Gallup did not poll for any political party. To emphasize the neutrality of his facts, he said he never voted in a presidential election after voting for Alfred Smith in 1928.

An affable and dynamic man, Gallup was still active in his eighty-third year. He continued to seek new fields for the use of surveys, urging, for example, their use in determining factors in the cause of disease. Gallup was survived by his wife, the former Ophella Smith Miller, whom he married on 27 December 1925, and their three children, a daughter and two sons who followed him in the polling business.

BIBLIOGRAPHY:
B. CB 1952, 200–202; EAB, 400–401; NYT 28 July 1984.

JUDITH A. SERRIN

GANNETT, FRANK ERNEST (b. 15 September 1876; d. 3 December 1957) was a newspaper editor, publisher, and founder of the Gannett Group (his preference over "chain"), which at his death included twenty-two newspapers, four radio stations, and three television stations, mostly in New York. His entrepreneurial expertise came not in starting but in acquiring newspapers, granting editorial autonomy, and consolidating business procedures. His legacy inspires professionalism and efficiency. In 1935 he established the Gannett Foundation to assure the continuation of the Gannett Group, safeguard employees' jobs, and provide philanthropic grants.

Gannett, the third son of six children, was born in a farmhouse about fifty miles southeast of Rochester, New York, to Joseph Charles Gannett and Maria Dixon Brooks Gannett. Hard times forced them to abandon farming and take up leasing small-town hotels. Joseph was innkeeper; Maria, cook. Gannett became self-supporting at nine. He delivered newspapers, did farm work, sold rubber address stamps to Italian laborers, scavenged and sold bones, and peddled picture books of the 1889 Johnstown flood. He earned his first dollar as a reporter for the *Buffalo News*. When the family moved to Oneonta, Gannett stayed behind, tended bar for room and board, and finished high school at Bolivar Union School and Academy in 1893. He worked a year as an accountant, then won a Cornell University scholarship, graduating with a bachelor of arts degree in 1898. Throughout college he hustled odd jobs to support himself, working on the student newspaper, as campus correspondent for *Ithaca Journal*, and reporter for *Syracuse Herald*. Gannett entered college with eighty dollars and left with $1,000.

In 1899 he served as secretary to the First Philippine Commission, learned Spanish and translated José Protasio Rizal's classic novel *Noli Me Tangere* (1900). In 1900 he worked briefly as editor of the *Cornell Alumni News*, then as city editor, managing editor, and business manager of the *Ithaca Daily News*. He left in 1905 to work on *Frank Leslie's Illustrated Weekly* and the *Pittsburgh Index*.

In June 1906, with $3,000 cash and $17,000 in loans, he began his newspaper group, becoming half owner of the *Elmira Gazette* with Erwin R. Davenport. Shortly he merged it for quarter interest with the *Evening Star* to become the *Star-Gazette*. In 1912 he bought the *Ithaca Journal* and, in 1919, merged it with the *News*, forming the *Journal-News*. In 1918, with Elmira associates Davenport and Woodford J. Copeland, Gannett bought Rochester's *Evening Times* and *Union and Advertiser*, forming the *Times-Union*, which, thereafter, was the only paper he edited, though his name appeared as president on the mastheads of all his newspapers. In 1921 the group bought and merged the *Utica Observer* and

Herald-Dispatch into the *Observer-Dispatch* and, in 1923, acquired Elmira's *Advertiser* and *Telegram*. In 1924 Gannett bought out his associates and went on to acquire thirty newspapers, merge ten, and sell three, but he never founded a single one.

Gannett insisted that the integrity of his newspapers never be questioned, that they be readily acceptable in the home, playing down crime and scandal. He was a champion of free press and a vigorous fighter for progress and reform. He was adamant in forbidding liquor advertising. He founded the Empire State School of Printing in Ithaca, New York, in 1922. He co-invented the Teletypesetter, heralded as 1929's outstanding printing-industry invention. He also developed a fast, inexpensive engraving process.

Politically, he was active on national, state, and local levels for more than thirty years. He opposed the New Deal and U.S. involvement in international problems. He supported labor unions, publically owned utilities, and Prohibition. In 1936 he was nominated for New York governor. In 1937 he founded and chaired the National Committee to Uphold Constitutional Government. In 1940 he was an unsuccessful candidate for the Republican presidential nomination. In 1942 he served as assistant chairman of the Republican National Committee.

Gannett was a pioneer in aviation advancement. He flew more than 1.7 million miles in his lifetime, including a flight around the world in 1947, when he interviewed leaders and wrote a series of articles on global problems of economics, peace, and prosperity, later published as a pamphlet. Other articles were collected in two more pamphlets and distributed complimentarily. Gannett was a citizen of the world, a global thinker, and an American patriot.

On 25 March 1920 he married Caroline ''Kyrie'' Werner. They had a daughter, Sarah ''Sally'' Maria, born in 1923, and adopted a son, Dixon, born in 1929. Gannett was a generous, loyal, quick-witted humanitarian, sympathetic, warm-hearted, sincere, and fearless. He died from complications of a spinal fracture and stroke. He was also a diabetic. His wife died 4 January 1979.

BIBLIOGRAPHY:

B. DAB Supp. 6, 226–227; NYT 4 December 1957; Samuel T. Williamson, *Imprint of a Publisher: The Story of Frank Gannett and His Independent Newspapers* (New York, 1948).

PATT FOSTER ROBERSON

GARDNER, ALEXANDER (b. 17 October 1821; d. 12 December 1882) was a photographer whose work covered a myriad of subjects including the Civil War and the nation's westward expansion following the war. Gardner was one of the finest photographers and photographic innovators of his era. Among his best-known works are the only photographs taken immediately after the battles of Gettysburg and Antietam, his portraits of Abraham Lincoln, the Lincoln conspirators, Indian chieftains, plus images of the railroad's expansion into Kansas after the Civil War.

Gardner was born in Paisley, Scotland, the son of James and Jean Glenn Gardner. The family later moved to Glasgow. Gardner's father died shortly after the move, leaving his mother with the task of raising the children. When Gardner was fourteen, he began a seven-year apprenticeship with a jeweler in Glasgow. Following this, Gardner worked as an editor for the *Glasgow Sentinel*, where he wrote about social problems, science, and art.

Upon emigrating to New York, Gardner took a job with Mathew Brady (q.v.), who recognized that Gardner's training and interest in physics and chemistry, plus his experience as a jeweler, would be valuable as a photographer. In addition, Gardner also brought to Brady's studio a sense of financial management and stability that had been lacking under Brady's management.

Two years later, in 1858, Brady sent Gardner to Washington, D.C., to manage another Brady studio. Gardner welcomed the move because his brother James was already living in the city. Shortly after his arrival, Gardner realized that there was money to be made in photographing common soldiers, a subject not considered to be worthy of portraiture by many photographers such as Brady.

Following a disagreement between Brady and Gardner in 1862 over copyrighting war photographs, Brady and Gardner ended their partnership. Brady felt that he had the right to copyright any photograph made by a photographer in his employ. Gardner felt that any photographer who used his own time and equipment should be allowed to copyright the photographs he took and make money from the images.

After leaving Brady's employ in early 1862, Gardner joined the headquarters staff of General George B. McClellan. With the title of "Photographer to the Army of the Potomac," Gardner made copies of maps and documents for McClellan's staff. He also had the opportunity to photograph other officers and soldiers, in addition to having his photographic equipment transported to military locations outside of Washington.

After McClellan was relieved of his command in November 1862, Gardner returned to Washington where he and his brother opened their own photographic studio just around the corner from Brady's studio. It was in this studio that Gardner made many of his now-famous images, including the photographs of Lincoln. Although Gardner did not venture into the field of combat very often after his return to Washington, he continued to collect war views by sending other photographers into the battlefields. On at least one occasion, however, Gardner left his studio and produced some of his most memorable images. After picking up his son from a seminary at Emmitsburg, Pennsylvania, Gardner went into the fields near Gettysburg, immediately following the final battle. Realizing the importance of the moment, Gardner shot the only series of photographs that captured the death and destruction of the Battle of Gettysburg.

Gardner's greatest contribution to the photographic record of the Civil War came in 1866 with the publication of his two-volume work, *Sketch Book of the War*. This was a collection of 100 actual photographs, not reproductions of photographs. It is of critical value to photo-historians because Gardner included the actual names of those who took the photographs, a practice not common among all collectors of Civil War photographs. Gardner also shot photographs of Indian delegations for the Office of Indian Affairs. He visited the Plains Indian Territory in 1867. Working for the Union Pacific Railroad, Eastern Division, Gardner visited every town along the line in Kansas. He made over 150 photographs on this trip, including everything from overviews to Kansas towns to key buildings, geographical points of interest, and even vegetation found along the railroad tracks.

Several years later Gardner made another contribution to his craft by establishing the first rogues gallery of criminals for the Washington, D.C., police department. Gardner's photographic efforts continued until shortly before his death.

BIBLIOGRAPHY

B. Josephine Cobb, "Alexander Gardner," *Image*, June 1958.

MICHAEL D. SHERER

GARRISON, WILLIAM LLOYD (b. 10 December 1805; d. 24 May 1879) was an activist opponent of slavery who used his journalistic skills with tremendous influence. Although not the earliest advocate, the publisher and his weekly, the *Liberator*, symbolized the movement in both North and South.

The son of a sea captain, Abijah Garrison, and Frances Maria Lloyd Garrison, William was born in Newburyport, Massachusetts. His father, a drunkard, deserted the family before William was three. In 1818 Garrison was apprenticed for seven years to Ephraim W. Allen, the editor of the *Newburyport Herald*. He developed into an expert compositor and wrote anonymously for the paper. Upon completing his apprenticeship in 1826, he became editor of the local *Free Press* until that paper failed. He was a journeyman printer until he met Benjamin Lundy (q.v.), a Quaker, who turned Garrison's attention to the evils of slavery.

During the summer of 1829, he joined Lundy in publishing the weekly *Genius of Universal Emancipation* in Baltimore. Garrison's comments grew more and more vehement; found guilty of libel and unable to pay a $1,000 fine, he was jailed for seven weeks. Upon his release after a friend raised the money, Garrison lectured in eastern cities against slavery and worked out a prospectus for the *Liberator*. First issued on 1 January 1831, the weekly was printed on a hand press with borrowed type.

Garrison admitted that his circulation never exceeded 3,000. So effective as an antislavery journal was the *Liberator* that the Georgia legislature offered a $5,000 reward for the arrest, prosecution, and conviction of the editor under that state's laws. In the fall of 1835, Garrison was seized by a Boston crowd and dragged through the streets with a noose around his neck. Only intervention by Mayor Theodore Lyman prevented even greater harm. Garrison spent the night in jail and left the city for several weeks. But the *Liberator* continued its weekly sledgehammer attacks, and popular opposition to slavery increased.

Garrison's abrasive manner featured a zealot's determination to support innovative causes that often lacked majority public support. In addition to abolition of slavery, he favored prohibition, women's rights, clairvoyance, and spiritualism, and opposed capital punishment, the use of tobacco, and imprisonment for debt. Even his ardent supporters in opposing slavery rebuked him.

Garrison also was active in formation of the American Anti-Slavery Society and served for twenty-two years as its president. When he learned that women were excluded from the World's Anti-Slavery Convention in London during June 1849, he refused to participate. In January 1843 the Massachusetts Anti-Slavery Society, pressured by Garrison, resolved that the U.S. Constitution, with its acceptance of slavery as an institution, represented "a covenant with death and an agreement with hell" and the delegates called for its annulment. A rallying cry for the *Liberator* was "No union with slaveholders." During 1847 the editor went on a northern tour with Frederick Douglass (q.v.). On 4 July 1854 at Framingham, Massachusetts, Garrison publicly burned a copy of the Constitution at an abolitionist meeting. "So perish all compromises with tyranny," he exclaimed.

Favoring peaceful separation of the states, Garrison could not condone John Brown's raid on Harpers Ferry. After initial coolness toward President Abraham Lincoln for what Garrison considered an undefined policy toward slavery, the editor prevented abolitionist societies from openly condemning the federal government. He well understood the importance of the Emancipation Proclamation. In January 1865 the American Anti-Slavery Society rejected his proposal to dissolve, and he declined to head the organization for another term. When the Thirteenth Amendment was ratified, he concluded his mission was completed and put out the final issue of the *Liberator* on 29 December 1865.

He married Helen Eliza Benson on 4 September 1834, and the couple settled in a home called Freedom's Cottage in Roxbury, Massachusetts. They had seven children, two of whom died in infancy. In December 1863, Mrs. Garrison was stricken with paralysis and lingered until she died of pneumonia on 28 January 1876. The editor died at the New York City home of his daughter Helen, wife of Henry Villard (q.v.). He was buried in Forest Hills Cemetery in Boston. His surviving sons were Wendell Phillips Garrison of the *Nation*, George F. Garrison, William Lloyd Garrison, Jr., and Francis J. Garrison.

BIBLIOGRAPHY:

B. DAB 7, 168–172; NYT 25 May 1879; Wendell Phillips Garrison and Francis J. Garrison, *William Lloyd Garrison 1805–1879: The Story of His Life Told by His Children*, 4 vols. (New York, 1885–89); John L. Thomas, *The Liberator: William Lloyd Garrison, a Biography* (Boston, 1963).

HILLIER KRIEGHBAUM

GARVEY, MARCUS MOSIAH (b. 17 August 1887; d. 10 June 1940) was to many a "Black Moses" pointing the way to nationalism for blacks in the United States and abroad. He communicated his ideas in his rousing speeches, his newspapers, and his magazine. Garvey's newspaper *Negro World* attempted to redefine black journalism. Garvey drew some of the leading writers and editors to his paper, including T. Thomas Fortune (q.v.). The *Negro World* had thousands of readers in the United States, the Caribbean, and Africa.

Born in St. Ann's Bay of north Jamaica, Garvey was the son of Marcus Garvey, a stonemason, and Sarah Garvey. The younger Garvey described his father as a man of great intellect and courage who took chances and died poor. He called his mother a gentle Christian, the direct opposite of his father. He also described his parents as "black Negroes," a distinction not only of race, but also of skin-color. The emphasis on shade of blackness was later significant in Garvey's nationalist crusade.

Garvey's education consisted of grammar school in St. Ann's Bay. He left school when he was fourteen years old to work as a printer's apprentice. By the time he was seventeen he moved to Kingston, where he polished two skills of communication: he observed great preachers and practiced speaking, and he continued work as a printer.

In 1912, after holding a number of jobs and traveling in Central America, Garvey went to London. There he studied, probably taking courses at the Birkbeck College of the University of London. Garvey developed an interest in the struggle for freedom by Africans and Afro-Americans. He wrote for *African Times and Orient Review*, and he was stirred by Booker T. Washington's book *Up From Slavery*. Filled with a desire to unite blacks throughout the world, Garvey returned to Jamaica in 1914 and formed the Universal Negro Improvement Association (UNIA). Two years later he moved to the United States to further his organization.

Black America of 1916 was receptive to a movement such as Garvey's. There had been an intellectual awakening brought on by a crop of graduates from black universities, and by the philosophical debates of Booker T. Washington and W.E.B. Du Bois (q.v.). There was a continued problem of violence against blacks, including riots and lynchings. A southern crop failure and job openings in war-related industries had caused a migration of blacks from the South to northern cities. Whether in military service or civilian life, blacks experienced humiliating discrimination. These conditions created a closely grouped populace that was ripe for a new approach to racial progress.

Some blacks worked for political change through the National Association for the Advancement of Colored People (NAACP) and similar organizations. Others found release in the self-expression of the Harlem Renaissance, a literary movement. Blacks in both of these movements, however, tended to be better educated and of lighter complexion. Marcus Garvey appealed to many of the poorer, darker Negroes. He praised black skin and negroid features. He called for a coming together of blacks, through his UNIA, to finance and operate industries such as shipping and printing. Garvey also called for control of Africa by Africans and the establishment of a government in Africa that would offer protection for blacks around the world.

To communicate with his followers, who were centered in Harlem but stretched throughout the United States and abroad, Garvey started the weekly newspaper

Negro World. The paper, started in January 1918, was designed to set a new standard for black journalism. Garvey criticized other papers, particularly the *Chicago Defender*, because of its extensive use of advertisements for hair straighteners and skin lighteners. The *Negro World* refused such ads, stressed black history and heroes, praised the beauty of blackness, and campaigned for the independence of Africa. Garvey usually wrote a front-page editorial. At its peak, the paper had a circulation of 50,000 and had sections in French and Spanish. Visitors to Africa reported seeing the paper there, and some political leaders mentioned the influence that the paper had in shaping their beliefs. Many of the nation's black journalists contributed to the paper, most notably T. Thomas Fortune. He was editor from 1923 until his death in 1928.

The UNIA collected about $10 million between 1919 and 1921 to buy ships, goods, and services. The Black Star Line of ships was started to allow commercial exchange between blacks of various nations. By 1922, however, the company was bankrupt and Garvey was indicated for mail fraud. He acted as his own lawyer, and used the trial as an opportunity to espouse his beliefs, but was convicted. He appealed, lost, and began serving a five-year sentence in an Atlanta penitentiary in 1925. His sentence was commuted in 1927 and he was deported to Jamaica.

Garvey was resilient. He dabbled in Jamaican politics and regularly sent editorials to the *Negro World*. He published a daily paper, the *Black Man*, but by the 1930s the depression had crippled his organization. The *Black Man* ceased publishing, and by 1933, so did the *Negro World*. Garvey moved to London in 1935 and published the *Black Man* as a monthly magazine. He died after a severe stroke at age fifty-two.

BIBLIOGRAPHY:

B. NYT 19 August 1924; Edmund David Cronon, *Black Moses: The Story of Marcus Garvey and the Universal Negro Improvement Association* (Madison, Wis., 1968).

KAREN FITZGERALD BROWN

GAUVEREAU, EMILE HENRY (b. 4 February 1891; d. 15 October 1956) edited the staid *Hartford Courant*, claimant to the title of oldest continuously published paper in the United States, the ribald tabloid *New York Graphic*, and other newspapers. He was a writer of popular fiction and nonfiction books and a keen observer of national and international politics.

He was born in Centerville, Connecticut, the son of French-Canadian immigrants, Alphonse Gauvereau, who worked in an arms factory, and Malvina Perron Gauvereau. At age six his right leg was crippled in an accident. He credited his handicap with turning his interests toward literature and music. For a time his family returned to Canada, and he was educated at the Jesuit-run Provencher Academy in Montreal. When the Gauvereaus returned to the United States, he entered public schools.

At eighteen, Gauvereau dropped out of high school and his studies as a flutist to work on the *New Haven Journal-Courier*, evincing a talent for developing sensational news. His exploits earned him the attention of the managing editor of the *Hartford Courant*, and in August 1916 he moved. Before leaving New Haven, he married Sarah Welles Joyner, *Journal-Courier* society editor. They had three children and were divorced in 1936.

He showed his mettle on the *Courant*, rose to assistant managing editor and became managing editor in 1919. His energetic, sometimes sensational, news policies placed him in conflict with Charles Hopkins Clark, majority stockholder and editor. When Gauvereau refused to terminate a series of stories about a traffic in fake medical diplomas, Clark forced him to resign.

Gauvereau was hired by Bernarr Macfadden (q.v.) to start a daily newspaper, the *New York Graphic*, which appeared 15 September 1924. Even in the "jazz journalism" era the *Graphic* was bizarre. It was lurid and used "composographs," manufactured illustrations that looked like real-life photos. His doctored picture of Rudolph Valentino on his deathbed was credited with having raised the paper's circulation by 100,000. Gauvereau toiled for five years to put the *Graphic* (dubbed the Porno-*graphic* by some) on a secure, profitable basis but failed.

William Randolph Hearst (q.v.) lured him to the *New York Mirror* in 1929. As managing editor, Gauvereau found himself in a circulation struggle with the successful *Daily News*. Scandal was the *Mirror's* métier. Racing information, promotional contests, and Broadway columnist Walter Winchell (q.v.) were the long suits of the *Mirror*. Gauvereau wrote a cutting novel, *The Scandal Monger* (1932), about Winchell. Gauvereau didn't get along with Arthur Brisbane (q.v.), whom Hearst installed as editor in 1934.

Gauvereau was a special observer with a congressional mission to Russia studying whether the United States should recognize that country. He returned in 1933 and urged recognition. In 1935 he published *What So Proudly We Hailed*, which contrasted the USSR and the United States. Hearst mistakenly believed the book to be pro-Communist, and Gauvereau was fired.

A friend obtained Gauvereau a position as staff investigator for the House Committee on Patents. One assignment dealt with patent pooling in the aircraft industry; this investigation led to an acquaintance with General William Mitchell, the advocate of air power who had been court-martialed for expressing his opinions. Gauvereau was a coauthor of a biography of Mitchell, and he crusaded for a restoration of honors to the airman.

In 1936 Gauvereau went to work at the *Philadelphia Inquirer*, which had been acquired by racing-news magnate Moses Annenberg. Placed in charge of the rotogravure section, Gauvereau produced features in the gaudiest Sunday-supplement tradition. In 1938 Annenberg named Gauvereau editor of *Click*, one of the many photo magazines founded in the late 1930s. Underpaid and overloaded with assignments, he resigned in 1940.

He married Winifred C. Rollins, his secretary at the *Mirror*, on 5 December 1936. He was adviser to the official delegation of the Korean provisional government to the United Nations in San Francisco in 1945. He was handicapped by a deteriorative brain condition in his later years. He died in Suffolk, Virginia.

In his autobiography, *My Last Million Readers* (1941), Gauvereau wrote: "I was part of that strange race of people aptly described as spending their lives doing things they detest to make money they don't want to buy things they don't need to impress people they don't like." Despite the self-contempt he was recognized as a skilled journalist.

BIBLIOGRAPHY:

A. With Mary Macfadden. *Dumbbells and Carrot Strips: The Life and Times of Bernarr Macfadden* (New York, 1953).

B. DAB Supp. 6, 231–232; NYT 17 October 1956; Lester Cohen, *The New York Graphic* (New York, 1964); John Bard McNulty, *Older Than the Nation: The Story of the "Hartford Courant"* (New York, 1964).

ROBERT E. BLACKMON

GEORGE, HENRY (b. 2 September 1839; d. 29 October 1897) was a journalist, economist, and philosopher, best known as the founder of the single-tax movement. George began his career as a printer and was in his late twenties before he began writing. His early articles were followed by pamphlets and several books. His major work, *Progress and Poverty* (1880), made him an instant public figure. He started his own weekly newspaper and was twice a candidate for mayor of New York City.

The oldest son among the eight children of Richard Samuel Henry George and Catherine Pratt Vallance George, he was born in a small brick house in Philadelphia. His father published and sold Protestant Episcopal books, and his mother ran a small private school before her marriage. The family attended church regularly and held daily Bible readings, practices which were said to have strengthened George's idealism and sense of justice. He attended both private and public schools and graduated from Philadelphia High School at the head of his class before turning fourteen.

Next he worked as an office boy in a crockery importing house for two dollars a week. Having a grandfather who was a sea captain inspired him to go to New York at fifteen and embark on a fourteen-month voyage to Calcutta. When he returned to the United States in 1856, he got a job in a printing office to learn typesetting. The next year he sailed for California and spent some unsettled years moving from the gold fields to British Columbia and back and forth between San Francisco and Sacramento. When he could not find work as a compositor, he did odd jobs. At one point he and five other young printers bought a small paper, the *Evening Journal*, but it failed.

Despite the fact that he was destitute, he married Annie Corsina Fox on 3 December 1861. George set type at the *San Francisco Bulletin*, the *Sacramento Union*, and other established papers when he could, but times were grim for the young couple. George's writing career began blossoming in 1865. Articles on public issues that he sent anonymously to newspapers and journals started to attract attention and comment. The editor of the *San Francisco Times* was so impressed that he gave George a job on the editorial staff. George worked his way up to managing editor before leaving in 1868 to be managing editor of the *Chronicle*, where he stayed only three weeks.

Also in 1868 he published an article, "What the Railroad Will Bring Us," in the *Overland Monthly* that contained the seeds of his ideas on how more population and business activity would bring greater wealth for a few and greater poverty for many. After a disappointing business trip to New York later that year, he returned West to become editor of the new *Oakland Transcript*. An unsuccessful candidate for the California assembly in 1869, George devoted much of the next couple of years to laying the groundwork for the single-tax thesis he expounded the rest of his life. In 1871 he wrote a forty-eight-page pamphlet called *Our Land and Land Policy* in which he said the value of the land belongs to the whole community and that all revenues should be raised by taxes on it.

Another venture in starting a newspaper followed. The *San Francisco Evening Post* was an initial success but was turned over to creditors after about four years, and George was broke again. In 1876 the governor appointed him state inspector of gas meters. With the publication of *Progress and Poverty* in 1880, George moved to New York for good. The book, which attributes poverty to rent and proposes a tax on land as the remedy for social ills, brought him fame both in the United States and abroad. He wrote several magazine articles and was in demand as a lecturer. The next year *The Irish Land Question* was published, and he sailed to Ireland as a correspondent for the *Irish World* of New York. He stayed for nearly a year.

Two more books, *Social Problems* (1883) and *Protection or Free Trade* (1886), followed, and in 1886 he lost in his first bid to become mayor of New York City, although he came in second, ahead of Theodore Roosevelt. The next year he began his own weekly newspaper, the *Standard*. His next book, *The Condition of Labor; An Open Letter to Pope Leo XIII* (1891), was in response to a papal encyclical of 1891 and is considered some of his best writing. Next came *A Perplexed Philosopher* (1892), an answer to Herbert Spencer's criticism of George's beliefs on the land question; however, it was not as widely read or translated as his other books. By 1892 George decided the *Standard* was too much of a burden, financially and otherwise, and that he would rather devote his time to other projects, so publication was suspended.

Described as an amiable man, only five feet six inches, and very domestic in his tastes and habits, George was finishing *The Science of Political Economy* in 1897 when he was persuaded to run for mayor again. His wife warned him about his rigorous schedule, but to no avail. He died of a stroke after making four campaign appearances in one evening.

BIBLIOGRAPHY:

B. DAB 8, 211–215; NYT 30 October 1897; Jacob Oser, *Henry George* (New York, 1974).

KAY MARIE MAGOWAN

GIBBINS, FLOYD (b. 16 July 1887; d. 24 September 1939) was a restless, roving journalist who gained international prominence as a war correspondent and radio personality. Covering many of the world's armed conflicts from 1914 to 1939, Gibbons, with his hand-knitted eye patch concealing a World War I wound, became the stereotypical dashing reporter for a generation of readers and listeners.

He was born Raphael Floyd Phillips Gibbons in Washington, D.C., the first of five children of Edward Thomas Gibbons and Emma Theresa Phillips Gibbons. His father built a successful retail produce business in Washington, then left it to establish an even more successful trading-stamp company in Des Moines and Minneapolis.

The family sent Gibbons back to a college prep program at Georgetown University, but his dismissal following a prank ended his formal education. He returned to the Midwest, eventually took a job as a police reporter on the *Minneapolis Daily News*, jumped to the *Milwaukee Free Press* for a few months, and then returned to Minneapolis, this time with the *Tribune*. In 1912 he moved to Chicago, where his first job was with the socialist *World*. Within a few months he had talked his way onto the *Chicago Tribune*. Gibbons married Isabell Pherrman of Minneapolis in February 1914. It was a generally unpleasant union that produced no children and ended in divorce in 1924.

Late in 1914 the *Chicago Tribune* sent him to cover revolutionary conflicts in northern Mexico. There he established a reputation as a colorful war correspondent, gained the confidence of Pancho Villa, who outfitted a special car on his train for the reporter, and later rode with Major General John J. ''Blackjack'' Pershing when a U.S. expedition was sent to punish Villa for raids into New Mexico.

With a keen eye for detail and a vivid, splashy writing style, Gibbons was sent in 1917 as *Tribune* London correspondent to cover World War I. Choosing to sail through quarantined Atlantic waters on a British ship, Gibbons was aboard the SS *Laconia* when it was torpedoed. His 4,000-word eyewitness account was widely reprinted throughout the United States. In June 1918 Gibbons was wounded while following a marine assault in the Belleau Wood, losing his left eye and gaining his famous eye patch.

After the war he returned to Europe as chief of the *Tribune*'s foreign-news service, for which he recruited an outstanding corps of correspondents, and editor of the paper's Paris edition. Continuing his own reporting, in 1920 he was the only journalist on the front in the Polish-Russian skirmish; in 1921 he scooped his rivals by slipping into Russia to cover a devastating famine; in 1923 he crossed the Sahara Desert for the *Tribune* to ''obtain true pictures of sheiks and their appeal to Anglo-Saxon and American women''; and in 1925 he covered French-Riff battles in Morocco.

In 1926, for no definite reason, Robert McCormick (q.v.) terminated Gibbons's fifteen-year employment with the *Tribune*. Almost immediately, however, McCormick's partner, Joseph Medill Patterson (q.v.), hired Gibbons to write a biography of Baron Manfred von Richthofen, the German air ace, for Patterson's nickel magazine *Liberty*. Later Gibbons wrote his first fiction—*The Red Napoleon*—for *Liberty*. While researching the novel, he met M. H. Aylesworth, president of NBC, who suggested that Gibbons try radio.

In 1929 he contracted with NBC for a program called "The Headline Hunter." Its immediate success and his reputation as the fastest talker on radio—he was once timed at 217 words a minute—led to other radio shows and an enlarged national following. Always on the lookout for a war to cover, Gibbons from time to time dropped his NBC affiliation to roam the world for Hearst's International New Service. In 1931 he reported the Chinese-Japanese conflict; in 1935 he covered Italy's invasion of Ethiopia; and in 1936 he reported on the Spanish Revolution.

Through this period, Gibbons was an internationally recognized personality, palling with Will Rogers (q.v.) and actor John Barrymore, making news himself in the gossip columns of the New York press, and lecturing throughout the nation.

Although Gibbons had been aware of a heart problem since 1934, he refused to slow his globetrotting pace and died of a heart attack in 1939 at his farm in Stroudsburg, Pennsylvania.

BIBLIOGRAPHY:

B. DAB 22, Supp. 2, 230–231; NYT 25 September 1939; Edward Gibbons, *Floyd Gibbons, Your Headline Hunter* (New York, 1953); Douglas Gilbert, *Floyd Gibbons: Knight of the Air* (New York, 1930).

ROBERT L. HOSKINS

GITLIN, IRVING JOSEPH (b. 16 July 1918; d. 12 December 1967) was one of the most highly regarded originators of documentary programs in the history of network television. For his work he received more than twenty awards from fourteen different national organizations. His commitment to bringing major social and political issues to the public through television was well recognized.

Irving Gitlin was a true "native New Yorker" who was born in the city, grew up and was educated there, spent most of his working life in Manhattan, and at the age of forty-nine died there. His life, though shortened, was a full one. He was born to Jacob and Celia Keen Gitlin, and received his education through the New York City public schools. He graduated from City College with a B.S. degree and went on to finish a master's at Columbia University in 1941. He took the position of principal of a school in the Virgin Islands for one year before he served four years in the U.S. Marine Corps during World War II.

In 1946 Gitlin returned home and to his alma mater, where he taught freshman biology. His education had been directed toward science and during his tour of duty he studied radar and communications at Harvard and Massachusetts Institute of Technology. This background led him to a position with CBS radio as a science reporter. He was to stay at CBS for the next fourteen years, holding positions that ranged from research-writer to network news executive. Within one year after moving into broadcasting, Gitlin married Louise Ziskind. They had three children, a son, Peter, and two daughters, Betty Ann and Barbara Jane.

"The Nation's Nightmare," a CBS radio documentary broadcast in 1951, was to bring Gitlin his first major recognition, the prestigious George Foster

Peabody Award. It dealt with crime in America. In 1954 he was again awarded a Peabody and also a Sylvania award for his television series "The Search." In that same year he was named director of public affairs for CBS News and given supervision over all public affairs broadcasts. In this position, Gitlin was in charge of the creation of such award-winning television programs as "Out of Darkness," about a young woman who recovers from mental illness, and "Conquest." He was responsible for other successful programs, notably "The Twentieth Century," "The Last Word," and "The Great Challenge" for television, and "Unit One" and "Who Killed Michael Farmer?" for radio.

In 1959 Gitlin was promoted to the position of program executive for creative projects. He had proven himself by the success of his work, but that may not have been enough. He was a restless man who wanted to continue to produce meaningful programs that would serve the public's interest. In 1960 he left CBS for NBC, perhaps because his production team at CBS was overshadowed by Edward R. Murrow's (q.v.) documentary group. He was named executive producer of creative projects for NBC News and moved quickly to assemble his team of documentarians to create and produce the highly acclaimed "NBC White Paper" series. The programs in this series that went on to capture some twelve awards included "The U–2 Affair"; "Sit-In," which was a moving and sensitive examination of the Southern black's battle against discrimination; "Panama: Danger Zone"; and "Angola: Journey to a War," among many others.

One of Gitlin's "White Paper" programs, "The Rise of Khrushchev," caused an international incident in early 1963 when Soviet authorities, angered over the "candid appraisal" of Khrushchev, forced NBC News to shut down its Moscow bureau. It was not until a year and a half later that NBC News personnel were allowed back into Russia. Gitlin went on to oversee production of many other highly regarded documentaries, including the discussion series "The Nation's Future"; "Purex Special for Women," a series documenting women's difficulties in a rapidly changing world; and the "Dupont Show of the Week." This latter series "developed a new technique of using highly mobile camera and sound equipment to cover the action as it develops in real life." It included such programs as "Police Emergency," "Fire Rescue," and "Emergency Ward."

In 1965 Gitlin resigned from NBC News to start his own independent production company. His success continued with both documentary and drama programs, at least two of which would be broadcast over his third network, ABC, on "Stage 67." Unfortunately, Gitlin had only two and a half years to experience program production for which he had sole responsibility. He died of leukemia.

BIBLIOGRAPHY:

NYT 13 December 1967; Les Brown, *The New York Times Encyclopedia of Television* (New York, 1977).

DAVID M. GUERRA

GOBRIGHT, LAWRENCE AUGUSTUS (b. 2 May 1816; d. 14 May 1881) was a reporter in Washington, D.C., from the 1830s until shortly before his death. He is best remembered as an agent for the Associated Press (AP) and for his coverage for the AP of the assassination of President Abraham Lincoln in April 1865.

Most records claim that Gobright was born in Baltimore and learned the printing trade in that city. (His obituary in the *Washington Evening Star* states he was born in Pennsylvania in 1813.) He operated a campaign paper in Batavia, Ohio, that supported Martin Van Buren. The date of his first employment as a journalist in Washington is lost in history, but he was one of the *Globe* reporters in the winter of 1839–40, and he reported in the capital for the *Baltimore Clipper*. In addition, he was an editor of the *Republic* and the *Union*, both in Washington. He was also associated with the *Washington Evening Star* prior to his employment by the AP. During the summer of 1845, he edited the short-lived *Washington Daily Bee*.

Gobright cannot be linked for certain with the Associated Press until 1853. Several sources claim that Gobright was the agent in charge of the Washington bureau only after it was organized in 1856. Exact dates are not to be found in the existing records. Gobright's often-quoted comments about his AP duties give an operational description of the functions of an "objective" reporter:

> My business is to communicate facts. My instructions do not allow me to make any comment upon the facts which I communicate. My dispatches are sent to papers of all manner of politics, and the editors say they are able to make their own comments upon the facts which are sent to them. I therefore confine myself to what I consider legitimate news. I . . . try to be truthful and impartial. My dispatches are merely dry matter of fact and detail. (Quoted in Benjamin Perley Poore's "Washington News" in *Harper's Monthly*, January 1874, pp. 225–236.)

Gobright's most famous story was his bill of particulars that followed the assassination of Lincoln by John Wilkes Booth. The story of his reportage that grim night is repeated in many books. A personal account appears in *Recollection of Men and Things* (1869).

Gobright accompanied the body of the late president on its way to entombment in Springfield, Illinois, and filed moving and emotional accounts of that journey. In 1866 he was the AP reporter who accompanied President Andrew Johnson on his "swing around the circle," the trip that resulted in the further alienation of Johnson from the Radical congressional leadership. Gobright testified (about Johnson's sobriety) in the impeachment hearings before the House Judiciary Committee on 24 May 1867.

In the spring of 1867 Gobright was elected president of a short-lived Washington Correspondents' Club. In 1869 he published his memoirs, and in 1873 he published a book of verse for children, *Jack and Jill*.

Gobright remained in charge of the Washington bureau of the AP until early summer of 1878, when he was replaced by Walter Polk Phillips. Gobright's retirement was announced in August 1879. He was connected with the *Telephone*, a weekly newspaper, after he left the AP. He published another book of verse for children called *Echoes of Childhood* in 1879. Indeed, he is described as a poet in the *Dictionary of North American Authors*. He died 14 May 1881 in Washington.

Of his family there are few records. His obituary and a tribute published in the *Washington Evening Star* stated that he was survived by a daughter and grandchildren. His wife preceded him in death.

BIBLIOGRAPHY:

A. *Recollection of Men and Things at Washington During the Third of a Century* (Philadelphia, 1869).

B. NCAB 5, 355–356; NYT 15 May 1881; *Washington Evening Star*, 16 and 25 May 1881; F. B. Marbut, *News from the Capital* (Carbondale, Ill., 1971).

ROY HALVERSON

GODDARD, MORRILL (b. 7 October 1865; d. 1 July 1937) was a newspaper editor, an exponent of ''yellow journalism,'' and father of the *American Weekly*, the first of the syndicated Sunday supplements.

He was the third of seven children of Charles William Goddard and Rowena Caroline Goddard. His mother was a daughter of Governor Anson P. Morrill of Maine. His father was president of the Maine state senate, a jurist, and postmaster of Portland. Both parents were descendants of English immigrants of the late 1660s. Goddard attended public schools in Portland and then Bowdoin College, but was expelled in his sophomore year because of a prank. He transferred to Dartmouth as the youngest member of the class of 1885. Except for work on student publications he kept to himself. His father had arranged for him to study law, but he left for New York after the June graduation ceremony without notifying his family.

He was turned down for a staff position of Joseph Pulitzer's (q.v.) *New York World* but roamed the streets of the city looking for stories acceptable on a space-rate basis. He was successful, and was hired full-time by the *World*. He was not yet twenty. Goddard was relentless in his search for news, brazenly making his way into the funeral cortege of General Ulysses S. Grant and making up part of the pack of reporters who dogged President Grover Cleveland on his honeymoon.

Promoted to city editor, he distinguished himself by developing unusual feature stories out of seemingly routine material. After four years Pulitzer named him editor of the *Sunday World*. With a keen eye for graphics and a grasp of popular psychology, Goddard used his own staff of artists and writers—something new in Sunday journalism—in layouts that featured blazing headlines and illustrations that sometimes made up entire pages. Circulation soared, but Pulitzer was unhappy with the extravagance. In the end, however, Goddard was given the free hand he wanted. In 1894 Goddard persuaded the *World* management to use comic drawings on their color presses. Richard F. Outcault (q.v.) was hired, and the colorful *Yellow Kid* strip evolved. Sunday circulation under Goddard mounted by the thousands per week.

Goddard was thirty and William Randolph Hearst (q.v.) thirty-one, when the two met in the Hoffman House late in January 1896. Hearst made Goddard an offer as editor of the *Sunday Journal.* A relationship began that lasted forty years. At one point Goddard was earning $5,000 a week. In the meantime, Arthur Brisbane (q.v.) had assumed the reins at the *Sunday World*, and the two fought it out with displays of pyrotechnics and sensationalism that led to the coining of the term *yellow journalism.*

Hearst was interested in a magazine that would challenge, surprise, and entertain readers, but also educate them—a ''People's University,'' he called it. On 15 November 1869 the first issue of the *American Sunday Magazine, Popular Periodical of the New York Journal* was published. In time the magazine absorbed all of Goddard's energies. Retitled the *American Weekly*, it could boast that it was the most widely distributed editorial product in the world, exceeding six million in circulation just before his death.

Goddard's editorial philosophy was expressed in *What Interests People—And Why* (1935):

> Man's emotions are more frequently stirred than his intelligence. The really intelligent mind is a mind willing and capable of thinking. But many are incapable of real thinking, and to others who are capable, the process of thinking is painful. But the emotions, on the other hand, are quickly and painlessly stirred. The dog has an emotional mind—capable of little or no thought—and, like man's faithful friend, a large majority of America's 100,000,000 react to emotional appeals of word or picture, but fall asleep when you present something requiring them to think.

Goddard was a solitary. He shied away from social contacts, declining even Hearst's invitations to San Simeon. He shunned publicity to the point of destroying pictures of himself. He married Jessamine Rugg of Hot Springs, Arkansas, on 28 December 1899. They had five children: Morrill, Dewitt Rugg, Mary Rowena, Jessamine, and Rowena. Goddard lived in New York and for many summers at Naskeag Point, Maine, where a heart attack ended his life.

BIBLIOGRAPHY:

B. NYT 2 July 1937.

ROBERT E. BLACKMON

GODDARD, SARAH UPDIKE (b. ca. 1700; d. 5 January 1770) was a printer and newspaper publisher in colonial America. Her son, William (q.v.), established the *Providence Gazette* in 1762 with funds advanced by his mother. She ran the paper and the print shop, assisted by her daughter, Mary Katherine, from 1765 to 1768 and then moved to Philadelphia to operate William's print shop there, as well as the *Pennsylvania Chronicle and Universal Advertiser*, from 1768 until her death.

Born at the family estate on Narragansett Bay, Rhode Island, Goddard was one of six children of Lodowick and Abigail Newton Updike. Her father, a land developer, provided tutors for the children, who grew up with unusual advantages both financially and academically. Goddard was married on 11 December 1735 to a physician from Groton, Connecticut, Giles Goddard. He soon moved his practice to New London, where he also became postmaster. Two of their four children, Mary Katherine and William, survived infancy.

Before Giles's death on 31 January 1757, the couple had decided to apprentice William to a printer in New Haven, Connecticut. In 1761 William chose Providence, Rhode Island, as a likely place to set up shop and became the first printer in that community. His mother not only supplied the necessary capital but also moved to Providence to assist in establishing the business.

The first issue of the *Providence Gazette; and Country Journal* appeared on 2 October 1762. The shop also published printed forms, broadsides, and pamphlets. In 1764 William obtained the postmastership and early in 1765 joined with three partners to establish a paper mill. However, he was unable to win the government printing contract, and financial difficulties led him to suspend the paper in May 1765 and travel to New York, leaving the Providence business and the partnership in the hands of his mother and sister.

They expanded the printing operation, using "S. and W. Goddard" as their imprint, and in August 1766 revived the *Providence Gazette* as "Sarah Goddard and Company." Goddard used items calculated to entertain, as well as to inform, her readers, including local and foreign news, essays, poetry, notices, and advertisements. The paper had an increasingly pro-Whig political stance. Goddard added *The New-England Almanack* and the letters of Lady Mary Wortley Montagu to the works produced by the print shop and offered books for sale and book-binding services. She hired an assistant, Samuel Inslee, in 1766. He stayed for a year and was replaced by John Carter. By this time the paper was making money, and so was the paper mill.

In the meantime, William had become a partner in a Philadelphia printing operation and was embroiled in the personal and financial feuds that seemed to be his lot. At the request of his partners, he wrote his mother to suggest sale of the Providence shop and a move to Philadelphia for her and Mary Katherine. She was reluctant; she had worked to build the newspaper, the businesses, and the community, and hesitated to spend the end of her life in "a strange part of the world," as she replied (Henry, 1980). A personal visit accomplished what the letter had not, and the Goddards sold the printing shop and the paper to Carter at the end of 1768.

Difficulties with William's Philadelphia partners continued; they reneged on their promise to provide a house for Goddard and Mary Katherine and protested when they started a small print shop in the house William found for them, forcing its closure. At the end of 1768 Goddard turned over to William her interest in her husband's estate and canceled his debt to her in return for a promise that he would take care of her with the proceeds from his business. While William traveled to Connecticut and Rhode Island, trying to collect money owed him, the two women again found themselves running his print shop and the newspaper connected with it, the *Pennsylvania Chronicle and Universal Advertiser*.

Goddard wrote her son in December 1769 that the number of subscribers to the paper was increasing daily and that soon it could support two families. Shortly after he received this letter another came, notifying him that his mother had died on 5 January 1770. She had made William's failing Providence business profitable, kept his Philadelphia business going, and demonstrated a commitment to printing as a community service that surpassed her son's.

BIBLIOGRAPHY:

B. NAW 2, 56–57; Richard L. Demeter, *Primer, Presses, and Composing Sticks* (New York, 1979); Susan Henry, "Sarah Goddard, Gentlewoman Printer," *Journalism Quarterly*, Spring 1980.

SHERILYN COX BENNION

GODDARD, WILLIAM (b. 29 October 1740; d. 23 December 1817), who established four newspapers in the colonial period, was fiercely independent and a strong believer in a free press. He fought both the Tories and the Patriots to maintain his freedom of expression. Goddard also established the first American postal system to replace the British system.

Goddard was born to a well-do-do family in New London, Connecticut. His father, Dr. Giles Goddard, was a physician and his mother, Sarah Updike Goddard (q.v.), a well-educated woman for that time who backed her son financially in his printing ventures. After he received some schooling at home and at a local school, William, at fifteen, was apprenticed in July 1755 to James Parker (q.v.), who had launched the *Connecticut Gazette* in New Haven. The young apprentice also received some printing experience in Parker's New York shop in 1758. His apprenticeship ended in 1761 and he became a journeyman at the *American Chronicle* in New York. Goddard later moved to Providence, Rhode Island, to start his own printing business with the financial aid of his mother. On 2 October 1762 Goddard issued the first number of the *Providence Gazette*. His sister, Mary Katherine, and his mother assisted in the operation.

After three years in Providence, Goddard left for New York, where he went to work for John Holt (q.v.) and became a silent partner in Holt's shop. He joined the Sons of Liberty and was responsible for the publication of the *Constitutional Gazette* in Woodbridge, New Jersey, which opposed the Stamp Act. Goddard returned to Providence briefly, but soon turned his eye toward Philadelphia. With the aid of silent partners, Joseph Galloway and Thomas Wharton, Goddard opened a print shop in June 1766. He was promised the printing of the Pennsylvania assembly if Galloway won a seat.

Goddard rented one of Benjamin Franklin's (q.v.) old presses and issued the *Pennsylvania Chronicle and Universal Advertiser* on 26 January 1767. He hoped to lure away readers from the *Pennsylvania Gazette* while supporting the candidacy of his friend Galloway. His partners persuaded him to bring his mother and sister to Philadelphia to help him run the shop. A newspaper war involving Goddard's *Chronicle*, the *Gazette*, and the *Pennsylvania Journal* helped

Goddard. His paper's circulation reached 1,000 in a short time and grew to 2,200, one of the largest in the colonies.

A bitter quarrel soon broke out between Goddard and his partners, especially Galloway, who had become conservative in his views regarding British-American relations. The partners withdrew their support and the *Chronicle* fell on lean days. Goddard looked toward Baltimore, and by the time the last issue of the *Chronicle* was published on 8 February 1774, Goddard had begun the *Maryland Journal or Baltimore General Advertiser* on 20 August 1773.

Goddard believed that it was important to the Patriot cause, and the interests of newspaper publishers, to establish an American postal system. He hired riders and laid out postal routes. The Continental Congress took over his postal system on 26 July 1775, but instead of being appointed postmaster general, Goddard was named surveyor of routes, a disappointment to him.

The publication of an ironic letter in the *Maryland Journal* on 25 February 1777 espousing the acceptance of a British peace proposal led to Goddard's being beaten and his shop wrecked by the Whig Club when he refused to reveal the writer's name. A group of Patriots threatened to tar, feather, and hang Goddard after he printed an attack on George Washington on 6 July 1779. When Goddard recanted his "transgression" he was released.

Goddard married Abigail Angell, a wealthy heiress, on 25 May 1786, and later took her brother, James Angell, into partnership. Goddard's wife disliked Baltimore, so Goddard sold his interest in the *Journal* to James Angell and moved back to Providence, where he spent his last years.

BIBLIOGRAPHY:

B. DAB 5, 314–315; Sidney Kobre, *Development of American Journalism* (Dubuque, Iowa, 1969); Ward L. Miner, *William Goddard, Newspaperman* (Durham, N.C., 1962).

SIDNEY KOBRE

GODEY, LOUIS ANTOINE (b. 6 June 1804; d. 29 November 1878) was founder and publisher of the *Lady's Book*. It was the leading woman's magazine of its day and set many precedents in magazine publication. Godey's interest in magazine publication extended to at least four other magazines before his retirement in 1877.

Godey's parents, Louis and Margaret Carel Godey, left Sens, France, for America at the beginning of the French Revolution. They settled in New York City, where Louis Antoine was born. They were too poor to provide their son with formal education, but he later educated himself through extensive reading and practical experience. Godey began working early; reportedly, by the time he was fifteen he had a small enterprise of his own, a combined newsstand and bookshop.

In 1828 Godey went to work in Philadelphia as a clerk for the *Daily Chronicle* under Charles Alexander. In 1830 Godey and Alexander brought out the first issue of the *Lady's Book*, a fifty-six-page monthly, which was made up almost entirely of reprints of fiction, poetry, and short articles from British magazines. Godey made a special effort to appeal to his audience by including at least one colored illustration of the latest fashion, a page of music, embroidery patterns, and sketches of fashionable hats. Alexander soon gave up his interest in the magazine, leaving Godey sole proprietor. In 1837 Godey bought *Ladies' Magazine*, a successful Boston publication, and put Sarah Josepha Hale (q.v.), former editor of *Ladies'*, in charge of the combined magazines, *Godey's Lady's Book*.

With expert help from Hale, Godey depended less and less on reprints from other magazines; he began to solicit and pay liberally for pieces written by American authors, particularly women. In 1843 he published an issue produced entirely by women. Among his many contributors were Sara Lippincott (q.v.) and Harriet Beecher Stowe. Godey also purchased work from Edgar Allan Poe, Washington Irving, Nathaniel Hawthorne, Oliver Wendell Holmes, and dozens of other men and women writers who later achieved fame in American letters. Godey's back-cover advertisements boasted that the *Lady's Book* was "devoted to American Enterprise, American Writers, and American Artists," a claim that few other magazines could make at that time.

From 1840 to 1860 the *Lady's Book* was the most popular and influential magazine in America. When other magazine editors began to reprint articles that Godey had paid his contributors for, Godey decided to copyright the *Lady's Book*. Other publishers were angered at this precedent, but soon began to copyright their own magazines.

By 1851 circulation of the *Lady's Book*, at 63,000, had surpassed that of any other magazine, and by 1858 it reached 150,000. Godey estimated that his readership was one million by 1860. Circulation began to drop as the Civil War approached, and throughout the war years the magazine declined. In 1877 Godey sold the magazine.

Godey's other magazine ventures came fairly early in his career. In 1836 he began the weekly *Saturday News and Literary Gazette* with Joseph C. Neal and Morton McMichael. With McMichael he started two other publications: *Young People's Book, or Magazine of Useful and Entertaining Knowledge*, in 1841, and *Lady's Musical Library*, in 1842. All three publications had brief histories.

Although Godey avoided political and religious controversies, he was well acquainted with his contemporaries in literature, art, government, and religion. Godey spent most of his life in Philadelphia. He married Maria Catherine Duke on 31 August 1833. They had five children: Louise, Louis, Frank, Marion, and Harry. When Godey died he left an estate worth over a million dollars. During his last years, Godey spent winters in St. Augustine, Florida, because of ill health. On 29 November 1878 he died from a complication of diseases.

BIBLIOGRAPHY:

B. DAB 7, 343–344; NCAB 22, 39; NYT 30 November 1878; Ruth E. Finley, *The Lady of "Godey's": Sarah Josepha Hale* (Philadelphia, 1931).

SHIRLEY M. MUNDT

GODKIN, EDWIN LAWRENCE (b. 2 October 1831; d. 21 May 1902), for decades the influential editor of the *New York Evening Post* and the *Nation*, achieved a national reputation for his impulsive, inconsistent, and often intolerant editorial stridency and his combative, conservative elitism that appealed to the prejudices of the Gilded Age's genteel intelligentsia. An Anglophile by temperament and training, Godkin was tutored in mid-nineteenth-century British political economy, idolized the "laws of trade," distrusted democracy, and criticized Americans' penchant for chauvinistic patriotism.

Godkin was born near Moyne, County Wicklow, Ireland, the first child of Sarah Lawrence Godkin and James Godkin, an itinerant dissenting clergyman and journalist who advocated home rule for Ireland. His parents sent him to a preparatory school at Armagh when he was seven, and three years later he entered Silcoates School at Wakefield near Leeds, England, where he studied a classical curriculum for four years. For a brief period, he studied at the home of his uncle, the Reverend John Edge, and was admitted to Queens College at Belfast in 1846 on a legal scholarship.

At Queens College, Godkin immersed himself in the study of political economy, chiefly David Ricardo, John Stuart Mill, and Jeremy Bentham, who left an indelible stamp on his political, economic, and social philosophy. Throughout his life, Godkin was a vociferous champion of representative government controlled by the "intelligent classes," laissez-faire entrepreneurial capitalism, and the moral expediency of "the economic man." In his third year, he was elected president of the college literary society, and after an otherwise undistinguished academic career, he received a degree in 1851.

Godkin moved to London in 1851 to begin a three-year course of study to prepare for the English bar. He cut his legal studies short, however, to become a subeditor of the *Workingmen's Friend*, a penny weekly that published Godkin's series of historical sketches on Hungary in 1851–52. Later expanded, rewritten, and published as *The History of Hungary and the Magyars* (1853), the 380-page book was well received and reprinted several times, including an American edition. Godkin served as a special correspondent for the *London Daily News* during the Crimean War, returning to England in 1855 and to Ireland in 1856. For a few months, Godkin was a contributing editor to the *Northern Whig* of Belfast, resigning in October 1856 to travel to America. He arrived in the United States in November 1856.

Shortly after his arrival in America, Godkin made a two-month horseback tour of the South, returning to New York City in January 1857 to resume his legal studies. He read law under David Dudley Field, a New York lawyer, passed the New York bar examination in 1858, and was admitted to practice in 1859. Godkin practiced law only briefly, preferring to continue his journalism career with contributions to newspapers in New York and London. With introductions he brought from Ireland, Godkin soon became acquainted with members of the New England elite, including Samuel E. Foote, who had acquired a fortune in the insurance business. Godkin married Foote's daughter, Frances "Fanny" Elizabeth Foote, in Trinity Church, New Haven, Connecticut, on 27 July 1859, and they had three children: Lawrence, born in 1860; Lizzie, born in 1865; and Ralph, who died in infancy in 1868. Lizzie died after a short illness in April 1873, and Fanny died two years later. After Fanny's death, Godkin suffered a period of despondency during which he withdrew from the *Nation*. He returned to New York City in the late 1870s, joined the *Evening Post*, and resumed direction of the *Nation*. He married Katharine B. Sands, a wealthy New York socialite, in 1884.

Established in July 1865, the *Nation* was founded as a joint-stock company by a group of New England abolitionists who sought to make the weekly an organ for freedmen's rights. Under Godkin's leadership, the *Nation* addressed a wide variety of public issues, prompting dissension among the shareholders. The *Nation* was losing about $4,000 a month at the end of its first year when the stock company was dissolved and Godkin took over financial control. The *Nation* was written for the "cultivated class" that shared Godkin's distaste for immigrants, evangelists, reformers, and anyone who advocated universal suffrage and government intervention in the marketplace. Godkin gave the *Nation* a tone of sober moral respectability laced with wit, reason, and genteel culture, a formula that earned the admiration of the American intelligentsia.

In 1881 Godkin sold the *Nation* to Henry Villard (q.v.) for $40,000, and the *Nation* became the weekly edition of the *New York Evening Post*. Villard and Horace White (q.v.) bought the *Evening Post* in May 1881, naming Godkin and Carl Schurz (q.v.) associate editors. Like the *Nation*, the *Evening Post* was addressed to an influential genteel audience that distrusted the masses who read the city's more flamboyant penny papers. In 1883 Godkin succeeded in pressuring Schurz to resign from the *Evening Post*, leaving him in editorial control. Under Godkin, the *Evening Post* supported civil service reform and joined the Mugwump movement in support of Grover Cleveland in 1884. Two years later Godkin unsuccessfully attempted to buy the *Evening Post*.

In the 1880s and 1890s Godkin became increasingly more conservative and disenchanted with the United States. He fulminated about "the mental trouble known as 'Americanism,' " concluding that "the patriotism which has been diffused among the masses during the past thirty years, and even taught to the children in the schools, is a species of madness" (Armstrong, 1957, 1978; Nevins, 1922). In the 1890s Godkin took long vacations in England and Europe. Upon his return from Europe in 1899, Godkin agreed to relinquish his editorial duties on the *Evening Post*, effective 1 January 1900.

Already in ill health, Godkin suffered a stroke in February 1900, and a year later he returned to England, where many of his old friends, including William and Henry James, visited him. Godkin died at Greenway House, Brixham, on 21 May 1902 and was buried in the Hazelbeach Churchyard, Northhampton, England.

BIBLIOGRAPHY:

B. DAB 7, 347–350; NYT 23 May 1902; *New York Evening Post*, 21 May 1902; *Nation*, 22 May 1902; William M. Armstrong, *E. L. Godkin and American Foreign Policy, 1865–1900* (New York, 1957); William M. Armstrong, *E. L. Godkin: A Biography* (Albany, N.Y., 1978); Allan Nevins, *The "Evening Post": A Century of Journalism* (New York, 1922).

ARTHUR J. KAUL

GRADY, HENRY WOODFIN (b. 24 May 1850; d. 23 December 1889) was the managing editor of the *Atlanta Constitution* during the 1880s, and in nine brief years he achieved national renown as a journalist and an orator. He was less well known as a political manipulator, although his talents in that field were the equal of his gifts in the other two. He is principally remembered as the "Spokesman of the New South," which meant that he advocated a diversification of the southern agricultural economic base while adding manufacturing to it.

Grady was born in Athens, Georgia, on 24 May 1850 to William Sammons Grady and Ann Gartrell Grady. His father was a prosperous Athens businessman and an adept manager, but the outbreak of the Civil War took him away from his business and his family. During the war, he died of wounds received in battle. Although the Grady family was not plunged into poverty, its fortunes became guarded. The mother became the head of the family, which consisted of three children including Henry, who was about fifteen years old when the war ended.

Grady entered the University of Georgia when it reopened in 1866 and was graduated in 1868. He studied at the University of Virginia in 1868 and 1869 but did not take a degree. He briefly considered law as a profession, but he had written several letters for the *Atlanta Constitution,* signed "Hans King," and these brought him widespread encouragement for a career in journalism.

In 1869 Grady began work on the *Rome* (Georgia) *Courier,* but he soon left it and acquired part interest in the *Rome Southerner and Commercial,* which he combined the next year with the *Rome Daily and Weekly*. His work had been a critical success but a more limited financial one, so he left Rome. In 1872 he acquired a one-third interest in the *Atlanta Daily Herald,* which collapsed in 1876. Other attempts to start newspapers also failed, and Grady was on the point of leaving Atlanta when he was offered a reporting position on the *Atlanta Constitution*. By then, Grady was a married man and he needed a steady income. He had married Julia King of Athens on 5 October 1871 and they had two children, Henry Woodfin Grady, Jr., and Augusta Evans Grady.

For the *Atlanta Constitution* Grady did some distinguished reportorial work, such as the coverage of the Hayes-Tilden election dispute in 1876, but it was generally uneven. At times he would work with energy and imagination, then do little for long periods. His chance to change the status of his employment came in 1880 when the promoter of the Atlantic cable, Cyrus W. Field, lent Grady the money to buy a one-fourth interest in the *Atlanta Constitution*. A railroad friend helped Grady with some successful investments and the Field loan was repaid. Evan P. Howell was editor in chief of the *Atlanta Constitution* in 1880, and with the acquisition of one-fourth ownership, Grady became managing editor. Atlanta had, in 1868, become the capital of Georgia, wresting the seat of government away from Milledgeville in central Georgia, a switch resented by the central and southern portions of the state.

For his first six years as managing editor, Grady devoted the greater part of his energies and abilities to promoting and protecting the city of Atlanta, whose dominance in Georgia was indicated by the 1880s but was not established. Augusta and especially Macon were challenging Atlanta for preeminence. At times, Grady permitted his correspondents to attack Augusta in the *Constitution* in a way which could damage that city's credit. Always, Grady was careful to see that the principal offices in state government were occupied by Atlantans or by persons sympathetic to Atlanta. In that way, attempts to thwart the development of the city could be contained, and moves to help it could be encouraged. Grady himself organized international expositions to attract attention to Atlanta. He also encouraged the development of Atlanta's system of railroads.

But his most concentrated effort between 1880 and 1886 lay in the political arena. Grady, in effect, became head of the Atlanta Ring, a loose-knit political organization aimed at keeping in power politicians sympathetic to Atlanta. He assumed that role in 1880 when he successfully managed the reelection campaign of Alfred H. Colquitt for governor just after maneuvering former Governor Joseph E. Brown into the U.S. Senate. Both were Atlantans. By 1886 he had managed six statewide campaigns and had achieved a grand sweep—two Atlantans in the U.S. Senate and one in the governor's chair.

The year 1886 was the pinnacle of Grady's political power, for the man he had had elected to the governorship, General John B. Gordon, was seriously irked when it was suggested, as it often was, that Grady had put him into office. He turned away from Grady and declined to help Grady in 1888 when the newspaperman apparently had a secret but powerful urge to be elected to the U.S. Senate himself.

In one of the ironies that could occur only in real life, Grady received the most important telegram of his life three days before his candidate Gordon was inaugurated as governor in 1886. The telegram asked Grady to speak to the New England Society in New York that December, responding to the toast, "The New South." Grady had long espoused the principles of the New South movement. Industrialization, an indispensable part of the New South concept, meant attracting northern money to help finance the factories. It meant that northern financiers must be assured that the Civil War was over, that the South accepted its result, that the South could handle its racial problems, and that northern money, once invested, would be safe. There were many New South leaders in Georgia and elsewhere, including Grady's principal newspaper rivals, Patrick Walsh in Augusta and John F. Hanson in Macon. Before 1886 Grady had been a prominent New South leader, but one among many.

What happened at Delmonico's Cafe in New York City on 22 December 1886 belongs to history. In the presence of an audience that could have been unfriendly just as easily as it could have accepted his message, Grady made a speech that is found in most anthologies of great American addresses. With humor, pathos, and passion, he summed up the New South themes better than anyone had ever done before. The national acclaim that followed was such that it was seriously suggested that Grady should run for vice president of the United States. In one evening, Grady was transformed from a spokesman of the New South into the "Spokesman of the New South."

He spoke in support of New South ideas during the next three years, most notably in Boston on 12 December 1889, where he achieved another oratorical triumph. No one knew when they heard that address that Grady would die eleven days later with the applause of the nation figuratively ringing in his ears. He had had a heavy cold when he went to Boston, and it turned into pneumonia. When he reached Atlanta for the last time, he could not walk without help. He died on 23 December 1889 at the age of thirty-nine. His eloquence, his youth, the power of his message, and the suddenness of his departure made him a national legend in short order, and ever thereafter he was acclaimed as the Spokesman of the New South. His role as a political manipulator was less specifically remembered; yet his monumental efforts in that vein were devoted to the advancement of his city, not to the advancement of the South as a whole.

BIBLIOGRAPHY:

B. DAB 7, 465–466; NYT 24 December 1889; *Atlanta Constitution*, 23 and 24 December 1889; Raymond B. Nixon, *Henry W. Grady, Spokesman of the New South* (New York, 1943).

HAROLD E. DAVIS

GRAHAM, PHILIP LESLIE (b. 18 July 1915; d. 3 August 1963) was a publisher of the *Washington Post* for seventeen years, but in some ways he considered himself politically frustrated in the nation's most political town.

Graham was born in Terry, South Dakota, one of four children. The family moved to the Florida Everglades while Philip Graham was still young. His father, Ernest Graham, was a miner with some difficulties breaking into another line of work. There were some rough times, and the Grahams even lived on a houseboat for a period. Despite the poverty, Florence Graham, a former schoolteacher, made certain her children were not intellectually deprived. Money for groceries was tight, but there was apparently no shortage of money for magazine subscriptions. Mrs. Graham wanted *Time* and the *New Yorker* available for her children.

Eventually Ernest Graham hit upon the right business at the right time. He bought a dairy as south Florida began to experience its population boom. The political bug bit Ernest Graham, and he was elected to the state senate. An attempt for the governor's office was unsuccessful. Philip Graham enrolled at the University of Florida, and he coasted through the university with a 4.0 average. Wanting a career in law or politics, he went off to Harvard Law School, where he again starred.

Graham was taken under the wing of Professor Felix Frankfurter, for whom he was a prized student and a surrogate son. During his years at Harvard, Graham excelled and was made editor of the *Harvard Law Review*. He was determined to jump head first into Florida politics upon graduation. But Frankfurter was nominated to the Supreme Court by President Franklin Roosevelt, and Frankfurter arranged for Graham to serve an unprecedented two stints as Supreme Court clerk—first for Justice Stanley Reed, then for Frankfurter.

Graham was intoxicated by Washington's New Deal atmosphere. At a party he was introduced to Katharine Meyer, daughter of *Washington Post* publisher Eugene Meyer (q.v.). Graham's first words to Katharine were an invitation to be married, followed by a promise that he would take her to Florida where they would live in poverty, and that he would work his way up the political ladder.

Not all of that was to be. They were married on 5 June 1940, but Graham so charmed Eugene Meyer that the old man talked his son-in-law out of a political career, and into a career as publisher of the *Washington Post*. Graham realized it would be difficult to give up the glamour of Washington, but he later came to regret not following his first instinct.

After serving in World War II, Graham set about trying to make the *Post* a better newspaper. He crusaded for self-government in Washington and was an early and strong advocate of civil rights. After a six-year battle, Graham was able to buy out the *Washington Times-Herald*, second only to the *Washington Star* in circulation and prestige in the nation's capital. Eventually the *Post* moved ahead of the *Star* in both categories.

Graham's business deals were legendary. He bought *Newsweek* in a swift, startling deal crafted in 1961, largely through stock trading. Only $75,000 in cash actually changed hands. He also established the Los Angeles Times–Washington Post News Service, and brought distinguished columnist Walter Lippmann (q.v.) to the pages of *Newsweek* to boost that magazine's prestige and to give it some ammunition with which to fight its competitor, *Time*.

Graham was also a political power figure. David Halberstam offers an account of how Graham put together the 1960 Democratic ticket of John F. Kennedy and Lyndon Johnson. But Graham did not want to be on the sideline while Kennedy, Johnson, and others of his generation exercised their real power. Graham felt that he had been forced into a publishing career and regretted that he had not entered politics. He suffered a mental illness, dating back to his early days as a publisher. Yet in the midst of his problems, he could still function as a brilliant journalist and businessman. He was institutionalized for a time, but was at his country home for a weekend when he took his life on 3 August 1963.

BIBLIOGRAPHY:

B. Howard Bray, *The Pillars of the "Post"* (New York, 1980); David Halberstam, *The Powers That Be* (New York, 1979); Chalmers Roberts, *The Washington Post: The First 100 Years* (Boston, 1977).

WILLIAM MCKEEN

GRAHAM, SHEILAH (b. 1908?) was one-third of a powerful triumverate of Hollywood gossip columnists. Although Louella Parsons (q.v.) and Hedda Hopper have had greater historical staying power, Graham outdistanced her journalistic rivals in several ways. Not only was Graham syndicated in more newspapers than Parsons and Hopper combined, but as a novelist, biographer, journalist, lecturer, and broadcast commentator, she had more creative versatility. Graham had one other thing her rivals lacked—F. Scott Fitzgerald. The writer was Graham's mentor, as well as her lover, during the last four years of his life.

Graham's journey from a London slum to Hollywood was as romantic as anything ever seen on film. (In fact, it was seen on film in *Beloved Infidel*, the celluloid version of Graham's autobiography.) Born Lily Shiel in 1908, Graham was raised in an orphanage, as her destitute mother (her father died shortly after Graham's birth) was unable to care for her. Graham was a bright child, and her teachers hoped to get her a scholarship to trade school. But Graham's mother was dying and needed her daughter's nursing. At fourteen, Graham left the orphanage and ended her formal education.

On her own after her mother's death, Graham demonstrated toothbrushes in a London department store. One of her customers was Major John Graham Gilliam, DSO. He gave her an office job and then an offer of marriage. The major, twenty-five years Graham's senior, enrolled her in the Royal Academy of Dramatic Arts. She was not talented enough to be an actress, but was pretty enough to be a show girl. Thus, she joined the cast of *One Damn Thing After Another* as Sheilah Graham. With her husband's encouragement, Graham also started writing short features for the smaller London newspapers and a lightweight novel, *Gentlemen-Crook*. When illness ended Graham's stage career, she decided to become a full-time writer. Class barriers, Graham believed, would prevent her from succeeding in England. She determined to try her luck in the United States.

Graham spent two years in New York writing for the *Mirror* and the *Evening Journal*. Then she moved to Hollywood when the North American Newspaper Alliance (NANA) offered her a syndicated column. Graham felt that the only way she could compete with Parsons and Hopper was to write a candid, outspoken column. The result was catastrophic. She was called the "biggest bitch in Hollywood." Some of her nastiness, she later admitted, was caused by the insecurities that developed during her orphanage years. While that feeling never disappeared, it did dissipate, and the column accordingly toned down as Graham became a recognized member of the film community.

On the personal side, Graham and her long-suffering husband were divorced in 1937. Almost immediately she became engaged to the Marquess of Donnegal. It was at a Hollywood party celebrating that engagement that she met F. Scott Fitzgerald. At this time, Fitzgerald's literature and life were both on their final downside. Not only had his work gone out of fashion, but he was sliding in and out of bouts of alcoholism. Fitzgerald also was hacking away at filmwriting to support a daughter at Vassar and a wife in an insane asylum. According to both Graham and Fitzgerald, it was love at first sight. Their relationship was stormy, but it lasted nearly four years. The two seemed to be good for each other. She stopped his slide and encouraged him to write *The Last Tycoon*. (The novel's heroine is said to have been inspired by her.) He educated her, improving her writing and mind by creating a classical course of study for her, which she outlined in her book *College of One* (1967).

When Fitzgerald died in 1940, Graham sought a change of scenery. At her request, she went to England as NANA's war correspondent. There she met Trevor Westbrook, whom she married in 1941. The couple had two children, Wendy and Robert.

Divorced in 1946, Graham returned to Hollywood and her career. In the ensuing years, she reached the top of her profession. Graham's gossip was delivered through all the media—in her syndicated newspaper column, in an additional column for *Daily Variety,* in pieces for *Photoplay* magazine, and in radio and television programs.

Meanwhile, a resurgence of interest in Fitzgerald produced several biographies of the writer. Graham found these to be inaccurate and unflattering. Thus she published her own reminiscences of Fitzgerald, *Beloved Infidel,* coauthored with Gerold Frank in 1959. Encouraged, Graham produced her own post-Fitzgerald autobiography, but *The Rest of the Story* (1964) was not very successful.

In 1969 Graham decided to change the format of her column. Henceforth she would cover the world, rather than just Hollywood; celebrities rather than just stars. But her books maintained the same focus. Sheilah Graham, her life, opinions and memories were the subject of *The Garden of Allah* (1970), *A State of Heat* (1972), *How to Marry Super-Rich* (1974), and *The Real F. Scott Fitzgerald, Thirty-five Years Later* (1976). Following the publication of her last book, Graham gave up her literary pursuits. She now lives on the East Coast with her grandchildren and her memories.

BIBLIOGRAPHY:

B. CB 1969, 175–177; *Who's Who of American Women,* 1972 and 1974; *Time,* 10 March 1952 and 29 May 1964.

LYNNE MASEL-WALTERS

GRANDIN, THOMAS BURNHAM (b. 19 July 1907; d. 19 October 1977) was among the first radio foreign correspondents to cover Europe on the eve of World War II. Joining Edward R. Murrow and William L. Shirer (qq.v.), Grandin began regular reporting for CBS during the Munich Crisis of 1938, and continued to report to America until the fall of France in 1940. He was the first radio correspondent to study the uses of radio by world governments. Grandin's radio reporting also included D day coverage for the NBC-Blue network.

Grandin was born in Cleveland, Ohio. His father, George Wilbert Grandin, was a banker. His mother, Mable Gordon Burnham Grandin, was a housewife. Grandin attended Hawken School in Cleveland, and Kent School in Kent, Connecticut, from which he graduated in 1926. He went to Yale, was editor of the *Yale Daily News*, and graduated in 1930. Grandin had concentrated on English and philosophy at Yale, but in 1931 he began studying international law, political science, and economic geography at the École des Sciences Politiques in Paris. In 1932 Grandin took social science courses at the University of Berlin.

In 1933–34 Grandin worked for the International Chamber of Commerce in Paris, researching an article on international transportation, and doing free-lance writing. He returned to America in 1934, working at the Council on Foreign Relations in New York. He married Ruth Thompson on 15 September 1934, but they had no children and were divorced in 1937.

Grandin returned to Europe in 1938, supported in part by Geneva Research Center Fellowship, to work on a plan for a radio monitoring facility in America. Grandin also traveled to a half-dozen European countries researching the way governments used radio. *The Political Use of Radio* was published in 1939. By then, Grandin was working for CBS. He had first broadcast for the network on 27 September 1938, identified as "United Press correspondent in Paris, France." Grandin told of the evacuation of Paris, fears of a German bombing attack, and storage of great artworks.

Murrow, who was in charge of the CBS European operation, had been looking for someone to cover southern Europe. One of Grandin's first assignments was the election of a new pope in March 1939. He joined Murrow and Shirer in the summer of that year to make plans for network coverage of the coming war. They decided more staff should be hired, and so Eric Sevareid (q.v.) was secured to share the Paris reporting with Grandin. In February 1940 Grandin went to the Balkans to cover a diplomatic conference. He met Natalia Parligras and they were married in Belgrade on 8 February 1940.

Returning to Paris with his wife, Grandin reported on French preparations for the expected German onslaught in the spring of 1940. When the blitzkreig began, he made arrangements for his wife to evacuate. Grandin went to Bordeaux to see her off, but was apparently persuaded by his pregnant wife to leave as well, with Sevareid abandoned to report the fall of Paris and the retreat of the French government.

In 1941 Grandin became acting chief editor of the Foreign Broadcast Intelligence Service for the Federal Communications Commission. In 1943 he went on a special mission for Elmer Davis's (q.v.) Office of War Information, visiting six foreign cities. His task was to improve foreign monitoring facilities and to increase the flow of information to the United States. Early in 1944

Grandin resigned his government position and joined the NBC-Blue network, which was soon to become ABC. Assignments included coverage of Normandy on D day, with Grandin reportedly giving the first eyewitness account of the landings at Omaha Beach.

A month later, still in Normandy, Grandin was injured in a jeep accident. He suffered head injuries which ended his career as a foreign correspondent. For a brief time in 1945, he was a special assistant to the news director at ABC. Grandin then became an account executive at D'Arcy Advertising Company in 1946, held several other business positions in the next few years, and then moved to Arizona, where he was involved in ranching. Natalia Parligras Grandin died in 1968, survived by her husband and three children, Thomas Jr., George, and Natalia. Grandin married Beulah Thompson Paul on 21 March 1970. Grandin died while visiting his sister in Philadelphia.

Grandin had labored beside men who would become some of America's best-known broadcast journalists at the beginning of the Golden Age of radio. His career in radio lasted less than a decade, yet he was there at the beginning, when the standards for broadcast foreign correspondence were established for decades to come.

BIBLIOGRAPHY:

B. *Arizona Republic,* 22 October 1977; David H. Hosley, *As Good As Any* (Westport, Conn., 1984).

DAVID H. HOSLEY

GRANT, HARRY JOHNSTON (b. 15 September 1881; d. 12 July 1963) engineered the transfer of ownership of the *Journal* in Milwaukee, Wisconsin, to its employees. Following Lucius W. Nieman (q.v.) as publisher of the *Journal,* Grant led it to its reputation for excellence among midwestern newspapers. It became famous for editorial independence and enormous advertising linage. It also was among the leaders in technological innovations, especially in color printing.

Grant was born in Chillicothe, Missouri, to Benjamin T. Grant and Ida Belle Grant. Grant was only fifteen when he went to work after his father's suicide. He never finished high school. He spent two years (between 1903 and 1906) at Harvard as a special student but never earned a degree. He did, however, come into contact with journalism at Harvard—as an advertising salesman for student publications. Later he worked for N. W. Ayer and Son and as the European representative of the Rubberset Brush Company.

During his association with Rubberset, Grant and his wife (they had married in 1910) were living in England. Wishing their first child to be born in the United States, Grant booked passage on the *Titanic* for the westward voyage, but circumstance delayed their departure and they sailed on a later ship, a happy coincidence.

Grant later joined the American Viscose Corporation, a rayon manufacturing firm. Both Grant and the firm prospered. Financially independent by 1914, Grant retired at thirty-three, but found idleness unrewarding. He joined O'Mara and Ormshee, a newspaper national advertising representative, and became vice president in charge of the firm's Chicago office. There he became acquainted with Nieman, publisher of the *Journal*. Nieman hired Grant as advertising manager in 1916. He later acquired 20 percent of the *Journal's* stock for $100,000 and became a director and treasurer of the Journal Company. In 1919 he assumed the title of publisher as well. When Nieman died in 1935, Grant became editor.

His idea about employee ownership came to fruition after Nieman's death Nieman's will directed that his stock be sold within five years to someone who would continue to conduct the *Journal* according to his principles of independence and social service. Mrs. Nieman's death in February 1936 complicated the transfer of ownership. She left the bulk of her estate to Harvard, and that bequest funded the Nieman Fellowships.

Grant's plan involved the formation of a trust to hold shares of stock in the Journal Company. Eligible employees of the *Journal* would buy shares in the trust that carried voting rights, and dividends would accrue to employees. They or their heirs would be required to sell back the shares after retirement or death.

The Journal Company with Grant in charge offered $3,500 per share to Harvard, holder of the shares. The total was about $825,000 less than Moses Annenberg, owner of the *Philadelphia Inquirer,* had offered for the Nieman shares. Harvard accepted. The stock was split, 100 to 1, to lower the price to $35, within the reach of employees. The first shares in the trust were offered to employees in 1937. In 1947 some 55 percent of shares were in the hands of employees. By 1964, just after Grant's death, 80 percent of shares of stock in the trust were owned by *Journal* employees.

In 1927 the Journal Company purchased a radio station that became WTMJ. It founded WTMJ-TV in 1947. In 1962 the company absorbed the Hearst-owned *Milwaukee Sentinel,* a morning newspaper. Grant stepped down as publisher in 1937, but remained as chairman of the board until his death. He was a director of the Associated Press in 1940 and 1941 and a member of the American Society of Newspaper Editors. His marriage in 1910 to Dorothy Glyde Cook ended in divorce in 1915, and Grant never remarried. She died in 1923. Their child, Barbara, married Donald Albert, who was executive vice president and general manager of the Journal Company at the time of Grant's death.

BIBLIOGRAPHY:

B. NYT 13 July 1963; *Milwaukee Journal,* 13 July 1963; Will C. Conrad, Kathleen Wilson, and Dale Wilson, *The Milwaukee "Journal": The First Eighty Years* (Madison, Wis., 1964); Robert W. Wells, *The Milwaukee "Journal": An Informal Chronicle of Its First 100 Years* (Milwaukee, 1981).

ROY HALVERSON

GRASTY, CHARLES HENRY (b. 3 March 1863; d. 19 January 1924) worked forty-four of his sixty years on newspapers as reporter, managing editor, publisher, general manager, and foreign correspondent. His greatest influence was in Baltimore, Maryland, where he was publisher and partner of the *Evening News* from 1892 to 1908, and general manager of the Sunpapers from 1910 to 1914. He also worked for the *Kansas City Star*, the *St. Paul* (Minnesota) *Dispatch* and *Pioneer Press,* and the *New York Times*. Grasty's chief interest always was in the news and editorial rather than the commercial aspects of journalism.

Grasty was born in Fincastle, Virginia, to a Presbyterian minister, the Reverend John Sharshall Grasty, and the former Ella Giles Pettus. The family moved to Mexico, Missouri. Unusually bright, Grasty entered the University of Missouri in 1876 to study law, but dropped that ambition, and formal education, after he was hired as a reporter on the *Mexico Intelligencer* in the summer of 1880. In 1882 Grasty joined William Rockhill Nelson's (q.v.) *Kansas City Star* as a reporter at $7 a week. At twenty-one he became the *Star*'s managing editor, probably the youngest managing editor in the country. During the seven years he held that post, Grasty made Nelson's fearlessness and independence the model for his own career.

On 29 May 1889 Grasty married Leota Tootle Perrin of St. Joseph, Missouri. In 1890 they moved to Baltimore, where Grasty was general manager of a weekly business journal. However, he preferred daily journalism, and in 1891, with the help of backers, bought the faltering *Baltimore Evening News*. He restyled it from a mouthpiece for the Gorman-Rasin Democratic machine that had dominated Maryland politics into a fighting, independent newspaper. His leadership at the *News* forced the more staid morning *Sun,* owed by the Abells, to join Grasty's crusade against corruption that brought the downfall of Gorman-Raisin. His sixteen years at the *Evening News* were the most fulfilling of his career.

The *Evening News* did not prevail in every crusade, however, and after it failed to get its candidate elected governor in 1907, Grasty sold the paper to chain publisher Frank A. Munsey (q.v.). In 1908 he moved to St. Paul, and bought control of the evening *Dispatch* and the morning and evening *Pioneer Press*. He combined the evening newspapers, giving him both morning and evening circulation leadership. Unable to turn these papers away from stockholder and advertiser influence, he sold them back to the previous owners and returned to Baltimore, where he hoped to gain control of the family-owned *Sun* because of differences among the owners, descendants of founder Arunah S. Abell.

Fearful that he might buy back the *News* if they turned him down, the Abells granted Grasty full control of the *Sun*. He then attempted to gain dominance in both morning and evening by creating the *Evening Sun* from remnants of the declining *Baltimore World* and forcing subscribers to take the morning, evening, and Sunday *Suns*. However, the *Evening Sun* never made money and became a dangerous drain on the profits of the morning paper. Because he so feared interference with the paper's editorial independence, Grasty refused to consult knowledgeable people in the company about circulation and advertising. When the losses reached nearly $1 million, the other directors asked Grasty to relinquish his control of the papers' business affairs, which he did on 12 September 1914, then resigned on 30 November.

In 1915 he went to Europe as a war correspondent for the *Kansas City Star* and the Associated Press. In 1916 he served for a short time as treasurer of the *New York Times,* a position he did not like and relinquished to return to Europe as a roving correspondent for that newspaper. He was respected as a crack reporter by such leaders as American General John J. Pershing and British Prime Minister David Lloyd George, who would speak to him while holding other reporters at bay. Following his death in London of hardening of the arteries, the *Sun* said "he was probably the best-informed journalist in Europe."

BIBLIOGRAPHY:

A. *Flashes from the Front* (New York, 1918).

B. DAB 7, 503; NYT 20 January 1924; *Baltimore Sun,* 20 January 1924; Gerald W. Johnson, Frank R. Kent, H. L. Mencken, and Hamilton Owens, *The Sunpapers of Baltimore* (New York, 1937).

DANIEL W. PFAFF

GRAVES, ELEANOR MACKENZIE (b. 21 September 1926) had a long and distinguished career at *Life* magazine, where she started right after her graduation from college. She is perhaps best known for the "Great Dinners" series which she authored during the 1960s while modern living editor of *Life*. It was described by Time editor in chief Henry Grunwald as "among the most successful features in *Life*." She was later one of those responsible for reviving *Life* as a monthly magazine, retiring in 1982 as its executive editor.

The daughter of Luther MacKenzie, a physician, and Rena Glogau MacKenzie, Graves was born and raised in New York City. She attended Barnard College, where she was a member of Phi Beta Kappa, and received her B.A. degree cum laude in 1948. Her marriage in 1949 to William White Parish produced two children, William White Parish II and Alexander MacKenzie Parish.

Beginning at *Life* as a trainee, she worked her way to the top, serving along the way as assistant fashion editor, assistant science editor, modern living editor, and senior editor. She found the transition from fashion to science challenging, coming as it did when the nation was preoccupied with developments in the scientific world. It was, however, a transition characteristic for *Life* reporters, who were expected to be generalists. Graves's first marriage ended in divorce in 1956, and in 1957 she married fellow *Life* staff member Ralph Graves (q.v.). They had two children, Andrew and Sara. Sara is on the staff of Time Inc., publication *People* magazine.

Photographed primarily by John Dominis, the popular "Great Dinners" series written by Graves was made into a book, published in 1968. Another *Life* series authored by Graves was "New Ideas in Houses," which focused on design and introduced to a mass audience such architects as Richard Meyer and Charles Gwathmy. In 1968 Graves left *Life* to work on development of a series of new magazines for Time. The venture was intended to revive the declining fortunes of *Life* by creating several satellite magazines, one of which was to have food as its topic. When the satellite magazine venture was scrapped, Graves transferred to the video division of Time, during the time that her husband was serving as managing editor of *Life*. She became involved with the moving image, helping to produce two weekly television shows. In 1974 she was appointed vice president of programming for Time-Life films. When the decision to reintroduce *Life* was made in 1977, Graves was asked to help institute it as a monthly magazine. She was made executive editor in 1980. In 1981 she received an award from the YWCA as woman of the year.

At the time of her retirement in 1982, Time editor in chief Grunwald called Graves instrumental in putting the monthly version of *Life* on the road to success. After her retirement in 1982, Graves pursued her interest in nineteenth-century American art by running the Tiasquam Gallery, dividing her time between New York City and Martha's Vineyard.

BIBLIOGRAPHY:

B. W. A. Swanberg, *Luce and His Empire* (New York, 1972).

BROOKS ROBARDS

GRAVES, RALPH A. (b. 17 October 1924) spent thirty-five years as a Time writer and editor, primarily at *Life* magazine, where as managing editor he had the unhappy task in 1972 of closing down the prototypical photomagazine. When he took over as managing editor of *Life* in 1969, Graves vowed to revive its emphasis on photographs and make it a ''hot'' magazine for advertisers. While advertising revenues may have continued their decline in the face of competition from television, during his stewardship the magazine was in the news frequently for its hard-hitting, first-on-the-scene reporting and pictures. He followed his career at *Life* with corporate duties for Time, retiring in 1984 as editorial director.

Born in Washington, D.C., to Ralph and Elizabeth Evans Graves, Graves spent part of his childhood in the Philippines where his stepfather, Francis B. Sayre, was serving as U.S. high commissioner. He wrote about the experience twenty-five years later in the pages of *Life* on the occasion of an anti-American demonstration in front of the residence where he had grown up. After attending the Brent School in the Philippines, he spent three years in the Army Air Corps and then entered Harvard, graduating Phi Beta Kappa in 1948.

Graves wrote his first novel, *Thanks for the Ride* (1949), in college and planned to work in publishing, but ended up instead as a research trainee at *Life*. After a year he moved to Time-Life's San Francisco bureau. He married Patricia Monser in 1950 and had two children, William and Katherine. Graves's second novel, *The Lost Eagles,* was published in 1955. After spending three years in New York as a *Life* writer, he became Chicago bureau chief in 1953 and then returned to New York in 1955 to work in the articles department.

He found the work of reporting deeply satisfying and especially relished a month-long assignment with photographer Margaret Bourke-White (q.v.) in 1949 which resulted in a photo-essay on social class in Illinois and a 1952 assignment on Everglades wildlife with photographer Alfred Eisenstaedt (q.v.). In 1958 he began his second marriage to *Life* staffer Eleanor MacKenzie; they had two children, Sara and Andrew. Graves was named senior editor of the articles department in 1959 and served as assistant managing editor from 1961 until his appointment as senior staff editor for Time in 1967.

When the corporation decided to replace George Hunt as managing editor of *Life* in 1969, Graves was named to the position. He was known as a perceptive editor and a good administrator. During his editorship, *Life* was caught up in the scandal over Clifford Irving's bogus biography of Howard Hughes, parts of which he had contracted for *Life* to publish. He commanded more favorable, if still controversial, publicity by publishing Khrushchev's memoirs in 1970, as well as running an investigative piece that eventually led to Supreme Court Justice Abe Fortas' resignation. He said his favorite story was an eleven-page photo-essay on GI's killed in Vietnam. *Life's* photo coverage of Vietnam during his editorial reign represented a significant contribution to the history of that period.

In the final issue of the weekly magazine, Graves wrote, "We didn't want to reach you as skiers, or teenagers, or car-owners, or tv-watchers, or single women, or as surburbanites, or inhabitants of New York City, or blacks, or whites. Instead, we wanted to talk to you as people, who share the common experience of humanity. I still believe that such talk is important to our country." Once *Life* suspended publication, Graves became editor for film and cable, then in 1975 associate publisher for *Time,* corporate editor, and, finally Time editorial director and deputy to editor in chief Henry Grunwald in 1979. He stayed in that position until his retirement in 1984.

Graves's sense of civic responsibility is illustrated by his role in founding and serving as chairman of the Citizens Crime Commission, a New York City watchdog group, along with his organization in 1984 of a journalistically star-studded Power and Politics Symposium for charitable purposes on the island of Martha's Vineyard, where he made his home after retirement. Having retired at age fifty-eight, Graves began work on his sixth novel after a thirty-year hiatus.

BIBLIOGRAPHY:

B. David Halberstam, *The Powers That Be* (New York, 1979).

BROOKS ROBARDS

GREELEY, HORACE (b. 3 February 1811; d. 29 November 1872) was a man of little formal education who became during his lifetime the most popular and influential newspaper editor in the United States. This was largely because of the nationally circulated *Weekly Tribune,* which he founded five months after establishing the daily *New York Tribune* on 10 April 1841. Other reasons for his renown where his persistent efforts to achieve elective office and his popularity as a lecturer.

The oldest of five children, Greeley was born in Amherst, New Hampshire, to Zaccheus Greeley, a poor farmer and day laborer, and Mary Woodburn Greeley. Though he was often kept from school to work, his mother encouraged him to read, promoting his lifelong interest in ideas. Critics have attributed Greeley's editorial inconsistency to the fact that he was largely self-educated.

It was natural for so avid a reader to decide to become a printer. Greeley started a four-year apprenticeship in 1826 at fifteen on a Vermont newspaper. When the paper failed in 1830, he went to New York City, where he got his first job in 1831. On 1 January 1833, using savings and borrowed funds, Greeley and partner Francis V. Storey issued the *Morning Post,* a penny newspaper. The paper failed, but they continued to do job printing. Following Storey's death in 1833, Greeley and another partner on 22 March 1834 brought out the *New Yorker,* a weekly literary and political newspaper. It had 9,000 subscribers before the economic collapse of 1837.

Greeley married Mary Youngs Cheney, a schoolteacher from Cornwall, Connecticut, on 5 July 1836. They had five children, only two of whom lived to adulthood. In addition to editing the *New Yorker,* Greeley also contributed through the 1830s to the *Daily Whig* newspaper and got to know New York Whig leaders Thurlow Weed (q.v.) and William H. Seward. He became editor of two highly successful Whig campaign newspapers in 1838 and 1840. Then followed the *Tribune,* the first penny paper with Whig loyalties, and the *Weekly Tribune*.

To self-made Greeley, the Whig doctrine of thrift and industry had a natural appeal. Yet, while advocating self-reliance generally, he was drawn to new ideas, many of which he promoted vigorously in the *Tribune* until some newer idea appealed to him. Some of these, such as socialism and collective bargaining, were antithetical to Whiggery. In 1850 he became the first president of the New York Printers' Union. However, Greeley biographer Glyndon G. Van Deusen concluded that the editor "was not half the reformer that he was supposed to be. There was a Greeley who yearned to build the New Jerusalem and whose sword leaped lightly to his hand, but there was also another Greeley who was calculating, conservative and full of shifts and evasions, not to mention a third Greeley who could seek refuge from reality in Utopia."

More positively, it is undisputed that the *Tribune*'s openness to ideas advanced the democratic conception of the newspaper as a forum for competing viewpoints. Some of the best minds of the nineteenth century, including Karl Marx and Margaret Fuller (q.v.), were *Tribune* contributors. Charles A. Dana (q.v.), the acclaimed editor of the *New York Sun,* and Henry J. Raymond (q.v.), founder of the *New York Times,* had worked under Greeley.

The *Tribune* had many departments, including marine, financial, literary, and agricultural; a large staff of reporters in and outside New York; and numerous correspondents in Europe. Greeley himself wrote news and editorials for the paper and sometimes served as a correspondent. In 1859 he made an overland journey from New York to San Francisco, sending back dispatches and interviews. Much of his travel and other writing was collected in book form, including a two-volume Civil War history and an autobiography. He was a facile writer whose work needed little editing. A teetotaler and optimist, he spoke and wrote often on the theme of moral uplift as well as political economy, agriculture, and other technical subjects. He popularized the slogan "Go West, Young Man, Go West," originated by an Indiana editor.

As did other penny papers, the *Tribune* built circulation by publishing sex and crime stories, which Greeley justified as being cautionary tales. The paper's popularity was demonstrated when its price was raised to two, three, and four cents, with little loss of readership. Circulation leveled off at about 40,000 daily and 100,000 weekly. At times during the Civil War circulation was 65,000 daily and 250,000 weekly.

A believer in an ever-brighter future for the United States, Greeley was astonished by the Civil War, at first denying it could happen. He vacillated in his support of the Northern and Southern causes and on the slavery issue, at first arguing that the union must be saved, not that slavery should be abolished. When the war turned in the favor of the North, his opposition to slavery increased, and on 20 August 1862 his most famous editorial, "Prayer of Twenty Millions," was published. Many thought it forced President Lincoln to issue the Emancipation Proclamation the next month—earlier than planned. Though perplexed by Greeley's inconsistent support, Lincoln recognized the *Tribune*'s hold on public opinion.

Except for a seat in the 1867 New York constitutional convention, Greeley never won an election. He first tried in 1850 for a U.S. House of Representatives seat he had held briefly to fill an unexpired term. He then lost elections for New York lieutenant governor and comptroller, U.S. Senator and, in 1872, as the Liberal Republican and Democratic candidate for president.

With 43.8 percent of the vote, Greeley's final defeat came just days after his wife's death on 30 October. He died within a month, on 29 November, of brain fever. He had given control of the *Tribune* to Whitelaw Reid (q.v.) when the campaign began, so at the end had lost all he cared for. His funeral procession down Fifth Avenue was watched by thousands. The president, vice president, and chief justice were among many notables present as the nation bade farewell to "Uncle Horace."

BIBLIOGRAPHY:

A. *Recollection of a Busy Life* (New York, 1868).

B. DAB 7, 528–534; NYT 30 November 1872; James Parton, *The Life of Horace Greeley* (Boston, 1896); Don C. Seitz, *Horace Greeley: Founder of the "New York Tribune"* (Indianapolis, 1926); Glyndon G. Van Deusen, *Horace Greeley: Nineteenth Century Crusader* (Philadelphia, 1953).

DANIEL W. PFAFF

GREELEY-SMITH, NIXOLA (b. 5 April 1880; d. 9 March 1919) was a feature writer for the *New York Evening World* for eighteen years and was known for her intelligent, perceptive interviews and her lucid, empathetic, and descriptive writing style. She was a suffragist, and this was reflected in her writing and in her concern for women's problems.

Nixola was born in Chappaqua, New York, the second child of Colonel Nicholas Smith and Ida Lillian Greeley Smith. Mrs. Smith was Horace Greeley's (q.v.) eldest daughter, and Nixola was born at the Greeley estate which her mother had inherited. Colonel Smith was a native of Shelbyville, Kentucky, and was raised in Leavenworth, Kansas. He attended Dartmouth College and was an 1859 graduate of the Harvard Law School. After serving with the Union army in the Civil War, he opened a law practice in New York City. Nixola's older brother, Horace Greeley Smith, became a well-known bacteriologist; her younger sister, Ida Lillian, became an actress on the New York stage.

Mrs. Smith died when Nixola was two, and part of Nixola's childhood was spent in Kentucky. At age six, she was enrolled in the school of the Convent of the Sacred Heart in New York City. Her father served as American consul at Three Rivers, Quebec, from the fall of 1889 to February 1893, then spent two more years as consul at Liège, Belgium. Nixola continued her education in both places; as a result, she was bilingual, reading French and speaking it fluently.

Upon the family's return from Belgium, Nixola began looking for work. She was soon hired by Joseph Pulitzer (q.v.), initially working on the staff of the *St. Louis Post-Dispatch*. In 1901 she returned to New York to join the staff of Pulitzer's *Evening World*. Except for a brief period just before World War I when she worked for the Newspaper Enterprise Association syndicate, Greeley-Smith continued on the *World* until her death. On 1 April 1910 she married Andrew W. Ford, city editor of the *New York Evening Telegram*. They had no children.

Greeley-Smith was an expert at the popular journalism which Pulitzer had introduced, and was particularly successful with human interest, description, the personal interview, and with material for women readers. She was equally good with straight news assignments and was a fast, accurate reporter. She wrote several survivor stories, including one on the *Empress of Ireland* steamship disaster in 1914, in which more than 1,000 people were killed. In addition, she wrote poetry and short stories for various magazines. During World War I she wrote many articles publicizing women's activities in the war effort. She supported the woman suffrage movement by personal participation and in her writing.

Greeley-Smith was often able to successfully interview people who had previously refused all interviews, such as Mrs. Astor. She charmed Sarah Bernhardt by asking all questions in flawless French. She was the only woman granted a statement by General Joseph Joffre when he visited the United States. She interviewed Mrs. William Howard Taft, the first Mrs. Woodrow Wilson, and most notables and visiting dignitaries of the time.

Her writing was lively and personal. An example of her style may be seen in her coverage of Evelyn Nesbit during the Thaw-White murder trial. Greeley-Smith wrote, for the issue of 25 January 1907: "To me, as I studied her face during the long hours of yesterday's session, she seemed neither [a victim nor a vampire] but simply a wistful child who had been caught in some peccadillo and was being publicly punished for it.'' Greeley-Smith and the three other women reporters who covered that highly emotional trial, Dorothy Dix, Winifred Black Bonfils (qq.v.), and Ada Patterson, were labeled ''sob sisters,'' a term that stuck.

According to her contemporaries, Greeley-Smith's personality was one factor in her success. She brought a sophisticated touch to the dullest assignment. Her questions were knowledgeable, surprising, amusing, and sometimes impertinent, taking people off guard. She was an intellectual, but was not afraid to take an academic subject and turn it into good newspaper copy.

Nixola Greeley-Smith's career came to a premature end when, at the age of thirty-eight, she died in a New York hospital following an operation for acute appendicitis. She was buried in the Greeley family plot in Greenwood Cemetery, Brooklyn. Her husband died 28 December 1937.

BIBLIOGRAPHY:

B. NAW 2, 78–79; NYT 10 and 11 March 1919; *New York Evening World,* 10 and 11 March 1919; *Who Was Who in America,* 144; Ishbel Ross, *Ladies of the Press* (New York, 1936.

NORA BAKER

GREEN, ANNE CATHERINE HOFF (b. ca. 1720; d. 23 March 1775) was official printer for the colony of Maryland and publisher of the *Maryland Gazette,* one of the first colonial newspapers, for eight years prior to the Revolution. Forced into her career by economic necessity after the death of her husband, Green displayed extraordinary competence. Her life illustrated the way in which colonial women frequently assisted their male relatives in printing and publishing and succeeded them in business following their deaths. It also testified to her innate ability and intelligence displayed in the pages of the *Gazette* during the turbulent prerevolutionary period.

Little is known of her early life. She is believed to have been born in Holland and to have come to Pennsylvania as a child. The first known fact is that she was married on 25 April 1738 in Philadelphia to Jonas Green, a journeyman printer from Boston who was a member of a prominent colonial printing family. The couple moved to Annapolis the following October. Jonas Green became printer to the colony of Maryland that same year, and beginning in 1745, publisher of the *Maryland Gazette*. (This publication was a revival of the original *Maryland Gazette,* started by William Parks (q.v.) in 1727. A newspaper of that same title still is published today in Annapolis, crediting its origin to Parks and Jonas Green.)

Anne Catherine Green had fourteen children, only six of whom lived to maturity. From advertisements in the *Maryland Gazette,* it appears she sold chocolate, coffee, and European merchandise at the family home, which also housed the print shop and town post office since Jonas Green was Annapolis postmaster. In spite of her domestic burdens, she must have joined in the printing operation during her husband's lifetime. Following his death in 1767, she announced in the *Gazette* her intention of carrying on the business with the help of her son William, who died two years later. Another son, Frederick, joined in after she had run the enterprise alone for two years.

As editor of the *Gazette,* she continued it without a break following her husband's death. She also issued the official proceedings of the colonial legislature on schedule, performing so well that the colonial assembly appointed her to succeed her husband as official printer. She received the same compensation as he had—48,000 pounds of tobacco annually when the assembly was in session.

In the newspaper, she kept her readers abreast of the political developments sweeping the colonies. Under Jonas Green, the paper had played a key role in fighting British authority by protesting the Stamp Act. Anne Catherine Green printed letters from the northern colonies protesting the Townshend Acts to tax the colonies, and published John Dickinson's ''Letters from a Pennsylvania Farmer,'' an early attack on British rule. She also ran accounts of the Boston Tea Party. Dependent on public support, however, the widow could not afford to antagonize readers by pressing causes too vehemently. She opened her columns to various points of view and refused to print a scurrilous attack on a political figure even though the author was an influential citizen.

Excelling in the printer's art, she issued almanacs, pamphlets, and *The Charter and Bye-Laws of the City of Annapolis,* a beautifully printed volume of 52 pages. The circumstances of her death are not known, although it presumably occurred in Annapolis. The *Gazette* obituary praised her in conventional terms for displaying ''conjugal Affection'' and ''parental Tenderness.''

BIBLIOGRAPHY:

B. NAW 2, 80–81; *Maryland Gazette,* 30 March 1775; Leona M. Hudak, *Early American Women Printers and Publishers, 1639–1820* (Metuchen, N.J., 1978).

MAURINE H. BEASLEY

GREEN, DUFF (b. 15 August 1791; d. 10 June 1875), entrepreneur, politician, and publisher, actively used the press to advocate often-inflammatory political, social, and economic causes during the volatile period between 1820 and 1860. A propagandist and antagonist of Andrew Jackson, Green was a member of Old Hickory's inner circle of advisers, the Kitchen Cabinet, until he switched his allegiance to John C. Calhoun, nullification, and states' rights—issues that led to Civil War. His editorial support of the southern cause, coupled with incendiary attacks on abolitionists and other political enemies, led opponents to label him a firebrand and a supporter of slavery.

Green was born near Versailles, Woodford County, Kentucky, a son of William and Lucy Ann Marshall Green, and was educated in the classics at a neighborhood school and at the Danville Academy. In 1812 he joined the army at Jeffersonville, Indiana. He earned the rank of captain before his discharge, and married Lucretia Maria Edwards on 26 November 1813. They had eleven children. He moved to Missouri to survey public lands in 1816, engaged in profitable land speculation and a mercantile business in St. Louis, and contracted for carrying the mails. Green became postmaster of a town he founded, Chariton, Missouri, and set up the first stage line west of the Mississippi River. He was admitted to the bar, practiced law, was a member of the Missouri constitutional convention, and served in both houses of the state legislature.

In 1823 Green bought the *St. Louis Enquirer* from one of Missouri's first U.S. senators, Thomas Hart Benton, who used the paper to support Henry Clay. Under Green's ownership, the *Enquirer* was allied with Calhoun and supported Jackson for the presidency in 1824. At the urging of Jackson, Green sold the *Enquirer* in 1825 and moved to Washington, D.C., to editorially oppose the reelection of John Quincy Adams. He bought the *United States Telegraph* from John S. Meehan in 1825, investing about $45,000 in the paper. The pro-Jackson *Telegraph,* with its motto declaring that "Power is always stealing from the many to the few," denounced the Adams administration and the Federalists as "monarchists" who were "opposed to elective government" and "the common people." Green and the *Telegraph* set the tone for the pro-Jackson press, which credited them for Jackson's election in 1828.

As a reward for his editorial support, the Jackson administration awarded Green patronage contracts for congressional and executive department printing between 1829 and 1833. Meanwhile, the *Telegraph* continued to be a party organ, although Green insisted that he and his newspaper were not the administration's "humble apologists." In 1830 Green found himself enmeshed in the political dissension between Jackson and Calhoun over nullification and other issues, and Green sided with Calhoun. The Jackson administration, angered over what it regarded as Green's disloyalty, replaced the *Telegraph* with Francis P. Blair's (q.v.) *Globe* as the party organ and withdrew government printing patronage. The *Telegraph* then became a staunch supporter of southern interests, including slavery, and the paper vehemently opposed the abolition movement. After losing government patronage amounting to an estimated $50,000 a year, Green turned the editorship of the foundering *Telegraph* over to Richard K. Cralle in 1836, and the paper ceased publication in February 1837.

Between 1837 and 1857 Green pursued his private business interests and founded four short-lived partisan newspapers: the *Washington Reformer* (1837–38) to advocate states' rights; the *Baltimore Pilot* (1840–41) to support the Harrison-Tyler ticket; the *New York Republic* (1844) to bolster James K. Polk's candidacy; and the *American Statesman* (1857) in Washington to attack the abolitionist movement. Green was made an unofficial government messenger under the Tyler administration, his task to improve trade relations with England and to influence opinion concerning slavery. He wrote many lengthy letters to newspapers prior to the Civil War, continuing his support of slavery and the southern cause.

During the Civil War he actively assisted the Confederacy by operating ironworks in Alabama and Tennessee and by advising the Confederate government concerning finances and foreign relations. After the war he wrote his memoirs, briefly published the *People's Weekly* (1868) to oppose Radical

Reconstruction, and helped to finance several ventures designed to rebuild the South. He died at his Hopewell estate near Dalton, Whitfield County, Georgia. The *Atlanta Constitution* called him a ''gentleman of pure character and sterling integrity'' and a ''fearless, caustic and tireless commentator upon public men and measures.''

BIBLIOGRAPHY:

A. *Facts and Suggestions, Biographical, Historical, Financial, and Political Addresses to the People of the United States* (New York, 1866).

B. DAB 7, 540–542; DLB 43, 273–277; *Atlanta Constitution,* 11 June 1875; Gretchen Garst Ewing, ''Duff Green, Independent Editor of a Party Press,'' *Journalism Quarterly,* Winter 1977; Fletcher M. Green, ''Duff Green, Militant Journalist of the Old School,'' *American Historical Review,* January 1947.

ARTHUR J. KAUL

GRIMES, (J.) FRANK (b. 13 October 1891; d. 28 July 1961) was the leading editorial writer of the Southwest during his forty-two-year career as editor of the *Abilene Reporter-News* of Texas, 1919–61. He was one of the last of the personal journalists and a forerunner of the editorial page editor. In 1951 he was a finalist in the Pulitzer Prize editorial writing contest, but was denied the prize by the committee because the members did not think that one man could write six editorials a day of the quality produced by Grimes. Late in his career his editorials also were printed by other newspapers in the Harte-Hanks newspaper group.

Grimes was born in Pendleton, Texas, the son of Lewis Gantt Grimes, a Methodist circuit rider, and Xantha Rosalie Wootton Grimes. Grimes was self-educated, with the exception of some schooling in small Texas communities. The eleventh of twelve children in his family, Grimes abandoned formal education at age fourteen and became a printer's devil for the *Belton Evening News*.

In 1906 he left newspapers for about two years to pick cotton and work cattle in Texas and Oklahoma. Grimes returned to Texas newspapers as a tramp printer, including periods at the *Copperas Cove Banner* and a Lampasas paper. In 1909, at eighteen, he accepted his first editor's job, the editor-managership of the weekly *Holland Progress* in Texas.

His first entry into west Texas was in 1911 when he became the printer-pressman of the *Aspermont Star,* but he returned to central Texas to work for papers in Moody and Belton before going in 1913 to the *Temple Daily Telegram* as cub reporter and later city editor. Then came short editorships of the *Temple Mirror* and *Brenham Banner-Press,* which he left in December 1914 to make a permanent move to west Texas as he became city editor of the *Abilene Daily Reporter*. In June 1919 publisher George Anderson, who was also training a young business manager named Bernard Hanks (q.v.), made Grimes editor. Hanks later became the publisher, and would be the cofounder of Harte-Hanks Newspapers, and he named Grimes editor in chief when a sister *Morning News* was started in 1926.

Grimes was known for the insightfulness of his national defense editorials; his ability to translate international and national affairs for his west Texas readers; his change-of-pace, folksy, and humorous editorials; and his willingness to challenge the national pundits appearing on his page, including Walter Lippmann (q.v.).

Grimes won four Texas Associated Press editorial awards: in 1949 for "He Sat Down to Play" about Harry Truman; in 1956 for "Christmas at Copperas Cove," a change-of-pace masterpiece; in 1958 for community service editorials about a city council-manager election; and in 1959 for community service editorials about an urban renewal bond election. Also a recognized poet, his editorial poem "The Old Mesquites Ain't Out" has become a part of west Texas meteorological folklore. His one-act folk opera, *Mesquites Under Thunder,* was produced at McMurry College, which he helped found in 1923.

Grimes married a widow, Mary Ellen Feutrelle Senter, in 1913. In addition to his stepson, W. Oscar Senter, who became an air force lieutenant general, she gave birth to four Grimes children—a stillborn daughter; a son, Rudyard Kipling, a West Point graduate who died after the Bataan Death March; and two other daughters, Mary Xantha and Frances. After a 1939 divorce, Grimes married another widow, Edith Lovett Harris. He died in 1961 after a long illness in San Angelo, the victim of tuberculosis and advanced age.

BIBLIOGRAPHY:

B. Charles H. Marler, "Often a Bridesmaid, Never a Bride: Frank Grimes and the Pulitzer Prize for Editorial Writing," *Southwest Journal of Mass Communication,* Fall 1985; Charles H. Marler, "Abilene Editor," Ph.D. diss., Univ. of Missouri, 1974.

CHARLES H. MARLER

H

HAGERTY, JAMES CAMPBELL (b. 9 May 1909; d. 11 April 1981), press secretary under President Dwight D. Eisenhower, is widely regarded as history's most influential and effective White House press secretary. He modernized presidential press operations, breaking the barrier against direct quotation of the president, then putting press conferences on radio, newsreel film, and television. He also was a master at making his boss look good, at times orchestrating the news to produce the semblance of presidential activity when there was little. In both respects, Hagerty set the framework for the struggle between the White House and reporters in the last half of the twentieth century.

Hagerty was born in Plattsburg, New York, the son of Katherine Kearney Hagerty, a schoolteacher, and James A. Hagerty, a reporter who spent a total of fifty-five years covering politics, thirty-four of them with the *New York Times*. The family moved to New York City when James was young, and he attended public schools there, finishing up at the Blair Academy in Blairstown, New Jersey. Upon graduation in 1928, Hagerty went to work on Wall Street, but the depression led him to reconsider his career plans. He enrolled in Columbia University. While there he became the campus correspondent for the *New York Times*. He joined the staff upon graduation in 1934, first as a police reporter. In 1938 he was sent to cover the state capitol at Albany.

In 1943 Governor Thomas Dewey asked Hagerty to become executive assistant and press secretary. Hagerty held the job for nine years, through Dewey's presidential tries, and he did much to improve Dewey's relations with the press. Dewey loaned him to Eisenhower before the Republican convention of 1952. Hagerty stayed on for the campaign and was named White House press secretary in 1953. On both jobs, Hagerty said, his policy with reporters was to help them to get what they wanted and not to lie.

Hagerty won points for the president many ways. He conducted daily briefings of his own and scheduled regular press conferences, usually weekly, for the president. He cultivated the press corps, provided advance texts of speeches, and, remembering deadlines, was available around the clock. He took care of reporters on trips; the word was that he once filed a story for a reporter who was too drunk to do so. As a close adviser to Eisenhower, he could give authoritative answers to questions. He was also good at manufacturing news, channeling routine reports of executive departments through the White House, for example, to give the president maximum exposure.

Hagerty realized the advantage that would come to a president who appealed directly to the public, and he reasoned that the advantage outweighed the potential for damage from a presidential blunder reported in the press. He allowed stenographers to take down quotes and supplied transcripts, then in 1954 allowed press conferences to be taped for radio. Making use of newly developed, less obtrusive lights, Hagerty let in newsreel and television cameras in January 1955, thereby putting the president on the nightly news. Newspaper reporters who objected were told that the electronic age had arrived.

Hagerty's most notable performance was during the aftermath of Eisenhower's September 1955 heart attack. Called to the president's bedside and told to take care of things, Hagerty conducted five news briefings a day, seven days a week, for three weeks, earning the nickname "Iron Man Hagerty." He deluged the press with details, such as presidential breakfast menus and bowel movements, previously considered strictly personal. Within five days, Hagerty organized Eisenhower's first official act, the initialing of a routine list of appointments, and for the next weeks he kept up a string of visitors and announcements designed to demonstrate that the president was in charge. Such openness did much to reassure the public and Hagerty was praised by reporters. But the next year, when the president had an attack of ileitis that raised questions about his second term, Hagerty downplayed the illness. Some reporters felt that was a coverup.

Hagerty served throughout Eisenhower's two terms. After leaving the White House, he became vice president of news, special events, and public affairs for ABC, and within three years became the firm's executive vice president for corporate relations. He retired from ABC in 1975, after a stroke, and lived in retirement in Bronxville, New York, until his death. He was survived by his wife, the former Marjorie Lucas, whom he married 15 June 1937, and two sons.

Unlike many of his successors, Hagerty wrote little about his White House days. An edited version of his diaries of the Eisenhower years was published in 1983.

BIBLIOGRAPHY:
A. *Eisenhower in Mid-Course, 1954–55* (Indianapolis, 1983).
B. NYT 13 April 1981; "Ike's Man Jim Hagerty," *Newsweek,* 6 August 1956; C. Phillips, "Speaker of the White House," *New York Times Magazine,* 12 August 1956.

JUDITH A. SERRIN

HALE, DAVID (b. 25 April 1791; d. 20 January 1849) was co-owner, editor, and publisher of the *New York Journal of Commerce*. He was known as an innovative news gatherer who drew from Christian doctrine principles of journalistic accuracy and objectivity.

Hale, only son of the Reverend David Hale and Lydia Austin Hale, and nephew of Nathan Hale, was born in Lisbon, Connecticut. He left school at sixteen to be a store clerk in nearby Coventry, then went to Boston to work on the *Daily Advertiser* and to start his own business. He was married to his first cousin, Laura Hale, on 18 January 1815, but she died in 1824. On 22 August 1825 Hale married Lucy S. Turner of Boston.

Early in 1827 Hale became business manager of a new newspaper, the *New York Journal of Commerce;* later that year he became co-owner and began to write frequent editorials. Hale became known for his innovations in news gathering. He set up a semaphore signaling device to announce the arrival of ships from Europe so that a *Journal of Commerce* pilot boat could head to the ships and bring back foreign newspapers. Under Hale's leadership the *Journal of Commerce* continually refined its news-gathering techniques. During the 1830s a pony express from Philadelphia to New York, with six relays en route, allowed the *Journal* to print congressional news and southern news a day ahead of the competition. Six *Journal* newsboats went out as far as 100 miles from shore and raced back with European news.

Hale as editor demanded a careful regard for facts and a careful avoidance of both sensationalism and partisan political coverage. "Everybody says the press should be independent," Hale wrote in 1840, "yet how few there are who mean by this anything but a press which will reiterate just what they themselves think and believe, the falsehoods, vituperation, and personal blackguard of the party press" (Thompson, 1850). Hale argued that since "all have sinned and fallen short of the glory of God," newspapers should cover virtues and vices in various political camps and let individuals, not editors, decide elections.

Hale was a Christian libertarian politically and economically. "Governments were instituted to secure the *inalienable rights* of men," he wrote in 1847. "Life, liberty, and pursuit of happiness. Yet our community think government should inspect fish, measure corn, and almost be the market-man and cook of every family." He forecast that governmental welfare systems "will be but rottenness in the bones of the commonwealth" and advocated personal and church charity; as Hale's wealth increased, he gave away most of it. He wrote of "the rights God has given us'' and saw governments threatening individual independence.

Hale was also famous for strict Sabbath observance—no *Journal of Commerce* writer worked on Sunday, so the Monday morning edition came out an hour late—and for his refusal, at considerable revenue loss, to print ads for lotteries and other activities he considered wrongful. Costs of covering the Mexican War in 1847 (through pigeon express, pony express, newsboat, and telegraph) were so high that he proposed to other New York publishers the formation of a cooperative effort to gather and transmit news. The proposal was accepted, and in 1848, Hale was elected first president of the Associated Press. Hale died of influenza one year later. He was survived by his second wife. They had no children.

BIBLIOGRAPHY:

B. DAB 4, 98–99; John M. Havas, ''Commerce and Calvinism: The *Journal of Commerce,* 1827–65,'' *Journalism Quarterly,* Winter 1961; Joseph Thompson, *Memoir of David Hale* (Hartford, Conn., 1850).

MARVIN N. OLASKY

HALE, SARAH JOSEPHA BUELL (b. 24 October 1788; d. 30 April 1879) was the founder of Thanksgiving Day as an annual holiday and is widely known as the woman who edited and wrote for the most important of early women's magazines. She opened the doors for respectable women to enter the field of journalism, yet she was no feminist. She did crusade for education for women, perhaps because of her own experience of being forced to support herself and her family, perhaps because she obtained her own education the hard way.

The daughter of Captain Gordon Buell, an American Revolution soldier, Sarah Buell moved with her mother, Martha Whittlesey Buell, from Connecticut to a farm owned by her great-grandfather, in Newport, New Hampshire, where she was born. Sarah Buell grew up there, married there, and never thought of working outside her home until she was past thirty.

Possessed of a good mind, she always liked to study and to write. Like so many of her generation, she was educated by her mother, whom she credited with giving her a love of books. Also like most ''educated'' women of her generation, she was instructed in more advanced subjects, such as Latin and philosophy, by an older brother who was privileged to attend Dartmouth College, where doors were closed to women. In October 1813 she married David Hale, an attorney, who encouraged her to continue her education as well as to begin writing articles for periodicals in the area. Nine years later her husband died suddenly, forcing her to a decision about how she could support herself and their five children.

Her first writing efforts were poems, published under the pen name ''Cornelia'' because it was not yet respectable for a woman to write under her own name. In 1826 one of her poems won a prize, and that same year she published a novel, *Northwood, a Tale of New England,* which did put her name before the public. Because of the attention this and other early works brought, she was offered the position of editor of *Ladies' Magazine* in Boston. So began her active life as a writer and promoter of certain reforms for women. She became a role model for female journalists as she did her best to promote the ideal of what a woman could and should be in the society of her time. She wrote articles about life in America, poems, essays and literary criticism, all wholesome, positive, and uplifting. She used her position to espouse her favorite theme: education for women. She also became involved in various benevolent and patriotic activities in Boston, such as the Seaman's Aid Society. She played an important role in raising money for the Bunker Hill Monument.

She continued to write poetry for the magazine she edited and for others. There is no question that she is the author of "Mary Had a Little Lamb," more properly entitled "Mary's Lamb," although some others claimed it along the way.

Sarah Hale reached her peak as a journalist as literary editor of Louis A. Godey's (q.v.) *Lady's Book,* which required that she move to Philadelphia. Her gentility, moral principles, and devotion to things cultural and educational made the periodical the best known to American women. She not only edited it, but wrote at least half of it each month with the intention of guiding her readers' tastes. She wrote that it was the mission of women to bring morality to the world, not by being activists in public affairs, but by example and gentle influence. She thought it was appropriate for women to be trained as teachers, since such work made it possible for them to extend their influence. Her writing influenced the founding of Vassar College for women, according to its founder, Matthew Vassar.

Mrs. Hale had to be a woman of considerable stamina, since she reared five children as well as worked full-time. Little is written about how much help she may have had at home, but certainly live-in help was more easily obtained then than later. Of her five children, a son, Horatio Emmons Hale, distinguished himself as an American ethnologist who led expeditions to the Northwest territories and wrote on Chinook jargon and other American-Indian languages.

Besides the vast amount of work Mrs. Hale did on *Godey's Lady's Book,* she found time to write annuals and anthologies of verse as well as prose, cookbooks, and other works dealing with women and the home. Mrs. Hale retired from the editorship in 1877—her ninetieth year—and died two years later in Philadelphia.

BIBLIOGRAPHY:

B. NYT 2, 4, and 12 May 1879; Marion Marzolf, *Up From the Footnote: A History of Women Journalists* (New York, 1977).

JUNE N. ADAMSON

HALLOCK, GERALD (b. 18 March 1800; d. 4 January 1866) was the editor, and for all but three years a co-owner, of the *New York Journal of Commerce* between 1828 and 1861, a leader, until the appearance of the telegraph, in operating harbor and overland expresses to speed the gathering of news. An energetic and enterprising editor, Hallock in the early 1830s introduced the extra edition for New York City, based on late news. He was president of the New York Associated Press from the AP's founding in the late 1840s until he retired from journalism in 1861.

Born in Plainfield, Massachusetts, Hallock was the second of four sons of Moses Hallock and Margaret Allen Hallock. His father, pastor of the Plainfield Congregational Church for forty-five years, also operated a preparatory school in his home. Hallock with only a few months' preparation entered Williams College in 1815, distinguished himself in language studies, and graduated with high honors in 1819. After two years of teaching at the Amherst Academy and a year of study at Andover Seminary, Hallock opened a private school at Salem, Massachusetts, in 1822.

At the urging of several friends, who also provided small loans for the venture, Hallock on 1 January 1824 found the *Boston Telegraph*, a weekly paper with religious emphasis, which was so successful that within a year it absorbed the *Boston Recorder,* founded in 1816 as one of the nation's first religious newspapers. Hallock became editor of the resulting *Telegraph and Recorder,* but sold his interest in this paper in 1826 to become editor of the *New York Observer,* that city's first religious paper. On 2 June 1825 Hallock married Eliza Allen, a cousin.

Meanwhile, Arthur Tappan, a religious activist, founded the *New York Journal of Commerce* in 1827 as a moral, Sabbatarian daily, employing, at Hallock's suggestion, David Hale (q.v.), a Connecticut minister's son, as business manager. The next year at Hale's suggestion Hallock was hired as editor to boost the paper's sagging circulation. Having made the paper successful with an aggressive news-gathering policy that appealed to mercantile readers, Hale and Hallock formed a partnership in 1831 and purchased control of the *Journal of Commerce*. When Hale died in 1849, Hallock continued the partnership with Hale's heirs.

Challenged for news supremacy by his chief mercantile and political rival, James Watson Webb's (q.v.) *New York Courier and Enquirer,* in the early 1830s Hallock operated two rangy schooners to intercept inbound transatlantic ships and gather the European news. A semaphore message that one of the paper's schooners was headed up the harbor with fresh news would cause crowds of businessmen to gather at the *Journal of Commerce* office, where the schooner's news would be printed in an extra edition. Hallock's competition with Webb also extended to horse expresses which brought news from Philadelphia and later Washington, D.C., in the 1830s.

Such news-gathering enterprise foreshadowed formation of the New York Associated Press, originally a partnership of the city's six leading dailies, including the *Journal of Commerce,* during the late 1840s, prompted by the arrival of telegraph in the city a few years earlier. While Hale is credited with first suggesting the idea of an AP in a meeting with *New York Herald* publisher James Gordon Bennett (q.v.), Hallock, esteemed as a scrupulously fair and sincere man, served as president of the New York AP from its beginnings until he left journalism in 1861.

A consistently forceful and independent editorialist, Hallock favored the Union and slavery and opposed abolition and Lincoln's war policy, causing the *Journal of Commerce* to be cited, along with four other papers, by a grand jury in August 1861 for encouraging rebel sentiment in the North. When a few days later the U.S. postmaster general ordered these papers excluded from the mails, Hallock ended his editorship of the paper on 31 August 1861 to preserve the paper's mailing privileges.

Although he kept the extent of his philanthropy a secret, it is widely reported that Hallock privately purchased and liberated about 100 slaves, providing for their transportation to Liberia. He also gave substantial amounts for the building and maintenance of the South Congregational Church in New Haven, Connecticut, the Hallock family's residence after June 1836 and which Hallock visited on weekends after spending his workweek in New York City. After leaving journalism, Hallock oversaw extensive real estate holdings in the New Haven area. He died at home.

BIBLIOGRAPHY:

B. DAB 8, 157–158; NYT 7 January 1866; *New York Herald*, 7 January 1866; William H. Hallock, *Life of Gerald Hallock, Thirty-Three Years Editor of the ''New York Journal of Commerce''* (New York, 1869).

RICHARD A. SCHWARZLOSE

HALSTEAD, MURAT (b. 2 September 1829; d. 2 July 1908) was a nationally prominent Republican editor of the Gilded Age. Under his leadership, the *Cincinnati Commercial* became one of the nation's most important political newspapers. A prolific writer, Halstead published over twenty books on history, politics, and current affairs.

Halstead was born in Paddy's Run, in rural southern Ohio, the son of Griffin Halstead, a farmer, and Clarissa Willet Halstead. He graduated from Farmer's College in Pleasant Hill, Ohio, in 1851, then moved to Cincinnati to pursue a career in newspapers. He worked briefly for the *Atlas* and the *Cincinnati Enquirer,* made an abortive attempt at running a Sunday paper called the *Cincinnati Leader,* then worked for two years on the popular literary weekly *Columbian and Great West*. In 1853 he jumped to the *Commercial,* where he worked for the next forty years.

Prior to Halstead's working at the *Commercial,* his bent was literary. But as a reporter/correspondent he quickly became immersed in politics. His coverage of the numerous presidential conventions of 1860 earned him a national reputation as a political commentator; his columns, later published as a book, are still used as a historical source. He was also known as a brilliant war correspondent for his coverage of the Civil and Franco-Prussian wars.

Halstead's career as a political editor was characterized by a gradual but mostly continual turn from reformist idealism to partisan pragmatism. He emerged from the Civil War a staunch liberal and an opponent of the corruption of the Grant administration. He was one of the leaders behind the liberal insurgency that culminated in the nomination of Horace Greeley (q.v.) in 1872. But this support was costly to the *Commercial* in terms of both circulation and advertising revenue, and it was to be Halstead's last experiment in independent politics. From 1872 on, he was to be a loyal supporter of the Republican nominee.

In terms of issues, also, Halstead's political outlook became less reformist as the 1870s yielded to the 1880s. Once a supporter of tariff reform, he came to support protectionism. Once a proponent of civil service reform, he came to see a danger in the creation of a class of professional bureaucrats.

As a loyal Republican, Halstead achieved great influence. In the election of 1876, he backed Hayes, chanting the party line over disputed electoral votes. He remained on intimate terms with his fellow Ohioan over the next four years, and was instrumental in choosing Hayes's cabinet. Halstead's importance was again demonstrated in 1884, when he was chosen to edit the *New York Extra,* a campaign paper designed to turn out the vote in what Republicans rightly considered to be the key state in the presidential election. In 1888 Halstead's support of Benjamin Harrison won him nomination for the post of minister to Germany, though the Senate refused to confirm.

As a newspaper editor and proprietor (Halstead acquired control of the *Commercial* in 1866), he was dynamic and progressive. He invested in the newest presses and equipment, making his paper a leader in innovation west of the Alleghenies in the 1860s and 1870s. He was also a leader in the Western Associated Press, and was influential in the Gilded Age movement for a journalism independent of partisan control. But like his political reformism, Halstead's leadership in progressive journalism was to wane after the 1870s. His commitment to "independent" journalism was to yield to partisanship, and the dynamism of the *Commercial* was hampered by financial difficulties, partly the result of union walkouts inspired by his open-shop policies. Gradually he lost his controlling interest in the *Commercial,* which was merged with its Republican rival, the *Gazette,* in 1884, and was finally bought out by Washington McLean, who also owned the city's leading Democratic organ, the *Enquirer*.

Halstead left Cincinnati in 1890. In the next decade, he edited the *Brooklyn Standard-Union,* published dozens of articles in the leading magazines of the day, and became well known on the lecture circuit as a champion of American imperialism during the time of the Spanish-American War. He also wrote and published over a dozen works of history, biography, and public affairs, the most famous of which was a biography of William McKinley that sold over 700,000 copies in the wake of his assassination.

Halstead's personal life seems to have been felicitous. He married Mary Banks, the daughter of a well-to-do Cincinnati family, in 1857. This fertile union produced twelve children over the next quarter-century. Four of his seven sons found careers in journalism. Halstead returned to Cincinnati in 1899. He spent his remaining years there, dying in 1908.

BIBLIOGRAPHY
A. *Caucuses of 1860* (Columbus, Ohio, 1860).
B. DAB 8, 163; DLB 23, 155–160; NYT 3 July 1908; *Cincinnati Commercial Gazette*, 3 July 1908; Donald W. Curl, *Murat Halstead and the "Cincinnati Commercial"* (Boca Raton, 1980).

JOHN NERONE

HANKS, MARSHALL BERNARD (b. 19 September 1884; d. 12 December 1948) was publisher of the *Abilene Reporter-News* in Texas and cofounder with Houston Harte (q.v.) of Harte-Hanks Newspapers, the foundation of Harte-Hanks Communications. Hanks rose from paperboy to publisher of the Abilene newspaper, established it as a regional voice in central-west Texas, introduced commercial radio into the area, became a part of the cadre of newspaper friends of Lyndon B. Johnson, and with Harte spread his influence through other parts of Texas via joint ownership of several newspaper properties.

Hanks, who was known as Bernard, was born in Dallas, Texas, the son of Dr. and Mrs. R. T. Hanks; his father was pastor of the Dallas First Baptist Church. He was educated in the Simmons College schools in Abilene and attended Baylor University for a year. During his third semester, with a fever and against a doctor's order, he played in a football game, and the resulting serious illness ending his college career.

At age eight Hanks began to throw papers for the *Abilene Daily Reporter* from the back of a pony he bought with money earned from odd jobs. The publisher of the newspaper, who had become a family friend, was George S. Anderson, who hired Hanks as a bookkeeper after he did not return to Baylor. The only other formal education he received was completion of a course in bookkeeping. Anderson then made Hanks in succession his business manager, advertising manager, general manager, and eventually he became publisher.

Hanks, the businessman, met Houston Harte, the journalist-publisher, in 1924, and the two became friends and newspaper partners. Harte bought the *San Angelo Standard-Times,* his first Texas newspaper property, in 1920. After the meeting of Hanks and Harte in Dallas in 1924, they entered into a joint ownership of newspapers in Lubbock, which ended in 1928. But they decided to continue a partnership under Harte-Hanks Newspapers, excluding the Abilene and San Angelo newspapers. The *Corpus Christi Times* became the first paper held by the corporation in March 1928. Eventually, the pair acquired the *Harlingen Daily Star,* the *Paris News,* the *Big Spring Daily Herald,* the *Marshall Evening Messenger* and *Morning News,* the *Denison Herald,* and a one-third interest in the *Wichita Falls Times* and *Record-News.* They also were engaged in some joint ownerships with Charles Marsh and E.S. Fentress under Texas Newspapers from 1929 to 1932.

Harte and Hanks had high journalistic and business standards, and they did not interfere in each local operation. They operated on the philosophy that a newspaper's special responsibility is to the market it serves. Hanks, additionally, in his own operation, the *Reporter-News,* gave his editor Frank Grimes (q.v.) broad editorial freedom and established an organizational structure in which the editor did not run the newsroom but devoted his time to producing an outstanding editorial page. Hanks helped bring into Abilene the first commercially viable radio station in 1937, KRBC, owned by the Reporter Broadcasting Company.

Politics drew Hanks into local, state, and national affairs. He gave the first sizable contribution to Lyndon B. Johnson in 1937 when he ran for Congress. Generally, Hanks worked behind the scenes in such projects as the securement in 1940 of Camp Barkeley, in which he called upon Johnson, Speaker Sam Rayburn, and Senator Tom Connally for help. After Hanks's death his widow and others would repeat this process in winning Dyess Air Force Base for Abilene.

During Hanks's career the circulation of the Abilene paper increased from a few hundred to about 40,000; he added a morning edition and expanded to a seven-day paper during World War II; he three times expanded the facilities and presses of the paper to keep it apace of technology and community growth; he and Harte ordered a pioneering readership study by the Belden Associates in the early 1940s. Additionally, Hanks and Harte developed a unique model of newspaper groups that protected local autonomy, and they established the framework for one of the nation's largest communication companies.

Hanks married Eva Marie Hollis in 1906. They had one daughter, Patty, who is married to A. B. "Stormy" Shelton. Mrs. Hanks succeeded her husband as publisher, and Shelton became publisher in 1964. Hanks had a heart attack in 1938 and suffered a fatal heart failure in 1948.

BIBLIOGRAPHY:

B. Charles H. Marler, "Abilene Editor," Ph.D. diss., Univ. of Missouri, 1974; Hugh Morgan, "The Acquisition of Newspapers by Houston Harte," M.A. thesis, Univ. of Oklahoma, 1967; Sally Post, "With or Without Offense . . . Bernard Hanks and the *Abilene Reporter-News,*" M.A. thesis, Texas Tech Univ., 1984.

CHARLES H. MARLER

HAPGOOD, NORMAN (b. 28 March 1868; d. 29 April 1937) was a reporter, drama critic, and magazine editor who came to prominence as a crusading editor of *Collier's Weekly* during the era of muckraking magazines. Although he had a law degree and practiced law for several years, once he turned away from that profession to work for midwestern newspapers, he never went back. In addition to his journalism, he wrote several books, including four biographies.

The Hapgood family had deep New England roots and could claim both Patriot and Tory for the family tree. Despite strong eastern ties, Hapgood's father, Charles Hutchins Hapgood, moved in 1859 to Chicago, where he chose business over law and manufactured farm plows. In 1867 he married Fanny Louise Powers and a year later Norman was born. They had three other children, Hutchins, William, and Ruth, who died in childhood. By 1875 Charles Hapgood had established his family in Alton, Illinois, where he successfully operated a farm implement business.

Eventually all three Hapgood brothers graduated from Harvard. Hutchins later wrote for the *New York Commercial Advertiser* and was columnist for the *New York Globe*. William returned to the Midwest and took over a canning company that became a pioneer in worker ownership, social welfare, and guaranteed employment.

At Harvard, Norman wrote for the *Harvard Monthly* and was its editor, but after graduation he entered Harvard Law School instead of pursuing a literary or journalistic career. Although he next worked for a Chicago law firm, he could not resist the pull of a writing career and worked for a short time for the *Chicago Evening Post* and then on the *Milwaukee Sentinel*. Hungering for a crack at the country's journalistic hub, Hapgood used a Harvard connection to land a job as a reporter at E. L. Godkin's (q.v.) *New York Evening Post*. He learned quickly, and by 1896 he was considered one of the paper's best reporters.

Frustrated by Godkin's approach to news coverage, he jumped to the *Commercial Advertiser* after it was purchased by two *Post* employees. He had always wanted to combine journalism with a literary career by writing critical essays, and he began to do that for magazines. That led to publication of his first book in 1897, *Literary Statesmen and Others*. Also in that year, he became drama critic for the *Commercial Advertiser,* producing "The Theatres" column for the paper three times a week. A year later he started the "Drama of the Month" feature in *Bookman* magazine. Another book, *The Stage in America, 1897–1900* (1901), was largely a compilation of his theater articles. During his time at the *Commercial Advertiser* he wrote biographies of George Washington, Abraham Lincoln, and Daniel Webster. He resigned from the paper following a short advertising boycott that was prompted by his theater criticism in October 1902.

After a year in Europe, he returned to New York to become editor of *Collier's Weekly,* having been recommended for the post by Finley Peter Dunne (q.v.). At *Collier's* he quickly became known for his reasoned, middle-of-the-road editorials that were short and tightly constructed. But his moralism and distrust of wealth led him to increasingly progressive and democratic views, and soon the magazine became an active player on the muckraking scene. It was involved in a libel suit with *Town Topics,* a New York scandal sheet, took on the patent medicine industry, argued for pure food and drug legislation, entered the fight over the conservation policies in the Taft administration, and pushed for limiting the powers of the Speaker of the House. Under Hapgood's direction *Collier's* became a magazine of some weight and influence in national affairs, and a staunch advocate of high journalistic ethics. After 1910, however, the influence and reputation of the magazine slipped, as did its financial status, and Hapgood resigned after putting out the 19 October 1912 issue.

Hapgood then obtained backers to purchase *Harper's Weekly,* which he edited and managed until the spring of 1916. He promised to restore the magazine to its nineteenth-century prominence, but his close attachment to Woodrow Wilson made the publication little more than a voice for Wilsonian policies. Its lack of independence and its shaky finances contributed to its takeover by the *Independent* in 1916. After that, Hapgood's energies were increasingly spent promoting Wilson and his policies. His devotion was rewarded with an interim appointment as U.S. minister to Copenhagen. His appointment failed to gain Senate approval, however, because he was accused of Bolshevik leanings.

During the 1920s Hapgood wrote for the Hearst press, and was editor of *Hearst's International Magazine* from 1922 to 1926. The magazine reflected Hapgood's continued progressivism as it exposed the Ku Klux Klan and Henry Ford's anti-Semitism. In 1925 he and Henry Moskowitz wrote *Up From City Streets,* a biography of Al Smith. In the late twenties he worked for United Features and started a newsletter.

His journalism slacked off in the 1930s until he became editor of the *Christian Register,* a Unitarian publication in Boston. He died unexpectedly at age sixty-nine, following prostate surgery. He had been married twice, first to Emilie Bigelow, whom he divorced in 1915, then to Elizabeth Kempley Reynolds, and had one child by the first marriage and three by the second.

BIBLIOGRAPHY:

B. DAB 22, 280–82; NYT 30 April and 2 May 1937; Louis Filler, *Crusaders for American Liberalism* (New York, 1939); Hutchins Hapgood, *A Victorian in the Modern World* (New York, 1939); Michael D. Marcaccio, *The Hapgoods* (Charlottesville, Va., 1977).

THOMAS CONNERY

HARD, WILLIAM (b. 15 September 1878; d. 30 January 1962) was an interpreter of public affairs for sixty years, primarily as a creative and prolific writer of magazine journalism. His career also included work for newspapers and in radio. But his main work was producing hundreds of articles for dozens of popular, special interest, and opinion and comment periodicals, principally *Everybody's, New Republic, Nation,* and *Reader's Digest,* on subjects ranging from child labor to global war.

Hard, the eldest of three children, was born in Painted Post, New York, to the Reverend Clark Pettengill Hard and Lydia E. van Someren Hard. When he was four, Hard went with his parents to India, where his father, a Methodist minister, was a missionary. He received his schooling in Lima, New York, public schools and in India and London, before attending Northwestern University. He earned a B.A. in history in 1900 and lectured in medieval history at Northwestern for one year.

Hard was appointed head resident at the Northwestern University Settlement House in Chicago in 1901 and wrote about local issues for the settlement house's monthly newsletter. In 1902 he was hired by the *Chicago Tribune* to write editorials. He and Ann Nyhan Scribner, assistant city editor of the *Chicago Post,* were married on 3 November 1903. They had one son and one daughter. After three years at the *Tribune,* Hard left in 1905 to become an assistant for a brief time to Joseph Medill Patterson (q.v.), Chicago's commissioner of public works, with whom Hard had worked at the newspaper.

By 1906 Hard's articles were being published regularly in *Saturday Evening Post, Outlook,* and *American*. Hard became Chicago editor for *Ridgway's Weekly*, starting in late 1906. The magazine, an offshoot of *Everbody's,* folded in early 1907, and Hard wrote for *Everybody's* and *Delineator,* another Ridgway publication, until 1917. His work included notable muckracking articles on child labor and unsafe conditions in industry and several series on women's status. He was editor of *Everybody's* in 1915.

Hard also wrote for other magazines and after 1914 was a Washington correspondent for *Metropolitan* and, from 1917 to 1920, a weekly contributor to *New Republic*. His account of a longtime friend's eighteen months in revolutionary Russia, *Raymond Robins' Own Story,* was published in 1920.

In the 1920s Hard wrote for several magazines, including *Asia* and *Collier's,* and wrote the "Weekly Washington Letter' from 1923 to 1925 for the *Nation*. He also served as a Washington correspondent for newspaper clients of his Hard News Service and the Consolidated News Service operated by David Lawrence (q.v.). He was a friend and early supporter of Herbert Hoover and in 1928 wrote a biography, *Who's Hoover*? Following Hoover's election, Hard for a time was a participant in Hoover's early-morning "Medicine-Ball Cabinet."

Hard became a regular commentator and correspondent on the NBC network in 1928. From January to April 1930 he reported by radio on the London Naval Disarmament Conference and also covered the 1932 Republican National Convention and international conferences in Geneva and Berlin. In 1936 Hard, by then a vocal critic of the New Deal, worked for the Republican party as a daily radio commentator on the presidential campaign. He was appointed executive assistant to the chairman of the Republican National Committee in February 1937 and was later secretary of the Republican Program Committee.

He resigned from political party work in October 1938 with a statement that he wanted to resume independent journalism. Hard began writing regularly for *Reader's Digest* in 1939. He was a roving editor for the *Digest*, covering labor, politics, and international affairs, until his death in 1962 at his New Canaan, Connecticut, home. Hard's journalistic integrity and his brilliance as a writer were widely acknowledged among contemporaries.

BIBLIOGRAPHY:

B. DAB Supp. 7, 320–321; NCAB 56, 42–43; NYT 1 February 1962; Erman J. Ridgway, "Conversazione," *Delineator,* September 1911.

RONALD S. MARMARELLI

HARDING, WARREN GAMALIEL (b. 2 November 1865; d. 2 August 1923) was the only publisher to become president in U.S. history, although his career in neither politics nor journalism was particularly distinguished; in fact, his administration is better remembered for its scandal than its achievement, and his newspaper, the *Marion* (Ohio) *Star*, is better remembered for his association with it than its good journalism. In journalism history, his presidency was the subject of much good political reporting, but the lack of serious scholarship about his life and administration (caused primarily by the destruction of his papers by his widow) leaves historians with considerable mystery.

Harding, the oldest of eight children, was born to George ''Tryon'' Harding and Phoebe Dickerson Harding on a farm at Blooming Grove in Morrow Country in north-central Ohio. His father, a lifelong frustrated entrepreneur, practiced homeopathic medicine, and his mother practiced midwifery, children's medicine, and obstetrics, but neither had much training. Dr. Harding's practice was not highly regarded in Caledonia, where the family moved when Warren was eight, or in Marion, where the family finally settled in 1882.

Tryon Harding, in one of many failed ventures, bought the short-lived *Caledonia Argus* in 1875, and Warren became an accomplished printer's devil, earning his lifelong lucky charm, a 13-em makeup rule and the craft sign of a bona fide printer. In the autumn of 1880, Warren Harding, fourteen, entered Iberia College, supporting himself with work at the *Union Register* printing shop. In 1882 he and a classmate started a four-page college fortnightly, the *Iberia Spectator*. The unprofitable paper died when Harding graduated in 1883. He taught school, studied law, and sold insurance, but he preferred card games, loafing, and playing in the Marion town band.

In 1884 his father bought the weakest of the three papers in Marion, the independent daily *Star*. Warren Harding was named editor. After several starts and stops, including a period during which Harding worked for the weekly Democratic *Mirror*, the *Star* came to permanent life and prospered after Warren Harding became the sole proprietor. In 1885 Harding started the weekly *Star*, a Republican paper that successfully competed for the legal advertising contract.

Except during the depressions of 1882 and 1891, Marion grew, and so did Harding's papers. On 5 July 1891 Harding married Florence Kling DeWolfe, a manipulative divorcée who became a major motivating force in Harding's life. She was given credit as circulation manager for helping to improve the business of the paper. She was affectionately called ''Dutchess'' by the tobacco-chewing Harding and his friends because of the clash between her stern will and his philandering ways. He had at least two mistresses after his marriage and had his only child, Elizabeth, by Nan Briton, thirty years his junior, in 1919.

In 1882 Harding issued his newspaper creed that included nice-sounding journalistic tenets of the day, but they were regularly violated. Harding's papers covered up important news that was embarrassing to some residents. He carried out a vindictive character assassination against the rival Republican editor. He was sued in 1890 for criminal libel, a charge that was probably true, but Harding eluded punishment. Some published items brought physical confrontations that prompted Harding to buy a guard dog. Generally his newspaper career paralleled his political career—huge successes built on luck and frequent compromise and marred by scandal and ineffectual leadership.

Harding's papers thrived, and they could have been more profitable had he not been so enamored with innovations in printing, which he regularly brought to the *Star*. In 1909 he incorporated the paper and sold 25 percent to his employees. In 1912 the powerful and conservative *Ohio State Journal* in Columbus withdrew its support for William Howard Taft, so Harding, a strong Taft supporter, started the *Ohio Star* in the state capital to combat the *Journal*. His paper survived for a year.

He became involved in Republican politics in the early 1880s, losing an election for country auditor in 1882. His oratorical abilities, noble physical appearance, association with political wheeler-dealers, and Republican loyalty, however, kept him in politics, and in 1900 he was elected to the first of two terms as state senator in the corrupt Ohio assembly.

After his entry into full-time politics, he became more of a politician than a journalist and more of a publisher than an editor. He was elected lieutenant governor in 1904, lost an election for governor in 1910, and was elected U.S. Senator in 1914. From 1918 he considered selling the *Star*, and finally, in 1923, he sold it to the Brush-Moore chain for $550,000.

In his campaign for and election to the presidency in 1920, he frequently recalled his newspaper days favorably. He restored full press conferences at the White House and demonstrated good public relations skills in opening up the administration to the press and public. He was occasionally criticized by the press during his time in office, but overall he was a favorite of reporters. His cabinet became infamous only after his death.

On a transcontinental speaking tour, Harding appeared fatigued and betrayed by the knowledge that confidants in the administration had been caught in scandal. On his way from Alaska to San Francisco, he suffered from suspected food poisoning and other ailments and suddenly died in San Francisco on 2 August 1923. The cause was never firmly established. His editor's chair in Marion was draped in black when he died. After destroying most of his papers, his wife died on 21 November 1924.

BIBLIOGRAPHY:

B. Charles L. Mee, *The Ohio Gang* (New York, 1981); Robert K. Murray, *The Harding Era* (Minneapolis, 1969); Francis Russell, *The Shadow of Blooming Grove* (New York, 1968).

THOMAS A. SCHWARTZ

HARRIS, BENJAMIN (dates unknown; fl. 1673–1716), a Boston printer and bookseller, published the first attempt at a newspaper in the colonies. His *Public Occurrences, Both Foreign and Domestick* appeared on 25 September 1690, but was suppressed by colonial authorities after a single issue.

No details are known of Harris's early life prior to his involvement in London religious and political controversies. Harris began his publishing career in London with a religious book, *War With the Devil,* in 1673. This was followed by numerous religious works, chiefly opposing Roman Catholics and Quakers. He was fined £500 for publishing and selling a Protestant work, but he defaulted on the fine and was sent to King's Bench Prison. Commons petitioned for his release, and when this was denied, Harris was illegally discharged from prison anyway.

On 7 July 1679 he began a newspaper, *Domestick Intelligence: Or News from Both the City and Country,* later retitled the *Protestant (Domestick) Intelligence.* Harris was publisher and editor of the journal, which appeared with several interruptions until it was suppressed on 15 April 1681. Harris also opened a coffeehouse, selling religious propaganda (including playing cards with theological themes) and patent medicines.

A devout Anabaptist, Harris joined with Shaftesbury, the Whigs, and Titus Oates in opposing what they considered to be a ''popish plot'' in 1679. When Monmouth's rebellion failed and James II ascended to the throne, Harris was arrested for possessing seditious literature and sentenced to the pillory. His wife defended him from assault by the mob. He was jailed, but continued to edit his paper from his cell. His shop was raided again in 1686, and Harris fled to Boston.

Within a year of his arrival, Harris was a success as a bookseller, and in 1690 he opened the London Coffee House, a social center whose visitors included the Mathers, whose works Harris often published, and jurist and diarist Samuel Sewall.

He published the *Boston Almanack* in 1687 and *The New England Primer* in 1690. That same year, after the downfall of Governor Edmund Andros, Harris began *Publick Occurrences, Both Foreign and Domestick,* although it was suppressed after a single issue. Sewall reported in his diary that the government had moved against Harris because he did not obtain a license to publish the paper, and because the issue contained offensive references to the French king and the Indian wars (*Bookman,* 1933).

However, Harris was still a success at his other printing ventures and published at least ten books that year. In 1691 he entered into a partnership with John Allen and was named official printer to the governor and council in 1692. He printed *The Acts and Laws of Massachusetts* in 1692 and 1693. A year later Bartholomew Green succeeded him as official printer.

Harris returned to London about 1694, although the reasons for his return are not known. He left his son, Vavasoar, and partner, John Allen, to close up his Boston business. There is no record of his ever returning to New England. Back in London, he found a climate more sympathetic to newspapers than New England's had been. He founded the *Intelligence Domestick and Foreign* in 1695. But although the political climate was favorable, Harris did not find an audience or advertisers, for this journal, and the three that followed it, failed.

Harris was a remarkably determined individual, however, and he finally succeeded with a newspaper, the *London Post*, which he published from 1699 to 1706. He also founded a later paper, the *Protestant Tudor*. Much of the information extant about Harris results from his fiery temper and frequent disputes, which were prominently mentioned in diaries.

BIBLIOGRAPHY:
B. DAB 4, 303–305; "The First American Newspaper and the 'New England Primer,' " *Bookman,* January 1933; Worthington Chauncy Ford, "Benjamin Harris, Printer and Bookseller," *Proceedings of the Massachusetts Historical Society,* 1924.

CAROLYN G. CLINE

HARRIS, JOEL CHANDLER (b. 9 December 1848; d. 3 July 1908), a Georgia journalist, columnist, editorial writer, and newspaper editor for thirty-five years, most of that with the *Atlanta Constitution,* is better known as a talented southern folklorist and creator of Uncle Remus, an aged Negro narrator who recounted tales of plantation life published in the *Constitution* and later in books.

Harris was born in Eatonton, Georgia, fifty miles southeast of Atlanta, and attended the Eatonton Academy for Boys. His mother, Mary Harris, had eloped with a young Irish laborer, only to be deserted by him before their child was born. During his boyhood, the Harrises lived in an antebellum plantation environment, where his mother provided support as a dressmaker.

At age fourteen, Harris became a printer's apprentice for the *Countryman,* a weekly newspaper published on a nearby plantation. At seventeen he took a job as typesetter on the *Macon Telegraph,* where he was allowed to review books and magazines and compose humorous paragraphs. After a six-month sojourn in New Orleans, where he worked as secretary for a magazine publisher, Harris accepted a position on the staff of the *Monroe Advertiser,* a weekly newspaper published in Forsyth, Georgia.

In 1870 Harris became the assistant editor of the *Savannah Morning News,* where his primary assignment was to write a humorous column, "Affairs in Georgia." He was married on 21 April 1873 to Esther LaRose, the daughter of a French Canadian couple who had temporarily moved to Savannah. A serious outbreak of yellow fever in Savannah during 1876 caused Harris to move his wife and their two children to Atlanta. What was planned as a temporary stay became permanent when Harris was offered a job as assistant editor of the *Constitution*.

Harris's first Uncle Remus story appeared in the *Constitution* in October 1876. The old Negro narrator, whose wit and wisdom were portrayed as inherent qualities of his race, immediately became popular with readers. Harris's first book, *Uncle Remus: His Songs and His Sayings,* followed in 1880. During the next twenty-four years, Harris's literary career evolved from his journalistic efforts on the *Constitution,* where he wrote daily editorials, feature articles, and book reviews, as well as fictional stories. Nine other books of Uncle Remus's songs, sketches, and sayings were published during these years. Harris also produced several volumes of children's stories and two inchoate novels, as well as short stories and other writings depicting Georgia life for national magazines.

As Harris's literary fame increased, he found that he could not entirely escape the spotlight of publicity. More and more he made a habit of attending the morning meeting of the editorial staff at the *Constitution,* after which he returned home to complete his writing assignments. At home in West End, Mrs. Harris protected her husband, always shy, from interruptions by strangers who admired Uncle Remus and wished to meet his creator. Harris finally resigned from the *Constitution* in September 1900 to devote his time to more literary writing.

Two other events climaxed Harris's long career as a journalist, humorist, and folklorist. One was the visit of President Theodore Roosevelt to Atlanta in October 1905, who singled out Harris for public praise. The other was Harris's last publishing venture as editor of *Uncle Remus's Magazine,* a monthly periodical launched in June 1907 by his eldest son, Julian, and a group of young Atlanta businessmen.

In May 1908 the magazine absorbed the *Home Magazine,* and Harris promised his readers that henceforth the magazine would be called *Uncle Remus's—The Home Magazine*. But Harris's health began to fail during the spring of 1908. During April and May he continued to give his attention to his editorial work, but he grew more listless. He died on 3 July 1908 of cirrhosis of the liver.

BIBLIOGRAPHY:

B. DAB 4, 312–314; NYT 4 July 1908; R. Bruce Bickley, Jr., *Joel Chandler Harris* (Boston, 1978); Julia Collier Harris, *The Life and Letters of Joel Chandler Harris* (Boston, 1918).

HARRY W. STONECIPHER

HART, FRANCIS BRETT (b. 25 August 1836?; d. 5 May 1902), known to readers as Bret Harte, pioneered a distinct California literary tradition that established the local color short story as a leading fictional form in late nineteenth-century America. His writing smoothly blended frontier humor with Dickensian sentiment and characters. The gamblers, schoolmarms, stage drivers, and miners who inhabited the picturesque gulches of the Sierra foothills became our most popular literary stereotypes. On the strength of some humorous verse and a few short stories, Bret Harte found himself one of America's Gilded Age idols. But his fame proved short-lived in this country. Constrained by his own creation, he was destined to tiredly repeat himself.

One of four children, Harte was born in Albany, New York. But there is disagreement as to the correct year of birth. Harte biographers Edgar T. Pemberton and George R. Stewart maintain 1839 and 1836 respectively. His father, Henry Philips Hart, a schoolteacher and improvident head of household, added an "e" to the family name to differentiate it from that of a well-known New York politician. His mother, Elizabeth Rebecca Ostrander Hart, possessed deep love for literature and nurtured her son's writing. A frail child, he was first taught at home by his parents. He quit school at age thirteen and worked as a clerk in New York and Brooklyn for the next five years.

In February 1854 Harte journeyed to Oakland, California, to join his mother, who had recently remarried after his father's death. He was soon hired as a tutor for a family in the San Ramon Valley. In the summer of 1857 he sailed up the coast to Union, about 300 miles north of San Francisco, where he learned the printer's trade on the *Humboldt Times*. He worked the same year as a compositor and assistant editor on the *Northern California,* published in nearby Eureka.

Harte returned north to San Franciso in late 1857 and worked as a compositor on the *Golden Era*. Occasional prose of his own appeared in the weekly magazine; his first contribution, "My Metamorphosis," introduced readers to the signature "Bret Harte." After about six months he begin writing a column entitled "Town and Table Talk"—comment on current happenings and life. Through it he became recognized locally as a satirist and humorist.

In October 1860 "The Man of No Account" appeared in the *Golden Era*—Harte's first attempt to fashion California background into his writing. But his impulse toward local color developed slowly. As late as 1865 he scoffed at remarks carried in the *Sacramento Union* that the "grand gold-hunting crusade" was a commendable literary theme. The Forty-Niners he met struck him as crude, rough, and oafish. They, in turn, responding to his patent-leather shoes, cane, and prissy manner, dubbed him an "Eastern dude."

By 1861 his prose had begun to attract influential patrons who secured a clerkship for him in the surveyor general's office that provided him with needed supplemental income. In May 1863 Harte was awarded a better paying job in the U.S. Branch Mint; he held the post, which seldom impinged on his writing, until he left San Francisco eight years later. On 11 August 1862 he married Anna Griswold. The unhappy union produced four children and suffered unreconciled separation after 1878.

In July 1868 Harte was made editor of a new San Francisco literary magazine, the *Overland Monthly*. With typical procrastination he failed to complete an article for the first issue, but the appearance of "The Luck of Roaring Camp" in the next grabbed the public's attention. Californians initially objected to the frankness of a story written about a prostitute's baby and to such language as a coarse miner's "the d—d little cuss!" But many weeks later when a steamer brought the piece to the East Coast, Harte was enthusiastically heralded by Boston and New York newspapers. By the end of two years, he had published and collected in a book seven stories under the title *The Luck of Roaring Camp, and Other Sketches*. (1870). Then in September 1870 he slipped into the *Overland,* as filler, a dialect poem generally known as "The Heathen Chinee." This account by Truthful James of a three-handed game of euchre provided the greatest impetus to Harte's career.

On 2 February 1871 Harte relinquished his position at the *Overland* and a professorship in literature at the University of California to further his career in the East. A lucrative job offer to edit the *Lakeside Monthly* in Chicago fell through, but he did enjoy brief success on the East Coast. In Boston he signed a one-year contract with the *Atlantic Monthly* for an unprecedented $10,000. A dispute followed with the magazine over the number and quality of his contributions, and the contract was not renewed. With no income except his book royalties and no reserve funds, Harte turned to the lecture circuit in 1873.

He went on three separate tours, at considerable cost in fatigue and with diminishing financial returns. His hopes of writing assignments and editorial posts came to nothing. With his reputation on the wane, he sold less, and to less profitable journals.

Nearly destitute, he accepted an appointment a year later as consular assistant in Crefeld, Germany—never to return to his homeland from self-imposed exile. In May 1880 he was made consul of Glasgow, Scotland, at $3,000 annually. He resigned his post in July 1885 and spent the last years of his life in London, an honored expatriate American writer. Almost until his death of throat cancer on 5 May 1902, Harte continued to pour out variations of the stories that had made his reputation more than thirty years earlier.

BIBLIOGRAPHY:

A. *Condensed Novels* (Boston, 1871); *A Protegé of Jack Hamlin's and Other Stories* (Boston, 1894).

B. DAB 4, 362; NYT 7 May 1902; Margaret Duckett, *Mark Twain and Bret Harte* (Norman, Okla., 1964); Richard O'Connor, *Bret Harte: A Biography* (Boston, 1966).

DAVID C. COULSON

HARTE, ROBERT WILLIAM HOUSTON (b. 12 January 1893; d. 14 March 1972) was publisher of the *San Angelo Standard-Times* in Texas, cofounder with Bernard Hanks (q.v.) of Harte-Hanks Newspapers, the forerunner of Harte-Hanks Communications, and vice president of the Associated Press in the 1930s and 1940s.

Unlike his future partner Hanks, who was trained as a businessman, Harte earned a bachelor's degree in journalism from the University of Missouri. Harte was one of the earliest college-trained journalists to become a publisher, and he received the Medal of Merit in 1931 from the University of Missouri School of Journalism for distinguished service to journalism. He used a small inheritance from his stepmother to launch his lifetime of newspaper acquisition even before finishing college, and he migrated to San Angelo in 1920 and bought the *Standard-Times*. Harte turned the paper into a leading voice of central-west Texas, brought broadcasting to the market, and with Hanks influenced other areas of Texas by jointly buying other newspaper properties.

The Missourian, who was known as Houston, was born in Knob Noster, the son of Edward S. Harte, a lumber company operator, and Lizzie Houston Harte, a schoolteacher who died a few days after Houston's birth. His stepmother was Mary Shafer Case, who died in 1907. Harte was educated in Knob Noster and graduated from high school there in 1911. Intending to become an architect, Harte entered the University of Missouri at Columbia but was led into journalism by Mary Bidwell Breed, a freshman English teacher. He attended the University of Southern California one year and was graduated from Missouri in 1915.

The adventuresome Harte bought his first newspaper in 1914, which was the *Knob Noster Gem*, by selling a building left to him by his stepmother.

Subsequently, during his senior year, he and classmate John D. Ferguson bought the *Central Missouri Republican,* a weekly in Boonville, Missouri, and Harte sold the *Gem*.

World War I led Harte into the infantry, and he left the *Republican* to be run by college friends. The young publisher was assigned to Camp Lee, Virginia, where he served as a first lieutenant and assistant adjutant. After the war he returned to Boonville and in 1919 started a daily companion to the weekly *Republican,* the *Boonville Daily Republican,* both of which he sold the next year.

Harte purchased in the spring of 1920 the *San Angelo Standard-Times* and moved to Texas. Within two years he purchased other newspaper properties in nearby Sweetwater and Roby. Ninety miles to the northeast another young newspaperman, Bernard Hanks, was running the *Abilene Reporter-News*. They met in 1924 at a Dallas gathering of Texas publishers. This meeting led to their participation in a joint newspaper ownership in Lubbock for a brief time—but more important to a partnership that would lead to Harte-Hanks Communications.

During Hanks's lifetime the pair would buy together the *Corpus Christi Times, Harlingen Daily Star,* the *Paris News,* the *Big Spring Herald,* the *Marshall Evening Messenger* and *Morning News,* the *Denison Herald,* and a one-third interest in the *Wichita Falls Times* and *Record News*. They also participated with Charles Marsh and E. S. Fentress in 1929–32 in some joint ownerships under Texas Newspapers. Harte and Hanks ordered in the early 1940s a pioneering readership survey by the Belden Associates of their group. At Harte's death the group included nineteen newspapers in six states with a total circulation of 600,000, several broadcast properties, and other media companies.

Harte was a close political ally of Lydon B. Johnson; Texas governors Dan Moody, Price Daniel, and John Connally; Speaker Sam Rayburn; and other Texas politicians. He was a member of the board of directors of the Associated Press in 1937–43 and served as a vice president for various periods between 1935 and 1946. Although he developed extensive business interests of other types, particularly transportation companies that were needed to help circulate his newspaper over San Angelo's broad west Texas market territory, his primary contributions were his development with Hanks of a unique ownership pattern for autonomous small newspapers within a group, the framework they built for Harte-Hanks Communications, and his service to AP and his community.

Harte was married to Caroline Isabel McCutcheon in 1921. They had two sons, Edward Holmead and Houston Harriman, who both became officers in Harte-Hanks. Harte died 14 March 1972 in San Angelo, after fifty-two years as publisher of the *Standard Times*.

BIBLIOGRAPHY:

B. NYT 14 March 1972; Hugh Morgan, "The Acquisition of Newspapers by Houston Harte," M.A. thesis, Univ. of Oklahoma, 1967; Wayland Yates, "An Historical Survey of the Development of the *San Angelo Standard-Times* as a Regional Newspaper,'' M.A. thesis, East Texas State Univ., 1969.

CHARLES H. MARLER

HEARN, PATRICK LAFCADIO (b. 27 June 1850; d. 26 September 1904) was a literary man of diverse and arcane interests. He began his career as a reporter and editorial writer for newspapers in Cincinnati and New Orleans, but he achieved a reputation for graceful translations from French literature and for his own novels. Hearn also published travel books and collections of folk tales, but his best works are his criticism of English literature and his attempt to interpret Japan for American readers.

Hearn was born on the Greek island of Leucadia, now Levkas, the son of Charles Bush Hearn, a surgeon in the British army, and of Rosa Antonia Cassimati. She was Greek; he was Irish. When Charles was transferred to the West Indies, wife and son remained behind until the opportunity came to send them to Dublin to live with Hearn's relatives. Lafcadio—so named after the Greek pronunciation of the isle of his birth—was only two when he began the Irish phase of his life. His mother could not adjust to this new life, and she returned to Greece in 1854, leaving the child with his great-aunt, a widow. In 1856 Lafcadio's father had the marriage annulled, and Lafcadio was never again to see his mother. Charles Hearn also remarried, and fathered several children. Lafcadio never met any of these, nor was he ever again to see his father after his remarriage. He was in effect orphaned—cared for only by his wealthy great-aunt, Sarah Brenane. She had the means to send Lafcadio briefly to school in France and later to England, where, as a result of a playground accident, Lafcadio was blinded in one eye, a disfigurement which affected his personal relationships. When Mrs. Brenane lost her fortune in poor investments, Lafcadio was withdrawn from school and sent to Cincinnati, where there were acquaintances. He thus entered the American phase of his life at eighteen, virtually destitute and thrown on his own resources in a strange land.

After a period of odd jobs, including a stint in a printer's shop, Hearn landed a job on the *Cincinnati Enquirer*. There he wrote book reviews and feature articles before becoming a full-fledged member of the staff in 1874. He became known as the *Enquirer*'s ''sensational reporter'' after his reports on the Tanyard murder case were published. But his marriage in 1874 to a mulatto led to his dismissal from the *Enquirer,* despite the admiration of the man who had hired him, John A. Cockerill (q.v.). He found work with the *Commercial,* however, and continued writing his descriptive accounts of Cincinnati's lowlifes and their miseries. He also added translations from Théophile Gautier to his repertory. But his marriage—probably invalid, anyway, because of an Ohio law forbidding interracial unions—was falling apart; Mattie Foley was absenting herself from their home unpredictably, and final separation seemed inevitable. Hearn left Cincinnati in 1877, bound for New Orleans and warmer surroundings. Publisher

Murat Halstead (q.v.) was reluctant to let him go, but agreed to accept some pieces written about the South.

Hearn found work with the *New Orleans Item* after the *Commercial* found that it no longer needed its correspondent. When he began writing for the *Item* in June 1878, it was barely surviving. Hearn's skills helped the *Item* to earn respectability. He wrote "fantastics," little features about the quaint and exotic aspects of the city, and he illustrated his own stories with woodcuts he carved on the backs of old wooden type that had been used for advertisements. Hearn acquired a special interest in the Creole heritage—an interest fostered by his friend George Washington Cable—and he began gathering Creole tales and rhymes and recipes and words. Eventually he would publish a recipe book, *La Cuisine Créole,* and a dictionary of Creole proverbs, *Gombo Zhèbes,* along with his pieces in the *Item*.

The *Times* and the *Democrat* merged in 1881, and Hearn was invited to become literary editor of the new paper. Besides his translations, published under the heading "The Foreign Press," and his "fantastics," he wrote many editorials. He was also beginning to publish in magazines, like *Harper's Weekly,* and in 1887 he finished his first novel, *Chita,* the story of a Louisiana Gulf storm and how it swept out to sea all who had been on the Île Dernière except one lone survivor, a child. He knew now that his literary talent was mature and that he had outgrown journalism. Accordingly he resigned from the *Times-Democrat* in 1887 and traveled to New York.

Hearn remained in New York—with time out for stays in the West Indies—for nearly three years, while writing prolifically. But New York frustrated him, and he proposed to write a book on Japan. Harper and Brothers expressed interest, and in 1890 Hearn arrived within sight of Mount Fuji to begin the Japanese phase of his career.

In Japan Hearn supported himself at first as a teacher of English in Matsue. He adapted easily to Japanese ways— so easily, in fact, that within a year of his arrival he married young Setsu Koizumi and undertook the support of her parents and grandparents. Although he enjoyed the area around Matsue, he was happy to accept another teaching position in Kumamoto at twice the salary. In Kumamoto his son, Kazuo, was born, and Hearn finished his first book about Japan, *Glimpses of Unfamiliar Japan.* But he was dissatisfied with the school where he taught, and when he was offered a position on the English-language *Kobe Chronicle,* he accepted. He wrote editorials by day, and by night he worked on his books. His one good eye suffered from the strain, and he was ready to leave Kobe when he received in December 1895 an offer from Tokyo Imperial University for a position as chair of the English language and literature department.

He also became a Japanese citizen, adopting the name Koizumi Yakumo—Koizumi being his wife's family name, and Yakumo chosen because of its meaning, "Eight clouds." His tenure at the university was a fruitful one: before he left the university in 1903 he fathered two more boys, Iwao and Kiyoshi, and a girl, Suzuko; and his books about Japan were appearing at the rate of about one each year. Hearn left Tokyo Imperial University, accepting an offer to lecture on English literature at Waseda University, also in Tokyo. He lectured briefly in the spring of 1904 and anticipated the next term. But he succumbed to a heart attack on 26 September at home.

BIBLIOGRAPHY:

A. *The Writings of Lafcadio Hearn,* 16 vols. (Boston, 1922).

B. DAB 8, 484–487; NYT 29 September 1904; Jon Christopher Hughes, *The Tanyard Murder: On the Case with Lafcadio Hearn* (Washington, D.C., 1982); Arthur E. Kunst, *Lafcadio Hearn* (New York, 1969); Kathleen M. Webb, *Lafcadio Hearn and His German Critics* (New York, 1984).

WHITNEY R. MUNDT

HEARST, WILLIAM RANDOLPH (b. 29 April 1863; d. 14 August 1951) was a towering presence, both physically and figuratively, on the landscape of American journalism for more than a half century. A man of tremendous ambition and ego to match, he not only aspired to be the greatest newspaper publisher in the United States, but to be the nation's president. The journalism Hearst's newspapers practiced was simple, straight-ahead sensationalism, but the man behind the journalism remains a complex and enigmatic person to this day.

Hearst remains a problematic figure in the history of American journalism because his name is often associated with what the profession considers its lowest form, "yellow journalism." Yet it is Hearst, whose media empire included not only dozens of daily and Sunday newspapers, but magazines, radio, television, and motion picture industry holdings along with nonmedia holdings in mines, ranches, and real estate, who was a prototype of the modern-day media capitalist and entrepreneur. But unlike most of his rivals in the news business, Hearst was born into wealth. He was the only son of George and Phoebe Apperson Hearst of San Francisco. His father struck it rich with investments in copper and silver mines and land speculation. George Hearst married when he was forty: Phoebe Hearst was twenty-two years his junior. George's political ambitions carried him to the California legislature and to national recognition as a U.S. senator. With his father absent much of the time, William was raised by his mother and her female friends. Biographers have seen this as a very significant influence in Hearst's development and personality as an adult.

The first time Hearst was separated from his mother was when he journeyed East in 1882 to enter Harvard University. He was expelled after his junior year for various pranks, including delivering chamber pots to his professors with their names etched inside, and a general indifference toward his studies. However, he was a smashing success as the business manager of the *Harvard Lampoon,* a financial drain that he turned into a profit-maker.

During what would have been his senior year, he ventured to New York and became a reporter for Joseph Pulitzer's (q.v.) *New York World* and studied Pulitzer's circulation-building techniques firsthand. He also admired and studied the sensationalism of Charles H. Taylor's *Boston Globe*. In 1887 he returned to San Francisco to take over the *Examiner,* a dull, lifeless newspaper his father had purchased in 1880 to boost his political career. While losing $300,000 in his first year, Hearst began to boost circulation and infuse life into the *Examiner*. He brought the best talent money could buy, regardless of cost, and took up crusades against big money and corrupt politics. A special target of his was the Southern Pacific Railroad.

Within a few years, Hearst was the Pulitzer of the West Coast, but he was not satisfied with that. He wanted to beat Pulitzer at his own game, so in 1895 he entered the New York market by purchasing the *Journal,* ironically, a paper originally owned by Pulitzer's brother Albert. The circulation battle, a free-wheeling, no-holds-barred, alley fight, between the *Journal* and the *World* created the style of journalism coined ''yellow journalism.'' As if planned, the Spanish-American War arrived on the scene in 1898 to fuel the battle between the two newspapers. Circulations topped one million for the first time in American history and journalism entered into a new era.

Soon after the war, Pulitzer, whose financial resources were outstripped by Hearst's, withdrew from the war and pushed his *World* into the respectable realm of journalism occupied by papers such as the *New York Times*. Hearst continued to dominate the market for sensational news and began to turn his interests actively toward politics. His political ambitions repeatedly were thwarted. Hearst aligned himself with the Democratic party; however, he did organize an independent party when he could not secure Democratic support. He sought the governorship of New York on several occasions, but the closest he came was 1906 when he lost to Charles Evans Hughes by 58,000 votes. Hearst was the only Democrat on the ticket to lose. At the 1904 Democratic National Convention, Hearst received 263 votes for nomination as presidential candidate, but he never came closer than that to the White House. He was elected to two terms in Congress as a Democrat (1903–1907). It was his only political success. His loss in the New York mayoral election in 1909 ended his political career as an office seeker, but he remained a political force in the country for most of his remaining life.

Hearst's political clout came from his newspaper and magazine holdings. He owned at least one newspaper, and sometimes two or three, in major cities such as New York, Chicago, Washington, D.C., Los Angeles, Boston, San Francisco, Baltimore, Seattle, Syracuse, Milwaukee, Fort Worth, Rochester, Omaha, Pittsburgh, and Detroit. He also owned popular magazines such as *Cosmopolitan, Good Housekeeping, Harper's Bazaar*, and the Sunday supplement, *American Weekly*. To this he added the International News Service, King Features, newsreel and motion picture companies, and broadcasting properties. Until the empire began to crumble during the Great Depression, there was scarcely an American city of any size that was beyond the reach of Hearst's media empire. In national Democratic politics, Hearst controlled the California delegation for many years and is credited with breaking the deadlock at the 1932 Democratic National

Convention by releasing the California delegation's votes to Franklin Roosevelt in order to stop his old political enemy, Alfred Smith, from gaining the nomination. However, Hearst would become a bitter critic of the New Deal in the 1930s.

At one time, Hearst's fortune had assets totaling between $200 million and $400 million. He owned one of the world's greatest private art and antique collections, as well as several castles, including the majestic San Simeon in California, overlooking the Pacific. At San Simeon he lived out a storybook romance with actress Marion Davies. Their relationship lasted more than three decades, but they were never married. Hearst was married to Millicent Willson, a Broadway dancer, on 28 April 1903. The marriage produced five sons: George Randolph, William Randolph Jr., John Randolph, Elbert Willson, and Randolph Apperson. Hearst's wife would never agree to a divorce; they remained married. Hearst lived with Davies; Millicent lived with her sons.

After World War II, Hearst's health declined and he was forced to leave San Simeon for a smaller home in Beverly Hills. He had a serious heart condition and became an invalid. He died in his home in Beverly Hills.

BIBLIOGRAPHY:

B. DLB 25, 98–116; W. A. Swanberg, *Citizen Hearst* (New York, 1961).

JOSEPH P. MCKERNS

HEATTER, GABRIEL (b. 1890; d. 30 March 1972) was a prominent network radio commentator known for the emotional and optimistic tone of his news broadcasts. His radio career spanned the depression, World War II, the Korean conflict, and the cold war era. He also engaged in newsreel commentary, newspaper reporting, and speech writing.

Heatter was born in New York City's Lower East Side, one of five children of Henry and Anna Heatter, Jewish immigrants from Austria. When he was four, the family moved to Brooklyn. His parents provided a warm, loving home environment and encouraged their children to study hard to escape the ghetto. As a child, Gabriel suffered from anxiety and depression, a condition that plagued him periodically throughout his life. He attended public school in Brooklyn, where he played ball and participated in school debates and literary clubs. At age fifteen, he worked as a Brooklyn stringer and messenger for William Randolph Hearst's (q.v.) *New York American*. As a youth, his voice was rich and strong. When Hearst ran for mayor in 1906, Heatter was hired as a "boy orator" to precede the candidate's platform speeches. This association with Hearst prompted Heatter's desire to become a newspaper reporter. He held a series of part-time jobs on the *East New York Record* and the *American* before joining the *Brooklyn Times* as a full-time reporter in 1909. Heatter attended New York University Law School, but his law ambitions were soon eclipsed by the thrill of getting a newspaper scoop.

From 1910 to 1915 Heatter continued his newspaper work in New York. From the *Brooklyn Times* he went to Hearst's *New York Journal*, where he covered crime and the city's slums and won a major journalistic award for his article "Children of the Crucible." Next, he and two other young journalists attempted to establish their own newspaper. However, the *Weekly Reporter* lasted only seven issues. After the paper's failure, Heatter returned briefly to the *Journal* and then moved to the *New York Hearld,* working as its political correspondent in Albany.

In 1915, at age twenty-five, Heatter married Saidie Hermalin, the daughter of David Hermalin, editor of the Yiddish daily *Der Tag* (The Day). Saidie, a former schoolteacher, provided the strong emotional support Gabriel needed. They had two children—a daughter, Maida, and a son, Basil. Soon after their marriage, the Heatters moved to France, where he worked as Paris representative for the Foreign Language Publishers' Association. In 1920 Heatter held a temporary publicity job in the Warren Harding (q.v.) presidential campaign; he often did ghostwriting for prominent Americans. After the campaign, Heatter wrote for *Forest and Stream* magazine. His next job was editor of the *Shaft*, a steel industry trade magazine. Despite his own anxieties, Heatter developed a writing style that inspired others, giving his readers hope and cheer. As a result, Heatter often traveled for the magazine, making what today are called "motivational speeches" to steel executives. It was this optimistic style in his writing and speeches that latter endeared him to his radio listeners.

In 1932 Heatter engaged in a series of debate-type articles for the *Nation,* taking issue with Norman Thomas on the subject of socialism. This series led to his first radio job in 1932 as a commentator for WMCA, New York. In 1933 he moved to WOR, New York, one of the founding stations of the Mutual Broadcasting System (MBS), where he did a fifteen-minute nightly newscast. In 1935 MBS sent Heatter to New Jersey to cover the Bruno Hauptmann trial for the kidnapping of the Lindbergh baby. This series of broadcasts won enormous public acclaim for Heatter. The high point of his career came the following year when he spoke for almost an hour on Mutual without notes or script while awaiting Hauptmann's electrocution.

Heatter continued his nightly commentaries on MBS until 1965. His radio style was unique—a blend of a choice story, very simple language, and a soothing vocal style. He traditionally opened each newscast with the phrase, "Ah—there's good news tonight!" Even during the darkest hours of World War II, he spoke optimistically that things would get better, bringing hope to millions of listeners. In part, Heatter achieved his tone of optimism through careful selection of stories related to hope and heroism, sprinkled among the serious news items. Although he avoided any slant on domestic politics, Heatter expressed staunch anti-Nazi, anti-Communist, and anti-Fascist sentiments. He advocated improved social security benefits and better wages for civil servants. Heatter appealed to all demographic groups, but especially to the elderly and people of low and moderate income.

In addition to his news commentaries, Heatter was in great demand to voice his own commercials. He also hosted a human interest interview show, "We, the People,'' on CBS for several years. In 1951 the Heatters moved to Miami Beach, where he continued to do his nightly radio broadcasts on MBS until 1965. He also did local TV work in Miami for a while and wrote a newspaper column six days a week for the *Miami Beach Sun* until 1968. Saidie Heatter, the newsman's wife of fifty-one years, died in 1966. Heatter suffered a stroke in 1968 that paralyzed his right side, forcing his retirement. He died in Miami Beach in 1972 at age eighty-two.

BIBLIOGRAPHY:

A. *There's Good News Tonight* (Garden City, N.Y., 1960).

B. NYT 31 March 1972; Irving E. Fang, ''Gabriel Heatter,'' *Those Radio Commentators!* (Ames, Iowa, 1977).

HERBERT H. HOWARD

HECHT, BEN (b. 28 February 1894; d. 18 April 1964), a master of the human interest story, a newspaper columnist, novelist, and screenwriter, was a pivotal figure in the Chicago Literary Renaissance whose prolific forty-year filmwriting career began during the Golden Age of Hollywood. His play, *The Front Page* (1928), coauthored with ex-reporter Charles MacArthur (q.v.) and later adapted into a film, portrayed the absurdly raucous world of Chicago-style journalism. A classic of the newspaper film genre, *The Front Page* continues to be one of the most comical stereotypes of the reporter as prankster and literary rogue in the popular culture of pre–World War II journalism.

Hecht was born in New York City, the son of Joseph and Sarah Swernofsky Hecht, Jewish peasants who emigrated from Russia in the 1890s. Joseph Hecht, a tailor, moved his family to Racine, Wisconsin, where he set up a small clothing factory. Hecht graduated from Racine High School in 1910, but his formal education ended after three days at the University of Wisconsin.

In 1910 Hecht joined the *Chicago Journal* as a $12.50-a-week ''picture chaser'' assigned to find photographs of criminals for use in the newspaper. By his own admission, Hecht's first stories were sometimes admixtures of fact and fiction. His success led to a higher-paying job at the *Chicago Daily News* in 1914, then under the editorship of Henry Justin Smith (q.v.). Before leaving the *Daily News* in 1923, Hecht had been a reporter, a foreign correspondent in Germany, and a widely acclaimed columnist. He began column writing in June 1921, a few months before the publication of his first novel, *Erik Dorn* (1921), a Kafkaesque portrayal of a cynical journalist. His *Daily News* columns, collected and published as *1001 Afternoons in Chicago* (1922), won Hecht a national reputation as an imaginative literary stylist and the finest human interest story writer in America.

Hecht's iconoclasm and literary assaults against conventional American morality prompted criticism and legal action. The federal government charged Hecht with obscenity for his novel *Fantazius Mallare* (1922). Unsuccessfully defended by attorney Clarence Darrow, Hecht and Wallace Smith, who illustrated the novel, were each fined $1,000 for sending obscene material through the mails. A year later, Hecht left the *Daily News* to devote himself full-time to a promising literary career.

With poet Maxwell Bodenheim as his assistant editor, Hecht founded the *Chicago Literary Times* in 1923. The tabloid, financed by bookseller-publisher, Pascal Covici, was a breezy literary version of 1920s-style jazz journalism complete with streamers and scareheads. Hecht's editorial policy for the *Chicago Literary Times* was blunt and simple: "attack everything." Although the tabloid's strident irreverence and inconoclasm gained some literary notoriety, the paper folded in June 1924. A year later, Hecht left Chicago.

In Chicago, Hecht married his first wife, Marie Armstrong, on 30 November 1915. They had a daughter, Edwina, but the marriage ended in divorce nine years later. Hecht married Rose Caylor in Miami, Florida, on 26 March 1925, and they had a daughter, Jenny. Hecht's divorce and remarriage, along with his move from Chicago to New York, was a turning point in his career. He left Chicago in 1925 and embarked on a prolific and successful stage and filmwriting career in New York City and in Hollywood.

With Charles MacArthur, Hecht wrote *The Front Page,* which was staged by George S. Kaufman at the Times Square Theater in New York City on 14 August 1928. The critically acclaimed production enjoyed a successful run on Broadway, made celebrities of its authors, and was adapted into a movie in 1931. Another Hecht-MacArthur collaboration, *Twentieth Century* (1932), became a Broadway hit and movie. A friend sent a telegram from Hollywood inviting Hecht to write scripts for the burgeoning film industry. Hecht accepted the lucrative offer, joining other writers in the Hollywood "gold rush" of the 1920s.

Hecht met with instant success in Hollywood, winning an Oscar for best original story for the film *Underworld (1927),* and another for *The Scoundrel* (1935), coauthored with MacArthur. During his forty-year filmwriting career, Hecht received credits for about seventy films (stories or screenplays), although he contributed to many other films for which he received no credit. He often worked on several scripts simultaneously, earning as much as $125,000 for a script.

In 1940 Hecht joined the newspaper *PM* in New York as a columnist, writing sketches about urban life and about the Nazi extermination of Jews in Europe. His columns were published as *1001 Afternoons in New York* (1941). He returned to Hollywood in 1941, ending his career as a newspaper journalist. His outspoken support of Jewish resistance movements in Palestine in the late 1940s led to a boycott of his films by British exhibitors, and for five years his film credits were removed from movies shown in England.

During the 1950s and 1960s he wrote his autobiography and other reminiscences of his film and newspaper careers while continuing to produce screenplays. Hecht died of an apparent heart attack while working on a filmscript in his New York City apartment at age seventy.

BIBLIOGRAPHY:

B. DAB Supp. 7, 331–332; DLB 25, 116–124; NYT 19 April 1964; *Chicago Daily News,* 18 April 1964; Doug Fetherling, *The Five Lives of Ben Hecht* (Toronto, 1977).

ARTHUR J. KAUL

HEISKELL, JOHN NETHERLAND (b. 2 November 1872; d. 28 December 1972) was editor of the *Arkansas Gazette* at Little Rock for seventy years beginning in 1902, president from 1902 to 1970, and then board chairman. His was an editorial voice of reason and good manners that made the *Gazette* a moderating influence on an often unruly and sometimes violent state. Heiskell approved the course that brought two Pulitzer Prizes, for editorial writing and meritorious public service, to *Gazette* staff members during the 1957 desegregation crisis at Little Rock.

Heiskell was born in Rogersville, Tennessee, in the home of his maternal grandfather, John Netherland, a prominent lawyer. He grew up in Memphis, to which his father, Carrick White Heiskell, a lawyer and former Confederate officer, and his mother, Eliza Ayre Netherland Heiskell, migrated shortly after the Civil War. Heiskell attended private and public schools at Memphis and graduated from the University of Tennessee in 1893 with an A.B. degree.

Heiskell's newspaper career began on the *Knoxville Tribune* and *Knoxville Journal* and blossomed on the *Memphis Commercial Appeal* as a reporter assigned to local news. In May 1889 he joined the Associated Press in Chicago, and after a year was transferred to Louisville, Kentucky, as correspondent. (He was a vice president of the AP in 1926–27.) Early in 1902, Heiskell and his parents invested in the *Gazette* (founded 1819). In June of that year, Heiskell became its editor.

He battled the power-hungry and demagogic Jeff Davis, the state's leading political figure, and wrote a detailed analysis of Davis's political style, which appeared as a long (seven and one-half columns) editorial on 1 April 1906 and is considered one of the best contemporary commentaries on Davis. After the death of Davis, then a U.S. senator, on 3 January 1913, Heiskell was appointed senator for twenty-two days. In a Senate speech, Heiskell pleaded for tolerance of the southern ''redneck'' and ''hillbilly,'' then objects of popular scorn.

As editor, Heiskell supported many of the political and economic reforms of the Progressive movement. Though he did not challenge the status quo of segregation, he condemned race-baiting and lynching. During World War I, Heiskell joined enthusiastically in the movement to ''rally 'round the flag'' but opposed the more extreme forms of superpatriotism such as the banning of German as a language taught in public high schools. To help make Little Rock more attractive he campaigned for city planning and establishment of a public library and subsequently served as Planning Commission chairman and president of the library board. In the 1920s he joined in the opposition to an effort to ban the teaching of evolution in state-supported schools, and in 1935 he opposed a state antisedition bill as a threat to individual rights. Under Heiskell, the *Gazette* consistently supported Democratic candidates and remained neutral in party primaries. In general, his editorials were constructive; he argued issues and eschewed personal attacks.

Heiskell married Wilhelmina Mann on 28 June 1910, and she bore him four children. A son, Carrick W. Heiskell, was groomed as his father's successor but was killed in World War II. In 1947 Heiskell brought Harry S. Ashmore to the *Gazette* and eventually turned over to him most responsibilities for news and editorial content.

However, Heiskell continued to be consulted on editorials, and he claimed to have read and approved virtually every one published during the 1957 crisis at Central High School, during which Governor Orval E. Faubus called out the National Guard to block court-ordered integration. Because of the *Gazette*'s call for obedience to the courts, it suffered a boycott that reduced circulation from 100,000 to 83,000 and caused some small advertisers to withdraw support.

Heiskell died 28 December 1972 at age 100 as a result of congestive heart failure. At the time of his death, he was said to be the oldest active newspaper editor in the United States. His widow died 23 March 1979.

BIBLIOGRAPHY:

B. NCAB 53, 627; NYT 29 December 1972; *Arkansas Gazette,* 29 December 1972; Wesley Pruden, ''Mr. J.N. and a Legend at the *Gazette,*'' *National Observer,* 28 September 1964; John A. Thompson, ''Gentleman Editor: Mr. Heiskell of the *Gazette:* The Early Years, 1902–1922,'' M.A. thesis, Univ. of Arkansas–Little Rock, 1982.

JOHN A. THOMPSON

HELLINGER, MARK (b. 21 March 1903; d. 21 December 1947) was, according to his biographer, Jim Bishop, ''The first of the Broadway reporters.'' Unlike fellow Great White Way columnists Walter Winchell (q.v.), Mark Sullivan, Earl Wilson (q.v.), and others, Hellinger's forte was not gossip, but rather storytelling and character sketches based sometimes on real, sometimes on composite, events and personages. He was himself a major figure on that half-make-believe, half-real ''Broadway Scene''—the reporting of which, together with lurid crime, comprised the volatile chemistry which fueled the New York City tabloids of the 1920s and 1930s and which, through column syndication, was followed in virtually every daily throughout North America.

Hellinger's career divided into two parts: as Broadway chronicler from 1921 to 1937; and as full-time Hollywood motion picture producer and part-time journalist—he continued to write a widely distributed Sunday column—until his death in 1947 from a heart attack.

Mark Hellinger was born into a comfortably upper-middle-class, New York City, Orthodox Jewish family, the son of Paul Hellinger and Millie Rinaldo Hellinger. His father hoped that his eldest son would follow him into the practice of law; but a precocious writing talent and an equal disinterest in academics led to the boy's dropping out of both a public and a private high school and onto, in 1921, the editorial staff of *Zit's Weekly*, a struggling show business periodical where he served an apprenticeship as journalistic jack-of-all-trades.

A campaign Hellinger orchestrated to bring himself to the attention of Philip Payne, managing editor of the spectacularly successful, pioneering New York City tabloid, the *Daily News*, resulted, in 1923, in an offer from Payne for Hellinger to work on the *News*. By 1925 Hellinger was writing a Sunday column, heavy with personality sketches; in 1928 a daily version was added. While Hellinger's columns enjoyed wide readership and popularity, *Daily News* editor and publisher Joseph Patterson (q.v.) was never happy with them. Patterson wanted a Broadway column with the kind of gossip which Walter Winchell was offering to readers of the *News*'s afternoon, tabloid competitor, the *Evening Graphic*. When Patterson, in late 1929, ordered Hellinger to stop the sketches, and to limit himself to short items of gossip, Hellinger left the *News* to join its other tabloid competitor, the Hearst-owned morning *Daily Mirror*. Here he remained, continuing to write daily and Sunday columns (both receiving wide syndication through Hearst's King Features) until he left for Hollywood in 1937.

As a Hollywood producer, Hellinger made films for Warners, Twentieth Century-Fox, again for Warners, and finally for Universal–which he left to set up his own independent production company in conjunction with United Artists, the very week of his death. He is best known in Hollywood for such realistic movies as *The Killers, Brute Force,* and *Naked City*—films characterized by the hard-nosed reality Hellinger supposedly came to know while working the Broadway beat.

Hellinger's significance, if any, would seem to rest mainly with his pioneering of contemporary American movie realism, rather than in any journalistic endeavors. Indeed, much of his newspaper reputation seems more a function of the wide personal popularity he enjoyed among his nightclubbing newspaper, sports, and entertainment colleagues than the result of any solid writing or reporting achievements. (He was, for example, one of the few close associates of Walter Winchell never to find himself on the mercurial Winchell's "Drop Dead" list. Winchell, in his autobiography, *Exclusively Yours*, refers to Hellinger at various times as "my best pal" and "my only real pal.")

Hellinger twice married Ziegfeld show-girl Gladys Hand, first on 11 July 1929, and then, after a brief divorce, again on 11 July 1933. They were the adoptive parents of a boy and a girl. Two compilations of Hellinger's columns have been published. A legitimate Broadway theater is named after him.

BIBLIOGRAPHY:

A. *Moon Over Broadway* (New York, 1932); *The Ten Million* (New York, 1934).

B. NYT 22 December 1947; James Bishop, *The Mark Hellinger Story* (New York, 1952).

DAVE BERKMAN

HEMINGWAY, ERNEST MILLER (b. 21 July 1899; d. 2 July 1961), one of the major fiction writers of his time, was an active journalist throughout his adult life. He distinguished himself with sports and war reporting as well as with his world-famous novels and short stories.

The son of Clarence Edmonds Hemingway, a physician, and Grace Hall Hemingway, a music teacher, Hemingway was born in Oak Park, Illinois, and grew up there, an outgoing, active youth. The family spent summers in northern Michigan, and young Ernest's experiences of hunting and fishing there were formative. At the Oak Park High School, his activities prefigured the three major aspects of his adult life of action and writing: he played sports wholeheartedly, he reported on sports for the student newspaper, and he wrote fiction for the literary magazine.

After graduation, he got his initiation into professional writing on the *Kansas City Star*, covering hospitals and police and other spot news, and following the paper's stylebook injunction: "Use short sentences. Use short first paragraphs. Use vigorous English." After six months on the *Star*, Hemingway joined the American Red Cross ambulance service, went to Italy, was badly wounded, and spent several months recuperating in hospitals. This experience formed the basis for several short stories and for one of his best novels, *A Farewell to Arms* (1929).

Back in the United States in 1919, Hemingway worked on his fiction and poetry, and became a part-time feature writer for the *Toronto Star*. In the fall of 1921, accompanied by his bride, Elizabeth Hadley Richardson, he set off for Paris to work at space rates as a foreign correspondent for the Toronto paper. His dispatches read today as exceptionally vivid, and some of them, in their use of dramatic techniques, anticipate the New Journalism of the 1970s. He often used them as a basis for his short stories. One of the best examples of this relationship is his transformation of three fairly short journalistic paragraphs describing the Greek evacuation from Thrace in the Greco-Turkish War. Hemingway trimmed this cable into a single, indelible paragraph and used it for one of the episodes of *In Our Time* (1925), his first major book of short stories.

The Sun Also Rises (1926) established Hemingway's reputation as a major new force in American literature, and as one of the spokesmen for the "lost generation," a phase he borrowed from Gertrude Stein for use in the novel. Hemingway and Elizabeth Hadley Richardson were divorced in early 1927, and shortly thereafter he married Pauline Pfeiffer, another American woman, whom he had met in Europe. After residence in Switzerland and Italy, the Hemingways moved to Key West, Florida, and made it their headquarters, though they continued to travel frequently.

In 1933 Hemingway began a series of articles for *Esquire*, writing on hunting in Africa, fishing in the Gulf Stream, and on war, revolution, and politics. In 1937 he went to Spain to report the civil war there for the North American Newspaper Alliance. Articles like "The Fall of Tereul" are classics of brilliant scenes and the laconic irony that was Hemingway's trademark as a journalist.

While in Spain Hemingway had become increasingly close to the journalist Martha Gellhorn, and this relationship ended in the dissolution of his marriage to Pauline Pfeiffer. In 1940, *For Whom the Bell Tolls*, based on his experiences in the Spanish civil war, was published and widely acclaimed as one of his best works. Hemingway and Gellhorn were married the same year.

In World War II, Hemingway was a correspondent in China, covering the Sino-Japanese fighting for the newspaper *PM*. After a lengthy period of antisubmarine patrolling in the Caribbean, using his refitted yacht the *Pilar,* Hemingway agreed to go to Europe as a war correspondent for *Collier's*. After the June 1944 invasion of Normandy, he acted both as a reporter and leader of an informal combat group of Free French volunteers. He was one of the first Americans in liberated Paris.

Once again, a marriage broke up during wartime as he became friendly with another woman journalist, Mary Welsh, while his wife was elsewhere. Divorced from Martha Gellhorn at the end of 1945, he married ''Miss Mary'' a few months later. They made their principal home in Cuba thereafter. Hemingway's greatest postwar achievement was *The Old Man and the Sea* (1952), a symbolic tale based on a story he had heard about a fisherman's encounter with a huge marlin. In 1954, two years after the publication of this short novel, Hemingway was awarded the Nobel Prize.

One of the writer's last journalistic achievements was his 1959 coverage of a bullfighting rivalry in Spain for *Life* magazine. His physical health and mental stability were deteriorating drastically, however, and this story, ''The Dangerous Summer,'' was one of his last efforts. In a hunting lodge in Ketchum, Idaho, in July 1961, Hemingway took his own life with a shotgun blast to the head.

BIBLIOGRAPHY:

A. *By-Line, Ernest Hemingway,* ed. William White (New York, 1967); *Ernest Hemingway, Cub Reporter,* ed. Matthew Bruccoli (Pittsburgh, 1970).

B. DAB Supp. 7, 333–339; NYT 3 July 1961; Carlos Baker, *Ernest Hemingway* (New York, 1969); Charles Fenton, *The Apprenticeship of Ernest Hemingway* (New York, 1954); Andre Hanneman, *Ernest Hemingway: A Comprehensive Bibliography* (Princeton, N.J., 1967).

EDWARD A. NICKERSON

HERRICK, GENEVIEVE FORBES (b. 21 May 1894; d. 17 December 1962) was one of the best-known front-page women reporters in the 1920s and 1930s. Her articles on local and national politics, crime, education, visiting royalty, and celebrities, as well as a variety of emerging social problems and life-styles, appeared regularly in the *Chicago Tribune*. Later she wrote for several national magazines. She also worked in a number of capacities for the federal government, particularly through the war years.

Herrick, one of three children, was born in Chicago, Illinois. Her mother was Carolyn D. Gee Forbes; her father, Frank G. Forbes, was a salesman who eventually became president of a tailoring company on Chicago's west side. Herrick attended Chicago schools, graduating in 1916 from Northwestern University, where she was the first woman editor in chief of the school's daily newspaper. A year later she received her master's degree in English from the University of Chicago.

After teaching high school English in Waterloo, Illinois, for one year, Herrick came to the *Chicago Tribune* in 1918 as assistant to the exchange editor; in 1920 she was made assistant literary editor. In October 1921 she made her reputation as a front-page reporter with a thirteen-part exposé of the U.S. immigration service. She had gone to Ireland and then returned, steerage class, posing as an immigrant. Her articles and testimony provided the basis for a congressional investigation of Ellis Island.

At the *Tribune* Herrick became best known for her crisp, jazzy articles about crimes and criminals. She was the first to get an interview with Al Capone after his release in 1930 from a Philadelphia prison; she also interviewed wives of notorious Chicago mobsters. She met her husband, John Origen Herrick, another *Tribune* writer and the son of a prominent Chicago doctor, while they were both covering the Leopold-Loeb trial in 1924. The Herricks occasionally worked together; in 1925 they quickly put together a rather shallow biography of William Jennings Bryan. They had no children.

Although she continued to write on a wide variety of subjects, once she became a Washington correspondent for the *Tribune,* Herrick's specialty became politics, especially women candidates and officeholders and other aspects of "the women's angle." But she also published straightforward discussions of congressional activities, as well as more lighthearted, mocking assessments of the intersection of society and politics.

Herrick was an enthusiastic regular at the women-only press conferences of Eleanor Roosevelt, and her articles reveal admiration for the New Deal. This approach was unpopular with the *Tribune*'s vehemently anti-Roosevelt publisher. Herrick resigned from the *Tribune* and from her radio show on *Tribune*-owned WGN in 1934 after Colonel Robert McCormick (q.v.) criticized her.

After leaving the *Tribune* Herrick briefly wrote for its sister paper the *New York Daily News,* and for the North American Newspaper Alliance. Her articles, usually about politics or the Washington scene, appeared in many magazines, including *Collier's,* the *Independent Woman,* and *Redbook.* Between 1935 and 1942 she had a regular column, "Women in the News," in *Country Gentleman*.

During World War II she did public relations work for the Treasury and War departments. She was a writer for the news division and then assistant chief and ultimately chief of the magazine and book division of the Office of War Information. In 1946 she toured Women's Army Corps facilities in Europe, an experience she turned into several speeches and articles.

In 1951 the Herricks moved to New Mexico, where John worked for a newspaper chain. Herrick did publicity for a number of organizations, and wrote for local papers. Because of both increasingly serious ill health and complications resulting from a 1935 automobile accident, she did little significant writing, especially after John's death in 1955. Genevieve Herrick died of cancer in Sante Fe in 1962.

BIBLIOGRAPHY:

B. *Chicago Tribune,* 18 December 1962; Ishbel Ross, *Ladies of the Press* (New York, 1936); Linda Steiner, ''Genevieve Forbes Herrick: A *Chicago Tribune* Reporter Covers Women in Politics,'' unpublished paper, 1984.

LINDA STEINER

HIBBS, BENJAMIN SMITH (b. 23 July 1901; d. 30 March 1975) was editor of the *Saturday Evening Post* from March 1942 to January 1962. The magazine had fallen on hard times and was in deep trouble with its readers and advertisers when Hibbs assumed the *Post* editorship. He masterminded a remarkable turnaround and provided unique leadership for twenty years to a magazine that was the essence of American values. Under Hibbs's editorship, the *Post* reached unprecedented circulation, carrying advertising to all-time highs. It is estimated that the magazine in Hibbs's time earned profits in excess of $100 million.

Hibbs, second of three children, was born in Fontana, a tiny village in eastern Kansas. His family moved shortly after his birth to Pretty Prairie, a town of about 500 persons on the high plains some fifty miles west of Wichita. It was there he spent his boyhood years. His father, Russell Hibbs, was an accountant for a lumber business. His mother, Elizabeth Belle Smith Hibbs, had been a mathematics teacher in a boys academy in Fayette, Missouri.

After high school, Ben Hibbs studied journalism at the University of Kansas. Upon earning his bachelor's degree in February 1924, Hibbs took a job as a reporter with the *Pratt Daily Tribune* in Kansas. In the summer of 1924, he accepted a teaching position at Fort Hays State College and taught there until June 1926. For a year after that he worked as a reporter on the *Goodland News Republic* before being named managing editor of the *Traveler,* a newspaper in Arkansas City, Kansas. His column writing while he was working on the *Traveler* brought him to the attention of William Allen White (q.v.) of the *Emporia Gazette*. Hibbs's columns and editorials were reprinted in White's *Gazette,* the *Kansas City Star,* and in many other papers throughout Kansas.

In 1929 Hibbs left Kansas to become a reporter for the *Country Gentleman,* a Curtis Publishing Company magazine. Hibbs left Kansas for Philadelphia with a rousing send-off. Newspapers from around the state, while ballyhooing his appointment to the *Country Gentleman* staff, lamented his leaving Kansas. William Allen White wrote: ''Philadelphia is taking from us the white-headed boy of Kansas journalism.'' Hibbs became fiction editor and then managing editor of the *Country Gentleman* before being named editor of the magazine in 1940. He remained in that position until he became editor of the *Saturday Evening Post* in 1942.

On 3 June 1930 Ben Hibbs married Edith Doty, a Kansas schoolteacher. They had one child, Stephen Doty, born in 1935.

The *Saturday Evening Post* that Hibbs became editor of in 1942 was a magazine with a glorious past. Hibbs introduced changes in the magazine that brought the publication new successes. He discarded most of the antiquated typefaces, dressed up the layouts, and emphasized nonfiction articles that stressed personalities and human interest features. In Hibbs's new *Post,* there were more stories and articles, and they were shorter. Unlike his predecessors, Hibbs gave favored treatment to nonfiction. He made changes which went beyond the physical aspects of the *Post,* announcing new policies which shaped a more modern editorial formula. George H. Lorimer (q.v.) and Wesley W. Stout had ignored Europe's war, but Hibbs set about to hire a corps of foreign correspondents for the *Post*. He asked the inimitable Marty Sommers to assist him on this task. Sommers and his staff performed brilliantly during World War II, providing readers with account after account of America's involvement in the war. These war pieces, along with Norman Rockwell's memorable covers—the Willie Gillis series and the Four Freedoms—gave the *Post* the character that brought it millions of loyal readers. During Hibbs's editorship, the magazine reached the extraordinary circulation of seven million copies a week.

Hibbs's last months at the *Post* were not happy ones. He was persuaded that the *Post* was in need of a different look. So, in the spring of 1961, Kenneth Stuart, art editor; Robert Fuoss, executive editor; and staff member Clay Blair, Jr., began planning a new *Post*. One million dollars was budgeted to promote it. The "new" *Post* hit the newstands on 16 September 1961 with a thud. Thousands of readers disapproved, as did Madison Avenue advertising executives. Hibbs wanted to retire before the new magazine came out, but he was persuaded by Curtis executives to stay on. He said later that he should have followed his first instincts.

After his retirement from the *Post,* Hibbs served for a time as senior editor to the magazine, but in time it became the kind of magazine he felt he could not serve, so he resigned in 1963 and accepted a similar position with *Reader's Digest*. There he became former President Dwight D. Eisenhower's editor, and the two became close personal friends.

At the end of 1971, Ben Hibbs submitted his resignation to *Reader's Digest* and ended his career as an active journalist. Shortly after Christmas in 1974, Hibbs entered the hospital where he was treated for leukemia. After a short hospital stay he returned to his home in Narberth, Pennsylvania, and died there.

BIBLIOGRAPHY:

B. NYT 31 March 1975; *Time,* 14 April 1975; Otto Friedrich, *Decline and Fall* (New York, 1970); Deryl R. Leaming, "A Biography of Ben Hibbs," Ph.D. diss., Syracuse Univ. 1969; B. R. Manago, "*The Saturday Evening Post* Under Ben Hibbs, 1942–1961," Ph.D. diss., Northwestern Univ., 1968.

DERYL R. LEAMING

HICKOK, LORENA A. (b. 7 March 1893; d. 1 May 1968) was a leading woman journalist of the early 1930s who left her job with the Associated Press to work as a confidential investigator of relief programs for the Roosevelt administration. A close friend of Eleanor Roosevelt, Hickok also made an impact on journalism by advising Mrs. Roosevelt to hold press conferences in the White House limited to women reporters only.

Poverty and unhappiness marked Hickok's childhood. The oldest of three daughters, she was born in East Troy, Wisconsin, to Anna W. and Addison J. Hickok. An unstable, violent individual, the father, a buttermaker, lost one job after another and abused his family while moving throughout the upper Middle West in search of employment. The mother, who had been a dressmaker before she ran away to be married, died in Bowdle, South Dakota, when Lorena was thirteen. The next year Hickok was forced to leave home to earn her own living as a "hired girl." After living with nine different families in the next two years, she went to live with her mother's cousin, Ella C. Ellis, in Battle Creek, Michigan, where she finished high school.

Hickok started her newspaper career on the *Battle Creek Journal*, meeting trains and collecting "personal" items. She took the cub reporter job after flunking out of Lawrence College, Appleton, Wisconsin. After a second unsuccessful try at Lawrence, she moved on to the *Milwaukee Sentinel* where she succeeded in getting herself transferred from the society pages, the customary assignment for women of her era, to the city staff. In 1917 she switched to the *Minneapolis Tribune* where, after a brief stint in New York, she was promoted to Sunday editor and then to star reporter, covering murder trials, football, and politics. Her success, unusual for a woman, stemmed from opportunities provided by Thomas J. Dillon, the managing editor. Hickok gratefully called him "The Old Man," and credited him with teaching her about the newspaper business. While working in Minneapolis, she enrolled at the University of Minnesota, but she soon abandoned college to concentrate on her job.

In 1926 Hickok was stricken with diabetes and left Minneapolis for San Francisco to try unsuccessfully to become a writer. When her money ran out, she moved to New York in 1927. She worked briefly on the *Daily Mirror* and then shifted to the Associated Press where she was credited by Ishbell Ross in her *Ladies of the Press* (1936) with "achieving standing . . . no other woman has matched." Known as a "front-page girl," the term given women reporters who competed directly with men for sensational stories, Hickok won prize assignments such as the Lindbergh baby kidnapping case and political news.

While covering the presidential campaign of Franklin D. Roosevelt in 1932, Hickok decided Eleanor Roosevelt would make good news copy. Assigned to Mrs. Roosevelt, Hickok, who soon became a confidante, wrote news stories that introduced Mrs.Roosevelt to the American public as a "different kind of First Lady," who would not be bound by traditions that limited presidents' wives to ceremonial functions. Urging Mrs. Roosevelt to break precedent and to play a public role, Hickok advised her to publicize the New Deal through her press conferences and related activities.

After her friendship with Mrs. Roosevelt compromised her reportorial objectivity, Hickok took a job in 1933 as chief investigator for the Federal Emergency Relief Administration (FERA), making fact-finding tours through thirty-two states from 1933 to 1936. She reported her findings directly to Harry L. Hopkins, head of the FERA, and to Mrs. Roosevelt, both of whom passed on her observations to President Roosevelt.

After leaving Hopkins's agency in 1936, Hickok was a publicist for the New York World's Fair from 1937 to 1940 and executive director of the women's division of the Democratic National Committee from 1940 to 1945. Her last employment was with the New York Democratic State Committee from 1947 to 1952.

Partially blind, Hickok, who suffered from obesity, moved to Hyde Park, New York, in the 1950s to be near the Roosevelt estate there. She coauthored a book with Mrs. Roosevelt on women in politics and also wrote a biography of her as well as books for young people. Hickok never married. She died in Rhinebeck, New York, in 1968 of pneumonia following amputation of a leg.

BIBLIOGRAPHY:

A. Richard Lowitt and Maurine Beasley, eds., *One Third of a Nation: Lorena Hickok Reports on the Great Depression* (Urbana, 1981).

B. NAW 4, 338–340; NYT 3 May 1968; Maurine H. Beasley, "Life as a Hired Girl in South Dakota, 1907–1908: A Woman Journalist Reflects," *South Dakota History,* Summer/Fall 1982; Maurine H. Beasley, "Lorena A. Hickock: Journalistic Influence on Eleanor Roosevelt," *Journalism Quarterly,* Summer 1980; Doris Faber, *The Life of Lorena Hickok: E.R.'s Friend* (New York, 1980).

MAURINE H. BEASLEY

HIETT, HELEN (b. 23 September 1913; d. 22 August 1961) was one of the first female foreign correspondents to report for NBC, scoring radio scoops during the fall of France in 1940 and the bombing of Gibraltar later that year. She was the first woman to win the National Headliners Award. Hiett also organized *New York Herald Tribune* public forums for over a decade and appeared on a number of television network public affairs programs in the 1950s.

Hiett was born in Chenoa, Illinois. Her father, Asa B. Hiett, was the superintendent of schools in nearby Pekin. Her mother, Estelle Erb Hiett, was a housewife. As a high school student, Hiett became the protégée of F. F. McNaughton, the editor of the *Pekin Daily Times*. She obtained her political science degree from the University of Chicago in 1934, having graduated in three years instead of the normal four. Granted a scholarship to study the League of Nations in Geneva, Hiett left for Europe the day after college graduation.

She applied for a press pass upon arrival in Switzerland, probably so she could gather material to send back to the Pekin paper. While on scholarship, Hiett studied public opinion of the league, and when her support ended, she got a job as a secretary at the Geneva Research Center. Because of staff shortages, she found herself editing the center's newsletter. Hiett left that job in 1936 to travel to Italy, and went home to America in 1937, returning to Europe later that year to begin a Ph.D. program at the London School of Economics. When the war began in 1939, she abandoned the program and moved to France.

Hiett briefly broadcast over Paris Mondial, the French government's foreign broadcasting facility. In January 1940 Hiett and several friends started the *Paris Letter,* a compilation of letters from the front and columns designed to show Americans what the war was like. Wanting to spread the message in person, Hiett sailed in April 1940 for the United States, and began a lecture tour which ended in Rochester, New York, 10 May 1940. She had learned of the Nazi invasion of the Low Countries before speaking, and her impassioned talk before an advertising club was carried on a local radio station. Members of her audience encouraged Hiett to go to New York and seek a position in radio so that she could talk about the war as a foreign correspondent on radio.

Initial interviews at CBS and NBC were not promising, and after a week Hiett planned to return to Illinois. But NBC news director Abel A. Schechter (q.v.) decided he needed reporting help in Paris, and dispatched Hiett on a Clippership flight, with Hiett arriving 21 May 1940. She assisted Paris bureau chief Paul Archinard, learning about broadcasting as she did it. When the French government fled Paris, so did reporters for the American networks. Hiett and Archinard departed 10 June 1940, winding up in Bordeaux four days later. They continued reporting on the lone shortwave transmitter still accessible to them until the government transferred power to the Vichy group. Her final broadcast from France was on 22 June 1940. Hiett fled with some friends from the *Paris Letter* days, driving southeast and reaching Geneva on 4 July 1940.

After conferring with NBC officials in New York, Hiett went to Madrid, where she found few stories of interest to the network, and the Spanish censorship so severe that getting dispatches out was nearly impossible. She did manage to score a scoop when British Gibraltar was bombed, and her report won the National Headliners Award. In 1941 Hiett returned to America and became a daily news commentator for NBC. She left that position to become a lecturer at Stephens College in Missouri, and then in 1944 returned to Europe as a correspondent for the Religious News Service. She was in Milan two days before the U.S. Army arrived, and witnessed Mussolini's corpse hanging from a lamppost. In 1945 she accompanied 1,500 displaced persons being taken on a ship back to the Soviet Union against their will.

Immediately after the war, Hiett joined the *New York Herald Tribune,* coordinating the paper's annual forum which gathered world experts to discuss the issues of the time. She also ran one for students, and moderated a number of forums on television. Hiett married publishing executive Theodore Waller in March 1948, and thereafter was professionally known as Helen Hiett Waller. They had three children: Jonathan, Mark, and Margaret Ann. From 1958 through 1961 she hosted the CBS television series "Young Worlds" in addition to her work for the *Herald Tribune*.

Helen Hiett Waller died 22 August 1961 following a mountain-climbing accident near Chamonix, France.

BIBLIOGRAPHY:
B. NYT 23 August 1961; *New York Herald Tribune,* 23 August 1961; David H. Hosley, *As Good As Any* (Westport, Conn., 1984).

DAVID H. HOSLEY

HIGGINS, MARGUERITE (b. 3 September 1920; d. 3 January 1966), the reporter, author, and columnist, was the first and only woman to win a Pulitzer Prize in journalism for war correspondence.

Higgins, an only child, was born in Hong Kong to Irish-American Lawrence Daniel Higgins and his French war bride, Marguerite de Godard. She grew up in Oakland, California, where her father was a stockbroker, her mother a housewife. After attending a prestigious local girls school and graduating cum laude with a B.A. in French from the University of California at Berkeley in 1941, she graduated with an M.S. in journalism from the Graduate School of Journalism of Columbia University in 1942.

Her newspaper experiences began with the *Daily Californian,* the university newspaper, and a summer's employment with the *Vallejo Times Herald* that whetted her appetite for big-city reporting. Unable to find a newspaper job in New York, she enrolled in Columbia, became a stringer for the *New York Herald Tribune,* and started a career with the paper that stretched over two decades. At twenty-four, she was assigned overseas to the paper's London and Paris bureau, where she demonstrated uncommon competence and energetically pursued the news, assisted by a fluency in French. She was gifted with appealing good looks, often saying that her femininity evened the score in a time of flagrant sexism.

Her descriptions of the closing days of World War II often appeared on the front pages of the *Paris Herald* and the *New York Herald Tribune.* At twenty-five, she was named Berlin bureau chief, earning front-page bylines and numerous awards for her coverage of Dachau and Buchenwald, the capture of Munich and Berchtesgaden, the Nuremberg war trials, and the Berlin blockade.

Named Tokyo bureau chief in 1950, Higgins, with three male reporters, flew from Tokyo into Korea on word of the North Korean attack. She was the only woman correspondent in the country at the time and established herself as a credible war correspondent, despite the impediment of sexism. She became a cause célèbre when the senior U.S. military officer in Korea ordered her out because he felt the front line was no place for a woman. On appeal, General MacArthur reversed the orders, setting an unparalleled precedent and marking a dramatic breakthrough for all women war correspondents. She was fearless and asked no quarter because of dangers and combat discomforts. As a result of frontline bloodcurdling reporting, she shared the Pulitzer with five male correspondents.

She returned to the United States a celebrity, and was in great demand as a speaker. Her 1951 best-selling book, *War in Korea: The Report of a Woman War Correspondent,* was also serialized in a popular women's magazine, and by her account, she received more than fifty awards. In 1952 she married Brigadier General William E. Hall, USAF, who earlier had been head of military intelligence in Berlin (her 1942 marriage to philosophy professor Stanley Moore ended in divorce in 1948). After several years of traveling together on military assignments, the two settled in Washington, D.C. Their premature infant daughter, Sharon Lee, died five days after birth. In Washington, a son and daughter, Lawrence O'Higgins Hall (1958) and Linda Marguerite (1959), were born. Here she wrote *News Is a Singular Thing* (1955), an early autobiography, and *Red Plush and Black Bread* (1955), detailing her 13,500-mile trek through Russia.

Throughout her career she had written for periodicals, beginning in the forties with *Mademoiselle* magazine. In the fifties and sixties, many of her articles continued to appear in popular magazines such as *McCall's* and *Reader's Digest* and, later, in journals of opinion such as *America*. She also opened the *Herald-Tribune's* short-lived Moscow bureau in the mid-fifties, and wrote a juvenile book, *Jessie Benton Fremont*. For a lark, she and colleague Peter Lisagor (q.v.) collaborated on *Overtime in Heaven: Adventures in the Foreign Service* (1964).

In 1963 she left the *Herald Tribune* to write a thrice-weekly column which was syndicated to ninety papers by *Newsday*. Assigned to cover Vietnam, she was in vehement disagreement with U.S. foreign policy as implemented in Vietnam. Her study, *Our Vietnam Nightmare* (1965), outlined her analysis and objections. She was particularly critical of the U.S. involvement she perceived in the overthrow of Diem and inaccuracies in accepted descriptions of the war, the Buddhist population, and their then widely publicized self-immolations. On one of her trips to this part of the world, she contracted *leischmaniasis*, a tropical disease, and, after returning to the United States, died of complications at age forty-five.

BIBLIOGRAPHY:

B. NYT 4 January 1966; *New York Herald Tribune*, 4 January 1966; Kathleen Kearney Keeshen, "Marguerite Higgins: Journalist, 1920–1966," Ph.D. diss., Univ. of Maryland, 1983; Antoinette May, *Witness to War: A Biography of Marguerite Higgins* (New York, 1983).

KATHLEEN K. KEESHEN

HILL, EDWIN CONGER (b. 23 April 1884; d. 12 February 1957) parlayed a career as a newspaper reporter and newsreel director into fame as a radio commentator who entertained listeners with mellifluous accounts of human interest features. In his newspapering years alone, he interviewed about 1,000 personalities in the news. Hill was the author of three books, including a novel.

The son of Harvey Boone Hill and Mary Conger Hill, he was a native of Aurora, Indiana, whose down-home, small-town customs were celebrated in broadcasts and repeated for twenty years on Thanksgiving holidays. Hill received a B.A. degree from Indiana University in 1901 and began graduate studies at Butler University. His first newspaper job was on the *Indianapolis Journal*, which he left to become a "space writer" on the *New York Sun* in 1904. He married Jane Gail, a motion-picture actress, on 20 July 1922. The following year, Hill resigned as a reporter and became director of Fox News Reel, where he remained until his appointment as scenario editor of Fox Film Corporation in 1924. He resigned in 1926 to return to the *New York Sun*, this time as a feature writer, for another five-year stint.

During more than a quarter-century of reporting and writing in New York, Hill was an eyewitness to sensational criminal events and trials, as well as an insider in national political controversies and campaigns. He covered the 1912 trial of a police lieutenant, Charles Becker, who murdered a gambler named Herbert Rosenthal. In Madison Square Garden, Hill saw Harry K. Thaw shoot to death the architect Stanford White. Equally lurid was the Ruth Snyder–Henry Judd Gray murder trial which Hill covered. He reported on the trial of Joseph J. Hines, former chieftain of Tammany Hall, who was accused of protecting gamblers and racketeers by corrupting justice.

Hill wrote a widely published series of exposés entitled "The Rise and Fall of Tammany Hall." In politics, he covered presidential campaigns beginning with Theodore Roosevelt's, earning the latter's declaration that Hill was a member of his unofficial cabinet. Similarly, Hill was credited with boosting the stock of Franklin D. Roosevelt when FDR first ran for governor of New York in 1928. Among the major world figures interviewed by Hill were Benito Mussolini, David Lloyd George, and Ramsay MacDonald.

But it was as a radio broadcaster that Hill became known to millions between the beginning of the New Deal and the mid–1950s. His daily program, "The Human Side of the News," was delivered in a deep, rich, sonorous voice that many felt superior to print news in conveying emotion, color, and movement which lay behind events. Critics said his stories, while colorful, were not particularly subtle and verged on the florid, and that his popularity was achieved by an excess of sentimentality. It was also noted that over the years, his broadcasts became increasingly political, as well as more politically conservative. Hill, however, insisted that his commentaries were a legitimate form of reporting. At the peak of his career, in 1951, Hill was doing five programs each week for two national radio networks simultaneously. His final broadcasts took place in the summer of 1956, when he replaced Walter Winchell (q.v.) for eight weeks on the Mutual System.

An Episcopalian and a Republican, Hill at his death was a member of the social fraternity Sigma Chi and of three country clubs. When he died in St. Petersburg, Florida, at age seventy-two, his wife was the only immediate survivor. A veteran of radio work with Mutual, ABC, and NBC networks, he had recorded fifty-two human interest broadcasts which were never used. Only his Thanksgiving and Christmas programs continued to be broadcast.

BIBLIOGRAPHY:

A. *The American Scene* (New York, 1933); *Human Side of the News* (New York, 1934).

B. DAB Supp. 6, 290–291; NYT 13 February 1957; Irving E. Fang, *Those Radio Commentators!* (Ames, Iowa, 1977).

DAVID L. ANDERSON

HINE, LEWIS WICKES (b. 26 September 1874; d. 3 November 1940) was one of the best-known social documentary photographers of the early twentieth century. His photographs appeared in *Charities and the Commons* and six volumes of the *Pittsburgh Survey*. He was the official photographer of the National Child Labor Committee from 1911 to 1916, a photographer with the American Red Cross, and chief photographer for the Works Progress Administration during the depression. He also documented the construction of the Empire State Building.

Hine was one of four children born in Oshkosh, Wisconsin, to Douglas Hull Hine and Sarah Hayes Hine, both natives of New York State. His father operated a coffee shop and restaurant and his mother was a homemaker. Hine studied at the University of Chicago and Columbia University. He taught nature studies and botany at the Ethical Culture School in New York City.

In 1904 he returned to his hometown to marry Sara Ann Hayes, a schoolteacher. They returned to New York City so Hine could finish a master's degree in education at New York University, which he did the following year. In 1907 he again enrolled in graduate school to study sociology at Columbia University.

Hine's first major photographic project involved immigrants at Ellis Island, resulting in 200 plates dating from 1904 to 1909. This project, published in 1908 in *Charities and the Commons* (later called *Survey*), was the first photographic documentary to combine text and photographs. In 1909 he was hired as a staff photographer for the journal, a position he held for several years.

During this time he also began free-lancing for the National Child Labor Committee (NCLC), and was appointed in 1911 as official photographer to explore child labor conditions in the United States. For the next five years he produced portraits and group shots of children working in factories, mines, textile mills, fields, and canneries which were used in the NCLC's pamphlets and brochures and in a variety of muckraking and reform journals during the early 1900s. Hine is credited with providing shocking evidence of the need for legislation to protect children and to encourage them to receive an education before going to work. The Hines had a son, Corydon, in 1912.

Hine's attitude toward photography changed around this time; rather than concentrating on what needed to be corrected, he turned his camera on things that had to be appreciated. The relief activities of the American Red Cross in Europe at the end of World War I was Hine's next project (photographs appeared in *Red Cross Magazine*).

Upon returning to the United States in 1919, Hine turned his attention to men and their machines. Believing that his earlier photographs had emphasized only the negative aspects of industrialization, he decided to focus on the affirmative aspects of the machine age. In 1924 the Art Directors Club of New York awarded Hine a medal for his portrait of an engineer at the Exhibition of Advertising Art. Five years later the National Child Labor Committee honored Hine at an anniversary dinner.

Hine's ongoing interest in man and machinery ultimately led him to document the day-by-day construction of the Empire State Building in 1930–31. These straightforward yet dramatic photographs appeared in Hine's book entitled *Men at Work* (1932). It is considered the forerunner of photographic books so commonplace today. During the early part of the depression, Hine recorded life in the Clinch Valley, which had been flooded by Norris Dam waters, for the Tennessee Valley Authority (photographs appeared in several issues of the *Survey* in 1932 without a credit line). From 1936 to 1937 he was chief photographer for the National Research Project of the Works Progress Administration.

It was difficult for Hine to make a living as a photographer during the late 1930s. He tried unsuccessfully to be hired by Roy Stryker of the Resettlement Administration (later known as the Farm Security Administration), and no other government agency seemed interested in his work. On Christmas Day in 1939 his wife died after a siege of pneumonia and grippe. The next year Hine tried unsuccessfully for the second time to interest the Guggenheim Foundation in a project on American craftsmen. Hine had an operation in the fall of 1940 for an intestinal obstruction, and died 4 November in Hastings-on-Hudson, New York, where he had lived with his family since 1918.

BIBLIOGRAPHY:

A. With A. E. Seddon and W. H. Ulm, *Child Labor in the Carolinas* (New York, 1909).

B. DAB 22, 305–306; NYT 4 November 1940; Judith Mara Gutman, *Lewis W. Hine and the American Social Conscience* (New York, 1967); Walter Rosenblum and Naomi Rosenblum, *America and Lewis Hine, 1904–1940* (New York, 1977).

C. ZOE SMITH

HOBBY, WILLIAM PETTUS (b. 26 March 1878; d. 7 June 1964) was the patriarch of one of the most influential families in twentieth-century Texas. One of many Texas journalists who also followed an active political career, he served as governor from 1917 to 1921. In 1939 Hobby bought the *Houston Post,* with which he had been associated on and off since 1895. His wife, Oveta Culp Hobby, was first secretary of Health, Education and Welfare in the Eisenhower administration. She earlier had served as commander of the Women's Army Corps during World War II. Hobby's family retained control of the *Post* until selling it to the Toronto Sun Corporation in 1983. One of Houston's two major airports, Hobby Field, is named for him.

Hobby, born in Moscow, Texas, was one of four sons of Captain Edwin Hobby and Eudora Adeline Pettus Hobby. His father, a former Confederate army officer, was a lawyer and a politician in southeast Texas, where Hobby spent his childhood. Just before Hobby's fifteenth birthday his family moved to

Houston, where, at age sixteen and against his parents' wishes, Hobby quit school for an $8-a-week job in the *Post*'s circulation department. Seven years later he became business writer for the *Post*. Two years later he became city editor and, a year later, managing editor. As his newspaper career advanced, Hobby began promoting his political career. He helped found the Young Men's Democratic Club of Houston and, in 1904, served as secretary of the state's Democratic party executive committee.

In 1907 Hobby left the *Post* to become manager and part owner of the *Beaumont Enterprise,* which he shortly afterward acquired. He became active in Beaumont's social and political affairs, laying the groundwork for the political career that began in 1914 with his election as Texas lieutenant governor. He was reelected in 1916 and became governor the following year when Governor James Edward Ferguson was impeached. Hobby won a full term of office in 1918 after defeating Ferguson in a bitter primary battle. As governor Hobby successfully pursued a progressive legislative program. His administration succeeded with such measures as drought relief legislation, woman suffrage, appointment of the first highway commission, and state aid for schools and highways.

Resisting pressures to run for the U.S. Senate, Hobby returned to the *Beaumont Enterprise* in 1921 and shortly afterward acquired the *Beaumont Journal*. Hobby owned both newspapers for more than a decade. He was part of a syndicate that bought the *Houston Post* three years later, becoming president of the newspaper. On 9 May 1925 his radio station KPRC, Houston's first, began broadcasting. In 1939 Hobby bought the *Post* outright.

In 1915 Hobby had married his first wife, Willie Cooper, daughter of former U.S. Congressman Samuel Bronson Cooper. She died in 1929. On 23 February 1931 he married Oveta Culp of Houston, a former parliamentarian of the Texas legislature. The second Mrs. Hobby made the couple's home a center of Houston society, decorating it with works by Picasso and Modigliani. She quickly assumed an active role with the *Post*, becoming executive vice president in 1938 and, following Hobby's death, chairman of the board. The couple had two children, Jessica and Will Jr. Their son followed in his father's footsteps in state politics, serving several terms in the 1970s and 1980s as lieutenant governor.

The *Houston Post* under the Hobbys established a consistent conservative editorial record. Hobby had few personal affiliations, but he was civic- and political-minded. The paper broke with the Democratic party in 1940 over the issue of a third term for President Franklin D. Roosevelt, and again broke with the party in 1952, when the *Post* supported Dwight D. Eisenhower over Democratic nominee Adlai Stevenson. Hobby added television station KPRC to his newspaper and radio holdings in 1951. He was board chairman of the *Houston Post* when he died in 1964 at age eighty-six. He had been in failing health since 1957, when he underwent surgery for a hemorrhaging ulcer.

BIBLIOGRAPHY:
B. NYT 8 June 1964; *Houston Post,* 8 June 1964; James A. Clark, with Weldon Hart, *The Tactful Texan: A Biography of Governor Will Hobby* (New York, 1958).

JAMES DANIEL WHITFIELD

HOLT, ELIZABETH HUNTER (b. 1727 or 1728; d. 6 March 1788). **HOLT, JOHN** (b. 1720 or 1721; d. 30 January 1784). John Holt was the most important Radical printer and newspaper editor and publisher outside Boston during the late colonial and revolutionary war era. As publisher of the weekly *New-York Journal; or General Advertiser,* John Holt became the major conduit to other colonial publishers for the Radical propaganda of Sam Adams (q.v.) and the New England–based Sons of Liberty. After the war Elizabeth Hunter Holt, his wife, succeeded him as editor and publisher of the newspaper and was the first woman in New York to be named official printer.

Holt was born in Virginia, probably at Williamsburg. His date of birth is uncertain, as is information about his parents. The colonial press historian Isaiah Thomas (q.v.) in his *History of Printing in America* (1810) said Holt "received a good education, and was instructed in the business of a merchant." Holt was elected mayor of Williamsburg and made a fortuitous marriage. On or about 1 October 1749 he married Elizabeth Hunter, daughter of another Williamsburg merchant, John Hunter, and sister of William Hunter, public printer at Williamsburg and, with Benjamin Franklin (q.v.), deputy postmaster general for America. Holt probably learned the printing business from his brother-in-law. The Holts had one son, John Hunter Holt, who became a printer and publisher of Holt's newspaper in Norfolk, Virginia; and one daughter, Elizabeth, who married the printer-publisher Eleazar Oswald and became a printer-publisher after his death.

In 1754 Holt suffered financial reverses as a merchant and went to New York City where, through family connections to Franklin, he went into business with the well-known printer, publisher, and postmaster James Parker (q.v.), one of Franklin's associates. Holt also secured appointment as one of the two deputy postmasters general for America. In 1755, after Parker acquired Franklin's printing establishment in New Haven, Connecticut, Parker sent Holt to manage the print shop and publish the *Connecticut Gazette,* the first newspaper printed in Connecticut, launched by Parker on 12 April 1755. Holt also was made deputy postmaster at New Haven. On 13 December the *Gazette* appeared with Holt named as the newspaper's editor and resident co-partner of James Parker and Company. In July 1760 Holt closed the New Haven shop and began managing Parker's printing business in New York. On 31 July 1760 their newspaper, the *New York Gazette; or the Weekly Post-Boy,* appeared, listing Holt as Parker's junior partner. On 6 May 1762 the partnership was dissolved when Parker, in ill health, leased the newspaper and printing house to Holt. Holt continued until

May 1766, when he left and started his own printing house. From 29 May 1766 Holt published his own weekly newspaper, at first keeping the same name. On 16 October 1766 he changed the name to the *New-York Journal; or General Advertiser*. During these years Holt gained a reputation as "a firm whig, a good writer, and a warm advocate of his country," according to Thomas. Though Holt founded the *Journal* as a Whig newspaper, he was drawn by events into collaborating with Sam Adams and Paul Revere in the Sons of Liberty propaganda network. In 1768 and 1769 the unidentified authors of the *Journal of Occurrences,* working under Adams's direction, compiled a record of alleged misdeeds of British troops in Boston and sent this to Holt to publish in his *Journal*. Holt printed the dispatches two months before the alleged events were reported in Boston papers. Other colonial newspapers picked up these items. Holt also forwarded Radical arguments to publishers, including Peter Timothy (q.v.) of the *Gazetee of South Carolina* in Charleston and William Goddard (q.v.) of Baltimore's *Maryland Journal*.

In the tradition of John Peter Zenger (q.v.), Holt championed the free press. "The great Use of News papers," he wrote to Adams at Philadelphia on 26 January 1776, "is that they form the best opportunities of Intelligence, that could be divised [sic]. . . . It was by the means of News papers, that we received & spread the Notice of the tyrannical Designs formed against America, and kindled a Spirit that has been sufficient to repel them" (Murphy, 1965).

Holt was one of the first to print the Declaration of Independence, and he continued publishing the *Journal* in New York until 29 August 1776, the eve of the occupation of the city by British troops. Holt fled to New Haven, losing much of his property. In 1777 he left Connecticut, again forfeiting property, to become New York's public printer at Kingston, where on 7 July 1777 he revived the *Journal* and published it until 13 October, three days before the British burned Kingston. Again he fled, this time losing most of his belongings, but saving two fonts of type. On 11 May 1778 Holt resumed the *Journal* in Poughkeepsie. On 6 November 1780 he suspended publication, resumed on 30 July 1781, and suspended again on 6 January 1782 when he began printing the New York Laws. When the war ended, he resumed publication in New York on 22 November 1783 as the *Independent New-York Gazette; or The New-York Journal*. On 30 January 1784 Holt, "worn out" and ill for some time, died in New York. He was buried in St. Paul's Churchyard in New York City, where his tombstone, cut in letters of printing type, states in part: "He merited Every Esteem."

Elizabeth Hunter Holt succeeded him as official state printer. On 5 February 1784 the first issue of the *Independent Gazette; or the New-York Journal Revived* was published. She continued publication for thirteen months until 3 March 1785, when she retired. Her son-in-law, Eleazar Oswald, published the newspaper for her under the title the *New-York Journal and the General Advertiser*. On 23 June Oswald assumed proprietorship of the paper. On 14 July Mrs. Holt publicly relinquished full control to Oswald, stating in the paper that she thanked her friends "for their generous encouragement since she became . . . the editor of this old established and patriotic Journal." She moved to Philadelphia, where Oswald had another print shop and newspaper. On 6 March 1788 she died in Philadelphia. On 8 March Oswald's newspaper, the *Independent Gazetteer,* noted that she was buried at Christ Church.

BIBLIOGRAPHY:

B. DAB 9, 180–181; NCAB 23, 280–281; Leona M. Hudak, *Early American Women Printers and Publishers, 1639–1820* (Metuchen, N.J., 1978); Layton Barnes Murphy, "John Holt, Patriot Printer and Publisher," Ph.D. diss., Univ. of Michigan, 1965; Victor Hugo Paltsits, "John Holt—Printer and Postmaster," *Bulletin of the New York Public Library,* September 1920.

LEONARD RAY TEEL

HORGAN, STEPHEN HENRY (b. ? February 1854; d. 30 August 1941) was the inventor of the halftone engraving process, a method that made it possible to publish a photograph in a newspaper without first having to have the photograph converted to a woodcut illustration. This new process meant that the published image could be obtained directly from a photographic negative, or as was noted at the time, "direct from nature."

Horgan was born on a sugar plantation near Norfolk, Virginia, the son of an overseer of slaves. Soon after his birth, Horgan's family moved to England and then Ireland. In 1863 the Horgan family returned to the United States, settling in Nyack, New York. At the age of sixteen, Horgan was introduced to photography by a Methodist clergyman.

The *New York Daily Graphic* employed Horgan as a photographer in 1873, a position that would eventually lead to his development of the halftone process. Three years later, in 1876, Horgan took over management of the newspaper's photomechanical printing operation. As supervisor, Horgan noted that the women in the department were making wall mottoes by running colored threads through perforated cardboard. This observation gave Horgan the idea that stamped metal could be used to publish photographs in newspapers.

Horgan's idea came to realization on 4 March 1880, when the *New York Daily Graphic* published for the first time a photograph that had been converted by screening to a halftone without the use of a wood-engraving process. The image, which depicted a series of run-down houses in the city and was entitled "A Scene in Shanty Town, New York" was carried on the lower lefthand corner of the editorial page. Although the newspaper noted that the process had not been perfected, the photograph was clearly readable. The newspaper continued to produce other halftone images after this, but problems with the technique did not make the method suitable for use on a regular basis.

Horgan, meanwhile, moved on. After ten years of service with the *Graphic,* he became the art manager of the American Press Association in

1883. During this time, Horgan continued to advocate the use of photographs in newspapers, in spite of the continued use of the wood-engraving process by many newspapers. In an address to the Photographic Section of the American Institute in New York in 1886, Horgan said that photographers of the period, both amateur and professional, were not oriented to thinking of photography as a newsworthy form of communication. Horgan said that most photographers were inclined to take photographs, show them to immediate friends, and then turn their attention to other subjects, thus not sharing their images with a larger audience. Horgan argued that the newspaper was the best medium for letting the public see the images produced by photographers. Horgan also argued that photography was a medium that could tell a whole story in a glance, quicker than could be done through the use of columns of type.

Horgan's advocacy of photography in newspapers was not without its consequences. One of Horgan's favorite stories centered around his brief stint as the art director for the *New York Herald,* a position that he obtained in 1893. As art director, Horgan told his publisher, James Gordon Bennett, Jr. (q.v.), that the halftone method should be used by the newspaper. Bennett then took this suggestion to the pressroom superintendent. The superintendent, upon hearing Horgan's suggestion, informed Bennett that anyone who would recommend the use of halftone cuts in a newspaper press was an idiot. On this recommendation Horgan was fired.

This career setback did not last long, for Horgan soon sold his idea to the publisher of the *New York Tribune,* Whitelaw Reid (q.v.). The *Tribune* became the first newspaper to publish a halftone cut on a web perfecting press on 21 January 1897. Following a ten-year period of employment with the *Tribune,* Horgan again moved on to another venture, this time setting up the art and printing facilities of the *Newark Star*. For a brief period of time, Horgan also served as editor of the *Catholic Monitor*.

In addition to his interest in printing photographs in newspapers, Horgan was also involved in the development of wire transmission of photographs. As early as 1879, one year before the publication of the "Shantytown" image, Horgan had invented a method of transmitting photographs via telegraph wires. Several years later, in the summer of 1924, the American Telephone and Telegraph Company successfully transmitted a color photograph from Chicago to New York over telephone wires. This achievement resulted from a suggestion that Horgan made to the company.

In recognition for his career efforts, Horgan received two special awards—gold medals from the American Institute of Graphic Arts in 1925, and from the Photographic Society of England in 1930. Horgan died at age eighty-seven after an extended illness. His first wife, Katherine Connor Horgan, died in 1920. His second wife, the former Della Van Houton, survived him. Horgan was also survived by his son, two daughters, and a sister.

BIBLIOGRAPHY:

B. NYT 31 August 1941; L. R. McCabe, "Beginnings of the Halftone: Taken from the Notebook of Stephen H. Horgan," *Inland Printer,* March-April 1924; "Horgan Awarded American Institute of Graphic Arts Medal," *Inland Printer,* January 1925.

MICHAEL D. SHERER

HOWARD, ROY WILSON (b. 1 January 1883; d. 20 November 1964) devoted more than sixty years to a newspaper career that saw him move up the ranks of news service reporting to become president of United Press, then chairman of the board of Scripps-McRae newspapers (later Scripps-Howard), and finally editor of the *New York World-Telegram and Sun.* His death came shortly before his eighty-second birthday when he suffered a massive coronary attack in his New York City office. He died later that day in a New York hospital.

Howard was born in a tollhouse on the Dayton turnpike, just north of Cincinnati, in the Ohio village of Gano. He was the son of William A. Howard, a Big Four Railroad brakeman, and Elizabeth Wilson Howard. The family moved to Indianapolis, Indiana, where Howard's father died from tuberculosis. Young Howard was up at dawn to deliver the *Indianapolis Star* and the *Indianapolis News* in the afternoon. He also worked for the *News* at space rates, making up to $35 a week. The newspaper found it more economical to hire him as a full-time reporter at $8 a week when he graduated from high school in 1902. He soon shifted to the morning *Star* to become sports editor.

Howard wanted big-city experience and he sought employment with the *New York World.* Failing there, he tried to get on with the *St. Louis Post-Dispatch,* believing that might open the door to New York. When these efforts failed, he went to the *Cincinnati Post* as assistant managing editor. His New York City chance came in 1906 when he became New York correspondent for the Scripps-McRae newspapers.

Then in 1907 E. W. Scripps (q.v.) merged Scripps-McRae Press Association, Publishers Press Association, and Scripps News Association (his West Coast news agency) into United Press Associations, both to compete with Associated Press and to service his own newspapers. Howard was named general news manager in New York and a year later was summoned to Scripps's Miramar ranch near San Diego to become West Coast news manager. Most subordinates who appeared before Scripps at his ranch adopted his rough western garb but Howard showed up in a Fifth Avenue–cut suit, spats, highly polished shoes, and a cane. Scripps found him to have confidence oozing from every pore but to be so frank that he could feel no resentment toward him.

Howard was a sleeves-rolled-up news manager. He increased the report coming to the West Coast from Chicago so that the wire moved from about 4,000 words a day to 12,000. He again and again insisted on a "today" angle on stories. During slack time, he ordered all bureaus to prepare feature or human interest stories. Bureaus carefully went over lists of coming events to prepare colorful details which could be released when the events occurred. In later years he promoted the transmission by wire of news pictures, extended news services to radio stations, and developed the feature syndicate Newspaper Enterprise Association.

Moved back to to New York City, Howard became president of United Press in 1920. Already he had traveled widely in an attempt to build up the news service. In the summer of 1908 he was in Chicago to cover the Socialist National Convention which nominated Eugene V. Debs for president, and later that year he covered the Democratic and Republican conventions too. He sent play-by-play accounts of World Series games and in 1910 was in Reno to cover the Jack Johnson—Jim Jeffries heavyweight championship fight. Later he was in Europe recruiting young, hungry Americans willing to report for small salaries but able to write the news without the foreign influence which he thought too often dominated Associated Press reports dependent upon foreign news services.

He was in Europe again during World War I and at the close of the war in 1918 was in Brest, France. Rumors were everywhere that the war was about to end. When he called on Admiral Henry B. Wilson, commander of American naval forces in France, in the afternoon of 7 November, the admiral told Howard he had a message from the U.S. naval attaché in Paris reporting the armistice. Howard was able to immediately dispatch a cable to New York which read: UNIPRESS, NEW YORK URGENT ARMISTICE ALLIES GERMANY SIGNED ELEVEN SMORNING HOSTILITIES CEASED TWO SAFTERNOON SEDAN TAKEN SMORNING BY AMERICANS HOWARD SIMMS. ''Simms'' was the United Press manager in France and his name and press card number were necessary on collect messages filed to United Press. Word was flashed around the world by United Press and wild rejoicing erupted. Two hours later the admiral told Howard he now had been told the report was unconfirmed, but Howard's message to this effect did not reach United Press until the next day. Howard insisted he had done what any reporter would have done under the circumstances and, of course, the official signing did come four days later. Howard later wrote that he believed the ''French official'' who had telephoned word to the American embassy was, in fact, a German agent who hoped for better terms from the Allies if the war could be declared over prematurely (Morris, 1957).

By 1920 the number of United Press clients had increased to more than 700 and Howard left the news service to become business director of Scripps-McRae newspapers. In 1922 he became chairman of the board and the name was changed to Scripps-Howard. The group embarked on a program of buying newspapers, but the purchase that gave Howard the most pleasure came in 1931: the purchase of the *New York World* (which had earlier denied him employment), the *Evening World,* and the *Sunday World*. He killed the evening and Sunday papers and merged the morning *World* and the *New York Telegram* to become the *New York World-Telegram*. With the purchase in 1950 of the *New York Sun*, the paper became the *New York World-Telegram and Sun*.

In 1936 he relinquished the title of chairman of the board of Scripps-Howard newspapers and became president. He held that title until 1953, his seventieth birthday. He continued as director of the newspapers' operating company and chairman of its executive committee. He retired as editor of the *New York World-Telegram and Sun* in 1960.

Scripps newspapers had been liberal in their editorial direction but were seen as more opposed to social reform when Howard took over. The newspapers supported Franklin D. Roosevelt for president in 1932 and 1936, but opposed him in 1940 and 1944. Relations between Howard and the Roosevelt administration became increasingly strained as the war years progressed.

Howard married Margaret Rohe, a reporter who at the time was performing in a London play, on 14 June 1909. They had two children, Jack Rohe Howard, later president and director of Scripps-Howard newspapers, and Jane Perkins Howard.

BIBLIOGRAPHY

B. DAB Supp. 7, 369–370; NYT 21 November 1964; Joe Alex Morris, *Deadline Every Minute* (Garden City, N.Y., 1957).

EARL L. CONN

HOWE, EDGAR WATSON (b. 3 May 1853; d. 3 October 1937) was a small-town newspaper editor and novelist. He was known as ''the village atheist'' who used his newspaper to attack Christianity, and as the author of *The Story of a Country Town* (1883), which was praised by those who saw hypocrisy behind every sentiment and realism in a depiction of what Howe called ''dull, boastful discontented people.''

E. W. Howe, the first of five children of Henry Howe and Elizabeth Irwin Howe, was born near Treaty, Indiana. Two older children from the father's first marriage were also at home. Henry Howe, a Methodist circuit rider and fervent abolitionist, seemed to care more about politics than about his own family; moving himself and his family to Missouri to crusade against sin and slavery just before the Civil War, he was tried and acquitted for inciting slave rebellion, but tried and found guilty by his son for domestic cruelty. When E. W. was twelve, Henry ran away with a woman from his congregation; when E. W. was fifteen, his mother died. After scant formal schooling, the boy was on his own.

As a teenaged tramp printer, Howe began work on the Gallatin *North Missourian* for five dollars a week and board, then joined the *St. Joseph Herald,* the *Council Buffs Nonpareil,* and the *Omaha Republican*. Looking for adventure and searching for a faith, Howe went west to Wyoming and Salt Lake City, where he worked for Brigham Young's Mormon church paper, the *Deseret News*. But Howe soon was on the road again: the Falls City, Nebraska, *Nemaha Valley Journal*; the *Rocky Mountain News* in Denver; the Golden, Colorado, *Eagle*; and Falls City once again.

Marriage in 1873 to Clara Frank of Falls City began to settle down Howe physically, if not spiritually. The Howes settled in Atchison, Kansas, at that time a railroad center, and Howe started his own newspaper, the *Atchison Globe,* in 1877. His family life, like that of his father, was not fulfilling. An increasingly bitter marriage eventually resulted in a divorce in 1901. Two of Howe's five children died young, and the other three became estranged from him. Son Gene, an Amarillo, Texas, newspaper editor, wrote in the *Saturday Evening Post* that Howe was the "most wretchedly unhappy man I ever knew."

Like his father, Howe ignored his family as he concentrated on saving the world from sin, except that in E. W.'s case, it was the sin of believing in God or anything else that could not be seen or counted. While editing the *Globe* from 1877 to 1910, Howe became well known for pessimistic epigrams such as "If you go slow others will overtake you; if you go fast, you will exhaust your strength and die young." He bluntly criticized preachers, populists, prohibitionists, labor unions, women's righters, and anyone else who wandered into his view.

In 1896 when Howe heard of Roentgen's discovery of X-rays, he wrote that "Prof. Roentgen is not a great scientist; he is simply a great liar," and added that, "Nine-tenths of the X-ray business is foolish, and the other tenth experiment." When Howe read about the invention of radio, he called it a "fraud" and wrote that "It will never be of practical use . . . Marconi is a joke. Mark the prediction from a little old country newspaper."

Howe sold his Atchison paper in 1910 and published *E. W. Howe's Monthly,* which he called "a journal devoted to indignation and information," from 1911 to 1933. After attacking higher education for five decades, Howe received honorary degrees in 1927 from Washburn College in Topeka and Rollins College in Winter Park, Florida. In 1937, two days after his former wife died, Howe died in his sleep at home in Atchison. Cause of death was given as gradual paralysis and infirmities of age, with complications of pneumonia. Howe had an Episcopalian funeral.

BIBLIOGRAPHY:

A. *The Indignations of E. W. Howe* (Girard, Kansas, 1933).

B. DAB Supp. 2, 326–327; NYT 4 October 1937; Gene A. Howe, "My Father Was the Most Wretchedly Unhappy Man I Ever Knew," *Saturday Evening Post,* 25 October 1941; Calder Pickett, *Ed Howe: Country Town Philosopher* (Lawrence, Kansas, 1968).

MARVIN N. OLASKY

HOWE, QUINCY (b. 17 August 1900; d. 17 February 1977) was well known for his work in several media. He was an author, an editor, and a radio and television news commentator. He also taught, and throughout his life he was an ardent defender of civil liberties.

Any listener to Quincy Howe could have told you that he was born in Boston. He was the first child of Mark Antony DeWolfe, who won a Pulitzer Prize as an author, and Fanny Huntington Quincy Howe, whose family line included a president of Harvard. Howe himself attended Harvard, after going to St. George's

School in Newport, Rhode Island. After he took his degree in 1921 he spent a year in Europe, traveling and studying at Christ's College, Cambridge.

Back in Boston, he became the editor of *Living Age,* an influential small monthly that translated and analyzed articles from the foreign press. In that decade of the Ku Klux Klan, the Wobblies, and the Red scare, he also developed and expressed his strong feelings in favor of civil rights.

He worked as editor in chief at Simon and Schuster from 1935 to 1942, and beginning in 1941 he edited *Atlas* magazine for twenty-four years. But, he said his life began at age 39 in 1939 when he became a radio commentator. For three years he worked at WQXR in New York City, delivering fifteen-minute news commentaries, and in 1942 moved to CBS as a commentator. He helped make commentary an accepted and popular part of radio, and worked in the days—the 1940s—when commentators were at their peak. Turning out a daily script for a commentary—upwards of 1,500 words of informed and thoughtful opinion—is a heavy burden, and Howe's colleagues said he accomplished it partly because he was an excellent writer, partly because he was an excellent extemporaneous speaker and rarely worked from a complete script, and partly because he worked on the basis of established principles—a few maxims and theorems about world affairs that served to guide his thinking and open any new topic of the day to consistent and coherent analysis. Howe could read and write fluently in three languages—English, French, and German—and that, his colleagues said, was a considerable help to him.

During his broadcasting career Howe narrated a number of documentaries and educational programs. He did some television reporting, but never became fully comfortable with that medium. A sponsor succeeded in persuading CBS to remove Howe from the early evening commentary spot in 1947, and Howe left the network. He taught journalism at the University of Illinois, but returned to broadcasting, working for ABC from 1954 to 1968 and occasionally after his official retirement in 1968.

In 1932 Howe married Mary Post of Boston. They had a son, Quincy Jr., and a daughter, Tina. Mrs. Howe died in late 1976.

BIBLIOGRAPHY:

A. *How to Understand the News* (New York, 1940).

B. NYT 18 February 1977.

LAURA NICKERSON

HOWELL, CLARK (b. 21 September 1863; d. 14 November 1936) was editor of the *Atlanta Constitution* for thirty-nine years, guiding it through difficult and competitive times: yet he is much less well known than the man who preceded him—Henry W. Grady (q.v.)—and the man who succeeded him a few years after his death—Ralph McGill (q.v.). He was a state officeholder as a young man, unsuccessful candidate for governor of Georgia, a lifelong Democrat active in his party, and an aggressive editor who led a variety of editorial crusades, including one that won for his newspaper a Pulitzer Prize.

Although he was a lifelong Georgian, he was born in South Carolina because of the fortunes of war. His mother had returned to her home there while her husband, Evan P., was commanding a Confederate artillery battery. Captain Howell returned to Atlanta after the war, conducted a successful lumber business that profited from the ruined city, turned briefly to work as a journalist and then resumed his prewar law practice. In October 1876 Evan Howell purchased a half-interest in the *Constitution,* hired Henry W. Grady and Joel Chandler Harris (q.v.), and began to guide the successful fortunes of his newspaper.

Clark graduated from the University of Georgia in 1883 and served brief editorial apprenticeships in New York and Philadelphia before joining the editorial staff of the *Constitution*. Shortly after he returned to Georgia, he was nominated for the state legislature and elected to the first of five terms in the House of Representatives. His first of three marriages occurred in 1887, when he was wed to Harriet Glascock Barrett of Augusta. They had one child, Clark Jr.

Howell was assistant managing editor of the *Constitution* when Grady died in 1889. The apprenticeship was a professionally profitable one; his editorial responsibility and authority increased in Grady's frequent absences, as he took an increasingly larger role in the editorial direction of the newspaper. In 1897 Howell became editor in chief when his father retired. He proved to be a forceful, dedicated, and competent editor. Among other campaigns, the *Constitution* aggressively fought the state's convict lease system, supported caring for refugees from a yellow fever epidemic in Savannah, and was one of the few voices against the move to ban football at his alma mater after a player died during a game.

Howell was elected to the state senate in 1890 and made its president. In 1898 his first wife died. The following year he gained a majority control over the newspaper's stock and married Annie Comer of Savannah, the daughter of a railroad president. They had three sons: Hugh, Albert, and Julian. His political eye was on the governorship, but he was soundly defeated in the 1906 Democratic primary by Hoke Smith, former owner of the *Atlanta Journal,* who had been secretary of the interior under President Cleveland. It was his last run for office, but he served in the Democratic party as an active committeeman for many years and was consulted by presidents of both parties. In 1921 Warren Harding (q.v.) appointed him to the National Coal Commission, and President Coolidge appointed him to the National Transportation Commission. His second wife died in 1922, and in 1924 he married Margaret Conner Carr of Durham, North Carolina.

His thoughtful reading of a story on the Atlanta City Council led to an investigative series uncovering corruption in bidding practices and a 1931 Pulitzer Prize, the newspaper's first. President Franklin Roosevelt, a longtime friend and correspondent, offered him minor ambassadorships after the 1932 election, but Howell declined. In 1934, however, he accepted the chairmanship of the Federal Aviation Commission. Although he was an unlikely pick in terms of aviation experience, he managed the commission's work to a fruitful conclusion, resulting in a blueprint for development and regulation of a budding industry. He was a member of the U.S. delegation to the Philippines in 1935 when its first president, Manuel Quezon, was installed. In 1936, only a few months before his death, he was named a chevalier of the French Legion of Honor.

Shortly before he died of cancer he dictated one of his last editorials, trumpeting the reelection of Roosevelt. He was buried in Atlanta.

BIBLIOGRAPHY:

B. DAB 22, 329; NYT 15 November 1936; Wallace B. Eberhard, ''Clark Howell and the *Atlanta Constitution,*'' *Journalism Quarterly,*, Spring 1983.

WALLACE B. EBERHARD

HOWELLS, WILLIAM DEAN (b. 1 March 1837; d. 11 May 1920), who at the age of nine began to set type in his father's printing office, had become a dominant figure in the world of literature and widely recognized as the chief exponent of realism in American literature by the time of his death in 1920 at the age of eighty-three. He had produced 35 novels and more than 100 other volumes of criticism, poetry, plays, and reminiscences. Much of this writing had appeared serially in the leading periodicals for some forty years.

Howells was born in Martins Ferry, an Ohio River town, the second of eight children. His father, William Cooper Howells, was a migratory abolitionist journalist with little formal education. His mother, Mary Dean Howells, whose uncles were profitably engaged as riverboat pilots, helped make the early years at Martins Ferry more bearable for the Howells family.

Howells's boyhood was passed in various Ohio towns, including Hamilton, Dayton, Ashtabula, and Jefferson. He received what little formal education he had during the earlier years in Hamilton, but he continued to learn from books that came into his possession, an eclectic course of development that he discusses in *My Literary Passions* (1895). He describes other aspects of life during those early years with humorous candor in *A Boy's Town* (1890), *My Year in a Log Cabin* (1893), and *Years of My Youth* (1916).

In 1856 Howells's father was appointed as a legislative clerk in Columbus, and Howells went along to write daily letters on the legislative proceedings for several Ohio newspapers. He later was offered the job of city editor for the *Cincinnati Gazette,* but he gave it up after a brief trial and returned to Columbus where he was employed by the *Ohio State Journal*, recently organized to serve the growing Republican party. Between 1856 and 1861, he served as a reporter, exchange editor, editorial writer, and city editor for the *Journal.* During the summer of 1860, Howells compiled materials for a book on the life of Lincoln, and the grateful president named Howells to the consulate in Venice. During his four years in Venice Howells found time to study the language and literature of Italy, which later bore fruit in two books of observations, *Venetian Life* (1866) and *Italian Journeys* (1967), as well as in various novels.

Howells was married to Elinor Gertrude Mead, whom he had met earlier in Columbus, on 24 December 1862, in the American embassy in Paris. She came from a talented Vermont family and was the second cousin of Rutherford B. Hayes, to whose presidential campaign Howells contributed a biography in 1876. The couple had two daughters, Winifred and Mildred, and a son, John.

The Howellses returned from Venice in 1865, and he was employed by the *Nation* in New York. After a few months, Howells accepted a position as assistant editor of the *Atlantic Monthly* in Boston, where he was to spend the next fifteen years, the last ten as editor. In Cambridge, where Howells lived for several of those years, he became friends with James Russell Lowell and Henry James as well as other literati. While Howells became an adopted son of the Brahmin culture of Boston, he retained the egalitarianism of the Ohio frontier which was fostered by his lifelong friendship with Samuel L. Clemens (q.v.). That friendship began in 1869 when Clemens visited the *Atlantic* office to thank the anonymous reviewer of his first book, *Innocents Abroad*.

Howells's first novel, *Their Wedding Journey,* was published in 1872, followed by six other books published during the 1870s, most of which were serialized in the *Atlantic*. He resigned from the *Atlantic* in 1881 and during the next decade wrote several novels for serialization in *Century Magazine*. In these novels Howells departed from his earlier comedies of manners to begin a series of realistic studies of characters grappling with ethical problems. These included two of Howells's better novels, *A Modern Instance* (1882) and *The Rise of Silas Lapham* (1885).

In 1885 Howells signed a lucrative contract with Harper and Brothers calling for a novel a year and the writing of a new feature in *Harper's Monthly,* "The Editor's Study." In New York, where he finally moved in 1888, Howells became interested in the larger problems of industrialism, and his reading of such social reformers as Henry George (q.v.) caused him to turn toward socialism. *A Hazard of New Fortunes,* published in 1890, a book many critics view as Howells's best novel, reflects the author's attempt to adapt his views of realistic fiction to the problems of the machine age.

Howells quit "The Editor's Study" for *Harper's* in 1892 to serve for a time as coeditor of *Cosmopolitan*. In 1895 he began regular contributions to *Harper's Weekly,* and in 1898 took a position he held for twenty years writing the "Editor's Easy Chair" for *Harper's Monthly*. Howells wrote at least fifteen books after the turn of the century, but most were undistinguished, with the exception perhaps of *The Leatherwood God* (1916). Howells died in his New York apartment on 11 May 1920, of influenza.

BIBLIOGRAPHY:

B. DAB 5, 306–311; NYT 12 May 1920; Van Wyck Brooks, *Howells: His Life and World* (New York, 1959); Kenneth S. Lynn, *William Dean Howells: An American Life* (New York, 1971).

HARRY W. STONECIPHER

HOYT, EDWIN PALMER (b. 10 March 1897; d. 25 June 1979) caught the *Denver Post* when it was on its last legs and transformed it into a successful newspaper. One of his editors called his performance "a great demonstration of how one man can change the shape of a newspaper."

The man who came to be known to his friends as Ep Hoyt, and to everyone else as Palmer Hoyt, was born in Roseville, Illinois, the son of Edwin Palmer Hoyt, a clergyman, and Annie Tendler Hoyt. He attended William Jewell College prep school in Kansas City and McMinnville (now Linfield) College prep school in Oregon. In 1923 he received his A.B. from the University of Oregon, where he had been a reporter and editor for the *Daily Emerald*. During his senior year he was sports editor for the *Eugene Register*. After graduation he spent two months on the copy desk of the *Portland Oregonian,* then moved to Pendleton to be telegraph editor of the *Eastern Oregonian*. He returned to the *Oregonian* in 1926 as copy editor and continued on the staff of that paper as reporter (1928), drama editor (1929), night city editor (1930), executive news editor (1931), managing editor (1933), general manager (1938), and editor and publisher (1939).

He left the *Oregonian* for six months in 1943 to rejuvenate the troubled domestic branch of the U.S. Office of War Information. After World War II he became one of the founders of Radio Free Europe. He served terms as president of the Oregon Press Conference and of the Oregon Newspaper Publishers Association.

In 1946 Hoyt became editor and publisher of the *Denver Post*. The *Post* at that time was a discredited organization, being drained by its stockholders. Hoyt saved it. He separated fact from opinion in the paper, and gave the *Post* an editorial page that earned distinction as a forum. He sent *Post* writers overseas and throughout the United States, and he expanded the paper's circulation throughout the Intermountain West, making it a regional newspaper. In the process he helped remove Denver from provincialism and make it a modern city.

Hoyt was a civil liberties advocate. He was one of the first publishers to question the tactics and claims of Senator Joseph McCarthy, and he won an award from the NAACP for service to that organization's goals. He served as a director of the Associated Press from 1944 to 1945. In the 1960s he directed the national advisory committee for Stanford's Professional Journalism Fellowship program. He was a director of the American Newspaper Publishers Association and of the Bureau of Advertising. Hoyt was also a writer of fiction; he published several western novels and more than fifty short stories.

In 1921 Hoyt was married to Cecile DeVore of Heppner, Oregon. They had two sons, Edwin Palmer and Charles Richard. They were divorced in 1949. In 1950 Hoyt married Helen May Lininger Taber of Denver. They had one son, Lincoln, and Hoyt adopted his wife's three sons from her earlier marriage: Monty, Gregory, and Wesley. At the age of eighty-two, after many years of poor health, Hoyt died at the Beth Israel Hospital in Denver.

BIBLIOGRAPHY:

B. NYT 27 June 1979.

LAURA NICKERSON

HUDSON, FREDERIC (b. 25 April 1819; d. 21 October 1875), managing editor of James Gordon Bennett's (q.v.) *New York Herald* and leader in Associated Press management for fifteen years, also wrote the first comprehensive account of the history of journalism in the United States. His contributions to journalism were in three areas: (1) refining methods of collecting news; (2) developing the position of managing editor and establishing newsroom organization; and (3) initiating a journalistic historical record.

Hudson was born in Quincy, Massachusetts, and early attended the Mayhew School in Boston, then public schools in Concord. When his mother died in 1836, he went to New York to work for Hudson's News Rooms, a news-gathering agency established by his older brother, Edward. Frederic's job was to obtain foreign news, and in searching for the news at the waterfronts he met James Gordon Bennett, who hired Hudson in 1837.

Hudson's first exposure to the news world, therefore, was focused on collection, and he regarded speed in collection of news as critical to the development of a good newspaper. After his retirement as managing editor of the *Herald*, Hudson noted in an interview published in the *Herald* that "Enterprise in getting news is the thing of prime importance in journalism, and by it the New York journals will always maintain their supremacy, as they can afford to give better reports than any other journals." In the 1875 interview Hudson said if he were editing a newspaper at that time, he would rely on the telegraph rather than the mails, and predicted that electricity one day would do all the work of gathering the news.

Hudson and Bennett, if not instrumental in, were certainly major characters in, the development of cooperative news gathering, again an attempt to improve the collection of news. In his history of journalism, Hudson credits David Hale (q.v.), editor of the *New York Journal of Commerce,* with approaching James Gordon Bennett about 1845 to establish a cooperative news-gathering association. Hudson wrote that this initial approach by Hale led to cordial relations between the two papers and that the *Herald* was of great service to the *Journal of Commerce* during the Mexican War.

Although Bennett was in Europe during much of the Mexican War, Hudson set up lines of communication with New Orleans for the transmission of war news partly by horse express, partly by railroad, and partly by telegraph.

In addition to his emphasis on gathering news, Hudson felt strongly that newspapers should be nonpolitical, saying no "great journal can be a party organ." He did not "overvalue" editorial writing, but said more important was the "mode in which the news is collected and presented. It is the *tout ensemble* of the newspaper every day that makes or mars its power as a public organ."

The title of managing editor, which Hudson eventually assumed on the *Herald,* represented a new style of newspaper organization. Although even the early penny newspapers did not have extensive reporting staffs, by the 1840s and certainly by the Civil War, newspapers were building extensive staffs. Individuals like Hudson assumed the role of directing reporters in the field, coordinating copy and managing the newspaper. For Bennett, Hudson answered voluminous correspondence and "entered the duties of each reporter in the daily journal kept for their inspection and guidance." He also edited copy.

When James Gordon Bennett, Jr. (q.v.), assumed his father's position as editor of the *Herald,* Hudson retired and moved to Concord. There he wrote *Journalism in the United States from 1690 to 1872*. This book, published in 1873, contains some historical inaccuracies but provides a firsthand account of the development of news as an institution.

Hudson died in 1875 in a railroad accident. He was married in 1844 to Eliza Woodward, a Concord schoolteacher. They had one son, Woodward, who became a prominent railroad attorney.

BIBLIOGRAPHY:

B. *New York Herald,* 22 October 1875.

JEAN FOLKERTS

HUNTLEY, CHET (b. 10 December 1911; d. 20 March 1974) was a broadcast journalist, advertising agency partner, and broadcast group station owner and program syndicator. Along with fellow newscaster David Brinkley, he appeared nightly on the NBC news program "The Huntley-Brinkley Report." The fifteen-year partnership is credited with molding the nightly national newscast into the principal daily news source for a great number of Americans. The show's sign-off, "Good night, David—Good Night, Chet," was so well known that it became part of everyday conversation. A consumer research company in 1965 found that Huntley and his co-anchor were recognized by more Americans than Cary Grant, James Stewart, John Wayne, and the Beatles, although they were not always certain which was which. When once asked whether he was Huntley or Brinkley, Chet quipped: "I'm not sure. Sometimes it's hard even for me to keep us straight."

Born Chester Robert Huntley in Carwell, Montana, he spent his boyhood on his grandfather's sheep ranch near the Canadian border. His father, P. A. Huntley, was a railroad telegrapher, and descendant of Presidents John Adams and John Quincy Adams. His mother, Blanche Wadime Tatham Huntley, was the daughter of W. R. Tatham, who crossed the Plains in a covered wagon. Huntley had three sisters.

Huntley attended Whitehall High School in Whitehall, Montana. He played basketball and football at school, and enjoyed debating and oratory. In 1929 he attended Montana State College in Bozeman on a scholarship, and for three years pursued a premedical program. Another scholarship took him to the Cornish School of Arts in Seattle, Washington, and a year and a half later he transferred to the University of Washington. While still in school he got his first broadcasting job at radio station KPCB, Seattle. He was hired as program director and soon became announcer, writer, salesperson, and janitor. He received his B.A. from Washington in 1934.

After college the young broadcaster spent time at two local radio stations—KHQ in Spokane (1936), and KGW in Portland (1937)—before moving to the NBC affiliate, KRI in Los Angeles (1937–39). This was followed by a twelve-year association with CBS radio as newscaster and correspondent. It was here that he received his first Peabody Award (1942) for a broadcast on Mexican-Americans. Huntley remained West Coast–based for CBS until 1951. Then he joined ABC as a newscaster, correspondent, and analyst. Throughout the entire period Huntley was recognized as a hardworking reporter, not afraid to interject commentary. His tendency to go deeper into a story presented problems occasionally, like the time he was attacked by anticommunists bothered by his critical report on Senator Joseph R. McCarthy. In a related incident, he went to court and won a sizable settlement and public apology in a slander judgment.

Huntley joined NBC in June 1955, when he began doing West Coast programs for the network. His first New York program was "Chet Huntley Reporting," a ten-minute radio commentary which started 26 March 1956. A Sunday afternoon news-in-depth program, "Outlook," began on television a few days later. He also had a slot on the WRCA-TV Saturday evening news program. That summer he was assigned to do NBC coverage of the political conventions in Chicago and San Francisco—assignments which found him teamed with David Brinkley. The combination worked. Thus came a fifteen-year partnership when both were selected to replace John Cameron Swayze for the fifteen-minute nightly network newscast. A hallmark of the new partnership was the great effort placed in straightforwardly reporting news. Each man actively wrote his own stories, a practice not always found among television news anchors.

Huntley's reporting style also included commentary, although he was quick to note he was not interested in advocacy journalism. Still his career was dotted with controversy. He scrutinized Richard Nixon before most other journalists did. He also refused to honor picket lines of the American Federation of Radio and Television Artists in 1967 while Brinkley did.

Following his retirement in 1970, Huntley returned to his much-loved Montana. Here he organized the building of a $25 million Big Sky recreational complex near Bozeman, a project which was attacked by environmentalists. In addition, he became a full partner in Levine, Huntley, Schmidt advertising agency in New York and did syndicated news commentaries. He contracted lung cancer and died in March 1974 at age sixty-two. He was survived by his second wife, the former Tipton Stringer, who was a television weather broadcaster (they were married in 1959), his mother, and two daughters by his first marriage to Ingrid Rolin (they were married in 1936; divorced in 1959). Throughout his career, he had received many awards and honorary degrees, including four Peabody awards, two Overseas Press Club awards, and seven Emmy awards.

In a fitting salute, his longtime co-anchor made one final sign-off to Huntley. In a low-keyed, emotion-filled tribute, Brinkley concluded, "I really don't want to say it, but the time has come. And so for the last time, good luck, and good night, Chet."

BIBLIOGRAPHY:
A. *The Generous Years: Remembrances of a Frontier Boyhood* (New York, 1968).
B. NYT 21 March 1974.

RICHARD C. VINCENT

HUSING, TED (b. 27 November 1901; d. 10 August 1962) was among the most famous and gifted sports announcers during the golden age of radio. His career spanned three decades, from 1924 to 1954. Although he is best remembered for his dramatic and colorful accounts of football and baseball games, the Kentucky Derby, and the like, his voice and mastery of descriptive reporting brought him to cover all manner of public affairs including inaugurations, political conventions, and funerals.

Husing was born in a room above a saloon in the Bronx, New York, to Henry Frederick Husing and Bertha Hecht Husing. His father was a headwaiter, and his convivial nature was passed on to his son. He was named Edward Britt Husing after a prizefighter his father admired. The boy adopted the name Ted during his teens.

He was not enthusiastic about formal education, but was a voracious reader. He loved sports and even was a semiprofessional football player for a time. He was the mascot of Columbia University's football, basketball, and baseball teams before World War I. He enlisted in the National Guard in 1917 and was discharged in 1918. He married Helen M. K. Gelderman, his beloved "Bubs," on 24 June 1924. That year, Husing answered an advertisement for radio announcers at WJZ in New York which appeared in the *New York Times*. Some 600 applied for the position, which required a college degree and a knowledge of music. Husing got the job, which paid $45 a week, despite his lack of a degree.

His first on-the-air performance was with Milton Cross. His entry into sports reporting was at the side of Major Andrew J. White at a University of Pennsylvania–Cornell game at Philadelphia on Thanksgiving Day in 1925. Subsequently, he went to WRC in Washington, D.C., and WHN in New York among others. In 1927 he helped organize WBET for the *Boston Transcript*. He was well known for his organizational ability as well as for his dramatic baritone voice.

Husing joined CBS, the network with which he would gain his greatest fame, on Christmas Day of 1927. The network was tiny at first. Husing claimed in his autobiography, *Ten Years Before the Mike* (1935), that the network gained great fame the following year from his broadcast of the funeral of Floyd Bennett, a war hero who had died trying to locate three missing German aviators.

Husing grew with CBS. He broadcast football games, baseball games, and the Kentucky Derby. He reported the exploits of Babe Ruth, Bill Tilden, Jack Dempsey, Bobby Jones, and scores of other sports heroes, at the same time lending his dulcet voice and masterful use of the language to elections and inaugurations. He even went on a tour with the jazz great Paul Whiteman. Husing claims that he introduced Rudy Vallee and Harry von Zell to big-time radio and that he was instrumental in bringing Bing Crosby to the close attention of Whiteman.

But he was especially adept at broadcasting football games. He developed his "annunciation board," an electric device that allowed him to identify football players with absolute accuracy even though he worked without binoculars. He studied the game and often attended practices. Coaches gave him playbooks, which he used to make his descriptions more detailed and accurate.

He was named the outstanding radio sports broadcaster by United Press every year from 1931 to 1938. And he was the Radio Daily Poll's All-American radio sports broadcaster in 1937, 1938, and 1940. He was a member of the Sports Broadcasters Association and president in 1942–43. He became a disk jockey, and in 1947, with "Ted Husing's Bandstand" on WMGM in New York, his income soared.

Husing lived intensely. He loved Broadway and was a habitué of its nightclubs. He earned as much as $300,000 a year late in the 1940s and early 1950s and spent lavishly. His three marriages ended in divorce. His marriage to Francis Sizer in 1934 lasted only months, and his last, to Iris Lemerise in 1944, ended in 1958. He was the father of one child from his first marriage, Pegge Mae, and a son, David Edward Britt, from his third marriage.

During the early 1950s, he suffered from recurring dizzy spells and double vision. He underwent a nine-hour operation for a brain tumor in 1954 that left him blind and nearly paralyzed. He never fully recovered. He attempted a comeback in California in 1954, but retired late that year.

BIBLIOGRAPHY:

A. *My Eyes Are in My Heart* (New York, 1959).

B. NYT 11 August 1962.

ROY HALVERSON

— I —

IRWIN, WILLIAM HENRY (b. 14 September 1873; d. 24 February 1948) had a long and varied career as a magazine and newspaper editor and writer, lecturer, playwright, propagandist, and author or editor of thirty-seven books of fact and fiction. His achievements included writing a classic *New York Sun* tribute to fire-ravaged San Francisco, establishing standards for modern press criticism, covering World War I for the *Saturday Evening Post* and the *New York Tribune,* crusading in print and on platform for international cooperation to end war, and writing the first biography of Herbert Hoover. Although he was eulogized as a jack-of-all-letters, he is best remembered as a reporter.

Irwin, the oldest of three children, was born in Oneida, New York. His father, David Irwin, was a bookkeeper and lumber salesman from Erie, Pennsylvania. His mother, Edith Greene Irwin, was the daughter of a Canandaigua, New York, poet and painter. In 1879 the Irwins moved to Leadville, Colorado, high in the Rocky Mountains. While his father unsuccessfully tried several occupations, Irwin excelled in school and worked for the *Herald-Democrat,* first as a printer's devil then as a carrier. In the late 1880s the Irwins, including younger brothers Wallace and Herman, moved to Denver. In 1892 Irwin graduated from West High School. He worked odd jobs, including punching cattle and barnstorming in melodramas, until his high school mentor loaned him money for college.

In 1894 he entered Stanford University. There he began a lifelong friendship with Herbert Hoover, won prizes for stories and poetry, participated in debate and theater, became editor of the student paper, and majored in classics. In the spring of his senior year, he withdrew from the university rather than be expelled for writing rowdy lyrics to a drinking song. While waiting for reinstatement, he secretly married Harriet "Hallie" Hyde, a classmate. He finally was allowed to receive a B.A. degree on 24 May 1899.

The next month he began editing and writing for a San Francisco literary weekly, the *Wave*. When it was sold in 1900, he became a general assignment reporter for the *San Francisco Chronicle*. In 1902 he became Sunday editor. Irwin was also writing stories and articles for other publications and collaborating with Charles K. Field and Gelett Burgess. In a formal ceremony Irwin and Hallie were remarried in 1901, and in October 1903 she gave birth to a son.

Leaving his family in California, Irwin in June 1903 began reporting for the *New York Sun*. He continued to free-lance, and by 1906 decided he wanted to do something more literary than newspaper reporting. An editorship on *McClure's Magazine* seemed to offer that opportunity. While he learned his new job, he worked for both S. S. McClure (q.v.) and the *Sun*. During this transitional period, Irwin wrote from memory a vivid description of San Franciso before the earthquake and fire. When "The City That Was" appeared in the 21 April 1906 *Sun,* it drew international acclaim. The feature was polished for book publication and often reprinted.

Irwin was unable to get along with McClure, and after about a year, first as managing editor then as the editor, he quit to free-lance full-time, mainly for *Collier's Weekly*. In 1911 *Collier's* published his fifteen-part series on "The American Newspaper," which provided a history of the medium and exposed unethical practices, setting standards for modern press criticism.

In 1914 Irwin gave up journalism to write fiction, but catastrophic events in Europe that August lured him abroad to cover the war. Back in the United States briefly, he helped Hoover publicize the work of the Commission for Relief in Belgium. Reporting for the *New York Tribune* and the *London Times* and *Daily Mail* in 1915, he revealed the heroic, strategic victory of the British at Ypres, kept secret by the British War Office for three months. In April 1915 he reported his second Ypres story, a poison-gas attack by the Germans, and was himself made ill by effects of lingering gas.

Having been divorced by Hallie in 1908, he married writer Inez Haynes Gillmore in 1916 and returned with her to Europe as a correspondent for the *Saturday Evening Post*. At Gorizia, Italy, with other correspondents, he was knocked down when a shell exploded nearby. The blast injured his right eardrum, and he eventually lost his hearing in that ear.

Irwin continued to cover the war except for six months in Washington as chairman of the new foreign division of the Committee on Public Information. In 1920 he returned to the United States to campaign in lectures, articles, and books for international cooperation to end war forever. During this time he wrote his best-selling *The Next War* (1921) and switched from the *Saturday Evening Post* to *Collier's* so he could champion the League of Nations. He also wrote other journalism as well as fiction, including his best novel, *Youth Rides West* (1925), set in a wild west mining town like his childhood Leadville. When Hoover ran for president, Irwin, once labeled a radical, fully supported his old friend. He not only wrote the campaign biography of Hoover, but also delivered speeches in his behalf. For the rest of his life, Irwin remained unwaveringly loyal to Hoover.

During the depression and World War II, Irwin wrote for newspaper syndicates, including the North American Newspaper Alliance, for magazines, including *Liberty,* and for book publishers, including McGraw-Hill and Putnam's. Two of his best remembered books written in this period were *Propaganda and the News* (1936), suggested by Hoover as a counterattack on his Democratic critics, and *The Making of a Reporter* (1942), an anecdotal memoir emphasizing people Irwin had met. Working with dramatist Sidney Howard, he adapted an ancient Chinese play, *Pi-Pa-Ki,* which eventually became the 1945 Broadway musical *Lute Song*.

Irwin was active in professional organizations, serving as president of both the Authors Guild and the Authors League of America, was a lobbyist for fair copyright laws for writers, and the recipient of many honors, most notably the Legion of Honor from France, King Albert Medal from Belgium, and the Olympic Games medal from Sweden. He died on 24 February 1948 of a cerebral occlusion.

BIBLIOGRAPHY:

B. DAB Supp. 4, 417–419; DLB 25, 136–143; NYT 25 February 1948; Robert V. Hudson, *The Writing Game: A Biography of Will Irwin* (Ames, Iowa, 1982); Robert V. Hudson, "Will Irwin's Pioneering Criticism of the Press," *Journalism Quarterly,* Summer 1970.

ROBERT V. HUDSON

IVES, FREDERIC EUGENE (b. 17 February 1856; d. 27 May 1937) was an inventor who perfected halftone photoengraving and several methods for processing and printing color photographs. Seventy patents were granted to him by the U.S. Patent Office. Ives was born to Hubert Leverit Ives and Ellen A. Beach Ives, near Litchfield, Connecticut. His father was a farmer and a storekeeper. He attended the public schools in Litchfield, Norfolk, and Newtown, Connecticut. His father died while Frederic was quite young. At age thirteen he signed on for a three-year apprenticeship in printing at the *Litchfield Enquirer*.

In 1873 he was hired as a journeyman printer by a print shop in Ithaca, New York. Within months he left the shop and went into business as the operator of a photography studio. His work as a photographer and printer was quickly noticed in upstate New York, and in 1875 he was employed as head of the photography laboratory at Cornell University. Here he was allowed to conduct experiments. It was while he was at Cornell that he successfully demonstrated a "swelled gelatin" method of making line photoengravings; and then introduced a workable halftone photoengraving process in 1878.

On 15 June 1879 Ives married Mary Elizabeth Olmstead. They had one child, Herbert Eugene Ives (1882–1953). Frederic Ives lived to see his son become a physicist with Bell Telephone Laboratories. Mary Elizabeth Ives died in 1904. Ives married Mrs. Margaret Campbell Cutting on 15 November 1913. She died in 1928. In 1879 Frederic Ives moved to Philadelphia and worked with a manufacturer of printing plates. In 1881 he began the manufacture of commercial printing plates using a mechanical halftone process. The U.S. government bought his first plates. After further experiments, in 1886 he perfected the type of halftone photoengraving process now used by printers worldwide.

Some of his other inventions were a color-photography process for still cameras using three negatives; a tint photometer; several key elements of motion photography in color; and the short-tube, single-objective binocular microscope.

His autobiography noted that Ives was a member of the following organizations: the American Association for the Advancement of Science, the American Academy of Arts and Sciences, the American Physical Society, the Royal Photographic Society, the Optical Society of America, the American Institute of Graphic Arts, the Photographic Society of Philadelphia, the New York Camera Club, the Society of Motion Picture Engineers, and others.

Ives received many awards. Among them were awards presented by the International Inventions Exhibition in London, and the Franklin Institute, in 1885 for the halftone photoengraving process; and awards for color photography from the Photographic Society of Philadelphia, and the Society of Arts in London (1892), the Photographische Gesellschaft in Wien (1893), the Royal Scottish Society of Arts (1896), and the American Academy of Arts and Sciences Rumford Medal for both photoengraving and color photography (1912).

He died on 27 May 1937 at Hahnemann Hospital in Philadelphia following a long illness. He was eighty-one years old.

BIBLIOGRAPHY:

A. *The Autobiography of an Amateur Inventor* (Philadelphia, 1928).

B. NYT 28 May 1937.

DONALD L. MCBRIDE

— J —

JOHNSTON, JAMES (b. 13 August 1738; d. 4 October 1808) was the first newspaper editor-publisher in Georgia. On 7 April 1763 the twenty-four-year-old Scotsman put out issue number one of the *Georgia Gazette,* which became the first focused medium of news in the British colony. He continued an active newspaper career in Georgia until 1802 with only brief interruptions.

James Johnston was born in Edinburgh, Scotland, the son of James and Jane Nisbet Johnston. Not much is known about his parents except that his father died when Johnston was six. An older brother, Lewis, moved to Savannah, Georgia, in 1752, where he was a physician, farmer, and retailer of medicines. James Johnston appears to have joined his brother in the colony in the early 1760s.

At that time, there was no printer in Georgia and the royal government felt that one was needed. Johnston, whose educational qualifications are unknown but who seems to have done an apprenticeship in printing, was encouraged financially by the Georgia government to set up a shop, which he did on Broughton Street in Savannah. The *Georgia Gazette* was probably its first product, although Johnston shortly thereafter printed other things such as government forms, proclamations, laws passed by the general assembly, and occasional pamphlets. For a time, he had a stipend from the government, which was also his biggest client. Johnston declined to be postmaster in Savannah except for a brief time when no one else would have the job.

At some point early in the 1760s, he married Sarah Lawrence and they had nineteen children, seven of whom lived to adulthood. One son, Nicholas Johnston, later became a newspaper figure in Georgia and worked with his father. In colonial times, James Johnston had personal as well as financial ties to the government of Georgia. His brother Lewis rose rapidly in the colony and became an important member of the council of the royal governor.

With this family connection in addition to his business interests, it is not surprising that James was an editor loyal to the British. A study of the surviving issues of the *Georgia Gazette* suggests, however, that Johnston tried to be impartial in his coverage of prerevolutionary public events. Toward the end of the colonial era, a party of revolutionaries visited Johnston and roughly chastised him for not being more accommodating to their point of view.

Finally in 1776, Johnson left his print shop and retired from Savannah, going eventually to St. Vincent in the West Indies. He had put out the last issue on 7 October 1776. Except for six months during the Stamp Act controversy in 1765–66 when he suspended publication, readers could look forward to receiving the *Georgia Gazette* on schedule.

James Johnston was not a great printer. What he produced was technically acceptable, but was not exceptional in quality. Neither did he make a mark as a writer. He and the *Georgia Gazette* are important not because they were innovative or imaginative, but because they gave Georgia its first newspaper. The *Gazette* was like other rather conservative papers of the time. It reprinted items from other publications and ran many advertisements, a column of local news, letters to the editor, occasional moral essays, a bit of poetry, the texts of important laws and governmental proclamations, the proceedings of public bodies, shipping news, prices current, and reports on the assize of bread. Almost always, there was editorial silence on local issues.

After Johnston departed the colony in 1776, he was accused of high treason by the revolutionary government then in charge in Georgia. When the British army recaptured Savannah in December 1778, Johnston was not slow in returning also. By August 1779 he was back publishing the *Royal Georgia Gazette* on a new printing press bought for him by British authorities. When the revolutionaries won the war and the British departed Georgia in 1782, Johnston left briefly but soon returned to be forgiven by the victors. The new state of Georgia needed a printer and Johnston was the candidate who came most readily to hand. In January 1783 he became the official printer of the state. The same month he issued the first edition of the *Gazette of the State of Georgia,* a new newspaper. Five years later, he readopted his old title, the *Georgia Gazette*. Late in life, he was assisted by his son Nicholas. James Johnston published the final issue of the *Georgia Gazette* on 25 November 1802, shortly after Nicholas's death. Johnston died at age seventy. He lies buried in the colonial cemetery in Savannah.

BIBLIOGRAPHY:

B. Louis T. Griffith and John E. Talmadge, *Georgia Journalism, 1763–1950* (Athens, Ga., 1951); Alexander Lawrence, *James Johnston: Georgia's First Printer* (Savannah, Ga., 1956).

HAROLD E. DAVIS

JONES, GEORGE (b. 16 August 1811; d. 12 August 1891) was one of the nation's first modern newspaper proprietors. Under his guidance, the *New York Times* developed a reputation for respectability, factual reporting, and an informative style that contrasted sharply with the prevalent sensationalism of the day. Though Jones wrote almost nothing for newspaper publication, his interest in cleaning up New York city government was responsible for the *Times*'s contribution to the 1872 overthrow of the Tweed Ring. Under Jones, the activities of the business office were kept separate from editorial policy-making. This was one of Jones's most significant contributions to modern journalism.

Born in Poultney, Vermont, Jones was the son of woolen manufacturer John Jones and his wife Barbara Davis Jones. When the boy was thirteen, both of his parents died. Jones was educated in country schools, and supported himself by working in a general store kept by Amos Bliss. In addition to owning the store, Bliss published a newspaper, the *Northern Spectator*. In 1824 Bliss hired Horace Greeley (q.v.), another local boy, as a printer's apprentice. Greeley and Jones became friends, and, in 1841 when Greeley founded the *New York Tribune*, he asked Jones to become a partner. Jones refused, but did accept a post in the business office. While working for the *Tribune*, he became acquainted with Henry J. Raymond (q.v.), Greeley's editorial assistant, and future editor of the *New York Times*. Later in the 1840s Jones moved to Albany, New York, where he took advantage of the lucrative free banking laws and went into business for himself. There he met influential Whig politician Thurlow Weed (q.v.), who in 1848 offered to sell the *Albany Evening Journal* to Raymond and Jones. Though the deal fell through, both men remained interested in the idea of establishing a daily newspaper.

In 1851 Raymond and Jones had that opportunity. According to *Times* office lore, the two men were walking across the icy Hudson when Jones commented that Greeley's *Tribune* was rumored to make $60,000 a year. This, combined with the impending regulation of the New York banking industry, convinced Jones to close up his Albany business and move to New York City. The two men formally associated into Raymond, Jones, and Company on 5 August 1851, and published the first issue of the *New York Times* on 18 September. Henry Raymond was the paper's editor; Jones was the publisher and financial manager. Under Raymond and Jones, the *New York Times* was highly successful as first a moderate Whig and then Republican newspaper.

When Henry Raymond died on 19 June 1869, Jones assumed control of both the *Times*'s business management and editorial policy. Though he did not own a controlling interest in the Times company, Jones was responsible for hiring the paper's editors. In September 1870 Jones began what was the *Times*'s best known nineteenth-century campaign—its attempt to overthrow the Tweed Ring. The *Times,* along with *Harper's Weekly* illustrator Thomas Nast (q.v.), were the city's most vehement opponents of the "Boss." The paper's publication of excerpts from Controller Richard B. Connolly's account books marked the beginning of the end of the Tweed Ring. Though Jones's *Times* prided itself on the success of its effort to unseat the Boss and his ring, some revisionist historians, most notably Leo Hershkowitz, have challenged the nineteenth-century paper's claim to rectitude. There is evidence to support the contention that Jones's crusade was akin to a partisan witch-hunt, and that the Republican newspaper toppled the ring with ardor and innuendo instead of fact. Regardless of the extent of the ring's culpability, the *New York Times* under Jones served the interests of New York's respectable Protestant establishment that felt threatened by the influx of "outsiders" and foreigners into the city.

Throughout the 1870s Jones increased his number of shares of *Times*'s stock, and gained complete control in 1876. In 1884 the paper bolted the Republican party over its nomination of James G. Blaine, and supported Grover Cleveland as the presidential candidate of the Independent Republicans. From that time until after Jones's death, the *New York Times* was known as the newspaper of New York City's "Mugwumps."

Very little is known about Jones's private life. He married Sarah M. Gilbert of Troy, New York, in 1836. He belonged to no organizations other than the Episcopal Church and the Union League Club. George Jones died in South Poland, Maine, on 12 August 1891.

BIBLIOGRAPHY:

B. DAB 5, 171; NYT 12 August 1891; Meyer Berger, *The Story of the "New York Times," 1851–1951* (New York, 1951); Elmer H. Davis, *History of the "New York Times," 1851–1921* (New York, 1921); Leo Hershkowitz, *Tweed's New York, Another Look* (New York, 1978).

JANET E. STEELE

JORDAN, MAX (b. 21 April 1895; d. 28 November 1977) was NBC's first European representative. He arranged for broadcasts from all over Europe to be heard in America on NBC's Blue and Red networks, and in the late 1930s and early 1940s, was the chief European correspondent for the network. Jordan was also a regular contributor to several Catholic journals and the National Catholic Welfare Conference (NCWC) News Service.

Jordan was born in San Remo, Italy, the son of parents with international ties. His mother and father, Tecla J. (Hauelsen) and Herman Jordan, were from Württemberg, Germany, but Jordan had both French and Austrian ancestors. His father was operating a pharmacy at the time of Jordan's birth, then became a Kodak representative for Italy and Switzerland. By the time Jordan finished high school, his family had lived in three countries, settling in Stuttgart in 1912. Jordan attended college at the Universities of Frankfort, Berlin, and Jena, receiving his Ph.D. in religious philosophy from the latter.

He had contributed to the *Berliner Tageblatt* while in college, and joined the staff of that paper in 1920, working on the foreign desk. Wooed away by the Hearst chain in 1922, Jordan soon became assistant bureau chief in Berlin, assisting Karl von Wiegard. In 1924 he went to New York to be in charge of Hearst's foreign coverage. Jordan fell in love with America, and when Hearst officials wanted to send him back to Europe, Jordan resigned. He became Washington correspondent for his old Berlin paper, and got his first glimpse of radio news in 1928, when NBC moved its Washington office across from Jordan's in the National Press Building.

Jordan left Washington to travel around the world, a journey which lasted nearly three years. In 1931 he was hired by NBC to represent the company in Europe. CBS already had Cesar Saerchinger in London. The network representatives were not foreign correspondents so much as they were program procurers. They combed Europe for interesting broadcast material, arranging for live performances of such groups as the Sistine Chapel Choir. They also arranged for talks by politicians, and at times would introduce the shortwave broadcasts. But they did little actual broadcasting until the threat of war caused the networks to want their own reporters, and not the newspapermen who moonlighted with commentaries for the networks.

The transition to foreign correspondent was finalized during two crucial periods in 1938, the Anschluss and Munich Crisis. Jordan made the first broadcast to America from occupied Austria on 12 March 1938. There was a lull in developments during the summer, but in the fall, the Munich Crisis brought hundreds of live broadcasts. Jordan was able to use superior connections with the German broadcast authorities to beat CBS on several key developments, including the terms of the agreement between Britain and Germany. Both networks built up their European staffs as war seemed imminent, but Jordan remained the chief European correspondent. After war was declared, Jordan found Nazi censorship to be unbearable and he moved the network's operations to Switzerland. He was also under suspicion for anti-Nazi actions. Prior to the war, he had gotten on a blacklist for associating with members of a democratic luncheon club, and had apparently helped Jews escape from Germany. He also is believed to have smuggled in restricted goods to friends. When Paris fell to the Nazis, in June 1940, German authorities came into possession of information Jordan had collected about religious persecution under Hitler. He had left it with a friend, who had abandoned the documents in his flight. Jordan had been a correspondent for several Catholic agencies, including the NCWC News Service. The material was apparently meant for publication in America. Also after war was declared, but the U.S. was still officially neutral, Jordan, who had become an American citizen, passed along information to U.S. representatives in Germany.

Whether Jordan felt he could no longer report from Europe, or whether he feared reprisals from the Nazis, is not known. But he left for America in late 1941. He wrote several articles on the war, as well as a book. NBC appointed Jordan director of a new department of religious broadcasts on 1 February 1943. He left NBC in 1945, and returned to Europe as correspondent for the NCWC News Service.

Jordan became a seminarian at Beuron, Germany, in 1947, and was ordained there on 8 December 1951. He wrote four books on religious topics: *Antwort auf das Wort* (1969); *The Divine Dimension* (1970); *Vom Innewerden Gottes* (1971); and *Die Toschter Gottes* (1973).

BIBLIOGRAPHY:

A. *Beyond All Fronts* (Milwaukee, 1944).

B. *Catholic Authors,* 1948; David H. Hosley, *As Good as Any* (Westport, Conn., 1984).

DAVID H. HOSLEY

— K —

KALTENBORN, HANS VON (b. 9 July 1878; d. 14 June 1965) was a pioneer news broadcaster and one of the leaders in that field for three decades. He was born in Milwaukee. His father, Rudolph von Kaltenborn, was a former Hessian army officer who claimed to be a baron. His mother, Bertha, died after Hans was born, and the boy was raised by a stepmother.

When he entered his teens, the family moved to Merrill, Wisconsin, where Hans began his writing career with a letter to the editor. The editor suggested the fourteen-year-old report for the paper, without pay. Later, the paper put him on salary. When the Spanish-American War began he enlisted, became a sergeant, and supplemented his pay by writing about army life for the Merrill and Milwaukee papers. He saw no action, but got in some domestic travel as a soldier. That whetted his appetite for travel; he worked his way to Europe and toured France and Germany. He found work as a salesman in Paris and continued to free-lance.

Back in the United States in 1902, Kaltenborn found a job with the *Brooklyn Eagle*, but left in 1905 to get his degree at Harvard. He traveled around the world as tutor to Vincent Astor, married Olga von Nordenflycht (a German baroness), and returned to the *Eagle*. He covered Washington for that paper, then Paris, then returned to Brooklyn to become the *Eagle*'s war editor.

He delivered a series of weekly talks about news topics in the newspaper's auditorium. Kaltenborn had practiced oratory and won prizes at it, and had developed a clipped, precise delivery that would become familiar to American radio listeners. In 1922 he was invited to deliver over radio station WYCB on Bedloe's Island what amounted to a half-hour editorial about a labor strike. The next year he began a weekly commentary on WEAF on Long Island. The popular program attracted a Washington station to what became a two-station network, making Kaltenborn the first ''network'' newscaster. In 1938, by introducing and commenting upon reports from European correspondents for CBS, he became, in effect, the first network anchorman.

In 1930 Kaltenborn left the *Eagle* to devote full time to radio. He joined CBS. He traveled occasionally, and interviewed leading world figures. He came to prominent attention in September 1938, when European leaders including Hitler and Chamberlain negotiated the fate of Czechoslovakia. CBS broadcast several special reports a day for nineteen days; Kaltenborn was the anchor and slept at the office. He ad-libbed for quarter-hours and longer at a time.

Two years before that, Kaltenborn acquired some notoriety by broadcasting from a haystack between the lines of a Spanish civil war battle. It was reporting "live" in a sense more dramatic and precarious than usual. He gained more notoriety late in his career, when he broadcast on election night 1948 that Harry Truman's million-vote lead meant nothing, that Truman would surely be defeated, and Truman mimicked the performance at a dinner for the Electoral College.

In 1940 Kaltenborn switched from CBS to NBC. He remained on the air, sometimes in a semiretired capacity, until 1958; his last regular broadcast was in 1953. Kaltenborn frequently worked from notes rather than from a script. He had some difficulties with sponsors because of his bluntness, and he resisted the movement of radio news in the 1940s away from commentary toward "objective" reporting; at that time he founded the Association of Radio News Analysts in a losing effort to stop the trend.

The Kaltenborns had a daughter, Anais, and a son, Rolf. H. V. Kaltenborn died at age eighty-seven of a heart attack.

BIBLIOGRAPHY:

A. *Fifty Fabulous Years* (New York, 1950); *It Seems Like Yesterday* (New York, 1956).

B. DAB Supp. 7, 408–410; NYT 15 June 1965; David Culbert, *News for Everyman* (Westport, Conn., 1976); Irving E. Fang, *Those Radio Commentators!* (Ames, Iowa, 1977).

LAURA NICKERSON

KELLOGG, ANSEL NASH (b. 20 March 1832; d. 23 March 1886) was a newspaper editor and publisher who became known as "the father of the newspaper syndicate." In this role he helped to revolutionize the content and technological processes used by the rural weekly press in America.

He was born in Reading, Pennsylvania. When Kellogg was young his family moved to New York where he was educated. After graduating second in his class from Columbia College in 1852, Kellogg studied one year to become an architect, but an interest in journalism took him to Wisconsin, where he went to work for the *Northern Republic* in Portage. In 1854 he moved to Baraboo, where he published the *Baraboo Republic*, a four-page weekly.

Kellogg, a staunch Republican, was elated at the election of Abraham Lincoln in 1860. "The People Want Honest Abe for President!" read part of the nineteen-deck headline over the election story. Lincoln's inauguration, however, brought civil war in its wake, and Kellogg soon lost his journeyman printer who joined the Union army.

Kellogg found out that he could not issue a full-sized newspaper on a regular publication-day basis without assistance. Out of necessity, he arranged to have the *Wisconsin State Journal* in Madison furnish him with half-sheet supplements printed on both sides with war news. These were folded within his own half sheets, but one issue was sufficient to convince Kellogg that this was too awkward an arrangement. For the next issue he ordered full sheets printed on one side from the *Journal*, and on 10 July 1861 the *Republic* appeared as a four-page paper, pages two and three consisting of war news printed by the *Journal* and pages one and four printed by Kellogg.

This was the first use of "patent insides" (also called "ready-print"). Other weekly publishers followed Kellogg's lead and ordered printed sheets from the *Journal*. By 1862 the number of papers using this economical device had grown to nearly two dozen. From the very first, some editors were alarmed at the prospect of a loss of independence, and of content control from a central source. Others, however, asserted that the arrangement made for better newspapers with a more diversified fare.

The *Journal*'s syndicate grew to some thirty papers; a competing syndicate in Milwaukee had the same number. In Baraboo, Kellogg saw the possibilities of a syndicate service, independent of any parent-newspaper affiliation. He sold the *Republic* and moved to Chicago in 1865 to launch a news business. He purchased the weekly *Western Railroad Gazette* as a financial backstop if his planned syndicate did not flourish. By August Kellogg had eight orders for his service from midwestern papers. On 19 August Kellogg started the first continuous independent syndicate to print from type set exclusively for weekly papers.

Clients of Kellogg's syndicate received the same undated seven-column folio sheets. Content (called "evergreen matter") was made up primarily of features and other miscellaneous items. In a short while Kellogg added advertising and news. To promote his product, Kellogg produced the first issue of the *Publisher's Auxiliary*, two pages of syndicated material and two pages of trade news and ads. By the end of 1865, Kellogg was furnishing fifty-three papers in four states with sheets at a price of seven cents per quire. The economy of the service attracted publishers so that by 1869 some 193 papers were using Kellogg's ready-print.

The operation grew to the point where Kellogg hired J. M. Edson in 1867 as the first syndicate editor. By 1871 Kellogg's syndicate had 240 clients. Nationally, competition had sprung up, and by 1872 some 1,000 papers were being supplied syndicate material. The great Chicago fire of 1871 almost put Kellogg out of business. His plant was engulfed in flames and left a charred ruin, but despite this setback Kellogg rebuilt the business. He pioneered technological changes that improved the service. Stereotyped plates supplemented the ready-print sheets to be later replaced by lightweight celluloid plates.

In 1876 Kellogg was invited to prepare an exhibit for the Centennial Exposition in Philadelphia of all the newspapers served by his syndicate. The 583 papers were published in twenty-five states and one Canadian province. He continued to expand. He moved to New York City in the 1880s in semiretirement but retained the presidency of the A. N. Kellogg Newspaper Company.

He became an invalid and died in Thomasville, Georgia, in 1886, leaving his wife, the former Annie E. Barnes, whom he had married in 1859 at Baraboo, and adult daughters. By the time of his death his syndicate had become a corporation serving nearly 1,400 papers with ready-print and thousands more with stereotyped plates. In 1906 the Kellogg company was bought out by its rival, the Western Newspaper Union.

BIBLIOGRAPHY:

B. DLB 23, 180–183; J. M. Edson, *History of the A. N. Kellogg Newspaper Company* (Chicago, 1890); Elmo Scott Watson, *A History of Newspaper Syndicates in the United States: 1865–1935* (Chicago, 1936).

ROBERT E. BLACKMON

KELLOGG, MARCUS HENRY (b. 31 March 1833; d. 25 June 1876) was the sole reporter to accompany Lieutenant Colonel George A. Custer on the fatal expedition that ended when the 7th Cavalry charged a coalition of Indian nations camped along the Little Big Horn River in southeastern Montana Territory. Kellogg died among the about 250 soldiers killed with Custer's immediate command.

Mark Kellogg was the third of ten children—four of whom died during early childhood—born to Simeon and Lorenda Whelpley Kellogg who were married in Kingston, Ontario, in 1829. In the 1850s Mark studied in Kenosha, Wisconsin, to become a telegraph operator. In 1851 his family moved to La Crosse, Wisconsin. He became one of the first commercial telegraph operators for the Northwestern Telegraph Company in La Crosse around 1858. In 1865 he was a partner in a flour and feed store.

As a telegrapher, Kellogg handled news for the first La Crosse daily in 1859, and he later met Marcus M. "Brick" Pomeroy, editor of the *La Crosse Democrat*. Pomeroy was a Copperhead editor whose vitriolic attacks on President Lincoln went so far as to suggest that the "widow maker" president be planted in "some nigger's grave." Kellogg went to work first as a cashier for Pomeroy, but became local editor in a short time.

Kellogg married Martha L. Robinson of La Crosse on 19 May 1861. The couple had two daughters: Cora Sue was born 5 February 1862, and Martha "Mattie" Grace was born 20 August 1863. The family was hit by a series of tragedies in 1867. After a long illness, Simeon Kellogg died in January. Mark's wife, Martha, died 17 May at the home of her father, Charles Robinson, after what the newspaper described as "a long and painful illness."

In March 1867 Mark Kellogg made his first run for political office. He received the Democratic party and newspaper endorsement for city clerk, but he lost the election by fifty-seven votes. Out of a job, Mark left his daughters, ages five and three, with their aunt and grandmother and set out to find work. By fall he arrived in Council Bluffs, Iowa, where the following spring he became assistant editor of the *Daily Democrat*, established in May 1868 by Alf S. Kierolf and Company. The *Democrat* had difficulty surviving in a patriotic Union town. When one of their colleagues purchased Kellogg's and Kierolf's interests in the paper, they left.

By 1870 Kellogg was back in La Crosse, where he lived with his daughters and his wife's parents. The federal census listed his occupation as printer, and the city directory said he was a telegraph operator. Beginning in the early 1870s, he contributed articles under the pen name "Frontier" to the *St. Paul Pioneer* and worked as a stringer for other newspapers as he followed the construction of the Northern Pacific Railroad from Duluth to Bismarck working as a telegraph operator. In 1872 he ran a close but unsuccessful race for the state legislature in northern Minnesota, and according to Professor Warren E. Barnard of Indiana State University, he published a campaign newspaper for presidential candidate Horace Greeley called the *Greeley Wave* in Brainerd, Minnesota.

The following year he worked for the *Bismarck Tribune* in Dakota Territory, and from then until his death, he alternated between working as a staff writer and a stringer for the newspaper. Custer and Kellogg met near Bismarck. Disobeying an order that he take no newspapermen with him, Custer invited C. A. Lounsberry (q.v.), the *Tribune*'s publisher, to tag along on the expedition which originated at Fort Lincoln near Bismarck. Lounsberry sent Kellogg in his place. Upon his death, Kellogg was claimed by at least five newspapers. He did write for both Bismarck and St. Paul newspapers and probably contributed to the Western Associated Press. Lounsberry forwarded his dispatches to the *New York Herald*, which had the most extensive coverage of the Little Big Horn. In his often quoted last dispatch, Kellogg wrote: "We leave the Rosebud tomorrow and by the time this reaches you we will have met and fought the red devils, with what result remains to be seen. I go with Custer and will be at the death."

Lounsberry wrote an obituary filled with factual inaccuracies and he claimed to be unable to locate Kellogg's survivors. Subsequent historians regarded Kellogg's past as "mysterious." Not until 1950 did historians begin to ask questions about the reporter killed in one of the most written about battles in American history. In a series of papers in 1983 and 1984, Professor Barnard suggested that Lounsberry and another Bismarck businessman who knew Kellogg well deliberately obscured details of Kellogg's past to avoid forfeiting a field diary which may have contained damaging information about Custer, their friend and fellow Civil War veteran. The last words that Kellogg, the Copperhead, wrote about Custer, the Union's "boy general," remain among the many mysteries of the Little Big Horn.

BIBLIOGRAPHY:

B. Oliver Knight, *Following the Indian Wars: The Story of the Newspaper Correspondents among the Indian Campaigners* (Norman, Okla., 1960); Lewis O. Saum, "Colonel Custer's Copperhead: The 'Mysterious' Mark Kellogg," *Montana, the Magazine of Western History*, October 1978.

WILLIAM E. HUNTZICKER

KELLY, FLORENCE FINCH (b. 27 March 1858; d. 17 December 1939) was a newspaperwoman whose career spanned fifty-six years and ranged across the United States. Her *New York Times* obituary credited her with doing "about everything a newspaperwoman or newspaperman could do." From 1906 until her retirement in 1936 she was associated with the *Book Review* of the *Times*, with her own column during most of those years.

Florence Finch was born at her family's farm on the outskirts of Girard, Illinois, youngest of the eight children of James Gardner Finch and Mary Ann Purdom Finch. Early memories of discussions about the Civil War implanted both an interest in public affairs and an intense patriotism. At fourteen, determined to be a writer of fiction, Kelly saw her first short story published in a fiction periodical. By this time she had completed elementary school. To support herself at high school in Paoli, Kansas, she did housework and child care, obtaining a teacher's certificate in six months. Although she disliked teaching, she spent two years at it to earn money for college. She was graduated from the University of Kansas in 1881.

In the meantime she had decided to try writing for magazines and newspapers, and she obtained summer work on the *Topeka Commonwealth* after her junior year. She then traveled to San Francisco, where she sold a story but was unable to find a satisfactory position. After returning to Kansas to graduate, she went to Chicago. At this time, she wrote later, few women worked on newspapers, "and the few who had been able to make an entrance, mainly by butting their heads against a stone wall until they had battered a hole through which they could creep, were not welcome." She stayed in Chicago only long enough to save money for a discount train ticket to Boston. There she found work at the *Boston Globe*, with assignments including millinery openings, society events, straight news, art criticism, a column called "The Woman's Hour," a series on American humor and humorists, and editorials.

During her three years at the *Globe* she became well acquainted with the chief editorial writer, Allen Kelly. He proposed marriage, and she accepted, but the wedding was postponed until 9 December 1884, after she had worked briefly for the *Morning Telegram* in Troy, New York, and then joined Allen to start a paper at Lowell, Massachusetts. The *Lowell Bell* was a venture for which Kelly had little enthusiasm; her pessimism seems to have been justified, for it failed after three months. In Fall River, Massachusetts, she worked as editorial assistant to her husband, who was managing editor of the *Globe* there, but she resigned in the fall of 1885 to give birth to a son. He died four and a half years later.

A move to New York provided opportunity for free-lance work, but Kelly's only newspaper staff position for the next several years was a brief stint at the *San Francisco Examiner* while Allen was city editor there. She had two romantic novels published during her five years in San Francisco.

The couple's next home was New Mexico, where another son, Sherwin, was born in 1894. Two years later Allen became city editor of the *Los Angeles Times*, and during 1899 Kelly was a columnist and literary editor for that paper. She also finished a novel set in New Mexico. In 1900 she returned to the East, seeking what she believed was a more healthy climate for herself and her son. Allen had positions in Philadelphia and New York but returned to the *Times*. Kelly joined him for a trip to New Zealand and Australia in 1905, investigating social and economic legislation there. He died in Los Angeles of tubercular problems on 16 May 1916.

Kelly decided that writing for the ten-year-old *New York Times Book Review* would be ideal and persuaded the editor to try her out in September 1906. She also wrote feature stories and interviews for the *Times*. Four more novels, a volume of short stories, and a history of the U.S. war effort in World War I were published during the next fifteen years. A leave of absence from the *Times* in 1916 found her working in Kansas to win support for Woodrow Wilson and the Democrats. She died three years after her retirement in New Hartford, Connecticut.

BIBLIOGRAPHY:

A. *Flowing Stream: The Story of Fifty-Six Years in American Newspaper Life* (New York, 1939).

B. NAW 2, 323–324; NYT 18 December 1939.

SHERILYN COX BENNION

KENDALL, AMOS (b. 16 August 1787; d. 12 November 1869), journalist, postmaster, and noted politician, was born in Dunstable, Massachusetts, son of Zebedee Kendall and great-grandson of Francis Kendall. His major effort and reputation were made during the Jackson and Van Buren presidencies. A significant member of Jackson's Kitchen Cabinet, Kendall used his writing skills and ability to adjust to the political climate and served both presidents as a government reformer.

His parents never did enjoy success as farmers. Kendall worked long hours with his older brother, who had taken over the family farm when the father became ill. His early education was in the academy at New Ipswich, New Hampshire, in 1806. Kendall prepared for college under Caleb Butler at Groton Academy, and entered Dartmouth College in 1807. He was graduated with honors in 1811. He studied law from 1811 to 1814, and then in 1814 he traveled to Kentucky to serve as a tutor to Henry Clay's family. He remained in Kentucky until 1829.

Kendall moved in 1815 to Georgetown, Kentucky, where he served as postmaster. He then moved to Frankfort, Kentucky, in 1816 to manage the *Argus of Western America*. He also edited the Georgetown *Patriot*, 1815–16. During the time he worked with the newspaper he wielded political support for Andrew Jackson, after breaking with Henry Clay in 1826. He remained with the *Patriot* until 1829. When Jackson moved to Washington he appointed Kendall the fourth auditor of the U.S. Treasury. He served from 1829 to 1835.

He was twice married, first, in October 1818, to Mary B. Woolfolk of Jefferson County, Kentucky, who died 11 October 1823; in 1826 he married Jane Kyle of Georgetown, Kentucky, who was twenty years younger than he.

During Jackson's term in office Kendall exerted a major influence in the administration, and was largely responsible for having the *Globe*, the administration newspaper, supersede the *Telegraph*. The similarity of Jackson and Kendall's thoughts can be found in his handwritten notes to Jackson, and in the president's speeches. In June 1835 Kendall was appointed postmaster general and found the department in debt. He reorganized the department and paid off the debts. He also approved the exclusion of abolitionist propaganda from the mails by southern postmasters.

However, Kendall's larger reputation came from his writing ability. He expressed opinions in the newspapers through his essays, columns, and editorial pieces which helped Jackson gain public support for his policies. As a member of the Kitchen Cabinet, he wrote most of Jackson's speeches and in July 1832 drafted Jackson's veto of the bill to recharter the Second Bank of the United States. He was reappointed postmaster by Van Buren on 4 March 1837, but resigned 9 May 1840 due to ill health.

In 1841 in Washington, D.C. he founded *Kendall's Expositor* which was a small sheet publication with 11,000 subscribers. It closed in October 1844. He founded the *Union Democrat* also in September 1841, which was "devoted to the preservation of the Union and the support of the democracy" (Kendall, 1872). He published the *Union Democrat* until it ceased publication in May 1842. The paper had only 1,600 subscribers.

In 1845 Kendall began a partnership with Samuel F. B. Morse, the inventor of the telegraph. Morse had engaged Kendall for his business sense and his knowledge of the workings of the government. Kendall worked on a percentage basis for Morse while looking after Morse's interest in the dozens of lawsuits involving patent debts. Through his efforts both men by 1859 were considered wealthy for that period. With the growing danger of civil war, Kendall embarked on a writing career which resulted in his *Letters on Secession* in 1861. He vigorously denied the right of the South to secede. The writings first appeared in the *Washington Evening Star*.

A philanthropist in later years, Kendall helped establish the Columbia Institution for the Deaf and Dumb, now Gallaudet College, in October 1856 with a gift of a house and two acres of ground adjoining Washington. He served as president of the institution until 1864 when Edward M. Gallaudet was named in his place. Kendall died in Washington, D.C.

BIBLIOGRAPHY:
A. *Autobiography of Amos Kendall* (Boston, 1872).
B. ACAB 3, 513; DAB 10, 325–327; EAB, 609–610.

JOHN M. BUTLER

KENDALL, GEORGE WILKINS (b. 22 August 1809; d. 21 October 1867) was the cofounder of the *New Orleans Picayune*, the "first great war-correspondent," author of two successful books, and the "most successful sheep raiser in the Southwest" (Copeland, 1943).

He was born in Mount Vernon, New Hampshire, and was the oldest of five children of Thaddeus Kendall, a storekeeper, and Abigail Wilkins Kendall. Because of illness in the family, George lived most of his youth with his grandfather in nearby Amherst, where he served an apprenticeship on the *Herald*. He also worked as an apprentice on the *Boston Statesman*. Later, while working his way around the country as an itinerant printer, he met Francis Asbury Lumsden at the *National Intelligencer* in Washington. They renewed acquaintances in New Orleans while Kendall was working for the *True American* and Lumsden for the *Standard*. The two young men decided to establish their own newspaper, after noting the instant success of Benjamin Day's penny newspaper, the *New York Sun*.

The *Picayune* appeared on 25 January 1837, and sold for a "Picayon," a Spanish-American coin worth six and a quarter cents. Other newspapers in New Orleans sold for at least ten cents. Like Day's *Sun*, the *Picayune* was an instant success—due partly, no doubt, to its price, but also due to Kendall's witty and sprightly writing. The partners gained another advantage by getting the news into print faster than their competitors. Kendall bought a horse to meet railroad and steamboat connections to beat the government mail service. On occasion Kendall sailed upriver to Baton Rouge or Memphis, transferring to passenger steamers for the trip back to New Orleans. He interviewed persons on their way south, and using his skill as a printer with a small press and type case, he had their stories ready to distribute at their arrival in the Crescent City.

Kendall, who was clearly the dominant partner because of his writing skills, organizational ability, energy, and the force of his personality, decided in 1841 to travel west of New Orleans in search of stories. He joined a group from the Republic of Texas which was ostensibly seeking to open trade routes to the West. But some leaders expected to confirm claims of jurisdiction over territory extending to the Rio Grande. The group was beset with trouble almost immediately, and was captured by armed Mexicans near Santa Fe in September. Most of the group were released, finally. Kendall obtained his freedom from the Mexico City prison in April, and returned to New Orleans in May 1842. The story of his Mexican adventure makes exciting reading even today; published in 1844 under the title *Narrative of the Texan Santa Fe Expedition*, it has been republished many times since, most recently in 1966 as *Across the Great Southwestern Prairies*.

When war was declared on Mexico in May 1846, Kendall resolved to cover it from the field of battle. He joined Captain Ben McCulloch's Rangers in June at Matamoros. He also organized a courier system to get his dispatches back to New Orleans, using relay riders from the interior to the Gulf Coast, where chartered boats picked up his dispatches for the final leg of the trip across the Gulf and into Lake Pontchartrain, just north of New Orleans. The *Picayune* set up an agreement with the *Baltimore Sun* to forward Kendall's war news north by rail and steamer to Mobile, and from there by pony express to Baltimore. From there it could be sent by telegraph to Washington, often beating the official dispatches. Kendall was credited with several notable news beats, leading to his being called ''the father of the 'scoop.' '' The biggest scoop of his career as a war correspondent was his story that the war had ended.

Kendall wrote *The War Between the United States and Mexico Illustrated*, which was published in 1851 with hand-colored lithographs by Carl Nebel prepared by artisans in Paris. While overseeing the work in Paris, Kendall met his future wife, Adeline de Valcourt. The couple had four children: Georgina, William, Caroline, and Henry. Their marriage in 1849 was not known to Kendall's mother, who would have objected to a Catholic daughter-in-law. She died in 1852, and Kendall brought his family to their new home, near San Antonio, Texas, in 1856.

Although Kendall continued to maintain his relationship with the *Picayune*, contributing articles and occasionally venturing to New Orleans to take an active hand in the operation of the paper, he spent most of his time on the ranch in Texas, where he raised sheep. He became known as the foremost sheep rancher in the Southwest, and his annual articles on sheep farming, published in the Texas *Almanac*, drew hundreds of immigrants to Texas. Kendall's reputation became so firmly established that in 1859 he was urged to run for governor—a draft he quickly discouraged. Although he declined the honor of political office, he was honored by his fellow Texans when they named Kendall County after him in 1862.

The exertion required to run a sheep ranch, while maintaining his correspondence with the *Picayune*, must have taxed his energies. He did not have the stamina which carried him through the forced march from Santa Fe to Mexico City and through the battles of the war with Mexico. He became ill, and, while writing, died of congestion of both lungs in 1867. Adeline was only thirty-seven; she remarried several years later and died at age ninety-four.

BIBLIOGRAPHY:

B. DAB 10, 327–328; Fayette Copeland, *Kendall of the ''Picayune''* (Norman, Okla., 1943).

WHITNEY R. MUNDT

KILGALLEN, DOROTHY MAE (b. 3 July 1913; d. 8 November 1965) was a star reporter and columnist for the Hearst organization. As a young reporter, she became a modern-day Nellie Bly when she flew around the world on commercial aircraft when aviation was still in its infancy. Later, she covered many of the major stories of her era and became a Broadway columnist. In addition, she wrote articles for the Hearst-owned *Cosmopolitan* magazine. She also was widely known as a panelist for the popular television show ''What's My Line?'' She and her husband, Richard Tompkins Kollmar, also starred in a radio talk show, ''Breakfast with Dorothy and Dick.''

Kilgallen was born in Chicago but spent most of her earliest years in Wyoming and Indiana while her father, James Lawrence Kilgallen, worked on newspapers in those states. Her mother, Mary Jane ''Mae'' Ahern Kilgallen, was originally from St. Louis. The only other child, Eleanor, was born six years after Dorothy, while the family was in Indiana. The father, better known as Jim Kilgallen and later to become a famous and remarkably long-lived reporter, moved the family back to Chicago and then to New York City after he joined the Hearst-owned International News Service. In New York City, Dorothy attended Public School 119 and Erasmus Hall High School, where she wrote for the school literary magazine, the *Erasmian*. In 1930 she entered the College of New Rochelle, a school for young Catholic women operated by the Ursulan nuns. She left the college after one year to enter newspaper work.

Kilgallen began her journalism career during the summer of 1931 on the Hearst-owned *New York Evening Journal*. As ''Jim Kilgallen's daughter,'' she was accorded special treatment by some but not by an assistant city editor who assigned her to the morgue so she would become accustomed to the sight of dead bodies. Although only a teenager, Kilgallen quickly developed into a competent reporter and writer. She was soon covering murder trials and out-of-town assignments.

In September of 1936 the twenty-three-year-old Kilgallen was given an assignment that was to make her a celebrity. She was assigned to fly around the world on commercial aircraft in competition with H. R. ''Bud'' Ekins of United Press and Leo Kieran of the *New York Times*. This was the beginning of the ''air age'' and such a stunt was considered daring. Kilgallen lost the race but completed her itinerary in twenty-four days. Her trip, which included a transatlantic flight on the German dirigible *Hindenburg*, made her famous. Upon her return, she received hundreds of congratulatory letters including one from the first lady, Eleanor Roosevelt. She endorsed products, appeared on coast-to-coast broadcasts, and lectured at the Columbia School of Journalism. She wrote a book, *Girl Around the World* (1936), with the help of a colleague, and a motion picture, *Fly Away Baby*, was made loosely based on her experiences. Kilgallen also was given a screen test which resulted in a bit part in a film.

The *Journal-American* then decided to make Kilgallen its Hollywood columnist. The column, ''Hollywood Scene as Seen by Dorothy Kilgallen,'' put her into competition with another Hearst newswoman, Louella Parsons (q.v.), who happened to be a particular favorite of William Randolph Hearst (q.v.). Friction developed between the upstart Kilgallen and the veteran Parsons. The actress Constance Bennett sued after one of Kilgallen's barbed comments about her, and Kilgallen was forced to write a retraction. She was happy when her newspaper recalled her to New York.

After her Hollywood sojourn, Kilgallen was sent to London to cover the coronation of George VI. She then was given a column, "The Voice of Broadway," and the Hearst newspapers in full-page advertisements hailed her as "the first and only woman Broadway columnist." Her column not only appeared in the *Journal-American* but also was syndicated by the Hearst-owned King Features Syndicate. In several of her early columns, she lavished praise on a young actor and singer named Richard Kollmar who would become her husband. They were married on 6 April 1940 in a Catholic wedding in New York City that was attended by more than 800 people, including a number of celebrities. A daughter, Jill (later Mrs. Larry Grossman), and two sons, Richard Jr., and Kerry, would be born to the couple.

Kilgallen became even more famous after she became a panelist on "What's My Line?" She was on the show from its start in 1949 until her death. The radio show with her husband was discontinued in 1945. In addition to her column and television appearances, she continued to cover some major stories, often causing controversy. She, for instance, once outraged many by describing the visiting wife of Soviet Premier Nikita S. Khrushchev as looking "dismal" in a dress that covered her "like a homemade slip cover on a sofa" (Israel, 1979). She went to Dallas after the Kennedy assassination and was the only reporter able to get a private interview with Jack Ruby, the killer of assassin Lee Harvey Oswald. She also obtained a transcript of testimony Jack Ruby gave members of the Warren Commission before this information was made public.

Dorothy Kilgallen died in her sleep on 8 November 1965 at her town house in New York City. The medical examiner's office reported that she died of an overdose of alcohol and barbiturates but did not determine whether the death was accidental or intentional. At the time of her death, Kilgallen was completing a book, *Murder One* (1967), which was published two years after her death. Her husband, who remarried, died on 9 January 1971.

BIBLIOGRAPHY:

B. NYT 9 November 1965; Lee Israel, *Kilgallen* (New York, 1979).

JAMES S. FEATHERSTON

KILGORE, BERNARD (b. 9 November 1908; d. 14 November 1967) was best known for changing the *Wall Street Journal* from a small financial newspaper into the nation's first national daily. While the newspaper committed itself to thorough reporting of business news, it also offered a paper of expanding general news, solidly reported and comprehensively presented with craftmanship. Kilgore also was responsible for the creation of the *National Observer*, a national weekly newspaper; the success of *Barron's*, a financial weekly; and expansion of the Dow Jones News Service.

Kilgore was born in Albany, Indiana, to Tecumseh Kilgore and Lavina Elizabeth Bodenhorn Kilgore. His father was superintendent of schools but left that to sell insurance, moving the family to South Bend, Indiana. Following his graduation from South Bend High School in 1925, "Barney," as he was known to the journalism world, enrolled in DePauw University at Greencastle, Indiana. He later said he found the most interesting people on campus associated with the school newspaper, the *DePauw*, so he joined the staff, becoming, in order, a proofreader, copy editor, and editor. During his junior year he also was editor of the campus yearbook, the *Mirage*.

With his graduation from DePauw in 1929 and supported by the prestige of a Phi Beta Kappa key, Kilgore fired off letters to prospective newspaper employers. One caught the eye of Kenneth Hogate, another DePauw alumnus and at that time general manager of the *Wall Street Journal*. In short order, Kilgore was assigned to the new San Francisco edition of the paper and was made news editor in 1931. It was in San Francisco that he started a column, "Dear George," which reduced difficult financial and economic problems to plain language, an ability which caught the attention of *Journal* editors. By late 1932 he was back in New York at age twenty-four writing a regular editorial page column.

Kilgore attracted the further attention of the *Journal* and other newspapermen when President Franklin D. Roosevelt identified himself as one of Kilgore's readers. Asked to explain a difference between two plans to pay a soldiers' bonus, President Roosevelt told reporters to read Kilgore's story in *The Wall Street Journal* on the subject. President Roosevelt referred reporters to Kilgore again when asked to comment on a Supreme Court decision. In 1935 Kilgore was the Washington bureau chief for the *Journal*, then managing editor in 1941, vice president of Dow Jones in 1943, and president in 1945. When he retired in 1966 with inoperable cancer, he was named chairman of the board.

It was in San Francisco and later in Washington that Kilgore began to exert his influence on the *Journal*. His goals were to simplify news coverage and to keep the reader interested. In Washington as bureau chief, he urged his reporters to avoid government jargon and to tell their stories simply but in sufficient detail. At the same time he was doing battle with New York to get enough space for these stories to appear. Later in New York he pioneered in a new front-page story, called a "leader," which dealt with current events but was not restricted to yesterday's news. He also developed the "What's News" capsules of important events, also on page one.

Circulation grew from 33,000 in 1941 when he became managing editor to 102,000 in 1947. At the time of his death in 1967 circulation had passed the million mark. These increases were due in part to establishment of regional publishing sites so the *Journal* could be delivered daily to its national reading audience.

At the same time, Kilgore was creating the *National Observer* in 1962, which reached a circulation of about 500,000 at the time of Kilgore's death. Dow Jones News Service had expanded to clients in 742 cities in forty-nine states and Canada, as well as supplying an international report in cooperation with the

Associated Press. *Barron's* circulation at Kilgore's death had reached more than 200,000. Kilgore believed the press needed a strong financial basis to succeed, and saw Dow Jones earnings rise from about $200,000 in his first year as president to more than $13 million in 1966.

Kilgore was married 1 October 1938 to Mary Louise Throop of Greencastle. They had three children, Kathryn, James Bernard, and John Harvey. Kilgore was active in professional journalism organizations, served as president of the DePauw board of trustees, published six New Jersey weekly newspapers, started the Newspaper Fund in 1958 to encourage young people to enter newspapering, and was considered by his peers to be one of America's leading reporters and editors.

BIBLIOGRAPHY:

B. NYT 15 November 1967; *Wall Street Journal*, 16 November 1967; Winthrop Neilson and Frances Neilson, *What's News—Dow Jones: Story of the "Wall Street Journal"* (Radnor, Pa., 1973).

EARL L. CONN

KLAUBER, EDWARD (b. 24 February 1887; d. 23 September 1954) has been called one of the founding fathers of broadcast journalism. A *New York Times* writer and editor in the 1920s known for his perfectionism, Klauber joined CBS in 1930 and became William S. Paley's (q.v.) righthand man, helping Paley turn CBS into a major corporation. Klauber also impressed upon CBS some of the high standards of journalism he learned at the *Times*, preventing CBS News from modeling itself on the sensational press of the 1930s. Klauber hired and trained some of the best writers and reporters in CBS's first generation of radio journalists, among them John Daly, Robert Trout, and Elmer Davis (qq.v.) By World War II, Klauber had helped build CBS into the preeminent broadcast journalism operation in the United States, free of the domination of advertisers who controlled radio's programming.

Klauber was born in Louisville, Kentucky, to Morris Klauber and Ray Forst Klauber. He attended the University of Louisville and the University of Pennsylvania. His early aspirations were to be a doctor, but the study of medicine did not appeal to him as much as the "romance" of journalism. He worked briefly for a Louisville newspaper but decided to try his luck in journalism in New York where his uncle, Adolph Klauber, was drama critic for the *New York Times*. Klauber joined the staff of the *New York World* in 1912. His assignments at the paper were varied, and he gained a reputation that allowed him to move to the more prestigious *New York Times* on 15 July 1916. For the next twelve years, Klauber remained with the *Times*, starting out as a reporter and writer. In the early 1920s, Klauber became one of the first staff reporters to be assigned regularly on night rewrite, a job that was customarily given to reporters on a rotating basis. On the night rewrite desk, he polished writing and editing skills that were to serve him at CBS as he guided the early efforts of the news operation in the 1930s. In August 1927 he was promoted to night city editor of the *Times*.

He filled the position for only a year. Public relations interested Klauber, and he left the *Times* in 1928 to work as public relations director of the Lennen and Mitchell advertising agency. There also only a year, Klauber then moved to the Edward L. Bernays public relations organization, one of whose clients was the newly formed Columbia Broadcasting System. CBS was being run by the relatively inexperienced, twenty-eight-year-old, former cigar magnate William S. Paley. Bernays suggested to Paley that he employ Klauber.

Klauber was hired as a CBS vice president, and he became Paley's assistant, a function Klauber relished and Paley appreciated. Klauber handled some of the administrative tasks Paley found unpleasant, including the reprimanding and firing of CBS executives. Klauber's administrative methods were firm and occasionally heavy-handed, but he had the good judgment—and the requisite background in journalism to recognize talent—to let newsman Paul White (q.v.) turn CBS into the most effective and efficient news operation in radio. White was a careful, precise writer who believed that excellent standards of ethical conduct and objectivity should be applied to the practice of broadcast journalism. The lesson stuck on virtually the entire first generation of CBS newsmen, and the influence of Klauber and White extended to the second and third generations of CBS: Edward R. Murrow, Eric Sevareid, and Walter Cronkite (qq.v.), among others. With Paley's blessing, Klauber had helped establish the tradition of excellence in news that Paley—and others inside and outside journalism—came to respect and emulate.

In 1937 Klauber was elected to the board of directors of CBS and, in 1942, was made chairman of the board's executive committee. The following year, however, Klauber retired due to ill health. In 1943, Klauber's wife, Gladys Gustafson Klauber, whom he had married 23 February 1925, died after a long illness. Despite his poor health, Klauber took a position as associate director of the Office of War Information from 1943 to 1945, working under his former colleague at CBS News, Elmer Davis. In April 1945 Klauber married his second wife, Doris E. Larson.

Following the War, Klauber helped reformulate the National Association of Broadcasters (NAB) Code of Standards and Ethics. It was fitting that his last major contribution was in broadcasting standards, for he had throughout his career a reputation for the highest quality of performance and reliability. Klauber died in New York.

BIBLIOGRAPHY:

B. NYT 24 September 1954; Gary Paul Gates, *Air Time: The Inside Story of CBS News* (New York, 1978); Robert Metz, *CBS: Reflections in a Bloodshot Eye* (New York, 1975).

JOHN P. FREEMAN

KNOX, WILLIAM FRANKLIN (b. 1 January 1874; d. 28 April 1944) was a newspaper editor and publisher. He was also active in politics for nearly forty years. Late in life, as secretary of the navy, he presided over the unprecedented expansion of the U.S. fleet and effectively administered his office for four years following American entrance into World War II.

Born in Boston, Massachusetts, Frank (as he was known in youth and throughout his life) was the eldest child and only son of William Edwin Knox and Sarah Collins Barnard Knox. Both of his parents, though born Canadians, had come to the United States early in their lives. When Frank was seven the family moved to Grand Rapids, Michigan, where his father worked as a grocer but failed to prosper. Frank grew up in a frugal Presbyterian home; he attended public schools and worked at various jobs. After the depression of 1893 wiped out a job he had at the time, he entered Michigan's Alma College and managed to earn enough at temporary jobs to pay his expenses. Before graduating from college, he enlisted in the army during the Spanish-American War. He became one of Theodore Roosevelt's Rough Riders and served with that outfit in all of its important engagements including the Battle of San Juan Hill. Afterwards he returned to Michigan, completed his degree at Alma College, and married Annie Reed, his college sweetheart. They had no children.

Throughout his professional life, Knox pursued two parallel careers, one in journalism and the other in politics. His first job in journalism was with the *Grand Rapids Herald*. Beginning in 1898 as a reporter, he advanced in four years to become the city editor and then circulation manager of that paper. In 1902 he and John A. Meuhling, a printer, purchased the Sault Sainte Marie *Lake Superior Journal*. Knox was editor and joint publisher of the *Journal*, and under his direction it prospered. The paper was converted into a daily; its circulation doubled; and it surged past and eventually acquired its only rival, the *News-Record*. In the process, Knox gained a reputation as a crusading editor. Knox also became increasingly active in Republican party politics in Michigan, and, in 1910, managed the campaign of Chase S. Osborn, who was elected governor in that year. Following that, Knox became chairman of the Republican State Central Committee and a leader in Michigan state politics. In 1911 and 1912 he was one of Theodore Roosevelt's political lieutenants and supported him in his bid for the presidency in 1912 by serving as his campaign manager in the Midwest. At the Progressive party's Bull Moose convention in Chicago in 1912, Knox headed the Michigan delegation and served as chairman of the convention's credentials committee. After Roosevelt's defeat, however, Knox lost his political power in Michigan and decided to leave that state.

He moved to Manchester, New Hampshire, where he and Meuhling founded a new Progressive paper, the *Manchester Leader*. Again prosperity followed. With Knox as editor and publisher, the *Leader* soon acquired the *Union*, its major competitor. In control of Manchester's newspaper field, Knox again became politically involved. He left the Progressive party and returned to regular Republican ranks. He worked hard for Charles Evans Hughes in the presidential election of 1916 and consistently attacked President Wilson's "too proud to fight'' stance during the period of American neutrality in World War I. When the United States entered the war in 1917, Knox enlisted as a private at the age of forty-three. He advanced rapidly in rank, serving as a major in France. Mustering out in 1919 with the rank of lieutenant colonel, he was commissioned a colonel in the reserve corps.

After the war Knox returned to his newspapers and to politics. Grown more conservative in his views, he became chairman of the New Hampshire delegation to the Republican National Convention in 1920 and was the floor leader for Leonard Wood in his unsuccessful bid for the party's nomination. In 1924 he made his own first quest for public office when he ran unsuccessfully for the New Hampshire gubernatorial nomination. After that, he left active politics for ten years. He continued to prosper in journalism, however, and became an acknowledged master of newspaper management. It was this quality that attracted him to William Randolph Hearst (q.v.). After rejecting several offers to join the Hearst organization, he finally did so in 1927. Retaining his own Manchester papers, he took charge of Hearst's failing Boston papers. Less than a year later, Hearst made him general manager of all of his papers. Knox's association with Hearst lasted until 1 January 1931, when he resigned over differences in business judgment.

Later that year, with the assistance of Theodore Ellis, a New York financier, Knox purchased the controlling interest in the *Chicago Daily News*. This was the climax of his newspaper career, for the *Chicago Daily News* was one of the country's premier newspapers. It is generally recognized that as its editor and publisher, he contributed to the *Daily News*'s survival during the difficult depression years by his careful management. There is some question, however, whether he did so without sacrificing some of the paper's quality. Regardless, with the acquisition of the *Chicago Daily News*, he once again became active in politics. Beginning in 1933, he became one of the strongest critics in the country of President Franklin D. Roosevelt's New Deal programs. In 1936 Knox received the Republican nomination for vice president on the ticket headed by Alfred M. Landon.

The final phase of Knox's long career in journalism and politics occurred after the 1936 election. Though Knox continued to oppose the president on domestic issues, he supported his foreign policy and naval preparedness program. When Roosevelt took steps to create a bipartisan cabinet as war spread across Europe in 1940, he invited two Republicans, Knox and Henry L. Stimson, to become respectively secretary of navy and secretary of war. Both accepted. The four years Knox spent as secretary of navy were critical ones in this country's history. He presided over that office at the time of the Japanese attack on Pearl Harbor and for the first three years of this nation's involvement in World War II.

He died in Washington, D.C., on 28 April 1944 at the age of seventy, after a series of heart attacks.

BIBLIOGRAPHY:

A. *We Planned It That Way* (New York, 1938).

B. DAB Supp. 3, 424–426; NCAB 3, 12–14; NYT 29 April 1944; Norman Beasley, *Frank Knox: American* (Garden City, N.Y., 1936); George Henry Lobdell, Jr., "A Biography of Frank Knox," Ph.D. diss., Univ. of Illinois, 1954.

JAMES D. STARTT

KOENIGSBERG, MOSES (b. 16 April 1878; d. 21 September 1945) established the Newspaper Feature Service in 1913 and King Features Syndicate in 1915, and in so doing helped establish syndicated features as a staple of American newspaper journalism. He was born to Harris Wolf Koenigsberg and Julia Foreman Koenigsberg in New Orleans, Louisiana, the youngest of three sons. The family moved to San Antonio, Texas, when Moses was an infant.

Koenigsberg began his newspaper career at age nine when he printed and published his own newspaper, the *Amateur*. He matured early and at age thirteen was a reporter for the *San Antonio Times*. There followed positions on literally dozens of newspapers in Houston, New Orleans, Kansas City, St. Louis, Chicago, Pittsburgh, New York, and Minneapolis. While at the *St. Louis Globe-Democrat* in 1898, he volunteered to carry a message to General Calixto Garcia, the insurgent leader in Cuba. His goal was to score a news beat by interviewing the popular hero. Failing to get the assignment, he joined the Alabama volunteers to fight in Cuba. Forced to train in a disease and insect-infested area outside Miami, Koenigsberg wrote an exposé of army mismanagement. It was published as *Southern Martyrs* (1898) hours after he was discharged.

His long association with Hearst started in Chicago. He served four years as city editor of the *Evening American*, from 1903 to 1907. He was summoned to New York, and then to Boston as general manager of the *Boston American*. After indifferent success there, he was sent by Hearst around the country seeking additional properties to be added to the Hearst empire.

The Newspaper Feature Service was incorporated in 1913 as a semi-independent part of the Hearst company. Two years later he established King Features Syndicate ("Koenig" is "king" in German), which proved to be very profitable. Despite Koenigsberg's penchant for features and sensational news, he is to be remembered for "A Newspaperman's Seven Commandments" that have elements of social responsibility. Three are quoted here:

> a. The gathering and reporting of news constitute a function affecting the progress of civilization. Performance should be limited to those fitted for the responsibility. Such fitness is inseparable from singleness of devotion to newspaper duty. It can subsist only in complete independence from divergent accountability or commitment.
>
> b. News traversing any matter of public concern or impinging on any individual right is not eligible for publication unless it includes an identification of its source.
>
> c. At all times and in all things the editor must serve the reader to the exclusion of everyone else (Koenigsberg, 1941).

In addition to establishing the aforementioned feature services, Koenigsberg was president and general manager of the International Feature Service, the Star Adcraft Service, Cosmopolitan News Service, and the Premier Syndicate, all for Hearst. In 1919 he became manager of Universal Service and International News Service, at that time in debt and in danger of failure. He gradually brought them to profitability.

He represented the Hearst organization at a League of Nations conference of press experts in 1927 and successfully fought a resolution by the Associated Press that would recognize news items as private property. For his work at the conference the French government awarded him a cross of the Legion of Honor. Hearst forbade his employees to accept honors from foreign governments, and Koenigsberg resigned rather than turn down the award. He returned the award in 1933 when France defaulted on its war debts.

After leaving Hearst, he resumed his wandering ways. He served for a time as general manager of the *Denver Post* and purchased the *Havana Post*. In 1923 he married Virginia Vivien Carter of New Haven, Connecticut. They had one daughter, Virginia Rose. At the time of his death, he was editor of a weekly magazine, *Now*, in New York. He died of a heart attack at his home.

BIBLIOGRAPHY:

A. *King News* (Philadelphia, 1941).

B. DAB Supp. 2, 427–428; NYT 22 September 1945; *New York Journal-American*, 21 September 1945.

ROY HALVERSON

KRAFT, JOSEPH (b. 4 September 1924; d. 10 January 1986) was one of the best-known foreign policy columnists, called by some the only visible replacement for Walter Lippmann (q.v.). His strong academic background contributed to his work on international affairs for several newspapers and national magazines, five major books, and a nationally syndicated column. Kraft, who was credited with inventing the term "Middle America," served as a speech writer for John F. Kennedy during the 1960 campaign, was one of two columnists to accompany President Richard M. Nixon to China in 1972, and was the only columnist selected as a member of the 1976 presidential debate panels.

Kraft, the elder of two sons of David Harry Kraft and Sophie Surasky Kraft, was born in South Orange, New Jersey, but at an early age moved with his family to Manhattan, New York, where he lived until his late teens. Kraft's father was a businessman and his mother a housewife. His grandfather, Louis Surasky, occasionally wrote for the *Jewish Daily Forward* and may have inculcated in the young Kraft, if not an interest in, at least an awareness of journalism as a profession.

At age fourteen, Kraft began writing occasional stories for the *New York World-Telegram* on private school sports; this lasted for only one year—it was more than a decade before Kraft would return to the field of journalism. In 1943 Kraft volunteered for the U.S. Army where, stationed in Washington, D.C., he served as a cryptanalyst and Japanese translator, rising to the rank of sergeant before being honorably discharged in 1946. His military experience introduced him to a wide range of foreign affairs matters and appears to have stimulated interests he would follow throughout his life. After the war, Kraft entered Columbia University and graduated in 1947 with an A.B. degree, first in his class. In 1948 he began postgraduate work at Princeton, then continued at the Institute for Advanced Study at Princeton, where he completed his course work and oral examinations, but not his thesis requirements, for a Ph.D. In 1951, following a brief period of study at the Sorbonne in France, Kraft returned to Princeton, where he planned to accept an appointment as a history professor at the Institute for Advanced Studies and was to serve as an assistant to historian and diplomat George F. Kennan. These plans were soon abandoned, however, when Kraft accepted his first regular newspaper position in Washington, D.C.

During the late 1940s and early 1950s Kraft wrote an occasional article for the *New Republic* and the *New York Times Book Review*, but it wasn't until the summer of 1951 that he signed on to a full-time job in journalism. During a weekend trip to Washington, Kraft was introduced to Herbert Elliston, then editor of the *Washington Post*, who offered him summer employment. He stayed with the *Post* for the summer as a writer, then in the fall of that year was hired by the *New York Times*. With this, he turned his back on a career in academics.

His position with the *Times* involved writing for the ''News of the Week in Review,'' which essentially provided a weekly news summary and analysis. This five-year stay with the *Times* provided Kraft the opportunity to work with some of the best foreign affairs writers and thinkers in journalism of the day, and so provided an exposure that helped him mature and cultivate the analytic style for which he was well known. Also during this period he had occasion to work again with his mentor George Kennan, who instilled in Kraft a keen interest in Soviet affairs and policy. Kraft's growing expertise in French politics enabled him to obtain assignments in Algeria with the *New York Times* during the troubled period before independence from France. Much of his writing for the *Times* during this period concerned French politics and international economics related to the Algerian situation.

He left the *New York Times* in 1957 to write *The Struggle for Algeria* (1961) and to work as a writer for a brief period at the *Saturday Evening Post*. In 1958 he received the Overseas Press Award for distinguished reporting from abroad (and did so again in 1973 and 1980). Due in part to his growing reputation in foreign policy analysis, Kraft was asked to join the 1960 Kennedy campaign, initially to advise on international matters, but by the end of the campaign as a writer working closely with the candidate. Following the election, Kraft returned to New York where, in 1962, he completed *The Grand Design*, which served as a credo for the Kennedy administration with respect to Atlantic relations. Also, during this time, he provided advice to the administration on the Trade Act of 1962 and contributed to speeches of Secretary of State George Ball.

In addition to occasional consultation with members of the administration, as a well-established foreign policy analyst, writer, and Washington insider, Kraft became involved in a variety of other professional activities. He was the Washington correspondent for *Harper's* for three years beginning in 1962, and a regular contributor to the *New Yorker*, writing features for "Letters from Far Off Places." In 1963 he started writing a column for the *Washington Star*, and during the same year began syndicating the column on his own. A year later, the Field Newspaper Syndicate picked up the column and has carried it ever since. Many of his columns for *Harper's* were published as a collection in 1966, titled *Profiles in Power*. During the 1970s and 1980s Kraft continued writing his syndicated column. He was married in 1960 to Rhonda Winton, and had two stepchildren, Mark and David.

BIBLIOGRAPHY:

B. NYT 11 January 1986.

GARY W. SELNOW

KROCK, ARTHUR (b. 16 November 1886; d. 12 April 1974) was the senior Washington political writer for the *New York Times* from 1932 to 1966. As Washington bureau chief, correspondent, and columnist, Krock was an influential observer of politics and presidents and commanded unusual access to Washington newsmakers. Exclusive interviews with Presidents Franklin D. Roosevelt and Harry S. Truman resulted in columns which earned Krock nominations for two of his four Pulitzer Prize awards.

Krock was born and raised in Glasgow, Kentucky, the son of Joseph and Caroline Morris Krock. He was educated in public schools in Kentucky and Chicago, and in 1904 attended Princeton University for a year until financial difficulties forced him to return to Chicago. He received an associate of arts degree from Lewis Institute in 1906.

His first job in journalism, which he obtained by feigning experience, was as police reporter for the *Louisville Herald*. As a legman for a veteran reporter, he covered the 1908 Democratic National Convention in Denver, beginning a career in political reporting which spanned sixty years. Krock briefly served as deputy sheriff of Jefferson County, Kentucky, following the loss of his newspaper job because of budget cuts, but he reentered the field as night editor for the Louisville office of the Associated Press. In 1910 Krock became Washington correspondent for the *Louisville Times*, a paper owned by George N. Haldeman, who also published the *Louisville Courier-Journal*. He returned to Louisville in 1916 as editorial manager for both papers. From 1918 to 1919 he covered negotiating sessions at the Versailles Peace Conference following World War I.

Because of disagreements over editorial policy between the Haldeman family and legendary journalist and part owner Henry Watterson (q.v.), Krock was asked to arrange for the sale of the papers to Robert Worth Bingham. Bingham reassigned Krock to become editor in chief of the *Louisville Times*. Disagreements over reorganization of the papers and disputes between Bingham's handling of Watterson's editorial differences with the paper led Krock to resign in 1923. Krock temporarily left newspaper work for a public relations job with the Motion Pictures Producers and Distributors Association in New York. Later that year he was hired as assistant to publisher Ralph Pulitzer on the staff of the *New York World*.

Krock began his association with the *New York Times* in 1927 when publisher Adolph S. Ochs (q.v.) hired him to write editorials. In 1932 he became Washington bureau chief and correspondent, a position he held until he was succeeded by James Reston in 1953. His column "In the Nation" appeared several times a week until his retirement in 1966. Krock began his second stint as a political correspondent in Washington with the advent of the New Deal. He compared his relationship with President Roosevelt as a cat-and-dog affair: "they endure each other and for periods display affection and even admiration. . . . but every so often nature asserts the innate conflicts of the species" (Krock, 1966).

Krock received the Pulitzer Prize for general excellence for his coverage of the New Deal in 1935. His second prize came after he was granted an exclusive interview with President Roosevelt in 1937. Because reporters from other newspapers charged the president with favoritism, he promised never to grant a private interview to a reporter again. In 1950 Krock arranged exclusive sessions with President Truman and wrote about the interviews in his columns. Krock declined to accept the award that year because he was a member of the Pulitzer Prize advisory committee, a position he occupied from 1940 to 1953. He received a special citation from the Pulitzer committee in 1955 for distinguished correspondence from Washington.

Known as "Mr. Krock" to even his closest associates, Krock adopted a formal, dignified, and seldom brief writing style. Although he was a Democrat, his political philosophy was conservative. He and the *Times* opposed the third-term candidacy of Roosevelt. In his later years he criticized the growing power of labor unions and lamented the loss of discipline and values which he saw as responsible for student demonstrations in the 1960s. Yet he opposed the commitment of American ground troops to Vietnam as intervention into Asian affairs.

Krock's first wife, Marguerite Polleys, whom he married 22 April 1911, died in 1938. They had a son, Thomas Polleys Krock. On 14 June 1939 he married Martha McCullough Granger Blair, who wrote a society column for the *Washington Times-Herald*.

BIBLIOGRAPHY:

A. *In the Nation, 1932–1966* (New York, 1966); *Memoirs: Sixty Years on the Firing Line* (New York, 1968); *Myself When Young: Growing Up in the 1890's* (Boston, 1973).

B. NYT 13 April 1974.

ELIZABETH FRAAS

— L —

LANGE, DOROTHEA MARGARETTA (b. 25 May 1895; d. 11 October 1965) was a documentary photographer best known for her work during the depression as a member of the Farm Security Administration (FSA). Beginning her career as an assistant in several photography studios, photofinisher, and free-lance photographer, Lange documented the internment of Japanese Americans in 1942 and worked for the Office of War Information in San Francisco during World War II. After briefly working for *Life* in the mid–1950s, she turned again to free-lancing because of ill health.

Born in Hoboken, New Jersey, Lange was one of two children of a German immigrant family. While she and her younger brother Martin were still in elementary school, her father, Heinrich "Henry" Nutzhorn, a lawyer, abandoned the family. Her mother, Joanna Caroline Lange, moved the family to live with her mother so she could work as a librarian. A bout with polio at age seven left Lange with a crippled right leg and an increased sensitivity to human suffering.

She attended public school on the Lower East Side of New York City, graduating in 1913 from the uptown Wadleigh School for Girls. From 1914 to 1917 she went to the New York Training School for Teachers, but during this time she also pursued her interest in photography by working for Arnold Genthe at his New York studio and studying with Clarence H. White at Columbia University.

In 1918 she adopted her mother's maiden name and left for California, settling in San Francisco where she first worked as a photofinisher and then opened a photography studio a year later. She married artist Maynard Dixon, twenty-seven years her senior, on 21 March 1920. Lange gave birth to Daniel Rhodes Dixon in 1925, and a second son, John Eaglefeather Dixon, was born three years later.

Lange continued to run her studio until 1934 when the depression slowed her business and opened her eyes to the suffering on the street. In 1935 she was commissioned by the California State Emergency Relief Administration to photograph migrant agricultural workers, and she collaborated with economist-author Dr. Paul S. Taylor. Lange and Taylor divorced their spouses and were wed 6 December 1935. They spent much of their married life working together on important projects, publishing a book on migrant workers entitled *An American Exodus: A Record of Human Erosion* (1939).

Although her career spanned more than half a century, Lange is best remembered for the black-and-white images she created from August 1935 to November 1939 for Roy Stryker's FSA. She excelled at documenting ordinary people in their environment; her FSA photograph of the "Migrant Mother" has become synonymous with the Great Depression. Lange's FSA photographs were widely exhibited and published with the others in newspapers and magazines in the United States and overseas.

In 1941 she was the first woman and third photographer to receive a prestigious Guggenheim Fellowship, but partway through the project she indefinitely postponed completing it to join the War Relocation Authority in April 1942. Her images of the evacuation and internment of Japanese Americans living on the West Coast formed the basis of an exhibition and book entitled *Executive Order 9066* (1972).

From 1943 to 1945 she worked for the Office of War Information in San Francisco, but chronic illness kept her from seriously photographing for the next eight years. Lange contributed to *Life* during the mid–1950s, publishing photo essays on Mormon towns and Irish country people. She free-lanced while traveling with her husband in Asia, South America, Egypt and the Middle East in the late 1950s and early 1960s. In 1957 she also taught photography at what is now known as the San Francisco Art Institute.

During the last few years of her life, Lange completed a book (and later exhibition) entitled *Dorothea Lange Looks at the American Country Woman* (1967). She also organized the first retrospective exhibition given to a woman photographer at the Museum of Modern Art. On 11 October 1965 Lange died of cancer in Berkeley, California. Three months later the exhibit opened in New York City.

BIBLIOGRAPHY:

A. *Dorothea Lange* (New York, 1966).

B. DAB Supp. 7, 455–457; NYT 14 October 1965; Christopher Cox, *Dorothea Lange* (New York, 1987); Milton Meltzer, *Dorothea Lange: A Photographer's Life* (New York, 1978).

C. ZOE SMITH

LARDNER, RINGGOLD WILMER (b. 6 March 1885; d. 25 September 1933) was one of America's outstanding journalist-humorists. With a complete mastery of the American vernacular and a sardonic twist to his humor, Ring Lardner wrote sports columns, magazine articles, collections of short stories, and plays from 1905 to 1933. In his famous "Jack Keefe" letters, Lardner expressed his disdain for the hero status accorded sports figures by the public.

Lardner, the youngest of nine children, was born in Niles, Michigan. His father, Henry, who had inherited a farm from his father and money from his cousin, was able to provide a comfortable living for his family. His mother, Lena Bogardus Phillips, a woman of literary and musical interests, educated her children at home. At an early age Lardner became interested in baseball. His only formal education consisted of four years at Niles High School and a term at the Armour Institute of Technology in Chicago.

From 1902 to 1905 Lardner worked at a variety of jobs in Niles and in Chicago. In 1905 he left his job as a meter reader for the Niles Gas Company to be a sports reporter for the *South Bend Times* in South Bend, Indiana. Lardner worked as a sports reporter on the *Chicago Inter Ocean*, the *Chicago Examiner*, and the *Chicago Tribune* from 1907 to 1910. Lardner went on the road with the Chicago White Sox where he learned not only about baseball but about the players. A careful observer, Lardner began to focus on the personalities of the players as well as inserting humor into his stories. In 1910 he became managing editor of the *Sporting News* in St. Louis. Lardner began to write dialogue in the vernacular of the baseball players. In February 1911 he became a baseball writer for the *Boston American*.

On 28 June 1911 Lardner married Ellis Abbott of Goshen, Indiana. They had four sons: John Abbott, born in 1912; James Phillips, in 1914; Ring Wilmer, Jr., in 1915; and David Ellis in 1918. Shortly after his marriage he was named sports editor of the *Boston American*.

When Lardner and his brother Rex went off to cover the World Series the fall of 1911, they were fired from the *Boston American*. Lardner became a copyreader with the *Chicago American* and then a sports reporter for the *Chicago Examiner*. He began to write with more humor, and he occasionally told stories in crude verse. From 1913 to 1919 Lardner wrote a feature sports column, "In the Wake of the News," for the *Chicago Tribune*. He often had ghostwritten stories with athletes speaking in the language of the dugout.

In 1914 Lardner began submitting a series of letters to the *Saturday Evening Post*. The series was based on "Jack Keefe," a fictitious White Sox rookie pitcher whose mind was as small as his ego was large, who wrote to friends back home. These were collected into the book *You Know Me, Al* (1916). This title became a catch phrase for admissions of personal stupidity. In 1917 Lardner became a war correspondent in Europe writing "In the Wake of the War" for the *Chicago Tribune*. In 1919 Lardner moved his family to New York where he began an eight-year contract for the Bell Syndicate covering major sports events. Lardner published approximately 125 short stores in magazines which were later collected in books. *Round Up* (1928) contained some of his best stories.

In addition to writing fifteen books, Lardner wrote two plays—*Elmer the Great* (1928) with George M. Cohan and *June Moon* (1929) with George S.

Kaufman. In 1932 he wrote a series of autobiographical articles for the *Saturday Evening Post*. He published a series of columns on radio for the *New Yorker* in 1933. In 1926 Lardner learned that he had tuberculosis. Years of heavy drinking and two heart ailments also weakened him. He died of a heart attack on 25 September 1933 at East Hampton, Long Island, New York, at the age of forty-eight. Since his death, Lardner has been widely praised as a short story writer of penetrating satire. Many critics have failed to realize that it was his success as a journalist that first brought him fame. Although his journalistic career was relatively short, he will be remembered for his humorous sports columns which demonstrated his mastery of common speech.

BIBLIOGRAPHY:

B. NYT 26 September 1933; Donald Elder, *Ring Lardner, A Biography* (Garden City, N.Y., 1956); Ring Lardner, Jr., *The Lardners: My Family Remembered* (New York, 1976); Jonathan Yardley, *Ring: A Biography of Ring Lardner* (New York, 1977).

C. JOANNE SLOAN

LATIMER, JAMES WELLINGTON (b. 27 December 1826; d. 6 April 1859) was cofounder and copublisher of the *Dallas Herald*, the first newspaper in Dallas, and editor of the *Herald* during its first ten years and until his death. The *Dallas Morning News* dates its volume number from the *Herald*, which it purchased in 1885. Though only in his twenties during most of his editorial responsibilities, Latimer enjoyed a reputation among his peers at Texas newspapers as an effective journalist and writer, particularly in behalf of the Democratic party and states' rights.

Latimer was born in Tennessee, the son of James L. Latimer and Jane Hamilton Latimer. Wellington, as he was called by his family to distinguish him from his father, was one of eleven children and more than fifty slaves to accompany the elder Latimer and his wife in 1833 to Clarksville in the frontier area of northeast Texas. As a youth, Latimer displayed considerable promise writing articles that attracted attention. He studied law, probably under two brothers who were attorneys, and was admitted to the bar at nineteen. On 22 February 1847 he and Lucy Jordan of nearby Bowie County were married. Lucy Jordan Latimer, a native of Danville, Virginia, was her husband's intellectual equal. Like Wellington, she was a talented writer, often preparing copy for the *Herald* when he was ill or away. The two were persons of culture, as articles in the *Herald* often revealed. Lucy was an accomplished pianist and gave lessons in Dallas. They had three children. During the war with Mexico, Latimer served with the First Division of Texas.

In 1849 Latimer became a partner in and editor of the *Texas Times*, published in Paris. In the fall of the year, the newspaper was moved to Dallas, a town of 2,500 people established only ten years earlier. Renamed the *Dallas Herald*, the newspaper appeared for the first time about 15 December. Latimer gained the respect of his colleagues in the Texas press, primarily through his support of the Democratic party and his defense of states' rights. His most brilliant essay on these subjects, entitled "The Charleston Convention," was published on 29 January 1859, less than three months before his death. It accurately predicted the political steps which led to the Civil War. Speaking of the 1860 presidential election, Latimer called the upcoming Democratic National Convention

> the most important convention of politicians that has ever met in this Union. Upon its action may and in all probability will depend the destinies of this government for weal or woe—the perpetuity of this glorious confederacy. If the Southern delegates go into that convention with a sullen determination to nominate for the Presidency none but a man, committed to the most ultra views of the Southern school of statesmen—none but a fire-eater, they may nominate their favorite, but their nominee will be beaten as certain as the fates.

Latimer's interest in the law and politics led him to run successfully for chief justice in Dallas County. In his only other bid for public office, he was defeated for state printer in 1855. A mason, Latimer held all offices in Dallas Tannehill Lodge and, at age thirty-one, was grand orator for the annual communication of the Texas Grand Lodge in 1858. On 5 April 1859 Latimer stumbled while carrying wood. Part of the load fell on him, and he died early the next day of a fractured skull. He was buried in the Masonic Cemetery in Dallas.

BIBLIOGRAPHY:

B. H. Bailey Carroll and W. P. Webb, eds., *The Handbook of Texas*, vol. 1 (Austin, 1952); Bruce W. Roche, "Wellington Latimer: Frontier Editor," M.A. thesis, Univ. of Texas, 1957.

BRUCE ROCHE

LAURENCE, WILLIAM LEONARD (b. 7 March 1888; d. 19 March 1977) was one of the nation's outstanding science and medical writers during the period of exploding information before and after World War II. Undoubtedly his most spectacular coverage was the dawn of the nuclear age. Known as "Atomic Bill" to distinguish him from a *New York Times* political correspondent with a similar name, William Lawrence, the science writer, was loaned to the government to witness—and then report through an official news release—the initial Alamogordo, New Mexico, atomic explosion. He also witnessed from an accompanying plane the atomic bomb drop on Nagasaki that led to Japan's surrender and the end of World War II.

Born in Salantai, Lithuania, 7 March 1888, he was the son of Lipman Siew and Sarah Preuss Siew. He fled his homeland to Berlin hidden in a hogshead and came to the United States in 1905. He became a naturalized citizen in 1913. His flattened nose, he claimed, was caused when it was smashed by a Cossack rifle butt in his native Lithuania. His original name was Siew and he chose Laurence in tribute to an elm-covered street in Cambridge where he lived when he was a Harvard student. He was so successful as a tutor in college that less gifted students were willing to contribute five dollars each to hear his cram session answers to anticipated examination questions. During World War I, he served overseas with the Army Signal Corps. He won a bachelor of laws degree from Boston University in 1925 and received an honorary doctor of science degree in 1946.

Laurence is said to have gotten his first journalism job because of his brilliant performance in a word game at the home of Herbert Bayard Swope (q.v.), executive editor of the *New York World*. He was hired as a general assignment reporter and named associate aviation editor in 1927. He joined the *New York Times* in 1930 and served for thirty-four years. He succeeded Waldemar Kaempffert as science editor in 1956. One of the few journalists to win two Pulitzer Prizes, Laurence shared the first with four others for coverage of the 1936 Harvard University tercentenary conference at Cambridge. The second was in 1946 for his eyewitness account of the atom-bombing of Nagasaki and subsequent ten articles on development, production, and significance of the atomic bomb.

Laurence had a special ability of gaining the confidence of scientists that was not common among his contemporaries. He told of listening to a then-young and little-known Dr. J. Robert Oppenheimer lecture on higher mathematics at the Massachusetts Institute of Technology. The newsman went up to ask the scientist to explain a point. Oppenheimer replied that the abstruse talk was ''not for the lay public.'' Laurence explained that then he would have to write the news as he understood it. Oppenheimer asked, ''And what is that?'' Laurence recited portions of the lecture in lay terms. ''I never thought of it that way,'' the scientist commented, rather pleased (Laurence, 1951). After that, Laurence said he never again had trouble getting Oppenheimer's cooperation during a long career.

Laurence's reporting on early research in ''splitting the atom'' led to his selection by the War Department to write the official version of the Alamogordo tests. In the spring of 1945, Laurence disappeared and only his wife, his editor, and his publisher knew in general terms where he was. In addition to seeing the test at Alamogordo that would prove the atomic bomb was ready, the correspondent witnessed the bomb drop on Nagasaki. He also covered the 1955 Geneva conference on peaceful uses of atomic energy and the 1956 hydrogen bomb test.

After he retired from the *New York Times* on 1 January 1964, he was science consultant for the 1964–65 New York World's Fair and scientific consultant to the National Foundation–March of Dimes. With his wife, the former Florence Davidow, whom he had married in 1931, Laurence moved to Majorca in 1968. He died there on 19 March 1977 of complications from a blood clot on the brain.

BIBLIOGRAPHY:

A. *Dawn Over Zero* (New York, 1946); *The Hell Bomb* (New York, 1951); *Men Over Atoms* (New York, 1959).

B. NYT 19 March 1977; Meyer Berger, *The Story of the New York Times, 1851–1951* (New York, 1951).

HILLIER KRIEGHBAUM

LAWRENCE, DAVID (b. 25 December 1888; d. 11 February 1973) ranked at the top of his profession as a reporter, columnist, editor, and publisher for some sixty years. His tireless dedication to enlightening his readers with information about public affairs earned him the respect and high regard of his colleagues as well as his readers.

Lawrence was born to Harris and Dora Cohen Lawrence in Philadelphia, Pennsylvania, in the family living quarters above his father's tailor shop. Soon after his birth, the family moved to Buffalo, New York, where he attended public schools. He got his first newspaper work selling sports photographs to the *Buffalo Express*, then worked as a reporter for the newspaper while on vacations from school. Lawrence worked his way through Princeton University as an Associated Press correspondent and campus stringer for seventeen newspapers. His first major achievement as a reporter was getting out the story of former President Grover Cleveland's death at Princeton in June 1908. This and his other work for the Associated Press earned him a summer job in the Philadelphia bureau of the AP in 1908 and 1909 and a full-time job there in 1910 after he received his bachelor's degree from Princeton.

A few months later, Lawrence was transferred to the AP bureau in Washington, D.C., where he quickly developed a reputation for relentless reporting effort, integrity, and clarity of presentation of the news. Several times between 1911 and 1917, Lawrence, who spoke Spanish, went to Mexico to cover developments there in the series of disputes between that country and the United States that erupted in those years. In 1911 the twenty-two-year-old reporter received a gold watch from AP chief Melville Stone (q.v.) for his work covering a battle in Juárez between Mexican government forces and rebels. He also served as an unofficial adviser on Mexican affairs to President Woodrow Wilson on several occasions.

His relationship with Wilson dated from his undergraduate days at Princeton, where Wilson had been a professor and university president. In 1912 Lawrence was assigned to cover the Wilson presidential campaign for the AP and in 1913 was assigned to the White House beat. Although he was viewed by many as a confidant of the president, Lawrence often insisted he received and gave no favored treatment. He saw personal relations with the president as compromising his impartiality as a newsman. He obtained one of his biggest scoops in June 1915 with the story of the resignation of Secretary of State William Jennings Bryan.

In December 1915 Lawrence left the AP to become special Washington correspondent for the *New York Evening Post*. As such he developed a style of interpretive reporting that was considered unique at the time. His articles were syndicated by the *Post* starting in 1916, and he covered the major stories out of Washington relating to preparedness, the war, and the postwar peace settlement. He married Ellanor Campbell Hayes on 17 July 1918. They had two sons and two daughters.

In 1919 Lawrence covered the peace conference at Versailles, Wilson's visits to European capitals, and the president's cross-country trip in support of the Versailles Treaty, which ended with Wilson's collapse. His own career took a new path in 1919 when Lawrence organized the Consolidated Press Association to syndicate his Washington column. He and Mark Sullivan and Frank Kent are said to have pioneered the modern American newspaper political column. Lawrence's service also supplied general news and feature material, financial news, and market quotations. By late 1920 it served about 100 newspapers. In 1926 Lawrence began publishing the *United States Daily*, a newspaper containing reports of activities of the federal government and texts of official actions. Three years later the daily added news about state governments. Its circulation reached a peak of 41,000 in 1930. Lawrence also wrote for magazines and became a regular radio commentator in the late 1920s.

A reorganization in 1933 ended the Consolidated Press Association and changed the daily into a weekly, the *United States News*, which contained a broadened mix of content, including an editorial page. Circulation reached 85,000 in 1940, when the newspaper was converted into a magazine with expanded coverage of national news. The magazine's circulation was 240,000 by 1943. Lawrence founded the *World Report* in 1946 to cover international news and merged his two magazines in 1948 to create *U.S. News and World Report*. Its circulation that year was 379,000, and when Lawrence died in 1973 it was nearly two million.

From the 1930s on, Lawrence's viewpoint, as expressed in his columns and editorials, was consistently conservative. He was a vocal and frequent critic of the New Deal, a staunch anticommunist, and a supporter of U.S. policy in Vietnam. Coupled with this conservative viewpoint, his financial success as a publisher brought Lawrence criticism from some quarters. But when he died, he was widely eulogized by journalists for his integrity, personal kindness, and unrelenting adherence to the highest standards of responsible public affairs journalism.

BIBLIOGRAPHY:

A. *Diary of a Washington Correspondent* (New York, 1942).

B. DLB 29, 158–167; NYT 12 February 1973; " 'Won Respect of Millions': Life Story of David Lawrence," *U.S. News and World Report*, 26 February 1973.

RONALD S. MARMARELLI

LAWSON, VICTOR FREMONT (b. 9 September 1850; d. 19 August 1925) was one of his generation's most prominent and influential newspaper publishers. As owner of the *Chicago Daily News*, Lawson was responsible for building that paper's circulation as well as its reputation for nonpartisan journalism and fine writing. As a member of the board of directors and as president of the Associated Press, Lawson staunchly defended the principle of cooperative news gathering.

Lawson's father, Iver Lawson, moved to Fox River Valley, Illinois, from Norway in 1837, and to nearby Chicago two years later. Like many enterprising immigrants who came to Chicago in the 1830s, the elder Lawson ended up making his fortune by buying and selling real estate. His wealth raised him to social prominence as well, and he later would serve as city marshal, Chicago alderman, and Illinois state legislator.

Iver Lawson married Melinda Nordvig, also a Norwegian emigrant, and they had three children, of whom Victor was the oldest. In 1869 Victor Lawson went east to attend private school, as did many children of Chicago's wealthy citizens. He entered Phillips Academy in Andover, intending to prepare for Harvard, but poor health forced him to leave the following year. After his father's death in 1872, Lawson took charge of his family's estate, which included the daily paper *Skandinaven*. In July 1876 Lawson bought the *Chicago Daily News*, an afternoon daily that had been founded several months earlier as one of the first penny newspapers in the West. Lawson retained as editor Melville E. Stone (q.v.), one of the paper's founders, thus beginning a lifelong professional collaboration and personal friendship. Lawson purchased the *Post and Mail* in 1878 to acquire that paper's Western Associated Press franchise. In 1881 the *Daily News* began a six-day morning newspaper called the *Chicago Morning News*, which in 1893 became the *Record*.

The *Daily News*, under Lawson and Stone's guidance, quickly earned a reputation as a popular, well-written, independent-minded daily. When many American papers were calling for military and police suppression of the 1877 railroad strikers, Lawson urged the public to recognize workers' plight. A sober, devout man, Lawson supported nonpartisan civic reforms of all sorts. But he was also an astute businessman, especially in his relations with his paper's advertisers. The *Daily News* favored no advertisers with special rates, nor did it offer free space. Lawson's paper sponsored a number of progressive and profitable advertising policies, such as refusing fraudulent ads, establishing drugstore agencies to accept classified ads, employing copywriters to service advertisers, and encouraging full-page ads by department stores.

During the 1890s Lawson's morning paper, the *Record*, became arguably the best and brightest daily in America. Among the brilliant writers who worked for that paper were George Ade, Eugene Field, Ray Stannard Baker, John T. McCutcheon, and Edward Price Bell (qq.v.). Lawson sold the *Record* in 1901 to Herman Kohlsaat, owner of the *Chicago Times-Herald*, in order to concentrate on his afternoon publication.

Lawson played a key role in bringing about the modern form of the Associated Press. He headed the Western Associated Press committee that uncovered a conspiracy by the United Press and members of the New York Associated Press executive committee to monopolize American news. It was under his guidance that the Associated Press reincorporated in 1893 as a cooperative enterprise. From 1894 to 1900 Lawson served as president of the Associated Press, and he remained a member of that organization's board of directors from 1893 till his death in 1925.

Lawson married Jessie S. Bradley, a socially prominent young Chicago woman, on 5 February 1880. She died 2 October 1914, leaving no children. After suffering throughout his life from poor health and nervousness, Lawson died quietly from heart disease in 1925.

BIBLIOGRAPHY:

B. DAB 11, 60–61; NYT 20 August 1925; Charles H. Dennis, *Victor Lawson: His Life and His Work* (Chicago, 1935); Robert C. Tree, "Victor Fremont Lawson and His Newspapers: A Study of the Chicago 'Daily News' and the Chicago 'Record,' " Ph.D. diss., Northwestern Univ., 1959.

JOHN J. PAULY

LEESER, ISAAC (b. 12 December 1806; d. 1 February 1868) worked prodigiously in his lifetime to establish traditional Jewish institutions in America. Through his activities as rabbi, author, translator, editor, and publisher, Leeser attempted to mold the 12,000 to 15,000 American Jews into a coherent Jewish community. To achieve his religious and social goals he worked to strengthen the synagogue and Jewish educational systems and to establish communication through Jewish publications. He promoted the first American congregational union, established the first Hebrew college, and organized the first Jewish publication society. His translation of the Hebrew Bible into English became an authorized version for Jews in America.

Leeser was born in Nevenkirchen in the province of Westphalia, Prussia, to the family of Uri Leeser, a successful merchant. After the death of his mother, Leeser, age eight, moved to the home of his grandparents to be reared. His father died when he was fourteen. As a youth Leeser attended the Gymnasium of Munster. He also studied Bible and Talmud privately with an ardent traditionalist, Abraham Sutro, chief rabbi of Munster and Mark.

At age seventeen, Leeser emigrated to America, arriving in Richmond, Virginia, in May 1824. The young Prussian took up residence with his uncle Zalma Rehine, a Richmond merchant, and for a short while attended private school until it closed ten weeks later. Leeser worked in his uncle's countinghouse for five years. During that time he volunteered on weekends as assistant religion teacher at the synagogue. At age twenty-two, he became hazzan of Mikveh Israel, the old Sephardic Congregation in Philadelphia. Leeser's election came after he published in the *Richmond Whig* a widely publicized rebuttal to an attack on Jews that had appeared in the *London Quarterly Review*. Lesser said later in his life that he would not have taken a position as hazzan of America's oldest synagogue had there been more trained rabbis in America. But, as there were no seminaries for the training of rabbis in 1830, congregations were dependent upon a few unordained ministers to lead them.

Upon taking office, Leeser enthusiastically embarked upon a series of ministerial activities. He conducted services, taught religion, and maintained a free Jewish school in his home. He staunchly advocated measures to strengthen Jewish structures. At the sufferance of his congregation, Leeser introduced the English sermon to American Judaism on 2 June 1830, and instituted the first Jewish Sunday school soon after.

In all, Leeser wrote, translated, and published more than three dozen religious books between 1830 and 1868, including ten volumes of his own sermons. Since many publications required printing in Hebrew, Philadelphia became the center of Hebrew publishing in America.

In 1843 Leeser began publishing the *Occident and American Jewish Advocate*, a monthly magazine intended to provide religious instruction for nonobservant, untrained American Jews. In its later years of publication the *Occident* focused primarily on countering pro-change attitudes of the Jewish Reform press.

Leeser traveled, particularly in the South and West, organizing and dedicating synagogues. In 1850 he retired from Mikveh Israel Congregation, never having married. In 1857 his supporters formed a new congregation, Beth El Emeth, to be a center from which Leeser could carry on his work. The culmination of his career came with the founding of Maimonides College, which Leeser headed for the last year of his life.

For all of Leeser's effort in organizing American Jewish institutions, few he organized survived his death. His indomitable will and bluntness made him a controversial figure in his lifetime as he pitted his energies against Reform. But he never gave up his belief that Jewish Reform would be a transient phenomenon, even though the final issues of the *Occident* reflected Leeser's disillusionment as religious change became more the rule than the exception.

BIBLIOGRAPHY:

B. DAB 7, 137–138; *Jewish Encyclopedia*, 7; *Universal Jewish Dictionary*, 6; Kathryn T. Theus, "From Orthodoxy to Reform: Assimilation and the Jewish English Press in Mid–19th Century America," M.A. thesis, Univ. of Maryland, 1982.

KATHRYN T. THEUS

LEGGETT, WILLIAM (b. 30 April 1801; d. 29 May 1839) was assistant editor, under William Cullen Bryant (q.v.), of the *New York Evening Post*. He is known for his fiercely libertarian editorials, published in book form during the 1840s and again during the 1980s. John Greenleaf Whittier wrote of Leggett that "no one labored more perseveringly, or, in the end, more successfully, to bring the practice of American democracy into conformity with its professions (Nevins, 1922).

Leggett was the son of Abraham Leggett, an American officer during the Revolution, and his second wife, Catherine Wylie of New Rochelle. William attended Georgetown College but, without graduating, joined the navy and became a midshipman in 1822. In 1825 he was court-martialed for dueling with another midshipman, and instead of sailing the oceans published two volumes of sea poetry.

In 1828 Leggett became part owner and assistant editor of the *Evening Post*. His ability to write a fluent daily editorial of 1,000 to 2,000 words in the crowded newspaper room, with presses crashing about him, amazed all. Leggett's editorials consistently opposed governmental economic activities of all kinds. He fought business-government partnerships to build turnpikes or railroads, charging that they would redistribute income to those with political clout. He opposed tariffs because they favored some industries and hurt others. He believed that those who wished to come together to build either companies or labor unions were entitled to do so without governmental help or hindrance.

Leggett's hatred of governmental power drove him into a fervent campaign against the Bank of the United States. Along with other Jacksonians he viewed it as a monopolistic source of privilege. He fought the Jackson administration, though, when it agreed to stop abolitionist newspapers from circulating through the postal system. "If the government once begins to discriminate as to what is orthodox and what heterodox in opinion, what is safe and what's unsafe in tendency," Leggett wrote, "farewell, a long farewell, to our freedom."

Day after day Leggett proclaimed that a libertarian position would most benefit the poor: "The only enemy they have to fear as yet in this free country," he wrote of those in need, "is monopoly and a great pauper system that grinds them to the dust. . . . " Fearing governmental economic control, Leggett favored sound money and attacked inflationary speculation, worrying in 1835 that the nation "is plunging deeper and deeper into the bottomless pit of unredeemed and irredeemable obligations." But in 1835 an overworked Leggett himself plunged into a pit of illness—"bilious fever," they called it—that was found to have no bottom. Although he reduced his work load, leaving the *Evening Post* in 1836 to edit the weekly *Plaindealer* (through 1837) and sometimes write for the daily *Examiner*, Leggett died in 1839.

Had only his sea poetry and the memory of some editorials survived his death, Leggett would be long forgotten. It is the survival of his political writings in book form that leaves him second only to the authors of the *Federalist Papers* as a writer whose ideas did not go as stale as yesterday's newspaper. Bryant's memorial tribute to Leggett included these lines:

> The words of fire that from his pen
> Were flung upon the fervid page,
> Still move, still shake the hearts of men,
> Amid a cold and coward age.

BIBLIOGRAPHY:

A. *Democratick Editorials: Essays in Jacksonian Political Economy*, ed. Lawrence H. White (New York, 1984); *A Collection of the Political Writings of Wm. Leggett* (New York, 1840).

B. Charles I. Glicksberg, "William Leggett, Neglected Figure of American Literary History," *Journalism Quarterly*, March 1948. DAB 6, 147–148; Allan Nevins, *The "Evening Post": A Century of Journalism* (New York, 1922).

MARVIN N. OLASKY

LEONARD, WILLIAM A. (b. 9 April 1916) went from being "bitten by the radio bug" at the age of twelve to the presidency of CBS News ("On the Record;" 1978). His broadcasting career, spent entirely with CBS, spanned thirty-seven years, during which he "excelled" as a "reporter, writer, programmer, producer, executive and industry leader." Leonard was responsible for bringing to television "60 Minutes," and his selection of Dan Rather to replace the retiring Walter Cronkite (q.v.) on the "CBS Evening News" proved highly successful. He was a leader in developing CBS News' political campaign and election coverage. For his network accomplishments, Leonard received the George Foster Peabody Award in 1981.

A native New Yorker, Leonard was born on Manhattan's west side to James Garfield Moses, an attorney, and to Ruth Leonard Moses, who later became Mrs. Richard C. Harrison. Leonard spent most of his boyhood in Orange, New Jersey, and Westport, Connecticut. It was in the latter state that he received his college preparatory education at the Avon School, where he lettered in baseball, football, track, and hockey. He was also an amateur boxer, who, years later, would fight exhibition rounds with two world champions.

Sociology was his major at Dartmouth, where he graduated with a B.A. degree in 1937. He was the managing editor of the *Daily Dartmouth*, president of the Amateur Radio Club, and even acted with the Dartmouth Players. Within a few months of graduation, he found a job with the *Bridgeport* (Connecticut) *Post-Telegram*. He moved to New York City in 1940 to work in radio research at the Cunningham and Walsh advertising agency. World War II intervened, and he entered the navy as an ensign a year later, serving as a communications officer in charge of electronic countermeasures aboard destroyers in the Mediterranean. By the time of his discharge in 1945, he had achieved the rank of lieutenant commander, and had been awarded both the Presidential Unit Citation and the Secretary of the Navy Commendation.

Leonard once said he "wanted to be at CBS from the time [he] was 15," and with help from a friend of the family, CBS President Frank Stanton (q.v.), he was hired by the network-owned New York radio station WCBS within a few months of leaving the service. He developed the highly popular "This is New York" radio program on which he covered the metropolis as a roving reporter. The television version, "Eye on New York," went on the air in 1954, and Leonard became known as "Mr. New York." He was a floor reporter for CBS at the 1952, 1956, and 1960 national political conventions.

One of his "Eye" programs, on the mentally retarded, received the Albert Lasker Award for Medical Journalism in 1956. That year his fourteen-year marriage to Adele Wilde ended in divorce. They had six sons, David M., William A., Andrew H., Nicolas D., James M., and Oliver L. On 11 May 1957 he married Norma Kaphan Wallace, the former wife of television newsman Mike Wallace. She brought two sons to the marriage, Peter, who died in a climbing accident in Greece in 1962, and Chris, who later became an NBC news correspondent.

In 1959 Leonard joined CBS News as correspondent and producer. He worked closely with Edward R. Murrow and Fred W. Friendly (qq.v.). His "CBS Reports" program "Trujillo—Portrait of a Dictator" won the Overseas Press Club's Ed Stout Award. In 1962 Leonard was named executive producer of the CBS News election unit, with charge over all policies, plans, and on-air broadcasts of political coverage. Added to his responsibilities in 1963 was the job of executive producer of WCBS-TV's expanded news program during the New York newspaper strike.

In 1964 he became vice president and director of news programming. Next, as senior vice president and director of public affairs broadcasts, he supervised all documentary and political broadcasts, along with children's and religious news programs, and administered several departments. He moved out of news for three years when the network assigned him to Washington as CBS vice president in 1975 in charge of all the corporation's government relations.

In 1978 he was brought back to New York and named executive vice president and chief operating officer, and at the same time it was announced that he would succeed Richard Salant (q.v.) as president of CBS News when Salant reached mandatory retirement age in April 1979. CBS would break its retirement policy in Leonard's case when he was asked to remain as president of CBS News for one year beyond his scheduled retirement. He handled the transition from Walter Cronkite (q.v.) to Dan Rather as anchor of the "CBS Evening News," brought Bill Moyers back to CBS, restructured "CBS Morning News," and put the Cronkite anchored "Universe" program on the air.

After his retirement on 1 March 1982, he served as a Washington-based consultant for CBS.

BIBLIOGRAPHY:

B. "On the Record: An Interview with Bill Leonard," *Washington Journalism Review*, September/October 1978; "At Large: The Way We Were, and Should Be," *Broadcasting*, 1 March 1982; Les Brown, "Incoming Chief of CBS News Describes Plans," NYT 1 August 1978.

DAVID M. GUERRA

LESLIE, FRANK (b. 29 March 1821; d. 10 January 1880) was the pioneer of pictorial journalism in the United States. His reputation as a journalist and publisher rests primarily on his weekly, *Frank Leslie's Illustrated Newspaper*. In that magazine Leslie added a new dimension to news coverage of the day by using words and pictures, in many cases a series of related pictures, to illustrate current news events with a promptness that was unmatched by other publications. He scorned the ornamental use of illustrations in what he called "picture papers" and gave his readers "the current news, thus bringing the genius of the pencil and pen promptly to illustrate the recorded events" (Mott, 1967). Leslie's use of words and illustrations foreshadowed the picture magazines of the 1930s.

Leslie was born Henry Carter in Ipswich, England, the son of Joseph Leslie and Mary Elliston Carter. His father was a prosperous glove manufacturer, and in 1838 young Leslie was sent to London to learn the glove business. Leslie, however, had developed a strong interest in drawing and engraving during his schooldays in Ipswich, and a few years after arriving in London he began to submit his drawings to the *Illustrated London News* signed with his pseudonym, Frank Leslie. While in London Leslie met Sara Ann Welham and married her on 14 February 1842. They had three sons, Henry, Alfred, and Scipio.

Leslie saw that his opportunities were limited in England, and he decided in 1848 to come to the United States. He arrived 6 July in New York, where he was joined a year or so later by his family. During the next six years he worked both as an independent engraver and on two of the early picture magazines—*Gleason's Pictorial Drawing-Room Companion*, published in Boston, and Barnum and Beach's short-lived *Illustrated Weekly*.

After successes with his first two publishing ventures, *Frank Leslie's Ladies' Gazette of Fashion* (started in 1854) and the *New York Journal of Romance*, Leslie was ready to launch his *Illustrated Newspaper*. In the first issue, dated 15 December 1855, Leslie told how he had anticipated and overcome the problems his predecessors had failed to solve—the lack of skilled artists and engravers and the printing difficulties caused by attempting lengthy press runs from large woodcuts.

During the *Illustrated*'s difficult first years, the publication was saved by two events—its sensational coverage in 1857 of the Burdell murder case and the effective crusade in 1858–59 against the "swill milk" racket. The weekly's popularity depended largely on the appeal of its illustrations, especially its cover and center-spread pictures which frequently were full-page in size. The *Illustrated*'s pictures and text took its readers to the Arctic with the explorer Dr. Elisha Kent Kane, to the American West, and to the Orient with Admiral Matthew Perry. The paper's extensive coverage of the Civil War became what journalism historian Frank Luther Mott called "a great pictorial history" of the conflict (Mott, 1967).

Leslie and his wife separated in 1860 and were divorced 18 July 1872. Two years later, on 13 July 1874, he married Miriam Florence Squier, the editor of several of his periodicals including *Frank Leslie's Lady's Magazine*.

By 1875 the Frank Leslie Publishing House was issuing twelve periodicals, and Leslie was at the peak of his career. He and the new Mrs. Leslie (*see* Leslie, Miriam) lived in luxury, dividing their time between a lavish estate in Saratoga and a house in New York. By the fall of 1877, his business was heavily in debt. That, combined with the financial crisis of that year and expenses of the couple's extravagant style of living, forced Leslie into bankruptcy. His business was turned over to an assignee, but Leslie continued to oversee its operation until his death three years later.

Leslie had become a U.S. citizen on 26 April 1856, and the following year was granted the right to use the name Frank Leslie by special act of the New York legislature. He was awarded a gold medal by Napoleon III for his service as a U.S. commissioner to the Paris Universal Exposition of 1867.

Leslie died of cancer 10 January 1880 at his home in New York. Leslie's motto in publishing was "never shoot over the heads of the people," and his periodicals are proof that he lived up to that motto. Yet while catering to the tastes of a mass public, Leslie's *Illustrated Newspaper* helped to usher in a new kind of journalism.

BIBLIOGRAPHY:

B. DAB 11, 186–187; NYT 11 January 1880; Frank Luther Mott, *A History of American Magazines, 1850–65* (Cambridge, Mass., 1967); Donald C. Peterson, "Two Pioneer American Picture Magazines," M.S. thesis, Univ. of Wisconsin, 1953; Madeleine B. Stern, *Purple Passage: The Life of Mrs. Frank Leslie* (Norman, Okla., 1953).

DONALD C. PETERSON

LESLIE, MIRIAM (b. 5 June 1836; d. 14 September 1914) was widely respected as eventual owner, editor, and publisher of *Frank Leslie's Illustrated Weekly*, published 1855–1922.

As Miriam Squier, the wife of Ephraim George Squier, the friend whom Frank Leslie (q.v.) appointed as an editor, she wrote for *Frank Leslie's Lady's Magazine* and was considered "a lady of highest achievement" (Stern, 1953). Much is known about her flamboyant personal life because she loved the limelight she was so often in. However, it is for her reporting and editing abilities as Mrs. Frank Leslie, and later as Frank Leslie herself after her husband died 10 January 1880, that gives her a place in journalism history. She changed her name to his legally, thus eliminating the necessity of using "Mrs." Undoubtedly the change also eliminated the fact of her gender for many readers, something women of her generation did. However, she was an ardent feminist and contributed much of her wealth to that cause. She wrote several books, including *Rents in Our Robes*, *Are Men Gay Deceivers?*, and *God Bless the American Man*. She also wrote a play, *The Froth of Society*.

Miriam Leslie developed and reported for the *Chimney Corner*, a magazine intended to be "a family fireside friend." She traveled widely in Europe, South America, and the American West, and wrote extensively about such things as interviewing Brigham Young in Utah, and going down into the Bonanza mine in Nevada for the *Illustrated Weekly*.

"Oh, if I could only find a woman with $50,000 to lend!" she said, when as Leslie's widow, she was faced with pulling the publishing business back into the black. Creditors laughed, but she found what she wanted and managed to pay back the loan ahead of time, largely because of the success of her coverage of President Garfield's assassination. It was a journalistic coup perhaps comparable to television coverage of President John F. Kennedy's death eighty-two years later. Her motto was always to give readers "the newest news."

Miriam Leslie was born in New Orleans, Louisiana. Her father was Charles Follin (his name often spelled Folline), a dealer in cotton, tobacco, and hides. There is no evidence that he ever married her mother, Susan Danforth, although she took his name and the two stayed together. As an adolescent, Miriam became the legal ward of her paternal uncle, Adolphus Follin, when her father's business failed. At her death, she was listed as "Baroness de Bazas," a name she had given herself, and said to be "from a noble Huguenot family," a myth she had perpetuated herself (Stern, 1953). She was educated in seminaries and female academies in Cincinnati, Ohio, and in New York, but most of her learning came from her father, who insisted that she learn several languages, a skill valuable to her in reporting travels.

She was married four times: first to David Charles Peacock in a kind of shotgun wedding after he had taught her to love the diamonds he "borrowed" for her. The ceremony took place on 29 March 1854; the marriage was formally annulled 24 March 1856. She married E. G. Squier, a journalist who was also a well-known archaeologist, on 22 October 1857, and divorced him 31 May 1873. Frank Leslie lived in the Squier home, employed Mr. Squier as well as his wife, and the classic triangle caused much gossip. Miriam once wrote: "there is probably none more dangerous, none more alluring, none more contagious, than the practice of flirtation among married people." She married Leslie on 13 July 1873, after he obtained a divorce. Leslie died 10 January 1880. His widow married William C. Kingsbury Wilde, Oscar Wilde's brother, on 4 October 1891, when she was fifty-five, and divorced him 10 June 1893. It was said he was drunk on their wedding night, and that she supported him during the time they were married. She had no children, but was known to have been pregnant by Squier.

Besides her marriages, she was involved with other men and seemed on the verge of a fifth marriage at least once. She was known to have been the mistress of William Montgomery Churchwell, a Tennessee congressman, before she married Squier, but the liaison was short-lived. She expected to marry Don Teodoro, the count of Villaverde de Alta, but he died before it could happen. After more years of playing the publishing grand dame, Miriam Leslie died at seventy-eight in New York of accute dilation of the heart following chronic endocarditis.

BIBLIOGRAPHY:

B. NYT 19 September 1914; Madeline B. Stern, *Purple Passages: The Life of Mrs. Frank Leslie* (Norman, Okla., 1953).

JUNE N. ADAMSON

LEWIS, FULTON, JR. (b. 30 April 1903; d. 21 August 1966) was for thirty years a conservative radio commentator of the Mutual Broadcasting System. Many Americans listened loyally to his fifteen-minute broadcasts each Friday evening which always began: "Good evening, ladies and gentlemen. This is Fulton Lewis, Jr., speaking to you from Mutual studios in Washington, D.C." The close was consistent, too: "That's the top of the news as it looks from here."

Lewis was born in Washington, D.C., to Fulton and Elizabeth Saville Lewis. He traced his ancestry to Mordecai Lewis, revolutionary war financier, and he was the fifth generation of the Lewis family to live in the District of Columbia. Lewis was an accomplished musician, having studied piano, voice, harmony, and composition for fourteen years. He attended the University of Virginia for only two years. In 1924 he joined the *Washington Herald* as a fishing columnist and national news writer. After becoming city editor he left the *Herald* in 1928 to become assistant bureau manager of Hearst's Universal News Service and International News Service.

Lewis was married on 29 June 1930 to Alice Huston, the daughter of former Republican national chairman and assistant secretary of commerce C. H. Huston. They had two children, Alice Elizabeth and Fulton III, and lived on a 275-acre farm in Maryland. For nine years he was chief of the Universal Washington bureau, and he wrote the syndicated column "The Washington Sideshow" from 1933 to 1936. The column was run by King Features in about fifty newspapers. Lewis frequently scooped his competitors. His investigations covered government airmail contract irregularities, and espionage by a navy lieutenant. In some cases he was instrumental in gathering data for congressional investigations.

In 1937 Lewis left Hearst to take a $25-a-week job as a substitute on Mutual radio's WOL in Washington. Within two months his broadcasts had become a "fixture," as the *New York Times* said in its obituary of Lewis. His nightly commentary was first carried coast to coast on 27 December 1937. In addition, Lewis chaired the "American Forum of the Air," and successfully pushed to gain radio proper recognition in congressional press galleries. He was subsequently elected first president of the Radio Correspondents Association. After war broke out in 1939, he invited Charles A. Lindbergh to speak on his program, and he and Lindbergh became known for their strong isolationism. In October a new program debuted with Lewis as a roving reporter covering such things as the Congress of Havana in Cuba and the two major American party conventions.

During his lifetime Lewis was known for his firsthand sources. He used these with a vengeance to attack favorite targets, usually anyone connected with the Roosevelt New Deal, such as former vice president Henry Wallace, former Atomic Energy Commission chairman David Lilienthal, and secretary of commerce Harry Hopkins. Lewis was a staunch supporter, too, of Senator Joseph McCarthy. His attacks were colorful characterizations: "piddle-paddle, double-talking, CIO-Communist-backed, left-wing crackpots" is one such. No matter what the verbiage, though, Lewis firmly believed he was right and completely truthful. Others agreed, including fellow journalists. In 1943 Lewis won an award from Mrs. Alfred I. duPont and the Florida National Group of Banking Institutions as the year's best radio commentator.

"The voice with the snarl," or "the golden stutter," as some came to call him, was an avid organ-builder who spent devoted hours reconstructing the instrument in St. David's Episcopal Church. It was played at his funeral. Lewis died at Doctor's Hospital in Washington after surgery for pancreatitis caused two heart attacks. For a few years his son, Fulton Lewis III, continued his broadcasts.

BIBLIOGRAPHY:
B. NYT 22 August 1966; Irving E. Fang, *Those Radio Commentators!* (Ames, Iowa, 1977).

JONATHAN L. YODER

LEWIS, LILLIAN ALBERTA, or **BERT ISLEW** (b. 1861; d. ?), the youngest of the early black newspaperwomen, obtained journalistic prominence as society editor for the black-owned *Boston Advocate*. Lewis was nationally recognized as one of a small group of black journalists to earn a position as a paid reporter for a major American newspaper.

She was born in the Boston home of abolitionist and underground railroad operator Lewis Hayden. Her mother was probably a fugitive slave. Lewis attended Bowdoin Grammar School in Boston until 1874. There she acquired an interest in literature and composition. At age thirteen she entered an essay contest and claimed third prize. Many of her competitors were high school graduates.

While a student at Boston's Girls High School in 1875, she began writing lectures and essays on social issues. For three months she traveled throughout Boston lecturing to temperance societies and other local groups. "The Mantel of the Church Covereth A Multitude of Humbugs" was her most popular exposition. Demanding classes forced her to cancel appearances after one season.

In 1878 she wrote an unpublished novel entitled *Idalene Van Therese*. What occurred in Lewis's professional and private life from 1878 to 1888 is unknown. Sometime during 1889 she became a columnist for the financially troubled *Boston Advocate*. She initiated the newspaper's "They Say" column, which was designed to report the ideas of persons of all ages and classes. Her columns, signed with the pseudonym Bert Islew, rapidly became popular and the newspaper's subscriptions increased. The first columns were written in a terse, breezy, reportorial style. Comments and criticism were added to later columns.

She received a promotion in 1893 and became the *Boston Advocate*'s society editor at age thirty-two. Her column was designated the society department. She also began contributing regular articles to the *Richmond Planet*, an aggressive Virginia newspaper. Concurrently, she served as Boston correspondent for the monthly *Our Women and Children*, an Afro-American magazine. She was hired by the *Boston Herald* as Max Elliot's private secretary and special writer in 1895. As a *Herald* staffer she became one of the first blacks to be hired by a white publication.

Lewis's reputation as a stenographer was highly acclaimed. She became a *Herald* reporter when she was thirty-nine and worked as a Boston journalist until 1901. No further information is available on Bert Islew's personal life or career beyond 1901.

BIBLIOGRAPHY:
B. *Boston Directory* (Boston, 1890, 1893, 1895, 1900, 1901); Marianna W. Davis, "Shaping of the Black Press By Critical Events," in *Contributions of Black Women to*

America (Columbia, S.C., 1981); Henry Davenport Northrop, Joseph R. Gay, and I. Garland Penn, "Noted Afro-American Women and Their Achievements," in *The College of Life* (New York, 1893); I. Garland Penn, *The Afro-American Press and Its Editors* (Springfield, Mass., 1891); Lucy Wilmot Smith, "Some Female Writers of the Negro Race," *Journalist*, January 1889.

NORA HALL

LIEBLING, ABBOTT JOSEPH (b. 18 October 1904; d. 28 December 1963) was a gifted and prolific New York magazine writer. A stylish reporter who often probed the urban underworld of boxers, con men, and touts, Liebling became a model for a later generation of New Journalists. His press criticism for the *New Yorker* continues to be widely read and admired.

Liebling was born in New York City to middle-class Jewish parents. His father, Joseph, was an Austrian immigrant who began as a furrier's apprentice in the gritty Lower East Side Jewish ghetto and eventually came to own a wholesale fur business. Liebling's mother, Anna Slone, was from San Francisco. Liebling's Upper West Side upbringing was genteel and well-to-do. German servants did the family's housework, and Liebling's parents frequently took him on trips to Europe as he grew older. But Liebling was a rebellious and mischievous youngster who admired the street life of the lower classes that his father had left behind.

A precocious student who voraciously read literature as well as newspapers, Liebling graduated from high school early and entered Dartmouth at age sixteen. Though he soon developed a reputation there as a literary man and raconteur, Liebling was bounced twice, the second time permanently, for not attending compulsory chapel. In fall 1923 he entered Columbia University's Pulitzer School of Journalism and graduated two years later.

Liebling's first professional job was as a copyreader at the *New York Times*, work he found rather dull. In March 1926 the *Times* fired him for changing a reporter's middle name as a prank. Liebling quickly found a job as a general assignment reporter at the *Providence Evening Bulletin* and soon after moved to the *Journal*, the *Bulletin*'s morning sister paper. In fall 1926 Liebling left for a year in France, at his father's expense. Liebling took a few classes at the Sorbonne, but spent most of his time imbibing French culture and gastronomy. After a year he returned to his old job at the *Providence Journal*.

In 1930 Liebling quit the *Journal* and returned to New York City. He began writing feature stories for the *New York World*, and when that paper folded in February 1931, he moved to Roy Howard's (q.v.) new *World-Telegram*. He left the *World-Telegram* in 1935, worked briefly for Hearst's King Features Syndicate, then landed a job at the *New Yorker*.

Liebling did his best work for the *New Yorker*. He developed a controlled but jazzy style that combined slang and extravagant metaphor. His gift for hearing and recalling street talk is apparent in his stories about New York lowlife, which were later collected in *Back Where I Come From* (1938), *The Telephone Booth Indian* (1944), and *The Honest Rainmaker: The Life and Times of Colonel John R. Stingo* (1953). His reporting on boxing, collected in *The Sweet Science* (1956), was some of the best ever written. During World War II Liebling covered the London blitz and the invasions of North Africa and Normandy for the *New Yorker*, and he was present in August 1944 for the liberation of his beloved Paris. His war reportage was collected in *The Road Back to Paris* (1944) and *The Republic of Silence* (1947). In recognition of his work during the war, Liebling was awarded France's Legion of Honor medal in 1952.

Liebling's stories frequently used first-person narrative—one of the features that would make his work attractive to later New Journalists. The autobiographical touch is particularly apparent in two later collections of reminiscences, *Normandy Revisited* (1958) and *Between Meals: An Appetite for Paris* (1962). In May 1945 Liebling wrote his first ''Wayward Pressman'' column. A charter member of the Newspaper Guild, Liebling often excoriated the penny-pinching policies and reactionary attitudes of newspaper publishers. Sometimes he would compare the inconsistencies of newspaper coverage of a single event; other times he would show how newspapers had ignored or downplayed an important story. His criticism was later collected in *The Wayward Pressman* (1947), *Mink and Red Herring: The Wayward Pressman's Casebook* (1949), and *The Press* (1961).

In the 1950s and 1960s, aside from his work for the *New Yorker*, Liebling wrote occasional book reviews for *Esquire* and sports stories for the *Observer*. He wrote *Chicago: The Second City* (1950) after spending a miserable year there on an abortive assignment for *Collier's*. In 1961 he published one of his best works of reporting, *The Earl of Louisiana*, about Governor Earl Long, Huey Long's erratic but politically liberal brother.

Liebling was married three times, and his personal life was often unhappy. In 1934 he married Ann McGinn, a poor Irish-Catholic girl from Providence. She was severely schizophrenic, however, and had to be hospitalized, first periodically then later permanently. Even after Liebling divorced her in 1949. he continued to support her and occasionally correspond. She committed suicide a few months after his death. In 1949 Liebling married Harriet Lucille Barr Spectorsky, a model who had previously been married to writers Stephen Barr and August Spectorsky. He divorced her in 1959 and married the writer Jean Stafford. He had no children by any of his marriages.

A gourmand of startling excess, Liebling remained seriously overweight most of his life and often suffered from gout. In 1963 he caught viral pneumonia and died a few days later, on 28 December, from congestive heart failure and renal collapse.

BIBLIOGRAPHY:
A. *Liebling Abroad* (New York, 1981).
B. DAB Supp. 7, 472–474; NYT 29 December 1963; Raymond Sokolov, *Wayward Reporter: The Life of A. J. Liebling* (New York, 1980).

JOHN J. PAULY

LIPPINCOTT, SARA JANE CLARKE (b. 23 September 1823; d. 20 April 1904), who published under the name Grace Greenwood, was one of the first women correspondents reporting from Washington, D.C., and was editor of one of the first—perhaps the first—of the magazines for children published in America.

She was born in Pompey, New York, the youngest daughter and one of eleven children of Dr. Thaddeus Clarke and Deborah Clarke. She grew up in Pompey, Fabius, and Rochester, New York. When she was about nineteen, the family moved to New Brighton, Pennsylvania.

Her articles began to be published in 1844 in the *New York Mirror*. She said many years later that it was easy for her to get published when she was young, but hard to get paid for it. She published a variety of work—poems, stories, reportage, travel, biography—most of it light in tone. In 1853 she married Leander K. Lippincott (a relative of J. B. Lippincott, the publisher). The couple had one daughter, whose name seems to be lost to the mores of the times; she is identified in biographical material as Mrs. Herbert Winslow Hall.

During the decade or so before the Civil War, Sara Lippincott lived sometimes in Philadelphia, sometimes in Washington. She began writing children's stories at the suggestion of Chief Justice Salmon P. Chase, a family friend, and published a number of books for children. She and her husband purchased a newsletter directed to children, moved it to Philadelphia, called it *Young Pilgrim*, and published it for several years. Louisa May Alcott made her literary debut in the publication, or so it is claimed, and Longfellow and Whittier were published in it. The magazine reached a circulation of 12,000 by 1861, but went out of business for financial reasons soon after that.

During the Civil War she began writing the "Washington Letter" in the *Philadelphia Weekly*. Newspapers in New York, Chicago, and California began publishing the letter, which she wrote for a number of years, sometimes from Washington, sometimes from Europe. Her friends liked to call her the first woman Washington correspondent, but that claim is difficult to maintain. It is also claimed that she was the first woman lecturer to appear on the college lyceum circuit; those appearances began during the Civil War. Abraham Lincoln paid tribute to her patriotism, and she apparently led an active social life among political and literary leaders. She was a supporter of various movements for women's rights, but was never a leader nor an ardent worker in those movements.

She contributed to the *Times*, the *Tribune*, and the *Independent* in New York City, to many other newspapers, and to *Hearth and Home*, *Atlantic*, *Harper's*, and other American and English magazines. One of her last works was an account of the inaugural preparations for President McKinley. Even by 1893, when her eighteen books were displayed at the Chicago World's Fair, it was hard to find copies of her work, and by the early twentieth century it had all but disappeared from view. She died at New Rochelle, New York.

BIBLIOGRAPHY:

B. DAB 6, 288; NYT 21 April 1904.

DWIGHT JENSEN

LIPPMANN, WALTER (b. 23 September 1889; d. 14 December 1974) was a noted columnist, editor, and author who played a unique role in political journalism. Best known for his interest in foreign affairs, Lippmann believed that journalists comprise an integral part of both the discussion and the formulation of policy ideas. He was a founding editor of the *New Republic*, helped author President Woodrow Wilson's Fourteen Points, and wrote numerous books, among them *Public Opinion* (1922), a work still considered seminal by mass communications researchers.

Lippmann was born in New York City, the only child of Jacob and Daisy Baum Lippmann. Although his father, a wealthy clothing manufacturer, provided a comfortable, even luxurious life, Lippmann was not close to him, preferring to seek strong male mentors in his teachers, statesmen, and other leaders. Lippmann attended the predominantly Jewish Sachs School for boys, the Sachs Collegiate Institute, and finally enrolled in Harvard in 1906. By that time he had traveled extensively in Europe and considered himself a cosmopolitan. His Jewish background was indeed just that; he, along with his parents, held high the value of assimilation. This value had a lifelong effect on Lippmann's public work and his private life.

Lippmann's class of 1910 was considered one of Harvard's most distinguished. It included journalists John Reed and Heywood Broun (qq.v.), as well as T. S. Eliot, Robert Edmond Jones, Hans von Kaltenborn (q.v.), Bronson Cutting, and other students who were later to become distinguished in fields ranging from architecture to literature. Lippmann sought out star professors, and was especially influenced by William James and George Santayana. Lippmann was awarded Phi Beta Kappa, and remained at Harvard for an extra year as Santayana's graduate assistant.

In May 1910 Lippmann took his first job as a journalist, working for Ralph Albertson, a Congregational minister and socialist reformer who founded the *Boston Common*. Soon dissatisfied with both the lack of journalistic professionalism and the naïvete of the *Common*'s political stance, Lippmann left for *Everybody's Magazine*, where he was Lincoln Steffens's (q.v.) secretary, researcher, and companion. Within a year, Lippmann became associate editor there, and he was fast gaining a reputation among progressives and socialists as a young man of note.

His first book, *A Preface to Politics* (1913), was critically acclaimed chiefly because of its unusual application of Freudian psychological insights to the problems of politics. Among other things, Lippmann advocated strong leadership and big government to serve as a foil for and regulator of an endemic part of American society, big business. Much of Lippmann's political philosophy at this time was influenced by Herbert Croly (q.v.), and when the two met it was for Croly to suggest that Lippmann join him in founding a new journal devoted to spreading the ideas of "constructive nationalism," a weekly that would cover politics and the arts. Croly's vision was for a radical, pragmatic journal that would challenge the status quo without being socialistic or doctrinaire. The *New Republic* was first published on the eve of World War I, and it is from Lippmann's involvement with the *New Republic* that his reputation as an expert in foreign affairs was established. By 1916 even President Wilson was an avid reader of Lippmann's editorials, and it was rumored that Wilson's "peace without victory" speech to the Senate in 1917 was penned by Lippmann.

Lippmann married Faye Albertson, daughter of Ralph Albertson, on 24 May 1917. They had no children although Jane Mather became their ward and she remained close to Lippmann throughout his life. The Lippmans shared a long but cool marriage and were divorced in 1937. Lippmann then married Helen Byrn Armstrong on 26 March 1938.

Lippmann spent the war years as a captain in military intelligence. By 1920 he had resigned from the army and was writing a regular column for *Vanity Fair*. In 1922 he joined the editorial staff of the *New York World*, and became the director of the editorial page in 1924. The *World* differed markedly from the elegant sophistication of the *New Republic*; its roots were in exposé and yellow journalism, and although by this time the *World* had moved toward journalistic respectability, the paper still served a blue-collar market. Lippmann wrote over twelve hundred editorials during his tenure there, one-third of those on foreign affairs.

It was also during this period that Lippmann's famous *Public Opinion* was published. It was a critical success. John Dewey called it "perhaps the most effective indictment of democracy as currently conceived ever penned." The central thesis of *Public Opinion* is that the ordinary citizen is unable to understand, let alone synthesize, the vast, complex issues of national and international politics. Lippmann explored the process of opinion formation and the nature of public opinion, creating what C. Wright Mills termed a definitive statement on public opinion theory (Steele, 1980). It was here that Lippmann coined the term "stereotype" to refer to a fixed preconceived notion, a word he borrowed from the printer's mold.

By 1929 Lippmann had moved to the *New York Herald Tribune* and initiated his "Today and Tomorrow" column. Initially syndicated by the *Washington Post* and *Los Angeles Times*, it was later syndicated in over 275 papers around the world. As Lippmann became increasingly involved politically, he moved to Washington, D.C., there writing his column which ran from 1931 through 1967. During that time Lippmann was a friend and adviser to numerous political figures. His politics became increasingly conservative.

The Johnson years created a significant conflict for Lippmann, and affected his journalistic career. Lippmann viewed Lyndon Johnson as the natural successor to Franklin Roosevelt, the man who would in fact implement the great reforms of the New Deal by way of the Great Society. Lippmann felt he had a strong relationship with the Democratic president, but he increasingly believed that the Vietnam involvement was misplaced, that it distracted from the more important thrust of the Johnson presidency. Because of the special nature of Lippmann's relationship with the president (a vantage point that some argued interfered with Lippmann's journalistic objectivity), Johnson courted Lippmann in an effort to appease the press, to affect the tone of Lippmann's columns. Lippmann later interpreted the consultation as a betrayal, and finally retired from his long-held position as writer of "Today and Tomorrow."

For the greater portion of his career Lippmann was in touch with presidents, both U.S. and foreign, ambassadors, and other influential contemporary people. He wrote biweekly columns for *Newsweek* as well as numerous books and articles. By the early 1970s, however, Lippmann's health began to fail. He stopped writing and spent his remaining years in New York City. His wife, Helen, died on 16 February 1974; Lippmann died later that year, on 14 December of cardiac arrest. His body was cremated and his ashes scattered, as were those of Helen, off the Maine coast where they had shared a summer house. He was survived by his ward, Jane Mather Wilmerding.

BIBLIOGRAPHY:

A. *A Preface to Morals* (New York, 1929); *Essays in the Public Philosophy* (Boston, 1955).

B. NYT 15 December 1974; Ronald Steele, *Walter Lippmann and the American Century* (New York, 1980).

ELLI LESTER-MASSMAN

LISAGOR, PETER "PETE" IRVIN (b. 5 August 1915; d. 10 December 1976) was Washington bureau chief of the *Chicago Daily News*, and a frequent guest journalist on network television public affairs programs.

Lisagor was born in Keystone, West Virginia, to Paris and Fanny Simpkins Lisagor. His father was manager of a general store in Keystone. Lisagor studied for a year at Northwestern University (1933), and then enrolled at the University of Michigan, where he received a B.A. in 1939. While in Ann Arbor he served as a sports reporter for the local newspaper.

He worked as a sports reporter for the *Chicago Daily News* from 1939 to 1941. He joined United Press as a general assignment news reporter in 1941. He married Myra K. Murphy on 14 February 1942, and then enlisted in the army. During World War II he was managing editor of the London edition of

Stars and Stripes from 1944 to 1945, and served as editor of *Stars and Stripes* magazine in Paris in 1945. Lisagor worked briefly as news editor of the *Paris Post* in 1945. Late that year he returned to the *Chicago Daily News* and remained with the paper until his death.

He received a leave of absence to accept a Nieman Fellowship at Harvard University during the 1948–49 academic year, and studied international affairs. When he returned to the *Daily News* in 1949 he was named U.N. correspondent. In 1950 he became diplomatic correspondent in Washington, D.C., and remained in that position until he was promoted to Washington bureau chief in 1959. While he was in Washington, Lisagor reported firsthand the domestic and foreign trips taken by every president beginning with Dwight Eisenhower. He covered John Kennedy's meeting with Khrushchev, Richard Nixon's trips to Russia and China in 1972, and Gerald Ford's trip to China in 1975.

Peter Lisagor was a leader among journalists in the nation's capital. At various times he served as president of the Gridiron Club (1975), the Overseas Writers' Club (1960–61), the State Department Correspondents' Association, and the White House Correspondents' Association. In addition, he was a member of the board of governors of the National Press Club. Lisagor frequently served as a guest journalist on the network television interview programs "Meet the Press" and "Washington Week in Review." He wrote a syndicated newspaper column and was coauthor, with Marguerite Higgins (q.v.), of *Overtime in Heaven* (1964), a compilation of stories of heroism among American Foreign Service officers.

He received numerous awards for his reporting and commentary, among them a George Foster Peabody Award (1974), and the Edward Weintel Prize for Diplomatic Reporting presented by the Georgetown University School of Foreign Service (1976). Lisagor and his wife had two children: P. Scott Lisagor and Diane Meredith Lisagor. Lisagor died at Northern Virginia Doctors Hospital in Arlington at age sixty-one. He had been suffering from cancer for almost a year before his death.

BIBLIOGRAPHY:

B. NYT 11 December 1976; *Washington Post*, 11 December 1976; *Newsweek*, 20 December 1976.

DONALD L. MCBRIDE

LOCKE, DAVID ROSS (b. 20 September 1833; d. 15 February 1888) was better known as the Reverend Petroleum Vesuvius Nasby, bigot par excellence. Through the satire of Nasby, Locke excoriated slavery, the Confederacy, and the Democrats, and was one of the leading literary spokesmen for the Union cause during the Civil War.

Born in Vestal, Broome County, New York, the seventh of eight children of Nathaniel Locke and Hester Ross Locke, David Ross Locke grew up in a home filled with considerable intellectual stimulation. Although the senior Locke was a craftsman rather than a man of letters—when David was born his father was operating a tannery and had worked as a shoemaker and at other trades—he was a man of strong convictions who encouraged David in his interest in reading.

The youth's formal schooling ended at age twelve when he was apprenticed to the *Cortland Democrat*, where he learned not only to set type but also to like the alcohol that gave him problems throughout his life. In discussions around the poker table he also honed the liberal ideas planted by his father. From Cortland he moved on to a succession of newspapers, sometimes as a compositor, sometimes as a writer. In 1853 he and a friend bought a newspaper in Plymouth, Ohio, and called it the *Advertiser*. This was the first of several small newspapers in which Locke owned an interest.

On 20 March 1856 Locke bought the Bucyrus, Ohio, *Journal*. During his five and a half years as editor and publisher of the *Journal*, he experimented with different kinds of writing, including the satire—and the phonetic spelling—he was later to use in the Nasby letters. Throughout this period Locke was also becoming more and more involved with Republican politics and increasingly opposed to slavery. A trip through the South served to harden his antipathy to the Confederate cause, and when the guns fired on Fort Sumter, he tried to recruit a company to join the Union army. He was rejected as physically unfit, but he served the Union side ably with his pen.

In 1861 Locke bought the *Hancock Jeffersonian* in Findlay, Ohio, a Republican newspaper in a Democratic stronghold. On 25 April 1862 the first Nasby letter, "Letter from a Straight Democrat," was published in the *Jeffersonian*. Nasby was a caricature of an overbearing, bigoted, unsavory slob who defended the South, slavery, and the "Dimekratic" party, damning them in the process.

Although Locke had a talent for humorous writing, his goal in the Nasby letters was not to amuse; rather he sought through satire to move his readers, to influence them to reject the ideas he found so repugnant. In this he was moderately successful. By 1865 the Nasby letters had a wide audience. President Abraham Lincoln was a Nasby enthusiast, and Locke's satire was seen as a valuable weapon in marshaling opinion in the North.

From the *Jeffersonian* Locke moved on to other small newspapers, tried his hand at selling medicines and advertising, established the short-lived *Locke's Monthly* in New York City, and worked for a few years as the managing editor of the *New York Evening Mail*. All the while he continued the Nasby letters, his principal forum being the *Toledo Blade*, which he joined in 1865 and returned to whenever his other ventures weakened. The *Blade* had both daily and weekly editions, and at its peak, the weekly edition had a circulation as high as 200,000 around the country.

Locke continued the Nasby letters almost until his death, although in later years he worked to establish his reputation separate from Nasby, resenting the fact that he was so closely identified with the unlikable character. In his later years Locke also took an uncharacteristic temperance stand and campaigned vigorously in the 1880s to "Pulverize the Rum Power."

Locke was popular on the lecture circuit; wrote novels, short stories, verse, and hymns; and had a theatrical success in *The Widow Bedott*. His newspaper articles, both as Nasby and as Locke, were published in several collections. His various writing enterprises and his Toledo properties brought him financial security.

On 7 March 1865 Locke married Martha H. Bodine of Plymouth, Ohio. They had three sons. Locke died in Toledo on 15 February 1888 from complications of tuberculosis and diabetes.

BIBLIOGRAPHY:

A. *The Nasby Papers* (Indianapolis, 1864); *Swingin' Round the Cirkle* (Boston, 1867); *Nasby in Exile; or, Six Months of Travel* (Toledo, 1882); *The Nasby Letters* (Toledo, 1893).

B. DAB 11, 336; NYT 16 February 1888; James C. Austin, *Petroleum V. Nasby (David Ross Locke)* (New York, 1965); John M. Harrison, *The Man Who Made Nasby, David Ross Locke* (Chapel Hill, N.C., 1969).

BARBARA CLOUD

LOCKE, RICHARD ADAMS (b. 22 September 1800; d. 16 February 1871) wrote one of the most fantastic and entertaining newspaper stories of the first half of the nineteenth century. In it he said that British astronomers, working with a large telescope in South Africa, had seen the moon and its mountains, valleys, trees and other vegetation, and its wildlife. They had also seen manlike creatures moving about very much like men on earth move. The story was the most famous newspaper hoax of a journalistic era given to entertainment more than journalism.

Locke was born in 1800 in East Brent, Somersetshire, England, a collateral descendant of the philosopher John Locke. He was the son of well-to-do parents, Richard Locke and Anne Adams Locke. He was educated by his mother and private tutors during early life. When he was nineteen, he went to Cambridge, and while a student there, he contributed to several publications, including the prestigious *Imperial Magazine* and the *Bee*.

After leaving Cambridge, he started the London *Republican*, a publication with decided sympathies for the American government. The *Republican* drew only a few readers, and Locke had to abandon it. He edited a periodical devoted to science and literature called *Cornucopia* for about six months, but it too failed financially. He championed the cause of Catholic emancipation in the *Somersetshire Herald* for nearly two years and wrote for a number of other publications.

In 1832 Locke brought his wife, Ester Bowering, whom he had married in 1826, and infant daughter to New York, where he became a writer for the *Courier and Enquirer*. He covered a variety of stories, including the sensational murder trial of Matthias the Prophet in White Plains, New York. There he met the editor of the *New York Sun*, Benjamin Day (q.v.), who recognized him as the best reporter at the trial. Day asked Locke to write a series of articles on the trial for the *Sun*. Locke did, and soon found himself in trouble with the owner of the *Courier and Enquirer*. Day offered Locke twelve dollars a week to become an editorial writer for the *Sun*, an offer which Locke found generous.

Locke came to the *Sun* just as it was blazing a new trail in American journalism. It was the leader of the "penny press," papers characterized not only by their cheap price, which made them affordable to people who could never before buy a newspaper, but also by their nonpolitical and human interest content. Locke could write the short, breezy items that characterized the "penny press."

The moon hoax saga began on 21 August 1835 with a short paragraph on the second page of the *Sun*. It quoted the *Edinburgh Courant* saying that "some astronomical discoveries of the most wonderful description" had been made by Sir John Hershel on the Cape of Good Hope. No hint was given as to the nature of these "discoveries" until the next article appeared four days later. On 25 August an article credited to the supplement of the *Edinburgh Journal of Science* presented readers a long treatise about the philosophy of man, the technical details of Sir John's telescope, and a history of the astronomer's work. The *Edinburgh Journal of Science* was also a figment of Locke's imagination. Although there had once been such a journal, it had died several years before. Like the first article, this second one gave no real indication of what was in store for the readers.

The next day, however, the picture Locke was drawing for the readers began to focus. The first descriptions of what the scientists had seen appeared. They included lunar vegetation, water, beaches, hills, and valleys. Later in the article, the astronomers were said to have seen animal life, including bison, goats, birds, and some sort of amphibian. During the next week, readers were treated to descriptions of human-like creatures and other lunar wonders. Some believed the story immediately and praised or reprinted the stories. Others expressed interested skepticism. The *Sun*'s chief rivals, the *Courier and Enquirer* and the *Journal of Commerce*, said nothing at this point.

Locke probably wrote the stories with no intention to deceive. They were simply meant to be entertainment. Yet many people believed the stories because they were so authoritative. The revelation of the hoax came when a reporter for the *Journal of Commerce* sought copies of the articles so his paper could reprint them. Locke confessed to the reporter—a good friend of his—that he was the author. The next day, the *Journal*, seeing a way to get back at its rival for stealing its circulation, denounced the articles as a hoax.

Locke's revelation did not end the excitement that his articles had caused, nor did it greatly damage his reputation as a journalist. The articles inspired a panorama and stage play and remained the main topic of conversation for some time afterwards. The *Sun* gave him other choice assignments, but Locke's tenure with the paper was to last only a year more. In the fall of 1836, he left the *Sun* to begin a new paper known as the *New Era*. He attempted to do the same thing for this penny paper that he had done for the *Sun* by writing another hoax, "The Lost Manuscript of Mungo Park." No reader was fooled by this second series, and the paper itself eventually died. Locke, who had become a contributor to the *New York Mirror*, then spent a short time as editor of the *Brooklyn Eagle*. His journalism career ended in 1841 when he got a job in a New York custom house. He lived quietly and died at his home on Staten Island on 16 February 1871.

BIBLIOGRAPHY:

B. DAB 11, 338–339; William N. Griggs, *The Celebrated Moon Story, Its Origins and Incidents* (New York, 1852); Frank M. O'Brien, *The Story of the Sun* (New York, 1918).

JAMES GLEN STOVALL

LORD, CHESTER SANDERS (b. 18 March 1850; d. 1 August 1933), known as "Boss" Lord to his associates, spent thirty-three years (1881–1913) as managing editor of the *New York Sun*. Under his leadership, the *Sun* became a training ground for journalists and influenced newspapers across the country. While at the *Sun*, Lord helped to organize the Sun News Service, which competed for a short time with the Associated Press. After retiring from the *Sun* in 1913, Lord devoted two decades of his life to improving education in his home state.

Lord was born in Romulus, Seneca County, New York, but grew up in Fulton and Adams, New York. His mother was the former Mary Jane Sanders; his father, the Reverend Edward Lord, a Presbyterian clergyman. Chester Lord attended the Adams Collegiate Institute, the Worcester (Massachusetts) Military Academy, and the Fairfield (New York) Seminary before entering Hamilton College in 1869. He had planned to follow the ministry, but after a year at Hamilton his finances were depleted and he was forced to leave. Lord's interest in journalism began while he was still at Hamilton; he contributed a few pieces on miscellaneous subjects to the *Utica Herald*. In 1871, after leaving college, he became a staff reporter for the *Oswego Advertiser* (later *Oswego Times*).

On 18 October 1871 Lord married Katherine Mahala Bates. A few months later they moved to New York, and Lord persuaded Amos J. Cummings, managing editor of the *Sun*, to give him a job. His reporting of the whiskey-ring frauds and his coverage of Horace Greeley's (q.v.) campaign for the presidency helped him to move up quickly to suburban editor, then to assistant night editor, and on to assistant managing editor. *Sun* owner Charles A. Dana (q.v.), impressed with Lord's reporting skills and executive ability, made him managing editor on 1 January 1881—an enviable post for a man of thirty with less than ten years in the newspaper business.

When in 1897 Dana became angry with United Press and Associated Press, and withdrew from both, Lord devised an independent international news service for the *Sun*. Lord sent messages to correspondents around the world, collecting news enough to fill his columns. Dana was so pleased with the success of the project that he called Lord "the John L. Sullivan of newspaperdom." Lord built up the service, calling it the Laffan Bureau and later the Sun News Service.

According to Lord's contemporaries, he had "unfailing resourcefulness," "sound judgment," "fairmindedness," "inspiring leadership," and "great personal charm." Upon his retirement, an editor of the *Kansas City Journal* wrote: "In a technical sense he [Lord] did more for the upbuilding of American journalism than any other one man, for his influence is found in every decent newspaper office in America."

Before Lord's retirement in 1913, he was joined at the *Sun* by his son Kenneth, who served as city editor from 1912 to 1922. Lord had three other sons—Chester, Edward Roy, and Richard Sanders Lord—and one daughter, Mrs. C. W. Merritt.

Lord's second career was in education. In 1897 he became a regent of the University of the State of New York. His main interests were in improving vocational education in high schools and in consolidating rural schools. He became chancellor of the State Board of Regents in 1921 and served twelve years.

Lord's first wife died in 1910. He was married again on 20 January 1926 to Mrs. Elizabeth Brown Riggs and was living with her in Garden City, Long Island, at the time of his death. In the last three years of his life, Lord suffered from diabetes. He died 1 August 1933 and was buried in Greenwood Cemetery, Brooklyn.

BIBLIOGRAPHY:

A. *The Young Man in Journalism* (New York, 1922).

B. DAB Supp. 1, 509–510; NCAB 25, 11–12; NYT 2 August 1933.

SHIRLEY M. MUNDT

LORIMER, GEORGE HORACE (b. 6 October 1867; d. 22 October 1937) was the man who made the *Saturday Evening Post* what its motto claimed it was—"An American Institution." When Lorimer became editor in 1899, the *Post* had only recently been saved from certain death by new publisher Cyrus Curtis (q.v.). When Lorimer resigned nearly forty years later, the *Post* was America's most popular magazine.

Lorimer, who often gave 1868 as his birthdate so he could brag that he became *Post* editor at thirty, was born in Louisville, Kentucky, the son of a Baptist minister. He grew up in Chicago and attended Yale. But one of his father's parishioners—meat-packing baron P. D. Armour—suggested that young Lorimer give up the schooling nonsense and go to work. After his sophomore year, Lorimer accepted a $10-a-week job with the Armour company.

Lorimer, who married during his stint with Armour, soon became a minor executive and was seen as a "golden boy" within the company. But he left to become a reporter for the *Boston Standard*. The *Standard* folded after Lorimer had been on the staff for a few months, and he returned to school at his father's urging—this time at Colby College in Portland, Maine. He then returned to the field, working for the *Boston Post* and the *Boston Herald*. He had become an excellent journalist and one of the most respected reporters in Boston.

While working at the *Herald* one day in 1898, Lorimer came across an announcement that Philadelphia publisher Cyrus Curtis, owner of the *Ladies' Home Journal*, had purchased the remains of the *Saturday Evening Post* and was in need of an editor. Lorimer wired Curtis within the hour and suggested he was the man. Curtis met Lorimer in Boston, but hired him as literary editor. William George Jordan was hired as editor. Curtis was not happy with Jordan's work, however, and fired him. Curtis sailed to Europe to find a new editor and left Lorimer in charge. Curtis returned from his trip without an editor, but he saw what Lorimer had done with the *Post* and realized he was the right man for the job.

Lorimer was often at odds with Edward Bok (q.v.), editor of the *Ladies' Home Journal* and Curtis's son-in-law. Bok was jealous of the attention Curtis lavished on the *Post*, and suggested to Curtis that Lorimer was going to drive the company into debt. But Curtis backed Lorimer, even though the *Post* lost nearly $1 million before taking off.

Lorimer believed a magazine should be something like a restaurant menu—there should be something for everyone. Throughout his tenure as editor, he ran how-to pieces next to works of literature, and philosophical essays next to potboilers. His list of contributors is astonishing: William Faulkner, Babe Ruth, Thomas Wolfe, Buffalo Bill, Stephen Crane (q.v.), Groucho Marx, Leon Trotsky, and O. Henry. In addition, *Post* "characters" (from serialized novels) became favorites with American readers: Hercule Poirot, Charlie Chan, Mr. Moto, Tugboat Annie, and Nero Wolfe.

Lorimer identified his magazine so strongly with traditional American values that it almost seemed unpatriotic not to subscribe. The *Post* had Independence Square, Philadelphia, as its mailing address and claimed Benjamin Franklin as its founder. (The connection to Franklin is tenuous at best; that tie was largely due to Curtis's clever public relations. On the editorial page, Lorimer anonymously offered the viewpoint from middle America, and nine presidents therefore sought his counsel.

Under Lorimer, the *Post* set trends and did not follow them. Lorimer said the best way for him to edit the magazine was to ignore all competitors, but to keep in touch with readers by reading every bit of mail addressed to him. Most letters he answered personally. One of the few exceptions to that rule came after an episode in a serialized novel ended one week with a man having a drink at home with his secretary, and began the next week with the two having breakfast. Readers were outraged and flooded the *Post* editor with protests. Lorimer had to resort to a form letter: "*The Saturday Evening Post* is not responsible for what happens to our fictional characters between installments." (Tebbel, 1948).

When Curtis had made Lorimer editor of the *Post*, it was little more than a weekly newspaper trading on its famous name. Lorimer made the *Post* into the biggest magazine in the country. At one time in the 1920s, forty-eight cents of every dollar spent on advertising in the United States went to the *Post* and the other Curtis magazines. Lorimer retired with the last issue of 1936 and died within the next year of throat cancer.

BIBLIOGRAPHY:

A. *Letters from a Self-Made Merchant to His Son* (New York, 1907).

B. John Tebbel, *George Horace Lorimer and the "Saturday Evening Post"* (New York, 1948).

WILLIAM MCKEEN

LOUNSBERRY, CLEMENT AUGUSTUS (b. 27 March 1843; d. 3 October 1926) was a frontier editor who in July 1873 founded the *Bismarck Tribune*, the first newspaper of significance in present-day North Dakota. His article "Massacred," published 6 July 1876, provided the first complete news account of the defeat of Lieutenant Colonel George A. Custer, who was killed with 261 men of the U.S. Seventh Cavalry at the Battle of the Little Big Horn on 25 June 1876, in southeastern Montana. He also provided telegraphic reports of the legendary Indian battle to the *New York Herald* and other eastern newspapers. In mid-life, after selling the *Tribune*, Lounsberry held a wide variety of journalism and governmental positions. Late in life he wrote *North Dakota: History and People* (1917), an early account of the state's history.

Lounsberry, one of six children, was born near Newville in Wilmington Township, De Kalb County, Indiana. His father, Rufus Rodman Lounsberry, and his mother, Sarah Weeks Lounsberry, had migrated from the Binghamton area of New York state in the mid–1830s. His father was a farmer and a community leader; his mother was a schoolteacher. By age seven, Lounsberry was orphaned.

At the outbreak of the Civil War, Lounsberry, a farm laborer in Michigan, enlisted as a private in Company I, First Michigan Volunteers. Wounded and taken prisoner 21 July 1861 at the First Battle of Bull Run, he spent a year in Confederate hands. Exchanged in June 1862, he received an officer's commission and moved up the promotion ladder quickly. As a colonel commanding two regiments, the First Michigan Sharpshooters and the Second Michigan Infantry, he received the surrender of Petersburg, Virginia, on 3 April 1865.

On 27 July 1864 he married Lucretia V. Hoskins and they had five children. After the war, he moved to Martin County, Minnesota, where in 1868 he began publishing his first newspaper, the *Martin County Atlas*, which he moved to Wells, Minnesota, in 1870. By 1872 Lounsberry had joined the *Minneapolis Tribune* as an editorial writer and legislative reporter. Even after he established his newspaper in Bismarck, he spent winters in Minneapolis, covering the legislature for its *Tribune*.

On 11 July 1873, with the first copy of the *Bismarck Tribune* off the press, he fulfilled a longtime goal to establish a newspaper at the site of the Northern Pacific Railroad's crossing of the Missouri River in Dakota Territory. Lounsberry, a boomer, shared the expansionist goals of his fellow residents in the rough and rowdy pioneer village that was 1870s Bismarck. Lounsberry envisioned Bismarck as the region's commercial, industrial, and political center, and devoted his personal and editorial efforts toward achieving that end. He also played a key role in the movement to divide the massive Dakota Territory into north and south units and to open the Black Hills to white settlement. Lounsberry was appointed Bismarck's postmaster in March 1876.

Lounsberry, a staunch Republican, operated the *Tribune* for about ten years (except for a year in the late 1870s). When he sold the paper in 1884, Lounsberry hoped to be appointed governor of Dakota Territory, but lost out to another newspaperman, Gilbert A. Pierce of the *Chicago Daily News*.

His next twenty years found him involved in a bewildering series of journalistic and other ventures. In 1884 he launched a new newspaper in Bismarck, the *Journal*. In 1886 he began publication of the *Duluth Evening News*, but broke with his partners in 1887 to establish a weekly, the *Saturday Evening Journal*. A year later he merged this paper with the *Duluth Daily Herald*. However, by July 1888 he had disposed of all his newspaper interests and was back in Fargo as North Dakota editor for the *Minneapolis Tribune*.

In 1889 he first obtained a political appointment as a special agent of the U.S. General Land Office. Ousted by the Democrats in 1893, he was reappointed in 1897 with another change of administration. In 1894 he was instrumental in organizing the North Dakota Historical Society and was elected its first president. In 1895 he launched a monthly historical magazine at Fargo, the *Record*, which enabled him to gather information about the state. This material later served as the foundation for his book, *North Dakota: History and People*, which first appeared in January 1917 and was republished in 1920 as the *Early History of North Dakota*. After his reappointment to the land office, he continued the magazine's publication with varied success.

In 1903 Lounsberry was accused of taking bribes in return for making favorable reports in land cases which he investigated. He eventually was cleared. In 1905 Lounsberry moved permanently to Washington, D.C., to work as a clerk in the General Land Office. He died on 2 October 1926 in Washington and was buried in Arlington National Cemetery.

BIBLIOGRAPHY:

B. NYT 5 October 1926; Frank E. Vyzralek, "Clement A. Lounsberry, Journalist & Historian," *Plains Talk*, Summer 1971.

WARREN E. BARNARD

LOVEJOY, ELIJAH PARISH (b. 9 November 1802; d. 7 November 1837) was a martyred abolitionist editor now renowned for his staunch defense of press freedom, specifically the right to publish unpopular views. He was killed while defending his press against a racist, anti-abolitionist mob.

Lovejoy, born on a farm near Albion, Maine, was the oldest of nine children. His father, Daniel Lovejoy, was a Presbyterian clergyman and farmer. His mother, Elizabeth Pattee Lovejoy, was a native of Maine of Scotch descent. As a youth, Elijah attended public schools and private academies in the nearby towns of Monmouth and China, Maine. He was graduated from Waterville (now called Colby) College, a Baptist college in Waterville, Maine, in 1826.

After graduation, Lovejoy taught school in Maine and then St. Louis until 1827 when he became editor of the *St. Louis Times*, a Whig party newspaper. In 1832 he experienced a religious conversion and left St. Louis to study at the Princeton Theological Seminary, and received a license to preach from the Philadelphia Presbytery in 1834. He immediately returned to St. Louis as editor of a weekly Presbyterian newspaper called the *St. Louis Observer*. He became an outspoken reformer who wrote against Catholicism and slavery, even though St. Louis had a sizable population of Catholics and pro-slavers. On 4 March 1835 Lovejoy married Celia Ann French, daughter of a planter from nearby St. Charles, Missouri.

Lovejoy left St. Louis in July 1836. Pressure from local citizens for him to leave reached a peak after he had labeled a judge an "Irish papist" in an editorial published in June. He had denounced the judge's decision not to prosecute a mob that had burned alive a black man being held on charges of murdering a white man. Lovejoy moved his printing equipment across and twenty-five miles up the Mississippi River to Alton, Illinois. The equipment arrived in Alton on a Sunday, and while it lay unguarded a mob pushed it—press included—into the river. He raised money locally for a new press, and was publishing again by September, but even those who donated asked him to stop publishing antislavery articles. Nevertheless, he took an increasingly hard line against slavery, and his press was destroyed twice more, on 21 August 1837 and 21 September 1837. Each time he bought a new press with help from the Ohio Anti-Slavery League. In October 1837, while waiting for his fourth press to be delivered, Lovejoy participated in the formation of the Illinois Anti-Slavery Society.

"Respectable" citizens who demanded that Lovejoy resign his editorship prompted a campaign by Lovejoy in which he forcefully defended freedom of speech. He has been cited as addressing a meeting of his opponents in the following words: " . . . as long as I am an American citizen, and as long as American blood runs in these veins, I shall hold myself at liberty to speak, to write and to publish whatever I please on any subject. . . . "

On 26 October 1837, one night after his fourth press was delivered to a riverside warehouse in Alton, a mob attacked the guarded building. Lovejoy, who had rushed into the street to stop members of the mob from setting fire to the building, was shot and killed.

BIBLIOGRAPHY:

B. DAB 11, 434–435; Edward Beecher, *Narrative of the Riots at Alton: in Connection with the Death of Elijah P. Lovejoy* (Alton, Ill., 1838); Merton L. Dillon, *Elijah P. Lovejoy: Abolitionist Editor* (Urbana, 1961); Joseph C. Lovejoy and Owen Lovejoy,

Memoir of Elijah P. Lovejoy: who was Murdered in the Defense of the Liberty of the Press at Alton, Illinois, November 7, 1837 (reprint. Freeport, N.Y., 1970).

GORDON BILLINGSLEY

LOWER, ELMER W. (b. 7 March 1913) reached the summit of the broadcast news media when he was named president of ABC News in 1963. His leadership, from that post, and from news positions at NBC and CBS in prior years, was widely recognized and respected. On the occasion of his retirement after forty-five years in the news field, Lower was lauded by the Radio-Television News Directors Association as among the staunchest defenders of the First Amendment's free press guarantees.

Lower was and is a Missourian. His parents, Elmer Lower and Eva McConnell Lower, settled in the central part of the state near Sedalia. He spent his childhood in Kansas City. He attended the University of Missouri School of Journalism and graduated in 1933. After college Lower went to work for ten dollars a week as a reporter with the Louisville, Kentucky, *Herald-Post*. Over the next twenty years he moved up the print media ranks from reporting with the Flint, Michigan, *Journal* to United Press bureau manager in Jefferson, Missouri, and Cleveland, Ohio. In 1937 he became UP's overnight news editor in Washington, D.C. A year later he joined the Newspaper Enterprise Association, covering the Munich Crisis from Europe. Lower went to work for the Associated Press in Chicago as photo assignment editor, setting up coverage of the 1940 Democratic convention. He stayed with AP until 1942, serving in a similar position in New York City.

He joined the U.S. Office of War Information, following Allied forces through North Africa and Europe, where he set up a radiophoto network and photo coverage of the Normandy invasion. After the war Lower moved back to the private sector as a foreign correspondent for *Life* magazine, heading the Paris bureau, before returning home as West Coast editor in 1948. He was sent abroad once again, eighteen months later, as chief correspondent for the Far East, based in Tokyo.

In 1951 he was named U.S. information chief in Germany and supervised the biggest propaganda effort the U.S. has ever made in another country. That position lasted two years, and in 1953 Lower began his broadcast news career as director of news and public affairs for CBS in Washington. A year later he became director of special projects for CBS radio and television, and finished out his time with CBS as director of operations, adding film production and sports to his responsibilities. In mid–1959 he was working for NBC, bringing with him his developing system for election tabulation which enabled the network to beat the wire service for the first time. Five years later Lower cofounded the National Election Service (NES) while he was ABC News president. NES brought together the three major networks and both wire services to provide raw vote tabulations to all five organizations for major primaries and elections.

Lower's stint with NBC News ran four years, during which time he headed up coverage of the first "live" presidential press conference, and planned the pooled coverage of Soviet Premier Nikita Khrushchev's visit to Washington. Before moving over to ABC, Lower became vice president and general manager of NBC News in New York. During his presidency at ABC News, the network expanded its nightly news program from fifteen minutes to a half hour and "more than doubled the number of stations carrying the newscast." He organized his network's coverage of the assassination of President John F. Kennedy and its aftermath, as well as the news of President Johnson's decision not to run and Martin Luther King's assassination.

He became vice president for corporate affairs for ABC in 1974. His career has been one of significant accomplishment, aided and supported by his family for more than forty years. Lower married the former Gilberta M. Stengel of France in 1938. They had two children: John W., who has served as an overseas field producer for ABC News, and Louis G., a Chicago business executive.

Elmer Lower retired on 1 April 1978, and immediately began his second career as a professor of journalism. In 1978 he taught at three universities, including his alma mater, and spoke to groups at home and abroad. He had pursued graduate study at Northwestern and Georgetown universities during his earlier years, and earned an M.A. degree in public law and government from Columbia in 1970. Since his retirement, Lower has taught in the School of Journalism at the University of Missouri, where he was named interim dean of the school.

BIBLIOGRAPHY:

B. "Elmer W. Lower," *ABC Biography*, 1969–70; "Lower Named Interim Dean," *Editor and Publisher*, 17 July 1982; "A Triple-Threat Media Star," *St. Louis Globe Democrat*, 21 October 1978.

DAVID M. GUERRA

LUBELL, SAMUEL (b. 1911; d. 16 August 1987) is the ex-newsman who pioneered in the public-opinion reporting that brought him national acclaim. He introduced the concept that American political parties rest on coalitions of identifiable streams of voters. He developed this theme in his award-winning *The Future of American Politics* (1952), which was widely used both as a reference and a college textbook. Five books followed. He was also a nationally syndicated columnist, magazine writer, an election-night radio and television analyst, and an educator.

Lubell, youngest of nine children, was born in 1911 near Sosnowiec, Poland, date unknown, but he later picked an election day, 3 November, as his birthday. In 1913 Mollie Reitkop Lubell brought Lubell by steerage to New York to be with his father, Louis Lubell, a tailor. The youngster then attended Lower East Side and Bronx schools, and evening classes at College of the City of New York, 1927–31. In 1933 he earned his B.S. from Columbia University School of Journalism, winning a Pulitzer traveling scholarship. His mother, who made possible his education, died a week before graduation.

His first job in 1935 was as a *Long Island Daily Press* reporter; he worked successively for the *Washington Post*, *Richmond Times-Dispatch*, and *Washington Herald*. In 1938 he began free-lancing, especially for the *Saturday Evening Post*. In twenty-one years he contributed forty-four articles, including coverage of the war in China-Burma-India. In December 1941 he joined the Office of Facts and Figures, then was White House assistant to Office of Economic Stabilization director James F. Byrnes and chief aide to Bernard M. Baruch on all his wartime studies. He was with Baruch on a presidential mission to Winston Churchill when Roosevelt died.

In 1948 the *Saturday Evening Post*'s assigning him to analyze Truman's surprise victory began Lubell's twenty-eight years of public-opinion reporting. He studied voting patterns starting with the 1892 Populist offensive by (1) analyzing election returns for each of more than 3,000 counties and big-city wards; (2) identifying economic, religious, and ethnic characteristics of major streams of voters; and (3) interviewing voters in every walk of life in specific areas.

"The invention I introduced to polling was to do interviewing and analysis in specific precincts, matching interview results with the past vote, to report *how much change had taken place and why*," Lubell wrote in his last book *The Future While It Happened*. He used this precinct approach in his first preelection survey in 1952. On CBS on election night he ignored two computers, and predicted that Eisenhower had cracked the South and was on his way to a landslide based on returns from three Richmond, Virginia, precincts. This precinct approach was later adopted by most networks and still serves as the basis of election-night projections.

His innovation led to *The Future of American Politics*, which won the 1952 Woodrow Wilson Foundation Award of the American Political Science Association. He wrote that for the third time in American history a majority party had been transformed into a minority party when, in 1932, Roosevelt formed a new majority coalition comprised of such distinct streams of voters as big-city workers, some—like Lubell himself—the offspring of immigrants, and of such clashing elements as Negroes and white Southerners.

Five books followed; his work was aided by Guggenheim Fellowships. A 1976 alumni award and a fiftieth anniversary medallion were presented by Columbia's Graduate School of Journalism. United Features syndicated his column from 1952 to 1966. By 1960 clients included the Scripps-Howard, Gannett, Knight, and Cowles chains; in 1964 more than 130 newspapers printed his column.

Lubell organized the Opinion Reporting Workshop at Columbia's Graduate School of Journalism from 1958 to 1968; taught at American University (1969), the University of Connecticut (1976), and the University of California at Irvine (1981); and in 1974 was a Kennedy Fellow at Harvard's Institute of Politics. In

1976 Lubell retired, giving his papers to Georgetown University, and began his memoirs. He married Helen Sopot on 22 March 1941; they had two sons. He died of a stroke in a Los Angeles nursing home in 1987.

BIBLIOGRAPHY:

A. *Revolution in World Trade* (New York, 1954); *Revolt of the Moderates* (New York, 1956); *White and Black: Test of a Nation* (New York, 1964); *The Hidden Crisis in American Politics* (New York, 1970): *The Future While It Happened* (New York, 1973).

B. *Editor and Publisher*, 24 February 1962; *Providence Evening Bulletin*, 5 November 1952; *Time*, 15 October 1956.

BEVERLY KEEVER

LUCE, HENRY ROBINSON (b. 3 April 1898; d. 28 February 1967) was the giant of magazine journalism in the twentieth century. His partnership with Briton Hadden (1898–1929) created *Time* newsmagazine and later led to an empire in his lifetime that included *Fortune*, *Life*, *Architectural Forum*, and *Sports Illustrated* magazines; *March of Time* on radio and film; book publishing; and broadcast stations. After the death of his partner, Luce gained control of *Time* and remained active in the editorial rooms of his publications until resigning as editor in chief in 1964.

Luce, the oldest of four children, was born to Presbyterian missionary Dr. Henry Winters Luce and Elizabeth Middleton Root Luce in Tengchow, China; his mother was related to Elihu Root, the statesman. Luce attended a British boarding school and then spent a year in England at St. Albans before studying on a scholarship at the Hotchkiss School in Lakeville, Connecticut, where he met Hadden, from a banking family in New York. Both attended Yale, where Hadden was chairman and Luce managing editor of the *Yale Daily News*. Both were in military service together in the States in 1918–19 and graduated with the class of 1920.

Luce studied at Oxford, then worked briefly for Ben Hecht (q.v.), a columnist for the *Chicago Daily News*. He rejoined Hadden in 1921 as a reporter on the *Baltimore News*. Discussion of starting a weekly newsmagazine led both of them to New York, where they succeeded in 1922 in raising $86,000 out of a planned $100,000 to finance the venture. *Time*'s first issue, dated 3 March 1923, summarized "the week's news in the shortest possible space." Timestyle emerged as coined words like *cinemacter* and *bookritic*; the subject and predicate were exchanged in sentence structure as Wolcott Gibbs wrote in a *New Yorker* parody: "Backward ran sentences until reeled the mind." Narrative and human interest were employed by a small staff of writers whose raw material was the nation's newspapers.

Luce and Hadden alternated yearly as editor and business manager. The magazine became profitable in 1927. With the demise of the *Literary Digest* in 1938, *Time* absorbed its remaining readers and continued to build its circulation past three million at the time of Luce's retirement. Luce's plan of a high-priced new monthly magazine reached the newstands as *Fortune* in February 1930, shortly after the stock market crash, and was successful almost immediately. The ''March of Time'' radio program began on CBS on 6 March 1931, after previous experiments titled ''Newscasting'' and ''Newsacting.'' It transferred to NBC in 1937 and left the air in 1945. *The March of Time* on film began in 1935 and eventually was booked into 5,000 U.S. movie theaters as well as hundreds overseas.

Luce had married Lila Ross Hotz on 22 December 1923. They had two sons, Henry III, born 28 April 1925, and Peter Paul, born 18 May 1928. He was divorced in 1935 and married a divorcée, Mrs. Clare Boothe Brokaw (b. 10 April 1903) on 23 November. She had been a writer on *Vogue* and an editor of *Vanity Fair*. After marriage, she wrote three Broadway plays which were also made into films, served two terms as a Republican congresswoman from Connecticut, and became the first American woman to be an ambassador in an important capital, serving in Italy (1953–57). She was later appointed by Eisenhower to be ambassador to Brazil during a controversy involving *Time*. After being confirmed by the Senate, she resigned before serving in the post.

Life, a weekly devoted to photojournalism, was a newsstand sellout from its first issue 19 November 1936. Because the advertising rates were calculated on a base of 250,000 copies a week while Luce increased the press run to meet demand, the extra costs of paper and printing resulted in a $6 million loss before advertising contracts could be revised to reflect the higher circulation. Despite the depression, his magazines produced millions of dollars in profits. *Architectural Forum* was purchased in 1932, the only magazine in the empire not created by Luce. However, *House & Home* was spun off as a separate magazine in 1952. Another Luce creation was *Sports Illustrated* on 16 August 1954. It was revised in focus several times before it became extremely profitable after ten years of losses.

At its peak in the 1950s, *Life* was taking a fifth of all revenues in magazine advertising. However, network television was becoming more cost-effective to national advertisers. By the 1960s *Life*'s advertising revenues began to diminish. Starting in 1969, *Life* became unprofitable and was suspended in 1972 after losing $30 million. (It was revived as a monthly in 1978.)

Beginning with a book produced by the *Life* staff in 1950, book publishing became a major corporate activity. In addition to Time-Life books, the company acquired Little, Brown and Company, Silver Burdett Company, and several book clubs. It purchased radio and television stations and made films for television and education. Luce's major expansion outside of journalism was East Texas Pulp and Paper Company in 1952, which became wholly owned later as Eastex. International editions of *Time* and *Life* became important.

Luce became a world traveler beginning in the 1930s and met heads of state, diplomats, and politicians. He often gave his editors written impressions of these contacts even after retiring as editor in chief in 1964. He was impressed by Hitler's Nazis at first and supported Franklin Delano Roosevelt's early presidential policies. Later, he became antifascist, pro-Republican, and anticommunist. His early upbringing in China and later visits convinced him of the eventual success of Chiang Kai-shek in the Chinese civil war against the Communists. Luce used his prestige and publications to tilt U.S. policy favorably to Chiang and later toward the government on Taiwan. Luce's publications began supporting Republican presidential candidates in 1940. They were unsuccessful until they influenced a draft for Eisenhower. *Life* for the first time endorsed a Democrat, Lyndon Johnson, in 1964.

A major reorganization of responsibilities was completed by 1960, resulting in more autonomy for each publication. There was less criticism of political bias thereafter. Luce's influence remained, but he found less occasion to involve himself in the editorial operations and increasingly was away from the Time-Life Building in New York. He died on 28 February from a coronary occlusion after being stricken at his Phoenix home.

BIBLIOGRAPHY:

B. NYT 1 March 1967; Robert T. Elson, *Time Inc.: The Intimate History of a Publishing Enterprise, 1923–1941* (New York, 1968); Robert T. Elson, *The World of Time Inc.: The Intimate History of a Publishing Enterprise, 1941–1960* (New York, 1973); Wolcott Gibbs, "Time . . . Fortune . . . Life . . . Luce," *New Yorker*, 28 November 1936; John Kobler, *Luce: His Time, Life and Fortune* (Garden City, N.Y., 1968); W. A. Swanberg, *Luce and His Empire* (New York, 1972).

SAM KUCZUN

LUNDY, BENJAMIN (b. 4 January 1789; d. 22 August 1839) is credited with introducing publication of antislavery periodicals. While there is some evidence that others published antislavery periodicals before him, there is no figure that stands out above Lundy in his unflagging opposition to slavery and his long struggle for emancipation of American slaves.

Lundy was born the only child of Joseph Lundy and Elizabeth Shotwell Lundy. His parents were farmers in Sussex County, New Jersey. Lundy was five when his mother died, and he was subsequently reared by his stepmother, Mary Titus Lundy. A desire for education had been planted by his mother, and Lundy attended school before her death. After that, however, his schooling was erratic, consisting of a brief session prior to puberty, and a return to school "to learn mathematics" at age sixteen.

Lundy was small for his age and was in somewhat poor health most of his childhood. Although his father urged him not to, Lundy insisted on working in the fields alongside hired men, a practice to which he later attributed partial deafness which developed early and remained with him all his life. Raised in the Society of Friends (Quakers), Lundy was to follow the teachings of that religion throughout his life. The Quakers' belief in the equality of all men formed the basis for Lundy's abhorrence of slavery.

At age nineteen, Lundy left Sussex to travel and to try to build his strength. He ultimately settled at Wheeling, Virginia, where he apprenticed himself to a saddle maker. Wheeling was a trade center for slavery, and Lundy's early impressions of the injustice of that practice were reinforced during his stay.

Lundy spent four years apprenticing in Wheeling and an additional eighteen months practicing his trade before relocating in Mount Pleasant, Ohio, a community comprised mostly of Quakers. He married a young Quaker girl named Esther Lewis, and they soon moved to St. Clairsville, Ohio, where Lundy set up his saddle shop. He founded the Union Humane Society in St. Clairsville. Originally comprised of half a dozen members, the ranks soon swelled to several hundred, including many influential leaders of that area. As part of his work as founder of the society, Lundy authored essays calling for the end of slavery.

At about that same time, Charles Osborne called for the establishment of an abolitionist newspaper at Mount Pleasant and agreed to sponsor the publication. Lundy responded to the call by selecting articles and forwarding them for publication in the *Philanthropist*. This led to a request that Lundy assist with the publication, which Lundy agreed to do, and to a subsequent offer from Osborne for Lundy to join in the publication of the newspaper.

Lundy set out for St. Louis. He arrived in Missouri at the time when controversy raged over whether Missouri ought to be admitted to the Union as a free or slave state. Lundy became involved in that controversy, contributing to newspapers in Missouri and Illinois. He returned home to Ohio after nearly two years. He learned that Elihu Embree had begun publication of the antislavery periodical *The Emancipator* in Jonesborough, Tennessee. When Embree died, Lundy decided to begin publication of the *Genius of Universal Emancipation* in January 1821 at Mount Pleasant.

At the urging of friends of the deceased Embree, Lundy transferred publication of the *Genius* to Embree's printing office in Jonesborough. By 1822 Lundy was publishing not only the *Genius* but a weekly newspaper and a monthly agricultural publication as well. In 1824 Lundy moved the *Genius* to Baltimore. In 1829 Lundy was joined at the *Genius* by William Lloyd Garrison (q.v.) as associate editor. They soon parted company, however, after Garrison involved the paper in several lawsuits. During 1830–31 Lundy often published the *Genius* in local printing shops during his journeys to find subscribers. By the end of 1835 the *Genius* had ceased publication.

Lundy next began to publish the *National Enquirer and Constitutional Advocate of Universal Liberty* in Philadelphia in which he sought to expose what he considered a plot by slave owners to take Texas from Mexico. This was followed by publication of Lundy's pamphlet *The War in Texas* (1836). In 1838 Lundy traveled to Lowell, Illinois, to visit with his children who had settled there. He remained in Lowell and again began to publish the *Genius*. In 1839, following a brief illness, Lundy died.

BIBLIOGRAPHY:
A. *The Life, Travels and Opinions of Benjamin Lundy* (Philadelphia, 1847).
B. DAB 11, 506–507; Merton L. Dillon, *Benjamin Lundy and the Struggle for Negro Freedom* (Urbana, 1966).

JOHN A. LEDINGHAM

LYON, MATTHEW (b. 14 July 1749; d. 1 August 1822) was a printer and publisher, soldier and politician, inventor and businessman. He helped bring the state of Vermont into existence, and he founded the town of Fair Haven in that state. He was elected to Congress from Vermont and from Kentucky. He was the first victim of the Sedition Act of 1798. And he cast the ballot which made Thomas Jefferson president of the United States.

It is a notable list of achievements for a poor Irish immigrant who left his homeland without parental permission in 1764 and who paid for his passage by signing his own letters of indenture upon his arrival. A resourceful youth, he bought his freedom, and by the time he was twenty-three he was a landowner in Cornwall, Connecticut, and a husband. He had married Mary Horsford on 23 June 1773, and she was to bear him four children—Ann, James, Pamelia, and Loraine—before her death at thirty-two on 29 April 1784.

They had moved shortly after their marriage to the New Hampshire Grants—the territory which was to become Vermont. There Lyon joined the Green Mountain Boys, and with them on 10 May 1775 he took Fort Ticonderoga from the British in one of the first confrontations of the American Revolution. In the summer of 1776 he was court-martialed and discharged for cowardice, over his indignant denials. But he returned to service and was a captain during the operation which forced Burgoyne to surrender at Saratoga with 5,000 British troops in 1777.

Following the death of his wife, Lyon married a young widow, Beulah Chittenden Galusha, daughter of Thomas Chittenden, the first governor of Vermont. She was the mother of an infant son, Elijah. The Lyons lived in Fair Haven, a town Matthew Lyon had founded and in which he operated a sawmill and gristmill. As his business interests expanded he established a tavern, a slitting mill, and a paper mill. He is credited as the first American to use wood pulp for the manufacture of paper. Lyon invented the process by which paper was made from the bark of the basswood tree.

In 1791, after Vermont became a state, Lyon was defeated in Vermont's first congressional race. In an effort to publicize his political views after his loss, Lyon founded the weekly *Farmers' Library* on 1 April 1793. He sold that newspaper the following year, and it was renamed the *Rutland Herald*. Rutland was a larger town a few miles east of Fair Haven, and perhaps Lyon wanted to operate a paper closer to home. At any rate, he established the *Fairhaven Gazette* in 1795, and renamed it the *Farmers' Library* that same year. It continued publication until 1798. Lyon also established a publishing house, called

Voltaire's Head, and the Fairhaven Library Society. His interest in the printed word was quite remarkable for one whose schooling was limited. He had served an apprenticeship to a printer and bookbinder in Dublin as a teenager, but had attended school only briefly as a child in his hometown south of Dublin.

He ran again for Congress, was elected, and took his seat in 1797. In 1797 fear of war with France prompted the Federalist Congress to give President John Adams power to expel foreigners and to imprison those who criticized the president or the Congress. Lyon, a Republican, was opposed to these measures. He criticized the president publicly before the Sedition Act was passed on 14 July 1798, but he was convicted of violating the act and was sentenced in October to serve four months in jail and was fined $1,000. He ran for reelection from his cell and was victorious. Upon his release on 9 February 1799, he set out for Philadelphia, where Congress was in session.

When in the election of 1800 Thomas Jefferson and Aaron Burr each received seventy-three electoral votes, the election was thrown to the House of Representatives, where each of the sixteen states had one vote and a majority of nine votes was required to elect the president. Through thirty-five ballots Jefferson garnered the votes of eight states; Vermont was split, with Lyon voting for Jefferson and Vermont's other representative casting his vote for Burr. On the thirty-sixth ballot, Lewis Morris, a Federalist, cast a blank ballot, and Lyon, a Republican, committed Vermont to Jefferson's column with his vote. Lyon thus had the honor of electing Thomas Jefferson president. Jefferson, like Lyon, was opposed to the Sedition Act, and it was allowed to expire. Ultimately, Lyon—the first victim of the act—was pardoned and his fine returned.

In 1801 Lyon and his family moved to Eddyville, Kentucky. Here Lyon set up various businesses, and he used his government contacts to obtain a shipbuilding contract, a mail route, and a post as commissary general for the Western army. He also established the first printing office in Kentucky. Despite his many commercial interests, he was not too busy to run for Congress, and in 1803 his Kentucky constituents voted to send him as their representative. He served until 1811.

Lyon's family had grown with the addition of eight children by his second wife, Beulah. (Another child was stillborn.) The number of his dependents, together with the fact that a shipload of meat spoiled while stuck on a sandbar in the Mississippi River, left Lyon in reduced circumstances. He turned over his business holdings to his son Chittenden, who eventually paid off all creditors.

In 1820 Lyon petitioned President James Monroe for a federal appointment. The President named Lyon U.S. Factor to the Cherokee Indians, and Lyon moved to Spadra Bluffs, in Arkansas Territory. His job was to supervise a trading post. In 1822 he built a flatboat and set out for New Orleans with Indian goods to trade and sell. The roundtrip of over 3,000 miles—much of it on horseback—took its toll, and Matthew Lyon died at Spadra Bluffs on 1 August 1822.

BIBLIOGRAPHY:

B. Aleine Austin, *Matthew Lyon: "New Man" of the Democratic Revolution* (University Park, Pa., 1981); Adolph O. Goldsmith, "The Roaring Lyon of Vermont,"

Journalism Quarterly, Spring 1962; DAB 11, 532–34; J. Fairfax McLaughlin, *Matthew Lyon: The Hampden of Congress* (New York, 1900).

WHITNEY R. MUNDT

LYON, ROBERT (b. 15 January 1810; d. 10 March 1858) is known as the "Father of the Anglo-Jewish weekly newspaper in America." Actually, the New York publisher was not the first to publish a Jewish English-language weekly. Isidor Bush of New York published a Reform weekly, *Israeld Herold*, for a brief period in 1848. But Lyon's *Asmonean* was the first to be published for an extended period—from 26 October 1848 until the journalist's death in 1858. In it he emphasized "general news" of the American-Jewish community, as well as religious and literary information useful to its growing population.

Little more is known of Lyon, an emigrant to the United States, than his place of birth. Born in London, England, Lyon pursued a brief business career before emigrating to the United States in 1844. For five years after his arrival he ran a small manufacturing business in New York City, but when that failed, he launched the *Asmonean*, and the *New York Merchantile Journal*, a trade publication. From his offices at 112 Pearl Street, Hanover Square, editor-publisher Lyon directed the affairs of his newspapers.

Lyon hoped the *Asmonean* would become the chief organ of American-Jewish opinion. Writers such as Rabbi Isaac Mayer Wise (q.v.) contributed regularly to the *Asmonean* during its existence. But the paper never achieved the prominence Lyon hoped. Its editorials showed specific concern with religious reform, civil liberties, formation of Jewish organizations, and forwarding of Jewish education. The paper also carried information on world Jewish affairs. Lyon's writing reflected the trend toward journalistic objectivity beginning to take hold in the secular press, rather than the personal journalism of his Jewish journalist contemporaries. He urged political action in his columns and proposed the use of Jewish group pressure to achieve goals. He suggested the use of resolutions, petitions, lobbying, and block voting, and endorsed politicians who he thought would work for the betterment of Jews in the United States.

While he did not often describe the American-Jewish community in his newspaper, Lyon frequently made references to its state of flux. He remained editorially neutral on the issue of religious reform even though the reform movement was very high on the list of issues confronting Jews. He encouraged Jewish participation within the larger, non-Jewish community, especially through politics and the arts. His columns supported development of an "American" yet ethnically and religiously Jewish citizen.

In 1856, two years before his death, he established a German-language page in the *Asmonean*, in response to the growth of the German-speaking Jewish population in the United States. He probably did so also because his chief competition, Rabbi Wise of Cincinnati, had recently begun publishing a German supplement to the *Israelite*. No circulation figures are available for either the *Asmonean* or the *Journal*, but subscription lists showed that *Asmonean* readers hailed from as far south as New Orleans and as far west as Ohio. That circulation was widespread may be inferred, as national Jewish associations ordered their minutes to be printed only in the *Asmonean* and two other prominent Jewish journals of the day, the *Israelite* and the *Occident and American Jewish Advocate*, published by Rabbi Isaac Leeser (q.v.) of Philadelphia. The *Asmonean* held an important position, if not the leading position, among Jewish publications during the decade of its publication.

Lyon was married to Dinah Mawson, probably in England. They had two sons, Gerald and Edmond Robert.

BIBLIOGRAPHY:

B. M. H. Stern, *First American Jewish Families, 1654–1977* (Cincinnati, 1978); Kathryn T. Theus, ''From Orthodoxoy to Reform: Assimilation and the Jewish English Press in Mid–19th Century America,'' M.A. thesis, Univ. of Maryland, 1982.

KATHRYN T. THEUS

M

MACARTHUR, CHARLES GORDON (b. 5 November 1895; d. 21 April 1956) was the quintessential big-city newspaperman during the decade of the 1920s. Although he became best known as a playwright and screenwriter, it was as a reporter in Chicago and New York that he influenced the style of journalism for generations to come. He himself was as much a colorful character as those he wrote about.

One of seven children, MacArthur was born on a farm in Scranton, Pennsylvania, to William Telfer MacArthur, a self-ordained evangelist, and Georgiana Welstead, the daughter of an English remittance man. He attended the Wilson Academy, a Nyack, New York, training school for ministers and missionaries. After the death of his mother in 1915, MacArthur left home to work for *Oak Leaves*, published by his brother Telfer in a Chicago suburb. He was hired away by the Chicago City News, a news-gathering agency, for ten dollars a week.

MacArthur enlisted in the First Illinois Cavalry in 1916, was with Pershing's expedition to the Mexican border, and served with the 149th Field Artillery, 42nd (Rainbow) Division during World War I. In 1919, never having risen above the rank of private, he returned to Chicago and landed a job with Walter Howey on the *Herald-Examiner*. He became Chicago's first $100-a-week reporter in the heyday of sensationalism and circulation wars. Rival reporters on the police beat often found official channels closed to all but MacArthur, a situation Ben Hecht (q.v.) attributed to the resignation letters of several high state officials Howey held in his desk drawer.

It was at Howey's instigation that MacArthur wrote "It's A Wonderful World," a front-page feature about efforts to rescue a little girl locked in an old railway station safe. The child was actually at home asleep, but MacArthur dictated for an hour about the people who *believed* there was a little girl in the safe. Howey ran the story the next morning under a seven-column headline.

MacArthur left the *Herald-Examiner* in 1921 for a job on the *Chicago Tribune*. Sent on a routine interview with Spanish novelist Vicente Blasco Ibáñez, whose *Blood and Sand* was being made into a movie, MacArthur arrived three hours late to find the nightgown-clad writer in bed with his toes sticking out from under the covers. MacArthur listened attentively while Blasco Ibáñez railed against American culture, then wrote a thousand words, some of them reporting what Blasco Ibáñez said, but most of them describing his toes. It was another front-page feature.

In 1924 MacArthur moved to New York as a reporter for William Randolph Hearst's (q.v.) *New York American*. His roommate for the next three years was humorist Robert Benchley, who drew MacArthur into a circle of friends that included Dorothy Parker and Alexander Woollcott (q.v.). MacArthur began contributing to Harold Ross's (q.v.) new magazine, the *New Yorker*, and eventually left the *New York American* in hopes of becoming a free-lance writer. In collaboration with Edward Sheldon, Sidney Howard, and Ben Hecht, he turned instead to writing plays.

It was with Hecht that MacArthur wrote his two most successful plays, *The Front Page* (1928) with characters based on Walter Howey and the cadre of police reporters they had known in Chicago, and *Twentieth Century* (1932). MacArthur made the transition to screenwriting in 1929. He teamed up with Hecht again to write a series of screen plays that have become film classics, including *Crime Without Passion* (1934); *The Scoundrel* (1935), which won an Academy Award for Best Original Story; *Gunga Din*; and *Wuthering Heights*. MacArthur's best-known screenplay was *The Sins of Madelon Claudet* (1931), which starred his wife Helen Hayes in her Academy Award–winning film debut.

MacArthur's first marriage in 1920 to Carol Frink, the *Examiner*'s "Little Girl Reporter," ended in divorce in 1926. Although the marriage soured almost immediately, Frink held out against divorce for more than six years. MacArthur and Hayes were married 17 August 1928 in New York. Their daughter Mary, born 15 February 1930, was an aspiring actress herself when she died of polio at nineteen. James MacArthur, their adopted son, is an actor.

During World War II MacArthur accepted a commission as major and served in both European and Asian theaters of conflict as a military observer. He rose to the rank of lieutenant colonel before the end of the war. From 1948 to 1950 he edited *Theatre Arts*, a financially unstable magazine he salvaged through reorganization, fund-raising, and innovative editing.

By the mid–1950s his health was failing, and he and his wife were spending much of their time at their Nyack home. He continued to write, however, and during the last year of his life he was working on a new play for Helen Hayes with Anita Loos and Ludwig Bemelmans. It was never completed. MacArthur died in a New York hospital in 1956 of nephritis and anemia.

BIBLIOGRAPHY:

A. *Bug's-Eye View of the War* (Oak Park, Ill., 1919); Arthur Dorlag and John Irvine, eds. *The Stage Works of Charles MacArthur* (Tallahassee, Fla., 1974).

B. DAB Supp. 6, 400–401; DLB 25, 173–178; NYT 22 and 24 April 1956; *Time*, 30 April 1956; Helen Hayes, "The Most Unforgettable Character I've Met," *Reader's Digest*, September 1947; Ben Hecht, *Charlie: The Impossible Life and Times of Charles MacArthur* (New York, 1957).

MARY SUE F. POOLE

MCCARTHY, JOSEPH WESTON (b. 6 March 1915; d. 30 January 1980) chronicled many leading celebrities, political leaders, and business leaders of the post–World War II United States, including Grace Kelly and Clark Gable, Harry Truman, the Kennedy clan, and Henry Ford II. He was managing editor of *Yank* magazine during World War II, in charge of twenty-one editions distributed throughout the African, European, and Asian theaters of war. His memoirs, published after his death, provide a treasure trove of anecdotes, reminiscences, and observations about prominent twentieth-century Americans.

McCarthy was born in Cambridge, Massachusetts, to Dennis F. McCarthy and Elizabeth Doyle McCarthy. He grew up in the old university town and worked as a reporter and sportswriter for the *Boston Post* from 1936 to 1940 while also attending Boston College. He received an A.B. in 1939; in 1940 McCarthy left the *Post* to work as a radio and publicity writer in Boston.

Shortly after the outbreak of World War II, McCarthy married Mary Dunn on 21 December 1941. The couple had three daughters and one son. Entering the army as an enlisted man, McCarthy in 1942 was offered the position of sports editor of *Yank* because of his previous media experience. In his memoirs *Days and Nights at Costello's* he said he accepted because he wanted to "escape from service as a private in a pack artillery battalion. . . . Editing was better than that." Later the same year he became managing editor. He held that post through V-J Day, which the enlisted man's magazine celebrated by publishing a special edition on the same press that had printed a magazine for Japanese soldiers during the war.

By war's end, McCarthy held the rank of master sergeant, won the Legion of Merit, and was a member of the first party of American soldiers and war correspondents to visit nuclear-devastated Hiroshima—only a day after the Japanese surrender and against the express orders of General Douglas MacArthur. Following his discharge from the army, McCarthy went to work for *Cosmopolitan* magazine as articles editor. In 1948 he quit and embarked on the free-lance career that was to last the rest of his life.

As a free-lance writer based in the Long Island community of Blue Point, New York, McCarthy came to know many prominent political, business, and cultural figures of mid-century America. He was a contributor to magazines such as *Life*, *Look*, *Saturday Evening Post*, *Reader's Digest*, *This Week*, and *Holiday*. Among those he wrote about were former President Harry S. Truman, Clare Booth Luce, Jimmy Durante, Clark Gable, Mary Martin, Grace Kelly, Henry Ford II, and the Kennedy family. His best-known books were *The Remarkable Kennedys* (1960) and *Johnny, We Hardly Knew Ye* (1972), the memoirs of

President John F. Kennedy's advisers, Kenneth P. O'Donnell and David F. Powers.

McCarthy was author of a weekly humor column for *American Weekly* from 1959 until the magazine folded in 1963, and was author of the Life World Library book on Ireland in 1964. In 1965 he edited *Fred Allen's Letters*. McCarthy completed his memoirs, *Days and Nights at Costello's* (1980), shortly before he died of a heart ailment in Central Islip, Long Island, New York, on 30 January 1980. He was sixty-five years old.

BIBLIOGRAPHY:

B. NYT 31 January 1980; *Publishers Weekly*, 22 February 1980.

JAMES DANIEL WHITFIELD

MCCLATCHY, CHARLES KENNY "C.K." (b. 1 November 1858; d. 27 April 1936) edited and directed McClatchy Newspapers in central California for fifty-three years. He was known as a fighter of political corruption and a champion of many causes, including most of the Progressive reforms of the early 1900s as well as the preservation of trees in Sacramento. McClatchy's father, James, helped to found the *Sacramento Bee* in 1857. On James McClatchy's death in 1883, his sons C. K. and Valentine Stuart "V. S." McClatchy took over the paper, with C. K. as editor and V. S. as publisher. The brothers purchased full control of the newspaper three months later by buying out the one-third interest of John F. Sheehan. C. K. McClatchy continued the outspoken editorial policies of his father and in 1897 began a regular column, "Private Thinks," in which he campaigned for public ownership of utilities, direct election of the U.S. president and vice president, freedom of speech for minorities, collective bargaining by labor and management, and humanitarian social legislation, among other goals.

In his later years, McClatchy strongly opposed prohibition as well as U.S. membership in the League of Nations. He wrote from Geneva in 1927 that the league was rank hypocrisy and it had no intention of making the world safe for democracy or of protecting weaker nations.

Many of McClatchy's political and social goals paralleled those of the Progressives, who gained control of the California legislature and governorship in 1910. He was never a strict partisan, registering at different times as a Progressive, a Democrat, and a Republican. McClatchy exercised his influence from his newspaper's pages, and avoided seeking political office or joining any fraternal or political organization. The *Bee*'s position as a state capital newspaper also enhanced its editorial influence.

McClatchy's editorship of the Sacramento newspaper, and the later addition of radio stations and other newspapers to the company, coincided with major economic growth in California's Central Valley, one of the world's leading agricultural regions and the home of McClatchy news properties. McClatchy's support for public ownership of utilities extended to strong leadership in the construction of large federal projects to provide for power, irrigation, and flood control. These include the Central Valleys Project, Folsom Dam, Trinity River, and Feather River power and flood control projects and, outside central California, the Tennessee Valley Authority and Hoover Dam. He also campaigned successfully for creation of the publicly owned Sacramento Municipal Utility District.

James McClatchy, C. K.'s father, had worked for the *New York Tribune* under Horace Greeley (q.v.). He left for California in 1848 and continued to write for the *Tribune* until he moved from San Francisco to Sacramento. The elder McClatchy had been born in County Antrim, Ireland, arriving in America in 1842. C. K. McClatchy's mother was the former Charlotte McCormack, born on Prince Edward Island, Canada, of Irish parents. He was educated in Sacramento public schools and at Santa Clara College in California. McClatchy reportedly did well in literature, history, and similar subjects, but had trouble with mathematics. He was short in math credits for graduation and left college without a degree in 1875 at age seventeen, beginning work with the *Sacramento Bee* as a cub reporter. In 1901 McClatchy received an honorary degree from Santa Clara for meritorious public service as editor of the *Bee*.

In 1885 McClatchy married Ella Kelly. They had two daughters, Charlotte and Eleanor, and one son, Carlos, who was instrumental in starting the company's first radio station, KFBK, in 1922. It was one of the first newspaper-initiated radio stations in the country. In 1922 the McClatchy company launched the *Fresno Bee*, edited by Carlos McClatchy, and acquired the *Modesto Bee* shortly afterward. Carlos McClatchy died in 1933 of double pneumonia. At the time he was vice president and general manager of McClatchy newspapers and broadcasting and second in command to his father. After a thirty-nine-year partnership, C. K. and his brother, V. S. McClatchy, decided to go separate ways in 1923. C. K. McClatchy won complete control of the family company in a contest of sealed bids with his brother.

McClatchy suffered a fall in 1933 which forced him to curtail his activities. He continued his work, which included strong support of Franklin D. Roosevelt and the New Deal. The *Sacramento Bee* was awarded a Pulitzer Prize in 1934 for a series of stories exposing political corruption in Nevada. McClatchy died of pneumonia on 27 April 1936 at the age of seventy-seven.

BIBLIOGRAPHY:

A. *Private Thinks by C. K. and Other Writings of Charles K. McClatchy* (New York, 1936).

B. DAB Supp. 2, 400–401; NYT 27 April 1936; "The Bee Through 100 Years, C. K. McClatchy," *The Bee's Centennial Album, Part the Ninth, Sacramento Bee*, 3 February 1958.

JAMES BOW

MCCLURE, SAMUEL SIDNEY (b. 17 February 1857; d. 21 March 1949), book and magazine publisher, was one of the most prominent of the fomenters of the "magazine revolution" of the 1890s. As founder and creative genius of

McClure's Magazine, McClure infused it with his enthusiasm for the new and fascination with the great, creating a journalistic formula that helped to transform the world of serious magazine publishing. When he applied this formula to investigations of business and government, he launched the muckraking movement.

S. S. McClure, as he was generally known, was born on a tiny farm in County Antrim, in northern Ireland, the oldest of four sons. His parents, Thomas McClure and Elizabeth Gaston McClure, were Protestants of Scottish and French Huguenot background, respectively. Thomas McClure, a carpenter, died in an accident when Samuel was eight, and his mother brought her family to America the following year and settled in northwestern Indiana. McClure's childhood was one of constant hard work, both to aid his family and to support himself while he intermittently pursued an education in public schools. He put himself through preparatory school and college at Knox College in Galesburg, Illinois, finally receiving an A.B. degree in 1882.

While at Knox, McClure met and determined to marry Harriet Hurd, the daughter of a prominent professor, and courted her for seven years despite strong resistance from their families. After graduation he soon found a job editing and publishing the *Wheelman*, a magazine promoting the new pastime of bicycling for a bicycle manufacturer. With this in hand he was finally able to persuade Harriet to marry him despite her family's wishes, and they were married on 4 September 1883. They had three daughters and a son and later adopted another son.

In keeping with his ambitions to publish a serious literary magazine, McClure modeled the *Wheelman* after *Century Magazine*, and in 1884 he joined the staff of the latter's printer, the DeVinne Press. However, he quickly found at DeVinne, and during a brief period at the *Century* itself, that he was too restless and ambitious to be a mere employee, particularly for such a genteel institution. When he proposed that *Century* go into the business of syndicating its literature to American newspapers, he was quietly dismissed. Consequently, in October 1884, he launched his own enterprise, the McClure's Syndicate, to do just that. Relying heavily upon his powers of persuasion and his boundless energy, he created a successful business that brought fiction and nonfiction by many popular and some distinguished American and British writers to a wide newspaper public. In order to gain freedom from irksome editorial routine, he hired a Knox classmate, John S. Phillips (q.v.), who had worked briefly with him on the *Wheelman*. Establishing a pattern they would follow for the next two decades, Phillips ran the office while McClure traveled incessantly throughout America and Europe, gathering ideas and enlisting contributions.

In 1893, taking advantage of these acquisitions and fulfilling a longtime ambition, McClure founded his own monthly magazine. Despite a lack of capital and its appearance at the beginning of the severe depression of the 1890s, *McClure's Magazine* survived. Taking advantage of technological improvements in printing, such as the halftone process of reproducing illustrations, and the rise of national name-brand advertising, the magazine was one of a new generation that produced cheaper and livelier journals to attract larger audiences than had the elite genteel magazines of the Gilded Age. It featured photograph-laden personality profiles, breathless reports of the latest scientific breakthroughs, fiction and human interest perennials. Its first great circulation advances came with monumental illustrated biographies of Napoleon and Lincoln. Both were written by Ida M. Tarbell (q.v.), who quickly became one of the foremost of a group of journalists who could meet McClure's and Phillips's exacting demands for clear and accessible writing. By 1900 *McClure's* circulation was near 400,000, and it carried the largest amount of advertising of any American magazine. The McClure's organization also established a book-publishing company and briefly assumed ownership of the Harper and Brothers firm in 1899.

Despite his successes, McClure at the turn of the century suffered from physical exhaustion and depression, in part because he yearned for still-greater prominence. When Tarbell and staffers Lincoln Steffens and Ray Stannard Baker (qq.v.) began in 1901 to investigate corruption in business, politics, and labor unions, McClure saw the opportunity to make his magazine a major influence upon public opinion. Inspiring a wave of journalistic exposés that Theodore Roosevelt was to label "muckraking," *McClure's* was one of the leaders of the movement. However, it was rocked in 1906 by the departure of Phillips and much of his editorial staff over personal and organizational issues. Although McClure subsequently gathered new writing talents, particularly Willa Cather (q.v.), and continued to publish important articles, neither the magazine nor its owner was the same thereafter.

More important, the magazine industry entered a period of retrenchment and greater advertiser power, and McClure, heavily in debt, was forced to surrender control of his magazine to a group of financiers in 1911. Though *McClure's* had at its height drawn substantial revenues, its owner had paid lavish fees and saved little for himself. In subsequent years the magazine declined; McClure regained control briefly in the early 1920s but soon lost his financial backing. It was sold to Hearst International Publications in 1925 and ceased publication entirely in 1930.

McClure himself drifted in search of employment: from time to time he went on the lecture circuit, and he edited the *New York Evening Mail* from 1915 to 1917, joined Henry Ford's ill-starred Peace Ship, and wrote for the Committee on Public Information during World War I. Harriet McClure died in 1929. Until his death of a heart attack at ninety-two, McClure went every day to the library of the Union League Club, where he wrote about political philosophy. In 1944 the National Institute of Arts and Letters awarded him their Order of Merit for distinguished public service in the arts.

BIBLIOGRAPHY:
A. With Willa Cather, *My Autobiography* (New York, 1914).
B. NYT 23 March 1949; DAB Supp. 4, 516–519; Peter Lyon, *Success Story: The Life and Times of S. S. McClure* (New York, 1963); Harold S. Wilson, *McClure's Magazine and the Muckrakers* (Princeton, N.J., 1970).

SALLY F. GRIFFITH

MCCORMICK, ANNE ELIZABETH O'HARE (b. 16 May 1880; d. 29 May 1954) was the first woman to win a major Pulitzer Prize in journalism, in her case for European correspondence, in 1937, and the second in the history of the prize (the first was awarded to a Columbia journalism student, who was recognized with another student for a school paper, an award category never repeated). McCormick was also the first woman on the prestigious *New York Times* editorial board. She had an illustrious career in which she wrote countless articles interpreting the complexities of national and international events.

She began writing fiction, poetry, and essays, but soon abandoned these for newspaper writing. Initially, her free-lance work appeared in *Catholic World*, *Reader Magazine*, the *Saturday Evening Post*, and *Atlantic Monthly*; she also wrote poetry for *Smart Set*, *Bookman*, and other magazines, and even sold a sonnet to the *New York Times*. However, with the exception of a series on contemporary events in Europe that she wrote for the *Ladies' Home Journal* in 1933 and 1934, she wrote fairly exclusively for the *New York Times* from 1922 until her death in 1954.

Her only book, *The Hammer and the Scythe: Communist Russia Enters the Second Decade* (1928), presented her opinions on Russia based on observations and experiences on two trips. It was an exceptional forum for her; she preferred the immediacy of a newspaper column for expressing her views. Marion Turner Sheehan later edited two collections of her columns after her death: *The World at Home* (1956), her observations on American life, politics, and government; and *Vatican Journal 1921–1954* (1957), articles on the Catholic church, its papacy, and its organization.

She was the eldest of three daughters of Thomas J. and Teresa Beatrice O'Hare and was born in Wakefield, Yorkshire, England. The family moved to the United States when she was an infant, settling in Columbus, Ohio. She attended Catholic schools in Columbus, Ohio, first graduating from St. Mary of the Springs Academy and later from the College of St. Mary of the Springs, now the Ohio Dominican College. Her father, who had been a regional manager for the New York–based Home Life Insurance Company, deserted the family, apparently because of severe business setbacks. Anne O'Hare was then still attending the academy, and her mother struggled to support the small family, supplementing a dry-goods business income with her poetry, sold door to door.

The family moved to Cleveland after Anne graduated from college. Her mother, as a poet and writer, preceded her on the staff of the *Catholic Universe Bulletin* in Columbus. Here her mother was editor of the women's page and occasional columnist; Anne, the associate editor, until her marriage to Francis J. McCormick on 14 September 1910.

With the marriage, Anne moved to Dayton, Ohio. She was thirty; her new husband, thirty-eight; though newlyweds, they were a mature couple. McCormick, an engineer, had joined his father's plumbing supply, manufacturing, and import business upon finishing his engineering degree at the University of Dayton, and his business regularly took him out of the country. Anne accompanied him on many of these trips, occasionally submitting pieces of poetry and articles, while at the same time honing her skills and knowledge in observing and understanding international affairs. In 1922 she proposed sending columns from abroad to *New York Times* editor Carr V. Van Anda (q.v.). He encouraged her, and her thirty-two-year career with the New York paper was launched. The couple, long peripatetic, lived most of the forty-four years of their married life in hotels. At first his attentions were devoted to the business; later, in 1936, at sixty-four, he retired and, with roles reversed, accompanied her, often smoothing the way and handling the details of necessary travel arrangements.

Her thrice weekly column, ''Abroad,'' was characterized by keen analysis and impartial presentation of her views and was followed by world leaders and the general public who relied on her incisive interpretation of international events. In addition to the 1937 Pulitzer Prize, she received honorary degrees from a host of universities in recognition of her unique contributions to journalism, as well as journalism awards from a wide range of national and international professional societies. She died on 29 May 1954 in New York City of cancer, having lapsed into a coma from which she did not regain consciousness.

BIBLIOGRAPHY:

B. AWW 3, 73–75; DAB Supp. 5, 446–447; NAW (Modern Period), 439–440; NYT 30 May 1954.

KATHLEEN K. KEESHEN

MCCORMICK, ROBERT RUTHERFORD (b. 30 July 1880; d. 1 April 1955) built the *Chicago Tribune* into the leading newspaper in the Midwest. The newspaper reflected his rigid, sometimes eccentric political and social views. The *Tribune* bore his mark so unmistakably that he is linked more to the tradition of earlier great personal editors, like William Randolph Hearst, James Edmund Scripps, and Joseph Pulitzer (qq.v.), rather than to his contemporary publishers, who focused more on business than editorial considerations.

McCormick was born in Chicago to Robert Sanderson McCormick, who was wealthy from the Virginia reaper, and Katherine Van Etten Medill McCormick, daughter of longtime *Tribune* publisher Joseph Medill (q.v.). His father was named to the U.S. legation in London in 1889 and later was ambassador to Austria-Hungary, Russia, and France. A sister, Katrina, died in infancy before he was born. An elder brother, Joseph Medill McCormick, was groomed to take over the *Tribune*, but his interests turned to politics and he was elected to the U.S. Senate.

His family in England, ''Bertie'' was enrolled at Ludgrove School in Middlesex. In 1894 he was sent to Groton in Massachusetts. In 1899 he went to Yale University, where he embraced social Darwinism, which became a theme in his thinking the rest of his life. He graduated in 1903. McCormick, in fact, was the last significant person in American public life to espouse social applications of Darwin's survival-of-the-fittest theory. After Yale, McCormick drifted into law studies at Northwestern University, and in 1908 he passed the bar.

Still in law school, McCormick was elected in 1904 to the Chicago City council, where he advocated municipal reform to purge corruption. In 1905 he was elected president of the Chicago Sanitary District, which had built the canal that connected Lake Michigan with the Mississippi River drainage. McCormick avoided political bosses and ward-heelers by hiring technicians to expand the canal system. He lost a 1910 reelection bid.

In 1911 McCormick was elected president of the Tribune Company, and he and cousin Joseph Medill Patterson (q.v.) rebuilt the *Tribune* into the city's dominant newspaper. *Tribune* circulation peaked in 1946 at more than 1 million, making it the nation's largest broadsheet. Sunday circulation peaked at 1.5 million. McCormick put the *Tribune* on solid financial footing, acquiring vast Canadian timberland in 1912 and building a paper mill in Canada. *Tribune* steamers transported the newsprint to Chicago, relieving reliance on outside suppliers. By the 1950s the Tribune Company also had extensive power-generating, aluminum-smelting, and shipping operations in Canada.

On a Russia trip in 1915, McCormick stopped in London to marry Mrs. Amie de Houle Irwin Adams on 11 March. She had just divorced McCormick's second cousin in Chicago. She seems to have attempted little influence on *Tribune* affairs. She died in 1939. In 1944 McCormick married Mrs. Maryland Mathison Hooper, who survived him. There were no children. In 1916, a major in the Illinois National Guard, McCormick spent six months at the Mexican border. He returned to active duty in June 1917, and he took lifelong pride in his battalion's performance at Catigny, the first U.S. offensive of World War I. He was promoted to colonel in 1919, and thereafter was known as the Colonel.

Excited at the financial success of London tabloids during World War I, McCormick and Patterson established the *New York Daily News* in 1919. It became the nation's largest-circulation newspaper. In 1925 the cousins divided their interests, Patterson to New York, McCormick in Chicago. Editorially, the *Tribune* under McCormick was not only nationalistic but isolationist. He was distrustful of foreign powers. His Anglophobia led to *Tribune* attacks on U.S. cooperation with the British against Germany on the eve of World War II. The *Tribune* castigated President Franklin Roosevelt's New Deal regularly. While the newspaper tended to be Republican, McCormick's ultra conservatism precluded endorsement in 1952 of the party's presidential candidate, Dwight Eisenhower.

McCormick's politics were not confined to the editorial page. His reporters, especially in Washington, colored their coverage to reflect the Colonel's thinking. Opinionated editorial cartoons were a front-page fixture. The *Tribune* bore other McCormick idiosyncrasies, including simplified spelling—*thru*, *frate*, *burocrat*, *jaz*, and *iland*.

McCormick dabbled in radio in the early 1920s and eventually established clear-channel WGN, a pioneer station that later added television. Under McCormick, the Tribune Company also owned the *Washington Times-Herald*, which had been run by his cousin Eleanor Medill Patterson (q.v.). He bought the paper in 1949, after she had died, but sold it as a money-losing property to the *Washington Post* in 1954. A man of causes, McCormick spent $350,000 in legal fees for smear-sheet publisher Jay Near of Minnesota in a case that became a landmark against prior restraint. He died at Catigny, his estate west of Chicago.

BIBLIOGRAPHY:

B. DAB Supp. 5, 477–481; NYT 1 April 1955; Jerome E. Edwards, *The Foreign Policy of Col. McCormick's "Tribune"* (Reno, 1971); Joseph Gies, *The Colonel of Chicago* (New York, 1979); Philip Kinsley, *The Chicago Tribune*, 5 vols. (Chicago, 1943–46); John Tebbel, *An American Dynasty* (Garden City, N.Y., 1947); Frank C. Waldrop, *McCormick of Chicago* (Englewood Cliffs, N.J., 1966).

JOHN H. VIVIAN

MCCULLAGH, JOSEPH BURBRIDGE (b. ? November 1842; d. 31 December 1896) was one of the most respected newspaper reporters and editors of the Midwest during the last decades of the 1800s. As a reporter he was known as an energetic innovator of news-gathering techniques, as the inventor of the modern journalistic interview, and as the first reporter to interview a president of the United States. As an editor, he was one of the early shapers of the New Journalism.

McCullagh was born in Dublin, Ireland, to John and Sarah Burbridge McCullagh. Not much is known about his early childhood, except that he was one of sixteen children born to the couple. At eleven he left home and worked his way to New York as a cabin boy on a ship that arrived in 1853. Little is known of his first few years in America, except that for a time he worked as an apprentice in the printing office of the *New York Freeman's Journal*. At sixteen he left New York for St. Louis, where he worked as a compositor for the *Christian Advocate*, a Methodist weekly. Encouraged by mentors who recognized his potential, young McCullagh received religious instruction, began a lifelong habit of reading widely, and studied shorthand. His hard work and quick mind were noticed, and within a year he was offered a job with the *St. Louis Democrat*.

His early reporting assignments at the *Democrat* showed him to be energetic and resourceful. He quickly developed a reputation as a prolific writer, producing more news stories than expected, and as a reporter who valued accurate reporting and concise writing. Within a year he accepted an offer for a fivefold salary increase to join the *Cincinnati Daily Gazette*. But at the outbreak of the Civil War he left the *Gazette* and entered the Union army.

McCullagh resigned his commission and returned to the *Gazette* as a war correspondent. During subsequent years he gained a reputation as a competent and aggressive, but fair and reliable, war correspondent. He was with Grant's army at Pittsburg Landing in Tennessee, and was shocked by the poor judgment and bad conduct of some of the Union officers in the battle. He sent a report of their drunkenness and mismanagement to the *Gazette*, and resigned when the newspaper refused to print it.

Almost immediately he was offered a position at twice the salary and a promise of absolute editorial independence with the competing *Cincinnati Commercial*. He accepted and earned wide popularity with his dispatches. He reported the siege of Vicksburg and Sherman's march through Georgia. He left the army in 1863 to become a Washington correspondent for the *Commercial*. Because of his stenographic skills, he was also the Senate reporter for the New York Associated Press. Writing over the name of ''Mack'' he gained added fame and popularity with the public by making special use of the interview, and in particular, with the interviews of President Andrew Johnson.

McCullagh earned the respect of President Johnson because of the reporter's accuracy and fairness when writing about the president in spite of the fact that both political parties and much of the press did not support Johnson. Johnson often called the reporter to the White House to give interviews, and was generally pleased that McCullagh accurately reported him in his stories. The relationship between the two men grew, Johnson relying on McCullagh to keep informed of developments at the capitol and trusting him to at least acknowledge the president's side of the ongoing debate. During Johnson's Senate impeachment proceedings, McCullagh was even subpoenaed as a witness for the defense.

Until McCullagh's dispatches appeared in the *Commercial*, interviews were unusual in newspapers. The few newspaper interviews that were published before his time followed an obtrusive question-answer format. McCullagh was the first journalist to use the modern format. In 1868 he resigned as Washington correspondent for the *Commercial* to become managing editor of the *Cincinnati Enquirer*. He was there until 1870, when he and his brother bought an interest in the *Chicago Daily Republican*. In spite of improved economic and professional profiles of the newspaper, the effort was lost when the Chicago fire of 1871 destroyed the *Republican* office along with much of the city. McCullagh lost all of his personal belongings.

That same year he returned to the *St. Louis Democrat* as managing editor. Because of internal conflict among the group of owners about financing news-gathering activities, McCullagh left the newspaper. He went to work as managing editor of the recently launched *St. Louis Globe*, begun by disgruntled former owners of the *Democrat*. Under McCullagh's leadership between 1873 and 1875, the newspaper prospered and became strong by securing an Associated Press franchise, expanding solid local and regional news coverage, and generating a colorful editorial exchange among the St. Louis newspapers. The *Globe* outstripped its major competitor and purchased the *Democrat*. McCullagh was editor of the *Globe-Democrat* until his death. His vision, discipline, and devotion motivated and enabled him to make the *Globe-Democrat* the preeminent newspaper in St. Louis, and among the best in the nation.

McCullagh continued to rely on the Western Associated Press as a source of news. But he also expanded the staff of correspondents to form his own news service. In addition, McCullagh made the editorial pages of the *Globe-Democrat* a hotbed of debate. Social, political, and moral issues of the day were vigorously debated. His fundamental concern for the editorial independence of the newspaper helped him speak to the community with force and credibility for several years.

Many scholars credit McCullagh as the primary thinker and catalyst for the New Journalism of the period. Indeed, one biographer Charles C. Clayton, notes that "McCullagh was doing all the things Pulitzer [did] before Pulitzer became a publisher."

McCullagh's health began to fail during the last few years of his life. Because of an asthmatic condition, obesity problems, and kidney difficulties, he spent several of his last months living with his brother and sister-in-law. He never married. History is unclear about the cause of his death, some sources claiming that he deliberately committed suicide by jumping from an upstairs bedroom window because he was so depressed about his physical condition, others arguing that he fell from the window during an asthmatic attack. He did not work the last few weeks of his life.

BIBLIOGRAPHY:

B. DAB 6, 5; DLB 23, 201–211; NYT 1 January 1897; Charles C. Clayton, *Little Mack: Joseph B. McCullagh of the "St. Louis Globe-Democrat"* (Carbondale, Ill., 1969).

J. DOUGLAS TARPLEY

MCCUTCHEON, JOHN TINNEY (b. 6 May 1870; d. 10 June 1949) was best known for his cartoons, particularly those drawn for the *Chicago Tribune*, but in addition was a world traveler, writer, and war correspondent. His two best known cartoons, both drawn for the *Tribune*, were "A Wise Economist Asks a Question" and "Injun Summer."

"A Wise Economist Asks a Question" won the Pulitzer Prize in 1931. In it a squirrel addresses a man sitting on a bench, asking "but why didn't you save some money for the future, when times were good?" The man, bearing a tag, "Victim of bank failure," responds, "I did." "Injun Summer," first published on the front page on 30 September 1907, is in two parts. The top shows a boy and an elderly man looking over a cornfield. The bottom shows the scene transformed through the boy's eyes into an encampment of war-dancing Indians. It was published by the *Tribune* on its front page in the autumn for many years.

McCutcheon was born on a farm near South Rabb in Tippecanoe County, Indiana. The son of John Barr and Clara Glick McCutcheon, he lived on a farm until 1876, when the father became the director of the first Purdue University farm at Lafayette, Indiana. McCutcheon attended Purdue and graduated in 1889. He formed a lifelong friendship with George Ade (q.v.) at Purdue.

McCutcheon moved to Chicago, where he worked for the *Chicago Record* (1889–1901) as both a reporter and cartoonist. During the 1896 Democratic convention, he drew a sketch of William Jennings Bryan making his ''Cross of Gold'' speech in Chicago that called attention to his political cartooning. He was with the *Chicago Record-Herald* from 1901 to 1903, and then began his long association with the *Tribune* until his retirement in 1946.

While with the *Record*, McCutcheon sailed with the naval cutter the *McCulloch* to the Far East. He was at Manila Bay when that battle was fought during the Spanish-American War and is credited with being the first war correspondent there. He continued as a correspondent, traveling throughout the Far East and then returning to the Philippines for the insurrection.

By this time having a reputation as a war correspondent as well as cartoonist, he was in Africa for the *Tribune* covering the Boer War and later the Balkan conflicts, and the Boxer uprising in China. He was with American forces when they occupied Vera Cruz, Mexico, in 1914 and then went to Europe for World War I. In the early part of the war, he was with the Belgian and German armies and, in a German airplane, is thought to be the first correspondent to make a flight over the trenches. In the meantime, he also had gone to Africa for big-game hunting with Theodore Roosevelt and naturalist Carl Akeley. Later he crossed the Gobi Desert in an open automobile (1925); went down the Amazon after crossing the Andes (1929); and crossed the Atlantic on the *Graf Zeppelin* (1935).

McCutcheon's long friendship with fellow Hoosier George Ade was also a productive literary one. He provided the illustrations for many of Ade's stories and books. Both he and Ade were honored by Purdue in 1939 with the distinguished alumni award. Earlier he received a Purdue honorary doctorate in humane letters in 1926. The University of Notre Dame gave him another honorary doctorate in 1931, as did Northwestern University in 1943.

A collection of his cartoons, most of them nostalgic of his Indiana childhood, was published under the title *John McCutcheon's Book* (1948). His autobiography was titled *Drawn from Memory* (1950). After his death, originals of his cartoons were given to Purdue University by his widow. McCutcheon published fifteen books, including four novels.

McCutcheon married the former Evelyn Shaw on 20 January 1917. They had four children. McCutcheon's brother, George Barr McCutcheon, also was a reporter and the author of the Graustark series. McCutcheon died at his Lake Forest, Illinois, home.

BIBLIOGRAPHY:
B. NYT 11 June 1949; R. E. Banta, *Indiana Authors and Their Books, 1861–1916*.

EARL L. CONN

MACFADDEN, BERNARR (b. 16 August 1868; d. 12 October 1955) founded *Physical Culture* magazine in 1899 to promote his ideas on self-healing, exercising, dieting, and fasting as the means to good health. From this modest start, he built a publishing empire that created the confession magazine and founded the *New York Evening Graphic*, the most sensational and least credible of the tabloids of the 1920s. Under the guise of promoting health, he founded a beauty pageant, fought the law over the publication of sexual material, and advocated women's short swimsuits.

Macfadden was born Bernard Adolphus McFadden on a far near Mill Spring, Missouri. His father, farmer William R. McFadden, died from the effects of alcoholism, and his mother, Mary Miller McFadden, died from tuberculosis. By his own account, Bernard was a sickly orphan by age ten. At this tender age, he worked for relative on a farm and in a hotel in Illinois. In St. Louis he worked as a delivery boy in a grocery store owned by an uncle. After a chance visit to a gymnasium in the 1880s, he bought a pair of dumbbells for fifty cents and began exhaustive workouts. At fourteen, he went on the bum, walking and hopping freight trains around Missouri and Kansas where he slept in haystacks and hobo camps. He changed his name because he thought it was more masculine and distinctive.

When Macfadden founded *Physical Culture* magazine, he wrote nearly all of the articles under a variety of masculine and feminine pen names. The magazine promoted Macfadden's dozens of self-help books on such subjects as keeping one's hair, caring for the feet, quitting smoking, fasting for health, preparing for motherhood, preserving one's masculinity, and predetermining a baby's sex.

Typical stories—fiction and nonfiction alike—told variations on the Macfadden biography: the rise of a sickly person to success and strength on a disciplined diet with strenuous exercise. A line on the magazine's cover proclaimed: "Weakness A Crime—Don't Be A Criminal."

Before 1898 he ended his brief and seldom mentioned marriage to Tilley Fountaine. In 1901 he married Marguerite Kelly, a nurse from Canada. Their marriage ended in divorce after the birth of a daughter. In 1913 Macfadden's traveling show staged a competition for Great Britain's most perfect woman, and after measuring each contestant himself, Macfadden selected nineteen-year-old swimmer Mary Williamson as the winner. They were married 5 March. The couple adopted one child and produced seven others delivered by midwives; one son died in infancy. They separated in 1933 and were divorced in 1946. Two years later Macfadden married Jonnie Lee; they divorced in 1954. Fights over alimony landed him in jail for two brief periods.

Macfadden's first run-in with the law came when antipornography reformer Anthony Comstock seized posters for a 1905 Macfadden program. His arrest and release helped draw 20,000 spectators to Madison Square Garden where they saw women in tights posing in silhouette behind a muslin curtain. For publishing a 1907 article on venereal disease in *Physical Culture*, Macfadden paid a $2,000 fine for mailing obscene materials, but he avoided a two-year prison term when President William H. Taft granted clemency.

The confessional tone of the many letters Macfadden received sparked the idea for *True Story*, the first confession magazine, in 1919. Macfadden took such pride in the amateurish nature of the publication that he fired an editor for taking a college journalism course. The articles were illustrated with photographs of such models as Norma Shearer and Frederic March. The editor avoided legal difficulties by hiring a board of clergymen to read stories for potentially offensive passages. By 1926 the magazine claimed a monthly sale of nearly two million. Macfadden followed with *True Romances*, *True Experiences*, *Love and Romance*, *Movie Mirror*, *Radio Mirror*, *Love Mirror*, *True Detective Mysteries*, *Famous Detective Cases*, *Master Detective*, *Modern Marriage*, *Dance Lovers*, *Fiction Lovers*, *Movie Weekly*, *Sportlife*, *Muscle Builders*, *Your Car*, *Your Home*, *Model Airplane*, *Dream World*, and *Metropolitan*. Macfadden acquired *Liberty* in 1931 and *Photoplay* in 1934. Although he had sold up to fifteen million magazines a month, Macfadden failed at some ventures. *Brain Power* failed to ride the 1920's wave of self-improvement; *Beautiful Womanhood* also failed. *Babies—Just Babies*, edited by Eleanor Roosevelt, was born and died in 1932, and *Midnight* was discontinued after a complaint by the New York Society for the Suppression of Vice.

Macfadden applied his formula to daily journalism with several small Michigan newspapers, the *Philadelphia Daily News*, the *New York Investment News*, the *New Haven Times-Union*, and the *Automotive Daily News* in New York. Macfadden's most notorious entry into daily journalism was the tabloid *New York Evening Graphic*, founded in 1924. Readers who found a single line to be dull were asked to write Macfadden about it. Sex, violence, scandal, readers' confessions and self-help advice crowded out boring subjects covered by other newspapers. Some examples of headlines: "HE BEAT ME—I LOVE HIM," "MY BACK WAS BROKEN BUT I KEPT ON LAUGHING," "LOVE'S LURE LEADS LAD TO GATES OF DEATH," and "STICK TO WOMEN—THEY'RE SAFER THAN HORSES." The *Evening Graphic*'s most notable contribution was the composograph, a faked photograph. One composograph of a sensational divorce trial was created by posing actors and models in a courtroom scene re-created in the newspaper office. Photographs of the heads of actual trial participants were then imposed on the scene. Another composograph showed the ascent into heaven of recently deceased movie idol Rudolph Valentino. The paper died in 1932 after losing money.

After a dispute with his staff in 1941, he sold Macfadden publications to its employees, keeping only *Physical Culture* for himself. He died in Jersey City Medical Center after an attack of jaundice aggravated by a three-day fast.

BIBLIOGRAPHY:

B. DAB Supp. 5, 452–454; NYT 13 October 1955; Simon Michael Bessie, *Jazz Journalism: The Story of the Tabloid Newspapers* (New York, 1938); Mary Williamson Macfadden, *Dumb-Bells and Carrot Strips: The Story of Bernarr Macfadden* (London, 1956).

WILLIAM E. HUNTZICKER

MCGEE, FRANK (b. 12 September 1921; d. 17 April 1975) was a broadcast news commentator from 1957 until his death. After 1971 he was host of NBC's "Today" show. Best known for his calm, articulate, and objective delivery, McGee covered *Apollo* moonshots (including the orbital flights), political conventions, presidential elections, Pope Paul VI's New York visit, and events following the Robert F. Kennedy assassination. In 1967 he won a Brotherhood award from the National Conference of Christians and Jews for his close-up study "Same Mud, Same Blood," which depicted black-white soldier relations in the Vietnam conflict. He was said to be one of the most respected newsmen at NBC.

McGee was born in Monroe, Louisiana, to Robert Albert McGee and his wife, Calla Brown McGee. He attended school in Monroe and then Oklahoma, where his mother moved following a divorce and remarriage. His high school years were spent in Seminole and Norman. Upon graduation from high school he enlisted in the Oklahoma National Guard and spent five years in the army. In 1940 Frank wed Nialta Sue Beaird. They had two children. He received his discharge from the army in 1945, and enrolled at the University of California–Berkeley for one year. Then he transferred to the University of Oklahoma. While in school, McGee began a part-time job at a small radio station, KGFF, in Shawnee, Oklahoma. He performed a variety of jobs from sales to music librarian.

In 1950 McGee took a newscaster job at WKY-TV in Oklahoma City. The job included shooting and editing film and writing scripts. In 1955 he moved to WSFA-TV in Montgomery, Alabama. It was here that McGee was noticed by NBC executives for his performance while covering racial tensions. He was hired as correspondent for the network's Washington bureau, and one of his initial assignments was to cover the federal troop–backed integration of Central High School in Little Rock during 1957. Two years later he was transferred to New York.

It was out of New York that McGee was recognized for his skillful ability to cover unfolding events. Many of his reports were produced under an agreement where Gulf Oil Company sponsored fast-breaking unscheduled news reports at NBC. There were over 450 of these "Instant News Specials." In addition he was chosen as moderator for the second "Great Debate" between Vice President Richard M. Nixon and John F. Kennedy, and he hosted regularly scheduled news programs like "Sixth Hour News" and "Sunday Report."

McGee also is distinguished for an NBC telecast on 10 March 1968 in which he was first to note that it appeared the United States was losing the battle in Vietnam. He further suggested that to destroy Vietnam in an effort to "save" it might not be the best policy for the United States to follow. In 1971 Frank McGee became the fourth person to host the network's "Today" show, when he replaced Hugh Downs.

In his career McGee earned a wide variety of honors and awards. Among these were the Headliners Award (1958), Robert E. Sherwood Award (1959), George Foster Peabody Award (1966), and an Emmy for special events coverage (1967–68). He suffered failing health for four years before his death, but remained on the job. Such behavior characterized his personality. He concealed the severe pain he suffered from multiple myeloma, a rare type of bone cancer. Frank entered the Columbia-Presbyterian Hospital immediately after a regular "Today" show appearance, and died there one week later of pneumonia. He was fifty-two.

In paying tribute, Walter Cronkite noted that "behind Frank's soft-spoken, almost courtly, manner one sensed character and integrity of iron." John Chancellor added, "Frank McGee was one of the men who gave his life to television, and brought to it a significant measure of decency and integrity."

BIBLIOGRAPHY:

B. NYT 18 April 1974; *Broadcasting*, 22 April 1974, 61; *Congressional Record*, 24 April 1974, 11765–11766; Eric Barnouw, *The Image Empire* (New York, 1970).

RICHARD C. VINCENT

MCGILL, RALPH EMERSON (b. 3 February 1898; d. 3 February 1969) was a news executive and writer for the *Atlanta Constitution* for forty years who argued vigorously for change in the American South. Although he was first employed by the *Constitution* mostly to write sports, he did not confine himself to that subject. As the South moved painfully through the Great Depression of the 1930s and early 1940s, he showed an especial sympathy for those persons living on farms, and later his broad concerns fixed upon those who were discriminated against because of race. He was not an early advocate of integration, but after 1954 he contended forcefully that the South was a part of the American nation and that southern people were obligated to accept the ruling of the U.S. Supreme Court in the case of *Brown vs. Board of Education*, which mandated the integration of public schools.

McGill was born near Soddy, Tennessee, the son of Benjamin Franklin McGill and Mary Lou Skillern McGill. There was little in the family background to suggest that he would become an important journalist or that he would acquire more than the rudiments of an education. His father made a hard living from farming, coal mining, and clerking in a hardware store. Nevertheless, on borrowed money he attended McCallie Preparatory School in Chattanooga. Later he went to Vanderbilt University. At both institutions, he played football, took part in debate, and made a feeble attempt at amateur dramatics. Shortly before graduation, he was expelled from Vanderbilt for gleefully extending the invitations to a fraternity party to include Nashville's bootleggers, professional madames, and prostitutes.

McGill went to work in the sports department of the *Nashville Banner*, where he had sometimes worked while in college. In 1923 he became sports editor. A development that became a hallmark of his career then occurred. Sports was not broad enough to hold McGill. While doing his duty fully on that assignment, he also began to write about politics and to undertake important features. He first attracted national attention covering the ordeal of Floyd Collins, a mountain hunter trapped in a cave for many days before death came. the nation hung with fascination upon the details of the unsuccessful efforts to save Collins.

In 1929 McGill joined the *Atlanta Constitution* to write about sports and occasionally politics. As the depression deepened, he ranged through Georgia reporting on the plight of poor men and women who could scarcely live on the land, some of whom were abandoning the South for what they believed was greater opportunity in northern cities. His poignant writing about their plight, and about what bleak economic conditions were doing to the human spirit, attracted the attention of the Julius Rosenwald Fund, which was interested in improving rural education. It granted sums of money to encourage southern teachers and journalists who showed promise of becoming influential. From the Rosenwald Fund, McGill received a travel fellowship for a lengthy trip to Europe in 1938. He was to look into farming in Scandinavia and in Ireland.

McGill afterward said that the Rosenwald Fellowship and the European travel changed his life. In the six months or so that he was gone, he did write about farms, and more importantly, his trip coincided exactly with Hitler's preparations to annex Austria. McGill heard Hitler speak in Berlin. He was in Austria when it was absorbed into the Third Reich. He saw France during the final year of peace in Europe, and in Great Britain he heard Winston Churchill in the House of Commons denouncing the British government for appeasing Hitler.

McGill returned to Atlanta a broadened man, and ten days after his return he was made executive editor of his newspaper in charge of the news, society, and sports departments. His column, which formerly appeared on the sports page, now moved to the editorial page and was a daily essay on any subject he chose. Subsequently he became editor in chief (1942) and publisher (1961), and during his years of greatest influence, his daily effort ran in column one of page one of the *Atlanta Constitution*.

The subject which McGill took for his own emerged slowly. Race relations and the need for the South to accept Supreme Court rulings became the broad issue upon which McGill won the Pulitzer Prize in 1958. A Jewish temple had been dynamited in Atlanta, and in a stunning column written at breakneck speed, McGill rocked the political leadership of Georgia and the South by declaring that some southern governors, attorneys general, other important elected officials, and even some newspaper editors shared massively in the guilt for the bombing. They had created the climate in which such things were occurring. In the Georgia congressional delegation in Washington, reaction was as bitter as it was elsewhere. That column, "A Church—A School," published on 13 October 1958, was cited by the Pulitzer committee when McGill received the prize. Honorary doctoral degrees began pouring in, seventeen in all, and after receiving one from Harvard, McGill, who never graduated from any college, jocosely referred to "us Harvard men."

McGill made many trips abroad for the federal government, appeared often on radio and television programs, and was an indefatigable supporter of the Democratic party and of Democratic candidates for office. He wrote for national publications in addition to his work for the *Atlanta Constitution*, and after 1958 his column was syndicated nationally. He loved the English language, especially poetry. In 1964, invited to address the Atlanta professional chapter of Sigma Delta Chi, he spoke not on race relations as expected but on the poetry of Tennyson, of which he was reputed to know hundreds of lines from memory.

He was married twice. The first Mrs. McGill, Mary Elizabeth Leonard, died in 1962 after a difficult illness. In 1967 he married Dr. Mary Lynn Morgan, a children's dentist. He had one son, Ralph Emerson McGill, Jr., born in 1945. During the 1960s McGill was treated for an arterial condition, and he died suddenly of a heart attack on 3 February 1969 while dining at the home of friends. He was seventy-one years old. His funeral at All Saints Episcopal Church in Atlanta was the object of a bomb threat, but no bomb was found and the service was held on schedule.

BIBLIOGRAPHY:

A. *The South and the Southerner* (Boston, 1959); *The Best of Ralph McGill: Selected Columns*, ed. Michael Strickland, Harry Davis, and Jeff Strickland (Atlanta, 1980).

B. NYT 4 February 1969; *Atlanta Constitution*, 4 February 1969; Calvin M. Logue, *Ralph McGill, Editor and Publisher* (Durham, N.C., 1969); Harold H. Martin, *Ralph McGill, Reporter* (Boston and Toronto, 1973).

HAROLD E. DAVIS

MCINTYRE, OSCAR ODD (b. 18 February 1884; d. 14 February 1938) became a newspaper reporter, city editor, and managing editor, but gained his greatest fame for his syndicated column "New York Day by Day." At the time of this death the column was published in more than 500 newspapers.

McIntyre, who had two older sisters, was born at Plattsburg, Missouri, where his father, Henry Bell McIntyre, managed the local hotel. Odd's mother, Frances Young McIntyre, died when her son was three years old. After her death, the children went to live with their maternal grandparents on a farm near Plattsburg. Later they were sent to Gallipolis, Ohio, to live with their paternal grandmother.

Odd—whose name was pronounced "Ud"—was educated in local schools, where he was unpopular with his peers and developed a lifelong inferiority complex. Expelled for bad grades and truancy, he hated school where his only success was in publishing a school newspaper. He attended Barlett's Business College in Cincinnati, where he did poorly in everything except typing. Dismissed from school, he worked as a hotel clerk and then as a reporter for the *Gallipolis Daily Sun*. He went to the *Gallipolis Journal*, where he set type and wrote news items without pay. When a reporter became ill, McIntyre took over the newsbeat at $2 a week.

His career-minded father sent him to the Cincinnati business school. Because of his poor school record, he was ordered to return to Plattsburg to his father's hotel. He soon quit and in 1904 became a reporter on the East Liverpool, Ohio, *Morning Tribune* at $12 a week. In 1906 he returned to Plattsburg, where he did nothing until given $20 and told to look for employment. He was offered a job on the *Dayton Herald* as police reporter. Within three weeks he became city editor, and by 1907 he was managing editor, city editor, and telegraph editor at the same time.

Ray Long offered him a $25-a-week job on the *Cincinnati Post* which he accepted and became the telegraph editor and later city editor. While Odd was with the *Post*, he and Maybelle Hope Small, his childhood sweetheart, were married in Kentucky on 18 February 1908. The couple had no children. She was born at Gallipolis on 9 February 1884 to riverboat captain Charles Richard Small and Kate Lowry Gatewood Small.

In 1911 Odd left the *Post* and went to New York as assistant editor to Long, who had become editor of *Hampton Magazine*. The magazine soon folded and McIntyre became a copyreader on the *Evening Mail*, but he was fired for incompetence. Without a job, McIntyre suffered a return of old fears and phobias, and he was on the verge of a nervous breakdown. His wife and friends encouraged him to write a letter for publication which could be done at home, and at age twenty-eight he began the work which would bring him success.

To support the couple McIntyre took part-time publicity work, and his first letters containing material about his clients were sent free to newspapers. They were chatty, informal letters describing a small-town boy's look at New York. Filled with local names and occasional references to Gallipolis and Plattsburg, they appealed to his readers. Among his clients was Florenz Ziegfeld.

Since he often used sketches of successful young New Yorkers, he featured the Majestic Hotel manager. McIntyre sent him the clippings asking for a check for what it was worth to the hotel. The manager not only paid but asked him to become the hotel's press agent, for which the McIntyres received living quarters and an unlimited expense account. The couple moved to the hotel in 1915 which marked the beginning of a life of luxurious living.

As more newspapers printed his letters, he decided it was time to give up the publicity and get his column into syndication. When his friend Ray Long became editor of *Cosmopolitan Magazine* in 1918, McIntyre began writing a monthly article which continued until his death. By July 1922 his letters were in syndication and he was being paid $400 a week. At his death his earnings were more than $3,000 a week.

He died of a heart attack at his Park Avenue apartment on 14 February 1938 with his wife at his side. He had refused the aid of a physician in keeping with his Christian Scientist religion which he had practiced for the last twenty years of his life. Mrs. McIntyre died on 27 April 1985 at age 101.

BIBLIOGRAPHY:

A. *white Light Nights* (New York, 1924); *Twenty-Five Selected Stories* (New York, 1929); *Another Odd Book* (New York, 1932); *The Big Town: New York by Day* (New York, 1935).

B. DAB Supp. 2, 414–415; NYT 15 February 1938; Charles B. Driscoll, *The Life of O. O. McIntyre* (New York, 1938).

ADRIAN L. HEADLEY

MCNAMEE, GRAHAM (b. 10 July 1888; d. 9 May 1942) was an early radio announcer and sportscaster. McNamee began as a general announcer, but found popularity covering sports and special events, the first broadcast national political convention (1924), and Charles A. Lindbergh's return from Paris. He later was master of ceremonies for a variety of radio programs including the "RKO Hour," the "Rudy Vallee Show," and the "Texaco Program" starring Ed Wynn. McNamee also was a regular narrator for Universal Newsreels.

McNamee was born in Washington, D.C., and was an only child. His father, John Bernard McNamee, was a lawyer who worked as legal adviser to the secretary of the interior under President Cleveland, then was employed as counsel for the Northern Pacific Railroad, St. Paul, Minnesota. McNamee's mother, Annie Liebold McNamee, played piano and sang in local church choirs. The young McNamee was educated in St. Paul, graduating from Irving School and Cretin High School. After high school he held odd jobs as a Great Northern Railroad clerk, a salesman, and professional hockey and baseball player. McNamee's father hoped he would follow in his own profession, but his mother wished for a musical career. His father died around 1912, after which he moved with his mother, first to New Jersey, and then to New York City. There McNamee studied voice, sang in area churches, and made his concert debut as baritone at Acolin Hall, in 1920. Following this he performed in most major American cities.

In 1923, being without a performance engagement and short of money, the young McNamee walked into WEAF in New York City seeking a job. He improvised an audition and was hired immediately. In the new position he found that early radio required a great deal of versatility, requiring him to do singing, announcing, and general station chores including "escort[ing] unaccompanied ladies home after programs." In time, McNamee helped demonstrate that radio announcing indeed was a profession.

He soon was assigned to cover sporting events like boxing matches, the World Series, and fall football games. Particularly memorable were the 1925 World

Series for which he received some 50,000 fan letters, and the 1927 Rose Bowl game, the first game to be broadcast coast to coast. He was known for his colorful narratives and chatty style, all done with high-level enthusiasm. He also moved to political conventions and campaigns, presidential inaugurations, and other special news stories like the 1927 Lindbergh flight. Millions recognized his cheery opening: "Good evening, ladies and gentlemen of the radio audience." He spent nineteen years at NBC, the network which gained control of WEAF in 1926. This included work with Ed Wynn and Rudy Vallee, and on other popular network radio variety shows of the day. McNamee also found his pleasant voice was suited for motion pictures. He acted as newsreel commentator for some ten years.

McNamee was married twice, first to Josephine Garrett, a soprano from Macomb, Illinois, whom he met while giving a concert (married, 1921; divorced, 1932), and then to Ann Lee Sims (married, 1934), daughter of a Rayville, Louisiana, planter. Both marriages were childless. The pioneer radio announcer died of a brain embolism in St. Luke's Hospital, New York. He was fifty-three years old. McNamee was buried in a family plot in Columbus, Ohio.

BIBLIOGRAPHY:

A. With Robert G. Anderson, *You're on the Air* (New York, 1926).

B. DAB Supp. 3, 495–496; NYT 10, 13, and 17 May 1942; William P. Banning, *Commercial Broadcasting Pioneer: The WEAF Experiment, 1922–1926* (New York, 1946); John Dunning, *Tune in Yesterday: The Ultimate Encyclopedia of Old-Time Radio, 1925–1976* (Englewood Cliffs, N.J., 1976); Geoffrey T. Hellmann, "Profiles," *New Yorker*, 9 August 1930.

RICHARD C. VINCENT

MCWILLIAMS, CAREY (b. 13 December 1905; d. 27 June 1980) was an unrepentant radical who combined a law practice and a writing talent to become a social activist and a prominent participant in American social turmoil for half a century. During twenty years of that time, 1955–75, he edited the *Nation*. He also wrote more than twenty books detailing American social problems such as migrant labor and racial prejudice.

McWilliams was born in Steamboat Springs, Colorado, to Jeremiah Newby McWilliams and Harriet Casley McWilliams. His father was a rancher who wore a coat and tie on roundup. Jerry McWilliams became a state senator, and in the cattle boom brought on by World War I he fared well. But a farm depression followed the war, and Jerry McWilliams went broke because of cattle speculation.

Carey McWilliams was expelled from Denver University because of a St. Patrick's Day spree his freshman year. He moved to Los Angeles in the spring of 1922 and worked in the business office of the *Los Angeles Times*. He arranged his working hours so he could attend the University of Southern California, which he said did him no harm. He obtained a law degree in 1927. He began to contribute to California magazines and newspapers, then to national publications. He met and was influenced by H. L. Mencken (q.v.). In 1929 he published his first book, a biography of Ambrose Bierce (q.v.), another influence on him.

McWilliams joined a law firm in 1927. His law practice made him intimate with the depression. An increase in personal dissatisfaction and mounting social excitement helped shape his views. He wrote scholarly materials until 1932, but after that he wrote about social issues, labor, and politics. He was involved in California social protest politics during the 1930s.

From 1939 to 1942 he served as head of the California Department of Immigration and Housing. "For all practical purposes," he wrote, "the appointment marked the end of my career as a lawyer." He resigned from the job upon the election of Earl Warren as governor in 1942 and became a busy writer and lecturer, crisscrossing the country to talk about civil rights issues.

In January 1945 the *Nation* named him its West Coast contributing editor. In 1950 he published *Witchhunt*, a book about what became generally known as McCarthyism. He also took up the issue of anti-Jewishness. In 1951 he went to New York for one month to edit a civil liberties special issue of the *Nation*, and he remained a New Yorker the rest of his life. He got caught up in the *Nation*'s battle against both McCarthyism and a part of the liberal establishment.

In the fall of 1955 he began his twenty-year stint as editor of the *Nation*. He tried to revive the muckraking tradition and took special pride in his work of recruiting contributors. Following Mencken's example, he answered with a personal note every submission sent to the magazine. One of his strengths as an editor is illustrated by the fact that several of his books, such as the one about migrant labor, hit the books stores just as that issue was coming to public attention; his timing was unusually acute. Besides editing his magazine and writing books, McWilliams continued to write for other publications.

In 1930 McWilliams married Dorothy Hedrick of Los Angeles. They had one son, Wilson Carey McWilliams. They separated in the mid–1930s and were later divorced. In 1941 he married Irish Dornfeld of Roseville, California, a novelist. They had one son, Jerry Ross McWilliams. He continued to be a political activist, and he continued to write, for several years after his retirement. He produced his regular column until a few days before his death on 17 June 1980 at University Hospital in New York City. In a posthumous article he warned of the danger of authoritarian control over the United States.

BIBLIOGRAPHY:

A. *The Education of Carey McWilliams* (New York, 1979).

B. NYT 28 June 1980.

DWIGHT JENSEN

MALCOLM X (b. 19 May 1925; d. 21 February 1965), also known as Malcolm Little and El-Hajj Malik El-Shabazz, was an important black spokesperson, leader, journalist, editor, and writer who sought to forge a new sense of group identity among Afro-Americans and to fashion a relationship among the world's black population. Among his strongest written statements is his autobiography, written with the assistance of Alex Haley.

Malcolm X was born Malcolm Little in Omaha, Nebraska, but soon moved to Lansing, Michigan. His father, the Reverend Earl Little, preached Marcus Garvey's (q.v.) back-to-Africa thesis; his mother, Louise Little, was originally from the West Indies. One of Malcolm's earliest memories was watching the Little home burning to the ground; the fire was set by white racists. Later his father was found dead on a railroad track; murder was suspected, but never proved.

Louise Little, with eleven children, strove to keep the family together, but after several years the children were placed in foster homes. Mrs. Little was sent to a state mental hospital. Malcolm himself was sent to reform school. In spite of that, he was allowed to attend public school, where he, the only black student, distinguished himself by earning high grades and being elected class president. But although he showed both academic promise and leadership ability, he was advised to pursue the carpenter's trade rather than the lawyer's profession, his expressed preference.

After completing the eighth grade in Lansing, Malcolm left Michigan to live with his half-sister in Boston. There, and later in New York City, Malcolm entered the street scene, eventually becoming involved in drug sales, pimping, numbers running, and an expensive cocaine habit. After a series of burglaries in Boston, Malcolm was sent to prison at age twenty-one.

It was in prison that Malcolm first heard of Elijah Muhammad and his version of the Muslim religon, whose adherents became known as Black Muslims. Malcolm became a follower of Elijah Muhammad, a leader who required that all his followers eschew drugs, liquor, dancing, and other aspects of Malcolm's preprison life. Malcolm took advantage of an excellent prison library, reading voraciously in a wide variety of fields. By the time he emerged from prison, he had discarded the name Little; he became the chief spokesperson of the Black Muslims, with articles and interviews appearing in numerous publications. He urged black independence in every sphere of life, encompassing both economics and philosophy.

His most important journalistic accomplishment was founding *Muhammad Speaks*, the national tabloid weekly newspaper of the Nation of Islam. The newspaper grew out of a combination of a magazine founded in 1960 by Malcolm for the Black Muslims called the *Messenger*, and a Harlem newspaper. *Muhammad Speaks* was begun in Chicago in 1961 and quickly became a strong voice of protest against racism. Its forced-sale operation (distributors purchased nonreturnable papers for sale in black communities) pushed its circulation to a reported 850,000 a week by the early seventies. The name of the publication was changed to the *Bilalian News* in the mid–1970s.

In 1958 Malcolm married Sister Betty X, a member of the Muslim mosque in New York. They had four children. After a trip to Mecca, Malcolm X recanted the black supremacy notions of Elijah Muhammad, embracing instead traditional

Islamic beliefs and the notions of a brotherhood of man. He established his own Muslim mosque and the Organization for Afro-American Unity. The rupture with the Black Muslims was serious, almost as controversial as Malcolm's own teachings. Shortly before his death, Malcolm predicted that adherents of Elijah Muhammad would murder him.

Malcolm X was shot to death at the Audubon Ballroom in Harlem as he began to make a speech to a group of followers. To many Americans he had become a symbol of a strong, articulate black leader, a man throwing off the yoke of repression. To others he was feared as a dangerous black racist. Writing for the *Saturday Evening Post*, he said, "I dream that one day history will look upon me as having been one of the voices that perhaps helped to save America from a grave, even possibly fatal catastrophe" (Malcolm X, 1966).

BIBLIOGRAPHY:

A. *The Autobiograhy of Malcolm X* (New York, 1964); *Malcolm X Speaks: Selected Speeches and Statements* (New York, 1966).

B. NYT 22 February 1965; Peter Goldman, *The Life and Death of Malcolm X* (New York, 1973).

ELLI LESTER-MASSMAN

MANNING, MARIE (b. 22 January 1873?; d. 28 November 1945), once eulogized by a biographer as America's ranking purveyor of advice to the lovelorn, was the innovator of the oldest surviving uninterrupted newspaper love forum in the country. Every day almost 1,400 sentimental buffs confessed their transgressions and woes to Manning's column, "Letters from the Lovelorn," in the *New York Evening Journal*. In return, they received advice from a person they knew only as Beatrice Fairfax, a name that became something of a national legend.

The name Beatrice Fairfax was a pseudonym, and the column, in fact, was the creation of Marie Manning, daughter of Michael Charles Manning and Elizabeth Barrett Manning. After a fairly sheltered education in private schools in Washington, D.C., New York, and London, acquiring, as she once observed, "such oddments as were considered meet for a young gentlewoman to know," she "stumbled" into journalism following a chance encounter with Arthur Brisbane (q.v.), then editor of the *New York World*.

In 1898 she joined the exodus of Pulitzer (q.v.) employees to the *New York Evening Journal* with her mentor, Brisbane. At the *Evening Journal*, she edited the women's page for an "amiable Victorian world," added the appropriate "women's angle" to sensational trials, and did some celeberity interviews. One day, after receiving three letters for that women's page, Manning proposed to Brisbane that the newspaper start a public confessional, a column inviting people to write about their personal problems. The column made its debut on 20 July 1898, featuring a tiny pen-and-ink drawing of its gawky, six-foot columnist in the upper left-hand corner.

The column was an instant success. Few social agencies existed at the time, and Victorian prudishness precluded practical solutions to common domestic and marital problems. For many people with personal problems Manning's column was the only place to turn. No sentimentalist herself, her advice was always strong and practical. Bewildered and heartbroken correspondents were firmly told, ''Dry your eyes, roll up your sleeves, and dig for a practical solution, battle for it; if the law will help, invoke the law . . . pick up the pieces and keep on going.'' Very soon other newspapers founded ''heart clinics'' of their own (Manning, 1944). Beatrice Fairfax was eulogized in song and legend.

Manning quit the column in 1905 to marry an old friend, Herman Gasch, with whom she had two sons, Oliver and Manning. For twenty-five years, except for a brief reunion during World War II, Manning was separated from her column and devoted herself to her family. Meanwhile, the column went through a succession of hands, remaining longest under Lilian Lauferty.

Manning returned to the column in 1930 and edited it until her death. The column was syndicated to 200 newspapers all over the country by William Randolph Hearts's (q.v.) King Features. She simultaneously worked for the International News Agency, another Hearst enterprise, covering Eleanor Roosevelt's White House press conferences and the woman's angle in Washington.

Manning was also a prolific short story writer, writing mostly for *Harper's*, *Harper's Weekly*, *Collier's*, and the *Ladies' Home Journal*. Her stories involved characters confronting problems similar to those of correspondents to her column. She published two compilations of her advice columns and authored two novels and an autobiography. Manning was a founding member of the Women's National Press Club and the Newspaper Women's Club, and she was active in the woman suffrage movement.

In an age when love forums are almost the quintessence of American newspapers and psychological counseling is almost a national obsession, it would be easy to underestimate Manning's contribution. Her innovation can be appreciated only if cognizance is taken of the fact that Manning's column preceded the theories of Sigmund Freud and Carl Jung and modern psychology and psychiatry. Her common-sense advice to correspondents stood in contrast to the almost maudlin responses of her competitors. For its times, her column was almost radical. Manning's true achievement is not a matter of public record for even she, most likely, had no knowledge of the solace she gave the anonymous thousands with her ''saccharine answers to the sentimental missives that blossomed'' in her column every day.

BIBLIOGRAPHY:

A. *Ladies Now and Then* (New York, 1944).

B. CB 1944, 193–196; DAB Supp. 3, 1503–1504; NYT 30 November 1945; Ishbel Ross, *Ladies of the Press* (New York, 1936).

ACHAL MEHRA

MARBLE, MANTON MELONE (b. 16 November 1834, d. 27 July 1917), though not so well remembered as other leading editors of his time, was well fitted to take his place with Horace Greeley, Henry Jarvis Raymond, William

Cullen Bryant, and James Gordon Bennett (qq.v.). Marble is remembered best as editor of the *New York World*, the newspaper closed by President Lincoln for three days in 1864 because of the publication of a forged government draft call.

Marble, who had one brother and one sister, was born in Worcester, Massachusetts, into a family of yeomen and artisans. His father, Joel Marble, was a schoolteacher who was instrumental in his son's education. His mother, Nancy Coes, was the daughter of the town's blacksmith. Marble's education was financed by a family friend who was a Baptist Sunday school teacher. Marble was a brilliant student and he was graduated from the Albany (New York) Academy in 1853. After two years Marble was graduated from the University of Rochester in 1855 and had chosen journalism to be his career.

Before Marble became editor and full owner of the *New York World* in 1869, he was assistant editor of the *Boston Journal* for a year beginning in 1855. He then went to the *Boston Traveller* and remained there a year as editor. He joined the staff of the *New York Evening Post* in 1858 and continued with that newspaper until 1860. Marble joined the *World* in 1860 as night editor and in 1862 became its controlling owner and editor, and continued as such through the period of Reconstruction. Marble was a heavy believer in political journalism and used his paper to advocate his views, yet the *World* under Marble was as well edited, in both news and editorial departments, as any newspaper in the country.

Marble was engaged to marry Delia Bishop West, and the date was set for 19 May 1864. Then on 18 May federal troops seized the *World* and suppressed its publication. The suppression resulted from the *World*'s publication of a forged presidential proclamation, announcing the failure of Grant's Richmond campaign and calling for 400,000 additional draftees. Careful checking by most of the dailies exposed the hoax before the papers went to press, but at the *World* the night editor allowed it to slip by. The subsequent arrest of Marble postponed the couple's marriage until 25 May. The Marbles had two children, Frank Marble and Delia West Marble. Marble's wife died on 17 June 1868, when she failed to regain her strength after their second child was born in April.

Under Marble, the *World* emphasized hostility against President Lincoln and the more radical members of his cabinet. It condemned the Emancipation Proclamation as fanatical, unconstitutional, and impossible to execute. It predicted that emancipation could only be carried out by treating the South as conquered territory because the national government lacked proper constitutional authority to free the slaves in 1863. The *World* became the leading spokesman for the Peace Democrats before Marble sold it in 1876 to a group of men headed by Thomas A. Scott, president of the Pennsylvania railroad.

Marble had a keen interest in politics, and his views were embodied in many state and national platforms of the Democratic party as he wrote the Democratic state platform in 1874. Two years later he wrote the national platform of the party on which Samuel J. Tilden was nominated for president in 1876, as well as much of the national platform of 1884.

In 1879 Marble remarried, taking as his wife Abby Williams Lambard, the widow of a New England railroad owner. As a result of his marriage, Marble became a foreign traveler. The Marbles began traveling to Europe and residing for long periods in Switzerland and Holland. Marble was sent abroad by President Cleveland in 1885 to sound out European governments on bimetalism, and conferred with William Gladstone, Otto Bismarck, and other public figures. After extensive investigation he reported to the president that the resumption of bimetallic coinage would not be carried out by any European government without the cooperation of Great Britain, which he saw no prospect of obtaining. He advised Cleveland against further purchases of silver by the U.S. Treasury Department.

Marble's second wife Abby died of complications from influenza on 10 April 1909. After his son's suicide in 1911, Marble's grip on life began to wane. Marble had been living in England the last twenty years of his life when he died on 24 July 1917 at the age of eighty-three.

BIBLIOGRAPHY:

B. DAB 11–12, 267; NYT 25 July 1917; George T. McJimsey, *Genteel Partisan: Manton Marble, 1834–1917* (Ames, Iowa, 1971); Sister Mary Cortona Phelan, *Manton Marble of the "New York World"* (Washington, D.C., 1957).

JULIA CRAIN ZAHAROPOULOS

MARCOSSON, ISAAC FREDERICK (b. 13 September 1876; d. 14 March 1961) was one of the highest-paid correspondents of the 1920s and 1930s and a well-known interviewer of world dignitaries. He was considered by some to be the foremost interviewer in American journalism. For more than twenty years, Marcosson was the *Saturday Evening Post*'s European correspondent. He was also the author of twenty-three books, many of which praised businessmen and capitalism.

Marcosson was born in Louisville, Kentucky, the son of Louis and Helen M. Marcosson. His father was a traveling salesman. He began work at the *Louisville Times* at eighteen. "I knew what I wanted to do once I went to work," he wrote about journalism in his autobiography, *Before I Forget* (1959). He worked at the *Times* from 1894 to 1903; he was an assistant city editor and a book reviewer. During this time he began writing reviews and stories for national magazines. After a dispute with the *Times* city editor, Marcosson quit and moved to New York City in search of a journalism job.

From 1903 to 1907 Marcosson worked as an associate editor for *World's Work*, a business-oriented monthly magazine. He usually wrote three articles per issue. While on the staff of *World's Work*, Marcosson interviewed famous people—"head hunting," as it was called—and wrote profiles of Theodore Roosevelt and Andrew Carnegie. In this period Marcosson married his childhood sweetheart, Grace Griffiths, even though he knew she was in the last stages of a fatal illness.

After a salary dispute, Marcosson left *World's Work* and joined the staff of the *Saturday Evening Post*, the largest-circulation periodical of its time. He served as its financial editor from 1907 to 1910 and wrote 124 weekly articles under the column title "Your Savings." He developed cordial relationships with Wall Street businessmen which led some in journalism to deride him as being too close to the financial interests. His first book was *How to Invest Your Savings*. Ironically, it was Marcosson who helped Upton Sinclair (q.v.) get his muckraking novel *The Jungle*, a critique of industry, published in 1906.

In 1910 Marcosson became an associate editor at *Munsey's* magazine, but returned to the *Post* in 1913 to become a foreign correspondent. For twenty-five years he interviewed virtually all of the world's leading statesmen and became known as a reporter who could get an interview when others would fail. For example, despite fourteen cancellations, Marcosson was able to arrange an interview in 1917 with Britian's wartime leader Lloyd George. He interviewed most of the leading Allied figures for the *Post*, then traveled to Russia to view the Kerensky government. When he returned to the United States, he went on a lecture tour warning the nation about Bolshevism. Marcosson said his life was regularly threatened while he was on tour.

During the 1920s and 1930s Marcosson was an important source of information for the American public about the thinking of European political and industrial leaders. Reporters often interviewed Marcosson for his impressions of conditions in Europe. Marcosson said he never took notes during his interviews, and consequently his profiles provided more color than direct quotations.

In 1932 Marcosson wrote a biography of his friend, David Graham Phillips (q.v.), a leading muckraking novelist and journalist who had been assassinated in 1911. In 1932, Phillips's sister, Carolyn Frevert, left Marcosson $729,286, nearly all of her estate. She described Marcosson as her loyal friend. In 1931 Marcosson married Frances Barbarey. She died of cancer in 1936, after which Marcosson abandoned all other work for the study of cancer. He became the first director of public relations for a New York hospital specializing in cancer treatment. He wrote often about cancer. In 1942 he married Ellen Petts, who became his assistant and helped him write a series of corporate biographies. He died in New York City.

BIBLIOGRAPHY:

A. *Adventures in Interviewing* (New York, 1919); *David Graham Phillips and His Times* (New York, 1932).

B. DAB Supp. 7, 512–513; NYT 15 March 1961; John Tebbel, *George Horace Lorimer and the "Saturday Evening Post"* (New York, 1948).

ROBERT MIRALDI

MARQUIS, DONALD ROBERT PERRY (b. 29 July 1878; d. 29 December 1937) established himself as an American humorist whose newspaper columns featuring the characters of archy and mehitabel outshone his contributions as a poet, short story writer, novelist, and playwright. Marquis, had enormous popularity during his time using satire to attack pretensions and fads. His humor reflected a bitterness which may have arisen from a number of personal disasters and an earthy quality which came from growing up in a typical midwestern town.

The youngest of four children of James Stewart Marquis, a physician, and Virginia Elizabeth Whitmore Marquis, he was born in Walnut, Bureau County, Illinois. He was a graduate of Walnut High School and attended Knox College in Galesburg, Illinois, for part of one semester in 1898. He worked as a country schoolteacher and a railroad section hand before joining the weekly Walnut newspaper where he had his first column featuring fictitious stories and poetry.

In 1899 he went to Washington, D.C., where he was a clerk with the Census Bureau and did some work for the *Washington Times*. Unable to get his own column and keep his political position, he left Washington and, after a brief stay in Philadelphia, joined the newly formed *Atlanta* (Georgia) *News* as an associate editor in 1902. Two years later he switched over to the *Atlanta Journal*, where he became a friend of Joel Chandler Harris (q.v.).

Harris enticed the columnist to join *Uncle Remus's Magazine* in 1907, and Marquis developed his literary style of parody, verse, and use of a wide variety of voices. After two years and the death of Harris, he left Atlanta for New York City. His wife, free-lance writer Reina Melcher Marquis, whom he had wed on 8 June 1909, joined him the next year.

After brief stints with the *American* and the *Brooklyn Eagle*, he joined the *New York Evening Sun*, where after a year he began the column ''Sun Dial'' in April 1913. Deviating from the trend for columnists of the day to use contributions, he wrote the bulk of the column himself six days a week. For the next nine years Marquis used his personal writing style to create a number of characters who delighted readers both inside and outside New York.

Much of his national reputation came from his books, beginning with *Danny's Own Story* (1912). As the first wave of his twenty-six books came out, Marquis left the *Evening Sun* in 1922 to join the *New York Tribune*, where he wrote a column called ''The Lantern'' for three years. His literary successes were clouded by the death of his only son, Robert Stewart Marquis, at the age of five in 1921, and of his wife, Reina, on 2 December 1923. As he saw new opportunities for his talents developing, he abandoned his newspaper column in 1925 to devote himself to his other literary pursuits.

In 1924 Marquis had been the author of *The Old Soak's History of the World* based on a column character, *The Awakening and Other Poems*, and the drama *The Dark Hours* demonstrating his versatility. He hoped his play about the Crucifixion would achieve the success of his earlier comedy, *The Old Soak*, which had run for 423 performances on Broadway in 1922–23. It would not be until 1932 that the drama would be produced with his financing and the direction of his second wife, actress Marjorie Vonnegut, whom he had married on 2 February 1926. It ran eight performances.

His lack of continued success in theater was joined by a number of unsuccessful stays in Hollywood, which had made *The Old Soak* into both silent and sound motion pictures. Yet his comic characters continued to live on in the pages of

Collier's and the *Saturday Review of Literature*, especially archy and mehitabel whose creation he sometimes rued for overshadowing his other work.

The popularity of the cockroach and cat characters was attested to by the books which featured them: *archy and mehitabel* (1927), *archy's life of mehitabel* (1933), and *archy does his part* (1935). Despite his literary success, Marquis continued to be plagued by his personal life. The early deaths of son and first wife were followed by the death of his only daughter, Barbara, in 1931, at the age of thirteen, and his second wife on 25 October 1936. Beset by financial problems throughout most of his later life, he suffered a heart attack in 1929, was blind for a time after a cerebral hemorrhage in 1932, and became an invalid in 1936. He died at the home of his two sisters, whom he had supported since 1916, in Forest Hills, New York, on 29 December 1937. An unfinished autobiographical novel *Sons of the Puritans* (1939) and *the lives of archy and mehitabel* (1940) were published posthumously.

BIBLIOGRAPHY:

B. DAB Supp. 2, 430–432; NCAB 30, 80–81; NYT 30 December 1937; Lynn Lee, *Don Marquis* (Boston, 1981).

SAMUEL V. KENNEDY III

MATTHEWS, HERBERT LIONEL (b. 10 January 1900; d. 30 July 1977) was with the *New York Times* from 1922 to 1967, mostly as a foreign correspondent and then an editorialist. His informed, interpretive coverage of the Republican side in the Spanish civil war earned him criticism as a partisan, but Matthews responded that he had reported things as he saw them. His controversial coverage of the early Castro revolution in Cuba, including an exclusive 1957 interview that confirmed the guerrilla leader still alive, drew criticism and the *Times* itself turned down some of his later coverage although he remained on the newspaper's editorial board until his retirement in 1967.

Matthews was born in New York City to Samuel Matthews and Frances Lewis Matthews. After World War I service as a private, he entered Columbia University and was graduated in 1922. He joined the *New York Times* as a business stenographer, worked his way to the cable desk, and in 1931 was sent to the Paris bureau. That same year, on 21 February, he married Nancie Edith Cross of Massingham, England. They had a son and a daughter.

His *Times* assignments were the Paris bureau, 1931–34; Abyssinian War, 1935–36; Spanish civil war, 1936–39; Rome bureau, 1939–41; India, 1942; Allied campaign in Sicily and Italy, 1943–45; chief of the London bureau, 1945–49; and member of the editorial board, 1945–67. Matthews, with a career-long penchant for on-the-spot reporting, scooped other reporters with the news that foreign warplanes were being used in Spain. He was first with reports that Italy and Germany were heavily supporting the Franco side of the conflict. He viewed events on a moral basis, which flavored his reporting. The Catholic Press Association and other Nationalist partisans alleged unfair reporting, but the *Times* was comforted that it received about the same volume of complaints about stories from its correspondent on the Nationalist side.

In Rome, his report that the Axis powers favored Franklin Roosevelt's defeat in his 1940 presidential reelection bid prompted the Mussolini government to evict him briefly. When Italy declared war on the United States, he was jailed for three days and then held five months in loose internment.

Matthews had concentrated on humanities at Columbia and sometimes characterized himself as bookish, but he also acknowledged an "urge to go out and fight, to pit one's strength and wits against the forces of nature, to seek adventure, risk life and take joy in comradeship and danger" (Matthews, 1946). In World War II he narrowly missed death by a German shell that killed three British colleagues.

On the *Times* editorial board Matthews specialized in Latin America and crusaded against dictatorships. His sympathetic 1952 coverage of the Bolivian revolution earned him a decoration from the revolutionary government in 1959. In 1957, after Castro had escaped a fumbled invasion of Cuba, Matthews and his wife posed as tourists and tracked him to a Sierra Maestra hideaway. In a three-part *Times* series, Matthews reported that Castro was friendly to the United States and desired democracy for Cuba. He also reported that Castro had an impressive 3,000 troops ready to move against the Batista dictatorship.

When the Cuban revolution succeeded and assumed a clear communist dimension, Matthews was widely criticized. The Senate Internal Security Subcommittee declared that he had made Castro a Robin Hood. The *Times* was picketed by Cuban exiles, and Matthews was put under government protection after life threats. He was dropped from the board of the Inter-American Press Association, shunned at the Overseas Press Club, and driven from the podium by a bomb threat at the University of New Mexico. At the *Times* itself, the book editor refused a Matthews review, and other articles were declined. He claimed that publisher Orvil Dryfoos (q.v.) pressed him to stay out of Cuba to avoid embarrassment for the *Times*.

Matthews stood by his coverage, saying it was not until 1960 that Castro entered the rapprochement with Cuban communists that led to the island's close Soviet ties. In some respects, Matthews had been duped by Castro. The guerilla leader had only eighteen men with him in the Sierra Maestra and had paraded them before Matthews over and over to add credibility to his claim of 3,000. Matthews died after a short illness in retirement in Adelaide, Australia.

BIBLIOGRAPHY:

A. *The Education of a Correspondent* (New York, 1946).

B. NYT 13 July 1977; Jerry W. Knudson, "Herbert Matthews and the Cuban Story," *Journalism Monographs* 54 (February 1978).

JOHN H. VIVIAN

MEDILL, JOSEPH (b. 6 April 1823; d. 16 March 1899) was editor of the *Chicago Tribune* during the period in which it became "The World's Greatest Newspaper." Medill and his newspaper were influential in the effort to abolish slavery, the election of President Lincoln, and the development of the upper Midwest. Following the great Chicago fire, Medill was elected mayor of that city, and remained active in its civic affairs, as well as management of the *Tribune*, the remainder of his life.

One of five children—three boys and two girls—Joseph Medill was born on a farm near St. John in New Brunswick, Canada. His parents, William Medill and Margaret Corbett Medill, were Irish immigrants. When Joseph was nine, the Medills moved to a farm in Stark County, Ohio. There Joseph lived with his family until he was twenty-one. Although he had been graduated from a college preparatory academy, Massillon Village, Medill was unable to attend college because of a fire that left the family in financial straits.

Medill obtained most of his education from books that he borrowed. On weekends he obtained lessons in philosophy, science, and Latin from a minister in Canton, Ohio. In addition, Medill read Horace Greeley's (q.v.) newspaper, the *New York Tribune*, for which he served as a subscription solicitor.

Having developed an interest in the law, Medill began studying it, and was admitted to the bar in 1846. For the next few years, Medill practiced law at New Philadelphia, Ohio. While practicing law, Medill developed an intense interest in the newspaper at New Philadelphia. He learned to set type, operate a press, and peform other newspaper jobs. In addition, he began contributing editorial matter.

Leaving the law, Medill bought a small newspaper in northwestern Ohio, the *Coshocton Whig*. He appointed himself editor in chief and made his three younger brothers assistants. The newspaper became deeply involved in the antislavery movement as well as politics and exerted great influence in its area. After only two years in newspapering, Medill moved to Cleveland and founded the *Daily Forest City*. With John C. Vaughan, a South Carolina abolitionist and editor of a Free-Soil paper, Medill entered into a merger that resulted in a new newspaper, the *Cleveland Leader*. The paper crusaded steadfastly against slavery and for the creation of a national political alignment that became the Republican party.

Although that party was conceived at an earlier meeting at Ripon, Wisconsin, a meeting instrumental in organization of the party was held about a month later in the office of the *Cleveland Leader*. Arranged by Medill, the meeting was attended by antislavery activists similar to those who had attended the meeting at Ripon. Following a suggestion by Medill, those present adopted "Republican" as the name of their movement.

While editing the *Leader*, Medill married Katharine Patrick, of New Philadelphia. The marriage, 2 September 1852, produced three daughters. One of the daughters, Elinor, married Robert W. Patterson; and another, Katharine, married Robert Sanderson McCormick, creating the McCormick-Patterson union that made the *Chicago Tribune* and *New York Daily News* one of America's most powerful newspaper enterprises. The Medills' third daughter, Josephine, remained unmarried.

With the responsibilities of marriage and his increasing knowledge of journalism, Medill began looking for greater opportunity. At the suggestion of Horace Greeley, who according to some stories gave his famous "Go West, Young Man, Go West" advice to Medill himself, the ambitious journalist decided to move to Chicago. Greeley arranged for Medill to meet another friend of his—Charles H. Ray, former editor of a newspaper at Galena, Illinois—to talk about starting a paper in Chicago.

At a historic meeting in Chicago's Tremont House, where they were introduced to one another through letters from Greeley, Ray and Medill decided to purchase a part of the eight-year-old *Chicago Tribune*. By virtue of their investment in the *Tribune*—Medill bought a third and Ray a fourth—Ray and Medill became partners in its publication. From 1855 to 1863 Medill held the position of general manager or managing editor. He became editor in chief in 1863 and held that position until 1866, except for brief periods during which he served as the newspaper's correspondent in Washington.

During its early years under Medill, the *Tribune* crusaded against liquor, advocated the abolition of slavery, promoted the Republican party's organization, opposed secession of the South, fought for preservation of the federal union even if it meant civil war, was instrumental in the nomination of Lincoln, supported Lincoln's presidency, championed General U.S. Grant's command of a Union army, defended "radical" reconstruction of the South, and tried to inspire a "simplified" spelling movement.

From 1866 until 1874 Medill devoted himself to public service of several kinds, serving as a member of the Illinois constitutional convention, a member of the U.S. Civil Service Commission, and mayor of Chicago. Returning to active leadership of the *Tribune* in 1874, Medill assumed direction of both the editorial and business operations.

In Medill's later years the *Tribune* opposed trade unionism and government regulation of business, was instrumental in obtaining the World's Fair of 1893 for Chicago, and promoted other civic projects. Medill's death, from heart disease, which occurred as he was visiting his ranch near San Antonio, Texas, gave rise to one of journalism's most often told stories. Medill's last words according to the story, were "What's the news?" The Medill School of Journalism at Northwestern University is named in his honor.

BIBLIOGRAPHY:

B. DAB 12, 491–492; DLB 43, 318–325; NCAB 1, 131–132; NYT 17 March 1899; H. I. Cleveland, "A Talk With . . . The Late Joseph Medill," *Saturday Evening Post*, 5 August 1899; Phillip Kinsley, *The Chicago Tribune* (New York, 1943); John Tebbel, *An American Dynasty* (Garden City, N.Y., 1947).

JOHN DE MOTT

MEEMAN, EDWARD JOHN (b. 2 October 1889; d. 15 November 1966) founded the *Knoxville News* for the Scripps-Howard newspapers, edited the *Memphis Press-Scimitar* during its influential era, and served many years as journalism's foremost spokesman for protection of the environment. Every year, Scripps-Howard gives awards, in Meeman's memory, for journalistic achievement in conservation.

One of four children, Meeman was born in Evansville, Indiana. Meeman's father, John Henry Meeman, was a cigar maker; and his mother, Mary Elisabeth Schulte Meeman, a housewife. Meeman was educated in the public schools of Evansville and graduated from its high school in 1907. Upon graduation, at seventeen, Meeman became a reporter for the *Evansville Press*, which he later served as managing editor. In the interim, he served as a reporter for the *Terre Haute Post*, another Scripps-Howard paper, and the Newspaper Enterprise Association.

In 1921, Scripps-Howard selected Meeman to create the newspaper in Knoxville. Under his editorship, the newspaper bought out older competition and became today's *News-Sentinel*. Meeman led the effort to establish today's national park in the Great Smoky Mountains and, also, today's Tennessee Valley Authority (TVA).

Moving to Memphis, Meeman continued his campaign for TVA, spearheaded a successful crusade against the Crump political machine, was instrumental in establishment of Shelby Forest State Park, and created the Meeman Foundation to promote conservation, good journalism, and democratic government. In 1959 Meeman served as a member of the U.S. delegation to the Atlantic Congress. In 1960 he received the Roy S. Howard award of the Scripps-Howard newspapers. In 1963 he received the human relations award of the National Conference of Christians and Jews.

Following a 1962 retirement, Meeman served as editor emeritus of the *Press-Scimitar* and conservation editor of Scripps-Howard until suffering a stroke and subsequent fatal heart attack. After Meeman's death—he never married—his $2-million-plus estate created an endowment for the Meeman conservation awards, fostered education for journalism, and benefited other interests. His papers were given to Memphis State University, where the journalism building is named in his memory.

BIBLIOGRAPHY:

A. *The Editorial We: A Posthumous Autobiography by Edward J. Meeman Compiled, Edited and With an Introduction and Afterword by Edwin Howard* (Memphis, 1976).

B. NYT 16 November 1966; Alan Bussel, "The Fight Against Boss Crump: Editor Meeman's Term," *Journalism Quarterly*, Summer 1967.

JOHN DE MOTT

MELLETT, DONALD RING (b. 26 September 1891; d. 16 July 1926), cited in 1975 by the Society of Professional Journalists, Sigma Delta Chi, as one of the "three martyrs to American press freedom in our history" (Himebaugh, 1978), was assassinated while waging a vigorous editorial campaign that had exposed a corrupt police department, public apathy, and a firmly entrenched underworld doing a thriving business in illicit liquor, gambling, prostitution, and drugs in Canton, Ohio, where he was publisher of the *Canton Daily News*, owned by James M. Cox (q.v.), Democratic nominee for the presidency in 1920. Mellett carried on his crusade, for the last five months at least, with full knowledge his life was in danger. Because of his courageous effort, the *Daily News* received the 1927 Pulitzer gold medal for community service. Mellett was enshrined in the Ohio and Indiana journalism halls of fame, Indiana University named a room in Ernie Pyle Hall after him, and Sigma Delta Chi placed a historic journalism site plaque in Canton. Prior to arriving in Canton, in January 1925, Mellett had served as managing editor of the *National Enquirer*, a Prohibition weekly published in Indianapolis; co-owned the daily *Columbus* (Indiana) *Ledger*; and worked in advertising for Scripps-Howard's *Akron* (Ohio) *Press*.

Mellett, next to the youngest of seven sons of Jesse and Margaret Ring Mellett, was born in Elwood, Indiana, where his father, a former schoolteacher, had purchased a struggling weekly newspaper, the *Elwood Free Press*, in 1886 and turned it into a daily. While Don was a youngster, the family moved to Muncie, where Jesse Mellett published the *Indiana Bimetallist*; then to Anderson, Indiana, where Don attended grammar school; and finally to Indianapolis, where Don graduated from Shortridge High School in 1909 and met his future wife, Florence Evans. They would marry 24 December 1913 and have a son and three daughters. (Florence died 20 September 1971 and is buried with Don in Crown Hill Cemetery, Indianapolis.)

Mellett grew up surrounded by journalists. Five of his brothers entered the profession, with Lowell, the best known, serving as editor of the *Washington Daily News* and manager of Scripps-Howard Newspaper Alliance. At Indiana University, which he attended on and off between 1909 and 1914, Mellett became a serious journalist. As editor of the *Indiana Student*, a daily, during spring quarter 1914, he waged editorial campaigns seeking reform of the campus Greek system and urging Bloomington officials to improve the city's inadequate water supply to the university. Exhausted and suffering from nephritis, Mellett published his last issue on 12 June and withdrew without graduating. For a year and a half, he operated an orchard in Brown County, Indiana.

Mellett returned to Indianapolis and, after working briefly in his brother Roland's print shop and for the *Indianapolis News*, became managing editor of the *National Enquirer*, a temperance weekly published by former Indiana Governor J. Frank Hanly, the National Prohibition party's presidential candidate in 1916. Mellett worked there from December 1915 to March 1917. Late in 1917, Mellett became general manager of the *Columbus Ledger*, a morning daily founded in 1915 by Paul Poynter with financial backing by prominent local Democrats to combat the dominant *Columbus Evening Republican*; Mellett stayed until July 1923, becoming publisher and acquiring more than half the stock by selling out when it became apparent the paper would fail.

At the urging of his boyhood friend, Wendell Willkie, Mellett moved to Akron, Ohio, where Willkie was practicing law, and sold advertising for the *Akron Press*, a dead-end job that frustrated him. He met James Cox at a state press meeting and accepted his invitation to publish the *Canton Daily News*. Canton was saddled with apathy that permitted organized crime to run rampant while police accepted payoffs. Mellett did his best to expose the situation and rally the public, publishing 243 local editorials, a third of them about law enforcement issues, between October 1925 and July 1926. The campaign ended on 16 July when, after parking his car at home, Mellett was shot to death by a hired thug. Five men, including a city detective and the police chief, were convicted; the chief was found innocent in a second trial. The case created a national furor and was reported for five days on the front page of the *New York Times*.

BIBLIOGRAPHY:

B. NYT 17 July 1926; Glenn A. Himebaugh, ''Donald Ring Mellett, Journalist: The Shaping of a Martyr,'' Ph.D. diss., Southern Illinois Univ., 1978; John Bartlow Martin, ''Murder of a Journalist,'' *Harper's*, September 1946; Boyden Sparkes, ''Jungle Days in Journalism,'' *World's Work*, December 1926.

GLENN A. HIMEBAUGH

MENCKEN, HENRY LOUIS (b. 12 September 1880; d. 29 January 1956), newspaper journalist, magazine editor, and an iconoclastic critic and essayist, had a strong influence on American thought and letters between 1910 and the middle 1930s. In often savage language he satirized public figures and the pet beliefs of what he called ''boobus Americans'' during the era following World War I. As a self-taught linguist he also won renown for his research and analysis embodied in *The American Language*, published in several editions between 1919 and 1963.

Mencken was born in Baltimore, Maryland, the eldest son of August Mencken, a cigar maker, and Anna Margaret Abhau Mencken, the daughter of European emigrants. Three other children were to follow: two brothers, August Jr., and Charles, who both became engineers; and a sister, Gertrude. Mencken's paternal grandfather, Burkhardt Mencken, a native of Saxony, was also a cigar maker, a trade the family expected young Henry to follow.

After graduation from Baltimore Polytechnic, a public high school, as class valedictorian in 1896, Mencken deferred to his father's wishes and went to work in the family cigar factory. But only a few months after his father's death in 1899, the youth pursued his ambition to become a journalist, joining the *Baltimore Morning Herald* as the youngest reporter on the news staff. After stints as police and political reporter, he became Sunday and city editor respectively.

On the *Evening Herald*, which replaced the morning newspaper in 1904, Mencken was soon promoted from city editor to managing editor, but a financial crisis forced the paper to close in 1906. After serving as news editor of the *Evening News* for a brief period, Mencken joined the *Baltimore Sun* as Sunday editor, an association that was to last, with only occasional interruptions, for the rest of his life. He wrote editorials and columns, covered political conventions, and during 1916–17 served as war correspondent in Germany.

While pursuing a newspaper career, Mencken was also cultivating a growing literary interest. As a member of the Saturday Night Club, which met to play classical music, talk, and drink beer, he made new literary friends. He contributed verse, articles, and short stories to popular magazines. In 1908 he became book reviewer for *Smart Set*, a New York literary monthly. As coeditor of that magazine from 1914 to 1923 with George Jean Nathan, a New York drama critic, Mencken gained a following among intellectuals and writers. His collaboration with Nathan continued during the early years of the *American Mercury*, which they founded in 1924 and which Mencken edited until 1933. One biographer notes that Mencken is best known for the aggressive iconoclasm of his editorial policies in these magazines, especially during the decade following World War I, exhibiting a savagely satirical reaction against the blunders and imperfections of democracy and American culture.

Upon America's entry into the war, Mencken's pro-German sentiments brought trouble for his newspaper career. Upon his return from Germany as war correspondent in 1917, he became the subject of much personal harassment, and the *Sun* gave him no further assignments. He immediately launched into research for *The American Language* (1919), which helped to establish him as an agent of literary revolt, and the first of his series of *Prejudices* (1919), which helped to establish him as a mentor to many young intellectuals. In 1919 Mencken also resumed his formal connection with the Sunpapers, this time as editorial adviser to the publisher and weekly contributor to the editorial page of the *Evening Sun*.

Mencken's editorial column, "The Free Lance," became one of the best read features in the *Sun*. The column dealt with everything from politics to new trends in writing and from the deplorable sewage system to the barbarous condition of the national culture. During this period, one critic has noted, Mencken was offering what the times needed—a clearinghouse for the cynicism and discontents of the postwar years.

All this changed, however, with the Great Depression of the 1930s. Mencken continued to write, railing against the New Deal politics of Franklin D. Roosevelt, but he was no longer being listened to. In retrospect, his criticism appears to be highly perceptive, but the tone of his writing was out of touch with the worsening financial depression, and his pro-German views grew increasingly unpopular with the rising tide of Hitlerism and the threat of war in Europe.

One blow after another came to Mencken during the 1930s. With the onset of the depression, the *Mercury* began to falter, and it was abandoned by Mencken in 1933. He had married Sarah Powell Haardt, a promising novelist and short story writer, on 27 August 1930 in Baltimore. His marriage surprised friends, both because Mencken was fifty years old and because he had railed against the institution of marriage more than a decade earlier in an ironically titled treatise, *In Defense of Women*. Mrs. Mencken died just five years later, and though she had been gravely ill when they were married, it was a cruel blow to Mencken. Another blow came from literary critics. His *Treatise on Right and Wrong* (1934) received bad reviews. Mencken's national reputation was clearly entering an eclipse.

Despite such personal and professional setbacks, Mencken continued to write. He tapped a new lode of his personality in a series of reminiscent sketches for the *New Yorker* that were later collected in three volumes of autobiography, *Happy Days* (1940), *Newspaper Days* (1941), and *Heathen Days* (1943). Mencken's last political assignment was to cover the national presidential conventions in 1948. Shortly afterward, on the evening of 23 November 1948, he suffered a massive stroke and cerebral hemorrhage which impaired his memory and speech to the point he could no longe read or write. He died seven years later at the age of seventy-five in his sleep, apparently from coronary occlusion.

BIBLIOGRAPHY:

B. DAB Supp. 6, 443–447; NYT 30 January 1956; Charles Angoff, *H. L. Mencken: A Portrait from Memory* (New York, 1956); Carl Bode, *Mencken* (Carbondale, Ill., 1969); George H. Douglas, *H. L. Mencken: Critic of American Life* (Hamden, Conn., 1978); William Manchester, *Disturber of the Peace: The Life of H. L. Mencken* (New York, 1950); Douglas C. Stenerson, *H. L. Mencken: Iconoclast from Baltimore* (Chicago, 1971).

HARRY W. STONECIPHER

METCALF, JAMES MARCUS (b. 11 May 1927; d. 8 March 1977) produced for WWL-TV, the CBS affiliate in New Orleans, a highly regarded thirty-minute artistic feature program entitled "Sunday Journal" from 1973 until his death. In 1976 he won a George Foster Peabody Award for one of his programs. Metcalf also wrote four books of poetry, much of which became a substantial part of "Sunday Journal."

Metcalf was the son of James Henderson Metcalf, an inventor and oil field speculator, and Edna Eugene Metcalf, a part-time nurse. He was born in Burkburnett, Texas, but was raised in Eastland. After entering the Army Air Corps in 1942, he served in Europe and participated in the Normandy invasion. On 11 December 1946 Metcalf married Mary Ann Jones in Ranger, Texas. Three years later he received a bachelor of arts degree in speech and dramatics from North Texas State in Denton, Texas.

After one year of teaching high school English in La Marque, Texas, Metcalf began his broadcasting career in 1950 as station announcer for KTLW radio in Texas City, Texas. From 1951 to 1953 he served as station announcer and newsman for KABC radio in San Antonio, Texas. From 1953 to 1966 Metcalf worked as a news broadcaster for WOIA-TV in San Antonio except for a two-year period from 1959 to 1961 when he worked as news director for KRGV-TV in Weslaco, Texas. Beginning in 1961, Metcalf produced and wrote a show which may have been the forerunner of the award-winning "Sunday Journal." "Early Evening Report" was a thirty-minute interview program which garnered enough audience support that by 1963 it was revamped into a sixty-minute news-talk show.

In May 1966 Metcalf came to WWL-TV in New Orleans as newsman and news anchor. In 1972 he began writing and producing ''Jim Metcalf's Scrapbook'' a unique two- or three-minute segment within the news broadcast that combined news and aesthetics. The positive audience response to ''Scrapbook'' essentially ended Metcalf's career as a news anchor when in 1973 he wrote and produced his first ''Sunday Journal,'' a thirty-minute program about Louisiana, people, and nature.

Metcalf brought an array of talents to the program. The combination of proven journalistic skills with poetry and music (Metcalf was also an accomplished musician) helped make the show such a local success that it competed, and often won, against network programming during prime time. (Although the time slot varied, the show was broadcast primarily at 6:30 P.M. or 9:30 P.M. on Sundays.)

One key element of the show's consistently high rating was Metcalf's ability to rewrite poems, or write original ones, to suit the televised format. The result was often a visual poem which painted the moods of people and places. Unlike the more traditional topical human interest programs, ''Sunday Journal'' was the interweaving of information and art. No subject was too obscure. In 1976 Metcalf won the George Foster Peabody Award for a story about Holy Thursday in the small town of Lacombe, Louisiana.

Four books of Metcalf's poems were printed: *Jim Metcalf's Journal* (1974), *In Some Quiet Place* (1975), *Please to Begin* (1976), and *Follow Another Star* (1979). Although Metcalf's work brought him acclaim within the broadcasting industry and with the public, he avoided public attention and led a quiet life. At the time of his death he had been married for thirty-one years and had four children, two boys and two girls. In March 1977 he died in New Orleans of lymphoid cancer.

BIBLIOGRAPHY:

B. *New Orleans Times-Picayune*, 9 March 1977; and *New Orleans States-Item*, 9 March 1977.

LLOYD CHIASSON

MEYER, EUGENE ISAAC (b. 31 October 1875; d. 17 July 1959) was a financier and newspaper publisher. He enjoyed a long and distinguished career in banking, public service, and publishing. He purchased the *Washington Post* and built it into a respected and influential independent newspaper.

Meyer was born in Los Angeles, California, to a well-to-do Alsatian-French immigrant, Eugene Meyer, and his German-English wife, Harriet Newmark Meyer. His father, a Jewish merchant, had emigrated from France by himself when he was sixteen years old, settled in Los Angeles, and eventually engaged in commercial banking in San Francisco and New York.

Young Eugene was educated in the public school system of San Francisco. He went to the University of California for a year (1892–93), transferred to Yale, and graduated in 1895 at nineteen with a B.A. degree. After working for a year in his father's banking firm, he studied languages, international finance, and foreign banking in the firms of his father's relatives in Paris, London, Berlin, and Frankfurt.

When he returned to America he worked for a time in his father's banking firm and in the New York offices of Lazard Freres as a clerk. He opened his own banking house in 1901, Eugene Meyer, Jr., and Company. He bought a seat on the New York Stock Exchange in 1901 at the age of twenty-six. His investment activity was in railroads, oil, copper, and chemicals. He also became director of a growing number of corporations in his first few years of business.

On 12 February 1910 Meyer married Agnes Elizabeth Ernst in a Lutheran ceremony. Their marriage was vibrant and at times boisterous and rocky. Agnes, like her husband, was strong-willed, full of opinions about social and political issues, and eager to express them. The Meyers had five children: Florence (Mrs. Oscar Homolka), Elizabeth (Mrs. Pare Lorentz), Eugene III, Katharine (Mrs. Philip Graham), and Ruth.

In 1917 Meyer accepted an invitation to go to Washington to serve as adviser on nonferrous metals to the Council of National Defense. He held many important governmental assignments through 1933 with only a few interruptions. He was special assistant to the secretary of war (1918); member of the War Finance Corporation (1918), and managing director of the corporation (1919, 1921, 1925); Federal Farm Loan commissioner (1927); governor of the Federal Reserve Board (1930–33); and first chairman of the Reconstruction Finance Corporation (1932).

In 1933 Meyer purchased the *Washington Post*, one of five Washington dailies, at auction for $825,000. The newspaper was near bankruptcy. When he purchased the *Post*, rumors circulated that his major interest in the newspaper was to further the prospects of the Republican party. The newspaper had been losing $1 million a year for some time before Meyer's purchase. The paper's printing plant was in shambles, and its editorial reputation was a disaster. Very possibly, its Associated Press franchise, exclusive in the morning field, was the most valuable of the *Post*'s assets.

Under Meyer's leadership the newspaper's circulation went up 173 percent within eight years, and more than tripled its circulation by 1946. Its advertising income enjoyed similar increases, going up 111 percent within eight years, and nearly tripling by 1946. The newspaper was editorially independent, and developed vigorous editorial and op-ed pages, in the main supporting the Roosevelt administration's foreign policy, but criticizing many of its other policies and programs. Meyer took strong exception to Roosevelt's effort to "pack" the Supreme Court of the United States.

Meyer created a national news staff. A new typeface was selected to give the paper a more contemporary, cleaner look. Meyer brought columnists of stature to the *Post*, including Walter Lippmann, Dorothy Thompson, and eventually Drew Pearson (qq.v.). The paper added reviews of books, art, theater, movies, and music. It expanded its coverage of sports.

In 1946 he relinquished his position as editor and publisher to return to limited governmental service. He turned over operations of the newspaper to his son-

in-law, Philip Graham (q.v.). On the occasion of Philip Graham's suicide in 1963, his wife Katharine Meyer Graham became publisher and controlling owner.
BIBLIOGRAPHY:

B. NYT 18 July 1959; Chalmers M. Roberts, *The Washington Post* (Boston, 1977).

J. DOUGLAS TARPLEY

MICKELSON, SIG (b. 24 May 1913) was the first of only a select few who can say they held the prestigious post of president of CBS News. He has been a dominant figure in the growth of television news, and a leading spokesman in its evolution. He is credited with bringing Walter Cronkite (q.v.) to millions of CBS viewers, and establishing the ''anchorman'' concept in coverage of presidential elections. He has authored two books, served as president of Radio Free Europe and Radio Liberty, received a master's degree from the University of Minnesota, and held the position of director of the Medill School of Journalism at Northwestern University. Mickelson was a founder and past president of the Radio Television News Directors Association, and was bestowed that group's 1983 Distinguished Service Award for ''outstanding achievement in broadcast journalism.''

Mickelson's roots center in the Upper Midwest. He was born to Olaf Mickelson and Harriet Reinholdson Mickelson in Clinton, Minnesota. His parents moved to Sioux Falls, South Dakota, where he attended public school and, in 1934, graduated from Augustana College. He began his news career while still in school, working as a part-time reporter for the *Sioux Falls Argus Leader* and as a newscaster for KSOO radio. After graduation he stayed with the newspaper as a full-time reporter-editor until 1937, when he began his graduate studies. He also taught in Minnesota's School of Journalism. From 1939 through 1946 he held successive teaching positions at Louisiana State University, the University of Kansas, and again at the University of Minnesota.

In 1943, while still teaching, Mickelson joined WCCO, the CBS-owned station in Minneapolis, as a consultant in establishing a news department. During his six years at the station he became director of news and special events, and eventually director of public affairs and production manager. CBS transferred him to New York, where he was named director of the division of discussion in early 1950. The following year he was moved to director of news and public affairs for CBS television, and then, in 1954, was promoted to vice president of CBS and general manager of CBS News.

Mickelson's influence on CBS News became most evident in October 1959 when he was named by then CBS head, Dr. Frank Stanton (q.v.), to the CBS News presidency. Under his leadership, news, public affairs, and sports programming grew in importance, including ''CBS Reports,'' ''The Twentieth Century,'' and ''Face the Nation,'' along with major league baseball and football, and religious programs. However, Mickelson would hold his post for only a year and a half before resigning and moving to an executive broadcast position with Time Inc. The ratings for CBS's 1960 presidential election coverage were not good, and may have led to his downfall at the network.

Mickelson stayed with Time throughout the 1960s, serving as a vice president and director of overseas development in New York. Mickelson and the former Maybelle Brown were married in 1940. They have two children, Karen Ann and Alan.

The Encyclopaedia Britannica Educational Corporation attracted Mickelson in 1970, electing him to the position of vice president, international and television. He also served as chairman of the board of trustees of the International Broadcast Institute. Mickelson moved back to teaching, and administered Northwestern's journalism program before taking over the "often embattled" Radio Free Europe and Radio Liberty in 1975. The public propaganda agencies based in Munich, broadcasting to Soviet-block countries, were "removed from dependency on the Central Intelligence Agency in 1971." The CIA once again became an issue in 1977, and Mickelson was a focal point of the controversy. His successor as CBS News president, Richard Salant (q.v.), disclosed that the network, during the 1950s and early 1960s, "worked closely" with the clandestine agency. Mickelson, who held the top post at the time, admitted to "sharing information" with the CIA, a policy that apparently had the "blessings" of CBS chairman William Paley (q.v.). Salant ended the arrangement, but he and Mickelson "defended it as a by-product of the Cold War" (Brown, 1977).

Mickelson retired from broadcasting in 1978, moved to California, and returned to teaching. He became executive director of the Center for Communications at San Diego State University. Within a few months he had joined forces with his old friend Walter Cronkite in developing a daily current events national television program to be fed by satellite to high school students. They formed a production company, Satellite Education Services, of which Mickelson became vice president and general manager.

In April 1981 Mickelson was appointed Hoover Research Fellow at Stanford University, where he would research and write *America's Other Voice* (1983) on his experiences with Radio Free Europe and Radio Liberty.

BIBLIOGRAPHY:

A. *America's Other Voice: The Story of Radio Free Europe and Radio Liberty* (New York, 1983); *The Electric Mirror: Politics in an Age of Television* (New York, 1972).

B. Les Brown, "Ex-CBS News Chief Tells of Sharing Information With C.I.A. in '50's," NYT 28 May 1977.

DAVID M. GUERRA

MILLER, FRANK (b. 28 March 1925; d. 17 February 1983) was editorial cartoonist for the *Des Moines Register*. His work usually appeared at the top of the front page, and his subjects ranged from politics to wry and gentle humor about Iowa life. Miller won a Pulitzer Prize in 1963 for a cartoon showing only a fragment of Earth remaining, with the caption. "I said—we sure settled that dispute, didn't we?"

Newsweek magazine called Miller's cartoon style "an affecting mix of homespun humor and populist outrage." One 1977 cartoon noted that many Iowa farm women were taking jobs in town or becoming more involved in community activities. The drawing showed one hog talking to another, saying, "The last thing this farm needs is feminism." During the 1960s and 1970s Miller followed civil rights issues and the Vietnam War closely. A 1964 cartoon showed a white sheriff standing on the back of a black man. The sheriff was holding a civil rights worker by the collar. "Caught him trespassin' on private property," the caption read.

Miller was born in Kansas City, Missouri, where his father was an artist for the *Kansas City Star*. The younger Miller studied art at the University of Kansas and at the Kansas City Art Institute. He worked for two years as an editorial artist for the *Star* after serving with the U.S. Third Army in World War II in Europe. He was recalled to duty in the Korean War with the U.S. Seventh Division Artillery, where he also drew for Pacific *Stars and Stripes*.

In November 1951 *Register* editor Kenneth MacDonald wrote Miller about a possible job. Karl Mattern, an artist and Miller's former teacher, had recommended him. The letter reached Miller in San Francisco, just as he was about to ship out for Korea, but he replied to MacDonald and sketched a GI on the letter with the accompanying words, "Damn—An I always did like Des Moines."

Miller joined the *Register* staff eighteen months later, on 3 August 1953. Front-page editorial cartooning had already been established on the paper by Jay N. "Ding" Darling (q.v.). Both cartoonists often drew political subjects, but Miller tended to avoid siding with a politician individually. Miller's colleague, political editor James Flansberg, said the cartoonist never expressed much interest in meeting the great and near-great—except for Eugene McCarthy. Miller was a student of the life of Abraham Lincoln and drew a portrait of him for the paper every 12 February, Lincoln's birthday. Other favorites of Miller were the New York Yankees, along with a series of recurring themes in his cartoons—Old Man Winter, farm animals chatting about politics or other wordly affairs, Iowans from many walks of life, and a number of national and international figures. Miller's style ranged from reverent drawings of Pope John Paul II on his visit to Iowa in 1979 to darker ink and sharper-lined cartoons of Richard M. Nixon.

Miller also drew landscape watercolors of Iowa scenes, and they were displayed in a Des Moines gallery. His love for Iowa was clear in delicately drawn lines of rolling farm land, barns, and silos. Miller enjoyed sailing on reservoirs near Des Moines and on Lake Superior. He spent time, also, trying to help alcoholics, for he was a recovered alcoholic himself. Dr. Stanley Haugland, director of a Des Moines alcoholism treatment program, said Miller was "sensitive to other people . . . I believe he was a great man who walked with humility."

Miller's cartoons were syndicated in fifty other newspapers at the time of his death. He had collapsed in the parking lot of a shopping mall and was prounounced dead of a heart attack at a hospital about an hour later. Miller was survived by his wife, Catherine, and two daughters, Melissa and Melinda, a staff artist for the *Des Moines Register*.

BIBLIOGRAPHY:

B. *Des Moines Register*, 18, 19, and 20 February 1983; *Newsweek*, 23 February 1983; *Frank Miller, Cartoons as Commentary: Three Decades at "The Register"* (Des Moines, Iowa, 1983).

JAMES BOW

MILLER, WEBB (b. 10 February 1892; d. 7 May 1940) was a foreign correspondent for most of his twenty-eight years as a journalist until his accidental death in the wartime blackout of London.

He was born on a farm near Pokagon, a small town in southwest Michigan, the son of Jacob H. and Charlotte Miller, one of five children. When not in school, he helped his father work the fields of a tenant farm. His upbringing included a ten-mile roundtrip walk to school and a self-imposed vegetarianism, which he abandoned only after he began his newspaper career. After graduation from Dowagiac (Michigan) High School, he worked briefly as an excursion boat pilot on a nearby lake, and taught eight grades at a one-room school for a year. His ambition to enter newspapering led him in 1912 to use a vactioning Chicagoan as an intermediary to land—without experience in journalism or knowledge of the Windy City—a job as a cub reporter on the *Chicago American*.

He progressed from legman to court reporter to police reporter (he had changed his given name of "Webster" to "Webb" to build a new self-identity), covering executions with the competitive and crafty Chicago press corps which included, among others, the legendary Ben Hecht (q.v.). He became a focal point of a story when he was kidnapped while trying to interview salt millionaire Mark Morton, whose daughter had eloped. Like many other reporters of the day without a college background, he learned by experience and by reading voraciously. When Pancho Villa raided Columbus, New Mexico, in 1916, he was ready to strike out alone. Miller left the security of a reporter's salary and a growing reputation to work as a free-lance covering the Mexican expedition led by General John Pershing. He joined the company of reporters like Walter Noble Burns and Floyd Gibbons (q.v.), and found new skill, daring, and zeal in following the elusive Villa through the harsh Mexican mountains.

A job with the United Press Association followed his solid work as a war correspondent, first in Chicago, then in Washington. When World War I broke out, he was posted to London. He was resourceful, not only in reporting and writing but in developing lines of communication that enabled him and other UP reporters to score many beats on other correspondents. The end of the war found him exhausted and disillusioned, but seasoned, as a foreign correspondent. In 1920 he married Marie Alston of London and became Paris bureau chief for

UP, launching twenty years of peripatetic service in what may have been the golden age of foreign correspondents. After five years in Paris, he moved to London as assistant to Ed L. Keen, UP's general European news manager.

Before his career ended, he had logged an estimated 400,000 miles practicing his profession. He watched the American Army of Occupation move into Germany, and reported the Sein Fein uprisings in Ireland. In 1925 he was in Morocco to cover the Riff revolts. A perilous 12,000-mile air journey in 1930 brought him to India to report the Gandhi-led civil disobedience, riots, and bloodshed. He joined the Italian army in Ethiopia in 1935, and sat atop a sandbag parapet when the invasion officially began. Messages relayed by runners and telegraph gave Miller and UP a clear beat on the actual launching of hostilities.

His next conflict was the Spanish civil war, and he moved from there to the Munich conference involving Hitler, Mussolini, Chamberlain, and Daladier. He had been named in 1938 as UP's general European manager, and is credited with helping to develop lines of communication that enabled UP to cover the Nazi blitzkrieg through the Low Countries, with reports that sometimes beat competitors by three hours. After a brief tour of the Finish-Russian front he returned to cover the debates over Chamberlain's policies in 1940. He was preparing to join the British forces in Norway when, after a night debate in Parliament, he apparently fell from a moving train while heading for his home in the London suburb of Walton-on-Thames. A coroner ruled his death accidental. His funeral in London was attended by the elite of the European press corps, as well as by U.S. Ambassador Joseph Kennedy. His ashes were returned to his native state for burial near the farm where he grew up. His wife and son Kenneth survived him.

BIBLIOGRAPHY:

A. *I Found No Peace* (New York, 1936).

B. DAB Supp. 2, 457; NYT 9 May 1940.

WALLACE B. EBERHARD

MITCHELL, JOHN, JR. (b. 11 July 1863; d. 1 December 1929), was referred to by the *New York World* as "one of the most daring and vigorous Negro editors" of his time.

An example of Mitchell's courage was displayed in 1887. As editor of the *Richmond* (Virginia) *Planet*, he launched a vicious editorial campaign against lynchings in the state. After editorially attacking a mob for the lynching of a black, Richard Walker, in Charlotte County, he received a letter containing a piece of hemp and a warning that the same thing could happen to him unless he remained silent. Mitchell informed his readers that he would not only continue his campaign, but would personally visit the site of Walker's lynching. Armed with a brace of Smith and Wesson revolvers and the Bible, Mitchell mounted a mule, rode bareback to Charlotte County, rested in the shade under the tree where Walker's lynching took place, returned to his office in Richmond, and wrote another anti-lynching editorial.

Mitchell was born of slave parents in Henrico County, Virginia. His father was a coachman and his mother a seamstress. Following their freedom, they encouraged their son to get an education. He entered Richmond Normal School in 1876 and graduated in 1881, earning several awards for scholarship. The young Mitchell displayed talent in art but chose to become a schoolteacher. For three years he taught in the public school systems of Fredericksburg and Richmond. After losing his teaching position, for protesting against the treatment of black teachers in the system, Mitchell found himself on the path of a career in journalism.

Mitchell had become a correspondent for the *New York Freeman* in 1883 while teaching. After the loss of his teaching job, he gained some experience as a reporter for the *Freeman* and the *Richmond Planet*, a paper that had been founded by thirteen former slaves in 1882. On 5 December 1884 Mitchell was appointed editor of the paper. Under his leadership, within two-years the *Planet* was transformed from a monthly tabloid into a full-sized weekly with a circulation of over 13,000. By 1887 the paper was classified as one of the largest-circulation black newspapers in the South.

Unafraid to speak, or write, his thoughts, Mitchell challenged Jim Crow laws in the South and was an articulate voice calling for an end to lynchings, discrimination, and prejudice in the United States. He also had his views on Indian affairs in the United States. While some Americans cheered at the death of Sitting Bull in 1890, Mitchell gave credit to the Sioux chief who had outsmarted George A. Custer.

Mitchell opposed America's expansionist policies following the Spanish-American War. He challenged the motives of the U.S. government in the Philippines, Cuba, and Hawaii. He expressed concern for the "colored" people in these areas. Mitchell accused the United States of hypocrisy and believed the money spent on these ventures, under disguise of freeing the oppressed, could well be used at home to help black citizens overcome their economic and social oppression. However, despite his objections to America's expansionist policies, Mitchell remained loyal to the Republican party and supported William McKinley in the 1900 presidential campaign.

Mitchell's crusade for justice for his race put him in the forefront of a nonviolent protest against segregated seating on public transportation in Richmond during the early 1900s. This eight-month economic boycott resulted in the Virginia Passenger and Power Company being placed in the hands of a receiver appointed by the court. For a short time thereafter, blacks in Richmond enjoyed the privilege of being able to ride unsegregated public transportation.

Elected vice president of the Colored Press Association in 1891, Mitchell was also active in other areas, some not directly connected to his duties as editor of the *Planet*. He was elected to the Richmond city council in May of 1890. Probably his greatest achievement outside the realm of journalism took place on 8 May 1903 when he established the Mechanics Savings Bank in Richmond. This venture led to his becoming the first black member of the American Bankers Association.

However, in 1923, when all looked well for the bank, things began to fall apart. Mitchell was charged with making false entries concerning $83,000. He was later charged and convicted. But in November the Virginia Court of Appeals unanimously ruled that the error was due to an auditor's mistake, and Mitchell was cleared of all charges. The ordeal had taken its toll on Mitchell's health. He became fragile and began to lose weight, but he managed to keep the *Planet* alive and growing and continued as editor until November 1929. A bachelor all of his life, Mitchell died in December of a heart attack. In 1938 the *Planet* was merged with the *Richmond Afro-American*.

BIBLIOGRAPHY:

B. Willard B. Gatewood, "A Negro Editor on Imperialism: John Mitchell, 1898–1901," *Journalism Quarterly*, Spring 1972; I. Garland Penn, *The Afro-American Press and Its Editors* (New York, 1969); "John Mitchell," *Quill*, May 1977; Clay Perry, "John Mitchell, Virginia's Journalist of Reform," *Journalism History*, Winter 1977–78.

J. WILLIAM SNORGRASS

MORGAN, EDWARD PADDOCK (b. 23 June 1910) was a leading radio and television news reporter for over thirty years and, as a radio news commentator, long outlasted other such journalists by continuing into the late 1960s his daily quarter-hour network program of news and commentary, "Edward P. Morgan and the News." Before becoming a broadcast journalist, Morgan had learned his profession in a series of print media positions, dating from the 1930s. He covered firsthand the major news events of four decades bridging several distinct historical eras—from the death of Leon Trotsky to the death of John F. Kennedy.

The prime of Morgan's career revolved around his twelve-year tenure as an ABC news commentator, during which time he was responsible for the Monday through Friday afternoon program sponsored by the AFL-CIO. Thus, his work has become associated with interest in labor issues, although Morgan could not accurately be called a labor reporter. He was never employed by the labor movement, and although in general political and economic philosophy his and organized labor's views were often akin, he frequently criticized labor and its policies or its positions on major public issues.

Morgan's first taste of journalism came during his undergraduate days (1928–32) at Whitman College (Walla Walla, Washington), where he worked as a reporter and editor for the school's weekly student newspaper, the *Pioneer*. He also serveed as campus correspondent for the *Spokane Spokesman-Review*. Following his graduation in 1932, Morgan worked for a half year as an unpaid sports writer for the *Seattle Star*. He then began receiving $15 a week and moved into a slot as a police reporter and as assistant city editor (1933–34).

Morgan's first professional post with national scope came in 1934, when he began as a correspondent for the United Press. For the next nine years, he reported from San Francisco, Los Angeles, Portland, Honolulu—where his first radio broadcast, describing a major volcanic eruption, originated from KGU—and Mexico City, where he scooped the attempted, and later the successful, assassination of Leon Trotsky in 1940.

During World War II Morgan became a foreign service roving reporter for the *Chicago Daily News* (1943–46). He covered many major events including the American liberation of Rome in 1944 and the German V–2 attacks on London during 1944–45. After the war (1946–48), Morgan took a post as an associate editor and roving foreign correspondent for *Collier's* magazine and did news broadcasts from Europe for CBS. Then he worked for two years (1948–50) as a free-lance journalist based in Paris.

Morgan returned to the United States in 1950 and spent the first half of that decade working in various positions for CBS News—in 1950 with Edward R. Murrow (q.v.) on "This I Believe" at WCAU in Philadelphia, from 1951 to 1954 as a correspondent, and during 1954–55 as director of news for radio and television.

But soon Morgan went back to the microphone, this time for ABC, beginning his long association with the AFL-CIO–sponsored "Edward P. Morgan and the News" (1955–67). During these dozen years, his home base was Washington, D.C., but he covered many major events around the world—with then Vice President Nixon in Africa and the Soviet Union, and with President Eisenhower on his 1959 goodwill tour of eleven nations in Africa, Asia, and Europe. Morgan began to appear frequently on ABC television news and public affairs programming during the 1960s. With Howard K. Smith (q.v.), he co-anchored the 1964 political convention coverage.

From 1967 to 1969 Morgan served as chief correspondent for the Public Broadcasting Laboratory, and in 1969 he returned to ABC News to serve as a correspondent and to do commentary. Since 1975 he has worked as a free-lancer and has broadcast a series of radio commentaries, "In the Public Interest," for the Fund for Peace, heard on some 400 stations. He lives in McLean, Virginia.

Morgan was born on 23 June 1910 in Walla Walla, Washington. His father, Arthur Henry Morgan, was a banker and businessman. His mother, Pansy Eledice Paddock Morgan, was the daughter of a prominent clergyman. After graduation from the Intermountain Institute, a private secondary school in Weiser, Idaho, Morgan entered Whitman College in 1928 as a premedical student. He changed his major to political science and graduated cum laude, and with a Phi Beta Kappa key. For a time he pursued graduate studies in journalism and political science at the University of Washington (1932–33).

On 31 December 1937 Morgan married Jane Stolle. The couple had one child. They divorced in November 1945. Morgan married again, on 18 July 1960, to Katherine Burden Sohier, who had two daughters by her previous husband.

Morgan has received many professional honors for news broadcasting, including a Peabody Award (1956), and Alfred I. duPont and Headliner awards (both 1960).

BIBLIOGRAPHY:
B. *Printer's Ink*, 24 February 1961; *Time*, 29 April 1957; James Walter Wesolowski, "A Quantitative Analysis of Commentary on Labor Issues of 1958 by Edward P. Morgan," M.S. thesis, Univ. of Wisconsin, 1962.

JAMES WESOLOWSKI

MOSSELL, GERTRUDE BUSTILL, or **MOSSELL, N. F.** (b. 3 July 1855; d. 21 January 1948) was well known for her columns offering advice on woman suffrage and civil rights. She was a correspondent and editor for several black publications, and frequently contributed to white-owned newspapers. Mossell was one of the best-known black women journalists of the nineteenth century. Her essays, poems, and short stories were also featured in newspapers. She was the author of two black American history books. In addition to her contributions as a writer, her career included positions in the public school system, and a job as a fund raiser. She was very active in women's clubs.

Gertrude Bustill was born in Philadelphia, Pennsylvania, before emancipation. However, her parents, Charles H. and Emily Robinson were free blacks. As a free citizen Gertrude attended the Institute for Colored Youth and the Robert Vaux Consolidated Grammar School in Philadelphia. Bishop Henry McNeal, a black editor, recognized her literary talent while she was in grammar school. He helped launch her newspaper career by publishing her valedictorian address in the *Christian Recorder* around 1872. Shortly thereafter Gertrude Robinson became a regular correspondent for the newspaper.

Robinson began teaching public school immediately after graduating from grammar school. She started teaching in Philadelphia and later taught in New Jersey, then Kentucky. She acknowledged journalism as a profession following seven years of teaching. At age twenty-five Robinson became women's department editor for two newspapers, the *New York Freeman* and *Philadelphia Echo*. In 1885 she initiated the women's column for the *New York Age*. Her first *Age* article called upon readers to support woman suffrage. Women's columns edited by Robinson also appeared in the *Indianapolis World* and the *Woman's Era*. From 1880 to 1887 she also wrote regularly for three Philadelphia newspapers: the *Times*, *Press*, and *Inquirer*. By 1891 she was contributing articles to the *Indianapolis Freeman*, *Richmond Rankin Institute*, and *Our Women and Children* magazine.

She married Nathaniel F. Mossell, a Philadelphia physician, in 1893. Shortly after her marriage she began signing her columns Mrs. N. F. Mossell or N. F. Mossell. The Mossells had two children, Mazie and Florence. Mrs. Mossell's book *The Work of the Afro American Woman* (1894) highlights the contributions of black women in a number of fields. In 1895 she coordinated a Philadelphia fund-raising project for the Frederick Douglass Hospital. Her efforts brought in $30,000. Her second book, a fictitious account entitled *Little Dansie's One Day at Sabbath School*, appeared in 1902. During that same period, Mrs. Mossell coedited the *Lincoln Alumni Magazine*, a publication founded by her husband. Articles carrying her byline were also featured in the *A.M.E. Church Review*.

Mossell was interested in every facet of the newspaper business. She never failed to offer sound advice to black publishers whenever she was given the opportunity. She challenged them to upgrade newspaper content, and to improve circulation by using newsboys to distribute papers. During her lifetime she founded two organizations: the Bustill Family Association, and the Philadelphia branch of the National Afro American Council. At age ninety-two, she died following a three-month illness.

BIBLIOGRAPHY:

A. "My Mother," *New York Freeman*, March 1886.

B. DANB, 457, NYT 25 January 1948; Penelope L. Bullock, "After Reconstruction General Periodicals," *The Afro American Periodical Press* (Baton Rouge, 1981); Henry Davenport Northrop, Joseph R. Gay, and I. Garland Penn, "Noted Afro American Women and Their Achievements," *The College of Life* (New York, 1893); I. Garland Penn, *The Afro American Press and Its Editors* (New York, 1891).

NORA HALL

MOWRER, EDGAR ANSEL (b. 8 March 1892; d. 2 March 1977), a columnist, foreign correspondent, and lecturer whose career spanned both World Wars, had the distinction of being expelled from Germany, Italy, and Russia.

He was born in Bloomington, Illinois, the younger of two sons of businessman Rufus Mowrer and his wife, Nell Scott Mowrer. While attending Hyde Park High School in Chicago, he was active in sports and edited the school annual. Mowrer attended the University of Chicago, but went to Paris to enroll at the Sorbonne. Upon his return to the United States, he entered the University of Michigan and was graduated with a B.A. in 1913.

After graduation he returned to Paris to pursue a literary career, but at the outbreak of World War I he was employed by the Paris bureau of the *Chicago Daily News*. Mowrer's life became one of adventure as he covered battles in Belgium, was arrested and deported to England, and arrested again as he returned to Belgium. He always found difficulty in separating reporting from activism. Offered a permanent position by the *Chicago Daily News*, he was sent to Rome in May 1915. During his tenure he met Benito Mussolini, who was then encouraging Italy to support the Allies.

While in Italy he wrote to Lilian Thomas, an English girl he had met five years earlier, and asked her to marry him immediately. They were married in London on 8 February 1916. They lived in Rome until 1923 during which time their daughter, Diana Jane, was born in May 1923. Mrs. Mowrer was born in London and studied at Liverpool University, the Sorbonne, and Sapienza, Rome. She was also a writer and has written about the theater, politics, and life as a war correspondent's wife.

When Italian Fascists began to riot, the Mowrers left for Berlin. From 1923 to 1933 Mowrer was chief of the Berlin bureau and watched Germany's Weimar

Republic commit suicide. During 1932 he won a Pulitzer Prize for best foreign dispatches, which were published as a book entitled *Germany Puts the Clock Back* (1933). It appeared a month before Hitler became chancellor, and German sales were large until the book was banned.

Mowrer was elected president of the Foreign Press Association in 1933 and refused to resign as the Nazis demanded. The *News* decided to transfer him to Tokyo. When the Nazis arrested an Austrian newspaperman, Mowrer offered to resign in exchange for the writer's release. The offer was accepted. Instead of Tokyo, Mowrer was assigned to the Paris bureau to replace his brother, Paul (q.v.), who had been made editor of the newspaper. Mowrer remained in Paris from 1934 until 1940 but spent time covering the early days of the Spanish civil war and visiting the Soviet Union, where he reported on the adoption of the new constitution.

He returned to Washington as a correspondent during 1940–41. From 1942 to 1943 he served as deputy of the U.S. Office of War Information, a position which he resigned because of his anti-Vichy stand. From 1943 to 1969 he was a syndicated columnist and a prodigious writer of magazine articles. Mowrer also served from 1957 to 1969 as North American editor in chief of *Western World*, an international monthly. He was the author of numerous books, the first being *Immortal Italy* (1922), and the last being his autobiography *Triumph and Turmoil* (1968).

Mowrer retired in 1969 and lived near Wonalancet, New Hampshire, where his widow resides. While the couple was vacationing on the Portuguese island of Madeira, Mowrer died in his sleep on 2 March 1977, six days short of his eighty-fifth birthday.

BIBLIOGRAPHY:

B. NYT 4 March 1977; Lilian T. Mowrer, *Journalist's Wife* (New York, 1937).

ADRIAN L. HEADLEY

MOWRER, PAUL SCOTT (b. 14 July 1887; d. 7 April 1971) was born in Bloomington, Illinois. His mother's maiden name became his middle name. He had an early interest in journalism, and at the age of eighteen landed a job on the *Chicago Daily News*. He attended the University of Michigan from 1906 to 1908, but a trip to Europe in 1907 made him impatient to begin his career as a foreign correspondent. Although many young men of his generation harbored dreams of becoming correspondents, few showed the precocity or dedication of Mowrer.

In 1908 he abandoned his academic career and, making use of his contacts at the *Chicago Daily News*, became its Paris correspondent during the years 1907–10. The arrangement was fortuitous: the paper was one of the few with a continuing interest in European affairs and offered the young writer an opportunity to publish his work; for his part, Mowrer was diligent, fair and, although he clearly had good prospects in more conventional careers, dedicated to his craft.

In 1914 the *News* named him a war correspondent and assigned him to French General Headquarters, a post he held until 1918. The years he spent in Europe before the war gave him a perspective on events denied those who arrived after the war was underway. Those who knew him during this period described him as unusually mature and trusted, evidently by both his colleagues and the French military commanders. In 1919 he became, successively, diplomatic correspondent, political analyst, and head of the European service of the *News*. He held his post until 1933.

Although he had established himself as a trusted journalist, his reputation as a skillful analyst of European affairs was not clearly established until the publication of his first nonfiction book, *Balkanized Europe* (1921). In it he argued that the war had not settled the problems of Europe, but rather had set the stage for a further series of contests. His second book, *Our Foreign Affairs* (1924), examined the role of the United States in European politics and was one of the earliest critiques of the emerging isolationist sentiment in this country. This phase of his career received formal recognition when, in 1928, he received the Pulitzer Prize for his work as a foreign correspondent. His European work came to an end in 1933 when the depression caused the *News* to cut back on its overseas coverage. He returned to Chicago in 1933 and became associate editor and, in 1935, editor in chief of the *Chicago Daily News*. In this post he continued his interest in international affairs, and during World War II helped the *News* develop its reputation for political coverage of Europe.

He left the *Chicago Daily News* in 1944 and joined the *New York Post* as European editor for four years beginning in 1945. His autobiographical book, *The House of Europe* (1945), is the best single source for an understanding of his patriotic but internationalist outlook, for his sense of the cultural links between Europe and the United States, and for his opinion of the function of the foreign correspondent.

Mowrer was a practicing poet throughout his adult life. His first book, *Hours of France* (1918), was a collection of his poems, and the first of eleven books of poetry. He and his first wife, Winifred Adams, shared an interest in creative writing. Socially, he was a part of the community of expatriates who lived, wrote, and painted in Paris in the 1920s. In 1933 he married Hadley Richardson, the former wife of Ernest Hemingway. He was particularly productive when, after leaving the *Post*, he and Hadley retired to Tamworth, New Hampshire, where they lived in a country home with a view of Mt. Chocorua.

As a poet Mowrer made no secret of his dislike of obscurity, nor of his love of the muscial quality of the traditional rhythms and rhyme schemes of English poetry. He felt alienated from the revolution Ezra Pound and T. S. Eliot brought about in English poetry. He knew there was a negligible contemporary audience for his poetry, but that he wanted it to be placed on library shelves because he was confident that future generations would rediscover the wonders of English lyric verse.

Although his journalistic work reported some of the darkest days and cruelest events of the century, his poetry was in the service of his joy in friendships, the natural world, and the pleasures of knowing oneself as one grows older. In "True Joys," found in *Twenty-One and Sixty-Five* (1958), he wrote:

> This faith I trow beyond all time's unmaking:
> True joys are free to all men for the taking.

BIBLIOGRAPHY:

B. DLB 29, 256–261; "Mr. Mowrer Remembers," *Time*, 24 September 1945.

ROBERT RUTHERFORD SMITH

MULLEN, FRANK ERNEST (b. 10 August 1896; d. 20 February 1977) was a pioneer in radio and the first full-time farm broadcaster in the United States. He created the "National Farm and Home Hour," the longest-running network program in the history of radio, and became a top executive of the Radio Corporation of America and the National Broadcasting Company.

Mullen was born in Clifton, Kansas, to Frank Everton Mullen, a teacher, lawyer, and county judge, and Nelly Hakes Mullen, who died when Mullen was a child. Mullen got his early schooling near Presho, South Dakota, where he grew up on a homesteaded farm with his father, stepmother Anna Margaret Mullen, brother, three half-sisters, and a half-brother who died in childhood.

He studied forestry at Iowa State College (now University) in 1916, but left to join a World War I overseas forestry regiment in 1917. When he returned to school in 1919 he changed his major to agricultural journalism. Mullen earned his degree in 1922 and in July became the first farm page editor of the *Sioux City Journal* in Iowa. On 25 February 1922 he married Lois V. Coulter, a teacher whose parents were among the early homesteaders of Iowa. They had one son.

On 24 March 1923 Mullen was hired by the *Pennsylvania and Ohio Farmer and Stockman* magazine as its radio editor. He had full-time responsibility for farm news on KDKA radio in Pittsburgh, which only one and one-half years before had made some of the first broadcasts in America. In 1924 he went on the KDKA payroll. While there, he served on the first national radio advertising study group. He had been credited with founding the first agency to sell radio time.

In 1926 Mullen joined the fledgling National Broadcasting Company (NBC) as its director of agriculture at station KFKX in Hastings, Nebraska. Six months later he moved NBC's rural broadcasting operations to KYW in Chicago. There he created the "National Farm and Home Hour," first broadcast on 2 October 1928. It included an unsponsored fifteen-minute segment by the U.S. Department of Agriculture that probably represents the only time a government agency ever controlled part of the news on commercial radio stations. The show aired daily for sixteen years and weekly from 1945 to 1960 for more than 4,700 shows. Mullen also created a dramatic-educational series, "Uncle Sam's Forest Rangers." It ran from 1932 to 1943.

In December 1934 Mullen went to New York as manager of the department of information at NBC's parent company, the Radio Corporation of America (RCA). On 2 August 1940 he was appointed vice president and general manager of NBC and elected to the company's board of directors, where he planned NBC's budding television network. During this time, Mullen and his wife, Lois, were divorced. On 23 January 1940 he married Florence Wilcock, whom he had met in New York when she was the top assistant to David Sarnoff, head of RCA. They had two sons.

Mullen left NBC in 1948 and moved to Los Angeles to become president of the G. A. Richards radio group, which owned stations in Detroit, Cleveland, and Los Angeles. In 1949 he became chairman of the board for the television film company Jerry Fairbanks, Inc.. He formed his own consulting firm—Frank Mullen and Associates—in 1952 and, in 1957, formed a company called Scenic Backgrounds to construct scenery for TV and films.

Mullen was a director of the Izaak Walton League of America, vice president of the American Forestry Association, and a trustee of the Farm Foundation of Chicago. He founded the National Radio Conservation Council and was president of Radio Pioneers in 1950. He earned the National Association of Farm Broadcasters' Meritorious Service Award in 1960.

Mullen retired in 1968, after suffering a stroke when his auto was struck from behind. On 25 March 1975 Mullen entered the Veterans Administration Hospital in Sepulveda, California, with brain damage caused by a fall related to his earlier stroke. He was hospitalized until his death from pneumonia two years later.

BIBLIOGRAPHY:

B. NYT 24 February 1977; John C. Baker, *Farm Broadcasting: The First Sixty Years* (Ames, Iowa, 1981); "Broadcasting's Veterans, Frank E. Mullen, Radio-TV's Foremost Prophet," *Advertiser*, April 1950; Ronald Howard Greenfield, "The National Farm and Home Hour: Voice of Agriculture," M. S. thesis, Univ. of Illinois, 1966; "A Prophet with Honor in His Own Business," *Advertiser*, October 1941.

GORDON BILLINGSLEY

MUNSEY, FRANK ANDREW (b. 21 August 1854; d. 22 December 1925) was a pioneer in the application of industrialism to the world of journalism. Primarily a businessman, he utilized the methods of big busines in managing his publications, founding, buying, modifying, merging, or killing some of the most prestigious newspapers and magazines of his day. Munsey also wrote several novels, established a chain of grocery stores, a bank, a hotel, and several office buildings.

Munsey, the fourth of six children, was born on a farm outside of Mercer, Maine. His father, Andrew Chauncey Munsey, was a farmer and carpenter from Quebec, Canada, who moved to several different farms in the area while Munsey was still a boy. His mother, Mary Jane Merritt Hopkins Munsey, could claim eight Mayflower passengers as ancestors, including John Alden and Priscilla

Mullens. Munsey was educated in public schools around Mercer, and attended Poughkeepsie Business College for a few months in 1881.

In 1882 Munsey arranged a partnership with an Augusta stockbroker and a friend in New York to begin *Golden Argosy*, a youth's magazine. Spending most of his own money for manuscripts, including one by Horatio Alger, Jr., Munsey arrived in New York on 23 September 1882 with $40 in his pocket. When one of his partners backed out of the deal, Munsey decided to publish the magazine himself, the first issue dated 9 December 1882. The first ten years were a terrible struggle for Munsey, who tinkered constantly with his magazine before he found the right formula. Unable to pay for much new material, Munsey began writing his own serials.

He began *Munsey's Illustrated Weekly* on 6 September 1884 as a "party organ" in New York to support the Republican presidential candidate, James G. Blaine, whom he had met in Augusta. The magazine died after the election, and its subscription list was given to *Golden Argosy*. The $8,000 debt it had accumulated was sufficient to require his creditors to keep him going. By May 1887 Munsey was able to pay off all his debts, only to fall $95,000 in debt later that year from a nationwide advertising campaign. He converted *Golden Argosy* into *Argosy*, a magazine for adults, in 1888, and in March 1889 founded *Munsey's Weekly*, a comic paper modeled after *Life*. It failed, and in October 1891 he tried his first newspaper, buying the *New York Star* and publishing it as a tabloid titled the *Daily Continent* from 1 February to 7 June 1891, when he killed it.

In September 1893, $100,000 in debt and in the middle of his fourth and most ambitious serialized novel, *Derringforth*, Munsey reduced the price of *Munsey's* to a dime, advertised heavily, and began his rise to success. By 1898 he could claim the largest circulation of any magazine in the world and earnings of over $380,000. Munsey continued to add to his magazine empire, founding *Puritan* in 1887, into which he merged *Godey's Lady's Book* in 1898, and *Junior Munsey* in 1900. Always restless, Munsey also diminished his empire, eventually merging both *Puritan* and *Junior Munsey* into *Argosy*. He established *All Story* magazine in 1904, only to merge it with *Argosy* and *Peterson's* in 1906, then he split it in 1912 into an all-fiction edition and an all-pictures edition, which he later added to *Live Wire*. Similar fates befell his other magazines such as *Cavalier*, *Railroad Man's*, *Woman*, the *Quaker*, and *Ocean*. By the time of his death, Munsey published only *Argosy All Story Weekly*, *Munsey's*, and *Flynn's Weekly Detective Fiction*.

Munsey had a vision of a chain of newspapers across the great cities of the East, modeled somewhat after the other giant industries of the time, and he tried to operate them with similar methods. Financed by millions in profits from his magazines, grocery chain, stock market speculations, and banking, he returned to the newspaper business with the purchase of the *Washington Times* and the *New York Daily News* in 1909, and the *Boston Journal* in 1902. He experimented with them just as he had with his magazines, adding and killing editions and features, changing prices and number of pages, without waiting for the changes to have an effect. He killed the *Daily News* in 1904, sold the *Journal* in 1913 and the *Times* in 1917.

Munsey continued the pattern in 1908, founding the *Philadelphia Times* and buying the *Baltimore News*; the former he killed in 1914 and the latter he sold twice, first in 1915 to Stuart Olivier, getting it back in 1917, and second in 1923 to W. R. Hearst (q.v.). He bought the *New York Press* in 1912 and merged it with the *New York Sun* when he purchased it in 1916. The *Morning Sun* was merged with the *New York Herald* when he purchased it in 1920, while he retained the *Evening* edition. That year he also bought the *Baltimore American*, *News*, and *Star* (which he merged into the *News* and sold to Hearst in 1923), and the *New York Evening Telegram*. In 1923 Munsey bought the *New York Globe*, which he promptly merged with the *Evening Sun*. The *New York Evening Mail* came to a similar end in 1924 when he bought and merged it with the *Evening Telegram*. Failing to compete with or buy the *New York Tribune*, Munsey sold the *Herald*, including the Paris edition, to the Whitelaw Reid (q.v.) family in 1924. He subsequently purchased no additional newspapers, much to the relief of journalists everywhere.

Although a respected businessman and well-known in conservative political circles, Munsey was detested by newspapermen for his casual attitude toward revered journalistic institutions, which he evaluated only by the ''bottom line.'' Eliminating weak papers may have made the survivors stronger, but it also eliminated thousands of jobs. Never married, and unfulfilled in either his journalistic or political ambitions, Munsey died on 22 December 1925 after two operations for appendicitis.

BIBLIOGRAPHY:

A. *Getting On In Journalism* (Ottawa, 1898); *The Founding of the Munsey Publishing House* (New York, 1907); *The Daily Newspaper: Its Relation to the Public* (Boston, 1910).

B. DAB 13, 334–335; NYT 23 December 1925; George Britt, *Forty Years—Forty Millions* (New York, 1935); Erman Jesse Ridgeway, *Frank A. Munsey: An Appreciation* (Chula Vista, Calif., 1926).

JACK H. COLLDEWEIH

MURROW, EDWARD (EGBERT) ROSCOE (b. 25 April 1908; d. 27 April 1965) was for a long time the best-known American radio and television news personality. As a news broadcasting pioneer he set the standards for the profession, and was especially known for his radio coverage of the bombing of London during World War II and for his exposé of Senator McCarthy on ''See It Now.'' Following a distinguished career with CBS, where he was a vice president and a member of the CBS board of directors, he was appointed by President John F. Kennedy as director of the U.S. Information Agency. By the time of his death in 1965 he had become the most honored man in American broadcast journalism.

Egbert, his given name, was born on a farm outside Greensboro, North Carolina. His family moved in 1913 to Blanchard, Washington, where his father became a logging-locomotive engineer. The son of Roscoe C. Murrow and Ethel Lamb, Murrow attended Edison High School from 1922 to 1925, where he was student body president and a member of the debating team. He spent the summer of 1925 in lumber camps and changed his name to Ed. He became Edward at Washington State College, which he attended from 1926 to 1930. There he took the first-ever college course in radio broadcasting and continued his involvement in student politics.

In 1929 Murrow was elected president of the National Student Federation (NSF), and after graduating in 1930 with a B.A. in speech, he went to New York to head that organization. His job entailed traveling to college campuses throughout the United States to make speeches and attend conventions, and he also traveled abroad to arange student travel and exchanges with foreign schools. He had a further task, that of obtaining speakers for the CBS program "University of the Air." On the way to an NSF convention in New Orleans he met Janet Huntington Brewster, a delegate from Mount Holyoke College. They were married on 27 October 1934 and eventually had a son, Charles Casey Murrow.

In 1932 Murrow became assistant director of the Institute of International Education (IIE). His work included arranging student exchanges between the United States and other nations, including the Soviet Union. With the rise of Nazism in Germany however, he began bringing persecuted German scholars to the United States. His career with CBS truly began in 1935 when he was named "director of talks," meaning he had to find participants for radio discussions. In 1937 CBS sent him to Eruope to be in charge of transmitting special events, such as the coronation of Britian's King George IV.

Murrow's journalistic work began in 1938 when he went to Vienna to cover Adolf Hitler's arrival there following the annexation of Austria. From the beginning Murrow's journalistic style was that of descriptive detail and personal observation. He developed the "news round-up" in which he arranged live broadcasts from various European cities on the same program. Correspondents recruited by him for this CBS foreign news staff included Howard K. Smith and Eric Severeid (qq.v.). However, Murrow's most memorable work in radio was his coverage of the bombing of London. He would often stand on rooftops and describe the bombings, while in the background listeners could hear the sounds of bombs, antiaircraft guns, and air-raid sirens. Murrow later reported the other side of the war as he accompanied crews in twenty-five bombing missions over Germany. Upon his return to the United States in 1946 he was named CBS vice president and director of public affairs.

Murrow's nightly radio news and commentary program advocated support for a pluralism of ideas, and he expressed hope that radio would be used as an educational tool and not necessarily as a tool for making profit. When television came along Murrow made an easy transition to it from radio. The weekly radio program "Hear It Now," which he produced with Fred W. Friendly (q.v.), also made the transition to television in 1951 as "See It Now." The most famous edition of that program was the 9 March 1954 broadcast in which Murrow combined live narration and various film clips to expose Senator Joseph R. McCarthy. McCarthy's crusade against the so-called communist conspiracy had touched Murrow personally. In addition to some CBS employees being blacklisted, Murrow himself had been accused of having communist ties because of his past work in arranging student exchanges between the United States and the Soviet Union. In addition, one of Murrow's close friends from the IIE days committed suicide as a result of being falsely accused of having communist connections. More than that, however, Murrow's personal beliefs in free speech and free thought motivated him to broadcast the McCarthy exposé.

Generally on "See It Now" Murrow, with his ever-present cigarette, explored various topics ranging from the dangers of smoking to the decolonization of Africa. Murrow also worked on a different type of television series called "Person To Person" (1953–59), in which he visited a celebrity at home each week. He also did "Small World" (1958–60), in which he talked to various world personalities.

Nevertheless, television was changing rapidly, and by 1958 "See It Now" was replaced by entertainment shows which attracted larger audiences. Television was becoming exactly what Murrow believed it should not. In a speech at the Radio and Television News Directors Association Convention in October 1958, Murrow criticized the networks for producing programs which insulated the public from the realities of the world and fostered decadence and escapism.

Even though Murrow had great freedom at CBS, he was slowly becoming disenchanted with commercial broadcasting, and in 1961 he resigned and took a large cut in pay to join the Kennedy White House as director of the U.S. Information Agency. Although he sought to present a realistic image of America abroad, Murrow never quite got accustomed to his more restrictive job.

In January 1964 after he was diagnosed as having cancer, he submitted his resignation to President Lyndon Johnson. On 14 September 1964 President Johnson awarded Murrow the Medal of Freedom, and on 5 March 1965 Queen Elizabeth II named him an Honorary Knight Commander of the Order of the British Empire. In his career Murrow had won four Peabody Awards for excellence in broadcasting, in 1943, 1949, 1951, and 1954. He died of lung cancer on 27 April 1965 in Pawling, New York.

BIBLIOGRAPHY:

A. *In Search of Light: The Broadcasts of Edward R. Murrow 1938–61* (New York, 1967).

B. DAB Supp. 7, 565–567; NYT 28 April 1965; Alexander Kendrick, *Prime Time: The Life of Edward R. Murrow* (Boston, 1969); R. Franklin Smith, *Edward R. Murrow: The War Years* (Kalamazoo, 1978).

THIMIOS ZAHAROPOULOS

N

NAST, THOMAS (b. 27 September 1840; d. 7 December 1902) was a cartoonist, caricaturist, and artist who was influential in arousing sympathy for the Union cause during the Civil War and in exposing corruption during the years following the war. His works were published primarily in *Harper's Weekly*, but he also illustrated a few books, drew giant caricatures of public figures for the "Opera Ball," and even published a magazine of his own for a short time. At the end of his life he was serving as consul general in Guayaquil, Equador.

Nast was born in Landau, Bavaria, son of a German musician whose name was also Thomas. His mother was the former Apollonia Apres. The senior Nast, a trombone player in the Ninth Regiment Bavarian Band, left Germany when the German revolution began to foment and went to France. In 1846 he wrote to his wife, instructing her to meet him in America; then he enlisted on an American ship. Young Thomas, his mother, and his sister emigrated to America, where they waited almost four years for the senior Nast to finish his tour of duty. Once in America, he continued his career as a musician, playing with the Philharmonic Society of New York City and later at the Burton Theatre on Chambers Street.

Young Thomas Nast attended public schools at first, later enrolled in two German schools in New York, and finally entered Forty-Seventh Street Academy. But he was not a scholar; his interest was in art. In 1854 he began studying under Theodore Kaufmann, a German artist with a studio on Broadway. When Kaufmann's place burned about six months later, Nast entered the Academy of Design on Thirteenth Street.

Nast became serious about journalistic art when he was about fifteen. He had been copying artworks at Bryant's Gallery of painting while working there as a doorkeeper. One day he gathered some of his drawings and took them to Frank Leslie (q.v.), owner of *Leslie's Weekly*. Leslie, impressed with what he saw, gave Nast his first assignment: cover the crowd scene at Christopher Street Ferry on Sunday morning. On Monday when Nast delivered his sketch, Leslie hired him at four dollars a week. Nast stayed with *Leslie's* until it began to have financial difficulties three years later; then he looked elsewhere for journalistic work.

In March 1859 Nast prepared a page of cartoons in which he depicted the New York Police Department as abusive and self-serving. The page was significant in that it was the first of many statements that he would make against social ills and it was the first of his drawings accepted by Fletcher Harper, owner of *Harper's Weekly*, which would later become Nast's forum.

November 1859 saw Nast on the staff of a new weekly, the *New York Illustrated News*. He had been with the *News* only three months when he was assigned as "special artist" to cover the Heenan-Sayers fight in England. After the fight, he hurried to southern Italy to follow Giuseppe Garibaldi in his triumphant march from Genoa to Capua. Nast's drawings of the battle scenes were published in New York, London, and Paris. When Nast returned to America in February 1861, his reputation as an illustrator was well established. The *News* had given much publicity to its "special artist" but had not managed its business well. Nast had no money waiting for him, and the *News* was soon taken over by its creditors.

On 26 September 1861 Nast married Sarah Edwards, whom he had met before his trip abroad. Throughout their forty-one years of marriage she was extremely supportive of Nast, often reading to him as he worked, discussing political ideas with him, and occasionally suggesting captions for his cartoons. They had five children: Julia, Thomas, Edith, Mabel, and Cyril.

Harper's Weekly hired Nast as a staff artist in July 1862. Until this time most of Nast's drawings had been simple illustrations of events, but Fletcher Harper urged him to present political and social ideas in his sketches. It was exactly what Nast wanted to do with his talent. And the timing was perfect—for Nast and for *Harper's*. Nast's feelings about slavery and other Civil War issues led to some of his best work, and *Harper's*, as his forum, became one of the most popular weeklies of the day.

Nast's detailed drawings depicted the pain, sorrow, and destruction of war. Pictures like "The War in the Border States" and "Emancipation," both published in *Harper's*, prompted President Lincoln to say: "Thomas Nast has been our best recruiting sergeant. His emblematic cartoons have never failed to arouse enthusiasm and patriotism, and have always seemed to come just when these articles were getting scarce." And Ulysses S. Grant said: "He [Thomas Nast] did as much as any one man to preserve the Union and bring the war to an end" (Paine, 1904).

By the time the war ended Nast was turning to political satire. In 1864 the Democratic convention took as its theme "Peace at Any Price." Nast bitterly attacked this goal in his "Compromise with the South" cartoon, published in

Harper's. The Lincoln administration bought all available copies of the weekly and even bought the plates of the cartoon to print copies for campaign literature. The cartoon was said to have played a major role in Lincoln's reelection.

In 1869 Nast's attention was drawn to corruption in New York City government. He began a cartoon crusade to expose William M. "Boss" Tweed, commissioner of public works, and his Tammany Ring. For four years Nast depicted the fraudulent practices of Tweed and his men, using caricatures that brought the nation's attention to Tweed and to Nast. The cartoon entitled "Tweed-le-dee and Tilden-dum" characterized Tweed so accurately that he was recognized and arrested in Vigo, Spain.

During the height of his career Nast created many caricatures and symbols: the round figure of Tweed with a moneybag for a face, the eyeglasses of A. Oakley Hall, the Tammany tiger, the Republican elephant, the Democratic donkey, and others. Nast continued his political satire until the presidential election in 1892. His cartoons in *Harper's* did much to sway public opinion at election time; they capsulized questionable practices in which the candidates had been involved. Nast was a close friend and loyal supporter of Grant; he supported Rutherford B. Hayes; and even at a time when his poplarity seemed to be declining, he was believed to have been helpful in securing votes for Cleveland. He depicted Andrew Johnson as an Iago, deceiving the black man of Reconstruction days; his attacks on Horace Greeley (q.v.) were so bitter that Nast himself was pictured in a cartoon called "Mixing Day at *Harper's*—Making Mud to Fling at Greeley."

Nast's genial side was most often shown through his Christmas pictures for *Harper's*. In the early 1860s he first drew his conception of the cheery, fat, bearded Santa with a pack of toys on his back, and almost yearly this Santa would appear on the cover or in the centerfold of *Harper's* December issue. The last picture he drew for *Harper's* was "Santa Claus and His Works," published Christmas 1886.

After leaving *Harper's* Nast published a few drawings in the *Illustrated America*. In 1892 he took over the *New York Gazette*, promptly changing the name to *Nast's Weekly*. He borrowed money to keep the paper going for a few months, but by the spring of 1893 it was dead. The failure of his paper left Nast a poor man. He had lost everything except his home in 1884 through unwise investments, and now he was in debt. His cartoons were not much in demand anymore, and although he had made three successful lecture tours earlier, he was unable to get a fourth one on the road.

In May 1902 Nast accepted an appointment as consul general at Guayaquil, Equador. The position offered $4,000; Nast needed the money. He served only seven months at his new post. He became ill with yellow fever the first of December and on 7 December he died.

BIBLIOGRAPHY:

B. DAB 13, 391–393; NCAB 7, 461; NYT 8 December 1902; Albert Bigelow Paine, *Th. Nast: His Period and His Pictures* (New York, 1904).

SHIRLEY M. MUNDT

NELSON, WILLIAM ROCKHILL (b. 7 March 1841; d. 13 April 1915) founded the *Kansas City Star* and served as its owner and editor throughout the newspaper's first thirty-five years. Though he had little previous experience in journalism, Nelson made the *Star* one of the most respected newspapers in the country, and a powerful influence in the early growth of Kansas City and its surrounding area.

His father, Isaac DeGroff Nelson, was engaged in farming and politics. His mother, Elizabeth Rockhill Nelson, was the daughter of a farmer who became famous as the first to plant 1,000 acres of corn in the United States. William was born at Fort Wayne, Indiana. He attended schools there and the University of Notre Dame in South Bend. Following his years at Notre Dame, Nelson studied law and obtained admittance to the bar. He practiced law only a short time, however, before deciding to enter the construction business.

While in construction, Nelson was approached by Samuel E. Morss, an editor for the *Fort Wayne Sentinel*, and persuaded to join in a partnership to purchase the newspaper. With Morss, Nelson published the *Sentinel* about a year and then sold it to found a paper in Kansas City. Although Morss served as first editor of the paper at Kansas City, he retired after a year as a result of poor health, and Nelson assumed sole control.

Kansas City's *Evening Star*, originally a two-cent, four-page paper ridiculed as the ''little twinkler,'' prospered and soon became that city's most influential daily. Although Nelson, then forty years of age, was not really a journalist at that time—he rarely wrote anything himself, throughout his career—the *Star* became nationally known as a paper of high quality and devotion to good government.

From the beginning, almost, Nelson took a position that the *Star* should be independent politically. Although a Democrat originally, Nelson supported Republican candidates from time to time—particularly Theodore Roosevelt and his Bull Moose movement. The *Star*'s overriding priority, however, was the best interests of Kansas City. With his builder's enthusiasm for growth and progress, Nelson advocated the development of modern streets, parks, utilities, and other services. Whenever political interests appeared to impede such improvement, Nelson's newspaper crusaded against such interests. The *Star*'s persistence became legendary, and even defeat failed to deter Nelson. Responding to one defeat, Nelson observed that ''the *Star* never loses'' (Johnson, 1925).

Because of its editor's strong character, and its independence, the *Star* blazed its own path to journalistic success. ''What the other fellow does doesn't interest me,'' Nelson said. ''Newspapers that are edited with a view to attract attention from other newspapers are failures. We are running the *Star* for our readers, not for other newspapers.'' Upon another occasion, Nelson advised his staff to remember this: ''The *Star* has a greater purpose in life than merely to print the news. It believes in doing things.'' Through numerous crusades, campaigns, and controversies, the *Star* continued to fight for what Nelson considered best for Kansas City and its region.

One of Nelson's chief interests in his later years was art. He founded the Western Gallery at Kansas City, and supported other cultural projects. In 1902 Nelson was elected vice president of the Associated Press and he served as a director of the AP from 1905 to 1914.

Nelson's death, from uremic poisoning, followed a long illness. During its latter stages, aware that he was being kept alive by artificial means, Nelson objected, saying, ''You are keep me alive for no purpose. The next time let me go.'' For eleven years following Nelson's death, the *Star* was published by its staff, under the direction of Nelson's widow, Ida Houston, whom he had married 29 November 1881, and their only child, Laura. Mrs. Nelson died in 1921, leaving the *Star* in the charge of Laura and her husband, Irwin Kirkwood, who served as editor. Following Mrs. Kirkwood's death, the paper was purchased by its employees and the proceeds used to found Kansas City's William Rockhill Nelson Art Gallery.

BIBLIOGRAPHY:

B. DAB 13, 427–428; NCAB 5, 170–171; NYT 13 April 1915; Icie F. Johnson, *William Rockhill Nelson and the ''Kansas City Star''* (Kansas City, 1925).

JOHN DE MOTT

NEWCOMB, JAMES PEARSON (b. 31 August 1837; d. 16 October 1907) was one of the leading political journalists in nineteenth-century Texas. During his career he owned part or all of twenty-two newspapers, including the forerunners of the present-day *San Antonio Express-News* and *San Antonio Light*. Newcomb was active in Radical Republican causes in post–Civil War Texas, was registrar of voters in the state during Reconstruction, and served as secretary of state during the Davis administration from 1870 to 1874.

Newcomb, the older of the two sons, was born in Amherst, Nova Scotia, to Captain Thomas Newcomb and Martha Margaret Pearson Newcomb. Captain Newcomb settled his family in the Republic of Texas in 1839, forming a law practice in Victoria. His wife died in March 1841, and following a second marriage, Captain Newcomb moved his family to San Antonio in 1848. He died the following year; his wife boarded James and his brother, John, with the wife of a Presbyterian church official and left San Antonio, never to return. In 1864 Newcomb married Jeanie Davis in San Francisco. She and the couple's infant son both died in 1866. In 1872 he married Antoinette Hitchcock, a native of Vermont, who bore him four children.

Newcomb began his journalism career at the age of twelve as printer's devil for the *Western Texan*, the state's first English-language newspaper. The following year he worked for the *San Antonio Ledger*. In 1854 the sixteen-year-old Newcomb began his first publishing venture, the *Alamo Star*. He discontinued publication in January 1855 and in April founded the weekly *San Antonio Herald*, his first entry into political journalism. The following year he sold the paper to attend the University of Vermont. He returned to Texas in 1858.

Newcomb rejoined the *Herald* as editor and quickly became embroiled in the secession movement. He used the *Herald* to promote his pro-Union sentiments. In August 1860 he published the first edition of the *Alamo Express*. His antisecessionist sentiments were unpopular, and in the summer of 1861, after Texas voters approved an ordinance of secession, the *Alamo Express* was razed by a Confederate mob. Newcomb left San Antonio the following day and eventually made his way to San Francisco, California, by way of Monterrey and Mazatlán, Mexico.

Newcomb served six months in 1862 with Colonel J. H. Carleton's California Column as a scout on an expedition to New Mexico. Disenchanted over a lack of plans to invade Texas, he returned to California, where he edited the *San Jose Tribune* and *San Francisco American Flag*, wrote and published two pamphlets, and made several unsuccessful forays into the gold fields in Arizona.

Newcomb returned to Texas in 1867 and immediately became embroiled in Reconstruction politics. He joined the *San Antonio Express* as a joint proprietor and coeditor, and acquired a one-third interest in the *Freie Presse feur Texas*, a German-language paper. In 1868 he published a Negro newspaper, the *Free Man's Press*, which folded after two months.

He was a delegate to the Texas Constitutional Convention of 1868–69, and was named Texas secretary of state in 1870. That same year Newcomb became editor of a new Austin paper, the *Daily State Journal*, which advocated Radical Republican causes and quickly gained the largest combined circulation of any paper in the state. In 1872 Newcomb traded his one-third interest in the *San Antonio Express* for a similar share of the *Journal*. Soon afterward, he started a new San Antonio political newspaper, the *Prospectus*. It was short-lived, and Newcomb, for the remainder of E. J. Davis's governorship, devoted his efforts to the *Journal*, finally ceasing publication in April 1874 after the Democrats took power.

Returning to San Antonio in 1874, Newcomb survived a politically motivated fraud charge and founded the *Republican*, a newspaper restricted to party propaganda. In 1877 he became associated with a monthly immigration newspaper, the *Texas Sun*, eventually becoming editor. In January 1881 Newcomb left the *Texas Sun* and cofounded, with Ed. P. Gifford, the *Evening Light*, whose first edition was published on 20 January. After a few months, city circulation of the *Light* surpassed that of the *Express*. The *Light* was the first San Antonio paper to feature a weekend supplement and offer extensive local news coverage.

Newcomb shared little in the newspaper's success. In the spring of 1883, while he was serving as San Antonio postmaster, the *Light*'s ownership was changed to exclude him. Although Newcomb threatened legal action to recover his half-interest, he never followed through. The *Light*, like the *Express* before it, continued to prosper and grow without Newcomb. Newcomb made several other ventures into San Antonio journalism with the *Plumed Knight* in 1884, the *Evening Paper* in 1886, the *Campaign News* in 1888, the *Times* in 1889, the *White Republican* in 1890, and the *National Liquor Dealer* in 1895, which outlived him. He died of injuries from an accident in October 1907.

BIBLIOGRAPHY:

A. *Sketch of Secession Times in Texas* (San Francisco, 1863).

B. Frederick Chabot, *With the Makers of San Antonio* (San Antonio, 1937); Dale A. Somers, "James Pearson Newcomb, Texas Unionist and Radical Republican," M.A. thesis, Trinity Univ., 1964.

JAMES DANIEL WHITFIELD

NEWHOUSE, S. I. (b. 24 May 1895; d. 29 August 1979) was a self-effacing little man who came out of Manhattan's Lower East Side, and painstakingly built one of the largest newspaper and broadcasting chains in American history. Unlike more flamboyant press lords, Newhouse avoided the trappings of wealth, the limelight, editorial control, and political influence. Instead, he emphasized the moneymaking aspects of journalism as a business, concentrated on new acquisitions, and enriched the industry through substantial educational philanthropies.

Newhouse was born at a time and place of social ferment, in a tenement to Meier and Rose Arenfeldt Neuhaus, recently arrived, impoverished Jewish immigrants from Russia and Austria, respectively. Reared in Bayonne, New Jersey, Newhouse was the eldest of eight children. His family was so poor that he had to stop going to school at thirteen, when his father's health failed, and get a job at $2 per week with Hyman Lazarus, a judge and businessman. Having completed a three-month business course, Newhouse was able to make himself useful as a clerk, then business manager.

Before long, Newhouse became the judge's protégé. He worked days as general manager of the judge's financially decrepit *Bayonne Times*, and in the evenings attended the New Jersey College of Law for four years, passing the bar in 1916. Newhouse put the paper in the black, and learned the business, advertising, and circulation ends of newpapering from the bottom up. Lazarus was so pleased with Newhouse's passing the bar that he bought Newhouse a new suit of clothes.

As the Bayonne paper gained circulation and profits, Newhouse put his relatives on the payroll, and negotiated a share of the profits for himself. By 1922 Newhouse was able to purchase controlling interest in his first paper, the *Staten Island Advance*. In five years he owned it outright, and began accumulating the money to buy another paper, the *Long Island Press*, in 1932. Working with his brothers Theodore, Louis, and Norman, Newhouse continued the pattern of media acquisitions that he had thus established.

The benchmarks of his progress included the year 1939, when he ventured beyond the New York metropolitan area to establish his chain on a regional basis by buying the *Syracuse Herald Journal*. In 1950 he established his chain on a national basis with the purchase of the *Portland Oregonian*, a quality paper then considered the best on the West Coast. In 1959 Newhouse moved into magazines when he bought the Condé Nast line, which included the prestigious women's periodicals *Vogue* and *House and Garden*. Along the way he also bought broadcasting properties, and he appeared on the cover of *Time* magazine in 1962.

In 1964 Lyndon Johnson, the president, and Nelson Rockefeller, governor, were present when Newhouse dedicated the $15 million Newhouse School of Public Communications at Syracuse University. In all, his philanthropies amounted to $25 million including donations to the Newhouse Center for Law and Justice at Rutgers University, and the Mitzi Newhouse Theater at Lincoln Center. His wife Mitzi, as socially outgoing as Newhouse was shy, brought out his personality and maintained an active social life, and interest in the arts. They were married in 1924, and had two sons.

In 1967 Newhouse broke the record paid for newspapers when he bought the *Cleveland Plain Dealer* for $50 million. Though in a major market, it was a mediocre newspaper, and did not enhance Newhouse's reputation as a businessman. In 1976 Newhouse impressed the industry with the purchase of Booth Newspapers—eight Michigan dailies and the Sunday supplement *Parade*—for $305 million, the largest newspaper transaction ever. When Newhouse died, he had amassed a chain worth hundreds of millions of dollars, amounting to thirty-one newspapers in eleven states, five broadcasting outlets, seven domestic magazines, and foreign magazines.

His formula for acquisitions was to stringently cut costs (regarding editorial as a good place to economize), to boost revenues by finding new sources of advertising, and to insist on a sound circulation operation.

Newhouse had a bad reputation with the American Newspaper Guild for his crude discriminatory treatment of union members and his harsh strikebreaking tactics. At the *Long Island Press* in 1937 Newhouse was charged with having the police beat up strikers, creating lasting enmity. In 1959 Newhouse provoked a guild strike at the *St.Louis Globe-Democrat* by utterly refusing to grant a pension plan, then broke the strike by selling the newspaper building. In the same year Newhouse tried to break a strike at the *Portland Oregonian* by importing shotgun-toting strikebreakers, touching off management violence and a five-year strike.

As long as his chain was small, Newhouse managed his papers through regular visits to monitor operations. He ran his operations out of a battered brown briefcase. His extravagances were few. He had a large Park Avenue apartment and a 140-acre country estate in New Jersey. After Newhouse had a stroke in 1978, two of his brothers, Norman and Theodore, and his two sons, Samuel I. Jr., and Donald E., ran the chain. After lapsing into senility, Newhouse died of a stroke in August 1979.

BIBLIOGRAPHY:

B. NYT 30 August 1979; Richard H. Meeker, *Newspaperman: S. I. Newhouse and the Business of News* (New Haven, 1983).

WILLIAM Q. PARMENTER

NEWMAN, CECIL EARL (b. 25 July 1903; d. 7 February 1976) had little doubt as a youth what career he wanted to pursue in life; journalism. In the seventh grade he ''edited'' and ''published'' his first newspaper, a handwritten sheet he passed out to his classmates. However, he would work at many occupations before his dream became a reality.

Newman was born in Kansas City, Missouri. His father, Horatio Oscar, was a chef at a leading hotel in the city and his mother, Cora, was a domestic worker. The only boy of four children, young Newman was the family favorite. Elementary school offered no real excitement for Newman. He had been taught to read by his father at a very young age, and prior to entering school at the age of seven, he was reading newspapers and magazines his father brought home from the hotel. High school, however, offered more excitement.

Although he received no encouragement from his teachers, journalism remained foremost in his mind. At thirteen he became the distributor for three national black publications. He employed a number of his schoolmates to help in distributing some 4,000 newspapers weekly. He also took a job performing various tasks at a local black newspaper, the *Call*. It was here he managed to get his first news story published.

In 1920, a year before finishing high school, Newman married Willa Coleman, a schoolmate. He finished high school in 1921 and in 1922 they became parents of Oscar Horatio. This was to be Newman's only child. Following high school he tried his hand at many occupations including ownership of a baseball team, which he purchased for $600. However, none of these were roads to his ultimate goal, a career in journalism. In 1922 he decided to move to Minneapolis, Minnesota.

Newman's first job in Minneapolis was as a bellhop at the Elks Club. Still with his goal in mind, he took on another job part-time selling subscriptions for the *Northwestern Bulletin*, a local black newspaper. He also became a stringer for the *Pittsburgh Courier* and the *Chicago Defender*, two leading black newspapers of the time. After about two years Newman gave up his job at the Elks Club and became a Pullman porter on the railroad.

In 1927, at the age of twenty-four, Newman got his first real taste of journalism. He and Joshua Perry, a black printer in Minneapolis, teamed with five other residents of the city to found the *Twin Cities Herald*. Newman served as editor and Perry as publisher. However, the paper was started on a weak financial base, and Newman kept his job as a Pullman porter. He wrote stories, editorials, and other materials for the paper while on the road and used part of his pay to help support the paper. He did not draw a salary for his duties as editor. This dedication to the *Herald* contributed to the breakup of his marriage.

In 1931 Newman decided to try his hand at publishing a magazine. He founded the *Timely Digest*, a monthly magazine which sold for fifteen cents. This venture lasted until February 1932. Newman now felt he had to make a grave decision, either give up his job as a Pullman porter or give up journalism. He gave up his job to devote his full time to journalism, win, lose or draw. He had severed his relationship with the *Herald* and was now on his own.

Newman admitted he was not a good writer and was looking for ways to sharpen his journalistic skills. On a visit to the University of Minnesota he met Professor Ralph Casey, head of the Department of Journalism. Casey was impressed with Newman and later gave him a set of books covering all phases of journalism. Newman studied them avidly. By 1934 Newman was ready to go it alone. He had unsuccessfully tried to buy the *Herald*. He decided to establish two newspapers at the same time, the *Minneapolis Spokesman* and the *St. Paul Recorder*. He once commented: "I didn't have enough money to start one newspaper so I started two."

The *Spokesman* and *Recorder* grew slowly but finally became entrenched among the leading black newspapers of the Midwest. During this period C. A. Franklin, owner and publisher of *Call* newspapers in Kansas City and St. Louis, offered Newman $100 a week to go to St. Louis and pump some life into his paper there. Newman accepted, sending most of his earnings back to Minneapolis to help suport his papers. He returned after five months with new ideas of how to increase his own advertising revenue and circulation. During this period (1937) Newman married DeVelma Hall, one of his part-time workers.

Using a community approach, Newman's papers began to grow rapidly and reach the white community as well as the black community. His editorials, whether concerning segregation, discrimination, or other subjects, were vigorous and to the point but not offensive, thus earning him a reputation as a rational and fair editor. During World War II, Newman became a consultant and director of negro personnel at an arms plant. However, he managed to keep his papers alive and prospering during the war.

Following the war Newman became noted for his public and community services. He and his papers were also involved in the civil rights movement of the 1960s and early 1970s. He supported the nonviolent philosophy of Dr. Martin Luther King, Jr., and disagreed with the violent philosophy of Rap Brown and Stokely Carmichael. He supported Muhammad Ali in his fight against entering military service but chided blacks for rioting and destroying their neighborhoods and black businesses. He was a longtime friend of Hubert Humphrey and an associate of Walter Mondale.

Divorced for a second time, Newman married Launa Quincy in April 1965. The two worked hand in hand at the *Spokesman* and *Recorder* until his death. In 1971 Newman suffered a stroke. He was forced to slow down but never completely recovered and died of a heart attack in 1976.

BIBLIOGRAPHY:
B. L. E. Leipold, *Cecil E. Newman: Newspaper Publisher* (Minneapolis, 1969); "Publishers," *Ebony*, November 1949; "Cecil E. Newman—1903–1976," *Minneapolis Spokesman*, 12 February 1976.

J. WILLIAM SNORGRASS

NICHOLSON, ELIZA (b. 11 March 1849; d. 15 February 1896) was a twenty-seven-year-old widow when in 1876 she became editor-publisher of the *New Orleans Picayune*, then the largest daily in the South. In her twenty years with the *Picayune* she helped make journalism a viable career for women.

Born in Hancock County, Mississippi, on the banks of the Pearl River, she wrote poetry using the pen name Pearl Rivers, and was published in John W. Overall's *The South*, the *New York Journal*, the *New Orleans Times*, and the *Picayune*. In 1869 she became a $25-a-week literary editor for the *Picayune*, the first newspaperwoman in conservative New Orleans and among the first in the South. She expanded the literary features of the morning paper and the Sunday edition, and also did more conventional reporting.

In 1872 she married sixty-four-year-old *Picayune* publisher, Colonel Alva Morris Holbrook. When he died in 1876, the paper was $80,000 in debt. Instead of declaring bankruptcy and claiming a $1,000 widow's allowance, Eliza took over as editor, and showed, from the first day, that she had learned well in her apprenticeship and short marriage to the dedicated newspaperman.

But in 1895 she told an Atlanta gathering of the International League of Press Clubs that women who aspired to manage and edit newspapers should think twice about it. In 1886 she was elected president of the Women's National Press Association and later was made first honorary member of the New York Women's Press Club founded in 1889 by Jennie June, editor and syndicated columnist otherwise known as Jane Cunningham Croly (q.v.). She hired Elizabeth Gilmer and introduced her to the world as columnist Dorothy Dix (q.v.). She also hired Martha Field, who wrote as Catherine Cole, a special correspondent for the *Picayune*.

Convinced that a newspaper could be an instrument for social change and civic improvement, she established, in March 1879, a society column, "Society Bee"; added separate fashion columns for men and women; introduced the "Green Room Gossip," in which former Yankee Major Nathaniel Burbank discussed entertainment and entertainers; and developed a youth section, "In Lilliput Land," featuring fiction, poetry, illustrations, advice, and subtle admonitions to proper conduct.

Other innovations at the *Picayune* included a column for homemakers, "Women's World and Work," later renamed "Household Hints"; a sports column; a medical column, "The *Picayune*'s Family Physician"; scientific and agricultural columns; a humor column by Burbank; and "The *Picayune*'s

Telephone,'' which commented on such public concerns as the shabby condition of certain streets, and minor and not so minor mismanagement by city officials.

Striving to make the *Picayune* a southern family newspaper, she kept independent of political parties, and excised scandals, affairs, divorces, pregnancies, and sensationalism from her paper. While avoiding coverage of violence and scandals, the paper was often squarely in the middle of burning issues. The paper supported the development of the New Orleans harbor and the draining of the swamps, and urged construction of an artesian water system and the electrification of the city's lighting system. The *Picayune* also campaigned in support of Sunday closing laws for saloons in 1884 and the years following.

The paper was well received. Circulation grew from 6,000 combined daily and Sunday circulation in 1878 to 40,000 for the annual business review issue in 1880. By 1891 the combined daily and Sunday figures topped 49,000, and the carnival editions at Mardi Gras time claimed a circulation of 100,000.

Married in 1878 to George Nicholson, longtime *Picayune* staff member, she shared leadership of the paper. He ran the business side and she the editorial. The Nicholsons had two sons, Leonard and Yorke, born 1881 and 1883, respectively. Nicholson died of influenza ten days after her husband died of the same disease. She was forty-six years old.

BIBLIOGRAPHY:

B. *New Orleans Daily Picayune*, 16 February 1896; Thomas Ewing Dabney, *One Hundred Great Years, the Story of the ''Times-Picayune'' from Its Founding to 1940* (Baton Rouge, 1944); Elsie S. Farr, *Pearl Rivers* (New Orleans, 1951); James Henry Harrison, *Pearl Rivers, Publisher of the ''Picayune''* (New Orleans, 1932); Lamar W. Bridges, ''Eliza Jane Nicholson of the *Picayune*,'' *Journalism History*, Winter 1975–76.

SHARON MURPHY

NIEMAN, LUCIUS WILLIAM (b. 13 December 1857; d. 1 October 1935) took over the fledgling *Milwaukee Journal* in 1882. He built a nonpartisan, crusading, community-minded reputation for the *Journal*. By the turn of the century, it was Milwaukee's leading newspaper. The *Journal* earned a Pulitzer Prize for Nieman's campaign aganist German propaganda in the U.S. German-language press during World War I.

Nieman was born at Bear Valley in south-central Wisconsin, the son of Conrad Nieman and Sara Elizabeth Dalameter Nieman, of pioneer farm families. His father died when he was two, and young Lute, as he was known, and his sister Violette, three years older, grew up with their maternal grandparents on a Mukwonago farm southeast of Milwaukee. Schoolteacher boarders encouraged Lute to become interested in current events. By age twelve he wanted to be a newspaper editor.

Almost thirteen, he went to the *Waukesha Freeman* as a printer's devil. Publisher Theron E. Haight, with whom Nieman lived, nurtured his journalistic interests. In two years Nieman became a journeyman printer at the *Milwaukee Sentinel*. While attending Carroll College in Waukesha, he was a correspondent for the *Sentinel*. After a brief reporting stint in Milwaukee, Nieman was sent to Madison to cover the legislature for the *Sentinel*. On returning, he became city editor and then managing editor.

In 1880, at age twenty-two, he was named manager of the St. Paul, Minnesota, *Dispatch* and offered one-third ownership if he could restore the newspaper to leadership, which he did. Within a year, however, he returned to his native Wisconsin and the *Sentinel*.

At age twenty-five, he acquired part interest in the *Journal*, a small newspaper launched a few months earlier to promote a congressional candidate. Nieman told *Journal* readers that his newspaper would be "an outspoken, independent organ of the people against all that is worng and unworthy." That made it distinctive among Milwaukee's seven dailies, and he soon had a dramatic opportunity to demonstrate his commitment. Within a month, on a freezing January morning, the prominent Newhall House hotel was destroyed by fire. Seventy-one persons died. Recognizing a major story, Nieman went all out. The *Journal* demanded investigations and prosecutions. The dominant Milwaukee newspaper, the *Sentinel*, was strangely accepting of the tragedy, and it later came out that some *Sentinel* owners had part interest in the hotel. Years later, Nieman would say: "Our handling of the Newhall fire made the *Journal* a newspaper." Although circulation claims were dubious in this period, the *Journal* probably was dominant in Milwaukee by 1900, certainly by 1905.

As World War I began in Europe, Nieman was suspicious of subversion in German-language newspapers in the United States. In 1915 he hired linguist F. Perry Olds to translate the German-language newspapers. As Nieman had suspected, many were carrying unadulterated German propaganda. Nieman published Olds's translations in the *Journal* and made them available nationwide to other newspapers to expose the internal menace. There were temporary circulation and advertising setbacks, for Milwaukee was heavily Teutonic, but Nieman's persistence helped seal the fate of the Milwaukee German-language press. In 1915 a Milwaukee German daily had 31,600 circulation and the weeklies many times that. They never recoverd, opening new opportunites for *Journal* circulation growth.

Nieman was a recognized business genius. His *Journal* was innovative with technology, establishing pioneer radio station WTMJ in 1927 and making an early commitment to colorgravure. In 1911 he began to motorize circulation, and in 1912 dabbled with airplanes for circulation.

Nieman died in Milwaukee at age seventy-seven. His widow, Agnes Elizabeth Guenther Wahl Nieman, whom he had married on 28 November 1900, died in 1936. There were no children. His estate included $1 million to Harvard University to establish the Nieman Fellowships for experienced newsmen to further their studies. Also, a Nieman chair in journalism was set up at Marquette University in Milwaukee.

BIBLIOGRAPHY:

B. DAB 21, Supp. 1, 576–577; NYT 2 October 1935; Jean L. Berres, *Local Aspects of the "Campaign for Americanism": The Milwaukee "Journal" in World War I*

(Carbondale, 1978); Will C. Conrad, Kathleen Wilson, and Dale Wilson, *The Milwaukee "Journal": The First Eighty Years* (Madison, 1964); Robert W. Wells, *The Milwaukee "Journal": An Informal Chronicle of Its First 100 Years* (Milwaukee, 1981).

JOHN H. VIVIAN

NILES, HEZEKIAH (b. 10 October 1777; d. 2 April 1839) founded and edited the United States' first weekly newsmagazine, *Niles' Weekly Register*, in Baltimore, Maryland. With this influential, nationally circulated periodical as his vehicle, Niles provided unbiased coverage of ten presidential elections, fought for a protective tariff for U.S. industry, gave his readers a wealth of facts and statistics on the American economy, and was an ardent spokesman for U.S. nationalism. As a repository for the public documents, important speeches, and major news stories of its day, *Niles' Register* was unsurpassed.

Born on 10 October 1777 near Chadd's Ford, Pennsylvania, to Quaker parents, Niles was named for his paternal great-grandfather, who had immigrated from England in 1682. Niles's father, also Hezekiah, was a carpenter and assistant burgess in Wilmington; his mother, Mary Way Niles, was the daughter of a Wilmington merchant. The couple had one other child, their first, whose name was Samuel.

Niles's formal education was brief; he is thought to have attended the Friends School in Wilmington. At age seventeen he was apprenticed to Philadelphia printer-bookseller Benjamin Johnson. Here in 1794 Niles wrote his first published articles, some on business topics, others in support of Thomas Jefferson for the presidency. Several in the latter category appeared in the respected *Aurora*. After being released from apprenticeship, he returned to Wilmington in 1797 and entered into a brief printing partnership with James Adams, Jr. Niles's older brother died, leaving him a modest estate, yet a subsequent partnership in Wilmington with Vincent Bonsal plunged Niles into debt by 1815.

In 1798 Niles maried Anne Ogden, daughter of a Philadelphia tavern keeper. The couple had twelve children, of whom five died as infants and another, Samuel, at age twenty-two. Anne Ogden Niles died on 2 June 1824, and in 1826 Niles took a second wife, Sally Ann Warner of Wilmington, and fathered an additional eight children, all of whom survived him. One, Henry Clay Niles, was named for Niles's good friend, the well-known Kentucky statesman.

Niles was politically active during his years as a Wilmington printer. He was town clerk in 1801 and again in 1804 and was twice an assistant burgess, in 1803 and 1805. From 12 February to 24 August 1805 he published his first magazine, an eight-page literary periodical titled the *Apollo, or Delaware Weekly Magazine*. Following this venture Niles moved to Baltimore and for five years was co-owner of the *Evening Post*, a four-page daily. A series of his *Post* editorials was published in book form in 1809 under the title *Things As They Are; or Federalism Turned Inside Out!! Being a Collection of Extracts from Federal Papers, & c. and Remarks Upon Them*.

Two weeks after the June 1811 sale of his interest in the *Post*, Niles issued the prospectus for his *Register*, the magazine that made him a famous man. Its maiden issue was in September 1811, its last in September 1849. The thirty-four-year-old Niles began his new magazine as the *Weekly Register*, but in March 1814 changed the title to *Niles' Weekly Register*. Years later the title was altered again to *Niles' National Register*. He pledged that his periodical would stay clear of political partisanship and divided its content into the following departments: politics; history; biography; geography; notices of the arts, sciences, manufacturing, and agriculture; miscellany; and a "neat summary of the news." Niles provided his readers a massive body of facts and statistical information, presented with grace and even wit. His impartiality, objectivity, and accuracy made the *Register* the unrivaled journal of record of its time so long as Niles himself edited it. While editing the *Register*, Niles published another book, *Principles and Acts of the Revolution in America* (1822), and an array of pamphlets.

On 3 September 1836 Niles announced his retirement, having been partially paralyzed by a stroke. The editor's chair was assumed by his eldest son, William Ogden Niles, who moved the magazine from Baltimore to Washington, D.C. After Hezekiah Niles's death on 2 April 1839, the *Register* passed out of family ownership and was later moved to Philadelphia, where it, too, died in 1849. In his personal political leanings Niles was a Jeffersonian Democrat until 1829, when he became a Whig in protest of President Andrew Jackson's policies.

BIBLIOGRAPHY:

B. DAB 7, 521–522; Norval Neil Luxon, *Niles' Weekly Register; News Magazine of the Nineteenth Century* (Westport, Conn. 1970).

SAM G. RILEY

NOYES, FRANK BRETT (b. 7 July 1863; d. 1 December 1948) was one of the founders of the Associated Press and served as its president for thirty-eight years. He was business manager of the *Washington Evening Star* from 1886 to 1901 and president from 1910 to 1948. In the interim, from 1901 to 1910, he was publisher and editor of the *Chicago Record Herald*.

Noyes, born in Washington, D.C., grew up in a family of newspapermen. His father was Crosby Stuart Noyes, part owner and editor of the *Star*; his mother, the former Elizabeth S. Williams. Theodore William Noyes, his oldest brother, was associated with the *Star* for sixty years and succeeded Crosby Noyes as editor in chief. Thomas C. Noyes, another brother, worked in the *Star's* news department.

Frank Noyes was graduated from a Washington, D.C., high school in 1878 and briefly attended the preparatory department of Columbian (later George Washington) University and Spencerian Business College. He began his career in journalism at thirteen, selling newspapers for his father; he continued working for the *Star*, moving up to business manager and treasurer by the time he was twenty-three.

On 17 September 1888 he married Janet Thruston Newbold. They moved to Chicago in 1901, and Noyes took over as publisher and editor of the *Chicago Record Herald*. He was there nine years, returning to the *Star* as president in 1910. Under Noyes's expert management the *Star* rose from a circulation of 48,000 in 1910, when he returned to its business office, to 211,000 at the time of his retirement in 1948—the largest circulation in the District of Columbia. The *Star*'s advertising linage became the highest in the United States and remained so for many years.

In 1893 Noyes and two associates, Victor F. Lawson and Melville E. Stone (qq.v.), realized that the Western Associated Press, forerunner of the present Associated Press, was about to be put out of business by a privately owned news service. Fearing that private ownership would mean biased news, Noyes and his friends fought to preserve a service which would be nonprofit, impartial, and cooperative. Noyes was elected a director of the newly formed Associated Press and helped to formulate policies for the new service. In 1900 he became president and continued until his death to regard collection and dissemination of news as a public trust and to believe that the news service was obligated to give the people reliable information so that they might form their own conclusions. He retired as president in 1938 but remained as a director until 1947.

Upon his twenty-fifth anniversary with the Associated Press, Noyes was presented with a small volume of testimonials written for the occasion. In it he is praised by his peers for his winning personality, unflagging energy, knowledge of details, high sense of justice, strong convictions, and determination to maintain the highest standards of the Associated Press.

Noyes outlived all three of his children: two daughters, Frances and Ethel; and one son, Newbold, who was associate editor of the *Star* from 1919 to 1942. His wife died on 8 November 1942. When he died of arteriosclerotic cardiovascular disease on 1 December 1948, he was survived by six grandchildren, including Newbold Noyes, Jr., who became editor of the *Star* in 1963.

Frank Noyes was buried in Rock Creek Cemetery, Washington, D.C.

BIBLIOGRAPHY:

B. DAB Supp. 4, 630–631; NCAB E, 81–82; NYT 1 December 1948; ''Frank B. Noyes Dies at 85; He Guided AP for 38 Years,'' *Editor and Publisher*, 4 December 1948.

SHIRLEY M. MUNDT

NYE, EDGAR WILSON (b. 25 August 1850; d. 22 February 1896), better known as Bill Nye, was an acclaimed journalistic humorist of his day who rose to national prominence on the strength of his newspaper humor and several books. Some see in his writing a ''new American analysis of traditional and conventional ideas.'' Some just enjoy laughing.

Nye was born in Shirley, Maine (he said he never heard of the place until he was born there), the son of Franklin and Elizabeth Mitchell Loring Nye. When he was two the family moved to Wisconsin, and he grew up in a log cabin on a farm. He completed secondary school and worked as a miller's helper, a law clerk, a teacher, and a part-time reporter.

In 1876, when he was twenty-five, he moved to Wyoming Territory and a job as a reporter on the *Laramie Daily Sentinel*. He contributed occasionally to the *Cheyenne Daily Sun* and the *Denver Tribune*. Late in 1877 he quit the *Sentinel* to practice law. He got few clients and claimed he could not mail his letters because he could not afford the postage. In 1881 he became editor of the new Republican paper in Laramie, the *Boomerang*. He stayed with the paper three years, and won for it a national reputation. He was appointed postmaster of Laramie, but kept his editor's job, too.

Nye's humor depends for its effect on the easy building of a yarn; he did not write one-liners. But a few lines chosen at random will at least give the flavor of his work:

> Laramie hogs . . . have a deep and abiding love for home, all of them, and they don't care whose home it is either.

> Last week I visited my birthplace in the State of Maine. I waited thirty years for the public to visit it, and as there didn't seem to be much of a rush this spring, I thought I would go and visit it my self.

Nye returned to the East after he fell ill with spinal meningitis and was told to leave Laramie's 7,200-foot altitude. In 1884 he moved to Hudson, Wisconsin. His reputation enabled him to begin selling articles to the *Boston Globe* in 1885 and to the *New York World* the next year. Then his column was syndicated to about sixty papers. After 1886 he lived at times in New York City and at times in Arden, North Carolina, but spent much of his time on the road. He took up the lecture circuit, often teaming with James Whitcomb Riley for appearances. He turned out several books and wrote two unsuccessful plays.

His health never did built up to full strength, and his tour schedule did nothing to help. He suffered a stroke in 1896 and died ten days later, at the age of forty-five. He is buried at Fletcher, North Carolina. Nye married Clara Frances Smith of Chicago on 7 March 1877. They had two sons and two daughters.

BIBLIOGRAPHY:

A. *Bill Nye: His Own Life Story* (New York, 1926).

B. DAB 13, 598; NCAB 6, 26; T. A. Larson, *Bill Nye's Western Humor* (Lincoln, Neb., 1968).

LAURA NICKERSON

O

OCHS, ADOLPH SIMON (b. 12 March 1858; d. 8 April 1935), who often noted that "the printing office was my high school and university," was publisher of the *Chattanooga Times* by age twenty. He later bought the bankrupt *New York Times* and transformed it into an international institution.

He was born in Cincinnati to Julius and Bertha Levy Ochs, Bavarian immigrants who raised him and his five younger siblings in a home wealthy in progressive politics but often poor in material goods. His mother, who had come to America to escape arrest for her connections with revolutionary committees, was an ardent Confederate during the Civil War; his father, an abolitionist, enlisted in the Union Army.

After the war the family moved to Knoxville, Tennessee, where Julius, a teacher fluent in six languages, emerged as a Jewish and civic leader but a less than successful provider. To help support the family, the eleven-year-old Adolph's elementary education at Bradford's Hampden-Sydney Academy was cut short, and he was sent to work as a copyboy at the *Knoxville Chronicle*. A year later he went to Providence, Rhode Island, to work as a cash boy in his maternal uncle's grocery store. Back in Knoxville by 1871, he worked briefly as a drugstore clerk before returning to the *Chronicle*, first as a printer's devil, later as an apprentice. He attended East Tennessee University's preparatory department as his job permitted.

In October 1875 Ochs found work in the job-printing department of the *Louisville Courier-Journal*. Six months later a homesick Ochs was back in Knoxville working in the composing room of a new daily, the *Tribune*. He was quickly promoted, first to reporter and then to assistant to the business manager, who took Ochs with him to Chattanooga in the fall of 1877 to serve as advertising solicitor on his new paper, the *Chattanooga Dispatch*. When the paper failed within six months, the unemployed but resourceful Ochs noted that the city lacked a directory and published one. With the profits from this venture and a small loan, Ochs purchased controlling half-interest in the failing *Chattanooga Times*. With only $37.50 in working capital, he became publisher on 2 July 1878. His brothers George and Milton joined the paper as reporters, and with their help Ochs made it a financial success; he bought the outstanding interest in the paper in 1880.

On 28 February 1883 Ochs married Effie Miriam Wise, who was soon working as the paper's book reviewer and drama critic. In 1891, dissatisfied with the wire services, Ochs, as secretary of the Southern Press Association, organized the Southern Associated Press. He served as general manager and executive committee chairman until it was dissolved in 1894, when he joined the Associated Press.

On 18 August 1896 Ochs bought a morning paper he once said represented the opportunity of a lifetime—the *New York Times*. To help raise circulation and decrease its deficit, Ochs offered his readers a pictorial Sunday magazine to rival the penny papers' comic supplements and established the *Review of Books*. But a decline in advertising—he refused to accept ''objectionable'' advertising—and the expensive coverage of the war with Spain brought the paper to the economic edge. In October 1898, believing that many of the penny papers' readers were loyal only to the price, Ochs went against all advice and lowered the *Times* price to one cent; circulation more than tripled within a year.

On his twenty-fifth anniversary as publisher of the *Times*, Ochs noted that during those years less than one percent of the paper's gross income had been withdrawn as dividends; the rest had been reinvested in the paper. Indeed, Ochs was always researching the latest printing technology. And he firmly believed in fulfilling the motto which first appeared in the *Times* masthead on 25 October 1896: ''All The News That's Fit To Print.'' Ochs had brought the paper into the Associated Press in 1896, joining its board of directors and executive committee in 1900. He held these positions until his death. In 1901 the *Times* began exchanging news with the *London Times*, and with its cooperation six years later, Ochs arranged with Marconi the first transatlantic wireless news service. During World War I the paper published in full the official statements of the various European governments; for its ''disinterested and meritorious service,'' the *Times* was awarded the first Pulitzer Gold Medal in Journalism in June 1918.

Ochs had bought the *Philadelphia Times* in 1901 and the *Philadelphia Ledger* a year later, but he sold them in 1913. He had established several subsidiaries to the New York Times Company: in January 1913, the *Annalist*, a weekly financial review; in August 1914, the *Current History Magazine*, a monthly survey of world affairs; in September 1914, the *Mid-Week Pictorial*, an illustrated review of the week's news; and in 1919, the Wide-World Photo Service. Devoted to humanistic studies, Ochs helped launch the American Council of Learned Societies' *Dictionary of American Biography* in the late 1920s.

In 1931, having lived for many years in New York City, Ochs moved to Hillandale, an estate in nearby White Plains. He and his wife summered at Abenia, their home on Lake George in the Adirondacks since 1915, where Ochs had engraved over the mantles "Unless the Lord build the house, they labor in vain that build it." While opposed to Zionism, he had long patronized Jewish causes. He gave the Chattanooga congregation a temple in memory of his parents. It was there, on 10 April 1935, that Ochs's funeral services were held. He had died of a cerebral hemorrhage two days earlier after visiting the *Chattanooga Times* for the first time in three years, having been kept away by ill health. One month later, Arthur Hays Sulzberger, husband of the Ochses' only daughter, Iphigene Bertha, became publisher of the *New York Times*.

BIBLIOGRAPHY:

B. DAB 1, 17–21; NYT 9 April 1935; Meyer Berger, *The Story of the "New York Times"* 1851–1951 (New York, 1951); Elmer Davis, *History of the "New York Times," 1851–1921* (New York, 1921); Gerald W. Johnson, *An Honorable Titan* (New York, 1946).

KRISTEN DOLLASE

OGDEN, ROLLO (b. 19 January 1856; d. 22 February 1937) entered the newspaper industry from the Presbyterian pulpit. After ten years of ministerial work, he resigned and began a career as a free-lance writer. In 1891 he joined the staff of the *New York Evening Post* and remained on the editorial side until joining the *New York Times* in 1920. He became editor in 1922 after the death of Charles Ransom Miller and remained editor until his death at age eighty-one.

Ogden was born at Sand Lake, New York, on 19 January 1856, the son of the Reverend Isaac Gray Ogden, a Presbyterian minister, and Emma Huntington. The precocious Ogden received most of his formal education from his parents, both former schoolteachers. Besides a quest for knowledge, the young Ogden possessed a rententive memory that would impress colleagues throughout his life.

He worked his way through Williams College by tutoring. He was able to transmit his exceptional powers of concentration to his pupils; there is the record of one student that he successfully prepared for a college entrance examination in Greek in the course of a single summer! But it wasn't all work for Ogden—he was pitcher for the Williams College baseball team.

After graduation in 1877, he spent two years at Andover Theological Seminary and another year at the Union Theological Seminary in New York. After a year as assistant pastor at Cleveland's Old Stone Church, he was ordained a Presbyterian minister in 1878. During that year he gave Greek lessons to the two daughters of the minister of Old Stone, the Reverend Arthur Mitchell. On 30 November 1881 he married one of those daughters, Susan.

Soon after the wedding, the couple left for Mexico City where Ogden served on the staff of the theological institution maintained by the Presbyterian Mission

Board. Though only there for two years, Ogden became proficient in Spanish which he later put to use in his works relating to Spanish-American history. (He translated from the Spanish, Jorge Issacs's *Maria, a South American Romance*.) After two years, they returned to Cleveland because of a serious illness which overtook his wife. After four years as minister of the Case Avenue Presbyterian Church, he resigned his position and retired from the ministry in 1887 because of a change in religious outlook and a growing inclination for literary work.

The family moved to New York, where Ogden began his career as a free-lance literary writer. He regularly contributed book reviews and special articles to the *New York Evening Post* and the *Nation*. In 1891 Ogden joined the editorial staff of the *Evening Post*, and for the next thirty years, he contributed daily editorial comment and wrote a column of literary chronicle and criticism. The *Evening Post*, under the leadership of Edwin Lawrence Godkin (q.v.), was among the foremost representatives of independent journalism. Ogden's contributions during the Godkin and Horace White (q.v.) eras continued to grow in scope and weight. He also served as correspondent for the *Manchester Guardian*.

Ogden succeeded White as chief editor in 1908. Like his predecessors, Ogden and the *Evening Post* continued to oppose the Bryan leadership, stood firm against a policy of overseas expansion, and assailed the protectionist policies of the Republican party, while at the same time campaigning for civil service reform and progressive policies for the underprivileged classes. The *Post*'s editorial policies also favored woman suffrage, protective legislation in industry, international cooperation for peace, and the defense of blacks' rights. It was through the leadership of Ogden, a staff of writers including Alexander Dana Noyes, Fabian Franklin, Paul Elmer More, and Hammond Lamont, and publisher Oswald Garrison Villard (q.v.) that the *Evening Post* shaped public opinion.

Ogden resigned as chief editor on 6 May 1920 and became associate editor of the *New York Times* on 7 May 1920. After the death of Charles R. Miller in 1922, Ogden was named chief editor. Under his guidance, the editorial page of the *Times* continued to uphold national expansion, denounce Tammany Hall, and call for honesty and efficiency in city government. He was given unlimited freedom by publisher Adolph S. Ochs (q.v.) to search for truth and to advocate what principles and policies he felt were right.

Ogden remained in touch with daily and periodical journalism in the United States and abroad, and with the world of books, reading everything from fiction to general scientific works. He was the author of the standard life of historian William H. Prescott in the American Men of Letters Series (1904) and *Life and Letters of Edwin Lawrence Godkin* (1907).

From 1912 to his death, Ogden's energies were given mainly to his daily editorial labors. He was reluctant to halt his daily exercise of scrupulous and candid judgment. He died on 22 February 1937 from complications resulting from a cold. He was the father of three children, Nelson, Alice and Winifred.

BIBLIOGRAPHY:
B. NYT 23 February 1937; Meyer Berger, *The Story of the "New York Times"* 1851–1951 (New York, 1951).

CHRISTINE M. MILLER

OLDER, FREMONT (b. 30 August 1856; d. 3 March 1935) was one of America's most prominent and controversial newspaper editors. While at the helm of the *San Francisco Bulletin* (1895–1918) he gained a reputation among admirers as a brilliant crusader for justice and reform. But to others he was an oppportunistic yellow journalist whose prime concern was building newspaper circulation. A dynamic man, Older was also a civic reformer, a leader in the California progressive movement, and a champion of the underdog.

Older was born in Freedom Township near Appleton, Wisconsin, the son of Joseph Emory and Celia Marie Augur Older, pioneer Presbyterian farm folk and abolitionists. He was named for the explorer John C. Frémont. His father, a Civil War private, died in 1864 after being released from a Confederate prison camp. His mother then sold books to support her two sons, Fremont and Herbert.

Older attended grammar schools in Appleton and Omro, Wisconsin, for about three years, then enrolled in 1868 in the preparatory department of nearby Ripon College. He attended for one term. He set out at thirteen, inspired by Horace Greeley (q.v.), to make his way in the world, principally as a printer's devil and newspaper compositor.

In 1873 he went West and worked chiefly as a compositor on newspapers for eight years in California and Nevada. In 1881 he became a reporter and city editor of the weekly Redwood City, California *Times-Gazette*. On 2 June 1881 he maried Emma Finger, a music teacher, and they had two children: a daughter, born in 1882, and a son in 1885. They were divorced, probably in 1885.

For the next ten years Older was a reporter and city editor on at least three San Francisco papers. On 22 August 1893 he married Cora Miranda Baggerly, a Syracuse University student, who was a prolific writer during their forty-two-year marriage. Two years later he became editor of the *San Francisco Bulletin* and set out, emulating William Randolph Hearst's (q.v.) yellow methods, to turn the conservative, declining evening daily into an exciting, financially successful newspaper.

Although at times ruthless and unscrupulous, Older crusaded for muncipal reform. When the city later lapsed into corruption under Mayor Eugene Schmitz and the notorious boss Abraham Ruef, Older was primarily responsible, through a "holy war" crusade, for the celebrated graft prosecution (1906–08) and for Reuf's imprisonment and a purified city government. He gained national prominence when he was kidnapped at gunpoint during the prosecution. Older was also a leading voice for the California progressive movement. This brought reform to the state government through the administration of his close friend, Governor Hiram Johnson.

Older turned the *Bulletin* into a journalism school, discovering and developing talented writers, many of them women. They wrote the scoops, exposés, and confession stories that made the *Bulletin* famous. Older is credited with the first use of the words *gangster* and *higher-up*.

As champion of the underdog, he worked for prison reform; justice for prostitutes, political radicals, and ex-convicts; and for abolition of capital punishment. Unlike most progressives, he supported unions and strikes and maintained his opposition to World War I. Influenced by the Social Gospel, he had a change of heart about Ruef's guilt and campaigned to have him released from prison. It was opposed by many, but along with his other crusades, it was good for circulation.

In 1917 Older began his last major crusade—to free Tom Mooney and Warren Billings, anarchists convicted in San Francisco's Preparedness Day bombing. Convinced they were convicted by perjured testimony, Older worked tirelesly for their release. His publisher objected, and he left the *Bulletin* in 1918 to work for his rival, W. R. Hearst, as editor of the *San Francisco Call*. He remained there and later as editor of Hearst's *Call-Bulletin* until he died of a heart atack in 1935.

Older was an impetuous, unpredictable man with a lively intellectual curiosity and a deep humanitarian concern for his fellowman. Although he wrote little until his later years, he cultivated the art in others. During World War II a U.S. Navy liberty ship was named for him, as was an elementary school in Cupertino, California, in 1966.

BIBLIOGRAPHY:

A. *My Own Story* (Oakland, Calif., 1919); *Growing Up* (San Francisco, 1931).

B. DAB 21, Supp. 1, 580–582; DLB 25, 235–243; Robert W. Davenport, ''Fremont Older in San Francisco Journalism, 1856–1918; a Partial Biography,'' Ph.D. diss., Univ. of California, Los Angeles, 1969; NYT 4 March 1935; *San Francisco Call-Bulletin*, 4, 5, and 6 March 1935; Evelyn Wells, *Fremont Older* (New York, 1936).

ROBERT W. DAVENPORT

OSBON, BRADLEY SILLICK (b. 16 August 1827; d. 6 May 1912) was a Civil War correspondent for the *New York World* and the *New York Herald* who earned celebrity status for his eyewitness accounts of major naval battles. He reported the outbreak of the Civil War with the bombing of Fort Sumter, the battles of New Orleans and of Port Royal, South Carolina, and the ironclad *Montauk* engagements in Georgia before establishing a naval news syndicate. His swashbuckling career included imprisonment for alleged violation of the Articles of War and the founding of America's first maritime newspaper, the *Nautical Gazette* (1871).

Born in Rye, Westchester County, New York, Osbon was a youthful delinquent, and thus a source of consternation and embarrassment to his father, Abiathar Mann Osbon, a Methodist minister. He repeatedly ran away from home, first at the age of eleven when he went to work on Hudson River Canal boats.

At thirteen, Osbon joined the crew of a ship sailing between New York and Liverpool, England, bringing Irish immigrants to America on the return trip. Upon his return to New York City, he enrolled in a private school in Brooklyn to study navigation.

A self-described "sailor of fortune," Osbon later joined the U.S. Navy, but he found service on storeships so boring that he mustered out of the navy in search of more adventure. He signed on a whaling ship en route to the Arctic and Antarctic oceans in 1847, disembarking in Hong Kong in 1851, when he joined the Anglo-Chinese navy to fight pirates in the South China Sea. After a short stay in the United States in 1852, Osbon joined the Argentine navy in 1853 as a schooner captain, resigning to become a quartermaster on a steamship in 1857. A year later, he ended his merchant marine career and returned to the United States.

In the United States, Obson made a tour of the lecture circuit, telling stories of his exotic travels and seafaring adventures. Newspaper editors often asked him to write his lectures for publication, tasks that Osbon enjoyed and which kindled an ambition for a journalism career. He contributed to many New York newspapers before joining the *New York World* in 1860. Obson claimed to be the first reporter the *World* hired.

Serving in a dual capacity as a *World* correspondent and ship's signal officer, Osbon was aboard a U.S. naval cutter off Charleston Harbor on 12 April 1861 when Fort Sumter was bombarded, forcing the surrender of Union forces and the outbreak of civil war. Osbon's dispatch to the *World* began with a terse lead: "The ball is opened. War is inaugurated" (Paine, 1906). His stunning account of the dramatic event gained him fame in newspaper circles.

Osbon joined the staff of the *New York Herald* as naval editor in 1861, earning a $25-a-week salary that nearly tripled his $9-a-week income from the *World*. As a *Herald* correspondent, Osbon also received a roving commission from the secretary of the navy to accompany naval expeditions "in any staff capacity to which the commanding officer may see fit to appoint him." He used his commission to cover the Battle of Port Royal in November 1861; in 1862 David Farragut appointed Osbon clerk of his flagship for the expedition against New Orleans; and he served as a clerk and signal officer on the ironclad monitor *Montauk*'s expedition against Fort McAllister, Georgia, in March 1863. Obson resigned from the *Herald* in 1864 to establish a naval news syndicate.

With headquarters in New York City, Osbon's bureau of naval intelligence supplied stories to nearly twenty newspapers. His stories based on advance information about an impending Union attack on Wilmington, North Carolina, were prematurely released in December 1864, by newspapers in Boston and Philadelphia. Because the reports were reprinted in Richmond's newspapers, Osbon was arrested on 1 January 1865, and charged with violating the Articles of War for giving information to the enemy. He was imprisoned for six months in the Capitol Prison, Washington, D.C. Osbon steadfastly maintained his innocence, won acquittal, and was released after six months of confinement.

A brief stint in the Mexican navy near Brownsville, Texas, in 1866, was followed by work for the New York Associated Press as a boarding officer at New Orleans in 1867 and Osbon's marriage to Eliza Balfour on 14 February 1868. With his wife, he traveled in Europe and sent reports about maritime activities to American newspapers.

With a captial investment of $4,000, Osbon founded the *Nautical Gazette* in New York City in 1871. Two years later, the weekly *Gazette*'s circulation had reached 7,000 and its size had doubled to sixteen pages. Osbon sold the newspaper in 1884, effectively closing his newspaper career and using the proceeds from the sale to engage in a series of unsucessful international business ventures. Osbon died impoverished at the Post-Graduate Hospital in New York City at the age of eighty-four, his only source of income being an inadequate government pension of twenty dollars a month.

BIBLIOGRAPHY:

A. *Visitor's Hand Book, or, How To See the Great Eastern* (New York, 1860); *Handbook of the United States Navy* (New York, 1864).

B. DLB 43, 330–333; *New York Herald*, 7 May 1912; *New York World*, 7 May 1912; Albert Bigelow Paine, *A Sailor of Fortune: Personal Memoirs of Captain B. S. Osbon* (New York, 1906).

ARTHUR J. KAUL

O'SULLIVAN, TIMOTHY H. (b. ca. 1840; d. 14 January 1882) was a pioneer in the field of photography, documenting the Civil War as Mathew Brady's (q.v.) employee and the frontier landscapes in California, Nevada, Utah, Arizona, and Panama as a member of various geological expeditions. Two years before his death he was appointed chief photographer for the U.S. Department of the Treasury. His photographs are remarkably clear and aesthetically pleasing for their time. O'Sullivan primarily used large-format (11" × 14") cameras and the collodian wet-plate process.

There is uncertainty about O'Sullivan's birthdate and whether he was born in Ireland or New York City. His parents, Ann D. and Jeremiah O'Sullivan, reportedly emigrated to New York around 1842 and settled in Staten Island. Little else is known about his background or formal education. At the age of sixteen he began an apprenticeship in photography under Alexander Gardner (q.v.) at the nationally renowned portrait studios of Mathew Brady. Around 1856 O'Sullivan was living in Washington, D.C., and working in Brady's studio there, coming in contact with the city's educated and elite.

In April 1861 when the Civil War erupted, Brady and several assistants (including O'Sullivan) left the studio and went into the field to photograph the federal troops protecting the nation's capital. In the fall O'Sullivan went to South Carolina to document General W. T. Sherman's expedition, photographing military activities and the local scenery until May 1862. Upon returning to Washington, O'Sullivan went back to Brady's studio, but left soon afterwards to work for Gardner, who had gone into business for himself. O'Sullivan was named "superintendent of the field or copy work to the Army of the Potomac." Some of the most memorable images of the Civil War are O'Sullivan's photographs of the aftermath of battles at Gettysburg, Fredericksburg, Petersburg, and Appomattox.

Having proven himself an accomplished technician and able to withstand grueling fieldwork, O'Sullivan was ready for further challenges. In April 1867 he was hired at $100 a month as the official photographer on the U.S. Geological Survey led by Clarence King. It was his job to help produce a geological and topographical survey of territory between the Rocky Mountains and the Sierra Nevada. For the next two years O'Sullivan traveled with the expedition, risking his life by using magnesium powder ignited in an open tray 900 feet underground at the Comstock Lode mines in Virginia City, Nevada. In September 1870 he was hired to photograph Lieutenant George Montague Wheeler's exploration of the Southwest, which began in the spring of 1871.

O'Sullivan returned to Washington to marry Laura Virginia Pywell on 11 February 1873, but a few months later went back to Wheeler's geographical survey in Arizona and New Mexico. For the next year he made trips back and forth to Washington to print what he had photographed, but did not resume a normal life there until late in 1874. The following year he continued printing for Wheeler in Washington. On 13 September 1876 O'Sullivan's wife delivered a son stillborn.

Two years later he worked as a photogapher for William J. Armstrong and Company, but in 1880 he became a temporary employee of Clarence King at the newly formed U.S. Geological Surveys. With recommendations from Mathew Brady and Alexander Gardner, O'Sullivan was appointed chief photographer for the U.S. Treasury Department on 6 November 1880.

However, in March 1881 O'Sullivan contracted pulmonary tuberculosis, which forced him to leave his job with the Treasury Department and return to his parents' home on Staten Island, New York. His wife died on 18 October 1881, and he attended her funeral in Washington. After returning to Staten Island, O'Sullivan died on 14 January 1882 at the age of forty-one or forty-two.

BIBLIOGRAPHY:

B. Alexander Gardner, *Photographic Incidents of the War* (Washington, 1882); James D. Horan, *Timothy O'Sullivan: America's Forgotten Photographer* (New York, 1966); *Macmillan Biographical Encyclopedia of Photographic Artists and Innovators* (New York, 1983); Nancy Newhall and Beaumont Newhall, *T. H. O'Sullivan: Photographer* (Rochester, 1966); Joel Snyder, *American Frontiers: The Photographs of Timothy H. O'Sullivan, 1867–1874* (Millerton, N.Y., 1981).

C. ZOE SMITH

OTIS, HARRISON GRAY (b. 10 February 1837; d. 30 July 1917), born near Marietta, Ohio, the son of Stephen and Sarah Dyar Otis, claimed descent from Boston patriot James Otis. He married Eliza A. Wetherly, probably on 11 September 1859 (one source says 1857). They had three daughters. His wife died in 1904.

Otis enlisted in the Union army during the Civil War and rose from the rank of private to lieutenant colonel, was decorated and twice wounded. After the war he worked at a series of federal and local government jobs in Ohio, Washington, D.C., and Alaska. He also published a newspaper at Marietta for a time, and was the Washington correspondent for the *State Journal*, a Columbus, Ohio, newspaper. For five years he ran the *Grand Army Journal*, a paper for Civil War veterans.

Otis moved to California in 1876, and for four years he ran the *Santa Barbara Press*. Then he went to Alaska as a treasury agent, and in 1882 moved to Los Angeles and purchased a one-fourth interest in the *Los Angeles Times*. He bought more shares in the next few years, and in 1886 he took over control of the *Times*. He became editor, manager, and president.

Otis was known for his firm anti-union policies, which were among the factors leading to a multi-fatality bombing at the *Times* in 1910, the conviction of the McNamara brothers for the bombing, and jury tampering charges against defense counsel Clarence Darrow. Otis helped found the Los Angeles Chamber of Commerce and was well known as a vigorous promoter of growth in and around Los Angeles.

Otis has been described as a man always looking for his next enemy and his next fight. It is said that even his purchase of a controlling interest in the *Times* from H. H. Boyce was undertaken as a contest between opponents. The *Times* he ran was not regarded by the American newspaper establishment as a good newspaper, and Otis barely receives more than passing mention in many standard histories of American journalism. His significance is that he bought the paper early in its history, kept it alive, helped build a prosperous region in which it could grow, and fought unions so effectively that the *Times* printing plant never was unionized, allowing it to move into technological change more rapidly than some papers could.

Otis returned to military service during the Spanish-American War, was commissioned a brigadier general, and served in the Philippines during the insurrection of 1898–99. He died in Los Angeles.

BIBLIOGRAPHY:

B. NYT 31 July 1917; David Halberstam, *The Powers That Be* (New York, 1979).

DWIGHT JENSEN

OTTENBERG, MIRIAM (b. 7 October 1914; d. 9 November 1982), a Pulitzer Prize–winning investigative reporter, set a snappy pace for Washington reporters. Ottenberg was the first woman police reporter for the *Washington Star*, an unusual assignment for a woman at the time. In addition to a wide range of front-page exposés uncovering abortion rings, unethical used car sales operations, and underworld figures, Ottenberg wrote two books, one of which examined the disease that forced her early retirement, multiple sclerosis; it was the first comprehensive text on the subject.

Ottenberg, one of three children, was born in Washington, D.C., to Louis Ottenberg, an attorney and a founder of the Anti-Defamation League of B'nai B'rith, and Nettie Podell Ottenberg, a social worker involved in a wide variety of causes. Ottenberg described her mother in an unpublished biography as "the mother of childcare," noting that although she never went to high school, she was an alumna of Columbia University. Her grandfather, Isaac Ottenberg, founded the prosperous Ottenberg Bakery in the city.

She attended old Central High School in Washington and Goucher College near Baltimore, as well as Columbia University in New York before graduating from the University of Wisconsin with a B.A. in journalism in 1935. Ottenberg worked for a Chicago advertising agency following her college graduation and a year later became a reporter in the women's department for what was then the *Akron Times-Press*. Joining the *Star* in 1937, she launched an investigation immediately. By the time a decade was out, she was known for her specialty, crime reporting, and her stories covered phony marriage counselors, a multi-state abortion ring, high food prices, juvenile crime, sex offenders and narcotics addicts.

She was awarded a Pulitzer Prize in journalism in 1960 for her seven-part series "Buyer Beware," which had appeared in the *Star* the previous year and which culminated three months of painstaking investigation. Alerting Congress and the public to shabby practices of unscrupulous used-car dealers and finance companies, the series led to wide-ranging legislation outlawing the unethical practices revealed. Only four women had won a journalism Pulitzer before her in its more than forty-year history.

Several years later, she broke a page-one story that appeared not only in the *Star* but in newspapers throughout the country. Joseph Valachi's testimony painted what was then as yet unseen pictures of the underworld "Cosa Nostra," the Mafia, significant because it was the first time an insider was willing to talk and confirm the group's existence.

Ottenberg was an early investigative reporter of white-collar crime and consumer fraud, and in a long-standing journalistic tradition, she often worked under cover in the guise of a potential victim. Many of her stories led to subsequent corrective legislation and accolades from governmental officials; on one occasion Washington law enforcement agencies even honored her with a testimonial reception and plaque recognizing her contributions. When Robert F. Kennedy, then attorney general, swore her in as president of the Washington Press Club in 1960, he said, "Justice is usually pictured as a tall woman, blindfolded; but the *Star*'s adaptation is a small slender woman, who is certainly not blindfolded."

In addition to her countless day-to-day stories in the *Washington Star*, she had written *The Federal Investigators* (1962), as well as a study of multiple sclerosis, *The Pursuit of Hope: A Pulitzer Prize-winner Tells the Story of How She and Many Others Fought and Conquered the Fear, Uncertainty and Despair of Multiple Sclerosis* (1978).

On learning that she had cancer, she proceeded to write a definitive study from the point of view of its victims, as she had done in 1978 on multiple sclerosis. This time, however, the disease conquered. She died of cancer at Washington's Georgetown Hospital on 9 November 1982, the book unfinished.

BIBLIOGRAPHY:

B. *Foremost Women in Communication* (New York, 1970); *Washington Post*, 10 November 1982; John Hohenberg, *The New Front Page* (New York, 1966); Marion Marzolf, *Up From the Footnote: A History of Women Journalists* (New York, 1977).

KATHLEEN K. KEESHEN

OUTCAULT, RICHARD FENTON (b. 14 January 1863; d. 25 September 1928) was a comic artist best known for his creation of *The Yellow Kid* and the characters of Buster Brown and Tige. Outcault drew the Yellow Kid for both Joseph Pulitzer and William Randolph Hearst (qq.v.) and unintentionally gave the era of yellow journalism its name.

Outcault was born in Lancaster, Ohio, the son of Jesse Pugh Outcault and Catherine Davis Outcault. He studied art at McMicken University (which later became the University of Cincinnati) from 1877 to 1878, and then received further training in Paris. Upon his return to the United States, Outcault settled in New York, where he was forced to take up commercial illustration to earn a living. For three years he worked as a draftsman for *Electrical World* and then the *Street Railway Journal*, but technical illustration bored the young artist. As a creative outlet, Outcault drew comics for some of the popular magazines of the time, including *Truth*, *Judge*, and *Life*.

His comic cartoons were extremely popular, and this new exposure came at a fortuitous time. Pulitzer's *New York World* had finally developed a usable color-printing process and wanted to introduce color into the paper. Sunday editor Morrill Goddard (q.v.) decided to use color for a comic section, but the established cartoonists he sought were already under contract to other publishers, so Goddard turned to Outcault.

The artist began his strip *Hogan's Alley* on 18 November 1894, with a page-wide drawing featuring caricatures of kids from the New York tenements. *Hogan's Alley* was an occasional feature until the *World* color-man dabbed bright yellow ink on the billowing nightshirt of the central kid and the strip became a weekly hit. Outcault incorporated contemporary events into the strip, and its popularity caught the eye of the brash young publisher, William Randolph Hearst.

As part of Hearst's assault on Pulitzer's audience, he hired away star reporters and editors, including Goddard and most of his staff for his *New York Journal*. In 1896 the *Journal* added a color page; since Goddard had brought Outcault with him to Hearst's paper, at a tremendous salary, *Hogen's Alley* and its central kid appeared in Hearst's *Journal*. Not willing to give up, Pulitzer hired cartoonist George Luks to draw his own Yellow Kid for the *World*.

The grinning, bald child with the yellow nightshirt was featured in advertising of both Hearst and Pulitzer, and a circulation war centered around which paper had the better—and the real—Yellow Kid. Ervin Wardman of the *New York Press* referred to the papers of Pulitzer and Hearst as the ''Yellow Press,'' and Charles Dana (q.v.) took up the nickname in the *Sun*. Eventually, the term *yellow journalism* came to describe the whole era of sensationalism.

Outcault moved to yet another New York paper, the *New York Herald*, in 1901. During his two years there he developed his most popular characters, based upon his own children: Buster Brown and Mary Jane. Along with Buster's dog, Tige, the characters were wildly popular and spawned fads in clothing and children's (and dogs') names. The success of the characters brought Outcault a fortune and offers of employment abroad. He published books on Buster and Tige, and founded the Outcault Advertising Company in Chicago to syndicate his drawings. He also developed another strip, *Pore Li'L Mose*, but it never came close to Buster's popularity.

Outcault returned to the *Journal* in 1905, and retired from active newspaper work in 1918. While in retirement he worked as president of his advertising company and continued the Buster series, including a play about Buster which he coauthored.

Outcault married Mary Jane Martin in 1890, and had two children, Richard Fenton and Mary Jane, who married a nephew of General John Pershing. Outcault died in 1928 at his home in Flushing, New York, after an illness of about ten weeks.

BIBLIOGRAPHY:

B. DAB 7, 112; NYT 26 September 1928; R. L. McCardell, ''Opper, Outcault and Company: The Comic Supplement and the Men Who Make It,'' *Everybody's Magazine*, June 1905.

CAROLYN G. CLINE

PAINE, THOMAS (b. 29 January 1737; d. 8 June 1809), magazine editor, revolutionary political pamphleteer, radical Deist agitator, and author, remains today a controversial public figure. His *Common Sense* in 1776 helped to rally public support for an immediate declaration of independence from Great Britain. In his other writing he took an extreme, partisan stand on two major issues which still divide Americans: in politics he stood with the Jeffersonians against the Hamiltonians and in religion he stood with the modernists against the funadmentalists.

Paine was born in Thetford, England, the son of Joseph Paine, a poor Quaker corset maker, and Frances Cocke Paine, an Anglican and the daughter of an attorney. Young Thomas attended grammar school until he was thirteen, when the family's poverty made it necessary to apprentice him as a staymaker. He left home at nineteen, shipping on the *King of Prussia* for a brief career as a privateer at the outbreak of war in 1756. After trying numerous occupations, including that of teacher, tobacconist, and grocer, in 1762 Paine became an exciseman, a post from which he was twice dismissed.

In England Paine went through two brief, childless marriages. He was married to Mary Lambert at Sandwich on 27 September 1759. She died within a year of their marriage. He was married to Elizabeth Ollive on 26 March 1771 while stationed at Lewes as exciseman. They were legally separated in 1774, due more to temperamental difficulties on both sides than to any scandal. The facts surrounding the separation, however, later proved to be a boon to Paine's enemies.

In November 1774, bearing letters of introduction from Benjamin Franklin (q.v.), whom he had met in London, Paine sailed for America. For eighteen months he edited and wrote for the new *Pennsylvania Magazine* in Philadelphia, aligning himself with the radical camp. He agreed, for example, with Samuel Adams (q.v.) that American subjects of the Crown were entitled to every right enjoyed by Englishmen. He advocated emancipation of slaves, the abolition of dueling, the extension of equal rights to women, the prevention of cruelty to animals, the establishment of national and international copyright laws, and the establishment of rational, equitable divorce laws.

In a forty-seven page pamphlet, *Common Sense*, published anonymously in 1776, Paine marshaled his arguments for independence, urging the immediate declaration of independence as a practical gesture that would help unite the colonies as well as fulfill America's moral obligation to the world. The pamphlet originally was sold for two shillings, but the demand was so great that attempts to sell it were abandoned. With Congress paying for printing costs, an estimated half million copies were printed and distributed.

After the authorship of *Common Sense* became known, Paine defended himself against Loyalist attacks in the *Pennsylvania Journal*. He also enlisted in the Continental army in time to join in the retreat across New Jersey. At Newark, he set to work on his first *Crisis* paper, which appeared in the *Pennsylvania Journal* on 19 December 1776 and was printed in pamphlet form on 23 December. The pamphlet, which began with the sentence "These are the times that try men's souls," was ordered read to every corporal's guard by General Washington. During the next six years, Paine published a total of sixteen *American Crisis* pamphlets in support of the rebelling American colonies. During this time he was appointed secretary to the Congressional Committee on Foreign Affairs, where he served for two years before being forced to resign in 1779 following his involvement in a letter-writing controversy.

In November 1779 Paine was appointed clerk of the Pennsylvania Assembly, continuing to work on his *Crisis* papers. He accompanied John Laurens to France in 1779 in a successful search for money and stores to wage the war. The end of the war, however, found Paine honored but poor. New York gave him a confiscated Loyalist farm at New Rochelle, and Pennsylvania rewarded him with £500 in cash. Until 1787 he lived in Bordentown, New Jersey, where he worked on a model for an iron bridge.

Paine sailed in 1787 for Europe, where he hoped to get his bridge erected. He spent two pleasant years, partly in France and partly in England, where he was made welcome as the author of *Common Sense* and as the friend of George Washington. The fall of the Bastille found him in Yorkshire making arrangements for his bridge to be built. He left for Paris late in 1789, and for the next three years alternated between Paris and London, a self-appointed missionary of world revolution. Paine hoped that his *Rights of Man* (1791–92), a two-part defense of the French Revolution against the attacks of Edmund Burke, would do in England what *Common Sense* had done in America. Instead, the work was suppressed, and Paine, now safe in France, was tried for treason in December 1792 and outlawed.

In Paris, Paine became a French citizen and was elected to the Revolutionary Convention, where he allied himself with the moderate republicans. After they lost power during the Terror in 1793, Paine's citizenship was revoked, and he was arrested as an enemy Englishman. While in a Luxembourg jail, Paine completed *The Age of Reason*, (1794–96), his "deistic Bible," which aroused great indignation in America as well as England. While many of his associates lost their heads to the guillotine, Paine was never brought to trial, and after the Terror had ended he was released in November 1794 at the request of James Monroe, the new American minister.

Paine finally returned to America in 1802, but his last years in Bordentown, New Jersey, New York City, and New Rochelle were marked by poverty, declining health, and social ostracism. Paine's enemies circulated stories accusing him of being a drunkard, a coward, an adulterer, and a "tavern atheist." He died in New York on 8 June 1809 as a social outcast and was buried in a corner of his farm in New Rochelle. In 1819 William Cobbett (q.v.), to atone for his bitter attacks on Paine in the 1790s, had Paine's bones dug up and transported to England, intending to raise a monument to honor the author of *Rights of Man*. After Corbbett's death in 1835, the bones passed into the hands of a receiver in probate and were lost.

BIBLIOGRAPHY:

A. *Agrarian Justice* (New York, 1797).

B. DAB 7, 159–166; Philip S. Foner, *The Life and Major Writings of Thomas Paine*, 4 vols. (New York, 1967); David Freeman Hawke, *Paine* (New York, 1974).

HARRY W. STONECIPHER

PALEY, WILLIAM SAMUEL (b. 28 September 1901) the broadcast executive, founded and helped build CBS, Inc. into a highly profitable American entertainment network. He is credited with organizing the CBS news organization. Under his leadership, Edward R. Murrow (q.v.) built a European news department which has been credited as a principal factor in establishing CBS as leader in the radio news field. The dominance continued into television news. In the late 1940s Paley raided NBC and signed such major stars as Edgar Bergen, Charlie McCarthy, Jack Benny, Red Skelton, Frank Sinatra, and Amos 'n' Andy. Other ventures were not so successful, like a brief ownership of the New York Yankees baseball team in the late 1960s, and an early move into the home video recording industry.

William Paley was born in Chicago in 1901 to cigar manufacturer, Samuel Paley, and his wife, Goldie Drell Paley. In 1918 he graduated from Western Military Academy, Alton, Illinois. He then attended the University of Chicago from 1918 to 1919 before transferring to the Wharton School of Business at the University of Pennsylvania. He received his B.S. degree in 1922. Soon after college he was named vice president of the family business, the Congress Cigar Company, where he had been working while in school. His interests in radio were aroused when he once invested $50 a week in advertising on WCAU, Philadelphia. His father and uncle were away on business. When they returned they forced him to cancel, but letters from the public soon caused them to reconsider their move. When a family friend bought the young Columbia

Broadcasting System, the Paleys were among the early sponsors. Financial troubles soon forced the young network's sale, and with his father's and uncle's help, William Paley managed to buy the company in 1928.

Running CBS proved more time-consuming than the young Paley originally anticipated, but under his leadership the network prospered. One innovative idea which led to its growth was a decision to offer programming free to affiliates (NBC was charging a fee). In exchange Paley received an option to buy any part of the affiliate's schedule for sponsored network series. This enabled him to sell time to a network sponsor and then instruct all affiliates to clear the time. The method was thorough and covered advertising rates, AT&T line charges, and time-sale revenues for stations. As broadcast historian Erik Barnouw notes in *The Golden Web*, the plan's neatness was quite characteristic of Paley.

Paley quickly moved to sign programming. He entered a cooperative effort with the U.S. Department of Education in the program ''Columbia School of the Air.'' Other programs were a New York Philharmonic-Symphony Society broadcast, ''Church of the Air,'' and a dramatic series, ''The Columbia Workshop.''

With the aid of Edward Klauber, Paul W. White (qq.v.), and Edward R. Murrow, Paley soon began the creation of a news operation which would become second to none. Murrow was the first to be widely recognized by the public, but soon other personalities emerged. Larry Lesueur was sent to the Soviet Union, Howard K. Smith (q.v.) went to Berlin, and Charles Collingwood (q.v.) joined the London-based staff.

The young CBS president spoke out against the Federal Communications Commission when it investigated alleged monopoly in network broadcasting between 1938 and 1941. Paley said the adoption of new regulations removed freedom of independent lawful action without which radio itself cannot remain free.

He traveled to Europe in 1943, serving as a civilian in the Office of War Information. In 1945 he was commissioned a colonel in the U.S. Army. He served as deputy chief of the Psychological Warfare Division of the Eisenhower headquarters. Upon returning to New York in November 1945, Paley started corporate reorganization. Frank Stanton (q.v.) was named president in January 1946, when Paley assumed the chairmanship of the board. In the late 1940s, a $5 million loan helped Paley raid NBC by signing many of its top stars. The move helped propel CBS over NBC, and it was to retain this ratings supremacy until 1976.

Paley stepped down as chief executive officer of CBS in April 1977, and as chairman in 1983. He remained a member of the CBS board of directors and executive committee chairman. In 1982 Paley became a partner of Whitcom Investment Company. The company is part owner of the Paris-based *International Herald Tribune* (with the New York Times Company and the Washington Post Company), and in March of that year he was named cochairman of the newspaper.

William Paley has been recipient of some of broadcasting's most coveted awards. In 1958 he was personally cited when CBS won the George Foster Peabody Award for excellence in "the news and news documentary fields." The same happened in 1961 when CBS was awarded another Peabody. He also has been active on the civic front. In recent years he has held positions on the New York City Task Force on Urban Design; the boad of trustees of North Shore University Hospital; the Museum of Broadcasting board of directors; and the Commission for Cultural Affairs, New York City.

Paley married Dorothy Hart Hearst on 11 May 1932. They were divorced in July 1947. He then married Barbara Cushing Mortimer, whom he fondly called "Babe," five days later on 28 July 1947. The couple particularly enjoyed traveling together. Babe died of cancer on 6 July 1978. There was a son and a daughter by each mariage.

BIBLIOGRAPHY:

A. *As It Happened: A Memoir* (Garden City, N.Y., 1979).

B. Erik Barnouw, *The Golden Web* (New York, 1968); Erik Barnouw, *Tube of Plenty* (New York, 1975).

RICHARD C. VINCENT

PARKER, JAMES (b. ca. 1714; d. 2 July 1770) was a Patriot printer-postmaster who, like many in his profession, founded several newspapers. One was the *Connecticut Gazette* (1755), the first in that colony. The outstanding printer of his day, surpassing both William Bradford and Benjamin Franklin (q.v.), Parker set up printing houses in three colonies.

Parker was born at Woodbridge, New Jersey, about 1714, to Janet Ford (about whom little is known) and Samuel Parker, a cooper. James Parker married Mary Ballareau and they had two children: Samuel Franklin, who succeeded his father in business, and Jane (Jenny) Ballareau. On 1 January 1727 James Parker became apprenticed to William Bradford in New York for an eight-year period. Apparently finding his service trying, the boy ran away in the spring of 1733. Bradford offered a reward for the runaway, advertising him in his *New York Gazette* as "of a fresh Complection, with short yellowish Hair." In Philadelphia, young Parker probably found work in the establishment of the eminent printer-postmaster, Benjamin Franklin, who became his lifelong mentor. On 26 February 1742 the two formed a six-year partnership.

Early the next year, the twenty-eight-year-old Parker launched his journalistic career by starting New York's third newspaper, the *New York Weekly Post-Boy* (renamed the *New York Gazette, Revived in the Weekly Post-Boy* in 1744 when Bradford's *Gazette* expired). At first a quarto, it became a small folio in 1753, and three years later a regular-sized paper. Parker's paper showed independence and boldness, and emerged as New York's leader for some years. Like other Patriot papers of the day, the *Gazette* appeared in mourning, with heavy black column margins, to protest the Stamp Act.

Parker succeeded Bradford as public printer of New York on 1 December 1743 (a post he held until about 1760), and the New Jersey assembly made him public printer in 1758. (Seven years earlier, he had started a printing house in his New Jersey birthplace, Woodbridge.) Before long, Parker's name also stood for quality printing and journalism in Connecticut. By 1754 he was printer to Yale College and the postmaster of New Haven. There, on 12 April 1755, Parker founded the *Connecticut Gazette*, the first newspaper in the colony. Like many of its counterparts in other colonies, it offered much shipping news and many advertisements. As tensions between England and the colonies intensified, the *Gazette* championed the Patriot cause and publicized the activities of the Sons of Liberty.

Parker founded the first newspaper in New Jersey, printed by his Woodbridge press on 21 September 1765. The single-issue *Constitutional Courant* protested against the Stamp Act with this imprint by a fictitious publisher: "Printed by Andrew Marvel, at the Sign of the Bribe refused, on Constitution-Hill, North America." Centered was the familiar illustration of a snake divided into parts to represent the colonies, with the words "Join or Die." The issue sold briskly and was reprinted in New York and Boston.

In 1756 the New York assembly had Parker arrested for publishing in his *Gazette* some "Observations on the Circumstances and Conduct of the People in the Counties of Ulster and Orange." He was released only after he identified the author, apologized, and paid fees. In December 1769 Parker printed a paper addressed "To the Betrayed Inhabitants of New York," signed by "A Son of Liberty" (Alexander McDougall). The assembly judged it "a false, seditious, and infamous libel," and had Parker arrested; but he died before the case was resolved.

Probably Parker's most well-known venture in magazine publishing was the *New American Magazine*, printed at Woodbridge. A successor to Franklin's short-lived *American Magazine*, Parker's venture included twenty-seven issues (January 1758–March 1760). But like other early colonial magazines, it languished financially, and in December 1768 Parker offered to sell the remainders below cost.

Parker also printed four magazines in New York: the *Independent Reflector* (20 November 1752–22 November 1753, fifty-two weekly issues); the *Occasional Reverberator*, a folio weekly (7 September–5 October 1753, four issues); the *Instructor*, a quarto weekly (6 March–8 May 1755, ten issues); and *John Englishman*, a folio weekly (9 April–5 July 1755, ten issues).

In his last years, Parker suffered increasingly from gout. He died at a friend's home in Burlington in 1770, and was buried in the family plot in Woodbridge's Presbyterian churchyard. He bequeathed his presses—one at Burlington, one at New Haven, one at Woodbridge, and two at New York—to his son.

BIBLIOGRAPHY:

B. DAB 14, 226–227; Alan Dyer, *A Biography of James Parker: Colonial Printer* (Troy, N.Y., 1982); William H. Benedict, "James Parker, the Printer, of Woodbridge," *Proceedings of the New Jersey Historical Society*, July 1923.

NANCY L. ROBERTS

PARKS, WILLIAM (b. ca. 1698; d. April 1750) was printer of the first newspapers in Maryland and Virginia. He is remembered as an excellent craftsman and as one of the printers who used their presses to encourage colonial writers. He was a promoter of the usefulness of printing and advertising.

Little is known about Parks's life except his work as a printer. The date of his birth is uncertain. He was born in Ludlow, Shropshire, England. He established a printing business there in 1719, moved to Hereford two years later, and moved again in 1723 to Reading. He was the first printer in each town and started newspapers in Ludlow and Reading. The Maryland assembly encouraged Parks to settle there by offering him work as official printer. He arrived in Annapolis in 1726 and began printing the acts of the assembly the next year. Also in 1727 he began the *Maryland Gazette*, the first newspaper in the Southern colonies.

His paper carried news from the other colonies and from England and the Continent. On a trip to England he arranged for a supply of correspondence from Europe to keep his readers informed of developments there. However, he also used essays, satires, poems, and other literary works, many by his colonial readers. Like James Franklin's (q.v.) *New-England Courant*, he used the *Spectator* and *Tatler* of Addison and Steele as his models more than the court papers followed by other colonial printers, perhaps because he was recently from England and knew the popularity of such material. He encouraged his readers to write for his paper. He also published their works in pamphlets and books.

In 1730 Parks opened a second printing shop in Williamsburg so he could print the acts of the House of Burgesses. He left his Annapolis shop in the hands of a partner, Edmund Hall. Parks printed *A Collection of all the Acts of Assembly, Now in Force in the Colony of Virginia* in 1737. It was a fine work of craftsmanship which helped establish his reputation as one of the best colonial printers. His Virginia business drew his attention away from Annapolis. The *Maryland Gazette* was discontinued in 1731 and then revived the next year. It stopped publication in 1734. He moved his entire business to Williamsburg in 1737, and for a time Maryland did not have a printer.

The *Virginia Gazette* was begun in 1736 by Parks and had much the same character as his Maryland paper. He became a warden of Bruton Parish Church and an alderman of Williamsburg. Two of Parks's Virginia productions are of special interest to journalism historians: *Typographica. An Ode to Printing* (1730), by John Markland, an attorney in the colony, is considered the first publication about printing in the colonies; "Advertisement, concerning

Advertisements'' (8 October 1736) appeared in the *Virginia Gazette* and was probably the first promotion of newspaper advertising.

Parks was accused of libel twice by the Burgesses in Williamsburg. One account is given by Isaiah Thomas (q.v.) in his *History of Printing in America.* The other appears in the *Journal of the House of Burgesses* (1749). Thomas relates that Parks libeled a member of the House by saying he had been convicted of stealing sheep years before. The printer was released when he had the records brought out which showed his report was true. The second charge was made when Parks printed a report on the actions of the House that seemed to ridicule their actions. He got off again when evidence was produced showing that he printed what had been ordered. These two early instances of using truth as a defense in libel came soon after the famous acquittal of John Peter Zenger in New York. They reflect the common-sense approach evidently taken sometimes by colonial citizens when presented with such situations, even though it was years before truth would be recognized as a complete defense in libel.

An excellent example of the native literature encouraged by Parks and his own printing skill is *The History of the First Discovery and Settlement of Virginia* by the Reverend William Stith, Henrico Parish. Lawrence C. Wroth in his biography of Parks said it was ''the most elaborate production of its kind in the first half of the century.'' Parks enlarged his craftsmanship by establishing his own paper mill (with assistance from Benjamin Franklin) and by doing his own bookbinding. His papermill was the first one in the South and helped supply printing shops in other colonies. At the time of his death Parks's Williamsburg shop was one of the best equipped in the colonies. He died in 1750 on board a ship sailing to England. He had started the first newspapers in two English towns and in two English colonies.

BIBLIOGRAPHY:

B. DAB 7, 250–251; Lawrence C. Wroth, *A History of Printing in Colonial Maryland, 1686–1776* (Baltimore, 1922); Lawrence C. Wroth, *William Parks, Printer and Journalist of England and Colonial America* (Richmond, 1926).

ROGER YARRINGTON

PARSONS, LOUELLA OETTINGER (b. 6 August 1881; d. 9 December 1972) was the most powerful woman in Hollywood for nearly forty years. That power was based on fear. The industry's first moguls, stars, starlets, and agents all courted Parsons because they were afraid of what she would—or would not—write in her widely syndicated column of film colony gossip. In those years, publicity was the lifeblood of the movie industry, and Parsons, with her twenty million readers, was its biggest donor. All the denizens of Hollywood worked hard to ensure that she would keep it flowing their way.

Parsons was successful with all her constituencies. Her success with her fans was due to her ability to think and write like them, as one fan to another. Her success with her sources was due to her belief that Hollywood's products and people were important and to her constant defense of the film industry. Her success with her boss, William Randolph Hearst (q.v.), was due to her relentless and generally triumphant pursuit of the scoops they both treasured. This success on all fronts was great enough to negate Parson's fatal flaw—her inaccuracy. One critic said that 50 percent of the items in Parsons's column were fictitious or erroneous; others set that percentage even higher.

Parsons first fell into the pattern of fabrication when she began changing the details of her own story. Not only did she shave thirteen years off her life, but she altered the circumstances of her birth, her first marriage, and other details of her pre-Hollywood days. Parsons even wrote her second husband, riverboat captain Jack McCaffrey, out of her autobiography.

The record does show that Louella Oettinger was born in Freeport, Ilinois, in 1881 to Helen Stine Oettinger and Joshua Oettinger, owners of a dry-goods store. Her 1905 mariage to John Parsons was brief and unhappy, and he deserted his young family several years before his 1914 death. In 1910 Louella Parsons took her four-year-old daughter Harriet to Chicago, where she started her journalistic career as a reporter for the *Tribune*. Fascinated by the movie business, Parsons wrote screen scenarios at night. This led to a full-time job with Essanay Studios. When that job was eliminated in an efficiency move, Parsons was hired by the *Herald Record* to write about the movies. This job, too, was short-lived. Hearst bought the paper to merge with his *American* and her position was eliminated.

Parsons decided to move to New York to see whether her luck would be better there. It was. After a short stint with the *New York Morning Record*, Parsons once again met up with Hearst. She probably came to the publisher's attention when she said some flattering things about Marion Davies. Impressed by Parsons's popularity and news sense, as well as her good taste, Hearst made her the motion picture editor of the *New York American* in 1923 and later of the Universal News Service.

In 1925 Parsons's steady rise appeared to be at an end when she came down with a serious case of tuberculosis. A generous Hearst sent her to California to recuperate. At the end of her six-month vacation, Parsons was fully recovered. She also had decided to stay on the West Coast and write her column from there. For the next forty years, Lolly Parsons was the undisputed (except by Hedda Hopper) queen of Hollywood. Her writing was idiosyncratic, her prejudices obvious, and her spelling erratic. But she was a shrewd and tough-minded newswoman who always got her story and usually got it first. This dogged determination made Parsons a top-notch newspaper reporter. She was less successful in other media, although her radio program, "Hollywood Hotel," spawned a movie and a moderately popular touring review that once included Ronald Reagan.

Nor were the postwar years kind to Parsons. The glamour had gone out of Hollywood and television trivialized the content of her columns. She also was personally devastated by the death of her third husband, Dr. Henry Martin, and professionally hurt by the death of her boss, William Randolph Hearst.

In 1964 Parsons's own health began to deteriorate and she gave up her column. A year later she went into a nursing home, where she remained until her 1972 death.

BIBLIOGRAPHY:

A. *How to Write for the Movies* (Chicago, 1915); *The Gay Illiterate* (Garden City, N.Y., 1944); *Tell It to Louella* (New York, 1961).

B. NYT 10 December 1972; George Eells, *Hedda and Louella* (New York, 1972)

LYNNE MASEL-WALTERS

PARTON, SARA WILLIS (b. 9 July 1811; d. 10 October 1872), newspaper columnist, novelist, and author of children's books, wrote under the pseudonym Fanny Fern, providing the *New York Ledger* with weekly columns from 1855 until one week before her death. Her favorable review of Walt Whitman's *Leaves of Grass* made her the first woman to publicly acknowledge the poet's genius. She was a champion of woman suffrage, criticized organized religion, and expressed revolutionary ideas about the rights of children. With Jane Cunningham Croly (q.v.), she was one of the founders, in 1868, of New York City's pioneer women's club, Sorosis.

Born in Portland, Maine, the future Fanny Fern was the fifth of nine children of Nathaniel and Hannah Parker Willis. She was originally named Grata Payson Willis, but the family soon changed her first name to Sara. Her father moved the family to Boston the year after Fanny's birth, and set up a printing business. In 1816 he founded the *Boston Recorder*, and in 1827, established the *Youth's Companion*. Fanny's older brother, Nathaniel Parker Willis, was a poet and editor of the *New York Mirror*. Her younger brother, Richard Storrs Willis, was a composer and editor of the *Musical World and Times*. Fanny attended schools in Boston, but received most of her education at Catharine Beecher's seminary in Hartford, Connecticut. She contributed pieces to the *Youth's Companion* during this period.

On 4 May 1837, at the age of twenty-six, Fanny married Charles H. Eldredge, a bank cashier. They had three children: Mary, born in 1839; Grace Harrington, born in 1840; and Eleanor (Ellen) Willis, born in 1844. At the age of seven, Mary died, and on 6 October 1846 Eldredge followed her, leaving his widow penniless with two children to support.

The Willis and Eldredge families provided minimal support. Fanny was unable to find employment and was under constant pressure. On 15 January 1849 she married Samuel P. Farrington, a Boston merchant and a widower with two daughters. Three years later, they were divorced. Against her family's wishes, Fanny tried to become self-supporting by sewing and teaching, but her earnings were so small that she was, at this time, forced to give up her daughter Grace to the Eldredge grandparents.

She finally turned to writing, hiding her identity under the names Olivia Branch and Fanny Fern, although she soon dropped the former. In 1851 her work appeared in the *Mother's Assistant*, the *True Flag*, and the *Olive Branch*, all small Boston magazines. Soon, many newspapers reprinted her short sketches. An Auburn, New York, publisher, James C. Derby, became aware of her popularity and, in 1853, collected her writing in *Fern Leaves From Fanny's Portfolio*, which became an immediate best-seller in both America and England. A second series of *Fern Leaves* appeared the following year, as did a children's book, *Little Ferns for Fanny's Little Friends*. These three books brought her sales in the United States to 132,000 and to 48,000 overseas. Within two years, she received more than $10,000 in royalties.

This astonishing popularity prompted Robert Bonner, owner of the *New York Ledger*, to hire her as a contributor in 1855. She was paid the then-exorbitant sum of $100 for each weekly column. Having relocated to New York, she stayed with the *Ledger* for the remainder of her life, never missing an edition. Her weekly audience numbered half a million readers. In addition to her work for the *Ledger*, she contributed to other newspapers, and this made her output equivalent to an article or sketch per day. In the next fifteen years, she published four editions of her collected *Ledger* writings: *Fresh Leaves* (1857), *Folly as it Flies* (1868), *Ginger-Snaps* (1870), and *Caper-Sauce: a Volume of Chit-Chat about Men, Women, and Things* (1872). In addition, she wrote two more children's books, *The Play-Day Book: New Stories for Little Folks* (1857) and *A New Story Book for Children* (1864); and two novels, *Ruth Hall* (1855) and *Rose Clark* (1856).

The publication of *Ruth Hall* created a minor literary scandal. The bitterness from her earlier struggles erupted in this book, a thinly disguised account of her treatment at the hands of her relatives. By her account, they had withheld adequate support in her time of need and had snubbed her literary endeavors.

On 5 January 1856 Fanny married James Parton, the biographer, eleven years her junior. The marriage lasted sixteen years, until her death, of cancer, in New York City at the age of sixty-one. Fanny Fern was buried in Mount Auburn cemetery in Boston. On 3 February 1876 Parton married his stepdaughter, Ellen Eldredge. He died on 17 October 1891.

BIBLIOGRAPHY:

B. DAB 7, 280–281; *New York Daily Tribune*, 11 October 1872; *New York Evening Post*, 11 October 1872; James Parton, *Fanny Fern: A Memorial Volume* (New York, 1873); Elizabeth B. Schlesinger, ''Fanny Fern: Our Grandmothers' Mentor,'' *New York Historical Society Quarterly*, October 1954.

NORA BAKER

PATTERSON, ALICIA (b. 15 October 1906; d. 2 July 1963) created *Newsday* and, as its editor and publisher, developed the Long Island tabloid daily into one of the most successful and influential newspapers in the United States.

Patterson combined her knowledge of the newspaper business with a willingness to innovate. She established a new format, which used three columns instead of the traditional five-column size and modular advertising. She also emphasized strong community content which concentrated considerable resources on coverage of all Long Island. One measure of the success is that no other daily newspaper exists on the island to serve the population of 2.6 million.

Her knowledge of newspapers can be traced to her youth as the daughter of Joseph Medill Patterson (q.v.), publisher of the tabloid *New York Daily News*, and Alice Higinbotham Patterson. Alicia Patterson was twelve when her father founded the *Illustrated Daily News* after he left the *Chciago Tribune*, of which her paternal grandfather, Robert Wilson Patterson, was editor and publisher. She attended several private secondary schools before joining the promotion department of the *Daily News* in 1927. The next year she became a reporter, but her career was cut short by a libel suit.

After returning to Chicago in 1928, she married James Simpson, Jr. After a year's "trial," they separated in 1929 and were divorced in 1930. A year later she wed Joseph W. Brooks, but that marriage lasted only seven years. Her third marriage was to Harry F. Guggenheim on 1 July 1939, but an estrangement resulted from her father's opposition. Nonetheless, Guggenheim was a positive force in making her a leading publisher. In 1928 she had joined *Liberty* magazine as a staff writer using the name Agnes Homberg, and in 1932 had also become a literary critic for the *New York Daily News*. However, the marriage to Guggenheim created a new opportunity.

They pooled his money with her drive to create and manage a newspaper into the purchase of the defunct *Nassau County Journal* and renamed it *Newsday*. On 3 September 1940 the first 15,000 copies came off an old press in a converted garage in Hempstead. Within two years the circulation had doubled and went up in quantum jumps, reaching more than 300,000 by the 1960s. The attractive appearance of the newspaper—it won several awards for excellence—was coupled with the emphasis on local community news. It won a Pulitzer Prize for public service in 1954 by exposing corruption at racetracks.

Patterson also went against the isolationism of other family members including her cousin Robert R. McCormick (q.v.), editor and publisher of the *Chicago Tribune*; her aunt Eleanor "Cissy" Medill Patterson (q.v.), editor and publisher of the *Washington Times-Herald*; and her father. She opposed Senator Joseph R. McCarthy, backed recognition of Red China, and urged moderation in race relations. A Republican, she often supported Democrats on Long Island.

Although the newspaper had early monetary difficulties, especially during wartime when Guggenheim was in the navy, *Newsday* used four zoned editions to build its financial success. It is one of the few newspapers in the United States in which news space takes precedence over advertising. Alicia Patterson showed this commitment to news coverage when the first edition declared: "Our first, second, and final object is to present the news. That is why *Newsday* is our slogan as well as our name. If we present the news honestly, we know we will have readers. If we have readers, it will be profitable for advertisers to use our columns whether they agree with our policy or not."

A volatile woman, she took an active role in the operation of her newspaper and in professional organizations. Alicia Patterson died in 1963 in New York

City after a number of operations for a stomach ulcer. She had no children, and Guggenheim became publisher of *Newsday* after her death.

BIBLIOGRAPHY:

B. NCAB 7, 603–604; NYT 3 July 1963; Gene Balliet, ''*Newsday*'s First Two Decades,'' *Quill*, January 1961; Charles Wertenbaker, ''The Case of the Hot-Tempered Publisher,'' *Saturday Evening Post*, 12 May 1951.

SAMUEL V. KENNEDY III

PATTERSON, ELEANOR MEDILL (b. 7 November 1881; d. 24 July 1948), née Elinor Josephine Patterson, was once divorced, once widowed, forty-nine, and at loose ends in her life when she became editor-publisher of the *Washington Herald* in 1930. It was her first real experience in journalism. Born in Chicago, ''Cissy'' was the daughter of Elinor Medill and Robert Wilson Patterson, Jr., and granddaughter of Joseph Medill (q.v.), owner of the *Chicago Tribune*. She had no formal education until she entered Miss Hersey's School in Boston at the age of fifteen. Two years later she was enrolled at Miss Porter's School in Farmington, Connecticut, but withdrew because of nervous tension.

Cissy was presented to Chicago society in 1901 and the following year was presented to the Austro-Hungarian court by her aunt and uncle, Kate Medill and Robert Sanderson McCormick, ambassador to Austria. She was introduced to Count Josef Gizycki of Poland, whom she married on 14 June 1904 over the protests of her family.

By December 1908 the marriage had failed. After a custody battle over their daughter Felicia, in which president-elect Taft and Czar Nicholas personally intervened, Cissy and Felicia returned to the United States on 18 August 1909. Cissy was granted a divorce on 18 June 1917. In 1925 she married Elmer Schlesinger, an attorney she met while campaigning for Theodore Roosevelt in 1912. Schlesinger died of a heart attack in 1929.

At the death of her grandfather Medill, control of the *Tribune* passed to Cissy's brother Joseph Medill Patterson (q.v.) and their cousin Robert McCormick (q.v.). Patterson so angered his editor, Walter Howey, that Howey quit to become managing editor of Hearst's (q.v.) *Chicago Herald-Examiner*. Howey then hired Cissy for two special assignments: the 1920 Republican National Convention and a series on big-game hunting. Howey made certain her byline identified her as Joe Patterson's sister. Patterson and McCormick still refused to let Cissy write for the *Tribune* or for their new tabloid, the *New York Daily News*, until 1927 when she persuaded her brother to let her cover the Ruth Snyder murder trial.

By 1928 Cissy was seriously considering a career in journalism for herself and wanted to buy Hearst's *Washington Herald*. Both McCormick and Arthur Brisbane (q.v.) counseled against the purchase, and Hearst was reluctant to part with the property. However, in 1930, at Brisbane's urging, Hearst hired Cissy as editor and publisher of the *Herald*, then running fourth in the five-paper Washington market. Her salary was $10,000 a year plus one-third of the net profit on a three-year contract.

She was innovative, unorthodox, and unfamiliar with the word *impossible*. She wrote her first editorial on the back of a telephone book and ran it, signed and boxed, on the frong page. "Be sure it's on the front page. Mr. Hearst says that's the only place people will read it." From her front-page vantage point she took potshots at Alice Roosevelt Longworth and waged circulation wars against Eugene Meyer's (q.v.) *Washington Post*. Inside, she established "Page 3," where she published Washington society's spiciest gossip. Cissy herself interviewed Al Capone and Albert Einstein and, dressed in rags, went underground to see how the street people lived. She feuded in print with her ex-son-in-law Drew Pearson (q.v.) and pirated Tribune-News syndicated comic strips from the *Post* until Meyer won them back in a two-year court battle.

In the third quarter of 1935 the *Herald* had the largest gain in advertising of any Washington paper. By early 1937 Hearst was again considering selling the *Herald*, this time to Cissy's rival Eugene Meyer. Cissy countered with an offer to lease both the *Herald* and its companion evening paper, the *Times*, for a period of five years with an option to buy. On 28 January 1939 she bought both papers and merged them into the *Times-Herald*, Washington's only round-the-clock newspaper.

The next several years saw Cissy using her growing political influence against American intervention in the war. Cissy, Joe Patterson, and Robert McCormick continued to support Roosevelt in his third presidential race, but made certain he understood their isolationist position. After the attack on Pearl Harbor, Joe Patterson, then sixty-two, went to Roosevelt personally and offered his services to the war effort. Roosevelt responded with a lecture on how Patterson and his sister had negatively influenced Congress and delayed his efforts. Patterson was stung, but Cissy was furious. Roosevelt had made two powerful enemies, and they both campaigned against him in 1944.

When her daughter "divorced" her in 1945, Cissy turned her attentions to her niece, Alicia Patterson (q.v.), a talented editor at *Newsday*—although Joe was opposed to Cissy's idea of having Alicia take over the *Times-Herald*. After Joe's death in 1946, Cissy lobbied for Alicia to be named to the board of the News Syndicate Company. McCormick opposed the idea but eventually gave in and named Alicia to the board of the parent organization, the Tribune Company, on the condition that Cissy resign, which she did. She was getting tired of responsibility, and no longer looked forward to the challenge of publishing.

Cissy was lonely, estranged from her relatives; her old friends Evalyn Walsh McLean and Tom White were dead; and her own health was debilitated by drugs and alcohol. On 24 July 1948 a servant, concerned that Cissy had not rung for breakfast at the usual time, found her still in bed, slumped over a novel she had been reading. She was dead at the age of sixty-seven of renal failure.

Cissy left the *Times-Herald* to seven of her employees. Within a year the seven had sold the paper to Robert McCormick, who revamped the style. In 1954 Eugene Meyer bought the *Times-Herald* and turned the building into a warehouse.

BIBLIOGRAPHY:
A. *Glass Houses* (New York, 1926); *Fall Flight* (New York, 1928).
B. DAB Supp. 4, 643–645; DLB 29, 265–268; NYT 25 July 1948; Paul F. Healy, *Cissy: The Biography of Eleanor M. "Cissy" Patterson* (Garden City, N.Y., 1966); Alice Albright Hoge, *Cissy Patterson* (New York, 1966); Ralph G. Martin, *Cissy* (New York, 1979).

PERRY J. ASHLEY

PATTERSON, JOSEPH MEDILL (b. 6 January 1879; d. 25 May 1946) was a creative and independent editor and publisher whose ability to identify and to provide what people wanted in a popular newspaper enabled him to achieve phenomenal success with the *New York Daily News* soon after its founding in 1919. His tabloid formula of high-interest news, features, comics, and pictures produced the newspaper that for decades had the highest daily and Sunday circulation in the nation.

Patterson was born in Chicago into a newspaper family, the first of two children of Robert W. Patterson, Jr., an editor at the *Chicago Tribune*, and Elinor Medill Patterson, daughter of Joseph Medill (q.v.), principal owner and editor of the *Tribune*. Joseph's younger sister was Eleanor "Cissy" Patterson (q.v.), later editor and publisher of the *Washington Times-Herald*; his cousins were Robert McCormick (q.v.), *Tribune* editor and publisher for some thirty years, and Joseph Medill McCormick, a newspaperman and U.S. senator.

Patterson was educated in private schools in Chicago and France, then at Groton and Yale. He received an A.B. from Yale in 1901, after spending part of 1900 assisting correspondents covering the Boxer Rebellion in China. When Joseph Medill died in 1899, his two daughters inherited an estate of $2 million plus *Tribune* stock placed in trust for them and their heirs. Robert Patterson moved up to president and editor. Joseph Patterson joined his father's staff as a reporter in 1901 and also worked as an editorial writer and assistant Sunday editor. On 19 November 1902 he married Alice Higinbotham. They had three daughters and an adopted son.

In 1903 Patterson was elected a Republican member of the Illinois legislature. Upon learning his election had been rigged by his father and Republican party leaders, he resigned from the newspaper in 1905. He joined a successful Democratic reform campaign in Chicago and was appointed public works commissioner. In February 1906 he resigned, declaring he was now a socialist. Patterson then took up farming and writing—magazine articles, Socialist party literature, novels and plays.

His father's death in April 1910 brought Patterson back into an active role in the newspaper. Patterson and Robert McCormick took charge of the company, agreeing to share power. They rejuvenated the *Tribune*, and by 1920 its circulation had doubled. One of Patterson's contributions was the introduction in 1917 of *The Gumps*, a comic strip by Sidney Smith.

In 1915 Patterson spent three months in Europe observing the war. Later that year he enlisted in the Illinois National Guard. In February 1917 he accepted a commission and by November his unit was in France, where it served for thirteen months. Patterson attained the rank of captain. While in Europe he noted the success of British tabloids and began thinking about the tabloid newspaper for New York City. He and McCormick, a colonel, discussed the idea in France in July 1918 and agreed to go ahead. In May 1919 the Tribune Company board of directors authorized the project, with Patterson heading it, while also continuing to manage the *Tribune*.

The *Illustrated Daily News* debuted on 26 June 1919. It promised that further editions of "your newspaper" would provide appealing pictures and brief stories about "the interesting things that are happening in the world." The first-day editorial also noted the tabloid size would be easier to read in subways and pledged an editorial policy with "no entangling alliance." First-day circulation was 150,000; by the end of the year, after a decline, circulation rose to almost 100,000, helped by a popular limerick contest. On its first anniversary, circulation was 233,000, sixth among the city's dailies.

Its success has generally been linked with the flamboyant nature of the 1920s. But Patterson's instincts and hard work were as important as timing. He practiced his belief in newspapers getting close to the people to find out their interests. He talked with them and watched what they read on streets and subways and at newsstands and lunch counters, and he insisted his staff do the same.

His work continued to pay off after the first issue of the *Sunday News* on 1 May 1921. In 1925, Patterson, who had been maintaining day-to-day supervision from Chicago, moved permanently to New York. Sunday circulation was averaging one million. Daily circulation topped that figure for good in 1926. Patterson continued to develop and prompt ideas for comics. Two of the biggest successes were *Little Orphan Annie* in 1924 and *Dick Tracy* in 1931. His hand was also evident in the distinctive *News* editorial page, whose plain, forthright style was said to directly reflect Patterson's personality.

Two new tabloids, William Randolph Hearst's (q.v.) *Daily Mirror* and Bernarr Macfadden's (q.v.) *Evening Graphic*, challenged the top position of the *News* in New York in the mid–1920s and heightened the "jazz journalism" of the period. The *News* kept pace in competition for the mass audience with sensational coverage of crime and celebrities. In January 1928 it published a front-page photograph of convicted murderer Ruth Snyder's execution in the electric chair. Patterson had reportedly suggested getting the photograph.

With the onset of the depression, Patterson saw readers wanted news with more substance about real problems and steered the *News* in that direction, without changing its basic style. In 1930 Patterson moved his newspaper into a $10 million thirty-six-story building on East 42nd Street, built to his specifications. On 5 July 1938, after a divorce from his first wife, Patterson married Mary King, who had worked with him at the *Tribune* and *News* for more than twenty years. The *News*, on its twentieth anniversary, had a daily circulation of 1.8 million with 3.3 million on Sunday.

In the 1930s Patterson, unlike most publishers, supported Franklin D. Roosevelt. He broke with Roosevelt over U.S. response to the war in Europe and Asia. He abhorred war because of his experience but supported preparedness. When Roosevelt asked for lend-lease authority after the 1940 election, however, Patterson joined Robert McCormick and "Cissy" Patterson in opposing administration policy and attacking lend-lease, which he called the "dictatorship bill." Roosevelt supporters branded the cousins the "McCormick-Patterson Axis."

Patterson resolved after Pearl Harbor to support the war effort. He requested reappointment in the army and went to the White House to offer support. Roosevelt rebuked him for his criticism, and Patterson felt he had been humiliated. He remained bitter, and during the war the Pattersons and McCormick were often critical of administration policy.

Patterson died of a liver ailment on 26 May 1946. He was buried with military honors at Arlington National Cemetery. When he died *News* circulation was more than 2.2 million daily and more than 4.5 million Sunday.

BIBLIOGRAPHY:

A. *A Little Brother of the Rich* (Chicago, 1908); *The Note Book of a Neutral* (New York, 1916).

B. DAB Supp. 4, 645–646; NCAB 36, 8–9; NYT 27 May 1946; *Chicago Tribune*, 27 May 1946; *New York Daily News*, 27 May 1946; John Chapman, *Tell It to Sweeney: The Informal History of the "New York Daily News"* (Garden City, N.Y., 1961); Leo McGivena, *The News: The First 50 Years of New York's Picture Newspaper* (New York, 1969).

RONALD S. MARMARELLI

PEARSON, ANDREW RUSSELL "DREW" (b. 13 December 1879; d. 1 September 1969) has been acclaimed as a pioneer of investigative reporting and criticized as a sloppy journalist; he was sued for libel more than 120 times, but lost only one suit; he was called a "chronic liar" by President Franklin D. Roosevelt and an "S.O.B." by President Harry Truman. To many he was a hero; to just as many others, he was a character assassin. Whatever he was, he established one of the most widely read columns in America—a column that continues even today. When he died, Pearson's "Washington Merry-Go-Round" was published in about 600 newspapers and scores of governmental misdeeds had been uncovered by the relentless columnist.

Pearson was born in Evanston, Illinois, to Edna Wolfe Pearson and Paul Martin Pearson. His father, later governor of the Virgin Islands, soon left Northwestern University to join the faculty of Swarthmore College, where he established a roving educational enterprise called Chautauqua. At various times, Pearson, his two brothers, and his sister worked for Chautauqua. Pearson attended Phillips Exeter Academy and was graduated from Swarthmore in 1918. He served a two-year hitch as a member of the American Friends Service Committee, assigned to Serbia, before beginning a miscellany of jobs.

On March 12, 1925, he married Felicia Gizycki, daughter of Eleanor Medill "Cissy" Patterson (q.v.), of the wealthy Medill-Patterson newspaper family and later publisher of the *Washington Times-Herald*. They had one daughter, Ellen, before the marriage ended in divorce in August 1928 and Felicia fled to Poland to live with her father. Shortly after the marriage, Pearson, who had spent much time traveling in Europe and the Far East and peddling articles to newspapers back home, became foreign editor of *United States Daily*. The publication was primarily a repository for government documents, but became *U.S. News and World Report*. Pearson's salary was low, but he was allowed to free-lance, and the free-lancing led to a job with the *Baltimore Sun*'s Washington bureau. While at the *Sun*, Pearson met Robert S. Allen of the *Christian Science Monitor*, who later approached Pearson with an idea for a book. The two men combined the gossip they had collected on their beats and, in 1931, anonymously published *Washington Merry-Go-Round*. A year later, they published a sequel. The books were immensely popular, but the identities of the authors were uncovered, and both men lost their jobs.

The books gave birth to the column of the same name, however. The column first appeared on Pearson's birthday in 1932, distributed by United Features to about a dozen newspapers. By the time Allen left the column to join the army in 1942, more than 350 papers were subscribing and a radio program featuring the columnists had been born. In 1936 Pearson married Luvie Abell after she received a divorce from George Abell, who had been Pearson's best friend.

Pearson's popularity and notoriety continued to grow. He was one of the first journalists to attack the methods of Senator Joseph McCarthy and, for his troubles, was assaulted by McCarthy. Pearson reported that Senator Robert F. Kennedy, as attorney general, had authorized electronic surveillance of the Reverend Martin Luther King. And his reporting led to the censure of Senator Thomas J. Dodd of Connecticut and to the ouster of Representative Adam Clayton Powell for financial misdeeds. Not all Pearson's revelations were so dramatic, however. He also reported, for example, that Secretary of War Patrick J. Hurley rehearsed ballroom entrances before a mirror.

Pearson, whose office was in his home, was a tireless reporter, continuously cultivating his excellent crop of sources. He was not satisfied with reporting, however, and attempted to affect government. By strategically planning his disclosures he attempted to affect elections and decisions of government officials. During the Kennedy administration, following detailed interviews with Nikita Khrushchev, he attempted to persuade the president to soften his stance toward the Soviets. Later, Pearson was an active adviser to Lyndon B. Johnson.

About ten years before Pearson's death, Jack Anderson joined the Pearson staff and began sharing the byline of the "Washington Merry-Go-Round." He took over the column at Pearson's death. Pearson died of a heart attack at age seventy-one.

BIBLIOGRAPHY:

A. *Diaries, 1949–1959* (New York, 1974); "Confessions of an S.O.B.," *Saturday Evening Post*, 3, 10, 17, 24 November 1956.

B. NYT 2 September 1969; Morris A. Bealle, *All-American Louse: A Candid Biography of Drew A. Pearson* (Frenchtown, N.J., 1965); Herman Klurfeld, *Behind the Lines: The World of Drew Pearson* (Englewood Cliffs, N.J., 1968); Oliver Pilat, *Drew Pearson: An Unauthorized Biography* (New York, 1973).

W. WAT HOPKINS

PEGLER, FRANCIS WESTBROOK (b. 2 August 1894; d. 24 June 1969) for three decades was one of America's best-known columnists. Called journalism's "angry man" and "master of the vituperative epithet," Pegler was known for his brutal attacks on public figures. And at the peak of his career, when his column was carried by 186 newspapers and reached approximately twelve million readers, to be "Peglerized" was almost a honor.

Pegler was born in Minneapolis, the second son of a hard-drinking English journalist and a churchgoer from a respectable, middle-class family. He was named for his mother, Frances Nicholson Pegler, but discarded his first name and used James Westbrook or J. Westbrook, after his father, until he shortened his name to Westbrook Pegler. Arthur James Pegler, who came to the United States in 1884 and worked on a number of newspapers, was a boisterous storyteller who was credited with the invention of the "Hearst style" of newswriting. He was also responsible for his son's interest in journalism.

As a student, first in the community of Excelsior near Minneapolis, and later in Chicago, Westbrook Pegler found little that held his interest. At Loyola Academy, Pegler briefly considered the priesthood, but left school suddenly in 1912 to take a job with the International News Agency (INA). He had been an office boy with United Press for a brief time, but the INA job was his first as a reporter.

Over the next seven years Pegler held a variety of newspaper jobs and served two stints in the navy. In 1919 he joined United Press in New York as a general assignment reporter making forty dollars a week. In New York, Pegler met Julie Harpman, a reporter for the *New York Daily News*. They were married 29 August 1922. Julie abandoned her career as a journalist, but only after she wrote a widely published story on Gertrude Ederly's swim across the English Channel.

Pegler's reputation grew when he began writing sports, first for UP, then for the Chicago Tribune News Syndicate. In 1933, however, Pegler joined United Features Syndicate, owned by Scripps-Howard, as a commentator. His column, "Fair Enough," was displayed opposite that of Heywood Broun (q.v.) on the second front of the *New York World-Telegram*, the Scripps-Howard flagship.

Pegler displayed his knack for controversy with his first column, in which he defended lynching. His mastery of words and flowing style, coupled with his vituperation, brought him instant recognition. Few public figures escaped his attacks. President Franklin D. Roosevelt was called a "feeble-minded fuhrer";

vice president Henry A. Wallace was ''Old Blubberhead,'' a ''slobbering snerd''; J. Edgar Hoover was called ''a nightclub fly-cop.'' In 1937 Pegler won a National Headliners Club award for exposing income tax evasion, and in 1941 he won the Pulitzer Prize for exposing labor union corruption. He was listed, in a poll by the University of Wisconsin School of Journalism, as the best adult columnist in 1942.

In 1949, four years after he switched to the Hearst-owned King Features Syndicate and changed the name of his column to ''As Pegler Sees It,'' Pegler viciously attacked writer Quentin Reynolds (q.v.). Reynolds had written a book review of a biography of Heywood Broun. Pegler interpreted a portion of the review as a charge that a Pegler column caused Broun's death. Reynolds sued and in 1954 a jury awarded Reynolds one dollar in compensatory damages and $175,000 in punitive damages.

The trial seemed to be the turning point in Pegler's career. Though he did not pay the award—Pegler was one of two columnists, the other was Walter Winchell (q.v.), powerful enough to be exempt from libel payments as a part of his contract—he was publicly humiliated. His influence waned, and he began having more disagreements with the Hearst organization. Julie, his wife of thirty-three years, died 8 November 1955 of a heart attack. Pegler married twice more. On 11 May 1959 he married Pearl Wiley Doane of Hollywood. They were divorced 30 October 1961. Three weeks later, 22 November 1961, he married his former secretary, Maude Towart.

Pegler reduced his work load from six columns a week to three following Julie's death, but more and more of his columns were being cut or killed. Then, at the August 1962 convention of Billy James Hargis's Christian Crusade, he made a speech attacking the Hearst organization. Pegler was not aware that a stringer for *Newsweek* was at the by-invitation-only speech. On 14 August the *New York Journal-American* announced the termination of Pegler's contract by mutual consent.

For the next two years, Pegler wrote a monthly column for *American Opinion*, a publication of the John Birch Society. The columns stopped, however, when a piece on Chief Justice Earl Warren was rejected in 1964. For the last years of his life, Pegler had little outlet for his writing. He died at his Tucson, Arizona, home of a heart seizure.

BIBLIOGRAPHY:

A. *'T Ain't Right* (New York, 1936); *The Dissenting Opinions of Mister Westbrook Pegler* (New York, 1939).

B. NYT 25 June 1969; Finis Farr, *Fair Enough: The Life of Westbrook Pegler* (New York, 1975); Oliver Pilat, *Pegler, Angry Man of the Press* (Westport, Conn., 1963).

W. WAT HOPKINS

PHILLIPS, DAVID GRAHAM (b. 31 October 1867; d. 24 January 1911) was a muckraking journalist and novelist whose 1906 magazine articles criticizing the U.S. Senate caused Theodore Roosevelt to coin the word ''muckraking'' to describe a particular type of journalistic writing. Phillips worked for thirteen years as a newspaper reporter and editorial writer. After leaving daily journalism he wrote twenty-three novels, many of which were near best-sellers. His early novels were of the muckraking variety, detailing corruption in business and government. Phillips's later novels had a feminist tone and explored the role of women in an industrial society.

Phillips, the fourth of five children, was born in Madison, Indiana, a city on the Ohio River, ninety miles northwest of Cincinnati. The son of Margaret Lee and David Graham, a successful banker, Phillips was educated in public schools in Madison. From 1883 to 1885 he attended Indiana Asbury College (now DePauw University). He left to finish his education at the College of New Jersey (now Princeton University), where he graduated in 1887 at the age of twenty.

Phillips's first newspaper job was at the *Cincinnati Times-Star*. He quickly won acclaim for his writing skill and was hired in 1888 by Murat Halstead's (q.v.) *Cincinnati Commercial-Gazette*, considered the best paper in Cincinnati. Under Halstead, he experimented with a variety of writing styles, becoming a star in Queen City journalism. In 1890 he headed East where he became a reporter for Charles A. Dana's (q.v.) *New York Sun*, a newspaper known for its talented writing staff. For the next eleven years Phillips worked in journalism in New York City.

At the *Sun* Phillips covered a wide variety of issues and events and began in earnest the education he said he would need before writing novels. During this time he also wrote numerous colorful features for *Harper's Weekly*. In 1893 he joined the staff of Joseph Pulitzer's (q.v.) *New York World*, the nation's largest-circulation newspaper. Pulitzer made Phillips the *World*'s London correspondent. After a short time in England, Phillips had a dispute with Pulitzer over whether he should be given a byline on his dispatches, and he returned to New York City, threatened to quit, was convinced to stay, and subsequently became a well-known feature writer.

In 1896 Phillips, who had become a confidant of Pulitzer's, began to write editorials for the *World*'s influential editorial page. Phillips wrote all the *World*'s editorials on foreign affairs. Occasionally Pulitzer gave Phillips special assignments—in 1897 he covered the month-long Greco-Turkish War, and in 1899 he toured the country with presidential aspirants.

In 1901, after publishing his first novel, *The Great God Success*, a critical look at the newspaper industry, Phillips left daily journalism to become a free-lance writer. In the next ten years Phillips, who never married, wrote twenty-three novels, a book of essays, a play, and dozens of magazine articles, most of them for the *Saturday Evening Post*, the largest general-circulation periodical of the day.

Phillips's novels between 1901 and 1907 detailed corruption in various industries and sketched out a newly developed symbiotic relationship between industrial tycoons and elected officials. Phillips's ideals were generally consistent with the principles of progressivism that had emerged after 1900, and his books suggest the need for reform and government regulation. However, Phillips portrayed the businessman as typical of both the best and the worst of industrial capitalism. In his novels *The Master Rogue* (1903), *The Cost* (1904), *The Deluge* (1905), and *Light-Fingered Gentry* (1907), he showed industrial corruption as pervasive. In *The Plum Tree* (1905), Phillips muckraked American politics, creating characters who were puppets of various industrial combines and who had characteristics similar to those of real elected officials.

Phillips also wrote notable nonfiction during this period. His book *The Reign of Gilt* (1904) focused on concentrated wealth and on education's role in a democracy. In 1906, for William Randolph Hearst's (q.v.) *Cosmopolitan* magazine, Phillips wrote nine articles on "The Treason of the Senate," a nonfiction exposé of the business-political alliance that he had written about in fiction. The articles also implied the need for direct election of U.S. senators. In response, on 14 April 1906 President Roosevelt criticized the growing number of writers who, he said, looked too much down into the "muck" of society. This was the beginning of the use of the work *muckraking* to describe journalistic exposé.

Stung by the criticism, Phillips turned mostly to fiction after 1907, writing several controversial and well received novels about male-female relationships. The sexuality in the novels made them risqué but popular. H. L. Mencken (q.v.) called Phillips "the leading American novelist." On 23 January 1911 Phillips was shot in New York City by a deranged man who felt that a Phillips novel was a satire of his family. Phillips died on 24 January. In 1917 Phillips's novel *Susan Lenox: Her Fall and Rise*, generally considered his best work, was published. Today most of his novels are forgotten, and he is perhaps best remembered because of his criticism of the Senate.

BIBLIOGRAPHY:

B. DAB 17, 539; NYT 25 January 1911; Louis Filler, *The Voice of Democracy* (University Park, Pa., 1978); Isaac F. Marcosson, *David Graham Phillips and His Times* (New York, 1934); Robert Miraldi, "The Journalism of David Graham Phillips," Ph.D. diss., New York University 1984.

ROBERT MIRALDI

PHILLIPS, JOHN SANBURN (b. 2 July 1861; d. 28 February 1949), magazine editor and publisher, was the quiet guiding force behind *McClure's* magazine, one of the first and most influential mass-circulation magazines in America. When *McClure's* emerged after 1903 as a leading muckraker, Phillips's astute direction protected the magazine's reputation for accuracy even as it assailed the evils of American society.

Phillips was born in Council Bluffs, Iowa, the second of four children of Edgar L. Phillips and Mary Lavinia Sanburn Phillips. His father, a physician, served as an army doctor during the Civil War. Thereafter, he moved his family to Galesburg, Illinois, where he was one of the organizers of Knox County. John Phillips was educated in local schools and at Knox College in Galesburg, where he received the A.B. in 1882.

At Knox he formed a close friendship with a dynamic student named S. S. McClure (q.v.), and the two worked on student publications together. In the summer of 1882 McClure was hired to publish the *Wheelman*, a magazine promoting the new sport of bicycling, and he asked Phillips to be his assistant. Though Phillips left the next year to attend Harvard College, this was the beginning of a publishing partnership that would continue for more than two decades.

Phillips studied literature at Harvard, received an A.B. magna cum laude in 1885, and went to the University of Leipzig in Germany for further work in philology, phonetics, and literature. He returned to the United States late in 1886 and soon resumed his work with McClure, who had meanwhile launched a syndicate to distribute fiction to American newspapers. Phillips headed the New York office, except for a short period in London in 1890–91. Phillips had married Emma Delia West of Galesburg on 25 August 1885; she committed suicide in 1888. On 2 October 1890 he married Jennie Beale Peterson of Boston; they were the parents of four daughters and one son.

In 1893 Phillips and McClure launched *McClure's* magazine, with Phillips providing much of the initial capital. After several years' struggle to survive amid the depression of the 1890s, *McClure's* flourished, drawing by 1900 a circulation over 350,000 and more advertising than any other magazine. As they had done before, the two men assumed complementary roles: McClure traveled restlessly in search of new ideas, and Phillips ran the office. He also gathered and trained a staff of talented journalists, including Ida M. Tarbell, Ray Stannard Baker, and Lincoln Steffens (qq.v.). Among them and a host of other young free-lance writers, Phillips was known for his sympathy and effectiveness as an editor. He managed the Harper and Brothers publishing house when the McClure organization acquired it briefly in 1899; in 1900 he was made head of McClure, Phillips and Company, a new book publishing firm.

In 1903 *McClure's* began a series of investigations of corporate, political, and labor corruption that launched the muckraking movement among American magazines. Throughout, Phillips carefully curbed his writers' reforming zeal and helped to maintain *McClure's* reputation for accuracy and fairness. However, in 1906 Phillips broke with McClure, not over muckraking but over financial and temperamental differences; many of the magazine's staff, including Tarbell, Baker, and Steffens, were loyal to Phillips and left with him. Together they founded the Phillips Publishing Company and purchased the *American Magazine*, pursuing there many of the same policies they had developed at *McClure's*. However, the magazine was consistently plagued by undercapitalization, and in 1911 the group sold its interests to the Crowell Publishing Company. Four years later, after conflicts with the more conservative management, Phillips resigned, though he continued as advisory editor until 1938.

From 1917 to 1920 Phillips edited the *Red Cross Magazine*, in which he promoted America's efforts to rehabilitate war-torn Europe. His health had long been troubled by a heart condition, and after 1920 he returned to semiretirement, dividing his time among New York City, his family's suburban home in Goshen, New York, and his summer home in Duxbury, Massachusetts. During his retirement, he wrote a column for the *Goshen Independent-Republican* which generally was on books but occasionally was autobiographical. He died in Goshen on 29 February 1949. Knox College had awarded him an honorary Litt.D. in 1910.

BIBLIOGRAPHY:

B. DAB Supp. 4, 661–663; NYT 2 March 1949; Kathleen Brady, *Ida Tarbell: Portrait of a Muckraker* (New York, 1984); Peter Lyon, *Success Story: The Life and Times of S. S. McClure* (New York, 1963); Harold S. Wilson, *McClure's Magazine and the Muckrakers* (Princeton, N.J., 1970).

SALLY F. GRIFFITH

POORE, BENJAMIN PERLEY (b. 2 November 1820; d. 29 May 1887) was one of the first nationally known Washington correspondents. His articles on political, military, and social affairs at the capital were published in newspapers and magazines throughout the United States. Poore also wrote on subjects as diverse as agriculture and autograph collecting; edited several newspapers; wrote biographies and novels; edited the *Congressional Directory*, the *Congressional Record*, and other government publications; and served as clerk of several congressional committees.

Poore, the oldest of four children, was born at Indian Hill, his family's 400-acre farm near Newburyport, Massachusetts, thirty-six miles northeast of Boston. Poore's father, Benjamin Poore, was a dry-goods merchant whose business extended into the Deep South. Poore's mother, Mary Perley Dodge Poore, was a native of Georgetown, D.C., but the family originally was from Hamilton, Massachusetts. Poore was educated in schools near Newburyport and in New York City, and he traveled extensively in Europe with his parents.

In January 1839, Poore became the editor of the *Southern Whig* in Athens, Georgia, a newspaper his father had purchased and planned to make the voice of the Whig party in the South. Poore made the *Whig* bright and vigorous, but it was no match for its Democratic rival, the *Southern Banner*. By January 1841 the paper was losing money and editorial battles to the *Banner*, and Poore left the paper after August 1841.

For the next six years Poore traveled throughout Europe and wrote letters that were published in the *Boston Atlas* and the *Hartford Courant*. Also, until 1844 he was an attaché to the American legation in Brussels. He returned to the United States in 1847 and served as Washington correspondent for the *Atlas* until he took a leave in 1848 to write a campaign biography of Zachary Taylor at the request of Thurlow Weed (q.v.).

Poore tried his hand, unsuccessfully, at editing several papers: the *Boston Daily Bee* (1848–49), *Perley's Sunday Picnic* (1849), and the *Sunday Sentinel* (1849–51). For a brief period in 1849, Poore was again the *Atlas*'s Washington correspondent. He also published several serialized novels in *Gleason's Pictorial*

Drawing-Room Companion, a Boston weekly, between 1851 and 1854. On 12 June 1849 he married Virginia Dodge, a cousin, of Georgetown. The Poores had two daughters, Emily (b. 19 March 1850), and Alice (b. 27 August 1854).

In 1854 Poore went to Washington as the correspondent of the *Boston Journal*, a position he held until 1883. Poore covered the entire Washington scene for the *Journal*. He sent condensed daily proceedings of Congress, usually by mail, and daily news dispatches by telegraph. Also, several times a week the *Journal* published letters from Poore that commented on important news and contained some gossip items. These letters, signed ''Perley'' were published under a standing headline, ''Waifs From Washington.''

To supplement his *Journal* income, Poore wrote for other publications, among them the *Chicago Tribune*, *Harper's* and the *Atlantic*. He also served as the clerk of the Foreign Relations Committee of both houses of Congress, and as clerk of the Senate Committee on Printing and Records. Poore left the *Journal* in 1883 because the paper refused to pay him a year-round salary instead of paying him only when Congress was in session. During the last four years of his life he corresponded from Washington for the *Boston Budget*, the *Albany Evening Journal*, and the *Omaha Republican*.

Poore was a jovial and popular man who became a fixture in Washington society. He was respected by his colleagues in the press and was elected the first president of the Gridiron Club in 1885. Poore died of complications from Bright's disease.

BIBLIOGRAPHY:

A. *Perley's Reminiscences of Sixty Years in the National Metropolis* (Philadelphia, 1886).

B. DAB 15, 73–74; NYT 29 May 1887; *Boston Evening Journal*, 31 May 1887; Josephine P. Driver, ''Ben: Perley Poore of Indian Hill,'' *Essex Institute Historical Collections*, January 1953; Joseph Patrick McKerns, ''Benjamin Perley Poore of the *Boston Journal*: His Life and Times as a Washington Correspondent, 1850–1887,'' Ph.D. diss., University of Minnesota, 1979.

JOSEPH P. MCKERNS

POYNTER, NELSON PAUL (b. 15 December 1903; d. 15 June 1978) built the once small, financially troubled *St. Petersburg Times* into a large, robust daily ranked among the best in the country. He also emerged as one of American journalism's most conspicuous figures—a liberal in a conservative community, an innovator in an industry resistant to change, and a loner in a field increasingly dominated by newspaper chains. To insure that the *Times* would remain free from chain ownership and under the control of a single individual, the publisher willed his newspaper and other media holdings to a small, nonprofit educational institution, the Poynter Institute for Media Studies.

The younger of two children, Poynter was born into the newspaper business in Sullivan, Indiana. His father, Paul, was the publisher of a string of ten small papers, including the *St. Petersburg Times*. But Poynter patterned himself more after his strong-willed mother, Alice Wilkey, an early feminist.

Poynter skipped two grades in the Sullivan public schools and went on to Indiana University where he was editor of the campus newspaper, the *Daily Student*. At the end of his junior year in 1923, he and classmate Ernie Pyle (q.v.) worked as reporters on the Scripps-Howard *Washington Daily News*, and upon graduation he covered the 1924 Democratic National Convention for the *Indianapolis Star*. He then traveled abroad and worked for a time in 1925 as news editor on the English-language *Japan Times* in Tokyo. He earned a master's degree in economics at Yale in 1927.

Over the next decade, Poynter gained editorial and business experience on seven newspapers in Florida and the Midwest. While assistant general manager of the *St. Petersburg Times*, he bought the *Clearwater* (Florida) *Sun* in 1928 and later sold it for a profit. Next he purchased the *Kokomo* (Indiana) *Democrat* from his father, but depression-era debts forced him to sell to his local competitor in 1930. The following year he went to work again for Scripps-Howard: first briefly as an advertising salesman on the *Cleveland Press* and then once more on the *Daily News*, this time as advertising manager. The chain promoted him in 1935 to editor and publisher of the *Columbus* (Ohio) *Citizen*; he was fired two years later for supporting President Roosevelt's "court packing" plan for the Supreme Court. He completed a brief stint as the *Minneapolis Star*'s business manager before returning to St. Petersburg as general manager in 1938. Within a year he became editor of the *Times*.

Beginning in December 1940, Poynter worked in the federal government's wartime propaganda program—initially as codirector of the U.S. Communication Bureau's press section in Washington. In the summer of 1941 he was chosen to help activate the new office of coordinator of information. In 1942 Poynter was divorced by his first wife, Sara Catherine Fergusson. They were married 28 December 1927 and had two daughters, his only children. On 8 August 1942 he married Henrietta Malkiel, a Columbia School of Journalism graduate, who was a feature editor of *Vanity Fair* and a foreign editor in Europe for *Vogue*. She became associate editor of the *St. Petersburg Times*, and with Poynter cofounded *Congressional Quarterly* in 1945. She died in January 1968 at age sixty-six. On 4 May 1970 Poynter married Marion E. Knauss, then a *Times* editorial writer, who serves on the paper's board of directors.

When Poynter gained controlling interest in the *Times* in 1947, he published fifteen "Standards of Ownership." Like much of his writing, the document is wordy and clumsily phrased. But the goals he set are exemplary. They included vows to avoid selling to a chain owner and to avoid forming a chain, to achieve financial stability so as to maintain editorial strength, to hire above-average staff members and to pay higher than normal salaries, to provide attractive pensions, and to set up a profit-sharing plan.

Poynter became president of the Times Publishing Company in 1953 and chairman of the board in 1969, a post he held until his death from a cerebral hemorrhage. Among the company interests he oversaw were *Editorial Research Reports*; Semit, a research and development subsidiary; and Modern Graphic

Arts, a commercial printing concern. Poynter entered the broadcasting field in 1940 when he bought St. Petersburg radio station WTSP, which he sold in 1956. He became a reluctant monopolist in 1962 when he acquired his afternoon competitor, the *Evening Independent*, to keep it from shutting down.

He withstood the public's wrath over his controversial editorial stances: the *Times*, for example, spoke out against racial discrimination long before the Supreme Court school decision in 1954. Under his direction the paper won a Pulitzer Prize in 1964 for public service.

BIBLIOGRAPHY:

B. NYT 17 June 1978; *St. Petersburg Times*, 16 June 1978; David C. Coulson, "Nelson Poynter: Study of an Independent Publisher and His Standards of Ownership," Ph.D. diss., University of Minnesota, 1982.

DAVID C. COULSON

PRICE, BYRON (b. 25 March 1891; d. 6 August 1981) combined careers as a reporter, bureau chief, and news editor with the Associated Press; director of the Office of Censorship during World War II; vice president of the Motion Picture Association of America; and ranking American member of the United Nations Secretariat when the international group moved its headquarters to New York City.

Price was born in Topeka, Indiana, where his father, John, farmed, and his mother, Emaline Barnes Price, was a homemaker. He graduated from Topeka High School in 1908 and enrolled in Wabash College at Crawfordsville, Indiana. While in college, he worked as a part-time reporter for the local *Journal and Review* as well as the nearby Indianapolis dailies, the *Star* and *News*. His Wabash College academic performance earned him election to Phi Beta Kappa.

Upon completion of his college degree in 1912, Price worked briefly with United Press in its Chicago and Omaha bureaus and then joined the Associated Press for a twenty-nine-year period. He was assigned to the Atlanta, Washington, D.C., and New Orleans bureaus and then went to Washington (1927–37) as news editor and bureau chierf. He was shifted to New York City in 1937 as executive news editor.

Price's career with the Associated Press had been interrupted in 1917 when he joined the army. As a first lieutenant and later a captain, he served in France, where his regiment was cited for conspicuous service in the Meuse-Argonne offensive which helped end the war. His second period of government service came on 16 December 1941 when President Franklin D. Roosevelt asked him to organize and direct the government's Office of Censorship, balancing wartime security with constitutional freedom of the press.

Price's censorship office for the most part was widely approved by the American news media. Voluntary in nature, the code worked well enough to keep secret the Allied 1942 invasion of North Africa, the time and place of the invasion of Europe, and the development of the atomic bomb. Price directed a staff which ultimately totaled 14,500 persons who censored all forms of communication with foreign countries and coordinated efforts of the U.S. news media to withhold information which might affect the war effort. His office had one million pieces of mail and more than 50,000 cable and radiotelegraph messages available daily for censorship purposes.

Price in 1942 described censorship as a military weapon that is a "necessary evil" in wartime. He said he wanted to impose the minimum restrictions so that Americans could accurately follow the progress of the war. His major task, however, was the regulation of international communications. Price reported only to President Roosevelt and was given by executive order "absolute discretion" to deal with communications. One objective was counterespionage, and through cooperation with other Allied censorship and intelligence agencies, the first worldwide counterespionage organization was formed.

In August 1945, with the war over, President Harry S. Truman named Price his personal representative to investigate relations between U.S. occupation forces and the German people. Near the end of the year he became vice president of the motion picture censorship body, the Motion Picture Association of America. Later he assumed other Hollywood offices including the chairman of the Association of Motion Picture Producers, Inc.

His country requested his services once again in 1947, and he became the ranking American member of the United Nations Secretariat. He was a major figure in the move of the U.N. headquarters from Lake Success, Long Island, to its permanent offices in New York City. He terminated his work with the United Nations in 1964. Price was married 3 April 1920 to Priscilla Alden. They had no children. She preceded him in death in 1978.

BIBLIOGRAPHY:

A. With Elmer Davis, *War Information and Censorship* (Washington, D.C., 1943).

B. NYT 8 August 1981.

EARL L. CONN

PULITZER, JOSEPH (b. 10 April 1847; d. 29 October 1911) revolutionized American journalism by combining the news crusade with editorials advocating progressive reform. His *New York World* was one of the most influential U.S. newspapers and became a model for twentieth-century dailies. Part of Pulitzer's fortune was left to establish a school of journalism at Columbia University and to endow the Pulitzer Prizes.

Pulitzer, one of four children, was born in Mako, Hungary, to Philip and Louise Berger Pulitzer. His father was a grain merchant. Joseph was educated by private tutors and was attracted to a military career. After being rejected because of poor eyesight and a slight physique by the military of Austria, France, and Great Britain, he was encouraged by a recruiter for the Union army of the United States.

Landing at Boston in 1864, and collecting a bounty for enlisting, he served for less than one year with a New York regiment and saw limited action. Penniless after the war, he set out for St. Louis, performing odd jobs on his arrival and learning the language. He read law and was admitted to the Missouri bar. In 1868 he was hired as a reporter for the leading German-language daily in the region, the St. Louis *Westliche Post*.

Despite his tall, gangling frame and thick glasses, which caused some to ridicule him, he applied common sense and energy to a pursuit for news. In 1869 he was elected as a Republican to the Missouri legislature in a heavily Democratic district. Championing anticorruption legislation, he became involved in a dispute with a lobbyist whom he shot and wounded. Friends paid the court costs and his fine. His work earned him part ownership of the *Westliche Post*, but he sold his interest in 1873 to travel.

Back in St. Louis in 1874, he bought and sold a German-language newspaper at a profit. He practiced law and worked as a Washington correspondent for the *New York Sun* for a time. On 19 June 1878 he married Kate Davis, a distant relation of Jefferson Davis. They had seven children: Ralph, born 11 June 1879; Lucille, 30 September 1880; Katharine, 30 June 1882, Joseph II (q.v.), 21 March 1885; Edith, 19 June 1886; Constance, 13 December 1888; and Herbert, 20 November 1895.

In 1878 Pulitzer purchased the nearly defunct *St. Louis Dispatch* and combined it with the *Post* to pursue his "new journalism" as proprietor of the *Post-Dispatch*. He began crusades against lotteries, gambling, and tax evasion. The paper's circulation increased so that it soon became profitable. Another shooting, this one in self-defense by his chief editorial assistant, John Cockerill (q.v.), killed a prominent lawyer in 1882. The resulting ill will against the *Post-Dispatch* slowed its progress. On a trip to New York the next year, Pulitzer purchased the marginal *New York World* on what would turn out to be favorable terms. A small down payment was made, and the remainder of the price was paid out of the *World*'s profits.

Beginning 11 May 1883, Pulitzer combined sensationalism in news, with active crusading and an aggressive editorial page to attract the working class. He wrote that the *World* would "expose all fraud and sham, fight all public evils and abuses, [and] . . . battle for the people with earnest sincerity."

His Sunday edition under Morrill Goddard (q.v.) broke away from the daily mold to add more features, sports, and comics to become the precursor of the present-day Sunday newspaper with its many supplements. Contests and stunts promoted circulation. His campaign among adults and children for small donations raised the necessary $100,000 to erect the Statue of Liberty that had been given to the United States as a gift from the French people. In October 1887 he founded the *Evening World*, which continued sensational while the morning *World* became the most substantial and thorough newspaper in the country. Circulation reached 100,000 in 1884 and went on to 250,000 in 1887. Combined circulation of both newspapers was 374,000 in 1892.

William Randolph Hearst (q.v.) arrived in 1896 from San Francisco to purchase the *New York Journal*. The two became bitter rivals for mass circulation at a penny a paper with similar methods of crusading and exploiting news of crime and society. The term *yellow journalism* was used to characterize this competition. It derived from the promotion of the *Yellow Kid* comic after Hearst hired away its creator from the *World* while Pulitzer continued the Sunday feature with another artist.

All facets of journalism were advanced in the heightened competition covering the Spanish-American War. Pulitzer was drawn into the jingoistic war coverage and emulated Hearst's sensationalism after the war as both publishers attempted to sustain the high circulations reached during the short conflict. Pulitzer sensed the developing public backlash against sensationalism and began toning down excesses. On some days, each publisher had sold a million copies a day from all editions of their papers.

Because of his absence due to ill health, Pulitzer delegated more responsibility to his subordinates. His neuroses required absolute quiet, which he found on his yacht *Liberty*. Although he sailed a solitary life away from family and associates and was nearly blind, Pulitzer kept active in editorial management by using secretaries to read to him and communicate his orders to subordinates. The morning *World*, particularly, was influential in national and world affairs after withdrawing from yellow journalism. The editorial leadership was supplied by Frank I. Cobb (q.v.), who was hired by Pulitzer after a national search. It no longer sought support only from blue-collar workers, but supported democratic policies and was against government by and for the privileged and the "plutocrats."

Pulitzer's will left $2 million to create a school of journalism at Columbia University (founded in 1912). He also left funds in trust for what became known as the Pulitzer Prizes to encourage "public service, public morals, American Literature, and the advancement of education." His will also decreed that his newspapers could not be sold, but were to continue as independent journals. The New York papers declined under the management of his sons, and a court in 1931 broke the prohibitions against their sale. They were sold to Scripps-Howard and disappeared as separate entities. Pulitzer died on his yacht in Charleston, South Carolina, on 29 October 1911.

BIBLIOGRAPHY:

A. "The College of Journalism," *North American Review*, May 1904.

B. DAB 15, 260–63; NYT 30 October 1911; James Wyman Barrett, *Joseph Pulitzer and His World* (New York, 1941); George Juergens, *Joseph Pulitzer and the "New York World"* (Princeton, N.J., 1966); Julian Rammelkamp, *Pulitzer's "Post-Dispatch" (1878–1883)* (Princeton, N.J., 1967); Don C. Seitz, *Joseph Pulitzer: His Life and Letters* (New York, 1924); W. A. Swanberg, *Pulitzer* (New York, 1967).

SAM KUCZUN

PULITZER, JOSEPH II (b. 21 March 1885; d. 30 March 1955) was the second son and namesake of the founder of the *St. Louis Post-Dispatch* and proprietor of the *New York World*. He succeeded as editor and publisher of the *Post-Dispatch* in 1912 and held the positions forty-three years, until his death.

During that time the *Post-Dispatch* achieved national and international stature as a crusading and thoughtful newspaper that based its news reports and editorials on penetrating investigation and careful research. The second Joseph Pulitzer considered himself the trustee of his father's pledge in founding the paper in 1878 to fight corruption and promote democratic decision making. When the *World*, under his brothers, Ralph and Herbert Pulitzer, failed in 1931, the son in whom the elder Pulitzer had shown the least confidence became the keeper of his ideals.

Joseph was born in New York City, the fourth of seven children of Joseph Pulitzer (q.v.) and Kate Davis Pulitzer. He attended Harvard University from 1904 to 1906, but because he was an indifferent student his father took him out of college and put him to work, first at the *World* and then at the *Post-Dispatch*. He was required to observe other people at work and write reports to his father on what he saw. The news and editorial departments interested him much more than the business aspects of newspapering. On his first opportunity to gather news—at the *World* in 1906–he wrote his father: ''Reporting suits me right down to the ground, and I am learning every day. I hope you will not think of transferring me to any other job.''

However, he did work in a variety of capacities in St. Louis between August 1906 and his father's death in October 1911 that amounted to an apprenticeship. Aided in his first years as editor and publisher by such experienced hands as editorial page editor George S. Johns and managing editor Oliver K. Bovard (q.v.), young Pulitzer gradually enlarged his directorial role. He communicated by a steady stream of dictated memos, letters, and telegrams from wherever he might be—including duck hunting in Arkansas and salmon fishing in Canada, sports he passionately pursued—to the various managers and editors. In nearly all instances the usually politely worded suggestions were regarded as direct orders. Like his father, he had gradual loss of sight that made it necessary for others to read aloud to him, though he retained some vision in his right eye. In 1929 he established a system to keep deceptive and objectionable advertising out of the *Post-Dispatch*, something he had tried unsuccessfully to convince his father to do. As a result, the paper turned away millions of dollars in advertising over the years because Pulitzer believed the paper should never knowingly deceive its readers.

Though he headed the advisory board for the Pulitzer Prizes, established by his father at Columbia University, Pulitzer saw to it that no favoritism was shown the *Post-Dispatch* and took no part in decisions involving his paper. During his editorship five Pulitzers for Meritorious Public Service went to the paper and six went to staff members.

No member of Pulitzer's editorial staff was required to write anything contrary to that person's convictions. Consequently, when Pulitzer committed the usually Democratic paper to presidential candidates Alf Landon in 1936 and Thomas E. Dewey in 1948, the writing and editorial cartooning were done only by staff members who agreed. In 1938, when Pulitzer refused to commit the *Post-*

Dispatch to a socialistic course advocated by Bovard, the managing editor resigned. Thereafter, Pulitzer was more active in determining news policy. In 1945 Pulitzer was one of a select group of editors taken on a U.S. government–sponsored trip to inspect the liberated German concentration camps. He wrote a series of articles for his newspaper and on his return addressed the Missouri legislature and had his articles published in book form for free distribution. The *Post-Dispatch* sponsored an exhibit of photographs taken in the camps that toured a number of U.S. cities. Many distinguished journalists served under Pulitzer, including Raymond P. Brandt and Marquis W. Childs (q.v.) of the paper's Washington bureau and editorial cartoonist Daniel R. Fitzpatrick (q.v.).

BIBLIOGRAPHY:

A. *A Report to the American People* (St. Louis, 1945).

B. DAB Supp. 5, 551–552; NYT 1 April 1955; *St. Louis Post-Dispatch*, 31 March 1955; Jack Alexander, "The Last Shall Be First," in *Post Biographies of Famous Journalists*, ed. John Drewry (New York, 1942); James W. Markham, *Bovard of the "Post-Dispatch"* (Baton Rouge, 1954).

DANIEL W. PFAFF

PULLIAM, EUGENE C. (b. 3 May 1889; d. 23 June 1975) was a publisher who felt his newspaper ought to say what was right—not just what was correct. He was a publisher with an extremely personal feeling about his newspapers, and felt that a newspaper could be an instrument of change. He fought against corruption and for moral decency. His approach was not unlike that of William Rockhill Nelson (q.v.) of the *Kansas City Star*; but that's no surprise, because one of Pulliam's first newspaper jobs was with the *Star* under Nelson.

Pulliam's first newspaper job came in college, at DePauw University in Greencastle, Indiana. He and a group of fellow collegians took the campus newspaper out of campus politics and steered it on a more professional course. Their model was Joseph Pulitzer's (q.v.) *New York World*. This group of enterprising collegians converted the semiweekly into a daily. (Pulliam served as the business manager.) They also formed an organization that would grow to become one of the most important in journalism—Sigma Delta Chi.

Just before graduation Pulliam left school. He moved back to his native Kansas (he was born in Ulysses) and took a job with the *Atchison Champion*. After a few months he moved on to the *Star*. After a year at the *Star* Pulliam got an itch that was to shape his whole career. He wanted to be his own boss, so he returned to Atchison and bought in. His crusading editorials, though, made him unpopular in so conservative a town. The paper failed. It proved to be his only financial failure, though, and he prided himself on never having sold out to special interests.

After marriage to his college sweetheart, he debated whether to accept a reporter position with the *Indianapolis News*. He opted instead for the position of managing editor of the *Franklin Evening Star*, just down the road from Indianapolis. He modernized the paper, toned his crusades somewhat, and made it a success. By 1920 he had purchased all of the paper and was ready to start on a career of buying and selling newspapers that would see him own or edit forty-six different newspapers. He sold his Franklin paper in 1923 and bought one in Lebanon, Indiana.

Pulliam purchased what proved to be his flagship paper, the *Indianapolis Star*, in 1944. In buying it, he outbid Roy Howard (q.v.) of Scripps-Howard; Marshall Field of the *Chicago Sun*; Col. Robert McCormick (q.v.) of the *Chicago Tribune*; Samuel Newhouse (q.v.), by now a chain owner; George Ball, an industrial magnate from nearby Muncie; the Cowles brothers, who owned papers in Des Moines and Minneapolis; and, finally, the Fairbanks family, who owned the rival *News*.

When he took over the *Star*, it was running third in Indianapolis behind the *News* and the *Times*, a Scripps-Howard newspaper. Through improvements in content and a more vigorous approach to the market, Pulliam moved the *Star* into first place in less than four years. Editorially Pulliam treated the *Star* much as he did the *Atchison Champion*. He returned to a more vigorous editorial policy, stressing moral issues and fighting corruption. Pulliam later outbid several prospective buyers to gain the *News*. He also acquired the newspapers in Muncie, Indiana, and later the two dailies in Phoenix, Arizona.

Late in his career Pulliam became more conservative than he had been in his youth. His fascination with political amateurs and reformers was replaced with an ever-increasing regard for skilled professional politicians. This is best marked by the 1964 candidacy of Barry Goldwater. In Phoenix, Pulliam had met the young Goldwater and urged him to enter political life, but by 1964 Pulliam had become more fascinated with career politicians and supported Lyndon Johnson—about the only time he actively supported a Democrat for the White House. Pulliam died in Phoenix on 23 June 1975 at the age of eighty-six.

BIBLIOGRAPHY:

B. NYT 24 June 1975.

RICHARD C. GOTSHALL

PYLE, ERNEST (ERNIE) TAYLOR (b. 3 April 1900; d. 18 April 1945) was best known by American newspaper readers during World War II for his stories about the day-to-day lives and battle experiences of the common soldier. Although Pyle spent a number of years in conventional writing and editorial assignments with various newspapers, he was happiest and did his best work when given the opportunity to travel and select those stories that uncovered the heroic character of ordinary people. In 1944 he was awarded the Pulitzer Prize for distinguished correspondence, and in 1945, posthumously, the U.S. Medal of Merit.

Pyle, the only child of William Clyde and Maria Taylor Pyle, was born on the family farm near Dana, Illinois, a small town about seventy miles west of Indianapolis. He was always a frail boy (as an adult he weighed no more than 110 pounds and stood about five feet tall), who never adapted well to the rigors of farm life. Despite his evident dislike for farm labor, he continued to work with his father until in his late teens when, as World War I was drawing to a close, he joined the Naval Reserves.

The Armistice ended Pyle's short enlistment, and in the fall of 1919 he enrolled in Indiana University, where he spent the next three and a half years. During his student days, Pyle served as writer and then editor for the student paper. In January 1923, just months before he would have graduated, he accepted a position with the *La Porte Herald* as a cub reporter and left the university.

After only several months with the *Herald*, Pyle was recruited by Earle E. Martin, editor of the newly formed *Washington Daily News*. Pyle later became a deskman and stayed with the paper until 1926. On 7 July 1925 Pyle married Geraldine Siebolds, originally from Minnesota, but at the time working in Washington as a clerk with the Civil Service Commission. ''Jerry'' would later figure prominently in Pyle's syndicated travel stories as ''that girl who rides beside me.''

In 1926, tired of the routine, the couple quit their jobs, invested their savings in a Model-T Ford roadster, and took a casual cross-country trip that, no doubt, set the pace for a life-style they would adopt several years later when Pyle worked as a roving columnist for Scripps-Howard. They ended this first trip in New York when Pyle signed on for a brief period as a copyreader with the *New York Evening World* and the *Evening Post*.

Pyle left New York in 1928 when he was hired again by the *Washington News*, first as a telegraph editor, then as aviation columnist, and finally as managing editor. During the four years in which he wrote the aviation column, he was able to develop the skill—for which he later became so well known—of presenting the personal, human side of events.

In 1935 he and Jerry began traveling throughout the world in search of stories that provided a glimpse of events from a human viewpoint. Over the next five years the couple crossed the country twenty-four times by plane, automobile, and train, and traveled extensively in North, Central, and South America, sending back stories that were syndicated by the Scripps-Howard chain.

Pyle's account of the London blitz on 1 January 1941 stirred great excitement among readers and critics, and was called the best column of the year. Within a few months his first book, *Ernie Pyle In England* (1941), was published. By this time all of Pyle's stories originated from the battlefields of Europe, North Africa, and later the Pacific theater. Unlike many correspondents of the day who wrote about generals and grand strategies, Pyle was known for his stories about the ''G.I. Joes'' who carried their rifles and mess kits into battle. He traveled with the foot soldiers, ate field rations with them, and slept in their trenches on the front lines, and always his stories provided a view of the war from the soldiers' perspective. A reprint of his articles from North Africa was released as *Here Is Your War* (1943).

Pyle continued to cover the war through the liberation of Paris; then he took a short rest in Albuquerque, New Mexico. In 1944 he was awarded the Pulitzer

Prize, and later that year another collection of his articles was published as *Brave Men*. He joined the Pacific fighting in 1945 where he covered activities of the U.S. Navy and Marines. He was reporting on a campaign of the 77th Infantry Division in the Ryukyus Islands on 18 April 1945 when an advance team he was with became pinned down by Japanese machine-gun fire. Pyle was struck in the head by a bullet and killed. He was buried on the island, but after the war his body was moved to the National Memorial Cemetery near Honolulu. Two books published posthumously were *Last Chapter* (1946) and *Home Country* (1947).

BIBLIOGRAPHY:
B. Lee G. Miller, *The Story of Ernie Pyle* (New York, 1950).

GARY W. SELNOW

— R —

RALPH, JULIAN (b. 27 May 1853; d. 20 January 1903) was widely regarded among his peers in late nineteenth-century journalism as the best reporter of his time. His achievements in reporting and writing, mostly for the *New York Sun*, were memorable, even for one who thought, as Ralph did, that he was born to be a reporter.

He was born in New York City to Dr. Joseph Edward Ralph, a physician, and Selina Mahoney Ralph. He attended private schools but left at fifteen to work as an apprentice at the weekly *Standard* in Red Bank, New Jersey, and soon moved up to become a reporter and local editor. In quick succession he founded a short-lived competing newspaper in Red Bank and worked as local editor of the *Courier* in Tom's River, New Jersey, and as editor of the *Times* in Webster, Massachusetts. In 1873 he joined the staff of the *New York Daily Graphic* as a reporter. His daily coverage of the adultery trial of Henry Ward Beecher (q.v.) brought him to the attention of *Sun* editor Charles A. Dana (q.v.), who hired him for the *Sun* in 1875. In 1876 he married Isabella Mount. They had three sons and two daughters.

On Dana's "newspaperman's newspaper" for two decades, Ralph achieved a solid reputation for being hardworking and persistent and having a deep commitment to accuracy and attention to detail. He loved his work as a reporter and special correspondent who traveled widely throughout the nation and world covering major events. Ralph's assignments included national political conventions and presidential inaugurations, legislative scandals and major trials, including the Lizzie Borden murder trial in 1893. For the funeral of Ulysses S. Grant in August 1885, Ralph wrote, in pencil, a story of about 11,000 words in seven hours. He also wrote for the *Sun* a long-running series of sketches featuring a German barber commenting in a dialect on matters of current interest.

In 1890 Ralph undertook publication of a weekly literary paper, *Chatter*, but financial problems ended it after six months. In that year he also began a secondary career as a regular contributor to *Harper's Monthly* and *Harper's Weekly* and other magazines. Much of his work consisted of regional color articles on the United States, Canada and Asia, while he was still a member of the *New York Sun* staff. He traveled extensively from 1891 to 1894 on assignments for the *Harper's* publications, covering some 75,000 miles in all. Several collections of his articles were subsequently published, as were a number of volumes of fiction, both short stories and novels.

William Randolph Hearst (q.v.) hired Ralph in late 1895 to work for the *New York Journal*, and Ralph went to London in 1896 to serve as European editor for the *Journal*. He covered the coronation of Czar Nicholas II, the Greco-Turkish War, and the Diamond Jubilee of Queen Victoria's reign for the *Journal*. After leaving that paper in 1898, Ralph stayed in London as a correspondent for the *New York Herald* and the *Brooklyn Eagle*. In 1899 he covered the Dreyfus court-martial in France, then went to South Africa to cover the Boer War as a correspondent for the *London Daily Mail* and *Collier's* magazine. Ralph and other correspondents with the British forces in March and April 1900 edited the *Friend*, a daily field newspaper. Among the contributors were Rudyard Kipling and Arthur Conan Doyle.

The experience was hard on Ralph's health. He was wounded, injured in a riding accident, and stricken with fever. He returned to London, then came back to the United States in 1902. Ralph served as eastern representative for the St. Louis World's Fair, wrote occasionally for the *New York Times*, and completed his personal account of his journalistic career, *The Making of a Journalist*, which was published in 1903 after his death at forty-nine following a prolonged illness.

As a journalist, Ralph had been one of those who, as he wrote of all journalists, "see their strained, exciting, never-halting toil through glasses colored by sentiment or through the heatwaves of excitement. They are forever stimulated by competition and freshened by constant novelty."

BIBLIOGRAPHY:

A. *War's Brighter Side. The Story of "The Friend" Newspaper Edited by the Correspondents with Lord Roberts's Forces, March–April 1900* (New York, 1901).

B. DAB 8, 332–333; NYT 21 January 1903; Frank M. O'Brien, *The Story of the Sun* (New York, 1918); Frederic Remington, "Julian Ralph," *Harper's Weekly*, 24 February 1894.

RONALD S. MARMARELLI

RAYMOND, HENRY JARVIS (b. 24 January 1820; d. 18 June 1869) was an influential politician in New York and the nation, but more important were his establishment and editing of the *New York Times* and his conception of the modern approach to news reporting that embraces accuracy, truth, fairness, and objectivity as the highest values in journalism. Raymond's deliberate passionlessness in his newspaper columns belied his influence in Whig and Republican party politics and the reform in government he fervently sought. His notions of the role of the press in society inspired the mystique long associated with the *New York Times*.

Raymond was the first of six children born to Jarvis Raymond and Lavina Brockway Raymond in Lima, New York. His parents were farmers. Raymond's father was a minor officeholder and ruling elder for Lima's First Presbyterian Church. Raymond excelled in district and elementary school and at Genesee Wesleyan Seminary. He taught school briefly, and in 1836 enrolled at the University of Vermont at Burlington. Upon his graduation at age twenty-one, Raymond was considered a scholarly and popular orator and writer.

Raymond unsuccessfully sought work as a teacher and then went to New York City in 1840 to work for Horace Greeley's (q.v.) *New Yorker* magazine. In 1841 Greeley started the *New York Tribune*, a Whig newspaper, and Raymond was named chief assistant. Raymond excelled at covering everything from lectures to murders in the competitive journalistic atmosphere of New York. Philosophical conflict between Greeley and Raymond was frequent, but they parted cordially in 1843 when Raymond took a job as editorial assistant for James Watson Webb's (q.v.) *Morning Courier and New York Enquirer*. Also in 1843, Raymond, twenty-four, married Juliette Weaver, a strong-willed and puritanical farmer's daughter, in Winooski, Vermont.

He helped elevate the *Courier* into a more cultural paper with special features about arts, sciences, and travel. He became active in Whig party politics, and associated with Webb; Greeley; Henry Clay; Zachary Taylor; William Henry Seward, U.S. senator from New York; and Thurlow Weed (q.v.), political boss and editor of the *Albany Journal*. Raymond gave and wrote speeches. His political and journalistic fortunes rose. In 1850 he was named managing editor of *Harper's New Monthly Magazine*, a literary journal. He kept the post until 1856. Also in 1850, Raymond, thirty, was elected state assemblyman from New York. The next year he was elected speaker of the house.

In 1851 Webb instigated a separation from Raymond even though Raymond had guided the *Courier* well during Webb's frequent absences. Raymond's antislavery and other positions were too extreme for Webb, who also was offended that Raymond did not support Webb for U.S. senator.

Raymond and George Jones (q.v.), a former colleague at the *Tribune*, revived a five-year-old plan for a new daily newspaper. Edward N. Wesley, an Albany broker, joined Jones and Raymond in forming the *New York Daily Times* (the *New York Times* after 1857). In his prospectus, editor Raymond announced the moderate ideology that would become the hallmark for the paper. Raymond controlled the editorial department; Jones controlled the business department. The first issue was published for 18 September 1851 at one cent a copy. A year later, the paper had a circulation of about 25,000 and a good toehold in the New York newspaper market. The *Times* faltered dangerously at one point when Jones took ill, but Wesley's business acumen rescued the paper.

In 1852 Raymond lost some enthusiasm for Whig politics, but his public life was not over. He withdrew his name as a candidate for governor and congressman from New York. The political, philosophical, and professional animosity between Greeley and Raymond flared. Raymond's ties to the Whigs were strong, especially after Weed loaned Raymond $5,000 to expand the physical plant for the *Times* in 1854. Whig leaders rejected Greeley as a candidate and nominated Raymond for lieutenant governor in 1854. He won.

Raymond was instrumental in establishing the Republican party in 1855–56. He wrote the party statement of principles at the Republican National Convention in 1856 in Pittsburgh. He discouraged a new movement to support him for governor, preferring to write and give speeches for John C. Frémont for president in 1856 and for Seward in 1860. The *Times*, however, gave its full support to Lincoln when he emerged as the party leader.

By 1859, with the *Times* entrenched as a leading New York newspaper, especially with its outstanding coverage of Europe, Raymond went to Italy to cover the French and Italian war with Austria. The *Times* and Raymond received extensive fame for his quick and moving report of the Battle of Solferino. Raymond also covered the Battle of Bull Run for the paper, which supported Lincoln's conduct of the Civil War.

Raymond was elected to the state assembly in 1861 and again was named speaker in 1862. He was chosen president of the New York Union Party Convention in Syracuse in September 1862, and in 1864 he was chosen to head the New York delegation to the national Union convention. He was elected chairperson of the executive committee and was the primary writer for the platform. Lincoln called Raymond "my lieutenant general in politics."

Raymond lost the Union-Republican nomination for U.S. senator in 1863, but he was elected in 1864 to the U.S. House of Representatives. In Congress, Raymond was associated with the unpopular administration, and he was no match for the Radical Republicans. He led a group of moderate Democrats and Republicans who met in Philadelphia in 1866 to support the administration's proposals for reconstruction. His reward later was nomination by President Andrew Johnson for U.S. minister to Austria, but the Senate, controlled by the Radicals, rejected all of Johnson's nominations. The Radicals also ousted Raymond from national committee leadership.

In 1867 Raymond withdrew from public life and busied himself with the newspaper, which he said he wanted to make into a truly national paper. The paper crusaded for monetary and civil service reform and tariff reduction and against the infamously corrupt Tweed Ring. Raymond was also involved with the Associated Press.

Raymond never recovered from the political blows he suffered, which coincided with the onset of a serious nervous condition. When several friends and his son Walter, fourteen, died, he grew despondent. His relationship with his wife was strained from at least 1857, when she took their children to Europe for school. They had seven children, two of whom died before Raymond. Raymond's ambitions often exceeded his diminutive size and his ability to achieve them. Even as a young man, he frequently had spells of illness, usually caused by overwork and stress. Raymond, forty-nine, died on 18 June 1869 of a stroke. Mrs. Raymond died on 13 October 1914.

BIBLIOGRAPHY:

B. (Ernest) Francis Brown, *Raymond of the "Times"* (New York, 1951); Dorothy Dodd, *Henry J. Raymond and the "New York Times" during Reconstruction* (Chicago, 1936).

THOMAS A. SCHWARTZ

READ, OPIE POPE (b. 22 December 1852; d. 2 November 1939) was a pioneer journalist, co-owner and editor of the *Arkansaw Traveler*, author of over fifty romantic novels and other books, and lecturer on the Chautauqua circuit.

Born in Nashville, Tennessee, youngest of eleven children, Opie Read grew up in Gallatin, Tennessee, where his parents, Guilford and Elizabeth Wallace Read, moved just after his birth. In Gallatin, Guilford Read set up a carriage shop with his brother David, but later took up farming.

Opie Read detested farm work and took every opportunity to escape it. He attended neighborhood schools in Gallatin and in his late teens began working with the *Franklin* (Kentucky) *Patriot*. He left newspaper work for two years to attend Neophogen College (now defunct) in Gallatin. At Neophogen, he paid expenses for his education by setting type for the college magazine, the *Pen*.

Leaving college in 1873, Read began a ten-year period in which he moved from one town to another, setting type, writing, and editing. He returned briefly to the *Patriot* as a reporter. Then he moved on. In Scottsville, Kentucky, he was co-owner and editor of the *Scottsville Argus*; in Bolivar, Tennessee, he was reporter for the *Bulletin*; in Carlisle, Arkansas, he helped to start (and finish) the *Prairie Flower*; in Bowling Green, Kentucky, he edited the *Bowling Green Pantagraph*; in Louisville, he was reporter for the *Louisville Courier Journal*; in Little Rock, Arkansas, he was city editor of the *Evening Democrat*; in Memphis, he was on special assignment for the *New York Herald*; back in Little Rock, he edited the *Daily Arkansas Gazette*; and in Cleveland, Ohio, he was reporter for the *Cleveland Leader*. During these years, Read established a reputation as a whitty yarn spinner, who, when news was limited, might even make up a story to print. He specialized in character pieces about poor whites, uneducated blacks, and pretentious society folk of Arkansas, Kentucky, and Tennessee.

On 30 June 1881 Read married Ada Benham in Little Rock. Shortly afterwards, Ada's brother, Philo D. Benham, proposed to Read that they begin a weekly humor sheet, which they would call the *Arkansaw Traveler*. Read would write and edit; Benham would manage the finances. They began publication on 4 June 1882. By 1885 subscriptions were up to 85,000. It was Read's first success.

Read's sketches delighted Midwesterners and city dwellers, but rural readers in Arkansas believed Read was holding hillbillies up for the country to laugh at. Their criticism of the *Traveler* became so bitter that in 1887 Read and Benham moved their base to Chicago.

Once in Chicago, Read spent much of his time socializing with celebrities at the Chicago Press Club and the Whitechapel Club, playing golf, and writing fiction, which he began to serialize in the *Traveler*. He and Ada now had six children: Philo Benham, Leslie Opie, Guilford, Harriet Veronica, Elaine Elizabeth, and Enid Ada; two other children had died as infants.

In January 1892 Read left the *Traveler* to write fiction full-time. Between 1891 and 1906 he published thirty-eight books, mostly novels. The romantic plots were thin, the characters flat; but his novels and short stories were well received by the turn-of-the-century readers, one novel selling over a million copies. By 1912 Read had become so popular as a storyteller that he joined the Chautauqua circuit and toured the country, reading from his novels and recounting anecdotes he had earlier included in the *Traveler*.

On 24 July 1928 Ada Benham Read died in Chicago, and Read moved into an apartment at 5000 Harper Avenue. In 1930 he published his autobiography, *I Remember*, but it attracted little attention. World War I and the onset of the depression had changed public taste. Read's brand of humor was passé.

In August 1939 Read fell in his apartment and injured himself. For three months he lapsed in and out of consciousness, never completely recovering from the fall. On 2 November 1939 he died; his ashes were placed in Oak Woods Cemetery, Chicago.

BIBLIOGRAPHY:

B. DAB Supp. 2, 549–550; NYT 3 November 1939; Maurice Elfer, *Opie Read* (Detroit, 1940); Robert L. Morris, *Opie Read: American Humorist* (New York, 1965).

SHIRLEY M. MUNDT

REED, JOHN SILAS (b. 22 October 1887; d. 19 October 1920) was a magazine and newspaper correspondent known for courage in pursuing stories. His highly descriptive writing style involved him with his subjects and laid out his point of view. His view that the United States should abstain from World War I put him at odds with the U.S. government. The alienation worsened when he lectured favorably on the Russian revolution after a reporting trip to Russia. *His Ten Days That Shook the World* (1919) is the definitive firsthand account of the Bolshevik revolution.

Reed was born in Portland, Oregon, the older son of Charles Jerome Reed, a businessman, and Margaret Green Reed, of a wealthy Portland family. Reed attended Portland schools, Morristown Academy in New Jersey, and Harvard College, from which he graduated in 1910. Muckraking journalist Lincoln Steffens (q.v.) found him a temporary job at the *New York Globe* and then an assistant editing job at *American* magazine. Reed became known in New York literary circles. While at the *American* from 1911 to 1913 he wrote also for other magazines. In 1913 he privately published *The Day in Bohemia*, among his best poetry, about artistic life in the Greenwich Village section of New York where he was living.

His politics gradually took a radical bent, and in 1913, bored with the *American*, he joined the *Masses*, which was being overhauled by socialist Max Eastman (q.v.). Covering a New Jersey strike in 1914, Reed attempted to speak for the strikers and was arrested. It marked Reed's attachment to his subjects, as well as an outrage at class divisions.

In 1913 *Metropolitan* magazine and the *New York World* sent Reed to cover the Mexican revolution. He tracked down guerrilla leader Pancho Villa and then followed his forces through four months of combat. His articles, sympathetic to the peon cause, softened the American view of Villa. The *World* promoted Reed to readers as "America's Kipling." Twice *Metropolitan* sent Reed to cover World War I. He reported on men in the trenches and war's impact on ordinary life. His stories sounded a theme he had been hammering at in the *Masses*, that the war was a commercial, not ideological, conflict.

Reed was married to aspiring journalist Louise Bryant in November 1916. She accompanied him in 1917 on a reporting trip to Russia for the *Masses*, the magazine *Seven Arts*, and the socialist *New York Call*. While in Russia, he was indicated at home for sedition in connection with his work at the *Masses*. The trial ended in a split jury.

Back in the United States, Reed lectured enthusiastically about the Bolshevik revolution and against U.S. involvement in World War I. He led the splinter Communist Labor party in 1919 and edited its paper, the *Voice of Labor*. Several times he was arrested, and he was indicted for incendiary speech. In this period he wrote *Ten Days That Shook the World*, his greatest literary and journalistic accomplishment. It was widely translated.

Facing new federal prosecution, he fled the United States for Russia and threw himself into revolutionary activities. He ignored his health, and after an exhausting trip to Baku, he died of typhus. A hero, he was buried in the Kremlin. In a 1926 edition of *Ten Days*, Lenin, a friend since Reed's 1917 reporting trip to Russia, wrote the introduction.

BIBLIOGRAPHY:

A. *Insurgent Mexico* (New York, 1914); *The War in Eastern Europe* (New York, 1916); "Almost Thirty," *New Republic*, 15 and 29 April 1936.

B. DAB 15, 450–451; NYT 19 October 1920; Barbara Gelb, *So Short a Time: A Biography of John Reed and Louise Bryant* (new York, 1973); Granville Hicks, *John Reed: The Making of a Revolutionary* (New York, 1930); Tamara Hovey, *John Reed: Witness to Revolution* (Los Angeles, 1975).

JOHN H. VIVIAN

REID, HELEN ROGERS (b. 23 November 1881; d. 27 July 1970), publisher and once president of the *New York Herald Tribune*, was a forceful influence in her thirty-seven years with the paper. Combining business judgment and editorial talents, Reid established herself among the influential leaders in newspaper and social circles of her time. Her contributions ranged from enhancing the *Herald Tribune*'s advertising and features to probing and explaining the nation's political and economic issues through highly regarded forums sponsored by the paper. An ardent feminist, she was instrumental in raising $500,000 for early New York suffrage campaigns and retained a lifelong interest in advancing the interests of working women.

Helen Rogers was the eleventh child of Sarah Louise Johnson Rogers and Benjamin Talbot Rogers, a former store proprietor from a Michigan copper-mining district who had moved to Appleton, Wisconsin, to buy into a hotel and to be near Lawrence College for the children. He failed in the hotel investment. Helen Reid had five older brothers and five older sisters; her father died when she was three. She attended local public schools and at eleven, entered Grafton Hall, a college preparatory boarding school in Fond du Lac where her brother, the Reverend Benjamin Talbot Rogers, was headmaster. Following her graduation, she entered Barnard College in New York in 1899, where she worked her way through school by working in the bursar's office, managing a dormitory, and tutoring.

Originally a Greek and Latin major who later switched to zoology, she had intended to teach. Instead, on receiving her B.A. in 1903, she became social secretary to New York grande dame Mrs. Whitelaw Reid, the wife of the wealthy financier, diplomat, and publisher of the *New York Tribune*. Eight years later, on 14 March 1911, she married the Reids' only son, Ogden Mills Reid. On graduating from law school, Ogden Reid became managing editor of the paper, and on his father's death in 1912, he assumed ownership and became its editor.

Helen Reid was little involved with the newspaper during the first six years of her marriage, her time given instead to the cause of woman suffrage and to the management of the Reids' Manhattan house and 800-acre property in nearby Westchester County, which she restored from a picturesque gentleman's estate to a profitable working farm. In these years, too, three children—Whitelaw, Elisabeth (who died in childhood), and Ogden—were born.

Her career with the paper began in 1918 when, at her husband's request, she joined him in its advertising operations. She worked in one advertising role or another until Ogden Mills Reid's death in 1947, when she became the *Herald Tribune*'s president. Gifted with astute financial acumen, she is credited with being responsible for the increases in the paper's advertising and circulation between 1918 and 1923 that put the paper on a competitive footing with the then-leading morning dailies, the *New York Times*, the *World*, and the *American*. Its advertising space more than doubled.

At her prompting, the paper acquired Frank Munsey's (q.v.) *Herald* in 1924 and entered into a new era, one that would see the *Herald Tribune* grow to recognition as one of the world's great newspapers. She is credited with developing suburban features, often focusing on gardening and other subjects of interest to women and a suburban public, further increasing circulation. She also introduced the Home Institute, a feature presenting recipes developed by the paper's own experimental kitchens, a first, and was responsible for introducing "Books," the literary section, and "This Week," featuring Sunday fiction and articles. She sought new writers, attracting columnists such as Dorothy Thompson and Walter Lippmann (qq.v.) to the paper's editorial pages, and was responsible for nationwide attention to issues of the day through the Current Events Forum which she initiated and the paper sponsored. She planned each program and personally selected the speakers over the years. She remained active with the paper until 1955, when, at seventy-two, she resigned as chairman, but remained a member of the board. Her son Whitelaw succeeded her as chairman, and her second son, Ogden, assumed its presidency. In retirement, she continued an active social life from the Reids' Fifth Avenue apartment and died at home at eighty-seven of arteriosclerosis.

BIBLIOGRAPHY:

B. NYT 28 July 1970; Harry W. Baehr, Jr., *The "New York Tribune" since the Civil War* (New York, 1936); "Helen Rogers Reid," *Foremost Women in Communication* (New York, 1970); Kenneth Stewart and John Tebbel, *Makers of Modern Journalism* (New York, 1952).

KATHLEEN K. KEESHEN

REID, WHITELAW (b. 27 October 1837; d. 15 December 1912), first recognized nationally during the Civil War as the correspondent "Agate," became a leading newspaper editor, Republican politician, and diplomat during the remaining fifty years of his career. Through his newspaper and political involvement, he became the conscience of conservative Republicanism, confidant and adviser to presidents, and ambassadors to two major allies of the United States.

Reid was born near Xenia, Ohio, the second child of Robert Carlton Reid and Marion Whitelaw Ronalds Reid. He was educated at Xenia Academy under the tutelage of an uncle, entered Miami (Ohio) University at fifteen, and graduated with honors in 1856. After attempting schoolteaching and other pursuits, he began a career in journalism as owner and editor of the *Xenia News* in 1858, a financially unsuccessful venture which he abandoned in 1860.

The following year Reid became a capital reporter for the *Cincinnati Gazette* but was soon assigned to the field to cover the early engagements of the war in Virginia and Tennessee, where his coverage of the Battle of Shiloh first brought him national attention with his thoroughness and attention to detail. However, in 1862 he was sent by the *Gazette* to cover the war from the national capital. It was here he first came in contact with national politics and met Horace Greeley (q.v.), famous editor of the *New York Tribune*. While in Washington, he also served as librarian for the House of Representatives.

After the war he toured the South for several months on a secret mission with Chief Justice Salmon Chase and compiled his classic observations into his first book, *After the War* (1866). While in the South, he became attracted to cotton farming and attempted two unsuccessful plantation operations in Louisiana and Alabama before reentering journalism with the *Gazette* in 1867.

In the fall of 1868 Reid finally accepted the long-standing offer to join Horace Greeley's *Tribune* as an assistant to the editor and editorial writer. The next year he was advanced to managing editor with the freedom to run the newsroom without restrictions. He went to Cincinnati to cover the moderate Republican convention in 1872 and first became active in the party movement to nominate Horace Greeley for the presidency.

When Greeley died within weeks of his disastrous defeat by Grant, Reid borrowed money from Jay Gould to buy controlling interest in the *Tribune* and, thereby, launch himself into national prominence through America's best-known newspaper. He became a leader of Republican editors of his time. While Joseph Pulitzer and William Randolph Hearst (qq.v.) were waging a sensational circulation war in New York for the readership of the working class, Reid kept the *Tribune* Republican, conservative, and appealing to the upper-class leadership.

Even though always supportive of the Republican party, Reid insisted he should be free to criticize both the party and its leadership from within and established himself and his newspaper as "keeper of the Republican conscience." As the result of party support, Reid was appointed, and served three years, as ambassador to France; nominated in 1892 as the vice presidential candidate in the second-term bid of Benjamin Harrison; and served as a member of the commission to negotiate peace with Spain in 1898.

His greatest political achievement was in 1905 when he was named ambassador to Great Britain, where he served until his death in London in 1912. At the time of his appointment, Reid gave up, for the first time, the editorship of the *Tribune*, a position which his son, Ogden Mills Reid, assumed in 1913.

Whitelaw Reid was an innovator in news gathering and newspaper printing. He was one of seven owners of the New York Associated Press; Richard Hoe's first web press was in the basement of the *Tribune*; and Ottmar Mergenthaler's first "line-o-type" machine operated in the Tribune building. He constantly was looking for ways to improve his newspaper's content and production. During his career he wrote forty-one books, many of which were his speeches and addresses. His two best-known publications were *After the War* (1866) and *Ohio in the War* (1868).

BIBLIOGRAPHY:

B. DLB 23, 292–305; Royal Cortissoz, *The Life of Whitelaw Reid* (New York, 1921); Bingham Duncan, *Whitelaw Reid, Journalist, Politician, Diplomat* (Athens, Ga., 1975).

PERRY J. ASHLEY

REMINGTON, FREDERIC SACKRIDER (b. 4 October 1861; d. 26 December 1909) was a writer, illustrator, painter, and sculptor whose best-known work depicted action in the American West. In less than twenty-five years, Remington completed more than 100 articles and stories and about 2,700 illustrations for such publications as *Harper's Weekly*, *Collier's*, *Scribner's*, and *Century*. His illustrations appeared in forty-one different magazines and 142 books; many of them helped the nation define its vision of the disappearing frontier.

Born in Canton, New York, Frederic Remington was the only child of Seth Pierre Remington and Clara Bascomb Sackrider Remington. The Remingtons were politicians and writers; the Sackriders owned the local hardware store. When the baby was eight weeks old, the father, an accomplished horseman and storyteller, sold his Republican newspaper in Canton to become a Civil War cavalry officer with a reputation for leading costly heroic charges. Except for a year in Bloomington, Illinois, the Remingtons lived in Canton and Ogdensburg, New York, where the father published newspapers and became the United States Customs officer in Ogdensburg.

After Remington did poorly in elementary school, his parents sent him to the discipline-oriented Vermont Episcopal Institute at Rock Point for the 1875–76 school year and the Highland Military Academy in Worcester, Massachusetts, for the two subsequent years. In 1878 he entered the Yale School for Fine Arts in a three-year course to become a painter. However, the only activity to which he applied himself was the football team for the 1879 season, after which he dropped out of school. His first published illustration was on football in the *Yale Courant* in 1878.

Remington failed at a succession of political and business jobs; he lasted only thirty minutes on one of them. He survived five months in 1880 as a reporter for the *Albany Morning Express*. In 1881 he took his first trip West. He did a sketch on wrapping paper of cowboys in Montana or Wyoming and submitted it to *Harper's Weekly*, where a staff artist redrew it and published it the following year as a full-page illustration of Arizona cowboys. Bitten by speculators' claims, Remington invested his inheritance in a Kansas sheep ranch only to discover in less than a year that he disliked ranching. To recover his loss, he became the silent partner in a Kansas City, Missouri, saloon. With his new income, he made the down payment on a house and married Eva Adele Caten, daughter of a railroad superintendent of Gloversville, New York. She understood neither his drinking nor his drawing, and upon discovering his source of income in 1885, she left him.

The couple were reunited when Remington enrolled for the spring 1886 term at the Arts Students League in New York. By the end of the term, he landed an assignment to the Southwest for *Harper's Weekly*. Illustrations from the outing appeared for two years. In 1886 Remington published twenty-five illustrations in periodicals and books to earn $1,200—a high income which he doubled the second year. In 1887 he also illustrated Theodore Roosevelt's *Ranch Life and the Hunting Trail*, which helped establish his national reputation. He was elected an associate of the National Academy of Design in 1891, but he never received the desired title of academician.

As a free-lance illustrator, Remington traveled to Germany, Russia, England, Mexico, and Cuba. Longing to witness a war, he went to Cuba in 1896 for William Randolph Hearst's (q.v.) *New York Journal*. Remington failed to find the insurrection the *Journal* had described, but Hearst's famous response supposedly was: "Please remain. You furnish the pictures and I'll furnish the war." Nevertheless, Remington returned to New York, where the *Journal* received a story of a woman searched by Spanish officials. To illustrate it, Remington published a provocative picture of a naked woman being inspected by three clothed male Spanish officers before he learned that the victim had been respectfully searched by female officers. Pulitzer's *New York World* outbid Hearst in 1897 for exclusive newspaper rights for one year to Remington's illustrations.

Remington usually took pride in accuracy. He did studies on the anatomy of the horse at the Sackrider farm near Canton. Despite his denials, he was surely influenced by Eadweard Muybridge's photographs of the horse in motion. Remington had an eye for detail, collecting artifacts on his trips which models used in his studios. Observers commented on his ability to reproduce a scene without notes or sketches. He frequently used a snapshot camera, and his figures had an earthy realism and tension about them. Yet Westerners could spot errors.

In 1895 he cast his first and most popular bronze, the Bronco Buster, the first of this three-dimensional adaptations of realistic horse-and-rider illustrations. In 1903 *Collier's* gave him an exclusive contract which provided him financial security to pursue his serious painting and sculpturing, but the obligatory illustrations were often hastily drawn and poorly researched. By 1908 he had developed a personal form of impressionistic painting.

Remington did most of his work on a free-lance basis in his New York homes. In 1890 he and Eva built a mansion and studio near New Rochelle, New York, and in 1900 they purchased a summer retreat at Ingleneuk, an island in the St. Lawrence River. They moved into a new home at Ridgefield, Connecticut, in May 1909. There in December Remington suffered an attack of appendicitis and died. Eva moved into an Ogdensburg mansion which eventually became the Remington Art Memorial. She died on 3 November 1918. Remington's mother, whom he had not seen since her second marriage in 1888, died in 1912.

BIBLIOGRAPHY:

A. *The Collected Writings of Frederic Remington*, ed. Peggy Samuels and Harold Samuels (Garden City, N.Y., 1979).

B. DAB 8, 496–497; Peter H. Hassrick, *Frederic Remington* (New York, 1973); Estelle Jussim, *Frederic Remington; The Camera and the Old West* (Fort Worth, Texas, 1983); Peggy Samuels and Harold Samuels, *Frederic Remington: A Biography* (Garden City, N.Y., 1982).

WILLIAM E. HUNTZICKER

REYNOLDS, FRANK (b. 29 November 1923; d. 20 July 1983), an American broadcast journalist, was best known for his political reporting which included covering the Senate Watergate Committee hearings in 1973, and anchoring ABC's "Evening News" in 1968 and "World News Tonight" from 1978 through 1983.

Reynolds was born in the industrial community of East Chicago, Indiana, to Frank James Reynolds, a steelworker, and Helen Duffy Reynolds. He was the third of four children, and the only boy. He described his upbringing as strict, even conservative. This background would often surface in later life as Reynolds was known to get emotionally involved in his stories, particularly when he thought certain stories were in poor taste.

The young Reynolds attended Wabash College, but after a year left school completely. He entered the army and fought in World War II. He received the Purple Heart while serving in Germany, and was later promoted to sergeant. On 23 August 1947 he wed Henrietta Mary Harpster, a marriage that produced five sons. One son, Dean, was a Washington correspondent for Cable News Network at the time of his father's death in 1983.

Once back in the Chicago area, Reynolds began his broadcast career by joining radio station WJOB in Hammond, Indiana, as a news reader and sports announcer from 1947 to 1950. In 1950 he left to work as a newscaster at the station which later became WBBM, the Chicago CBS-owned television station. He remained until 1963, when he moved to ABC's KBKB. While at KBKB he went to Vietnam to film a special report. The program was well received in Chicago and also was aired on the ABC network.

Reynolds left Chicago in 1965 to be ABC's Washington correspondent. Three years later ABC named him "Evening News" co-anchor, a post he shared with Howard K. Smith (q.v.). In 1970 the network decided to replace Reynolds with Harry Reasoner, who left CBS to join ABC. Some feel that Reynolds had suffered from the network's uneasiness when Vice President Spiro T. Agnew began criticizing TV news coverage of the Nixon administration.

After this Reynolds spent eight years as a correspondent, first in New York narrating documentaries, and then in Washington covering major stories like political conventions, U.S.-manned space flights, and the Senate Watergate hearings. He was one of the three television representatives to ask questions during the Carter-Ford presidential debates in 1976.

With the arrival of Roone Arledge as ABC News president, there was a push to revamp the network's evening news program. Barbara Walters and Harry Reasoner were dropped as co-anchors, and a new three-anchor format was conceived. Frank Reynolds was selected for the pivotal Washington post (other co-anchors were Peter Jennings and Max Robinson), and with the format change ratings began to climb. Reynolds held this job from 1978 until he took ill in April 1983. When he left, the show fell back to third place in the ratings. Reynolds also pioneered the ABC late-night news show "Nightline," which began to offer extended daily network news coverage during the Iran hostage crisis.

Reynolds's most memorable performance may have come in 1981 when during the assassination attempt on President Reagan, Reynolds's friend, presidential press secretary, James Brady, was shot. An early report suggested that Brady had died. Later news came through that the press secretary indeed was still alive. Frank turned off camera and angrily said, "get this straight . . . nail this down."

The newsman was fifty-nine years old when he died in Washington. He had been ill with multiple myeloma, a form of bone cancer, for several years. Only close friends apparently knew. The immediate cause of death was diagnosed as viral hepatitis, believed contracted from a blood transfusion received during surgery on a fractured left femur a few months earlier. Throughout his career Frank Reynolds was the recipient of the industry's most prestigious awards. In 1969 he was awarded the George Foster Peabody Award for television news broadcasting, an Emmy in 1980 for an ABC special post-election report, and he received the Robert S. Ball Memorial Award.

BIBLIOGRAPHY:

B. *Encyclopedia of American Journalism*, 426; NYT 21 July 1983; *Broadcasting*, 25 July 1983, 97; Barbara Matusow, *The Evening Stars* (New York, 1983); Av Westin, *News-Watch: How TV Decides the News* (New York, 1982).

RICHARD C. VINCENT

REYNOLDS, QUENTIN JAMES (b. 11 April 1902; d. 17 March 1965), a prolific writer of books and articles, fiction and nonfiction, was one of America's most popular war correspondents in World War II. Six feet, six inches tall and weighing 220 pounds, the gregarious, hard-drinking writer became known for his bravura in covering combat and his effusive coverage of the British.

Reynolds was born in Bronx, New York, the son of James J. Reynolds, a public school superintendent, and Katherine Mahoney Reynolds. The family moved to Brooklyn, where Quentin grew up in a comfortable, middle-class home. He completed Manual Training School in 1919 and in 1924 received the Ph.B. degree from Brown University, where he was an outstanding athlete.

Reynolds then drifted from job to job, including a season as a professional football player. He began taking night classes at Brooklyn Law School in 1928, but gave up taking the bar exam for a job with the *New York World-Telegram* covering the spring training camp of the Brooklyn Dodgers. An economy move forced Reynolds out of work in 1932, but with the help of Heywood Broun and Damon Runyon (qq.v.), he landed a job with the International News Service (INS).

Reynolds left INS to report the war for *Collier's*, establishing a relationship that would last until 1949. He plied every trick he knew, including attempting to pass himself off as the nephew of Franklin D. Roosevelt, to get close to the action. His reporting of the Battle of Britain made him a national hero in England. He also became popular in the United States and was widely in demand for lectures.

Though Reynolds was prolific—he wrote about one book a year and hundreds of articles—his admitted lack of research helped cause a major literary hoax in 1952. He wrote a *Reader's Digest* article and a book on George DuPre, a Canadian who claimed to have been a British secret agent during the war. DuPre was an imposter. *Reader's Digest* and Reynolds were embarrassed, but Bennett Cerf, head of Random House, reclassified the book as fiction and told Reynolds, "I've always wanted you to write a novel for us. Now you've done it, and it's a good one."

The embarrassment, however, could not have come at a worse time for Reynolds. In 1949 he wrote a review of a biography of Heywood Broun. In the review, Reynolds noted that Broun, late in his life, had been told by physicians to get complete rest. Because of a Westbrook Pegler (q.v.) column attacking Broun, however, Broun was unable to rest and died. In response to the review, Pegler wrote a column charging Reynolds with cowardice, with being an absentee war correspondent, and with being a war profiteer. The column also charged that Reynolds was a member of the "parasitic, licentious lot" which surrounded Broun, that Reynolds was seen "nuding" down a country road with a girlfriend, and that Reynolds had proposed marriage to Broun's widow as the two were riding to Broun's funeral together. Pegler called Reynolds a sneak, a dirty fighter, a hypocrite, a sorry mediocrity.

As a result of the column, Reynolds, already in debt $44,000 to the Internal Revenue Service, lost his position with *Collier's*, lost radio and television jobs, and lost lecture opportunities. He sued, and in 1954 a jury awarded him $1 in compensatory damages and $175,000 in punitive damages. At the time it was the largest libel verdict ever returned.

In 1960 Reynolds's marriage to actress Virginia Paine ended in divorce. The two were married 30 March 1942, and had no children. In 1965 Reynolds went to Manila to prepare a biography of former President Diosdado Macapagal of the Philippines. He was stricken with abdominal cancer and died at Travis Air Force Base in California.

BIBLIOGRAPHY:

A. *By Quentin Reynolds* (New York, 1963).

B. DAB Supp. 7, 642–643; NYT 18 March 1965; John Jakes, *Great War Correspondents* (New York, 1967); Louis Nizer, "Reputation," *My Life in Court* (Garden City, N.Y., 1961).

W. WAT HOPKINS

RHETT, ROBERT BARNWELL, SR. (b. 21 December 1800; d. 14 September 1876), was owner and chief editorial writer for the Charleston, South Carolina, *Mercury* during the early years of the Civil War. Called by some historians the "Father of Secession," Rhett served in the U.S. House of Representatives from 1836 to 1849, in the Senate from 1850 to 1852, and as a member of the Confederate Congress before returning to Charleston to promote his secessionist philosophy through the *Mercury*.

Born Robert Barnwell Smith in Beaufort, South Carolina, he was the eighth of fifteen children born to James and Marianna Gough Smith. His father was admitted to Middle Temple Bar in London in 1781, "an accomplished scholar and gentleman, but poor planter of rice." Marianna Gough was the great-granddaughter of Colonel William Rhett, known for his adventures against pirates, and it was to perpetuate his name that Barnwell and his brothers changed their surname in 1837.

Robert entered Beaufort College in 1811, and in 1819 began studying law. He was admitted to the South Carolina bar in 1821. Rhett married Elizabeth Washington Burnet, the seventeen-year old niece and ward of Chancellor De Saussure of Charleston, in 1827. She died on 14 December 1852 giving birth to their twelfth child. His second wife was Catharine Herbert Dent, daughter of Elizabeth Ann Horry Dent and John Herbert Dent of Maryland.

Rhett's political career began in 1826 when he was elected to the state legislature from St. Bartholomew's parish in Colleton County. He mustered enough support in 1832 to nullify the protective tariff he opposed, but when John C. Calhoun himself joined forces with Henry Clay in compromise, South Carolina delayed action. In March 1833 the state repealed the nullification, and Rhett urged the convention to consider a confederacy of Southern states. Rhett knew he did not have the support necessary to bring about secession, and since he had just been elected attorney general of the state, he resigned from the legislature. For a time he withdrew from politics. Between 1833 and 1836 he devoted his time to church and civic affairs. Rhett continued to support Calhoun throughout the early 1840s, taking over as editor of Calhoun's organ, the *Spectator*, in 1843.

When Calhoun died in 1850, Rhett won the vacant Senate seat. Because of party discord in South Carolina, Rhett left Washington before the end of the session but was unable to win acceptance for the sovereignty of the state. He resigned his Senate seat and divided his time between his law practice in Charleston and his plantation on the Ashepoo River. Rhett offered himself as a candidate for governor in 1856 and was backed by the *Mercury*, but the *Mercury* was no longer influential in state politics and Rhett's nomination was ignored by the legislature.

In 1857 the *Mercury* was controlled by John Heart and Rhett's son, Robert Barnwell Rhett, Jr. Heart's supporters urged him to let Rhett Jr. take over the paper. The Rhetts then tried to sell the *Mercury*, but they could not find a buyer. Father and son then took over the *Charleston Standard*, combined the two papers, and aligned the new publication with the Democratic party, a move secessionists saw as a turn toward nationalism.

When the war began, Rhett started writing editorials for the *Mercury*, although most of his editorials were unsigned. His criticism of Jefferson Davis's administration was relentless. By 27 May 1862 Rhett was convinced that the South could not establish a separate nation. Rhett used the *Mercury* to keep Southern passions running high, sometimes reprinting stories and editorials from Northern papers for the incendiary effect they had on his readers. Only once, however, in his editorials did Rhett deal with the issue of slavery, writing on 29 November 1862 that "slavery is the best condition for the African; for he is incapable of rising pupilage and, in his master, he obtains a permanent and interested guardian."

A cancerous growth was discovered on Rhett's face in 1864 during a visit to Flat Rock, North Carolina. The treatment was debilitating and disfiguring, requiring surgery four times by 1875. He went to New Orleans in 1872 where Rhett Jr. was editing the *Picayune*, and then moved to St. James Parish with his son-in-law, Colonel Alfred Roman. He wrote editorials for Rhett Jr., and turned out a few magazine articles and essays, contenting himself mostly with tutoring his grandson. Rhett died on 14 September 1876 in St. James Parish, Louisiana, and was buried in Magnolia Cemetery in Charleston, South Carolina. His grave is unmarked.

BIBLIOGRAPHY:

B. DAB 8, 526–528; NYT 15 September 1876; Laura A. White, *Robert Barnwell Rhett: Father of Secession* (Gloucester, Mass., 1931).

PERRY J. ASHLEY

RICE, HENRY GRANTLAND (b. 1 November 1880; d. 13 July 1954) was one of the best-known and most highly regarded American sports writers of the early twentieth century, and one of the primary reasons that the 1920s are considered a golden age of sports writing in American newspapers. For years, Rice was "the dean of American sports writers."

Grantland Rice was born in Murfreesboro, Tennessee, the son of Bolling Hendon Rice and Beulah Grantland Rice. He attended the Nashville Military Academy and the Wallace University School and was a Phi Beta Kappa graduate of Vanderbuilt University in 1901. During his university days he played college and semi-professional baseball.

Immediately after graduation, he got a job as a capitol and courthouse reporter for the *Nashville News*. During that time he also wrote for the *Forester* magazine. From 1902 to 1904 he was on the staff of the *Atlanta Journal*, where he wrote the article that led to the discovery of Ty Cobb by major league baseball. In 1905 Rice moved to the *Cleveland News*. The next year he was back in Tennessee and remained with the *Nashville Tennessean* until 1910, when he went to New York and the *New York Mail*. In 1914 he switched to the *New York Tribune*, where he stayed until 1930.

Rice took a year off from newspapering in 1918–19 to serve as a first lieutenant in the 115th Regiment Field Artillery, 80th Division, in France. He also wrote for *Stars and Stripes*. In 1920 Rice formed Grantland Rice Sportlights and was its president. In 1922, the first year the World Series was broadcast in its entirety, he was the play-by-play announcer.

After 1930 he was essentially self-employed, although he did go on payrolls with such jobs as editor of a golfing magazine. His column, "The Sportlight," was syndicated by North American Newspaper Alliance to more than 100 newspapers. His company produced sports features accompanied by his commentary. He won an Academy Award for best one-reel picture in 1943. He broadcast radio programs, too.

Rice also wrote verse:

> When the Great Scorer comes to mark against your name,
> He'll write not "won" or "lost," but how you played the game.

During World War II he toured army camps and lectured about sports. In 1951, to mark his fiftieth anniversary as a sports writer, an anonymous donor established the Grantland Rice Fellowship in journalism at Columbia University. In 1906, Rice married Katharine Hollis of Americus, Georgia. They had one daughter, Florence.

His colleagues described him as "kindly" and his prose as "over-rich" and said he "was always kind to those he wrote about." He coined the nickname "Galloping Ghost" for Red Grange, and it was Rice, in one of those flows of rich prose, who identified the Notre Dame backfield of Don Miller, Harry Stuhldrher, Elmer Layden, and Jim Crowley with the Four Horsemen of the Apocalypse. (It was some other writer who called their linemen the Seven Mules.)

Late in his career, Rice estimated that he had turned out one million words a year for fifty years—that would average about 3,000 words a day—and had traveled 15,000 miles a year in pursuit of sports stories. He was in his office, working on yet another column, when he suffered the stroke that killed him; he died at Roosevelt Hospital in New York City. Sports columnist Red Smith (q.v.) said of Rice, "He put us all in white collars."

BIBLIOGRAPHY:

A. *The Tumult and the Shouting: My Life in Sport* (New York, 1954).

B. NCAB 41, 19; NYT 14 July 1954.

LAURA NICKERSON

RIDDER, HERMAN (b. 5 March 1851; d. 1 November 1915) founded the family that founded the Ridder newspaper chain, and was himself an important publisher and a leader in the newspaper industry.

Ridder was born in New York City to German immigrants Herman and Gertrude Tiemann Ridder. He had little education. He went to work at eleven as an errand boy, and at thirteen became a messenger on Wall Street. Soon after that he joined the Tradesmen's Fire Insurance Company and remained with them until 1878.

He left that job to establish the *Katholisches Volksblatt*, a German Catholic weekly in 1878. In 1886 he founded the *Catholic News*, which became the leading U.S. Catholic journal. In 1890 he became a 10 percent shareholder, a director, the treasurer, and the business manager of the *Staats-Zeitung*, a New York City German-language newspaper. The *Staats-Zeitung* took over the *Abendblatt* in 1892. By 1906 the *Staats-Zeitung* was the nation's most influential German paper, and Ridder was its editor and publisher.

Ridder was president of the American Newspaper Publishers Association during the early twentieth century and led its fight to get tariff barriers reduced to allow Canadian newsprint to enter the United States. His effort eventually succeeded. Ridder directed the development of the Intertype version of the Linotype, which was introduced in 1913 and was produced by Ridder's International Typesetting Company. That company went bankrupt, but Ridder had friends who assumed the debts of his newspaper in order to keep it alive.

He was ill the last year of his life—his son Bernard Herman wrote a column that appeared under Ridder's byline—and he died in 1915 of arterial sclerosis.

Ridder married Mary C. Amend on 6 April 1880, and they had five sons: Herman, Bernard Herman, Victor F., Joseph E., and William. The three middle sons became partners in what was to be the Ridder newspaper chain. Ridder left the *Staats-Zeitung* to his sons, and they built upon that by purchasing in 1926 the *Journal of Commerce*, a New York City paper dating back to the 1820s. (The *Wall Street Journal* purchased it in 1951.) Starting in 1927 the Ridder brothers expanded to the Midwest, then to the Far West and elsewhere.

Ridder participated in politics as a Democrat and served as treasurer of the Democratic National Committee in 1908. He was also active in other businesses and in charitable organizations. He was a director of the Associated Press.

BIBLIOGRAPHY:

B. NYT 3 November 1915.

DWIGHT JENSEN

RIDDER, HERMAN HENRY (b. 25 June 1908; d. 15 September 1969) was born in New York City, the son of Bernard Herman and Hilda Luyties Ridder, and grandson of Herman Ridder (q.v.). He received his A.B. at Columbia University in 1929. His grandfather died in 1915 and willed to young Ridder's father and his two uncles the *Staats-Zeitung*. In 1926 the uncles purchased the old *New York Journal of Commerce*, and in subsequent years they expanded that into a chain of newspapers.

Herman became publisher of one of those papers, the *St. Paul Daily News*, in 1937. He also became publisher of the *St. Paul Dispatch* and *Pioneer Press* in 1942, and continued to publish those papers until 1952. Then he moved to California and published the *Long Beach Independent* and the *Long Beach Press-Telegram*. In addition, he became president and director of Ridder Publications; vice president and director of Twin Coast Newspapers; and vice president of Northwest Publications. Ridder Publications was an operating company that owned the other two companies.

He has been credited with building the Long Beach papers into respected dailies. He was an active booster of the Long Beach area and used his newspapers to promote the oil, aircraft, and shipyard industries in the community. He promoted hospitals, education, and culture as well. He was a trustee of the California state college system, and was an art and antiques collector.

From 1942 to 1945 Ridder served in the U.S. Marine Corps, attaining the rank of major. Her served as a group intelligence officer on Okinawa and elsewhere in the Pacific theater. Ridder married Virginia Randolph on 11 February 1938. They had one daughter, Marsha, and were divorced in 1944. His second marriage, on 18 April 1953, was to Florence Murphy Pearson of Montclair, New Jersey. They adopted a son, Thomas Payne LeBosquet. Ridder died in Long Beach.

BIBLIOGRAPHY:
B. NCAB 58, 248; NYT 16 September 1969.

DWIGHT JENSEN

RIIS, JACOB A. (b. 3 May 1849; d. 26 May 1914) was a late nineteenth-century crusader and reformer whose work inspired the generation of reporters known as the muckrakers. Most of Riis's work predates the major works of Lincoln Steffens, Ida Tarbell, David Graham Phillips (qq.v.), and the others, but he was regarded as something like the elder statesman of the muckraking movement. Riis spent his career as a journalist-photographer-reformer exposing the living and working conditions of the slum dwellers and child laborers in New York City. He was passionately committed to his work and referred to journalism as the noblest of all professions.

He was one of sixteen children born to a part-time reporter and schoolteacher in Ribe, Denmark. He spent his young manhood working as a carpenter until he emigrated to the United States. The voyage to America may have played some part in making Riis into a great reformer. He was packed in the ship's sinkhole for weeks, knee-deep in people, and began to see the world in terms of victims and victimizers. It was miserable, but it was only a preview of coming attractions in America.

Riis lived a hand-to-mouth existence in New York for three years, working mostly as a carpenter, until he secured a job with the *South Brooklyn News*. He was a natural reporter and wrote about what he saw: small-time merchants losing profits to police graft, sweatshop conditions, homeless children of the streets, and the appalling life of the immigrant in the promised land.

Riis saved enough money to buy the *South Brooklyn News*, but sold it within a year. After a trip home, during which he married his childhood sweetheart, Elizabeth Neilsen, Riis became a reporter for the *New York Tribune*. He worked there from 1877 to 1888. Riis left the *Tribune* for the *New York Evening Sun*, and worked there until 1899. It was in those last two decades of the nineteenth century that Riis did the work that inspired the next generation of reporters. Mulberry Bend was Riis's beat, and as if he were not already familiar with them, his research for stories on poverty and crime there reacquainted him with the deplorable conditions in the city's slums.

Riis was credited with helping the city avoid a cholera epidemic when he reported waste dumping in New York City's major water supply. He used a camera to document the dumping, and the broad of health intervened. By a fortuitous set of circumstances, Riis and the photo-engraving process arrived in journalism nearly simultaneously.

The reformer-journalist caught the attention of Theodore Roosevelt. Roosevelt had been merely an interested reader of Riis's work, but was so moved by the book *How the Other Half Lives* (1890) that he sent Riis a card that said, "I have read your book and I have come to help" (Alland, 1974). When Roosevelt became president of the New York City Police Board, he sought Riis's counsel, and they developed an informal partnership in an enterprise to clean up New York. Their focus was, in large part, on the corrupt police force, and their nocturnal wanderings to surprise policemen sleeping on the job became legendary.

Riis is remembered today largely for his contribution to documentary photography. His harrowing pictures of slum life—particularly of the tenement children—stand today as classic works of photojournalism. His work provided a link between the experiments of the nineteenth century and the realization of documentary photography in the twentieth century.

Paying tribute to Riis in a 1903 *McClure's* article, Steffens wrote, "If a rich man could mark a city with as many good works as Jacob A. Riis has thrust upon New York, his name would be called good and himself great." Riis was devastated by his wife's death in 1905, and it may have aggravated his already poor health. He remarried and retired from active work as a journalist. He became a popular lecturer, but his rigorous schedule also took its toll on his health. He died in 1914, aged fifty-five.

BIBLIOGRAPHY:

A. *Children of the Poor* (New York, 1892); *Out of Mulberry Street* (New York, 1898); *The Making of an American* (New York, 1901); *The Battle With the Slum* (New York 1902); *Children of the Tenements* (New York, 1903).

B. Alexander Alland, Sr., *Jacob A. Riis: Photographer and Citizen* (New York, 1974).

WILLIAM MCKEEN

RIND, CLEMENTINA (b. ca. 1740; d. 25 September 1774) inherited her husband's printing and newspaper business in Williamsburg, Virginia, and operated it successfully for just over a year, until her own death. She designed her paper to appeal to both women and men, and became increasingly supportive of the Patriot cause, even while upholding her paper's motto, "Open to ALL PARTIES, but Influenced by NONE."

Nothing is known about Rind's early life, not even her date and place of birth, although she probably was born in Maryland. She was married to William Rind sometime between 1758 and 1766, while he was the partner of Jonas Green, a printer and publisher of the *Maryland Gazette* in Annapolis, Maryland, to whom William had been apprenticed prior to that time. At the urging of Thomas Jefferson and others, William moved in 1766 to Williamsburg, Virginia, where he established the *Virginia Gazette*. Another *Gazette*, which regularly supported the royal governor, already existed there. William soon became public printer for Virginia as well.

William died on 19 August 1773, and Rind assumed control of both the paper and the printing business, appealing in the *Gazette* for the goodwill of the public and for divine aid: "May that All Ruling Power, whose chastening Hand has snatched from my dear Infants and myself our whole Dependence, make me equal to the Task!" He appeals were answered, apparently, because the paper prospered under Rind's direction. In May 1774 the Virginia House of Burgesses appointed her printer to the colony. Even earlier, in April, she announced that she had purchased "an elegant set of types from London."

Rind had promised at the outset of her editorship to make the paper both useful and entertaining. Content of the few numbers still extant indicates that she was true to her word. She printed foreign and domestic news, essays, poems, and advertisements, with an emphasis on science, education, and philanthropy. Letters written by or addressed to ladies, as well as poetic tributes to them, show an attempt to appeal to female readers.

Rind took seriously the motto she inherited from her husband, using contributions from both Royalists and Patriots. Editorially, however, she supported the revolutionary cause. In May 1774 she wrote, "The printer of this paper conceives herself obligated to convey to the public the late despotic proceedings of h——e of c——s in the most ample manner, and to brand with infamy those unprecedented resolves which they have so precipitately entered into." She urged support for the people of Boston after closure of Boston's port in May 1774 in retaliation for the Boston Tea Party. Suggesting that the colonies boycott all British goods, she published the name of each colony as it joined this campaign.

Rind's shop printed books, pamphlets, sermons, statutes, and broadsides, as well as the newspaper. She also sold books and used her shop as a lost-and-found bureau. She had taken on boarders when William was alive and continued to supplement her income in this way.

In mid-August 1774 Rind began running a request for continued public support with the assurance "that she shall shortly, should Providence be pleased to restore her health, to be enabled to conduct her business with more ease," the first indication in her paper of her ill health. This she followed with a statement of her editorial philosophy, noting that she would endeavor "to amuse and instruct" in spite of the "extreme hurry" in which she generally was involved. She died on 25 September after what one obituary referred to as "a tedious and painful illness." It may have been her assistant, John Pinkney, who reported the progress of delegates traveling "to join the grand AMERICAN CONGRESS" on 15 September, but it is tempting to credit Rind with appending "God send them safe."

Pinkney continued the paper until 1776, helping to support the Rind children during this period. The Masonic Lodge of Williamsburg made regular payments for their board, schooling, and clothing after that time. One son, William, published the *Virginia Federalist* at Richmond during 1799 and 1800, then served as the first printer to the District of Columbia.

BIBLIOGRAPHY:

B. NAW 3, 161–162; Richard L. Demeter, *Primer, Presses, and Composing Sticks* (New York, 1979); Leona M. Hudak, *Early American Women Printers and Publishers, 1639–1820* (Metuchen, N.J., 1978); Norma Schneider, "Clementina Rind: 'Editor, Daughter, Mother, Wife,' " *Journalism History*, Winter 1974–75.

SHERILYN COX BENNION

RIPLEY, GEORGE (b. 3 October 1802; d 4 July 1880) was one of the first Americans who truly could be called a man of letters. During the last twenty years of his career he received wide recognition for his lucid writing on literature and philosophy. Yet Ripley was not always so honored by the literary establishment. For much of his life he was regarded as a dangerously unorthodox critic of established religion and society. As a Transcendentalist minister, the organizer of Brook Farm, and a leading American Fourierist, Ripley earned nothing from his early social criticism but opprobrium from those who later lionized him.

Ripley was born in Greenfield, Massachusetts, to Jerome and Sarah Franklin Ripley. His father was a substantial merchant and leading citizen of Greenfield. A sickly boy, Ripley demonstrated notable aptitude for learning, and was sent to preparatory school at Huntington's Academy in Hadley, Massachusetts. He entered Harvard College in September 1819. Though Ripley had been brought up in orthodox Calvinism, his exposure to Unitarianism convinced him upon graduation to enter the Harvard Divinity School in 1823. Ripley was ordained the minister of Boston's Purchase Street Church in 1826, and married Sophia Dana, the niece of Richard Henry Dana, on 22 August 1827.

In 1836 Ripley helped to organize the Transcendentalist Club, a group of loosely affiliated individuals who rejected Unitarian formalism in favor of an intuitive philosophical method. That same year, Ripley became embroiled in a theological controversy with conservative minister Andrews Norton, who attacked him in the *Christian Register* for his unorthodox view of Christian miracles. This debate, which lasted for several years, resulted in severance of ties between Unitarians and Transcendentalists.

In 1840 Ripley joined with other Transcendentalists in founding the *Dial*, a monthly magazine. Ripley edited the *Dial* along with Margaret Fuller (q.v.) until its collapse in 1844. In spite of this activity, Ripley never fully accepted the Transcendentalist emphasis on individualism, and in 1841 he abandoned the ministry in hopes of organizing a community that would practice radical economics based on simplified Christianity. In April 1841 he founded what was probably the best-known American utopian community, Brook Farm.

From the beginning, Ripley hoped that Brook Farm would be a model for the radical transformation of society. In the 1840s he was strongly influenced by the ''socialist'' philosophy of Charles Fourier, called ''Association'' in America, which was popularized by Horace Greeley (q.v.) in the *New York Tribune*. When the American Union of Associationists decided to publish a Fourierist journal at Brook Farm, Ripley became its chief editor. This journal, the *Harbinger*, was first published in June 1845. Serious financial troubles, an unreceptive public, and an 1846 fire led to the collapse of Brook Farm, but not the *Harbinger*. Internal struggles within the Associationist movement resulted in a vote to move the *Harbinger* to New York in 1847, and Ripley became one of four assistant editors. Unsatisfied with the new arrangement, Ripley resigned from his post in 1849. The journal expired shortly thereafter.

The end of Brook Farm and the *Harbinger* brought what most scholars have agreed was a new conservatism to Ripley's thought. He began part-time work on the *New York Tribune* in May 1849, writing articles on a wide range of topics: public events, personalities, and ''Gotham Gossip.'' In 1852 he published a book with *Tribune* travel writer Bayard Taylor called the *Handbook of Literature and the Fine Arts*. Later in the decade he helped to found *Harper's Monthly*. At the same time he was involved with Charles A. Dana (q.v.), also of the *Tribune*, in editing the *American Cyclopaedia*, a multi-volume reference work completed in 1862. The several editions of the *Cyclopaedia* received warm reviews, and brought Ripley his first real financial security and independence. In the 1860s Ripley began to write book reviews in literary criticism for the *Tribune*, an endeavor that occupied him for the last twenty years of his life. One of the first American book review editors, he became widely recognized as a powerful figure in nineteenth-century American letters.

In 1861 Ripley's wife Sophia died of breast cancer. On 18 October 1865 Ripley married a young German widow named Louisa Schlossberger. Ripley suffered from a number of minor ailments during the last two years of his life, and died on 4 July 1880, his reputation cemented as the scholarly and popular dean of American literary and philosophical criticism.

BIBLIOGRAPHY:

B. DAB 8, 623–625; NYT 5 July 1880; Charles Crowe, *George Ripley; Transcendentalist and Utopian Socialist* (Athens, Ga., 1967); Octavius Brooks Frothingham, *George Ripley* (Boston, 1882); Henry L. Golemba, *George Ripley* (Boston, 1977).

JANET E. STEELE

RITCHIE, THOMAS (b. 5 November 1778; d. 3 July 1854) was one of the first generation of nationally important partisan editors. During a career that spanned nearly half a century, "Father Ritchie" turned his *Richmond Enquirer* into a major Democratic organ and achieved great personal influence in party councils. He was the preeminent Democratic editor in the South throughout the first half of the nineteenth century.

Thomas Ritchie was born in Tappahannock, Virginia, the son of Archibald Ritchie, the chief local businessman and a native of Scotland, and of Mary Roane, whose family was to provide many important political connections. Ritchie read in law and then studied medicine, but neither field appealed to him. He then took charge of an academy in Fredericksburg. He was an enthusiastic educator, but found teaching too physically demanding. In 1803 he moved to Richmond and bought a bookstore. The next year, with encouragement from Thomas Jefferson, he began to publish the *Richmond Enquirer*.

When the *Enquirer* appeared in 1804, it was a biweekly with a circulation of 1,500. By 1830 it had achieved a circulation of 5,000. A large part of its financial support came from official patronage: Ritchie was awarded Virginia's public printing contract. He was inept at finance, however, and was chronically in debt, a fact which his opponents used to impugn his editorial independence.

As an editor, Ritchie was authoritative. He represented Virginia's Jeffersonian and Jacksonian factions, and was the editorial voice of the Richmond Junto, the political clique that controlled the southern end of the New York–Pennsylvania–Virginia axis that dominated Democratic politics until the 1840s. In addition to the *Enquirer*, he edited two campaign papers: the *Crisis* in 1840—on behalf of Martin Van Buren—and the *Campaign* in 1848. But Ritchie was neither a partisan ideologue nor an astute organizer. He was a forceful and original editorialist who had wide appeal, popular in both eastern and western Virginia, among both the lowland aristocracy and ordinary farmers. He was particularly Virginian in outlook, and his regionalism placed a limit on his national effectiveness.

The evolution of Ritchie's political views is best interpreted in terms of concrete local and regional interests. For example, he was sternly anti-Tariff and anti-Bank, but favored the statewide monopoly of the Bank of Virginia. He was a unionist, but remained vehemently opposed to the nationalist goals of Henry Clay—he and Clay were notorious political enemies after 1825. He was a strict constructionist in terms of states' rights, but was also an opponent of the nullifiers. He was a champion of Texas annexation and opposed any attempt to limit the expansion of slavery into the territories. He was a proponent of scientific agriculture—a movement led in Virginia by his cousin Edmund Ruffin (q.v.). He was also a proponent of free public education. His views were progressive, but well within the boundaries of mainstream Virginia politics.

The development of Ritchie's views on slavery demonstrates the gravitational pull of regional interests. He harbored instinctive doubts about the peculiar institution, and in his earlier years seemed to favor some form of emancipation. But whenever slavery became a North-South issue he took a pro-slavery stance. Thus he opposed the Missouri Compromise in 1820. In 1831 he came out in favor of gradual abolition for Virginia, depicting the rising slave population as a threat to the future of the South, especially in the wake of Nat Turner's rebellion, and his stand was influential in the famous debate on slavery in the Virginia legislature in 1832. But his hostility to northern abolitionism hardened his attitudes, and after 1832 he was to be ardently anti-emancipationist for the rest of his career.

Ritchie's importance in national politics was established early and remained constant up to his final years. He was a logical choice to head up Jackson's national press elite, but was passed over in favor of Francis Preston Blair (q.v.), reportedly because Jackson resented Ritchie's opposition to his invasion of Florida a decade earlier. Ritchie's career in national politics reached its zenith in 1845 when he was drafted by James K. Polk to replace Blair as editor of the *Globe* (which Ritchie renamed the *Union*). This position included a large contract for government printing awarded by the Democratic Congress.

Ritchie's effectiveness as Washington editor was limited by his financial carelessness and his inability to overcome regional and sectional animosities. At one point his paper was censured by senatorial resolution and barred from Senate chambers. Ritchie's outspoken opposition to the Wilmot Proviso outraged northern Congressmen, and David Wilmot actually called for his resignation in a speech to the House of Representatives.

The sterling accomplishment of Ritchie's Washington years was the passage of the Compromise of 1850. In an act of shrewd political magnanimity, he reconciled himself with his bitter enemy Henry Clay, and Ritchie's editorial support was recognized as crucial to the apparent success of the compromise. Shortly afterward, Congress voted him an appropriation to bail the *Union* out of financial embarrassment. At this point, vindicated politically and financially solvent, Ritchie decided to retire. He continued to live in Washington, where he died a few years later.

Ritchie's private life was more serene than his public one. His home was a center of genteel Richmond society. He was a personable man, well connected with prominent Virginians through his mother's family and later through his children's spouses. He married Isabella Foushee, the daughter of a Richmond physician, when he was twenty-nine, and had twelve children. Two of his sons, William Foushee and Thomas Jr., took over the editorship of the *Enquirer* when Ritchie moved to Washington. Thomas Jr. was killed in a celebrated duel just before his father's death, but William continued to edit the *Enquirer* until well into the Civil War.

BIBLIOGRAPHY:

B. DAB 15, 628–629; Charles Ambler, *Thomas Ritchie: A Study in Virginia Politics* (Richmond, 1913).

JOHN NERONE

RIVINGTON, JAMES (b. 17 August 1724; d. 4 July 1802) was a printer, bookseller, editor, and publisher who was the leading Tory propagandist of the American Revolution. His skillfully edited newspaper, the *New York Gazette*, became a Tory bible in the colonies, but was hated and feared by the Patriots. His loyalist views were not tolerated and brought Rivington censure from the colonial government and violence from the Patriot mob.

Born in London, Rivington was the seventh son and ninth child of Charles and Eleanor Pease Rivington. His father was the head of a prosperous publishing house that had made its reputation printing mostly religious works, but also was responsible for publishing Samuel Richardson's *Pamela*. When his father died in 1742, James and his brother John took over the business and kept it thriving until the early 1750s, when the two separated. In 1756 Rivington entered into a printing partnership with James Fletcher, and by 1757 they published their first significant work, Tobias Smollett's *Complete History of England*, which was a huge success.

High living and gambling losses quickly ate up Rivington's earnings, and racing losses and a number of lawsuits for pirating books nearly led him to financial ruin. In 1760 he declared bankruptcy, and with £300 from his father-in-law's estate and a cargo of books, he left for New York, where in September he opened a bookstore and announced himself as the only London bookseller in the Colonies.

It was probably in 1761 or early 1762 that he entered into partnership with Samuel Brown, opened another bookstore in Philadelphia, where he had moved, and opened a third bookstore in Boston. By 1765 Rivington was again living in

New York, and after that year he confined his business activities to that city. Within three years he was again bankrupt. Yet he apparently was able to continue operating a bookstore, and in 1772 he added a printing office.

Then on 22 April 1773, just as the differences between the colonies and England were about to erupt into open revolt, Rivington started a newspaper that had the rather pretentious title of *Rivington's New York Gazetteer, or the Connecticut, New Jersey, Hudson's River and Quebec Weekly Advertiser*. He quickly earned a reputation for being a master printer and was considered by some to be the finest editor in the colonies. By 1775 he claimed 3,500 subscribers for his paper, and its influence extended beyond New York as it drew the ire of Whigs and Patriots.

Initially, Rivington strove for objectivity in his paper, as he had in his broadsides and pamphlets, although even that bothered the Patriots, and in one issue Rivington stressed to his readers that his press "has been open to publication from ALL PARTIES." His Royalist views became more pronounced by 1775, and he soon became the consummate Whig-baiter and his paper the principal voice of the Tories. In May of that year he survived an attack on his press by a mob led by Isaac Sears, the head of the Sons of Liberty in New York. But when Sears and the Patriots attacked again in November, Rivington was not as lucky. They destroyed his press and carried away his type, melting it down into bullets for the rebels. Although many Whigs condemned the attack, Rivington was unable to obtain compensation for his losses and returned to England.

Crucial to Rivington's success as a printer-publisher, and as a bookseller, was his ability to know just what would appeal to his readers. Furthermore, despite the partisan nature of his paper, it had no equal in the colonies in foreign coverage, and contained transcripts of the debates in Parliament as well as information from Europe. More than 50 percent of the paper's content was advertising.

When Rivington returned to New York in October 1777, he resumed publishing a newspaper, first calling it *Rivington's New York Loyal Gazette* and then the *Royal Gazette*. However, the issues were numbered consecutively with his earlier paper, suggesting that he considered this a resumption rather than a new publication. Publishing as "Printer to His Majesty," Rivington considered his paper a persuasive organ designed to serve the interests of the British. He took relish in printing rumors about the patriots and their leaders, who called the paper "Rivington's Lying Gazette."

Although there has been speculation that in the later years of the war he was a spy for Washington, that has not been clearly proved. As victory came closer for the Americans, his attacks on the revels became fewer and less vitriolic. Shortly after the British troops left New York, he changed the paper's name to *Rivington's New-York Gazette and Universal Advertiser*, indicating he was ready to set aside his Tory views and remain in the country. But he continued to be threatened and harassed, and on 31 December 1783 the last issue appeared. He returned to selling books and achieved some affluence before again facing bankruptcy and spending 1797 to 1801 in debtor's prison. Defeated at last, he died July 4, 1802.

BIBLIOGRAPHY:

B. DAB 15, 637–638; Bernard Bailyn and John B. Hench, eds., *The Press and the American Revolution* (Worcester, 1980).

THOMAS CONNERY

ROBB, INEZ CALLAWAY (b. 1901; d. 4 April 1979) was best known as a nationally syndicated columnist, but was also a World War II correspondent and a society editor, first covering small towns near Boise, Idaho, and later the world for International News Service in a column of general news called "Assignment America." Her later opinion column for Scripps-Howard and United Press International appeared in as many as 140 newspapers and won her the New York Newspaper Women's Club award for the "best column in any field" in 1957. She also contributed to magazines, notably the *Saturday Evening Post*, *Saturday Review*, and *Vogue*. A compilation of her columns was published in *Don't Just Stand There* (1962).

Robb was born Inez Callaway in Middleton, California, but grew up on her maternal grandfather's 15,000-acre ranch in Caldwell, Idaho. Her mother was Adah M. Asbill Callaway; her father, Abner Kenton Callaway, was in the fruit-packing business. A sister, Catherine Callaway McCune, was a woman's editor of the Tulsa, Oklahoma, *Tribune*, and a brother, Stephen Kenton Callaway, was a lawyer in Galveston, Texas.

Inez Callaway began her newspaper career as a high school student reporter for a Boise newspaper, won a scholarship to the University of Idaho, and earned the B.A. from the University of Missouri's School of Journalism in 1924. After graduation she became a general assignment reporter on the *Tulsa Daily World* at $40 a week. Then Joseph M. Patterson (q.v.) hired her at the *Chicago Tribune*. He later paid her $75 a week to work as assistant editor, then society editor, for the *New York Daily News*. She continued her work after she married Major J. Addison Robb, a New York advertising executive, in 1929. The couple had no children.

Robb covered such historic events as the coronation of King George VI and the wedding of Princess Elizabeth to Philip Mountbatten. She was again one of the few reporters allowed in Westminster Abbey when Elizabeth II was crowned. She covered the first Pan-American Airlines roundtrip flight across the Atlantic in 1939; she did a series on England at war, then wrote of the arrival of the first American forces in Britain during World War II. She wrote of postwar Germany and interviewed Juan Perón in Argentina. In 1953 she switched to opinion writing, covering a wide variety of subjects until her retirement in 1969.

During her years in New York, she and her husband owned a country house in Flemington, New Jersey. After her retirement, the Robbs lived in Tucson, Arizona, where she died at seventy-eight. Although she had suffered from

Parkinson's disease for several years, she always believed she had a wonderful life.

BIBLIOGRAPHY:
B. NYT 6 April 1979.

JUNE N. ADAMSON

ROCK, HOWARD (SIQVOAN WEYAHOK) (b. ? August 1911; d. 28 April 1976) was the founding editor of Alaska's *Tundra Times*, the first statewide newspaper independently owned, operated, and published by Aleut, Eskimo, and Indian natives of Alaska and designed to address their social and political concerns. Under Rock's guidance from 1962 to 1976, the newspaper was an outspoken advocate for the state's native peoples and covered such topics as land claims, living conditions in native villages, racial discrimination, and poverty, and stressed the importance of education and pride in heritage and culture.

Articulate and knowledgeable about non-native culture, artist and sculptor Rock found himself a spokesman at Inupiat Paitot (''people's heritage''), a conference held at Point Barrow in November 1961. Concerned representatives from twenty arctic villages organized the meeting in response to Project Chariot, an Atomic Energy Commission plan to excavate a harbor by exploding the northwest arctic villages of Point Hope (Rock's ancestral home), Noatak, and Kivalina.

Friends, relatives, and community leaders convinced him to accept what he considered an overwhelming task, and at age fifty-one, Rock changed careers. With no formal training, the new editor persuaded *Fairbanks Daily News-Miner* reporter Tom Snapp to sign on as assistant editor and introduce him to the world of print journalism. They secured funds for publication and a place to work. Inexperience quickly gave way to confidence, and responding to Snapp's questions about Eskimo and Indian cultures, Rock wrote award-winning columns depicting native life in Alaska.

Rock used well-honed artistic skills to design the newspaper's masthead and layouts, first for semiweekly, then for weekly publication. Snapp initially researched and wrote lead articles; Rock produced editorials whose topics matched the leads.

During the peak years of Alaska native land claims, 1966–71, Rock saw to it that the *Tundra Times* was a medium of political organization and enlightenment for native groups. Public officials read it to gauge native attitudes toward their actions. Native leaders used it to plan and implement political strategies. Constituents read it to assess the best ways to support their leaders.

Some of the editor's most successful series included a 1964–65 investigation of living and working conditions of Aleut seal hunters, employed on Alaska's Pribilof Islands by the U.S. Fish and Wildlife Service. The coverage caused a 1965 investigation by federal, state, and local officials into racial discrimination and unfair labor practices. This finally led to federal legislation which improved living conditions there.

Rock encouraged and praised native leadership, spoke against the destructive effects of in-fighting, and stressed the benefits of a unified native political front. The success of the *Tundra Times* during Rock's tenure shows that the editor, even with no initial writing or editorial experience, was in other ways well suited to his task. Many of Rock's editorials reveal a sharp awareness of the structure and function of American politics.

Born fifth in a family of eight children at Point Hope, Alaska, Rock was the descendant of generations of renowned arctic hunters. His father, Weyahok, continued the family tradition, and was first in the village to accept Christianity. Keshorna (Emma Rock), his mother, was described as kind and generous with a good sense of humor. An aunt and uncle, Mumangeena and Nayukuk, two people delightfully brought to life in several of his ''Arctic Survival'' columns, also helped to raise him.

Boyhood and youth were filled with hunting, training and mushing dog teams across the arctic tundra, and learning the games, songs, and stories that were an integral part of his heritage. At three, he attended a one-room, eight-grade school run by Episcopal missionaries. In 1925 he enrolled at White Mountain, a Bureau of Indian Affairs vocational school, and was inspired by the lives of famed artists—Rembrandt, Gauguin, Michelangelo—and chose an artistic career.

Rock studied with Belgian artist and Oregon homesteader Max Simes, spent three years at the University of Washington, Seattle, and in the early 1940s became a sculptor and jewelry designer. During World War II, Rock spent eighteen months in Tunisia as a radio operator.

Rock helped organize the June 1964 Conference of Native Organizations, a forerunner of the Alaska Federation of Natives, the group that fought for and won a historic 1971 land claims settlement. He was a pioneer member of the American Indian Press Association. A personal battle with leukemia lasted nearly two years. He is buried near Point Hope.

BIBLIOGRAPHY:

B. *Tundra Times*, 28 April 1976; John Fischer, ''God Rest Ye Merry Gentlemen, Ladies and a Few Others,'' *Harper's*, December 1962; S. E. Fogarino, ''The *Tundra Times*: Alaska Native Advocate, 1962–1976,'' M.A. thesis, Univ. of Maryland, 1981.

SHIRLEY FOGARINO

ROGERS, WILLIAM PENN ADAIR (b. 4 November 1879; d 15 August 1935) was known worldwide as a writer, philosopher, movie star, and humanitarian. His daily ''piece for the papers'' was read by millions, and his weekly articles, books, and other writings also found an eager audience.

Known as Will, Rogers was born at Rogers Ranch, north of Claremore in Indian Territory, now Oklahoma. His father, Clement Vann Rogers, was a rancher and politician who served on the committee that wrote the constitution for the state of Oklahoma. Rogers's mother, Mary America Schrimsher Rogers, a housewife, died when Will was ten years old. Rogers attended schools in the Indian Territory and went to Missouri to attend Scarritt College in Neosho in 1895–96 and Kemper Military Academy, Booneville, in 1897–98.

Rogers worked as a rancher and ranch manager following college, and after winning roping contests, he toured Australia and New Zealand with Wirth Brothers Circus. He did his roping act at the St. Louis Exposition in 1904, and on 17 October that year he gave his first vaudeville performance in Chicago. Vaudeville shows, including performances in the Wintergarten in Berlin and for the king of England in London, occupied the next several years. In the meantime, he was married on 25 November 1908 to Betty Blake (b. 1880; d. 1944) at the bride's home in Rogers, Arkansas. The Rogerses had four children, the first of whom was born in 1911 and named Will Rogers, Jr.

After joining the Ziegfeld Follies in 1916, Rogers began his movie career in 1918 with *Laughing Bill Hyde*, a silent film, and continued making movies until his death seventeen years later. His impressive literary output included six books, beginning with *Cowboy Philosopher on Prohibition* in 1919, weekly and daily syndicated newspaper columns, and travel articles for *Saturday Evening Post*. He covered the presidential conventions in 1924, 1928, and 1932, and some of his most memorable lines were barbs at politicians and the political parties. He noted, "You could transfer the Senate and Congress over to run Standard Oil or General Motors and they would have both things bankrupt in two years." Using California as his home base, he traveled widely, giving benefit performances for victims of floods, fires, drought, and earthquakes. His first talking film, *They Had to See Paris*, was made in 1929, the year he published the book *Ether and Me*.

A love for flying led him to become, in 1927, the first civilian to fly coast to coast with airmail pilots. It was on a flight in Alaska with master navigator Wiley Post that he died on 15 August 1935. Their plane crashed into a river bank near Point Barrow and both were killed. Rogers's funeral was in California with burial in a temporary vault there. In 1944 funeral services were held for him in Claremore, Oklahoma, and he was permanently interred in a tomb at the Will Rogers Memorial. Preserved there are such statements as "I joked about every prominent man of my time, but I never met a man I didn't like."

Newspapers reported that news of Rogers's death shocked the world and that cars pulled off the highways, businesses closed, and families gathered around their radios, hoping it was not so. His many honors include the dedication of a bronze of Rogers in the Capitol Rotunda in Washington, D.C., in 1939 and the issuing of a commemorative stamp in 1979 honoring his hundredth birthday. In 1970 the Franklin Mint issued a commemorative medal honoring Rogers as one of twelve to be placed in the Gallery of Great Americans.

BIBLIOGRAPHY:

A. *Autobiography of Will Rogers* (Boston, 1949); *Will Rogers' Daily Telegrams* (Stillwater, Okla., 1979); *Will Rogers' Weekly Articles* (Stillwater, Okla. 1980).

B. DAB 21, 635; NYT 17 August 1935; Margaret Axtell, *Will Rogers Rode the Range* (Phoenix, 1972); Donald Day, *Will Rogers; A Biography* (New York, 1962).

DENNIE HALL

ROSS, ALBION (b. 29 April 1906; d. 26 June 1988), a foreign correspondent associated mostly with the *New York Times*, covered the rise of Hitler, post–World War II Europe, and the Middle East and Africa. Ross went beyond official sources for insights from a wide range of sources that included peasants, streetwalkers, and everyday people. In his 1957 autobiography, he argued that enduring truths could not be found in the event-oriented reportage of his era.

Ross, an only child, was born in Ashland, Wisconsin, to Albion H. Ross, an Episcopal priest, and Elizabeth Ella Nicholson Ross, of Irish descent. He grew up in rectories in Marion and Gallipolis, Ohio, and Hollidaysburg, Pennsylvania. He attended Pennsylvania State University and Swarthmore College before taking a degree at Dartmouth College, his father's alma mater, in 1929.

Ross was an apprentice reporter with the Altoona, Pennsylvania, *Tribune* the summer of 1929. That fall he began graduate journalism studies at Columbia University, but disillusioned with the mundane lives of newspapermen at his lodginghouse, he sailed for Europe in February 1930. After one semester at the University of Berlin and having exhausted his money on travel, Ross returned to New York. He was hired as a cub reporter by the *Evening Post* but did not get the hang of the job and was fired in December.

Back in Berlin in 1931, Ross was hired hastily by the *Post*'s correspondent, who neglected to check with the newspaper's home office where he had just been fired. In 1933 he was named bureau chief, but within weeks the *Post* collapsed, and its partner, the *Philadelphia Public Ledger*, shut the bureau shortly thereafter. Ross, by then with a reputation for covering Germany's economic and political problems, was picked up quickly by the *New York Times* Berlin bureau where he remained until 1938. By his own estimate, Ross covered 200 meetings at which Hitler spoke. He traveled extensively, and his reporting included examinations of peasant life in Central Europe.

Disgusted with events in Germany, Ross was lured to the *San Francisco Chronicle* as foreign editor in 1938. He assembled a daily foreign section of the recently compartmentalized newspaper. In 1939 he went to Europe for the series "Will War Come?" and also wrote for United Press. He was in Berlin when the Nazis invaded Poland. For the *Chronicle* he also made two major trips to the Far East, in 1938 to Japan, Korea, Manchuria, and Japanese-occupied China, and in 1940 to the Philippines and Indochina. Ross rejoined the *Times* in New York in 1941 on the war summary and foreign desk, but quickly put on a uniform and served the duration of World War II uneventfully as an army captain.

The war over, he was back in Central Europe for the *Times*. He was expelled by the Tito government after exposing misuse of U.N. aid to Yugoslavia, but he continued his coverage of Czechoslovakia, Austria, and Hungary. In 1948 he was named chief correspondent of the volatile Middle East, specifically covering the Arab states and Iran. In 1953 he became Southern Africa correspondent, covering South Africa, Rhodesia, Tanganyika, Mozambique, Kenya, and the Congo. In 1954 he returned to Germany as Bonn correspondent.

Consistent with *Times* policy, Ross was rotated to New York in 1955, but he disliked the city and left the newspaper in 1956 for a brief magazine venture in Montreal. From 1957 to 1959 he was deputy director of information for the International Cooperation Administration in Iraq, then until 1962 was chief of the communications media division in the U.S. mission in Cambodia.

In 1962 he became a visiting lecturer at the University of Illinois. The next year he was named to the Nieman chair in journalism at Marquette University. Upon retirement in 1973 he moved to Switzerland as a translator and editor for the Bethlehem Missionary Fathers. A linguist, he was master of German, French, Spanish, and Italian, and could get along in Portuguese, Afrikaans, Dutch, and Japanese. After bouts of illness, Ross moved to Tampa, Florida, in 1979 to be near relatives.

Ross and Cecilia Grossi had married. There were no children, and little was known of the marriage. Ross himself declined to discuss the marriage even among friends and colleagues in later years. The death certificate, when he died in Tampa, Florida, said he had never married.

BIBLIOGRAPHY:

A. *Journey of an American* (Indianapolis, 1957).

B. James W. Arnold, "The Journeys of Albion Ross," *St. Anthony Messenger*, September 1980.

JOHN H. VIVIAN

ROSS, HAROLD WALLACE (b. 6 November 1892; d. 6 December 1951) founded and for twenty-six years edited the *New Yorker* magazine. That publication was so much the product of Ross's abrasive, driven personality that many expected it to fail after his death. But it has continued to thrive and has remained synonymous with wry humor and witty comment. The man who guided the sophisticated metropolitan weekly was himself unsophisticated. He distrusted anything he suspected of being intellectual, for instance, dismissing painting and music as "phony arts." According to James Thurber, among the few books that Ross had read and enjoyed were Mark Twain's *Life on the Mississippi* and a book about eels. His ignorance of literature is the basis for the most famous of all Ross stories: he once asked a member of the magazine's checking department, "Is Moby Dick the whale or the man?"

Ross was born in Aspen, Colorado, the son of George and Ida Martin Ross. His father, an Irish immigrant, worked as a contractor, mining engineer, and house wrecker. Before her marriage, his mother had worked as a schoolteacher. When Aspen's silver boom faded, the family moved to Salt Lake City. Though he was a good student, Ross quit school at fourteen for a job on the *Salt Lake City Tribune*, and by the time he was twenty-five, he had written for newspapers in Sacramento, San Francisco, New Orleans, and Atlanta.

When the United States entered World War I in 1917, Ross enlisted in the Eighteenth Engineering Regiment and was sent to France. But he was no better suited to army life than to school, and within a few weeks, he went AWOL. He talked his way out of imprisonment and into the editorship of *Stars and Stripes*, whose staff included Alexander Woollcott, Grantland Rice, and, for a time, Franklin P. Adams (qq.v.). Because of his success with the AEF newspaper, he was offered the editorship of a new magazine for returning veterans, the *Home Sector*. It lasted for only four issues. In 1919 it was merged with the *American Legion Weekly*, which Ross edited until 1924.

For less than a year, he edited the weekly humor magazine *Judge*, because, he said later, he wanted the experience for his own humor magazine, which he envisioned as an American *Punch*. In his prospectus he wrote that the magazine "will be what is commonly called sophisticated, in that it will assume a reasonable degree of enlightenment on the part of its readers." He had refined his concept of the magazine in discussions with some of his fellow members of the Algonquin Round Table: Dorothy Parker, Robert Benchley, Alexander Woollcott, and Heywood Broun (q.v.). Many of them lent their names to a list of "advisory editors" and later lent their writing talents. Ben Hecht (q.v.) recalled Ross at this time as "looking like some stranded cowhand, ringing doorbells, and asking for funds to start the *New Yorker*." He raised only half of the $50,000 he needed for the magazine. Ross found a backer among the poker players at Franklin Adams's Thanatopsis Literary and Inside Straight Club. Raoul Fleischmann, heir to a banking and yeast fortune, agreed to invest $20,000 in the magazine; within a few years, his investment had swelled to $75,000.

The first issue, with the now famous Rea Irvin dandy, Eustace Tilley, on the cover, went on sale 21 February 1925 and sold a meager 15,000 copies. Even F.P.A., his friend from the Algonquin, dismissed it as "frothy." By April the magazine was losing $800 a week. Ross set about correcting his initial mistakes by sharpening the focus and the editing and by assembling a staff that could make the magazine as he wanted it: witty, offhand, and informative. With a staff that came to include James Thurber, E. B. White, and Katherine Angell White, he refined such *New Yorker* trademarks as "The Talk of the Town," the profiles, and the one-line cartoons. A now-forgotten article by Ellin Mackay, Irving Berlin's wife, on the dullness of Park Avenue society, generated headlines and an increase in circulation and advertising sales. Within three years, the magazine showed a profit. While its circulation has always remained relatively small—under 50,000—it has remained unmatched in advertising revenue and literary merit.

Ross was notoriously tightfisted with his writers, but was generous with criticism, often salted with expletives. In his rasping voice, he would tell an offending writer that he demanded nothing less than perfection; a staff writer once quipped that Ross saw perfection as his personal property, "like his watch or his hat." Every galley bore Ross's impatient demands for writing that was clear, direct, and grammatical. Only in the last months of his life, when he was fighting lung cancer, did he relinquish some of his responsibilities to William Shawn, who succeeded him as editor.

Ross's devotion to the magazine often strained his personal relationships. He was married three times: in 1920 to Jane Cole Grant; in 1934 to Marie Francoise Elie, who bore his only child, Patricia; and in 1940 to Ariane Allen.

Just a day after Ross died on an operating table in a Boston hospital, E. B. White wrote an eloquent tribute for the *New Yorker*. He said that Ross's boisterous temperament and his pursuit of excellence had totally shaped the magazine. "Ross, even on this terrible day," he wrote, "is a hard man to keep quiet."

BIBLIOGRAPHY:

B. DAB, Supp. 5, 593–594; NYT 7 December 1951; Brendan Gill, *Here at the "New Yorker"* (New York, 1975); Dale Kramer, *Ross and the "New Yorker"* (New York, 1952); James Thurber, *The Years with Ross* (New York, 1959).

HARRIS E. ROSS

ROSS, ISHBEL (b. 15 December 1895; d. 21 September 1975) earned her reputation as New York City's best female reporter in the 1920s during her fourteen-year career at the *New York Herald Tribune*, but she first gained national prominence as the author of *Promenade Deck* (1933), a best selling novel that was sold to the movies. While she wrote several more novels, she concentrated primarily on the biographies of notable American women. She also authored a variety of magazine articles and worked for the Office of War Information during World War II.

Ross was born and raised in Sutherlandshire, Scotland, fifty miles north of Inverness, capital of the Scottish Highlands. Her parents were David and Grace McCrone Ross. She admitted to a lack of talent for mathematics and science, and during her schooling, she immersed herself in the classics. After graduating from Tain Royal Academy in 1916, Ross moved to Toronto and worked for a year as a publicist for the Canadian Food Board. In 1917 she accepted a clerical position at the *Toronto Daily News*, and she was given her first chance as a reporter six weeks later when the paper's editor assigned her to cover the arrival in Canada of British suffragist leader Emmeline Pankhurst. Ross traveled to Buffalo, New York, met Pankhurst's westbound train, and obtained an interview with her before other Canadian reporters approached the famous Britisher in Toronto. Her editor was pleased enough with her story to offer her a permanent reportorial position.

After a year and a half as a reporter in Toronto, Ross moved to New York and went to work for the *New York Tribune* (later called the *New York Herald Tribune*) as a general-assignment reporter. She later became a member of the editorial staff. During her fourteen years with the *Tribune*, Ross competed with the top reporters in New York City. She was a competent reporter who sometimes scooped her rivals, and in the 1920s, when tabloid journalism swept the city, she was assigned to cover sensational stories, including the Halls-Mills murder case and the Lindbergh kidnapping. While covering the two-year divorce trial of James A. Stillman, Ross met Bruce Rae, a reporter for the *New York Times*. They were married on 10 January 1922, and because Rae was an American, Ross became a naturalized citizen later that year. The couple had one child, Catriona, who was born in 1935. Rae went on to become an assistant managing editor for the *Times* and a director of the New York Times News Service. He died of a stroke on 12 March 1962. Ross continued to cover news for the *Tribune* until 1933, when she became a full-time author. Her first book had been published in 1931.

Although she intended to be a novelist, especially after the success of *Promenade Deck*, the *Tribune's* copy editor, Stanley Walker, suggested that she write about famous newspaperwomen of the 1930s. Ross completed *Ladies of the Press* in 1936, which was a compilation of the lives of famous newspaperwomen in the nineteenth and twentieth centuries. This launched her career as a biographer of famous women, particularly U.S. presidents' wives. Although her subjects included Mary Todd Lincoln, Edith Bolling Wilson, and Grace Coolidge, she also wrote about famous professional women such as physician Elizabeth Blackwell, nurse Clara Barton, and Confederate spy Rose O'Neal Greenhow. Other nonfiction efforts included *Taste in America* (1967), an illustrated history of the evolution of architecture, furnishings, fashions, and customs of the American people; and *The Expatriates* (1970), a 200-year survey of Americans abroad. Four of her nonfiction books received uniformly positive reviews, while the rest received mixed reviews.

In addition to twenty-one works of nonfiction, Ross completed four novels during her career. While love and marriage are recurrent themes in her novels, several of her characters experience existential searches for meaning and for values. As was true for most of her nonfiction work, her novels also received mixed reviews.

While pursuing her writing career, Ross published a number of magazine articles in the most popular magazines of her day. She wrote for *Scribner's*, the *Saturday Evening Post*, and *Independent Woman*, and several of her works appeared in *Reader's Digest*, either in original or condensed form. From 1941 to 1944, she wrote numerous magazine articles about art, books, and music for the Office of War Information's overseas division.

Ross died from injuries she received in a fall at her New York City residence on 21 September 1975, shortly after her last book was published. She was seventy-nine years old.

BIBLIOGRAPHY:

B. NYT 23 September 1975; Barbara A. Bannon, ''Ishbel Ross,'' *Publishers Weekly*, September 1975; Harry R. Warfel, ''Ishbel Ross,'' *American Novelists of Today* (New York, 1951).

BRUCE L. PLOPPER

ROTHSTEIN, ARTHUR (b. 17 July 1915; d. 11 November 1985) is widely recognized as one of the finest photojournalists of modern times. With his career spanning over five decades, Rothstein took photographs in the dust bowl days of the Great Depression through World War II and into the modern era of magazine photojournalism. His subjects ranged from the most powerless rural farmers fighting the winds of erosion to the most powerful world leaders fighting the winds of war.

Rothstein was born in New York City and later attended Columbia University. While a student at Columbia, Rothstein founded the University Camera Club and served as photo editor of the *Columbian*. It was his efforts as a student photojournalist that caught the attention of Roy Emerson Stryker. Stryker felt Rothstein's photographic skills and his ability to work with people, gaining their confidence and capturing them in striking settings and meaningful moments, were valuable traits.

Following Rothstein's graduation from Columbia in 1935, Stryker issued an invitation to Rothstein to be the first of several photographers to document programs sponsored by the Farm Security Administration (FSA). The photographers, including Rothstein, were briefed on what information was needed, and were then given extensive freedom to operate on a creative basis. In the spring of 1936, Rothstein was sent to document the dust bowl tragedy that covered more than a thousand miles of desolate landscape.

Out of this assignment came one of Rothstein's most memorable images, a photograph of a father and his two sons struggling to reach a shed half buried by blowing soil. This picture was used by newspapers and magazines across the country. Rothstein spent five years, from 1935 to 1940, working on the FSA project.

After completing his FSA assignment, Rothstein held a series of positions: first as a staff photographer for *Look* magazine; next, shortly after the outbreak of World War II, a position with the Office of War Information, and then with the U.S. Army. During his military assignment, Rothstein went to the China-Burma-India theater, and remained in China after his discharge in 1945. While in China, Rothstein was the chief photographer for the United Nations Relief and Rehabilitation Administration.

The opportunity to rejoin *Look* magazine as the technical director of photography drew Rothstein back to the United States in 1946. After holding this position for several years, Rothstein was promoted to director of photography for *Look* in 1969, a position he held until 1971. *Parade* magazine offered Rothstein his next key position. Appointed as an associate editor for *Parade* in 1972, he was responsible for the supervision and selection of photographs, picture research, feature story production, and editorial illustration.

Rothstein has served on the faculty of the Graduate School of Journalism at Columbia University. In 1983 he was named Spencer Chair Professor at the S. I. Newhouse School of Public Communication at Syracuse University. He was the first photographer to be honored with the position. Rothstein also taught at Mercy College and Daytona Beach Community College.

BIBLIOGRAPHY:

A. *The Depression Years* (New York, 1978); *Photojournalism* (New York, 1979); *The American West in the Thirties* (New York, 1981).

MICHAEL D. SHERER

ROWELL, CHESTER HARVEY (b. 1 November 1867; d. 12 April 1948) was editor and publisher of the Fresno, California, *Republican* from 1898 to 1920. He unsuccessfully sought election as mayor of Fresno in 1901 and for the next ten years played an increasingly significant role in state politics. Rowell was president of the Lincoln-Roosevelt League, a coalition of California Progressives who gained control of the state's governorship and legislature in 1910. Rowell expressed his support for Progressive aims on the editorial pages of the *Republican*. He sold the newspaper in 1920 for $1 million, served on state and national commissions and boards, and traveled. From 1932 to 1935, Rowell edited the *San Francisco Chronicle*. He served as editorial columnist for the paper from 1935 to 1947. In 1914 Rowell ran unsuccessfully for the Progressive party nomination for U.S. Senator from California.

Rowell was born in Bloomington, Illinois, son of Jonathan and Maria Sanford Rowell. His father was a lawyer and U.S. congressman from 1883 to 1891. Rowell graduated from the University of Michigan, after three years, in 1888. He stayed in Ann Arbor for a year's postgraduate study, then took a job his father had secured for him as clerk for the Committee on Elections of the U.S. House of Representatives. He spent his spare time preparing a digest of contested election cases, published in 1901.

Rowell's interest at this time was not journalism but college teaching. He spent two years in Europe, chiefly at the German universities of Halle and Berlin studying political economy and philosophy with the aim of eventually receiving a Ph.D. His money ran out before he could achieve this goal, and he returned to the United States in 1894, spending the next four years teaching at small schools and colleges in Kansas, Wisconsin, California, and Illinois. While serving as instructor at the University of Illinois, Rowell married Myrtle Marie Lingle of Webb City, Missouri, on 1 August 1897. They eventually had five children, two of whom died in infancy

Because of his wife's poor health Rowell sought work in a better climate and accepted an offer from his uncle, Dr. Chester Rowell, a physician, to take over a newspaper the uncle had founded in Fresno, California. Rowell became involved in politics soon after his arrival. Rowell was angered by the political control of the Southern Pacific Railroad over California. He helped to found the Lincoln-Roosevelt League in 1907, along with other newspaper editors, attorneys, and businessmen. They sought to take over the state Republican party and carry out Progressive goals, ending the railroad's dominance. In 1910 the league's candidate for governor, Hiram Johnson, won the Republican nomination and the election. A Progressive majority won the legislative seats. Rowell used his editorial pages to campaign because the *Republican* was distributed in other California cities.

Rowell shared the rhetoric of many Progressives, but as a newspaperman and a political participant, he appeared to possess the stance of the scholar he once hoped to be. His editorials were serious, sometimes jocular, but seldom humorous. Rowell throughout his life spoke French and German fluently and, in one associate's report, could read six more languages.

By 1916 Progressive party members had returned to Republican ranks, and Rowell's most active days in politics were over. After selling his newspaper in 1920, he served on the state railroad commission and as a regent of the University of California (1914–48). He reported on China to the League of Nations and to President Herbert Hoover. Rowell was a supporter of the league in direct opposition to his friend and political ally, U.S. Senator Hiriam Johnson, who led the fight against the international body.

Rowell began a second newspaper career in 1932 as editor and then editorial page columnist with the *San Francisco Chronicle*, a newspaper once strongly aligned against the *Fresno Republican* politically.

Rowell died at his home in Berkeley, California, at the age of eighty. The cause of his death was listed as cerebral vascular thrombosis. His wife had died in 1942. They had three surviving children; a son, Jonathan A. Rowell, a San Francisco attorney; and two daughters, Cora Winifred (Mrs. J. A.) Givens of Berkeley and Lois (Mrs. W. D.) Laughlin of Fairfield, California.

BIBLIOGRAPHY:

A. *"Chester H. Rowell, Autobiographical Manuscript"* (unpublished), Rowell Collection of Letters and Private Papers, Bancroft Library, University of California, Berkeley.

B. DAB Supp. 4, 707–708; NYT 13 April 1948; Gregg Layne, "The Lincoln Roosevelt League: Its Origin and Accomplishments," *Quarterly of the Historical Society of Southern California*, September 1943, George E. Mowry, *The California Progressives* (Berkeley and Los Angeles, 1951).

JAMES BOW

ROYALL, ANNE NEWPORT (b. 11 June 1769; d. 1 October 1854) was a traveler when few women ventured outside the home, an author when most women did not write, an eccentric when most Americans were content not to rock the boat, and quite probably the first genuine American newspaperwoman. In her later years she was a nuisance to many who knew her, a scold of those who opposed her views, an aggressive freethinker, and probably the original muckraker. Scandals in government were a stable in her two Washington, D.C., newspapers. Her eccentric and powerfully held views led to her becoming the only person ever convicted in America of being a "common scold."

Anne Royall was born in Baltimore, the elder of two daughters of William and Mary Newport. Little is known of Mary Newport, but several biographers have suggested that William was the illegitimate son of one of the Maryland Calverts and that royal Stuart blood flowed in his veins. However, there appears to be no support for the claim. William Newport moved his family to the Pennsylvania frontier when Anne Royall was three years old. The family remained on the frontier for ten years. William Newport died about 1775 and Mary Newport married Patrick Butler. Butler died in July 1782 during an attack by a band of Indians and British soldiers on Hanna's Town, Pennsylvania. Anne Royall's mother had a son, James, from her marriage to Butler. After Butler's death she took Anne and James to Virginia. Anne's sister remained with a family in Pennsylvania.

Mary Newport became the housekeeper for a wealthy landowner in Staunton, Virginia, and Anne Royall joined the indentured servants in doing household chores. No doubt much of her later life was colored by the events of that period. She was snubbed by the children of the landowners and was not permitted to enter the society of the gentry.

The most rewarding period in Anne Royall's life began in 1785 when her mother was employed in the household of Major William Royall, a revolutionary war hero and a descendant of Tidewater aristocracy. He introduced Anne Royall to his large library, took on the role of tutor, and devoted himself to teaching his young protégée the great ideas current in literature and philosophy. Among the ideas Royall pressed on Anne Royall was Freemasonry.

After living in the Royall household for ten to fourteen years (the sources vary on the time span), Anne and Royall were married on 18 November 1797. The bride was twenty-eight and her husband 55. For the next sixteen years Anne Royall lived the life of a southern belle. When Royall died in 1913, his widow began travelling throughout the South. However, her life of leisure ended abruptly in 1823 when relatives of her late husband succeeded in breaking his will, thus leaving Anne penniless at the age of fifty-five.

From 1823 to 1831, Anne Royall traveled continuously through the country east of the Mississippi River. During the period she wrote and published ten travel books, which are still valuable resources on the society in which she lived. The books were *Sketches of History, Life and Manners in the United States* (1826), *The Black Book; or A Continuation of Travels in the United States* (3 vols., 1828–29), *Mrs. Royall's Pennsylvania* (2 vols., 1829), *Mrs. Royall's Southern Tour* (3 vols., 1830–31), and *Letters from Alabama* (1830).

It is for her journalism, however, that she is most remembered. On 3 December 1831 the first edition of the four-page *Paul Pry* was issued. The editor was then sixty-two years old. It was clearly a new brand of journalism, and the years had not mellowed Anne Royall at all. At the time most newspapers of the country clipped and reprinted material from other newspapers, and there was little local news. The newspapers in Washington were no different. However, *Paul Pry* and its successor, the *Huntress*, were different. They were gossipy, and Anne Royall held so many strong beliefs that it was rarely necessary to reprint material from other newspapers. Interviews were a regular feature of both newspapers.

She defended Sunday transportation of mails (probably in opposition to Sunday blue laws) and states' rights. Anne Royall was an advocate of sound monetary policy and education and tolerance for Catholics. She fought graft and corruption in government, the Bank of the United States, anti-Masons, and evangelicals. She favored separation of church and state, and justice for immigrants and Indians. She favored abolition during her early years but was vehement in her opposition in later life, probably because the movement was associated with established churches. It was the established church which came under her most scathing criticism. Two years before the appearance of *Paul Pry*, a name-calling episode between Anne Royall and the Presbyterians had led to her being convicted in 1829, under an antiquated law, as a "common scold."

Anne Royall's newspapers have been described as crude, amateurish, and in general poor productions. This seems an unfair assessment, based more on her personality than on the design and execution of the newspapers. Both *Paul Pry* and the *Huntress* were as good visually as most newspapers being printed at the time and better than many. They were readable both in terms of content and in design.

BIBLIOGRAPHY:

B. DAB 16, 204–205; Maurine Beasley, "The Curious Career of Anne Royall," *Journalism History*, Winter 1976–77; George Stuyvestant Jackson, *Uncommon Scold* (Boston, 1937); Bessie Rowland James, *Anne Royall's U.S.A.* (New Brunswick, N.J., 1972.

DONALD R. AVERY

ROYSTER, VERMONT CONNECTICUT (b. 30 April 1914) was a reporter and correspondent for the *Wall Street Journal* when it was a small financial daily in the 1930s. As the paper grew in size and influence following World War II, Royster became associate editor, then editor. He took strong editorial stances, declaring that "a newspaper should be a nuisance to our conscience and a disturber of our ways," but his commentary was always civilized. For his editorial writing and commentary, Royster won the Pulitzer prize in 1953 and 1984.

Royster was born in Raleigh, North Carolina, to Wilbur High Royster and Olivette Broadway Royster. His unusual given names are the same as his grandfather's. Wilbur Royster was a professor of classics and law at the University of North Carolina, and he began teaching his eight-year-old son Latin. Royster continued his study of classics at what he called an "old fashion" college preparatory, Webb School in Bell Buckle, Tennessee. Upon graduating in 1931, he entered the University of North Carolina at Chapel Hill, where he studied classics, English literature, and history. He found time to act as editor of the student newspaper, to contribute to the campus literary magazine, and to become a "radical" political activist who tried the patience of university officials. Royster graduated Phi Beta Kappa in 1935.

Royster went to New York to find a journalism job and worked as a reporter for the City News Bureau in 1935–36 when he could not find a position on a newspaper. In 1936, however, the *Wall Street Journal* offered Royster a job, and within a few months he was in Washington as a correspondent covering the Congress and the White House. On 5 June 1937 he married Frances Claypoole. The couple raised two daughters, Frances Claypoole and Sara Eleanor. Royster continued with the *Journal* in Washington until World War II broke out, and he was called to active duty in the naval reserve in 1941. He served as an officer in the Atlantic, Caribbean, and Pacific, an experience he found "exhilarating." He ended the war as a lieutenant commander.

Royster returned to his Washington correspondent's job for the *Wall Street Journal* in 1945. He became chief of the Washington bureau in 1946, but, in his own words, "inevitably drifted toward the editorial page out of a natural frustration at recording events with no license to express my opinions about them." In 1948 Royster became an associate editor of the *Journal*, and in 1951, a senior associate editor. During this period, Royster wrote a daily editorial column, "Review and Outlook." His subjects were diverse—from economics to politics and politicians to foreign policy and war. For the body of his editorial work, Royster was awarded his first Pulitzer Prize in 1953. Royster became editor of the *Wall Street Journal* in 1958 and continued in that position until 1971. Upon retirement from his daily duties with the *Journal*, he continued to be active with the paper as a public affairs commentator.

Between 1971 and 1980, Royster was William Rand Kenan Professor of Journalism and Public Affairs at the University of North Carolina. He also contributed articles to scholarly and popular periodicals, served as a director of Dow Jones and Company, and appeared regularly on the CBS "Spectrum" radio and television programs. In his distinguished career, Royster received numerous awards and honors. He was president of the American Society of Newspaper Editors in 1965–66. A longtime member of the National Press Club, Royster was awarded that organization's prestigious Fourth Estate Award in 1978 for his lifetime contributions to journalism. Royster continued writing a weekly column for the *Wall Street Journal* in the 1980s. He won his second Pulitzer Prize for his commentary in 1984.

BIBLIOGRAPHY:

A. *Journey Through the Soviet Union* (New York, 1962); *A Pride of Prejudices* (New York, 1968); *My Own, My Country's Time: A Journalist's Journey* (Chapel Hill, 1983).

B. CA 21 (1969–71), 754; CB 1953, 549–550.

JOHN P. FREEMAN

RUFFIN, EDMUND (b. 5 January 1794; d. 18 June 1865) was an intense southern nationalist who used the press to defend slavery and encourage secession in the years before the Civil War. Before 1855, he was a respected agriculturist who founded and edited the influential *Farmer's Register*, and who published the results of numerous agricultural experiments in journals and newspapers throughout the region. After 1855, his new interests became apparent in increasingly strong utterances urging secession, and eventually war, in such newspapers as the *Charleston Mercury*, published by Robert Rhett (q.v.), who was often called the "father of secession." For his part, Ruffin earned the title of "preacher of secession." As time passed, Ruffin's words gave way to strong action, and when he was nearly seventy, he was chosen by General P.G.T. Beauregard to pull the lanyard of the cannon that sent the first ball into Fort Sumter.

Edmund was one of six children of George Ruffin, a descendant of a family which had arrived in Virginia in 1666, and which had prospered in farming. His mother, Jane Lucas Ruffin, died soon after his birth, and his father married Rebecca Cocke. Edmund received a typical education by parents and tutors, and he was sent off to William and Mary College in 1810, when he was sixteen. He stayed only two years, and he left to serve as a private in the War of 1812. He married Susan Travis in 1811, and she bore his eleven children; she died in 1846.

He served a short time in the Virginia State Senate (1823–26), but politics did not seem to be an honorable calling, and he resigned to experiment in farming. His aim was to rejuvenate soils which had become depleted from two centuries of tobacco farming. He eventually discovered that marl had a beneficial effect, and presented his findings to agricultural societies in the state; he collected his papers in *An Essay on Calcareous Manures* (1832).

He began a periodical, *Farmer's Register*, in 1833, and used it to spread his ideas on crops throughout the region. He widened his interests to include all things that affected farming, and in 1841 he began a second, much more radical periodical, *Bank Reformer*, in which he railed against harsh banking practices. These efforts caused him to neglect his *Farmer's Register*, and he was forced to suspend both periodicals in 1842. He withdrew from public life, bitter and disillusioned.

He soon received a new lease on public life when the governor of South Carolina looked to Ruffin to help the Deep South become independent of the North and seek alliances overseas. His own cherished opinions on the rightness of slavery and the superiority of his race dovetailed precisely with the intentions of southern nationalists in the Deep South. He once again began to contribute to newspapers and periodicals.

Although he at first couched his discussions in the framework of agriculture, defending slavery as an agricultural imperative, by 1855 he was arguing directly for secession—peaceful if possible, but armed if necessary. He published four pamphlets in 1858, with the aim of crystallizing for their readers the necessity of slavery, and the harmful effects of a northern-dominated Congress on southern life. He sent fiery letters to periodicals such as *DeBow's Review*, and to "fire-eater" newspapers in Charleston and Richmond, which were themselves trying to inculcate and maintain secessionist sentiments in their readers.

By 1860 Ruffin was a popular hero, sought out to speak at Southern secession rallies. When *Leslie's Weekly* called him the "preacher of secession," he agitated even harder, although he was nearly seventy. He referred to his call for Southern independence as the one great idea of his life. He lived to see the Confederacy collapse, and soon after news of Appomattox reached him, he took his own life rather than live with the "perfidious, malignant and vile Yankee race."

BIBLIOGRAPHY:

B. DAB 8, 214–216; NYT 22 June 1865; Avery Craven, *Edmund Ruffin: Southerner* (Hamden, Conn., 1964).

GARY COLL

RUNYON, DAMON (b. 8 October 1880; d. 10 December 1946) was a widely read New York reporter, short story writer, and chronicler of Broadway. His slangy, irreverent tales of show business, the sporting life, and the underworld gained him international fame and later were adapted for a series of Hollywood films as well as for the musical *Guys and Dolls*.

Born Alfred Damon Runyan in Manhattan, Kansas, he was the only son of Alfred Lee Runyan and Elizabeth J. Damon Runyan. Runyon's childhood was tempestuous. His father, an itinerant printer and would-be publisher, founded a series of short-lived newspapers. Runyon's mother died of tuberculosis when he was nine, just after the family had moved to Pueblo, Colorado. Following her death, Runyon's three sisters went to live with in-laws in Abilene, but young Runyon stayed with his alcoholic father.

A tough, street-smart boy, Runyon was expelled from school in the sixth grade. He took his first newspaper job at age thirteen—as errand boy for a series of Pueblo newspapers. By age fifteen he had become a hard-drinking reporter for the *Pueblo Evening Press*. (The spelling of Runyon's original name now changed; when a printer substituted an "o" for an "a," Runyon kept the new spelling.. Later a New York copy editor would trim the "Alfred" from his byline.) At age thirty Runyon would renounce alcohol for marriage, but he remained a chain-smoker all his life.

Runyon served eighteen months in the army, most of it in the Philippines, during the Spanish-American War. After his discharge Runyon bummed around San Francisco for a time, then rode the railroad back to Colorado. For the next few years Runyon worked at newspapers in Colorado, Missouri, and San Francisco, before returning to Denver in 1906 to begin work at the *Rocky Mountain News*. His reputation there grew quickly because of a series of humorous commentaries he did with caricaturist Frank "Doc Bird" Finch to promote the *News* in small towns around the state. As the *News* star reporter, he soon began covering politics and business as well as crime and sports.

In 1910 Runyon moved to New York, supporting himself by writing plots for fiction writer Charles Van Loon and magazine stories. The following year he won a job in the sports department of William Randolph Hearst's (q.v.) *New York American*. He would work as a sportswriter, columnist, war correspondent, and crime reporter for the paper till the *American* folded in 1937. He gained fame by accompanying General John J. Pershing on the search for the bandit Pancho Villa in 1916, and in 1918 he traveled to France to cover the American Expeditionary Force. After the war his articles and columns were syndicated through Hearst's King Features and International News Service. By 1946 his column was appearing in over 100 papers and being read by over ten million people each day.

Though widely known as one of his generation's greatest sportswriters, Runyon is remembered today as the preeminent recorder of Broadway life. In the 1930s his tales of showgirls, touts, crapshooters, and thugs began appearing regularly in *Cosmopolitan, Collier's*, and other magazines. From 1929 to 1946 he would write eighty Broadway stories, later collected in *Guys and Dolls* (1931), *Blue Plate Special* (1934), *Money from Home* (1935), *Take It Easy* (1938), and *Runyon à la Carte* (1944). Runyon's distinctive and slangy style even came to be tagged "Runyonese" by readers and critics.

In 1932 Columbia Pictures made his story "Madame La Gimp" into the movie *Lady for a Day*, which won four Academy Award nominations. During the 1930s Runyon became one of America's most financially successful writers, selling a number of his stories to Hollywood. By 1933 *Collier's* was paying him $5,000 per story, and movie producers were offering upwards of $10,000 for screen rights to individual stories. In the 1940s he would even produce films for RKO and 20th Century-Fox.

In 1935 Runyon wrote, with Harold Lindsay, a Broadway play called *A Slight Case of Murder*, and after his death three of Runyon's Broadway stories became the basis for the musical *Guys and Dolls* (1950). During the 1930s Runyon's newspaper columns also began to appear in collections. *My Old Man* (1939), *My Wife Ethel* (1939), and *In Our Town* (1946) featured fictional sketches based on his Colorado experience. *Short Takes* (1946) and *Trials and Other Tribulations* (1948) collected some of his best crime reporting.

The strain of Runyon's difficult temperament and night-owl habits helped break up both of his marriages. In 1911 he had married Ellen Egan, a former society editor for the *Rocky Mountain News*. They separated in 1928 and she died in 1931. Their daughter, Mary, was institutionalized after a mental breakdown in 1944, and their son, Damon Jr., a newspaperman who battled alcoholism much of his life, killed himself in 1965. In 1932 Runyon married Patrice Amati Del Grande Gidier, a dancer, in a ceremony performed by his friend, New York City Mayor Jimmy Walker. Runyon and she divorced in 1946.

After suffering hoarseness and throat pain for years, Runyon discovered in 1944 that he had cancer of the larynx. Following his death and cremation two years later, Runyon's ashes were scattered over Manhattan by aviator Captain Eddie Rickenbacker. Runyon's friend, the columnist Walter Winchell (q.v.), established a fund for cancer research in his name.

BIBLIOGRAPHY:

B. DAB Supp. 4, 708–709; NYT 11 December 1946; Tom Clark, *The World of Damon Runyon* (New York, 1978); Patricia Ward D'Itri, *Damon Runyon* (Boston, 1982); Jean Wagner, *Runyonese: The Mind and Craft of Damon Runyon* (Paris, 1964).

JOHN J. PAULY

RUSSELL, BENJAMIN (b. 13 September 1761; d. 4 January 1845) was a longtime newspaper editor and publisher with a proclivity for turning a phrase. Among the terms he coined which have taken a place in the American lexicon are "Gerrymandering" and "The Era of Good Feeling." Russell played an important role in the Federalist party for many years through his excellent and popular newspaper, the *Columbian Centinel.* The *Centinel* was noted for its excellent news coverage and advertising as well as for its political content. Russell himself for years wrote summaries of news from foreign newspapers (instead of just reprinting articles from overseas as most editors did). These, as well as many of Russell's original stories, were frequently reprinted by other American newspapers.

A native of Boston, Benjamin Russell was the son of John Russell, a mason. At age thirteen he ran away from school to join the army at Lexington at the outbreak of the American Revolution. Finally collared by his father three months later, he was soundly thrashed and then was apprenticed to Isaiah Thomas (q.v.) to learn typesetting at the *Massachusetts Spy.* When Thomas subsequently was called to arms, he ironically sent young Benjamin as his substitute, and Russell (although he never saw action) eventually returned as a major.

Russell married Esther Rice of Worcester, Massachusetts, on 21 September 1783, about the time he finished his journeyman printer service under Thomas. The following year, on 24 March, Russell established the *Massachusetts Centinel* in Boston in partnership with William Warden. A small sheet with moderate patronage, the paper was enlarged in 1786. In 1790, now on his own as publisher, Russell enlarged the newspaper again and renamed it the *Columbian Centinel,* reflecting its increased circulation and influence.

At first Russell had proclaimed himself a neutral in politics, but he soon used his paper to argue strongly for adoption of the proposed Federal Constitution. He devised a cartoon showing each state as a column for the new federal edifice, enthusiastically adding a new column as each state in turn ratified the constitution. Thus, he became known as a leading Federalist even beyond the boundaries of New England.

The paper succeeded commercially as well, and by the 1790s had a circulation of 4,000 at a time when most papers had fewer than 1,000 subscribers. Russell's paper supported the Washington and Adams administrations at every step, and no newspaper editor stood higher in Federalist party circles. The Jeffersonian Republican opposition was referred to by the *Centinel* as "ridiculous, despicable, weak-minded, weak-hearted Jacobins." With Jefferson's ascendancy to the presidency, Russell printed a long "Inscription for a Monument to the Deceased," in which he eloquently recounted the achievements of Federalism, now killed by "the secret arts and open violence of foreign and domestic demagogues." His first wife having died, Russell in 1803 married a widow, Guest Campbell. They had two sons and one daughter.

In the early 1800s Russell became more active in civic and social affairs, serving as president of a printers' mutual protection society and of the Massachusetts Charitable Mechanic Association (which he had founded in 1795). He also served as president of the Boston board of health, as a member of the school committee and the Common Council, and as an alderman, and began his long service in the Massachusetts House of Representatives with an unbroken term from 1805 to 1821.

When the War of 1812 broke out, Russell opposed it in the *Centinel*, calling it a "waste of blood and property" in a "useless and unnecessary war." His newspaper spearheaded New England Federalist opposition to the government and endorsed a movement for the secession of the region from the Union in the *Centinel* of 13 January 1813.

However, with the coming of peace and the virtual dissolution of the national Federalist party following the election of 1816, Russell turned to conciliation. He welcomed President Monroe's visit to Boston in 1817 with an editorial titled "The Era of Good Feeling," a label that since has been applied to the period in general. Russell endorsed John Q. Adams for the presidency in 1824, but when Adams failed in his bid for reelection in 1828, Russell sold his interest in the *Centinel* and retired from the newspaper business.

He continued to be active in politics, serving again in the state House of Representatives from 1828 to 1835 and as a member of the Executive Council in 1836–37. Russell died on 4 January 1845.

BIBLIOGRAPHY:

B. DAB 8, 238–240; Frank Luther Mott, *American Journalism*, 3d ed. (New York, 1962); Robert A. Rutland, *The Newsmongers* (New York, 1973).

ROBERT M. OURS

RUSSELL, CHARLES EDWARD (b. 25 September 1860; d. 23 April 1941) was a prominent muckraking writer in the first decade of the twentieth century, a well-known activist in the American Socialist party, and the winner of a Pulitzer Prize for a 1927 biography. Russell was one of five founding members of the National Association for the Advancement of Colored People in 1909. For nearly twenty years of a fifty-year career, Russell was a newspaper and magazine reporter, editor, and publisher, often allying his work with reform causes. In 1908 he became convinced that reform would not solve the problems caused by monopolies, however, and he turned in the later years of his life to democratic socialism. Although one of the more radical muckrakers, he always held to gradualism as the way to achieve socialism.

Russell was born in Davenport, Iowa, one of four children of Edward and Lydia Rutledge Russell. Edward Russell was the editor of the *Davenport Gazette*, an ardent abolitionist, and a steadfast Republican. Charles Russell was educated at St. Johnsbury Academy in Vermont. Upon graduation in 1881, he worked at the *Gazette* for two years. In 1884 he married Abby Osborn Rust of St. Johnsbury, the same year he left Davenport to begin a series of newspaper jobs.

From 1884 to 1886 Russell worked successively as a reporter at the *St. Paul Pioneer Press*, night editor at the *Minneapolis Tribune*, and managing editor at the *Minneapolis Journal* and then the *Detroit Daily Tribune*. In the summer of 1886 he came to New York City, where he wrote fillers for various newspapers until landing a reporting job in May 1887 with the *Commercial-Advertiser*, a trade paper. He was assigned to the police beat. In his autobiography, *Bare Hands and Stone Walls* (1933), he wrote: "The only education I ever had that amounted to anything was when I was a police reporter on the East Side of New York."

In Manhattan Russell saw slum life and began to question the system of private capital that allowed poverty to exist. In 1889 Russell became a reporter and subsequently city editor for the *New York Herald*, where he worked until 1894 when he became city editor for Joseph Pulitzer's *New York World*. Russell, known as "Iron Face Charlie" because he was a tough city editor, said: "To be king or president is nothing compared to being the city editor of a New York paper." William Randolph Hearst (q.v.), engaged in a circulation battle with Pulitzer, hired Russell in 1897 to be the managing editor of his *New York Journal*. In 1901 Russell moved to Chicago to become publisher of Hearst's newspaper, the *American*.

In 1901, after his wife died, Russell's health broke and he left daily journalism. He took a year off from work and then plunged back into reporting, joining with, among others, Lincoln Steffens and Ida Tarbell (qq.v.) in the muckraking movement. He was one of the most versatile, prolific, and best known of the muckrakers, mastering difficult subjects and writing with clarity and controlled passion. His topics included the beef trust, the railroads, slum landlords, legislative graft, election frauds, race relations, prison conditions, and pure food and drugs. Although most muckraking had waned by 1912, Russell kept up his exposés for another six years, detailing pressure brought to bear on magazines that continued to muckrake.

Russell's research led him to believe that the competitive systems forced duplicitous behavior and that socialism was the cure. Russell ran as the Socialist party candidate for governor of New York in 1910 and 1912, for mayor of New York City in 1913, and for U.S. Senate in 1914. He was formally expelled from the party in 1917 when he accepted President Wilson's invitation to join a peace mission to Russia.

In his final years Russell turned to poetry and biography. His 1927 biography of Theodore Thomas, the founder of the American grand orchestra, won a Pulitzer Prize. But it was his muckraking exposés that were most important. Russell died in 1941 from a coronary occlusion.

BIBLIOGRAPHY:

B. DAB Supp. 3, 674–676; NYT 24 April 1941; Donald H. Bragaw, "Soldier for the Common Good: The Life and Career of Charles Edward Russell," Ph.D. diss., Syracuse Univ., 1970; David Chalmers, *The Social and Political Ideas of the Muckrakers*, (New York, 1964); Louis Filler, *Crusaders for American Liberalism* (New York, 1939).

ROBERT MIRALDI

RUSSWURM, JOHN BROWN (b. 1 October 1799; d. 17 June 1851) had a brief but very significant career in American journalism as cofounder and editor of *Freedom's Journal*, the first black newspaper published in the United States.

Russwurm also edited a newspaper in Liberia and served as governor of the Maryland Colony in Liberia from 1836 to 1851.

Russwurm was born in Port Antonio, Jamaica, to a Jamaican woman and a white American man. His father sent him to schools in Canada and in Maine, and he was enrolled in Bowdoin College, from which he was graduated in August 1826. For a long time it was believed that Russwurm was the first black to graduate from an American college, but it now appears certain that another black, Edward A. Jones, was graduated from Amherst College a few days before Russwurm.

After graduation, Russwurm went to New York City where he and Samuel Cornish published the first issue of *Freedom's Journal* on 16 March 1827. The paper was dedicated to the struggle of blacks for freedom and citizenship, but Russwurm was soon disillusioned and he emigrated to Liberia in either 1828 or 1829. In Liberia, Russwurm was appointed superintendent of public schools. He became colonial secretary and, by virtue of that office, editor of the *Liberia Herald* in 1830. He served in those capacities until 1834. In 1836 he was appointed governor of the Maryland Colony in Liberia and served effectively in that office until his death.

BIBLIOGRAPHY:

B. Martin Dann, ed., *The Black Press, 1827–1890* (New York, 1971).

JOSEPH P. MCKERNS

— S —

SALANT, RICHARD S. (b. 14 April 1914), a lawyer without professional journalistic experience, took command of CBS News in 1961 and presided over it during the tumultuous civil rights, Vietnam, and Watergate eras when electronic journalism came of age. It is Salant more than any other figure who can be called the architect of modern television news. A staunch opponent of jazzed-up news and an outspoken champion of serious TV reporting, he expanded TV news to a half hour, gave Walter Cronkite (q.v.) his job as anchor, oversaw the birth of "60 Minutes" and "The CBS Morning News," defended such controversial documentaries as "Hunger in America" and "The Selling of the Pentagon," and developed the CBS Election News Unit, which provided the basis for the Vote Profile Analysis system that revolutionized election reporting.

Salant was born in New York City, the only son of lawyer Louis Salant and Florence Aronson Salant. While at Phillips Exeter Academy in New Hampshire, he served as editor of the schools' newspaper, the *Exonian*, and campaigned, unsuccessfully, to have students allowed to keep radios in their rooms. After graduation in 1931, Salant went on to Harvard, where he majored in English and won a $500 prize for his honors thesis on the influence of the moon on romantic poets. He was Phi Beta Kappa and graduated magna cum laude in 1935. He then entered Harvard Law School, serving on the board of editors of the *Harvard Law Review*.

Once he received his law degree in 1938, Salant went to Washington to serve on the staff of the National Labor Relations Board. After two years there, he served as acting director of the attorney general's Committee on Administrative Procedures and then worked as an attorney in the solicitor general's office of the Department of Justice from 1941 to 1943. He married Rosalind Robb in 1941, and the couple had four children. In 1943 Salant entered the navy and served until 1946, when he was discharged as a lieutenant commander.

Salant's career first turned toward communications when he joined the law firm of Rosenman Goldmark Colin and Kaye. CBS was one of the firm's leading clients, and Salant soon found himself representing the broadcasting corporation in such cases as the legal battle with RCA over compatible color television. He joined CBS in July 1952 as a vice president, and rapidly made the transition from law to broadcast journalism, joining the CBS Editorial Board in 1955. He married his second wife, Frances Trainer, in 1956; his first marriage had ended in divorce in 1954. His fifth child was a product of this second marriage. In late 1960 Salant was appointed chairman of the CBS News Executive Committee, formed to oversee CBS News.

In February 1961, CBS appointed Salant president of CBS News. Although looked on with some skepticism at first because of his lack of experience as a journalist, Salant pruned the news operation of such non-news programming as sports and beauty pageants and quickly developed a reputation for his commitment to serious journalism.

In 1964 Fred Friendly (q.v.) replaced Salant, who became vice president of corporate affairs and special assistant to Frank Stanton (q.v.). But Salant was brought back as CBS News president in 1966 when Friendly resigned; his tenure the second time lasted until his mandatory retirement in 1979. These were historic years for broadcast journalism, and Salant built a solid reputation for the number one network news operation of the time as courageous and hard-hitting. Salant refused to waver under increasing government criticism of CBS News. In one now-notorious incident, Salant was said to have rejected John Ehrlichman's attempt to get him to fire Dan Rather. Under Salant's tutelage, CBS led the way in broadcast coverage of the Watergate affair.

It was Salant who had a full evening's news script typeset in newspaper columns and pasted on the front page of the *New York Times*, discovering that the script covered only about one-third of the page. Salant often made news himself by supporting such broadcast causes as the full application of the First Amendment to broadcasting, the repeal of the equal time provision, television coverage of Supreme Court cases, and limits on presidential access to the airwaves. He refused to accede to international attempts to manage the news, turned down an offer to buy Nixon's television memoirs, and threatened to boycott the 1976 presidential debates when he felt that the League of Women Voters was permitting itself to be manipulated by the candidates. Salant said one of his biggest regrets was buying the television memoirs of H. R. Haldeman. He was sharply critical of ABC when it named Barbara Walters as news anchor, and of CBS when it chose Phyllis George, without journalistic experience, as co-host of "The CBS Morning News."

No sooner did Salant reach mandatory retirement in 1979 than he took the unusual step of joining CBS's rival NBC as vice chairman. He hoped to expand the evening news there to one hour, but his attempt was unsuccessful. He was an NBC senior adviser from 1981 to 1983. In 1983 he was appointed president of the National News Council, and in 1984 had the unpleasant duty of presiding over its demise because of lack of support from the press. The year he retired from CBS, Salant won the George Polk Memorial Award, the Alfred I. DuPont–Columbia University Award, and the George Foster Peabody Award.

BIBLIOGRAPHY:

B. Marvin Barrett, *Rich News, Poor News* (New York, 1978); Fred Friendly, *Due to Circumstances Beyond Our Control* (New York, 1967); Robert Metz, *CBS: Reflections in a Bloodshot Eye* (New York, 1976); "Never a Newsman, Always a Journalist," *Broadcasting*, 26 February 1979; Robert Lewis Shayon, "The Pragmatic Mr. Salant," *Saturday Review*, 11 March 1961.

BROOKS ROBARDS

SALISBURY, HARRISON EVANS (b. 11 November 1908) is a prolific Russian specialist whose interviews with world leaders, and articles and books on the political and social realities of life under communism have been widely read. He also has visited, and written both contemporary and historical pieces on, most of the other communist nations. He has written two novels, and the diverse subjects of his other eighteen books include the civil rights movement of the 1960s and juvenile delinquency. Salisbury was also a member of the *New York Times* editorial staff.

He was born in Minneapolis and raised in his paternal grandfather's home in Oak Lake, an Orthodox Jewish section of the city. His father, Percy Pritchard Salisbury, was an intellectual and an artist who supported his family as a bag factory executive. His mother, Georgianna Evans Salisbury, was a Victorian housewife who aspired to be a writer. Salisbury was graduated from high school in 1925, two years ahead of his class, and attended the University of Minnesota. Within weeks of his enrollment in the fall of 1925, he was a cub reporter on the campus paper, the *Minnesota Daily*; he was named editor in the fall of 1929. Lacking funds, Salisbury left school for short periods in 1928 and 1929 to work as a full-time reporter for the *Minneapolis Journal*. In January 1930, expelled by the university because of one of his newspaper crusades, he joined the United Press as a correspondent in St. Paul, Minnesota.

A year later, he transferred to the Chicago bureau, and on 1 April 1933 he married Mary Jane Hollis; they had two sons. In February 1934, eleven months into the New Deal, Salisbury joined the UP's Washington bureau. His pay frozen for joining a newspaper guild, he turned to free-lancing in his spare time, writing under assumed names—most often Michael Evans—for *Coronet*, *Newsweek*, *Ken*, and others. Salisbury was assigned to the foreign desk in the New York City office in early 1940. Believing he could best serve the Allied effort as a journalist, he transferred to London as bureau manager in February 1943. He covered the war in England, North Africa, the Middle East and, from January to September 1944, in Moscow. At the end of 1944, he returned to New York as the UP's foreign news editor. There he wrote *Russia on the Way* (1946), the first of twenty books.

The frustrations of his job and his marital problems mounted, and at the end of 1948 Salisbury took a leave of absence to enter a psychiatric clinic. In January 1949, instead of returning to the United Press, he moved into the *New York Times*'s only available opening as a correspondent in the Moscow bureau. It was a post he did not want, but during the next six years he grew to know and love Russia. Upon his return to New York in 1955 as a general staff member, he wrote a series of articles on Russia under Stalin and Khrushchev that won him the 1955 Pulitzer Prize for international reporting. In 1957 his articles on the Iron Curtain countries earned him the George Polk Memorial Award for foreign reporting; in 1958 he won the Sigma Delta Chi Award for foreign correspondence.

Salisbury joined the editorial ranks of the *Times* in February 1962 as the director of national correspondence. In April 1964, having divorced his wife in the summer of 1950, he married Charlotte Young Rand. Although he had been named assistant managing editor in September 1964, Salisbury continued to make occasional trips abroad for the *Times*. From 12 December 1966 to 7 January 1967, he reported from Hanoi, the first American reporter allowed in North Vietnam during the war. Salisbury earned several awards for these dispatches in 1967, including the Overseas Press Club Asian Award and another Polk Award. In 1970 he was named editor of the *Times*' op-ed page, and in May 1972 was also named associate editor. He retired from the paper in 1973, having reached the mandatory retirement age.

Salisbury continued to travel and write. He replaced Brendan Gill as the host of television's "Behind the Lines" in the fall of 1974, and in 1975 Xerox commissioned a series of articles for *Esquire*, "Travels Through America."

BIBLIOGRAPHY:

A. *A Journey for Our Times* (New York, 1983).

B. Turner Catledge, *My Life and "The Times"* (New York, 1971); Gay Talese, *The Kingdom and the Power* (New York, 1966).

KRISTEN DOLLASE

SANDBURG, CARL AUGUST (b. 6 January 1878; d. 22 July 1967) was a noted poet and biographer who became a seasoned observer of the human condition after more than twenty years as a newspaperman in Milwaukee and Chicago. Early on he covered a variety of labor issues for socialist publications before joining E. W. Scripps's (q.v.) experimental adless newspaper, the *Day Book*, in 1913. He joined the *Chicago Daily News* in 1917 and spent most of the next fifteen years there first covering labor and race conditions, then serving as motion picture editor, and finally writing a twice-a-week column. During World War II, he came out of retirement to write a widely syndicated weekly column for the *Chicago Times*.

Sandberg, the fourth of nine children, was born at Galesburg, Illinois. Sandburg's father, August, was a railroad blacksmith, and his mother was the former Clara Mathilda Anderson. Both his parents were originally from Sweden.

Sandburg quit school at the end of eighth grade, but in 1898 he was enrolled as a "special student" at Lombard College. Four years later, after editing both the student yearbook and newspaper, he dropped out of school again.

In July 1898, while serving with the army in the Spanish-American War, Sandburg contributed his first journalistic efforts in the form of letters sent from Puerto Rico to the *Galesburg Daily Mail*. After leaving Lombard, Sandburg went East and for six weeks in 1902 was a police reporter for the old *New York Daily News*. He returned to the Midwest and wrote poetry and a few prose pieces and settled down in Wisconsin, where he became an organizer for the Social Democratic party. On 15 June 1908 he married Lilian Steichen, sister of Edward Steichen (q.v.), who was to become famous later for his photography. The Sandburgs had three daughters: Margaret, born in 1911; Janet, born in 1916; and Helga, born in 1918.

In 1909 Sandburg became a reporter for the *Milwaukee Sentinel* and later that year for the *Milwaukee Daily News*, where he wrote a highly regarded editorial on the significance of the Lincoln penny for the common man. The next year he became secretary to the Socialist mayor of Milwaukee but dropped that position to become city editor of the *Milwaukee Social-Democratic Herald*. In 1912 he joined the *Chicago Evening World* staff. The next year he became chief reporter for the adless tabloid, the *Day Book*, which was run by N. D. Cochran, a man Sandburg regarded as having a strong sense of social justice.

When E. W. Scripps decided to stop publication of the *Day Book* upon the United States' entry into World War I, Sandburg went over to the *Chicago Daily News* to begin an association that would last about fifteen years with a couple of exceptions. For three weeks, he was employed on William Randolph Hearst's (q.v.) *Chicago Evening American* to write editorials for $100 a week, the most money he ever made. But he returned to the *Daily News* for half the salary. For three months in 1918, he went to Stockholm, Sweden, as a correspondent for the Newspaper Enterprise Association, and there he wrote on the declining days of World War I as well as the turmoil of the Russian Revolution.

However, Sandburg was to find his way back to the *Daily News*. An investigative series on the Chicago race riots of July 1919 was so highly thought of that it was collected, bound, and published in book form. From 1920 to 1927 he served as motion picture editor of the *Daily News*. The position allowed him some free time to go after his own literary pursuits. The first two volumes of his monumental six-volume Lincoln biography appeared in 1926, and after they were serialized in the *Pictorial Review*, Sandburg realized he no longer needed a regular newspaper assignment to assure his family's well-being. However, he did write a personal column that appeared twice a week until 1932.

A majority of Sandburg's newspaper writings related to social problems, labor disputes, and workers' rights. But during the years that he was earning a living as a newspaperman, he was also writing poetry dealing with many of these same issues. Sandburg was a popular writer who is in his later years gave lectures and sang folk songs in his own highly individual, yet American, way. He won the Pulitzer Prize for history in 1940 and for poetry in 1951. In 1964 he received the Presidential Medal of Freedom—the nation's highest civilian honor. Sandburg died on 22 July 1967, following a lengthy illness.

BIBLIOGRAPHY:

A. *The Chicago Race Riots* (New York, 1919).

B. NYT 23 July 1967; *Chicago Daily News*, 23 July 1967; North Callahan, *Carl Sandburg: Lincoln of Our Literature* (New York, 1970); Harry Golden, *Carl Sandburg* (New York, 1961).

ROBERT L. BAKER

SAVITCH, JESSICA (b. 1 February 1948; d. 23 October 1983) spearheaded the movement of women into network television news broadcasting. Her determination to achieve brought her to the pinnacle of television news, earning approximately $500,000 a year and anchoring NBC's Saturday edition of the nightly news. She served as a principal reporter for "Prime Time Sunday" on NBC, was a featured reporter on "NBC Magazine" and anchor for the sixty-second prime-time updates, "NBC News Digest." Savitch was recognized with numerous awards for her work, including four Emmys and the prestigious Alfred I. DuPont–Columbia University Award.

She was born in Kennett Square, Pennsylvania, to Florence and David Savitch, a registered nurse and a clothing store merchant, respectively. She was the oldest of three daughters who faced her first misfortune at age twelve when her father died.

The family moved to Margate, New Jersey, and she attended Atlantic City High School. She studied broadcast communications at Ithaca College, and there met discrimination head on when she was denied a position with the campus radio station by the faculty adviser who told her there was "no place for broads in broadcasting." This drove her to seek financing for college as a model, filmstrip narrator, and on-camera commercial announcer through which she was seen locally as the "Dodge Girl." She landed a position as disk jockey with WBBF-AM and became something of a local celebrity with the nickname "The Honeybee." She received her B.S. in 1968.

In September 1968 she was hired by the personnel director at CBS, a woman, to work as an assistant in the various divisions of the network. From there she worked for WCBS Newsradio while taking political science courses at New York University. She continued to apply for a television news position at stations across the country without success until the CBS Houston affiliate, KHOU-TV, was impressed enough to hire her. She held the positions of general assignment reporter and weekend anchor for two years before moving to Philadelphia, a major broadcasting market. At KYW-TV, an NBC affiliate, she worked first as a general assignment reporter, then weekend anchor. In 1974 she became co-anchor of the evening news and a year later anchored the noon news.

Savitch joined NBC News in 1977 after being courted by all three major networks. She served in the Washington bureau as a correspondent assigned to cover the Senate and anchor the weekend edition of "NBC Nightly News." She held other important positions at NBC News and earned the respect of many of her male colleagues.

In 1980 NBC News named Savitch the podium correspondent for coverage of the national political conventions. Just prior to the conventions, she married Melvin Korn, a Philadelphia advertising executive. The marriage ended in divorce in less than a year. After remarrying in March 1981, Savitch learned that her husband, Donald Rollie Payne, a gynecologist, was seriously ill with incurable cancer. He could not live with his condition and committed suicide. She found his body. Only a few weeks earlier Savitch had suffered a miscarriage, and also was victimized by a "scare letter."

These tragedies rocker her emotional stability, and she developed physical maladies including a severe ulcer and a deviated septum. By 1982 her career at NBC News was on the wane, particularly after she turned down the anchor position for the "Sunrise" program. She signed a new contract with NBC in August 1983, and the network planned for her to play a significant role in NBC's coverage of the 1984 primaries, conventions, and election.

Savitch's career was again on the rise, but tragedy was still to befall her. On a Sunday night in a heavy downpour, she and a male companion drowned in an apparent freak accident when their car drove off a road in New Hope, Pennsylvania, and into the muddy Delaware Canal.

BIBLIOGRAPHY:

A. *Anchorwoman* (New York, 1982).

B. NYT 25 October 1983; "Milestones: Tragic Sign-Off for a Golden Girl," *Time*, 7 November 1983; Judith Adler Hennessee, "All in a Day's Work: What it Takes to Anchor the News," *Ms*, August 1979.

DAVID M. GUERRA

SCHECHTER, ABEL ALAN (b. 10 August 1907) was the first news director of NBC and the first executive producer of NBC television's "Today" show. He helped establish broadcast news standards during the first decade of regular radio newscasts, and many of those standards have endured.

Schechter was born in Central Falls, Rhode Island, just a few miles outside Providence. His father, George Schechter was a merchant in Pawtucket. His mother, Celia Riven Schechter, was a housewife. In 1924, as a senior at Central Falls High School, Schechter worked election night for the *Providence Journal*. After graduation, he joined the paper full-time while carrying a full course load at Boston University. Schechter would usually work from 6:00 P.M. to 2:00 A.M. at the paper, grab a few hours of sleep, then take a forty-five-minute train ride to Boston for school. Upon graduation in 1929, Schechter worked for the *Newark Star Eagle* briefly, and then the *New York Journal*. When that paper folded, he became night city editor of the International News Service.

In 1932 Schechter joined NBC's press department. Originally hired to write publicity releases, Schechter became a one-man news department when a dispute between the networks and the press associations resulted in wire service being cut off. He worked out of a converted closet, and set up a system for obtaining news from NBC-owned stations and affiliates, and the network's European representatives. Soon director of news and special events, Schechter oversaw the development of regularly scheduled newscasts, with Floyd Gibbons, Lowell Thomas (qq.v.) and Sam Hayes among the presenters. Schechter became known for his innovative techniques and detailed planning of coverage for special events.

As the threat of war increased in the late 1930s, the demand for news, especially from abroad, greatly increased. Network news staff were increased to meet the demand. Schechter favored Americans as foreign correspondents because they could relate developments to the American character. Competition between NBC and CBS was especially fierce, and the two networks battled for scoops. The reporting on radio during this time showed the advantage of instant communication, and eliminated the need for newspaper extra editions. And it made household names of the people who reported for the networks.

Schechter left NBC after Pearl Harbor, joining the Office of War Information in 1942 as a captain. He helped draw up the censorship code for radio in the United States and was in charge of Army Air Force Radio. In 1943 Schechter transferred to General Douglas MacArthur's Southeast Pacific Area General Headquarters to oversee press relations. He left the military as a colonel in August 1945, and decided to join Mutual Broadcasting as director of news and special events. He became a vice president in 1946, and remained with Mutual until 1950, when he joined Crowell-Collier as a vice president. The publishing firm produced such magazines as *Collier's*, *American Magazine*, and *Woman's Home Companion*.

Schechter once more got in on the ground floor of broadcasting history when he returned to NBC in 1951 as the first executive producer of the "Today" show. Despite his role as a key figure in the precedent-setting days of both radio and television news, Schechter did not see himself as an innovator. He says that he and other broadcast news pioneers such as CBS's Paul White (q.v.) formulated coverage "on gut instinct."

In 1952, Schechter founded his own company, A. A. Schechter Associates, providing consultation to corporations and media-related companies. His firm became a wholly owned subsidiary of Hill and Knowlton in 1970, and Schechter became a director of the parent firm. Schechter lives in retirement in Palm Beach, Florida, with his wife, the former Fritzi B. Breger, whom he married 24 July 1941.

BIBLIOGRAPHY:

A. *Go Ahead, Garrison!: A Story of News Broadcasting* (New York, 1940); with Edward Anthony, *I Live On Air* (New York, 1941).

B. David H. Hosley, *As Good As Any* (Westport, Conn., 1984).

DAVID H. HOSLEY

SCHURZ, CARL (b. 2 March 1829; d. 14 May 1906) was minister to Spain under Abraham Lincoln, major general in the Civil War, U.S. senator from 1869 to 1873, and secretary of the interior under Rutherford B. Hayes. Throughout his political career Schurz took positions on newspapers and magazines which would allow him freedom to express his views on the abolition of slavery, black suffrage, just treatment of minority groups, civil service reform, and anti-imperialism. He was a Washington correspondent for the *New York Tribune* (1865–66); editor of the *Detroit Daily Post* (1866–67); editor and part owner of the *St. Louis Westliche Post* (1867–1906); editor in chief of the *New York Evening Post* (1881–83); and editorial contributor for *Harper's Weekly* (1892–97).

Schurz was born in Liblar, near Cologne, to Christian Schurz, a schoolmaster who later started a small hardware business, and Marianne Jüssen Schurz, whose father was tenant-in-chief on a feudal estate. At ten, young Schurz entered Marcellen Gymnasium at Cologne; he did not finish the nine-year program there, but was allowed to take his final exams anyway in August 1847 so that he could enter the University of Bonn as a full-time student.

At the university, Schurz met Professor Gottfried Kinkel—revolutionary leader and publisher of *Bonner Zeitung* (later *Neue Bonner Zeitung*). Schurz, influenced by Kinkel, threw himself wholeheartedly into the revolutionary movement. When Kinkel left Bonn in February 1849, Schurz took over the leadership of student revolutionaries and the management of *Neue Bonner Zeitung*, but in May he left the university himself to join the fighting. His records of the twenty-three-day siege preceding the fall of the revolution at Rastatt in July 1849 were later published in the *Neue Bonner Zeitung*. When the revolutionists were overthrown, Kinkel was taken prisoner; Schurz escaped to Switzerland, returning in November 1850 to rescue Kinkel—a feat for which he became internationally famous.

In London in 1851 Schurz met Margarethe Meyer, daughter of a wealthy Hamburg merchant. They were married on 6 July 1852; in August they sailed for America, reaching New York on 17 September 1852. Settling in Watertown, Wisconsin, in the midst of a thriving German-American community, Schurz bought land in 1856 and sought positions in local and state government, even before his final citizenship papers came through in late 1857. With subsidies from the newly established Republican party, he acquired two Watertown papers, the *Chronicle* and the *Deutsche Volkszeitung*. Margarethe, with the help of relatives who had joined them in Watertown, set up a kindergarten, the first of its kind in America.

Schurz was quick to take sides on the slavery question. He used the Watertown papers to voice his opposition to slavery and took every opportunity to speak (in German or in English) for abolition and to campaign for the Republican candidates who shared his view. His enthusiastic campaigning for the Republican party led to his meeting Abraham Lincoln. The two became friends, and when Lincoln was elected in 1860, he appointed Schurz minister to Spain.

During the war, Lincoln appointed Schurz brigadier general in June 1862, and promoted him to major general in March 1863. After the war, Schurz returned to journalism. He continued to be outspoken in political controversies, but he needed a source of income. Horace Greeley (q.v.) hired him as Washington correspondent for the *New York Tribune* in November 1865. In March 1866 Zachariah Chandler urged him to move to Detroit and edit the *Daily Post*;

prospects for the new paper looked good, and Schurz needed greater financial stability. He took the job. But when the *Post* proved financially disappointing, he borrowed money from German friends and in April 1867 bought half interest in the *St. Louis Westliche Post*, a leading German newspaper.

Two years after moving to Missouri, Schurz was elected to the U.S. Senate. His duties as senator took him away from St. Louis and active editing of the *Westliche Post*, but he continued to write editorials for several years and owned stock in the paper until his death. Schurz was defeated in his second campaign for the Senate, but he continued to campaign for liberal candidates, whether Republican or Democrat.

On 12 March 1876 Margarethe died from illness following the birth of their fifth child. Schurz's greatest political achievement came a year after her death. On 4 March 1877 Rutherford B. Hayes appointed him secretary of the interior. In this office his accomplishments included civil service reform, national forest preservation, and settling of territorial disputes among American Indians. His term ended in 1881, and although he did not hold public office again, he continued to be a leader in the liberal Mugwump movement.

In 1881 Henry Villard (q.v.) asked Schurz to head the editorial team for the *New York Post*, with E. L. Godkin and Horace White (qq.v.) sharing responsibilities. It was Schurz's most prestigious position, but by the end of 1883 he and Godkin were in such disagreement over editorial policies that Schurz gave up the editorship. From 1892 to 1897 Schurz held his final editorial position: weekly editorial contributor to *Harper's Weekly*. To his long list of political interests he added opposition to the popular thrust toward Manifest Destiny. When he openly opposed the war with Spain, *Harper's* relieved him of his editorial duties.

Although Schurz never married again, his friendship with Fanny Chapman, whom he met in late 1879 or early 1880, was a comfort to him until his death. His unmarried daughters, Agathe and Marianne, lived with him after 1885. His son, Carl Lincoln, married, but his only child died as an infant. Two other children died before their father: Emma Savannah, at three; Herbert, at twenty-four.

Schurz suffered from gallstones and bronchial infections throughout his final years; he fell seriously ill in early May 1906 and died in his home in New York City on 14 May 1906.

BIBLIOGRAPHY:

A. *The Reminiscences of Carl Schurz* (New York, 1907–1908; London, 1909).

B. DAB 16, 466–470; DLB 23, 313–322; NCAB 3, 202–203; NYT 15 May 1906; C. M. Fuess, *Carl Schurz, Reformer* (New York, 1932); Hans L. Trefousse, *Carl Schurz, A Biography* (Knoxville, 1982).

SHIRLEY M. MUNDT

SCOTT, HARVEY WHITEFIELD (b. 1 February 1838; d. 7 August 1910), the editor and part owner of the *Portland Oregonian* for forty-five years, was one of the last of the great "personal editors." Scott's conservative editorial stance on woman suffrage, prohibition, state-funded secondary and higher education, labor reform, and "sound money" attracted national attention. Scott's forceful, personal style of journalism and his hard-hitting political editorials made the *Oregonian* one of the most widely quoted of Pacific coast newspapers of its day. He maintained an active role in state, regional, and national political affairs, and served as a director of the Associated Press from 1900 to 1910.

Scott, the older of two children, was born on the family farm near Groveland, Tazewell County, Illinois, just south of Peoria. His father, John Tucker Scott, a grain and livestock farmer, moved the family to the Pacific Northwest in 1852. His mother, Ann Roelofson, died on the Oregon Trail during the move. For two years the Scotts lived on a farm in Oregon's Williamette Valley. In 1854, the family moved north to a farm near Shelton, a small town on the southwestern edge of Puget Sound in the newly formed Washington Territory. During the Indian Wars of 1855 and 1856, Scott served with the territorial army. In the fall of 1856, the Indian unrest prompted the Scott family to return to a farm near Oregon City, Oregon. In December 1856, Scott enrolled in Tualatin Academy where he attended irregularly for three years because of lack of funds. In 1859, he began full-time studies at Pacific University, Forest Grove, Oregon, supporting himself by working part time as a teamster, woodcutter, and teacher. After his graduation in 1863, Scott taught school for one year, became a librarian at the Portland library, and studied law in the private law office of Judge Shattuck. Scott was admitted to the bar in December 1865. He married Elizabeth Nicklin of Salem, Oregon, 31 October 1865.

Scott's journalistic career began while he was studying law. The *Portland Oregonian*, still a struggling operation consisting of its publisher, Henry Lewis Pittock, one reporter, and two or three others after fifteen years of existence, regularly published the editorial opinions of Judge Shattuck. When Abraham Lincoln was assassinated, Shattuck asked his student, Scott, to supply the editorial copy of the *Oregonian*. His editorial, "The Great Atrocity," published in the 17 April 1865 issue of the *Morning Oregonian*, so pleased Pittock that Scott was asked to be the paper's regular editorial writer. Within a month, Pittock appointed Scott as the paper's editor.

He was still serving as editor in October 1870 when he agreed to serve as customs fee collector for the Port of Portland. By 1872 he decided to leave the *Oregonian* and pursue the customs position full-time. In May 1876, however, Scott was fired from his post by Oregon Senator John Hipple Mitchell. In an editorial published 5 July 1898 in the *Oregonian*, Scott claimed that he was fired because he refused to contribute financial support to the *Portland Bulletin*, the newspaper organ of Mitchell. It was during this period of political turmoil that Scott's wife died, leaving him one son. In June 1876, Scott married Margaret McChesney, of Latrobe, Pennsylvania, and by April 1877 he returned to the *Oregonian* as both editor and part owner, positions he held until his death.

During his final thirty-three years, Scott set a firm, conservative, predominantly Republican course for the *Oregonian*. From his very first editorial on Lincoln's assassination to his vigorous editorial campaigns against the Greenback and Free Silver movements, Scott showed himself to be a forceful, though somewhat dogmatic and abrasive, writer and editor.

By his own admission, Scott was not a gifted writer. What he lacked in style, he made up in passion, however. He wrote with such fervency that his editorials were frequently accused of being abusive. His self-confidence was also seen as unbridled arrogance. His abusive and arrogant tendencies notwithstanding, Scott had the ability to make even complex issues understandable and to offer thoroughly studied, logically sound, convincing opinions. He wrote more than 10,000 articles and editorials during his journalistic career.

In the latter half of his editorship of the *Oregonian*, the editorials became the work of several hands as Scott became more and more involved with political and professional activities at the state and national levels. From 1898 to 1901 he was the president of the Oregon State Historical Society. Though he never held elective office, he did make overtures to state Republican party leaders for a U.S. Senate seat in 1903. He also declined diplomatic appointments to Belgium in 1905 and to Mexico in 1909.

In the last years of his life, Scott became increasingly reclusive. He also became increasingly interested in religious and theological issues. He became a regular contributor to the Methodist periodical *Pacific Christian Advocate*. Scott died at Baltimore's Johns Hopkins University hospital following complications from prostatectomic surgery.

BIBLIOGRAPHY:

B. DAB 16, 491; NYT 8 August 1910; *Morning Oregonian*, 8 August 1910; George Turnbull, "The Schoolmaster of the Oregon Press," *Journalism Quarterly*, December 1938.

ROY ALDEN ATWOOD

SCOTT, WILLIAM ALEXANDER II (b. 29 September 1902; d. 7 February 1934) was the first black since the Civil War to publish a daily newspaper in the United States, and the first black to establish a national newspaper syndicate. His family-operated enterprise owned three newspapers in Atlanta, Birmingham, and Memphis, and contracted through his syndicate to do the printing for more than fifty undercapitalized black-owned newspapers from Florida to Oklahoma and Iowa. As a promoter, Scott stimulated and inspired a generation of newspapermen during the depression. As an editor, he championed the elimination of racial discrimination and focused attention on complaints about police brutality against blacks.

Scott, one of nine children, was born in Edwards, Mississippi, near Jackson. Scott's father, the Reverend William Alexander Scott, was a Christian Church minister and printer in Jackson and later in Johnson City, Tennessee, who printed church publications. Scott's mother, Emeline Southall Scott, was a native of Ohio. Scott was educated in Edwards and Jackson, and as a boy learned to set type and operate a Linotype in his father's printing operation.

In 1922 Scott left Jackson College as a sophomore and on 22 June 1922 married Lucile McAllister, the daughter of a minister in the Christ Temple Holiness Church. They had two sons, William Alexander III, born 15 January 1923, and Robert E., born 10 September 1924. In 1923, Scott, along with the oldest of his five brothers, Aurelius S., moved to Atlanta and studied business and mathematics at Morehouse College. Scott excelled in various endeavors, as a football quarterback, a band musician, and a champion debater; with Aurelius as his debate partner, his team was undefeated.

Scott left Morehouse in 1925 without graduating, and taught for one year at Swift College in Knoxville, Tennessee, then ventured into the printing business. Recognizing the need in the segregated black community for an exchange of information between black-owned businesses and black consumers, Scott sold advertising and published the *Jacksonville* (Florida) *Negro Business Directory* in 1927, and in 1928 the *Atlanta Negro Business Directory*.

In March 1928, Scott borrowed money and assumed a lien against the equipment of the Service Company Printing Office, which had gone into receivership, part of the black-owned Standard Life Insurance Company. On 3 August 1928 he published the first issue of the weekly *Atlanta World*, which carried his first editorial calling for an end to racism and police brutality; the news columns reflected his effort to inspire readers by reporting positive news about blacks. Scott also used his editorial columns to advance the causes of education and jobs for blacks. Assisted by another brother, Cornelius A., he began in 1930 to publish the *World* semiweekly and soon afterwards triweekly. On 12 March 1932 the *Atlanta Daily World* became the nation's first successful black-owned daily. In 1929 Scott and his wife of seven years, from whom he had been separated, agreed upon a divorce, and Scott wed Mildred Jones of South Carolina, from whom he was separated within months. In 1932 Scott wed Ella Ramsay of Atlanta, a marriage which lasted about a year. In 1933 he married Agnes Maddox of Atlanta.

During these early depression years Scott built his newspaper syndicate by motoring extensively across the country, especially in the South and Midwest, and personally concluding franchise-type printing contracts with local black businessmen. Each member of the Scott chain would receive the basic *Daily World* national news and sports pages, plus a different front page with local news and the local newspaper's masthead. The whole eight-page paper was printed in the Atlanta office and was shipped on scheduled freight trains and buses. Local owners earned revenue from local advertising and circulation sales, and the Scott Syndicate profited from the national advertising. By the time of Scott's death in February 1934, the Scott Newspaper Syndicate printed and shipped to fifty-five member newspapers, including the *Charleston Ledger Dispatch*, *Chattanooga Observer*, *Alabama Tribune*, *Atlantic City Eagle*, *Cleveland Guide*, *Peoria Informer*, *Iowa Observer*, and *Oklahoma Defender*. Most were weeklies, but many were semiweeklies. In 1933 Scott employed fifty-five full-time and twelve part-time employees in the main plant and in branch plants in Birmingham and Memphis.

Scott was an aggressive, self-confident personality who loved to excel even in his pastimes of swimming, bicycling, croquet, and parlor pool. In business he chafed at the barriers of segregated society but also found enterprising ways to encourage other blacks to venture into business during economic hard times, and he eventually knew many of the nation's most progressive blacks. In 1930 he was honored for establishing the first chain of black newspapers. Scott died at the Spelman University clinic in Atlanta on 7 February 1934 from abdominal peritonitis, eight days after he was shot in the back on 30 January while he was putting his car in his garage at night. On his deathbed he reportedly named a suspect; the man authorities later indicted for Scott's murder was acquitted by a jury and no one else was ever charged.

Scott's reputation as a pioneer newspaperman was underscored more than forty years after his death. In 1976 *Jet Magazine* named him as one of the nation's top 200 blacks during the 200 years of U.S. independence. In 1908 he was elected to the Howard University Hall of Fame for black journalists. The same year, the national professional organization for journalists, Sigma Delta Chi, honored him by designating the *Daily World*'s original building as a national historic site.

BIBLIOGRAPHY:

B. *Atlanta Constitution*, 8 February 1934.

LEONARD RAY TEEL

SCRIPPS, EDWARD WILLIS (b. 28 June 1854; d. 12 March 1926) forged a chain of newspapers that fought for reform and the common man. He also started a feature syndicate, known as Newspaper Enterprise Association, and a wire news service, called the United Press, which through a merger became United Press International (UPI).

Scripps, born on a farm near Rushville, Illinois, was the youngest of the five children of James Mogg Scripps and his third wife, Julia Adeline Osborn. James had been a bookbinder in England before coming to America, as a widower with six children, to take up farming. He married Julia, a schoolteacher, in Cleveland before going to Illinois, and it was her farm background that enabled them to make a living on the soil. Scripps, who felt he was not a wanted child, once said he was born "of an accident, the last expiring flame of passion burned to ashes in the aged bodies of my parents."

Named Edward Willis Scripps, he ordinarily signed his name as E. W. Scripps or Edward W. Scripps. Various family records show both Willis and Wyllis as his middle name, but he signed it Willis on the only occasion on record on which he wrote his full name in full—a will signed in 1906. Scripps attended a district school near his home and a private school conducted by his half-sister, Ellen Browning Scripps (q.v.), before leaving school at about fifteen to take over the family farm because his father had become ill.

Disliking farm work, Scripps hired boys his own age to work in the fields while he sat reading in a fence corner. At age eighteen he went to Detroit to work as an office boy at the *Detroit Tribune*, where a half-brother, James E. Scripps (q.v.), was editor and another half-brother, William A., was job shop foreman. James, nineteen year older, held Scripps in contempt, perhaps because of the age difference and perhaps because both had strong and opposite personalities. However, James allowed Scripps to join in a new venture he started, an experiment with a cheap new paper he named the *Detroit Evening News*. Scripps helped to build up the circulation of the new paper and became first a member of the news staff and then city editor.

Scripps was so attracted to the idea of a press for the masses that he borrowed money and established a paper of his own, the *Cleveland Penny Press*, in 1878. With his paper's entire operation housed in a four-room shack in an alley, he laid, at age twenty-four, the foundation for a career as owner of a chain of daily papers extending over the country. The *Penny Press* had a multitude of short stories and was politically independent. Cleveland, as a fast-growing city, was a perfect host to the venture. His "God damn the rich" philosophy appealed to the workingmen. He said, as his newspaper chain expanded, that his papers were designed for the common people. "Whatever is, is wrong," he maintained. While retaining the controlling interest in all his papers, he sold stock to members of the editorial and business staffs, and at the time of his death about two-fifths of the stock of his papers was in the hands of his employees. He took Milton Alexander McRae into partnership in 1889 and formed the Scripps-McRae League of Newspapers with McRae and George H. Scripps, a half-brother, in 1895.

In 1907 Scripps combined two news-gathering organizations he owned to form the United Press Association, generally known simply as the United Press. He formed Newspaper Enterprise Association in 1902. Scripps's empire took the name Scripps-Howard in 1922, with the Howard being Roy W. Howard (q.v.), who had been president of United Press.

Scripps built a villa, Miramar, near San Diego in 1891 and ran his papers by active, yet remote, control while he became reclusive. He outlined the maxims he had employed in his business. Included were these: Never spend as much money as you earn; it is more blessed to pay wages than to accept them; never do anything yourself that you can get someone else to do for you; never do anything today that you can put off till tomorrow; always buy, never sell; never do anything, if you can help it, that someone else is doing; when you become rich, don't let anyone know it; one of the greatest assets any man can secure is a reputation for eccentricity; never hate anybody.

In October 1885 Scripps married Nackie Benson Holtsinger, the daughter of a Presbyterian minister, and they had six children. She died in 1930, four years after her husband. Scripps often boasted of drinking a gallon of whiskey a day in his younger days and of his sexual conquests as a young man.

With his sister Ellen, Scripps endowed the Scripps Institution of Biological Research at La Jolla, California (later the Scripps Institute of Oceanography).

Scripps was ill the last years of his life. Four years before his death, after relinquishing control of his papers, he boarded his yacht, the *Ohio*, and roamed the world, gaining the title ''hermit of the seas.'' He died of apoplexy aboard his yacht as it was anchored in Monrovia Bay, Liberia, and was buried at sea in keeping with his instructions.

BIBLIOGRAPHY:

A. *I Protest: Selected Disquisitions of E. W. Scripps* (Madison, Wis., 1966).

B. DAB 16, 517–518; NYT 14 March 1926; Negley D. Cochran, *E. W. Scripps* (New York, 1933); Gilson Gardner, *Lusty Scripps* (New York, 1932); Charles McCabe, *Damned Old Crank* (New York, 1951).

DENNIE HALL

SCRIPPS, ELLEN BROWNING (b. 18 October 1836; d. 3 August 1932), a journalist and philanthropist who was a major participant in the founding of the nation's first newspaper chain, was born in London, England, the daughter of James Mogg Scripps and Ellen Mary Saunders Scripps. She was the sister of James (q.v.) and George Scripps, and the half-sister of Edward W. Scripps (q.v.).

She came with her family to the United States in 1844 and attended school at Rushville, Illinois. She took her A.B. at Knox College in Galesburg, Illinois, in 1859, and afterwards taught school for a time. She went to Detroit, where her brothers owned the *Evening News*, and worked as a proofreader, literary editor, and popular columnist, but she returned to Illinois to care for her father until he died in 1873. She then resumed her work in journalism.

In 1878 she helped her half-brother Edward (who she said possessed ''a man's mind'') found the *Cleveland Penny Press*. It is variously said that the genius Edward was grateful for his half-sister's help and helped her build a fortune, and that on several occasions Ellen bailed Edward out of financial trouble and helped him build his fortune. In any event, Edward built the Scripps-McRae League, which evolved into the Scripps-Howard chain. Ellen's ''Miscellany'' column, which she began writing in Detroit, developed eventually into the syndicate known as the Newspaper Enterprise Association.

In 1897, after the Scripps chain had expanded to California, Ellen built a house at La Jolla and lived out her life there. By that time she was wealthy, and spent the rest of her years heavily engaged in philanthropy. She converted the Scripps farm at Rushville, Illinois, into the Scripps Memorial Park, and helped found what became the Scripps Institution of Oceanography and the Bishop School for Girls at La Jolla. She established and endowed the Scripps College for Women at Claremont, California. Ellen Scripps, who never married, died at La Jolla.

BIBLIOGRAPHY:
B. NYT 4 August 1932.

DWIGHT JENSEN

SCRIPPS, JAMES EDMUND (b. 19 March 1835; d. 29 May 1906) was founder and for many years publisher of the *Detroit News*. A member of the famous newspaper family and older half-brother of Edward Willis Scripps (q.v.), he also was one of the founders of the *Cleveland Press* and the *St. Louis Chronicle* and one of the organizers of the *Cincinnati Post*.

Scripps, born in London, was a son of James Mogg Scripps and his second wife, Ellen Mary Saunders Scripps. James M. Scripps, a bookbinder, came to the United States in 1844 and settled on a farm near Rushville, Illinois. Young James, who was only nine when his family came to America, attended a district school and a Chicago business college and then worked a while as a bookkeeper. In 1857 he began work as a reporter on the *Democratic Press*, published by his cousin, John Locke Scripps, which was merged in 1858 with the *Chicago Daily Tribune*.

In 1859 Scripps became commercial editor of the *Detroit Daily Advertiser* and later bought an interest in the paper. The *Advertiser* merged with the *Detroit Tribune*, and Scripps was first business manager and then editor of the combined papers. On 23 August 1873 Scripps started the *Detroit Evening News*, a two-cent, four-page paper which followed his philosophy that there was room in Detroit for a cheap paper in which news and editorial comment were condensed for busy readers. The paper later was named the *Detroit News*.

Within a year the lively little paper had so interested the Detroit working men and their wives that it gained as large a circulation as any of its five-cent rivals. Scripps was elected to the Michigan State Senate in 1902 as an advocate of home rule for cities. He also was a director of the Associated Press. Scripps often was at odds with his half-brother, Edward Willis Scripps, and after some early business associations, they parted company.

Scripps was married on 16 September 1862 to Harriet Josephine Messinger of Peru, Vermont. She survived Scripps, as did three daughters and a son. Scripps, who was interested in art, architecture, and early printed books, served on the commission of the Detroit Museum of Art (later the Detroit Institute of Arts) contributed to it both money and paintings that he collected on trips abroad. He gave to the city of Detroit a park that bears his name.

Scripps's death, at age seventy-one, followed a long illness from myelitis, or inflammation of the spinal cord. He was buried in Detroit. His widow died on 6 March 1933.

BIBLIOGRAPHY:
B. DAB 16, 519–520; NYT 30 May 1906; *Detroit News*, 29 May 1906; M. A. McRae, *Forty Years in Newspaperdom* (New York, 1924).

DENNIE HALL

SEATON, WILLIAM WINSTON (b. 11 January 1785; d. 16 June 1866) was an editor of the Washington, D.C. *National Intelligencer* for half a century. The newspaper was the semiofficial organ of presidents Jefferson, Madison, Monroe, and Fillmore. With his brother-in-law, Joseph Gales, Jr. (q.v.), the firm of Gales and Seaton published three major political documentary history sources in book form for the nation's first fifty years.

He was the son of Augustine and Mary Winston Seaton. Both were from the earliest Virginia families. Seaton was educated by tutors and attended Ogilvie's Academy in Richmond. He began his career on the *Richmond Patriot* at seventeen. He edited the *Republican* in Petersburg and the *North Carolina Journal* in Halifax, North Carolina. Seaton worked for Joseph Gales, Sr., on the *Raleigh Register* and became a partner of Gales and Seaton in Raleigh in 1809. He married Gales's daughter Sarah on 30 March 1809.

In 1812, after Gales's son Joseph acquired the *National Intelligencer*, Seaton and his wife moved to the nation's capital where Seaton became a partner with the younger Gales. The partners divided the work equally. At first Seaton covered the Senate while Gales reported on the House proceedings. Other reporters were hired in later years.

The newspaper became a daily in 1813, keeping its triweekly as a separate publication. The *Intelligencer* had been the semiofficial voice of Jefferson under Samuel Harrison Smith (q.v.), who sold the paper to Gales in 1810. It continued to represent Jeffersonian politics and those of his two successors. The firm expanded its printing business when it became the official printer to Congress between 1819 and 1829. It also was to enjoy political patronage fitfully in subsequent decades. In spite of fluctuations in government printing contracts, the partners supervised the most extensive printing business in the country for decades.

The were partially financed by congressional appropriations in publishing in book form three documentary political sources which proved important to the nation's historians. Publication was begun in 1825 of the *Register of Debates in Congress* covering the period to 1837. In 1834 they began printing the *Annals of Congress* (forty-two volumes) covering the years 1789 to 1824. Material of earlier reporters was used as well as reports from the *National Intelligencer*. From 1832 to 1861 the firm printed thirty-eight volumes of the *American State Papers* which included the important historical documents of the early political life of the nation.

The emphasis on political news caused a steady decline in the circulation of the daily after the 1830s when most of the nation's dailies began broadening their news coverage of society. The Seatons were prominent in Washington society and entertained leading politicians and statesmen. In addition, Seaton served as Washington's mayor from 1840 to 1850. He was also involved in many public activities including establishing the Washington Monument and serving as an officer of the Smithsonian.

He continued the *National Intelligencer* after the death of Gales in 1860, but his own declining health led him to sell the firm and newspapers as of 31 December 1864. Seaton died of cancer on 16 June 1866.

BIBLIOGRAPHY:

B. DAB 16, 541–542; NTY 17 June 1866; William E. Ames, *A History of the ''National Intelligencer''* (Chapel Hill, N.C., 1972); Josephine Seaton, *William Winston Seaton of the ''National Intelligencer''* (Boston, 1871).

SAM KUCZUN

SELDES, GEORGE HENRY (b. 10 September 1890) has been a watchdog of the press for more than fifty years. He edited the nation's first successful journalism review, *In Fact*, for a decade and has written nineteen books, many of them harshly critical of the press. Seldes also worked as a correspondent in Europe during and after World War I. He now lives in Vermont, where he is working on his twentieth book.

Seldes was born in Alliance, New Jersey, the son of George Sergius Seldes and Anna Saphro Seldes. Alliance was a utopian colony started by his father, who served as its postmaster, teacher, and justice of the peace. The colony did not last long after Seldes's birth, however, so he was educated in conventional schools.

Seldes was eighteen when he first went to work as a reporter for the *Pittsburgh Leader* in 1909. He then worked as a copy editor and night editor on the *Pittsburgh Post* before spending a year at Harvard University in 1912–13. In 1916 Seldes became managing editor of *Pulitzer's Review* in New York City. In October of that year he went to England as a free-lance writer and became an assistant in the London office of the United Press. After the United States entered the war in 1917, Seldes became a member of the press section of the American Expeditionary Force, representing a syndicate that served the *Atlanta Constitution*, the *Los Angeles Times*, the *St. Louis Globe-Democrat*, and other newspapers. Among his colleagues were Damon Runyon, Heywood Broun, and Floyd Gibbons (qq.v.).

After World War I, Seldes remained in Europe as an assistant to the London correspondent of the *Chicago Tribune* in 1919, and then for ten years he was the chief European correspondent for that paper. Those were extremely important years of his career. He was thrown out of Russia in 1923 for his reports of the Bolshevik purge of anarchists and other opponents, and expelled from Italy in 1925 for his coverage of the rise of Mussolini and fascism in that country. These experiences contributed to the development of his deep and lasting loathing of fascism and press censorship, loathings reflected in much of his writing.

Seldes resigned from the *Tribune* in 1928 and the next year published his first book, *You Can't Print That, The Truth Behind the News*, in which he recounted suppressed stories about leading European political figures. In 1932 Seldes married Helen Larkin Wiesman, whose father was a chemist at Procter and Gamble, and one of the developers of Ivory Soap. Seldes and his wife lived and worked together until her death in 1979. They had no children.

During the 1930s, two of Seldes's books were on the best-seller list. They were major indictments of the press that were to have the greatest lasting importance—*Freedom of the Press* (1935) and *Lords of the Press* (1938). In *Lords of the Press*, Seldes attacked members of the American Newspaper Publishers Association, which he called the "house of lords," for using their papers to advance their own commercial and political interests.

From 1936 to 1937 he was a war correspondent in Spain for the *New York Post*. Then he returned to writing books until 1949 when he launched *In Fact*, in which he attacked journalists, their practices, and the economic structure of the press. He also was a pioneer in consumer news, crusading against the tobacco, automobile, and drug industries years before those were popular causes. A weekly publication, *In Fact* reached a circulation of 176,000 and influenced future generations of press critics and consumer advocates, including I. F. Stone, A. J. Liebling (qq.v.), Ben Bagdikian, and Ralph Nader.

Ironically, the feisty, personal *In Fact* was the cause of Seldes's downfall, as well as his most enduring journalistic contribution. Seldes's muckraking of the press caused him to be shunned by that group and ignored by book critics. In addition, the alleged Communist party membership of his financial partner in the venture resulted in Seldes's being questioned before the McCarthy committee in 1953. Seldes said he did not know his newsletter was underwritten by the Communist party, U.S.A., and he was cleared by the committee. However, the circulation of *In Fact* declined, and Seldes discontinued it in 1960.

After living in relative obscurity in rural Vermont for many years, outspoken as ever and writing a steady stream of books, Seldes was rediscovered by the journalistic community in the 1980s. In 1980 he received an award for professional excellence from the Association for Education in Journalism. Also, he received a George Polk Award in Journalism and an award from Temple University's Society of Professional Journalists chapter, both in 1982.

BIBLIOGRAPHY:

A. *Witness to A Century* (New York, 1987).

B. Paul Blanchard, "Battling for a Free Press, the Saga of George Seldes, Journalistic Muckraker," *Churchman*, February 1977; Everette E. Dennis and Claude-Jean Bertrand, "Seldes at 90: They Don't Give Pulitzers for that Kind of Criticism," *Journalism History*, Autumn/Winter 1980.

CATHY PACKER

SELDES, GILBERT VIVIAN (b. 3 January 1893; d. 29 September 1970), columnist, editor, and media critic, was one of the most influential celebrants of America's popular arts. His iconoclastic defense of popular culture against its highbrow detractors in the 1920s was one of the earliest efforts to examine seriously the aesthetics of mass media. More than a dozen books established his reputation as a media critic committed to the idealism of democratic aesthetics.

Born in Alliance, New Jersey, a utopian colony founded by his parents, George Sergius Seldes and Anna Saphro Seldes, he attended Central High School in Philadelphia and was a Phi Beta Kappa graduate of Harvard in 1914. After graduation, Seldes joined the *Philadelphia Evening Ledger*, serving as music critic (1914–16) and as a European correspondent during World War I. In addition, he was a political correspondent in Washington, D.C., for *L'Écho de Paris* (1918), associate editor of *Collier's* magazine (1919), and associate managing editor of the *Dial* (1920–23). With a year's leave of absence from the *Dial*, Seldes moved to Paris where he wrote *The 7 Lively Arts* (1924), a defense of popular culture. He married Alice Wadhams Hall of New York City on 21 June 1924; they had two children.

Seldes became drama critic in 1929 for both the *Dial* and the *New York Evening Graphic* and he was a columnist between 1931 and 1937 for the *New York Journal*. He edited *This Is America*, a 1933 documentary film that used excerpts from newsreels. In 1937, Seldes became director of television programs for CBS, a position he held until 1945 when commercial network television was still in its experimental stage. He joined the faculty of the University of Pennsylvania's Annenberg School of Communications in 1950, serving as its dean between 1959 and 1963. A writer of murder mysteries under the pseudonym Foster Johns, Seldes was also a radio commentator and a member of the National Institute of Arts and Letters.

His critical reputation rests largely on three influential books that comprise the first great trilogy on the aesthetics of popular culture in America: *The 7 Lively Arts* (1924), *The Great Audience* (1950), and *The Public Arts* (1956).

In *The 7 Lively Arts*, Seldes declared his manifesto, defending Al Jolson, Ring Lardner (q.v.), Florenz Ziegfeld, Mack Sennett, and Charlie Chaplin, among others. George Herriman's comic strip *Krazy Kat* "is easily the most amusing and fantastic and satisfactory work of art produced in America to-day," Seldes wrote, while "the circus can be and often is more artistic than the Metropolitan Opera House in New York." His modernity stood against "a tradition that what is worthwhile must be dull; and as often as not we invert the maxim and pretend that what is dull is high in quality, more serious, 'greater art' in short than whatever is light and easy and gay. We suffer fools gladly if we can pretend they are mystics."

Seldes shifted his attention in *The Great Audience* from the aesthetics of the popular arts to their social and cultural influence, the pessimism of his more mature voice muting the giddy tones of his youth. Without abandoning his admiration for the "lively arts," Seldes at mid-century had grown apprehensive about their cultural impact. The entertainment media had coalesced into an antidemocratic oligarchy, he argued, and radio, television, and film had engaged in "a determined, effort to perpetuate the adolescent mind," reducing America to "a nation of teenagers," "a robotized society." The uniformity of mass media content was the antithesis of his conception of democratic pluralism. The high ground of his criticism was the assertion that "the popular arts do not sufficiently reflect the ethics and aspirations of democracy," he wrote. Seldes's antidote: "to use the media as counterforces—against themselves."

In *The Public Arts*, Seldes reasserted the subversive democratic thesis that the people have valid, sovereign rights over their cultural institutions. The public arts had become a fulcrum for social change, he argued, and the public has a moral obligation to direct the change. Without self-criticism of mass media, Seldes wrote, "we are prevented from thinking about the process by which we are hypnotized into not thinking."

In many respects, Seldes's cold war–era media criticism anticipated and grounded themes that reemerged in the decade following his death. Seldes suffered a fatal heart attack at his home at 125 East 57th Street in New York City on 29 September 1970. His body was cremated.

BIBLIOGRAPHY:

B. NYT 30 September 1970; Norman Jacobs, ed., *Culture for the Millions?* (Boston, 1964).

ARTHUR J. KAUL

SEVAREID, (ARNOLD) ERIC (b. 26 November 1912), an American broadcast journalist, is well known for the urbanity, wit, and insight he has displayed throughout his career. Sevareid has served as a newspaper reporter, war correspondent, radio newscaster, television commentator, and author. In 1977 mandatory retirement forced him to sign off after thirty-eight years with CBS News. He continues to work as a consultant and maintains an office at CBS's Washington news bureau. In 1962, *New York Times* television critic Jack Gould labeled Sevareid, "CBS's commentator in charge of significance."

He was born in Velma, North Dakota, to Clare Hougen Sevareid and Alfred Sevareid. His father, a Norwegian immigrant, ran the local bank. Drought hit the wheat-growing region in the 1920s, and with farmers bankrupt, his father's bank closed. The family moved to Minneapolis; Sevareid's father became secretary of the St. Paul Federal Land Bank. He enrolled at Minneapolis Central High School, and worked on the school paper until graduation in 1930.

Soon after graduation the young Sevareid and a friend set off on a 2,200-mile canoe trip to York Factory on Hudson Bay. The venture received some financing from the *Minnesota Star*. Sevareid, in turn, wrote articles about the adventure. When eighteen years old, Sevareid got a job with the *Minneapolis Journal*. He began as copyboy and six weeks later was made reporter. He continued to work while majoring in political science and economics at the University of Minnesota. Sevareid also wrote for the *Star* and his campus paper. Throughout his college career the student often became identified with liberal causes.

He received his B.A. in 1935 and worked at the *Journal* until 1937. He then traveled to Europe, studying political science at the London School of Economics and attending the Alliance Française in Paris. He later likened the work of a news commentator to "the life of a perpetual graduate student. There's not enough time to get it all done." While in France, the young Sevareid was employed as a reporter for the *New York Herald Tribune*'s Paris edition, and was later named city editor. He also worked as night editor for the United Press.

In August 1939, Sevareid was hired by Edward R. Murrow (q.v.) to join a group of newsmen he was assembling to cover the war in Europe. Sometimes known as ''Murrow's boys,'' the newsmen chosen for this elite group helped make CBS a radio news leader. Sevareid has fondly referred to Murrow as ''the man who invented me.'' The new position kept Sevareid in France until that country fell to Germany. From there he moved to London, and in 1940 returned to the United States. He was assigned to the CBS Washington news bureau.

After numerous assignments that took Sevareid to Mexico and Brazil, he left to cover the China-Burma-India theater during the summer of 1943. With nineteen others he bailed out of a crippled plane and had to briefly live in the Assam jungle among head-hunting natives. Following this adventure he returned to Europe, where he covered the Italian campaign, accompanied the first American troops to land in southern France, and had a variety of assignments in Yugoslavia, France, Germany, and Britain.

Returning to the United States following the war, Sevareid again was assigned to CBS's Washington office. He played a major role in CBS News election coverage in 1948, 1952, and 1956. In 1959 he traveled to London and served as roving European correspondent. By 1961 he was back in the United States, this time New York, narrating a variety of programs. He appeared in CBS ''Reports'' and covered the 1964 national presidential conventions. He was again sent to Washington in November of that year, now as national correspondent for CBS News. Although Sevareid has claimed that he never was interested in a news anchorship position, privately he is said to have been quite angered when passed over in favor of Walter Cronkite (q.v.). Some believe that Sevareid simply came across as too much of an intellectual.

In 1966 Sevareid again returned to the battlefield, this time to Vietnam. His commentaries were broadcast on ''The CBS Evening News'' and on special reports. He did a series of ''Vietnam Perspective'' telecasts. In the 1970s he conducted two interviews with Presidents Richard Nixon and Gerald Ford, participated in special broadcasts on events of the Watergate scandal, and covered the resignations of Vice President Spiro Agnew and Richard Nixon. Of course, he kept his regular schedule of some three to five two-minute commentaries each week. He did these news commentaries for fourteen years. Sevareid retired formally from his regular CBS position on 30 November 1977.

Since retirement Sevareid has pursued a variety of activities including commentary for Mobil Oil's sixteen-part ''Between the Wars,'' WGHB-Boston Public Television's ''Enterprise'' series, and the twenty-four-episode syndicated ''Eric Sevareid's Chronicle.'' He also has appeared in a few motion pictures.

Sevareid has won professional honors including three George Foster Peabody Awards (1950, 1964, and 1967), and two Emmys for his role in CBS News coverage of the Agnew resignation and a report, ''LBJ: The Man and the President.'' His lengthy list of awards includes the Alfred I. Dupont–Columbia University Award, two Overseas Press Club Awards, and the George Polk Memorial Award.

Sevareid has had three marriages, first to Lois Finger (married, 1935; divorced, 1962), then to Belen Marshall, a musician (married, 1963; divorced 1974), and finally to Suzanne St. Pierre (1979). He has twin sons by the first marriage, and a daughter by the second.

BIBLIOGRAPHY:

A. *Not So Wild a Dream* (New York, 1946; reprinted, 1976).

B. "Sevareid Goes Gently into that Good-bye," *Broadcasting*, 5 December 1977; *Congressional Record*, 1 December 1977, S38249–50; David Halberstam, *The Powers That Be* (New York, 1979); Barbara Matusow, *The Evening Stars* (New York, 1983).

RICHARD C. VINCENT

SHAW, ALBERT (b. 23 July 1857; d. 25 June 1947), editor and publisher of the *Review of Reviews*, achieved distinction in several fields. The recipient of a Ph.D. from Johns Hopkins in 1884, he gained recognition in the next decade as an authority on municipal betterment and lectured on this subject in several universities and before various civic improvement clubs. Thereafter, his interests in reform broadened to embrace other progressive causes such as conservation, education, and the regulation of big business. A well-known public figure, he was both a friend and an adviser to President Theodore Roosevelt, as well as a leader in the American Publishing industry for more than a generation.

The son of Griffin Shaw, a physician and merchant, and Susan Fisher Shaw, housewife, he was born and brought up in the crossroads village of Paddy's Run, later named Shandon, in Butler County in the southwestern corner of Ohio. Although Griffin Shaw died when Albert was only six, the family never lacked the comforts of life. Albert was reared with a respect for education, religion, and civic responsibility. Influenced by the example of his cousin Murat Halstead (q.v.), editor of the *Cincinnati Commercial*, and an older friend who operated a paper in nearby Oxford, Ohio, Shaw grew up aspiring to enter the profession of journalism.

With his mother and older sister Shaw moved to Grinnell, Iowa, in 1875 to attend Iowa College (now Grinnell College), where he developed a particular interest in the study of government and history, subjects he believed would fit him for the profession of journalism. Following Murat Halstead's advice that the best preparation for journalism was to write for a country paper, Shaw acquired a half-interest in the *Grinnell Herald*, a biweekly Republican paper, in 1879. Shaw did most of the writing for it and maintained his association with the paper until 1883, when he sold his share and returned to Johns Hopkins University (where he had previously spent a semester) as a full-time graduate student in history and political economy.

Shaw had the makings of a distinguished scholar and while he was at Johns Hopkins made such friends among the other graduate students as Woodrow Wilson and J. Franklin Jameson, later a prominent historian. But despite the lures of the academic world, Shaw joined the *Minneapolis Tribune* as chief editorial writer in 1884. With breaks for travel and further study abroad, Shaw continued with the *Tribune* until late 1890 when he left for New York to set up an American edition of William T. Stead's (q.v.) London publication, the *Review of Reviews*.

Stead hoped to use his new periodical as a vehicle to unite the English-speaking peoples, and later introduced an Australian edition as well. The *Review of Reviews* represented something new in journalism: a magazine which would appeal to the busy professional man by presenting in each issue an analysis of current events titled "The Progress of the World," a character sketch, a selection of political cartoons, and two additional sections, "Leading Articles in the Reviews," which summarized the best writings in periodical literature, and "The Reviews Reviewed," which surveyed the contents of the leading English, American, and European magazines.

Stead and Shaw underestimated the expenses of establishing the *Review* in the United States, and Shaw borrowed in order to keep the magazine going. By 1892 Shaw had acquired majority ownership of the American edition which, although initially similar to the English prototype in departmentalization, emerged with its own distinctive style reflecting Shaw's judicious, scholarly approach to public affairs. By the middle of the 1890s Shaw's *Review of Reviews* had become a success and waxed prosperous until 1909 with a monthly circulation that rose as high as 205,000 and a substantial advertising income. Shaw, writing the editorial section of some twenty pages, "The Progress of the World," made the magazine into an advocate of good government and a voice for progressive republicanism as well as American assertiveness in international affairs.

In 1893 he married Elizabeth "Bessie" Bacon of Reading, Pennsylvania. They had two sons. Two years after Bessie's death in 1931, Shaw married Virginia McCall.

Magazines have their own life cycles, and the heightened interest in international affairs created by World War I masked the fact that the *Review* had begun to show signs of slipping. By the 1920s difficulties had become manifest: advertising revenues declined, and Shaw broke with his partner Charles Lanier, who had acquired Stead's share upon the Englishman's death in 1912. The growing success of the weeklies, especially the new *Time*, made it apparent that Americans now wanted their news analyzed more often, and in a more sprightly style than the staid *Review* offered. Frequent experiments with the format of the *Review* failed to halt the decline.

At last, Albert Shaw, Jr., Shaw's elder son, who had been the *Review*'s business manager for several years, suggested that the only way to survive was to publish weekly. Since most of the younger editors agreed with this advice, the reluctant Shaw authorized the purchase of the now-ailing *Literary Digest* in 1937. The merged periodicals appeared as a weekly under the name the *Digest*, but the new arrangement lasted only a few months.

Shaw had lost a substantial amount of his personal fortune trying to keep his magazine afloat, and suffered reverses on the stock market as well. Infirm in health after a bout with pneumonia, he sold out to younger associates for a nominal sum, and they in turn sold their interests to *Time* shortly thereafter. In retirement, Shaw was to live another decade. Less than a month before his ninetieth birthday, he died in a New York City hospital and was interred in the family plot in Sleepy Hollow Cemetery in North Tarrytown, New York.

BIBLIOGRAPHY:

B. DAB Supp. 4, 738–739; NYT 26 June 1947; Lloyd J. Graybar, *Albert Shaw of the "Review of Reviews": An Intellectual Biography* (Lexington, Ky., 1974).

LLOYD J. GRAYBAR

SHIRER, WILLIAM LAWRENCE (b. 23 February 1904) established such a reputation reporting about Hitler's Third Reich that it is often overlooked that he also covered Gandhi's India and spent many years in the United States as a writer and lecturer. He worked for newspapers and wire services and was a pioneer in foreign coverage by American network radio.

Shirer was born and spent his childhood in Chicago. His father, Seward Smigh Shirer, was an attorney and politician who became assistant U.S. district attorney in Chicago. When he died in 1913, Shirer's mother, Bessie Josephine Tanner Shirer, took the boy to her hometown, Cedar Rapids, Iowa, where he spent his youth. He earned his degree from Coe College in Cedar Rapids and edited the *Cosmos*, the college weekly. From high school on he wrote features and edited sports for the local daily, the *Cedar Rapids Republican*.

Upon graduation from college in 1925 he worked his way to Europe on a cattle boat for a two-month visit, but also sought work. On what was to be his last night there he received a note from the editor of the Paris edition of the *Chicago Tribune* and wound up staying in Europe to work for that paper. For two years he helped write the Paris edition, which was full of frequently fictitious stories conjured up by such men as James Thurber. They invented full-blown stories based loosely on terse cable summaries. Shirer became acquainted with Ezra Pound, Ernest Hemingway (q.v.), Gertrude Stein, and other famous people of that era, and with the Paris they knew.

He also was able to report. He covered Charles Lindbergh's landing in 1927, work that won him a job with the real *Chicago Tribune*. He covered a number of sports events, including the 1928 winter and summer Olympics. He covered the League of Nations and Mussolini's early years. The *Tribune* twice sent Shirer to India to cover Mahatma Gandhi's resistance movement. Between the two trips, on 31 January 1931, he married Theresa Stiberitz, a Viennese painter. They had two daughters, Eileen Inga and Linda Elizabeth.

Colonel Robert McCormick (q.v.), owner of the *Tribune*, fired Shirer in 1932. Shirer and his wife spent a year in Spain, then he went to work for the Paris edition of the *New York Herald*. In the late summer he became chief correspondent in Berlin for the Universal News Service and began his years of covering the Third Reich from within Germany. When Universal News Service closed, he worked for International News Service. He called his years in Hitler's Germany "the nightmare years" and wrote that "most Germans joined joyously in this Nazi barbarism'' that eventually killed seven million Jews and seven million Slavs.

CBS hired Shirer in 1937. He covered the Anschluss and the Sudeten crisis for them in 1938. He was in Vienna when the Anschluss began but had to fly to London to use the cable. CBS news director Paul White (q.v.) instructed him to set up a news roundup from Europe that night to cover the crisis and its implications. That had never been done, and it required Shirer in a few hours to arrange for reporters and shortwave transmitters in several European cities and to instruct them to time their broadcasts by the clock because there was no feedback or cueing system. The broadcast worked and set the pattern for overseas coverage that continued through and beyond World War II.

Shirer covered the early part of World War II from the German side, despite increasing censorship. When he could no longer effectively get the story past the censors, he left Germany. During the 1930s and the beginning of the war, Shirer suffered a series of accidents, beginning with a skiing accident and ending with being bombed by the British, that blinded him in one eye. From 1942 to 1948 Shirer wrote a column for the *New York Herald-Tribune* and its syndicate. He was a news commentator as well. In 1945, after twenty years overseas, he turned down an offer to become the chief European correspondent for CBS and returned to the United States.

He signed a friend of the court brief for the Hollywood Ten and was therefore blacklisted for five years. During that time he earned his living mostly by lecturing on college campuses. Since then he has written works and contributed to periodicals from his home in Lenox, Massachusetts. His work has appeared in the *Nation*, *Harper's*, *Atlantic Monthly*, and the *Saturday Review of Literature*, among other magazines.

His principal work since he covered World War II and the Nuremberg trials has been writing the history of the Third Reich and his own multi-volume memoirs, a work in which he extensively researches and describes the world he lived in, concentrating on that more than on himself.

BIBLIOGRAPHY:

A. *Berlin Diary* (New York, 1941); *The Rise and Fall of the Third Reich* (New York, 1960); *Twentieth Century Journey* (New York, 1976, 1984).

DWIGHT JENSEN

SINCLAIR, UPTON BEALL, JR. (b. 20 September 1878; d. 25 November 1968), was one of the most productive writers of the twentieth century, having published as many as ninety novels and many other papers, pamphlets, and magazine articles. Although Sinclair is better known as a novelist, his work as a muckraker is highly regarded. A dedicated reformist, Sinclair was a member of the Socialist party for about thirty years and one of the first board members of the American Civil Liberties Union.

Sinclair was born in Baltimore as the only child of Upton Beall Sinclair and Priscilla Harden Sinclair. His father worked as a salesman, but was an alcoholic and the family was poor. Sinclair's childhood would leave a lasting impression on him. Sinclair entered school in 1888 at the age of ten when his family moved to New York City. He was a bright student, and in 1892 he entered the College of the City of New York. To support himself he would write for comic papers and adventure magazines such as *Argosy*. He graduated in 1897 and briefly attended Columbia University to study law but soon dropped out.

In 1900 Sinclair married Meta H. Fuller and they moved to Quebec, where he wrote and published his first novel *Springtime and Harvest* (later republished as *King Midas*). The following year Sinclair's wife gave birth to a son, David, his only child. In 1902 he joined the Socialist party, and in 1906 he ran, unsuccessfully, for Congress from New Jersey as a Socialist party candidate.

In 1904 Sinclair visited Chicago for seven weeks to research *The Jungle*. Although this was published as a novel in 1906, it first appeared in serialized form in *Appeal to Reason*, the newspaper of the Socialist party. In *The Jungle* Sinclair described the unsanitary conditions in which poor immigrants worked in the Chicago stockyards. This novel made Sinclair a national figure. He was invited to the White House by President Roosevelt and was instrumental in the passage of the Federal Meat Inspection Act.

Sinclair continued writing as he moved around the United States and Europe, living first in a cooperative community and then in a single-tax colony. In 1912, while in Europe, he divorced his wife, and a year later he married Mary Craig Kimbrough. In 1915 Sinclair settled in California but left the Socialist party because of its opposition to American involvement in World War I. After the war Sinclair joined the party again and ran, unsuccessfully, for the House of Representatives in 1920, and for the Senate in 1922, and for governor of California in 1926 and 1930. Meanwhile, he continued writing muckraking novels including *King Coal* (1917), about a strike at a Rockefeller-controlled Colorado mineral company; *Oil* (1927); and *Boston* (1928), about the Sacco-Vanzetti trial. In his career Sinclair wrote exposés of Henry Ford, the Roman Catholic church, and the press, and campaigned for various causes including clean meat, unionism, birth control, and the abolition of child labor.

In 1934 Sinclair again left the Socialist party and ran for governor of California as a Democrat. He narrowly lost the election, and many believed the *Los Angeles Times* was instrumental in his defeat because it continuously attacked him and his platform, "End Poverty in California" (EPIC). In addition to writing about his political experiences, Sinclair later wrote a series of eleven novels centered around a journalist Lanny Budd, which painted a picture of twentieth-century life in the Western world. One such novel, *Dragon's Teeth* (1942), dealing with the rise of Hitler, won the 1943 Pulitzer Prize for fiction, Sinclair's only major literary award. Nevertheless, Sinclair's writings were influential in the United States, and very popular in Europe. In 1961 Sinclair's second wife died and he married Mary Hard. She died in 1967. Sinclair published his last work, *The Autobiography of Upton Sinclair*, in 1962. He died in 1968 at a nursing home in New Jersey.

BIBLIOGRAPHY:
A. *The Brass Check* (Pasadena, California., 1920).
B. EAB, 1001–1002; NYT 26 November 1968; William A. Bloodworth, *Upton Sinclair* (Boston, 1977); Leon Harris, *Upton Sinclair: American Rebel* (New York, 1975); Jon A. Yoder, *Upton Sinclair* (New York, 1975).

THIMIOS ZAHAROPOULOS

SMALLEY, GEORGE WASHBURN (b. 2 June 1833; d. 4 April 1916) was a distinguished Civil War correspondent for Horace Greeley's (q.v.) *New York Tribune*, and after 1866 was a precedent-setting European correspondent for the *Tribune*, usually operating from London. From 1895 until 1906 he was American correspondent for the *London Times*, working from New York City and Washington, D.C. Smalley is often cited by American historians American for his work as a Civil War correspondent; those who focus upon European matters prefer to recall his brilliant work there.

He was born in Franklin, Massachusetts, the son of a Congregational minister, the Reverend Elam Smalley, and his wife, the former Louise Jane Washburn. He received the A.B. degree from Yale in 1853 but made his principal undergraduate mark as an athlete. After graduation, he read law for a year at Worcester in the office of George Frisbie Hoar (later a U.S. senator), studied law at Harvard, was admitted to the bar in 1856, and parcticed law in Boston until 1861. He became a close friend of Wendell Phillips, the abolitionist.

As the Civil War was beginning, Smalley applied for work with and was accepted by Horace Greeley's *New York Tribune*. He was assigned to the Beaufort–Port Royal section of South Carolina which had been occupied by Union forces. In time, he was moved to the command of General John C. Frémont in Virginia. Newspaper reporters attempting to cover the war in Virginia operated under difficulties, and Smalley seems to have gotten an appointment as an aide to General John Sedgwick with the rank of captain. Sometimes he wore a U.S. Army uniform and sometimes he did not. When finally, in September 1862, General Robert E. Lee invaded Maryland, Smalley's position as an aide and a captain helped him gain access to the field of action and to information. During the Battle of Antietam, Smalley was pushed into service as aide to General Joseph Hooker and thus got a better than average understanding of what was going on in that crucial engagement. His account of Antietam is often cited as the best single piece of reporting done during the Civil War.

In 1862 he married the adopted daughter of Wendell Phillips. Smalley and Phoebe Garnaut Smalley in time had five children, two boys and three girls. They spent most of the remainder of the war in New York City, where Smalley wrote editorials and occasional items for the *Tribune*.

Smalley's manners were haughty, his demeanor was aloof, and Greeley did not care for him. Even so, his talents were recognized. In 1866 the Atlantic cable was completed after Smalley was already in Europe reporting on the Austro-Prussian War. He obtained a long and exclusive interview with Bismarck, the

Prussian leader. European statesmen rarely gave interviews in 1866. The accomplishment was regarded as phenomenal.

During the next year, 1867, Smalley was set up in London as the representative of the *New York Tribune*. In time, he came to know everyone. In the 1860s and 1870s he tended to be a Radical Republican who was mildly anti-British; but slow changes were taking place, and by the 1880s he had become somewhat conservative and pro-British. He was mildly critical of the royal family but was a master at describing state ceremonials. He covered Great Britain's troubles in Ireland with avidity. The *Tribune* regarded its newspaper responsibilities seriously and took even more seriously the huge Irish-American population in its own backyard.

Smalley insisted upon an independence in his operations that irritated the management of the *Tribune* in New York. In 1895 Smalley was offered a position by the *London Times* as that newspaper's man in New York. He took it. In New York he occasionally wrote for the *Herald*, which the *Tribune* regarded as its principal rival in international news. After six years, Smalley moved his base of operations to Washington, D.C.

There was a serious break (though not a divorce) with his wife and with four of his children; and finally irritations mounted with the *London Times* to the point where a separation from it occurred. The terms were fairly generous to Smalley. For the remaining ten years of his life, he lived in England, writing books and an occasional newspaper article or letter to the editor. He died in England in 1916, having set standards for war reporting and international correspondence during much of his working life.

BIBLIOGRAPHY:

A. *London Letters and Some Others*, 2 vols. (London, 1890); *Anglo-American Memories* (London and New York, 1911).

B. DAB 17, 223–224; NYT 5 April 1916; Joseph J. Mathews, *George W. Smalley, Forty Years a Foreign Correspondent* (Chapel Hill, N.C., 1973).

HAROLD E. DAVIS

SMITH, HENRY JUSTIN (b. 19 June 1875; d. 9 February 1936) was for ten years managing editor of the *Chicago Daily News* and in that capacity was instrumental in making it one of the best written newspapers in the United States. His encouragement of the literary pursuits of his reporters, however, did not get in the way of his vigorous crusades against gangsters whom he refused to have depicted as heroic figures. Smith also wrote fiction and historical works generally dealing with journalism and/or his native Chicago. Although he spent the bulk of his professional life working on the *Daily News*, for a few months he was editor of the little Chicago magazine, *Four O'Clock*, and for a couple of years worked in public relations at the University of Chicago where he later also taught journalism.

Smith was born in Chicago. His father, Justin, was a Baptist minister. His mother was the former Mary L. Grose. Smith was educated at Chicago's Morgan Park Military Academy and in 1898 received his B.A. with high honors in classical studies from the University of Chicago. In 1899 Smith became a reporter for the *Daily News*, which was then the world's largest afternoon newspaper, but it was third nationally in circulation to Joseph Pulitzer's (q.v.) *New York World* and William Randolph Hearst's (q.v.) *New York Journal*. Within a few months, editors realized Smith's good sense of news and command of the language, and he was appointed a deskman working with other reporters' copy. In 1901 he became city editor, a post he held until 1906, when he was appointed assistant managing editor. In 1913 he became news editor.

Smith developed a reputation for his ability to organize and cultivate his staff—making reporters out of cubs and fine writers out of reporters. Ben Hecht (q.v.), one of his protégés, claimed Smith equated the daily newspaper to "a daily dime novel written by a score of Balzacs. . . . Its news stories were reports of life to him."

When the later literary giant Carl Sandburg (q.v.) was recommended in 1917 as "a good reporter you ought to hire," Smith claimed that the newspaper was overstaffed. However, after learning that Sandburg wrote "superb poetry," as Hecht put it, Smith could not resist taking a look at Sandburg, and hired him. Others who worked under Smith's supervision included John Gunther, Charles Vincent Starrett, Robert J. Casey, Lloyd Lewis, Paul Scott Mowrer (q.v.), Robert Hardy Andrews, Junius Wood, Sterling North, Keith Preston, and Harry Hansen.

Smith remained as news editor until 1924 except for one year when he went to Paris to coordinate the *Daily News* corps of foreign correspondents who gained wide attention for their work during World War I. In June 1924 he left the newspaper to lead a pioneering effort in public relations, which as part of a strategic development campaign eventually netted the University of Chicago $7.5 million.

In 1926 Smith returned to the *Daily News*, this time as managing editor. Smith survived three ownership changes in his ten years as managing editor. Smith had become a "Saint" in the eyes of Sandburg, who stayed at the *Daily News* until 1932, but more importantly he garnered the respect of press colleagues throughout the nation for his promotion of clean government. In 1931 the Chicago Foundation for Literature Prize for fiction was awarded to him. He died in 1936 of complications from pneumonia.

On 9 September 1899 he married Katherine A. Smith, a cousin. They had no children.

BIBLIOGRAPHY:

A. *It's the Way It's Written* (Chicago, 1921); *Deadlines* (Chicago, 1922).

B. DAB Supp. 2, 619–620; NYT 10 February 1936 *Chicago Daily News*, 10 February 1936; Robert J. Casey, *Such Interesting People* (New York, 1943); Chi-Ying (Jim) Chu, "Henry Justin Smith (1875–1936), Managing Editor of the *Chicago Daily News*," Ph.D.

diss., Southern Illinois Univ., 1970; Ben Hecht, *A Child of the Century* (New York, 1954).

ROBERT L. BAKER

SMITH, HOWARD KINGSBURY (b. 12 May 1914) may be one of the last of the traditional editorialist-commentators. Smith's range of interests has always been broad, but many observers agree that his approach is fundamentally conservative—and motivated by a strong sense of civic duty. Smith's career has spanned now nearly fifty years, and his career began in some of the most exciting days of radio journalism.

Born in Ferriday, Louisiana, to nightwatchman Howard K. and Minnie Cates Smith, his early years were lived in depression poverty. Apparently a motivated young man, Smith enrolled at Tulane University in New Orleans in the 1930s to study journalism and German, gaining experience also in sports and student government. He received his B.A. in 1936. Smith was a track star: his record for the 110-meter race was unbeaten until 1975.

Adventuresome like H. V. Kaltenborn and Upton Close (qq.v.), Smith worked his way to Germany as a freighter deckhand, spending what must have been luminous but nervous times touring the country. Returning, he worked for the *New Orleans Item-Tribune* and worked his way from rewrite straight into analytical pieces on the changes in Nazi Germany in a relatively short time.

Smith's athletic abilities and strong academic standing won him a Rhodes scholarship to Merton College of Oxford University in May 1937. There he distinguished himself both in studying economics and by becoming the first American student elected head of the Labour Club.

When World War II broke out in September 1939, Smith worked in London and Copenhagen before he moved on to Berlin the very first day of 1940. In 1941 he joined CBS radio's growing staff and broadcast regularly from Berlin until December 1941. Moving to neutral Switzerland, Smith racked up hours as correspondent for CBS, *Time* magazine, and *Life*, and completed the classic book, *Last Train from Berlin* (1942).

Smith was married in March 1942 to Benedicte Traberg. They have two children, Jack Prescott Smith, who for a time wrote for the Chicago ABC affiliate, and Catherine Hamilton Smith.

Working as the 9th Army war correspondent in France, Holland, and Germany, and aggressively recruited at this point, Smith elected to stay with CBS and Ed Murrow's (q.v.) crew in Europe. In fact, Smith remained in Europe even after Murrow left, reporting from his London base for the next eleven years. He won four consecutive Overseas Club awards and much critical acclaim for his reporting from abroad.

He wrote regularly for the *Nation* and produced yet another book, *The State of Europe*, in 1949. Its so-called progressivism got him listed in *Red Channels*.

Nonetheless, the professional kudos continued. Smith received the DuPont award in 1955 and Sigma Delta Chi recognition in 1957 for radio journalism.

He returned to the United States in 1957 to do commentary and analysis for CBS television and radio, and began what became a solid career as broadcast moderator by hosting "The Great Challenge," a series of sixty-minute broadcast symposia on contemporary public issues. In 1960 he won the George Polk Award for his broadcast documentary on the population explosion. Moderating "Face the Nation" followed. Smith is also well-known for moderating the famous televised Nixon-Kennedy debates. Smith was named CBS Washington bureau chief in March 1961.

But Smith's stay with CBS would not last. He resigned in October 1961 after battle with CBS over his editorial stances, and moved to ABC to produce a proposed half-hour news analysis program. Smith in fact got his sponsor—Nationwide Insurance—and ABC to agree in his contract not to interfere with his "independence." His efforts in "Howard K. Smith—News and Comment" appeared first on Wednesday, 14 February 1962, at 7:30 P.M., but was soon moved to 10:30 P.M. Sundays. The Radio-Television News Directors Association praised him for his work on this program, giving him the Paul White Memorial Award—the first working journalist to receive it.

But awards do not feed networks, and Smith ran into serious trouble with a broadcast outlining the career of Richard Nixon shortly after Nixon lost the 1962 California governor's race. Smith's interview with Alger Hiss scraped a few nerves. ABC received more than 80,000 angry letters and telegrams, and Kemper Insurance and Schick threatened to pull more than $1 million in network advertising. Despite critical and network support and praise, Nationwide Insurance withdrew its backing and ABC cancelled the show.

Staying with ABC, Smith produced news and commentary for the network and local WABC-TV. He produced another Overseas Press Club Award–winning piece of analysis on the Vietnam involvement for ABC's "Scope" in 1966. Generally labeled "hawkish" on Vietnam, Smith explained that his views were based on what he had seen in pre–World War II Germany. He blamed the American divisiveness, in fact, on what he perceived to be a left-wing bias among U.S. journalists covering the war, including Harrison Salisbury (q.v.) of the *New York Times*.

Smith was assigned the co-anchor position on the network evening news in 1969, sharing the spotlight with Harry Reasoner. In 1975 Smith chose to leave the anchor seat for full-time analysis. After some disagreements with the ABC multiple-anchor news format which he called a "Punch and Judy show," Smith resigned from ABC in 1979, stating that his analysis was being cut to such an extent from the broadcasts that his job had no real function anymore. A Washington, D.C., resident, Smith moderated the 1980 Carter-Reagan debates and is still listed by some sources as an ABC "commentator."

BIBLIOGRAPHY:

B. *Washington Post*, 11 August 1974; *Saturday Review*, 11 December 1976.

JONATHAN L. YODER

SMITH, MERRIMAN (b. 10 February 1913; d. 13 April 1970) was White House correspondent for United Press International from 1941 until his death in 1970. He covered six presidents, wrote five books about the presidency, and won the Pulitzer Prize in 1964 for his coverage of the assassination of President John F. Kennedy. Smith was also a lecturer and wrote a column, "Backstairs at the White House," twice a week.

He was born in Savannah, Georgia, to Albert Clinton Smith and Juliet Merriman Smith and graduated from Savannah High School. In high school he edited the school newspaper and was suspended for a week for an editorial in which he labeled the school a firetrap. He attended Oglethorpe University in 1931–32, dropping out to become a sports writer for the *Atlanta Georgia-American* in 1932–33; subsequently Smith wrote features for the *Atlanta Journal*'s Sunday magazine (1934–35) and served as managing editor of the *Athens Daily Times* (1935–36). He joined the United Press in 1936, covering the Georgia and Florida legislatures and writing features. In 1937 he married Eleanor Brill, with whom he had three children: Merriman Jr., Timothy, and Allison.

Smith moved to Washington, D.C., in 1940 with United Press and became White House correspondent for the wire service in 1941. During the next four years he traveled with President Franklin D. Roosevelt to wartime conferences abroad and was at Warm Springs, Georgia, when Roosevelt died. Smith won the National Headliners Award in 1946 for his story on Roosevelt's death. In 1946 Smith published his first book, *Thank you, Mr. President*, and followed it in 1948 with his second, *A President Is Many Men*.

Known as "Smitty," Smith was an aggressive, competitive, enthusiastic reporter who, in the words of a rival, was "there, always there." In the midst of a victory celebration at Hyannis Port in 1960, President-elect John F. Kennedy introduced Smith to Jackie by saying, "I want you to meet Merriman Smith. We inherited him with the White House" (Smith, 1972).

Smith was reputed to be the fastest reporter of his time, capable of handling any White House story quickly and accurately. Smith took pride in getting the story first, and getting it out, keenly aware of the wire service's constant deadlines. Once, after a news conference held by President Roosevelt, Smith fell and broke his shoulder while running to the phone. Ignoring the pain, he called his office and dictated his story.

As the senior wire service reporter, Smith was riding in the front seat of the White House press "pool" car when President Kennedy was shot. Smith's bulletin from Dallas was the first to reach the world. After making his call to UPI over the radio telephone in the car, Smith hunched over the phone, protecting it from the frantic reach of his archrival, the Associated Press White House correspondent, in the back seat. Later that fateful afternoon, Smith witnessed the swearing in of Lyndon B. Johnson onboard Air Force One.

In 1966 Smith was divorced and married his second wife, Gailey L. Johnson. They had a daughter, Gillean. In 1967 his son Merriman Jr., an army captain, was killed in Vietnam when the helicopter he was flying struck a power line. President Johnson attended the funeral services at Arlington National Cemetery.

In 1968 an exhausted Smith accompanied Presidential-elect Richard Nixon to Florida. While there, his health gave way, and a physician who examined him said he had never seen anyone so terribly fatigued. Smith, described as a lonely man despite his garrulous nature, had a drinking problem that had grown worse over the years. On the night of 13 April 1970, he committed suicide. During his next news conference, President Nixon requested a moment of silence in honor of Smith, who had become a White House institution, though a fiercely independent one, in his three decades as a chronicler of presidents.

BIBLIOGRAPHY:

A. *Merriman Smith's Book of Presidents: A White House Memoir* (New York, 1972).

B. NYT 14 April 1970; *Time*, 27 April 1970; *Washington Post*, 14 April 1970.

JOSEPH E. LOFTON

SMITH, SAMUEL HARRISON (b. 1772; d. 1 November 1845) played an important role as a journalist and as a reporter of the debates of Congress during the first decade of the nineteenth century. As an ardent Republican, Smith's *National Intelligencer* not only supported the Jefferson administration, but the newspaper became a valuable organ for preserving a record of congressional debates.

Before moving to Washington, D.C., in 1800, Smith had spent his entire life in Philadelphia where he was born in 1772. His father, Jonathan Smith, was a successful Philadelphia businessman who had been an ardent anti-British delegate to the Provincial Congress. His mother, Susannah Bayard, was the daughter of Samuel Bayard, scion of a prominent Maryland family. Little is known of Samuel's early education or training, but he received a B.A. degree from the University of Pennsylvania in 1787 and an M.A. in 1790. He received another master's degree from the College of New Jersey (now Princeton University) in 1797.

That same year Smith established a printing business in Philadelphia, and later printed the *American Universal Magazine*, a literary publication which survived for only two years. He then entered the lively competition of Philadelphia journalism in 1796 with the publication of a tabloid news sheet, the *New World*, which ceased publication a year later. Smith purchased the *Independent Gazetteer* in 1797 from Joseph Gales, Sr., one of the first reporters to regularly cover sessions of Congress and who had taught Smith the art of shorthand. Smith changed the name of the paper to the *Universal Gazette* and set a moderate partisan policy, supporting the cause of Thomas Jefferson.

As the 1800 presidential election approached, Smith was faced with two important decisions. One was his plan to marry his second cousin, Margaret Bayard; the other was to improve his prospect as a husband by establishing a newspaper in Washington where the financial prospects for printing and publishing looked better. He was married on 26 September in New Brunswick, New Jersey, and the couple left by carriage for Philadelphia, from where they took the stagecoach to Washington City.

After a delay in receiving his printing equipment from Philadelphia, Smith published his first issue of the *National Intelligencer* on 31 October 1800, with a declaration that "the conduct of public men and tendency of public measures" would be "freely examined." For the next decade, Smith was a faithful but far from servile supporter of the Jefferson administration. The Smiths' home became a rendezvous for visiting statesmen, authors, musicians, and journalists. The Smiths often dined with Jefferson and visited him at Monticello.

As important as Smith's support of Jefferson may have been, his greatest contribution as a journalist was his reporting of the proceedings of Congress. Not only were *Intelligencer* readers supplied with column after column of congressional debates, newspapers throughout the country found these reports their most complete source of Washington news. The financial success of the newspaper, however, was due more to the new publisher's success in gaining a sizable share of the government printing contracts than to the editorial content of his newspaper.

Jefferson's retirement after his second term and the toll of the arduous tasks involved in publishing the *Intelligencer*, for several years virtually single-handedly, led Smith to sell the paper in 1810. The buyer was Joseph Gales, Jr. (q.v.), son of the former publisher of the Philadelphia *Gazetteer* which Smith had bought in 1797. Gales, joined by his brother-in-law, W. W. Seaton (q.v.), continued the *Intelligencer* until after the Civil War.

In 1809 Smith had been named director of the Bank of Washington, and the following year he became president. In 1813 he was appointed by President Madison as the first commissioner of the revenue for the Treasury Department, and he served a short term as secretary of treasury. He became president of the Washington Branch of the Second United States Bank in 1828, where he served until the branch closed in 1836.

The friendship between the Smiths and Jefferson continued after both had retired, primarily through correspondence. Smith also helped to negotiate the purchase of the former president's personal library after the Library of Congress was destroyed by the British during the War of 1812. Mrs. Smith died on 7 June 1844, and her husband on 1 November 1845. He was buried in Rock Creek Cemetery in Washington. Their deaths received only slight notice in the *Intelligencer*.

BIBLIOGRAPHY:

B. DAB 9, 343–344; William E. Ames, *A History of the "National Intelligencer"* (Chapel Hill, N.C., 1972); Constance McLaughlin Green, *Washington: Village and Cap-*

ital, 1800–1878, vol. 1 (Princeton, N.J., 1962); Margaret Bayard Smith, *The First Forty Years of Washington Society*, ed. Gaillard Hunt (New York, 1906).

HARRY W. STONECIPHER

SMITH, WALTER "RED" WELLESLEY (b. 25 September 1905; d. 15 January 1982) was for three decades the most widely syndicated newspaper sports columnist in the world. On his receiving the Pulitzer Prize for Commentary in 1976, the Pulitzer jury reported: "In an area heavy with tradition and routine, Mr. Smith is unique in the erudition, the literary quality, the vitality, and the freshness of viewpoint he brings to his work and in the sustained quality of his columns."

Smith was the second of three children born to Walter Philip Smith and Ida Richardson Smith. His father operated a wholesale produce business, and Red—then called "Brick" because of his red hair—had a comfortable boyhood in his Green Bay, Wisconsin, home. After high school he worked at a hardware company for a year, then went to the University of Notre Dame, where he studied journalism. Never the athletic type, the slightly build, five-foot-seven Smith tried out for the track team coached by Knute Rockne, but placed last in the only mile race he ever entered.

After receiving his B.A. in 1927, he took a job as a general reporter for the *Milwaukee Sentinel*, moving on a year later to the *St. Louis Star* to work on the copydesk. While in St. Louis he met Catherine (Kay) Cody, and married her on 11 February 1933. At the *Star* he got his nickname "Red" (from an editor) and his first work as a sportswriter. After moving in 1936 to the *Philadelphia Record*, he became a bylined sports columnist. Writing seven columns a week, he began drawing recognition from the New York press. Stanley Woodward, *New York Herald Tribune* sports editor, wooed Smith to his staff in September 1945.

By that time Smith was forty-one, but did not yet have a national reputation. Once he got to New York, and his work was syndicated to over 100 newspapers, he quickly rose to prominence. His column "Views of Sport" appeared six times a week, until the *Herald Tribune* folded in 1966. Thereafter he worked briefly for the *World Journal Tribune* and, from 1967 to 1971, for the Publishers Newspaper Syndicate. He was without a newspaper home base during those years, but in 1971, at age sixty-six, he was hired by the *New York Times*, which syndicated his four-times-a-week "Sports of the Times" column to over 500 newspapers in more than thirty nations. Though he rarely used his column as a forum for controversial issues, he was one of the first sportswriters to speak out about baseball's color line, and he was the first columnist to call for an American boycott of the 1980 Moscow Summer Olympics as an appropriate response to what he called the Soviets' "bloody work" in Afghanistan.

His wife Kay died in 1967. She and Red had two children, Catherine Halloran and Terence (who, like his father, became a *New York Times* reporter). Red Smith married again, in 1968, to Phyllis Warner Weiss. Though in the last few years of his life he was in failing health after surgery for cancer of the colon, he continued writing his column until his death. He died of heart failure at Stamford Hospital on 15 January 1982, and the next day American newspapers coast to coast were filled with tributes by other sportswriters. Dave Anderson of the *New York Times* wrote: "Red Smith was, quite simply, the best sportswriter. Put the emphasis on writer. Of all those who have written sports for a living, nobody else ever had the command of the language, turn of the phrase, the subtlety of the skewer as he did."

Smith's columns were characterized by his light and often wry humor and by clear, wonderfully economic prose that was virtually free of the clichés, jargon, and inflated diction that mar much sportswriting. During the last three decades of Smith's career, his columns were frequently collected in books—seven of them in all. And he received numerous awards—the National Headliners Club Award (1945), the Grantland Rice Award (1956), the Red Smith Award given by the Associated Press Sports Editors (APSE) to honor meritorious service to the profession, and multiple awards from the American Newspaper Guild. Five times he was voted by his peers the nation's best sportswriter.

BIBLIOGRAPHY:

B. NYT 16 January 1982; Dennis Jackson, "Sportswriter Red Smith's 'Jousts with the Mother Tongue,' " *Style*, Fall 1982; Roger Kahn, "Red Smith of the Press Box," *Newsweek*, 21 April 1958; John L. Kern, "Red Smith in the Final Innings" (Interview), *Writer's Digest*, June 1982.

DENNIS JACKSON

SMITH, WILLIAM EUGENE (b. 30 December 1918; d. 15 October 1978) was a photojournalist, among the world's ten best in the heyday of photo essay magazines. He was renowned for extensive black-and-white photography of World War II combat troops under shellfire, and the effects of postwar industrial society. He published in *Life* and other mass-circulation magazines.

Smith, the second son of William H. and Nettie Lee Smith, was born in Wichita, Kansas. Smith's father was a successful grain dealer. Smith was educated in the Wichita schools and by the age of sixteen published his photographs of local sports events in the *Wichita Eagle*. After graduation in 1936 he attended the University of Notre Dame for one semester, then studied briefly at the New York Institute of Photography.

In New York Smith was at the center of the new wave of photo reporting. In September 1937 and not yet nineteen years old, he started his forty-year career by working part-time at *Newsweek*. His subjects included a New Yorker who bred silkworms in his attic—one of many assignments he came to regard as trivial. From 1938 to 1943, *Black Star*, a worldwide agency, helped him publish more than 370 picture stories or single photographs in dozens of U.S. and European magazines. From 1939 to 1942 he contracted to shoot two weeks a month for *Life*. In 170 assignments, 81 articles were published with his photographs. As his career was accelerating, he married Carmen Martinez in

1940. From 1940 to 1942 he also worked for the affiliated *Collier's*, *American Magazine*, and *Woman's Home Companion*, and from 1942 to 1943 shot for the new Sunday magazine supplement, *Parade*.

In 1943 Smith became a war correspondent for *Flying* magazine and in five months flew sixteen combat missions in the Pacific, making photographs with dramatic aerial angles and harsh contrasts. He switched over to *Life* and in June 1944 photographed the horror experienced by civilians in the Battle of Saipan. He abandoned artificial lighting, placement, and composition, and tried to draw the viewer to share the "emotional space" of an action. In Okinawa during his thirteenth campaign, on 22 May 1945, he stood up to photograph soldiers driving from a mortar barrage and was severely wounded. He underwent surgery, spent two years recuperating, writing, and, in 1946, exhibiting his war photography at the Camera Club of New York, where he was acclaimed as a genius.

Smith used the camera as an extension of his conscience. For *Life* from 1946 to 1954, he became a respected artist, with varied photo essays including "Country Doctor" (1948), "Spanish Village" (1950), "Nurse Midwife" (1951), and "A Man of Mercy" (1954) in which he depicted Nobel Prize–winner Albert Schweitzer at his African hospital. When *Life* declined to give him more control over the Schweitzer essay, he resigned and resumed free-lancing for the last twenty-three years of his career.

He spent two years creating a photo epic of the people of Pittsburgh. During these years his career stalled, and his emotional and family life suffered. In 1957 he moved into a New York studio loft, leaving his wife, his much-photographed daughter Juanita; his son, Patrick; and two other daughters.

Smith traveled widely and photographed such subjects as the postwar industrial landscape of Japan (1961–62) and the Hospital for Special Surgery in New York (1966–68). In 1969 Smith obtained a divorce and in 1971 married Aileen Mioko Sprague, a Japanese-American. From 1971 to 1975 they lived at Minamata, Japan, and published dozens of photographs and articles—and a book—describing the catastrophic effects of mercury poisoning on the people in a fishing village. By 1975 Smith received worldwide honors. The same year he and Aileen divorced.

Smith was a dramatic and intense man with a thick chest and powerful arms, a thin face and a thin mustache and, later, a bushy gray beard. The lisping impediment in his speech, the result of a war wound in the larynx, combined with his intensity to make him an unforgettable teacher. In 1976, after extensive lecturing and several awards—including the Robert Capa Medal from the Overseas Press Club—he settled at Tucson to teach at the University of Arizona and to organize his archives of at least 100,000 negatives he donated to the university's Center for Creative Photography. He suffered a stroke and died on 15 October 1978.

BIBLIOGRAPHY:

A. *W. Eugene Smith: His Photography and Notes* (New York, 1969); *W. Eugene Smith: Let Truth Be the Prejudice* (Tokyo, 1971); *Minamata* (New York, 1975).

B. NYT 16 October 1978; William S. Johnson, ed., *W. Eugene Smith: Master of the Photographic Essay* (New York, 1981).

LEONARD RAY TEEL

SMITH, WILLIAM HENRY (b. 1 December 1833; d. 27 July 1896), after being the general agent of the Western Associated Press for thirteen years, helped combine the Western and New York City APs, serving as the combination's general manager from 1883 to 1893. In addition to vastly enlarging and speeding up the news service of AP, then the nation's largest news agency, Smith conducted significant historical research and participated in Republican party politics, a confidant of several party leaders, including President Rutherford B. Hayes and editor-ambassador Whitelaw Reid (q.v.).

Born in Austerlitz, New York, Smith, the second youngest of five children of William DeForest Smith and Almira Gott Smith, moved during 1834–35 with his family to a frontier settlement in Union County, Ohio, thirty miles northwest of Columbus. Smith's father was a farmer and the country's first carriage and wagon maker. After attending Ohio public schools and Green Mount Seminary in Indiana, Smith became a schoolteacher and college tutor. In 1855 he married Emma Reynolds of Wayne County, Indiana; the couple had one daughter, Emma Almira, and one son, Delavan.

Moving to Cincinnati, Smith reported and edited for the *Type of the Times* after 1855 and joined the *Cincinnati Commercial* as Columbus correspondent in 1858. Moving to the *Cincinnati Gazette* early in 1859 as an editor writer, Smith actively supported Lincoln's war policy and the successful Ohio gubernatorial candidacy of John Brough, who named Smith his private secretary. In 1864 Smith was elected Ohio's secretary of state, and although reelected in 1866, he resigned in early 1868 before his term expired to help establish the *Cincinnati Chronicle*. While in state office Smith helped nominate Hayes for Ohio governor and established Ohio's historical society.

Smith became the general agent of the Western AP on 26 October 1869, moving his headquarters from Cleveland to Chicago in 1870. This regional AP, with about sixty member newspapers, most of them located in the old Northwest Territory, relied on the New York City AP for most of its Washington, D.C., eastern, and European news, forcing Smith to negotiate constantly and aggressively with the New Yorkers over rates, territories, and the quality of news service. While serving as AP agent, Smith was also collector of the port of Chicago from 1877 to 1881 in the Hayes administration.

Relations between the two APs were strained throughout the 1870s, abating only when Smith, in league with some Western AP leaders, *New York Tribune* publisher and longtime friend Whitelaw Reid, *New York World* owner Jay Gould, and *New York Evening Mail and Express* owner Cyrus W. Field forged a joint committee in November 1882 to govern both APs simultaneously. The committee named Smith general manager of the combined agencies on 10 January 1883.

To improve the speed, length, and accuracy of AP's news service, Smith introduced automatic telegraph repeaters, telegraph circuits leased from Western Union but controlled by AP, duplex telegraphy by which two news dispatches could occupy the same line simultaneously, and typewriters for recording incoming news dispatches in bureaus and newspaper offices. Meanwhile, the unprecedented growth of a competitor, United Press, after 1882 forced Smith and AP's leaders to arrange several cartel agreements quietly with UP for news exchanges and exclusive territories. Although such pacts and a subsequent UP stock-pooling arrangement involving AP leaders were accepted business practice in the late 1880s, younger midwestern AP editors exposed this collusion, reorganized AP, and forced Smith to retire on 31 July 1893.

As literary executor, Smith after retirement turned his full attention to writing a biography of President Hayes, along the way assembling a two-volume *Political History of Slavery*, posthumously published in 1903. His biography of Hayes was completed by son-in-law Charles Richard Williams in 1914, and his controlling interest in the *Indianapolis News*, acquired in 1892, was passed on to his son, Delavan. Smith died of pneumonia at his Lake Forest, Illinois, home, Mrs. Smith having died in May 1891 and their daughter having died in May 1895. In most circumstances he used his full name, "William Henry Smith," but he used "Paul Crayne" in some early Ohio news reporting, and "Housatonic" in some political essaying.

BIBLIOGRAPHY:

A. "The Press as a News Gatherer," *Century Magazine*, August 1891.

B. DAB 17, 364–365; NYT 28 July 1896; *New York Tribune*, 28 July 1896; F[rancis] C[olburn] Adams, *President Hayes' Professional Reformers: The Two Smiths, Tommie and William Henry, Men after Hayes' Own Heart, How He Rewarded Them* (Washington, D.C., 1880); Edgar Laughlin Gray, "The Career of William Henry Smith, Politician-Journalist," Ph.D. diss., Ohio State Univ. 1951.

RICHARD A. SCHWARZLOSE

STANTON, ELIZABETH CADY (b. 12 November 1815; d. 26 October 1902) was a crusader, leader, and spokesperson for a number of reforms affecting women, especially suffrage. She wrote for a number of general-distribution and reform papers; between 1868 and 1870 she edited *Revolution*, a militant woman suffrage paper published in New York.

Stanton was born in Johnstown, New York, on 12 November 1815, the day her father, attorney Daniel Cady, was elected to Congress; he later became a New York State Supreme Court judge. Her mother, Margaret Livingston Cady, was the daughter of a revolutionary war colonel. Elizabeth, the fourth of six children, dated her interest in scholarship to 1826 when, mourning the death of his only son, her father told her, "I wish you were a boy." Judge Cady apparently refused to believe that a daughter could bring as much pride as a son, but Elizabeth threw herself into studies, first at home, then at Johnstown Academy. In 1832 she graduated from Emma Willard's Troy Female Seminary, which turned her against sex-segregating schooling.

During annual pilgrimages to Peterboro, New York, home of her cousin, the well-respected reformer Gerrit Smith, Elizabeth heard discussions of the antislavery and temperance movements as well as of women's rights. There she also met Henry Brewster Stanton, an abolitionist who wrote for several reform, political, and religious journals. They were married in 1840, honeymooning in London where Henry was a delegate to the World's Anti-Slavery Convention. There, controversy over exclusion of women delegates and conversations with Lucretia Mott, a liberal Quaker who was one of those excluded, aroused in Elizabeth a determination to improve the status of women.

Upon returning to the United States, the Stantons lived first in Johnstown, where Henry studied law with Judge Cady, and then in Boston, where Elizabeth enjoyed meeting preeminent abolitionists and reformers. They finally settled in Seneca Falls, New York. Between 1842 and 1859 they had seven children.

In July 1848 Stanton and Mott, renewing their friendship, planned the first women's right convention, using abolition conventions as their model. At that surprisingly well attended July 1848 convention Stanton introduced a resolution calling for women's enfranchisement. Although many opposed this, including her husband and Mott, the resolution was adopted.

The interest (and contempt) which greeted that and subsequent women's conventions prompted Stanton to begin writing letters about women's rights for various newspapers, including Horace Greeley's (q.v.) *New York Tribune* (later Henry Stanton wrote for the *Tribune*). She also wrote for reform papers such as the *Lily*, a Seneca Falls paper (begun by Amelia Bloomer as a temperance paper and then, under Stanton's influence, switched to women's rights), and for *Una*, a suffrage paper published in Providence, Rhode Island, by Paulina Wright Davis.

In 1851 Stanton and Susan B. Anthony (q.v.) met at an antislavery convention, and the two quickly became friends, colleagues, and partners for reform. The cheerful Stanton was known for her abilities as orator and writer. The more severe Anthony supplied the facts and organizational abilities. Stanton agreed with the prevailing belief that "I forged the thunderbolts and she fired them."

With the financial backing of the eccentric George Francis Train, in January 1868 Anthony and Stanton launched *Revolution*. Anthony was publisher and Stanton was editor, along with, briefly, the abolitionist Parker Pillsbury. Stanton's radicalism was instantly apparent. The popular press called the sixteen-page weekly "spicy" if not "militant." Some of the reform editors criticized *Revolution*'s connection with Train, a Copperhead, but Stanton claimed that abolitionists' desertion of women had forced it.

Stanton's editorials addressed a number of themes which had long interested her, including woman suffrage (and simultaneous enfranchisement of women and blacks) and liberalized divorce laws. Stanton thought drunkenness was grounds for divorce. More importantly, Stanton described and prescribed a new sort of woman, a "strong-minded" woman who was physically fit, educated, independent, and assertive, even belligerent.

Stanton's redefinition of womanhood, her New York–based National Women's Suffrage Association, and *Revolution* were discomfiting to more conservative suffragists, who formed a competing organization with its own organ. By May 1879 *Revolution*, having attracted immense publicity but only 3,000 paid subscribers, was given over to Laura C. Bullard, who turned it into a genteel literary magazine. Disgusted, Stanton soon reneged on her promise to write for the new editor.

In 1869 Stanton had begun lecturing, and she continued to do so, most often on "Our Girls." She often wrote for newspapers and magazines such as *Arena*, *Forum*, and *Westminster Review*, as well as for suffrage papers such as the *Woman's Tribune*, edited by her close friend Clara Colby. She and Anthony were corresponding editors of the *National Citizen and Ballot Box*, edited in Syracuse by Matilda Josylin Gage. Stanton, Anthony, and Gage also coauthored the first three volumes of the *History of Woman Suffrage* (1881–86). Stanton also continued to lead the National Woman Suffrage Association; and after the 1890 merger of the two suffrage groups, she was the first president of the National American Woman Suffrage Association.

Stanton had long felt that religion was an obstacle to woman's progress, and that women should demand equal status in the church. In 1895 she published the *Woman's Bible*, written with a group of friends; a second volume was issued in 1898. This aroused protest not only from clergy but among suffragists as well; Anthony herself did not agree with Stanton on the significance of religion. Although her eyesight failed her in her last years, Stanton continued to promulgate her ideas on suffrage, divorce, and religion as well as on various issues of the day. She died in her sleep on 26 October 1902.

BIBLIOGRAPHY:

A. *Eighty Years and More* (New York, 1898; reprinted, 1971); *Elizabeth Cady Stanton as Revealed in Her Letters, Diary, and Reminiscences*, ed. Theodore Stanton and Harriot Stanton Blatch, 2 vols. (New York, 1922).

B. DAB 9, 521–523; NYT 27 October 1902; Alma Lutz, *Created Equal: A Biography of Elizabeth Cady Stanton* (New York, 1940).

LINDA STEINER

STANTON, FRANK (b. 20 March 1908), an American broadcast executive, is known for the leadership he provided CBS during his career spanning almost four decades. For twenty-five years he served as president of CBS, and then was named vice chairman. Stanton holds a Ph.D. in psychology from the Ohio State University. In conjunction with his doctoral research, he invented the first device to document radio listening behavior automatically. A proponent of broadcast journalism, Stanton was instrumental in bringing about the 1960 presidential debate, and is known for his continuing efforts to repeal Section 315 of the Federal Communications Act, which requires television networks to grant equal time to all political candidates.

He also helped CBS expand its operations by decentralizing its administration and creating autonomous divisions, through Broadway show investments, and via a controversial purchase of the New York Yankees, to name some.

Born in Muskegon, Michigan, he was the first of two sons of Frank Cooper Stanton and Helen Josephine Schmidt Stanton. The family moved to Dayton, Ohio, where his father was a public school teacher. After graduating from Steele High School in Dayton, he entered Ohio Wesleyan University and graduated with a bachelor's degree in zoology in 1930. He then enrolled at Ohio State University and completed a master's degree in psychology in 1932 and a Ph.D. in 1935. He taught in the psychology department while working on his doctorate.

While earning the doctorate, Stanton wrote CBS requesting information. Upon completing the thesis, "A Critique of Present Methods and a New Plan for Studying Radio Listening Behavior," he sent it to CBS. Network executive Paul Keston was impressed with this and previous research of Stanton's. The young teacher was invited to work at CBS during the summer of 1934, and he never returned to Columbus. By 1938 he was named director of research at CBS, and held two academic appointments in the New York City area (Princeton and Columbia). Stanton became associated with Dr. Paul F. Lazarsfeld, of Columbia University, and together they developed the Stanton-Lazarsfeld program analyzer, a small mechanical device for measuring audience reactions to radio programs, music, and movies.

Stanton was promoted to vice president and general manager of CBS in 1945, and when William S. Paley (q.v.) resigned the presidency for board chairmanship, the thirty-eight-year-old administrator was named president. In this post Stanton guided CBS through an era of diversification and expansion.

Stanton also is known for his stance on television coverage of national elections. Often he defended the CBS Vote Profile Analysis, which used survey samples to project election winners before all polls closed nationally. He offered that a uniform twenty-four-hour voting day should exist across the country. On other fronts he asked Congress and the Supreme Court to open proceedings to broadcasters and worked to facilitate international satellite exchange of television programs. He has been active in educational television issues too.

Stanton has served as chairman of the American Red Cross (1973–79), overseer at Harvard University (1978–84), chairman of the Carnegie Institute of Washington, chairman of the U.S. Advisory Commission on Information under Presidents Johnson and Nixon, director of the Lincoln Center Institute, member of the National Portrait Gallery Commission of the Smithsonian Institution, and was a member of the President's Committee on the Arts and the Humanities for Ronald Reagan, to name a few public positions. In business, he served as director of Atlantic Richfield, New York Life Insurance, Pan Am, American Electric Power, and the (London) Observer, Ltd. In 1986 he was director of the New Perspective Fund, Euro-Pacific Growth Fund, the Interpublic Group, Chem Lawn Corporation, and the International Herald Tribune (Paris). He is co-owner of Access Press.

In 1961 Frank Stanton received the George Foster Peabody Award for his efforts leading to the "Great Debates," and in 1972 was awarded a special Peabody for his defense of broadcast journalism and "the people's right to know," growing out of a House committee investigation of "The Selling of the Pentagon." In 1971 he received the Paul White Memorial Award of the Radio Television News Directors Association for his efforts on behalf of constitutional rights of broadcast journalists. Following his retirement in 1973, he held the position of president emeritus at CBS.

Stanton married his childhood sweetheart, Ruth Stevenson, on New Year's Eve, 1931, while still a graduate student. The marriage remained childless.

BIBLIOGRAPHY:

A. *Journalism by Slide Rule* (Chicago, 1959); *Mass Media and Mass Culture* (New York, 1962).

B. NYT 15 November 1964.

RICHARD C. VINCENT

STEAD, WILLIAM THOMAS (b. 5 July 1849; d. 15 April 1912), a prominent British editor, achieved renown as a crusading editor and special correspondent in the United States. A Radical in politics, Stead was an ardent advocate of Anglo-American amity, world peace, women's rights, social and political reform, and a rational understanding of psychic phenomena.

The son of a Congregationalist parson, Stead was born in northeast England. He was educated at home and for two years at the Silcoates School, which he left for employment as a clerk in Newcastle-on-Tyne. Appointed editor of the Darlington *Northern Echo* in 1871, Stead quickly made this provincial daily nationally known as the voice of the nonconformist conscience and Gladstonian liberalism in north England by his use of the paper to launch the Bulgarian "horrors" agitation and unrelenting criticism of Disraeli's Tory government (1874–80). Following the electoral victory of Gladstone and the Liberals in 1880, Stead was rewarded by Gladstone with the appointment as assistant editor of the *Pall Mall Gazette* in London. On the election of his chief, John Morley, to Parliament in 1883, Stead assumed the editorial direction of the *Pall Mall Gazette* and immediately transformed the daily into a crusading journal which advocated social reform, woman suffrage, the New Imperialism, and Irish home rule by what he described as the "New Journalism."

In part inspired by James Russell Lowell's poem "The Pious Editor's Creed," Stead's "New Journalism" involved the use of sensationalism to mobilize public opinion for his causes and of such journalistic "mutations" (borrowed and perfected from American journalism) as the signed special article, the personal interview, and the use of crossheads, pictorial illustrations, indexing, special "extra" editions, and the "character sketch" to make the news more attractive to the reader. In his practice of the "New Journalism," Stead waged crusades or agitations which compelled the government to act on such issues as slum housing, the modernization of the Royal Navy, and the abolition of juvenile prostitution and white slavery. Indeed, until he left the *Pall Mall Gazette* in early 1890 to found the monthly *Review of Reviews*, Stead made the *Gazette* a power to be reckoned with in Britain.

It was following his establishment of the *Review* that Stead became directly involved in American affairs. In late 1890 he formed a partnership with the American academic Dr. Albert Shaw (q.v.) to found the American counterpart of the *Review*. This was especially important to Stead, who viewed his *Review* as the voice of the English-speaking peoples of the world and a device to promote Anglo-American unity. Unfortunately, Stead's collaboration with Shaw was uneasy and fraught with misunderstandings and friction until Shaw, weary of Stead's enthusiasms, established firm personal control over the *American Review of Reviews*. Shaw was especially irritated when Stead came to Chicago in 1893, inspired a crusade against sin and corruption in the city, and published the sensational *If Christ Came to Chicago* (1894). Nevertheless, Stead returned to London convinced that the United States was the great power of the future. It was this conviction and the ideal of English-speaking unity which moved Stead to strongly advocate arbitration of Anglo-American differences during the Venezuelan crisis of 1895–96.

During the late 1890s, Stead accepted William Randolph Hearst's (q.v.) invitation to contribute as a special correspondent to Hearst newspapers. Beginning with the First Hague Conference (1899), Stead continued to write on various political events for the Hearst syndicate until his death on the *Titanic* on 15 April 1912. Stead's demise was much mourned by his many friends and associates in the United States.

BIBLIOGRAPHY:

B. DNB Supp. 1912–1921, 506–508; *Times* (London), 18 April 1912; Frederic Whyte, *Life of W. T. Stead*, 2 vols. (London, 1924).

JOSEPH O. BAYLEN

STEFFENS, JOSEPH LINCOLN (b. 6 April 1866; d. 9 August 1936) was one of the first, best-known, and most influential of the American muckrakers. He has been called the foremost journalist of the first decade of the twentieth century. He was the professional skeptic who set aside his skepticism when he visited the young Soviet Union and reported that he had seen the future and it worked.

Steffens was born in San Francisco, California, the son of Joseph Steffens and Elisabeth Louisa Symes Steffens. The family moved to Sacramento in 1870. Joseph Steffens became a successful banker, the kind of typical businessman muckrakers would later condemn.

Lincoln Steffens proved himself a poor pupil in the Sacramento schools and at a San Mateo military academy. He worked as an exercise boy and an apprentice jockey at racetracks. He took his Ph.B. from the University of California at Berkeley in 1889, then studied at the Universities of Berlin, Heidelberg, and

Leipzig and at the Sorbonne. In 1891, while in Europe, he married Josephine Bontecou. They had no children. She died in 1911.

In 1892 Steffens became a reporter for the *New York Evening Post*. He became known as one of the best reporters in the city. He covered Wall Street during the panic of 1893, covered the 1894 hearings on New York City police corruption, found "human nature posing in the nude," and eventually became the assistant city editor. In 1897 he moved to the *New York Commercial Advertiser* (at $25 a week) as city editor. He also wrote for *Chap-Book*, the *New York Post* Saturday supplement, and *Youth's Companion*.

In 1901, this time at a salary of $5,000 a year, Steffens became managing editor of *McClure's Magazine* and, under the leadership of S. S. McClure (q.v.), joined the reporters Ida Tarbell and Ray Stannard Baker (qq.v.) on what would quickly become the flagship magazine of muckraking. Theodore Roosevelt, who was for a time a friend of Steffens, coined that term, and their friendship faded. To the Roosevelt criticism that the muckraker could not take his eyes off the filth even in exchange for a heavenly crown, Steffens replied that the purpose of the muckraker was to let in light and air. Steffens's special concern became city politics, then state politics. Some of his articles were published as the book *The Shame of the Cities* (1904). Steffens followed those articles with a series on state government corruption. In 1906, Steffens became a vice president of the *American Magazine*, joining several other McClure's writers in purchasing that publication.

By 1908 Steffens had left the *American*, and was hired by the Good Government Association of Boston to propose solutions to city problems. In 1910 he joined the editorial board of *Everybody's Magazine*. He hired Walter Lippmann and John Reed (qq.v.), whom he had met at Harvard. In 1911 Steffens worked briefly as editor of the *New York Globe*.

Steffens and others concluded that muckraking led to no structural changes, as he had hoped it would, but simply showed how things worked. For that and other reasons, after 1912 the United States fell out of the spell of the muckrakers, but Steffens raked on. He became sympathetic with the Bolsheviks and lectured about them; he testified in behalf of people arrested for obstructing the draft in World War I. He was blacklisted by many editors and published without byline by others.

Through his protégés Lippmann and Reed, Steffens acquired contacts in the Wilson administration and in the Soviet Union. Steffens became a member of William Bullitt's mission to Moscow, and it was upon his return from that journey that he developed the theme, and the slogan, "I have seen the future, and it works." For most of the 1920s Steffens, no longer warmly welcome in the United States, lived in Europe. In 1919 he met Ella Winter, who was then twenty-one. In 1923 he began living with her, and when she got pregnant he married her, in 1924. Peter Steffens was born when Lincoln was fifty-seven years old.

Steffens brought his family to the United States in 1927 and settled with the artists colony in Carmel, California. He resumed a lecturing career, "served as sage for the . . . young and as mentor in their move to the left," and became "guru of the left" (Steffens, 1931). He was vigorously denounced by anticommunist groups.

In 1933 Steffens collapsed in Chicago of a stroke. He was bedridden the rest of his life, but he wrote a regular column for the *Pacific Weekly* and was visited by artists, radicals, Reds, and students. He died in 1936.

BIBLIOGRAPHY:

A. *The Autobiography of Lincoln Steffens* (New York, 1931).

B. NYT 10 August 1936; Justin Kaplan, *Lincoln Steffens* (New York, 1974).

DWIGHT JENSEN

STEICHEN, EDWARD JEAN (b. 27 March 1879; d. 25 March 1973) was for more than half a century one of the world's outstanding photographers. His artistic portraits of such notables as Auguste Rodin, George Bernard Shaw, Theodore Roosevelt, Greta Garbo, and Charlie Chaplin, among others, found their way into such magazines as *Everybody's*, *Life*, *Vanity Fair*, and *Vogue*. Steichen was also a painter and noted picture editor, who showed off the artistic possibilities of photographs for the Museum of Modern Art in New York. He was also one of the pioneers in the use of aerial photography for reconnaissance in World War I.

Steichen, the oldest of two children, was born in Luxembourg, but he and his parents immigrated to Hancock, Michigan, when he was three. Steichen's father, Jean Pierre Steichen, worked in the copper mines while his mother, Marie Kemp Steichen, was a millinery store keeper. In 1888 Steichen moved to Milwaukee and the Pio Nono College Preparatory School, where a drawing class endeared him to art. Six years later, he dropped out of school to become an apprentice with the American Lithographing Company of Milwaukee. In 1895 he shot his first photographs with a Kodak Box 50 camera, but he was disappointed when only one of the fifty frames was clear enough to print.

His misfortunes did not last long, however. Within four years, Steichen not only had mastered basic photographic skills, but he had also discovered through experimentation that he could create artistic images with his camera. Exhibits of these images in 1899 gained the attention of Alfred Stieglitz (q.v.), then America's master photographer, who paid Steichen for three of his prints. By 1905, Steichen, Stieglitz, and others founded the Photo-Secession in New York as a place to emphasize the concept of photography as art and to secede from the prevailing idea of it merely as a technical skill.

When World War I broke out, however, Steichen became more and more concerned about technical skill. During the second battle of the Marne, he was made chief of the American Army Air Corps's photographic section, and in that capacity he was responsible for all aerial photography. It was up to Steichen to be sure that the best lenses and exposures were in operation from planes traveling as fast as 100 miles per hour and 15,000 to 20,000 feet above enemy terrain.

With the war over, Steichen returned to his idea of photography as art, but he never lost sight of the importance of technical preparation. Just after the war, for instance, he spent a year taking more than 1,000 shots of a single cup and saucer to determine the effects of various lighting arrangements. This extreme attention to detail was one reason that by 1923 Steichen commanded a $35,000 annual salary to do portrait and fashion photography for *Vanity Fair* and *Vogue*. He stayed with the Condé Nast publications as chief photographer until 1938. He also frequently did promotional work for the J. Walter Thompson advertising agency.

During World War II, the sixty-two-year-old Steichen reentered the service as a navy officer in charge of all navy combat photography. While on active duty Steichen also prepared two wartime exhibitions for the Museum of Modern Art and was praised by the press for his artistic selection and arrangement of photographs. In 1947 he began a fifteen-year stint supervising photographic exhibitions for the Museum of Modern Art. His most celebrated "Family of Man," which traveled to sixty-nine countries, including the Soviet Union, was the result of looking through millions of photographs to find 503 which served "as a mirror of the essential oneness of mankind throughout the world." The museum honored him in 1964 by opening its Edward Steichen Photography Center.

In 1903 Steichen married Clara E. Smith. They had two daughters, Mary and Kate. After a divorce in 1921, Steichen married Dana Desboro Gloves, an actress, who died in 1957. In 1960 he married Joanna Taub.

Steichen was a popular man who became a guiding light to American photographers. In 1945, 1949, and 1963, he was honored with the U.S. Camera Achievement Award. Also a holder of six honorary degrees, in 1963 he was named to receive the Presidential Medal of Freedom, the nation's highest civilian honor. Steichen died on 25 March 1973 following a lengthy illness.

BIBLIOGRAPHY:

A. *The Family of Man* (New York, 1955); *A Life in Photography* (Garden City, N.Y., 1963); *Steichen: The Master Prints 1895–1914, The Symbolist Period* (New York, 1978).

B. NYT 26 March 1973; Christopher Phillips, *Steichen at War* (New York, 1981); Carl Sandburg, *Steichen the Photographer* (New York, 1929).

ROBERT L. BAKER

STEINBECK, JOHN ERNST, JR. (b. 27 February 1902; d. 20 December 1965), author of *The Grapes of Wrath* (1939), one of the most socially influential novels of the twentieth-century America, was a prolific journalist, essayist, and writer for theater and film.

He was born in Salinas, California, the son of John Ernst Steinbeck, an accountant who was treasurer of Monterey County for a time, and Olive Hamilton Steinbeck, a schoolteacher. Young Steinbeck and his three sisters were raised in middle-class comfort, but not affluence, and Steinbeck's youthful friendships were with all classes of people. He majored in English at Stanford University, but never graduated.

In his early years he worked in a variety of jobs—chemical tester at a sugar-beet factory, ranchhand, carpenter's helper. These experiences helped put him in sympathy with the impoverished fruit-pickers whom he later immortalized. In 1925 he worked for a few months as a reporter for the *New York American*. As he explained later, when sent out to interview a bereaved family for the Hearst (q.v.) paper he "invariably got emotionally involved and tried to kill the whole story to save the subject." After being fired, he tried newspaper free-lancing, but with little success. By 1926 he was back in California, working on his fiction. His first published novels had little success, but his lighthearted tale of life among the poor Chicanos of Monterey, *Tortilla Flat* (1935), captured the public imagination in the middle of the depression. His short novel, *Of Mice and Men* (1937), made him famous.

In 1936 he did a series for the *San Francisco News* called "The Harvest Gypsies," based on his study of the lives of the Okies, the new immigrants from the dust bowl. In this return to journalism he laid the basis for *The Grapes of Wrath*, his epic story of the sufferings of the Joad family and their friends. A best-seller, *The Grapes of Wrath* focused national attention on the problem of the migrant workers, and brought Steinbeck widespread praise as well as some vilification as a "Communist" (he was not). The book won the Pulitzer Prize, and Steinbeck was admitted to the National Institute of Arts and Letters.

After *The Grapes of Wrath*, Steinbeck was productive in a number of areas. He did a documentary film script on Mexican life, *The Forgotten Village*, that won an international first prize; he wrote a short novel based on the German occupation of Norway, *The Moon Is Down*, and a promotional book for the air force, *Bombs Away*. In 1943 he went to Europe as special correspondent for the *New York Herald Tribune*. In 1945 the popular *Cannery Row*, about poor people in Monterey, appeared. He went back to journalism again to produce *Russian Journal*, with photographer Robert Capa (q.v.), for *Life* magazine in 1948. His most notable postwar fiction was the novel *East of Eden* (1952), but his informal, personal investigation of America, *Travels With Charley* (1962), rivaled it in popularity. His novel *The Winter of Our Discontent* provided the occasion for the Nobel Prize committee to reward his labors in 1962, but the prize was more the recognition of earlier work than of recent.

In the 1950s Steinbeck produced many magazine articles, and in 1952 was a speech writer for Democratic presidential candidate Adlai Stevenson. He also wrote an attack on Senator Joseph McCarthy, "How to Tell the Good Guys from Bad Guys," that was often cited.

Steinbeck was married three times. His first marriage, to Carol Henning, ended in divorce in 1942. His second, to Gwendolyn Conger, produced his only children, Thom, born in 1944, and John IV, born in 1946. But in 1948 his second marriage also ended in divorce. In 1950 he married Elaine Scott, former wife of actor Zachary Scott. She was with him at his death in his New York City brownstone in 1968.

BIBLIOGRAPHY:

B. NYT 21 December 1968; Jackson J. Benson, *The True Adventures of John Steinbeck, Writer* (New York, 1984); Warren French, *John Steinbeck* (Boston, 1975).

EDWARD A. NICKERSON

STIEGLITZ, ALFRED (b. January 1864; d. 13 July 1946) although born in Hoboken, New Jersey, is remembered as a New Yorker. He studied engineering at the City College of New York and, in 1881, enrolled at the Polytechnic Institute in Berlin, Germany. He remained in Berlin, eventually studying at the University of Berlin and returning to America in 1890. His father, a German immigrant who prospered in the wool trade, provided his son not only with a prolonged education, but with a sense of independence and confidence in his own opinions.

While Stieglitz was in Germany, he not only studied photography but began entering exhibitions. In 1887 he won a first prize in London. He returned to America to pursue his photographic interests with unusual vigor. In 1893 he married his first wife, Emeline Obermeyer, and became editor of the *American Amateur Photographer*. In 1897 he began a five-year term as editor of *Camera Notes*, the publication of the Camera Club of New York. During this time his career took a decisive turn. He used the publication and his influence on the exhibitions of the club to develop and publicize his notion—radical at the time—that photography was an art form as serious and potentially profound as painting or sculpture.

In 1902 he was one of a group known as "Photo Secession" who began to explore the artistic potential of the new medium. Another magazine, *Camera Work*, appeared the next year and continued under his editorship until 1917. In 1905, with Edward Steichen (q.v.), he opened the Little Gallery of the Photo-Secession ("291") at 291 Fifth Avenue. In May 1917, shortly before the gallery closed, he opened the first solo—and unauthorized—exhibition of the work of Georgia O'Keeffe.

During this time he developed an approach to photography in which the vision of the artist was the principal component. He disdained darkroom effects, multiple exposures, retouching, or odd camera angles. He depended instead upon a sense of composition, patience in waiting until the right light or action occurred so that his vision could be realized on the film plate, and an imaginative use of focus and depth of field.

In 1923 he divorced his first wife; and the following year he married O'Keeffe. In 1925 he opened the Intimate Gallery, and so, in his sixties, he entered the most influential period of his career. His wife matured as an artist, eventually finding an audience that was not dependent on Stieglitz's help. It was a distant marriage as she pursued her work in the Southwest while he truculently remained true to the muse he found in the metropolis.

In 1929 he opened another gallery, An American Place, on the seventeenth floor of a Madison Avenue skyscraper, in which his work, O'Keeffe's, and that of others who shared his vision was displayed. It became the mecca for some photographers, and it remains so for those who share his attitude toward photography.

A good editor, Stieglitz wrote vigorous prose:

> In order to obtain pictures by means of the hand camera it is well to choose your subject, regardless of figures, and carefully study the lines and lighting. After having determined upon these watch the passing figures and await the moment in which everything is in balance; that is, satisfies your eye. This often means hours of patient waiting. Personally, I like my photographs straight, unmanipulated, devoid of all tricks; a print not looking like anything but a photograph, living through its own inherent qualities and revealing its own spirit.

His technique was profoundly ethical. His objection to tricks, distortion, and laboratory enhancement of photographs now provides the basis of ethical photojournalism. Although advertising may use photographs of marvelous complexity, our daily newspapers have an unspoken definition of ethical photojournalism: to be like Stieglitz. In one respect, however, his model is not emulated by many: Stieglitz never accepted money for a photograph.

BIBLIOGRAPHY:

B. Dorothy Norman, *Alfred Stieglitz, an American Seer* (New York, 1960).

ROBERT RUTHERFORD SMITH

STONE, ISIDOR FEINSTEIN "I.F." (b. 24 December 1907) was for nearly twenty years the editor of *I. F. Stone's Weekly* (for a time, *I. F. Stone's Bi-Weekly*), a small but influential gazette that allowed him to "annoy some of the people all of the time, and all of the people at one time or another."

Stone, who was a pariah to one generation and a folk hero to another, was born in Philadelphia, to Russian immigrants. His father was a merchant, and when Stone was young the family moved to Haddonfield, New Jersey. Stone began his journalism career at fourteen, as editor of the *Progress*, a weekly that folded after three issues when Stone was forced back to school. Stone worked for several local newspapers during high school, and could not stay out of newsrooms while a college student. He quit the University of Pennsylvania after three years to work on the *Camden Courier*.

He was an editorial writer on the *New York Post* in the 1930s, and was the *Nation*'s chief Washington correspondent in the early 1940s. By the last half of that decade, he had moved to *PM*, and stayed with that newspaper and its successors until the last surviving descendant of that experimental paper folded in 1952.

Politically, though Stone had once considered himself a communist anarchist, by the 1950s his views had changed a good bit. But the atmosphere in the early 1950s did not tolerate much in the way of unconventional politics, and Stone found himself (as described in a documentary film about his life) "unemployed and unemployable. He was forty-four, had a family of four, and almost no savings."

Of course, he decided to start a newspaper. *I. F. Stone's Weekly* appeared in 1953. It was a four-page newspaper devoted almost entirely to reporting of the federal government. Stone's reporting style was to read official documents. More than a decade earlier, he had discovered he was going deaf, and he got into the habit of reading transcripts of public hearings, rather than suffering through long sessions, straining to hear every word. He found that by reading transcripts he was able to find things that other reporters missed, simply because they could not sustain the level of concentration necessary to follow the discussion during a four-hour hearing. Stone had better luck flipping through transcripts, finding the gems that reporters in attendance missed.

Aside from that physical disadvantage (he later regained his hearing), Stone had a political disadvantage. Because of his politics, he was regarded by much of official Washington (and the press) as something akin to the Antichrist. He was excluded from some functions, and found himself working in a hostile atmosphere. He knew that what he published would be denied and doubted unless he had the authority of the official transcript behind his work.

During much of the life of his *Weekly*, Stone found himself shunned. He rented an office near the Capitol, but in the two years he worked there he rarely had a visitor. He closed it down and worked out of a room in his home. His wife, Esther Stone, was the *Weekly*'s circulation manager, and she did much of her work on the dining room table.

As the war in Vietnam dragged on, and the nation's attitude toward the war changed, Stone emerged as a hero and something of a prophet. Stone had been one of only a handful of journalists to openly question President Johnson's version of events at the Gulf of Tonkin in 1964. Stone read the wire reports carefully, examined official documents, dug a little deeper, asked a few more questions, and came out with a different version of events—one that would be proved correct by history. The Americans, he wrote, had provoked the attack (if it was an attack) after a secret campaign of bombing North Vietnam.

Stone folded the *Weekly* in 1971, having become the folk hero he predicted he would one day be, and having won the George Polk Award. He was not through with writing, and continued to contribute articles to the *New York Review of Books*.

I. F. Stone's Weekly, a brilliant documentary film by Jerry Bruck, Jr., chronicled the last years of the *Weekly*. The film was released in 1973, and continues to appear frequently on college campuses, introducing Stone to a new generation.

BIBLIOGRAPHY:

A. *The Haunted Fifties* (New York, 1963); *The I. F. Stone's Weekly Reader* (New York, 1973).

WILLIAM MCKEEN

STONE, LUCY (b. 13 August 1818; d. 18 October 1893) was a feminist, abolitionist, and suffragist who persistently and persuasively argued these three causes in lectures and in her weekly suffrage journal. The *Woman's Journal* was the longest-lived of all suffrage papers, lasting, with some name changes, from 1870 until 1931.

Stone's family was well established in Massachusetts, one ancestor having come in 1635 for religious liberty. Her paternal grandfather was a captain during the American Revolution. Lucy was the eighth of nine children born on the prosperous West Brookfield, Massachusetts, farm of her father, Francis Stone. Although her mother, Hannah Matthews Stone, accepted a husband's divine right to rule his family, Lucy, even as a child, resented preferences shown to males at home, at school, and in the local Congregational church.

At sixteen she began teaching, using her rather meager salary to study briefly at Quaboag Seminary and Wesleyan Academy; in 1839 she entered Mount Holyoake Female Seminary, also in Massachusetts. In 1843 she enrolled at Oberlin College in Ohio, where Greek and Hebrew studies confirmed her childhood suspicion that various biblical passages dictating women's inferiority had been misinterpreted. Despite the severe headaches which were always to plague her, she graduated with honors in 1847, the first Massachusetts woman to receive a college degree.

She was soon hired to lecture for the American Anti-Slavery Society on weekends; she worked for women's rights during the week. She was apparently a popular, courageous, and eloquent speaker. In 1850 she led in calling the first truly national women's rights convention, in Worcester. She presided over the seventh such convention in 1856.

While on a lecture tour Stone met Henry Blackwell, a Cincinnati merchant and abolitionist who first won Stone's respect by befriending a fugitive slave. Elizabeth and Emily Blackwell, the pioneering women physicians, were his sisters; and his brother Samuel later married Antoinette Brown, the first American woman ordained as minister, and an Oberlin friend of Lucy. When Lucy and Henry married on 1 May 1855, she kept her own name and publicly protested marriage laws.

Upset by minor accidents that befell her daughter Alice, born in 1857, while she was away lecturing, Stone basically retired from major political activity until after the Civil War. (A premature son died soon after birth in 1859.) In 1858, however, living in Orange, New Jersey, she let some of her household goods be sold for taxes, as a protest of taxation without representation.

In 1866 she helped organize the American Equal Rights Association, to promote Negro and woman suffrage; and later worked with several other state and regional suffrage organizations. In 1869 she moved to Boston, and with others, founded the American Woman Suffrage Association. This group was formed largely in (negative) reaction to the more radical freewheeling organization, based in New York, of Elizabeth Cady Stanton and Susan Anthony (qq.v.).

Horrified by Stanton's strong-minded organization and organ, the *Revolution*, Stone quickly raised $10,000 to establish the more respectable *Woman's Journal*. "Devoted to the interests of Woman, to her education, industrial, legal, political equality, and especially to her right of Suffrage,'' the paper maintained a reasonable, decorous, and mild tone. It avoided many of the controversies (such as free love and easy divorce) with which *Revolution* was linked.

Mary Livermore, editor of the Chicago-based *Agitator*, was the editor in chief for the first two years, with Stone and others on a large board of contributing editors. Stone did everything from write editorials to solicit advertisements. In 1872 Lucy Stone took over most editorial responsibilities, although she was not formally recognized as editor in chief until 1880. By then, daughter Alice had also joined the staff. (Later, Alice became editor; Henry Blackwell served in many editorial capacities as well.) The paper had considerable advertising and already in 1873, according to Blackwell, had 4,500 subscribers.

The *Journal* continued as the organ of the National American Woman Suffrage Association after the 1890 merger of the two factions, with Stone chairing the executive committee. Several smaller suffrage papers merged into the *Journal* over the years. It maintained its ''responsible'' tone, trying to address and attract both old reformers and recent converts, both committed feminists and curious ''club women.''

At age seventy-five, a few months after delivering lectures at the 1893 World Columbian Exposition, Lucy Stone died, in Dorchester, Massachusetts, of a stomach tumor. She was the first person to be cremated in New England.

BIBLIOGRAPHY:

B. DAB 9, 80–81; NAW 3, 387–390; NYT 19 October 1893; *Boston Evening Transcript*, 19 October 1893; Alice Stone Blackwell, *Lucy Stone; Pioneer of Woman's Rights* (Boston, 1930); Elinor Rice Hayes, *Morning Star, A Biography of Lucy Stone* (New York, 1961).

LINDA STEINER

STONE, MELVILLE ELIJAH (b. 22 August 1848; d. 15 February 1929) was the founder of the *Chicago Daily News* and one of the most prominent newspapermen of his era. For nearly thirty years he served as general manager of the Associated Press; under his direction that organization established the principles of cooperative news gathering as well as of news organizations' property rights in news.

Stone was the second of six sons born to Elijah Stone and Sophia Louisa Creighton. Elijah Stone was a New Yorker of English descent who had moved west while still a boy and met Sophia Creighton while the two were students at Knox College in Galesburg, Illinois. The senior Stone was a Methodist Episcopal minister who also manufactured tools for sawmills. Between 1854 and 1859 Elijah Stone's duties took the family to a series of Illinois towns—Chicago, Libertyville, De Kalb, Kaneville, Naperville, and back to Chicago. As a result the younger Stone's formal education was frequently interrupted.

In 1868 Melville Stone began work as a reporter for the *Chicago Republican*, assisting the well-known reporter Franc Wilkie in covering the Democratic party convention in New York City that summer. Later that year Stone struck out on his own to publish his first paper, *Sawyer and Mechanic*, designed to cash in on Chicago's thriving lumber and grain trade. (Stone's business card also noted that he was a dealer in "Saw and Flour Mills and Furnishings" as well.) When that paper soon died, Elijah Stone bought his son an interest in an iron foundry and machine shop, much of whose work was manufacturing folding iron chairs for Chicago's new theater houses.

After the Chicago fire destroyed Stone's foundry business in October 1871, he worked on the fire relief effort over the winter. Shortly thereafter Stone was invited to run Jonathan Young Scammon's newly acquired *Chicago Republican*, which soon changed its name to the *Inter-Ocean*. Stone became first the managing editor, then later the city editor and editorial writer. When the stress of that job became too great, Stone traveled south on vacation and wrote a series of articles on the progress of Reconstruction for his paper. In June 1873 he was offered the managing editorship of the *Chicago Mail*, a two-cent afternoon daily. Two months later the *Mail* and the *Chicago Evening Post* were consolidated to acquire the *Post*'s Associated Press franchise, and the new paper was named the *Post and Mail*. Stone was named managing editor; later he became the paper's Washington correspondent, and got himself added as well to the Washington staff of the *New York Herald*.

On 1 Januaray 1876, with the help of two partners, Stone returned to newspaper publishing, putting out the first issue of the *Chicago Daily News*. That one-cent afternoon daily soon gained a reputation for its political independence and innovative business practices. In June 1876 Victor Lawson (q.v.), who had attended high school with Stone, bought half of the paper, and Stone stayed on as editor. For nearly a half century afterwards, the two would collaborate, first at the *Daily News* and later at the Associated Press.

Under Stone and Lawson's direction, the *Daily News* instituted a number of progressive editorial and advertising policies. During the violent railroad strikes of 1877, Stone used reporters on horseback as well as telephone and telegraph to gather news of the disturbances. The *Daily News*, often at Stone's personal instigation, became known for its "detective journalism," in which *Daily News* reporters would collaborate with police to help solve crimes. Stone's *Daily News* also hired specialists to cover the news, supported progressive civil service reforms, opposed the political influence of saloon owners, and generally offered the paper's largely working-class audience a model of independent news journalism. In order to promote the circulation of pennies with which to buy his paper, Stone imported barrels of pennies that he distributed to local merchants who agreed to mark their goods at prices like ninety-nine cents. The success of the *Daily News* encouraged Stone and Lawson, in 1881, to issue the *Chicago Morning News*, a six-day paper that became the *Record* in 1893.

The success of the *Daily News* made Stone a prominent figure both in Chicago society and in national journalism circles. From 1877 to 1880 Stone served as a member of the Chicago Board of Education, and in 1884 he was one of the Mugwumps who supported Grover Cleveland. Two years later Stone, in his most noted act of detective journalism, helped write up the charges under which the Haymarket anarchists were arrested and convicted. Ever a shrewd businessman, Stone was one of four prominent publishers to purchase Ottmar Mergenthaler's patents for a Linotype machine in the 1880s; Stone became the group's first chairman of the board, though he later sold his interest to Lawson.

When Stone's health failed again in 1888, he sold his share of the *Daily News* to Lawson and spent the next two years traveling in Europe. Upon his return he invested in the newly organized Globe National Bank of Chicago, serving first as a vice president and later as president. During the 1890s he continued to be one of Chicago's most active and powerful citizens.

But Stone's national reputation would result more from his administration of the Associated Press. In 1893 he left his bank job to begin work as general manager of the newly organized Associated Press of Illinois, a cooperative group designed to thwart the attempts of some New York papers to monopolize national news. (While at the *Daily News* Stone had served as a member of the board of directors and executive committee of the old Assocoiated Press.) When in 1898 the supreme court of Illinois ruled that the new Associated Press was bound by its charter to furnish news to any papers that applied for it, Stone supervised still another reorganization in 1900, this time under New York State statutes. In 1918 the organization won its biggest victory of all, however. Under Stone's management the Associated Press fought a series of court battles that led to the U.S. Supreme Court decision *International News Service v. Associated Press*, which established the legal principle that news is a commercial property protected by copyright laws. Stone also gained fame for widening the AP's coverage of European affairs, and for taking an important personal role in the peace negotiations that ended the Russo-Japanese War of 1904–1905.

Stone married Martha McFarland on 25 November 1869. They had three children—two sons, Herbert Stuart and Melville E., Jr., and a daughter, Elizabeth Creighton Stone. Herbert, who founded Stone and Kimball, publishers of the famous literary *Chap Book*, was one of those who died when the *Lusitania* was sunk in 1915; his brother Melville Jr. died in 1917. To celebrate his twenty-fifth year as general manager, the Associated Press in 1918 presented him with a memorial book entitled *"M.E.S."* Stone died in 1929 of hardening of the arteries.

BIBLIOGRAPHY:

A. *Fifty Years a Journalist* (New York, 1968).

B. DAB 18, 81–83; NYT 16 February 1929; Oliver Gramling, *AP, the Story of News* (New York, 1940); Victor Rosewater, *History of Cooperative News-Gathering in the United States* (New York, 1930).

JOHN J. PAULY

STOREY, WILBUR FISK (b. 18 December 1819; d. 27 October 1884) was a talented and vitriolic Chicago newspaper publisher. As the leading newspaper spokesman for the Democratic party in the Midwest, Storey was responsible for the early success of both the *Detroit Free Press* and the *Chicago Times*. His flamboyant and sensational style won for the *Times* a large readership and for Storey a nationwide reputation as a brilliant, eccentric crank.

Raised on a farm near Salisbury, Vermont, Storey was the fourth of six children born to Jesse Storey and Elizabeth Pierce. He received little formal schooling and was largely self-educated. When he was ten his family moved to Middlebury, and in 1831 Storey was apprenticed to the *Middlebury Free Press* as a printer. In 1836 he left Middlebury and began work as a printer with the *New York Journal of Commerce*. There he apparently absorbed the anti-abolitionist views of David Hale (q.v.), the *Journal*'s editor, and acquired a sense of effective typographical design that he used later in his own newspapers.

In 1838 Storey moved to South Bend, Indiana, where an older sister lived, and began his career as a newspaper publisher. He put out two small Democratic weeklies, the *La Porte Herald* from 1838 to 1841, and the *Mishawaka Tocsin* from 1841 to 1842. Unable to make money on the *Tocsin*, Storey moved to Jackson, Michigan, where a second sister lived. There he studied law for two years, then founded another paper in 1844, the *Jackson Patriot*, to support the Senate candidacy of Democrat General Lewis Cass. When James Polk won, Storey was named Jackson's postmaster, a job he held till the Whigs won in 1848. At this time Storey also operated a combination drugstore (which sold alcohol) and bookshop. In 1849 he served for several months as an inspector of state prisons.

In January 1853 Storey left Jackson to buy a half interest in the *Detroit Free Press*, the official state organ of the Democratic party, and in July he became the sole owner. Within a year he made that struggling paper into a bright and influential success, improving its typography, establishing a Sunday edition, and creating its first city news department. As editor of the *Free Press*, Storey also became a vigorous spokesman for his party's principles. Though not a proponent of slavery, he was an unabashed white supremacist and believer in states' rights. Storey particularly despised abolitionists, for he thought that they were undermining social values and fomenting civil war.

In May 1861 Storey moved again, this time to Chicago to buy the *Daily Times* from inventor and manufacturer Cyrus McCormick. Storey hoped to make the *Times*, a small Democratic paper, into the advocate of a presidential campaign for Stephen Douglas in 1864. Douglas died just a month later, but during the war Storey nevertheless made his paper the chief midwestern opponent of the Lincoln administration. An opponent of secession, Storey wholeheartedly supported Lincoln's attempts to preserve the Union, but vehemently opposed any plan to emancipate Negroes or establish the abolitionist social program. Storey's inflammatory diatribes led General Ambrose Burnside to shut down the *Times* on 3 June 1863 for "repeated expressions of disloyal and incendiary statements." Public uproar over Burnside's imprudent action, however, forced the reopening of the paper on 5 June.

The rest of Storey's career would be marked by similar retaliations by his outraged victims. In 1870 the burlesque queen Lydia Thompson and four of her dancers horsewhipped Storey in the street for his unkind comments about them. Storey's unrelenting criticism of Chicago city councilmen in 1875 produced twenty-one libel and three criminal actions against him in that year alone.

Storey believed that the purpose of a newspaper was "to print the news, and raise hell," and he did both. Though widely known for his harsh polemics, Storey also promoted the new styles of news gathering and writing. The *Times* coverage of the Western armies during the war was outstanding. Storey also spent enormous amounts for telegraph news (over $100,000 in 1878), and generously supported a European bureau in 1877 to provide news during the Russo-Turkish War. He introduced sleek typography, heavy doses of crime news, and outrageous headlines to hold the *Times* largely working-class audience. (He memorialized the victim of one hanging as being "Jerked to Jesus!")

Storey remained the editor of the *Times* till his death in 1884, but his last years were filled with sadness and insanity. In 1847 he married Maria Parsons Isham, a minister's daughter, but he divorced her in 1867 to marry Harriet Dodge. When she died suddenly of pneumonia in 1873, Storey became disconsolate and turned to spiritualism. A year later he married Eureka Pearson as a matter of social and sexual convenience (their prenuptial agreement provided her a yearly stipend but denied her any claim on Storey's estate). Storey's promiscuity during his first marriage had left him with a severe case of syphilis, however. In the 1870s he began exhibiting the first symptoms of paretic dementia. In 1878 he suffered the first of three serious strokes, and in 1884 he died, crippled and insane.

BIBLIOGRAPHY:

B. DAB 18, 97–98; NYT 28 October 1884; Justin E. Walsh, *To Print the News and Raise Hell! A Biography of Wilbur F. Storey* (Chapel Hill, N.C., 1968); Franc B. Wilkie, *Personal Reminiscences of Thirty-Five Years of Journalism* (Chicago, 1891).

JOHN J. PAULY

STOWE, LELAND (b. 10 November 1899) is a journalist, newspaper correspondent, and author. Stowe's achievements became more interesting in light of the fact that in the fall of 1939 the *New York Herald Tribune* told him he was too old to be a war correspondent. He left the *Herald Tribune* and covered World War II for the *Chicago Daily News*. He made the transition from newspaper work to radio commentator in 1945 and also served as director of the news and information service of Radio Free Europe. He is the author of eight books, including *Nazi Means War* (1933), *No Other Road to Freedom* (1941), and *The Last Great Frontiersman: The Remarkable Adventures of Tom Lamb* (1982).

Leland Stowe was born in Southbury, Connecticut, the son of Frank Philip Stowe and Eva Sarah Noe Stowe. While working on his bachelor's degree at Wesleyan University, Stowe held his first newspaper job as campus correspondent for the Springfield, Massachusetts, *Republican*. He graduated from Wesleyan in 1921 and landed a reporting job on the *Worcester Telegram* covering the Swedish community in Worcester. From 1922 to 1926 he reported for the *New York Herald* and served as foreign editor for Pathé News. In 1924 he married Dr. Ruth F. Bernot. They were the parents of a son, Bruce, and an adopted son.

Stowe was obsessed with the idea of becoming a foreign correspondent. Arthur Draper, the new executive editor of the *Herald*, offered him a position in Paris. His competitive reportorial style paid off. He worked long hours in Paris, learned French, German, and Spanish, and began to report on the developments in Spain.

In 1929 he set the wheels toward a Pulitzer Prize in motion. Negotiations for how Germany was to pay its World War reparations lasted five months. Stowe and Ralph Barnes of the *Paris Herald* established a rapport with experts from each of the major Western powers and the Japanese. Stowe concentrated on the Japanese, who were most likely to leak key information. He was awarded a Pulitzer Prize in 1930 and was decorated with the French Legion of Honor in 1931.

Beginning in 1931 he covered important world events from London to Istanbul. He reported on the Pan-American conferences at Buenos Aires and Lima, and he covered Franco in Spain, where his sympathies were with the Loyalist forces.

In September 1939 the *Herald Tribune* refused the white-haired thirty-nine-year-old Stowe a foreign position because he was too old to be a war correspondent. An hour later he received a telegram offering him a foreign post with the *Chicago Daily News*, which, at the time, had the best foreign service of any American newspaper.

He was first assigned to the London bureau but was transferred to Finland when it was invaded by Russia in early December 1939. He sent back eloquent dispatches on the Russo-Finnish situation—often cited as reportorial masterpieces—although he seldom came very near the scene of events.

He was in Stockholm in the spring of 1940 when he decided to travel to Oslo instead of Riga. Everything was peaceful until the morning of 8 April when Nazi bombers roared over the Norwegian housetops. That afternoon about 1,500 Nazi conquerors marched through the streets of Oslo, and the forty-year-old seasoned war correspondent escaped to Stockholm to cable his scoop. He also covered the war in Eastern Europe and the Balkans.

He was sent to China in the summer of 1941. He discovered massive theft, graft, and smuggling of precious supplies over the Burma Road to Rangoon. Stowe filed a series of articles exposing Chiang's regime in the *Daily News*, but they were halted because of pressure from Washington and from China's ambassador. Stowe was barred from China and was reassigned to the Soviet Union. He became the first Western correspondent to spend time with active Russian combat forces, filing twenty-two exclusive dispatches datelined "With the Russian Army."

Stowe tried his hand at radio, too. He worked as a commentator for ABC and the Mutual network from 1944 to 1946. He served from 1949 to 1950 as foreign editor of the *Reporter*, an elite New York magazine. From 1955 to 1976 he was a roving staff writer for *Reader's Digest*, and began in 1956 a half-time teaching position at the University of Michigan.

In 1952 he married Romanian-born Theodora ''Dollika'' F. Calauz, whom he had met at an embassy party in Bucharest in 1940 on the eve of the pro-Nazi coup in Romania. Their romance was interrupted by Stowe's reassignment to Greece. He helped engineer her escape from Romania in 1946 and married her in New York.

BIBLIOGRAPHY:

B. *Who's Who in America, 1984* (Chicago, 1984); ''The Extraordinary Career of Leland Stowe,'' *Ann Arbor Observer*, January 1985.

CHRISTINE M. MILLER

STROUT, RICHARD LEE (b. 14 March 1898) is one of those rare reporters who become idolized by their colleagues during their lifetime. He covered Washington for sixty years for the *Christian Science Monitor*, and for forty of those years he wrote the respected TRB column for the *New Republic*. The column was syndicated to about sixty newspapers. Strout is regarded by other journalists as one of the best minds in American journalism.

Strout was born in Cohoes, New York, and grew up in Brooklyn. His father, George Morris Strout, taught at Erasmus Hall High School, which young Strout attended. His mother was Mary Susan Lang Strout. Richard studied two years at Dartmouth College, then entered the U.S. Army as a second lieutenant in the infantry. After the war, Strout entered Harvard, worked on the *Crimson* and the *Harvard Advocate*, and earned his B.A. degree.

He went to England with a letter from one of his Harvard professors, Harold Laski, introducing him to editor C. P. Scott of the *Manchester Guardian*. Scott got Strout a job in England as a reporter on the *Sheffield Independent*. After two years in England, including some writing for the *Guardian*, Strout returned to the United States, worked briefly for the *Boston Post*, then began his long career with the *Monitor*.

He worked as a reporter and copy editor and studied at Harvard, earning his M.A. In 1925 he went to the *Monitor* bureau in Washington. Occasionally he left the capital on assignments; one of them was covering the D-day invasion in 1944. In 1943 he began writing the TRB column which had run in the *New Republic* since 1923. (TRB is a pseudonym. One story—Strout's favorite on the topic—is that editor Bruce Bliven used those initials when the column started because he was riding the subway and used the initials for Brooklyn Rapid Transit, but reversed them. A problem with the story is that there was and is no Brooklyn Rapid Transit.) Strout stopped writing the column forty years and one month later, in April 1983, but continued to write for the *Monitor*—even though he temporarily lost his press gallery card in 1975 because the governing committee of the gallery forbade members to accept any fees from public or private promotional organizations. Strout earned small amounts ($240 in 1973) as a commentator for the Voice of America, a public promotional agency.

Strout covered—and knew personally—every president from Harding to Reagan. He covered the Teapot Dome and the Watergate scandals. He was at the White House on the day Calvin Coolidge handed out slips of paper saying he did not choose to run for president in 1928. He covered Harry Truman's 1948 whistle-stop tour and Nikita Khrushchev's 1959 tour of the United States.

Strout did not accept happily all he saw transpire. In 1954 he attacked the idea of allowing television into presidential press conferences, saying it turned a useful contrivance into a public performance. In later years he criticized the workings of the government, arguing that a parliamentary system would serve the nation better.

Strout married Edith Rittenhouse Mayne in 1924. She died in 1932. The couple had three children: Alan, Phyllis, and Nancy. Strout married Ernestine Wilke on 4 September 1939. They have two daughters, Elizabeth and Mary.

BIBLIOGRAPHY:

A. *TRB: Views and Perspectives on the Presidency* (New York, 1979).

B. *NYT Book Review*, 21 October 1979.

DWIGHT JENSEN

SULLIVAN, EDWARD "ED" VINCENT (b. 28 September 1902; d. 13 October 1974) was a newspaper journalist and columnist, and master of ceremonies for a television variety show that became an essential part of each Sunday evening's viewing for millions. He is most noted for his twice-weekly *New York Daily News* syndicated column "Little Old New York" (1932–74) and his CBS programs "Toast of the Town" (1948–55) and "The Ed Sullivan Show" (1955–71), in which he introduced more performers to prime-time television than anyone else in show business.

Sullivan was one of seven children born to Peter Arthur Sullivan and Elizabeth Smith in East Harlem, New York. His father was a customs inspector. After the death of his twin brother Daniel and his sister Elizabeth, the family moved to Port Chester, a suburb of New York. Sullivan received his secondary education at Port Chester High School, where he was an outstanding athlete. After graduation, Sullivan became sports editor of the *Port Chester Daily Item* (1918–19) for the weekly salary of ten dollars. In 1920 he started a series of jobs as a sports reporter for the New York dailies: the *Evening Mail*, the *World*, and the *Morning Telegraph*. In 1927 he became a sports editor for the *New York Evening Graphic*. After almost twelve years of writing for the back pages, he became the Broadway columnist for the *Graphic* in 1929, a job that put him in contact with important show business personalities. When the *Graphic* stopped publishing in 1932, Sullivan moved to the *New York Daily News*, where he began his famous syndicated column, "Little Old New York."

It was during his work with the New York dailies that Sullivan met Sylvia Weinstein. They were marrried 28 April 1930. They had one daughter, Elizabeth. In the 1930s Sullivan branched out into radio, vaudeville, and film. On 29 March 1932 his ''Broadway's Greatest Thrills'' radio show premiered over CBS station WABC (later WCBS) in New York. The show business contacts Sullivan made for his *Daily News* column made it easy for him to attract performers. Sullivan introduced many of radio's most famous stars to the medium, including Jack Benny, Irving Berlin, and Jimmy Durante. During the 1930s, Sullivan's ''Dawn Patrol'' stage troup played nationwide and starred leading vaudeville performers. He also wrote several films, including *Big Town Czar* (1939).

During World War II, Sullivan staged numerous fund-raisers, and he also produced shows for wounded servicemen in New York. Following the war, Sullivan's work hosting the 1947 televised ''Harvest Moon Ball'' dance competition for the *Daily News* impressed Worthington Miner, then manager of programs development at CBS. A meeting between Miner and Sullivan was arranged. The result was the ''Toast of the Town'' television variety show that premiered Sunday, 20 June 1948, on CBS. The name was changed to ''The Ed Sullivan Show'' in 1955, and it continued to run until 1971, fifty-two weeks each year with only occasional preemptions.

Sullivan was an unlikely TV master of ceremonies. He seemed awkward and serious on camera, and he earned the nickname ''Great Stone Face.'' Audiences loved him, however, and he was an exceptional showman. His contacts from his years as a Broadway columnist, sports enthusiast, and radio show personality made him aware of how to spot and spotlight talent effectively. Sullivan said he succeeded because he ''surrounded himself with terrific acts.''

Sullivan received numerous awards and honors for his charitable and television work. ''The Ed Sullivan Show'' received the prestigious Peabody Award in 1956, 1959, and 1967. The Academy of Television Arts and Sciences honored Sullivan with its Trustees Award in 1971 for ''pioneering in the variety format which has become a backbone of television programming'' and ''for having the foresight and courage to provide national exposure for minority performers.'' CBS renamed its Broadway and 53rd Street studios the Ed Sullivan Theater in 1967.

Sullivan died in New York of cancer. His wife died on 16 March 1973.

BIBLIOGRAPHY:

B. NYT 14 October 1974; Jerry G. Bowles, *A Thousand Sundays: The Story of the Ed Sullivan Show* (New York, 1980).

JOHN P. FREEMAN

SWING, RAYMOND GRAM (b. 25 March 1887; d. 20 December 1968) was one of the most widely known (and, for a time at least, perhaps the highest-paid) radio news commentators of the 1930s and 1940s. Fred W. Friendly (q.v.) called him the Walter Lippmann (q.v.) of broadcasting.

He was born Raymond Swing in Cortland, New York. He was the son of the Reverend Alfred Temple Swing and Alice Mead Swing. He spent part of his childhood in Germany, where his father was a theology student. Oberlin College suspended him at the end of his freshman year, but effectively reversed that decision in 1940 when it awarded him an honorary doctor of laws degree.

Swing landed a reporting job with the *Cleveland Press*, was fired because he wanted a raise, and became a court reporter for the *Cleveland News*. Then he edited the weekly *Courier* in Orville, Ohio, and moved from there to Indiana—the staff of the *Richmond Item*, and managing editor (at the age of twenty-three) of the *Indianapolis Sun* (1910). Then back to Ohio in 1911 to the *Cincinnati Times Star*.

A wealthy relative financed a trip to Europe for Swing and his first wife, Suzanne Morin of France, whom he met and married in the United States. They went to Europe in 1912, and he became foreign correspondent for the *Chicago Daily News*, headquartered in Berlin. He covered the war from Germany, once hiring a student to memorize an 800-word story and type it out after his arrival in London—the only way Swing had to get the story past the German censors. He also reported from the Turkish front and from France, and on occasion engaged in diplomatic ventures extracurricular to his reporting activities. Because he perceived a conflict between such activities and his job, he resigned from the *Daily News*. After the war he worked briefly for the *Nation*, then returned to Berlin as correspondent for the *New York Herald*. He moved to London and the *Wall Street Journal*, then became head of the London bureau of the *Philadelphia Public Ledger*. He remained with that paper ten years. He also wrote two plays, composed some music, and became interested in radio. He began his broadcasting career in 1930 with the BBC and did some reporting from Europe for NBC.

In 1934 the *Public Ledger* closed its foreign service and Swing went home. He rejoined the *Nation*, wrote his first book, and became the American correspondent for, in succession, the *London News Chronicle* and the *Economist*. When President Roosevelt proposed an exchange of broadcasts between American radio and the BBC, Swing was selected (by the BBC) as the American broadcaster. He built up a large following in Britain; later, his voice became known worldwide.

In 1936 Mutual hired Swing as a commentator. His broadcasts became popular and more frequent, and his salary increased to $87,000 a year. In 1942 he moved to NBC's Blue network, and by 1944 he was on 120 stations and making $160,000. He reduced his work schedule after 1948 because of poor health. He worked sporadically for a time, with WOR in New York and the Liberty Network in New England. In 1951 he became the first political commentator for the Voice of America. After two years of that, he joined Edward Murrow's (q.v.) personal staff writing commentaries. He edited the CBS series "This I Believe." In 1959 he returned to the Voice of America. He retired at the end of 1963, but a heart attack had already curtailed his work.

Swing's first marriage broke up during World War I. After that war he married Betty Gram, a feminist who refused to change her name. Swing took her name as his middle name. When that marriage also ended in divorce, he intended to drop the middle name, but it had become part of his everyday identification to millions of listeners. By his first wife Swing had two children, Albert George and Elizabeth Francoise. His second marriage produced three children: Peter Gram, Sally Gram, and John Temple. He was married a third time, to Meisung Loh. They had no children. Swing died of a heart attack at the age of eighty-one.

BIBLIOGRAPHY:

A. *"Good Evening!" A Professional Memoir* (New York, 1964).

B. NYT 24 December 1968.

LAURA NICKERSON

SWISSHELM, JANE (b. 6 December 1815; d. 22 July 1884) was an abolitionist editor, one of the first female journalists to write for Horace Greeley's (q.v.) *New York Tribune*, the first woman to sit in the Senate press gallery in Washington, an enemy of alcoholism, a nurse in Civil War hospitals, a fiercely anti-Indian crusader, and a feared and respected lecturer on women's rights, abolition, and temperance.

She was born Jane Grey Cannon in the then frontier town of Pittsburgh, Pennsylvania. Left fatherless at a early age, she learned lace-making, and subsequently taught the art. At age fourteen she became a public school teacher in Wilkinsburg, a small town just outside of Pittsburgh.

In 1836 she married James Swisshelm and, in 1838, moved with him to Louisville, Kentucky, where she saw slavery firsthand and became committed to abolitionism. Though she avoided public statements as unseemly for women, she recognized the power of the press and, despite the stigma attached, launched a career which for over three decades used the press to further every cause she believed in, from abolition to women's rights. In 1842, when she was twenty-seven, she submitted stories and rhymes to the *Dollar Newspaper* and *Neal's Saturday Gazette*, both of Philadelphia. Under the pen name Jennie Deans she also wrote on abolition and women's rights for Pittsburgh's *Spirit of Liberty*.

Her own byline first appeared in 1844, over an antislavery piece in the *Spirit of Liberty*. When that paper was discontinued, she wrote for the *Pittsburgh Commercial Journal*. In January 1848 she introduced an abolitionist weekly, the *Pittsburgh Saturday Visiter*. It condemned slave catchers and the Fugitive Slave Law, using prose as well as poetry. It also crusaded for women's rights, but Swisshelm urged that activists not make unreasonable demands, or expect change too quickly. She urged better sense in women's fashions, and wrote regular columns later reprinted in book form, on reading, diet, makeup, gardening apparel, cooking, laundering, dress, and other topics.

In 1850 she also requested and received a seat in the Senate press gallery, while she was in Washington in late April 1850, to cover the vote on slavery for the Mexican Territory. She was representing the *Visiter* and Horace Greeley's *New York Tribune*. A *Tribune* column she wrote rumored that Daniel Webster had fathered a family of mulattoes, and led her to resign her press gallery seat. It was antislavery copy, preceding the presidential nominations, and she retracted the story two weeks later, but only after it had done its part in helping thwart Webster's 1852 Whig nomination.

In 1852, finances caused a merger of the *Visiter* with the *Family Journal and Visiter*, and Swisshelm became associate editor, continuing her crusade for abolition and for women's rights, especially their property rights. She found support from a young attorney, Edwin M. Stanton, who admired her writing and told her so. Much later, as secretary of war, he was to come to her aid in Washington.

Growing unhappiness in her marriage led her, in 1857, to resign from the *Visiter* and to leave her husband. With her daughter, Mary Henrietta, she moved to Minnesota and soon reestablished the *Visiter* in St. Cloud in 1858. Opposition by pro-slavery factions led to vigilante-style action, the wrecking of the *Visiter* press, and loss of the type, thrown into the river. The paper was reestablished as the *St. Cloud Democrat*.

Slavery, the rights of wives and widows, railroad development, and anti-Indian crusades made the *Democrat* a lively paper. On a trip to Washington, D.C., she visited wounded Union troops and wrote about their poor conditions. The welfare of the soldiers became a major issue for her, and she filed copy for Greeley's *Tribune* and her *Democrat*, urging public contributions to the war hospitals but also criticizing them as louse-ridden, poorly run, and ill-equipped.

She also briefly held a clerical job in Washington with the War Department after selling the *Democrat* to a nephew in 1863. She continued to write for the paper, fighting traditional constraints and what she saw as unfair practices throughout her career. For example, unable to afford printer union wages, she had learned and trained female assistants as typesetters. From 1858 to early 1863 she had been both editor and practical printer, issuing a weekly paper, doing a large amount of job work, acting as city and county printer for half a dozen counties, and publishing legal notices, tax lists, and extras.

After the war, she edited the short-lived *Reconstructionist*, which first appeared in Washington in December 1865. Her strong criticism of President Andrew Johnson, however, cost her her War Department job and with it her income. The *Reconstructionist* folded, too, and she returned to her Swissvale, Pennsylvania, home, claiming ill health and fatigue. She continued writing, usually for the *New York Independent* and especially when her interests surfaced in the common debate. In 1880 appeared her recollections and reminiscences, *Half a Century*, reflecting on her career as a crusader and an innovator.

BIBLIOGRAPHY:

B. NYT 23 July 1884; Kathleen Endres, "Jane Grey Swisshelm, 19th Century Journalist and Feminist." *Journalism History*, Winter 1975–76.

SHARON MURPHY

SWOPE, HERBERT BAYARD (b. 5 January 1882; d. 20 June 1958) was once referred to as "The *World*'s greatest reporter—*New York World* or the whole wide world" (Kahn, 1965). He started as a cub reporter on the *St. Louis Post Dispatch* at the age of eighteen and over the years held various positions including foreign correspondent, investigative reporter, chief correspondent, and executive editor of the *New York World.* He was a member of the executive committee of the Columbia Broadcasting System (CBS), and chairman of the New York State Racing Commission for ten years, making racing a respectable and popular sport in New York.

Swope was born in St. Louis, Missouri, to Isaac Schwab, a German immigrant watchmaker, and Ida Cohn Schwab. He was a high-spirited, unconventional, adventurous boy who loved football and tried his father's patience. After his father's death, he bypassed college for a trip to Europe, but the trip was cut short by a swimming accident in the Black Forest. He returned home to do odd jobs. A local department store was offering at that time a $100-prize for the best essay on why it was the fastest growing business in St. Louis. He captured the prize and the judges' commendation that he was "a good observer and writer."

Swope had a difficult time separating his professional and extracurricular activities. He took a job as a cub reporter on the *St. Louis Post Dispatch*, but he mixed football with routine work. He was suspended. After a brief stint at the *Chicago Tribune*, he moved to New York where fame was awaiting him. His early years in New York consisted of shuttling jobs on the *Herald* and the *Morning Telegraph*, and in 1909 he became a reporter for Ralph Pulitzer on the *New York World*. His reports on the Becker-Rosenthal case made him one of the top-ranking newspapermen of the city.

On 10 January 1912 he married Margaret Pearl Honeyman Powell of Far Rockaway, New York, with H. L. Mencken (q.v.) as their only attendant. Shortly afterward he left for Europe as the *World*'s foreign correspondennt. He dazzled New York with exclusive dispatches from Germany. Swope's interest in the war continued, and he made a second trip to Germany in 1916. In 1917 he received the first Pulitzer Prize for reporting. His articles were published as a book under the title *Inside the German Empire* (1917). When the United States entered the war, Swope was commissioned a lieutenant commander in the U.S. Navy and received an appointment to the War Industries Board as associate member and assistant to Bernard M. Baruch.

Swope returned to the United States and took a position created especially for him by Ralph Pulitzer. He was named the executive editor of the *World* in 1920, at a salary of $54,000 a year plus 2 percent of the profits from the morning and

Sunday editions. He knew the *World* could not compete with the *New York Times* in breadth of coverage, so he relied on in-depth stories. Over the next eight years the newspaper took on crusade after crusade, exposing the Ku Klux Klan, the peonage scandal in Georgia, and radium poisonings at a watch factory. Slum landlords, subway service, and the League of Nations were other favorite subjects for his crusades. The paper received three Pulitzer Prizes for public service during his tenure. However, despite the fact the newspaper was known for its courageously liberal tone, it began to show signs of failure. Some said fine writing had replaced hard news. The op-ed page was maintained at tremendous costs. Old advertisers grew skeptical of the elevated tone of the paper; when the price went from two to three cents, there was a major drop in circulation.

While at the *World*, Swope made inroads into the political scene. He succeeded in bringing the Democratic National Convention to New York in 1924, the first time one had been held in the city since 1868. Swope turned ''king-maker'' when he singled out Alfred E. Smith as a potential statesman. Swope was triumphant when Smith was nominated for the presidency in 1928 and crestfallen when he was defeated.

Swope left the paper in 1929 because it no longer matched his personal goals. Some people said he had edited the *World* from Belmont Park. Betting became legal in New York State in 1934, and Swope accepted the chairmanship of the New York State Racing Commission. He made racing a respectable and popular sport, and saw that part of the profits went to the state. He introduced such innovations as the electric eye, the camera finish, the saliva test to detect drugging of horses, and the Australian barrier for starting races. He was reappointed chairman in 1941 and, in the meantime, acquired a stable of his own. He was the father of two children, Jane Marion and Herbert Bayard. He died in New York City.

BIBLIOGRAPHY:

A. *Journalism—an Instrument of Civilization* (Geneva, N.Y., 1924).

B. DAB Supp. 6, 615–617; NYT 21 June 1958; Ely J. Kahn, *The World of Swope* (New York, 1965).

CHRISTINE M. MILLER

—T—

TAISHOFF, SOL JOSEPH (b. 8 October 1904; d. 15 August 1982). Although he functioned for more than a half century as a business periodical journalist—not as a broadcaster—Sol Taishoff was one of the persons largely responsible for the shape of broadcast journalism in the United States. He was, indeed, one of the principal shapers of the American broadcasting system, in general, and the first business journalist ever to receive the University of Missouri's Distinguished Service in Journalism Award (1953). Taishoff effected his influence as the head of Broadcasting Publications from 1931 until his death in 1982, as editor and publisher and as president of Broadcasting Publications, the source of the industry's most influential trade book, *Broadcasting* magazine. Taishoff always considered broadcasting, even during its infancy under the Federal Radio Commission, as a journalistic medium, which he dubbed "The Fifth Estate." Throughout his fifty-year tenure as the editorial guide of *Broadcasting*, the magazine promoted full First Amendment rights for radio, television, and other electronic mass media and fought against undue regulation.

Taishoff's interest in journalism began at age sixteen, while he was still in high school, when he worked the graveyard shift as a copyboy for the Associated Press in Washington (1920–21). Later he became a telegraph operator and eventually a member of AP's news staff (1922–26). In 1926 he began as a reporter for David Lawrence's (q.v.) *U.S. Daily* (the forerunner of *U.S. News and World Report*), where he worked with senior reporter Drew Pearson (q.v.). While Lawrence's employee, Taishoff began writing a column on radio, under the pen name Robert Mack, which soon began appearing daily in 250 newspapers as a feature distributed by Lawrence's Consolidated Press. He continued writing this column until 1934 even after leaving Lawrence to start a radio industry trade publication with Martin Codel.

The first issue of the new, semimonthly trade paper *Broadcasting* was published on a shoestring on 15 August 1931. As the radio industry grew, so did the magazine, which became a weekly in 1941. After a period of frequent battles, in 1944 Taishoff bought out Codel's interest for $750,000. Taishoff then took on the triple title of president, editor, and publisher. As broadcasting technology expanded following World War II, so over the years did *Broadcasting* magazine's coverage—to television, cable, and the latest associated media technologies. In his fifty years as a journalist covering broadcasting, Taishoff interviewed nearly all of the industry's leaders.

In 1960 Taishoff bought a monthly magazine, *Television*, which he hoped to turn into a *Fortune*-type publication for the television industry, covering people and events attractively and in depth. After *Television* had lost a sizable amount of money, even sapping the financial well-being of *Broadcasting*, it was terminated by Taishoff's son, Lawrence—by then an executive with the company—while his father was in the hospital for lung surgery made necessary by cancer.

Taishoff was born in Minsk, Belorussia, on 8 October 1904, the son of Joseph H. Taishoff and Rose Orderu Taishoff. In November 1904 the family moved to Germany, where they spent two years before emigrating to the United States (1907). The elder Taishoff was a wholesale grocery salesman and was later associated with the Metropolitan Life Insurance Company; he died at the age of thirty-nine, in 1916. Sol Taishoff was educated in the Washington, D.C., public schools. He married Betty Tash on 6 March 1927, and the couple had three children, the older son of whom, Lawrence, became president of Broadcasting Publications and publisher of *Broadcasting* magazine in 1982. Betty Tash Taishoff died of cancer in November 1977.

Sol Taishoff was known among his associates as a charming personality, one who could and did influence U.S. telecommunications policy in his role as adviser and confidant to leading broadcasters, Federal Communications Commission (FCC) commissioners, and even presidents, particularly Lyndon B. Johnson, to whom he was especially close. Some called Taishoff the "eighth commissioner" of the FCC. He died of cancer on 15 August 1982 at Georgetown Hospital in Washington, D.C.

BIBLIOGRAPHY:

B. NYT 16 August 1982; *Broadcasting*, 12 October 1981 and 23 August 1982; Jack Gould, "He Knows Where the Power Is," NYT 9 March 1969; James Walter Wesolowski, "Sol Taishoff's *Television Magazine*, 1961–1968," Ph.D. diss., Univ. of Wisconsin, 1971.

JAMES WESOLOWSKI

TAMMEN, HARRY HEYE (b. 6 March 1856; d. 19 July 1924) was the curio shop promoter who convinced Frederick G. Bonfils (q.v.) to purchase the *Denver Post*. The partners created one of the most sensational crusading newspapers in the West during the time of the yellow journalism battle between Joseph Pulitzer and William Randolph Hearst (qq.v.) in New York City. Tammen, as ignorant as his partner in journalism techniques, spurred the staff to cover and write sensational stories using red headlines and coined slogans which promoted the *Post* as "Your Big Brother." The *Denver Post* became the largest-circulation newspaper in the mountain states and continued sensational for decades after the partners died.

Tammen, one of several children, was born in Baltimore. His father, Heye Heinrich Tammen, was a pharmacist who married Caroline Henriette Piepenbruker. Both were natives of Hanover, Germany. The elder Tammen immigrated to the United States as an attaché at the Netherlands consulate. Tammen attended Knapp's Academy in Baltimore but had to support himself at age seventeen when his father died. He held a variety of jobs including work in a printing shop and as a bartender. Arriving in Denver in 1880, he presided over the bar at the Windsor Hotel. He opened a curio shop in the hotel the next year and expanded to mail order and wholesale, offering Indian artifacts, scalps, blankets, and other items that were fake or manufactured for sale to tourists. In connection with the business, he began publishing a small monthly in 1889 named the *Great Divide* to spur tourism and interest in the West.

In 1894 a financial panic stopped tourism and nearly wiped out the now substantial curio business. Tammen traveled to Chicago, where by chance he met his future partner, Bonfils, who was reputedly wealthy from years of conducting the Little Louisiana Lottery out of Kansas City until Kansas City newspapers under William Rockhill Nelson (q.v.) exposed its crookedness. Tammen convinced Bonfils that running a newspaper would be a profitable enterprise.

The *Evening Post* had appeared in Denver on 8 August 1892 as a Democratic party sheet but died a year later. The *Post* resumed publication in 1894 but was losing in the competition with four other Denver dailies. Tammen had become interested in buying the newspaper but had no capital. It was Bonfils who supplied the $12,500 purchase price on 28 October 1895, but the two were equal partners. Tammen was president and secretary of the venture and Bonfils the treasurer. In announcing themselves to the public, they stated the *Post* would be "thoroughly and emphatically the people's paper, without links to political parties, corporations or special interests of any kind."

From the beginning Tammen applied showmanship to journalism. To the staff, he compared a newspaper to a vaudeville show: "It's got every sort of act—laughs, tears, wonder, thrills, melodrama, tragedy, comedy, love and hate. That's what I want you to give our readers." Tammen pressed for larger and larger headlines. When they were not arresting enough, he ordered front-page headlines in red ink. Tammen peppered his staff with ideas for stories which would evoke emotion. In 1903 Tammen interested Bonfils in buying a circus as an investment for the newspaper.

The partners contrived a colorful, noisy newspaper with crusades supporting causes of the working and lower-middle classes such as keeping commuting fares low, lowering the price of coal to keep heating costs down, and ensuring the underdog his day in court. They were boosters of the growing city and state, but often criticized politicians and officials whose actions appeared to benefit private purses. Whether Tammen and Bonfils were aware or not, E. W. Scripps (q.v.) and Pulitzer had already proven that the techniques attracted readers and readers attracted advertisers. The *Post* increased its circulation from 4,000 to 24,213 in 1901 to become the Denver circulation leader.

Bonfils, who was well off from his earlier ventures in the Oklahoma land boom and the lottery business, insisted on plowing cash flow back into the *Post* and improving the equipment and hiring competent journalists. Thus Tammen had to continue to rebuild his curio business and other ventures to support himself. However, in 1908, they began drawing a salary of $1,000 apiece.

Strident editorial attacks and Tammen's braggadocio produced reaction. In 1900 both were shot and wounded in their office by an attorney who disagreed with them. Court suits were brought against them and the newspaper. Intimations that businesses were blackmailed into advertising in the newspaper were common in the early years, but never proved.

Tammen, a short, stocky blond, befriended many individuals privately and Children's Hospital in Denver, especially. His first wife, Elizabeth Evans of Baltimore, died in 1890. He was married in 1892 to Agnes Reid of Denver. Tammen contributed the total building cost of the Agnes Reid Tammen wing of the hospital. His will provided amply for his wife from an estate appraised at $2 million. Almost half of the estate went into a trust fund with income supporting the hospital. Tammen died of cancer.

BIBLIOGRAPHY:

B. DAB Supp. 1, 93–96; NYT 20 July 1924; *Denver Post*, 19 July 1924; Gene Fowler, *Timber Line* (New York, 1933); Bill Hosokawa, *Thunder in the Rockies* (New York, 1976).

SAM KUCZUN

TARBELL, IDA MINERVA (b. 5 November 1857; d. 6 January 1944), writer of magazine articles and books, won greatest fame for her exposé of the Standard Oil Company, but during a long and distinguished journalistic career she was widely respected for her biographies and her balanced and thorough investigations of issues of public importance. Tarbell was foremost among a generation of professional women writers who in the early twentieth century managed to break away from traditionally feminine subjects.

Ida Tarbell was born on a farm in Erie County, Pennsylvania, the oldest of three surviving children. She never married and remained very close to her family throughout her life. Her mother, Esther Ann McCullough Tarbell, had been a schoolteacher before her marriage to Franklin Sumner Tarbell. After working at a variety of occupations from carpenter to schoolmaster, he went into business in 1859 providing wooden barrels for the infant oil industry in western Pennsylvania; later he became an independent oilman. The Tarbells worked to build stable communities in Pithole and then Rouseville, Pennsylvania, amid the rough frontier boomtowns of the oil region. Later they moved to nearby Titusville, where Ida attended public high school. Influenced by her mother's fierce resentment of married women's subordinate position, she resolved to remain single and independent. She attended Allegheny College in Meadville, Pennsylvania, where she was one of five women students. Her scientific studies fostered a fascination with original research and skepticism toward her parents' Methodism.

Finding no opportunities in scientific research for women, Tarbell taught for two years following her graduation in 1880 at the Poland (Ohio) Union Seminary. Rejecting that career option, she soon found a job as assistant editor for the *Chautauquan*, a monthly magazine that supplemented the home study courses offered by the popular Chautauqua adult education movement. During her eight years with the magazine, in preparing articles suitable for its unschooled but serious readers, she learned to write in clear, unornamented prose as well as to understand the interests of ordinary Americans. In 1891 she adventurously moved to Paris to research the life of Madame Roland, a prominent figure in the French Revolution. There she drank deeply of cosmopolitan Parisian culture and met a diverse group of French and English intellectuals. Supporting herself through free-lance writing, she came to the attention of S. S. McClure (q.v.), who enlisted her contributions to his newspaper syndicate and soon to his new magazine, *McClure's*.

When Tarbell returned to the United States in 1894, McClure hired her to write a life of Napoleon to accompany a collection of photographs he had acquired for the magazine. Her biography was hugely successful and ensured the survival of the nascent publication. Becoming a permanent member of the staff, she wrote a biography of Abraham Lincoln that was even more popular. Thereafter, throughout her life she returned to Lincoln as her—and her readers'—favorite subject for numerous books and articles.

After the turn of the century, seeking a topic that would address public concern about the new industrial trusts, Tarbell decided to investigate the rise of one of the earliest and most powerful of them. The *History of the Standard Oil Company* ran in *McClure's* for two years beginning in November 1902 and was published as a book in 1904. Although widely praised at the time for its evenhanded tone and voluminous documentation, it was at basis a dramatic epic, pitting independent oilmen (including her father and brother) against an economic juggernaut built by a power-hungry John D. Rockefeller. This combination of factuality and morality helped to spawn a wave of journalistic exposés of corruption in American life, as well as inciting legal actions against Standard Oil that resulted in its breakup in 1912.

When John S. Phillips (q.v.), her close friend and the editor of *McClure's*, left the magazine in 1906, Tarbell and much of the magazine's staff went with him. They combined forces to purchase the *American Magazine* and there continued to publish exposés, including Tarbell's exhaustive study of how special interests manipulated the U.S. tariff. Wearying of controversy, she began in

1912 to search for cooperative answers to social problems, writing about welfare capitalism and scientific management as alternatives to economic conflict. Despite, or perhaps because of, her own single and childless state, she also became critical of feminism for encouraging in young women a distorted sense of priorities. She was similarly lukewarm to the issue of woman suffrage.

After she and her colleagues sold the *American Magazine* in 1915, Tarbell continued a prolific career as a lecturer and free-lance magazine writer. She reported on the Paris Peace Conference for the *Red Cross Magazine* and in 1921 covered the Washington Naval Disarmament Conference. She was also called upon to serve on several government commissions, including the Woman's Committee of the U.S. Council of National Defense during World War I, Wilson's Industrial Conference in 1919, and Harding's Conference on Unemployment in 1921.

Favorable biographies of "responsible" businessmen Elbert H. Gary and Owen D. Young, published in 1925 and 1932, demonstrated that her criticisms of Rockefeller arose from a hatred not of capitalism in general but of what she considered abuses of economic power. In 1926 she visited Italy to report on the effects of Mussolini's regime; she found the man attractive and his social welfare programs admirable, but she criticized fascist violence and repressiveness. In the 1930s she was a moderate supporter of the New Deal. In later years Ida Tarbell retired to her farm in Easton, Connecticut. Her autobiography, *All in the Day's Work*, was published in 1939. She died of pneumonia on 6 January 1944.

BIBLIOGRAPHY:

B. DAB Supp. 3, 761–763; NYT 7 January 1944; Kathleen Brady, *Ida Tarbell: Portrait of a Muckraker* (New York, 1984); Mary E. Tomkins, *Ida M. Tarbell* (New York, 1974); Harold S. Wilson, *McClure's Magazine and the Muckrackers* (New York, 1970).

SALLY F. GRIFFITH

THOMAS, ISAIAH (b. 19 January 1749; d. 4 April 1831) began the *Massachusetts Spy* in Boston when the revolutionary spirit was growing in the English colonies. He identified his paper with the Patriot cause and became a central figure in the newspaper war against Great Britain. After the Revolution he gained additional fame as printer of fine Bibles and other books. He established a network of printing partnerships from New Hampshire to Maryland which helped to make him wealthy. In later years he collected early American imprints and information from other printers which he used to write his *History of Printing in America*. He used the material he collected to establish the American Antiquarian Society in Worcester, Massachusetts.

Thomas was born in Boston when it was an English colony. His mother, Fidelity Grant Thomas, was soon a widow. Her husband, Moses Thomas, died in 1752 in North Carolina where he had wandered. He had been a restless soldier, farmer, and storekeeper. He left his widow with five children and no money. Isaiah, the youngest, was put out as an apprentice to Zachariah Fowle at the age of six. Fowle was not a careful printer, but it was in his shop that Thomas learned to set type, even before he taught himself to read. By the age of twelve he was a competent printer, carrying the responsibility of a journeyman because he was energetic and his master was lazy.

An argument with Fowle in 1765 provided the excuse Thomas wanted to run away. His ambition was to go to London and learn printing from skilled craftsmen. He worked as a journeyman in Halifax, Nova Scotia, and Portsmouth, New Hamphsire, before returning to Fowle's shop in Boston, only to leave again for South Carolina, where he worked as a journeyman to save money to get to England or to start his own printing business. In Charleston he married his first wife, Mary Dillon, on Christmas Day, 1769. The next year he returned to Boston and proposed a partnership to Fowle, who accepted. The partners began the *Massachusetts Spy* in July 1770, the same year as the Boston Massacre. By October Thomas had bought out Fowle and was the sole publisher of the *Spy*.

Thomas seems to have taken Benjamin Franklin (q.v.) as his model. The Philadelphia printer had gone to London to perfect his craftsmanship, just as Thomas tried to do. In 1773 Thomas set up the first of many printing partnerships, as Franklin had done. This one was in Newburyport. And in 1774 he began a magazine, again as Franklin had done. Thomas called his the *Royal American Magazine*. It had a short life before the Revolution broke out. But it lasted longer than Franklin's.

He allied himself and the *Spy* with the Patriots and his shop became a center for their discussions. His paper carried reports of British actions and responses by the Patriots in Boston and the other colonies. He printed essays on the rights of the colonists in the *Spy* and in pamphlets. He was threatened by the authorities, but with the help of his Patriot accomplices, he was able to argue his way out of trouble whenever the British tried to intimidate or prosecute him.

The publisher of the *Spy* saw that the newspaper war was about to become a shooting war, and he moved his press to Worcester, out of the reach of the British, just before the first shots were fired at Lexington and Concord. He had a remarkable sense of timing. He rose to warn the countryside the same night as Paul Revere and then made it to Lexington in time to witness the exchange of shots.

The move to Worcester brought hardships. In effect he had to begin his business again. But he kept his paper going. He also published almanacs, tracts, and books. Soon after the war he had a successful partnership in Boston with Ebenezer Andrews. He set up other partnerships, usually with his former apprentices, in Salem, Springfield, and Brookfield, Massachusetts; Londonderry and Walpole, New Hamphire; Albany and Troy, New York; Rutland and Windsor, Vermont; and Baltimore, Maryland. He and his partners established another half-dozen newspapers in these towns.

It was during the early difficult years of the Revolution and his struggle to get his business going in Worcester that his first marriage ended. He discovered his wife had been unfaithful, and he divorced her in 1777. They had two children,

Mary Anne and Isaiah Jr. Two years later he married Mary Thomas Fowle, a cousin. She died in 1818, and he married his third wife, Rebecca Armstrong, the next year. She preceded him in death in 1828.

His fortune was built by energy and skilled craftsmanship. The foundation stone was the *Spy*. It made him famous. The rest was accomplished through the numerous printing partnerships and a reputation for quality printing. He printed juvenile books, textbooks, law books, spellers, dictionaries, geographies, histories, music books, novels, and especially Bibles. His "standing Bible" was offered at an affordable price because he had succeeded in buying sufficient type to set the whole book and leave the type standing and still have sufficient type left to conduct his other business. This saved him the time and expense incurred by other printers who had to redistribute their scarce type into the case after printing a few pages of the Bible. Also, he printed beautiful Bibles with illustrations individually colored and inserted by hand. He was determined to show that he could produce the highest-quality work, and he became the new nation's premier printer.

In 1802 he began his retirement and also began collecting material for his *History of Printing in America*. He had conducted extensive business correspondence for many years with other printers in America. Now he asked them to send him lists and samples of the things they had printed. He published his history in 1810. The collection of imprints became the nucleus of the library he used to establish the American Antiquarian Society in 1812. Like Franklin, he accomplished many other civic and philanthropic good works. He was honored by fellow printers, his neighbors, and the statesmen of the new nation. Franklin called him "the Baskerville of America."

He died in 1831 with a reputation as a successful and skilled printer, a patron of the arts and civic improvements, and a patriot of the Revolution.

BIBLIOGRAPHY:

A. *History of Printing in America* (Worcester, 1810); *The Diary of Isaiah Thomas,, 1808–1828* (Worcester, 1909); *Three Autobiographical Fragments* (Worcester, 1962).

B. DAB 9, 435–436; Annie Russell Marble, *From 'Prentice to Patron* (New York, 1935); Clifford K. Shipton, *Isaiah Thomas: Printer, Patriot, Philanthropist* (Rochester, 1948); Roger Yarrington, "Isaiah Thomas, Printer," Ph.D. diss., Univ. of Maryland, 1970.

ROGER YARRINGTON

THOMAS, LOWELL JACKSON (b. 6 April 1892; d. 29 August 1981) was a world traveler, lecturer, prolific writer, and pioneer broadcaster. His network radio evening newscasts began in 1930 and continued until 1976, longer than those of any other broadcaster. He was responsible for many "firsts" in radio news, such as the first broadcasts from airplanes and ships. His resonant baritone voice and his distinctive sign-on, "Good Evening, Everybody," and sign-off, "So Long Until Tomorrow," made him famous. Thomas's broadcast style was so popular that he has been credited with instilling the American habit of turning to the radio as a source of news. He narrated the Fox Movietone News seen in movie theaters by millions during the 1930s and 1940s. Thomas also helped develop the Cinerama wide-screen film process which he used for travelogues in the 1950s.

Thomas was born to Colonel Harry G. Thomas, a physician and surgeon, and Harriet Wagner Thomas, a schoolteacher, in Woodington, Ohio. The family moved to Cripple Creek, Colorado, in 1900, a gold camp. Despite the cultural isolation, Colonel Thomas insisted that his son be well educated and learn how to speak clearly and distinctly. Thomas's oratorical skills served him well as a broadcaster and narrator in later years.

A bright student, Thomas was able to complete a B.S. degree in 1911 at the University of Northern Indiana at Valparaiso after only two years. He obtained both a B.A. and M.A. in 1912 from the University of Denver. Between 1912 and 1914 Thomas was a reporter for the *Chicago Journal* and attended the Kent College of Law in Chicago, where he also taught oratory. In 1915, Thomas completed another M.A. at Princeton University. He also taught English at Princeton.

In 1915 he took his first trip to Alaska, the beginning of numerous worldwide travels. The experience of Alaska was exhilarating, and his enthusiastic lectures about the territory upon his return were popular and made him well known. As a result of them, President Woodrow Wilson commissioned Thomas to make on-scene reports of World War I. His mission was to tell the American people what the country was up against. Travels to the European and Mediterranean theaters led Thomas to meet Colonel T. E. Lawrence, a British officer fighting the Turks in Palestine and best known as "Lawrence of Arabia." His reports and lectures on Lawrence following the war made both men famous. Thomas's first book, *With Lawrence in Arabia* (1924), remains his most popular, partly because of its romanticizing of Lawrence.

Thomas married his first wife, Frances Ryan, on 4 August 1917. Their son, Lowell Jr., was born 6 October 1923. He assisted his father on numerous projects beginning in 1939, and he later became a state senator and lieutenant governor of Alaska.

Thomas began his broadcast career in March 1925 over KDKA, Pittsburgh. It was an hour program in which he narrated the story of the first aerial circumnavigation of the globe. His network career began 29 September 1930 over CBS when he started a daily evening newscast. He left CBS to join NBC in 1932 and remained with that network until 1947, when he returned to CBS. Thomas's style was warm and folksy. His formula for the news has remained a model for broadcast: lead off with the top news of the day, mix in important stories in the middle, and end with a light or poignant story. Thomas continued his nightly newscasts for CBS until 14 May 1976.

In 1935 Thomas became the voice of Fox Movietone News, the newsreel service widely distributed throughout movie houses in the United States. He narrated the newsreels for the next seventeen years, and he was heard by an audience of almost 100 million a week.

Thomas's world travels continued, despite the pressures of his radio and newsreel work. He traveled to Australia, India, Burma, even the Arctic, and continued to write about his experiences. During his career, he wrote over fifty books, many of them travel guides or records of his journeys such as *Seeing Japan with Lowell Thomas*. He also filmed numerous travelogues such as *Borneo*.

In 1952 he became associated with the wide-screen process known as Cinerama. It was a natural vehicle for showing audiences the sights and sounds of the world. Thomas narrated several Cinerama films, including *This Is Cinerama* and *Seven Wonders of the World*.

Thomas broadcast the first television news program in the United States in 1939, but he preferred radio as a news and information medium. In the 1950s, however, he was cofounder of Capital Cities Communications, a broadcast group. He also became producer and host for a CBS television series during 1957–59 called "High Adventure," which stressed, like so much of his work, his pleasure at sharing the world with audiences. After he retired from CBS radio in 1976, Thomas worked on a PBS television series called "Lowell Thomas Remembers" that was essentially a personal approach to world history.

Thomas claimed he was not a journalist, but an entertainer. He often used hyperbole and subjective commentary in his newscasts. He felt audiences wanted to hear the color of a man who was the friend of kings, presidents, generals, and illustrious explorers. Thomas received numerous awards, including the National Association of Broadcasters Distinguished Service Award (1964) and a special Peabody Award for his contributions to broadcast news (1974).

Thomas died of a heart attack at his estate in Pawling, New York. His first wife had died 17 February 1975. His second wife, Marianna Munn, whom he married in January 1977, survived him.

BIBLIOGRAPHY:

A. *With Lawrennce in Arabia* (New York, 1924); *Good Evening, Everybody: From Cripple Creek to Samarkand* (New York, 1976); *So Long Until Tomorrow* (New York, 1978).

B. NYT 30 August 1981; Norman R. Bowen, ed., *Lowell Thomas: The Stranger Everyone Knows* (Garden City, N.Y., 1968).

JOHN P. FREEMAN

THOMPSON, DOROTHY (b. 9 July 1893; d. 30 January 1961) was a journalist and political pundit whose popularity reached its zenith just before World War II. At that time her column on world and national affairs reached about eight million readers through 170 newspapers.

She was born in Lancaster, New York, an upstate community served by her Methodist minister father, the Reverend Peter Thompson, a native of County Durham, England. Her mother, Margaret Grierson Thompson, from Chicagao, died when Thompson was eight, and her father married Eliza Abbott, his church organist. In 1908, because of strained relations with her stepmother, Thompson was sent to live with aunts in Chicago, where she completed public school and two-year Lewis Institute.

Thompson completed her formal education at Syracuse University, graduating cum laude in 1914. An active suffragette, she worked after college for the New York Suffrage Association and later gained writing experience as a publicist in New York and Cincinnati. With modest success as a free-lance journalist and with vague promises from editors to consider future material, she sailed for England in 1920. Shipmates bound for a Zionist conference in London helped Thompson secure an International News Service (INS) assignment to cover the event. Though the conference was routine, her INS contact assisted her in obtaining more substantive stories in Ireland and Italy, and she toured Europe selling news to a number of newspapers.

Working out of Vienna, she met *Manchester Guardian* correspondent Marcel Fodor, who helped her gain notable interviews with Central European leaders. With such stories to her credit and with her space-rate pay approaching a correspondent's regular salary, she was hired in 1921 by the *Philadelphia Ledger* as its full-time Viennese correspondent. By 1924 she had moved to Berlin as Central European bureau chief for Curtis Publications' *Ledger* and *New York Evening Post*.

One of Thompson's most memorable stories came in 1931 when she interviewed Adolph Hitler, concluding that he was "a man of startling insignificance" (Sanders, 1973). Later she candidly admitted her mistake and became a strident proponent of American intervention in Europe. Thompson's renown as an observer of world affairs boomed in 1936 when she was given a continuing column on the editorial page of the *New York Herald-Tribune*. "On the Record" was grounded in facts, aggressive, controversial, and emotional.

After World War II, as readers' interest in international affairs cooled, the popularity of her column diminished. Her views on the Middle East hurt, too. Thompson had consistently supported Zionism, but as Jews began to displace Arabs in Palestine, she voiced concern for treatment of Arab refugees and dismay at Jewish terrorist tactics. Readers and newspapers accused her of serving as propagandist for Arab interests. Refusing to alter her views, she helped found the American Friends of the Middle East, a pro-Arab group backed by oil interests, serving as its president in 1956.

At the height of her career, Thompson was in demand as a public speaker, was heard by five million listeners through an NBC radio program, and was regarded as one of the most influential women of her day. She was honored by the National Institute of Social Sciences and the American Women's Association. She served four years as president of American PEN Club, a writers group, and as a founder and president of Freedom House, an internationalist group with which she later broke.

During her Vienna period Thompson married (1922) Josef Bard, a Hungarian Jew with whom, it turned out, she had little in common. They divorced in 1927.

A year later Thompson married author Sinclair Lewis, whom she met in Berlin, and they returned to America to live in New York and Vermont. Although Thompson and Lewis had several happy periods, the relationship was stormy and they were separated frequently. They had one child, Michael, but divorced in 1942. A year later, Thompson married Maxim Kopf, an easygoing Austrian artist who died in 1958.

Following Kopf's death, Thompson discontinued her newspaper column. She continued to provide a monthly piece for *Ladies' Home Journal*, for which she had written since 1937, until her death, which resulted from a heart attack while visiting her daughter-in-law in Lisbon.

BIBLIOGRAPHY:

B. DAB Supp. 7, 739–741; NYT 1 February 1961; Margaret Case Harriman, "The It Girl," *New Yorker*, 20 and 27 April 1940; Marion K. Sanders, *Dorothy Thompson: A Legend in Her Time* (Boston, 1973); Madelon Golden Schilpp and Sharon M. Murphy, "Dorothy Thompson: Political Columnist," *Great Women of the Press* (Carbondale, Ill., 1983).

ROBERT L. HOSKINS

TIMOTHY, ELIZABETH (b. ?; d. April 1757), **PETER TIMOTHY** (b. 1725; d. 1782), and **ANN DONOVAN TIMOTHY** (b. 1727; d. 11 September 1792) were members of the most illustrious eighteenth-century printing family of South Carolina. In addition to serving as colonial government printers, Charleston postal officials, and colonial government officials, they turned out a variety of printed matter including tracts, pamphlets, books, and business forms. However, the centerpiece of Timothy printing was the variously named *South-Carolina Gazette*, which the family published for sixty-eight years.

Elizabeth Timothy, the mother of Peter and the mother-in-law of Ann, was the first female newspaper publisher and editor in colonial America. As was common among colonial women, she took over her husband's business after his death. Little is known of Elizabeth Timothy, born in Holland before 1731. Neither her date of birth nor her parents' names are known. What is known is that she married Louis Timothée, of Huguenot extraction, sometime in the early eighteenth century and that they had four children before sailing for Philadelphia in 1731. She had two more children after reaching America. Her husband, who anglicized his name to Lewis Timothy in 1734, joined with Benjamin Franklin (q.v.) to issue the first German-language newspaper in colonial America. The *Philadelphia Zeitung* failed, but the Franklin and Timothy families were associated in business for the remainder of the eighteenth century.

In 1733 Lewis Timothy contracted with Franklin to operate a printing business in Charleston, South Carolina, for a six-year period. Under the terms of the agreement, Franklin provided the type and press, assumed one-third of the maintenance costs, and received one-third of the profits. Elizabeth Timothy remained in Philadelphia with her children until the following spring. By the time she reached the South Carolina city, her husband had revived the *South-*

Carolina Gazette (2 February 1734), a weekly. It had been published until his death the previous year by another Franklin partner, Thomas Whitmarsh. The newspaper under Lewis was often late in making publication dates, and the amount of news from outside South Carolina was often sparse, due primarily to the absence of inland mail routes and Lewis's need to depend upon the arrival of ships carrying mail and newspapers.

In addition to printing the *Gazette*, Lewis's printing shop was busy with colonial government documents, Dr. Nicholas Trott's *The Laws of the Province of South-Carolina*, and a number of lesser works including sermons, hymns, and an almanac. However, much of the work of Lewis's press was official or at least subsidized by the colonial government. His connection with colonial authorities also included the office of postmaster, which was no doubt useful for newspaper exchanges, a primary source of newspaper content during the colonial period.

Disease, including yellow fever and smallpox, was a recurring scourge in Charleston in the eighteenth century. In the summer of 1738, a smallpox epidemic swept Charleston, taking with it the Timothys' youngest son. By December 1738, Lewis himself was dead, the victim of an accident. On 4 January 1739, only five days after Lewis's funeral, the *Gazette* appeared on time under the imprint of his son, Peter Timothy. However, Peter was only about fourteen years of age and the publisher was Elizabeth Timothy. In fact, Elizabeth Timothy would continue as editor and publisher of the *Gazette* until Peter reached the age of twenty-one in 1746.

When Lewis died, a year remained on his original contract and Franklin agreed to let Elizabeth Timothy complete its term. According to his *Autobiography*, Franklin was satisfied with her conduct of business. Where Lewis had been lax in reporting the affairs of the printing shop, his widow was prompt and exact in her reports. Elizabeth Timothy performed satisfactorily because business accounting was part of female education in Holland, Franklin said. There is no evidence that she had any formal training in printing, but she may have learned her husband's craft at his elbow as did many colonial women. At the end of the contract she bought the printing house from Franklin.

The quality of the *South-Carolina Gazette* at first suffered somewhat under Elizabeth Timothy's editorship. It was smaller, there was less news of Charleston, and Elizabeth Timothy depended to a greater extent on material lifted from the foreign press and colonial newspapers than had Lewis. Advertising appeared to hold its own. While Elizabeth Timothy experienced the usual problems of colonial printers—the lack of rags to make paper, typographical inaccuracies, collection of accounts, and circulation difficulties—the *Gazette* gradually improved over the seven years she published the newspaper.

The print shop under Elizabeth Timothy continued to turn out a range of printed material including the official publications of the colonial government, sermons, and other imprints of a religious nature. She also sold almanacs and other works produced by Benjamin Franklin along with various commodities such as tallow, beer, and flour. As had Lewis, she served as postmaster, and the printing shop handled local distribution of letters, packages, and newspapers. While Franklin had been satisfied with the way Elizabeth Timothy conducted her business, the colonial government decidedly was not. On at least one occasion the House of Assembly threatened to take its business elsewhere because of poor-quality printing, and several times she was taken to task for overcharging the colonial government for printing. However, she continued to do government printing as long as she ran the printing house.

In 1746 Elizabeth Timothy turned over the *Gazette* and the print shop to her eldest son, Peter, and was apparently never involved with the enterprise again. However, before the year was out she opened a bookstore next to the print shop. Little is known of her whereabouts during the remaining years of her life. She died in April 1757; the exact date is not known and the *Gazette* did not print an obituary. That she had been financially successful in life is clear from her will, which was probated in May 1757. She left three houses, eight slaves, household furniture, and money to her surviving children.

When Peter Timothy took control of the printing house in 1746, he was already well placed by virtue of his mother's stewardship of the business. It was common for a colonial woman, following the death of her husband, to hold the family business in trust for a son until he became of age. While all financial arrangements of the printing house were carried on by his mother, Peter Timothy was clearly the legal owner of the business and involved in its operations. In early 1741 a libel suit lodged against the *Gazette* named Peter Timothy as defendant and not his mother.

With the exception of his being named in a libel suit, little is known of Peter Timothy until his marriage to Ann Donovan, 8 December 1745. He became a leading citizen of South Carolina during the remaining thirty-seven years of his life. He continued his parents' business dealings with Franklin, buying printing matter, materials, and commodities for resale. As had Lewis and Elizabeth, Peter Timothy continued to serve the colony as the official South Carolina printer, although after 1758 he shared government printing with another Charleston printer. He succeeded his mother in the office of postmaster and in 1765 became deputy and secretary to the postmaster general of the southern provinces. Peter Timothy remained active in politics throughout his life. Indeed, he served as clerk of the South Carolina Assembly in the prerevolutionary period and during the early years of the Revolution.

However, much of the current knowledge of Peter Timothy is based on his editorship of the *Gazette*. Prior to 1768, the newspaper under his control remained neutral in the growing Anglo-American conflict. In fact, the stated editorial position of the *Gazette* was one of impartiality, and the newspaper appears to have maintained that position despite the editor's personal beliefs, which were pro-American. The nonpartisan viewpoint of the *Gazette* was demonstrated chiefly by the absence of editorial comment. The passage of the Stamp Act of 1765, which among other provisions levied taxes on advertisements and each copy of a newspaper, altered the newspaper's nonpartisan stance. By early 1765 the *Gazette* was commenting on the Stamp Act in virtually every issue. Despite being a Patriot, Peter Timothy came under considerable suspicion because of his connections with the postal system and because he suspended publication of the *Gazette* and refused to revive it immediately following the act's repeal as the Patriots wanted. Actually, Peter Timothy was criticized from both sides: by Loyalists because of his support of violence against the Stamp Act and by Patriots because he did not actively try to prevent the use of stamps in Charleston.

Throughout the 1770s, Peter Timothy grew closer to the Patriot cause and began to work actively for American rights, both in the *Gazette* and personally. He served in a number of extralegal Patriot organizations before the Revolution, and in 1776 he became secretary of the general assembly that created the state constitution of South Carolina. Not surprisingly, when the British fleet entered Charleston in 1780, he along with other Patriots was watched by the authorities and finally made a prisoner late in the year. Thus ended, on 9 February 1780, the publication of the *Gazette of the State of South Carolina* (as Peter Timothy had renamed the newspaper in 1777) until 16 July 1783, when it was revived by Ann Donovan Timothy. Peter Timothy and two daughters were lost at sea in 1782.

Following the death of her husband, Ann Donovan Timothy became the second female printer, publisher, and editor of a South Carolina newspaper. Before reviving the *Gazette of the State of South Carolina*, on 16 July 1783, Ann Timothy appears to have had little to do with publishing, although she probably learned printing from her husband. She spent most of her married life bearing children, perhaps as many as fifteen, although apparently only five survived after 1770. Only a son, Benjamin Franklin, and daughters Sarah and Elizabeth survived her.

Ann Timothy published the *Gazette* in partnership with at least two others. The format of the newspaper was attractive for the period with three-column pages, woodcuts, a variety of news both domestic and foreign, and advertising. Indeed, advertising was typically at least one-half the newspaper. During the nine years she published the *Gazette*, the newspaper steadily improved and was a successful publication when it was passed on to her son.

As had her mother-in-law and husband before her, Ann Timothy turned out a wide range of printed matter in her print shop. In addition to printing material for the state government as the official state printer, Ann Timothy printed books, pamphlets, business forms, and documents. There is no evidence that her printing caused any of the controversies that attended the work of her mother-in-law and husband, and her printing was first-rate.

Ann Timothy died 11 September 1792 at the age of sixty-five. Her concern that Timothys continue in the printing craft is evidenced by her will. Noting that her son's father and grandfather had been printers, and that the business was financially sound, she left Benjamin Franklin Timothy the rechristened *State Gazette of South Carolina*. In keeping with Timothy tradition, there was no obituary for Ann Timothy in the *State Gazette of South Carolina*. Benjamin Franklin Timothy, his brother-in-law William Mason, and his nephew Peter Timothy Marchant continued to publish the *Gazette* until 1802, when it ceased publication. It was replaced the next year by the *Charleston Courier*, with Marchant as part owner. The Timothy printing dynasty ended with Marchant's death.

BIBLIOGRAPHY:

B. Ira L. Baker, "Elizabeth Timothy: America's First Woman Editor," *Journalism Quarterly*, Summer 1977; Hennig Cohen, *The South Carolina Gazette, 1732–1775* (Columbia, S.C., 1953); Leona M. Hudak, *Early American Women Printers and Publishers 1639–1820* (Metuchen, N.J., 1978); J. Ralph Randolph, "The End of Impartiality: *South-Carolina Gazette*, 1763–75," *Journalism Quarterly*, Winter 1972.

DONALD R. AVERY

TROTTER, WILLIAM MONROE (b. 7 April 1872; d. 7 April 1934) became one of the leading black journalists of his time not by design but by chance. Trotter was born in Chillicothe, Ohio, to James Monroe Trotter and Virginia Isaacs Trotter. Although the Trotters were living in Boston at the time, Mrs. Monroe returned to her hometown for the birth of her third child. Two previous children had died in infancy.

James Monroe Trotter, born of a slave mother and her owner in Mississippi, had made his way to Boston and joined the all-black Fifty-Fifth Massachusetts Regiment. He distinguished himself by rising through the ranks from private to lieutenant. He was well known for his successful attempts to gain equal pay for black soldiers. Following his discharge from the army, he returned to Ohio and married Virginia. They returned to Boston, where he obtained a well-paying job in the post office, was later appointed recorder of deeds in Washington, D.C., and became a succesful businessman dealing in real estate.

Young Willliam and his two sisters, Maude and Bessie, were raised without the need for money in one of the better parts of Boston. Trotter graduated as president of his class in a predominantly white school. After working for a year as a shipping clerk, he entered Harvard University in the fall of 1891. In his junior year he was elected to Phi Beta Kappa. He graduated magna cum laude in June 1895 with an A.B. degree and an eye on a career in business. But he refused to use his father as a crutch.

Trotter was soon to find that the freedom allowed blacks in Boston was limited. After several jobs as a clerk for various businesses in Boston, he finally landed a job with a real estate firm and later went into business for himself. In 1899 he married Geraldine Louise Pindell. She would later become his right hand at the *Boston Guardian*. The two moved into a house in the Dorchester section of Boston, and it appeared that Trotter was well on his way to following in the footsteps of his father. However, he was soon to assume the role of a "protester" and fighter for the rights of his people.

In 1901 he formed the Boston Literary Historical Society, which was soon tagged as a ''militant'' organization concerned with race relations in the United States. During this period Trotter began to see Booker T. Washington, the undisputed leader of blacks at that time, as a threat to the progress of blacks in America. He vigorously disagreed with Washington's philosophy that ''in all that are purely social we [blacks and whites] can be as separate as the fingers, yet one as the hand in all things essential to mutual progress.''

Trotter and George W. Forbes decided they needed a voice to combat the rising tide of ''Washingtonism.'' This voice would come in the form of a newspaper—the *Boston Guardian*. Trotter had the capital and Forbes, who had some newspaper experience, had the expertise. The first issue of the *Guardian* appeared on 9 November 1901. The paper was dedicated to fighting for the rights of blacks in the United States; however, it was strongly anti–Booker T. Washington, an unusual stand for a black publication to take during this period. Trotter attacked Washington on his editorial pages on all fronts—his philosophy, person, and prestige. The paper disagreed with Washington on what type of education blacks should receive, on their involvement in politics, and on Washington's ''role'' as a leader of black people. Trotter spent thirty days in jail for disturbing the peace while Washington was attempting to make a speech in Boston in 1903.

Trotter was very active in organizing opposition to racial prejudice and discrimination. It was the *Guardian* and Trotter's editorials that were at the forefront of having the film *Birth of a Nation* banned in Boston. He was instrumental in forming the Niagara Movement in July 1905, which laid the groundwork for the NAACP. He helped W.E.B. Du Bois (q.v.) draft the ''Declaration of Principles'' which set forth the purpose of the organization. He also organized and headed the National Equal Rights League (NERL). During his tenure Trotter led delegations to the White House to discuss race relations with President Woodrow Wilson. Trotter was truly an independent in politics. He supported Republican presidential candidates in 1908, 1912, 1928, and 1932.

Around 1904 Trotter had to make a grave decision. His real estate business had prospered; however, the less prosperous *Guardian* demanded his full-time attention and support. He gave up his real estate business and devoted his full attention to the paper, the NAACP, and the NERL. This decision meant a change in life-style for the Trotters. In order to keep the *Guardian* afloat, Trotter mortgaged their Dorchester home. Mrs. Trotter gave up much of her ''social standing'' and became her husband's co-worker at the *Guardian*. She kept accounts, edited the society columns, and performed what other tasks were necessary to keep the paper alive. The Trotters had no children. During the influenza epidemic of 1908, Mrs. Trotter became ill and died on 8 October.

Alone, and his influence dwindling, Trotter managed to keep the *Guardian* on course. From its founding until his death, the paper missed only two issues. In ill health, Trotter received help from his sister Maude and her husband, Charles Stewart, to continue publication of the paper. Trotter was now living in an apartment, having lost the assets he had accumulated as a successful businessman. He had poured everything into the *Guardian*. Early in the morning of 7 April 1934, Trotter apparently fell from the roof of the three-story building. He died en route to a hospital.

Lerone Bennett, Jr., a noted historian of black history, was later to write of Trotter: "[He] laid the first stone of the modern protest movement," and "mobilized the forces that checked the triumphant advance of Booker T. Washington's program of accommodation and submission." Trotter's sister Maude continued to publish the *Guardian* until her death in 1957.

BIBLIOGRAPHY:

B. *Boston Guardian*, 14 April 1934; Lerone Bennett, Jr., *Pioneers in Protest* (Chicago, 1968); Stephen R. Fox, *The Guardian of Boston: William Monroe Trotter* (New York, 1970).

J. WILLIAM SNORGRASS

TROUT, ROBERT (b. 15 October 1908) has had one of the longest and most varied careers in broadcast journalism of anyone now in the trade. His career has spanned the White House years of at least six U.S. presidents.

Known for his insightful news commentary, Trout was born on a farm in Wake County, North Carolina, to parents Louis and Juliette Mabee Trout. His earliest ambition was to be a railroad engineer and cartoonist, but he turned early—after leaving home and graduating from Central High School in Washington, D.C.—to the fledging radio industry in 1931. He broadcast over WJSV in Vernon Hills, Virginia, doing news, announcements, scripts, commentaries, poetry readings, and even household tips. Indeed, the variety of Trout's personal experiences would be the envy of any would-be writer: he took a series of odd jobs at one point, and they included driving taxis, pumping gas, running messages on Wall Street, collecting bills, and working as a merchant seaman. In fact, Trout at one point entertained a writing career, but a drafty Greenwich Village apartment brought him pneumonia and a new sense of the importance of other, more secure, professions.

WJSV joined the CBS network in October 1932, close to Trout's twenty-fourth birthday, and moved to Washington. Staying with the staff as a news reporter, Trout became famous as the announcer who introduced President Roosevelt's "Fireside Chats."

Trout was married on 4 July 1938 to Catherine Crane of Toledo, Ohio. He developed an early reputation as being amazingly and tirelessly able to handle spontaneous, on-the-spot live news reports. Not surprisingly, Trout was soon asked to go to CBS's key New York station in 1935, and further built up his credibility as "The Iron Man of Radio."

He covered the Democratic and Republican conventions of 1936 and reported the Roosevelt-Landon campaign, and was once forced to ad-lib for almost an hour while awaiting FDR's arrival on a cruise ship. During this period, to appear old enough to announce presidents, Trout grew a mustache.

Something of a sailor (perhaps due to his experience in the merchant marine), Trout in 1936 won the Miami-to-Nassau yacht race with his fifty-foot schooner, the *Water Witch*. In May 1937 Trout went to London for CBS to cover the coronation of George VI, then was sent to France to report on the marriage of the Duke of Windsor and Mrs. Wallis Warfield Simpson.

Versatility marks Trout's work. He reported the Kentucky Derby, a submarine disaster, dam openings, floods, Easter egg rollings, and the New York 1939 World's Fair. Once he reported, from a blimp, as a Washington traffic official harangued motorists below. Another occasion saw him broadcast a Christmas party for homeless animals who made such a racket that even Trout's smooth ad-libs were impossible to hear. In 1940 he reported, from the air, the flight of the first transatlantic clipper.

In October 1941 Trout flew to London as CBS European news chief to be a vacation replacement for Ed Murrow (q.v.). While there he broadcast reports on the blitz and man-on-the-street interviews carried over the BBC and shortwaved here. Trout reported D day, the Allied invasion of France, spending at one point more than seven hours without a break in front of the microphone. His broadcast of the Japanese surrender capped a remarkable several days on mike.

After the war Trout's reputation grew to such an extent that he became a kind of radio news superstar, with a huge staff of correspondents and researchers, broadcasting the daily program "Robert Trout With the News Till Now." In 1948 Trout began as host of an early NBC television quiz program "Who Said That?" He returned to CBS after four years—in time once again to demonstrate his remarkable stamina while reporting the two major national political conventions.

Trout's ventures into television have never really replaced his first love, radio, and he can be said to have served during the television decade of the 1950s as CBS's most dedicated radio reporter. He did some documentary work, however, and critical reaction to his gentlemanly, dapper delivery was always positive. In the 1960s he worked mostly in documentaries.

In 1964 Trout and Roger Mudd were named co-anchors for the CBS coverage of the Democratic National Convention, mainly in response to favorable public reaction to the Huntley-Brinkley team's work during the Republican National Convention. Trout was praised for his smoothness and clear experience; nonetheless, Walter Cronkite (q.v.) returned to the screen as solo anchor on election night.

After working regular WCBS-TV evening newscasts, in 1965 Trout left CBS to become a "special roving correspondent" overseas. He has served in that capacity ever since, and is now special correspondent for ABC radio. In 1979 he received the George Foster Peabody Award "for his nearly sixty years as a broadcast commentator." Headquartered in Madrid and living in Spain, Trout returns to the United States now and again for special occasions and assignments.

BIBLIOGRAPHY:

B. CB 1965; *Newsweek*, 15 April 1946, 20 October 1947, 31 January 1949; NYT 15 July 1945, 28 May 1965, 20 April 1980, 30 April 1981.

JONATHAN L. YODER

— U —

UTLEY, CLIFTON MAXWELL (b. 31 May 1904; d. 19 January 1978) was a nationally prominent radio and television commentator and newspaper columnist from the 1930s through the 1950s. He specialized in commentary on foreign affairs.

Utley was born in Chicago, where he spent most of his working life. His parents were William Ross Utley and Reigh Hogue Utley. He had one sister who died as an infant before his birth. William Ross Utley, a businessman, was head of the sales division of Maxwell Wallpaper Company of Chicago, the largest distributor of wallpaper in the Midwest. Mrs. Utley was a native of Wisconsin.

Utley was educated at the University of Chicago, where he earned a Ph.B. degree in 1926. As an undergraduate student, Clifton majored in English and had secondary concentrations in history and economics. He continued his studies at the University of Chicago, completing all of the work for the Ph.D. except for the dissertation. As a graduate student, he majored in political science with a specialty in international affairs. Later Utley studied at the University of Munich and the University of Algiers, where he developed fluency in both German and French. He also spent time in Mexico, where he learned to read and speak Spanish. Utley also learned to read Russian.

Utley married Frayn Garrick in 1931. The couple met at the University of Chicago, where she earned the M.A. degree in political science. Mrs. Utley worked in radio news at WBBM and WMAQ, Chicago, at various times in the 1930s and 1940s. The couple had three sons—David, Garrick, and Jonathan. After Clifton and Frayn Utley were married, he served as director of the Chicago Council on Foreign Relations from 1951 to 1959. He has been credited with transforming that organization from a small elite group to a more broadly based public interest group in the Chicago area.

During the 1930s Utley held a series of news positions with the Chicago City News Bureau, the *Chicago Daily News*, the Chicago bureau of the Associated Press, and stations WGN and WBBM. It was Utley's style to use well-documented data presented objectively, followed by his commentary. He was a strong interventionist, advocating U.S. involvement in World War II. Utley was released by WGN after he criticized an editorial in the *Chicago Tribune*, the station's owner, which called for a limitation on free speech. Subsequently, he moved to WBBM, Chicago, where his news commentaries were continued until 1941. In 1942 Utley and his sponsor, the Charles A. Stevens Department Store, moved to WMAQ, NBC's Chicago facility, where the program continued to hold its top rating for several years. Utley remained with NBC until his retirement. While employed by NBC, Utley also served as an American commentator for the BBC from 1945 to 1953. He also wrote a syndicated column for the *Chicago Sun-Times* during the early 1950s.

Utley's television career began at NBC in Chicago when WMAQ-TV first went on the air in 1949. During the early 1950s he was a TV anchorman and commentator for the network. Utley was credited with helping to set the tone and shape of TV journalism for the 1960s and 1970s. In June 1953 Utley suffered an embolism, which left him partially paralyzed and forced his early retirement. When he was taken ill, Frayn Utley stepped in and handled the Sunday night news and a daily television commentaary program for a time. Between them, Clifton and Frayn Utley chalked up twenty-five years of news commentary for the same sponsor. Eventually, in 1957, Clifton Utley managed a partial recovery and returned to the air part-time.

Utley was the recipient of the DuPont Award for television and radio commentary in 1957. Honorary degrees included the LL.D. from Lawrence College (1945) and the doctor of humane letters degree from Illinois College (1946). After retirement, the Utleys moved to Hawaii in 1971, where he died in 1978. Utley's radio and TV scripts are preserved in the archives of the Wisconsin Historical Society and Mass Media Center in Madison, Wisconsin. One of the Utley sons, Garrick, became an NBC news correspondent.

BIBLIOGRAPHY:

B. NYT 21 January 1978.

HERBERT H. HOWARD

—V—

VAN ANDA, CARR VATTEL (b. 2 December 1864; d. 28 January 1945) began his journalism career in the composing room but soon moved up through the newsroom ranks of several Ohio papers and the *Baltimore Sun*. After sixteen years with the *New York Sun*, he joined the *New York Times* as managing editor. There he helped the new publisher build a paper whose coverage was unparalleled at the time.

He was born in Georgetown, Ohio, to Frederick C. and Mariah E. Davis Van Anda. His interest in journalism surfaced early. At age six he produced a paste-up newspaper which was bought by indulgent relatives, and four years later he built a makeshift printing press. When Van Anda was in his early teens, his father moved the family to Wapakoneta, Ohio, to establish a law practice. Van Anda's mother had died during his infancy, and his father had remarried. In Wapakoneta, Van Anda published the *Boy's Gazette* and did job printing on a regular press he had bought for five dollars.

His profits were spent on materials for experiments in chemistry and physics, subjects which he studied when he enrolled at Ohio University in Athens when he was sixteen. Within two years, Van Anda—who had been working outside the classroom as a correspondent for Cleveland and Cincinnati papers—decided he had enough of higher education. He returned home, taking a job as foreman for one of the village weeklies, the *Auglaize Republican*.

In 1883 he went to work for the *Cleveland Herald* as a typesetter. To supplement his income, Van Anda covered assignments for the paper, doing so well that he was promoted to telegraph editor. Soon after the paper merged with the *Cleveland Plain Dealer*, he moved to the *Cleveland Evening Argus* as a reporter. When it failed two years later, the twenty-two-year-old Van Anda decided his future was in the East, and he found a job as a night editor with the *Baltimore Sun*. Two years later, in 1888, Van Anda left to join the *New York*

Sun as a reporter and copyreader. He was named night editor on 1 January 1893, a post he held until 14 February 1904, when Adolph S. Ochs (q.v.) hired him to be managing editor of the *New York Times*.

Over the next twenty years the scholarly Van Anda helped establish the *Times* as a newspaper of record. He was one of the first to recognize the potential of the transatlantic wireless, using it to develop a network of staff correspondents abroad. He encouraged in-depth reporting of aviation, exploration, and science; Van Anda was the first editor to push coverage of Albert Einstein, and on one occasion discovered an error in one of Einstein's equations. The paper's coverage of World War I earned it the first Pulitzer Gold Medal in Journalism for "disinterested and meritorious service" by a newspaper in June 1918.

In February 1925, exhausted by years of twelve-hour workdays and rare vacations, Van Anda took a leave from the *Times*. Ill health kept him from returning to his duties, and he formally retired in the spring of 1932. The early years of his retirement were spent pursuing his lifelong interest in mathematics and astronomy at Oenteora Park, his Catskills farm near Tannersville, New York. In 1938 he bought "The Mount," a summer home in Lexington, Massachusetts, but he was able to enjoy it only a few years. His second wife, Louise Shipman Drane, died on 17 February 1942. They had married on 11 April 1898 and had one son. Van Anda's first marriage was to Harriet L. Tupper on 16 December 1885. She died giving birth to their daughter in December 1887. It was the shock of his daughter's death on 28 January 1945 that led to Van Anda's death of a heart attack two hours later.

BIBLIOGRAPHY:

B. NYT 29 January 1945; Meyer Berger, *The Story of the "New York Times" 1851–1951* (New York, 1951); Elmer Davis, *History of the "New York Times," 1851–1921* (New York, 1921); Barnett Fine, *A Giant of the Press* (Oakland, Calif., 1968).

KRISTEN DOLLASE

VANN, ROBERT LEE (b. 27 August 1879; d. 24 October 1940) rose from obscurity to make the *Pittsburgh Courier* one of the leading black newspapers in America.

Vann was born in Ahoskie, North Carolina, the son of Lucy Peoples, a highly skilled cook in the area. There is no "official" record of his father; however, some historians suggest he was Joseph Hall, who lived with Lucy during Vann's early life. Lucy Peoples bestowed upon her son the surname of Vann, which was the name of her employer, who was highly respected in the area. This naming custom was from earlier slave times. Lucy Peoples named her son Robert Lee in honor not of Robert E. Lee, the Confederate general, but of her son's grandfather.

After completing elementary school, Vann worked as a janitor and part-time clerk at the Harrellsville Post Office. He managed to save sixteen dollars, enough money to enroll at Waters Training School in Winston-Salem, North Carolina. By walking home on weekends, a round-trip of twenty-two miles, to save money, and with the help of Headmaster Calvin S. Brown, Vann managed to graduate from Waters in 1901. He was chosen as valedictorian of his class.

Following graduation, Vann was not satisfied with the education he received at Waters. He entered Wayland Academy, a preparatory school for Virginia Union University in Richmond. In 1902 he enrolled as a college student. Vann was not considered a very serious college student and built a reputation as a practical joker. In 1903 he was "given" a diploma and asked to leave. However, while at Virginia Union, Vann established a lifelong friendship with a fellow student who would also make his mark in the history of blacks in journalism—J. Max Barber, who would become editor of the *Voice of the Negro*, a leading black publication between 1903 and 1907.

After leaving Virginia Union, Vann decided he could no longer endure conditions in the South. With the help of a scholarship, he made his way to Pittsburgh in 1903 and enrolled at the Western University of Pennsylvania. Because of his light complexion, straight hair, and sharp features, it was suggested that he enroll as an "American Indian"; however, he insisted on being registered as Negro or colored person.

Vann's first exposure to journalism came during his time in Richmond, when he spent some time "hanging around" John Mitchell's (q.v.) *Richmond Planet*. However, at Western University he became seriously interested in the profession. He became a regular contributor to the university's newspaper, the *Courant*, and later was selected as its editor in chief, a first for a black student at the school. He was also encouraged in this profession by his friend Barber. However, there were other interests which came first.

After graduating from Western University in 1906, Vann stayed on to study law. He completed his studies in June 1909 and passed the bar in December. He immediately set up a private practice, but found the services of a black lawyer, even in the North, were not in great demand. In October 1908, while in his last year of law school, Vann met Jesse Ellen Matthews. She was born in Gettysburg and after finishing high school in Harrisburg had taught kindergarten. She later moved to Pittsburgh where the two met at a dance. After a courtship of almost sixteen months, they were married 17 February 1910.

In March of the same year, Vann became associated with the *Pittsburgh Courier*. He was first sought for his legal knowledge rather than his journalistic skills. He was approached by the owners of the *Courier* to draw up papers of incorporation for the group. He was later appointed treasurer and in the fall of the same year was offered the editorship. Vann accepted for $100 a year in *Courier* shares.

Vann inherited all of the problems of black publications during the time. Circulation was hampered because newsstands, mostly owned by whites, refused to display black newspapers; inadequate news-gathering techniques resulted in late, inaccurate, and secondhand news. Attracting "first-rate" advertisements was also a problem. However, Vann fought these problems, and by 1914 he was well on his way to making the *Courier* one of the leading black newspapers in the United States. He did so by making the paper socially responsible to its readers.

Through the pages of the *Courier*, Vann began to call for social justice for blacks under the law, proper housing conditions, equal voting rights, and improved educational facilities. He fought vigorously for an anti-lynching bill. By the early 1920s the *Courier*'s circulation had reached approximately 55,000. Vann took this as a sign for the future and began to make plans for expansion. He established a national edition of the *Courier* in addition to the city edition, and established branch offices in various parts of the United States. The next move for the *Courier* was its own printing plant in 1930. Under Vann's guidance, the paper became one of the most influential black publications in America.

Vann was also very active in the political arena. In 1932 he defected from the Republican party and committed the *Courier* to Franklin D. Roosevelt and his New Deal. However, he returned to the Republican camp in 1940 and supported Wendell Willkie. Vann held several appointed political positions in Pittsburgh and in 1933 was appointed U.S. special assistant attorney general. He was the first black to be appointed to this office.

In January 1940 Vann underwent surgery for abdominal cancer. It reappeared in October and could not be arrested. He died at Shadyside Hospital in Pittsburgh. Several posthumous honors were given Vann. A school was named for him in his hometown of Ahoskie, and one in Pittsburgh. Scholarships were established at Virginia Union University and the University of Pittsburgh. At Virginia Union, the Robert L. Vann Memorial Tower was also erected. In 1943 a Liberty ship was named in his honor.

Following Vann's death, his wife took control of the *Courier*. Although the paper prospered during World War II, it began to decline in the 1950s. In 1960 a board of directors took control of the *Courier* with Mrs. Vann remaining as a board member. She served in this capacity until she retired in 1963. In 1965 the paper was purchased by John H. Sengstacke, owner and publisher of the *Chicago Defender*. Mrs. Vann died on 9 June 1967. Apparently, she and her husband had no children.

BIBLIOGRAPHY:

B. BHB, 433–435; *Pittsburgh Courier*, 2 November 1940; Andrew Buni, *Robert L. Vann of the "Pittsburgh Courier"* (Pittsburgh, 1974).

J. WILLIAM SNORGRASS

VILA, JOSEPH SPENCER (b. 16 December 1866; d. 27 April 1934) was a sports writer and editor in New York for forty-five years and was credited with originating the play-by-play method of reporting football games. He was sporting editor of the *New York Sun* from 1914 until his death.

He was born to Spencer and Josephine Vila in Boston and attended Boston Latin School. He attended Harvard College in 1886–87 and the Harvard Law School for a time. During his brief stay at Harvard he was a member of the freshman baseball and football teams.

After leaving Harvard, he worked as a brakeman and baggage master for the Baltimore and Ohio Railroad. On one of his trips as a railroad employee he met Joseph I. C. Clark, managing editor of the *Morning Journal*, who persuaded him to become a cub reporter. In 1889 he was assigned his first sports event, the Harvard-Princeton football game, and his study described it play by play. He left the *Journal* in 1890 and joined the *New York Herald*, where he worked until 1893. That year he joined the *Sun* under Charles A. Dana (q.v.). He became sports editor in 1914.

Vila (whose name is spelled "Villa" erroneously by some authorities) was described as a reporter and a reviewer instead of a critic of sports. His writing was simple and to the point. His phenomenal memory caused his stories to be filled with allusions to past performances. He included dates and statistics of all kinds, batting averages, win-loss records, wins by knockouts, and anecdotes without number. For many years, some authorities say as many as twenty years, he wrote a daily column called "Setting the Pace."

He was a powerful influence behind the scenes in professional sports. He was instrumental in Andrew Freedman's 1902 sale of the New York National League baseball club to John T. Brush. He helped establish a New York club in the American League (the "junior circuit") in 1903. He is said to have introduced Jacob Ruppert, owner of the New York Yankees, to Joe McCarthy, who became a longtime manager of the club.

He always wrote his column in longhand, with a pencil, chewing a wad of tobacco. When he covered a sporting event, he rarely took notes, depending instead on his photographic memory. Some authorities credit him with introducing the typewriter to ringside reporters. He never used the instrument himself, but dictated the story to a typist as the fight went on.

Vila collapsed at his desk at the *Evening Sun* on 27 April 1934. He was taken to a hospital and then to his home at 1819 Avenue O in Brooklyn, where he died late that night of a heart ailment. Hundreds of sports figures attended his funeral. His wife, Edna, and their daughter, Josephine survived him. A son, Joseph Jr., died in 1930.

BIBLIOGRAPHY:

B. NYT 28 April 1934; *New York Herald Tribune*, 28 April 1934; Frank M. O'Brien, *The Story of the Sun* (New York, 1918).

ROY HALVERSON

VILLARD, HENRY (b. 10 April 1835; d. 12 November 1900) left his mark on American history principally as a railroad builder and financier, but only after he had established himself as one of the nation's most able political journalists.

Born Ferdinand Heinrich Gustav Hilgard in Speyer, Bavaria, on 10 April 1835, Villard was the son of a jurist, Gustav Leonard Hilgard, and Katharina Antonia Elisabeth Pfeiffer. Spending his youth in Bavaria, Villard was more sociable than scholarly, but he early became interested in literature and writing. He attended universities at Munich and Würzburg, but in 1853, resisting his father's efforts to push him into technical training, he borrowed some money and a schoolmate's surname, and ran off to the United States.

Arriving 18 October 1853, nearly penniless, speaking no English, Villard made his way from New York to relatives in Illinois. For the next few years, he worked at a variety of odd jobs. He also began contributing to local German-American newspapers. Villard opposed slavery and in the course of his antislavery activities was introduced to the Republican party. He became a staunch party member, briefly publishing a German-language party newspaper in Racine, Wisconsin.

In 1857 he moved to New York, where his work was accepted by German-American newspapers, but he was coolly received by the English-language papers. For a year, he taught school to make ends meet. In 1858 Villard covered the Lincoln-Douglas debates for the *New York Staats-Zeitung*, but he still wanted a connection with the English-language newspapers. He moved to Cincinnati and went to work for the *Daily Commercial*. When gold fever centered on Pikes Peak, Villard persuaded his editor to send him to Colorado.

Villard spent most of 1859 in Kansas and Colorado, visiting the mine sites, dabbling in Denver real estate, guiding Horace Greeley (q.v.) when that editor made his western trip, and writing stories about the region. Late that year he returned to Cincinnati to write a guide to the Pikes Peak region.

In 1860 he covered the Republican National Convention and the subsequent election for the *Commercial*, and after the election again tried his luck in New York. Finally the New York Associated Press sent him to Springfield, Illinois, to cover the new president's activities until he moved to Washington. By February 1861 Villard had established himself as a political writer. He moved to Washington, D.C., where he was the first to sell his articles in syndication. He even persuaded the *New York Herald* to print his pro-Republican articles. During the Civil War, Villard reported first for the *Herald*, later for Greeley's *Tribune*; his was the first report of the outcome of the Battle of Bull Run, resulting in a *Herald* "extra." He accompanied the Union army in various campaigns through most of the war.

On 3 January 1866, Villard married Helen Frances Garrison, the only daughter of abolitionist William Lloyd Garrison (q.v.). After a two-year sojourn in Europe with his family, Villard and his wife settled into the Garrison home in Boston. Villard became secretary of the American Social Science Association, contributed to the *Boston Daily Advertiser*, and helped pioneer civil service reform.

For the next years Villard traveled between the United States and Germany, both for his health and as a representative of German financiers who had invested in railroad building in the United States. In 1874 he was sent by a Frankfurt group to look into problems they were having in Oregon. Excited by the potential of the Pacific Northwest, Villard himself bought out the German creditors, gaining control first of the Oregon activities, later taking over the Northern Pacific Railroad. Thanks to Villard's efforts, the transcontinental line was completed to Tacoma, Washington, in 1883. Financial problems forced Villard from the railroad temporarily, but he returned to the board in 1888.

In 1881 Villard purchased the controlling interest in the *New York Evening Post*, but allowed the editorial department full independence. He also organized and invested heavily in the Edison General Electric Company. Villard died of apoplexy on 12 November 1900 at his home at Thorwood, Dobbs Ferry, New York. Among the survivors was a son, Oswald Garrison Villard (q.v.), who edited the *Nation* from 1918 to 1934.

BIBLIOGRAPHY:

A. *Memoirs of Henry Villard*, 2 vols. (Boston, 1904).

B. DAB 19, 273–275; *Who Was Who in America, 1607–1896* (Chicago, 1963); NYT 13 November 1900; James Blaine Hedges, *Henry Villard and the Railways of the Northwest* (New Haven, 1930; reprinted New York, 1967).

BARBARA CLOUD

VILLARD, OSWALD GARRISON (b. 13 March 1872; d. 1 October 1949) was a liberal reformer, author, thoughtful critic of the press, and editor. He was the owner and editorial leader of the *New York Evening Post* for two decades prior to World War I and then developed the *Nation* magazine into one of journalism's foremost liberal voices of the 1920s and 1930s. Villard spent his life fighting for peace, equal rights for blacks and women, and numerous other causes.

The third of four children, Villard was born in Wiesbaden, Germany, where his parents were vacationing for his father's health. Villard's father was Henry Villard (q.v.), a journalist and railroad baron who in 1881 obtained controlling interest in the *New York Evening Post* from its founder, Edwin L. Godkin (q.v.). At the same time, he obtained control of the *Nation*, then the *Post*'s weekly literary supplement. Villard's mother, Helen Frances "Fanny" Garrison Villard, was the daughter of abolitionist William Lloyd Garrison (q.v.). Following in the footsteps of her father and leading the way for her son, she spent much of her life crusading for liberal causes. The family home was in New York City, with a summer estate in Dobbs Ferry, New York.

Villard was educated in Germany and in private schools in the United States. He entered Harvard in 1889, graduated in 1893, traveled in Europe for a year, and then returned to Harvard to earn a master's degree in history in 1896. Rejecting an academic career as too passive, Villard then began a six-month apprenticeship as a cub reporter for the *Philadelphia Press* in 1896–97.

In 1897 he moved to the *Evening Post*, where he was editor of the Saturday supplement and a reporter. Godkin was the editor in chief. Villard inherited ownership of the paper in 1900 when his father died. Three years later, on 18 February 1903, he married the former Julia Breckinridge Sandford of Covington, Kentucky. They had three children.

In 1915 Villard went to Washington, D.C. as the *Post*'s capital correspondent. There he used editorials, cartoons, and interpretive news stories to try to prevent

U.S. entry into World War I. He later was an outspoken critic of the Treaty of Versailles, which he predicted would result in another European or worldwide war, and of U.S. participation in World War II. Meanwhile, he was a dominant figure in the new NAACP and served as chairman of its board.

Always, Villard was easily inflamed by injustice and oppression, but he paid a high price for his idealism. By 1918 his liberal, isolationist editorial course had cut into the circulation and financial resources of the *Post*, and he was forced to sell it to Thomas W. Lamont of J. P. Morgan and Company. Villard retained the *Nation*, however, and proceeded to develop it into a high-grade weekly journal of liberal opinion and literary criticism. He yielded control in 1932 to a board of editors and wrote a signed weekly essay, "Issues and Man." In 1935 he sold the magazine to Maurice Wertheim, a New York stockbroker long associated with liberal causes. In 1940 he ceased writing his column because the editors of the magazine had abandoned its traditional pacifist course.

After leaving the *Nation*, Villard wrote for the *Christian Century* and the *Progressive*, and continued to write books. He wrote eighteen in his lifetime, including three on Germany, a biography of John Brown, an autobiography entitled *Fighting Years* (1939), and *The Disappearing Daily* (1928). In the latter, Villard decried the trend toward fewer newspapers, their lack of individuality, their preoccupation with entertaining features, and the growing influence of their business departments over editorial decision making.

Devoted to the sea, Villard also owned the *Nautical Gazette* from 1918 to 1935, but was too busy to direct it. He founded *Yachting* magazine in 1907. In 1949 Villard suffered a stroke and died two days later on 1 October in his New York residence. He was seventy-seven. His wife died on 10 March 1962.

BIBLIOGRAPHY:

B. DAB Supp. 4, 849–852; NYT 2 October 1949; D. Joy Humes, *Oswald Garrison Villard, Liberal of the 1920s* (Syracuse, 1960); Allen Nevins, *The "Evening Post": A Century of Journalism* (New York, 1922); Michael Wreszin, *Oswald Garrison Villard: Pacifist at War* (Bloomington, Ind., 1965).

CATHY PACKER

W

WALLACE, WILLIAM ROY DEWITT (b. 12 November 1889; d. 30 March 1981), founder and, with his wife, Lila, longtime editor and publisher of the *Reader's Digest*, was an avid reader who built his own impatience with the length of magazine articles into the world's largest-circulation magazine.

"I have read hundreds of periodicals," Wallace once said in outlining the idea for his magazine, "and I'm convinced that the events of the world can be told far more simply and convincingly by economy of words. We're living in a fast-moving world, and people are impatient to get at the nub of all matters."

The first issue of the *Reader's Digest*, in February 1922, had a printing of 5,000 copies and promised on its cover, "Thirty-one articles each month from leading magazines—each article of enduring value and interest, in condensed and compact form." The number of articles changed, but the style never did. From the beginning, the magazine, with its distinctive, pocket-sized format, was a success. Circulation was 50,000 by 1926, a quarter of a million by 1929, and in 1984, *Reader's Digest* was printed in seventeen languages and had a worldwide circulation of 30.6 million in 168 countries. The U.S. circulation was 17.8 million.

Yet the magazine was frequently criticized. Some said it was middlebrow and socially conservative, a description Wallace acknowledged but did not regard as a fault; he said America was basically middlebrow and socially conservative. Others thought the *Digest* had a right-wing and anti-labor slant. Wallace denied the charges, but he was proud, he said, that the *Digest*, "more than any other mass circulation magazine, has constantly exposed the evils of communism and has as constantly portrayed the blessings of the free-enterprise system."

Politics, however, has been a minor part of the *Digest* contents. The magazine emphasized humor (with reader contributions solicited), science, sex, inspiration, and self-improvement. The *Digest* was a leader in printing articles about venereal disease, safe driving, family planning, and the dangers of smoking. ''The *Digest* opens windows on the world,'' Wallace said. ''It discusses problems that baffle us all, and it publishes articles that cheer us—progress articles.''

Wallace was born in St. Paul, Minnesota, the son of Dr. James and Janet Davis Wallace. His father was a minister, and taught at and was president of Macalester College. Wallace attended the college for two years, from 1907 to 1909, then transferred to the University of California for two years. He left without graduating and went back to St. Paul, where he found a job in the book department of Webb Publishing Company. He spent a year selling advertising for Brown and Bigelow, a calendar publisher, then, in 1917, with World War I, he joined the U.S. Army.

Wallace became a sergeant and was wounded during the Verdun offensive. While recovering, he said, he read many magazines and, convinced that the articles were too long, developed the idea for the *Digest* and practiced cutting stories. Back in St. Paul after the war, he put together a sample of his magazine but was unable to interest any publishers.

In 1921 Wallace decided to try the magazine for himself. He headed to New York, looked up Lila Bell Acheson, the sister of a college roommate, and convinced her to become his partner, both in founding the Reader's Digest Association and, on 15 October 1921, in marriage. With mostly borrowed money, they rented a basement room in Greenwich Village and sent out a circular asking for subscriptions. The cost was twenty-five cents a copy and three dollars a year. Then the couple went on their honeymoon. When they returned, they found 1,500 orders waiting and the *Digest* was launched. Early issues were produced from the New York Public Library, where the Wallaces spent days reading, copying, and condensing articles. The characteristics they looked for were that the article be significant, quotable, and discussable; that the subject relate to the average person's daily life; and that the article maintain interest a year or so in the future.

At first other magazine publishers did not charge for reprints, considering them good publicity. Before long, the *Digest* was seen as competition and magazines occasionally withheld reprint rights. Wallace started commissioning articles directly for the *Digest*. Sometimes these were planted first in other magazines to be reprinted later, a practice criticized as deceptive. He also began paying both authors and magazines for reprints. As the magazine grew, it acquired a reputation for being a generous place to work, both in the salaries it paid and in the amenities at its gracious Pleasantville, New York, headquarters.

Until 1955 the magazine did not accept advertising. But the company was quite profitable and expanded into publication of condensed books and operation of a record company. Still Wallace would sometimes say that the early struggling days of the company were the most fun. The Wallaces retired from active publishing in 1973. Eight years later, he died of pneumonia at their home in Mt. Kisco, New York, at the age of ninety-one. His wife died 8 May 1984, at the age of ninety-five. The couple had no children.

BIBLIOGRAPHY:
B. NYT 1 April 1981; John Bainbridge, *Little Wonder* (New York, 1946); James Playsted Wood, *Of Lasting Interest: The Story of the ''Reader's Digest''* (Garden City, N.Y., 1958).

JUDITH A. SERRIN

WALLER, JUDITH CARY (b. 19 February 1889; d. 28 October 1973) was a pioneer broadcaster and the first manager of radio station WMAQ, Chicago. Although she had never heard of a radio station when she was offered the manager's job, she proved to have enormous programming talent, and under her leadership WMAQ became one of the country's largest stations. She produced the first play-by-play coverage of a college football game; created ''Ding Dong School,'' the first successful television program for preschoolers; and was influential in the success of ''Amos 'n' Andy,'' which was aired first on WMAQ and then by NBC for more than twenty years.

Waller was born on Oak Park, Illinois, the oldest of four daughters of John Duke Waller, a physician and surgeon, and Katherine Short Waller. Waller was graduated from Oak Park High School in 1908, toured Europe for a year, attended business college, and then went to work. One of the firms she worked for was the J. Walter Thompson advertising agency in Chicago and New York. In 1922 Waller received a telephone call from an old friend, Walter Strong, the business manager of the *Chicago Daily News*. He said the *Daily News* had decided to start a radio station and asked her to run it. Although she conceded she had never heard of a radio station and doubted her ability to run one, she accepted.

From the start, Waller's interest was in quality programming. She chose a classical music format for her station as an alternative to the jazz and popular music aired by Chicago's other radio station, and her first guest performer was an opera star. Radio carried no advertising in those days, so Waller promised publicity in the *Daily News* to attract talent. Her job was to find talent, write the publicity, deliver the publicity to the newspaper, and then produce and announce the show. The station's only other employee was an engineer.

Waller's contribution to broadcast programming—both news and entertainment—were numerous. She produced the first play-by-play broadcast of a college football game—the University of Chicago vs. Brown in 1924. The next year she convinced William Wrigley, Jr., owner of the Chicago Cubs, to permit WMAQ to air all of that team's home games. The team's gate receipts soared. She was responsible for WMAQ's broadcasts of both 1924 political conventions, Coolidge's inauguration in 1925, the first broadcast of the Chicago Symphony Orchestra, and the first transatlantic broadcast in 1925.

For two years Waller negotiated with Charles Correll and Freeman Gosden, originators of the ''Sam 'n' Henry'' show, to move that program from rival WGN to WMAQ. In 1928 she succeeded, and on 19 March of that year the first broadcast of the renamed ''Amos 'n' Andy'' show was aired. It was the first radio show to run six nights a week, and it went on to become one of the most successful shows in both radio and television history.

Determined that broadcasting could be an educational as well as an entertainment medium, Waller broadcast lectures from Northwestern University and introduced a series of educational radio programs into the Chicago public schools. She created the "University of Chicago Round Table," the first radio discussion program. That show remained local for several years until NBC moved it to the network, where it ran continuously for more than twenty years and was widely imitated.

Waller also played an influential role in the development of government regulation of the broadcast industry. She participated in all four of Secretary of Commerce Herbert Hoover's national radio conferences in the 1920s. She joined with other broadcasters to form the National Association of Broadcasters (NAB) in response to a dispute with the American Society of Composers, Authors and Publishers (ASCAP) over payment of music copyright holders. She opposed the introduction of advertising into broadcasting and promoted radio news.

In 1931 Colonel Franklin Knox (q.v.) bought the *Chicago Daily News* and sold WMAQ to NBC. Under NBC ownership, Waller was reassigned from vice president and general manager of WMAQ to educational director for the network's central division and later public service director. While working for the network, she served on the congressionally appointed Federal Radio Education Committee, was one of the first members of the NAB's Education Standards Committee, and was a board member of the University Association for Professional Radio Education (UAPRE). In 1942 she set up the first radio institute for aspiring broadcasters. In 1946 she wrote a broadcasting textbook, *Radio, the Fifth Estate*.

In 1950 Waller represented the United States at a UNESCO conference on school broadcasting. She was the person most directly responsible for the first successful television program for preschool children, "Ding Dong School." The program ran in Chicago for several years until NBC put it on the network on 1953. It won a coveted Peabody Award.

Waller retired from NBC in 1957, but continued to pioneer broadcasting history. She headed an airborne television program through Purdue University that broadcast educational shows from an airplane over a six-state area. After her retirement, she also lectured at Northwestern University's School of Speech and served on the board of the Interlochen Music Camp. She never married. She died of a heart attack at age eighty-four in Evanston, Illinois.

BIBLIOGRAPHY:

B. *Chicago Tribune*, 29 October 1973; Mary E. Williamson, "Judith Cary Waller: Chicago Broadcasting Pioneer," *Journalism History*, Winter 1976–77.

CATHY PACKER

WARNER, CHARLES DUDLEY (b. 12 September 1829; d. 20 October 1900) was an essayist, editor, and novelist. Although probably best known for *The Gilded Age* (1873), a novel he wrote with Mark Twain (*see* Clemens, Samuel

Langhorne), Warner also was the editor of the *Hartford Courant* and a contributing editor of *Harper's Magazine*. His humor and ability to turn daily experiences into literature are exhibited in numerous essays on subjects ranging from his boyhood to Shakespeare. Considered a keen observer, he traveled extensively and wrote many articles and books on areas as diverse as the Nile and the Adirondacks.

The oldest of the two sons of Justus Warner and Sylvia Hitchcock Warner, he was born in Plainfield, Massachusetts. His father, who farmed 200 areas in western Massachusetts, insisted before his death in 1834 that Charles go to college one day. Young Warner attended Oneida Conference Seminary in Cazenovia, New York, and graduated from Hamilton College in Clinton, New York, in 1851 with the first prize in English. While in college he wrote for the *Knickerbocker Magazine* and in 1852 had some articles accepted by *Putnam's Magazine*. He expanded his commencement oration into his first book, *The Book of Eloquence*, which was published two years after his graduation.

Warner joined a Missouri railroad surveying party in 1853 but after a year returned to the East to study law. He graduated from the University of Pennsylvania in 1856. On 8 October of that year he married Susan Lee of New York City, and they lived in Chicago for the next four years while he practiced law. In 1860 he became assistant editor of the *Hartford Evening Press*. The next year the paper's editor went off to war, and Warner, who was too nearsighted to serve, became editor. When the *Press* and the *Courant* consolidated in 1867, Warner was named coeditor. He later became editor but eventually his connection with the paper was mostly literary. From 1884 to 1898 he was a contributing editor of *Harper's*.

Warner's first major literary success came in 1870 when a series of essays he had written for the *Courant* about his experiences as an amateur gardener was published in book form. *My Summer in a Garden* brought him recognition as a new American humorist. In 1873 he collaborated with his friend and neighbor, Mark Twain, on *The Gilded Age*, which gave its name to an era. The reading public loved the humorous story of western life, but the critics assailed it, and, friends said, Warner was mortified. Twain later bought the rights and it was transformed into a highly successful stage play.

Several of Warner's travel books evolved from letters home and sketches that appeared in many different magazines. *Saunterings* (1872), *My Winter on the Nile* (1876), *In the Levant* (1877), and *In the Wilderness* (1878) are considered his outstanding travel works. Many believe Warner's essays to be his best writing. The titles reflect a wide range of subject matter, for example, *On Horseback* (1888) and *The Relation of Literature to Life* (1896).

The humorous edge of his essays was absent from three novels published between 1889 and 1899. *A Little Journey in the World* (1889), *The Golden House* (1894), and *That Fortune* (1899) formed a trilogy about acquiring, misusing, and losing a great fortune. Warner also wrote biographies of Captain John Smith and Washington Irving, and was general editor of the American Men of Letters series, twenty-two volumes of critical biographies issued between 1881 and 1904. In addition, he edited a biographical dictionary and synopsis of books and, along with his brother, George, was coeditor of the *Library of the World's Best Literature*, a thirty-volume comprehensive literary dictionary.

Although his writings were popular during his lifetime, Warner never became wealthy, but he and his wife lived comfortably in Hartford, enjoying the company of neighbors such as Twain and Harriet Beecher Stowe. Because Warner's health suffered in his later years, the couple, who had no children, usually spent winters in the South. He never fully recovered from a 1898 bout with pneumonia and died suddenly two years later while out for a walk after attending a luncheon for friends. His complete works, edited by Thomas R. Lounsbury, were published in fifteen volumes in 1904.

BIBLIOGRAPHY:

B. DAB 19, 462–463; NYT 21 October 1900; Annie A. Fields, *Charles Dudley Warner* (New York, 1904).

KAY MARIE MAGOWAN

WASON, ELIZABETH (b. 6 March 1912) was a broadcast foreign correspondent for CBS during World War II, and is a prolific author of cookbooks and other nonfiction works, who has been published in a number of leading American magazines.

Wason was born in Delphi, Indiana. Her father, James Paddox Wason, was a lawyer, and later, a judge. Her mother, Susan Una Edson Wason, was a housewife. Elizabeth, known as Betty, attended Oberlin College, and then transferred to Purdue University. She graduated from Purdue in 1933 with a degree in home economics. She held a number of jobs during the depression, including copywriter, secretary, store clerk, annd home economist. When her position with the Kentucky Utilities Company was eliminated, Wason got a job at WLAP, Lexington. She organized inexpensive luncheons for local women, and broadcast the events on the radio. The entire commentary was ad-libbed. When she advanced to a Cincinnati station to do another woman's broadcast, scripts were required. Wason had trouble working with one, and was fired before a week was out.

In 1938 Wason moved to New York, where she became an assistant editor at *McCall's*, and then joined the public relations firm of Raymond C. Meyer. In 1938 she went to Europe "to see the world." Wason had cited her broadcasting and print experience when requesting press credentials from the Transradio Press Service prior to her departure. Transradio officials were establishing a stable of stringers who provided material that the service's editors wrote in broadcast style for its clients, which included American networks as well as local stations. When the Munich Crisis occurred, Wason was in Czechoslovakia. She says she became a foreign correpondent by being in the right place at the right time, and by having a natural instinct for knowing what news is.

After the crisis lessened, Wason found there was little work for her in Europe. In early 1939 she returned to the United States, obtaining a position with the

New York newspaper *PM*, which was in the planning stages. She helped formulate the paper's section on food, but left before it actually began publication. She returned to Europe in January 1940 and, at the suggestion of CBS News chief Paul White (q.v.), looked up William L. Shirer (q.v.), who was stationed in Berlin.

CBS was just expanding its European staff, having added Mary Marvin Breckinridge (q.v.) that winter to complement Edward R. Murrow, Eric Sevareid, Thomas B. Grandin (qq.v.), and Shirer. When the German invasion of Norway began in April, Shirer called Wason in Stockholm, and asked for a report. Her first broadcast for CBS was on 12 April 1940, and was a scoop on the Norwegian royal family fleeing a German bombing attack. Wason feels that she would not have gotten the assignment from CBS if a man had been available for the job. In fact, after a few more reports, Wason was asked to find a male to read her reports. She believes that CBS officials felt her voice sounded too young, although she was twenty-eight years old at the time (Hosley, 1984).

Wason recruited Winston Burdette, who had been working for Transradio in Stockholm. Soon he was hired full-time by CBS, and Wason was out of work. She went to the Balkans, and then to Greece, where the Nazis were pushing toward Athens. She broadcast for CBS from Athens, but was again asked to find a man to broadcast for her. This time she found a man who worked at the American embassy to read her reports, using the pseudonym Phil Brown. When the Germans captured Athens, Wason was stranded there for two months. After getting back to Western Europe, Wason found that CBS had no further use of her services, and she returned to America.

Wason wrote a book about her experiences in Greece, and followed that with a cookbook. She married Samuel Dashiell, a United Press and newspaper reporter, in 1945. They were divorced in 1948. Wason hosted a radio talk show on WINX in Washington in 1945–46, and was production manager for another Washington broadcast in 1947. From 1948 through 1952 Wason was women's editor of the Voice of America, often voicing the scripts she wrote and produced. In May 1953 she married Neville Hall, and they had a daughter, Ellen (Bannick), in 1954. That marriage ended in divorce in 1970.

Wason became kitchen editor for General Foods Corporation in 1954, and assistant food editor of *Woman's Home Companion* in 1955. She left that position in 1957, and has been a free-lance writer ever since. She lives in Arlington, Virginia.

BIBLIOGRAPHY:

B. David H. Hosley, *As Good As Any* (Westport, Conn., 1984); Marion Marzolf, *Up From the Footnote: A History of Women Journalists* (New York, 1977).

DAVID H. HOSLEY

WATTERSON, HENRY (b. 16 February 1840; d. 22 December 1921), one of the last of the great political newspaper editors, used the editorial pages of the *Louisville Courier-Journal* as his principal forum for fifty-one years. He said he knew personally all of the presidents from John Quincy Adams to Franklin

D. Roosevelt. He was involved in the nominations, and subsequent campaigns, of most of the Democratic presidential candidates from 1872 through 1916. As a principal spokesman for the South during those years, he was more widely quoted throughout the country than any other newspaper editor.

Watterson was born on Pennsylvania Avenue, Washington, D.C., next door to a printing plant, a happenstance of birth which he considered an omen of his future—his involvement in both newspaper editing and national politics. Politics seemed to be a way of life for the Watterson family. Henry's grandfather, William Watterson, was a neighbor and constant political supporter of Andrew Jackson. Harvey Watterson, Henry's father, was serving in the U.S. House of Representatives at the time Henry was born.

Henry Watterson began his journalistic career in 1852 at the age of twelve when he was named editor of the student newspaper at the Protestant Episcopal Academy in Philadelphia. Four years later his father bought him a printing press and he began publishing the *New Era*, which first brought him to prominence for his editorial in support of James Buchanan. In 1856 he went to New York to begin a literary career but discovered he needed to supplement his income by working part-time on the *New York Tribune* and the *New York Times*. He returned to Washington in 1958 where, at various times, he worked for the *Washington States*, served as capital correspondent for the *Philadelphia Bulletin*, was a stringer for the Associated Press, wrote for the *Democratic Review*, and served as a clerk in the Interior Department. In 1861 when the *States* went out of business, he returned to his native Tennessee, where he remained throughout the Civil War.

During the summer of 1861 he served for a few months in the Confederate armed forces, but in the fall of 1861 he resigned the service due to his poor eyesight and slight build and accepted the associate editorship of the *Nashville Banner*. When Nashville fell to the Union forces in early 1862, he rejoined the military, fled the city, and soon accepted the editorship of the *Rebel* in Chattanooga until forced from that city in the summer of 1863. Always moving ahead of the Union army, Watterson was later assistant editor of the *Atlanta Southern Confederacy* and the *Montgomery Mail*.

At the end of the war, Watterson joined friends in Cincinnati, where he served about six months as editor of the *Cincinnati Evening Times*. He found, however, that the Ohio city was no comfortable place for a former "rebel," and he returned in September 1865 to Nashville to become part owner and editor of the *Nashville Banner* and to marry Rebecca Ewing. For the next three years he campaigned for national reconciliation in a campaign he called "The New Departure." He argued for diversified farming and invited northern investors to help develop southern resources.

In the spring of 1868 Watterson was offered the editorship of the *Louisville Journal*, a position he readily accepted. Six months after arriving in Louisville, he persuaded Walter Halderman, publisher of the rival *Courier*, to buy the *Journal*, a merger which was completed on 7 November 1868. This gave Watterson one-third ownership and the editorship of the publication and began his rapid rise to national prominence. By 1880 Watterson had established himself, through his newspaper, as a major spokesman for the South and had gained a widespread, national reputation. Through his influence, the *Courier-Journal* could boast the largest circulation of any Democratic newspaper west of the Alleghenies with a combined daily and weekly circulation of 150,000. Watterson thought the editorial page was the heart and soul of a newspaper. Consequently, the *Courier-Journal* would have as many as ten editorial writers—more than the number of reporters usually found in the newsroom.

Watterson saw Louisville as the "Gateway to the South" and a perfect place to continue his campaign of national reconciliation. He thought Kentucky would play a pivotal role during the Reconstruction years and, consequently, attached himself to the Democratic party of the state.

In a sense the problems of twentieth century America passed Watterson by. His politics never changed from nineteenth-century concerns, and he failed to grasp the significance of the Progressive movement, which shifted national attention from politics to economic and industrial concerns.

When Walter Halderman died in 1901, his heirs began to disagree over the business policies of the newspaper. As a compromise, the owners gave Watterson full control of the *Courier-Journal*, but this proved too strenuous for the seventy-seven-year-old editor. As a consequence, one year later the Halderman heirs joined Watterson in seeking new owners for "the Old Lady at the Corner." Thus, after half a century of absolute control as editor, Watterson relinquished control of the *Courier-Journal* to Robert Worth Bingham, a wealthy and successful Louisville attorney. Realizing Watterson was the newspaper's greatest asset, Bingham encouraged him to stay with the newspaper as an editorial writer. Watterson's opposition to the League of Nations, which Bingham supported, brought an end to the relationship in 1919 and resulted in a request for Watterson's retirement, forcing him to express his opinions through occasional letters to the editor.

Watterson spent the summer of 1921 getting his affairs in order, wrote a will, prepared his papers for the Library of Congress, worked on his autobiography, and prepared for his last trip to Florida, where he died 22 December 1921. Throughout his career, Watterson's written influence exceeded that of the editorial page of the *Courier-Journal*. He frequently wrote for national publications such as *Century Magazine*, *Harper's Weekly*, *Collier's Weekly*, *Saturday Evening Post*, *Cosmopolitan Magazine*, and *American Magazine*.

BIBLIOGRAPHY:

A. *Marse Henry* (New York, 1919); *The Editorials of Henry Watterson* (New York, 1923).

B. NYT 23 December 1921; Joseph Frazier Wall, *Henry Watterson, Reconstructed Rebel* (New York, 1956).

PERRY J. ASHLEY

WAUD, ALFRED "ALF" RUDOLPH (b. 2 October 1828; d. 6 April 1891) sketched news events for several major illustrated newspapers for forty years after arriving in the United States in 1850. During the Civil War he was the leading "special artist" with *Harper's Weekly* and spent most of the war with the Army of the Potomac.

Waud (pronounced Wode) was born into an old Yorkshire family in London, England. As a youth, he was apprenticed to a decorator, but he dropped the occupation when he came of age and began studying art at the School of Design at Somerset House in London. After working as a scene painter for theaters in London, he sailed for the United States, arriving in New York in 1850. Failing to get work in a theater, Waud moved to Boston, where he learned to draw on wood blocks for engravers of books and periodicals. During the 1850s, he produced sketches for several publications in Boston and New York, including Barnum and Beach's *Illustrated Weekly*. His earliest surviving sketches date back to 1851 and illustrate New England, New York, and Washington.

In 1853 Waud was living in the first of several studios he would operate on Broadway in New York City. In the mid–1850s he married Mary Gertrude Jewett, and their first child, Mary, was born in 1856 in Boston. Their other children were Selina, Alfred, and Edith. In 1860 Alfred Waud became an illustrator for the *New York Illustrated News*, one of the nation's three top illustrated newspapers, and in May 1861 the *News* announced that Waud would sketch "the interesting and important events of the war." His illustrations were signed by the engraver Thomas Nast (q.v.), for whom Waud developed an intense dislike. By the time his last picture appeared in the *News* in early 1862, Waud had already left the publication for *Harper's Weekly*. Meanwhile, brother William Waud joined *Frank Leslie's Illustrated Newspaper* in 1860 and traveled far afield for it until he joined Alf at *Harper's Weekly* in 1864. Alf maintained a close relationship with his brother and a lifelong correspondence with three sisters who apparently never left England. William died in November 1878.

Alf Waud was one of the few artists to spend most of his time in the field, as opposed to a New York studio. Waud's sketches, which often received full front-page or double-truck inside treatment, were accompanied by first-person accounts of the artist's experiences on or near the battlefields. He scored a number of exclusives as he followed the Army of the Potomac from Bull Run to Appomattox, where he sketched the moment of Lee's surrender. He published 344 Civil War illustrations in the *News* and *Harper's*, making him the most prolific of the special artists. Many of his original sketches from which the engravings were made are preserved in the Library of Congress.

Following the war, *Harper's* sent Waud west and south through Cincinnati, Louisville, Nashville, Vicksburg, and New Orleans. Most of the sketches published in 1866 and 1867 portrayed the cities; others contained such subjects as Jefferson Davis's plantation and a Texas cattle drive. "A Drove of Texas Cattle Crossing a Stream," published in 1867 after he returned to New York, was probably the first nationally distributed illustration of a cattle drive. He remained at *Harper's* through 1870. He designed the invitations to President Grant's 1869 inaugural reception and ball.

In 1871 Waud and reporter Ralph Keeler reported on life in New Orleans and the Mississippi delta for the new but short-lived *Every Saturday*; the team covered the Chicago fire in October. He again returned to the South and West for the two-volume *Picturesque America* (1872–74), edited by William Cullen Bryant (q.v.).

His free-lance work was successful enough to send all of his children to boarding schools in Pennsylvania and to support a twenty-two-room New York home with servants and a governess for the children. He illustrated historic ships for *Harper's New Monthly Magazine* in 1886. He resided briefly in Bethlehem, Pennsylvania, in 1873–74, but he returned to a Broadway studio by the end of the decade. He drew political caricature for the pro-Blaine *Munsey's Weekly* during the 1884 presidential campaign. He was an early exhibitor at the National Academy of Design. He was among the contributing artists to the prestigious *Century Magazine* series that became the four-volume *Battles and Leaders of the Civil War*. He frequently did historical sketches.

Despite his failing health, he began an extended sketching tour of southern battlefields to illustrate war narratives for Joseph M. Brown of Marietta, Georgia, in whose home he died of heart disease after a short illness. Waud was a resident of South Orange, New Jersey, at the time of his death; his wife had died several years earlier.

BIBLIOGRAPHY:

B. NYT 10 April 1891; Frederic E. Ray, *Alfred R. Waud: Civil War Artist* (New York, 1974); Philip Van Doren Stern, *They Were There: The Civil War in Action as Seen by Its Combat Artists* (New York, 1959).

WILLIAM E. HUNTZICKER

WAYNE, FRANCES BELFORD (b. 1870; d. 16 July 1951) was a reporter for the *Denver Post* from 1909 to 1947. She also worked, briefly, for the *Rocky Mountain News* in Denver and for the *Chicago Examiner*. Frances Wayne's writing style was that of the times—often verbose, preachy, sometimes vague. Her talent was for investigation. Her instincts about people and about a good story were unbeatable. She had the respect of the owners of the *Denver Post*, Harry Tammen and Fred Bonfils (qq.v.), who seldom respected anyone. She had what all reporters hope for—the backing of a powerful metropolitan newspaper to investigate and write stories on concerns of her own.

As a result, she was instrumental in aiding social reform in Colorado and in setting patterns that were used as models nationwide. Her daily stories about the efforts of a young Denver teacher led to the establishment of the Emily Griffith Opportunity School in Denver, the first vocational-technical school for adults in the United States. She was a prime mover in the enactment of enlightened laws to protect women and children, and she worked closely with Denver's Judge Ben Lindsey, founder of the juvenile court concept. Other Colorado institutions she helped establish include the Myron Stratton Home in Colorado Springs, one of the first children's homes using the cottage concept of housing. She worked for years for the establishment of the Colorado Psychopathic Hospital, an institution set up to treat the insane as sick people rather than as criminals.

Frances Wayne was born in La Porte, Indiana, in 1870 to James B. Belford and Frances McEwen Belford. Her father was a lawyer in La Porte when he was appointed by President Grant to become a member of the territorial supreme court in Colorado in 1874. The family moved to Central City, Colorado, and then to Washington D.C., when Judge Belford served as a Colorado congressman from 1878 to 1885. Frances, with her three brothers, was educated in Central City, Washington, and, finally, in Denver, where her parents moved in 1886. Her mother served on the trustee board of what are now the University of Northern Colorado and Colorado State University, but there is no record of Frances's attending any institution of higher education.

Frances was married to John Anthony Wayne sometime in 1901 in Greeley, Colorado, but there is no evidence that she lived with him after 1906. She was extremely secretive about her private life, telling co-workers at various times that her husband had died or that they were separated. She was equally vague about her education and her birthday. When social security laws were enacted, she did not apply for benefits because a co-worker said, ''she would have had to list her exact birthday'' (Hause, 1982). Her temperament matched her red hair—fiery—and while she had many friends and thousands of acquaintances, few were confidants. Her nickname, which she sometime used in her byline, was ''Pinky'' because of her hair. (Her father, with bright red hair and beard, was known as ''the red-headed rooster of the Rockies'' during his years in Congress.)

At the *Denver Post*, Bonfils and Tammen usually backed her in whatever crusade she began. She repaid them with loyalty, devotion to the paper, and long hours of work for relatively low pay. In the early years of the twentieth century she was a feminist, chiding the women of Colorado in her stories and in a column she wrote for not being more active politically (they had had the vote since 1901), calling for day-care centers for children of working mothers, and lobbying for legal birth control.

In 1914 she was the only woman reporter in the country to cover the Ludlow Massacre, battles between the Colorado National Guard, representing the Colorado Fuel and Iron Company, and striking coal miners. Because of her well-written stories from Ludlow, President Woodrow Wilson sent Red Cross representatives into the area to aid miners' families.

In 1914 she was named a ''Representative Woman of Colorado.'' In 1918 she was appointed a National Red Cross Director to do publicity work in France until the end of World War I. In 1922 she received the University of Colorado recognition gold medal, the first journalist and one of the first women to do so. The Denver Women's Press Club awards a scholarship named for her, and in 1946 she was named ''Woman of the Year'' by the Colorado Business and Professional Women's Clubs. She left the *Post* in 1947 following a dispute with a new managing editor and went home to Central City, where she died of cancer in 1951.

BIBLIOGRAPHY:

B. Gene Fowler, *Timber Line* (New York, 1933); Nancy P. Hause, "The Unsinkable Frances Wayne," M.A. thesis, Kansas State Univ., 1982; Bill Hosokawa, *Thunder in the Rockies* (New York, 1976); Zoe Von Ende, "Frances Wayne, Star Reporter," *Denver Post*, 6 February 1972.

NANCY P. HAUSE

WEBB, JAMES WATSON (b. 2 February 1802; d. 7 June 1884) was for a third of a century ending in 1861 the strident, at times innovative, editor of the *New York Courier and Enquirer*, the city's most successful antebellum mercantile paper, a vociferous conservative journal following an early loyalty to Jackson. During the early 1830s Webb's paper had the nation's largest circulation, and throughout the 1830s Webb operated expensive and pioneering schooner and horse expresses to gather news, foreshadowing the appearance of wire services in the 1840s.

The eighth of nine children, Webb was born in Claverack, New York, the son of Samuel Blatchley Webb and Catherine Hogeboom Webb. His father, a merchant and land speculator, was General George Washington's personal aide during the revolutionary war. Orphaned at the age of five, Webb lived with relatives and worked for three years in a brother's store in Cooperstown, New York. Boldly approaching Secretary of War John C. Calhoun, Webb secured a second lieutenant's commission in 1819, stationed in turn in New York City, Detroit, Fort Dearborn (now Chicago), and back in Detroit over the next eight years.

In 1822 Webb volunteered to cross Illinois from Fort Dearborn to the Mississippi River on foot in bitterly cold weather to warn frontier forts of an impending Indian attack. Webb married Helen Lispenard Stewart, a daughter of a wealthy New York City merchant, on 1 July 1823. The couple had five children before Mrs. Webb died in 1848. Leaving the military in 1827, Webb with the financial help of his father-in-law acquired an interest in December 1827 in the *New York Morning Courier*, a seven-month-old mercantile paper being sold by subscription to members of the business community. Webb, then a staunch Jacksonian, became the paper's editor.

The *Courier* and its chief Jacksonian rival, Mordecai M. Noah's *New York Enquirer*, founded in 1826, were merged under Webb's control on 25 May 1829 to reduce party factionalism. The resulting *Courier and Enquirer* grew rapidly in the next three years, replacing printing presses three times in eighteen months to keep up with growing circulations that approached 5,000 daily, expanding page sizes, and demand for additional advertising space. Although careless with personal finances, Webb at the age of thirty was realizing one of the newspaper industry's largest revenues.

During the 1830s Webb invested heavily in horse expresses to speed political news from Washington, D.C., and schooners to deliver European market news from incoming transatlantic ships. Webb was the first publisher to devise such long-distance news networks for regular operation. Competition in these news-gathering enterprises between Webb and his chief rival, New York's *Journal of Commerce*, a mercantile paper with opposing political views, broke out sporadically from 1828 to 1846 when the arrival of telegraphy led the city's leading dailies to form the Associated Press. Webb's *Courier and Enquirer* was an AP partner until the paper ceased publication in 1861.

Ignored by the New York State Democrats with whom he disagreed over the rechartering of the U.S. Bank, Webb abandoned Jackson and the Democrats in August 1832, asserting a "principles, not men" motto, but subsequently finding comfort almost exclusively in Whig, and later Republican, principles. He quarreled with many politicians and editors, occasionally caning enemies in the street, causing one duel in which a participant was killed, and being wounded in another duel for which he was convicted and pardoned. Despite his sometimes quarrelsome traits and vitriolic editorials, Webb attracted many leading correspondents and associate editors, including James Gordon Bennett (q.v.), founder in 1835 of the *New York Herald*, and Henry J. Raymond (q.v.), a founder in 1851 of the *New York Times*.

On 9 November 1849 Webb married Laura Virginia Cram, a daughter of a wealthy brewer. The couple had five sons. A parade of successful penny newspapers beginning in 1833 superseded Webb and other mercantile editors who were unable to modernize their newspapers. The *Courier and Enquirer* was absorbed by the *New York World* on 1 July 1861, and two days later Webb left to become U.S. minister to Brazil, a post he held until 1869. He died in his New York home of a bladder inflammation. Tall, with a large head, bushy sideburns, and piercing eyes, Webb used the signature of "J. Watson Webb."

BIBLIOGRAPHY:

B. DAB 19, 574–575; NYT 8 June 1884; James L. Crouthamel, *James Watson Webb: A Biography* (Middletown, Conn., 1969); James L. Crouthamel, "James Watson Webb: Mercantile Editor," *New York History*, October 1960.

RICHARD A. SCHWARZLOSE

WEBSTER, NOAH (b. 16 October 1758; d. 28 May 1843) is America's foremost lexicographer. His name is synonymous with "dictionary," and his 1828 work, *An American Dictionary of the English Language*, was the most ambitious work completed in America at that time. Yet Webster's talents were many—scholarly, literary, and political—and he made a significant contribution to journalism in the early republic.

He was the fourth child of Noah and Mercy Steele Webster and was born in West Hartford, Connecticut. His father was a farmer and justice of the peace, and the young Noah showed a bent for books and scholarship. In 1774 he was admitted to Yale College and graduated four years later. His first inclination was to practice law, and he did so for a time, but by 1789 he had given up this career. Previously, he had earned a living as a teacher in Goshen, New York, and while there, in 1783, he published his first textbook, an elementary speller entitled *A Grammatical Institute of the English Language*. The *Institute* also contained a grammar book and a reader, which were published in succeeding years. These were the forerunners of his more famous later works, but they exemplified one of his life's works: responding to the needs of American teachers in American schools.

Almost from the moment of the first publication, Webster saw the need for a strong copyright law to protect authors, and he made such a law one of his lifelong quests. In 1785 his pamphlet *Sketches of American Policy* caught the interest of George Washington and James Madison, and he was soon among the writers to urge the adoption of the new constitution for the nation in 1787. One forum that he used was the editorship of the *American Magazine*, New York's first monthly. The magazine lasted only a year before its financial collapse, and Webster returned to Hartford and his law practice. During this decade, Webster had been traveling widely and had become a noted authority on the English language. He consulted with Benjamin Franklin (q.v.) about Franklin's simplified spelling scheme, and he was in demand as a lecturer on the American language.

During a stay in Philadelphia as supervisor of the Episcopal school, Webster met Rebecca Greenleaf, and they were married on 26 October 1789. Three years later, Webster returned to New York to found the *American Minerva*, a Federalist daily newspaper that was a staunch supporter of Washington. Here Webster had his greatest impact as a journalist. His series of articles signed "Curtius" was a vigorous defense of the Jay Treaty, and in general he was a most effective advocate of Washington's policies. Webster's writings for the *Minerva* are thought to be among the earliest true editorials—regular columns of opinion for a paper's editors.

In 1798 Webster gave up the daily management of the paper and went back to New Haven. He was tired of journalism and disenchanted with politics and some of the Federalist leaders, and he wanted to devote himself more fully to his scholarly pursuits. He had an active, curious, and agile mind, and he devoted himself to many subjects, not just politics and the language. In 1809, for instance, he published *Experiments Respecting Dew*, a scholarly essay on physical science; in 1799 he published *A Brief History of Epidemic and Pestilential Diseases*. He also brought out a revised edition of the Authorized Version of the English Bible in 1833.

Webster's first love was lexicography, of course. His first work after his retirement from journalism was *A Compendious Dictionary of the English Language*, published in 1806. It took him nearly twenty years to finish his large dictionary and more than that to have it published. Financially it was disappointing, though not unsuccessful, but critically and practically it was a success. He included 12,000 words and between 30,000 and 40,000 definitions that had not appeared in any earlier dictionary. Webster established the principle of recording nonliterary words and using American as well as British definitions. His definitions began with original or primary meanings and continued with other meanings derived from the originals. None could match Webster's work in volume or quality. No working dictionary that has been published since then has escaped its influence.

In 1812 Webster moved to Amherst, Massachusetts, where he helped found Amherst College, but he returned to New Haven in 1822. He worked there for the rest of his life except for a year in France and England in 1824–25 and a winter in Washington, D.C., in 1830–31. There he was successful in obtaining the passage of a revised copyright law.

Webster died in 1843 in New Haven. He was a man of vast intellect whose personality, prejudices, and proclivity for self-promotion often obscured his finer qualities from his contemporaries. Jefferson erroneously dismissed him as "a mere pedagogue, of very limited understanding and very strong prejudices and party passions." Others refused to support him in his quest to record and classify the American language. In time, however, he proved himself correct. His legacy to his nation was a recognition that its language was a living organism, to be reported upon rather than brought under control.

BIBLIOGRAPHY:

B. DAB 19, 594–597; Richard Moss, *Noah Webster* (Boston, 1984).

JAMES GLEN STOVALL

WEED, (EDWARD) THURLOW (b. 15 November 1797; d. 22 November 1882) used the *Albany Evening Journal* as a base for a career as a journalist and political leader. As editor of the *Journal*, he championed internal improvements, antislavery, and the social responsibility of government. In politics he was known as the "Dictator" and "governor of governors" because of the power he wielded. He led the New York State Whigs into the fledgling Republican party, but was unable to secure the Republican nomination of William H. Seward over Abraham Lincoln. Afterward he was a statesman who advised Lincoln and performed patriotic service during the Civil War.

But above all he was a newspaperman. The oldest child of Joel and Mary Ellis Weed, he was born in Cairo, Greene County, New York, in the Hudson Valley. With little education, he tasted journalism when he did odd jobs at the *Catskill Recorder* at age eleven. His father, an unsuccessful farmer, took the family soon thereafter to the frontier of Cincinnatus in Cortland County and then to the Onondaga Valley, where young Weed apprenticed at the *Lynx*.

After working at several newspapers and marrying Catherine Ostrander on 26 April 1818 in Cooperstown, he found his first newspaper, the *Republican Agriculturalist*, in Norwich. In this and then the *Manlius Republican*, he promoted the policies of Dewitt Clinton using the newspapers as political sheets. They failed, but Weed was undaunted as he went to work at the *Rochester Telegraph*, where he matured as a politician and a journalist. Following his purchase of the *Telegraph* he capitalized on the disappearance of William Morgan in 1826 to align himself with the anti-Masonic political movement. His influence grew both as publisher of the *Anti-Masonic Enquirer* and his election as assemblyman in 1828, the only office he would ever seek or hold.

With financing from leading anti-Masons, he founded the *Albany Evening Journal* in 1830. In the state capital he battled the "Albany Regency," creating victories for his friend Seward as governor in 1838 and William Henry Harrison as president in 1840. One of Weed's chief Regency adversaries was Edwin Croswell of the *Albany Argus*. He had been with Weed at Catskill, but the boyhood companionship turned into an adult antagonism. Weed countered Croswell by employing Horace Greeley (q.v.) to edit the *Jeffersonian*, a political journal. Together the two journalists joined the governor to form the political triumvirate of Weed, Seward, and Greeley, a force in Whig politics for almost two decades.

At home Thurlow and Catherine Weed had one son, James, who died at thirty, and three daughters, one of whom, Harriet, would help edit his autobiography. Another daughter was adopted. Catherine would die on 3 July 1858, when Weed was preparing to make his most ambitious political move—to secure for Seward the Republican nomination for president. During the 1840s and 1850s Weed was a dominant force in New York state and national politics, securing with one exception the nomination of his candidate by his party. He was successful by melding the traditional spoils system of patronage with journalistic support for the rights of the majority and the needs of the underdog. The result was a curious mixture of belief in reform but not reformers and a political philosophy that was conservative yet sometimes radical.

Weed astutely saw the declining power of the Whigs and carefully maneuvered the New York segment into the newly formed Republican ranks. His moment of truth came in his attempt to gain the Republican nomination for Seward, but his opponents including Greeley, who had broken the triad in 1854, prevailed. Beaten but unbowed, Weed supported Lincoln and consulted with the new president on his appointments. His political role now turned to that of a statesman as he went to Europe to rally support for the Union cause. At the same time his editorial voice weakened and after a semiretirement from 1854 to 1858 he sold the *Journal* in early 1863.

His political influence deteriorated, as he was a poor match for the Radical Republicans. His one attempt to get back into publishing with the *Commercial Advertiser* in New York during 1867–68 was curtailed by failing health. In his later years Weed concentrated on business, accumulating enough wealth to become a millionaire. He died in 1882 of old age in his eighty-sixth year.

BIBLIOGRAPHY:

A. *Autobiography of Thurlow Weed*, ed. Harriet Weed (Boston, 1886).

B. DAB 19, 12–13; NCAB 3, 598–600; NYT 23 November 1882; Glyndon G. Van Deusen, *Thurlow Weed: Wizard of the Lobby* (Boston, 1947).

SAMUEL V. KENNEDY III

WELLS-BARNETT, IDA BAKER (b. 16 July 1862; d. 25 March 1931) was known nationally and throughout Great Britain for her pugnacious articles documenting lynchings of black Americans, and other racial injustices. Her militant writings appeared in black and white newspapers and occasionally in black magazines. She owned two black newspapers and contributed to more than twenty-five other publications. Wells-Barnett was the first black American journalist hired by the *Chicago Inter Ocean*. She was well known in women's circles and active in politics.

Born a slave in Holly Springs, Mississippi, Ida was the oldest daughter of Jim and Elizabeth Wells. Her father, a skilled carpenter, grew up as his master's companion. He was never beaten or sold. Elizabeth, a Virginia native who worked as a cook, was sold to two different masters and never reunited with her family of origin. The Wells had eight children. Ida was educated in a Freedmen's Aid School (1866–78) and attended summer classes at Fisk University after high school. In 1887 Wells became editor of the Memphis, Tennessee, *Evening Star*. An article written for the *Star* about her controversial lawsuit against the Chesapeake, Ohio, and Southwestern Railroad drew national attention, and she received numerous requests for articles. Later she became editor of the *Living Way*, a Memphis church newspaper.

In 1889 she became one-third owner and editor of the *Memphis Free Speech*, a weekly newspaper with a circulation of 4,000. The newspaper grew in popularity under her editorship; by 1892 she was able to earn a living solely from subscriptions. Wells's anti-lynching campaign began in March 1892 after the lynching of three black businessmen. She was outraged by lynchings in Memphis and wrote numerous editorials to support her views. An angry mob demolished the *Free Speech* office and presses on 27 May 1892 while Wells was out of town. Her co-owner was told to leave Memphis, and a note left at the site promised death to anyone attempting to publish the paper again.

Wells moved to New York and acquired a one-fourth interest in the *New York Age*. She wrote two weekly columns for the *Age* until April 1893. She also wrote a pamphlet, *Southern Horrors: Lynch Law In All Its Phases*, published in 1892. An 1893 pamphlet, *The Reason Why the Colored American is Not in the World's Columbian Exposition*, was written by Wells and other noted black leaders. In February 1893 Wells began a two-month speaking tour in Great Britain. After the tour she moved to Chicago and became a writer for the *Chicago Conservator* and a leading women's rights activist. She returned to England to lecture for six months in 1894 and began writing the column ''Ida B. Wells Abroad'' for the *Chicago Inter Ocean*.

On 27 June 1895 Wells married attorney and *Chicago Conservator* owner Ferdinand L. Barnett. She purchased the *Conservator* shortly after their marriage and was its editor for two years. The Barnetts had four children: Charles Aked, Herman Kohlsaat, Ida B. Wells, Jr., and Alfred M. In 1909 Wells-Barnett investigated and reported on a lynching in Illinois for the *Chicago Defender*. She also covered race riots in two cities for the paper.

Wells-Barnett established several organizations from 1900 to 1930, met with President William McKinley and President Woodrow Wilson to protest discrimination against blacks, and was an independent Illinois senatorial candidate. She finished third in the senate race. Her autobiography, *Crusade for Justice* (1970), begun at age sixty-six, was never completed. She died of uremic poisoning. Her husband died in 1936.

BIBLIOGRAPHY:

B. DLB 23, 340–345; Madelon Golden Schilpp and Sharon M. Murphy, *Great Women of the Press* (Carbondale, Ill., 1983).

NORA HALL

WESTON, EDWARD HENRY (b. 24 March 1886; d. 1 January 1958) helped turn photography from simply a means of reproducing reality to a new way of seeing, from a craft to an art. While he stripped the artificial and the sentimental from his photographs, giving them an honesty and originality that was new in his day, he also demonstrated that the camera, with a creative person behind it, could show people, objects, and places from different perspectives.

Weston was born on 24 March 1886 in Highland Park, Illinois, the son of Edward Burbank Weston, a physician, and Alice Jeanette Brett Weston. His mother died before he was five, and his older sister, Mary Jeanette, shared in his upbringing. When Weston was sixteen his father gave him a Bullseye Kodak, which immediately fascinated him. Photography quickly overshadowed a career in retailing, started when he dropped out of high school. In 1906, after moving to Tropico (Glendale), California, where his sister was living, Weston bought a postcard camera and went door to door, offering his photographic services.

As his interest deepened, Weston in 1908 attended the Illinois College of Photography, then returned to California where he worked for commercial portrait studios. In 1911 he opened his own studio at Tropico, and rapidly built a reputation for the romantic, soft-focus portraits popular with the Hollywood stars and others in southern California. From 1914 to 1917 he held numerous one-man exhibitions and was honored by photographic societies. In 1917 he was elected to the prestigious London Salon.

At the height of his triumph as a pictorial photographer, however, Weston was also discovering modern art and literature, as well as modern, radical ideas. Increasingly unhappy with traditional approaches to photography, he began to experiment, working with extreme close-ups and unusual angles, and emphasizing forms. In March 1922 a friend, Tina Modotti, took some of Weston's experiments to Mexico for an exhibit. The enthusiasm of Mexican artists like Diego Rivera, José Clemente Orozco, and other leaders of the Mexican Renaissance encouraged Weston and in 1923, after a trip to Ohio, where he photographed steel mills, and to New York, where he was exposed to the work of Alfred Stieglitz (q.v.), Weston went to Mexico.

In Mexico he found a responsive audience for his work, and patronage for his realistic, sometimes stark portraits was sufficient for bare financial survival, giving him time to explore other forms with the camera, such as clouds and tiled rooftops. He returned to the United States permanently in 1928, settling on Wildcat Hill in the Carmel Highlands south of San Francisco the following year. In 1935 he moved to Santa Monica, but returned to Carmel three years later.

The man who has been called the ''Rembrandt of the Lens'' worked simply, using an 8'' × 10'' view camera and taking exceptional care to determine how the finished print would look before he made the exposure. He rarely made more than one negative of a photograph and by 1934 was not retouching any prints. He said he saw subjects for his photographs everywhere, as his first one-man show in New York bore witness, featuring the close-up studies of shells and rocks that resulted from his work at Point Lobos near Carmel.

In 1937 Weston was awarded a Guggenheim Fellowship, the first given to a photographer, to do a series about the West. In 1941 he was commissioned to provide photographs to illustrate a special edition of Walt Whitman's (q.v.) *Leaves of Grass*. During World War II he was involved in defense activities and prepared a traveling exhibition for the Office of War Information. His last one-man exhibition was at the Museum of Modern Art in New York in 1946.

Weston was married twice. His first marriage, to Flora May Chandler on 30 January 1909, ended in divorce in 1938. They had four sons, Chandler, Brett, Neil, and Cole. On 24 April 1938 Weston married Charis Wilson, with whom he had published *California and the West* (1940). They were divorced in 1946. Weston, stricken with Parkinson's disease, died 1 January 1958 in Carmel.

BIBLIOGRAPHY:

A. *The Daybooks of Edward Weston*, ed. Nancy Newhall, 2 vols. (New York, 1961, 1966).

B. DAB Supp. 6, 684–686; NYT 2 January 1958; Amy Conger, *Edward Weston in Mexico, 1923–1926* (Albuquerque, 1983); Beaumont Newhall, ''Edward Weston in Retrospect,'' *Popular Photography*, March 1946; Lew Parella, ed., Special Weston issue, *Camera* (Lucerne, April 1958).

BARBARA CLOUD

WHITE, HORACE (b. 10 August 1834; d. 16 September 1916) was a newspaper editor, businessman, and author of books on macroeconomics. A strong advocate of low tariffs and the gold standard, he improved newspapers' economic coverage and did much to shape party platforms and public opinion from the Civil War through World War I.

White was born in Colebrook, New Hampshire, to Horace White, a doctor, and Eliza Moore. White's father became an agent of the New England Emigration Company, which sent wagon trains westward. In 1838 he moved his family to the first log cabin in Beloit, Wisconsin. Horace entered Beloit College in 1849 and received a B.A. with honors four years later. In 1854 he became city editor of the *Chicago Evening Journal*, in 1855 the Chicago agent for the New York Associated Press, and in 1857 a reporter on the *Chicago Tribune*. Active in the abolitionist movement, he was assistant secretary of the National Kansas Commission and sent weapons to John Brown and others.

White was an early admirer of Abraham Lincoln; when he heard Lincoln attack the Kansas-Nebraska bill in 1854, White wrote that ''Lincoln is a mammoth. He has this day delivered a speech, the greatest ever listened to in the state of Illinois.'' In 1858 White covered the Lincoln-Douglas debates and also married Martha Root of New Haven, Connecticut. When the Civil War began, White became both Washington correspondent for the *Tribune* and clerk of the Senate Committee on Military Affairs. He left the *Tribune* in 1863 and, with Henry Villard (q.v.) and Adams S. Hill, started the Independent News Room Service in Washington, the first agency to compete with the Associated Press. White rejoined the *Tribune* in 1865 as editor in chief and part owner.

For White, the problems of Reconstruction were secondary to economic issues; he thought the granting of universal male suffrage would solve all problems of the ex-slaves. Horace Greeley (q.v.) had published Karl Marx in the *New York Tribune*, but the *Chicago Tribune* ran writings of John Stuart Mill and Frederic Bastiat. White himself edited in 1869 a translation of Bastiat's *Sophisms of Protection*, and warned that ''Communism is constantly gaining organization, and has all the desperation of those who have nothing to lose and everything to gain.'' But in 1873 White's wife died, and in 1874 he resigned his editorship.

Villard, president of the Oregon Railway and Navigation Company, made White his treasurer in 1875. That same year White married Amelia Jane McDougall of Chicago; they had three daughters. After six years in business and the gaining of a new fortune, White became part owner with Villard of the *New York Evening Post* in 1881. They made Carl Schurz (q.v.) editor in chief and E. L. Godkin (q.v.) of the *Nation* associate editor; the *Nation* was the weekly supplement of the *Post*. White took charge of the financial and economic policies of both. He opposed government fiat money and defended the gold standard. White's second wife died from an overdose of morphine in 1885, and White became coeditor of the *Post* with Godkin from 1885 to 1899, then editor in chief from 1900 to 1903.

A textbook White wrote in 1895, *Money and Banking*, went through ten editions and was used in college classrooms through the 1930s. His antitariff writings used both laissez-faire and social equity arguments to explain that higher taxes placed burdens on the poor. He had trouble with the problem of monopoly, but suggested that ''The Standard Oil Trust will be put to death somehow and sometime, most probably by its own vaunting ambition.'' White received an honorary doctor of laws degree from Brown University in 1906. When World War I began he wrote that it ''is too horrible for words. I dread to open a newspaper.'' White died in 1916 with the cause of death given as ''old age.''

BIBLIOGRAPHY:

B. DAB 10, 104–105; NYT 17 September 1916; Joseph Logsden, *Horace White, Nineteenth Century Liberal* (Westport, Conn., 1971).

MARVIN N. OLASKY

WHITE, PAUL WELROSE (b. 9 June 1902; d. 9 July 1955) was a pioneer of radio broadcast journalism and a founding father of CBS News. He organized the corporation's news-gathering operations in the 1930s and helped CBS News gain the reputation of being the most competent, objective, and alert in radio. With the support of CBS Vice President Ed Klauber (q.v.) and a superior staff of journalists including Edward R. Murrow, William Shirer, Elmer Davis, Robert Trout, and H. V. Kaltenborn (qq.v.), White turned CBS into a respected global news organization. In addition, White was largely responsible for the conversational and informal style of radio journalism, with its emphasis on clarity, conciseness, and simplicity.

White was born in Pittsburg, Kansas, to Paul W. White, a stone contractor, and Anna Pickard. During his years at Pittsburg High School, he worked as a reporter for the *Pittsburg Headlight* and the *Salina Sun*. Upon graduating in 1918, he continued to work in journalism, and he matriculated into the journalism program at the University of Kansas in 1919. During this period he was telegraph editor for the *Kansas City Journal*. In 1921 he entered the Columbia University School of Journalism and earned a bachelor's degree in 1923 and a master of science degree in 1924. After graduation, White worked briefly for the *New York Evening Bulletin* and then joined the staff of United Press, where he remained for the next six years in a variety of jobs. He became famous as a staff correspondent covering such stories as Lindbergh's flight across the Atlantic.

In 1930, he joined CBS as news editor in the publicity department, and he was promoted to publicity director in July 1932. White became director of public affairs in 1934 and director of news broadcasts in 1936, supervising all CBS News programs and CBS journalists. With the blessing of CBS President William S. Paley (q.v.), White energetically built CBS News over the next ten years, but he performed his job with such a sense of perfectionism that his health suffered permanently. White brought a rigorous, respectable background in print journalism to CBS, and he quickly recognized how different it was to *hear* news over the air rather than *read* it in the newspaper. Consequently, CBS journalists were instructed to write in a style more informal and appropriate to the medium of radio.

In 1938, following a trip to Europe, White felt that a war was likely, and he began organizing the CBS News operation on a global scale. White was able to set up live coverage of the Munich Crisis in September 1938 with Edward R. Murrow and William L. Shirer reporting live from Europe and H. V. Kaltenborn commenting from New York. CBS continued extensive, live coverage of the events leading to World War II, coverage which continued throughout the war with such now-famous names as Eric Sevareid, Bob Trout, John Daly, and Walter Cronkite (qq.v.). The coverage would earn CBS a Peabody Award in 1945.

From 1939 to 1946 White was an assistant professor of journalism at his alma mater, Columbia. Following the war and suffering from ill health resulting from overwork, White resigned from CBS and moved to the more moderate climate of California. He took a position as associate editor of the *San Diego Journal* from 1948 to 1950, then became news director of KFMB-TV in San Diego, where he remained until his death.

In 1947 White published a radio news textbook which formally presented many of the now standard principles of radio journalism. *News on the Air* was an authoritative text on objectivity, news judgment, and especially style. It was White's premise that radio's major contribution to journalism was the emphasis on clarity and conversationality.

White died after lengthy illnesses, including emphysema. On White's death, CBS President Frank Stanton (q.v.) paid tribute to White's great leadership in pioneering electronic journalism. The Radio-Television News Directors Association honors the memory of White with an annual award in his name. White married twice, to the former Susan Taylor and Margaret Miller. He had two daughters, Joan White Jenkins and Toni Suzanne.

BIBLIOGRAPHY:

A. "Radio News: Its Past, Present and Future," *Journalism Quarterly*, June 1946.

B. NYT 10 July 1955; Gary Paul Gates, *Air Time: The Inside Story of CBS News* (New York, 1978); Robert Metz, *CBS: Reflections in a Bloodshot Eye* (New York, 1975).

JOHN P. FREEMAN

WHITE, SALLIE JOY (b. 1847; d. 25 March 1909) was one of the pioneer newspaper women of New England because she was the first woman to work as a reporter on a Boston newspaper. She began by reporting on the woman suffrage campaign for the *Boston Post* and later wrote for the *Boston Herald* under the pen name Penelope Penfeather. White also was one of the founders and the first president of the New England Woman's Press Association.

White was born Sarah Elizabeth Joy in Brattleboro, Vermont, the daughter of Samuel Sargent Joy and Rhoda Elizabeth Ballou Joy. There were several writers in the family, including her great-grandfather, poet Silas Ballou, and her great-uncle, Nathan Sargent. Sargent, who wrote under the pen name Oliver Oldschool, was one of the first Washington correspondents. White was graduated from the Glenwood Seminary in 1865. Then from 1865 to 1868 she held a position with Loring's Circulating Library, a private, aristocratic book exchange in New England, and taught home economics in Charlestown, near Boston.

In 1869 White saw Lucy Stone (q.v.), a reporter from the *New York Tribune*, covering a suffrage convention and decided she wanted to do the same. She went to the *Post*, the only Boston paper giving the suffrage movement serious coverage at that time, and talked editor Nathaniel Green into giving her a job. But before he would hire her, Green assigned White to write about a roller-skating rink. She skated in a dress, wrote her story, and got the job. Then Green sent her "without masculine aid" to cover a suffrage convention in Vermont. She was the only woman at the press table. Furthermore, the first time she visited the *Post* city room the male reporters reportedly laid down a path of newspapers to protect her white satin gown from getting dirty.

On 2 June 1874 she married Henry K. White, an amateur musician. They had two daughters. In the same year as her marriage, White went to work for the *Boston Advertiser*. She moved to the *Boston Herald* in 1875 when *Advertiser* publisher Delano Goddard died. She worked for the *Herald* for ten years, writing a society column under the name Penelope Penfeather.

In 1885 White and five others founded the New England Woman's Press Association. She served as its first president from 1885 to 1891 and held that post again in 1907 and 1908. She also helped found the General Federation of Women's Clubs and served as president of the Daughters of Vermont and the Fortnightly Study Club of Dedham.

A smart and witty woman with a talent for public speaking and a love of literature, she lectured to women's clubs all over the country. Her best known lecture was entitled "Leaves From a Reporter's Notebook." She also wrote magazine articles and several books on the topics of home economics and careers for women. In 1891 the New England Woman's Press Association held a special dinner in Boston to honor White for her twenty-one years of service as a journalist. Two years before her death in 1909, White resumed writing for the *Boston Advertiser*. She died in Dedham near Boston.

BIBLIOGRAPHY:

B. *Dedham Transcript*, 27 March 1909; Mary R. Cabot, ed., *Annals of Brattleboro*, vol. 2; *1681–1895* (Brattleboro, Vermont, 1922); Myra B. Lord, *History of the New England Woman's Press Association* (Newton, Mass., 1932); Ishbel Ross, *Ladies of the Press* (New York, 1936)

CATHY PACKER

WHITE, THEODORE HAROLD (b. 6 May 1914; d. 15 May 1986) was a foreign correspondent and political analyst; his book *The Making of the President—1960* (1961) revolutionized the way journalists covered presidential elections. It spawned a school of political journalism based on meticulous detail and a novelistic perspective on political events, a school still dominant twenty-five years later.

White grew up in the poor Dorchester section of Boston, son of an impecunious lawyer, David White, and Mary Winkeller White. When his father died, sixteen-year-old White, a student at the Boston Latin School, dropped out of his after-school Hebrew classes and sold newspapers at a trolley stop. A newsboy's scholarship enabled him to attend Harvard, and he was graduated summa cum laude in 1938. Having studied history and Oriental languages in preparation for an academic career, White won a Shelton Traveling Fellowship and ended up in China. His career as a journalist began when he sent unsolicited dispatches to the *Boston Globe* and the *Manchester Guardian*.

John Hersey recruited White for *Time*, and he covered East Asia for the magazine until 1945, serving as chief of the China bureau. Disagreement with Henry Luce (q.v.) over the politics of China led White to leave *Time*. With Annalee Jacoby, he authored *Thunder Out of China* (1946), a best-selling Book-of-the-Month Club selection that stirred up controversy because of its criticism of the Chinese Nationalist government. He next served as senior editor at the

New Republic, but found working for that magazine even more constricting that working for *Time*.

After editing the World War II writings of General Joseph W. Stilwell and marrying Nancy Ariana Van der Heyden Bean of Connecticut, White moved to Paris in 1948 and wrote for the Overseas News Agency. He had two children, Ariana Heyden and David Fairbank. His best-selling *Fire in the Ashes* (1953) chronicled the postwar recovery of Europe.

When White returned to the United States in 1953, he began the second stage of his career, covering the U.S. political scene, first for the *Reporter*, and then for *Collier's*. After *Collier's* folded in 1956, White focused on fiction, writing a novel of China, and another on publishing called *The View from the 40th Floor* (1960). The income from his fiction allowed him to put into action a twenty-year plan for research and writings on the U.S. presidential elections. Two publishers turned down what was to become the phenomenally successful first in a series of books entitled *The Making of the President*. They argued that the public would not be interested in reading about the presidential campaign a year after it happened.

White doggedly covered the seven major candidates from the New Hampshire primary to the inauguration. The product of his exhaustive research described the campaign in dramatic, richly detailed terms, examining the underlying issues as well as building up the atmosphere so effectively that his style became known as the "milk and Total" school of reporting. A personal friend of John F. Kennedy as well as a chronicler of his presidency, White eulogized the assassinated president for *Life* magazine, using the Camelot mythology which became permanently associated with Kennedy.

The success of the campaign series continued in 1964 and 1968, but in 1972 many critics had become disenchanted with what they called White's compulsive hero worship and sometimes overwrought style. Relegating the Watergate break-in to a minor role, White viewed Nixon as one of the major presidents of the century. His book was all but written before the Watergate affair came to a head. He was subjected to severe criticism for his willingness to overlook Nixon's criminal activities in both *The Making of the President—1972* (1973) and the later *Breach of Faith: The Fall of Richard Nixon* (1975). The "Teddy White syndrome," in which reporters sanctified even the most trivial details of a candidate's life, was attacked. Having divorced his first wife in 1971, White married historian Beatrice K. Hofstader in 1974. His 1978 autobiography, *In Search of History*, was positively received, and he capped the Making of the President series in 1982 with *American in Search of Itself: The Making of the President 1956–1980*. In the mid–1980s he continued work on an ongoing project, a history of the world with the working title of "The Castle on the Hill."

BIBLIOGRAPHY:

B. NYT 16 May 1986; Rod Cockshutt, "In Search of Theodore H. White," *Journal of Popular Culture*, Fall 1981; April Koral, "Teddy White Says He's Not a Politician,"

Writer's Digest, July 1975; Howard J. Langer, "Confessions of a Second-Look Liberal," *Society*, July/August 1983; Joseph Nocera, "The Case for Teddy White," *Washington Monthly*, March 1983.

BROOKS ROBARDS

WHITE, WILLIAM ALLEN (b. 10 February 1868; d. 29 January 1944) was one of the best-known and most widely quoted newspaper editors in America. His shrewd and lively commentary in his newspaper, the *Emporia* (Kansas) *Gazette*, in twenty-four books, and in hundreds of magazine articles was believed to express the sentiments of midwestern, small-town, middle-class America. He epitomized for many the independence, crusading courage, and eccentricity of a disappearing breed of personal journalists.

White was born in Emporia, the only surviving child of Allen White, a physician and merchant, and Mary Ann Hatten White, who had been a schoolteacher before her marriage in 1867. In 1869 the Whites moved to the frontier town of Eldorado, Kansas, where young Will grew up. He was educated in public schools in Eldorado and attended the College of Emporia (1884–85, 1886) and the University of Kansas (1886–89), but he left without receiving a degree.

Beginning as a compositor, then as a reporter, White worked during his school years for newspapers in Eldorado, Emporia, and Lawrence. He managed the *Eldorado Republican* in 1890–91, and then wrote editorials and covered Kansas politics for the *Kansas City Journal*, a conservative Republican newspaper. Allen White had been a Democrat, but after his death in1882, his son gravitated toward the Republican party, which generally dominated Kansas politics. In 1892, after an editor mishandled an important story, White switched to the *Kansas City Star*, published by William Rockhill Nelson (q.v.).

Aspiring to be both man of letters and journalist, like his model E. W. Howe (q.v.), White wrote much poetry and fiction during these years. In 1891 he met Sallie Lindsay, a young schoolteacher with similar literary tastes; they were married on 27 April 1893. Throughout the rest of his life, Sallie White was his most important adviser on all matters, literary, political, and business. They had two children; William Lindsay (q.v.), who became a writer and publisher in his own right, and Mary Katherine.

Deciding he wanted to be his own boss, White bought the *Emporia Gazette* in 1895. With a circulation of 485, it was a faltering newspaper with an outmoded plant, but White got it for $3,000, all borrowed from political allies. Over the next decade he built the *Gazette* into a prosperous business. His success was due to both personal acumen and the general prosperity of the turn-of-the-century country press, brought by increased advertising, rural free delivery, and high farm prices. By 1910 the *Gazette* had a circulation of 3,500; by the 1940s it was around 7,000.

White first came to national attention when Republican political leaders blanketed the country with reprints of his editorial indictment of populism,

"What's the Matter With Kansas?" The publicity brought him to the attention of national magazine editors such as S. S. McClure and George Horace Lorimer (qq.v.). It also led to a meeting between White and Theodore Roosevelt. For over two decades White would be one of Roosevelt's most ardent and loyal followers.

White attributed his conversion from conservative to progressive Republican to Roosevelt's influence, but his shift was actually more gradual and was tied to the complexities of Kansas politics. Nonetheless, he did emerge by 1905 as a major leader of the "insurgent" wing of the party, and he skillfully used his connections with Roosevelt and reform-minded magazines to further both his political goals and his journalistic career. He also wrote several novels, including the best-selling *A Certain Rich Man* (1909), which expressed his belief that progressivism was fundamentally a "spiritual" movement. When Roosevelt's bid for another presidential term was defeated at the 1912 Republican National Convention, White helped to found the Progressive party. As a national committeeman, he struggled to build a new reform coalition, but after it collapsed in 1916, White returned to the Republican fold.

During World War I, White launched yet another career, as world citizen, when he visited European battlefronts as an observer for the Red Cross. He returned in 1919 to report the peace conference, and he actively supported the League of Nations. In 1930 Hoover appointed him to a committee to study conditions in Haiti, and the report's criticism of U.S. actions there helped inspire a Good Neighbor policy in Latin America. In the 1920s and 1930s the Whites traveled throughout the world, including the Soviet Union in 1933.

In reaction to the suppression of civil rights during World War I, in which he had concurred, White staunchly defended freedom of speech. In 1922 he clashed with Kansas Governor Henry Allen over whether he had the right to publicly support striking railroad workers. "To an Anxious Friend," an editorial written during the controversy, received the 1923 Pulitzer Prize. Two years later he ran for governor as an independent to protest the influence of the Ku Klux Klan in both parties. Otherwise he remained a progressive gadfly within the Republican party. To the chagrin of liberal friends, he endorsed all Republican presidential nominees, even after Franklin Delano Roosevelt carried the reform banner to the Democratic party. However, White did support many New Deal programs, and he assisted Roosevelt's war preparedness efforts, most notably in 1940 as the chairman of the Committee to Defend America by Aiding the Allies.

White's championship of tolerance and social justice, together with his virtuoso handling of the midwestern vernacular, his small-town folksiness, and his shrewd but genial wit, made him an American folk hero. This reputation was heightened by his 1921 editorial "Mary White," a moving tribute to his seventeen-year-old daughter who died in a horseback-riding accident. It was widely reprinted at the time and included in hundreds of anthologies over the next several decades. In an age when the ambitious flocked to big cities, White was respected by both urban and rural Americans for having chosen to stay in Emporia and remain his own boss, despite many lucrative job offers from national journals. His successful combination of diverse roles—journalist, businessman, man of letters, politician, world citizen—seems particularly impressive in this age of specialization. He was awarded nine honorary degrees and was president of the American Society of Newspaper Editors in 1937–38. He died, of a heart attack complicated by cancer, on 29 January 1944. His *Autobiography* received a posthumous Pulitzer Prize.

BIBLIOGRAPHY:

A. *The Autobiography of William Allen White* (New York, 1946).

B. DAB Supp. 3, 815–818; NYT 30 January 1944; Sally F. Griffith, *Home Town News: William Allen White and the ''Emporia Gazette''* (New York, 1989); E. Jay Jernigan, *William Allen White* (New York, 1983).

SALLY F. GRIFFITH

WHITE, WILLIAM LINDSAY (b. 17 June 1900; d. 26 July 1973), a noted author, journalist, and newspaper publisher, as well as war correspondent, was recognized also for his reporting skills during World War II. He replaced his famous father, William Allen White (q.v.), as editor and publisher of the *Emporia Gazette* upon the latter's death.

White was born in Emporia, Kansas, son of William and Sallie Lindsay White. When he was fourteen years old he began his journalism career as a reporter for the family newspaper. He attended the University of Kansas from 1918 to 1920 but was graduated from Harvard in 1924. He returned to the *Emporia Gazette* from 1924 to 1935. He married Katherine Klinkenberg on 29 April 1931. From 1931 to 1932, White served in the Kansas legislature but moved to the staff of the *Washington Post* briefly in 1935 and then to *Fortune* magazine from 1937 to 1939. In 1939 White became the war correspondent in Europe for the Columbia Broadcasting System and the *New York Post* while serving forty American newspapers as a correspondent.

While covering the Mannerheim Line in Finland, he received first prize from the National Headliners Club as the best European broadcaster of the year. In 1938 his novel *What People Said* appeared, a story about the effects of a bond scandal on the town and the lives of state officials. The story was based on the Finney scandal in Kansas. After the war White moved to the *Reader's Digest* and was made roving reporter in 1943.

While in London, England, during the war he adopted a three-year-old girl who became the source of his book *Journey for Margaret*. She was the Whites' only child. In 1942 White wrote *They Were Expendable*, a story about the MTB Squadron 3 in the Philippine campaign, as told in book-length interview fashion. It became a successful motion picture. He also wrote numerous articles during this time for the *Atlantic Monthly, Life*, the *New Republic*, the *Saturday Evening Post*, and others. At the same time he kept busy working for the *Reader's Digest*.

In 1943 *Queens Die Proudly* was published. It was the story of one of the original Flying Fortresses.

In 1945 he wrote *Report on the Russians*, which became controversial. Some reviewers spoke warmly of the book while other critics thought he may have touched up the events. In 1949 White wrote *Land of Milk and Honey*, about a young Russian flyer who escapes when the plane crashes while returning to Russia. In 1953 White detailed the actions and success of medical personnel in *Back Down the Ridge*. In 1953 he also wrote about the fate of war captives in *The Captives of Korea*. Many of White's books resulted from his travels throughout much of his life. In1969 White's last book, *Report on the Asians*, explored his impressions of India and the Far East.

Apparently White made a decision early in life to make his own mark in the world. He often said he did not really resent the fact that his father automatically received credit for many of the editorials he wrote in his early years on the family newspaper. As a result of his writing skills and his desire to move elsewhere for an education, his adult life involved him as an overseer for Harvard. He retained this relationship until his death in 1973. His son-in-law and daughter remain with the family newspaper. His wife is listed as publisher.

BIBLIOGRAPHY:

B. NYT 27 July 1973; *Time* 6 August 1973; *Washington Post*, 27 July 1973; *Twentieth Century Authors*, Supp. 1, 1075.

JOHN M. BUTLER

WHITMAN, WALT (b. 31 May 1819; d. 26 March 1892) was a leading poet of the nineteenth century whose newspaper work influenced his philosophy and poetry. His journalism exposed him to the social unrest of the times, the rough conditions of New York society, and to political corruption. He once claimed that his short stories and poetry, which also appeared in many of the newspapers and magazines of the day, were "of pure American breed, large and lusty . . . naive, masculine, affectionate, contemplative, sensual, imperious."

Whitman, the second oldest of nine children, was born at West Hills, on Long Island, New York. Whitman's father, Walter, was a carpenter and farmer. His mother was the former Louisa Van Velsor, whose parents were of Dutch and Welsh descent. In 1823 Whitman's family moved to Brooklyn, where young Whitman attended the public schools before dropping out at the age of thirteen.

In 1832 Whitman became an apprentice on the *Long Island Patriot*, the first of countless newspapers he was to be associated with over the next thirty years. But his association with journalism was interrupted intermittently from 1836 to 1841 by schoolteaching, although he continued to contribute to journals during this period and actually edited the *Long Islander* for a year. From 1841 to 1848 he worked on at least ten newspapers or magazines in New York and Brooklyn, the most important of which were the *Democratic Review* and the *Brooklyn Daily Eagle*. The former was a literary journal that afforded Whitman the literary company of Nathaniel Hawthorne, Edgar Allan Poe, William Cullen Bryant (q.v.), Henry Wadsworth Longfellow, and others.

In February 1846 he became editor of the *Daily Eagle*, a four-page daily for which he wrote one or two editorials and summaries of news daily. Later he called this position "one of the pleasantest sits of my life—a good owner, good pay, and easy work and hours." By 1848, however, he had fallen out of favor with those in control of the paper on the issue of slavery. He then spent three months on the *New Orleans Crescent* in a position similar to that of managing editor, but more importantly his trip South made it possible for him to become acquainted with America's vastness—an acquaintance quite evident in his *Leaves of Grass*. The relationship with the *Crescent* owners was a cool one, and later in 1848 Whitman was back in Brooklyn supporting the Free-Soil movement and editing the *Freeman* until its demise a year later.

For the next five or six years Whitman dedicated much of his life to poetry, and his journalism amounts to only an occasional contribution in one of the Brooklyn or New York newspapers. He became editor of the *Brooklyn Daily Times* in 1857 and in that capacity wrote less about politics but a great deal about society. His editorials on prostitution, abortion, and slavery were considered "daring" for his age. But after two years he lost his position on the *Daily Times* because of attacks by "certain orthodox deacons of what was then a smug, conventional town." It was Whitman's last role as editor, but his articles and poetry found their way into *Life Illustrated, Saturday Press*, the *Galaxy*, *Harper's*, *Scribner's*, and other journals of the day.

Whitman's contribution to journalism was not nearly as great as that of his contemporary William Cullen Bryant of the *New York Evening Post*, and some observers have recorded the poet's newspaper work as an editor was no worse, and perhaps slightly better than other editors of the 1840s and 1850s. However, Whitman found journalism a way to make a living and a training ground for an insight into the ways of America—an insight that gained his poetry immortality. He died on 26 March 1892 of emphysema.

BIBLIOGRAPHY:

A. *Leaves of Grass* (Brooklyn, 1855, and revised through 1892); *I Sit and Look Out: Editorials from the "Brooklyn Times"* (New York, 1932); *Walt Whitman of the "New York Aurora": Editor at Twenty-Two* (State College, Pa., 1950).

B. DAB 20, 143–152; NYT 27 March 1892; Thomas L. Brasher, *Whitman as Editor of the "Brooklyn Daily Eagle"* (Detroit, 1970); Justin Kaplan, *Walt Whitman* (New York, 1980); Paul Zweig, *Walt Whitman: The Making of the Poet* (New York, 1984).

ROBERT L. BAKER

WILE, FREDERIC WILLIAM (b. 30 November 1873; d. 7 April 1941) was a noted foreign correspondent, author, columnist, and radio commentator. Working as a correspondent in Europe from 1900 to 1919, he gained a reputation as an authority on Germany. After World War I, he returned to the United States where he spent the second half of his career as a news analyst in Washington and as one of the first radio commentators.

Born in the small, northern Indiana town of La Porte, Frederic was the son of Jacob Wile and Henrietta Guggenheim Wile. His father, who migrated to the United States in 1848, was one of those political immigrants whom history remembers as "the Forth-eighters." He was a banker in La Porte and a leader of the small Jewish community in that town. A scholarly man with a strong interest in politics, he became a figure of considerable importance in the local and state activities of the Democratic party in Indiana. Frederic attended the University of Notre Dame, but due to financial reasons did not graduate. That university, however, later awarded him his first LL.D. in 1924; he received a second one from Ursinus College in 1929. Wile married Ada Skakman of Chicago in 1901. They had two children, Frederic William II and Helen Isabel.

Wile spent the first half of his career as a reporter and foreign correspondent. In 1898 he acquired a position with the *Chicago Record*. Two years later, Edward Price Bell (q.v.), who had just been sent to London to develop the *Record*'s foreign news service there, requested that Wile be sent over to assist him. Thus began Wile's twenty years abroad. In 1901 the *Record* made him its Berlin correspondent, a position he held until 1906 when he became the correspondent in that same city for Lord Northcliffe's *London Daily Mail*. He remained with the Northcliffe organization for the next thirteen years. As Wile's reputation grew, so grew the demand for his services. Accordingly, in 1908, he became the Berlin correspondent for the *New York Times* as well as for the *Daily Mail*. Moreover, during the years before World War I, he was also commissioned to send occasional mail correspondence to the *Chicago Tribune*.

Although the outbreak of war in 1914 ended Wile's Berlin residency, it failed to make a break in his journalistic work abroad. At the start of the conflict, the German government arrested him as a suspected spy and forced him to leave the country. For that action, Wile later sued the German government, and in 1929 he was awarded $6,400 for false arrest, false charges of espionage, and the loss of personal property. During the war, however, Wile remained in Europe. He wrote a column entitled "Germany Day by Day," which was a digest of the German press. It appeared regularly on the main news page of the *Daily Mail* throughout the war. After the United States entered the war in 1917, he became a specialist on Germany for the Intelligence Section, GHQ, AEF, with the rank of lieutenant colonel. At the end of the war, he represented the *Daily Mail* in a small group of journalists who accompanied President Woodrow Wilson on his pre–peace conference tours through France, Belgium, England, and Italy.

Invited to give a series of speeches on the Chautauqua lecture circuit, Wile returned to the United States in 1919. Here he spent the second half of his career. The well-known owner of the *Philadelphia Public Ledger*, Cyrus H. K. Curtis (q.v.), appointed Wile to serve as chief of his Washington bureau, and Wile assumed that position on 1 January 1920. Three years later, however, he left the *Public Ledger*, became an editorial writer for the *Washington Star*, and began a column called "Washington Observations" that appeared in the *Star* and a number of other papers. Accordingly, he became one of the early columnists.

He also was a pioneer news commentator. In 1923 he introduced a weekly, fifteen-minute review of political affairs called "The Political Situation in Washington Tonight," first for NBC (1923–28) and later (1929–38) for CBS. He was the first radio commentator to broadcast from the Capitol, doing so with a short talk immediately preceding the inauguration of Calvin Coolidge on 4 March 1925. Later he became the first reporter to cover an event in Europe by radio when he did a series of transatlantic broadcasts from London during the London Naval Disarmament Conference of 1930.

Most of all, Wile was a reporter, and in that capacity he was one of the best of his time. He placed himself in superb positions to report on some of the most significant political news of the century, and he did so in a way that made him a trusted figure among the journalists of his day. His memoirs, *News Is Where You Find It* (1939), is an engaging and unpretentious record of his life's work and of the people, both in journalism and in public life, whom he knew. He died of a heart ailment in Washington, D.C., on 7 April 1941.

BIBLIOGRAPHY:

B. *Indiana Authors and Their Books 1816–1916*, 338–339; NYT 8 April 1941; *La Porte Herald-Argus*, 7 April 1941; *Who Was Who in America* 1. 1346–1347.

JAMES D. STARTT

WILSON, EARL (b. 3 May 1907; d. 16 January 1987) had been a nationally syndicated Broadway columnist for forty years when he retired on 25 March 1983. He was the author of a dozen books, several of which were produced from material published in the gossip columns he wrote for the *New York Post*. Besides keeping tabs on celebrities, especially entertainers, Wilson was credited with tracking down many front-page news stories. He also was a contributor to the *Saturday Evening Post*, *Collier's*, and *Esquire*.

The son of Arthur Earl Wilson and Cloe Huffman Wilson, he was an Ohio farm boy. Born in Rockford, a town of less than 1,500 in the northwestern part of the state, just over the Indiana border, Wilson was a choreboy for a country weekly at the age of twelve. He later taught Methodist Sunday school, and during the summer when he was sixteen he drove a team of horses that pulled a water wagon for a threshing crew for one dollar a day and board. He first studied at Heidelberg College and then graduated from Ohio State University in 1931.

Wilson got into the newspaper business as a sports writer on the *Piqua* (Ohio) *Daily Call* because he needed money for college. After graduation he was a reporter for the International News Service and the *Akron Beacon Journal* before joining the *Washington Post* as a copy editor. In 1935 the city editor for the *New York Post* told Wilson a rewrite job was open for him, but the city editor thought Wilson should go back to Ohio and be happy. Wilson replied, "I don't want to be happy. I want to work for you." When he got to New York he moved into a rooming house in Washington Square where he met Rosemary Lyons, a secretary from Kansas City. They were married on 10 January 1936, and several years later had a son, Earl Lyons Wilson, who grew up to become a writer of revues and songs. Wilson's career at the *Post* began to blossom when he became the wartime replacement for the amusement editor and he started to write a column called "It Happened Last Night" on the side. The 1,000-world column began appearing six days a week on 19 October 1942. At its peak it was syndicated by Field Newspaper Service in more than 200 dailies.

Wilson, who created the title "saloon editor" for himself, used notebooks, tape recorders, cameras, and typewriters on his Broadway beat or wherever else his quest for "what's hot and what's not" took him. Living and working in the Times Square area, he began his typical eighteen-hour workday shortly after 11:00 A.M. He would gulp down some orange juice and coffee and, as he once told an interviewer, was "at work in 30 seconds." The afternoon would be spent in his office at home, writing or interviewing. After eating dinner at Toots Shor's, he and his wife, who usually went with him and to whom he referred in his columns as B.W. (beautiful wife), would be out touring night spots by 8:00 P.M. He held himself to a maximum of two drinks a night and between 2:00 A.M. and 4:00 A.M. would be home again, going through his copious notes and writing his column. A taxi driver would pick it up in time to get it to the paper for the 7:00 A.M. deadline.

In addition to his Broadway rounds, Wilson followed stars to Las Vegas, Hollywood, and throughout Europe. During his most hectic times he traveled the equivalent of four times around the world annually. This feverish pace is evident in the fact that during the 1940s he wrote three books in four years. His first book, *Jungle Performers*, was written with Clyde Beatty, the famous animal trainer, in 1941. The next four, all published between 1945 and 1953—*I Am Gazing Into My Eight Ball, Pike's Peak or Bust, Let 'Em Eat Cheesecake,* and *Look Who's Abroad Now*—mostly contained material from his columns. Among his other books, the one to generate the most comment was *Sinatra: The Unauthorized Biography*, which, when published in 1976, prompted a $3 million suit by Frank Sinatra, who claimed it provided unfair competition for his planned autobiography.

Terms most often used to describe the five-foot-six Wilson were bland, mild-mannered, and sleepy-eyed, while his writing was called flip, terse, candid, and bizarre, but eminently readable. It was said that he had a penchant for bare facts and that he gave the readers what they seemed to like, what he called the three B's—booze, busts, and behinds. He defined a nightclub as a place where the tables are reserved but the customers aren't and bragged that he was the first newspaperman to get "stink" into type. Referred to by some as "Peck's Bad Boy" of journalism, he made himself at home in the dressing rooms and bedrooms of stars. He once interviewed a dancer as she sat in the nude and also covered a nudist convention "clad only in his crewcut." His popularity led to frequent appearances on the major television talk shows and the panel shows like "I've Got a Secret."

Wilson's columns and books contained tidbits on all sorts of celebrities, but some of his most memorable material came from breaking the story of Marilyn

Monroe's romance with Arthur Miller and their later divorce. He said the highlight of his career was learning from an actress in 1953 that the Salk polio vaccine was in the works and scooping the rest of the world with a front-page story.

Wilson had been suffering from Parkinson's disease for two years and had cut back to three columns a week before retiring from newspaper work, but not from writing, at the age of seventy-five. His last column, the 11,424th of his career, ended with the three words that had closed all of the others: "That's Earl, brother."

BIBLIOGRAPHY:

A. *Earl Wilson's New York* (New York, 1964); *The Show Business Nobody Knows* (Chicago, 1971); *Show Business Laid Bare* (New York, 1974); *Hot Times: True Tales of Hollywood and Broadway* (Chicago, 1984).

B. Mark Nichols, "Broadway's Nite Errant," *Coronet*, February 1957; "Long-time Broadway Columnist Retires at 75," *Editor and Publisher*, 26 March 1983; "Midnight Earl," *Newsweek*, 27 June 1949; "Saloon Editor," *Time*, 19 November 1945.

KAY MARIE MAGOWAN

WINCHELL, WALTER (b. 7 April 1897; d. 20 February 1972) was the father of the modern newspaper gossip column, which he transplanted to network radio. His weekly audience of readers and listeners at the peak of popularity numbered in the tens of millions. At first he wrote about Broadway stars and shows. Later, he expanded to the movies, Manhattan, politicians, world affairs, and even tips on stocks. Eventually, he became too eccentric for a mass audience.

Winchell (the family name had only one "l"), oldest of two sons, was born in New York City to Jacob and Janette Bakst Winchel. His father was a shopkeeper who went out of business and deserted the family. Walter dropped out of school in the sixth grade to supplement his mother's income by appearing in vaudeville shows. In 1910 he was part of a singing trio that included George Jessel and Eddie Cantor. After two years, he teamed with Rita Green in a song and dance routine. In 1917 he enlisted in the U.S. Navy, but returned to the stage after his service was completed. He married his partner in 1920.

He began writing up gossip for backstage bulletin boards. Some of his material was printed in *Billboard*. This caught the attention of *Vaudeville News* in 1922 and he was hired as a reporter. After a divorce, he married Jane Magee, a dancer, in 1923. Two children were born to the Winchells and they adopted an infant girl. Gloria was adopted in 1923 and died in 1932. A daughter, Walda, was born in 1927, and a son, Walter Jr., in 1935.

The newly created *New York Graphic* hired him in 1924 to be the drama critic, to solicit advertising on commission, and to write gossip columns. His distinctive style employed coined words and short items that used euphemisms to protect his often incomplete information. He invented expressions such as "Chicagorilla," "Lohengrined" for married, "on the verge" for contemplating divorce, and "cupiding" for romance.

He worked long hours because of his restlessness and nervous energy and his interest in Broadway gossip. The Stork Club became his nocturnal headquarters, and its proprietor, Sherman Billingsley, became a national celebrity through Winchell's columns. His columns became a reader magnet, and his celebrity status earned him admission to the famed literary Algonquin Round Table. His writing appeared in *Vanity Fair* and *Bookman*. His columns began appearing outside New York through syndication to other newspapers.

Even wider circulation of his daily columns under different titles came when he was hired by William Randolph Hearst's (q.v.) *New York Mirror* in 1929. His columns appeared in all the Hearst newspapers and received wider syndication. His first radio program began in 1929. Through the depression years his popularity and income continued to mount. His fifteen-minute Sunday night program on NBC began in 1932 and at its peak boasted of an audience of twenty million. Titled the "Jergens Journal," it opened with Winchell's famous line: "Good Evening Mr. and Mrs. North and South America and all ships at sea. Let's go to press. Flash!" The entire program was accompanied by the sound of a telegraph key which he operated. The sounds were an example of his showmanship because the dots and dashes were random so that Winchell could release some of his nervous energy. Jergens continued to sponsor the program for ten years, and it continued under various sponsors on ABC and Mutual until 1956.

His staccato style and reading speed of more than 200 words a minute were distinctive. But by 1956 his opinionated slurs, particularly against Democratic presidential candidate Adlai Stevenson, had lost him his sponsors and his audience. On television he hosted the "Walter Winchell Show" briefly in 1956, and in 1957, the "Walter Winchell File." He later became the narrator for "The Untouchables" on ABC (1959–63). At one time, 800 newspapers used his column. When the *Mirror* suspended in 1963, subscribers to his column continued to drop.

At times, much of his material was contributed by press agents and public relations practitioners who were rewarded with a favorable mention for their clients. Because of his popularity, he could sell books, buoy stocks, or make a movie into a hit with a favorable mention. He supported President Franklin Roosevelt and had meetings with him. J. Edgar Hoover and the FBI were made into national heroes. To honor his friend, he created the Damon Runyon Memorial Fund for Cancer Research in 1946.

As early as 1932 he was anti-Nazi. He promoted Senator Joseph McCarthy's red hunt in the 1950s. His feuds were countless and his opinionated comments often irritating to large numbers of people. After the suicide of his estranged son Walter on 25 December 1968, he announced his retirement on 5 February 1969. His wife died on 5 February 1970. Winchell died on 20 February 1972 in Los Angeles after undergoing cancer therapy for four months.

BIBLIOGRAPHY:

A. *Winchell Exclusive: Things that Happened to Me—and Me to Them* (Englewood Cliffs, N.J., 1975).

B. NYT 21 February 1972; Herman Klurfeld, *Winchell, His Life and Times* (New York, 1976); Bob Thomas, *Winchell* (New York, 1971); Ed Weiner, *Let's Go to Press: A Biography of Walter Winchell* (New York, 1955).

SAM KUCZUN

WISE, ISSAC MAYER (b. 29 March 1819; d. 18 March 1900), a rabbi, editor, and author, was considered during his lifetime to be one of the most prominent Jews in the United States. His organizational drive facilitated the development of the Jewish press and the Jewish Reform movement in America and the birth of the three major Jewish institutions in the United States where none had existed before. These included the Union of American Hebrew Congregations, Hebrew Union College, and the Central Conference of American Rabbis.

Wise wrote the first book of common prayer for Jews in America, and founded and edited one of the earliest and longest-lived Jewish-English publications of that period, the *Israelite*. He later founded a companion newspaper for German-speaking Jews, *Die Deborah*. In addition, Wise wrote numerous articles on historical and theological subjects, novels in both English and German, and several plays.

Born in Steingrub, Bohemia, to Leo and Regina (Weis) Weis, Wise began his Hebrew education under the tutelage of his father, a schoolteacher. Later he continued his religious and secular studies in Prague. In 1835 Wise entered the rabbinical school of Rabbi Aaron Kornfield in Jenikau, Bohemia. Two years later he returned to Prague to attend the gymnasium and the university, where he studied for two years. He also spent one year of study at the University of Vienna. At the age of twenty-three Wise appeared before the rabbinical court, Beth Din, and was awarded the title of rabbi. Six months later he was elected rabbi of the Jewish congregation in Radnitz, Bohemia (26 October 1843). There, he married Theresa Bloch on 26 May 1844; she was the daughter of a Jewish merchant in the neighboring town of Grafenreid. They had ten children.

Disgruntled by the restrictions still in force against Jews in Bohemia, Wise emigrated to the United States, arriving in New York on 23 July 1846. It was abut this time that he changed the spelling of his name. Rabbi Max Lilienthal of New York assisted Wise in gaining an appointment as rabbi of the Congregation Beth-El of Albany, New York, in the fall of 1846.

From the moment Wise began his American rabbinate, he demonstrated his sympathy with the German Reform movement. He supported innovations in worship such as introducing the organ, a choir, and mixed seating in the synagogue. He wrote articles in favor of Reform and published them in the two periodicals of American Judaism, the *Asmonean* and the *Occident and American Jewish Advocate*. As early as 1848 Wise urged the formation of a union of congregations and rabbis to put an end to religious individualism and anarchy. He persisted in his admonitions until, finally, twenty-five years later in 1873, the Union of American Hebrew Congregations was organized in Cincinnati.

When his radical ideas put him at odds with Orthodox rabbis in 1850, Wise founded a new congregation in Albany, Anshe Emeth, where he remained until he accepted a call to Bene Yeshurun congregation in Cincinnati in 1854. He officiated there as rabbi for the remaining forty years of his life. During his New York years Wise designed a stately order of worship, *Minhag America*, a Reform prayer book which became an authorized liturgy when the 1855 Cleveland rabbinical conference approved it with only a few changes. It remained in use until the 1894 Union prayer book was authorized.

Within a month after assuming the pastorate of his Cincinnati congregation, Wise began to publish the *Israelite*, a weekly newspaper intended to create a "sharp weapon" for Judaism in the reformed fashion. A year later he published the German edition. Both flourished for half a century. Wise claimed his newspapers were more read than any other Jewish journals. Only a year after its birth, the *Israelite* boasted some 2,000 subscribers nationwide. By 1860 *Die Deborah* claimed 1,800.

About the same time that the *Israelite* began publication, Wise set to work to establish a college where young men could receive a Jewish education. Although Zion Collegiate Association, founded by Wise in 1855, did not succeed in establishing a college, Wise continued for twenty years to press for an institution of higher learning and a theological seminary for the training of rabbis for American pulpits. It was not until 3 October 1875 that Hebrew Union College opened its doors to students. On 1 June 1883 Wise, the college's founder and president for life, conferred the title of rabbi on four young men who constituted the first class of rabbis to be ordained in the United States.

Throughout his rabbinate Wise publicized his views in his newspapers. He traveled throughout the United States lecturing, dedicating synagogues, and enlisting the interest of Jewish communities in his projects. He frequently took stands within a national political forum when issues affecting Jews became a concern. In his journals he did not give much space to the coverage of purely Jewish associations. Rather, he often solicited Jewish support for non-Jewish civic enterprises. He advocated public schooling for Jewish children, while recognizing the need for Jewish institutions of higher learning. And he welded the spirit of American Judaism with the spirit of America through a universalistic theological position. He maintained only one activist stance, that Jews should assert themselves to eradicate laws and customs that catered to Christians and impinged upon Jewish freedoms. These points were consistently promoted in the editorial pages of the *Israelite*.

After the death of his first wife in 1874, Wise married Selma Boudi of New York on 25 April 1876. She bore him four children. At the time of his death in Cincinnati, Wise was survived by his wife, five daughters, and six sons.

BIBLIOGRAPHY:

A. *Reminiscences* (Cincinnati, 1901).

B. DAB 20, 426–427; NYT 27 March 1900; Kathryn T. Theus, "From Orthodoxy to Reform: Assimilation and the Jewish-English Press in Mid–19th Century America," M.A. thesis, Univ. of Maryland, 1982.

KATHRYN T. THEUS

WISNER, GEORGE WASHINGTON (b. 1812; d. 10 September 1849) was the nation's first full-time police reporter, and a partner in Benjamin H. Day's (q.v.) *New York Sun*, the first successful "penny paper." Wisner's police reporting helped account for the paper's quick success, and was widely copied. But after twenty months with the *Sun*, he moved to Michigan. There, he became prominent in journalism, law, and Whig politics, and prepared the ground for the formation—after his death—of the Republican party in that state.

Wisner, tenth of sixteen children of Moses and Nancy Merwin Wisner, was born on the 117-acre family farm near Springport, Cayuga County, New York. The Wisner family was a relatively old one in New York, with an array of prominent members. His father, Wisner said, served as a militia colonel in the War of 1812. Like his siblings, Wisner received a "common school" education. At fifteen he was apprenticed to Ulysses F. Doubleday, printer-publisher of the *Cayuga Patriot*, at nearby Auburn. But Wisner ran away, and found employment on an anti-Masonic paper in Batavia, New York. When the Masons organized a raid on the paper, Wisner defended it, and was indicted for attempted murder. But Auburn attorney William A. Seward won him an acquittal.

Wisner then went to New York City, possibly joined by a younger brother, Ira G. Wisner, in 1834 publisher of the *Protestant Vindicator*. He worked in a variety of printing shops. His involvement with the *Sun* began in September 1833, about two weeks after Day had first issued it. Day had hired an editor who was not working out. Wisner, then unemployed, appeared and agreed, in return for $4 a week and a share of the paper, to attend police court, write what was interesting, and set type and other chores. Apparently, he took over the bulk of the editorial work, with Day concentrating on business details.

In his police reporting, Wisner had a sharp eye and ear for the appearance and speech of the defendants, and his treatment was variously sardonic, facetious, moralistic, and prurient. Sometimes he summarized tersely; sometimes he gave more extensive and even imaginative vignettes. His police column became a chief attraction of the paper, and caused other penny papers to seek to duplicate it. At the same time, it aroused criticism and caused problems.

The police court defendants did not like having their names publicized or being made the objects of fun and scorn. So a move developed to bar reporters from the court proceedings. The *Sun* contested the move and won a ruling that reporters had a right to be present. And more conservative members of society deplored the emphasis on the seamier sides of New York life.

Politically, at Day's insistence, the *Sun* was independent, and refused to endorse candidates or parties. Its treatment of national and international political events was terse, as events of little interest to its readers. Like other papers, it reprinted short passages of literary works of the era, so making them available to a growing and "literizing" group of readers. Wisner also may have pioneered in an early form of the crusade, against quack doctors, and in investigative reporting, by challenging official reports on the incidence of cholera.

Day and Wisner split amicably in June 1835 when Day bought out Wisner's share in the paper. Wisner, who had married Catherine Langan on 6 September 1834, moved with her and an infant son to Pontiac, Michigan. There he began to study of law, engaged in trade and land sales, became active in a radical wing of the Whig party, and helped found the Michigan Anti-Slavery Society. He also edited the *Pontiac Courier*. In 1837, the year Michigan became a state, he was elected a state representative. During his one term he moved that the University of Michigan be located in Ann Arbor, and headed a committee which authorized Douglas Houghton's epic geological survey of the state.

Subsequently, he practiced law with several partners, including a younger brother, Moses Jr. (a Republican governor of Michigan in 1860) and edited the *Pontiac Jeffersonian*. In 1842, 1844, and 1846, he was the unsuccessful Whig candidate for Congress. In 1847 he became editor of the *Detroit Daily Advertiser*, the party's chief organ in the state, and his attacks helped overturn Democratic rule in that city. His attitudes—nativist, antislavery, anti-Mason, temperance, and Whiggish—reflected those of the groups which joined to form the Republican party in 1854.

Wisner died of a lung disorder in 1849. He was buried in Pontiac's Oak Hill Cemetery, and was survived by his wife; three sons, Oscar, Henry C., and Charles; and a daughter, Frances. Charles and Frances died young, and Mrs. Wisner, in Detroit in 1891.

BIBLIOGRAPHY:

B. James Stanford Bradshaw, "George W. Wisner and the New York Sun," *Journalism History*, Winter 1979–1980; James Stanford Bradshaw, "George W. Wisner, a Forgotten Firebrand," *Chronicle of the Historical Society of Michigan*, Fall 1983; William David Sloan, "George W. Wisner, Michigan Editor and Politician," *Journalism History*, Winter 1979–80.

JAMES STANFORD BRADSHAW

WOODHULL, VICTORIA CLAFLIN (b. 23 September 1838; d. 10 June 1927), journalist and reformer, was a pioneer for women's rights and the first woman presidential candidate. She was the first suffragist to have an official hearing in Washington and is prominent in the annals of Wall Street, socialism, and spiritualism. Woodhull was a popular orator, addressing such subjects as constitutional equality, the social revolution, the principles of finance, and free love.

Victoria Claflin was born in Homer, Ohio, the seventh of ten children of Reuben Buckman Claflin and Roxana Hummel Claflin. The father plied various trades, including storekeeper, stableman, tavern keeper, and gristmill operator. Roxana Claflin, before their marriage, had been a maid. The family was poor, eccentric, and shunned by the community. In the late 1840s, when Victoria was still a child, her father was suspected of arson and the family was forced to leave town. Mrs. Claflin was a spiritualist, and as the family, moved from town to town, Victoria and her sister, Tennessee Claflin (q.v.), gave spiritualistic exhibitions. For a time, the family traveled as a fortune-telling and medicine show.

In 1853, at the age of fifteen, Victoria married Dr. Canning Woodhull. The couple had two children: Byron, born in 1854, and Zula Maud, born 23 April 1861. After her marriage Victoria continued to travel with the medicine show and as a clairvoyant with her sister. The Woodhulls were divorced in 1864, and Victoria began traveling with Colonel James H. Blood, whom she later married. A marriage license was issued on 14 July 1866 in Dayton, Ohio, but there is no record of when the marriage was actually performed. It is generally accepted that Blood was the major force in the education of Victoria.

In 1868 Victoria Woodhull and Tennessee Claflin managed to engage the attention of the elderly Cornelius Vanderbilt, who was interested in spiritualism. They opened a stock brokerage and, with Vanderbilt's guidance, made considerable profits in the stock market. At about the same time, Victoria became interested in socialism and in a cult called the Pantarchy, which advocated free love and which was headed by Stephen Pearl Andrews. From that time on, Victoria and the Claflin clan were constantly involved in scandal and litigation.

Victoria and Tennessee began *Woodhull and Claflin's Weekly* in 1870, launching a campaign in its pages which promoted equal rights for women, free love, a single standard of morality, and Victoria Woodhull for president. The newspaper condemned abortion and prostitution. Although it is generally accepted that Blood and Andrews wrote much of the material, the viewpoints expressed were those of Victoria Woodhull. The newspaper quickly turned to muckracking and to the sensational in an effort to boost circulation.

In the fall of 1871 *Woodhull and Claflin's Weekly* became the first American newspaper to print the *Communist Manifesto*. In 1872 Victoria Woodhull was nominated for the presidency by the Equal Rights party; the vice presidential candidate was Frederick Douglass (q.v.). In this election, Victoria went to the polls, but was not allowed to vote.

On 2 November 1872 *Woodhull and Claflin's Weekly* printed a story which precipitated one of the greatest scandals of the age. The article described the alleged intimacy between Henry Ward Beecher (q.v.) and the wife of Theodore Tilton, a young reporter. Because of the article, Anthony Comstock had the edition confiscated on the charge of sending obscene literature through the mail. Victoria and Tennessee were arrested and spent two periods of time in jail. They were later acquitted.

On 18 September 1876 Victoria Woodhull and Colonel Blood were divorced. The following year, Victoria and Tennessee moved to England. On 31 October 1883, Victoria married John Biddulph Martin, a wealthy English banker. He died 29 March 1897. Although her life in England was devoted to charitable works, Victoria Woodhull did not totally forsake journalism. There was the short-lived (one issue) *Woodhull and Claflin's Journal*, 29 January 1881, and, with her daughter, Zula, the *Humanitarian* (1892–1901). Woodhull died in her sleep at Bredon's Norton, Worcestershire, at the age of eighty-eight.

She lived to see many of her reforms implemented. American women were allowed to vote. Divorce and a single standard of morality were becoming accepted in the 1920s. Her work for the labor movement was remembered and honored. Her interests in eugenics and family planning were beginning to be taken seriously.

BIBLIOGRAPHY:

B. DAB 10, 493–494; NYT 11 June 1927; Johanna Johnston, *Mrs. Satan* (New York, 1967); M. M. Marberry, *Vicky: A Biography of Victoria C. Woodhull* (New York, 1967); Emanie Sachs, *The Terrible Siren* (New York, 1928).

NORA BAKER

WOOLLCOTT, ALEXANDER (b. 19 January 1887; d. 23 January 1943) was a witty, sarcastic, sentimental, charming, tyrannical, and eccentric print and radio journalist who specialized in theater, trivia, and sentimentality, with results that charmed many and irritated some.

Woollcott was born at the Phalanx, New Jersey, an eighty-five-room house built as part of a socialist living experiment and the property of some of Woollcott's maternal ancestors. He was the youngest of five children. His mother was Frances Bucklin Woollcott. His father, Walter Woollcott, moved several times in quest of work, so Alexander started school in Kansas City, continued it in Germantown, Pennsylvania, and, after the family returned to the Phalanx, boarded at Central High School in Philadelphia. He attended Hamilton College in upstate New York, becoming Phi Beta Kappa, the editor of the *Lit*, a devoted alumnus, and eventually a trustee and a generous donor to the school. His ashes are buried in the college cemetery.

Woollcott's father seems to have wandered off by the time the boy entered high school. Alexander supported himself partly by writing book reviews and doing odd jobs for the *Evening Telegraph* and the *Record* in Philadelphia. After his graduation from Hamilton in 1909 he got a job in the Chemical National Bank in New York City, but lost it when he came down with the mumps. When he recovered, he joined the *New York Times* as a reporter. He was neither happy nor especially good at reporting, but held on to the job until 1914 when, to their mutual relief and advancement, the *Times* appointed Woollcott its drama critic. He had loved the theater since his introduction to it as a child in Kansas City, where he also played his first stage role at the age of four.

Woollcott worked with theater the rest of his life, in various ways—as critic, playwright, actor, and as its ardent promoter. He himself was theatrical. As a critic he could be more dramatic than the play on the stage, entering the theater carrying a cane and wearing cloak and opera hat, sweeping down the aisle, waving to friends across the theater, and issuing greetings and luncheon invitations to those nearby without breaking stride.

He interrupted his newspaper career during World War I to join a hospital unit. He served in France, became a sergeant, and in 1918 was transferred to the staff of *Stars and Stripes*. He covered frontline action, remained in Europe six months after the war, then went back to New York and the *Times*.

In 1922 he moved from the *Times* to the *Sun*, and soon after that to the *Herald*. In 1925 he shifted to the *New York World*, joining a group of well-known writers including Walter Lippmann (q.v.). By that time he was also known as one of the wits at the Algonquin Round Table. A review he wrote in 1924 established the fame of the Marx Brothers.

He stopped writing newspaper criticism in 1928. He had already begun writing for magazines and turning out books, and it was after leaving the *World* that he began playwriting. He traveled, in Europe and later in the Orient. He began broadcasting, first with a local program called "The Town Crier," then with a program on CBS.

He became known to many who did not know of him already, including many who did not see the play George S. Kaufmann and Moss Hart wrote about him, *The Man Who Came to Dinner*. The play captured the Woollcott that Kaufmann and Hart knew from seeing him in his homes in New York and Vermont—the usually benevolent, always dramatic tyrant who could take over the lives and houses of others. It is said of him that when invited to stay at the White House, he greeted Eleanor Roosevelt's return from a trip by saying, "Come right in, Mrs. Roosevelt." Woollcott himself appeared for a time in the Pacific Coast company of the play, portraying himself, but left it in April 1940 when he suffered a heart attack.

Even after that he continued his social life, his passionate games of croquet, his broadcasting, and his travel. He broadcast in London during the early years of World War II, and the British found him to be a source of encouragement. He turned out more books and magazine articles.

On 23 January 1943, while appearing on radio on "The People's Forum," Woollcott suffered a fatal heart attack.

BIBLIOGRAPHY:

A. *The Portable Woollcott* (New York, 1946).

B. Samuel Hopkins Adams, *Alexander Woollcott* (New York, 1945); Wayne Chatterton, *Alexander Woollcott* (Boston, 1978).

DWIGHT JENSEN

WRIGHT (D'ARUSMONT), FRANCES (b. 6 September 1795; d. 13 December 1852) was a reformer, feminist, lecturer, and writer who for four years (1828–32) published and coedited the *Free Enquirer*, a seminal weekly for American dissidents.

A native of Dundee, Scotland, she was the daughter of James Wright, a Scots radical, and Camilla Campbell Wright. They died when she was two, and she and a younger sister, Camilla, were brought up by relatives in England. The family was wealthy, and she was very well educated. By the time she was in her early twenties, she had written a play, *Altorf* (1819), and a literary tract, *A Few Days in Athens* (1822). She also had been attracted to the United States, and had read widely about it.

In 1818 as a wealthy heiress, she came to America, meeting important personages of the time, and touring widely. She was delighted with what she saw (except for slavery) and put her observations into a book, *Views of Society and Manners in America*, published in England in 1822. The book brought her to the attention of the Utilitarian English philosopher Jeremy Bentham, and she became part of his liberal circle. Through him, she also met the old French hero, the Marquis de Lafayette, and lived with him—both insisted only as a daughter—in France.

When Lafayette made a nostalgic official visit to America in 1824, Miss Wright accompanied him, and visited with the aging Thomas Jefferson, as well as James Madison, corresponding later with both. Slavery, however, troubled her. She purchased land in Tennessee—so advised by Andrew Jackson—and established at Nashoba, near Memphis, a commune where ten slaves she had bought could work out their own freedom. By 1828 the settlement, a financial failure and marred by sexual misconduct by her administrator, had all but disintegrated.

At this critical time, she decided to change her life, to become an editor and teacher. She went to New Harmony, Indiana, where the industrialist Robert Owen had established a commune, and with his son, Robert Dale Owen, took over publication of the *New Harmony Gazette*, which had less than 300 circulation. The notoriety she had obtained, and liked, together with the novelty that a woman could be an editor, promptly increased the circulation list. In signed articles she attacked organized religion and advocated rationality and equality, with education as the key to progress.

Actually, much of the editorial work fell on Robert Dale Owen, since Wright that fall and winter undertook a famed lecture tour—almost never before had a woman appeared on a public platform—all the way to New York and Philadelphia. The *Gazette*, soon renamed the *Free Enquirer*, printed her responses to argumentative and largely theological letters written to her. It also reprinted abstracts from the works of other liberal thinkers, but had little real "news."

In early 1829 the paper was moved to New York City, with young George Henry Evans (q.v.) as its printer. Wright purchased an old church, renaming it the Hall of Science, where readings and lectures were presented, and launched a further attack, "The Christian Party in Politics." Owen and she quickly found some common ground with a nascent labor movement—whose members also were interested in better schooling for their children—and a result was the formation of the Workingman's party, which badly rattled the older parties with a small success in the 1829 elections. These groups termed the workingmen the "infidel" or "Fanny Wright" party, and so succeeded in splitting the movement.

Through Evans, however, Wright arranged for the publication of a series of liberal tracts—works by Voltaire, Paine (q.v.), and other freethinkers, and William Cobbett (q.v.). She also continued her lecturing—speaking out for the rights of women—and in 1830 went to Haiti, to see to the settlement of her slaves from Nashoba. She returned briefly to New York—her contributions to the *Free Enquirer* gradually dwindling—and then went again to Europe. There, on 21 July 1831, she married William Phiquepal D'Arusmont, a Frenchman who had been manager of her lecture tours. After the birth of a daughter, Sylvia, and their return to America, the marriage ended in a separation, with Phiquepal securing much of the remaining Wright wealth in a settlement.

Ultimately, she returned to lecturing and to political involvement in support of Andrew Jackson. She settled in Cincinnati and, after the divorce, lived in some poverty. In a fall, she broke her leg, was immobilized for months, and died.

BIBLIOGRAPHY:

A. *Biography, Notes and Political Letters of Frances Wright D'Arusmont* (Boston, 1849).

B. DAB 10, 549–550; NYT 18 December 1852; Celia M. Eckhardt, *Fanny Wright, Rebel in America* (Cambridge, 1984).

JAMES STANFORD BRADSHAW

—Y—

YANCEY, WILLIAM LOWNDES (b. 10 August 1814; d. 27 July 1863) is the man whom many credit as the driving force behind the secessionist movement and the creation of the Confederate States of America. As an Alabama politician, lawyer, and publisher of the *Wetumpka Commercial Advertiser* and the *Wetumpka Argus*, Yancey was uncompromising in his devotion to the principle of states' rights and to the consequences of that stand in the mid-nineteenth century. He knew what it would cost his nation, his state, and his own career, and even though he died in the midst of the Civil War, he held few illusions about its outcome.

Yancey was born to Benjamin Cudworth and Caroline Bird Yancey at his grandfather's home in Warren County, Georgia. Soon afterwards, his father began a law practice in Abbeville, South Carolina, but in 1817 he died, leaving his widow with two small sons, William, three, and Benjamin, one. His mother moved back to Georgia and married Nathan Sidney Smith Beman, a teacher and minister, in 1822. Beman took the family to Troy, New York, where he was pastor of the First Presbyterian Church and a leader of the New School Presbyterians. Yancey's stepfather thus became actively identified with the growing antislavery movement.

The stepson left home before this influence could take hold, however. He went to Williams College from 1830 to 1833 but left before graduation to join the law practice of Benjamin Perry, a friend of his father, in Greenville, South Carolina. The principle of nullification was the major topic of debate at the time, and Yancey entered into it as a Unionist editor of the *Greenville Mountaineer*. He married Sarah Carolina Earle, the daughter of a prominent Greenville farmer, in 1835, and became a part of the South Carolina plantation society. As that society accepted him, he accepted the prevailing thinking on slavery and states' rights and was soon to become its staunchest advocate. A year and a half later, the two moved to Dallas County, Alabama. While visiting his wife's family in Greenville two years later, he killed his wife's uncle in self-defense. He was fined $1,500 and sentenced to a year in jail, but the governor commuted the sentence to a $500 fine.

Back in Alabama in 1839, Yancey rented a plantation near Cahaba and along with his brother bought the *Wetumpka Commercial Advertiser* and the *Wetumpka Argus*. He also bought a farm near Wetumpka but went back to practicing law when his slave population was wiped out by poison. He quickly became prominent and was elected to the state legislature in 1841, the state senate in 1843, and Congress in 1844. He served there until 1846, when he resigned. He had been involved in a heated debate and subsequent duel with Thomas Clingman. Neither man was injured, and Yancey was relieved of responsibility for the duel by the Alabama legislature, but he felt it his duty to resign and leave public offices to others. He remained a private citizen until serving in the state secessionist convention in 1860.

In 1848 Yancey composed the Alabama platform written in answer to the Wilmot Proviso. The platform stated that the U.S. Constitution was designed to curb the powers of Congress and the executive and to preserve to the states' rights not expressly given to Congress. Yancey was attacked from all sides because of his stand, especially when he presented his platform for the national Democratic convention in 1848.

At the national convention of the Democratic party in 1860 in Charleston, South Carolina, Yancey once again pressed his principles, and his speech was followed by the withdrawal of the Southern delegates. The severed convention was reconvened in Baltimore, but by this time the northern Democrats were in complete control, and they refused to seat Yancey's Alabama delegation. Yancey withdrew and formed the Constitutional Democratic party, which nominated John Breckinridge for president. Yancey traveled all across the country delivering speeches in favor of this ticket, but to no avail. Lincoln's election brought on the secession of the Confederate states, and in March 1861 Yancey was sent to England and France as a commissioner for the new nation. He returned in 1862 and was elected to the Confederate Senate but died in Montgomery shortly thereafter.

BIBLIOGRAPHY:

B. DAB 20, 592–595; J. W. Dubose, *The Life and Times of William Lowndes Yancey* (New York, 1942).

JAMES GLEN STOVALL

YOUNG, ARTHUR "ART" HENRY (b. 14 January 1866; d. 28 December 1943) was an exceptionally talented political cartoonist who journeyed ideologically from republicanism to Marxism. In his secularized version of religious revival Young argued that the Soviet example showed the way for a world to enter an era of peace and happiness.

Art Young was born on a farm near Orangeville, Illinois, the third among four children of Daniel Stephen Young, a storekeeper and agnostic, and Amanda Wagner Young. After the family moved to Monroe, Wisconsin, Art Young's mother took him to church, but he later wrote, "All I remember about this religious experience is that one Sunday we each were given a colored card with tinseled angels on it." Young studied at the Academy of Design in Chicago from 1884 to 1886. After working as a staff artist on three Chicago newspapers—the *Evening Mail*, the *Daily News*, and the *Tribune*—he studied from 1888 to 1890 at the Art Students League of New York and the Académie Julian of Paris.

Young first became famous with daily cartoons drawn for the *Chicago Inter Ocean* beginning in 1892. He worked briefly on the *Denver Times*, then moved to New York and drew for *Judge, Life, Puck,* and William Randolph Hearst's (q.v.) *Evening Journal* and *Sunday American*. His cartoons were valued highly by Hearst's principal editor, Arthur Brisbane (q.v.), who would accept Young's increasingly frequent drawings of fat, silk-hatted figures but change the labels from "Capitalism" to "Greed."

Young married Elizabeth North on 1 January 1895. They had two sons and two separations before parting finally in 1905, with Young proclaiming, "I am an artist, and the duties and courtesies of married life are too much for me." They were never legally divorced, but Elizabeth moved to Los Angeles and the continental divide lasted.

During the final throes of married domesticity, Young spent many hours in the New York Public Library reading Marxist literature. His cartoons headed left, and he became a contributor to the new radical magazine *Masses* in 1911. Young also was Washington correspondent for *Metropolitan* magazine from 1912 to 1917, drawing caricatures and illustrating articles by Walter Lippmann (q.v.). Explaining in his autobiography, *Art Young: His Life and Times*, the turn to Marxism, Young wrote that he had long desired to learn "the truth," and had finally come to believe in the centrality of "the class struggle" to human misery. For the last thirty years of his life Young believed firmly that "the end of Capitalism is near."

Indicted for *Masses* cartoons in 1913 and 1918, Young never was convicted. The charge in 1913 was brought by the Associated Press for a cartoon which showed an AP man pouring into a vast reservoir labeled "The News" contents of bottles labeled, "Lies, Suppressed Facts, Prejudice, Slander, and Hatred of Labor Organizations." The charge in 1918 was antiwar sedition. Both trials ended in hung juries and Young seemed unfazed. He even fell asleep in one courtroom and snored away until his attorney, fearing contempt of court, whispered in his ear, "For God's safe, Art, wake up."

From 1919 to 1921 Young published his own weekly magazine, *Good Morning*, and contributed to the Marxist magazine *Liberator*. He opened a Connecticut art gallery in the 1920s and continued to draw cartoons for radical publications, and for the *New Yorker* during the 1930s. His favorite work, *Art Young's Inferno* (1933), depicted "the Hell of reality . . . Bosses, figures, paper shuffling. Back to discordant homes—debts and the Hell Blues.'' At Young's death in 1943 after a heart attack, he was contributing editor to the *New Masses*. Young ''is agreeable to know socially,'' one reporter had said of him, ''but he puts vitriol into his cartoons.''

BIBLIOGRAPHY:

A. *Art Young: His Life and Times* (New York, 1939).

B. DAB Supp. 3, 851–853; NYT 31 December 1943; Richard W. Cox, ''Art Young: Cartoonist from the Middle Border,'' *Wisconsin Magazine of History*, Autumn, 1977.

MARVIN N. OLASKY

YOUNG, PLUMMER BERNARD (b. 27 July 1884; d. 9 October 1962) became known as the publisher of one of the best edited and most influential black newspapers in the nation.

Young was born at Littleton, North Carolina, the son of Winfield and Sallie Adams Young. He attended St. Augustine's College in Raleigh. He worked for his father, who published a local paper, the *True Reformer*. Young worked as a printer's devil beginning in 1898, and continued in that job, and others, until 1910. That year he bought the *Lodge Journal and Guide*, a weekly published by the Knights of Gideon at Norfolk, Virginia.

Young dropped ''Lodge'' from the name and was the publisher-editor of the paper until 1949 when it was taken over by his sons. Young, however, remained as publisher. The *Journal and Guide* was the largest weekly south of the Mason-Dixon line.

A story goes that one day in 1933, while Young was looking out his window trying to think of a lead for an editorial about slum housing, a hovel collapsed on the family living in it. Young went out, got pictures, and wrote an illustrated editorial that began a successful campaign for slum clearance in Norfolk.

Young became involved in other business enterprises, and was active in political efforts to solve racial discrimination. He helped found the Southern Commission on Interracial Cooperation and its successor, the Southern Regional Council. President Franklin Roosevelt appointed Young to the Fair Employment Practices Commission. He was a trustee of Howard University, Hampton Institute, The Anna T. Jeannes Foundation, St. Paul's College (later St. Paul's Polytechnic Institute), and the Palmer Memorial Institute. He took an active role in education leadership in Norfolk.

In 1960 the National Newspaper Publishers Association named him distinguished editor of the year, one of many awards he received. A park and a school in Norfolk are named for him. Young married Eleanor White on 6 May 1906 in Raleigh, North Carolina. She died in 1946. He married Josephine Tucker Moseley of Norfolk on 11 February 1950. By his first wife, Young had two sons: Plummer Bernard, Jr., and Thomas White. Young died in Norfolk.

BIBLIOGRAPHY:

B. NYT 12 October 1962.

DWIGHT JENSEN

Z

ZENGER, ANNA CATHERINE (b. 1704?; d. 1751) was the publisher of the *New-York Weekly Journal* for about nine months while her husband, John Peter Zenger (q.v.), was imprisoned and charged with seditious libel. She also published the paper for two years following the death of her husband.

Little is known of Anna Catherine Maulin. She was born into a well-to-do family in New York. Her father was Dutch, apparently, and her mother, French. Anna was active in church work. Some sources credit her with starting the first Sunday School in New York. She married Zenger in the Old Dutch church in New York on 24 August 1722. They would have five children.

When Zenger was arrested in November 1734 for publishing seditious libel—material critical of William Cosby, New York's royal governor—Anna took over printing and publishing the *Journal*. She took meals to Zenger and received instructions through the jailhouse door. For the nine months of his imprisonment and trial she remained steadfast in her support.

Zenger was released from jail following his acquittal in August 1735 and resumed his printing duties. When he died in July 1746, Anna again took over printing and publishing the paper and continued until December 1748, when the duties were taken over by Zenger's son from a previous marriage, John.

Kent Cooper (q.v.), in what he called a "novelized biography" of Anna Zenger, gives her credit for the creation and editing of the *Journal*. According to Cooper, Anna, rather than James Alexander, William Morris, and other critics of the Cosby administration, pushed Zenger to begin the *Journal* and was the primary editor of and writer for the paper. Only after Zenger was released from jail, and had become more accomplished as a writer and editor, did he take over the actual editing of the paper.

Cooper's version has been attacked as myth by historian Vincent Buranelli who, while agreeing that Anna was publisher and printer of the paper during her husband's imprisonment, writes that there is no evidence that she was ever editor.

BIBLIOGRAPHY:

B. Vincent Buranelli, "The Myth of Anna Zenger," *William and Mary Quarterly*, April 1956; Kent Cooper, *Anna Zenger* (New York, 1946).

W. WAT HOPKINS

ZENGER, JOHN PETER (b. 1697; d. 28 July 1746), publisher of the *New-York Weekly Journal* and accused libeler of the governor of the colony of New York, is one of the best-known figures in the history of freedom of the press in the United States. In 1735 Zenger was acquitted of seditious libel when a jury returned an unprecedented verdict. Though the law required a guilty verdict when a defendant was shown to have published libelous material, and though Zenger admitted publishing material said to be libelous of the governor, a jury ignored the instructions of the judge and accepted arguments of Zenger's defense attorney that the material must be shown to be false before a publisher could be punished for libel. The case had no precedential value, but was highly inspirational and established that the press could criticize the government and escape punishment. There is dispute over the role Zenger played in the case, but it is likely that he was simply the printer of critical material supplied to him by a clique of colonists angry at the administration of the new royal governor.

Zenger was thirteen when, in 1710, he arrived in New York from Germany with his mother, sister, and brother. The exact place and date of his birth are not known, nor is anything known of his father. His father, however, may have been one of the more than 400 immigrants who died during the long ship voyage from Germany to the colonies.

On 16 October 1711 Zenger was apprenticed to New York's only printer, William Bradford. He fulfilled his eight-year term and moved to Maryland where, in the spring of 1720, he successfully petitioned the Maryland legislature for the right to print the county laws and other official records. On 27 October 1720 he was naturalized. While in Maryland, Zenger married. His wife, however, died giving birth to a son, who was named John. Zenger returned to New York in 1722 where, on 24 August, in the Old Dutch church, he married Anna Catherine Maulin. They would have five children.

Zenger was in partnership with Bradford briefly in 1725, before establishing his own print shop on Smith Street in 1726. In May 1734 he moved his print shop to Broad Street. In April 1732 William Cosby arrived from England to become royal governor of New York and almost immediately entered into dispute with acting governor Rip Van Dam and other colonists. Among other things, Cosby demanded additional payments from Van Dam and, when he was not supported by the courts, fired New York Supreme Court Chief Justice Lewis Morris. A group of colonists, including Morris and former attorney general James Alexander, recruited Zenger to print the *New-York Weekly Journal*. Morris and

Alexander were probably among the most frequent contributors to the *Journal*, which first appeared 5 November 1733.

A year later, following the publication of some particularly critical material, Cosby succeeded in having Zenger arrested for raising sedition. Zenger was jailed under £400 bail, a sum the critics of Cosby could have raised, but did not. Zenger would be in jail for more than eight months before trial. In the meantime he would have a number of legal setbacks, including the dismissal of his attorneys, James Alexander and William Smith, from the case.

When the case was finally called for trial on 4 August 1735, attorney John Chambers was appointed as Zenger's defense counsel. Chambers, apparently, was as surprised as anyone in the courtroom when Andrew Hamilton, a Philadelphia attorney with an excellent reputation, arose from his seat among the spectators and announced that he was representing Zenger. Hamilton, a business partner of Alexander and Smith, admitted that Zenger had published the material critical of Cosby. The prosecuting attorney believed the case was over, since, in a libel trial, the jury only determined the facts of the case—that is, whether the defendant published the material in question. Hamilton argued, however, that the published material was true, that truth was a valid defense for libel, and that both the facts and the law of libel should be decided by the jury. When the judge refused to hear the arguments, Hamilton addressed his remarks to the jury, which took only ten minutes to acquit Zenger.

Before the furor over the trial could settle, Cosby died. His replacement called in several critics of the former administration as advisers, and the disputes that brought about Zenger's arrest evaporated. In 1737 Zenger was made public printer of New York and a year later was appointed to the same position for New Jersey. He published the *Journal* until his death.

BIBLIOGRAPHY:

B. DAB 20, 648–650; James Alexander, *A Brief Narrative of the Case and Trial of John Peter Zenger* (Cambridge, Mass., 1972); James Wright Brown, "Life and Times of John Peter Zenger," *Editor and Publisher*, 14, 21, 28 March and 4, 11 April 1953; Vincent Buranelli, *The Trial of Peter Zenger* (Westport, Conn., 1975).

W. WAT HOPKINS

APPENDIX

NEWS MEDIA AND PROFESSIONAL FIELDS

Columnists

Willis J. Abbot
Franklin P. Adams
George Ade
Joseph Alsop
Stewart Alsop
Mary Clemmer Ames
Ray Stannard Baker
H. R. Baukhage
Edward Price Bell
Winifred Black
Emily Edson Briggs
Arthur Brisbane
Heywood Broun
Erwin D. Canham
James Cannon
Boake Carter
Marquis Childs
Raymond Clapper
Irvin S. Cobb
Bob Considine
Kenneth Crawford
George Creel
George W. Curtis
Elmer Davis
Mary Abigail Dodge
Dorothy Dix
Roscoe Drummond
W. E. B. Du Bois
Finley Peter Dunne
Eugene Field
Doris Fleeson
Sheilah Graham
Murat Halstead
Norman Hapgood
William Hard
Joel Chandler Harris
Bret Harte
Gabriel Heatter
Mark Hellinger
Ben Hecht
Genevieve Forbes Herrick
Ben Hibbs
Marguerite Higgins
William Dean Howells
Florence Finch Kelly
Dorothy Kilgallen
Bernard Kilgore
Joseph Kraft

Arthur Krock
Ring Lardner
David Lawrence
Fulton Lewis, Jr.
Lillian Alberta Lewis
A. J. Liebling
Sara Clarke Lippincott
Walter Lippmann
Peter Lisagor
Samuel Lubell
C. K. McClatchy
Anne O'Hare McCormick
Ralph McGill
O. O. McIntyre
Marie Manning
Isaac F. Marcosson
Don Marquis
H. L. Mencken
Gertrude Bustill Mossell
Edgar Ansel Mowrer
Edgar Wilson "Bill" Nye
Rollo Ogden
Louella Parsons
Sara Willis Parton
Drew Pearson
Westbrook Pegler
John S. Phillips
Benjamin Perley Poore
Ernie Pyle
Grantland Rice
Inez Robb
Howard Rock
Will Rogers
Chester H. Rowell
Vermont Royster
Damon Runyon
Carl Sandburg
Ellen Browning Scripps
Gilbert Seldes
Walter "Red" Smith
Richard L. Strout
Ed Sullivan
Sol Taishoff
Dorothy Thompson
Clifton Utley
Joe Vila
Oswald Garrison Villard
Frances Wayne
Ida B. Wells-Barnett
Sallie Joy White
Frederic William Wile
Earl Wilson
Walter Winchell
Alexander Woollcott

Editorial Cartoonists and Illustrators

Clifford K. Berryman
James T. Berryman
Otto L. Bettman
Jay N. Darling
Homer Davenport
Theodore Russell Davis
John Fischetti
Daniel Fitzpatrick
John T. McCutcheon
Frank Miller
Thomas Nast
Richard F. Outcault
Frederic S. Remington
Alfred Rudolph Waud
Art Young

Foreign Correspondents

Elie Abel
Hugh Baillie
H. R. Baukhage
Edward Price Bell
Frederick T. Birchall
Winifred Black
Margaret Bourke-White
Mary Marvin Breckinridge
Arthur Brisbane
Cecil Brown
Erwin D. Canham
Turner Catledge
Marquis Childs
Raymond Clapper
Samuel L. Clemens
Upton Close
John A. Cockerill
Charles Carleton Coffin
Charles Collingwood
James Creelman
Walter Cronkite
George W. Curtis
Elmer Davis

Richard Harding Davis
Rheta Childe Dorr
Roscoe Drummond
Walter Duranty
Doris Fleeson
Harold Frederic
Margaret Fuller
Wes Gallagher
Floyd Gibbons
Thomas Grandin
Charles H. Grasty
William Hard
Ben Hecht
Ernest Hemingway
Helen Hiett
Marguerite Higgins
Will Irwin
Max Jordan
H. V. Kaltenborn
Joseph Kraft
Arthur Krock
David Lawrence
Elmer W. Lower
Anne O'Hare McCormick
Isaac F. Marcosson
Herbert L. Matthews
Webb Miller
Edward P. Morgan
Edgar Ansel Mowrer
Paul Scott Mowrer
Edward R. Murrow
David Graham Phillips
Ernie Pyle
Julian Ralph
John Reed
Inez Robb
Albion Ross
Harrison E. Salisbury
Carl Sandburg
George Seldes
Gilbert Seldes
Eric Sevareid
William L. Shirer
George W. Smalley
Henry Justin Smith
Howard K. Smith
William T. Stead
John Steinbeck
Leland Stowe
Raymond Gram Swing
Herbert Bayard Swope
Ida Tarbell
Lowell Thomas
Dorothy Thompson
Robert Trout
Elizabeth Wason
Ida B. Wells-Barnett
Theodore H. White
William L. White
Frederic William Wile
Alexander Woollcott

Humorists

Franklin P. Adams
George Ade
Ambrose Bierce
Charles Farrar Browne
Samuel L. Clemens
Irvin S. Cobb
Mary Abigail Dodge
Finley Peter Dunne
Eugene Field
Benjamin Franklin
Joel Chandler Harris
Bret Harte
Ring Lardner
David Ross Locke
Don Marquis
Edgar Wilson "Bill" Nye
Opie Read
Will Rogers

Magazines

Willis J. Abbot
Lyman Abbott
Ansel Adams
Samuel Hopkins Adams
Stewart Alsop
Ray Stannard Baker
H. R. Baukhage
Henry Ward Beecher
Ambrose Bierce
Edward W. Bok
Andrew Bradford
William Bradford III
William Cowper Brann

Noah Brooks
Charles Farrar Browne
William Cullen Bryant
Burridge D. Butler
Willa Cather
Turner Catledge
Norman Chandler
Francis P. Church
Irvin S. Cobb
Fr. Charles Coughlin
Gardner Cowles Jr.
Kenneth Crawford
George Creel
James Creelman
Herbert Croly
Jane Cunningham Croly
Cyrus H. K. Curtis
George W. Curtis
Elmer Davis
Richard Harding Davis
Theodore Russell Davis
Dorothy Day
Joseph Dennie
Mary Abigail Dodge
Rheta Childe Dorr
Theodore Dreiser
Roscoe Drummond
W. E. B. Du Bois
Abigail Scott Duniway
Finley Peter Dunne
Max Eastman
George Henry Evans
Kate Field
John Fischetti
Daniel Fitzpatrick
Benjamin O. Flower
Josiah Flynt
Benjamin Franklin
Frederick A. Freed
Philip Freneau
Margaret Fuller
Marcus Garvey
Emile Gauvereau
Morrill Goddard
Louis A. Godey
E. L. Godkin
Philip L. Graham
Sheilah Graham
Eleanor Graves
Ralph Graves
Sara Josepha Hale
Norman Hapgood
William Hard
Joel Chandler Harris
Bret Harte
Lafcadio Hearn
William Randolph Hearst
Gabriel Heatter
Ernest Hemingway
Genevieve Forbes Herrick
Ben Hibbs
Marguerite Higgins
Edgar Watson Howe
Quincy Howe
William Dean Howells
Will Irwin
Florence Finch Kelly
Dorothy Kilgallen
Moses Koenigsberg
Joseph Kraft
Dorothea Lange
Ring Lardner
David Lawrence
Isaac Leeser
Frank Leslie
Miriam Leslie
Lillian Alberta Lewis
A. J. Liebling
Sara Clarke Lippincott
Walter Lippmann
Peter Lisagor
David Ross Locke
George Horace Lorimer
Clement A. Lounsberry
Elmer W. Lower
Samuel Lubell
Henry R. Luce
Charles MacArthur
Joseph W. McCarthy
S. S. McClure
Anne O'Hare McCormick
Benarr Macfadden
O. O. McIntyre
Carey McWilliams
Marie Manning
Isaac F. Marcosson
Don Marquis

H. L. Mencken
Edward P. Morgan
Gertrude Bustill Mossell
Edgar Ansel Mowrer
Frank E. Mullen
Frank A. Munsey
Thomas Nast
S. I. Newhouse
Cecil E. Newman
Hezekiah Niles
Adolph S. Ochs
Rollo Ogden
Richard F. Outcault
Thomas Paine
James Parker
Sara Willis Parton
Westbrook Pegler
David Graham Phillips
John S. Phillips
Benjamin Perley Poore
Julian Ralph
Henry J. Raymond
John Reed
Frederic S. Remington
Quentin Reynolds
Grantland Rice
George Ripley
Inez Robb
Will Rogers
Harold Ross
Ishbel Ross
Arthur Rothstein
Edmund Ruffin
Damon Runyon
Charles Edward Russell
Harrison E. Salisbury
A. A. Schechter
George Seldes
Gilbert Seldes
Albert Shaw
William L. Shirer
Upton Sinclair
Henry Justin Smith
Howard K. Smith
Samuel Harrison Smith
W. Eugene Smith
Elizabeth Cady Stanton
William T. Stead
Lincoln Steffens
Edward Steichen
John Steinbeck
Alfred Stieglitz
I. F. Stone
Leland Stowe
Richard L. Stout
Raymond Gram Swing
Jane Swisshelm
Sol Taishoff
Harry Tammen
Ida Tarbell
Isaiah Thomas
Dorothy Thompson
Henry Villard
Oswald Garrison Villard
DeWitt Wallace
Charles Dudley Warner
Elizabeth Wason
Henry Watterson
Alfred Rudolph Waud
Noah Webster
Ida B. Wells-Barnett
Horace White
Sallie Joy White
Theodore H. White
William Allen White
William L. White
Walt Whitman
Earl Wilson
Walter Winchell
Alexander Woollcott
Art Young

Newspaper Editors, Managing Editors, and Publishers

Willis J. Abbot
Robert S. Abbott
Samuel Adams
Riley H. Allen
Susan B. Anthony
Benjamin Franklin Bache
L. C. Bates
Moses Y. Beach
Henry Ward Beecher
Edward Price Bell
Philip A. Bell
James Gordon Bennett

James Gordon Bennett, Jr.
George Barry Bingham
Frederick T. Birchall
Francis P. Blair
Frederick G. Bonfils
George Booth
Elias Boudinot
O. K. Bovard
Samuel Bowles III
Hugh Henry Brackenridge
Andrew Bradford
John Bradford
William Bradford III
William Cowper Brann
Emily Edson Briggs
Arthur Brisbane
Noah Brooks
Heywood Broun
Cecil Brown
William G. Brownlow
William Cullen Bryant
Burridge D. Butler
Abraham Cahan
John Campbell
Erwin D. Canham
S. S. Carvalho
Turner Catledge
Harry Chandler
Norman Chandler
Tennessee Claflin
Cassius M. Clay
Samuel L. Clemens
Frank Cobb
Irvin S. Cobb
William Cobbett
John A. Cockerill
William Coleman
Ira Copley
Gardner Cowles
Gardner Cowles, Jr.
James M. Cox
George Creel
James Creelman
Jane Cunningham Croly
Cyrus H. K. Curtis
Charles A. Dana
Josephus Daniels
Benjamin H. Day
Dorothy Day
George B. Dealey
Martin R. Delany
Michael De Young
Frederick Douglass
Charles H. Dow
Margaret Draper
Roscoe Drummond
Orvil E. Dryfoos
William Duane
Abigail Scott Duniway
Finley Peter Dunne
Mary Baker Eddy
Benjamin Edes
George Henry Evans
Joseph Rider Farrington
Mary Elizabeth Pruett Farrington
Wallace Rider Farrington
John Fenno
Eugene Field
Kate Field
T. Thomas Fortune
Gene Fowler
Ann Franklin
Benjamin Franklin
James Franklin
Harold Frederic
Legh R. Freeman
Philip Freneau
Hugh Gaine
Joseph Gales, Jr.
Frank E. Gannett
William Lloyd Garrison
Marcus Garvey
Emile Gauvereau
Henry George
Floyd Gibbons
L. A. Gobright
Morrill Goddard
Sarah Goddard
William Goddard
E. L. Godkin
Henry W. Grady
Philip L. Graham
Harry J. Grant
Charles H. Grasty
Horace Greeley
Anna Catherine Green

Duff Green
J. Frank Grimes
David Hale
Gerard Hallock
Murat Halstead
Bernard Hanks
Warren G. Harding
Benjamin Harris
Joel Chandler Harris
Houston Harte
William Randolph Hearst
Ben Hecht
J. N. Heiskell
Ben Hibbs
Lorena A. Hickok
William P. Hobby
Elizabeth Hunter Holt
John Holt
Roy W. Howard
Edgar Watson Howe
Clark Howell
Edwin Palmer Hoyt
Frederic Hudson
Will Irwin
James Johnston
George Jones
A. N. Kellogg
Amos Kendall
George W. Kendall
Bernard Kilgore
William Franklin Knox
Arthur Krock
Ring Lardner
James W. Latimer
David Lawrence
Victor F. Lawson
William Leggett
Walter Lippmann
David Ross Locke
Richard Adams Locke
Chester S. Lord
Clement A. Lounsberry
Elijah P. Lovejoy
Benjamin Lundy
Mathew Lyon
Robert Lyon
C. K. McClatchy
S. S. McClure
Robert R. McCormick
Joseph B. McCullagh
Benarr Macfadden
Ralph McGill
O. O. McIntyre
Manton Melone Marble
Don Marquis
Joseph Medill
Edward J. Meeman
Donald R. Mellett
H. L. Mencken
Eugene Meyer
John Mitchell, Jr.
Paul Scott Mowrer
Frank A.Munsey
William Rockhill Nelson
James P. Newcomb
S. I. Newhouse
Cecil E. Newman
Eliza Nicholson
Lucius W. Nieman
Hezekiah Niles
Frank B. Noyes
Adolph S. Ochs
Rollo Ogden
Fremont Older
B. S. Osbon
Harrison Gray Otis
James Parker
William Parks
Alicia Patterson
Eleanor Medill Patterson
Joseph Medill Patterson
Benjamin Perley Poore
Nelson Paul Poynter
Joseph Pulitzer
Joseph Pulitzer II
Eugene C. Pulliam
Ernie Pyle
Julian Ralph
Henry J. Raymond
Opie Read
John Reed
Helen Rogers Reid
Whitelaw Reid
Robert Barnwell Rhett, Sr.
Herman Ridder
Herman Henry Ridder

Jacob A. Riis
Clementina Rind
Thomas Ritchie
James Rivington
Howard Rock
Chester H. Rowell
Anne Royall
Vermont Royster
Benjamin Russell
Charles Edward Russell
John Russwurm
Carl Schurz
Harvey W. Scott
William A. Scott II
Edward W. Scripps
James E. Scripps
William Winston Seaton
Henry Justin Smith
Merriman Smith
Samuel Harrison Smith
William Henry Smith
Elizabeth Cady Stanton
William T. Stead
Lucy Stone
Melville E. Stone
Wilbur F. Storey
Raymond Gram Swing
Jane Swisshelm
Herbert Bayard Swope
Harry Tammen
Isaiah Thomas
Ann Donovan Timothy
Elizabeth Timothy
Peter Timothy
William Monroe Trotter
Carr Van Anda
Robert Lee Vann
Henry Villard
Oswald Garrison Villard
Charles Dudley Warner
Henry Watterson
James Watson Webb
Noah Webster
Thurlow Weed
Ida B. Wells-Barnett
Horace White
William Allen White
William L. White
Walt Whitman
Isaac Mayer Wise
George W. Wisner
Victoria Woodhull
Frances Wright
William L. Yancey
P. B. Young
Anna Catherine Zenger
John Peter Zenger

News Services and Syndicates

Elie Abel
Samuel Hopkins Adams
George Ade
Joseph Alsop
Steward Alsop
Hugh Baillie
Frank Bartholomew
H. R. Baukhage
Moses Y. Beach
James Gordon Bennett
James Berryman
Winifred Black
Howard Blakeslee
Mary Marvin Breckinridge
Cecil Brown
James Cannon
Robert Capa
Boake Carter
S. S. Carvalho
Marquis Childs
Raymond Clapper
Charles Collingwood
Bob Considine
Kent Cooper
Ira Copley
Gardner Cowles
Daniel H. Craig
Kenneth Crawford
Jane Cunningham Croly
Walter Cronkite
Jay N. Darling
Michael De Young
Dorothy Dix
Rheta Childe Dorr
Charles H. Dow
Roscoe Drummond
Stephen T. Early

Alfred Eisenstaedt
John Fischetti
Daniel Fitzpatrick
Doris Fleeson
Wes Gallagher
Floyd Gibbons
L. A. Gobright
Morrill Goddard
Sheilah Graham
Thomas Grandin
Charles H. Grasty
David Hale
Gerard Hallock
Murat Halstead
Houston Harte
William Randolph Hearst
J. N. Heiskell
Mark Hellinger
Ernest Hemingway
Genevieve Forbes Herrick
Lorena A. Hickok
Stephen H. Horgan
Roy W. Howard
Edwin Palmer Hoyt
Frederic Hudson
A. N. Kellogg
Marcus H. Kellogg
Dorothy Kilgallen
Bernard Kilgore
Moses Koenigsberg
Joseph Kraft
David Lawrence
Victor F. Lawson
Fulton Lewis, Jr.
A. J. Liebling
Walter Lippmann
Peter Lisagor
Chester S. Lord
Elmer W. Lower
Samuel Lubell
S. S. McClure
Joseph B. McCullagh
Ralph McGill
O. O. McIntyre
Marie Manning
Edward J. Meeman
Frank Miller
Webb Miller
John Mitchell, Jr.
Edward P. Morgan
Edgar Ansel Mowrer
Paul Scott Mowrer
Frank B. Noyes
Edgar Wilson "Bill" Nye
Adolph S. Ochs
B. S. Osbon
Louella Parsons
Drew Pearson
Westbrook Pegler
John S. Phillips
Byron Price
Ernie Pyle
Henry J. Raymond
Whitelaw Reid
Quentin Reynolds
Grantland Rice
Herman Ridder
Inez Robb
Howard Rock
Will Rogers
Albion Ross
Damon Runyon
Harrison E. Salisbury
Carl Sandburg
A. A. Schechter
Harvey W. Scott
William A. Scott II
Edward W. Scripps
Ellen Browning Scripps
James E. Scripps
George Seldes
Eric Sevareid
William L. Shirer
Merriman Smith
Walter "Red" Smith
William Henry Smith
William T. Stead
Melville E. Stone
Richard L. Strout
Ed Sullivan
Sol Taishoff
Dorothy Thompson
Clifton Utley
Henry Villard
Elizabeth Wason
James Watson Webb
Horace White

Paul W. White
Theodore H. White
William L. White
Frederic William Wile
Earl Wilson
Walter Winchell

Photography, Documentary, and Newsreels

Ansel Adams
Margaret Bourke-White
Mathew Brady
Robert Capa
Louis de Rochemont
Nancy Dickerson
Stephen T. Early
Alfred Eisenstaedt
Frederick A. Freed
Fred W. Friendly
Alexander Gardner
Irving Gitlin
Edwin C. Hill
Lewis W. Hine
Stephen H. Horgan
Frederick E. Ives
Dorothea Lange
Frank Leslie
Elmer W. Lower
Graham McNamee
Timothy H. O'Sullivan
Jacob A. Riis
Arthur Rothstein
Gilbert Seldes
W. Eugene Smith
Edward Steichen
Alfred Stieglitz
Lowell Thomas
Robert Trout
Edward Weston

Radio and Television

Elie Abel
Hugh Baillie
H. R. Baukhage
Edward Bliss, Jr.
Mary Marvin Breckinridge
Cecil Brown
Burridge D. Butler
Erwin D. Canham
Boake Carter
Norman Chandler
Raymond Clapper
Upton Close
Charles Collingwood
Fr. Charles Coughlin
Gardner Cowles
Gardner Cowles, Jr.
James M. Cox
Walter Cronkite
John Charles Daly, Jr.
Elmer Davis
Nancy Dickerson
Frederick A. Freed
Fred W. Friendly
Frank E. Gannett
Floyd Gibbons
Irving Gitlin
Sheilah Graham
Thomas Grandin
Bernard Hanks
William Hard
Houston Harte
Gabriel Heatter
Genevieve Forbes Herrick
Helen Hiett
Edwin C. Hill
William P. Hobby
Quincy Howe
Edwin Palmer Hoyt
Chet Huntley
Ted Husing
Max Jordan
H. V. Kaltenborn
Dorothy Kilgallen
Edward Klauber
David Lawrence
William A. Leonard
Fulton Lewis, Jr.
Peter Lisagor
Elmer W. Lower
Samuel Lubell
Robert R. McCormick
Frank McGee
Graham McNamee
James M. Metcalf
Sig Mickelson

Edward P. Morgan
Frank E. Mullen
Edward R. Murrow
S. I. Newhouse
Lucius Nieman
Louella Parsons
William S. Paley
Drew Pearson
Nelson Paul Poynter
Frank Reynolds
Grantland Rice
Vermont Royster
Richard S. Salant
Harrison E. Salisbury
Jessica Savitch
A. A. Schechter
Gilbert Seldes
Eric Sevareid
William L. Shirer
Howard K. Smith
Frank Stanton
Leland Stowe
Ed Sullivan
Raymond Gram Swing
Sol Taishoff
Lowell Thomas
Dorothy Thompson
Robert Trout
Clifton Utley
Judith Cary Waller
Elizabeth Wason
Paul W. White
William L. White
Frederic William Wile
Walter Winchell
Alexander Woollcott

Sports Journalism

James T. Berryman
Heywood Broun
Burridge Butler
James Cannon
Bob Considine
Walter Cronkite
Finley Peter Dunne
Daniel Fitzpatrick
Gene Fowler
Wes Gallagher
Ernest Hemingway
Lorena A. Hickok
Roy W. Howard
Edwin Palmer Hoyt
Ted Husing
Ring Lardner
A. J. Liebling
Peter Lisagor
Elmer W. Lower
Joseph W. McCarthy
Ralph McGill
Graham McNamee
Edward P. Morgan
Westbrook Pegler
Frank Reynolds
Quentin Reynolds
Grantland Rice
Damon Runyon
William L. Shirer
Walter "Red" Smith
Ed Sullivan
Joe Vila

War Correspondents

Elie Abel
Hugh Baillie
Frank Bartholomew
Edward Price Bell
Margaret Bourke-White
Mathew Brady
Mary Marvin Breckinridge
Noah Brooks
Heywood Broun
Cecil Brown
James Cannon
Robert Capa
Marquis Childs
Raymond Clapper
John A. Cockerill
Charles Carleton Coffin
Charles Collingwood
Bob Considine
Stephen Crane
Kenneth Crawford
James Creelman
Walter Cronkite
John Charles Daly, Jr.
Richard Harding Davis

Theodore Russell Davis
Rheta Childe Dorr
Walter Duranty
Doris Fleeson
Margaret Fuller
Wes Gallagher
Floyd Gibbons
Sheilah Graham
Thomas Grandin
Charles H. Grasty
Murat Halstead
Ernest Hemingway
Helen Hiett
Marguerite Higgins
Will Irwin
Max Jordan
Marcus H. Kellogg
George W. Kendall
Ring Lardner
A. J. Liebling
Elmer W. Lower
Samuel Lubell
Herbert L. Matthews
Joseph W. McCarthy
Joseph B. McCullagh
John T. McCutcheon
H. L. Mencken
Webb Miller
Edward P. Morgan
Edgar Ansel Mowrer
Paul Scott Mowrer
Edward R. Murrow
Thomas Nast
B. S. Osbon
David Graham Phillips
Ernie Pyle
Julian Ralph
Henry J. Raymond
John Reed
Whitelaw Reid
Frederic S. Remington
Quentin Reynolds
Inez Robb
Damon Runyon
Harrison E. Salisbury
Carl Sandburg
George Seldes
Gilbert Seldes
Eric Sevareid
William L. Shirer
George W. Smalley
Henry Justin Smith
Howard K. Smith
W. Eugene Smith
John Steinbeck
Leland Stowe
Raymond Gram Swing
Herbert Bayard Swope
Lowell Thomas
Robert Trout
Henry Villard
Elizabeth Wason
Alfred Rudolph Waud
Theodore H. White
William L. White
Frederic William Wile
Alexander Woollcott

Washington Correspondents

Elie Abel
Joseph Alsop
Stewart Alsop
Mary Clemmer Ames
Hugh Baillie
H. R. Baukhage
James Gordon Bennett
Emily Edson Briggs
Noah Brooks
Erwin D. Canham
Turner Catledge
Marquis Childs
Raymond Clapper
Kenneth Crawford
George Creel
John Charles Daly, Jr.
Nancy Dickerson
Mary Abigail Dodge
Roscoe Drummond
Stephen T. Early
Joseph Rider Farrington
Kate Field
Doris Fleeson
L. A. Gobright
William Hard
Genevieve Forbes Herrick
Lorena A. Hickok

Max Jordan
H. V. Kaltenborn
Bernard Kilgore
Joseph Kraft
Arthur Krock
David Lawrence
Fulton Lewis, Jr.
Sara Clarke Lippincott
Walter Lippmann
Peter Lisagor
Elmer W. Lower
Joseph B. McCullagh
Frank McGee
Marie Manning
Joseph Medill
Edward P. Morgan
Edgar Ansel Mowrer
Harrison Gray Otis
Drew Pearson
Benjamin Perley Poore
Byron Price
Joseph Pulitzer
Whitelaw Reid
Frank Reynolds
Vermont Royster
Harrison E. Salisbury
Jessica Savitch
Carl Schurz
Gilbert Seldes
Eric Sevareid
George W. Smalley
Howard K. Smith
Merriman Smith
I. F. Stone
Melville E. Stone
Richard L. Strout
Jane Swisshelm
Robert Trout
Henry Villard
Oswald Garrison Villard
Henry Watterson
Horace White
Frederic William Wile
Art Young

WOMEN IN JOURNALISM

Mary Clemmer Ames
Susan B. Anthony
Winifred Black
Margaret Bourke-White
Mary Marvin Breckinridge
Emily Edson Briggs
Willa Cather
Tennessee Claflin
Elizabeth Cochrane
Jane Cunningham Croly
Dorothy Day
Nancy Dickerson
Dorothy Dix
Mary Abigail Dodge
Rheta Childe Dorr
Margaret Draper
Abigail Scott Duniway
Mary Baker Eddy
Mary Elizabeth Pruett Farrington
Kate Field
Doris Fleeson
Ann Franklin
Margaret Fuller
Sarah Goddard
Sheilah Graham
Eleanor Graves
Nixola Greeley-Smith
Anne Catherine Green
Sarah Josepha Hale
Genevieve Forbes Herrick
Lorena A. Hickok
Helen Hiett
Marguerite Higgins
Elizabeth Hunter Holt
Florence Finch Kelly
Dorothy Kilgallen
Dorothea Lange
Miriam Leslie
Lillian Alberta Lewis
Sara Clarke Lippincott
Anne O'Hare McCormick
Marie Manning
Gertrude Bustill Mossell
Eliza Nicholson
Miriam Ottenberg
Louella Parsons
Sara Willis Parton
Alicia Patterson
Eleanor Medill Patterson
Helen Rogers Reid

Clementina Rind
Inez Robb
Ishbel Ross
Anne Royall
Jessica Savitch
Ellen Browning Scripps
Elizabeth Cady Stanton
Lucy Stone
Jane Swisshelm
Ida Tarbell
Dorothy Thompson
Ann Donovan Timothy
Elizabeth Timothy
Judith Cary Waller
Elizabeth Wason
Frances Wayne
Ida B. Wells-Barnett
Sallie Joy White
Victoria Woodhull
Frances Wright
Anna Catherine Zenger

MINORITY AND ETHNIC JOURNALISM

Robert S. Abbott
L. C. Bates
Philip A. Bell
Elias Boudinot
Abraham Cahan
Martin R. Delany
Frederick Douglass
W. E. B. Du Bois
T. Thomas Fortune
Marcus Garvey
Victor F. Lawson
Isaac Leeser
Lillian Alberta Lewis
Robert Lyon
Malcolm X
John Mitchell, Jr.
Gertrude Bustill Mossell
James P. Newcomb
Cecil E. Newman
Herman Ridder
Howard Rock
John Russwurm
Carl Schurz
William A. Scott II
William Monroe Trotter
Robert Lee Vann
Henry Villard
Ida B. Wells-Barnett
Isaac Mayer Wise
P. B. Young

DuPONT AND PEABODY AWARDS IN BROADCASTING

Elie Abel
Cecil Brown
Charles Collingwood
Elmer Davis
Nancy Dickerson
Frederick A. Freed
Fred W. Friendly
Irving Gitlin
Chet Huntley
William A. Leonard
Peter Lisagor
Frank McGee
James M. Metcalf
Edward P. Morgan
Edward R. Murrow
Frank Reynolds
Richard S. Salant
Jessica Savitch
Eric Sevareid
Howard K. Smith
Frank Stanton
Ed Sullivan
Lowell Thomas
Robert Trout
Clifton Utley

PULITZER PRIZES

Ray Stannard Baker
Clifford K. Berryman
James T. Berryman
Frederick T. Birchall
Howard W. Blakeslee
Edward W. Bok
Willa Cather
Marquis Childs
Frank I. Cobb
Jay N. Darling
Walter Duranty
John Fischetti

Daniel Fitzpatrick
Ernest Hemingway
Marguerite Higgins
Arthur Krock
William L. Laurence
Walter Lippmann
Anne O'Hare McCormick
John T. McCutcheon
Ralph McGill
Frank Miller
Edgar Ansel Mowrer
Paul Scott Mowrer
Miriam Ottenberg
Westbrook Pegler
Byron Price
Ernie Pyle
Vermont Royster
Charles Edward Russell
Harrison E. Salisbury
Carl Sandburg
Merriman Smith
Walter "Red" Smith
John Steinbeck
Leland Stowe
Herbert Bayard Swope
Theodore H. White
William Allen White

INDEX

Page numbers in italics indicate dictionary entries.

Abbot, Willis J., *1–3*
Abbott, Lyman, *3–4*, 34–35
Abbott, Robert S., *4–6*
Abel, Elie, *6–7*
Abell, Arunah S., 141, 288
Abilene Reporter-News, 298–99, 309–10, 321
Abolitionist press, 21, 34, 111–12, 187, 260–61, 430–32, 437–39, 673–75, 685, 761
Adams, Ansel E., *7–8*
Adams, Franklin P., *8–10*, 81, 82, 604
Adams, John, 24, 131, 132, 213, 223, 361, 440, 616
Adams, John Quincy, 361, 617, 725
Adams, Samuel, *10–11*, 213, 347, 535–36
Adams, Samuel Hopkins, *11–13*
Ade, George, *13–14*, 405, 456
Agee, James, 61
Air Force Register, 32
Albany (Oreg.) *Evening Democrat*, 28
Albany (N.Y.) *Evening Journal*, 242, 371, 734–35
Alexander, Charles, 275–76
Allen, Riley Harris, *14–16*
Alsop, Joseph, *16–17*, 18, 104
Alsop, Stewart, 16, *17–18*
Alta California, 81
Alternative journalism, 93, 173–74, 190, 200, 202, 209, 215–17, 277, 576–77, 592–94, 625, 648, 760–62, 764–66
America, 342
American Broadcasting Company, 31, 32, 85, 167, 302, 343, 652–53, 681, 753; ABC News, 160, 286, 362, 432–33, 491–92, 582–84, 622, 653, 707
American Chronicle, 274
American Crisis, 536
American Magazine (Andrew Bradford), 67–68, 239, 540
American Magazine, 203, 313, 557, 576, 667, 693–94
American Magazine and Monthly Chronicle, 70
American Magazine, or General Repository, 70
American Mercury, 481
American Minerva, 733
American Newspaper Guild, 81, 83, 145, 229, 417
American Newspaper Publishers Association, 229, 359, 588, 640
American Opinion, 554

American Press Association, 349–50
American Press Institute, 104
American Sentinel, 231
American Society of Newspaper Editors, 3, 15, 57, 96, 104, 287, 746
American Spectator, 231
American Sun, 33
American Weekly, 271–72, 325, 446
American Weekly Mercury, 67–68, 70
Ames, Mary Clemmer, *18–20*
Anderson, Jack, 552
Anderson, Peter, 37
Annenberg, Moses, 264, 287
Anthony, Susan B., *20–22*, 77, 662, 674
Anti-Slavery Standard, 21
Arbeiter Zeitung, 93
Archinard, Paul, 340
Architectural Forum, 435–36
Arena, 230–31
Argus of Western America, 50–51, 381–82
Arizona Farmer, 90
Arkansas Gazette, 330–31
Arkansas State Press, 29–30
Arkansaw Traveler, 575–76
Arkansian, 60
Army and Navy Journal, 108
Army and Navy Register, 20, 32
Arp, Bill. *See* Smith, Charles Henry
Asmonean, 441–42, 754
Associated Press, 31, 32, 33, 52, 85, 129–31, 141–43, 183, 207–8, 214, 254–55, 269–70, 287, 289, 304, 306–7, 320, 321, 330, 337, 338, 359, 360, 379, 388, 403, 404, 405, 426, 432, 454–55, 484, 518, 522, 528, 561–62, 574, 580, 631, 654–55, 660–61, 675–77, 689, 732, 738, 765
Atchinson (Kans.) *Champion*, 567
Atchinson Globe, 354
Atlanta Constitution, 141, 279–81, 298, 317–18, 355–57, 460–62
Atlanta Daily Herald, 279
Atlanta Daily World, 633–34
Atlanta Journal, 356, 473, 587
Atlantic Monthly, 17, 108, 186, 187, 226, 319, 358, 419
Aurora, 23–24, 197–98
Austin (Tex.) *Iconoclast*, 74
Aylesworth, M. H., 267

Bache, Benjamin Franklin, *23–24*, 197
Baillie, Hugh, *24–26*
Baker, Ray Stannard, *26–28*, 232, 405, 449, 557, 667
Baltimore Evening News, 288, 435, 480–81, 500
Baltimore Evening Post, 516
Baltimore Sun, 141, 288, 480–81, 552
Baraboo (Wis.) *Republic*, 376–77
Barron's, 386, 388
Bartholomew, Frank H., *28–29*
Bates, Lucius C., *29–30*
Baukhage, Hilmar R., *30–32*
Beach, Moses Y., *32–34*, 161, 171, 173
Beaumont (Tex.) *Enterprise*, 346
Beecher, Henry Ward, 4, *34–35*, 55, 110, 571, 758
Bell, Edward Price, *35–36*, 405, 749
Bell, Philip A., *36–38*
Bell Syndicate, 230, 399
Benchley, Robert, 8, 444, 604
Bennett, James Gordon, 33, *38–40*, 306, 359–60, 470, 732
Bennett, James Gordon, Jr., 39, *40–41*, 148, 350, 361
Bernays, Edward L., 389
Berryman, Clifford K., *41–43*
Berryman, James T., *41–43*
Bettmann, Otto L., *43–44*
Bierce, Ambrose G., *44–45*, 466
Billings, Josh. *See* Shaw, Henry Wheeler
Bingham, Barry, Jr., 46
Bingham, George Barry, *45–47*
Bingham, Robert Worth, 45–46, 395–96
Birchall, Frederick T., *47–48*
Bismarck Tribune, 379, 429–30
Black, Winifred, *48–50*, 295
Black journalists, 4–6, 29–30, 36–37, 176–78, 188–90, 199–200, 233–35, 261–63, 415–16, 466–68, 489–91, 493–94, 511–13, 583, 618–19, 632–34, 704–6, 712–14, 735–37, 766
Black Man, 263
Black periodicals, 4–6, 29–30, 176–78, 188–90, 199–200, 233–35, 261–63,

415–16, 466–68, 489–91, 493–94, 511–12, 618–19, 632–34, 704–6, 712–14, 735–37, 766
Black Star, 658
Blaine, James G., 186, 187
Blair, Francis P., *50–52*, 297, 595
Blakeslee, Howard W., *52–53*
Bliss, Edward, Jr., *53–54*
Bloomer, Amelia, 21, 662
Bly, Nellie. *See* Cochrane, Elizabeth
Bok, Edward W., *54–56*, 154, 155, 428
Bonfils, Charles Alden, 49
Bonfils, Frederick G., *56–57*, 690–92, 729–30
Booth, George G., *57–59*
Boston Advocate, 415
Boston American, 392, 399
Boston Atlas, 80, 558
Boston Common, 419
Boston Gazette, 10, 95, 212–14, 240
Boston Globe, 230, 325, 380
Boston Guardian, 704–6
Boston Herald, 415, 427–28, 741–42
Boston Journal, 124–25, 499, 500, 559
Boston News-Letter, 94–95, 192–93, 240
Boston Post, 427, 741–42
Boston Standard, 427
Boston Telegraph and Recorder, 306
Boston Traveller, 64
Boudinot, Elias, *59–61*
Boudinot, Elias C., 60
Bourke-White, Margaret, *61–62*, 215, 290
Bovard, Oliver K., *62–63*, 107, 565–66
Bowen, Henry C., 20
Bowles, Samuel, 64
Bowles, Samuel III, 19, *63–65*, 190
Brackenridge, Hugh H., *65–67*
Bradford, Andrew, *67–68*, 70, 239
Bradford, John, *68–69*
Bradford, William, 67, 70, 539, 768
Bradford, William III, 68, *69–71*
Brady, Mathew B., *71–73*, 259, 528, 529
Breckinridge, Mary Marvin, *75–76*, 725
Briggs, Emily Edson, *76–78*
Brinkley, David, 153, 361–62
Brisbane, Arthur, *78–79*, 122, 272, 468, 547
Broadcasting, 689–90
Brooker, William, 95, 240
Brooklyn Daily Bugle, 54
Brooklyn Daily Union, 20
Brooklyn Eagle, 55, 375–76, 426, 747–48
Brooklyn Magazine, 55
Brooklyn Standard-Union, 308
Brooklyn Times, 326, 748
Brooks, Noah, *79–81*
Brother Jonathan, 171, 173
Broun, Heywood C., 9, *81–84*, 145, 419, 553, 554, 584, 585, 604, 639
Broun, Heywood Hale, 82
Brown, Cecil, *84–85*
Browne, Charles Farrar, *85–87*, 113
Brownlow, William G., *87–88*
Bryant, Louise, 577
Bryant, William Cullen, *88–89*, 126, 407, 469–70, 729, 748
Bucyrus (Ohio) *Journal*, 423
Bucyrus Telegraph-Forum, 53
Buffalo Express, 403
Bullard, Laura Curtis, 21, 663
Burr, Aaron, 125–26, 440
Butler, Burridge D., *89–91*

Cahan, Abraham, *93–94*
Campbell, John, *94–96*, 192, 240
Canham, Erwin D., *96–97*
Cannon, James, *97–98*
Canton (Ohio) *Daily News*, 478–80
Capa, Robert, *98–99*, 670
Carpet Bag, The, 86
Carter, Boake, *99–101*, 114, 115
Carter, Henry. *See* Leslie, Frank
Carter, Jimmy, 153, 653
Carvalho, S. S., *101–2*
Casey, Ralph, 512
Castro, Fidel, 475
Cather, Willa, *102–3*, 449
Catledge, Turner, *103–4*
Catholic Monitor, 350
Catholic Universe Bulletin, 450–51
Catholic Worker, 173–74
Century, 232, 448

Chancellor, John, 460
Chandler, Harry, *104–5*
Chandler, Norman, *105–6*
Charleston (S.C.) *Courier*, 38, 704
Charleston Mercury, 585–86, 612–13
Chattanooga Times, 521–23
Chatter, 571–72
Chautauqua Daily, 31
Chautauquan, 693
Cherokee Phoenix, 59–60
Chiang Kai-shek, 36, 434, 437
Chicago American, 2, 79, 102, 392, 399, 543, 625
Chicago Daily News, 15, 35–36, 203, 227, 228, 328, 391, 404–5, 421–22, 430, 492, 494–97, 624, 625, 650–51, 675–77, 679–80, 684, 710, 721, 722
Chicago Daily Republican, 454
Chicago Defender, 4–6, 263, 511, 714, 736
Chicago Evening Mail, 2
Chicago Evening Post, 203, 311, 312, 676
Chicago Examiner, 399
Chicago Herald, 203
Chicago Herald-Examiner, 443–44
Chicago Inter Ocean, 399, 676, 736, 765
Chicago Journal, 9, 203, 328, 738
Chicago Literary Times, 329
Chicago Morning News, 13, 224, 405
Chicago News-Record, 13
Chicago Post and Mail, 405, 676
Chicago Record, 13, 26, 35, 224, 405, 456, 749
Chicago Record Herald, 517–18
Chicago Sun, 103, 104, 227
Chicago Times, 1, 203, 624, 677–79
Chicago Times-Herald, 405
Chicago Tribune, 2, 49, 64, 82, 203, 267, 312–13, 334, 335, 399, 444, 451–53, 455–56, 475–77, 543, 546, 547, 548, 549–50, 639, 646, 710, 738–39, 749
Childs, Marquis W., *106–7*, 566
Christian Register, 312, 593
Christian Science Monitor, 1, 96–97, 195–96, 210–12, 552, 681–82
Christian Union, 4, 34–35
Church, Francis P., *107–8*
Churchill, Winston, 461
Cincinnati Chronicle, 660
Cincinnati Commercial, 64, 307–8, 322–23, 454, 555, 644, 660
Cincinnati Daily Evening Post, 34
Cincinnati Enquirer, 90, 307, 308, 322, 454
Cincinnati Gazette, 308, 357, 454, 578, 660
Cincinnati Journal, 34
Cincinnati Post, 351, 463
Claflin, Tennessee, *108–10*, 758
Clapper, Raymond, *110–11*
Clay, Cassius Marcellus, *111–12*
Clemens, Samuel L., 55, 86, 108, *112–14*, 722–23, 724
Cleveland, Grover, 157, 162, 242, 278, 356, 372, 403, 505, 676
Cleveland Leader, 476
Cleveland Plain Dealer, 86, 510
Cleveland Press, 635, 636, 684
Click, 264
Close, Upton, *114–16*, 652
Cobb, Frank I., *116–17*, 564
Cobb, Irvin S., *117–19*
Cobbett, William, *119–21*, 537, 762
Cobbett's Political Register, 120
Coburn, Catherine, 201
Cochrane, Elizabeth, *121–22*
Cockerill, John A., *122–24*, 322, 563
Coffin, Charles Carleton, *124–25*
Coleman, William, *125–26*
Collier's, 2, 12, 145, 146, 147, 203, 227, 228, 310, 311, 313, 334, 335, 366, 474, 492, 582, 584, 585, 615
Collingwood, Charles C., *126–28*, 538
Colored Press Association, 490
Columbia Broadcasting System, 100–101, 126–28, 135–36, 153, 159, 167, 243, 268, 328, 340, 355, 361–62, 363–64, 500–502, 537–39, 583, 612, 626, 663–65, 683, 684, 687, 698; "CBS Evening News," 53–54, 152–53, 409, 643; CBS News, 53–54, 75, 76, 84–85, 126–28, 152–53, 159–60, 183–84, 247–48, 269, 285, 361–62, 373, 376, 388–89, 408–10, 432–33, 485–86,

492, 500–502, 537–39, 621–23, 628, 642–44, 647, 652–53, 697, 706–7, 724–25, 739–41, 746, 750; "CBS Reports," 53, 248, 249, 409, 485, 643
Columbian Centinel, 616–17
Columbus (Ohio) *Citizen*, 53, 560
Columbus *Ohio Star*, 315
Columbus *Ohio State Journal*, 315, 357, 530
Coming Century, 202
Common Sense, 536
Condé Nast, 510, 668, 669
Congregationalist, 187
Congressional Globe, 51
Connecticut Gazette, 274, 347, 539–40
Connecticut Nutmeg, 83
Considine, Robert D., *128–29*
Consolidated Press Association, 403–4, 689
Constitutional Gazette, 274
Continental Press Association, 31
Coolidge, Calvin, 150, 356, 682
Cooper, Kent, *129–31*, 767
Cooper, Thomas, *131–33*, 198
Copley, Ira C., *133–34*
Cornish, Samuel E., 37, 619
Coronet, 227
Cosmopolitan, 45, 118, 194, 325, 358, 385, 445, 461, 556
Coughlin, Father Charles, 114, *134–36*
Council Bluffs (Iowa) *Daily Democrat*, 379
Country Gentleman, 335, 336
Cowles, Gardner, *136–38*
Cowles, Gardner, Jr., 137, *138–40*
Cowles Communications, 136–40, 256, 434
Cox, James M., *140–41*, 479–80
Craig, Daniel H., *141–43*
Crane, Stephen, *143–44*, 242, 428
Crawford, Kenneth Gale, *144–45*
Creel, George, *145–47*
Creelman, James, *147–49*
Crisis, 199–200
Crockett, Gibson, 43
Croly, David Goodman, 149, 150–51
Croly, Herbert D., *149–50*, 151, 420
Croly, Jane Cunningham, 149, *150–52*, 513
Cronkite, Walter, 53–54, *152–54*, 184, 248, 389, 409, 410, 460, 621, 643, 707, 740
Curtis, Cyrus H. K., 55, *154–56*, 427–29, 749
Curtis, George W., *156–57*
Curtis, Louisa, 55, 154–55
Custer, George A., 171, 378, 379, 429, 490

Dallas Herald, 400–401
Dallas Morning News, 175–76, 400–401
Daly, John Charles, Jr., *159–60*, 388, 740
Dana, Charles A., 101, 108, 150, *160–62*, 173, 233, 292, 426, 533, 555, 571, 594, 715
Daniels, Josephus, *162–64*
Darling, J. N., *164–65*, 487
Davenport, Homer C., *165–66*
Davis, Elmer, *166–68*, 285, 388, 740
Davis, Richard Harding, 144, *168–70*
Davis, Theodore R., *170–71*
Day, Benjamin H., 33, 39, 161, *171–73*, 424–25, 756–57
Day, Dorothy, *173–75*
Day Book, 624, 625
Dayton Evening News, 140
Dealey, George B., *175–76*
Delany, Martin R., *176–78*
Delineator, 313
Dennie, Joseph, *178–80*
Denver Post, 49, 56–57, 146, 235, 358–59, 393, 690–92, 729–30
Denver Republican, 235
De Rochemont, Louis C., *180–82*
Des Moines Register and Leader, 136–40, 164–65
Des Moines Register and Tribune, 136–40, 165, 486–88
Deseret News, 353
Detroit Daily Advertiser, 757
Detroit Daily Post, 629–30
Detroit Free Press, 116, 677–78
Detroit Journal, 52
Detroit News, 6, 57, 58, 635, 636, 637

De Young, Michael H., *182–83*
Dial, The, 249, 593, 641
Dickerson, Nancy H., *183–85*
Die Deborah, 754, 755
Dix, Dorothy, 49, *185–86*, 295, 513
Dixon (Ill.) *Telegraph*, 80
Dodge, Mary Abigail, *186–88*
Dorr, Rheta Childe, *188*
Douglass, Frederick, 176–77, *188–90*, 261
Douglass' Monthly, 189–90
Dow, Charles H., 65, *190–92*
Dow Jones News Service, 386, 387
Draper, Margaret Green, *192–93*
Draper, Richard, 192
Dreiser, Theodore, *193–95*
Drummond, Roscoe, *195–96*
Dryfoos, Orvil E., *196–97*, 475
Duane, William, 24, *197–99*
DuBois, W.E.B., *199–201*, 262, 705
Duluth Daily Herald, 430
Duluth Evening News, 430
Duluth *Saturday Evening Journal*, 430
Duniway, Abigail Scott, *201–2*
Dunne, Finley Peter, 146, *202–4*, 311
Duranty, Walter, *204–5*

Early, Stephen T., *207–8*
Eastman, Max, 173, *208–10*, 577
Eddy, Mary Baker, 103, *210–12*
Edes, Benjamin, *212–14*
Editor and Publisher, 208
Edwards, Douglas, 153, 184
Eisenhower, Dwight D., 97, 139, 301–2, 337, 346, 422, 434, 437
Eisenstaedt, Alfred, *214–15*, 290
Elizabethton (N.C.) *Whig*, 87
Emancipator, The, 438
Emporia (Kans.) *Gazette*, 744–46
Esquire, 227, 243, 333
Ethnic press, 64, 93–94, 327, 393, 405, 406–7, 441–42, 588–89, 599–600, 629–30, 700, 716, 754–55
Evans, George H., 172, *215–17*, 761
Everybody's, 312, 313, 419, 667
Ev'ry Month, 194
E. W. Howe's Monthly, 354

Fairfax, Beatrice. *See* Manning, Marie
Farm Security Administration, 245, 397, 398, 607
Farmers' Library, 439–41
Farmer's Museum, 179
Farmer's Register, 612–14
Farrington, Joseph Rider, *219–20*, 221
Farrington, Mary Elizabeth Pruett, 219, *220–21*
Farrington, Wallace, 15, 219, 220, *221–22*
Federal Communications Commission, 538
Fenno, John, 24, *222–24*
Ferguson, Alexander, 37
Fern, Fanny. *See* Parton, Sara Willis
Field, Eugene, 14, *224–25*, 405
Field, Kate, 151, *225–26*
Field Newspaper Syndicate, 227, 395, 751
Fillmore, Millard, 252, 638
Fischetti, John, *226–27*
Fitzpatrick, Daniel R., *227–29*, 566
Fleeson, Doris, *229–30*
Flint (Mich.) *Journal*, 432
Flower, Benjamin O., *230–32*
Flynt, Josiah, *232–33*
Ford, Gerald, 422, 643
Foreign language press. *See* Ethnic press
Forney, John W., 77
Fort Wayne (Ind.) *Sentinel*, 506
Fortune, 435–36
Fortune, T. Thomas, *233–35*, 262
Forum, 2
Fowle, Zachariah, 694–95
Fowler, Gene, *235–36*
Frank, Reuven, 243
Frank Leslie's Illustrated Newspaper, 72, 257, 410–11, 728
Franklin, Ann Smith, *236–37*, 241
Franklin, Benjamin, 23, 67, *237–39*, 240–41, 274, 347, 428, 535, 539, 540, 542, 695, 700, 701, 702
Franklin, James, 236, 237, 238, *239–41*, 541
Frederic, Harold Henry, *241–42*
Frederick Douglass' Paper, 189
Free Enquirer, 215, 760–62

Freed, Frederick A., *242–44*
Freedom's Journal, 618–19
Freeman, Legh R., *244–46*
Freeman's Journal, 246
Freneau, Philip, 23, 65, 223, *246–47*
Fresno Republican, 608–9
Friendly, Fred W., *247–49*, 409, 501, 622, 683
Frontier Index, 244–46
Fuller, Margaret, *249–50*, 292, 593
Fun, 45

Gaine, Hugh, *251–52*
Galaxy, 108
Gales, Joseph, Jr., *252–54*, 638, 656
Gallagher, Wes, *254–55*
Gallup, George H., 138, 139, *255–57*
Galveston Evening Tribune, 74
Galveston News, 74, 175
Gannett, Frank E., *257–58*
Gannett organization, 15, 139, 257–58, 434
Gardner, Alexander, 72, *258–60*, 529
Garfield, James, 77, 412
Garrison, William Lloyd, 112, 189, *260–61*, 716, 717
Garvey, Marcus, 233, 234, *261–63*, 467
Gauvereau, Emile H., *263–65*
Gazette of the United States, 222–23
General Magazine, 67, 239
Genius of Universal Emancipation, 260, 438
George, Henry, 2, *265–66*
Georgia Gazette, 369–70
Gibbons, Floyd, *266–68*, 488, 628, 639
Gill, John, 213
Gilmer, Elizabeth Meriwether. *See* Dix, Dorothy
Gitlin, Irving J., *268–69*
Gobright, Lawrence A., *269–71*
Goddard, Morrill, *271–72*, 563
Goddard, Sarah Updike, *272–74*
Goddard, William, 272–74, *274–75*, 348
Godey, Louis A., *275–77*, 305
Godey's Lady's Book, 151, 275–76, 305, 499
Godkin, Edwin L., *277–79*, 311, 524, 630, 717, 739
Golden Age, 30
Golden Era, 319
Grady, Henry W., *279–81*, 355
Graham, Katharine M., 282, 484–85
Graham, Philip L., *281–83*, 484–85
Graham, Sheilah, *283–84*
Grand Rapids (Mich.) *Herald*, 390
Grand Rapids Morning Democrat, 90
Grand Rapids Press, 58
Grandin, Thomas B., *284–86*, 725
Grant, Harry J., *286–87*
Grant, Ulysses S., 170, 504, 505, 571, 728
Grasty, Charles H., *287–89*
Graves, Eleanor M., *289–90*, 291
Graves, Ralph A., 289, *290–91*
Greeley, Horace, 19, 64, 156, 161, 216, 249, *291–93*, 294, 308, 371, 379, 426, 447, 469, 476, 477, 505, 573, 574, 579, 580, 593, 629, 649, 662, 685, 686, 716, 735, 739
Greeley-Smith, Nixola, 49, *293–95*
Green, Anne C., *295–96*
Green, Bartholomew, 95, 192
Green, Duff, 51, *296–98*
Green, Samuel, 192
Greenwood, Grace. *See* Lippincott, Sara Jane
Gridiron Club, 42, 111, 422, 559
Grimes, Frank, *298–99*, 310
Grinnell (Iowa) *Herald*, 644

Hadden, Briton, 435
Hagerty, James C., *301–3*
Hale, David, *303–4*, 306, 360, 678
Hale, Sara Josepha, 276, *304–5*
Hallock, Gerald, *305–7*
Halstead, Murat, 64, *307–9*, 323, 555, 644
Hamilton, Alexander, 89, 125–26, 223, 247
Hamilton, Gail. *See* Dodge, Mary Abigail
Hampden Post, 64
Hancock Jeffersonian, 423
Hanks, Bernard, 298, *309–10*, 320, 321
Hapgood, Norman, 235, *310–12*
Harbinger, 593

Harbor News Association, 33
Hard, William, *312–13*
Harding, Warren G., 111, 141, 150, 208, 222, *313–15*, 327, 356
Harper's Monthly, 4, 18, 156–57, 194, 358, 395, 419, 573, 594, 723, 729
Harper's Weekly, 2, 72, 157, 168–69, 170–71, 311–12, 358, 503–5, 555, 581, 629, 630, 728
Harris, Benjamin, *315–17*
Harris, Joel Chandler, *317–18*, 356, 473
Harrison, Benjamin, 308, 580
Harrison, William Henry, 51, 297, 735
Hart, Francis Brett (Bret Harte), 81, 86, 113, *318–20*
Harte, Houston, *320–22*
Harte-Hanks Communications, 298–99, 309–10, 320–21
Hartford Courant, 263–64, 723
Hawaii Star, 15, 221–22
Hayes, Rutherford B., 279, 308, 505, 628, 630, 660, 661
Hearn, Lafcadio, *322–24*
Hearst, William Randolph, 1, 2, 45, 49–50, 78, 79, 101–2, 148, 165–66, 169, 185, 264, 272, 287, 312, *324–26*, 385, 391, 392, 393, 444, 451, 469, 500, 525, 526, 532–33, 543, 547, 548, 550, 553, 554, 556, 563–64, 571, 580, 581–82, 614, 618, 666, 690
Hearst's International Magazine, 14, 312
Hearth and Home, 419
Heatter, Gabriel, 115, *326–28*
Hecht, Ben, 235, *328–30*, 435, 444, 488, 604, 651
Heiskell, John N., *330–31*
Hellinger, Mark, 97, *331–32*
Hemingway, Ernest, 98, *332–34*, 646
Henry, Carter, 2
Herrick, Genevieve Forbes, *334–36*
Hibbs, Benjamin S., *336–37*
Hickok, Lorena A., *337–39*
Hiett, Helen, *339–41*
Higgins, Marguerite, *341–42*, 422
Hill, Edwin C., *342–44*
Hine, Lewis W., *344–45*
Hitler, Adolf, 36, 47, 48, 436, 461, 501, 602, 646
Hobby, William P., *345–47*
Holland, J. G., 65
Holt, Elizabeth H., *347–49*
Holt, John, 274, *347–49*
Honolulu Advertiser, 15
Honolulu Evening Bulletin, 15, 219, 221
Honolulu *Pacific Commercial Advertiser*, 221
Honolulu Star-Bulletin, 14, 15, 219–22
Hoover, Herbert, 36, 96, 104, 135, 138, 204, 208, 313, 366
Horgan, Stephen H., *349–51*
House and Garden, 75, 510
House & Home, 436
Houston Post, 74, 152, 345–46
Howard, Roy, 83, *351–53*, 416, 567, 635
Howe, Edgar Watson, *353–54*, 744
Howe, Quincy, *354–55*
Howell, Clark, *355–57*
Howell, Evan P., 356
Howells, William Dean, 49, 93, 114, *357–58*
Howey, Walter, 443, 547
Hoyt, Edwin Palmer, *358–59*
Hudson, Edmund, 20
Hudson, Frederic, 40, *359–61*
Huntley, Chet, 153, *361–63*
Huntress, The, 610–11
Husing, Ted, *363–64*

Iconoclast, The, 73–75
I. F. Stone's Weekly, 672–73
Illustrated Christian Weekly, 4
In Fact, 639–40
Independent Woman, 335
Indianapolis Journal, 342–43
Indianapolis News, 351, 479, 566–67, 661
Indianapolis Star, 351, 567
International News Service, 28, 129–31, 152, 268, 325, 385, 393, 414, 584, 598, 614, 627, 646, 699
International Newsreel, 181
Interstate Reporter, 29
Irwin, Will, *365–67*
Islew, Bert. *See* Lewis, Lillian Alberta

Israelite, The, 441–42, 754–55
Ives, Frederic Eugene, *367–68*

Jackson, Andrew, 50–51, 89, 296–97, 381–82, 408, 517, 595, 731, 732, 761
Jefferson, Thomas, 132, 178–79, 198, 223, 247, 252, 439, 440, 616, 637, 638, 655–56, 761
Jet, 634
Jewish Daily Forward, 93–94, 393
Johnson, Andrew, 19, 77, 270, 453–54, 505, 574, 686
Johnson, Lyndon B., 184, 282, 309, 310, 321, 421, 433, 437, 502, 552, 567, 643, 655, 673
Johnston, James, *369–70*
Jones, Alexander, 142
Jones, George, *370–72*, 573
Jonesboro (Tenn.) *Whig and Independent*, 87
Jordan, Max, *372–74*
June, Jennie. *See* Croly, Jane Cunningham

Kaempffert, Waldemar, 402
Kalb, Marvin, 7
Kaltenborn, H. V., 115, 167, *375–76*, 419, 652, 740
Kansas City Call, 29, 511, 512
Kansas City Evening News, 1
Kansas City Journal, 427, 744
Kansas City Post, 56
Kansas City Star, 2, 56, 288, 289, 333, 487, 506–7, 566, 744
Kate Field's Washington, 225–26
Kaufman, George S., 8, 9
KCET, 85
Keats, John, 8
Keimer, Samuel, 238
Kellogg, Ansel N., *376–78*
Kellogg, Marcus H., *378–80*
Kelly, Florence Finch, *380–81*
Kendall, Amos, 51, *381–83*
Kendall, George W., *383–84*
Kennedy, John F., 16, 17, 18, 53, 176, 185, 282, 386, 393, 394, 412, 422, 433, 445–46, 460, 491, 500, 502, 552, 653, 654–55, 743
Kent, Frank, 403–4
Kentucky Gazette, 68–69
Keokuk (Iowa) *Daily Whig*, 77
Keokuk Gate City, 77
Khrushchev, Nikita, 104, 129, 184, 269, 291, 386, 422, 433, 552, 682
Kilgallen, Dorothy M., *384–86*
Kilgore, Bernard, *386–88*
King, Martin Luther, Jr., 433, 512, 552
King Features Syndicate, 43, 325, 332, 386, 392–93, 414, 416, 469, 554, 614
Kintner, Robert E., 16
Klauber, Edward, *388–89*, 538, 740
Kneeland, Samuel, 213
Knight-Ridder newspapers, 434, 588–89
Knox, William Franklin, *389–92*, 722
Knoxville Chronicle, 521
Knoxville Journal, 330
Knoxville News Sentinel, 477–78
Knoxville Tribune, 330, 521
Knoxville Whig, 87–88
Koenigsberg, Moses, *392–93*
Kohlsaat, Herman, 405
KOY, 90
Kraft, Joseph, *393–95*
Krock, Arthur, *395–96*
KTUC, 90

Labor press. *See* Alternative journalism
La Crosse (Wis.) *Democrat*, 378
Ladies' Home Journal, 54–55, 154–56, 428, 700
Ladies' Magazine, 276, 305
Lafayette (Ind.) *Call*, 13
Lafayette Morning News, 13
Lancaster (N.H.) *Weekly Democrat*, 85
Lange, Dorothea M., *397–98*
Laramie Boomerang, 519
Lardner, Ring, 235, *398–400*, 641
Latimer, James Wellington, *400–401*
Laurence, William L., *401–2*
Laurie, Annie. *See* Black, Winifred
Lawrence, David, 31, 313, *402–4*, 689
Lawson, Victor F., 35, *404–6*, 518, 676
Leeser, Isaac, *406–7*, 442
Leggett, William, *407–8*
Leonard, William A., *408–10*
Leslie, Frank, *410–12*, 503–4

Leslie, Miriam, 411, *412–13*
Leslie's Illustrated Weekly, 31, 411, 412, 503–4, 613
Lewis, Lillian Alberta, *415–16*
Lewsi, Fulton, Jr., 114, *413–15*
Liberator, The (Eastman), 209, 765
Liberator, The (Garrison), 189, 260–61
Liberty, 267, 367
Liebling, A. J., *416–18*, 640
Life, 44, 61–62, 75, 214–15, 289–91, 334, 398, 432, 435, 436, 437, 658–59, 670, 743
Lily, The, 21, 662
Lincoln, Abraham, 80–81, 89, 125, 189–90, 259, 270, 293, 307, 311, 376–77, 378, 449, 470, 476, 477, 487, 504–5, 574, 628, 629, 631, 632, 660, 678, 693, 734, 738–39
Lippincott, Sara Jane, 276, *418–19*
Lippmann, Walter, 9, 81, 117, 282, 299, 393, *419–21*, 484, 579, 667, 683, 760, 765
Lisagor, Peter, *421–22*
Literary Digest, 2, 36, 435, 645
Little Rock *True Democrat*, 60
Living Age, 355
Locke, David Ross, 87, *422–24*
Locke, Richard Adams, 33, 172, *424–26*
London *Daily Mail*, 111, 366, 749
London Post, 316
London Quarterly Review, 406
London *Times*, 2, 119, 366, 522, 649, 650
Long, Huey, 254, 417
Long Island Press, 509–10
Look, 44, 136, 138–40, 195, 256, 607
Lord, Chester S., *426–27*
Lorimer, George H., 337, *427–29*, 745
Los Angeles Herald, 25
Los Angeles Record, 25
Los Angeles Times, 104–6, 227, 381, 420, 529–30, 648
Louisville Courier-Journal, 45–47, 395, 725–27
Louisville Evening Post, 118
Louisville Herald, 395
Louisville Herald-Post, 432
Louisville Times, 45–47, 90, 395–96, 471
Lounsberry, C. A., 379, *429–30*
Lovejoy, Elijah P., *430–32*
Lowell (Mass.) *Bell*, 380
Lower, Elmer W., *432–33*
Lubell, Samuel, *433–35*
Luce, Claire Booth, 436, 445
Luce, Henry R., 215, *435–37*, 742
Lundy, Benjamin, 260, *437–39*
Lyon, Matthew, *439–41*
Lyon, Robert, *441–42*

MacArthur, Charles G., 235, 328, 329, *443–45*
McCall's, 221, 342, 724
McCarthy, Joseph Weston, *445–46*
McClatchy, C. K., *446–47*
McClure, S. S., 12, 27, 103, 233, 366, *447–50*, 557, 667, 693, 745
McClure's, 12, 26, 27, 102, 103, 194, 232, 233, 366, 448–49, 556–57, 591, 667, 693
McClure's Syndicate, 11, 12, 143, 448
McCormick, Anne O'Hare, *450–51*
McCormick, Robert R., 267, 335, *451–53*, 546, 547, 548, 549–51, 567, 646
McCullagh, Joseph B., 123, *453–55*
McCutcheon, John T., 13, 14, 405, *455–57*
Macfadden, Bernarr, 264, *457–59*, 550
McGee, Frank, *459–60*
McGill, Ralph, 355, *460–62*
McIntyre, O. O., *462–64*
McKinley, William, 169, 308, 490, 736
McLean, Washington, 308
McNamee, Graham, *464–65*
McWilliams, Carey, *465–66*
Macon Telegraph, 317
Mademoiselle, 342
Madison, James, 65, 198, 252, 637, 656, 761
Magnum, 99
Malcolm X, *466–68*
Manchester Union-Leader, 390
Manning, Marie, *468–69*
Marble, Manton M., *469–71*
March of Time, 180, 181, 435, 436
Marcosson, Isaac F., *471–72*
Marion (Ohio) *Star*, 314–15

Marquis, Don, *472–74*
Martin County (Minn.) *Atlas*, 429
Maryland Gazette, 295–96, 541, 591
Maryland Journal, 275, 348
Marysville (Calif.) *Daily Appeal*, 80
Massachusetts Centinel, 616
Massachusetts Spy, 10, 616, 694–96
Masses, The, 173–74, 209, 577, 765
Matthews, Herbert L., *474–75*
Medill, Joseph, 451, *475–77*, 547
Meeman, Edward J., *477–78*
Meir, Golda, 18
Meliss, David, 21
Mellett, Donald R., 478–80
Memphis Commercial Appeal, 330
Memphis Evening Star, 736
Memphis Free Speech, 736
Memphis Press-Scimitar, 477–78
Menace, The, 231
Mencken, H. L., 465, *480–82*, 556, 687
Meriwether, Elizabeth. *See* Dix, Dorothy
Metcalf, James M., *482–83*
Metropolitan, 313, 577, 765
Meyer, Eugene I., 282, *483–85*, 548
Michigan Cyclist, 90
Mickelson, Sig, *485–86*
Miller, Charles R., 65, 523, 524
Miller, Frank, *486–88*
Miller, Webb, *488–89*
Milwaukee Daily News, 625
Milwaukee Free Press, 267
Milwaukee Journal, 286, 287, 514–15
Milwaukee Sentinel, 311, 338, 514–15, 625
Minneapolis Daily News, 90, 267
Minneapolis Journal, 617, 623
Minneapolis Spokesman, 512
Minneapolis Tribune, 429, 430, 617, 644
Mishawaka (Ind.) *Tocsin*, 678
Mitchell, Edward P., 108, 173
Mitchell, John, Jr., *489–91*, 713
Monroe, James, 198, 252, 440, 617, 637
Monroe (Ga.) *Advertiser*, 317
Montreal Gazette, 6
Morgan, Edward P., *491–93*
Mossell, Gertrude Bustill (N. F. Mossell), *493–94*
Motor, 102
Movietone News, 181, 697–98
Mowrer, Edgar Ansel, *494–95*
Mowrer, Paul Scott, *495–97*, 651
Mudd, Roger, 707
Muhammad Speaks, 467
Mullen, Frank E., *497–98*
Munsey, Frank, 41, 288, *498–500*, 578
Munsey's, 2, 194, 499
Murrow, Edward R., 53, 75, 76, 126–28, 184, 247, 248, 269, 284, 285, 389, 409, *500–502*, 537, 538, 642–43, 652, 684, 707, 725, 740
Mussolini, Benito, 494
Mutual Broadcasting System, 32, 85, 110, 111, 115, 327, 343, 413–14, 628, 681
Mystery, The, 176–77

Nasby, Petroleum V. *See* Locke, David Ross
Nashville Banner, 726
Nast, Thomas, 125, 157, 165–66, 371, *503–6*, 708
Nation, The, 83, 261, 277–79, 327, 358, 465–66, 524, 672, 717, 718, 739
National Association of Broadcasters, 389
National Broadcasting Company, 31, 115, 135, 243, 248, 267–68, 269, 313, 343, 372–73, 464–65, 497–98, 538, 622, 628, 699, 707, 721–22, 753; NBC News, 7, 85, 115, 184, 243, 269, 285, 339–40, 361–62, 372–73, 432–33, 459–60, 626–28, 684, 697, 750; NBC "White Paper," 243–44, 269
National Enquirer, 479
National Era, 187, 190
National Gazette, 23, 66, 223, 246–47
National Headliners Club, 32, 84, 227, 340, 554
National Intelligencer, 252–54, 383, 637–38, 655–56
National Observer, 386, 387
National Press Club, 32, 111, 422, 612
Native American journalism, 59–60, 599–600
Nautical Gazette, 526, 528, 718
Negro World, 233, 234, 261–63

Neie Zeit, 93
Nelson, William Rockhill, 2, 288, *506–7*, 566, 691, 744
New American Magazine, 540
New England Courant, 95, 236, 238, 239–41, 541
New England Woman's Press Association, 741, 742
New Era, 425
New Harmony Gazette, 761
New Mexico State Journal, 42
New National Era, 190
New Northwest, 201
New Orleans Crescent, 748
New Orleans Item, 323
New Orleans Item-Tribune, 652
New Orleans Picayune, 185, 383–84, 513–14, 587
New Orleans Times-Democrat, 1, 323
New Republic, 2, 145, 149–50, 313, 394, 419–20, 681–82, 742–43
New York Age, 233, 234, 493, 736
New York American, 2, 84, 149, 166, 235, 326, 444, 543, 614, 765
New York *Colored American*, 37
New York *Commercial Advertiser*, 311, 617–18
New York *Correspondent*, 215
New York Courier, 38, 731
New York Courier and Enquirer, 38–39, 306, 424–25, 573, 731–32
New York Daily Advertiser, 246
New York Daily Graphic, 349, 571
New York Daily News, 229–30, 332, 335, 452, 546, 547, 549–61, 553, 682, 683
New York Evening Graphic, 263–64, 458, 550, 641, 682, 752–53
New York Evening Mail, 9, 166, 423, 449, 463, 500, 765
New York Evening Telegram, 41, 500
New York Examiner, 408
New York Extra, 308
New York Freeman, 234, 490, 493
New York Gazette, 67, 505, 539, 596–98
New York Globe, 39, 164, 233, 234, 311, 500, 576, 667
New York Herald, 33, 38–41, 124, 147–48, 327, 350, 359–61, 379, 429, 500, 526, 527, 533, 578, 680, 716
New York Herald Tribune, 9, 16, 196, 339, 340, 341–42, 420–21, 577–79, 605–6, 657, 679–80, 699
New York Illustrated News, 504, 728
New York *Independent*, 18, 20, 34, 419
New York *Independent Gazetteer*, 349
New York Journal, 1, 2, 40, 41, 45, 78–79, 121, 143–44, 148, 165–66, 185, 272, 283, 325, 326–27, 385, 468, 532–33, 563–64, 571, 581–82, 618, 641, 765
New York Journal American, 385–86, 554
New York *Journal of Commerce*, 303–4, 305–7, 360, 425, 589, 678, 732
New York Journal; or General Advertiser, 347–49
New York Ledqer, 34, 544–45
New York Man, 216
New York Mercantile Journal, 441–42
New York Mercury, 251–52
New York Mirror, 79, 235, 264, 283, 332, 338, 550, 753
New York Mirror (nineteenth century), 418, 426, 544
New York Morning Telegraph, 82, 235
New York Newspaper Guild, 81, 83, 227
New York Newspaper Women's Club, 230, 598
New York Observer, 306
New York Plaindealer, 408
New York *PM*, 329, 334, 672, 725
New York Post, 9, 84, 88–89, 125–26, 155, 277–79, 311, 403, 407–8, 523–24, 629, 630, 699, 717–18, 739, 750–51
New York Press Club, 124, 151
New York Review, 89
New York Sentinel, 172, 216
New York Staats-Zeitung, 588–89, 716
New York Sun, 2, 11, 12, 32–34, 39, 47, 78, 107–8, 160–62, 168–69, 171–73, 216, 343, 352, 366, 424–25, 426–27, 473, 500, 555, 563, 571, 590, 714–15, 756–57
New York Telegram, 83, 380

New York *Time Piece*, 247
New York Times, 3, 6, 39, 41, 47–48, 56, 65, 75, 81, 82, 98, 103–4, 148, 167, 196–97, 204–5, 227, 241–42, 288, 289, 301, 325, 363, 370–72, 380, 381, 385, 388–89, 394, 395–96, 401–2, 414, 419, 450–51, 474–75, 480, 521–25, 572–75, 602–3, 606, 622, 623–24, 657–58, 688, 711–12, 749, 759–60
New York Tribune, 1, 9, 13, 47, 81, 82, 161, 186, 187, 216, 226, 249–50, 291–93, 350, 365, 366, 371, 419, 473, 500, 573, 578, 579–80, 587, 590, 593, 605–6, 629, 630, 649–50, 662, 685, 686, 716, 765
New York Weekly Advocate, 37
New York Weekly Journal, 767–69
New York Weekly Post-Boy, 251, 347, 539
New York Weekly Sun, 33
New York World, 1, 9, 21, 40, 41, 63, 78–79, 82–83, 101–2, 116-17, 118, 121–24, 144, 148, 228, 271, 272, 293–95, 324, 325, 351, 388, 396, 402, 416, 420, 468, 469–71, 489, 526, 527, 532–33, 555, 562–66, 577, 582, 618, 687–88, 760
New York World-Telegram, 83–84, 393, 416, 553, 584
New York World-Telegram and Sun, 351, 352, 353
New Yorker, 281, 395, 400, 416–17, 444, 603–5, 765
Newark (N.J.) *Daily Advertiser*, 81
Newark Ledger, 84
Newark Star, 350
Newcomb, James P., *507–9*
Newhouse, S. I., *509–11*, 567
Newhouse newspapers, 57, 509–10
Newman, Cecil E., *511–13*
Newport Mercury, 237
Newsday, 342, 545–47, 548
Newspaper Enterprise Association, 227, 478, 625, 634, 635, 636
Newspaper Feature Syndicate, 392–93
Newsweek, 18, 145, 282, 421, 487, 554
Nicholson, Eliza Jane, 185, *513–14*
Nicola, Lewis, 70
Nieman, Lucius W., 286–87, *514–16*
Niles, Hezekiah, *516–17*
Niles' Weekly Register, 516–17
Nixon, Richard M., 17, 144, 185, 362, 393, 394, 422, 460, 583, 622, 643, 653, 655, 743
Noah, Mordecai M., 731
Norfolk Journal and Guide, 234, 766
North American Intelligencer, 246
North American Newspaper Alliance, 6, 31, 283, 335, 367, 587
North Star, The, 176–77, 188–90
Norway (Maine) *Advertiser*, 85
Noyes, Crosby S., 517
Noyes, Frank B., *517–18*
Noyes, Newbold, 518
Noyes, Newbold, Jr., 518
Noyes, Theodore W., 517
Nye, Edgar Wilson (Bill Nye), *518–19*

Occident and American Jewish Advocate, 407, 442, 754
Ochs, Adolph S., 104, 155, 175, 396, *521–23*, 524, 712
Ogden, Rollo, *523–25*
O'Hara, John, 9
Older, Fremont, *525–26*
Oldschool, Oliver. *See* Dennie, Joseph
Oreqon City Courier, 28
Osbon, B. S., *526–28*
O'Sullivan, Timothy H., *528–29*
Otis, Harrison Grey, 104–5, *529–30*
Ottenberg, Miriam, *530–32*
Outcault, Richard, 271, *532–33*
Overlook, 2, 4, 35, 313,
Overland Monthly, 81, 266, 319
Overseas News Agency, 6, 743
Overseas Press Club, 7, 84, 111, 129, 243, 362, 394, 475, 624, 653
Overseas Writers, 32, 422

Pacific Empire, The, 202
Paine, Thomas, 239, *535–37*, 762
Paley, William S., 388, 389, 486, *537–39*, 664, 740
Pall Mall Gazette, 31, 47, 665–66
Parade, 607

Paris Herald, 341
Paris Letter, 340
Paris Post, 422
Parker, Dorothy, 8, 9, 444, 604
Parker, James, 251, 274, 347, *539–41*
Parks, William, 295, *541–42*
Parsons, Louella, 283, 385, *542–44*
Parton, Sara Willis, *544–45*
Pathé News, 181, 680
Patterson, Ada, 49, 295
Patterson, Alicia, *545–47*, 548
Patterson, Eleanor Medill, 453, 546, *547–49*, 551, 552
Patterson, Joseph Medill, 267, 313, 332, 452, 546, 547, 548, *549–51*, 598
Paul Pry, 610–11
Pearson, Drew, 115, 484, 548, *551–53*, 689
Pegler, Westbrook, 235, *553–54*, 585
Pekin (Ill.) *Daily Times*, 339
Penfeather, Penelope. *See* White, Sallie Joy
Pennsylvania Chronicle, 272–75
Pennsylvania Gazette, 238–39, 274
Pennsylvania Journal, 69–71, 274, 536
Pennsylvania Magazine, 535
Pennsylvanian, The, 39
People's Advocate, 234
People's Rights, 216
People's Weekly, 297–98
Philadelphia Inquirer, 155, 264, 493
Philadelphia Ledger, 522, 640–41, 699
Philadelphia Press, 77, 155, 168, 493
Philadelphia Public Ledger, 684, 749
Philadelphia Times, 493, 500, 522
Philadelphia Weekly, 418
Philanthropist, The, 438
Phillips, David Graham, 232, 472, *554–56*, 590
Phillips, John S., 27, 448–49, *556–58*, 693
Philomathean Review, 55
Photo-Secession, 668, 671
Physical Culture, 457–58
Pierce, Gilbert A., 430
Pilgrim, The, 2
Pillsbury, Parker, 21
Pittsburgh Courier, 200, 511, 712–14
Pittsburgh Dispatch, 121
Pittsburgh Gazette, 65–66
Pittsburgh Press, 84
Pittsburgh *Saturday Visiter*, 685–86
PlYmouth (Ohio) *Advertiser*, 423
Plymouth Pulpit, 34
Political Censor, 120
Polk, James K., 51, 297, 595, 678
Pomeroy, Marcus M., 378
Poore, Benjamin Perley, 270, *558–59*
Porcupine's Gazette, 119–20
Port Folio, 178–80
Portland (Oreg.) *Bulletin*, 631
Portland Evening Telegram, 28
Portland Oregonian, 28, 201, 359, 510, 630–32
Poynter, Nelson Paul, *559–61*
Prairie Farmer, 89–90
Pratt (Kans.) *Daily Tribune*, 336
Prescott (Ariz.) *Journal-Miner*, 84
Price, Byron, *561–62*
Providence Evening Bulletin, 191, 416
Providence Gazette, 272–73, 274
Providence Journal, 191, 416
Publick Occurrences, Both Foreign and Domestick, 315–16
Publisher's Auxiliary, 377
Pulitzer, Joseph, 62–63, 78–79, 101–2, 116–17, 122–24, 148, 162, 271, 294, 324, 325, 451, 468, 532–33, 555, *562–64*, 565, 566, 580, 690, 692
Pulitzer, Joseph II, 63, 563, *564–66*
Pulitzer, Ralph, 83, 396, 563, 565, 687
Pulliam, Eugene C., *566–67*
Punch, 86
Putnam's Monthly, 156
Pyle, Ernie, 111, 560, *567–69*

Radical, The, 216
Radio Correspondents Association, 32, 414
Radio Free Europe, 486
Radio Liberty, 486
Radio News Analysts Association, 32, 376
Radio Television News Directors Association, 432, 485, 502, 653, 741

Raleigh News and Observer, 162–63
Ralph, Julian, *571–72*
Rather, Dan, 408, 410, 622
Raymond, Henry J., 292, 371, 469, *572–75*, 732
Read, O. P., *575–76*
Reader's Digest, 181, 195, 209, 313, 337, 342, 584, 681, 719–20
Reagan, Ronald, 583, 653
Reasoner, Harry, 583, 653
Reconstructionist, 686
Record, The, 430
Red Cross Magazine, 557, 694
Redbook, 335
Reed, John S., 81, 419, *576–77*, 667
Reid, Helen Rogers, *577–79*
Reid, Ogden Mills, 9, 578, 580
Reid, Whitelaw, 350, 500, *579–80*, 660
Religious News Service, 340
Religious press, 1, 3–4, 34–35, 55, 187, 312, 450–51, 453, 474–75, 493, 494, 588, 593, 632, 718, 754–55, 756
Remington, Frederic, *580–82*
Reporter, The, 681
Reston, James, 107, 197, 396
Review of Reviews, 644–46, 666
Revolution, 20, 21–22, 661–63, 674–75
Reynolds, Frank, *582–84*
Reynolds, Quentin, 554, *584–85*
Rhett, Robert Barnwell, Sr., *585–87*, 612
Rhode Island Gazette, 236–37, 241
Rice, Grantland, 9, *587–88*, 604
Richmond Enquirer, 594–96
Richmond Planet, 415, 489–91, 713
Richmond Whig, 406
Richter, Beatrice Olive, 100
Ridder, Herman, *588–89*
Ridder, Herman Henry, *589–90*
Ridgway's Weekly, 313
Riis, Jacob A., *590–91*
Rind, Clementina, *591–92*
Ripley, George, *592–94*
Ritchie, Thomas, 51, *594–96*
Rives, John C., 51
Rivington, James, 252, *596–98*
Robb, Inez, *598–99*
Rock, Howard, *599–600*
Rocky Mountain News, 57, 235, 353, 614, 615
Rogers, Will, 118, 268, *600–602*
Roosevelt, Eleanor, 17, 335, 337–39, 385, 458, 469, 760
Roosevelt, Franklin D., 16, 17, 36, 94, 100, 104, 115, 135–36, 141, 144, 147, 160, 163, 167, 207–8, 229, 230, 256, 282, 326, 335, 337, 338, 339, 346, 356, 357, 391, 395, 396, 414, 421, 434, 436–37, 447, 452, 475, 481, 484, 548, 551, 553, 560, 561, 562, 654, 684, 706, 714, 725, 745, 753
Roosevelt, Theodore, 55, 134, 165, 166, 318, 343, 390, 456, 471, 554, 556, 581, 590, 644, 667, 745
Rosedale (Ind.) *Bee*, 35
Ross, Albion, *602–3*
Ross, Harold W., 9, 444, *603–5*
Ross, Ishbel, *605–6*
Rothstein, Arthur, *606–8*
Rowell, Chester Harvey, *608–9*
Royal American Magazine, 695
Royall, Anne, *609–11*
Royster, Vermont C., *611–12*
Ruffin, Edmund, 595, *612–14*
Runyon, Damon, 97, 235, 584, *614–15*, 639, 753
Russell, Benjamin, 222, *615–17*
Russell, Charles Edward, *617–18*
Russwurm, John B., *618–19*

Sacramento Bee, 446–47
Sacramento Union, 79–80, 265, 319
St. Cloud (Minn.) *Democrat*, 686
St. Cloud Visiter, 686
St. Louis Enquirer, 297
St. Louis Evening Journal, 224
St. Louis Globe-Democrat, 74, 194, 392, 453–55, 510
St. Louis Observer, 431
St. Louis Post-Dispatch, 62–63, 106–7, 122–24, 227–29, 294, 351, 563–66, 687
St. Louis Star, 62–63
St. Louis Times, 431

St. Louis Westliche Post, 64, 563, 629–30
St. Nicholas, 81
St. Paul Pioneer, 379
St. Paul Recorder, 512
St. Petersburg (Fla.) *Times*, 559–61
Salant, Richard S., 53, 410, 486, *621–23*
Salisbury, Harrison, 152, *623–24*, 653
San Angelo Standard-Times, 320, 321
San Antonio Express, 74, 507–9
San Antonio Light, 507–9
San Francisco *Argonaut*, 45
San Francisco Bulletin, 215, 525–26
San Francisco Call, 526
San Francisco Chronicle, 182–83, 265–66, 366, 602, 608, 609
San Francisco Daily Times, 81, 265–66
San Francisco *Elevator*, 37
San Francisco Evening Post, 266
San Francisco Examiner, 45, 49, 165–66, 325, 381
San Francisco News, 670
San Francisco News Letter, 44
San Francisco *Pacific Appeal*, 37
Sandburg, Carl A., *624–26*, 651
Sarnoff, David, 498
Saturday Evening Post, 18, 118, 154–56, 195, 313, 336–37, 365, 366, 394, 399, 400, 427–29, 434, 468, 471–72, 555
Saturday Review, 10, 195
Saturday Spectator, 36
Sault Sainte Marie *Lake Superior Journal*, 390
Savannah Morning News, 317
Savitch, Jessica, *626–27*
Schechter, Abel A., 340, *627–28*
Schurz, Carl, 64, 278, *628–30*, 739
Scott, Harvey W., 201, *630–32*
Scott, William A., II, *632–34*
Scott Newspaper Syndicate, 633
Scribner's Monthly, 65, 81, 194
Scripps, Edward W., 58, 351, 624, 625, *634–36*, 637, 692
Scripps, Ellen Browning, 634, *636–37*
Scripps, George H., 58, 635
Scripps, James E., 58, 451, 635, *637*
Scripps-Howard organization, 58, 83–84, 111, 351–53, 434, 477–78, 479, 553, 568, 598, 634–37
Scripps-McRae Press Association, 130, 351,352, 635
Scull, John, 66
Seaton, William W., 253, *637–39*, 656
Seattle Post-Intelligencer, 15
Seldes, George H., *639–40*
Seldes, Gilbert V., *640–42*
Sengstacke, John H., 6, 714
Sengstacke, John Herman Henry, 5
Sevareid, Eric, 127, 285, 389, 501, *642–44*, 725, 740
Shaw, Albert, *644–46*, 666
Shaw, Henry Wheeler, 87
Shirer, William L., 76, 127, 284, 285, *646–47*, 725, 740
Sinclair, Upton, 11, 147, 232, 472, *647–49*
Smalley, George W., *649–50*
Smart Set, 481
Smith, Henry Justin, 328, *650–52*
Smith, Howard K., 248, 501, 538, 583, *652–54*
Smith, James McCune, 37
Smith, Merriman, *654–55*
Smith, Red, 588, *657–58*
Smith, Samuel Harrison, 638, *655–57*
Smith, W. Eugene, *658–60*
Smith, William Henry, *660–61*
Social Justice, 135–36
Society of Professional Journalists, Sigma Delta Chi, 25, 84, 85, 111, 129, 227
South Bend (Ind.) *Times*, 399
South Brooklyn News, 590
South Carolina Gazette, 348, 700–704
Southern Whig, 558
Spirit of Liberty, 685
Sporting News, 42, 399
Sports Illustrated, 435, 436
Springfield (Mass.) *Gazette*, 64
Springfield Republican, 19, 63–65, 226, 680
Springfield Union, 64
Stalin, Joseph, 204
Stallings, Lawrence, 82
Stanley, Henry M., 40, 147, 170

Stanton, Elizabeth Cady, 21, 22, *661–63*, 674
Stanton, Frank, 409, 485, 538, 622, *663–65*, 741
Stars and Stripes, 9, 31, 207, 227, 422, 487, 587, 604
State Department Correspondents Association, 422
Stead, W. T., 26, 645, *665–66*
Steffens, Lincoln, 27, 94, 232, 419, 449, 557, 576, 590, 591, 618, *666–68*
Steichen, Edward, 625, *668–69*
Steinbeck, John, *669–71*
Stieglitz, Alfred, 8, 668, *671–72*, 737
Stoddard, Henry, 9
Stone, I. F., 640, *672–73*
Stone, Lucy, *673–75*, 741
Stone, Melville E., 224, 403, 405, 518, *675–77*
Storey, Francis V., 292
Storey, Wilbur F., *677–79*
Stowe, Leland *679–81*
Straight, Dorothy, 149
Straight, Willard, 149
Strand, Paul, 7
Strout, Richard L., *681–82*
Suffragist, 188
Sullivan, Ed, *682–83*
Sullivan, Mark, 403–4
Sulzberger, Arthur Hays, 523
Swing, Raymond Gram, *683–85*
Swisshelm, Jane, *685–87*
Swope, Herbert Bayard, 82–83, 402, *687–88*

Taft, William H., 311, 315, 458
Taishoff, Sol, *689–90*
Tammen, Harry H., 56–57, *690–92*, 729–30
Tappan, Arthur, 306
Tarbell, Ida, 27, 232, 449, 557, 590, 618, 667, *692–94*
Taylor, Deems, 9, 82
Taylor, Zachary, 558, 573
Television, 690
Terre Haute (Ind.) *Express*, 35
Texas Times, 400
Thomas, Isaiah, 213, 347, 542, 616, *694–96*
Thomas, Lowell, 100, 115, 628, *696–98*
Thompson, Dorothy, 484, 579, *698–700*
Thurber, James, 9, 603
Time, 222, 281, 290–91, 435–37, 645, 742–43
Timothy, Ann, *700–704*
Timothy, Elizabeth, *700–704*
Timothy, Peter, 348, *700–704*
Toledo Blade, 423
Toledo Commercial, 86
Toronto Star, 333
Town and Country, 75
Tree of Liberty, 66
Trotsky, Leon, 98, 491
Trotter, William Monroe, 200, *704–6*
Trout, Robert, 153, 388, *706–8*, 740
True American, 111–12
Truman, Harry, 208, 229, 299, 376, 395, 396, 434, 445, 551, 562, 682
Tundra Times, 599–600
Tunica (Miss.) *Times*, 103
Twain, Mark. *See* Clemens, Samuel L.
Twin Cities Herald, 511–12
Tyler, John, 33, 51, 297

Uncle Remus's Magazine, 318, 473
United Features Syndicate, 25, 107, 111, 230, 312, 434, 553
United Press, 24–26, 28–29, 84, 110, 111, 127, 129–31, 144–45, 152, 351–53, 364, 385, 405, 426, 432, 488–89, 491–92, 553, 623, 624, 634, 635, 642, 725, 740
United Press International, 24–26, 28–29, 130, 598, 634, 654–55
United States Daily, 31, 404, 552
United States Magazine, 65, 246
United States News, 31, 404
United States Telegraph, 51, 297, 382
U.S. News and World Report, 31, 32, 404, 552
Utica (N.Y.) *Morning Herald*, 19, 426
Utica Observer, 241–42, 257
Utley, Clifton M., *709–10*
Utopian press. *See* Alternative journalism

Vallandigham, C. L., 123
Van Anda, Carr V., 47, 451, *711–12*
Van Buren, Martin, 50, 51, 89, 381, 382, 595
Vancouver (B.C.) *Sun*, 28
Vanity Fair, 86, 420, 436
Vann, Robert L., *712–14*
Vila, Joseph, *714–15*
Villard, Henry, 261, 278, 630, *715–17*, 739
Villard, Oswald Garrison, 524, *717–18*
Virginia Gazette, 541–42, 591–92
Vogue, 75, 436, 510
Voice of the Negro, 713

Waco (Tex.) *Daily News*, 74
Wall Street Journal, 65, 190–91, 386–87, 611–12
Wallace, DeWitt, *719–21*
Wallace, Lila, 719–20
Waller, Judith Cary, *721–22*
Ward, Artemus. *See* Browne, Charles Farrar
Warner, Charles Dudley, *722–24*
Washington, Booker T., 200, 262, 705
Washington, George, 23–24, 70, 246–47, 311, 597, 616, 733
Washington Chronicle, 77
Washington Correspondents Club, 270
Washington Daily Bee, 270
Washington Daily News, 479, 560, 568
Washington Farmer, 245–46
Washington Globe, 50, 51, 253, 297, 595
Washington Herald, 2, 128, 129, 414, 547–48
Washington Post, 42, 75, 111, 123, 128–29, 281–83, 394, 420, 453, 483–84, 548
Washington Star, 41–43, 82, 230, 270, 271, 282, 382, 395, 517–18, 530–32
Washington Times, 79, 499, 548
Washington Times-Herald, 282, 453, 546, 547–48, 549, 552
Washington Union, 595–96
Washington Union Democrat, 382
Wason, Elizabeth, *724–25*
Watterson, Henry, 395, *725–27*
Waud, Alfred, *727–29*
Wave, The, 365–66
Wayne, Frances Belford, *729–31*
WBBM, 709, 710
WEAF, 375, 464–65
Webb, James Watson, 39, 306, 573, *731–32*
Webster, Noah, *732–34*
Weed, Thurlow, 292, 371, 558, 573, *734–35*
Wells-Barnett, Ida B., *735–37*
Western Ideal, 30
Western Newspaper Union, 31
Western Texan, 507
Weston, Edward H., *737–38*
Wetumpka (Ala.) *Argus*, 763–64
Wetumpka (Ala.) *Commercial Advertiser*, 763–64
WGN, 335, 453, 710
WHAS, 46
Wheelman, The, 448, 557
White, Horace, 64, 278, 524, 630, *738–39*
White, Paul W., 389, 538, 628, 647, 725, *739–41*
White, Sallie Joy, *741–42*
White, Theodore H., *742–44*
White, William Allen, 15, 336, *744–46*
White, William L., 744, *746–47*
White House Correspondents Association, 422
Whitman, Walt, 108, 544, 738, *747–48*
Wile, Frederic William, *748–50*
Wilson, Earl, 331, *750–52*
Wilson, Woodrow, 25, 26, 27, 55, 116, 117, 140, 146, 150, 312, 390–91, 403, 419, 420, 618, 644, 697, 736
Winchell, Walter, 235, 331, 332, 343, 554, 615, *752–54*
Windsor (Ontario) *Star*, 6
Wisconsin News, 79
Wisconsin State Journal, 377
Wise, Isaac Mayer, 441, *754–56*
Wisner, George W., 172, *756–57*
WJR, 135
WLS, 89–90
WLW, 135
WMAQ, 36, 135, 709, 710, 721–22

WMAQ-TV, 710
Woman's Home Companion, 229, 230, 725
Woman's Journal, 21, 673–75
Women journalists, 8, 9, 18–20, 20–22, 48–50, 55, 61–62, 75–76, 76–78, 100, 102–3, 108–10, 121–22, 149, 150–51, 154–55, 172, 183–88, 192–93, 201–2, 225–26, 229–30, 235, 236–37, 249–50, 264, 272–74, 276, 282, 283–84, 289–90, 291, 293–95, 301–5, 334–35, 337–42, 347–49, 380–81, 384–86, 397–98, 411, 412–13, 415, 418–19, 436, 450–51, 468–69, 484–85, 493–94, 513–14, 530–32, 542–49, 551–52, 557, 560, 577–79, 598, 604, 605–6, 609–11, 615, 618, 622, 626–27, 634, 636–37, 661–63, 667, 673–75, 685–87, 692–94, 698–704, 709–10, 719–22, 724–25, 729–31, 735–37, 742–44, 757–59, 760–62, 767–68
Women's National Press Association, 78
Women's National Press Club, 230, 469, 513
Women's press, 18–20, 20–22, 54–55, 151, 154–56, 201–2, 275–76, 304–5, 335, 411, 412, 436, 469, 493–94, 510, 560, 598, 628, 661–63, 668, 669, 673–75, 685–86, 724, 725, 758–59
Women's Press Club of New York City, 151, 513
Woodhull, Victoria, 109–10, *757–59*
Woodhull and Claflin's Weekly, 109–10, 758–59
Woodville (Ga.) *Times*, 5
Woollcott, Alexander, 8, 9, 12, 81, 444, 604, *759–60*
WOR, 135, 327, 684
Working Man's Advocate, 215–17
Workingmen's Friend, 277
World's Work, 471–72
Wright, Frances, 172, 215, *760–62*
WWL-TV, 482–83

Yancey, William Lowndes, *763–64*
Yank, 445–46
Young, Art, *764–66*
Young, P. B., *766*
Young America, 216
Youngstown (Ohio) *Vindicator*, 84

Zenger, Anna Catherine, *767–68*
Zenger, John Peter, 348, 542, 767, *768–69*
Zit's Weekly, 332

ABOUT THE CONTRIBUTORS

JOSEPH P. MCKERNS is Associate Professor of Journalism at the Ohio State University in Columbus. His work on communication history has appeared in *Journalism History, Critical Studies in Mass Communication*, and other journals. He is the author of *News Media and Public Policy*, and former editor of *Journalism Monographs*.

JUNE N. ADAMSON is Professor of Journalism at the University of Tennessee in Knoxville where she has taught since 1971. She has published a number of articles on journalism history, which is her main interest.

DAVID L. ANDERSON is Associate Professor of Journalism and Mass Communication at the University of Northern Colorado. A major interest of his is news media performance from an ethical and critical perspective.

PERRY J. ASHLEY is Professor of Journalism at the University of South Carolina. He has edited several volumes on American newspaper journalists for the *Dictionary of Literary Biography* series.

ROY ALDEN ATWOOD is Associate Professor of Communication at the University of Idaho. He has published research on the history of early printing, the frontier and rural press, and rural telephone communication in the Progressive Era.

DONALD R. AVERY is Associate Professor and Director of the Advertising Program at the University of Southern Mississippi. His research on American colonial and party press history has been published in *American Journalism*, *Journalism Quarterly*, and other journals.

NORA BAKER is Assistant Professor of Mass Communications at Southern Illinois University at Edwardsville. Her major research interest is nineteenth-century American women journalists.

ROBERT L. BAKER is Assistant Professor of Communications at Pennsylvania State University. His primary interests are in the history of journalism/mass communication education, and the literary and visual aspects of journalism.

WARREN E. BARNARD is Associate Professor of Communication at Indiana State University. He is an authority on George A. Custer and has been widely published on the subject.

JOSEPH O. BAYLEN is Regents Professor of History Emeritus at Georgia State University. He is coeditor of the *Biographical Dictionary of Modern British Radicals since 1770*, 3 vols.

MAURINE H. BEASLEY is Professor of Journalism at the University of Maryland. Among her books are: *Women in Media: A Documentary Source Book; Voices of Change: Interviews with Pulitzer Prize Winners; One Third of a Nation: Lorena Hickok Reports the Great Depression;* and *The White House Press Conferences of Eleanor Roosevelt.*

SHERILYN COX BENNION is Professor of Journalism at Humboldt State University, and is the author of articles on early women journalists published in *Journalism Quarterly, Journalism History*, and other journals.

DAVE BERKMAN is Professor of Mass Communication at the University of Wisconsin–Milwaukee, and is the author of numerous articles on mass communication.

GORDON BILLINGSLEY is a public information specialist in the School of Agriculture at Southern Illinois University of Carbondale. His research interests include agricultural journalism history and curriculum development.

ROBERT E. BLACKMON is Professor of Journalism at California State University–Los Angeles. His research interest is the impact of the American press on urbanization, 1870–1900.

JAMES BOW teaches journalism at Central Michigan University, and has served on the faculties of Ohio State, Ohio Wesleyan, and Kent State universities, and the University of Iowa. He has studied graduate economics under a Sloan Fellowship at Princeton University.

JAMES STANFORD BRADSHAW is Professor Emeritus of Journalism at Central Michigan University. His main interest is nineteenth-century American press history.

DONALD F. BROD is Professor and Chairman of Journalism at Northern Illinois University and executive secretary of the International Society of Weekly Newspaper Editors. He is editor of *Grassroots Editor*.

KAREN FITZGERALD BROWN is Assistant Professor of Mass Communication at the University of South Florida. Among her research interests is black press history.

JOHN M. BUTLER is Associate Professor of Journalism at Louisiana State University. His research interests include nineteenth-century American press history.

THEODORE H. CARLSON is Associate Professor of Journalism at Oregon State University, and his research interests are in journalism history, especially the life of Elizabeth Cochrane.

LLOYD CHIASSON is Assistant Professor of Communications at Loyola University in New Orleans.

CAROLYN G. CLINE is Assistant Professor of Journalism at Southwest Texas State University.

BARBARA CLOUD is Associate Professor and Chair of Communication Studies at the University of Nevada, Las Vegas. She is past president of the American Journalism Historians Association and has published research in *Journalism Quarterly*, *Western Historical Quarterly*, and other journals.

GARY COLL is Associate Professor and Chair of Journalism at the University of Wisconsin–Oshkosh. His major research interest is in early American history, and his work has appeared in several books and in *Journalism History*.

JACK H. COLLDEWEIH is Associate Professor and Chair of Communications, Speech and Theatre at Fairleigh Dickinson University. His major research interest is in the history and technology of mass media, especially film and magazines.

EARL L. CONN is Professor and Chair of Journalism at Ball State University. His primary interests are in history, ethics, and issues of press and society.

THOMAS CONNERY is Assistant Professor of Journalism and Mass Communication at the College of St. Thomas in St. Paul, Minnesota. His interests are in the literary aspects of journalism.

DAVID C. COULSON is Associate Professor of Journalism and Director of Graduate Studies at the University of Nevada–Reno, and has taught at the Poynter Institute. His work has appeared in *Journalism Quarterly* and the *Newspaper Research Journal*.

ROBERT W. DAVENPORT is Associate Professor of History at the University of Nevada, Las Vegas.

HAROLD E. DAVIS is Research Professor of Communication at Georgia State University and the author of *The Fledgling Province: A Social and Cultural History of Colonial Georgia, 1733–1776*.

ANNA JANNEY DEARMOND is Professor Emeritus of English at the University of Delaware. She is the author of *Andrew Bradford, Colonial Journalist*.

JOHN DE MOTT is Professor of Journalism at Memphis State University. He has published in *Journalism Quarterly, Quill, Newspaper Research Journal*, and other journals.

KRISTEN DOLLASE is Assistant Professor of Journalism at the Univesity of Southern Mississippi. Her major interests are communications law, advertising, and public relations.

WALLACE B. EBERHARD is Professor of Journalism and Mass Communication at the University of Georgia. His research interests include media history and communication law. He has written for *Journalism Quarterly, Journalism History*, and *Jurimetrics Journal*.

JAMES S. FEATHERSTON is Associate Professor of Journalism at Louisiana State University. He worked on newspapers in Mississippi and Texas for nineteen years, and his research interests are in journalism history and biography.

SHIRLEY FOGARINO is a public information officer at Vista Community College in Berkeley, California. She holds an M.A. in journalism from the University of Maryland, where she wrote her thesis on the *Tundra Times*.

JEAN FOLKERTS is Associate Professor and Chair of Communication at Mount Vernon College in Washington, D.C.

ELIZABETH FRAAS is Associate Professor of Journalism at Eastern Kentucky University. Her research interests include Kentucky history, politics, and newspapers.

JOHN P. FREEMAN is Assistant Professor of Radio-TV-Film at Texas Christian University. His research interests include broadcast history and the history of television technology.

RICHARD C. GOTSHALL is a copy editor for the *Indianapolis Star*, and has taught at Franklin College in Franklin, Indiana.

LLOYD J. GRAYBAR is Professor of History at Eastern Kentucky University. He is the author of *Albert Shaw of the Review of Reviews: An Intellectual Biography*. His research interests include progressivism, early twentieth-century American journalism, and naval history of the World War II era.

SALLY F. GRIFFITH is Assistant Professor of History at Villanova University. A cultural historian, she is interested in the social influence of community journalism in America.

DAVID M. GUERRA is Professor of Radio, Television and Film at the University of Arkansas at Little Rock. Among his research interests are broadcast news, network news policies and the impact of technology on media.

DENNIE HALL is Assistant Professor of Journalism at Central State University in Edmond, Oklahoma, and directs the Oklahoma Journalism Hall of Fame.

NORA HALL is Assistant Professor and Coordinator of Special Projects for the Vice President for Academic Affairs at the University of Minnesota. She is interested in research on African-Americans in communications with special emphasis on African-American women in leadership roles.

ROY HALVERSON is Professor of Journalism at Arizona State University. He is involved in research on the impact of changing technology on American newspapers. He is also an accomplished fly fisherman.

NANCY P. HAUSE is a temporary assistant professor in the Department of Journalism and Mass Communication at Kansas State University.

ADRIAN L. HEADLEY was Assistant Professor of Journalism and Printing at Arkansas State University. He died in 1986.

THOMAS H. HEUTERMAN is Professor and former Chair of Communications at Washington State University. He is the author of *Movable Type: Biography of Legh R. Freeman* and is a past president of the American Society of Journalism School Administrators.

GLENN A. HIMEBAUGH is Associate Professor of Mass Communications and Acting Chairman of Journalism at Middle Tennessee State University. He is interested in Tennessee media history.

W. WAT HOPKINS is Assistant Professor of Communication Studies at Virginia Polytechnic Institute and State University, where he teaches media law and media history. His published work has appeared in *Journalism Quarterly* and *Journalism Monographs*.

ROBERT L. HOSKINS is Dean of the College of Communications and Professor of Journalism at Arkansas State University. His work has appeared in *Journalism Quarterly, Public Relations Review,* and *Journalism Educator*.

DAVID H. HOSLEY is station manager at KQED-FM in San Francisco, California, and was Program and News Director at WINZ-FM in Miami, Florida. He has taught at Stanford University, the University of Florida and Florida International University and is the author of *As Good As Any*, a social history of foreign correspondents on American radio to 1941.

HERBERT H. HOWARD is Professor of Communications and Assistant Dean for Graduate Studies and Research in the College of Communications at the University of Tennessee at Knoxville. He is the coauthor of books on broadcast advertising, broadcast programming, and broadcast ownership.

ROBERT V. HUDSON is Professor of Journalism at Michigan State University and is the author of *The Writing Game: A Biography of Will Irwin*, and *Mass Media: A Chronological Encyclopedia of Television, Radio, Motion Pictures, Magazines, Newspapers and Books in the United States*.

WILLIAM E. HUNTZICKER is a Minneapolis–St. Paul journalist who has taught journalism and American Studies at the University of Minnesota and the University of Wisconsin–River Falls. He holds a Ph.D. in American Studies and his research interests are the cold war, the American West, and mass media history.

DENNIS JACKSON is Associate Professor of English and Journalism at the University of Delaware. He has been editor of the *Irish Renaissance Annual* and the *D. H. Lawrence Review*. He coedited *D. H. Lawrence's "Lady": A New Look at "Lady Chatterley's Lover."*

DWIGHT JENSEN is Acting Director of the School of Journalism at Marshall University. His research interests include the intellectual history of freedom of the press, local television news, newspaper chain ownership, and Idaho history.

ARTHUR J. KAUL is Associate Professor of Journalism and Director of Graduate Studies in Communication at the University of Southern Mississippi. His interests are the cultural history of mass media, literary journalism, and the integration of history and social theory. His work has appeared in *American Journalism*, *Critical Studies in Mass Communication*, and other journals.

KATHLEEN K. KEESHEN is Communications and Community Relations Manager for IBM Corporation's Almaden Research Center in San Jose, California. Her primary research interest is women in journalism, and she has contributed to *American Women Writers* and other publications.

BEVERLY KEEVER is Associate Professor of Journalism at the University of Hawaii at Manoa.

SAMUEL V. KENNEDY III is Associate Professor of Public Communications and Chair of the Newspaper Department at Syracuse University.

SIDNEY KOBRE teaches at Cantonsville Community College in Cantonsville, Maryland. He holds the Ph.D. in Sociology from Columbia University and has taught at Florida State University and the University of Maryland. He is the author of many books on journalism history and practices, including *The Development of American Journalism*.

HILLIER KRIEGHBAUM is Professor Emeritus of Journalism at New York University and the author of several books on science news. He is also the author of *Pressures on the Press* and has contributed to *Saturday Review, Columbia Journalism Review*, and other periodicals and journals.

SAM KUCZUN is Professor of Journalism and Mass Communication at the University of Colorado at Boulder, and served for more than a decade as Associate Editor of *Journalism Quarterly*. His recent research has been in economic history, technology, and public policy.

DERYL R. LEAMING is interim Dean of the College of Liberal Arts at Marshall University. His work has appeared in a wide range of popular and scholarly publications, from the *Saturday Evening Post* to the *Tokyo Journal of Psychoanalysis*.

JOHN A. LEDINGHAM is Director of Market Research for the Davon Group in Columbus, Ohio. His work has appeared in the *Journal of Advertising Research* and other journals.

ELLI LESTER-MASSMAN is a doctoral student at the University of Wisconsin–Madison. Her research interests include transnational communications, African area studies, and critical cultural studies.

JOSEPH E. LOFTON is Associate Professor of Communication at Louisiana State University in Shreveport. His research interests include Scandinavian-American journalism and Southern journalism history.

ALFRED LAWRENCE LORENZ is Professor and Chair of Communications at Loyola University in New Orleans. He is the author of *Hugh Gaine: A Colonial Printer-Editor's Odyssey to Loyalism*.

DONALD L. MCBRIDE is Assistant Professor of Journalism and Mass Communication at South Dakota State University. His teaching and research interests are in broadcast journalism and journalism history.

WILLIAM MCKEEN is Assistant Professor of Journalism and Communications at the University of Florida. He has worked for newspapers and magazines, including the *Saturday Evening Post*. While at the *Post*, he edited an anthology called *The American Story*.

KAY MARIE MAGOWAN is a lecturer and print sequence coordinator in Mass Communication at the University of Wisconsin–Milwaukee.

CHARLES H. MARLER is Professor and Chairman of Journalism and Mass Communication at Abilene Christian University. His research interests include Southwest media, religious journalism, and First Amendment history.

RONALD S. MARMARELLI is Assistant Professor of Journalism at Central Michigan University and a doctoral student in American Studies at Michigan State University.

LYNNE MASEL-WALTERS is on the staff of the Houston Area Research Center, and adjunct faculty in the School of of Communication at the University of Houston. She holds the Ph.D. from the University of Wisconsin–Madison. Her research on women's history has appeared in *Journalism Quarterly* and *Journalism History*.

ACHAL MEHRA is on the staff of the Xinhau News Agency in Beijing, People's Republic of China. He holds the Ph.D. in Journalism from Southern Illinois University at Carbondale.

CHRISTINE M. MILLER is Management Associate, Community and Media Relations for Subaru-Isuzu Automotive, Inc., in Lafayette, Indiana. Her primary areas of research are MTV and audience perception, and media coverage of human rights.

ROBERT MIRALDI is Associate Professor and Coordinator of Journalism at the State University of New York at New Paltz.

WILLIAM RAY MOFIELD is Professor of Broadcasting and Journalism at Murray State University and the author of many journal articles. In 1985 he received the Regents' Prize as an outstanding teacher and in 1987, the Alumni Prize as Distinguished Professor.

SHIRLEY M. MUNDT is an instructor at Louisiana State University in Baton Rouge, and a former editor of the *Kenilworth Herald*. She has contributed to the *Dictionary of Literary Biography*.

WHITNEY R. MUNDT is Associate Professor of Journalism at Louisiana State University in Baton Rouge, and a former editor of *Media Law Notes*. He has contributed to the *Dictionary of Literary Biography*.

SHARON MURPHY is Professor and Dean of the College of Communications, Journalism and Performing Arts at Marquette University, and past president of the Association for Education in Journalism and Mass Communication. She is coauthor of *Great Women of the Press* and *Let My People Know: American Indian Journalism 1828–1978*, and author of *Other Voices: Black, Chicano and American Indian Press*.

MICHAEL D. MURRAY is Associate Professor and Director of the Mass Communication program at the University of Missouri–St. Louis, and past president of the American Journalism Historians Association. His primary research interest is the history of broadcasting.

JOHN NERONE is Assistant Professor of Communications at the University of Illinois.

EDWARD A. NICKERSON is Director of the Journalism program at the University of Delaware, and Associate Professor of English. He is writing a book on the newspaper experience of American novelists.

LAURA NICKERSON works in advertising and public relations and was a research assistant in the S. I. Newhouse School of Public Communications at Syracuse University.

MARVIN N. OLASKY is Associate Professor of Journalism at the University of Texas at Austin, where he teaches media history, media law, and public relations. His work has appeared in *Journalism Quarterly*, the *Wall Street Journal*, and other publications.

ROBERT M. OURS is Professor of Journalism at West Virginia University. He is the author of *College Football Almanac* and has contributed to *American Writers Before 1800*.

CATHY PACKER is Assistant Professor of Journalism at the University of North Carolina. She is the author of *Freedom of Expression in the American Military*. Her primary research interest is mass communication law.

WILLIAM Q. PARMENTER teaches at Fremont High School in Los Angeles, California. His work has been published in *American Journalism*, *Journalism Quarterly*, and other journals. He was a Fulbright Scholar in India in 1986.

JOHN J. PAULY is a member of the Faculty of Communication at the University of Tulsa. His research on the history and sociology of mass communication has appeared in *American Quarterly, American Journalism*, and other journals.

DONALD C. PETERSON is Associate Professor of Journalism at Northern Illinois University.

DANIEL W. PFAFF is Associate Professor of Communications at the Pennsylvania State University. His work on journalism history and communications law has appeared in *Journalism Monographs, Journalism Quarterly, Columbia Journalism Review*, and other publications.

BRUCE L. PLOPPER is Associate Professor of Journalism at Central Arkansas University. His research interests are in media history and law.

MARY SUE F. POOLE is on the staff of the College of Journalism at the University of South Carolina.

ALF PRATTE is Associate Professor of Communications and former head of the journalism sequence at Brigham Young University. His research on media history and media economics has appeared in *American Journalism*, the *Newspaper Research Journal*, and other journals.

SAM G. RILEY is Professor of Communication Studies at Virginia Polytechnic Institute and State University. He is the author of *Magazines of the American South*, and the compiler of *Index to Southern Periodicals*.

BROOKS ROBARDS is Associate Professor of Mass Communication at Westfield State College in Westfield, Massachusetts. She has worked for *Life, Ramparts*, and *Connecticut Magazine*. Her primary research interest is media criticism.

PATT FOSTER ROBERSON is Associate Professor of Mass Communication at Southern University in Baton Rouge, Louisiana.

NANCY L. ROBERTS is Associate Professor of Journalism and Mass Communication, and an adjunct faculty member in American Studies at the University of Minnesota. She is the author of *Dorothy Day and the "Catholic Worker"*, and coeditor of *"As ever, Gene": Letters of Eugene O'Neill to George Jean Nathan*.

BRUCE ROCHE is Associate Professor of Advertising and Public Relations at the University of Alabama. His principal interest is advertising history.

HARRIS E. ROSS is an Assistant Professor of English at the University of Delaware. He has written for journals such as *Style* and the *D. H. Lawrence Review* and is the author of a forthcoming book on the relationship of film to literature.

MARIANNE SALCETTI is an adjunct faculty member at Ursuline College in Cleveland, Ohio and a Ph.D. candidate in the School of Journalism and Mass Communication at the University of Iowa. Her principal academic interests are labor history, media professionalism, and twentieth-century journalism history.

THOMAS A. SCHWARTZ is Associate Professor of Journalism at Ohio State University in Columbus. His research and teaching interests include constitutional law and history.

RICHARD A. SCHWARZLOSE is Professor of Journalism at Northwestern University. His teaching and research interests are mass communications history and the law and ethics of journalism. His books are *Newspapers: A Reference Guide*, and *The Nation's Newsbrokers*, 2 vols.

GARY W. SELNOW is Associate Professor of Communication Studies at the Virginia Polytechnic Institute and State University. His work on interactive communication, mass media effects, media content, and communication education has been published in the *Journal of Communication*, the *Journal of Broadcasting*, and other journals.

JUDITH A. SERRIN is Assistant Professor of Journalism in the Graduate School of Journalism at Columbia University.

MICHAEL D. SHERER is Associate Professor of Journalism at the University of Nebraska at Omaha. His work on photojournalism and law has been published in *Journalism Quarterly, Communications and the Law*, and other journals.

C. JOANNE SLOAN teaches English at Tuscaloosa County High School in Northport, Alabama, and is a free-lance writer for diverse magazines.

C. ZOE SMITH is Associate Professor and head of the photojournalism sequence in the College of Communications, Journalism and the Performing Arts at Marquette University. Her research has been published in *Journalism Quarterly, American Journalism*, and the *Journal of American Culture*.

ROBERT RUTHERFORD SMITH is Professor of Communication and Dean of the School of Communication and Theater at Temple University. He is the author of *Beyond the Wasteland*, a guide to television criticism, and a past president of the Philadelphia chapter of Sigma Delta Chi, the Society of Professional Journalists.

J. WILLIAM SNORGRASS was Associate Professor of Journalism at Florida A&M University. He died in 1987. He was the coauthor of *Blacks and Media, A Selected Annotated Bibliography, 1962–1982*.

JAMES D. STARTT is Professor of History at Valparaiso University, and his primary interests include foreign correspondents, the press and foreign affairs, the press and the presidency, and British journalism. He is the author of *Journalism's Unofficial Ambassador: A Biography of Edward Price Bell, 1869–1943*.

JANET E. STEELE is a member of the faculty of the Department of Rhetoric and Communication at the University of Virginia. She was a research fellow at the Gannett Center for Media Studies at Columbia University. She received her Ph.D. in History from Johns Hopkins University.

LINDA STEINER is University Professor of Media Communications at Governors State University in Illinois. Her research on the history and theory of women's/feminist media has been published in *Journalism History, American Journalism*, and *Critical Studies in Mass Communication*. She is coauthor of *And Baby Makes Two: Motherhood without Marriage*.

HARRY W. STONECIPHER is Professor Emeritus of Journalism at Southern Illinois University at Carbondale. He is author of *Editorial and Persuasive Writing*; and coauthor of *Electronic Age News Editing*; and *The Mass Media and the Law in Illinois*.

JAMES GLEN STOVALL is Associate Professor and Director of the Communication Research and Service Center at the University of Alabama. He is the author of *Writing for the Mass Media* and coauthor of *On-Line Editing* and *Watergate: A Crisis for the World*.

J. DOUGLAS TARPLEY is Associate of Journalism at CBN University, Virginia Beach, Virginia. He is the author of *Student Publications*, and his research interests include the student press, communications law, and journalism history.

LEONARD RAY TEEL is Assistant Professor of Communication at Georgia State University. He is coauthor of *Into the Newsroom: An Introduction to Journalism* and *Erma: A Black Woman Remembers, 1912–1980*, and is working on a biography of Ralph McGill.

KATHRYN T. THEUS is Associate Director of the National Center for Post-secondary Governance and Finance at the University of Maryland. Her research has appeared in *Journalism History* and *Public Relations Review*. She is coauthor, with Maurine Beasley, of *The New Majority*, a study of gender shifts in journalism-related occupations.

JOHN A. THOMPSON is editor and part owner of the *Times*, a suburban weekly newspaper published at North Little Rock, Arkansas. He wrote his master's thesis on John N. Heiskell at the University of Arkansas at Little Rock.

RICHARD C. VINCENT is Assistant Professor of Communication at the University of Hawaii at Manoa. He is the author of *Financial Characteristics of Selected ''B'' Film Productions of Albert J. Cohen, 1951–1957*. His primary interests are media history, economics, and effects.

JOHN H. VIVIAN is Associate Professor and Chair of Mass Communication at Winona State University in Minnesota. His primary interests are newspaper style and design, chain ownership, and news-gathering practices.

IRENE M. WASSELL is a feature writer for the *Arkansas Gazette* in Little Rock.

JAMES WESOLOWSKI is Professor of Communication at Western Kentucky University and former Chair of the Department of Mass Communication. He has taught at the University of Wisconsin–Milwaukee, Villanova University, and the American University in Cairo, and was a Fulbright lecturer at the University of Jos in Nigeria for two years.

W. RICHARD (RIK) WHITAKER is Professor and Chair of Journalism, Broadcasting and Speech at State University College at Buffalo in New York. His research on twentieth-century American history and the role of the press in shaping attitudes and opinions has appeared in *Journalism History* and *Journalism Quarterly*.

JAMES DANIEL WHITFIELD is Professor and Director of Journalism at Texas A&I University. His research interests include history, international communications, and curriculum development.

ROGER YARRINGTON, formerly Associate Dean of the College of Journalism at the University of Maryland, is Editorial Director of Herald Publishing House in Independence, Missouri and adjunct lecturer in Journalism at the University of Kansas.

JONATHAN L. YODER is Manager of Employee Communications for Orange and Rockland Utilities in Pearl River, New York. He holds a Ph.D. in Radio-TV-Film from Northwestern University.

JULIA CRAIN ZAHAROPOULOS received a master's degree in Journalism at Southern Illinois University at Carbondale.

THIMIOS ZAHAROPOULOS is Assistant Professor of Communication and Director of Broadcasting at Pittsburg State University in Kansas. His research interests include news analysis and international communications.